THE HANDBOOK OF EMPLOYEE BENEFITS:

Design, Funding and Administration

The Handbook of Employee Benefits:

Design, Funding and Administration

Edited by
JERRY S. ROSENBLOOM
Professor of Insurance
Wharton School
University of Pennsylvania

DOW JONES-IRWIN
Homewood, Illinois 60430

ISBN 0-87094-406-1

Library of Congress Catalog Card No. 82-74070

Printed in the United States of America

1 2 3 4 5 6 7 8 9 0 D 0 9 8 7 6 5 4 3

Preface

No longer can employee benefits be considered "fringe benefits" but must be viewed as an integral and extremely important component of an individual's financial security. The most recent U.S. Chamber of Commerce study on employee benefits in the United States indicates that on average they account for 40 percent of a worker's total compensation. In light of the ever-increasing importance of benefit plans, those dealing with them must be well versed in the objectives, design, costing, funding, implementation, and administration of such plans.

While *The Handbook of Employee Benefits* is intended for students in the benefit field and for professionals as a handy reference, it can be a valuable tool for anyone with an interest in the field in general or in a specific employee benefits topic. The *Handbook* can be used either as a reference work for benefit professionals or as a textbook for college courses and professional education and company training programs. Each chapter of the *Handbook* stands alone and is complete in itself. While this produces some overlap in certain of the chapters, it eliminates the need for the reader to "check back" into other chapters, and it provides important reinforcement of difficult concepts.

The chapters of the *Handbook* are structured into eight parts, each covering a major component of the employee benefit planning process. These are: Part One, Environment of Employee Benefit Plans; Part Two, Designing Employee Benefit Plans—Death Benefits; Part Three, Designing Employee Benefit Plans—Health-Related Benefits; Part Four, Designing Employee Benefit Plans—Additional Benefits and Services; Part Five, Designing Employee Benefit Plans—Retirement and Capital Accumulation Plans; Part Six, Costing and Funding of Employee Benefit Plans; Part Seven, Administration of Employee Benefit Plans; and Part Eight, Issues of Special Interest in Employee Benefit Planning.

v

The *Handbook* consists of 60 chapters written by distinguished experts—academics, actuaries, attorneys, consultants, and other benefit professionals—covering all areas of the employee benefits field. Their practical experience and breadth of knowledge provide insightful coverage of the employee benefits mechanism, and the examples presented throughout the *Handbook* illustrate the concepts presented.

The *Handbook* also incorporates the changes in benefit planning caused by the Economic Recovery Tax Act of 1981 (ERTA) and the Tax Equity and Fiscal Responsibility Act of 1982 (TEFRA).

In such a massive project, many people provided invaluable assistance, and it would be impossible to mention them all here. Thanks must be extended, however, to the authors of the individual chapters and to the Editorial Advisory Board: Mr. Everett T. Allen Jr., Dr. Dan M. McGill, Dr. Robert J. Myers, Mr. Dallas L. Salisbury, and Mr. William G. Williams for their yeoman service. Thanks must go, too, to my colleague Dr. Jack L. VanDerhei, who read the entire manuscript and made many constructive comments and suggestions. I would like to thank Dr. Davis W. Gregg, the former President of the American College, for his encouragement over the years to undertake such a project. Appreciation also must go to my most able assistant Diana Krigelman, who spent many hours on all aspects of the manuscript and handled her duties in a totally professional manner.

In a work of this magnitude, it is almost inevitable that some mistakes may have escaped the eyes of the many readers of the manuscript. For these oversights I accept full responsibility and ask the reader's indulgence.

Jerry S. Rosenbloom

Contributors

Everett T. Allen, Jr., Vice President and Principal, Towers, Perrin, Forster & Crosby, Inc.

Preston C. Bassett, F.S.A., F.C.A., M.A.A.A., Consulting Actuary

Burton T. Beam, Jr., Associate Professor of Insurance, The American College

Henry Bright, F.S.A., Vice President, The Wyatt Company

Mary A. Carroll, CPCU, CEBS, ARM, Vice President and Assistant Secretary, Mack and Parker, Inc., and Consultant, Mass Insurance Consultants and Administrators, (MICA), Inc.

Joseph Casey, University of Central Florida

Robert W. Cooper, Ph.D., Dean, Solomon S. Huebner School, The American College

Donald J. Doudna, Ph.D., CLU, CPCU, Assistant to the President, Equitable Life Insurance Company of Iowa, Equitable American Life Insurance Company

Edmund W. Fitzpatrick, CFP, Ph.D., Director of Corporate Services, Legg Mason Wood Walker, Inc.

Linda Pickthorne Fletcher, Ph.D., CLU, CPCU, Chairman, Department of Finance, Old Dominion University

Arthur C. Folli, Manager, Executive Compensation, Mobil Oil Corporation

Mark R. Greene, Ph.D., Distinguished Professor of Risk Management and Insurance, The University of Georgia

Donald S. Grubbs, Jr., J.D., F.S.A., Consulting Actuary, George B. Buck Consulting Actuaries, Inc.

Charles P. Hall, Jr., Ph.D., Professor of Health Administration, Insurance and Risk, School of Business Administration, Temple University

G. Victor Hallman, Ph.D., J.D., CPCU, CLU, Dean - Examinations, American Institute for Property and Liability Underwriters/Insurance Institute of America; Lecturer, Wharton School, University of Pennsylvania

Carlton Harker, F.S.A., President, Aims Consulting Services, Inc.

David L. Hewitt, F.C.A., Partner, Hay Associates

Charles E. Hughes, D.B.A., CLU, CPCU, Vice President for Academic Affairs, The American College

Ronald L. Huling, Towers, Perrin, Forster & Crosby, Inc.

James D. Hutchinson, J.D., President, Capital Associates, Inc., Washington, D.C.

Lloyd S. Kaye, William M. Mercer, Incorporated

David R. Klock, Ph.D., Chairman, Department of Finance, University of Central Florida

Phyllis A. Klock, FLMI, Instructor and Coordinator of Graduate Programs, University of Central Florida

Harry V. Lamon, Jr., Esq., Partner, Lamon, Elrod & Harkleroad, P.C.

Robert T. LeClair, Ph.D., Dean, Graduate School of Financial Sciences, The American College

Claude C. Lilly III, Ph.D., Professor of Insurance, Florida State University

Zelda Lipton, FLMI, Second Vice President, Union Mutual Life Insurance Company

John T. Lynch, Towers, Perrin, Forster & Crosby, Inc.

Edward E. Mack, Jr., CLU, CPCU, Chairman of the Board, Mack and Parker, Inc. and Mass Insurance Consultants and Administrators (MICA), Inc.

Ernest L. Martin, Ph.D., FLMI, Manager, Examinations Department, Life Office Management Association (LOMA)

Ronald T. Martin, Esq., Partner, DeCarion, Roberts & Martin

Thomas Martinez, Assistant Professor, Villanova University

Harry McBrierty, The Wyatt Company

Dan M. McGill, Ph.D., Frederick H. Ecker Professor of Life Insurance and Chairman, Insurance Department, University of Pennsylvania

Morton D. Miller, Past President of the Society of Actuaries, Member of the Institute of Medicine, and Vice Chairman of the Board of Directors of the Equitable Life Assurance Society of the United States

Robert J. Myers, F.S.A., Professor Emeritus, Temple University, and Chief Actuary, Social Security Administration, 1947-70

Robert V. Nally, Associate Professor, Villanova University

Robert M. Neiswanger, Secretary, Group Department, The Travelers Insurance Company

Norma Nielson, Ph.D., Assistant Professor, Department of Finance and Business Economics, University of Southern California

Paul J. Ondrasik, J.D., Member, Steptoe & Johnson Chartered, Washington, D.C.

Bruce A. Palmer, Ph.D., CLU, Professor of Insurance, Georgia State University

William H. Rabel, Ph.D., FLMI, CLU, Vice President and Director, Life Management Institute, Life Office Management Association (LOMA)

James E. Roberts, Esq., Partner, DeCarion, Roberts & Martin

Jerry S. Rosenbloom, Ph.D., CLU, CPCU, Professor of Insurance and Academic Director, Certified Employee Benefit Specialist (CEBS) Program, Wharton School, University of Pennsylvania

Dallas L. Salisbury, Executive Director, Employee Benefit Research Institute

Carlton R. Sherman, Administrator, Local 1 and Local 4 Health Funds, Chicago, Illinois

Robert W. Smiley, Jr., L.L.B., Senior Consultant, Benefit Systems, Inc., Los Angeles, California

Gary K. Stone, Ph.D., Professor, Michigan State University

Richard L. Tewksbury, Jr., Vice President, Johnson & Higgins

Jack L. VanDerhei, Ph.D., CEBS, Assistant Professor, University of Pennsylvania

Charles A. Weaver, Consultant, Human Resources Development; Corporate Consultant, Love Care Med Centers, Inc., Indianapolis, Indiana

Bernard L. Webb, Professor, Georgia State University

William G. Williams, Director, Health Care Relations, Provident Mutual Life Insurance Company of Philadelphia

Joseph D. Young, Vice President, Employee Benefits, The Bank of California

Contents

able and Customary Charge Plans. Exclusions and Limitations. Types of Vision Care Providers. Conclusion.

chise Plans. Mass Merchandising Plans. True Group Plans. Advantages for Employees: *Lower Cost of Insurance. Greater Availability of Insurance. Payroll Deduction.* Disadvantages for Employees. Role of Employer. Federal Income-Tax Consequences. U.S. Labor Code. State Regulation: *Fictitious Group Regulations. Fictitious Group Statutes. Effectiveness of Rulings and Statutes. Enabling Legislation. Present Status.* Summary and Conclusions.

Funding Media: *Trusts. Life Insurance Companies. Mutual Funds. Government Retirement Bonds.* Factors Influencing Adoption of a Qualified Pension Plan.

Determination of Eligibility: *Special Problems*. Communications: *Communicating with Participants and Their Families. Communicating with Providers. Communicating with Other Plan Advisers and Government Agencies. Special Problems.* Processing of Claims: *Retirement Plans. Health Protection. Life and Accidental Death and Dismemberment (AD&D) Coverage. Loss of Income Protection. Special Problems.* Accounting for Plan Funds: *Special Problems*. Data Processing: *Special Problems.*

Minimum Requirements. Financial Implications. Analysis of Retention. Bid Cost Matrix. Qualitative Factors. Negotiating with Carrier. Presentation to Decision Makers.

The Implementing Process: *Approval of Top Management. Development of Plan Specifications. Legal Document Preparation. Announcement and Enrollment Materials. Record-Keeping and Reporting.* Reviewing Employee Benefit Plans: *Establishing Objectives. Management Review Committee. Analyzing Current Plans. Employee Sensing. Developing Alternative Plans or Amendments.*

Reasons for the Communication of Employee Benefits: *Legal Requirements.* Managerial Requirements. Responsibility for Communicating Employee Benefits: *Top Management. Employee Benefits Manager. Line Management. Employee Benefit Communication Events.* The Communication Process: *Steps of the Communication Process.* Effective and Ineffective Communications. Forms of Communication: *Written Communications. Overall Approach and Tone. Oral Communications.*

Introduction. General Considerations in Plan Choice—Types of Plan: *Regular Profit-Sharing Plans. Profit-Sharing Thrift Plans. Pension Plans. Combinations of Plans. Simplified Pension Plans.* Specific Qualification Aspects Relevant to Small Business Employers: *Eligibility and Minimum Participation Standards. Vesting and Benefit Accrual. Past Service. Integration with Social Security Benefits. Payment of Benefits.* Top-Heavy Rules: *Key Employee. Employees. Officers. Ownership. Determination Date. What Is a Top-Heavy Plan? Impact of Top-Heavy Rules.* Section 401(k) Cash-Deferred/Salary Reduction Plans Outline: *Basic Elements of a Cash-Deferred/Salary Reduction Plan. Discrimination Restrictions on Contributions to Cash-Deferred/Salary Reduction Plans.*

General Administration of the Plan. Reporting and Disclosure Requirements of ERISA: *Summary Plan Description. Participant's Benefit Statements upon Request. Furnishing Other Documents Relating to the Plan.* Adoption of Plans and Adoption of Amendments. Loans to Participants. Bonding Requirements of ERISA. Investments. Master Plans versus Individually Designed Plans. Prohibited Transactions. Contributions: *Nondeductible Voluntary Employee Contributions. Deductible Voluntary Employee Contributions.* Annual Addition Limitation. Qualifying Plans with the Internal Revenue Service. Discrimination in Operation: *Erroneous Administration of Plan Provisions. Improper Exclusion of Employees. Withdrawals from Qualified Plans. Opting Out. Definition of the Term Compensation. Employee Turnover. Tax Consequences of Disqualification.* Insurance: *Profit-Sharing Plans. Defined Benefit Pension Plans. Money Purchase Pension Plans. Tax Treatment.* Other Issues. Disposition of H. R. 10 Plans upon

Incorporation: *Freezing the H. R. 10 Plan. Termination of Plan and Distribution to Participants. Termination of Plan and Transfer of H. R. 10 Funds to Qualified Retirement Plans of the New Small Business.* Income and Estate Tax Consequences of Distributions on Termination: *Consequences of Lump Sum Distributions. Tax Consequences of Ten-Year Averaging. Rollover of Lump Sums. Receipt of Periodic Retirement Benefits from the Qualified Corporate Plan.* Affiliated Service Groups: *Revenue Ruling 68-370—The IRS States Its Position. Packard/Burnetta Cases—The Tax Court Approves the Service Position. The Kiddie Case—Pre-ERISA. The IRS Position after Kiddie. The Garland Case—Post-ERISA. Effect of Section 414(m). Reallocation of Income.*

PART ONE

Environment of Employee Benefit Plans

Employee benefits constitute a major part of almost every individual's financial and economic security. Such benefits have gone from being considered "fringe" benefits to the point where they constitute over 40 percent of an employee's compensation, and the plans under which they are provided are a major concern of employers.

Individuals responsible for the design, pricing, selling, and administration of employee benefits carry a very broad range of responsibilities. The role of the employee benefits professional has changed rapidly and radically in the past two decades. During that period the number of employee benefits has virtually exploded. Expansion has occurred in many of the more traditional benefits while at the same time new forms of benefits were added.

Part One of the *Handbook* is concerned with the environment in which employee benefit plans are designed and operated. Chapter 1 considers many important design issues. Chapter 2 extends the discussion of employee benefit plan design concepts by looking at the functional approach to employee benefit planning. This approach examines the various strategies for considering benefits on a risk-by-risk basis and as a part of total compensation.

The final chapter in this part is a brief overview of the regulatory environment surrounding employee benefit plans. Later chapters cover in greater detail the extremely important regulatory issues involved in employee benefit planning.

CHAPTER 1

Designing Employee Benefit Plans[1]

EVERETT T. ALLEN, JR.

Once upon a time, the first employee benefit plan was established. For our purposes, it does not matter much whether the first plan was a pension or a death benefit plan, nor is it very important to know which company took this important first step. What is important is that this step was taken—for it was the beginning of a major force that affects and protects the economic security of almost all Americans.

It is reasonable to speculate that the first employee benefit plans were established to serve specific purposes—for example, to avoid "passing the hat" among employees when someone died. For many years, the design of these plans was influenced largely by the insurance industry's attitude toward underwriting, funding, and administration—since most of the early plans installed were those made available by insurers under the terms and conditions they chose to utilize.

Over the years, many factors have influenced the design of employee benefit plans, and a body of law has emerged that affects these plans in terms of minimum requirements and permissible provisions. The taxation of contributions and benefits also has influenced plan design, and the process of collective bargaining and the interests of organized labor have been a major influence, as has the availability of alternate funding mechanisms. These, and other factors, including a growing degree of sophistication and knowledge of the field, have created an environment in which an employer has a wide degree of choice and flexibility in benefit plan design.

The cost of employee benefits is significant. A well-rounded program (including paid time off) can easily generate a total cost in the vicinity of 30 percent or more of an employer's base payroll. If the cost of statutory benefits also is included, total cost can easily reach 40 percent of payroll or

---

[1] Parts of this chapter are based on material that originally appeared in Everett T. Allen, Jr.; Joseph J. Melone; and Jerry S. Rosenbloom, *Pension Planning*, 4th ed. (Homewood, Ill.: Richard D. Irwin, 1981).

more. Indeed, some companies have total benefit costs that approach 50 percent of payroll. The amounts accumulated under these plans also are of major importance. For example, the assets accumulated by some companies in their pension plans alone exceed their net worth.

Given the substantial costs involved in employee benefits plans, the importance they have to millions of workers, and the complex legal, tax, and funding environment that exists, it is most important that such plans be designed with particular care and that they be fully supportive of the employer's philosophy, goals, and objectives.

In this chapter, some of the environmental considerations that can influence plan design are described first. Then employer philosophy and attitudes are discussed. The final portion of the chapter deals with specific employee benefit plan objectives.

ENVIRONMENTAL CONSIDERATIONS

Before passage of the Tax Equity and Fiscal Responsibility Act of 1982 (TEFRA), the employer's legal status often influenced plan design. Federal tax law was different as it applied to sole proprietorships, partnerships, Subchapter S corporations, nonprofit organizations, and regular corporations. For example, the defined *contribution* pension or profit-sharing plan generally has been adopted by unincorporated organizations and by Subchapter S corporations because of the deduction limits previously imposed on these organizations. However, these deduction limits and the potential benefits of a defined *benefit* pension plan often have caused such organizations to incorporate either on a regular basis or as a professional corporation or association. Section 501(c)(3) organizations also have availed themselves of the defined contribution approach because of the availability of tax-deferred annuities under Section 403(b) of the Internal Revenue Code. The parity provisions of TEFRA eliminate most of the distinctions in tax law that formerly applied to different organizations. However, precedents established by prior practice and on account of prior law may still continue to influence plan design for some organizations.

The basic characteristics of the employer and its industry also are part of the background for designing an employee benefit program. Is the firm a growing, young organization, or is it relatively mature? Is its history of profits stable and predictable, or have profits been, or likely to be, volatile? Does the firm anticipate moderate or significant growth, and what will be its needs for employees in the forseeable future? Is the industry highly competitive? Are profit margins narrow? Is the business cyclical? What are the firm's short- and long-term capital needs? The answers to these questions and others like them can be of great importance in structuring benefit plans that meet employee needs with funding patterns compatible with the employer's objectives and capabilities.

The characteristics of the individuals employed by the employer also play an important role in plan design. The distribution of employees by age, service, sex, and pay can have significant implications in terms of the type of benefit provided, cost levels generated, and similar matters. This distribution can be even more significant under certain funding methods and instruments.

An employer with diversified operations has special considerations when it comes to employee benefit plan design. For example, such an employer needs to consider whether the same benefit program is appropriate for all facets of the business. Factors such as cost, profit margins, competitive need, and geographic differences should be taken into account. Another factor related to this issue is the employer's attitude on the transfer of employees. A uniform program facilitates such transfers while different plans at different locations may create impediments. Obviously, the employer's basic policy concerning employee transfers, whether encouraged or discouraged, bears on the matter. One approach used by some employers is to establish a basic or "core" program that applies in all areas of the business, with a flexible or varying program of supplemental benefits to accommodate different industry needs.

The communities in which the employer does business also can be an environmental factor in plan design. This is less the case in large, urban areas but can become quite meaningful when the company is the dominant or a major employer in a discrete geographical area. In this case the design and structure of an employee benefit plan could reflect the employer's degree of concern over the image it wishes to create in the communities in which it does business. If such a concern exists, it often indicates the need for liberal benefit provisions—not only by the employer's own industry standards, but by the standards established by different employers involved in the same communities.

The presence or absence of collective bargaining units can be a significant consideration. The demands of labor, both on a local and national or "pattern" basis, can influence plan design, even for nonbargaining employees. Many employers follow the practice of extending bargained-for benefits to nonbargaining employees—or a practice of making the plans of the nonbargaining employees slightly better than those of the bargaining employees, to the extent that this does not violate labor laws. Others, however, treat the programs as totally separate, particularly in the context that benefit plans are part of total compensation (see Chapter 2) and that basic salary and wage structures also are quite different between the two groups.

The foregoing is not intended to be an exhaustive discussion of environmental factors that influence plan design. Rather, it is intended to give some indication of items that should be considered. With these in mind, it is appropriate to turn to a discussion of employer philosophy and attitudes.

EMPLOYER PHILOSOPHY AND ATTITUDES

Specific objectives for employee benefit plans should be set in the context of the employer's philosophy and attitudes for the management of human resources. The following list of questions and observations, again not all-inclusive, is designed to suggest the nature of some of the items that need to be considered.

1.   What is the employer's basic compensation philosophy? Many employers believe benefit plans are part of total compensation and that the cost and benefit structure of these plans should reflect the employer's basic attitude toward other compensation elements. Thus, the employer who has adopted a policy of paying high wages and salaries may very well adopt a liberal benefit program. On the other hand, an employer may choose to establish a benefit program that keeps total compensation costs at an acceptable level while presenting one element of compensation on a more favorable basis. For example, an employer may wish to establish highly competitive wages and salaries but, to keep total compensation costs in line, may provide only modest benefits. Such a compensation strategy, of course, can affect the type of employee attracted and also can influence matters such as turnover rates. It also is possible for an employer to adopt a reverse compensation strategy mix and have a liberal benefit program to go along with a cash compensation program that is not fully competitive. This type of compensation mix often is found in governmental units where cash compensation is fixed by law and where incentive compensation may not be payable. Here, it is common to find employees with a liberal benefit program.

2.   Is the employer's basic attitude toward providing employee benefits one that emphasizes the protection and maintenance of income in the event of economic insecurity? Or is its attitude oriented more toward providing additional current, although deferred, compensation? Most employers do not have a clear-cut and total preference for one or the other of these positions; however, one position might be of greater significance than the other. The employer's leaning toward one or the other of these two concepts can find expression in a number of plan decisions. For example, a preference for the income-maintenance approach could suggest the choice of a defined benefit pension plan integrated to the maximum extent with Social Security benefits or of a death benefit that provides an income benefit but only to survivors of the employee's immediate family. A compensation-oriented approach, though, might suggest the use of a defined contribution plan as the basic program for providing retirement benefits.

3.   Does the employer believe employees should share in the cost of meeting their own economic security needs? Many employers take the position that employees do have such a responsibility, and benefits in the event of medical expense needs, death, disability, and retirement should come from three sources—the government, the employer, and the employee's own savings. Where desired, employee involvement can be in the form of direct employee contributions, or it can be recognized in indirect ways as, for example, when income-replacement objectives in a non-contributory pension plan are consciously set below what might otherwise

be desired levels, or through the use of deductibles, coinsurance, or inside plan limitations in a medical expense plan. Also, an employer can view this issue from the perspective of the total employee benefit program, making some specific plans contributory and some noncontributory, with the overall employee contributions achieving a total level the employer feels is satisfactory.

4. A long-term, advance-funded retirement program involves certain risks. Two of the most important relate to the impact of inflation and investment results with respect to plan assets. The employer's attitude on who should bear these risks—the employer or the employees—can play a significant role in the choice between a defined benefit and a defined contribution pension plan. Under the former, these risks are assumed by the employer, although the risk of inflation can be tempered by the choice of a formula that is not pay-related or by the choice of a career-pay formula, while the employee in effect assumes both of these risks under a defined contribution plan.

5. The selection of specific retirement plan provisions (normal retirement age, early retirement age and subsidies, the treatment of deferred retirement, and the benefit levels provided under all these events) and the amount of postretirement life and medical expense insurance provided can influence the pattern of retirements in any organization. Many employers prefer to encourage employees to retire at or before normal retirement age, and for a variety of reasons, such as keeping promotional channels open. Others prefer to encourage deferred retirements and are reluctant to see skilled workers leave while still capable of making important contributions to the firm's profitability. Still other employers take a neutral position and do not seek to exert any influence on the pattern of retirements in their organizations. In any event, this issue has taken on added significance in view of the 1978 amendments to the Age Discrimination in Employment Act which protect employment rights through age 70.

6. A growing number of employers prefer to structure an employee benefit program on a basis which gives employees a wide choice of plans in which to participate and the extent to which they participate in these plans. This can be accomplished on the basis of before-tax credits in the form of flexible or "cafeteria" benefits, or it can be accomplished by developing various layers of aftertax contributory coverage. Such employers believe this type of flexibility makes the program more meaningful to employees and more efficient since benefits are delivered only when needed or desired. Other employers prefer not to become involved in the administrative complexities and cost associated with such flexibility, nor do they wish to absorb any additional costs associated with the adverse selection permitted by such choices. Also, those employers who have a paternalistic attitude might feel many employees would not want to make choices or would not be able to make the right choices.

7. An employer's position concerning the cost levels it can assume can

be a major determinant for a plan's benefit levels and the various ancillary benefits that might be included. The assumption of any given level of cost commitment also involves a balancing of employee interests with those of the organization's owners or shareholders. Another aspect relates to the employer's attitude about the need for maintaining controls over future cost levels. A high degree of concern in this area, for example, might lead to the selection of a career-pay or a defined contribution pension plan, to the use of pay-related deductibles in a medical plan, or to nonpay-related death benefits.

8. Whether the plan's benefits should be coordinated with Social Security benefits is a most important question. The employer's basic philosophy concerning this issue plays an important role in plan design. A great many employers believe that because of the very nature of Social Security benefits and their relatively larger value for lower-paid employees, it would be impossible to achieve an equitable balancing of benefits and costs for employees at all pay levels without integrating pension and disability income plans in some fashion with the benefits provided by Social Security. Others believe the communications and administrative difficulties associated with integrated plans are such that integration is not desirable.

9. Should an employer provide a benefit program for executives that differs from that provided for its employees in general? Over the years, the majority of benefit programs have been applied across-the-board to all employees, and many employers still believe executives or highly paid employees should be treated the same as all employees. An increasing number of organizations, however, believe the unique needs of executives cannot be met by plans which must meet the nondiscrimination requirements of federal tax law. For example, it may be difficult for a firm to recruit a needed executive in mid-career because of the loss of pension benefits he or she will experience since a large part of the executive's benefits will be frozen at the pay levels achieved with the prior employer. In such a case, a need may exist for the employer to have a retirement arrangement which restores the benefits such an executive might potentially lose. Similarly, an employer might find it desirable to provide executives with a supplemental pension that applies the basic pension plan formula to the executive's incentive pay, if the basic pension applies to base compensation only. Obviously, special benefits for executives such as those described cannot be provided through a qualified, nondiscriminatory pension or profit-sharing plan. Instead, these benefits must be provided through some form of unfunded, nonqualified supplemental pension arrangement. Many employers also provide executives with additional death benefits, both before and after retirement, funded either with supplemental group life insurance or with individual life insurance policies, as well as with additional disability income protection.[2]

---

[2] Group life insurance plans and medical expense plans that provide discriminatory coverage for executives might result in additional taxable income for certain employees; however, they are not prohibited by federal tax law.

10.   An important question, since the passage of the Employee Retirement Income Security Act of 1974 (ERISA), is whether the employer is willing to assume the plan termination obligations imposed upon the employer in the event of the termination of a defined benefit plan before all accrued and vested benefits have been funded. The potential exposure of up to 30 percent of net worth, and the impact this might have on credit ratings and the ability to raise capital, have caused a good deal of concern— particularly among small employers. This potential liability can be avoided if a defined contribution pension plan is adopted and, indeed, over 80 percent of all new tax-qualified plans adopted since the passage of ERISA have been of the defined contribution variety.

EMPLOYER OBJECTIVES

With the preceding in mind, it is appropriate to consider specific employer objectives. The following discusses major employer objectives, as well as some of the factors relating to such objectives. Obviously, not all these objectives apply to each employer and, if they do have application, it is likely their relative importance may not be the same for each employer.

Attraction and Retention of Employees

Most employers recognize they must maintain some form of employee benefit program to attract and retain desirable employees. This is particularly so when the employer must compete with other employers for personnel.

Even so, many employers believe the presence of an adequate benefit program is not a positive influence in their efforts to attract and retain employees—at least to any significant extent. Rather, these employers reason the absence of such a program could have a negative effect on their recruiting and retention efforts. Put another way, these employers are of the opinion that an inadequate program can hinder their efforts to recruit and retain employees, while an overly generous program will not produce a corresponding increase in their ability to attract and hold desirable workers.

While this might be true as a general concept, it is worth noting that some benefit plans might have greater impact than others as far as employees are concerned. Thus, for example, the presence of a generous profit-sharing plan might make employment with one employer more attractive than employment with another employer who maintains a more conventional benefit program. In the same vein, employees might find the choice and value of a flexible (or cafeteria) benefit plan of more interest than a plan which offers a standard fare of benefits.

Meeting Competitive Standards

The objective of having competitive employee benefit plans is closely related to the objective of being able to attract and retain good employees.

It is, however, somewhat broader in concept and can reflect employers' attitudes concerning their standing in their own industry, as well as in the communities in which they operate. This objective also recognizes that, unlike other forms of compensation, employee benefit plans are highly visible and readily subject to external comparison.

An employer who wishes to have competitive employee benefit plans must establish the standards to use for measuring these plans. Will competitiveness be measured against industry standards, local geographic standards, or both? Many employers have a preference for measuring their plans against industry standards. However, it should be recognized that such standards are most appropriate for skilled or professional workers and for management personnel—those whose capabilities are more related to the employer's own industry. For workers whose capabilities are more readily transferred from one industry to another, a more realistic standard would be the plans maintained by the local companies with which the employer competes on a local basis for human resources. Thus, as a practical matter, most employers seek to compare their plans both on an industry and geographic basis.

Having identified the standard against which the plans are to be measured, the employer also must decide the relative level of competitiveness to achieve. For example, the employer might decide the objective is to have an employee benefit program that meets the average of the companies that form its comparison base (or it can establish different positions for different plans). The employer also might decide it wishes to be a leader and have a program consistently among the best, or it might wish to rank somewhere between the 50th and 75th percentile. And, of course, the employer might elect to lag somewhat behind other companies because of cost or other considerations.

Even though the comparison base has been identified and the relative ranking within this base established, there remains the important matter of determining the technique to be used to establish the relative standing of the different plans. One method used quite frequently is to make comparisons of the benefits actually payable to representative employees under different circumstances. For example, the benefit payable under a retirement plan at normal retirement age might be projected for several employees with differing pay, service, and age characteristics. This method is relatively simple in concept but should be used with caution. First, it shows benefits only and does not necessarily give any true indication of the relative cost of the plans involved. Also, by isolating a specific benefit, the importance and value of other benefits included in the same plan are not taken into account. For example, a company might be ranked as the highest in terms of benefits payable at normal retirement, but the other companies in the comparison may have much more valuable early retirement or survivor income benefits. Even if other benefits are illustrated and compared in the same way, the aggregate value of all benefits within the same plan may not be readily ascertainable. This method also is sensitive to the assumptions used in making the illustrations. If retirement benefits are being illustrated, for example, and if future pay increases are not taken into account, the benefit differences attributable to career-pay and final-pay formulas will not be apparent (nor will there be any apparent difference between a final three-year average plan and a final five-year average plan).

Another method used for comparative purposes is to compare actual costs to the employer for different benefit plans. The material used for this purpose usually is information acquired from both published and private surveys about actual employer cost patterns. A major difficulty with this approach is there is often inconsistent reporting, by different employers, of the information requested. Also, actual contribution patterns do not necessarily reflect the real cost or value of the benefit involved. The cost reported, for example, might be the total annual cost of the plan including employee contributions and reflect the specific characteristics of the employee group involved. In the case of retirement plans, significant differences may exist in annual contributions because of the choice of a particular actuarial method and the combination of actuarial assumptions employed— for example, two employers with identical plans might report significantly different annual costs because of their different choices of assumptions for future investment earnings and growth in pay.

A third method is to measure plans on a basis that uses uniform actuarial methods and assumptions and focuses on the relative value of the different benefits provided. This technique establishes the value of specific plans, specific benefits within a plan, and the aggregate value of all plans. The method also can establish these relative values on the basis of employer cost only, or on the basis of combined employer and employee cost. By using uniform actuarial methods and assumptions, and by applying these to a data base of employees held the same for all employer plans in the study, the actual differences in the value of different benefits are isolated and their relative values established. It should be noted that this technique does not establish actual costs or cost patterns, it simply establishes whether one particular benefit or plan is more valuable than another and the extent to which this is so.

Cost Considerations

Earlier in this chapter, reference was made to an employer's attitude on costs and how this can play a major role in plan design. Since a retirement plan often represents the largest part of an employer's total benefit program cost, it is particularly important that the employer have specific objectives in this area.

It is important to distinguish between ultimate real cost and estimated annual accruals. With this distinction in mind, an employer may establish specific objectives for actual liabilities assumed under a plan and specific objectives for annual accruals. The employer also may establish objectives in terms of the budgeting pattern to be assumed. For example, does the employer desire an accrual cost that remains level, as a percentage of payroll, or would it be preferable to have a pattern that starts with relatively low accruals, gradually building to higher levels in the future?

The employer's objectives for these cost levels influence the choice of retirement plan formula as well as the inclusion and level of ancillary benefits. These objectives also may influence the decision on whether the plan should be contributory and, if so, the level of employee contributions required.

There are other objectives an employer could have for matters concerning cost. The need for contribution flexibility might be one such objective and, if desired, could influence the choice of actuarial funding method and assumptions and could even lead the employer to adopt a profit-sharing plan. Another objective could relate to the employer's willingness to assume the costs associated with future inflation. The extent to which the employer wishes to limit commitment might dictate the choice of a career-pay formula for a defined benefit plan or even the choice of a defined contribution plan of some type.

The need for a cost-efficient retirement program is an obvious objective. Thus, the employer wishes to avoid excessive or redundant benefits and to fund the plan in the most efficient manner possible. For this reason, many employers choose to coordinate benefits from all sources and, for example, integrate their retirement plan benefits with those provided by Social Security.

It also is possible an employer views a retirement plan as a tax shelter for the benefit of key employees. When this is the case, the employer's objective might be to maximize benefits and contributions within the limits permitted by federal tax law.

Other employee benefit plans also involve cost considerations. If postretirement death and medical expense benefits are to be provided, should these liabilities be prefunded, and if so, how? Should inflation-sensitive benefits—medical expense and pay-related death benefits—be subjected to some degree of control through plan design? What type of funding mechanism—minimum premium, retrospective premium, administrative services contract, and so forth—should be utilized to gain greater control over cash flow? Clearly, cost considerations are becoming an increasingly important factor in plan design and in plan funding.

Compliance with Legal Requirements

Employee benefit plans almost always have been subject to some degree of regulation and other legal requirements. This has become much more the case in the last decade with the advent of ERISA, antidiscrimination laws, and the like. The recent enactment of TEFRA will have a major impact on the design of plans—particularly in the case of small employers. Thus, the design and maintenance of employee benefit plans must meet the requirements of federal tax law, antidiscrimination laws, securities laws, labor laws, and state insurance laws. In several areas, state as well as federal laws must be taken into account. Thus, an implicit, if not explicit, objective of any employee benefit plan is that it must comply with these legal requirements.

However, an employer often has a choice in the manner in which compliance is achieved and, in some cases, may avoid compliance requirements by the design of the plan. For this reason, it is desirable that the employer formulate specific objectives in this regard. The following examples should give at least some indication of areas where compliance choices are available.

1. The Age Discrimination in Employment Act prevents discrimination in employment up to age 70. However, this does not require all benefit plans to treat all employees alike, regardless of age. It is possible, for example, to reduce life insurance coverage for active employees by reason of age (but only within cost-justified limits). It also is possible to terminate pension accruals in a defined benefit plan after an active employee has attained age 65 and to freeze the employee's benefit to what would have been payable at normal retirement age. An employer should establish basic objectives on how its over-65, active employees will be treated and whether compliance with this law should be at or above the minimum level. The employer's decision, of course, is influenced by other objectives and attitudes, such as whether it is desirable to encourage earlier or deferred retirements, its public relations posture, and the like.

2. Federal tax law permits the exclusion from a defined benefit pension plan of employees who have less than one year of service, who are under age 25, or who have been employed within five years of the plan's normal retirement age. Employers may include all employees in their plans or may seek to exclude the maximum number possible, depending upon their attitude on minimum compliance and other objectives.

3. An employer may wish to establish a defined pension plan that includes incentive compensation for executives as part of the compensation base used to determine plan benefits but may not want to include overtime pay and shift differential paid to other employees. It is unlikely the Internal Revenue Service would approve such a pay definition in a qualified pension plan. Compliance with the nondiscrimination requirements of federal tax law could be satisfied by designing the qualified plan with a compensation definition that relates to base pay only, and by instituting a nonqualified, supplemental executive retirement plan (SERP) that applies the base plan formula to incentive pay.

4. A savings plan can be designed so that some part of both employer and

employee contributions can be invested in employer securities. Securities and Exchange Commission (SEC) requirements are such that the plan will have to be registered before employee contributions may be invested in this manner. These requirements can be avoided if employer securities can be purchased only by employer contributions.

Achieving Optimum Tax Benefits

Federal tax law is such that many advantages exist for distributions from employee benefit plans. This is particularly so in the case of tax-qualified retirement and profit-sharing plans. For example: (1) investment income on plan assets is not taxed until it is distributed in the form of a benefit; and (2) qualifying lump-sum distributions are accorded special and favorable tax treatment. Indeed, on the one hand these tax advantages very often are the motivating force behind the adoption of a plan—particularly in the case of a small employer. Larger employers, on the other hand, are not as apt to give a high priority to achieving optimum tax advantages for plan distributions. Since these plans cover large groups of employees, the employer's objectives more often are oriented toward benefit levels and costs.

If an employer wishes to achieve maximum tax advantages for a retirement program, this can find expression in many areas—for example, the choice of benefit formula, the degree to which the plan is integrated with Social Security benefits, the level of funding chosen, the funding instrument chosen, the adoption of both a defined benefit and a defined contribution plan, the use of a target benefit plan, permitting voluntary employee contributions, and so on.

The desire to maximize tax advantages also may affect other benefits and how they are funded. For example, a preretirement spouse benefit may be included as part of a retirement plan, or it may be funded by a separate group term life insurance program. If funded by life insurance, most of the benefit payments will escape income tax; however, the annual cost of insurance can represent taxable income to the employees under Section 79 of the Internal Revenue Code.[3] Also, the benefit may be includable in the employee's estate for estate tax purposes if rights of ownership exist and have not been assigned more than three years prior to death. If the benefit is provided from retirement plan assets, the payments represent taxable income (except to the extent provided by employee contributions), but there will be no annual cost of insurance to be reported by the employee. Also, the value of a typical spouse benefit will qualify for the unlimited estate tax marital deduction. The emphasis to be placed on these various tax

---

[3] Life insurance proceeds generally are income-tax free. However, if paid in installments, the portion representing interest payments will be taxable, subject to a spouse's ability to exclude $1,000 of such payments from income each year.

considerations and the characteristics of the employee group involved influence the choice of how the benefit will be funded.

As mentioned earlier, lump-sum distributions from a pension plan can qualify for favorable tax treatment. This could be very important for highly paid employees, and a desire to achieve maximum tax advantages could lead to the inclusion, in a retirement plan, of a provision that allows such lump-sum distributions. However, since the option also would have to be extended to all employees, consideration needs to be given to possible misuse of this feature by some employees and whether this could defeat overall plan objectives.

Efficiency of Design

The overall cost of employee benefits is quite substantial and, as noted earlier, can amount to one third or more of an employer's payroll costs. For this reason, it is important for an employer to structure its employee benefit program so benefits are provided in the most efficient manner possible and overlapping or redundant benefits are eliminated or, at least, minimized.

One of the most effective ways of doing this is to recognize that while any particular benefit plan has a primary focus (e.g., retirement, death, or disability), all benefit plans and some statutory plans must function in some fashion in the case of an event covered primarily by another plan. For example, the primary plan dealing with retirement is, of course, the employer's retirement plan. However, Social Security can be a major source of additional retirement income. Supplemental retirement income also can be provided by the employer's savings or profit-sharing plan if such a plan is in existence. The employer's group life insurance and medical-expense plans may be the source of additional benefits for a retired employee. Viewing all these plans as a total retirement program can influence the choice of specific benefits and benefit levels. Thus, the existence of significant amounts of postretirement life insurance might suggest that, except for legally required joint and survivor protection, the normal form for payment of retirement benefits exclude any form of death benefit, such as a guarantee that benefits will be paid for a minimum period of time; otherwise, excessive or redundant postretirement death benefits might be provided.

The same approach can be applied to the events of preretirement death and disability. The primary plan in the event of preretirement death is the employer's group life insurance plan. However, additional death benefits may be provided by way of continuation of medical-expense coverage for the employee's dependents and, of course, the retirement plan may provide for additional life insurance or survivor income benefits. Social Security also can be a source of substantial survivor benefits, as can a profit-sharing or savings plan. In the case of disability, a need exists to coordinate the benefits available from the employer's plan (life insurance, short- and long-term disability income plans, savings and profit-sharing plans, and medical-expense plans) with those available from Social Security. Again, efficient plan design suggests the benefits from all these sources be coordinated to insure overall benefits in line with employer objectives.

Income-Replacement Ratios

Employer objectives as to income-replacement ratios are critical in the design of disability income and retirement plans.

In the case of disability income plans, the issues are not as complex. The benefit usually is not service-related (although some plans are), and it is generally designed to replace a percentage of current pay. There are no restrictions on the ability of a plan to integrate with Social Security benefits, and it is customary to offset 100 percent of the employee's primary Social Security disability benefit. In fact, most plans offset 100 percent of the total Social Security benefit payable, including family benefits. In general, the plan formula recognizes that Social Security benefits and some part or all of the plan benefits may be income-tax free, and that total aftertax income should provide adequate maintenance while at the same time creating an economic incentive for the employee to rehabilitate and return to active work. A typical formula might provide for a total gross before-tax benefit (including Social Security) of 50 to 60 percent of current pay.

Establishing income-replacement objectives for a retirement plan is more complex. Before selecting a specific benefit formula, it is important for an employer to identify the amount of an employee's gross income to be replaced by the retirement plan and under what circumstances.

From the employee's viewpoint, it would be desirable to have a situation where total retirement income permits the full maintenance of the standard of living the employee enjoyed just prior to retirement. For most employees, some or part of this income consists of Social Security benefits. Indeed, for employees at lower-income levels, a substantial portion of preretirement gross income will be replaced by Social Security benefits. This is illustrated by Table 1–1, which shows estimated Social Security benefits at different final pay levels for both a single individual and a married couple, assuming the employee (and spouse) are both age 65 at the beginning of 1983. As can be seen, the replacement ratios, relative to gross pay, can be as high as 51 percent for an individual whose final pay is $10,000 (77 percent for the married couple). At a final pay level of $20,000, Social Security can replace as much as 40 percent (60 percent for a married couple). Even at $32,000, the replacement ratio is 27 percent for a single individual (40 percent for a married couple). As is discussed later, the aftertax replacement ratios are even more significant.

An employee's personal savings, including equity in a home, also can be a source of retirement income. Also, many employers maintain supplemental profit-sharing and savings plans which can be a source of additional income.

Table 1–1
Social Security Replacement Ratios
(1983 retirement)

Final Pay*	Social Security Benefit as a Percentage of Final Pay	
	Single	Married Couple
$10,000	51%	77%
12,000	48	72
14,000	46	69
16,000	44	66
18,000	42	63
20,000	40	60
24,000	35	52
28,000	30	45
32,000	27	40

* Assumes pay has grown at the rate of 7 percent a year.

In the absence of any such plan, however, it must be recognized that many individuals will not be able to save meaningful amounts of money to assist in meeting their retirement needs.

Another factor that should be considered in setting income-replacement ratios is that some reduction in gross income can take place without causing a significant reduction in a retiree's standard of living. Tax considerations are one reason why this is so. First, a retired employee is no longer paying a Social Security tax (unless he or she is in receipt of earned income). Moreover, Social Security benefits are income-tax free except, beginning in 1984, for retirees with relatively high income. In addition, double federal tax exemptions are provided for individuals 65 or over. Finally, retirement income is not subject to state or local taxes in many jurisdictions.

Another reason why some reduction in gross income can be tolerated is the removal of work-related expenses, such as commutation costs, the expense of maintaining a second car, lunch and clothing costs, and so on.[4] Also, many retired individuals no longer face the costs associated with child-rearing (food, clothing, education, and the like) and many will have reduced housing costs because of the completion of mortgage payments and, in some localities, reduced real estate taxes.

With factors such as these in mind, most employers establish income-replacement objectives which generate something less than a 100 percent replacement of full preretirement gross income. Typically, these income-

---

[4] While it is difficult to estimate work-related expenses in any definitive way, it is interesting to note that the President's Commission on Pension Policy, in its Interim Report of May 1980, estimated these expenses to be 6 percent of aftertax preretirement income.

replacement objectives are set with several factors in mind:

1. They usually take full primary Social Security benefits into account.

2. The objectives usually are higher for lower-paid employees than for higher-paid employees.

3. The objectives usually are set for the employee's pay level during the final year of employment or over a three- or five-year average just prior to retirement when the employee's earnings are highest.

4. Full income-replacement objectives are set only for individuals who have completed what the employer considers to be a "career" of employment; individuals who have less than this amount of service with the employer have objectives proportionately reduced.

A few comments are appropriate for each of these points.

As indicated earlier, Social Security benefits can be of great importance to individuals at lower income levels, and they take on added significance since they are income-tax free. Further, the employer has shared in the cost of providing these Social Security benefits. Thus, even though the particular pension formula for the employer's plan may not directly reflect Social Security benefits, the accrual rates chosen can be designed to produce a net plan benefit which, when added to the employee's primary Social Security benefit, produces the desired result.[5]

At one time, it was not uncommon for an employer to have a single income-replacement objective for employees at all pay levels. However, it was soon recognized that lower-income employees need a higher level of income-replacement simply because of minimum income needs. Moreover, it was reasoned that higher-paid employees could accept lower income amounts without incurring a major reduction in living standards.

Most defined benefit plans utilize an employee's final average pay to determine benefit amounts. Typically, this is a five-year average, although there has been some trend toward the use of a three-year average. It is common for employers who have such a plan to state their income-replacement objectives in terms of the pay base used in the plan. Some employers, however, actually set objectives in terms of the employee's pay in the final year of employment, with the result that the plan benefit, when expressed as a percentage of the final average pay used in the plan, is somewhat higher than the employer's actual objective. It also should be noted employers who adopt career-pay plans or who adopt defined contribution plans often do so with final-pay income-replacement objectives in mind. Those that use career-pay plans frequently "update" accrued career-pay benefits to reflect current pay levels and to move benefits closer to objectives. Those with defined contribution plans find it more difficult to make such adjustments

---

[5] It is not customary to take the spouse's Social Security benefit into account in setting objectives. To do so would be difficult since a direct recognition of this benefit would not be permitted by the Internal Revenue Service, and to approximate its value on an across-the-board basis would result in inequities between employees who have a spouse and those who do not.

but often so set contribution levels that, under reasonable expectations for salary growth and investment return, final pay objectives might be achieved. Unfortunately, the inherent nature of defined contribution plans is that, in most situations, these objectives will either be exceeded or not met at all.

Understandably, most employers do not feel an obligation to provide a full level of benefits to short-service employees. Thus, it is common practice to set objectives and design benefit formulas so that proportionately smaller benefits are provided for those individuals who work for an employer for less than what the employer considers to be a reasonable career. The number of years involved, of course, varies from employer to employer and reflects the nature of the employer's business and the degree of maturity it has achieved. However, periods of from 25 to 35 years are common.

Table 1-2
Illustrative Income-Replacement Objectives
(employee with 30 years of service)

Final Pay	Retirement Income as a Percentage of Final Pay*
Under $15,000	80%–70%
$15,000 to $25,000	75 –65
25,000 to 35,000	70 –60
35,000 to 50,000	65 –55
Over $50,000	60 –50

* Including primary Social Security benefits.

With these factors in mind, Table 1-2 sets forth a typical set of income-replacement objectives. These objectives are merely examples. What is appropriate for one employer may be inappropriate for another and, in any event, what one employer might adopt as objectives necessarily must reflect that employer's own philosophy and environment.

Other Objectives

The foregoing has discussed some of the major employer objectives associated with employee benefit plans. Other employer objectives also play an important role in plan design. Some of these additional objectives are discussed below.

Social Obligations. Many employers feel a strong sense of social responsibility to their employees and to society in general. The adoption of adequate and meaningful employee benefit plans is a form of meeting this responsibility.

Employee Incentives. It would be a rare employer who is not interested in improving employee productivity. Profit-sharing plans and plans that involve ownership of employer securities are plans that can create employee incentives and, as a result, improve productivity. Beyond this, employee morale is an important factor that can influence productivity. As noted earlier, the presence of employee benefit plans may not be a positive force in recruiting and retaining employees, and they may not be a positive factor in creating improved morale. However, their absence could be a negative influence and, for this reason, most employers believe a benefit program, along with other compensation and personnel practices, is an important factor in maintaining employee morale at a proper level.

Corporate Identification. It may be desirable to have employees identify with overall employer business objectives. This might be accomplished by having employees acquire an ownership interest in the firm. Profit-sharing plans, savings plans, and employee stock-ownership plans can achieve this objective. By having all or part of an employee's account invested in employer securities, the employee is made aware of progress of the company and the importance of achieving satisfactory profit results. The employee also can have the opportunity to vote the shares credited to his or her account; and the employer has the additional opportunity of being able to communicate with the employee as a shareholder by sending annual reports, proxy statements, and the like.

Administrative Convenience. Generally, it is desirable that employee benefit plans be designed so that administrative involvement and cost are kept to a reasonable minimum. This objective has become especially important with increasing government regulations and requirements and as design and funding choices become greater and more complex. In this regard, employers should be aware of their own administrative capabilities, as well as those available from external sources. Also, while it is desirable to hold administrative costs to a minimum, these costs are not the most significant element of total plan costs. Thus, good plan design should not be sacrificed for the objective of holding down administrative costs.

CHAPTER 2

Functional Approach to Employee Benefits

G. VICTOR HALLMAN III

This chapter deals with the functional approach toward analyzing an existing employee benefit program and evaluating the need for new employee benefits. The functional approach can be defined as an organized system for classifying and analyzing the risks and needs of active employees, their dependents, and various other categories of persons into logical categories of exposures to loss and employee needs. These exposures and needs may include: medical expenses, losses resulting from death, losses caused by short- and long-term disabilities, retirement income needs, capital accumulation needs, needs arising out of short- and long-term unemployment, and other employee needs.

THE FUNCTIONAL APPROACH IN CONCEPT

As indicated above, the functional approach essentially is the application of a systematic method of analysis to an employer's total employee benefits program. It analyzes the employer's employee benefits program as a coordinated whole in terms of its ability to meet various employees' (and others') needs and loss exposures within the employer's overall compensation goals and cost parameters. This approach can be useful in overall employee benefit plan design, in evaluating proposals for new or revised benefits, for evaluation of cost-saving proposals, and in effective communication of an employer's total benefits program to its employees.

The functional approach to employee benefits is not really a new concept. In 1967, George C. Foust outlined the functional approach in the American Management Association book entitled *The Total Approach to Employee Benefits.*[1] Similarly, Robert M. McCaffery in his 1972 work on *Managing the Employee Benefits Program* stated:

---

[1] George C. Foust, Jr., "The Total Approach Concept," in *The Total Approach to Employee Benefits,* ed., Arthur J. Deric (New York: American Management Association, 1967), chap. 1.

The "package" or total approach to employee benefits is simply the purposeful management of an integrated program. Rather than continually reacting to current fads, outside pressures, and salesmen's pitches, the contemporary businessman relies on fundamental principles of management in developing, organizing, directing, and evaluating systems of employee benefits for his organization.[2]

The functional approach represents such systematic management of the employee benefits function.

NEED FOR THE FUNCTIONAL APPROACH

The functional approach is needed in planning, designing, and administering employee benefits for several reasons.

First, in most instances, employee benefits are a very significant element of the total compensation of employees. They have become an important part of the work rewards provided by employers to their employees. Therefore, it is important to employees, and hence their employers, that this increasingly important element of compensation be planned and organized so as to be as effective as possible in meeting employee needs.

Second, employee benefits currently represent a large item of labor cost for employers. Depending on the industry, the particular employer, and how employee benefits are defined, benefits may range from less than 18 percent to over 65 percent of an employer's payroll. Therefore, effective planning and hence avoidance of waste in providing benefits can be an important cost-control measure for employers.

Third, employee benefits, in the past, often were adopted by employers on a piecemeal basis without being coordinated with existing employee benefit programs. Thus, some benefit plans just "grew like Topsy." For this reason, it usually is fruitful to apply the functional approach in reviewing existing employee benefit plans to determine where overlapping benefits may exist and costs can be saved, and where gaps in benefits may exist and new benefits or revised benefits may be in order.

Fourth, since new benefits and coverages, changes in the tax laws, changes in the regulatory environment, and other developments in employee benefit planning have come about so rapidly in recent years, it is necessary to have a systematic approach to planning benefits to keep an employer's program in order.

Finally, a given employee benefit or program, such as a pension plan, often provides benefits relating to several separate employee needs or loss exposures. Therefore, an employer's benefit plan needs to be analyzed according to the functional approach so its various benefit programs can be integrated properly with each other.

---

[2] Robert M. McCaffery, *Managing the Employee Benefits Program* (New York: American Management Association, 1972), p. 17.

CONSISTENCY WITH AN EMPLOYER'S TOTAL COMPENSATION PHILOSOPHY

In designing its total compensation package, an employer should seek to balance the various elements of its compensation system, including basic cash wages and salary, current incentive compensation (current cash bonuses and company stock plans), and so-called employee benefits, to help meet the needs and desires of the employees on the one hand and the employer's basic compensation philosophy and objectives on the other. Thus, it is clear the functional approach to planning and designing an employee benefit plan must remain consistent with the employer's total compensation philosophy. A particular employer, therefore, may not cover a particular employee desire for benefits, or may cover it in a rather spartan manner, not because the desire is not recognized but because the employer's total compensation philosophy calls for a relatively low level of employee benefits or, perhaps, benefits oriented in a different direction.

Employers may adopt different business policies regarding the general compensation of their employees. For example, many employers want to compensate their employees at a level about in line with that generally prevailing in their industry or community, or both. They do not wish to be much above or below average compensation levels. The employee benefit programs of such employers also frequently follow this general philosophy. Other employers may follow a high-compensation philosophy (including employee benefits) with the goal of attempting to attract higher levels of management, technical, and general employee talent. This may be particularly true in industries where the need for a highly skilled workforce is relatively great. On the other hand, there may be employers which follow a low-compensation policy, feeling that, for them, the resultant lower payroll costs more than outweigh the resulting higher employee turnover and lower skill level of their workforce. An employer with this kind of philosophy also may want to adopt more modest employee benefit programs.

Type of industry and employer characteristics also will have an impact on an employer's total compensation philosophy and on the design of its employee benefit plan. Figure 2–1 is a grid presented by one employee benefit consulting firm showing the relationship between type of organization, working climate, and compensation mix.

Thus, a larger well-established employer in a mature industry, a financial institution, or a nonprofit organization may take a relatively liberal approach toward meeting the benefits needs and desires of its employees. But developing industrial firms and other growth companies, which may have considerable current needs for capital, may seek to rely more heavily on short-term-oriented incentive types of compensation. Further, industries that are highly competitive, subject to cyclical fluctuations, or perhaps in a currently depressed state, may not be willing to add to their relatively fixed labor costs by adopting or liberalizing employee benefits, even if there may

Figure 2-1
Organizational Style and Compensation Mix

Type of Organization	Working Climate	Reward Management Components				
		Cash		Noncash		
		Base Salary	Short-Term Incentives	Level	Characteristics	
Mature Industrial	Balanced	Medium	Medium	Medium	Balanced	
Developing Industrial	Growth, Creativity	Medium	High	Low	Short-Term Oriented	
Conservative Financial	Security	Low	Low	High	Long-Term, Security-Oriented	
Nonprofit	Societal Impact, Personal Fulfillment	Low	None	Low to Medium	Long-Term, Security-Oriented	
Sales	Growth, Freedom to Act	Low	High	Low	Short-Term Oriented	

Source: Hay-Huggins, member of the Hay Group.

be a functional need for them. In fact, such firms may seek to cut back on their employee benefit commitments when possible. However, even in these situations firms should attempt to allocate their available compensation dollars in as consistent and logical a manner as possible to meet the needs and goals of their employees as well as their own corporate compensation objectives. In fact, the functional approach may be even more appropriate in such cases because their resources for compensating employees are relatively scarce.

Another area of employer philosophy that affects the functional approach and how it is actually applied is whether the employer tends to follow a compensation/service-oriented benefit philosophy or a benefit- or needs-oriented philosophy. Employers having a compensation/service-oriented philosophy tend to relate employee benefits primarily to compensation or service, or both, in designing their employee benefit plans. Thus, the level of benefits would tend to be tied in with compensation level, and eligibility for benefits may be conditioned directly or indirectly on salary level. For example, separate benefit plans may be provided for salaried and for hourly rated employees with more generous benefits being made available to the former group. Further, some types of benefits may be available only to certain higher-paid employees or executives. In addition, such employers tend to emphasize service with the employer in determining benefit levels and eligibility for benefits. The theory of this approach is that employee benefits generally should be aimed to reward the longer-service employees who have shown a commitment to the employer. The benefit- or needs-oriented philosophy, on the other hand, tends to focus primarily on the needs of employees and their dependents rather than on compensation and service.

In practice, the design of employee benefit plans tends to be a compromise between these two philosophies. On one side, certain kinds of employee benefits, such as medical expense benefits, tend to be primarily benefit- or needs-oriented. On the other side, benefits like group life insurance and pensions customarily are compensation-oriented, at least for nonunion employees. Thus, this distinction in philosophy really is one of degree. However, the extent to which eligibility for benefits, participation requirements, and levels of employee benefits reflect compensation or service, or both, may affect the extent to which the needs of employees or certain categories of employees will be met by an employee benefit plan.

APPLICATION OF THE FUNCTIONAL APPROACH

While the functional approach to planning employee benefits has been actively discussed since the early 1960s, no clearly developed procedure or technique exists for the application of this approach to individual benefit plans. However, based on the underlying concept and the way it is applied in practice, the following are the logical steps in applying the functional approach to employee benefit plan design, revision, or review. For convenience of presentation, these steps can be listed as follows:

1. Classify employee (and dependent) needs or objectives in logical functional categories.
2. Classify the categories of persons (e.g., employees, some former employees, and dependents) the employer may want to protect, at least to some extent, through its employee benefit plan.
3. Analyze the benefits presently available under the plan in terms of the functional categories of needs or objectives and in terms of the categories of persons the employer may want to benefit.
4. Determine any gaps in benefits or overlapping benefits, or both, provided from *all* sources under the employer's employee benefit plan and from other benefit plans in terms of the functional categories of needs and the persons to be protected.
5. Consider recommendations for changes in the employer's present employee benefit plan to meet any gaps in benefits and to correct any overlapping benefits.
6. Estimate the costs or savings from each of the recommendations made in step 5.
7. Evaluate alternative methods of financing or securing the benefits recommended above, as well as the employee benefit plan's existing benefits.
8. Consider other cost-saving techniques in connection with the recommended benefits or existing benefits.
9. Decide upon the appropriate benefits, methods of financing, and sources of benefits as a result of the preceding analysis.
10. Implement the changes.
11. Communicate benefit changes to employees.
12. Periodically reevaluate the employee benefit plan.

Each of these steps is considered in greater detail below. Naturally, it must be recognized in applying this process to a particular employee benefit plan that some of these steps may be combined with others and some will be taken implicitly. However, each step represents a logical decision-point or consideration in the design or revision of an employee benefit plan.

Classify Employee and Dependent Needs in Functional Categories

The needs and exposures to loss of employees, their dependents, and certain others can be classified in a variety of ways, some being more complete than others. The following classification appears to cover most of the commonly accepted needs and exposures to loss that may be covered under an employee benefit plan:

1. Medical expenses incurred by active employees, by their dependents, by retired (or certain otherwise terminated or suspended) former employees, and by their dependents.
2. Losses due to employees' disability (short-term and long-term).
3. Losses resulting from active employees' deaths, from their dependents' deaths, and from the deaths of retired (or certain otherwise terminated or suspended) former employees.
4. Retirement needs of employees and their dependents.
5. Capital accumulation needs or goals (short-term and long-term).
6. Needs arising from unemployment or from temporary termination or suspension of employment.
7. Needs for financial counseling, retirement counseling, and other counseling services.
8. Losses resulting from property and liability exposures, needs for legal services, and the like.
9. Needs for child-care services.
10. Needs for educational assistance for employees themselves or for employees' dependents, or for both.
11. Other employee benefit needs.

Naturally, a given functional analysis often does not encompass all these needs or loss exposures. The above classification is intended to be more exhaustive than frequently is included in a functional analysis. However, the history of employee benefit planning, particularly since the end of World War II, has been one of continually expanding the areas of employees' (and others') needs for which the employer is providing benefits of various kinds. It seems likely, therefore, that additional categories of needs and loss exposures will be added to the above list from time to time. Also, some of those needs and exposures mentioned only incidentally above may become more important in the future.

Figure 2–2 provides an illustration of the functional approach to employee benefit planning, using the employee benefit plan of a large corporation and the functional categories used by that corporation. Note that the employee needs and exposures to loss are shown on the left-hand margin of the grid while the components of this corporation's employee benefit plan are shown across the top of the grid. This arrangement thus shows how each benefit plan applies to each of these employee needs or loss exposures. Any gaps or duplications in coverage (or need for further information) can be seen more easily through this systematic process of analysis.

Classify by Categories the Persons the Employer May Want to Protect

This step basically involves the issues of who should be protected by an employee benefit plan, for what benefits, for what time period, and under

Figure 2–2
Illustration of Functional Approach to Employee Benefit Planning

Employee Needs or Exposures to Loss	Health Care Plan	Basic Salary Continuation Plan	Extended Salary Continuation Plan	Long Term Disability Plan	Primary Life Insurance Plan	Basic Life Insurance Plan
Medical expenses	Provides comprehensive coverage of hospital and medical bills for employee and employee's eligible dependents					
Disability losses	Coverage continues while employee receives disability benefits under company plans	Up to 30 days of paid absence each year for illness or injury	After the basic allowance is exhausted, employee's full salary less offsetting benefits is maintained up to a maximum of 25 months depending on length of service	After extended allowance ends, 75 percent of employee's base monthly pay less offsetting benefits is maintained for a maximum of 25 months; 50 percent thereafter depending on length of service	Coverage continues while employee receives disability benefits under company plans	Coverage continues while employee receives disability benefits under company plans
In case of death	Dependent coverage continues for four months after employee's death. Dependents then have the option to convert the base plan to a nongroup policy	Coverage terminates	Coverage terminates	Coverage terminates	Provides beneficiary with a benefit of three times employee's current annual base pay. Employee also has the option to purchase additional life insurance at favorable group rates, up to three times current base pay	Provides beneficiary with a benefit of 3,000 dollars
Retirement	Portions of coverage continue if employee retires under the company pension plan	Coverage terminates	Coverage terminates	Coverage terminates	Continues after retirement with the amount and duration of coverage depending on the option employee chooses	3,000 dollars coverage continues after retirement under the company pension plan for as long as employee lives
Capital accumulation						

Travel Accident Insurance Plan	Savings Plan	Employees' Stock Purchase Plan	Retirement Plan	Social Security	Workers' Compensation	Supplemental Workers' Compensation	State Disability Benefits
					Pays if illness or injury is job-related under the workers' compensation laws		
Pays a benefit of up to three times employee's annual base pay if disability involves an accidental dismemberment while traveling on company business	Contributions are discontinued when long-term disability benefits begin. Participation may continue unless employee becomes permanently and totally disabled or until formal retirement. Withdrawals are permitted	Employee receiving disability benefits may suspend any payments being made to the plan for a period not to exceed six months nor a specified date in the offering	Participation continues while employee is receiving disability benefits under company plans. Service credits accumulate until the end of the extended disability period or three months, whichever is longer	Pays after five months of continuous total disability when approved by Social Security	Pays if disability is job-related under the workers' compensation laws	Increases disability income if employee receives workers' compensation benefits	Employee may receive supplemental disability income if the state of employment has a statutory disability benefit plan
Pays beneficiary a lump sum benefit of three times employee's annual base pay if death is the result of an accident while traveling on company business.	Beneficiary receives the amount credited to employee's account	Payment is made of any amount being accumulated during a "purchase period" with interest	Active employees: Employees age 55 or older may elect a preretirement survivor's benefit which covers their spouses if they die before actual retirement. For other employees coverage terminates. Hired employees: At retirement retiree may elect a pension option which will provide pension benefits to retiree's beneficiary in the event of retiree's death	Pays a lump sum death benefit and monthly survivor income to spouse and children	Pays if death is job-related under the workers' compensation laws	Coverage terminates	
Coverage terminates	Employee will receive the balance in the plan account upon retirement	Stock purchased under plan and owned by employees is, of course, available to them at retirement as well as before retirement. Retired former employees are not eligible to participate in future offerings	Pays regular retirement benefits at age 65 or reduced benefits as early as age 55	Pays regular retirement benefits at age 65 or reduced benefit as early as 62. In addition, health care expenses may be covered under Medicare	Coverage terminates in accordance with the workers' compensation laws	Coverage terminates	
	Balance in employee's account and employer/employee contributions accumulate. Employer contributions and investment earnings on balance of account are not currently taxable as income to employees. Employees may contribute up to 6 percent of salary and employer will contribute from 25 percent to 50 percent of the employee's contribution depending upon service	Eligible employees periodically can purchase specified amounts of company stock, based on their salary, at the lesser of 85 percent of the stock price when the offering is commenced or 85 percent of the price at the end of any purchase period. Payment for stock is in installments during each purchase period					

what conditions. These issues have become increasingly important in employee benefit planning as the scope of employee benefit plans has increased not only in terms of the benefits provided but also in terms of continuing to protect employees once the formal employment relationship has ended and of protecting dependents of employees in a variety of circumstances. It is a logical part of the functional approach since the needs and loss exposures of employees imply consideration not only of the kinds of benefits to be provided but also of the persons to be protected and when they will be protected. Thus, in designing its employee benefit plan the employer also should consider how the various functional categories of needs and goals will be met for different categories of persons under a variety of circumstances.

In this type of analysis, the following are among the categories of persons whom the employer may or may not want to protect under its employee benefit plan—under at least some circumstances and benefits:

1. Active full-time employees.
2. Dependents of active full-time employees.
3. Retired former employees.
4. Dependents of retired former employees.
5. Disabled employees and their dependents.
6. Surviving dependents of deceased employees.
7. Terminated employees and their dependents.
8. Employees (and their dependents) who are temporarily separated from the employer's service, such as during layoffs, leaves of absence, strikes, and so forth.
9. Other than full-time active employees (e.g., part-time employees, directors, and so forth).

The employer basically must decide how far it wants to extend its employee benefit program, and for what kinds of benefits, to persons who may not be active full-time employees. This represents a significant issue in employee benefit planning both in terms of adequacy of employee protection and of the cost implications for the employer. Some extensions of benefits, such as provision of group term life insurance and medical expense benefits to retirees and perhaps their dependents, can be quite expensive.

The extent to which employers may want to extend coverage of their benefit plans to one or more of these categories of persons varies with employer philosophy, cost constraints, union negotiations, and employee benefit practices in the particular industry and geographic area involved. Such extensions also vary considerably among the different kinds of benefits. For example, medical expense benefits may be extended to active employees, various categories of dependents of active employees, retired former employees, dependents of retired former employees, surviving spouses and other dependents of retired former employees, disabled employees, dependents of disabled employees, and surviving dependents of deceased active employees. Further, medical expense coverage may be provided for terminated employees, dependents of terminated employees, and dependents of active employees who no longer meet the definition of an eligible dependent under the regular employee benefit plan, through conversion of medical expense benefits to individual coverage or through the shifting of enrollment status to a direct payment basis from a group basis. Group term life insurance, however, may be provided to active full-time employees, disabled employees who meet the definition of disability under the plan, and retired employees in reduced amounts. Also, some plans provide dependents group life insurance in limited amounts to eligible dependents of active employees. At the other extreme, cash disability income benefits normally are provided only to active full-time employees.

Another factor to consider in this analysis is to what extent and on what contribution basis certain employee benefits will be provided or continued to various categories of persons. Benefits may be provided or continued without contribution by the employee or covered person in full or in a reduced amount. Or, the benefits could be provided or continued with contribution to the cost by the employee or covered person in full or on a reduced basis. Finally, benefits may be provided or continued to covered persons on an elective basis at the covered person's own cost. For example, group coverage may be converted to an individual policy or a direct payment basis by the covered person.

Analyze Benefits Presently Available

The next step in the functional approach is to analyze the benefits, terms of coverage, and plan participation by employees in terms of how well the existing or proposed employee benefit plan meets employee needs and desires in the various functional categories for those classes of persons the employer wants to protect or benefit. This step involves measuring the employee benefit plan against the objectives and coverage criteria set up for it under the functional approach outlined above.

Types of Benefits.   A common application of the functional approach to employee benefit planning is to outline the different types of benefits under an employee benefit plan that apply to each of the functional categories of employee needs and goals. This is often done in the form of a grid as shown in Figure 2–2. In that figure, for example, employee needs and exposures to loss are shown on the left-hand margin of the grid while the components of the corporation's employee benefit plan are shown across the top of the grid.

Levels of Benefits.   In a similar fashion, the levels of benefits under the various components of the employee benefit plan can be determined or shown, or both, for each of the functional categories of needs or goals.

To supplement this analysis, it may be helpful to use benefit illustrations to determine or illustrate the levels of benefits that would be provided under the various components of the employee benefit plan or proposed plan in the event of certain contingencies and using certain assumptions.

For example, it might be assumed an employee with certain earnings and using certain salary projections will retire at age 65 with 30 years of service with the employer. This employee's total retirement income then may be estimated from various components of the employer's employee benefit plan as well as from Social Security as of the assumed retirement date. This can be expressed as a percentage of the employee's estimated final pay, which often is referred to as the employee's retirement income "replacement ratio." The employee benefits used in such an analysis may include only the employer's pension plan and Social Security; but it would be more logical to include all potential sources of retirement income available through the employee benefit plan, such as a pension plan, profit-sharing plan, thrift or savings plan, supplemental executive retirement plans, and perhaps other kinds of plans or benefits intended primarily to provide capital accumulation or stock-purchase benefits. Naturally, assumptions must be made for a variety of factors if all these sources of retirement income are considered. Also, different assumptions as to employee earnings, year of retirement, final pay, years of service, and so forth may be used to test the adequacy of retirement income for employees under different conditions.

The same kind of analysis can be made for disability benefits from all sources under the employee benefit plan. When the analysis is made of disability benefits, it may be found that excessive benefits will be paid under certain conditions and for certain durations of disability, while inadequate benefits will be paid under other conditions. Thus, better coordination of disability benefits may be called for in making recommendations for changes in the plan. This approach also may prove fruitful for other employee loss exposures, such as death, medical expenses at various levels and under various conditions, and so forth. Finally, the adequacy of benefit levels can be tested for different categories of persons the employer may want to protect.

Another interesting kind of analysis in terms of benefit levels is to estimate the potential for capital accumulation available to employees under the various components of an employee benefit plan designed primarily for this purpose. These may include, for example, profit-sharing plans, thrift or savings plans, stock-purchase plans, stock options, employee stock ownership plans (ESOPs), and so forth. Employees often are pleasantly surprised to learn how much capital can be accumulated under such plans over a period even using relatively conservative investment assumptions.

In evaluating levels of benefits and benefit adequacy, consideration also may be given to optional benefits that may be available to employees under the employee benefit plan. Such options usually involve the opportunity for employees to purchase coverage or additional levels of coverage beyond a basic level of benefits. Through such optional benefits, the employer in effect is giving employees the opportunity at a given cost to themselves to make their total benefits more adequate in certain specific areas. As an example, the primary life insurance plan shown in Figure 2–2 allows eligible employees to purchase additional life insurance at favorable group rates up to three times their current base pay over and above an employer provided benefit of three times current annual base pay.

Probationary Periods. In assessing how well an existing employee benefit plan meets the needs and loss exposures of employees and certain other individuals, it also is helpful to analyze the probationary periods required for the various types of benefits contained in the plan. Such probationary periods, or the length of service otherwise eligible employees must have with the employer before they become eligible to participate in the various types of benefits, will have an effect on the plan's protection for employees, their dependents, and possibly others. The longer the probationary period required, the greater is the exposure of employees and others to a loss not covered by the plan. But, many employers believe only employees with certain minimum periods of service, and hence demonstrable connection with the employer, should be eligible for at least certain types of benefits.

Probationary periods by their nature create gaps in coverage for newly hired or newly eligible employees and their dependents. Thus, probationary periods should be analyzed as part of the functional approach to determine whether the resulting gaps in coverage are appropriate and consistent with the employer's objectives and the employees' needs.

It seems desirable that the use of probationary periods in an employee benefit plan should be based on a reasonably consistent employer philosophy. One possible philosophy in this regard is to divide employee benefits into "protection-oriented" benefits and "accumulation-oriented" benefits. *Protection-oriented* benefits would consist of medical expense benefits, life insurance benefits, short- and long-term disability benefits, and so forth. These benefits protect employees and their dependents against serious loss exposures which, if they were to occur, could spell immediate financial disaster for the employees or their dependents, or both. For such benefits, where the need/protection orientation is great, there might be no probationary period, or a relatively short probationary period. The rationale for this would be that the need for immediate coverage would overcome the traditional reasons for using probationary periods or longer probationary periods. *Accumulation-oriented* benefits, such as pension plans, profit-sharing plans, thrift plans, stock-bonus plans, stock-purchase plans, and so forth, could involve relatively long probationary periods if desired by the employer. The theory might be that these kinds of benefits should be a reward for relatively long service with the employer. Also, an employee who stays with the employer would have a relatively long time in which to accumulate such benefits and thus longer probationary periods would not really place the employee at any serious disadvantage or risk.

Eligibility Requirements. Requirements for eligibility for benefits, including definitions of covered persons, obviously affect those who may benefit from or be protected by various employee benefits. In this area, for example, the employer and union—or unions—with whom the employer negotiates should consider such issues as:

1. Which dependents of active employees (and perhaps dependents of retired former employees, disabled employees, and deceased employees—see 2, 3, 4, and 5 below) should be covered for medical expense benefits?
2. Should retirees (and perhaps their spouses and other dependents) continue to be covered and, if so, for what benefits?
3. Should survivors of deceased active employees continue to be covered and, if so, for what benefits and for how long?
4. Should survivors of retired former employees continue to be covered and, if so, for what benefits?
5. Should employees or former employees on disability (and perhaps their dependents) continue to be covered and, if so, for what benefits, how long, and under what conditions?
6. Should coverage be extended to employees during layoffs, leaves of absence, strikes, and other temporary interruptions of employment and, if so, for what benefits, how long, and under what conditions?
7. Should coverage be limited only to full-time employees (or employees meeting ERISA requirements) or should coverage or some coverage be extended to part-time employees as well?
8. What coverage should or must be continued or made available to persons after termination of their employment with the employer (or for the dependents of such persons) and on what basis?

The resolution of some of these issues depends in part on statutory or other legal requirements, insurance company underwriting rules, collective bargaining agreements, and similar factors. However, the philosophy or rationale of the employer and union concerning the employee benefit program will have a substantial impact on how some of these coverage and eligibility issues are resolved. At the heart of many of these issues is the basic question of how far should an employer (or union) feel obligated to go, either legally or morally, in meeting the various needs and loss exposures of its employees, their dependents, and persons who once were employees or dependents of employees but who now have various other relationships with the employer.

Employee Contribution Requirements.   If certain employee benefits under an employer's employee benefit plan are contributory (i.e., the employees or possibly their dependents must contribute to the cost of the benefit), this will have an impact on employee participation and hence on how well the plan meets the needs of the employee group as a whole. This really represents a trade-off: between the financing and other advantages of a contributory plan and the loss of employee participation in the plan, which results from requiring employee contributions, assuming employee participation in the contributory plan is voluntary. Thus, an employer, and union if the plan is negotiated, must decide whether a particular employee benefit will be noncontributory or contributory, and, if it is to be contributory, how much the employees will have to contribute toward the cost of the plan. Further, if the plan is contributory, the employer (and union) will have to decide whether participation will be voluntary or whether it will be mandatory as a condition of employment. Making a contributory plan mandatory solves the employee participation problem, but it may well create serious employee relations problems. Therefore, employers generally do not have contributory plans that are mandatory.

In the context of this cost/employee participation trade-off, one approach toward helping make this decision is to rank employee benefits in terms of the relative degree to which the employer feels that all employees and their dependents should be protected, and hence that the plan should aim for 100 percent participation, compared with plans where such a high level of participation is not deemed essential. This same kind of analysis also might be helpful in determining the level of employee contribution if it is decided to have the plan be contributory. Another factor bearing on this decision is whether other benefits in the employer's overall plan also may be available to meet the same functional need. For example, employee benefit plans frequently contain a number of kinds of benefits intended to help provide retirement income for employees. Still another factor to consider is the extent to which employees or their dependents, or both, may have similar benefits available to them elsewhere. Those employees or dependents who have an alternative source of similar benefits may opt not to participate if the plan is made contributory, thereby helping to avoid duplication of benefits. An example of this is the availability of multiple plans of medical expense benefits when both a husband and wife are employed outside the home.

There has been a trend over the years toward eliminating or reducing the extent of employee contributions to the cost of many employee benefits. As part of its benefit planning system, it will be helpful for an employer to make a benefit-by-benefit analysis, within the context of its overall benefit and compensation philosophy, to evaluate the desirability of any employee (and possibly dependent) contributions to the cost of the various employee benefits.

Flexibility Available to Employees.   The degree to which employees have flexibility in making such choices as whether they will participate in a given employee benefit; the amounts of additional coverage they may wish to purchase; the opportunity to select from among two or more alternative plans of benefits; and even the opportunity to structure their own benefit program, as under a cafeteria compensation approach, for example, clearly has an impact on the extent to which employees may tailor an employee benefit plan to meet their own needs and goals within the functional categories described previously. In fact, it may be argued that the more flexibility employees have, the more likely it is that the benefit program they select will meet their individual needs and goals. It thus can be argued, on the one hand, that flexibility in employee benefit plan design should facilitate the goals of the functional approach to employee benefit planning. On the other hand, it also can be argued that allowing too much employee flexibility in choosing types and amounts of employee benefits may work against the functional approach, because employees may misperceive or not understand their and their families' needs and hence leave some uncovered. This concern often is addressed in employee benefit planning by limiting the choices of employees or by specifying a core of benefits which are not subject to employee choice.

A distinct trend exists toward giving employees more flexibility in the structuring of their own employee benefits. As discussed above, this trend probably buttresses the functional approach, in that it may be presumed that rational employees will opt for those benefits and benefit amounts that will best meet their individual needs and goals.

Actual Employee Participation in Benefit Plans. It was noted above that under the functional approach an employer may analyze the types of benefits provided to employees and their dependents according to the various functional categories. The employer also may estimate or project benefit levels for the benefits in the different categories under certain assumptions and given certain contingencies or events. However, these analyses and estimates of benefits and benefit levels may not completely show how well certain employee benefits actually reach a given employee group. Therefore, an employer also may want to calculate the actual participation ratios of its employees and their dependents for given employee benefit plans. These ratios can be calculated in terms of the employees (and their dependents) actually participating in the plan as a ratio of total full-time employees, as a ratio of total eligible employees, or as both.

A given employee benefit plan may have many good features, and may even be quite liberal in some respects; but if the ratio of employee participation is low, the particular benefit may not be meeting the employer's objectives in terms of its total compensation system.

Of course, if a given employee benefit is noncontributory, and if its eligibility requirements are reasonably liberal, all the eligible employees will be covered and, probably, a reasonably high percentage of total employees also will be covered. However, when employee benefit plans are contributory and eligibility requirements are tighter, the participation ratios may drop significantly. When this is the case, an employer may wish to evaluate what steps it might take to improve participation in the particular plan or plans.

Determine Gaps in Benefits and Any Overlapping Benefits

From the preceding steps, it is possible to analyze more effectively any gaps in the employer's present employee benefit plan. These gaps may be in terms of the benefits available from all sources in the plan to meet the various functional categories of employee needs, in terms of the projected levels of benefits for those needs, in terms of the coverage of the various categories of persons the employer may want to protect, and finally in terms of the actual participation of employees in the various components of the employee benefit plan. In a similar fashion, the employer will want to determine any overlapping benefits that presently may be provided from all sources in its employee benefit plan to meet certain categories of needs.

Consider Recommendations for Changes in Present Plan

As a result of the functional approach described above, the employer may consider various recommendations or alternative recommendations for changes in its present employee benefit plan to eliminate gaps in benefits or persons covered and to avoid any overlapping benefits. This step involves the consideration of alternatives which is implicit in any decision-making system.

Estimate Costs (or Savings) for Each Recommendation

This is an important step before any recommendations for improvements, reductions, or changes in an employee benefit plan can be adopted. These cost (or savings) estimates are based upon certain assumptions and may be expressed in terms of ranges of possible cost (or savings) results. An employer normally will have certain overall cost constraints on its employee benefit planning. Therefore, recommended improvements or changes in the plan may have to be assigned certain priorities in terms of which ones the employer can afford to adopt.

Evaluate Alternative Methods of Financing Benefits

This step involves the evaluation of how the recommended changes in benefits for the present plan or existing benefits in the present plan, or both, should be financed or secured. While this may not strictly involve the functional analysis of benefits in relation to needs, it is an essential step in analyzing any employee benefit plan.

Consider Other Cost-Saving Techniques

At this point, the employer also should consider other cost-saving techniques concerning its employee benefits. These may involve changes in benefit plan design, elimination or reduction of certain benefits, use of alternative methods of financing certain benefits, changes in insurers or servicing organizations, changes in investment policies or advisors, the decision to self-fund or retain certain benefits as opposed to seeking insurance coverage, and other similar techniques. Again, while consideration of such techniques may not be directly involved in the functional analysis of an employee benefit plan, it is a logical step in the planning process once such a functional analysis is begun.

Decide upon Appropriate Benefits and Financing Methods

Once the preceding analysis is complete, the employer or union is in a position to decide upon the particular benefit recommendations it wants to adopt or bargain for. The employer also may decide upon appropriate financing methods. This is essentially the selection of the best alternative or alternatives in the decision-making process.

Implement Any Changes

This step involves the implementation of the changes or recommendations decided upon above. It is the implementation phase of the decision-making process.

Communicate Benefit Changes to Employees

The effective communication of employee benefits and changes in such benefits is a vital element in the overall success of any employee benefit plan. It often is a neglected element. An employer may go to a great deal of time, trouble, and expense in making improvements in its employee benefit plan, but all this effort and cost may not be as effective as it could be in terms of good employee relations and meeting the employer's personnel policies if the improvements are not effectively communicated to the employees.

Many employers communicate periodically to employees the current overall status and value of their employee benefits. This frequently is done annually. Such a communication concerning the status and total value of an employee's benefits may be accomplished at least in part by using categories of benefits similar to those classified in the functional approach described above. See Chapter 51 of the *Handbook* for a more detailed discussion of communications.

Periodically Reevaluate the Plan

Employee benefit planning is a task that is never complete. Concepts of employee needs, and the benefits available to meet those needs, are constantly changing. Therefore, the employee benefit plan must be constantly reevaluated and updated.

CHAPTER 3

Regulatory Environment of Employee Benefit Plans

DALLAS L. SALISBURY

The regulatory environment of employee benefit plans has changed dramatically over the past 35 years. Major legislation was passed in 1942, 1958, and 1974, with a continuous flow of regulations and rulings from then until the recent passage of the Economic Recovery Tax Act of 1981 (ERTA) and the Tax Equity and Fiscal Responsibility Act of 1982 (TEFRA). The combined effect of these laws and rules has been to make the administration of employee benefit plans increasingly complex.

This chapter briefly reviews the regulatory environment for private pension and welfare plans; insurance programs; federal, state, and local government pension plans; and disability programs. It is intended to heighten awareness of the complexity of the regulatory environment.

The chapter is not intended to provide legal guidance or to be a guide to compliance. There are several "loose-leaf" services available that should be consulted to keep abreast of the constant changes taking place.

PRIVATE PENSION AND WELFARE PLANS

Pre-ERISA

Before the enactment of the Employee Retirement Income Security Act (ERISA) on Labor Day 1974, only three principal statutes governed private pension plans: the Internal Revenue Code (IRC), the Federal Welfare and Pension Plans Disclosure Act of 1958 (WPPDA), and the Taft-Hartley Act, more formally known as the Labor Management Relations Act of 1947. The latter regulated collectively bargained multiemployer pension plans.

Amendments to the Internal Revenue Code enacted in 1942 established standards for the design and operation of pension plans. The principal purposes were to prevent plans from discriminating or disproportionately benefiting one group of employees over another and to prevent plans from

39

taking excessive or unjustified tax deductions. Until 1974, the Internal Revenue Service was not concerned with the actuarial soundness of plans.

The Federal Welfare and Pension Plans Disclosure Act of 1958 was enacted to protect plan assets against fraudulent behavior by the plan administrator. The act mandated that, upon request, participants concerned with plan malpractice would be provided with information concerning the plan. If misuse or fraud were suspected, it was up to the participant to bring charges against the administrator. A significant amendment to the WPPDA was enacted in 1962. That amendment authorized the Department of Justice to bring appropriate legal action to protect plan participants' interests and authorized the Department of Labor to interpret and enforce the Act. For the first time, the burden of plan asset protection was placed upon the government rather than the individual participants.

Employee Retirement Income Security Act of 1974 (ERISA)

The shift to government protection of participants' rights enacted in 1962 would carry through to ERISA. It reflected a concern for workers, which was confirmed by President John Kennedy in 1962 with appointment of a Committee on Corporate Pension Funds and Other Retirement and Welfare Programs. That committee, issued its report in 1965, concluding that private pension plans should continue as a major element in the nation's total retirement security program. The report advocated many changes in the breadth of private plan regulation.

The report received widespread attention and led to the introduction of a number of legislative proposals. Congress concluded that most plans were operated for the benefit of participants on a sound basis, but some were not. To solve this problem, Congress enacted ERISA. ERISA governs every aspect of private pension and welfare plans and requires employers who sponsor plans to operate them in compliance with ERISA standards.

TITLE I: PROTECTION OF EMPLOYEE BENEFIT RIGHTS

Title I of ERISA places primary jurisdiction over reporting, disclosure and fiduciary matters in the Department of Labor. The Department of the Treasury is given primary jurisdiction over participation, vesting, and funding. This "dual-jurisdiction" led to a number of problems for plans during the first years of ERISA, which were addressed in 1979 by Reorganization Plan Number 4, discussed in a later part of this chapter. As a result of reorganizations and administrative experience under ERISA, many requirements have been adjusted, resulting in a reduction of regulatory burdens.

Reporting and Disclosure

Plan sponsors are required to provide plan participants with summary plan descriptions and benefit statements. They also are provided access to plan financial information. Documents provided to participants are to be written in "plain English" so they can be easily understood.

Plan sponsors file an annual financial report (Form 5500 series) with the IRS, which is made available to other agencies. In addition, plan sponsors must file amendments when modifications to the plan are made. Taken together, these provisions seek to assure that the government has accurate information on employer-sponsored plans.

Fiduciary Requirements

Plan sponsors are subject to an ERISA fiduciary standard mandating the plan be operated solely for the benefit of plan participants. The fiduciary standard, or "prudent man standard," requires the plan fiduciary perform duties solely in the interest of plan participants with the care a prudent man acting under like circumstances would use. This means any person who exercises discretion in the management and maintenance of the plan or in the investment of the plan assets must do so in the interest of the plan participants and beneficiaries, in accordance with the plan documents, and in a manner that minimizes the risk of loss to the participant. The standard applies to plan sponsors, trustees, and cofiduciaries, and to investment advisors with discretionary authority over the purchase and sale of plan securities. Underlying the standard are prohibitions against business or investment transactions between the plan and fiduciaries or interested parties. Upon violation of the prohibitions, the fiduciary may be held personally liable to the plan for any misuse, fraud, or mismanagement. Exemptions can be applied for when parties feel that actions are not to the detriment of the plan and its participants and should be allowed. Both the IRS and the Department of Labor are responsible for enforcing the fiduciary standards. The Department of Labor may file charges on behalf of the participants if the fiduciary has breached or violated the standards imposed by ERISA. The IRS may fine the employer and revoke the plan's favorable tax treatment. Both civil and criminal actions may arise for violations.

TITLE II: MINIMUM STANDARDS

Title II of ERISA contains minimum standards for participation, vesting, and funding of benefits, which must be satisfied for qualification of a plan. It also contains amendments to the IRC that increase the scope of federal regulation over certain pension plans, whether tax qualified or not.

Participation

Although ERISA does not require every employer set up an employer pension or welfare benefit plan, it does impose requirements on those who do. For those employers sponsoring plans, the age of employee eligibility cannot be higher than 25. A maximum of one year of service and 1,000 hours of work also may be required for eligibility.

Vesting

Upon satisfying the participation requirements, further conditions must be met for the participant to become entitled to receive a benefit—that is, to have a vested right to the benefits. There are three alternative vesting requirements contained in ERISA:

Full vesting after 10 years of service, with no vesting before the 10-year requirement is met.

Graduated vesting from the time the participant completes 5 years of service (full vesting after 15 years).

Graduated vesting, which requires that vesting begins when the participant has completed at least 5 years of service and when the age plus years of service totals at least 45 or after 10 years of service, irrespective of the participant's age, full vesting occurs when the participant has at least 15 years of service or age plus years of service equal at least 55. (This is called the "rule of 45.") In addition, the IRS has specified a 4-40 graded vesting schedule which can be used by plans. This schedule has been adopted by many small plans.

Benefits

Under ERISA, benefits generally must be earned in a uniform manner while the participant is employed. This does not affect the levels of benefits provided by the plan, only the rate at which the benefits are earned.

Funding

The minimum funding standards attempt to ensure that plans will have sufficient assets to pay benefits. Those employers with plans subject to the standards must establish and maintain a funding standard account. The sponsor must annually contribute the normal cost—the annual cost of future pension benefits and administrative expenses—plus amounts necessary to amortize in equal installments unfunded past service liabilities and any experience losses less experience gains. The amortization period in the former case generally is 30 years, and in the latter case 15 years. The presence of these standards has changed the environment for pension plans, creating greater need for long-range planning.

Tax-Qualified Plans

Requirements for tax qualification of plans has not materially changed since 1942. Meeting these requirements allows the employer to deduct contributions from income and makes investment earnings on plan assets exempt from current taxation.

The structure of tax-qualified plans is determined by ERISA requirements. The terms of the plan must be set forth in a written document. Copies of the plan and related documents must be made available to participants. In addition, a summary of the plan must be made available. The plan sponsor must have created the plan with the intent of permanency.

The provisions of the pension plan also are dictated by the requirements of the IRC.

- As referred to above, the plan must meet minimum participation, vesting and funding standards and plan assets must be legally segregated from other assets of the sponsor.

- The plan must not benefit only a limited number of favored employees but must benefit employees in general in such a way as to be deemed nondiscriminatory by the IRS. This status must extend to contributions and benefits such that officers, shareholders, or highly compensated employees are not favored when the plan is viewed in its entirety.

- The pension plan must provide definitely determinable benefits.

Overall, the IRC implementing regulations and rulings have had the goal of fostering accrual and preservation of benefits for present and potential plan participants and beneficiaries.

The requirements for a tax-qualified profit-sharing plan are somewhat different in that the plan must cover all employees and the benefit is not determinable. In addition, the profit-sharing plan is not always a retirement income vehicle.

Fulfillment of all tax qualification requirements entitles the employer to a current deduction from gross income for contributions to the plan. The participating employee recognizes no taxable income until the funds are made available in the form of benefits or are distributed as a lump-sum distribution. When the distribution is made upon termination of service (an amount received as an annuity from a qualified plan) there are two applicable rules. If the employee's investment can be recouped from annuity payments within three years, all payments are tax free until the employee's investment has been recouped, at which time all future payments become fully taxable. If the investment cannot be recovered within three years, an exclusion ratio is used.

Employees may voluntarily be allowed, or in some cases required, to make contributions to qualified plans. The employee's required contributions are limited to the maximum amount provided in the plan and no tax deduction is allowed; in other words, the contribution is made with aftertax dollars. For voluntary contributions, up to $2,000 may be contributed on a tax-deductible basis.

Nonqualified Plans

Nonqualified employee benefit plans have not been designed to satisfy the IRC requirements and may either be funded or nonfunded. Under the funded plan, the employer agrees to make contributions to the plan for the benefit of the employee. Under an unfunded plan, the employer promises to provide a benefit to the participant at some future time. Most funded plans must satisfy ERISA, while unfunded plans must only meet ERISA's reporting and disclosure provisions.

TITLE IV: PLAN TERMINATION INSURANCE

Title IV of ERISA established the Pension Benefit Guaranty Corporation (PBGC), a governmental body that insures payment of plan benefits under certain circumstances.

Most defined benefit pension plans (those that provide a fixed monthly benefit at retirement) are required to participate in the program and pay premiums to the PBGC.

There are certain restrictions and limitations on the amount of benefits insured, which is adjusted annually to reflect the increasing average wages of the American workforce. The limit applies to all plans under which a participant is covered so that it is not possible to spread coverage under several plans to increase the guaranteed benefit. To be fully insured, the benefit must have been vested before the plan terminated and the benefit level must have been in effect for 60 months or else benefits are proportionately reduced. Further, the guarantee applies only to benefits earned while the plan is eligible for favorable tax treatment.

In an effort to protect against employers establishing plans without intending to continue them, ERISA introduced the concept of contingent employer liability in the event of plan termination for single-employer plans and for multi-employer plans in the event of employer withdrawal or insolvency. Additional complex requirements that apply to multi-employer plans also were established by Congress in 1980. Such changes may soon be adopted for single-employer plans.

The PBGC has served to change substantially the environment in which plans operate. For present sponsors, and for those thinking of establishing new defined benefit plans, Title IV should be carefully reviewed to assure its implications are fully understood.

ADDITIONAL REGULATORY AGENCIES

Labor Laws

A number of other laws, from both statutory and case law, give the Department of Labor authority to monitor and regulate employee benefit plans.

Among them is the National Labor Relations Act, which promotes collective bargaining between employers and employees' representatives. The Taft-Hartley Act contains specific provisions similar to ERISA and the IRC relating to plan structure and content. The landmark case of *Inland Steel Company* v. *the National Labor Relations Board* prohibits an employer from refusing to bargain with employees upon a properly presented demand to bargain regarding employee benefit plans.

Equal Employment Opportunity Commission (EEOC)

The EEOC's interest in employee benefit plans stems from various acts that prohibit discriminatory plan practices. The Civil Rights Act of 1964, Title VII, is interpreted by the EEOC as defining discrimination between men and women with regard to fringe benefits as an unlawful employment practice. The Equal Pay Act of 1963 makes employer discrimination between the sexes in the payment of wages for equal work unlawful. Benefits under employee benefit plans are a form of wages and must be free from discrimination, held one EEOC decision. The Age Discrimination in Employment Act of 1967 and its 1975 and 1979 amendments clearly prohibit discrimination on the basis of age and have moved towards elimination of mandatory retirement ages.

Securities and Exchange Commission (SEC)

Under the Securities Act of 1933, information concerning securities publicly offered and sold in interstate commerce or through the mails is required to be disclosed to the SEC. At first blush, the act does not seem to apply to employee benefit plans. However, a security is defined by the act as including participation in any profit-sharing agreement. The Securities Act of 1934 affects the administration of plans by imposing disclosure and registration requirements and antifraud provisions. The SEC has not actively enforced requirements, but the scope of legal SEC jurisdiction has been debated and litigated.

The Investment Company Act of 1940 regulates reporting and disclosure, structure, content, and administration of investment companies. A pension benefit plan could be subject to this act if it fits the definition of an investment company. An investment company, as defined by the act, is one engaged in the business of holding, trading, investing, or owning securities.

Other Acts and Agencies

The Small Business Administration (SBA) receives complaints from small businesses regarding the relationship of small business to agencies of the federal government.

Banking laws also apply. The National Bank Act permits national banks to act as trustees in a fiduciary capacity in which state banks or trust companies are permitted to act under the laws of the state where the national bank is located. This affects private employee benefit plans because banks act as fiduciaries. The Federal Reserve Act and the Federal Reserve System can affect pension and welfare plans, since plans may either be borrowers or lenders. Because there is regulation of interest payable on deposits in banks that are members of the Federal Reserve System, IRA and Keogh plans are affected in terms of possible rates of return. The Federal Deposit Insurance Act also affects these plans that are not covered by the PBGC since funds held by an insured bank, in its capacity as fiduciary, will be insured up to $100,000.

The Commerce Department is concerned with ERISA's impact on the health of the economy. The Department of Health and Human Services (HHS) tries to keep track of individuals with deferred vested benefit plans as well as administering Social Security and other public programs that have a substantial impact on private plan design.

EVALUATION OF ERISA ADMINISTRATION UNDER REORGANIZATION PLAN NUMBER 4

In 1978, President Carter mandated that the administration of ERISA be evaluated. Reorganization Plan Number 4 was developed to provide an immediate solution to some of the existing and potential problems caused by shared agency responsibilities under ERISA. The plan provides that the Department of Labor has rulemaking responsibility concerning employee benefit plan fiduciary matters and the Department of Treasury responsibility for participation, vesting, and funding standards.

An evaluation of Reorganization Plan Number 4 was released in 1980. It indicated improvements in the agencies' administration of ERISA. The plan was credited with leading to:

1. Speedier processing of requests for exemptions from prohibited transaction provisions.
2. Expediting the issuance of regulations by both the Labor and Treasury Departments.
3. Reduction of the paperwork associated with ERISA.

As a result of a recommendation coming from the evaluation of Reorganization Plan Number 4, President Carter signed a January 7, 1981, executive order which created an Interagency Employee Benefit Council. The council is composed of the secretaries of Treasury, Commerce, Labor, Health and Human Services, the attorney general, the director of the Office of Management and Budget, the administrator of the Small Business Administration, the chairman of the Equal Employment Opportunities Commission, plus representatives from the Federal Trade Commission, the Securities and Exchange Commission, and the National Labor Relations Board. Besides assisting in interagency coordination of proposals affecting employee benefits under ERISA, the council will seek to develop comprehensive long- and short-term policies applicable to plans covered by ERISA.

THE REGULATION OF INSURANCE

Both the individual state governments and the federal government regulate insurance. The states regulate rates, financial examination, formation of the company, qualification of officers, licensing, and taxing. The federal government provides for regulation as noted above in addition to the activity of the Federal Insurance Administrator, the Interstate Commerce Commission, and the Federal Trade Commission.

A growing concern exists over which level of government is the most appropriate for the regulation of insurance. It is felt by many that there should be greater federal involvement. Advocates of federal regulation argue that state regulation lacks uniformity and that multiple state regulation is more costly than federal regulation, that the state insurance commissioners are unqualified, and that the states cannot effectively regulate interstate companies. Those who favor state regulation feel the states are more responsive to local conditions and needs, that state regulation encourages innovation and experimentation, and that the decentralization of power is advantageous.

At present there exists an ongoing disagreement between the states and the federal government over the extent of preemption of state laws by ERISA. The federal government believes it could move towards greater regulation without legal difficulty. This is based upon the federal ability to regulate interstate commerce, to provide for the general welfare, and to tax. Section 514(a) of ERISA states that it shall supersede any and all state laws insofar as they may now or later relate to any employee benefit plan. The preemption does not apply to any state law that regulates insurance. But, to what extent does ERISA preempt laws enacted under the insurance codes of the states, when such laws are designed specifically to apply to the insurance-type functions of employee benefit plans?

The Department of Labor advocated a broad interpretation of Section 514, which would preempt most state statutes even if the laws deal with areas not explicitly covered by ERISA, such as the content of health benefit plans. The federal courts have not been so consistent in their interpretation of the statute. In one case, *Fleck* v. *Spannaus,* the court decided ERISA does not preempt causes of action occuring before January 1, 1975. But in another case, *Azzaro* v. *Harnett,* the court held that Congress intended absolute preemption in the field of employee benefits. Even the insurance exception found in section 514 is subject to limitations: "No employee benefit plan shall be deemed to be an insurance company or engaged in the business of insurance for the purpose of any law of any state purporting to regulate an insurance company."

In general, the courts have tended to preempt state regulation which relates to employee pension and retirement plans. This stems from the broad-based protections incorporated in ERISA for pension plan participants. The courts are less inclined to preempt state laws which apply to employee health and insurance plans. ERISA has had a more limited application to welfare plans and a more narrow view of the preemptive effect in the health and welfare plan area. When health insurance benefits are mandated in traditional insurance contracts, rather than through comprehensive health care legislation, claims of federal preemption will not hold. However, when an employer's prepaid health care plan satisfies the ERISA definition, state regulation is preempted.

Where the line eventually will be drawn between state and federal regulation of health and welfare plans is very uncertain. The debate will most likely center on the degree to which arrangements have insurance versus noninsurance characteristics. Ultimately, the courts can be expected to be heavily involved.

FEDERAL, STATE, AND LOCAL GOVERNMENT PENSION PLANS

Public plans represent a substantial level of retirement income promises for federal, state and local employees. Benefit levels promised in public plans exceed those of the private sector. Public plans exist free of federal regulatory controls like those imposed by ERISA. For practical purposes there is only a limited "regulatory environment."

Public employee pension programs are receiving a considerable amount of attention today because of the sharp increases in current appropriations necessary to support retirement programs. Federal regulation of private plans has given rise to a Congressional commitment to the study of public plans and to an assessment of whether a public plan version of ERISA should be enacted.

Research has revealed that large cities with their own pension plans are likely to provide some of the most generous benefits available in the public sector. Public employees generally have more liberal early retirement provisions in their pension plans than private employees, and public plans usually include a provision for automatic increases in retirees' benefits when the cost of living increases.

State and local plans are viewed by many as being substantially underfunded. Actuarial, financial, auditing, and disclosure requirements are viewed as deficient. Many charge that fiduciary standards are seriously breached. Other characteristics of public plans have led to criticisms, including:

- Their retirement benefits replace a substantial percentage of final pay after only 20 to 25 years of service.
- Their normal retirement ages are set well ahead of the end of productive working lifetimes.
- They are generous in granting a high proportion of early disability retirements in "high risk" professions (police, firemen, and the like), rather than retaining the workforce in less hazardous positions.

Substantial concern also is generated because some federal, state, and local employees currently are not covered by the Social Security program Because of noninclusion, or lack of integration when both programs are involved, there is a belief that public employees obtain "windfall" benefits or unnecessarily large benefits, or both. For example, a recent government study indicated that income replacement ratios for public employees serving 30 years at average wages received more than 100 percent of salary in 53 percent of all cases, and 125 percent of salary in more than 10 percent of all cases.

These and other issues have led to the development of state commissions to advise state legislators on pension issues. The threat of an impending federal intervention (in the form of PERISA—the Public Employee Retirement Income Security Act) has stimulated efforts in many states to monitor state and local pension funds more closely and to improve reporting and disclosure practices. As of 1979, 21 states had established pension commissions. Five more states have proposals for the creation of pension commissions pending. The existing commissions have suggested that there should be some redesign of public pension plans, that Social Security integration with public plans should be encouraged, that cost of living increases should be capped, and that there should be an increase in normal retirement ages.

DISABILITY PROGRAMS

In 1975, cash disability payments equaled 25 percent of all cash payments to retirees, survivors, and the disabled. Disability programs resemble pension programs in that the purposes are similar (both, generally, are intended to maintain the income of workers and their dependents or survivors when they are unable to work), program finances are intertwined, and disability programs are sometimes used to substitute for retirement programs.

Disability program trends indicate that cash disability programs have grown rapidly and that the federal role in disability programs has increased. Analyses indicate workers of all ages are being awarded disability benefits more frequently than in previous years. Per capita benefits generally have grown more rapidly than earnings and the difference in growth rates has been larger since 1970.

Social factors also add to the increase in disability payouts. Society is doing more to support the disabled. More and more people identify themselves as disabled. It is indicated that disability programs may be repeating the welfare crisis of the 1960s, the dramatic increase in beneficiaries largely representing a growing percentage of eligible persons claiming benefits.

State Disability Retirement Plans

Disability retirement coverage is available to state workers in 47 states. Arizona, Kansas, and Iowa provide employee coverage under an employer-paid group long-term disability insurance plan. Of all the states providing coverage, most do not require any minimum years of service for on-the-job disability but do require years of service for off-the-job disability. Workers in virtually all of the states are eligible for disability income only when the disability is classified as permanent, or long-term. Benefit levels are determined by several factors: age, years of service, numbers, and relevant pay figures. Half of the states impose upper limits on the benefits, expressed as a specific percentage of final pay. Others limit the combination of retirement and primary Social Security benefits. Most of the states with disability retirement coverage have payout arrangements incorporating certain features aimed at setting a floor level of benefits. The floors are designed to provide extra protection for the lower years-of-service worker.

Social Security Disability Benefits

To qualify for Social Security disability benefits, the wage earner must be unable to engage in any substantial activity by reason of medically determined physical or mental impairment that can be expected to result in death or to last for a continuous period. Total disability exists if the claimant's disability equals or exceeds the standards as established and is documented by a medical report using the language required by the regulations. The Social Security Act considers age, education, and previous work experience when applying the disability standard. The wage earner also must meet special earnings requirements to be covered. The wage earner must have performed 20 quarters of employment in the 40 quarters immediately prior to the alleged onset of disability. The benefit payout begins on the sixth month of disability.

CONCLUSION

The regulatory environment of employee benefit programs is far reaching and complex. It involves all levels of government in at least some areas, and numerous different agencies at each level, all with the purpose of protecting the potential recipient and adding security to the benefit promise.

The degree to which the environment is refined is constantly changing. There has been no rest from discussion of new legislative proposals or new regulatory initiatives. Some proposals aim at reducing regulation, others at increasing it. Frequently the short-term effect is the same: creation of uncertainty, which inhibits the growth and development of employee benefit programs.

The challenge for the practitioner is to understand the environment, to understand how it affects particular situations, and to affect it when the opportunity arises.

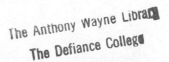

PART TWO

Designing Employee Benefits— Death Benefits

Some form of death benefit is provided by almost all employers, large and small, for their employees. Such death benefit plans must be designed in terms of the employer and employee objectives.

Part Two starts with a discussion of some of the most important considerations involved in the design of a death benefit plan and an overview of group term life insurance in Chapter 4. Following this is a discussion of Social Security and other governmental death benefits in Chapter 5 and permanent forms of group life insurance in Chapter 6. This part of the *Handbook* concludes with Chapter 7 on the retired lives reserve approach to providing death benefits.

CHAPTER 4

Some Issues Involved in the Design of Death Benefit Plans and An Overview of Group Term Life Insurance

JERRY S. ROSENBLOOM

INTRODUCTION

Death benefits are a nearly universal employee benefit in the United States. Almost all employers, regardless of size, provide as an integral part of their employee benefit program some form of death benefits for their employees. While death benefits are provided through workers' compensation, Social Security, and pension plans, most of this coverage is provided through group life insurance. Traditionally, death benefits through life insurance have paid benefits to beneficiaries of employees who die during their working years. The protection provided usually is one-year renewable group term life insurance, with no cash surrender value or paid-up insurance benefit. With the growth of retirement plans, other forms of death benefits, such as arrangements for the payment of a lifetime pension to the spouse of a career employee who dies before retirement, have developed.

In some cases, life insurance also is provided for dependents of employees, typically in small amounts such as $1,000 or $2,000. Moreover, many employee benefit plans continue a reduced amount of death benefits on retired employees. Additional death benefits may be established under special benefit plans for executives.

Survivor death benefit plans have been increasing in employee benefit plans in recent years. These plans differ from traditional employer-sponsored death benefit plans since a benefit is payable only to certain specified surviving dependents of the employee and is payable only in installments. Mandated survivor benefits to spouses also are available under certain conditions under the Employee Retirement Income Security Act of 1974

(ERISA).[1] The enactment of the Tax Equity and Fiscal Responsibility Act of 1982 (TEFRA) also has implications for the design of death benefit plans.

This chapter examines some of the issues involved in the design of death benefit plans provided through the employee benefit mechanism. The chapter then concentrates on the most popular method of providing death benefits, group term life insurance. Other chapters in this part of the *Handbook* describe death benefits provided by Social Security, permanent forms of group life insurance coverage, and the retired lives reserve approach to funding death benefits. Additional death benefits, such as those provided under pension and profit-sharing plans, are described in other parts of the *Handbook*.

PLAN OBJECTIVES

As described in Chapter 2, death benefit objectives are established in the same way as retirement income and disability income objectives. The level of income that will enable an employee's survivors to maintain appropriate living standards should be ascertained. Because of the large amounts involved, sometimes four or more times an employee's annual earnings, few employers set a death benefit income objective at levels that maintain predeath levels. Because of the availability of individual life insurance and Social Security, most employers believe an employee should assume a significant portion of the burden of income replacement at death.[2]

In designing a death benefit plan, it is necessary to consider the possibility of the employee's death before and after retirement. Once an appropriate benefit level is determined, the best method or methods for providing such benefits can be developed.

If death benefits are considered as a certain multiple of an employee's income, the need for death benefits typically decreases as the employee's age increases. The need generally is greatest for young, married employees with dependents. However, the death benefit provided by many firms increases as a multiple of pay as an employee grows older. Moreover, if the firm has a pension plan, it may provide a death benefit to a surviving spouse based upon the employee's accrued pension for employees who die within a certain number of years preceding normal retirement age, or after a certain number of years of service. Thus, it is possible for an employee's death benefit shortly before retirement to exceed the amount necessary for the employee's survivors to maintain their present living standards. Yet, it may be inadequate for younger employees with dependents who have the greatest death benefit needs. Appropriate design of death benefits can help prevent this situation.

---

[1] See Jerry S. Rosenbloom and G. Victor Hallman, *Employee Benefit Planning* (Englewood Cliffs, N.J.: Prentice-Hall, 1981), p. 36.

[2] Ibid., pp. 37–39.

Death benefit design objectives also may consider causes of death. Accidental death benefits are popular because they are "inexpensive" and appear to offer large death benefits.

Another basic death benefit design issue is whether a program providing death benefits serves a sound purpose from the employer's viewpoint. As mentioned earlier, since in practice almost all employers have death benefit plans, the question seems to have been answered. Reasons for employer-sponsored death benefit programs include:[3]

Recruit and retain employees.

Other employers have such programs.

Income and estate tax advantages to employees.

Employer-provided programs may make possible features that are impractical on an individual policy basis.

Since later chapters focus on death benefits provided through Social Security, permanent forms of group life insurance, death benefits available under retirement plans, and so on, the balance of this chapter concentrates on the most popular method of providing death benefits, namely, group term life insurance.

GROUP TERM LIFE INSURANCE

The importance of group term life insurance in employee benefit plans is shown by data in Table 4–1.[4] This table reveals that at the end of 1980, group life insurance in force in the United States totaled $1,579.4 billion. Most of this coverage is issued to employers to protect their employees.

Table 4–2 shows that 91.7 percent of group life insurance master policies in force at year-end 1978 covered employer-employee groups, accounting for 87.8 percent of the total amount of group life insurance in force. The average amount of coverage per employee was $16,753. Survivor income and dependent coverages accounted for $91.4 billion, as shown in Table 4–3. Thus, the death benefits in employee benefit plans, exclusive of pension plans, amounted to about 40 percent of all life insurance in force in the United States at the end of 1980.[5]

Further evidence of the importance of group term life insurance in employee benefit plans of major U.S. corporations is found in the reports of recent employee benefit surveys by the Conference Board, the Chamber of Commerce of the United States and *Fortune*. The Fortune Market Research study showed that in 1975, 95 percent of respondents in the top

---

[3] Ibid., pp. 38–39.

[4] A special note of thanks is due Dr. John Stinton, Professor of Insurance, University of South Carolina, for doing the background work for this section of this chapter.

[5] *1981 Life Insurance Fact Book* (Washington, D.C.: American Council of Life Insurance), pp. 30–31.

Table 4-1
Group Life Insurance in Force in the United States (selected years: 1940–1980)

Years	Number of Master Policies	Number of Certificates (000s)	Average Amount per Certificate	Amount in Force (millions)	Percent of Total Insurance in Force	Purchases Number of Certificates	Purchases Amount	Percent of Total Insurance Purchases
1940	23,000	8,800,000	1,700	$ 14,938	12.9%	285,000	691	6.4%
1950	56,000	19,288,000	2,480	47,793	20.4	2,631,000	6,068	21.1
1960	169,000	43,602,000	4,030	175,903	30.0	3,734,000	14,645	19.7
1965	234,000	60,930,000	5,060	308,078	34.2	7,007,000	23,585	20.6
1970	304,000	79,844,000	6,910	551,357	39.3	5,219,000	46,590	26.5
1975	378,000	96,693,000	9,360	904,695	42.3	8,146,000	93,490	32.4
1976	404,000	100,138,000	10,010	1,002,647	42.8	9,145,000	104,683	32.2
1977	437,000	105,649,000	10,550	1,115,047	43.2	9,599,000	115,839	31.3
1978	495,000	110,445,000	11,260	1,243,994	43.3	9,267,000	125,129	30.2
1979	559,000	114,893,000	12,350	1,419,418	44.0	9,245,000	157,906	32.0
1980	586,000	117,762,000	13,410	1,579,355	44.6	10,010,000	170,184	31.3

Source: *Life Insurance Fact Book.*

Table 4-2

Group Life Insurance in Force by Type and by Size of Insured Group in the United States 1978

	Master Policies		Insurance in Force		Average Amount of Coverage per Member
	Number	Percent of Total	Amount (millions)	Percent of Total	
Type of Group:					
Related to Employment or Occupation					
Employer-Employee	453,670	91.7	$ 945,891	87.8	$16,753
Union and Joint Employer-Union	5,250	1.1	35,209	3.3	5,175
Professional Society	960	.2	18,458	1.7	28,052
Employee Association	1,730	.3	19,911	1.8	13,703
Other—Related to Employee Benefit Program	3,290	.7	7,933	.7	11,497
Other—Not Related to Employee Benefit Program	130	*	2,095	.2	22,287
Total	465,030	94.0	1,029,497	95.5	15,561
Not Related to Employment or Occupation					
Fraternal Society	340	.1	2,517	.2	12,460
Savings or Investment Group	21,380	4.3	17,764	1.7	633
Group Mortgage Insurance	5,720	1.1	24,780	2.3	17,512
Other	2,370	.5	3,170	.3	6,108
Total	29,810	6.0	48,231	4.5	1,597
Total All Groups	494,840	100.0	$1,077,728	100.0	$11,183
Size of Group:					
Fewer than 10 Members	147,310	29.8	$ 7,223	.7	$11,802
10– 24 Members	136,400	27.6	25,816	2.4	11,837
25– 99 Members	135,800	27.4	68,265	6.3	12,074
100–499 Members	42,640	8.6	105,597	9.8	12,840
500 or More Members	32,690	6.6	870,827	80.8	10,927
Total All Groups	494,840	100.0	$1,077,728	100.0	$11,183

Note: Data exclude dependent coverage, Federal Employees' Group Life Insurance, and Servicemen's Group Life Insurance. Group credit life insurance on loans of over 10 years' duration is included.
 * Less than .05 percent.
Source: American Council of Life Insurance.

500 firms and 91 percent of those in the second 500 firms provided group term life insurance.[6]

---

[6] *Fortune, How Major Industrial Corporations View Employee Benefit Programs* (New York: Fortune Market Research, 1975). There were 245 of the top 500 companies included in the survey of which 157 (64%) responded and 299 of the second 500 companies of which 180 (60%) responded.

Table 4–3
Employee and Dependent Coverage under Group Life Insurance in the
United States 1980

	Number of Master Policies	Amount
Purchased during Year:		
Primary Coverage, Employee, and Other	140,260	$ 155,371
Survivor Benefit Coverage	N.A.	1,719
Dependent Coverage	8,620*	8,082
Mortgage Insurance Issued through a Lending Agency	1,160	5,012
Total	141,420	$ 170,184
In Force at End of Year:		
Primary Coverage, Employee, and Other	580,000	$1,454,637
Survivor Benefit Coverage	N.A.	33,601
Dependent Coverage	42,550*	57,775
Mortgage Insurance Issued through a Lending Agency	5,530	33,342
Total	585,530	$1,579,355

* These policies cover employees as well as dependents and are also included with
employee master policies.
N.A. = Not available.
Source: American Council of Life Insurance.

The Conference Board survey revealed that all of the 1,368 responding
companies provide group life insurance covering managers, only 2 percent
exclude nonoffice employees, and less than one half of 1 percent exclude
clerical employees.[7] Although this study did not distinguish between group
term and group permanent plans, no doubt the vast majority of these
companies provided group term life. The Chamber of Commerce 1980
survey showed that, among 983 reporting companies, 87 percent reported
payments for group life insurance, and an additional 9 percent reported
combined payments for life and health insurance.[8]

Benefits

Group term life insurance benefit amounts should be based on a plan
designed to avoid or minimize possible adverse selection either by the

---

[7] *Profile of Employee Benefits: 1981 Edition* (New York: The Conference Board, 1981),
p. 39. Of the 3,083 companies included in the survey, 1,368 (44.4 percent) responded.
Respondents included companies in commercial banking (16 percent), insurance (15.9
percent), large and small manufacturing (8 percent), retail and wholesale trade (8 percent),
electricity and gas (11 percent), construction (3.5 percent), and trucking and warehousing (1.6
percent). By number of employees, 14 percent of respondents reported fewer than 500, 15
percent reported between 500 and 999, 36 percent reported 1,000 to 4,999, and 35 percent
reported 5,000 or more.

[8] *Employee Benefits 1980* (Washington: Chamber of Commerce of the U.S., 1981), p. 17.

employees or the employer. Factors to consider in the selection of a benefit schedule include (1) the employees' needs, (2) the overall cost of the plan, and (3) the employees' ability to pay if the plan is contributory. The interrelationship of factors has resulted in the development of group term life insurance benefit schedules related to earnings, occupation or position, or a flat benefit amount for everyone covered, and length of service. Benefit schedules also exist which are a combination of two or more of the types of benefit schedules mentioned above.[9]

The most common benefit schedule bases the amount of insurance on the employee's earnings. An illustration of such a schedule in Table 4-4 follows:

Table 4-4
Sample Schedule Basing Benefits on Amount of
Employee Earnings

Monthly Earnings	Group Term Life Insurance
Less than $750	$10,000
More than $750 but less than $1,000	12,500
More than $1,000 but less than $1,500	15,000
More than $1,500 but less than $2,000	20,000
More than $2,000	25,000

Financing

Any employee benefit program, including group term life insurance, may be financed on either a noncontributory basis (where the employer pays the total amount for the insurance) or a contributory basis (where the employees share the cost with the employer). A number of advantages are claimed for each approach. The advantages claimed for the *noncontributory approach* follow:[10]

All Employees Insured. All eligible employees who have completed the probationary period and are actively at work have coverage. Thus, the plan has maximum participation and minimizes adverse selection.

Tax Advantages. Employer premium costs are deductible as an ordinary business expense for federal income tax purposes, whereas employee contributions under a contributory plan are not.

Simplicity of Administration. Records for individual employees are easier to maintain than under contributory plans primarily because no payroll deduction procedures are necessary.

---

[9] See Davis W. Gregg, "Fundamental Characteristics of Group Insurance," in *Life and Health Insurance Handbook*, 3d ed., eds. Davis W. Gregg and Vane B. Lucas (Homewood, Ill.: Richard D. Irwin, 1973), pp. 357–58.

[10] Ibid., pp. 358–60.

Economy of Installation. Since all employees are covered, it is not necessary to solicit plan membership among individual employees.

Greater Control of Plan. The employer may have more control over changes in benefits under noncontributory plans because, in the absence of collective bargaining, unilateral action may be more feasible when employees are not sharing in the cost of the plan.

The *contributory approach* to financing group term life insurance also has certain claimed advantages:[11]

Larger Benefits Possible. More liberal benefits are possible if employees also contribute.

Better Use of Employer's Contributions. A contributory plan may permit the employer to direct group term life insurance funds to the employees with the greatest needs. Employees who elect not to contribute, and hence are not covered, tend to be young, single individuals who may have few life insurance needs and among whom employee turnover also may be high. Therefore, if such is the case, a contributory plan allows employer funds to be used most effectively by sharing the cost of benefits for the employees who have greater needs and who also are most likely to be long-service employees.

Employees May Have More Control. The contributory plan may afford employees a greater voice in the benefits since they are paying part of the cost.

Greater Employee Interest. Employees may have a greater interest in plans in which they are making a contribution.

Important Group Term Life Insurance Provisions[12]

Beneficiary Designation. Under group term life insurance, an employee may name and change his or her beneficiary as desired. The only restriction is that the insurance must benefit someone other than the employer. If, at the death of the employee, no beneficiary is named, or if a beneficiary is named but does not survive the employee, the proceeds may be payable at the insurer's option to any one or more of the following surviving relatives of the employee: wife, husband, mother, father, child or children, or to the executor or administrator of the estate of the deceased employee. If any beneficiary is a minor or otherwise incapable of giving a valid release, the insurer is able to pay the proceeds under a "facility of payment" clause, subject to certain limits.

Settlement Options. The covered employee or the beneficiary may elect to receive the face amount of the group term life insurance on an

---

[11] Ibid.

[12] See William G. Williams, "Group Life Insurance," in *Life and Health Insurance Handbook*, 3d ed., eds. Davis W. Gregg and Vane B. Lucas (Homewood, Ill.: Richard D. Irwin, 1973), pp. 373–77.

installment basis rather than in a lump sum. The installments are paid according to tables listed in the group master policy. An insurer generally offers optional modes of settlement based on life contingencies. But the basis is seldom mentioned or guaranteed in the contract, and insurance company practices at the time of death govern.[13]

Assignment. Group term life insurance generally may be assigned if the master policy and state law both permit. Assignment of group term life insurance is important as a means for an employee to remove the group life insurance proceeds from his or her gross estate for federal estate tax purposes by absolutely assigning all incidents of ownership in the group term life insurance to another person or to an irrevocable trust. This has become an important estate planning technique for some employees whose estates potentially will be subject to federal estate taxation. (This subject is discussed in greater detail in Chapter 60.)

Conversion Privilege. If an employee's life insurance ceases because of termination of employment, termination of membership in a classification(s) eligible for coverage, or retirement, he or she may convert the group term insurance to an individual permanent life insurance policy. The employee must apply to the insurer in writing within 30 days of termination and pay the premium for his or her attained age, the type of insurance, and the class of risk involved; however, medical evidence of insurability is not necessary.

A more restricted conversion privilege may be provided for an employee if the group master policy is terminated or amended so as to terminate the insurance in force on the employee's particular classification.

Thirty-One-Day Continuation of Protection. This provision gives a terminated employee an additional 31 days of protection while he or she evaluates the conversion privilege or while awaiting coverage under the group life insurance plan of a new employer.

Continuation of Insurance. The employer can elect to continue the employee's group term life insurance in force for a limited period, such as three months, on a basis that precludes adverse selection during temporary interruptions of continuous, active, full-time employment. Upon expiration of the continuation period, premium payments are discontinued, and the employee's insurance is terminated. However, in this event, the insurance as well as the right to exercise the conversion privilege is still extended for 31 days after termination of the insurance.

Waiver of Premium Provision. Because employees may become disabled, group life insurance policies generally contain a waiver-of-premium provision. Under a typical waiver-of-premium provision, the life insurance remains in force if: (1) the employee is under a specified age, such as 60 or 65, at the date of commencement of total disability; (2) total disability commences while the person is covered; (3) total disability is continuous

---

[13] Ibid., p. 376.

until the date of death; and (4) proof of total and continuous disability is presented at least once every 12 months.[14]

The waiver-of-premium provision is one of three types of disability benefit provisions used for group life plans. The second, the maturity value benefit, pays the face amount of the group term life insurance in a lump sum, or in monthly installments when an employee becomes totally and permanently disabled. A third type of disability provision, the extended death benefit, pays group life insurance death claims incurred within one year after termination of employment. It requires the employee be continuously and totally disabled from the date of termination of employment until death occurs.

Dependent Coverage

The growth of dependents' group life insurance has been relatively slow. When provided, a typical schedule of benefits might provide the dependent spouse with life insurance equal to 50 percent of the employee's coverage but not more than $1,000 or $2,000. Typical benefits for dependent children often are graded from $100 between the child's age of 14 days to six months up to, for example, $1,000 or $1,500 between ages 5 and 19 years.

The death benefit normally is payable automatically in one lump sum to the insured employee or, in the event of the prior death of the employee, either to the employee's estate or, at the option of the insurer, to one of certain specified classes of "order-of-preference" beneficiaries.

Coverage of Employees after Age 65[15]

Retired Employees. Upon retirement, a former employee's group term life insurance often is discontinued and the high cost of conversion at the retiree's advanced age usually makes use of the conversion privilege impractical. Therefore, many employers are continuing reduced amounts of group term life insurance on retired employees under various types of reduction formulas. One formula reduces the insurance by 50 percent at retirement. Another uses a graded percentage system decreasing the amount of coverage each year after retirement age until a certain minimum benefit is reached; for example, 10 percent per year until 50 percent of the amount in force immediately prior to retirement is attained. Because continuing group life insurance on retired lives is costly, employers may consider funding coverage for retired employees through some other means such as group paid-up, group ordinary, or a separate "side fund" to pay the premiums at retirement. (See Chapters 6 and 7.)

---

[14] Ibid., pp. 374–75.

[15] Jerry S. Rosenbloom/G. Victor Hallman, *Employee Benefit Planning*, © 1981, pp. 46–49. Reprinted by permission of Prentice-Hall, Inc., Englewood Cliffs, N.J.

Active Employees.   These retirees are not current employees of the employer, and continuation of group term life insurance on their lives is a voluntary decision on the employer's part. In this section, the important issue of coverage requirements for active employees after age 65 under the Age Discrimination in Employment Act of 1967 (ADEA), as amended in 1978, is evaluated.

The main change made by the 1978 ADEA amendments was raising the upper age limit of the protected group from age 65 to age 70. Thus, the law now prohibits discrimination in employment on the basis of age against individuals from age 40 to age 70. This means employees between the ages of 65 and 70 generally are not subject to mandatory retirement and are protected by ADEA against employment discrimination.

With respect to group life insurance, the final Interpretive Bulletin (IB) on the act permits an employer to reduce the amount of group term life insurance for employees after a certain age, such as age 65, provided the reduction is no greater than is justified by the increased cost of providing life insurance coverage for the employee's specific age bracket encompassing no more than five years. That is, the reduction must be cost justified. It is permissible for ADEA purposes to begin reductions in life insurance benefits before age 65; this has not been the practice in the past. The IB points out, however, that a total denial of life insurance coverage for active employees on the basis of age would not be justified for ADEA purposes under a benefit-by-benefit approach to cost justifying reductions in benefits.

In applying these general guidelines, an employer (1) may reduce life insurance coverage each year starting at age 65 by 8 to 9 percent of the declining balance of the life insurance benefit, or (2) make a one-time reduction in life insurance benefits at age 65 of from 35 to 40 percent and maintain that reduced amount in force until age 70. The 8 to 9 percent annual reduction is justified by mortality statistics showing that, on the average, the probability of death increases by that amount each year for the age 60 to 70 group. The one-time 35 to 40 percent reduction is justified by the difference in mortality expected by employees in the age 65 through age 69 bracket, compared with the mortality expected in the age 60 through age 64 bracket. An employer also may be able to cost justify greater reductions in group term life insurance benefits on the basis of its own demonstrably higher cost experience in providing group term life insurance to its employees over a representative period of years.

The IB also permits use of a "benefit package" approach for making cost comparisons for certain benefits under ADEA. This benefit package approach offers greater flexibility than a benefit-by-benefit analysis as long as the overall result is no lesser cost to the employer and is no less favorable in terms of the overall benefits provided to employees. Under the IB, the benefit package approach is applicable to group term life insurance plans and certain other benefits under these plans, such as the waiver-of-premium benefit and accidental death and dismemberment benefits.

The IB also states it is not unlawful for life insurance coverage to cease at age 70, or upon separation from the employer's service, whichever occurs first.

Advantages and Disadvantages of Group Term Life Insurance

In summary, employers and employees are interested in evaluating the relative advantages and limitations of group term life insurance as an employee benefit.[16]

Advantages to the Employer. From the employer's perspective the following might be considered advantages of including a well-designed group term life insurance program as one of its employee benefits.

- Employee morale and productivity may be enhanced by offering this element of financial security.

- The coverage is necessary for competitive reasons, since most employers offer this form of protection.

- The life insurance protection is an aid to attaining good public and employer-employee relations.

Advantages to Employees. Group term life insurance dovetails into an employee's financial security planning.

- It adds a layer of low-cost protection to personal savings, individual life insurance and Social Security benefits.

- It helps reduce the anxieties about the consequences of the employee's possible premature death.

- Employer's contributions are not reportable as taxable to the insured employee for federal income tax purposes unless the total amount of group insurance from all sources exceeds $50,000, and then only the value of the amount which exceeds $50,000 is taxed according to the income tax regulations. However, the Tax Equity and Fiscal Responsibility Act of 1982 (TEFRA) requires that "key" employees must include the cost of the first $50,000 of group term life insurance as current income if the plan discriminates in their favor. A group term life insurance plan may be considered to discriminate in favor of key employees unless the plan benefits at least 70 percent of all employees, at least 85 percent of the participants are not key employees, the plan is part of a cafeteria type, or the plan complies with a reasonable classification system found by the Internal Revenue Service (IRS) to be nondiscriminatory. In applying these IRS rules, part time and seasonal workers as well as those with fewer than three years of service do not have to be considered. Employees covered by a collec-

---

[16] See W. G. Williams, "Group Life Insurance," pp. 377–78.

tive bargaining agreement where group term life insurance has been bargained for also may be excluded.

- If employees are contributing toward the cost, their contributions are automatically withheld from their paychecks, making it convenient and also reducing the possibility of lapse of the insurance.

- The conversion privilege enables terminated employees to convert their group term life insurance to individual permanent policies without individual evidence of insurability.

- Liberal underwriting standards provide coverage for those who might be uninsurable or only able to get insurance at substandard rates.

Disadvantages.   Despite its many advantages, group term life insurance has some disadvantages. First, the employee usually has no assurance the employer will continue the group policy in force from one year to the next. Group life insurance plans seldom are discontinued, but business failures can and do occur, and the conversion privilege upon termination of a group life policy may be of limited value to the employees because of the high cost of conversion on an attained-age basis.

Another limitation exists when employees change employers, because group term life insurance is not "portable." Only about one out of every hundred terminating employees uses the conversion privilege. In practice, however, most employees changing jobs expect to be insured for the same or a higher amount of group life insurance with their new employers. Group term life insurance provides "protection only," while employee needs, at least partially, may dictate some other form of life insurance that has a savings or cash value feature. Future chapters look at the more permanent forms of group life insurance, as well as other methods of funding death benefits under employee benefit plans.

CHAPTER 5

Social Security and Other Governmental Death Benefit Plans

ROBERT J. MYERS

Economic security for the survivors of deceased workers in the United States is, in the vast majority of cases, provided through the multiple means of Social Security, private pensions, and individual savings. This is sometimes referred to as a "three-legged stool" or the three "pillars" of economic security protection. Still others look upon the situation as Social Security providing the floor of protection, with private sector activities building on top of it, and with public assistance programs, such as Supplemental Security Income (SSI) and Aid to Families with Dependent Children (AFDC), providing a net of protection for those whose total income does not attain certain levels or meet minimum subsistence needs.

Some people believe that the Social Security program should provide complete protection for the survivors of deceased workers—children (and the remaining parent) and the aged surviving spouse. However, over the years, it generally has been agreed that Social Security should be only a floor of protection upon which private programs can build. Furthermore, private planning for survivor economic security often can adapt to special needs, such as periods when the surviving spouse has not reached age 60 and has no young children present, or when post-secondary education needs of children are present. In addition, the capital needs of industry for development funds are served by the accumulation of assets under private plans, whereas Social Security operates on a largely unfunded basis, with any investments being in government obligations.

As described elsewhere in this book, private pension and insurance plans have, to a significant extent, been developed to supplement Social Security. This is done in a number of ways, both directly and indirectly. The net result, however, is a broad network of survivor protection that serves the country well.

This chapter discusses the survivor-benefit provisions of the Social Security program, not only their historical development and present structure, but also possible future changes. Following this, other governmental programs in this area, the separate one for railroad workers and the numerous plans for governmental employees, are described. Then, the public assistance programs available to supplement other forms of survivor income, when necessary, are analyzed. Finally, the relationship of the Social Security program with governmental benefit plans which cover other risks, such as work-connected accidents, is evaluated.

The consideration of the Social Security program in this chapter deals only with the survivor-benefit provisions applicable equally to both active and retired insured workers. Actually, the program is a closely coordinated one, covering also the risks of long-term disability and retirement of the worker. These subjects are dealt with in Chapters 17 and 28, respectively.

"Social Security" as used here is the meaning generally accepted in the United States, namely, the cash benefits provisions of the Old-Age, Survivors, and Disability Insurance (OASDI) program. International usage of the term *social security* is much broader than this and includes all other types of programs protecting individuals against the economic risks of a modern industrial society, such as unemployment, short-term sickness, work-connected accidents and diseases, and medical care costs.

The term "widow" is used here to include also widowers. Until recently, the latter did not receive OASDI benefits on the same basis as widows, either being required to prove dependence on the deceased female worker or not being eligible at all. Now, because of legislative changes and court decisions, complete equality of treatment by sex prevails for OASDI survivor benefits.

OLD-AGE, SURVIVORS, AND DISABILITY INSURANCE PROGRAM (OASDI)

Historical Development of Survivor Provisions

When what is now the OASDI program was developed in 1934–35, it was confined entirely to retirement benefits (plus lump-sum refund payments to represent the difference, if any, between employee taxes paid, plus an allowance for interest, and retirement benefits received). It was not until the 1939 act that monthly survivor benefits were added, in lieu of the refund benefit.

The minimum eligibility age for aged widows was established at age 65. This figure was selected in a purely empirical manner, because it was a round figure (see Chapter 28 on why this was selected as the minimum retirement age).

Beginning in the 1950s, pressure developed to provide early-retirement benefits, first for widows and spouses and then for insured workers themselves. The minimum early-retirement age was set at 62, again a pragmatic political compromise, rather than being based on any completely logical reason. The three-year differential, however, did represent about the average difference in age between men and their wives (but, of course, as with any averages, in many cases the actual difference is larger). The benefit amounts were not reduced for widows when they claimed before age 65 under the original amendatory legislation, but this is no longer the case.

Persons Covered

OASDI coverage, for both taxes and earnings credits toward benefit rights, currently applies to somewhat more than 90 percent of the total work force of the United States.

Eligibility Conditions

To be eligible for OASDI survivor benefits, individuals must have a certain amount of covered employment. Eligibility—termed *fully insured status* or *currently insured status*—depends upon having a certain number of quarters of coverage (QC). (The number of QCs required for fully insured status is described in Chapter 28.) Currently insured status requires only 6 QC earned in the 13-quarter period ending with the quarter of death.

Beneficiary Categories

Two general categories of survivors of insured workers can receive monthly benefits (in all cases being based on the Primary Insurance Amount, or PIA). Aged survivors are widows aged 60 or over (or at ages 50–59 if disabled) and dependent parents aged 62 or over. Young survivors are children under age 18 (or at any age if disabled before age 22), children aged 18 who are full-time students in elementary or secondary educational institutions,[1] and the widowed parent of such children who are under age 16 or disabled. In addition, a death benefit of $255 is payable to widows or, in the absence of a widow, to children eligible for immediate monthly benefits.

The disabled widow receives a benefit at the rate of 50 percent of the deceased worker's PIA if claim is first made at age 50, and receives gradually larger amounts for older ages, up to 71.5 percent at age 60. The benefit rate for other widows grades up from 71.5 percent of the PIA if claimed at age 60 to 100 percent if claimed at age 65 or over. Any delayed-retirement credits the deceased worker had earned also are applicable to the widow's benefit. Widows, regardless of age, caring for an eligible child (under age 16 or disabled) have a benefit of 75 percent of the PIA. Divorced spouses, when the marriage lasted at least 10 years, are eligible for benefits under the same conditions as undivorced spouses.

---

[1] Post-secondary student benefits (up to age 22) were available before legislation in 1981. For those previously qualifying (before May 1983), these benefits are still available, but on a gradually phased-out basis on benefit amount, until being eliminated after April 1985.

Children under age 18 and children aged 18 or over and disabled before age 22, plus children attending elementary or high school full time at age 18, also are eligible for benefits at a rate of 75 percent of the PIA. Before amendments in 1981, child school-attendance benefits for all types of educational institutions were payable up to age 22.

An overall maximum on total family benefits is applicable (as discussed in Chapter 28). If a person is eligible for more than one type of benefit, e.g., both as a worker and as a surviving spouse, in essence only the largest benefit is payable.

Benefit Computation Procedures and Indexing

As indicated in the previous section, all OASDI benefits are based on the PIA. (The method of computing the PIA is described in detail in Chapter 28.)

Eligibility Test and Other Restrictions on Benefits

From the inception of the OASDI program, there has been some form of restriction on the payment of benefits to persons who have substantial earnings from employment. This provision is referred to as the earnings or retirement test. It does not apply to nonearned income, such as from investments or pensions. The same test applies to survivor beneficiaries as to retirement benefits. However, the earnings of one beneficiary (e.g., the widowed mother) do not affect the benefits of the other beneficiaries in the family (e.g., the orphaned children).

If a widow receives a pension from service under a government-employee pension plan under which the members were not covered under OASDI on the last day of her employment, the widow's OASDI benefit is reduced by the amount of such pension. This provision, however, is not applicable to women (or men who were dependent on their wives) who became eligible for such a pension before December 1982 but to individuals who became first so eligible from December 1982 through June 1983 and who were dependent on their spouses.

Financing

The survivor benefits are financed as a part of the OASI program. (Such financing provisions are described in detail in Chapter 28.)

RAILROAD RETIREMENT (RR) PROGRAM

The OASDI system covers virtually all nongovernment wage employment except for railroad employees, who are covered by the Railroad Retirement system. This separate system is coordinated closely with

OASDI, and its general structure is similar. The survivor benefit amounts, however, are significantly higher.

Eligibility Conditions

The eligibility conditions for all types of benefits require 120 months of railroad service. If a person does not meet the eligibility conditions, the earnings record is transferred to OASDI for whatever benefit rights it will produce. Survivor benefits are payable to the same categories of beneficiaries as under OASDI. The RR survivor benefit amounts are equal to what OASDI amounts would be on the same earnings record, plus an amount based on the Tier-II retirement benefit (as described in Chapter 28), e.g., 50 percent thereof for the widow at age 65 or with eligible child, 15 percent for a child, and 80 percent as the maximum family benefit. The automatic-adjustment provisions for changes in the consumer price index (CPI) apply in the same manner as under OASDI insofar as the OASDI portion of the benefit is concerned, but only a 32.5 percent increase is applicable to the Tier-II portion.

GOVERNMENT EMPLOYEE PLANS

Governmental employee retirement plans initially provided only retirement benefits; any survivor benefits were available only for retirees and then only if the retired had elected a joint-and-survivor option on an actuarial-equivalent basis. Later, survivor benefits for both active and retired workers were added. Many of these plans have provided survivor benefits by becoming coordinated with OASDI, as is common in the private sector, but others did so by merely adding OASDI on top, e.g., the military plan.

Civil Service Retirement System (CSR)

The basic nature and coverage of CSR is described later (in Chapter 28). If survivor benefits are desired after retirement, a reduction in the basic pension is made, but these benefits are automatically available for survivors of active workers. The reduction for widow's benefits is 2.5 percent of the first $300 of monthly pension, plus 10 percent of the remainder which is significantly lower than if on an actuarially equivalent basis. The reduction is restored if the spouse dies before the retiree. Nonmarried retirees can make a similar election for dependents with an insurable interest, but with larger deductions but still less than the actuarial equivalent.

The widow pensions under CSR are payable without regard to age. The child survivor benefits are payable under somewhat the same conditions as under OASDI, except that school-attendance benefits are available up to age 22.

The amount of the widow and widower pensions is 55 percent of the full pension for which the retired member was eligible, i.e., before any reduction on account of taking the survivor protection, or of the full disability pension for which the deceased employee would have been eligible if he or she had become disabled instead of dying in active service. The survivor pension in the case of nonmarried pensioners who have a beneficiary with an insurable interest is 50 percent of the *reduced* employee pension. Child-survivor pensions, when a widowed mother is present, were established in 1969 as flat-dollar amounts of $75 per month per child, with a maximum for all children of $225 per month. These flat-dollar amounts are subject to automatic adjustment for changes in the cost of living, as described hereafter, and they were $218 and $654, respectively, in early 1983. In instances where the only survivors are children, the pension amounts are 20 percent higher. Automatic cost-of-living adjustments for CSR pensions are made annually based on the percentage increase in the CPI over a 12-month period. In 1983–85, these periods were increased to 13 months for each of these years successively.

In addition to the monthly survivor benefits, a refund of accumulated contributions, without interest, minus monthly benefits paid, is available after all monthly benefits have ceased.

The cost of the CSR survivor benefits is included within the overall cost of the program (except for the portion of the cost of the elective postretirement survivor benefits met by the reduction in the retirement pension). (Chapter 28 gives details as to this overall financing basis.)

In addition to the survivor protection provided by CSR, a group life insurance program is available. It is underwritten by a consortium of about 250 insurance companies. The standard plan provides one year's salary during active service at ages 45 and over and two years' salary at ages 35 and under, with graded-in amounts at ages 36–44. For retirees, the full amount continues in force until age 65, and then it reduces by 2 percent each month until reaching 25 percent of salary, at which level it stabilizes. The employees pay about $.55 per month per $1,000 (except for postal employees, who do not pay anything), and the government pays the balance of the cost (about one third, currently, for general employees).

Several types of optional insurance, whose cost is borne entirely by the employees, are available. Employees may purchase additional insurance up to five times their annual salary. They also may purchase $5,000 of insurance on their spouses and $2,500 on each unmarried dependent child under age 22. Retirees may purchase insurance such that the reduction in the amount of protection after age 65 will not be as large as it would be if only the standard plan were taken.

Retirement Systems for Other Federal Civilian Groups

Both the Tennessee Valley Authority and the Board of Governors of the Federal Reserve Bank have established pension plans for their employees. In both instances, OASDI coverage, with the accompanying survivor-benefit protection, is applicable. The supplementary pension plans are quite similar to those of private employers.

Employees of the State Department and certain related agencies in the Foreign Service have a separate retirement system, which resembles CSR (including its survivor benefit provisions), but is significantly more liberal.

Supreme Court justices and other federal judges have a noncontributory retirement system. Survivor benefits are available only if the member elects such coverage and contributes thereto, with part of the cost for such benefits being paid by the federal government.

Military Retirement System

In addition to OASDI, members of the military services are covered by a noncontributory pension plan. This plan provides no survivor benefits for death in active service. However, after retirement, survivor protection is available if the retiree so elects and takes a reduction in the retiree's pay. Such postretirement survivor benefits are modeled after those under CSR, including automatic adjustment for changes in the CPI, except that the widow's benefits are reduced at age 62 in recognition of the availability of OASDI benefits then. The reduction for such survivor benefits is computed in the same manner as under CSR. As a result of the generally younger ages at retirement and the Social Security offset, these benefits often are not the same actuarial bargain as the similar ones under CSR.

Another program, Dependency and Indemnity Compensation, provides survivor benefits for death in active service and also for service-connected causes with regard to retirees, as an alternative to the benefits described in the previous paragraph. The benefit amounts for the widow vary with the rank of the individual, and a flat additional amount is paid for each child. These benefits are available on a noncontributory basis.

Life insurance, in amounts up to $35,000, is available on an individual election basis for those in active service and, later, for those leaving service. During active service, it is on a term insurance basis with small premiums payable by the member. After separation from service, the individual can retain the insurance and convert it to other forms, such as whole life; the extra cost is borne by the individual, except for the administrative expenses and any costs arising from service-connected causes. The entire program is administered by a consortium of life insurance companies.

Survivor pensions also are paid for veterans with nonservice-connected disabilities, subject to an income test.

Retirement Systems for State and Local Government Employees

There are many separate retirement systems for employees of state and local governments. A wide divergence exists among the various state and local systems on whether they have elected OASDI coverage which would provide some survivor-benefits protection.

These state and local plans are quite diverse about how they provide survivor benefits. Some have automatic survivor protection, with monthly benefits available in all cases of death in active service or after retirement. At the other extreme, some plans have no other survivor benefits than elective joint-and-survivor pensions on an actuarial-equivalent basis and refund of accumulated employee contributions.

Many state and local governments have separate group life insurance plans similar to those of private employers. The benefit for death in active service usually is some multiple of annual salary, while for death after retirement the amount often is limited to a relatively small flat amount.

PUBLIC ASSISTANCE PROGRAMS

Public assistance programs provide a financial backstop for survivors of deceased workers if OASDI and other governmental benefits, plus private-sector benefits, are insufficient. For aged widows (65 or over), this is done through the Supplemental Security Income program in the same manner as for any other aged person.

Widowed mothers with young children can receive payments under the Aid to Families with Dependent Children program, which consists of various state plans with part of the cost borne by the federal government. The vast majority of AFDC recipients are not survivor cases, but rather families where the father is absent from the home through divorce, desertion, or illegitimacy.

RELATIONSHIP OF OASDI PROGRAM WITH OTHER GOVERNMENTAL PROGRAMS

The survivor benefits payable under the OASDI program parallel those available under other governmental programs. OASDI benefits are coordinated with those under the Railroad Retirement program, but they generally are not coordinated with such survivor benefits as are available under other governmental insurance-type programs, including workers' compensation. Of course, there is coordination, in a sense, of OASDI benefits with public-assistance payments, because the latter take into account all other income, including OASDI benefits.

CHAPTER 6

Permanent Forms of Group Life Insurance

WILLIAM H. RABEL*

Most people, including retired persons, are inadequately insured at the time of their death. Even though most retired workers do not have dependent children, many of them have dependents, most often spouses, and some have problems of estate liquidity. A lifetime of work may not be sufficient to provide the legacy desired by many retirees, and their financial goals are made particularly elusive by the high level of inflation that has plagued most countries since World War II. Since group insurance is one of the principal means for meeting the economic security needs of our society, it is appropriate to consider it as one possible way to provide insurance after retirement.

Coverage can be continued on retired persons in a variety of ways. First, they can exercise the conversion privilege available under group term life and obtain an ordinary life policy. Another approach is for the employer to maintain the group term coverage on a former employee after retirement. This could be financed on a pay-as-you-go basis, with the likelihood of eventually paying very high premiums, or the employer could establish a deposit fund (sometimes called a side fund) to fund postretirement benefits during the working life of the employee.

Unfortunately, all the approaches mentioned above have one or more shortcomings. Conversion at or near age 65 involves a premium outlay most people cannot afford. In addition, tax factors (explained below) would probably prevent the employer from contributing to the purchase of the converted permanent insurance. Even under the best of circumstances, pay-as-you-go funding for term coverage on retired employees involves substantial cash outlays, which may result in undesirable cash-flow problems for an employer. Furthermore, although a deposit fund may solve some of the problems of pay-as-you-go funding, in most cases, the tax consequences

* The author would like to express his appreciation to John Crane, FLMI, Senior Associate, LOMA, for his assistance in preparing this chapter.

are either unsatisfactory or unclear and therefore unpredictable. Perhaps the most promising approach to deposit funding is the retired lives reserve (RLR), which is discussed in detail in Chapter 7 and will not be covered here. Less formal funding approaches may not engender the funds needed to provide coverage for retired persons.

In view of the limitations of the methods mentioned above, employers, employees, and insurers have sought other ways to provide group coverage after retirement. Prominent among the approaches tried have been group paid-up insurance, group permanent, and group ordinary. While such permanent products have developed over the years, primarily in response to income-tax law and regulation, it should be noted that the sale of all types of permanent has been far outstripped by group term.

GROUP PAID-UP LIFE INSURANCE

In the search for postretirement group life insurance, the least complex product and the clearest tax status are combined in group paid-up coverage. First written in 1941, it was the principal group permanent product until group ordinary was introduced in the 1960s. Today it retains its advantage from a tax standpoint, but competition from group ordinary and changing consumer demands are leading to the liberalization of its traditional rights of insureds, which are described below.

This approach allows all or part of an employee's scheduled group coverage to be so written that it will be fully paid up when the employee retires. During his or her working life, the employee makes a regular contribution that is used to purchase paid-up increments of whole life insurance. Each purchase increases the total amount of paid-up insurance owned. Figure 6–1 illustrates how units of paid-up insurance accumulate.

For tax reasons, discussed in the next section, employers do not purchase permanent insurance for their employees under this plan. Rather, they supplement the employees' purchases of permanent insurance with decreasing amounts of term insurance. After each contribution, the amount of term insurance decreases by exactly the amount that the paid-up insurance increases. Thus, the combined amount of both types of insurance remains constant at the amount set by the benefits schedule. Figure 6–1 illustrates the combination of coverages in this product.

Contributions

Employee contributions generally are designed to be level throughout the employee's working life. Naturally, because of actuarial considerations, the amount purchased with each contribution decreases as the employee gets older. Furthermore, costs are higher for individuals who enter the plan at older ages because they have fewer years in which to accumulate paid-up coverage. Therefore, in theory, a schedule of contributions should be

Figure 6-1
Interrelationship between Increasing Increments of Paid-Up
Group Life Insurance and Decreasing Increments of Group
Term Life Insurance

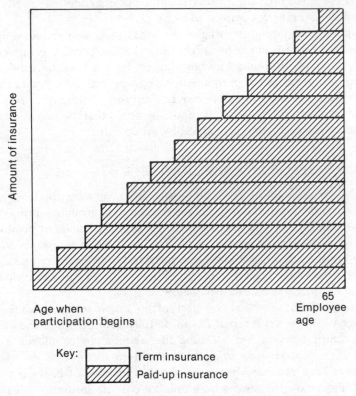

Key: Term insurance
     Paid-up insurance

graded for age and anticipated length of service, and this is a common practice. Consequently, older employees entering the plan typically will pay a higher periodic contribution than will young employees, although the contribution of both will be level.

To provide certain minimum benefits for all employees and to encourage a high level of participation (particularly among older employees), some employers set a single contribution rate for all employees. The rates are attractively low, frequently $1.00 to $1.30 per month per $1,000 of coverage. Table 6-1 illustrates the amounts of paid-up insurance that can be accumulated by workers at various ages with a monthly contribution of $1. When the flat contribution results in inadequate coverage for older employees, the employer may supplement the paid-up insurance by continuing the necessary amount of term insurance after the employee retires. Sometimes a flat contribution schedule is limited to those who are with a firm for a minimum time when the coverage starts, while new employees pay according to an age-graded schedule.

Table 6-1
Accumulated Amounts of Paid-Up Insurance Based
on $1 Monthly Contribution

	Number of Years in Plan				
Entry Age	5	15	25	35	45
20	$229	$609	$905	$1,139	$1,329
30	178	474	708	899	—
40	139	373	563	—	—
50	110	301	—	—	—
60	91	—	—	—	—

Source: Robert W. Batten et al., *Group Life Insurance*
(Atlanta, Georgia: Life Office Management Association,
1979), p. 111.

Plan Provisions

As is normal for group insurance, benefits are determined by a schedule.
In general, the provisions found in group term contracts also apply to the
term portion of the paid-up plan as well. These include conversion and
disability benefits (such as waiver of premium).

The employee-owned paid-up segment of the policy develops cash values, which are the greater of (1) the employee's contributions without
interest, or (2) the standard nonforfeiture values as shown in the policy. In
contrast to individual life policies, however, cash values are available only
when the worker's employment terminates. Except in the case of termination, most insurers will not permit a surrender of the policy, and contracts
do not contain a loan privilege.

The justifications for the constraints on loans and surrenders are that
the cost of administering these benefits would offset some of the savings
made possible through use of the group technique, and access to cash
values could lead to an undermining of the goal of the plan—to provide
post-retirement protection. Finally, it sometimes is maintained that access
to policy values could subject insurers to adverse financial selection on a
line of coverage for which contingency margins have not explicitly been
added. This, of course, begs the question why margins are not added, and
it becomes clear that the first two factors are the principal considerations
in support of the practice.

Under the provisions of most plans, the life company may delay paying
surrender values for up to two years after employment is terminated. This is
to prevent employees from quitting temporarily and then resuming their
jobs just to obtain the policy surrender values. Obviously, there may be a
great temptation to do so during a strike, layoff, or other period of economic stress for the worker. This restrictive provision is not applied when
employees terminate with small amounts of coverage (e.g., less than
$1,000). In such cases, policies are surrendered automatically for purposes
of administrative simplicity.

It is important to note that coverage is not surrendered, and cash values are not available, if the master contract terminates. Paid-up coverage remains intact as long as employment is not terminated.

Although the reasons for not including a policy loan provision in traditional group paid-up policies still seem valid, limitations on the availability of surrender values seem less justifiable in light of contemporary consumer standards. It seems likely that those still in force will be phased out in the face of competitive pressures.

Premium Rates and Experience Rating

As a rule, paid-up coverage is sold on a "net" basis. In other words, rates are based on mortality and interest assumptions alone; no specific loading is added for expenses or contingencies. It is assumed the cost of the plan will be met through margins in mortality and interest, and that the expense factor will be kept low because the paid-up coverage is administered automatically with the term coverage. Historically, this feature has contributed to the relatively low cost of paid-up coverage.

Group term policyowners (usually an employer) normally receive a dividend or "experience credit" each year if their experience has been favorable. However, with group paid-up plans, dividends usually are not paid until the combined experience of both the paid-up and term accounts are favorable for a particular case. This may take several years, because of start-up and early surrender costs under the paid-up account.

Until 1971, the allocation of experience credits varied among plans. Under the tax code, it was permissible for benefits of favorable experience to be divided proportionately between the term and paid-up accounts. Alternatively, they could be allocated to the term account until all its costs were returned, at which time they were shared with the paid-up account. (A similar practice is still common for contributory group credit life, where the policyholder—a financial institution—may receive a return of all its premiums before insureds share in the benefits of experience.) However, as a result of revenue rulings beginning in 1971, described below, as of 1982 each account must stand on its own feet. Thus, favorable experience credits must be allocated to the account from which they originate. Favorable experience may be passed on to the paid-up account in the form of a dividend to insureds, or as reduced rates for future purchases.

All normal or customary practices in experience rating are subject to change under the pressure of competition. When competition is intense, insurers may expand their tendency to pool the underwriting experience of different coverages or even different lines (e.g., group term and group permanent, or group life and group health). Pooling may lead to changes in the experience-rating practices enumerated above.

Uses of Group Paid-Up Insurance

Group paid-up tends to appeal to firms with fewer than 500 employees. Furthermore, it generally is underwritten only for groups that display certain characteristics. This limitation can be regarded as a disadvantage when compared with the greater flexibility associated with group term coverage.

As a first requirement, only those employers that provide stable employment can purchase group paid-up. Since strikes and layoffs interrupt employee contributions, and therefore interfere with the accumulation of paid-up coverage, they must be most unusual for the industry in which the policyowner operates. Furthermore, some carriers will not underwrite a case until the firm has been in business for a minimum period (e.g., three years).

Insurers also require that turnover be very low for the employer. To a degree, the turnover problem can be controlled by a long probationary period. However, the underwriting rules of some carriers exclude employers that have an annual turnover rate in excess of 5 percent. In addition, some establish minimum age requirements for participation (e.g., age 30–35).

Advantages of Group Paid-Up Life Insurance

Adherents of group paid-up life insurance claim it provides several advantages to employers or employees, or both. First and foremost, as contrasted with group term, it does provide permanent protection. Related to this is the advantage of cash value accumulations by the insured that can be made available when employment terminates. Both of these features are related to a third, which is that group paid-up provides a scientific way to fund postretirement coverage over the working life of the employee.

Group paid-up plans facilitate the conversion by long-service employees of any term coverage remaining at age 65, because it usually is a relatively small proportion of the scheduled amount, and because converted coverage is purchased at net rates. Thus, for these two reasons, retirees may end up being able to afford even more permanent coverage than they anticipate.

A sixth advantage to group paid-up is that employers electing to continue all or part of the coverage on retirees find the scheduled amount of term reduced well below the amount needed in the absence of paid-up insurance. This smaller financial burden may be easier for a business to justify.

A seventh advantage, when compared with other forms of permanent group coverage (discussed below), is that the status of these plans is well established with the Internal Revenue Service. They are a known commodity, and no serious modification of existing plans has been required by tax rulings to date. Therefore, it is highly unlikely that they will be subject to unfavorable rulings in the future. Another important tax factor is that the employer-purchased term coverage receives the favorable tax treatment accorded to all group term coverage.[1]

The group paid-up system provides still other advantages. Being contributory, the plan encourages participation only by those who need insurance. At the same time, in contrast to group term plans, employees may be more willing to contribute to the cost of group paid-up because they can see a permanent benefit growing out of their premiums.[2]

It is worth noting that insurers may be willing to offer higher limits on group plans containing permanent coverage than on term alone. The amount at risk for each individual continually diminishes throughout his or her working life. Furthermore, margins in interest earnings on reserves may support a more liberal benefit schedule.

Disadvantages of Group Paid-Up Life Insurance

Among the greatest disadvantages of group paid-up insurance is that the type of employer that can use it is limited, as explained above. Another limitation relates to the relatively high cost of administering the plan, when compared with term insurance. More professional advice is needed in designing, installing, and administering the plan. Furthermore, changes in benefits, eligibility status, and the like often require more record changes than would be required for term. A third disadvantage is that employer costs are higher in the early years of the plan than they would be for group term. Thus, the employer may delay the plan until it can be afforded. The high cost in the early years is due to start-up costs, as well as to the need to fund coverage for employees approaching retirement. In some cases, the employer may decide not to purchase a term plan to provide temporary protection with the result that there is no protection at all.

Finally, the principal advantage of group paid-up is also its principal weakness. Employee contributions purchase permanent coverage, and therefore afford less current protection for each premium dollar.

LEVEL PREMIUM GROUP PERMANENT LIFE INSURANCE

In exploring various approaches to providing postretirement coverage through the group mechanism, it was only a matter of time before someone suggested taking standard, level-premium, whole life insurance and writing

---

[1] See: William H. Rabel and Charles E. Hughes, "Taxation of Group Life Insurance," *Journal of Accounting, Auditing, and Finance* 1, no. 2, p. 177, for a thorough discussion of this topic.

[2] For a discussion of the advantages of contributory group life plans, see Robert Batten et al., *Group Life and Health Insurance* (Atlanta, GA: Life Office Management Association, 1979), p. 42.

it on a group basis. The idea was to have the employer pay all or part of the premium and to have the employee pay any amount not paid by the employer. However, before this approach could develop much of a following, the Treasury Department quashed it for all practical purposes in a 1950 tax ruling (Mimeograph 6477). The ruling required employees to include as current taxable income any employer contribution toward the cost of permanent insurance, unless the insurance is nonvested and forfeitable in the case employment is terminated. As a result of this ruling, the use of traditional level premium group life has been limited principally to qualified pension plans or to forfeitable group life plans. However, in the mid-1960s a new type of permanent group coverage was introduced that purported to conform with some newly introduced standards of the tax law. These products varied widely in design, but were known collectively as "group ordinary" or "Section 79" plans.

GROUP ORDINARY LIFE INSURANCE

In the most generic sense, group ordinary plans are a loosely knit group of plans under which the employee may elect to substitute permanent life insurance for all or part of his or her group term coverage. The permanent policy may be of the limited payment form (e.g., life paid up at age 65) or it may be ordinary life. As explained in greater detail below, designers of these plans tried to distinguish them from level premium permanent (described in the previous section) and to qualify them for favorable tax treatment, by purporting to allocate employer premiums to the purchase of term insurance. Usually, insurers denoted the amount at risk in a whole life policy as term insurance, although other approaches were used. Before analyzing various group ordinary designs, however, it is important to examine the tax environment that rekindled an interest in group permanent coverage other than group paid-up.

Group ordinary was fostered by the Revenue Act of 1964, which significantly modified the Internal Revenue Code. Section 79 of the revised code, as amplified through regulations issued by the Internal Revenue Service in 1966, gave the impression an employer could contribute to a level premium group contract without having the contributions become taxable to the employee. All that was necessary, it was assumed by many who interpreted the code, was to divide the premium in such a way that the employer was paying only for the amount at risk under the contract. This interpretation derived from the wording of the 1966 regulations, which permitted an employer to contribute to a permanent plan of insurance, without having premiums paid on behalf of an employee taxable to the employee, provided the following conditions were met: (1) the group policy set forth the proportion of the premium properly allocable to term insurance, (2) the employer's contribution did not exceed the proportion properly allocable to term insurance, and (3) each covered employee was eligible for such optional permanent insurance.

There were great differences of opinion as to what Section 79 permitted in the way of products, and a wide spectrum of products was designed. However, most of them followed one of three approaches as described below.

Group Ordinary Plans of the 1960s

Three approaches were used to allocate the cost of group ordinary insurance between the employer and employee. The first was to have the employer pay each year the amount it would pay if the employee had elected annually renewable term insurance (ART) instead of permanent coverage. The employee would then pay the rest of the level premium. As the cost of ART rose, the employer's share would increase until it reached 100 percent of the level premium. From that time forward, the employee would pay nothing and the employer would pay the full level premium.

A second approach required the employer to pay a premium that varied with the amount at risk under the policy and the age of the insured. The cost was determined by multiplying the average amount at risk in any given year by the mortality rate for the insured's age and adding a loading factor for expenses and contingencies. The increasing mortality was offset to some degree by the decreasing amount at risk, although if the employer were to fund coverage past retirement the cost would rise until age 100, or at least until the very highest ages in the mortality table. (Naturally, most employers stopped contributions at retirement.) The insured was required to provide for the increase in the reserve, and this could be done through either level or variable premiums, depending on the plan. Employers found the variable aspect of the premium somewhat undesirable.

A third approach, derived from the second, overcame the unattractiveness of the variable premiums of the employer. This approach recognizes that, even though the amount at risk and death rate vary under the second approach, there is no need for premiums to vary. After all, insurers had been providing level premium, decreasing term insurance contracts for many years. Therefore, the life companies computed a level cost for the employer's share. When subtracted from the premium for the policy, this left the employee with a level premium as well. Thus, the contribution of each party could be expressed as a fixed percentage of the premium.

Of all the forms of group ordinary, it was the third that caught on most widely. This was no doubt due to the ease with which it could be explained to policyholders and the attraction of the level premium. Before long, a great deal of group ordinary was being sold.

In short order, the IRS began to revisit the question of group ordinary insurance. The third form, in particular, became subject to review, because, having level premium insurance for both parties, employer contributions were in fact going into a plan that seemed quite close if not identical to those which were denied favorable tax treatments in the early 1950s under

Mimeograph 6477. At least the results were the same, despite the fact they had been reached in a different way. Furthermore, the IRS raised questions whether the costs on group ordinary contracts of any type were being fairly allocated among the parties. A suspicion existed that employers were bearing more than their fair share of the cost of coverage, which in fact represented an untaxed subsidy to employees.

Rule 71-360: An Effort to Clarify the Issue

As the decade of the 1960s closed, great uncertainty existed over the tax status of group ordinary plans. Finally, the situation was partly clarified with the issuance of Revenue Ruling 71-360 in 1971. Further guidance was provided with the adoption of additional rules over the years, but even a decade later the situation still remains somewhat vague.

Under 71-360, a group insurance plan could qualify for favorable tax treatment as provided by Section 79, if it met three conditions. First, the group term life coverage could not be based in any part on the net amount at risk under a permanent life insurance contract. In other words, the IRS took the position a permanent life insurance contract could not be divided into savings and protection constituents, although two contracts could be issued concurrently that would achieve similar results. Second, an employer's premium would not be considered properly allocable to group term insurance "if it [was] a level premium [i.e., did not vary with the attained age and amount at risk] or if the rate per $1,000 of term protection varied only as a function of the duration of some form of permanent insurance policy issued in conjunction with a term insurance policy." Finally, both the term and permanent segments of the plan had to stand on their own as to expense charges, loading, and dividends.

The IRS put teeth into the ruling by reserving the right to determine the amount of premium that was "properly allocable" to group term life insurance. If the amount "allocated" (charged) by the plan was higher than what was properly allocable, the excess was taxed to the employee as ordinary income. Furthermore, if the employer contributed more than the amount allocated to it and that amount exceeded the amount properly allocable (i.e., the employer openly subsidizes the employee), then the entire employer contribution was taxable to the employee.

While many of the first two types of group ordinary plans of the 1960s were modified to qualify under 71-360, none of the third, and most popular types, of plans qualified. Nevertheless, a few companies continued to argue the point and to try to qualify such plans throughout much of the decade of the 1970s. Some of these companies also continued trying to sell these plans. In the face of 71-360, however, most companies stopped marketing the third type of plan. For those plans in force, some insurers tried to develop substitute contracts that would qualify. This was not always possible or commercially feasible, and many policyholders had no option other

than to abandon their group ordinary plan or keep it in force with taxable
income accruing to the employee. Tax relief was given in certain cases to
the degree that only those contributions in excess of annually renewable
term rates were treated as taxable income, and some contracts favored in
that way remain in force today.

Contemporary Group Ordinary Products

Many life insurance companies dropped out of the group ordinary market during the 1970s, because the attractiveness of the product was substantially diminished by the requirements of the tax law. Nevertheless,
some interest remains in providing permanent group insurance other than
traditional group paid-up, and a few new products have been developed to
satisfy the law.

The IRS issued new regulations under Section 79 on May 14, 1979, after
lengthy hearings and much discussion. The regulations provide that a group
plan may contain permanent benefits and still qualify for favorable tax
treatment if it meets the following conditions:

(i)   the policy or the employer states in writing the portion of the death
      benefit that is group term life insurance;[3]
(ii) the term insurance benefit must not be less than the difference between
      the death benefit determined by the schedule and the permanent insur-
      ance owned by the employee;[4] and
(iii) the employee must have the right to decline or discontinue permanent
      protection without reducing the amount of term insurance provided by
      the plan.[5]

The new regulations provide that an employee must include as gross
income the cost of permanent benefits provided under a group plan, less
the amount, if any, that he or she paid for the benefits. Thus, as under
previous regulations, employer contributions for permanent benefits are
treated as taxable income to the employee. Formulas for computing the cost
of benefits are set forth in the regulations. It should be noted that all or a
portion of dividends paid under participating group permanent insurance
also may be includable in the employee's gross income. The amount is
determined by a formula designed to prevent an employer from subsidizing
permanent coverage for an employee through policy dividends.

Prior to the release of the 1979 regulations, some plans were written
with two contracts instead of one. The purchase of one contract was not
contingent on the purchase of the other. Insurers offering such plans did so
because they believed it was required by 71-360, and indeed that was what
the rule stated although some tried to interpret it in other ways. Also,

---

[3] Regulation Section 1.79-1 (b) (1) (i).
[4] Regulation Section 1.79-1 (b) (1) (ii).
[5] Regulation Section 1.79-1 (b) (1) (iii).

insurers felt that this market test would prove that one policy was not subsidizing the other. However, the new regulations do not require separate plans, and in fact the market test is not ipso facto proof that there are no subsidies. On the contrary, such dual plans covering a group of employees are deemed to be sold in "conjunction," and are subject to the formulas for computing the cost of benefits that were described above.

Most contemporary group products bear a strong resemblance to traditional group paid-up insurance, in that they combine decreasing increments of employer-purchased term coverage and employee purchased permanent coverage. Employee-owned coverage may make use of a variety of plans, including (1) group paid-up, (2) level premium, level benefit whole life, and (3) level premium, increasing-benefit whole life. The two elements frequently are so designed that at the employee's retirement age the reserve on the paid-up coverage is equal to the reserve on an ordinary policy issued at the date the coverage came into force. This permits a conversion of the term coverage at the entry age, rather than the attained age. If such a conversion is chosen, the cash value in the permanent segment of the plan is used to meet the reserve requirements involved in converting the term to permanent coverage. The periodic premium on the converted policy is the same as it would have been at the original age. This original age premium may be more affordable than the annual renewable term or the premium on a permanent policy obtained by conversion at the insured's attained age.

Another contemporary variation of group ordinary calls for level term insurance and increasing permanent insurance. Under this plan, the total amount of insurance increases by the amount of the increase in the permanent component. While this approach may meet the needs of random individual cases, as well as satisfying regulatory requirements, from the standpoint of insurance programming for the public in general it has little economic justification.

Plan Provisions

Both the term and permanent segments of the group ordinary contract have the standard policy provisions found when the coverages are sold separately. These include a conversion privilege for term insurance, a variety of disability benefits for both segments, and a policy loan privilege on the permanent coverage. In this sense, they are more flexible than the traditional group paid-up contracts which, with time and regulatory constraints, they have come to resemble.

FUTURE OF PERMANENT FORMS OF GROUP INSURANCE

In 1977, permanent forms of group insurance represented less than 1 percent of all group insurance in force. The proportion of the total had not

Table 6–2
Group Life Insurance in Force in the United States by Plan: 1974 and 1977

Plan of Insurance	1974			1977		
	Number of Policies (000s)	Amount ($ millions)	Percent of Amount	Number of Policies (000s)	Amount ($ millions)	Percent of Amount
Term:						
Decreasing	1,700	$ 27,300	3.3	2,000	$ 35,000	3.2
Other	90,200	793,600	95.9	102,000	1,071,800	96.1
Permanent:						
Whole life						
Premium paying	1,100	5,200	.6	1,100	6,200	.6
Paid-up	500	1,000	.1	500	1,100	.1
Endowment	*	100	†	*	100	†
Retirement income	100	400	.1	*	300	†
Total Group	93,600	$827,600	100.0	105,600	$1,115,100	100.0

* Less than 50,000.
† Less than .05 percent.
Source: American Council of Life Insurance.

changed since the previous survey in 1974. This percentage is so insignifi-cant, and the tax status so fluid, that is has not been possible to maintain statistics separating group ordinary coverage from other forms. Rather, more generic classifications have been used, as is illustrated in Table 6–2.

It seems safe to assert that no more than a handful of companies market permanent forms of group insurance aggressively. Probably fewer than 50 have a product in their portfolio.

The group paid-up business continues to attract a low, but steady level of interest in the market. However, given the tenor of recent tax regulations, and the history of group ordinary, it seems unlikely that it will again command the widespread interest as an employee benefit that it attracted in the 1960s. Nevertheless, group ordinary still remains very attractive to insureds who are substandard risks. Therefore, it seems likely that this will prove to be the market in which much group ordinary will be concentrated, and it will continue to provide an important benefit for those who cannot purchase insurance at standard rates.

CHAPTER 7

Retired Lives Reserve*

JAMES E. ROBERTS AND
RONALD T. MARTIN

Some group life insurance plans provide for insurance on an employee's life to be continued after the employee's retirement. A retired lives reserve (RLR) is a fund established and maintained by an employer to provide a means of prefunding the cost of continuing group insurance benefits for retired employees. The purpose of the retired lives reserve concept is to provide an employer with a vehicle through which he or she can allocate the cost of providing group term life insurance benefits to retired employees over the working lifetimes of those employees. Although this concept initially was used for group term life insurance plans insuring a large number of employees, the concept is applicable to large as well as small closely held corporations. In this chapter, the income-tax aspects involved in using the retired lives reserve concept are discussed, as are the various funding media available to fund postretirement benefits.

Deductibility of Contributions

The issue of the deductibility of premiums paid or incurred under life insurance policies providing group term life insurance for active or retired employees or both, where a portion of such premium is credited to an RLR fund is governed by Section 162(a) of the Internal Revenue Code, which allows a deduction for all ordinary and necessary expenses paid or incurred during a taxable year in carrying on a trade or business. However, to avoid distortions in a taxpayer's taxable income, such expenses are deductible

* Portions of the material in this chapter and in Chapter 59 have appeared in modified form in (1) "How to Cope with the New Regulations under Internal Revenue Code Section 79, 679," *The Insurance Law Journal*, 454, August 1979 and "57 Taxes," *The Tax Magazine*, 635, October 1979; (2) "Section 79—The New Regulations," CLU Journal, Vol. XXXII, No. 4, October 1979, American Society of CLU, Bryn Mawr, PA 19010; (3) "Group Life Insurance," Chapter 7, *Employees' Benefits in Florida*, CLE, The Florida Bar, 1979; (4) "Group Life Insurance," Bureau of National Affairs, Tax Management Portfolio, 1980; and (5) *Federal Taxation of Group Life Insurance after ERTA*, 2d ed. (Farnsworth Publishing Company, 1981) and appear here with permission of the publishers.

only for the year to which they are properly attributable. For example, a cash-basis employer, who pays a premium for fire insurance insuring his or her business property for a period of three years, must ratably deduct the premium paid over the three-year period even though the entire premium is paid during a single taxable year.[1] For a retired lives reserve fund, the Internal Revenue Service has taken the position that payments made to an RLR fund are deductible for federal income-tax purposes if:

1.   The balance in the reserve fund is held solely for the purpose of providing life insurance coverage for active or retired persons so long as any active or retired employee remains alive.

2.   The amount added to the retired lives reserve fund is no greater than an amount which would otherwise be required to fairly allocate the cost of the life insurance coverage provided over the working lives of the employees insured under the reserve.

3.   The sponsoring employer has no right to recapture any portion of the monies in the RLR fund so long as any active or retired employee remains alive.[2]

To avoid distortions in the employer's taxable income, payments made to a retired lives reserve fund must be actuarially determined and made on a level basis.[3] In other words, the contribution made by an employer on behalf of an employee must reasonably represent the cost of benefits "earned" by the employee under the employer's group term life insurance plan during the taxable year such contribution is made.

The Internal Revenue Code (IRC) provides that contributions to a deferred compensation plan shall not be deductible under Section 162 or Section 212 of the code unless (1) such plan is a qualified retirement plan, or (2) the amount of the contribution is includable in the employee's gross income in the taxable year of such contribution.[4] However, a retired lives reserve fund is an employee benefit plan, rather than a deferred compensation plan, even though some or all of the employees benefiting under it are retired. Therefore, the fund is not treated as a deferred compensation plan and is specifically excluded from the application of Section 404(a).[5]

The deduction for contributions to a retired lives reserve fund is limited to ordinary and necessary business expenses.[6] A contribution to the RLR fund on behalf of an employee is an ordinary and necessary business expense if the entire compensation, including fringe benefits, paid to or for

---

[1] Rev. Rul. 70-413, 1970-2 CB 103.

[2] Rev. Rul. 69-382, 1969-2 CB 28.

[3] Rev. Rul. 73-599, 1973-2 CB 40.

[4] I.R.C. §404(a).

[5] Treas. Reg. §1.404(a)-1(a)(2); Rev. Rul. 69-478, 1969-2 C.B. 29. According to the regulations, the following plans constitute employee benefits plans and not deferred compensation plans: dismissal wage plans; unemployment benefit plans; sickness, accident, hospitalization, medical expense, recreation, welfare, and similar benefit plans. See Treas. Reg. §§1.162-10(a) and 1.404(a)-1(a)(1).

[6] I.R.C. §162(a).

the benefit of that employee is reasonable.[7] In the event an employee's total compensation is unreasonable in light of the services actually performed for the employer, the deduction for the unreasonable portion of the compensation paid would be disallowed.

Tax-Free Accumulation of Funds

The IRS has taken the position that earnings on monies in a retired lives reserve fund do not constitute gross income to the sponsoring employer, even though such earnings, as well as the contributions to the fund, may be used to pay the current costs of providing group term life insurance for both its active and retired employees.[8]

In addition, the earnings on the amounts accumulated in the RLR fund are not subject to federal income tax if the funds are held (1) in life insurance or annuity products, as long as the contracts are not surrendered and no amounts are received under the contracts,[9] (2) in an account maintained by a life insurance company,[10] or (3) in an exempt employees' trust.[11] These items are discussed in greater detail under Alternative Funding Vehicles later in this chapter.

Monies Reverting to Employer

Any monies or property reverting to the sponsoring employer from the retired lives reserve fund, upon its termination or otherwise, would result in taxable income to the sponsoring employer to the extent contributions to the fund resulted in a tax benefit to the employer (i.e., to the extent the employer received an income-tax benefit from the deductions previously claimed for contributions to the fund).[12] In the event or to the extent that deductions for contributions to the fund were taken in a year or years in which the employer would have otherwise had no taxable income, the monies or property reverting to it from the fund as a result of such contributions would not represent income to the employer. However, any earnings on such contributions would be includable in the employer's gross income.

Taxability to Employees

Since the employee generally has no vested right to postretirement group term life insurance until retirement and has no right to monies contributed to the retired lives reserve fund, he or she will not be taxed prior to retirement on amounts contributed to the fund by the employer for

---

[7] Treas. Reg. §1.162-7(a).
[8] Rev. Rul. 69-382, 1969-2 CB 28.
[9] I.R.C. §§72 and 1035.
[10] I.R.C. §§801 et seq.; Rev. Rul. 69-382, 1969-2 CB 28.
[11] I.R.C. §501.
[12] Treas. Reg. §1.111-1.

postretirement group term life insurance coverage.[13] The taxability to the employee at retirement, when he or she first has a right to postretirement coverage, and thereafter, would be governed by Section 61, Section 79, or Section 83. The impact of these sections is discussed in the paragraphs below.

Section 83 was enacted as part of the Tax Reform Act of 1969, and was directed specifically to restricted stock. However, the language of the statute, entitled "Property Transferred in Connection with Performance of Services," is broad enough to reach transfers unrelated to restricted stock.

Section 83 provides rules for the taxation of property transferred to a person in connection with the performance of services by the person. Such property generally is not taxable until it has been transferred to the person and becomes substantially vested in the person.[14] A transfer of property occurs when a person acquires a beneficial ownership interest in such property.[15] Such property is substantially vested when it is either transferable or not subject to a substantial risk of forfeiture.[16] The rights of a person in property are transferable if the person can transfer any interest in the property to any person other than the transferor of the property, but only if the rights in such property of such transferee are not subject to a substantial risk of forfeiture.[17] A substantial risk of forfeiture exists when rights in property transferred are conditioned, directly or indirectly, upon the future performance (or refraining from performance) of substantial services by any person, or the occurrence of a condition related to a purpose of the transfer, and the possibility of forfeiture is substantial if such condition is not satisfied.[18]

Clearly, from the foregoing definitions, if a retired employee's vested right to postretirement group term life insurance coverage constitutes "property" for purposes of Section 83, such property will have been transferred to and substantially vested in the employee and, therefore, will be taxable to the employee under Section 83(a).

The proposed regulations promulgated under Section 83 stated that the term *property,* as used in connection with insurance contracts, was applicable only to the cash surrender value of such contracts.[19] Therefore, as the usual retired lives reserve product has no cash surrender value, it could be concluded, based on the definition of "property" in the proposed regulations, that Section 83 did not apply.

---

[13] I.R.C. §§61 and 83. A retired lives reserve plan should not have an early retirement option since, in the case of early retirement, Section 79(b)(1) cannot override Section 83. Treas. Reg. §1.79-2(b)(3). The importance of Section 79(b)(1) overriding Section 83 is discussed in the text at footnotes 21–24.

[14] Treas. Reg. §1.83-1(a).

[15] Treas. Reg. §1.83-3(a).

[16] Treas. Reg. §1.83-3(b).

[17] Treas. Reg. §1.83-3(d).

[18] Treas. Reg. §1.83-3(c).

[19] Proposed Treas. Reg. §1.83-3(e).

The definition of *property* for purposes of Section 83 was modified, however, in the final regulations. In the final regulations, the term property is defined in Treasury Regulation §1.83-3(e). That regulation provides, in pertinent part, as follows:

> . . . The term "property" includes real and personal property other than money or an unfunded and unsecured promise to pay money in the future. The term also includes a beneficial interest in assets (including money) which are transferred or set aside from the claims of creditors of the transferor, for example, in a trust or escrow account. . . . In the case of a transfer of a life insurance contract, retirement income contract, endowment contract, or other contract providing life insurance protection, only the cash surrender value of the contract is considered to be property. . . .

The foregoing definition in the final regulations changes in two respects the definition of "property" in the proposed regulations. First, the proposed regulations excluded from the definition of property an unfunded and unsecured promise to pay deferred compensation. As indicated by Treasury Regulation §1.404(a)-1(a)(2), a retired lives reserve fund is an employee benefit plan rather than a deferred compensation plan. Therefore, since the employer's promise to provide a retired employee with postretirement coverage is fully funded, the exclusion in the final regulations from the definition of property of an unfunded and unsecured promise to pay "money in the future," rather than "deferred compensation," may be significant. Second, the final regulations add to the definition of property ". . . a beneficial interest in assets (including money) which are transferred or set aside from the claims of creditors of the transferor. . . ." Under this new language, an argument could be made that the interest of the retired employee is in the retired lives reserve fund itself, rather than in the group term life insurance purchased by the fund.

It can be argued that several revenue rulings are inconsistent with the conclusion that the continuance, via a retired lives reserve fund, of group term life insurance on the life of an employee who has attained normal retirement age and whose employment has terminated results in taxable income to the insured employee under Section 83.[20] Section 83(h) provides that a deduction equal to the amount includable as compensation in the gross income of the employee is allowable to the employer only for the taxable year of the employer in which or with which ends the taxable year of the employee in which such amount is includable as compensation. As the employee generally has no vested right to postretirement group term life insurance until retirement, Section 83 could not tax the employee until that time. Therefore, the argument goes, if Section 83 applied to retired lives reserve products, the employer would be entitled to a deduction only at the time of the employee's retirement, rather than annually, as set forth in the revenue rulings. Under Treasury Regulation §1.83-6(a)(3), in the case of a transfer to an employee benefit plan described in Treasury Regulation

---

[20] Rev. Rul. 69-382, 1969-2 CB 28; 73-599, 1973-2 CB 40.

1.162-10(a), Section 83(h) does not apply. Thus, since, presumably, a group term life insurance program is a plan so covered, contributions to fund a retired lives reserve fund would be currently deductible notwithstanding Section 83(h).

The best argument against the taxability of an employee at or after retirement under Section 83 is that Section 79 overrides Section 83. Standard principles of statutory construction require that, where there are overlapping divisions within a statutory scheme, the more specific provisions should apply. Section 79 specifically is directed at employee taxability for group term life insurance and, therefore, should take precedence over any potentially overlapping provision in Section 83. As discussed in Chapter 59, Section 79(b)(1) provides that the inclusionary rule of Section 79(a) "shall not apply to the cost of group term life insurance on the life of an individual provided under a policy carried directly or indirectly by an employer after such individual has terminated employment with such employer and . . . has reached . . . retirement age. . . ."[21] Thus, Congress intended to continue for retirees the tax-free status of group term life insurance prior to the Revenue Act of 1964.[22] This is confirmed by the Senate Report on the Revenue Act of 1964 which, in discussing the new Section 79, provides "it was concluded that it would be undesirable to tax the aged or disabled individual who is no longer working for group term life insurance protection provided to him by his former employer."[23]

Under Section 61, an employee's gross income includes all income from whatever source derived, except as otherwise provided in the IRC. Under Section 451, an item of gross income is to be included in gross income for the taxable year in which the taxpayer receives it. Treasury Regulation §1.451-1 states that receipt can be actual or constructive in the case of a cash-basis taxpayer. Under the doctrine of constructive receipt, set forth in Treasury Regulation §1.451-2(a), income, although not actually reduced to a taxpayer's possession, is constructively received by him or her in the taxable year:

> . . . during which it is credited to his account, set apart for him, or otherwise made available so that he may draw upon it at any time, or so that he could have drawn upon it during the taxable year if notice of intention to withdraw had been given. However, income is not constructively received if the taxpayer's control of its receipt is subject to substantial limitations or restrictions.

Because an employee has no rights to monies contributed to the retired lives reserve fund, no amount would be includable in the employee's gross income under the doctrine of constructive receipt.

Notwithstanding the nonapplicability of the doctrine of constructive receipt, it is arguable that an employee who has attained normal retirement age and whose employment has terminated should be taxed under Section

---

[21] I.R.C. §79(b)(1).

[22] See discussion in text at footnotes 2 and 3 *supra.*

[23] S. Rep. No. 830, 88th Cong., 2nd Sess. (1964); 1976-1 CB (Part 2) 550.

61 pursuant to the doctrine of economic benefit. Under this doctrine, an individual will be taxed on any economic benefit conferred so long as and to the extent the benefit has an ascertainable fair market value. As in the case of Section 83, the best argument against inclusion at or after retirement under the doctrine of economic benefit is that Section 79 takes precedence.

The validity of the above discussion assumes, of course, that the life insurance provided under the retired lives reserve fund is group term life insurance.[24] Because the usual retired lives reserve product involves advance funding and the accumulation of funds, it is possible the Internal Revenue Service will contend the life insurance provided under the RLR fund is not group term life insurance on the ground that such funding and accumulation constitute permanent benefits.[25] This contention, if made, would seem contrary to the applicable Treasury regulations under Section 79. The examples of permanent benefits in Treasury Regulation §1.79-0 include "a paid-up or cash surrender value," neither of which is provided by the usual retired lives reserve product. Moreover, the same regulation excludes from the definition of a permanent benefit: "Any other feature that provides no economic benefit (other than current insurance protection) to the employee." It would seem that the usual RLR product does not at any time provide anything other than current insurance protection to the employee. Of course, in the event the possible contention referred to is made and upheld, Sections 83 or 61, or both, would apply.

What Constitutes a Retired Lives Reserve Fund

The purpose of a retired lives reserve fund is to accumulate monies to be used to pay all or part of the cost of providing group term life insurance on the lives of retired employees. To have an RLR fund that provides an employer and its employees the benefits described above, the fund must not provide anything other than group term life insurance to an employee. Money or property paid or made available to the employee under the fund would constitute gross income to the employee. Therefore, the fund may not, without adverse tax consequences to the insured employee, discharge its obligations to an employee insured thereunder by purchasing and distributing to the employee a paid-up insurance contract with a face amount equal to the amount of insurance the fund is obligated to provide the employee.[26] Also, the insured employee cannot be given the right at any time (i.e., at death, disability, retirement, or termination of employment) to receive monies contributed to the fund on his or her behalf. In addition, a provision allowing the employer to terminate the plan and distribute the monies in the plan to the employees then insured under the employer's

---

[24] See discussion in text at footnotes 21 through 34 in Chapter 59 for the requirements that must be met for life insurance to qualify as group term life insurance.

[25] Treas. Reg. §§1.79-0 and 1.79-1(b)(1).

[26] The fund, however, could prepay premiums on a group term life insurance contract, so long as the insured employee had no rights or interest in such prepaid premiums.

group term life insurance plan will not be approved by the national office of the Internal Revenue Service.

The plan also must contain a provision precluding the employer from recapturing a portion of the retired lives reserve fund so long as any active or retired employee remains alive. Following the death of the last employee, monies remaining in the fund, however, may revert to the sponsoring employer. As discussed above, such monies may constitute gross income to the employer.

Alternative Funding Vehicles

A retired lives reserve fund may be held by a nonexempt trust, an exempt trust, or an account maintained by an insurance company. As discussed below, each of these alternatives raises federal income-tax questions.

"Retired Lives Reserve" Maintained by a Nonexempt Trust. Section 61 of the IRC provides that ". . . gross income means all income from whatever source derived." The question to be resolved is whether the funds received by a trust, created to administer a group life insurance plan which provides prefunded, postretirement benefits, will be treated as gross income to the trust. In general, when an entity receives funds as a conduit or agent for the forwarding of such funds, the receipt by the entity is not gross income. In other words, if an intermediary is employed as a depository for funds in trust and is obligated, in a fiduciary capacity, to expend the funds in their entirety for a specified purpose, the benefit, profit, or gain does not accrue to the intermediary and, consequently, the funds received are not gross income. Even though the monies contributed to a retired lives reserve fund maintained by a trust are not required to be spent in one year, the sums remaining, if restricted as to future use, are not gross income to the trust.

Therefore, if the contributions by the employer to a retired lives reserve group life insurance plan are paid to an irrevocable trust and the trustees are required, under the trust agreement, to use the funds solely for the administration of the plan on behalf of the employer and its employees, the trust will recognize no gross income upon receipt of the contributions. However, any investment income received by the trust will constitute gross income within the meaning of Section 61 of the Code.[27]

---

[27] The following cases and rulings are authority for this conclusion. However, within the context of their factual situations, the conclusions were not necessarily the same (i.e., the funds were determined, in some cases, to be subject to general disbursements of the entity involved and, therefore, were gross income). *Concord Village, Inc.*, 65 TC 142 (1975); *Ford Dealers Advertising Fund, Inc.*, 55 TC 761 (1971), aff'd 456 F.2d 255, 72-1 USTC ¶9228 CA5, 1972), nonacq. Rev. Rul. 74-318, 1974-2 CB 14; *New York State Association of Real Estate Boards Group Insurance Fund*, 54 TC 1325 (1970); *Growers Credit Corporation*, 33 TC 981 (1960); *Seven-Up Company*, 14 TC 965 (1950), acq. in result only Rev. Rul. 74-319, 1974-2 CB 15; Rev. Rul. 75-370, 1975-2 CB 25; Rev. Rul. 74-318, 1974-2 CB 14; Rev. Rul. 74-321, 1974-2 CB 16.

"Retired Lives Reserve" Maintained by a Section 501(c)(9) Trust. If a trust, exempt from taxation pursuant to Section 501(c)(9) of the IRC, is utilized to administer a group life insurance plan, neither the contributions from the employer nor the investment income therefrom will be subject to federal income tax.[28]

To qualify for exempt status under Section 501(c)(9) as a voluntary employees' beneficiary association, the following requirements must be met:

1. The organization must be an employees' association.[29] In general, the organization must be composed of all individuals employed by a single employer. However, membership and, therefore, benefits may be limited to one or more classes of employees, as long as the classes are selected on the basis of criteria that do not limit membership to officers, shareholders, or highly compensated employees. In addition, persons other than employees may be included in the organization so long as they have an employment-related bond with employee members.[30]

2. The membership of the employees in the association must be "voluntary."[31] An association is not a voluntary association if the employer unilaterally imposes membership in the association on the employee as a condition of his employment and the employee thereby incurs a detriment (e.g., deductions from pay).[32]

3. The organization must provide for the payment of life, sickness, accident, or other benefits to its members, their dependents or designated beneficiaries and substantially all of its operations must be in furtherance of providing such benefits.[33] Generally, the providing of life benefits must be for current protection only. Thus, term insurance is an acceptable benefit. In addition, a permanent benefit, as defined in the regulations under Section 79, is acceptable.[34]

4. No part of the net earnings of the organization inures, other than by payment of the benefits described in paragraph 3 above, to the benefit of any private shareholder or individual.[35] The payment to highly compensated personnel of benefits that are disproportionate in relation to benefits received by other employees will constitute inurement and, therefore, will cause the plan to not qualify under Section 501(c)(9).[36] In addition, the return of contributions to an employer upon termination of the plan will constitute inurement.[37]

---

[28] I.R.C. §§501(a), 511, 512(a)(3) and 513.

[29] Treas. Reg. §1.501(c)(9)-1(a).

[30] Treas. Reg. §1.501(c)(9)-2(a)(1). Such members, however, may not exceed 10 percent of the membership of the organization.

[31] Treas. Reg. §1.501(c)(9)-1(b).

[32] Treas. Reg. §1.501(c)(9)-2(c)(2).

[33] Treas. Reg. §1.501(c)(9)-1(c).

[34] Treas. Reg. §1.501(c)(9)-3(b).

[35] Treas. Reg. §1.501(c)(9)-1(d).

[36] Treas. Reg. §1.501(c)(9)-4(b).

[37] Treas. Reg. §1.501(c)(9)-4(d).

Because of the eligibility requirement set forth in paragraph 1 above, and the broad definition of inurement contained in paragraph 4 above, an exempt trust normally will not be used to maintain a retired lives reserve fund.

Retired Lives Reserve Maintained by a Life Insurance Company. If an RLR is maintained by a life insurance company to prefund the postretirement group life insurance benefits, neither the contributions from the employer to fund future premium requirements nor the investment income will be subject to federal income tax.[38]

The employer's contributions, which are added to the retired lives reserve fund, are excluded from the insurance company's gain from operations and from life insurance company taxable income.[39] Interest credited to the RLR fund is treated as interest paid by the life insurance company and is excluded from taxable investment income under Section 804(a)(1), from gain from operations pursuant to Section 809(a)(1) and, ultimately, from life insurance company taxable income as defined by Section 802(b).[40] In addition, the earnings on the fund do not constitute gross income to the sponsoring employer, even though such earnings may be used to pay the current costs of providing group term life insurance for both its active and retired employees.[41]

---

[38] I.R.C. §801 *et. seq.* The text accompanying footnotes 39, 40, and 41 represents only a very simplified and incomplete summary of the Federal income taxation of accounts held by insurance companies.

[39] I.R.C. §§802(b), 809(b)(1), 809(d)(2) and 810(c)(6).

[40] I.R.C. §§805(a) and 805(e)(4), see *Occidental Life Insurance Company of California* v. *U.S.* 70-1 USTC ¶9225 (D.C. 1970).

[41] Rev. Rul. 69-382, 1969-2 CB 28.

PART THREE

Designing Employee Benefits— Health-Related Benefits

In this part, health-related benefits—including disability income and medical expense benefits—are explored. Of prime importance in any discussion of the design of health-related benefits is the subject of cost containment. This topic is discussed in the opening and closing chapters of this part of the *Handbook* and is referred to either explicitly or implicitly in the intervening chapters.

In addition to concerns regarding cost containment, another important issue in health-related benefits is the movement toward broadened benefits. Chapters dealing with newer benefit plans, such as dental and vision care plans, are therefore included in this part, in addition to chapters dealing with the more conventional medical, hospital, surgical, major medical, and comprehensive plans. Also, other plans—those providing coverage for prescription drugs, mental health, preventive care, and the like—are touched on in various chapters, and health maintenance organizations (HMOs) as an alternative delivery system for health care are discussed in Chapters 8, 10, and 20.

One chapter is devoted to a brief review of various health risk bearers, a subject described and evaluated in greater detail throughout the handbook, and governmental providers of health-related benefits are covered in two brief chapters, one dealing with medical and one with disability income benefits. Two chapters are devoted to considerations in the design of the latter.

CHAPTER 8

Designing Medical Care Expense Plans

CHARLES P. HALL, JR.

BACKGROUND

The severe and continuing escalation of health care costs over the past decade is a matter of growing concern to virtually all segments of our society. It has caused great financial stress to both public and private sponsors of health benefit plans, with the private sponsors being especially hard hit. Yet, despite much rhetoric, there is little evidence of lasting solutions being developed.

Nevertheless, as we enter the 1980s, it is safe to say that the two major issues concerning employee health plans will continue to be (1) broadened benefits, and (2) cost containment. Of the two, cost containment clearly occupies center stage at this time. As a result of the combined forces of a weak economy, continuing high interest rates, growing unemployment, and actual or threatened corporate failures, there recently has been an unprecedented series of renegotiated labor agreements in several industries. This has greatly reduced, at least for a while, the pressure to expand benefits; rather, the focus of many unions has turned to job security and a joint concern with management for cost containment.

Controlling the cost of medical care expense benefits can be accomplished either by controlling the factors that affect cost (e.g., the ordering and providing of care and services by doctors and hospitals; the existence of cost shifting to "charge paying patients" by Medicare, Medicaid, and some Blue Cross plans; and inflation) or by designing the benefit or plan to minimize the impact of changes in the various cost factors. The focus of this chapter is to identify some of the efforts to control costs through the design or redesign of medical expense benefit packages and to examine the potential for success offered by these approaches.

Despite the recent overriding concern with cost containment, it must not be forgotten that a major underlying purpose for employee health benefit plans is satisfaction of employee needs.[1] Obviously, much of the develop-

---

[1] Interview with Ernest Reach, U.S. Industries, New York, N.Y., February 7, 1981.

ment of benefits over the years has been in direct response to union demands, and continued pressure from this source undoubtedly will continue to play a role in benefit design, even if that role may be diminished by concern over rising costs.

Recognition of the Problem

An article in *Business Insurance*[2] began with the statement: "Armed with few surefire weapons, employers are nonetheless on the march to confine cost increases in today's $206 billion health care system.

"They are fighting the good fight individually within their own companies and collectively in employer coalitions that sometimes include health care providers."

The article recites the usual litany of horrors—average cost increases of 12.4 percent per year for the last 10 years (15 percent in 1979), projections that health care costs, at that rate of growth, will reach $2.4 trillion by the year 2000 ($4 trillion, if the 1979 rate is maintained), and so on.

Noting that employers pay about 25 percent of the nation's health care bills through group health insurance programs for employees, the article reports that the result has been "a time of tremendous experimentation by the employer. Only in the past decade has the mentality changed from one of acquiescent payer to participant . . . only recently has there been a shift from doing nothing to doing something . . . but there's not much data. It's kind of an iffy business."

Individual Responses

Many individual employers have approached this "iffy" business by redesigning their benefit packages, primarily to provide coverage for alternatives to hospital care. Naturally, benefit design has been combined with a number of other efforts to control costs, including, among others, more stringent auditing of claims and noninsurance "fitness" or "wellness" programs. In addition, there have been renewed efforts to educate employees about the more economic use of health benefits.

Insurers are cooperating with employers in searching for more effective cost control, sometimes leading the way and sometimes being carried along by the tide. Unions are a variable force, generally supporting broadened benefits and the concept of cost containment, but frequently opposing some of the more commonly used techniques, such as deductibles and coinsurance provisions, and seldom, until recently, even agreeing to any cutback in benefits which seem to have inflationary aspects.

---

[2] Maryann Matlock, "Employers Battle Health Care Costs," *Business Insurance,* June 2, 1980, p. 1, *et. seq.*

Collective Responses

On a collective basis, a variety of national and local organizations, usually consortia of business interests, have emerged in recent years with the avowed objective of working to contain health care costs. Many of these groups have overlapping memberships, and some branch out to include a broad range of interest groups, including union, hospital, medical, governmental, and other civic organizations. Blue Cross/Blue Shield and commercial health insurers are often prominently involved. Examples of such groups include the National Chamber Foundation, the Washington Business Group on Health, the Penjerdel Corporation, the Philadelphia Area Committee on Health Care Costs, and the Industrial Management Council (Rochester, N.Y.) to name but a few. Virtually all these organizations believe the design of employee medical care expense benefit programs can have a significant impact on overall health care costs.

Early Findings

Most of the organizations referred to have concluded that one serious problem that confronts them is an absence of an adequate information base.[3] Despite a plethora of national and local data on various elements of health care costs, insurance payments and general morbidity statistics, significant gaps in information exist when it comes to more useful questions, such as the impact of specific benefit provisions on cost and usage. Though some studies have found corporate employee benefits managers have definite ideas about what benefit provisions, claims procedures, and other techniques might be effective, they seldom have empirical data to back up their views. What is even more ironic, their corporate benefit programs often fail to incorporate those benefits believed to be most effective.[4]

RECENT BENEFIT INNOVATIONS

Some of the more popular new benefit provisions developed to be incorporated at the design or redesign stage of an employee benefit health plan to reduce hospital costs and meet employee needs include coverage for preadmission testing, a variety of forms of ambulatory care, second opinions on surgery, and increased availability of an HMO alternative. Though many claims have been made, relatively little substantiated evidence exists about the extent or duration of cost savings from these design features. However, since it is well known that in-hospital medical services are by far

---

[3] See, for example, the Penjerdel Council, Greater Philadelphia Chamber of Commerce, and Health Services Council, *Cost Effective Management of Health Benefit Programs* (Philadelphia: Health Services Council, Inc., c. 1979), pp. 1–5.

[4] Ibid., p. A–6.

the most costly, logic suggests any alternative should save costs. Following this logic, many basic hospital and medical benefit plans have been broadened in recent years to extend coverage to a variety of ambulatory services that had not typically been available under basic benefit plans, though at least some of them had been available under the "blanket" coverage of major medical insurance for some years.

Preadmission Testing

Since inpatient hospital care is notoriously expensive, one logical approach in designing benefits is to try to reduce the length of stay (LOS). Particularly for surgical procedures, it has been traditional for years to admit a patient one or more days in advance to perform all the necessary preoperative laboratory tests and, where needed, X-ray procedures. Interest has been growing in the concept of preadmission testing for well over a decade, and while various studies have reported mixed results, the consensus seems to be an efficiently administered plan does have the potential to reduce LOS. Furthermore, it may offer the potential, in extreme cases, of avoiding inappropriate hospitalization altogether.

It is difficult to obtain precise measures of the savings potential inherent in preadmission testing (PAT) because of the number of variables that have an impact on such a program. Convenience of scheduling—influenced at least by proximity of dwelling to hospital, availability of public or private transportation, and family circumstances—is certainly one major factor. Awareness and acceptance by both physicians and patients also is important. A substantial level of coverage has always been available under major medical policies for PAT, and explicit allowance for it is found increasingly in basic hospital plans; but many providers and insureds have not been aware of this. Furthermore, not all physicians are comfortable with the idea of uncontrolled fasting, for example, prior to certain critical tests. This concern is exacerbated by the present malpractice climate, which dims their enthusiasm for any procedure that may lack adequate quality control.

Despite the problems noted, PAT does have potential for cost savings both through reducing average LOS (perhaps by as much as one to two days per admission) and through the more subtle, indirect influence on hospital costs. At the Risk and Insurance Management (RIMS) meetings in Atlanta in April 1980, an insurance company actuary estimated that, if every group health insurance plan in the country required routine tests to be done on an outpatient basis, at best, $1.7 billion could be cut from health care bills. Unfortunately, the benefit is not always used effectively.

PAT can improve hospital efficiency by allowing for more effective use of beds and personnel. In areas of excessive bed supply, however, hospital administration may be less than enthusiastic about such a program, since it could conceivably lead to more empty beds than would otherwise exist.

Naturally, no hospital is likely to make PAT available unless third-party payors are willing to reimburse for it.

However, the trend seems to be toward more extensive coverage of PAT. Employers are likely, in cooperation with their health care providers, to put increased emphasis on informing their employees of this benefit and may, in some cases, even mandate that it be used for all elective surgical procedures.

Ambulatory Surgical Benefits

Means other than PAT exist by which to reduce the volume of inpatient care utilized under an employee benefit medical plan. One of the more popular of these goes by a variety of names, including "ambulatory surgery," "same-day surgery," and "outpatient surgery." In addition to the variety of titles, such procedures may be performed in a variety of institutional settings.

When run directly under hospital sponsorship, a variety of administrative and staffing patterns exist for these short procedure units (SPUs), each with its own ramifications for costs and equipment needs. In many cases, such a program is integrated into the normal hospital activities without any special designation of facilities or personnel. This has the major advantage of low start-up costs but presents a potential problem with scheduling. At the next level, the hospital may designate a discrete unit—a wing or a separate building on the same grounds as the hospital. Proximity to other hospital services and administrative support are advantages; but some costs are involved in dedicating discrete space, even if major renovations are not required.

Two other models include a hospital satellite or a free-standing "surgi-center." In both, all the needed services are located in a separate facility which, typically, was designed specifically for the purpose. Both suffer the potential danger of being some distance from the emergency backup facilities of a hospital in case of complications, a factor that may inhibit some patients. Each offers the potential of convenience for both patient and physician—depending on location. The hospital satellite model has both administrative and professional ties to the parent hospital, a factor some see as assuring quality. Presumably, a satellite would not duplicate facilities already available in the hospital, and it might free some beds in the parent facility for other needs. Concerns about freestanding units revolve around the lack of accreditation and licensure standards in some states and the danger, especially in fully bedded or overbedded areas, of unnecessary duplication of services.

Cost, however, is the major issue. All four settings can effectively lower costs of surgery for a wide and ever-growing range of surgical procedures by eliminating the need for overnight hospitalization with all its attendant costs. Employers and insurers are showing a growing interest in the potential savings that may be realized, though not entirely without reservation.

Most commercial insurance companies provide coverage for ambulatory surgery in either freestanding or hospital-based facilities, and the general experience has been the costs associated with freestanding units are considerably lower than those in hospital-based units.

However, some third parties (e.g., Blue Cross of Philadelphia) only cover same-day surgery when provided in a hospital-based facility. The rationale is that they do not want to be party to the construction of additional, costly ambulatory surgical centers when other suitable facilities already exist. They view the construction of additional centers as inflationary.[5] This argument, of course, may have merit in regions that already have adequate or excess hospital bed capacity. In areas where a limited supply of hospital beds exist, however, construction of ambulatory surgical centers may offer savings both in capital investment and in costs of care.

Another major insurer has established its own rather elaborate set of criteria, which must be met by any short procedure unit if it wants to be eligible for reimbursement. A regularly updated list of qualified facilities is provided to company claims managers.[6] It also should be noted that several states, by legislative or administrative fiat, have mandated that benefits be provided for procedures performed in SPUs, so long as they would have been covered in a hospital setting.

In conclusion, it is probably worth noting that a very substantial portion of existing coverage is not specifically identified in group insurance programs. Under many major medical policies it would be routinely covered under "reasonable and customary" surgical benefits. Unfortunately, where the benefit is not specifically identified, usage is likely to lag. Therefore, more and more employers and health care providers, as they become convinced cost-saving potential exists, are going to want SPU benefits made explicit.

Other Outpatient Alternatives

Many benefit plans in recent years have expanded coverage for other outpatient services—ranging from more extensive coverage of outpatient diagnostic services and home- and office-based medical protection, at one end of the spectrum, to fairly generous coverage of home health services at the other extreme. Short-run data, however, frequently reflect no decline in hospital usage with the introduction of institutional diagnostic and physician-oriented ambulatory care benefits. Indeed, costs often go up whenever

---

[5] Interview with John McMeekin, senior vice president, Blue Cross of Greater Philadelphia, December 12, 1980.

[6] Interview with Richard J. Mellman, vice president and actuary, Prudential Insurance Company of America, Newark, N.J., January 30, 1981.

such new services are covered. The apparent explanation is that a voluntary increase in the use of outpatient services often leads to "discovery" of conditions requiring hospitalization. Theory suggests over time this benefit should result in better overall health status of the covered group, with lower levels of hospitalization and, therefore, lower costs. The harsh reality of short-run cost concerns, however, has largely prevented, to date, empirical verification of this hypothesis. Many employers, with their "backs to the wall" already on employee benefit costs, have simply refused to offer these benefits in the absence of union concessions on other benefit provisions. These concessions have not, in general, been forthcoming. Undoubtedly, some of the recent data-gathering efforts (e.g., local and national consortia of business interests, referred to above) will shed further light on this issue in the near future.

In contrast to the "front-end" ambulatory services just discussed, home health services offer an opportunity for early discharge and the possible savings that can accrue because in virtually all circumstances, home health services are substantially less expensive than inpatient care. Some health care providers have simply inserted this coverage as a no-cost design experiment in large plans. Introduction of this benefit should be accompanied by some effort to educate covered workers about its availability and efficacy. The structure of health benefits over the last 40 years has left much of the public with the perception, however erroneous it may sometimes be, that hospital care is the best care. Since they frequently incur either no point of service costs for hospital care or, at best, minimal ones, they may view it as their right to utilize what they perceive to be the best care when treatment is needed. Furthermore, not all physicians are fully aware of the availability and quality of home health services, or they may be unhappy with the local administration of such programs. Unless encouraged by a physician to do so, not many patients will enter the home health care market. Therefore, these benefits may have to be aggressively marketed to local physicians if they are to have the desired impact on costs. Some insurers and employers have expressed reluctance to cover home health benefits because they feel there is a danger of getting involved with the provision of nonhealth "social services," which have not, traditionally, been part of employee benefit plans. Ultimately, again, the deciding factor is likely to be the potential for cost savings.

It should be noted that at least some health care providers view home health care benefits as being more important for Medicare beneficiaries than for actively employed workers. They see the benefit as being more directly concerned with "quality of life" than with cost savings.

Inpatient Alternatives to Acute Care

Coverage in skilled nursing facilities (SNFs) can hardly be classified as a recent benefit innovation any longer, since it has been widely provided by commercial insurers and Blue Cross at least since its introduction under Medicare in the mid-1960s. A large proportion of employee benefit plans provide the coverage as a matter of course—many insurers automatically include it as a supplement to hospitalization benefits. Typically, these plans count a day in an SNF as the equivalent of a half day in a hospital when determining benefit-period limits. Daily dollar limits, where stated, often are pegged considerably lower.

At the present time, virtually all SNF coverage requires at least three days of prior hospitalization as a prerequisite to eligibility. Though some feel this is unnecessary and serves only to raise costs, no evidence exists of any serious move to remove this stipulation. Major barriers to more widespread utilization of this lower-cost alternative are the inadequacy of many local referral patterns, the reluctance of some hospitals to reduce their census—especially by the early transfer of an insured (paying) patient—and the reluctance of many patients and their families to accept the nursing home alternative in the light of periodic "horror stories" about the quality of these facilities. A variety of forces (e.g., more extensive regulation and a growing sense of professionalism) are at work which may, in time, overcome these barriers, and more widespread utilization of this benefit can be expected in coming years.

Another extension of benefits, which is in a very preliminary experimental stage, is the provision of hospice coverage (either home care or institutionalized) for terminally ill patients. Blue Cross/Blue Shield, Aetna Life and Casualty, and Equitable, among others, are providing these benefits under experimental pilot programs at the present time—in some cases at no cost to the insured. The major effort seems to be in the electrical industry, where over 400,000 workers currently are covered. Most believe the very survival of hospice care is dependent upon the willingness of health care providers to provide coverage. That, in turn, may depend on the extent of market demand. There have been some recent signs that society's attitude toward death and dying is changing, however, and support for the allegedly less expensive (by a factor of one half) and more humane approach of the hospice is likely to grow. Strict controls may be needed, however, and virtually no data currently are available.

Second Surgical Opinions

Probably no single benefit introduced in the last 15 years has had more publicity than second surgical opinions. One reason for the "notoriety" of the benefit is the widespread belief that a lot of unnecessary surgery is performed in the United States. Though little doubt exists that some unneeded procedures are performed, there still is considerable controversy over the extent of the problem. Many, however, believe traditional insurance coverage for surgery has had a role in creating the problem—thus the interest in the new benefit.

While a few examples of this coverage have been around for longer periods, most such benefits are of relatively recent origin, and despite the widely hailed advantages of second opinions for elective surgery, it has not been clearly proven to be cost-effective. Some health providers claim potential savings would average as much as $2,000 for every procedure not performed as a result of such evaluation. While available data show a significant number of surgical procedures are not performed in a given time when a second opinion proclaims the surgery to be "unnecessary," it is difficult to confirm a cause-and-effect relationship, since many patients are known to reject recommendations for elective surgery even without a negative second opinion—simply out of fear. Furthermore, no definitive longitudinal study has been undertaken to determine the extent to which the surgery is merely deferred, nor to evaluate the relative cost and duration of alternative treatment, if any. An underwriter for one large health insurer has suggested that, if the major impact is merely to defer surgery, the ultimate result, given recent trends, will be to increase costs rather than to contain them. Furthermore, note that most second-opinion surgical coverage today is voluntary, none forbids the patient from going ahead with the surgery even if the second opinion says it is not necessary, and many go on to provide coverage for a third opinion if the first two are in disagreement.

There does appear, however, to be growing support for the hypothesis that mandatory programs are cost-beneficial. Recently, it was reported that a mandatory plan in New York City has documented a savings of $2.63 for every dollar spent. "The savings were a result primarily of surgery not undertaken because a consulting surgeon said it was not needed."[7] The same article reported that study of a voluntary program, offered by Blue Cross/Blue Shield of New York, not only reflected very limited usage but also suggested costs might be inflated by "encouraging patients to have needed operations they would otherwise have avoided."[8] The director of the study of the mandatory program stated no one had yet been able to prove patients were more likely to accept surgery when it is recommended by two physicians rather than one. It also was stated that the benefit-cost advantage of the mandatory program would be further enhanced if it were restricted to a small group of surgical procedures known to be frequently rejected by consultant physicians.

The largest commercial health insurer in the nation, Prudential, supports the above conclusions. After several years of experimentation, it concluded voluntary second-opinion programs are "virtually worthless," and since January 1, 1980, the Prudential has only sold its "incentive" second opinion program (though it will still provide the voluntary type on demand). The

---

[7] Jane E. Brody, "2nd-Opinion Plan for Operations Called a Success," *New York Times,* January 3, 1981, p. B-3.

[8] Ibid.

incentive plan makes a second opinion mandatory for all elective procedures. Under its plan, the Prudential pays 100 percent of reasonable and customary charges for confirmed operations, but only 80 percent of those charges if no second opinion or a nonconfirming second opinion was obtained. It was reported some incentive programs pay as little as 50 percent when there is no confirming second opinion. Naturally, in cases of conflict, payment also will be made for a third opinion to "break the tie." Moreover, some employers requested that penalties for unconfirmed surgical procedures also be applied to related hospital charges.[9]

To support its second opinion benefit plan, Prudential has about 13,000 board-certified physicians around the country under contract to provide a second (or third, as needed) opinion at a set fee, while agreeing not to perform the surgery even if they confirm the need. (These prearranged fees range from a low of $50 to a high of $100.) Some medical societies have resisted this effort, but most have been cooperative.

Though some unanswered questions remain about the cost-benefit relationship of second opinions, most experts agree the impact on quality must be positive. Unfortunately, some unions have failed to recognize the quality aspect as a plus for their members; too often they view second opinion benefits as purely cost-containment efforts, which offer little to make the employee happy.[10]

Finally, there are those who believe the most significant fallout from a second opinion benefit is the so-called sentinel effect: when doctors become aware their recommendations always will be reviewed, they presumably will be more careful with their initial diagnosis and suggestions. This effect, though potentially substantial, can never be measured accurately.

Despite the inconclusive evidence and some distaste on the part of unions, second opinion surgery benefits are widely perceived by employers to have cost-containment merit, and therefore are strongly considered in the design or redesign of a health plan. This virtually assures continued growth in the foreseeable future. A side benefit, as perceived by many surgeons, is insulation against malpractice proceedings.

Miscellaneous Benefits

A variety of other benefit-feature provisions recently have emerged or are under consideration. These are presented briefly.

Dental Benefits. Coverage of dental services has been one of the most rapidly growing benefits over the past decade. Because of the timing of the development of this benefit, cost-containing provisions are virtually always an integral part of plan design, but the major impetus for the benefit is

---

[9] Interview with John Cole, v.p.–group, and William Matusz, head underwriter, Prudential Insurance Company of America, Regional Home Office, Willow Grove, Pa., January 13, 1981.

[10] Ibid.

consumer demand/employee satisfaction. Most programs encourage prevention by providing full coverage for periodic checkups, and most also require preauthorization for orthodontia, when covered, and, sometimes, other major procedures. Preauthorization (or predetermination) of benefits has been particularly effective as a cost-control measure. It is especially suitable for dental services, moreover, because generally no need exists for great haste in receiving the treatment in question. A common position of insurers seems to be it is important to keep dental benefits distinct (separate) from medical benefits and to put a major emphasis on prevention. Monitoring of claims is, typically, very tight. Administrative costs are held down through extensive automation. Dental benefit plans are covered in detail in Chapter 14.

Vision Benefits. Here is another emerging benefit, as yet quite limited, designed mainly to produce employee satisfaction. Typically, the benefit package includes annual examinations, one pair of frames per year, and replacement of lenses every 12 to 24 months. From an insurer's point of view, it is important to try to develop a provider network, because huge discounts frequently can be negotiated. To monitor costs, it is important on all claims to identify the supplier. Continued slow, rather unspectacular, growth may be anticipated in this area. Vision care is discussed in detail in Chapter 15.

Prescription Drugs. There is a lot of discussion about the need for this benefit. Many unions negotiate very hard for it. Some coverage often is available under existing major medical benefit plans. Employers, however, frequently resist this benefit, fearing, among other things, potential abuse. At least one major employer addressed this issue by removing prescription drug coverage from its major medical policy and providing the benefit under a separate program, in which the employer directly provides the worker with a card specifically encouraging use of certain drug stores where prescriptions are available at lower cost.[11] The popularity of this benefit with workers strongly suggests continued expansion in its availability, but tight administrative controls are likely to remain.

Preventive Care Benefits. Specific coverage of such services as regular annual physicals, innoculation/immunization, including flu shots, well-baby care, and others generally viewed as prevention-oriented is very limited. Though a few major insurers have made such benefits widely available in recent years, there has been, in the experience of one major firm, "no action in terms of buying it."[12] This is not too surprising for several reasons, not the least of which is that the efficacy of these and other so-called preventive health services is much less recognized and apparent than is the value of preventive services in, say, dental care. Future growth in this area is likely to remain slow as far as general health insurance benefits

---

[11] Ernest Reach, February 7, 1981.
[12] Cole and Matusz, January 13, 1981.

are concerned. Nevertheless, such benefits have been widely available, generally on a voluntary basis, to top executives in many firms for years on an uninsured basis. This probably will continue.

Mental Health Benefits.   Considerable expansion and innovation in the field of mental health benefits took place from the mid-1960s until the early 1970s. This was especially true for ambulatory benefits. The United Auto Workers (UAW) plan, the Federal Employees' Health Benefit Plan, and others showed the way, along with several federal and state programs, by, in effect, bringing mental health care out of the closet. The UAW plan, for example, recognizing that social stigma already existed as a barrier to prompt and appropriate treatment, removed any further front-end financial screen by negotiating full coverage for an initial dollar range of outpatient services. This was followed by a second range of benefits, for which the patient was assessed a copayment until the limited ceiling on the outpatient mental health benefit was exhausted. (This contrasts with the pattern for most physical health benefits, in which an initial copayment or coinsurance provision is followed by a coinsurance cutoff, e.g., at the $1,000 level.) This implicitly recognized the catastrophic economic potential of long-term mental problems and accepted the principle that at some reasonable point such patients ought to become governments' responsibility.

There have been few, if any, dramatic innovations in mental health benefits in recent years. The most significant changes probably have been as a direct result of legislation, as discussed below. One discernable tendency, however, has been to broaden the definition of reimbursable services. For example, it is not unheard of to reimburse directly for services of a clinical psychologist or even, in the case of learning disabilities, an M.S. in education. These and other new provisions fit the prevailing concept of a multidisciplinary team approach to mental illness.

More recently, efforts by the federal government to contain its health expenditures have led to cutbacks in mental health benefits both under the Federal Employees' Health Benefits Plan and under various government financial "entitlement" programs. The effect of these actions on private plans remains to be seen.

While some evidence exists that more generous mental health benefits may lead to reduced costs for other medical services, continuing concern is apparent with the potential magnitude of mental health claims.

Mandated Benefits.   One development during the 1970s was relatively unheard of in earlier days. A growing army of special-interest groups, some of them having been unsuccessful for years in attaining their objectives through the marketplace, engaged in extensive lobbying efforts in an effort to mandate inclusion of their "pet" benefits in group health insurance programs. Thus, a number of states and the federal government mandate prescribed mental health benefits, maternity/abortion benefits, coverage of services provided by previously uninsured vendors of health services (e.g., chiropractors, psychologists, and others), and care delivered in specific centers (e.g., inpatient rehabilitation facilities for alcohol and drug treatment) not previously eligible for coverage.

As might be expected, these mandated benefits have their good and bad points. Unfortunately, in some cases, either because legislators or special-interest advocates had not done their homework, or because they encountered other difficulties, the mandated coverage fell short of existing benefits and served primarily as an excuse to cut back. On balance, most of these well-intentioned requirements have at least some merit, and some even have cost-saving elements. Needless to say, problems sometimes arise with benefit plans for firms with multi-state operations. It is not always easy to keep abreast of all the required benefits. This is a challenge for health care providers, employee benefit managers, and union negotiators alike. There is little reason to expect any abatement in the lobbying efforts of special-interest groups, so further changes of this sort are likely to continue. Hopefully, the main thrust of the 1980s will be to attain some uniformity of these mandated benefits rather than even further diversity.

Alternative Delivery Systems

A very large proportion of employers now provide a health maintenance organization option to their employees under their group health benefits program (they are required by federal law to do so under prescribed conditions), and mounting evidence exists that these organizations do reduce hospital utilization and costs. Nevertheless, enrollment in these plans is voluntary and, to date, only a modest proportion of the workforce has chosen to participate. For reasons not altogether clear, employers have been relatively slow to get involved, especially in the start-up and promotion of HMOs, where their support may be sorely needed. Some have suggested HMO penetration has been slow because employers see them as evidence of another federal intrusion and have, therefore, not encouraged them. As evidence of HMO cost advantage continues to accumulate, employer interest is expected to grow.

Insurers, on the other hand have evidenced considerable interest. Blue Cross/Blue Shield and several large commercial health insurers have been closely monitoring and nurturing the development of HMOs. Insurers view developments in this arena with more than passing interest, because if the idea ever really catches on, HMOs could threaten the survival of many insurers. At the same time, they are interested in evaluating those cost-saving attributes of HMOs that might be adaptable to insurer use.

Union leaders, long the vocal advocates of alternative delivery systems, have been somewhat frustrated by the relatively small proportion of their workers who have exercised their option to join HMOs across the nation. It is estimated that while about 25 percent of the American population could take advantage of this option, less than 10 percent have done so, despite extensive financial and moral support from the government for over a decade.[13] One explanation may be that several major unions have negotiated such rich packages of conventional health insurance benefits that there is simply no incentive to change. A union representative acknowledged "there are not many areas left for benefit breakthroughs . . . there is not much else we don't already have."[14] He went on to note full first-dollar coverage for visits to doctors' offices for primary care is still desired, but acknowledged "these are troubled times," and it will be tough to negotiate this benefit at the next industrywide contract renewal. (Note: Subsequent events showed this to be an accurate prediction. Indeed, even the normal historical pattern of industrywide contract negotiations failed to survive the economic pressures of early 1982. Instead, the major auto manufacturers separately negotiated a whole range of contract modifications with the UAW. These were more often characterized by "give-backs" than by "add-ons.") A representative of another union stated its members apparently ask themselves the question, "What's in it for me?" when confronted with an HMO option. They have largely concluded there is insufficient advantage to support a change.[15]

Part of the problem, at least until recently, was that the original federal HMO legislation actually was counterproductive to HMO growth, by establishing excessively tough standards for federal qualification. The original standards mandated such extensive benefits that the HMO involved a significantly higher cost to the employee, thus discouraging its election. Furthermore, without federal qualification, employers were not bound by the legislative mandate to provide a dual choice of plans for their workers. In response to this problem, the UAW's Social Security Department has established its own "Criteria for HMO Evaluation," which it views as more realistic. When it finds an acceptable HMO (by its standards) in operation, it attempts to force dual choice by contract.

The apparent gap between the support of national labor leaders for HMOs and the relatively low level of acceptance by individuals is not terribly surprising. Union leadership consistently has been clearly identified with more "liberal" political ideas for most of this century. Union leaders tend to support these kinds of "entitlement" programs as a matter of principle. Individual union members are more likely to go with short-term self-interest.

As the new idea on the block in most parts of the country, HMOs are faced with a need to overcome a great deal of inertia on the part of consumers who, though they may do a lot of general griping about the medical care system, frequently are satisfied with their own doctors. Commented one labor leader, "Outside of California, where the success of

---

[13] Ibid.

[14] Telephone interview with Patrick Killian, United Automobile Workers, March 9, 1981.

[15] Telephone interview with Thomas Duzak, United Steelworkers, March 6, 1981.

Kaiser has made it easy, we can only generate interest [in HMOs] where there is a seriously underdeveloped health care system to begin with."[16] It was also acknowledged that some poorly organized HMOs are not "doing the job." Some recent well-publicized HMO bankruptcies have done little for their image, and they have raised some concern about the absence of adequate financial guarantees for this form of alternate delivery system.

Naturally, employers, unions, and insurers have a significant stake in learning exactly what characteristics of HMOs can be profitably adopted by or incorporated into existing health benefit plans. Though HMOs should continue to grow despite threats of reduced funding, they are not likely to replace completely the traditional patterns of health and medical care in the foreseeable future. If they can acquire adequate resources, however, they should make for some very interesting confrontations as the nation moves toward at least a temporary flirtation with the concept of competition in the health care market.

One of the main advocates of competition, Professor Alain Enthoven, has proposed a "consumer choice health plan" which, if fully implemented, presumably would create true marketplace incentives for the consumer. In essence, the four basic components call for: (1) consumer choice among competing plans at regular intervals, (2) incentives for physicians and other health care providers to provide services at competitive price levels, (3) uniform rules for all health insurance carriers, and (4) a fixed-dollar subsidy from employers or the government, which could be used for the purchase of any health insurance plan. Among other things, the plan would require extensive changes in income-tax deductibility of health insurance premiums.[17] A more detailed discussion of HMOs appears in Chapter 10.

"Carve-out" Provisions

Since the advent of Medicare, but especially more recently, since Congress prohibited mandatory retirement at age 65, situations exist where employees are still actively working after they become eligible for Medicare benefits. In addition, numerous union-negotiated plans continue benefits for retired workers. In both cases, plan benefits usually differ in important respects from Medicare and in many cases are considerably more generous. In these circumstances, it is customary for the group plan to be tailored to take full advantage of the federal benefits to which the worker/retiree is entitled, while also assuring that no benefit available to other members of the group is forfeited. In colloquial terms, the Medicare benefits are "carved-out" of the group plan for those eligible for the federal program.

---

[16] Ibid.

[17] For a much more detailed discussion of his prototypical consumer choice health plan, see Alain C. Enthoven, *Health Plan* (Reading, Mass.: Addison-Wesley Publishing, 1980).

Preferred Provider Organizations

One of the latest developments, still in its infancy, is to identify Preferred Provider Organizations (PPOs). Insureds are assured of full coverage when they utilize the PPO, but may be penalized by way of deductibles, coinsurance, or other limitations, when care is obtained elsewhere. Initial concern over potential antitrust implications of these arrangements has eased somewhat with passage of "enabling legislation" in California in 1982. PPOs may be either known low cost providers or may actually contract to provide services at stated prices. Potential problems include inadequate data to identify low cost providers and/or inadequate market share to command a contract for low prices. There may also be some employee resistance if, for example, their doctor lacks privileges at a designated PPO facility. Despite some problems, however, this concept should grow.

SOME TRADITIONAL HEALTH BENEFIT PROVISIONS REVISITED

Along with the introduction of new benefit provisions, many employers are taking a closer look at some traditional design features to examine how they may be made more effective. (Chapters 19 and 20 address these matters in greater detail.)

Notable among these are the various cost-sharing provisions, including deductibles, coinsurance and copayments, and premium-sharing. More often than not, these provisions are applied in less-than-optimal fashion, often falling most heavily on just those services now thought to be most desirable (e.g., outpatient services), while frequently not applying at all to hospital costs. This may have been consistent with the historically sound concept that the hospital benefit was less likely to be abused because the patient could not self-admit, but it is clearly out of touch with the medical and economic realities of today. Many benefit managers today believe selective application of deductibles and copayments can reshape utilization patterns to favor less-costly outpatient services. This is not easy, however, since most unions are adamantly opposed to relinquishing any present benefits. The possible combinations of deductibles and coinsurance and copayment provisions—in terms of type, amount, and application—are almost limitless and deserve careful study by those who design benefit packages. Administrative costs of their application also must be considered. As one senior insurance executive stated, "In order to work, financial incentives cannot simply be made neutral. They must make outpatient and other less costly (than hospital) services more attractive."[18]

In keeping with the new vogue enjoyed by marketplace incentives, increasing interest is apparent in use of alternate premium-sharing formulas

---

[18] Richard J. Mellman, January 30, 1981.

to encourage employees to choose more economical health benefit packages. Little documentation is available in this area, but the idea is mentioned with increasing frequency by benefits managers. Again, most unions oppose premium-sharing as a matter of principle.

Though not always considered as cost-sharing provisions per se, such basic benefit design features as limitations on coverage clearly can be viewed as having a significant cumulative impact on the overall cost of a benefit program. Limitations take many forms, some of which are common and generally accepted, while others are more controversial. Preexisting conditions, commonly excluded under individual health insurance policies, usually have been granted more generous treatment in group plans since there is presumed to be less risk of "adverse selection." Nevertheless, there are some preexisting conditions whose potential impact, even on a group basis, might warrant exclusion. Exclusions on coverage for purely custodial care are almost universal, at present, and benefits for nursing homes face a variety of other limitations, ranging from the common need for prior hospitalization to various limits based on the level of care received. Coverage for certain "hospital extras" (e.g., television rental, air conditioners, telephone charges, bath massagers) has come under scrutiny, and some plans have very strict requirements regarding "cosmetic surgery." Provision of benefits for eye refractions and hearing aids, when offered at all, typically limit the frequency with which they are available.

Group insurance programs generally are careful to restrict coverage of treatment received in federal or state hospitals to those services the patient would be legally obligated to pay for in the absence of the insurance. To avoid duplication of benefits available under workers' compensation laws, virtually all group plans exclude coverage for occupational accidents and sicknesses. In addition, the nature of conversion provisions, termination and survivor health benefits influence cost. Cost, however, is by no means the only factor to be considered. Overall employee satisfaction and employer objectives also must be weighed.

It should be obvious, too, that benefit design always must be dovetailed with all new governmental actions, whether they be in the form of entitlement programs (e.g., Medicare), which could overlap, or of duplicate existing benefits, or of regulatory actions (e.g., mandated coverages, the Age Discrimination in Employment Act), which impose constraints on the form or extent of benefits, or of court actions, which establish guidelines or penalties, or both, for deviating from currently accepted norms (e.g., possible sex discrimination in the benefit package).

The ultimate in cost-sharing, of course, comes when the maximum benefit has been exhausted. With the soaring health care costs of the 1970s and early 1980s, maximum benefits under group health insurance plans reached unprecedented highs. By 1981, for example, of the nearly quarter million employees covered under new comprehensive major medical expense plans, 86 percent had available maximum benefits of $1 million or more, many with no limit.[19] Even these "jumbo" limits, however, frequently are conditioned with internal constraints imposing restrictions on certain daily charges (e.g., hospital room and board) or set lifetime maximums for certain conditions (e.g., mental disorders).

Other traditional features of group health benefits also are being studied more carefully. Though virtually all group plans already have coordination of benefits (COB) provisions, they seldom have been pursued vigorously. With the sharp increase in the number of two-income families during the past decade, many believe substantial savings could be realized through more careful implementation of COB. Often, this is made possible by sophisticated, modern computer programs.

A unique approach to cost-sharing has been introduced in California. In contrast to traditional deductibles and coinsurance programs, usually viewed by workers as cash penalties, the Mendocino County Office of Education has established a cash-incentive program. It deposits $500 per employee per year in a trust account. As medical expenses are incurred, the worker may draw against the $500 reserve. When expenses exceed the $500, the remaining costs are picked up by a Blue Cross/Blue Shield package. Any part of the $500 that is unused in any year is kept on deposit for the employer as a "savings" account. Upon retirement or departure from the district, workers may withdraw their accumulated savings. Note that a bad year never cuts into previous savings. In the meantime, as the trust fund grows, the interest from it is used toward the district's premium for the BC/BS coverage. Results to date, though limited, are very encouraging. The district has received interest on the trust account, BC/BS premiums have not been raised in two years, a "vision package" of benefits has been added to the coverage without charge, and it is believed the employees have learned to make more intelligent use of the health care system. There also has been a noticeable decline in the number of visits to doctors.

One traditional benefit provision currently undergoing particularly careful scrutiny by government, employers, and unions is that which limits the duration of coverage upon termination of employment to a relatively brief time period. Recent high levels of unemployment, the result of a serious national recession, have generated much anxiety. In a nation where the overwhelming majority of health insurace coverage is job related, and where individual coverages are typically less broad, more costly, and more difficult to obtain than group coverage, some means must be found to continue protection during troubled times. Similar concerns during the 1975–76 recession led to a flurry of bills in Congress, but recovery preceded action. As of early 1983, despite a variety of new proposals, no real solution had been found, but millions were without their usual coverage.

---

[19] *New Group Health Insurance, 1981* (Washington, D.C.: HIAA).

Indeed, it is not clear whether the ultimate responsibility will (or should) rest with government, the employer, or the individual. It does seem imperative, however, that some mechanism be developed to assure continuity of coverage.

"CAFETERIA" PLANS

"Cafeteria"-type employee benefit programs have been discussed for many years, but until recently, they have not attracted too much attention. That seems about to change. The general characteristics of cafeteria plans tend to have much in common with current proposals for various forms of consumer-choice health care plans. The idea is to provide a basic core of benefits, encompassing life and health insurance as well as pension, but to allow individual workers great latitude in the choice of specifics. Given a stipulated level of employer contribution, employees are able to select from a variety of "packages" covering more-or-less extensive ranges of benefits, and with a choice of deductibles, copayments, and absolute limits. Furthermore, they are permitted to change the mix of their benefits as their family circumstances change over time, usually on an annual basis.

Cafeteria plans present certain underwriting and administrative problems. Clearly, there is room for considerable adverse selection, and this could have some negative impact on costs. Modern computer technology, with appropriate software, should minimize the administrative difficulties. The biggest advantage of such plans in the eyes of most employers is that they may lead to a significantly higher level of employee appreciation for the benefits provided, something frequently lacking under conventional plans. Indeed, there is some danger that this alleged advantage could backfire. Unless employers are successful in effectively communicating the relative advantages and consequences of various choices to the employees, a strong possibility exists that unwise choices will be made and disappointment result at the time a claim is submitted. Even under the standardized programs of the past, few employers and even fewer employees have fully understood their coverage, especially concerning those elements relating to cost containment or cost control.[20]

Few, if any, expect cafeteria plans to solve all the problems in the employee benefit field, and union officials seem particularly wary of these and other "competitive" plans. For the moment, however, hard-pressed corporations and insurers reflect considerable interest in at least exploring the concept. A more detailed discussion of cafeteria plans appears in Chapter 26.

---

[20] For a thorough and enlightening discussion of this problem, see Allison Alkere, B.A., *Effective Communication of Cost Containment and Cost Control Elements in Employee Benefit Plans* (Master's thesis, the College of Insurance, New York, N.Y., January 1981).

BEYOND BENEFIT DESIGN

Though the focus thus far has been on benefit design, few expect that approach to be successful in and of itself. Employers will have to use every other means at their disposal if the cost crisis is to be brought under control. Among the other efforts currently in use are various financing controls ("minimum premiums," control over reserves, and the like), a more vigorous review of utilization, and interaction with providers (including concurrent hospital utilization review), hospital prompt payment discounts, hospital bill audit programs, monitoring of turnover and absenteeism, more intensive bargaining with carriers, and direct involvement in health systems agencies and other community-based health activities. (Again, see Chapters 19 and 20 for more detail.)

As noted above, the cost problem is particularly difficult for private insurers and employers as the proportion of the population covered by government-sponsored cost-reimbursement programs has increased. As government has tightened its definitions of costs in an effort to control its outlays for health care services, the discrepancy between health institutions' costs and charges has ballooned, and private plans have borne the brunt of this differential.

To review, in an effort to combat the problem, many groups of employers around the country have formed to sponsor joint health cost-containment programs. They have found very little good data exist on which to base careful analysis of the health care cost crisis. Insurers, primarily interested in the bottom line, generally have not kept good diagnostic-related or service-specific records of claims, and employers have not coordinated their efforts. Nevertheless, they have found, through the sharing of their experiences and the careful design of a data base for the future, that they have been able to improve their understanding of the issues, the problems of health care providers, and the available techniques for gaining some control over costs. This activist role, though belated, augurs well for the future.

If nothing else, it has made clear that, while everyone seems most concerned about cost, cost is not the only real problem. Our system of health care also is faulty. We are in an era of "lifestyle disease." The medical care system cannot do as much to control cancer, strokes, heart attacks, and automobile accidents as can the individual. The result, it seems, is a far greater awareness on the part of employers that they must play a major role in promoting good health or "wellness" in addition to providing benefits for the treatment of sickness. Unions, too, reflect an increasing awareness in this area.

Whether these new perceptions will result in including even more specific benefits under traditional health insurance programs, or whether an entirely new generation of employee benefits will spring up as a separate entity, is at this time not clear. However, it cannot be denied that interest is mounting in the area of physical fitness for employees. Programs promoting self-care, immunization, nonsmoking, control of alcoholism, exercise, and so on are proliferating. Employee assistance programs offering a wide range of counseling services also are growing in number, as are a variety of health-related educational programs such as, cardiac pulmonary resussitation (CPR), blood pressure control, diet, and others. Courses designed to make employees wiser users of the health care system and their benefit plans also are appearing. The cost-effectiveness of these and other programs will be closely monitored in coming years, and the most effective programs undoubtedly will become commonplace. Many will undoubtedly remain separate ad hoc initiatives, but some eventually may be incorporated into benefit packages.

Of one thing we can be sure: employers are not likely to be the idle bystanders of the past. The stakes are high, and so, too, is their awareness. Finally.

CHAPTER 9

Social Security and Other Governmental Health Benefit Plans

ROBERT J. MYERS

Health (or medical care) benefits for active and retired workers and their dependents in the United States is, in the vast majority of cases, provided through the multiple means of the Medicare portion of Social Security, private employer-sponsored plans, and individual savings. As mentioned in an earlier chapter, this is sometimes referred to as a "three-legged stool" or the three "pillars" of economic security protection. Still others look upon the situation as Social Security providing the floor of protection for certain categories, or, in other cases, providing the basic protection with public assistance programs, such as Medicaid, providing a net of protection for those whose income is not sufficient to purchase the needed medical care not provided through some form of prepaid insurance.

Private health benefit plans supplement Medicare to some extent. In other instances—essentially for active workers and their families—health benefit protection is provided by the private sector. The net result, however, is a broad network of health benefit protection.

This chapter discusses the provisions of the Medicare program, not only their historical development and present structure, but also possible future changes. Following this, various other governmental programs, including Medicaid, workers' compensation, and plans for government employees are treated.

MEDICARE

Historical Development of Provisions

Beginning in the early 1950s, efforts were made to provide medical care benefits (primarily for hospitalization) for beneficiaries under the Old-Age, Survivors, and Disability Insurance (OASDI) program. In 1965, such efforts succeeded, and the resulting program is called Medicare.

122

Initially, Medicare applied only to persons age 65 and over. In 1972, disabled Social Security beneficiaries who had been on the benefit rolls for at least two years were made eligible, as were virtually all persons in the country who have end-stage renal disease (i.e., chronic kidney disease). Since 1972, relatively few changes in the coverage or benefit provisions have been made.

Medicare is really two separate programs. One part, Hospital Insurance (HI),[1] is financed primarily from payroll taxes on workers covered under OASDI, including those under the Railroad Retirement system and, beginning in 1983, all civilian employees of the Federal Government, even though, in general, they are not covered by OASDI. The other part, Supplementary Medical Insurance (SMI), is on an individual voluntary basis and is financed partially by enrollee premiums, with the remainder coming from general revenues.

Persons Protected by Hospital Insurance

All individuals age 65 and over who are eligible for monthly benefits under the Old-Age, Survivors, and Disability Insurance program or the Railroad Retirement program also are eligible for Hospital Insurance benefits (as are federal employees who have sufficient earnings credits from their special HI coverage which began in 1983). Persons are "eligible" for OASDI benefits if they could receive them when the person on whose earnings record they are eligible is deceased or receiving disability or retirement benefits, or could be receiving retirement benefits except for having had substantial earnings. Thus, the HI eligibles include not only insured workers, but also spouses, disabled children (in rare cases where they are at least age 65), and survivors, such as widowed spouses and dependent parents. As a specific illustration, HI protection is available for an insured worker and spouse, both at least age 65, even though the worker has such high earnings that OASDI cash benefits are not currently payable.

In addition, HI eligibility is available for disabled beneficiaries who have been on the benefit roll for at least two years (beyond a 5-month waiting period). Such disabled eligibles include not only insured workers, but also disabled child beneficiaries, age 18 and over but disabled before age 22, and disabled widowed spouses, age 50–64.

Further, persons under age 65 with end-stage renal disease (ESRD) who require dialysis or renal transplant are eligible for HI benefits if they meet one of a number of requirements. Such requirements for ESRD benefits include being fully or currently insured (see Chapter 28 about requirements), being a spouse or a dependent child of an insured worker or of a monthly beneficiary, or being a monthly beneficiary.

Individuals age 65 and over who are not eligible for HI as a result of their

---

[1] Sometimes referred to as Part A (Supplementary Medical Insurance is Part B).

own or some other person's earnings can elect coverage, and then must make premium payments, whereas OASDI eligibles do not. The standard monthly premium rate is $113 for the first half of 1983 and $132 for the following 12 months.

Benefits Provided

The principal benefit provided by the HI program is payable for hospital services. The full cost for all such services, other than luxury items, is paid by HI during a so-called spell of illness, after an initial deductible has been paid and with daily coinsurance for all hospital days after the 60th one, but with an upper limit on the number of days covered. A spell of illness is a period beginning with the first day of hospitalization and ending when the individual has been out of both hospitals and skilled nursing facilities for 60 consecutive days. The initial deductible is $304 in 1983. The daily coinsurance is $76 for the 61st to 90th days of hospitalization. A nonrenewable lifetime reserve of 60 days is available after the regular 90 days have been used; these lifetime reserve days are subject to daily coinsurance of $152 in 1983. The deductible and coinsurance amounts are adjusted automatically each year after 1983 to reflect past changes in hospital costs.

Benefits also are available for care provided in skilled nursing facilities, following at least three days of hospitalization. Such care is provided only when it is for convalescent or recuperative care, and not for custodial care. The first 20 days of such care in a spell of illness are provided without cost to the individual. The next 80 days, however, are subject to a daily coinsurance payment, which is $38 in 1983, and which will be adjusted automatically in the future in the same manner as the hospital cost-sharing amounts. No benefits are available after 100 days of care in a skilled nursing facility for a particular spell of illness.

In addition, an unlimited number of home health service benefits are provided by HI without any payment being required from the beneficiary. Also, hospice care for terminally ill persons is covered if all Medicare benefits other than physician services are waived; certain cost restrictions and coinsurance requirements apply with respect to prescription drugs.

HI benefit protection is provided only within the United States, with the exception of certain emergency services available when in or near Canada. Not covered by HI are those cases where services are performed in a Veterans Administration hospital or where the person is eligible for medical services under a workers' compensation program. Furthermore, Medicare is the secondary payor in cases when (a) medical care is payable under any liability policy, especially automobile ones, (b) during the first 12 months of treatment for ESRD cases when private group health insurance provides coverage, and (c) for persons aged 65–69 (employees and spouses) who are under employer-sponsored group health insurance plans (which is required for all plans of employers with at least 20 employees) unless the employee opts out of it.

Financing of HI

With the exception of the small group of persons who voluntarily elect coverage, the HI program is financed by payroll taxes on workers in employment covered by the OASDI program. This payroll tax rate is combined with that for OASDI and is subject to the same maximum taxable earnings base ($35,700 in 1983, with automatic adjustment thereafter). Unlike OASDI, under which the employer and employee rates are the same, but the self-employed pay one and a half times the employee rate, the HI tax rate is the same for employers, employees, and self-employed persons. Such HI tax rate for each party is 1.3 percent in 1983–84, 1.35 percent in 1985, and 1.45 percent thereafter. It should be noted that long-range actuarial cost estimates indicate this tax schedule will not provide adequate financing after about a decade from now (or perhaps even sooner).

The vast majority of persons who attained age 65 before 1968, and who were not eligible for HI benefit protection on the basis of an earnings record, were nonetheless given full eligibility for benefits without any charge. The cost for this closed blanketed-in group is met from general revenues rather than from HI payroll taxes.

The HI Trust Fund receives the income of the program from the various sources and makes the required disbursements for benefits and administrative expenses. The assets are invested and earn interest in the same manner as the OASDI Trust Funds, described in detail in Chapter 28.

Although the federal government is responsible for the administration of the HI program, the actual dealing with the various medical facilities is through fiscal intermediaries, such as Blue Cross and insurance companies, which are reimbursed for their expenses on a cost basis.

Persons Protected under Supplementary Medical Insurance

Individuals aged 65 or over can elect coverage on an individual basis regardless of whether they have OASDI insured status. In addition, disabled OASDI beneficiaries eligible for HI and persons with ESRD eligible under HI can elect SMI coverage. In general, coverage election must be made at about the time of initial eligibility, that is, attainment of age 65 or at the end of the disability-benefit waiting period. Subsequent election during general enrollment periods is possible but with higher premium rates being applicable. Similarly, individuals can terminate coverage and cease premium payment at their own volition.

Benefits Provided under SMI

The principal SMI benefit is partial reimbursement for physician services, although other medical services, such as diagnostic tests, ambulance services, prosthetic devices, physical therapy, medical equipment, and home health services, are covered as under HI. Not covered are out-of-hospital drugs, most dental services, most chiropractic services, routine physical and eye examinations, eyeglasses and hearing aids, and services outside of the United States, except those in connection with HI services that are covered in Canada. Just as for HI, there are limits on SMI coverage in workers' compensation cases, medical care under liability policies, private group health insurance applicable to ESRD, amd employer-sponsored group health insurance for employees aged 65–69 and for employees' spouses aged 65–69.

SMI pays 80 percent of so-called reasonable charges, actually allowable charges, under a complicated determination basis that usually produces a lower charge than the reasonable and prevailing one, after the individual has paid a calendar-year deductible of $75. Special limits apply on out-of-hospital mental health care costs and on the services of independent physical therapists.

Financing of SMI

The standard monthly premium rate is $12.20 for the first half of 1983 and $13.50 for the next 12 months. The premium is higher for those who fail to enroll as early as they possibly can, with an increase of 10 percent for each full 12 months of delay. The premium is deducted from the OASDI benefits of persons currently receiving them, or are paid by direct submittal in other cases.

The remainder of the cost of the program is met by general revenues. In the aggregate, persons age 65 and over pay only about 25 percent of the cost, while for disabled persons such proportion is only about 15 percent. As a result, enrollment in SMI is very attractive, and about 95 percent of those eligible to do so actually enroll.

The enrollee premium rate is changed every year, effective for July. In practice, the rate of increase in the premium rate is determined by the percentage rise in the level of OASDI cash benefits in the previous year under the automatic adjustment provisions, although for the premium years beginning in 1983 and 1984, the premium rate is set at 25 percent of the cost for persons age 65 or over.

The SMI Trust Fund was established to receive the enrollee premiums and the payments from general revenues. From this fund are paid the benefits and the accompanying administrative expenses. Although the program is under the general supervision of the federal government, most of the administration is accomplished through fiscal intermediaries, such as Blue Shield or insurance companies, on an actual cost basis for their administrative expenses.

Possible Future Development of Medicare

Over the years, numerous proposals have been made to modify the Medicare program. Some of these would expand it significantly, while others would curtail it to some extent.

Among the proposals that would expand the program are those to establish some type of national health insurance program, having very comprehensive coverage of medical services applicable to the entire population. Somewhat less broadly, other proposals would extend Medicare coverage to additional categories of OASDI beneficiaries beyond old-age beneficiaries age 65 and over and disabled beneficiaries on the roll for at least two years—such as to early retirement cases at ages 62–64 and to all disability beneficiaries.

In another direction, liberalizing proposals have been made to add further services, such as out-of-hospital drugs, physical examinations, and dental services. Still other proposals have been made in the direction of reducing the extent of cost-sharing on the part of the beneficiary by lowering or eliminating the deductible and coinsurance provisions and by eliminating the duration-of-stay limits on HI benefit eligibility.

As to financing aspects, proposals have been made to eliminate the enrollee premiums under SMI and to replace them by complete financing from general revenues or by partial financing from payroll taxes, while at the same time reducing the HI tax rates and making up for this by partial general revenue financing of III. It also has been proposed that the HI program should be financed partially, or even completely, by general revenues.

Proposals concerning the reimbursement of physicians under SMI have been made to discourage or prevent them from charging the beneficiaries more than the so-called reasonable or allowable charge. Similarly, various proposals have been made to lower the cost of the HI program as far as reimbursement of hospitals and skilled nursing facilities is concerned, although this would have no effect on the Medicare beneficiary directly.

Recently, proposals have been made to reduce the cost of the Medicare program by increasing the cost-sharing payments made by the beneficiary. For example, the cost-sharing in the first 60 days of hospitalization could be changed from a one-time payment of the initial deductible to some type of daily coinsurance that would foster the incentive to shorten hospital stays. Another proposal is to adjust automatically, from year to year, the SMI annual deductible, which, unlike the HI cost-sharing payments, is a fixed amount, although it has been increased by ad hoc changes from the initial $50 in 1966 to $75 in 1982.

MEDICAID

Over the years, the cost of medical care for recipients of public assistance and for other low-income persons has been met in a variety of ways. Some years ago, these provisions were rather haphazard, and the medical care costs were met along with the public assistance payments. In 1960, a separate public assistance program in this area was enacted—namely, Medical Assistance for the Aged (MAA), which applied to persons age 65 and

over, both those receiving Old-Age Assistance (OAA) and other persons
not having sufficient resources to meet large medical expenses.

Then in 1965, the MAA program and the federal matching for medical
vendor payments for public assistance categories other than MAA were
combined into the Medicaid program. This new program covered not only
public assistance recipients, but also persons of similar demographic characteristics who were medically indigent.

The Medicaid program is operated by the several states, with significant
federal financing being available. Only one state, Arizona, does not have a
Medicaid program, although some states cover only public assistance
recipients.

Medicaid programs are required to furnish certain services, to receive
federal financial participation. These services include those for physicians,
hospitals (both inpatient and outpatient), laboratory and X-ray tests, home
health visits, and nursing home care. Most other medical services, such as
drugs, dental care, and eyeglasses, can be included at the option of the state,
and then federal matching will be made available. Also, states can pay the
SMI premiums for their Medicaid recipients eligible for that program, and
thus the states can have the advantage of the relatively large general revenues financing in that program.

The federal government pays a proportion of the total cost of the
Medicaid expenditures for medical care that varies inversely with the average per capita income of the state. This proportion is 55 percent for a state
with the same average per capita income as the nation as a whole. States
with above-average income have a lower matching proportion, but never
less than 50 percent. Conversely, states with below-average income have a
higher federal matching percentage, which can be as much as 83 percent,
although the highest ratio in actual practice currently is about 78 percent.
The federal government also pays part of the administrative costs of the
Medicaid programs; generally, this is 50 percent, but, for certain types of
expenses that are expected to control costs, the federal percentage is
higher.

WORKERS' COMPENSATION PROGRAMS

Workers' compensation programs provide benefits for injuries and occupational diseases that arise in the course of employment. These benefits
include both cash payments to the worker (and, in the case of death, to the
survivors) and payments for necessary medical expenses. The WC programs
have been established over the years by the states, with no participation by
the federal government except in plans it has for its own employees and for
longshoremen and harbor workers nationwide.

Some years ago, several state plans had limitations on the amount of
medical care that would be provided for WC cases. However, all plans
currently furnish complete medical care and with no waiting period, as
there often is for the cash benefits.

OTHER GOVERNMENTAL PROGRAMS

Medical care plans or programs of reimbursement for part or all of medical care costs have been established for employees of the federal government. Active members of the armed forces are provided full medical care by military personnel and facilities, without any payment being required from the individual; their dependents also can receive such services if sufficient facilities are available. Otherwise, if they are not near a military installation, they can receive medical care reimbursement benefits under a program operated by several private insurance organizations.

Retired members of the military services and their dependents can receive medical care in the same manner as for active members, although with certain nominal charges in military hospitals. Former members of the military services who did not serve long enough to attain retired status can obtain medical care through the Veterans Administration in all cases where this is necessary for service-connected cases or for those who are service-disabled, regardless of the cause. In other cases, medical care is available under a liberally administered means test. However, no medical care is provided by the Veterans Administration for dependents of veterans.

Federal civilian employees have a health insurance program for themselves and their dependents that consists of a choice of a large number of different plans provided by various types of health care providers. The program is financed by a flat monthly payment by the government for each covered person, varying only between single persons and those with eligible dependents. As a result, the covered individuals pay an amount that varies with the degree of comprehensiveness of the coverage. Thus, some of the plans provide, at a low cost to the employee, only basic benefits, while other plans that have comprehensive coverage require large contributions from the employee. In 1983, the government contribution was determined as 60 percent of the average of the premiums charged for the high-option basis in the six largest plans.

Employees of state and local governments generally have health insurance plans similar to those provided by private employers.

MATERNAL AND CHILD HEALTH PROGRAMS

The Social Security Act provides for grants of federal funds for consultation services in the area of maternal and child health services (including crippled children's services). Each state has programs in these areas and uses the federal funds for such things as maternity clinics, family planning services, home health visits of public health nurses, well-child clinics, school health programs, pediatric clinics, dental care, mental retardation clinics, immunization against preventable diseases clinics and various treatment programs for crippled children involving diagnosis and measures to prevent the development of conditions that lead to crippling.

CHAPTER 10

Types of Health Risk Bearers

LINDA PICKTHORNE
FLETCHER

The health risk exposures that confront individuals, along with their desire for comprehensive health care benefits, have created a continuing interest on the part of employees in the types of available health risk bearers. This interest, when combined with the constantly increasing cost of health care benefits, makes especially relevant any analysis of the alternative mechanisms for financing the costs of medical care expenses.

Among these alternatives are the indemnity or reimbursement approach traditionally associated with insurance companies, the service benefit approach associated with Blue Cross/Blue Shield associations, the health maintenance organization (HMO) approach, and the self-funding approach.

THE INDEMNITY OR REIMBURSEMENT APPROACH

Health care benefits provided by an insurance company traditionally were paid on an indemnity or reimbursement basis; that is, the insurer agrees to pay for the actual cost of the health care received by the employee up to the maximum dollar limit stated in the policy. Benefits were paid to the employee, unless the latter had assigned them to the health care purveyor.

An insurance company that writes health insurance generally makes available the so-called basic coverages, as well as major medical-type policies. The basic coverages include hospitalization, surgical, and regular medical benefits. The major medical contracts are issued on both a supplemental and comprehensive basis. The supplemental policy is written on the assumption there are underlying basic coverages in force. The comprehensive plan combines certain elements of basic benefits and the major medical concept in one policy.

As previously indicated, both the basic coverages and major medical policies traditionally make benefits available on an indemnity or reimbursement basis. Many insurers, however, increasingly are willing to pay for specified health care expenses in full, on the basis of their reasonable and customary cost. For these benefits—such as the cost of a given number of days in a semiprivate hospital room—a maximum dollar reimbursement is not applicable. In effect, then, this departure from the indemnity concept permits an insurance company to emulate the service-type benefits historically marketed primarily by Blue Cross/Blue Shield associations.

Competitive pressures, as well as the high cost of medical care, have caused insurers to further expand their product lines. They thus provide contracts that include all the services of a fully insured group policy, but permit premium deferrals, refund of the incurred but unreported claims reserve, or a retrospective premium agreement. Additional modifications include risk sharing by the employer, such as the minimum premium approach and the administrative services only contract (see Chapter 43 for a description of these plans).

Insurance companies are major health risk bearers, and benefits are provided by monoline health carriers, life insurers, and property-liability companies. In terms of legal form, both stock and mutual insurers sell health care benefits. It should be noted, however, that nothing inherent in the legal form of an insurance company makes one superior to another. It is how the insurer conducts its various functions and operations that should be the primary determinant in selecting a company. Such factors, therefore, as cost, financial stability and solvency, and quality of service should be reviewed before deciding from among various insurers.

THE SERVICE BENEFIT APPROACH

Blue Cross/Blue Shield associations, the "Blues," contract with purveyors of medical care services— hospitals and physicians—for certain health care services to be provided to the members of the associations. The members of the associations, referred to as subscribers, pay to the plans a fee, a premium. The plans, in turn, utilize these fees to pay the expenses of the health care provided the subscribers, the insureds, by the hospitals and physicians that have entered into contractual agreements with the Blues. In short, the Blues arrange for the prepayment of the expenses of health care services received by plan subscribers.

Blue Cross/Blue Shield associations are independent, nonprofit entities organized under special enabling statutes of the various states, and generally are subject to supervision by the state insurance department. This regulation, however, generally is not as comprehensive or extensive as that applicable to insurance companies.

Blue Cross plans provide hospitalization benefits, while Blue Shield plans provide surgical and medical services to subscribers. The plans are organized separately and restrict their operations to a specifically limited geographical area, such as a state or a large metropolitan area. There are approximately 70 Blue Cross and Blue Shield plans providing service benefits to their subscribers.

Each association is established by, or in conjunction with, the medical purveyors that furnish the contractual services to the plan's subscribers. For example, a Blue Cross plan will have been organized by or with the assistance of the hospitals in the geographical area where the association operates. The plan contracts with the hospitals, referred to as member hospitals, to provide hospital services to the plan subscribers. The plan reimburses the hospital directly for any services provided to members according to a prearranged formula. The same broad pattern of organization and purveyor relationship exists between Blue Shield associations and local medical societies.

Because of their limited geographical operation, the Blues are known as community-based organizations; that is, since they operate in a specifically defined area, they try to enroll as many individuals as possible as plan subscribers. To reinforce this community orientation, membership fees (premiums) are based on the cost of services provided to all subscribers in the area rather than being determined by a differentiation between the expenses incurred by given groups. For larger groups, however, experience rating has been used under many plans.

As stated above, the hospitalization benefits provided by Blue Cross and the surgical and medical benefits provided by Blue Shield generally are written on a service basis. Blue Cross plans, however, adhere more closely to the service concept than do the Blue Shield associations. Many Blue Shield plans provide for services to be provided to subscribers on the basis of the usual, customary, and reasonable charge made by the physician. If the latter accepts this amount as his or her fee, the subscriber, in effect, has been provided benefits on a service basis. Other Blue Shield plans, however, call for the payment of a stated sum for specific services rendered by a physician. If the latter's usual fee exceeds this allowance, the subscriber must pay the difference. In this situation, service benefits are not provided by Blue Shield.

In addition to the hospitalization, surgical, and regular medical benefits offered by the Blues, these plans also market the extended benefit coverages that expand the scope of their traditional offerings. The associations also are making available to subscribers major medical-type benefits. These products were created in direct response to the competitive pressures being exerted by insurance companies as the latter expanded their product lines.

Distinctive Characteristics of the Indemnity and Service Benefit Approaches

The Blues are the major competitors of insurance companies in financing the delivery of health care benefits. The early differences between the two types of health risk bearers were easily identifiable. The Blues provided benefits on a service basis; insurance contracts were written to indemnify or reimburse employees for health care expenses. The Blues emphasized first-dollar coverage of medical care costs; insurers instituted the concept of catastrophic or major medical-type benefits. The Blues adopted the philosophy of community rating and the absence of rate differentiation among groups of subscribers; insurance companies utilized experience rating techniques, so the payments made for the claims of a given group were reflected specifically in the premiums paid by that group. Over time, however, these differences became less distinct. Insurers now offer the equivalent of service-type benefits. The Blues offer extended basic benefit packages, as well as major medical-type coverages. Finally, although the Blues still endorse the concept of community rating, they, too, have begun to utilize experience rating on an increasingly frequent basis.

Despite the blurring of the early differences between the Blues and the insurance companies, various competitive distinctions still exist. These distinctions, in most cases, have a direct impact on the costs associated with each type of health risk bearer. For example, as previously indicated, the Blues are incorporated under state insurance laws as nonprofit organizations. These statutes recognize the nonprofit and community-oriented philosophy of the Blues by granting the associations exemption from certain taxes. The treatment varies by state; some states impose no taxes on the Blues, others provide some degree of exemption only from premium taxes. In addition, the associations pay no federal income taxes. Insurance companies, including mutual insurers that are legally organized as nonprofit corporations, receive no special tax treatment. This situation may result in a competitive pricing advantage for the Blues, compared to insurance companies.

Blue Cross associations have a further competitive advantage in the manner in which the reimbursement of hospital care costs is handled. Since Blue Cross is organized by or with the assistance of hospitals for the purpose of prepaying the cost of subscribers' hospitalization care, Blue Cross is able to negotiate special rates of reimbursement for hospital care. A common technique is for Blue Cross to pay a member hospital some percentage, such as 80 percent, of the actual daily charge for hospital benefits. The difference in the hospital's actual cost and the payment made by Blue Cross must be wholly or partially absorbed by patients who are not association subscribers. This situation also results in a competitive pricing advantage for Blue Cross plans, compared to insurance companies.

Insurers, though, have a certain competitive and therefore a possible cost advantage in terms of their product line. As referred to earlier, many insurance companies offer medical insurance contracts that permit an employer, with favorable loss experience, to directly benefit from this situation by providing for risk sharing by that employer. Other medical insurance contractual arrangements improve the cash-flow situation of employers by permitting flexible premium payment and reserve reductions. To the extent these product innovations result in cost savings for the employer, insurers may experience a competitive pricing situation compared to the Blues.

Finally, the difference in the effectiveness of the two types of health risk bearers should be evaluated on its impact on the cost of health care benefits. Because of their special relationship with area hospitals, on the one hand, Blue Cross associations have been somewhat effective in initiating and monitoring cost-control activities directed toward member hospitals. The relationship between Blue Shield associations and local medical societies, on the other hand, is not such that extensive cost-control efforts have been possible or effective with respect to physicians' charges. Insurers do not have the same advantageous relationship with hospitals as do Blue Cross associations. Insurance companies attempt to contain health care costs, however, through various means, including extensive monitoring of claims submitted on reasonableness of charges, patterns of charges, and the like. Generalizations about the effectiveness of health care cost-containment efforts are difficult to make. Any assessment probably should be made by an individual analysis of specific health risk bearers.

HEALTH MAINTENANCE ORGANIZATIONS (HMOs)

A health maintenance organization provides a broad range of health care services, including preventive care, for its members for which a fixed, per capita fee is prepaid on a periodic basis. An HMO generally confines its operations to a specific, restricted geographical area. Members receive all health care—or that care the HMO states it will provide—through the HMO. No additional charge, other than the periodically prepaid fee, is made to the members for that care.

The HMO may be established on a profit or nonprofit basis. The approximately 200 HMOs currently in existence have been initiated by a variety of sponsors including labor unions, insurance companies, Blue Cross/Blue Shield associations, consumer/employers, and physicians. Their creation was substantially encouraged by the enactment of the Health Maintenance Organization Act of 1973. This federal law encouraged the establishment of HMOs by overruling restrictive state laws that prohibited the organization of such plans and by providing certain grants and loans to aid in their development.

An HMO may be broadly categorized as a group practice prepayment plan or as an individual practice association (IPA) plan. The first HMOs established were organized as group practice prepayment plans. Under such plans members receive care at the HMO's facility from a number of physicians who have expertise in a variety of medical specialities. Patient records are maintained centrally. The physicians are compensated either by a salary or under a contract with the HMO. In some cases, the physicians may be on the HMO's staff, and also are paid by the HMO. Hospital care generally is provided through the HMO's own facility or through a hospital with which the HMO has contracted for benefits for its members. As previously indicated, members must utilize the physicians in the HMO's office. The members may choose, however, among the various physicians in the organization or transfer to another facility if the HMO maintains more than one facility at separate locations.

The IPA is a relatively new development in HMOs. Rather than being operated on a group practice prepayment basis, the HMO utilizes physicians engaged in individual practice. A member seeks care from these physicians at their offices; the HMO does not maintain a clinic. This type of HMO calls for a fixed, per capita payment by members, but the latter sometimes may be required to pay a small deductible each time care is received from a participating physician. The physicians are paid by the HMO on either a fee-for-service arrangement or on the basis of a fixed schedule of fees.

Distinctive Characteristics of the HMO Approach

HMOs represent an innovative concept in the delivery and financing of health care expenses. As such, they are a significant and viable alternative to the health risk bearers discussed previously. The unique characteristics of HMOs, compared to insurers and the Blues, have already been identified: the comprehensive services provided by the HMO, the emphasis on preventive care, and the fixed periodic charge to members for all services received. Perhaps the unique feature of the HMO, however, is the manner in which the HMO attempts to control health care costs.

The HMO receives a predetermined fixed payment for the services received by its members. If the cost of providing the health care exceeds the income of the HMO, then the latter incurs a financial loss. In effect, the HMO becomes a risk bearer. This situation results in an increased awareness by the HMO of cost-control techniques. Among these cost-control techniques are attempts to avoid the use of high-cost medical care services, especially unnecessary hospitalization, and to provide supportive peer review and assistance in avoiding unneeded treatment. Although increasing attention has been given by other types of health risk bearers to cost-containment techniques, HMOs probably have been the most successful in attempting to control constantly increasing health care expenses.

THE SELF-FUNDING APPROACH

An employer may choose to finance his or her employees' health care benefits through some form of self-funding arrangement. The employer formally establishes an employee benefit plan that includes specific health care benefits. All or part of the cost of these benefits is retained (paid) by the employer. No other health risk bearer is involved in that portion of the health care benefits that the employer has decided to self-fund.

Self-funding is of increased importance in providing health care benefits because of the perceived lower costs associated with the approach. One technique employers may adopt to facilitate a self-funded medical benefit plan is the creation of a 501(c)(9) trust. It is named after the section of the Internal Revenue Code that specifies the requirements for the creation of the trust. Once the trust is qualified under the code, contributions become deductible as a business expense and the income earned by the trust is not subject to federal income taxation. Benefits are paid by the trust according to the schedule outlined in the employee benefit plan.

Another approach to self-funding health care expenses is the use of a multiple-employer trust (MET). Small employers that do not wish to rely solely on the predictability of the medical expense loss experience of their employees might prefer the use of a MET. Under these circumstances, a group of generally small employers would agree to the creation of a trust fund for the purpose of administering their medical expense benefits. Contributions are made to the trust and benefits are paid from it. The services of a professional administrator probably are utilized to make such decisions as the level of each employer's contribution to the fund and the manner in which trust assets are invested. It also should be noted that while self-funding is viewed as a cost-saving technique, the MET may be the only option of small employers unable or unwilling to obtain health care benefits from traditional health risk bearers.

Distinctive Characteristics of the Self-Funding Approach

Self-funding does not involve the use of a traditional health risk bearer unless the employer decides to incorporate a form of stop-loss or catastrophe protection in the plan. In this situation, the employer is financially responsible only for a certain level or amount of claims; any medical expense benefits paid in excess of that amount would be absorbed by an insurer.

As indicated previously, self-funding generally is viewed by employers as a cost-saving technique. On the assumption the level of claims incurred under the employer's self-funded plan is the same as would have been incurred if a traditional health risk bearer were used, several areas exist where self-funding may lead to lower benefit costs or improvement, or both, in the employer's cash-flow position.

For example, a self-funded plan pays no state premium taxes. This may represent a substantial saving to the employer. In addition, through self-funding, the employer may be able to improve his or her firm's cash flow through the maintenance of contingency reserves and of reserves for incurred but unreported claims that have lower margins than those established by a traditional health risk bearer. The employer also can eliminate the charge made by the carrier to maintain a claims fluctuation margin and risk charge.

In addition, if the employer is able to execute better control over claims than a carrier—or more effectively tailor the benefit structure of the self-funded plan to fit the needs of the group—then additional cost savings may be achieved.

The potential for reduction in the cost of an employee benefit medical expense plan generally associated with a self-funded plan should not obscure, however, the existence of offsetting factors that may increase the costs of the plan.

The employer has to assume any administrative functions—such as actuarial, legal, and the processing of claims—previously performed by the traditional health risk bearer, as well as the resulting costs associated with those tasks. Despite the assumed improvement in relations with employees and the more effective claims control, the employer may find resentment being directed toward the firm if claims are denied. The "buffer" effect of the carrier in the claims process is lost. Similarly, the employer's employee-benefit plan administrative staff may lack the expertise needed to process and monitor effectively the payment of claims. The staff also may be ineffective in exercising cost-containment techniques with purveyors of medical care services.

In a related area, a self-funded plan lacks the financial stability of a plan provided by a carrier that guarantees payment of claims. To avoid unexpected claims fluctuations that could result in a catastrophic loss to the plan, the employer needs to incur the expense of stop-loss insurance.

Additional costs will be charged to the self-funded plan if a 501(c)(9) trust is established. Moreover, the trust is essential to the self-funded alternative if tax advantages are to be realized.

All such factors must be thoroughly reviewed before the employer decides to implement a self-funded plan as an alternative to providing benefits through a traditional health risk bearer. A more detailed discussion of self-funding appears in Chapter 43.

CHAPTER 11

Hospital Plans

CHARLES P. HALL, JR.

INTRODUCTION

Group hospitalization insurance was the first of the now diverse health-related employee benefits to appear in the United States. Though there were a few isolated earlier examples, it is customary to identify the modern origin of health insurance with the Baylor University Hospital prepayment plan, which emerged in the late 1920s and ultimately gave birth to Blue Cross.

In general, commercial insurance companies were not active in medical care expense insurance until about a decade later. Beginning in the 1940s, growth accelerated, spurred by such factors as the wage and price stabilization programs of World War II and the identification of these benefits as appropriate matters for collective bargaining just after the war.

Because of their pioneering role, the early Blue Cross plans had a profound and lasting impact on the nature of hospitalization benefits. Aside from insisting on distinguishing their "prepayment" method from traditional commercial insurance, they were philosophically wedded to the concepts of "service benefits," first-dollar coverage and community rates, as mentioned in the preceding chapter on Health Risk Bearers.

SERVICE BENEFITS

Service benefits were possible because of the special relationship that Blue Cross plans had (and have) with hospitals. Blue Cross operated through contracts with both subscribers and hospitals. Typically, the hospital fixed the price for its services in its contract with Blue Cross; this enabled Blue Cross to compute an appropriate subscription fee (premium) for its members, while defining benefits in terms of days of coverage. Commercial insurers, lacking direct contracts with hospitals, typically promised their insureds, instead, a certain fixed maximum number of dollars per day up to a specified number of days. The clear result of this disparity was that Blue Cross subscribers always knew exactly how many days of hospitalization were available to them without cost, while commercial insureds knew only how many days they would be eligible to collect up to some stated number of dollars. They had no assurance the number of dollars available would be adequate to fully pay the hospital. As a result, commercially insured patients always carried a residual financial risk avoided by Blue Cross subscribers. In recent years, however, many commercial insurers also offer a service benefit in the form of full coverage for the cost of semiprivate room accommodations. This still entails some pricing problems, but these are not too serious in experience-rated programs.

As the proportion of patients covered by cost-based reimbursement arrangements has grown, so, too, have the financial problems of hospitals. To remain solvent, hospitals have had to make up the short-fall from charge-based (e.g., primarily commercially insured) patients. As the number of cost-based patients increases, of course, the proportion of charge-based patients from which hospitals are able to recover dwindles, and the differential necessarily grows. This has had a devastating impact on the ability of commercial health insurers to compete in the marketplace, with differentials exceeding $100 per day for identical services in some areas. The aggregate Medicare/Medicaid "shortfall" (underpayment to hospitals) in fiscal year 1982 was estimated as high as $5.8 billion, a figure which is projected to grow. Clearly, while this may represent cost savings for the government programs, it is only cost shifting for society and represents an enormous hidden tax on parts of the private sector. (See, also, the section on Changing Market Forces, below.)

The uninitiated observer must wonder why commercial insurers have not emulated the cost payors, but there is really no mystery. Lacking either the geographical monopolies enjoyed by Blue Cross plans or the "clout" inherent in government programs, few commercial insurers ever obtained the economic leverage necessary to negotiate similar discounts (though there were a few minor exceptions, e.g. in "company town" situations), and they are barred from collective action by antitrust restrictions.

The latest innovation is to identify "preferred provider organizations" (PPOs), where group members are to seek their care if they want assurance of full coverage; penalties are possible when treatment is obtained in other facilities. The PPO, typically, will simply be a known low cost provider or it might promise benefits at some negotiated price for a contract period. The concept is an outgrowth of the procompetition school of thought, the premise being that hospitals and/or medical groups will compete for PPO status, thus providing incentives for real cost-containment. Despite some initial fears of antitrust implications, interest in PPOs is growing, especially since special legislation in California explicitly authorized the concept in 1982. Continuing problems frequently include inadequate market share to obtain favorable rates and insufficient data to select the best PPO.

FIRST-DOLLAR BENEFITS

Initially, Blue Cross plans were at least as interested in assuring hospital solvency as they were in protecting patients from financial strain. Furthermore, the plans tried to distinguish their operation from traditional insurance by emphasizing they were prepayment plans, providing service benefits from the first moment of hospitalization. Their direct contractual relationship with hospitals helped make this feasible.

Initially, commercial insurers followed rather blindly the same pattern of first-dollar benefits. Later, it was the commercial insurers who introduced some of the traditional "trappings of the trade," such as deductibles and coinsurance. Nevertheless, the pattern of first-dollar coverage had been established and, perhaps because of the incorporation of these benefits in many of the early union-negotiated contracts, the pattern has persisted on a wide front until today. Frequent allegations by some that, though originally well intentioned, such benefits are uneconomical and also may promote abuse or overuse of benefits are certainly not shared by all. The substantial premium savings achieved by placing some initial burden of cost on the subscriber/insured have led to wider use of cost-sharing provisions in recent years, even by Blue Cross plans.

COMMUNITY RATING

Community rating, a uniform rate for all subscribers/insureds in a given area, though still the philosophical favorite of many, especially in Blue Cross ranks, has long since become insignificant in the group insurance market. The competitive pressures from corporate insurance buyers and unions to obtain rates commensurate with their real or perceived "preferred risk" status were simply too great to be resisted in most cases. Most Blue Cross plans still use community rates for their individual subscribers, and some also may use them for small groups, but all have some form of experience rating available to large group customers.

OTHER HEALTH INSURANCE

After the initial breakthrough in hospital insurance, a series of "named peril" health insurance coverages followed—first surgical benefits, and then nonsurgical medical benefits, both in and out of hospital settings. Blue Shield emerged in these areas as the prepayment counterpart to Blue Cross. In the late 1940s a few companies also introduced "dread disease" policies, with quite high limits of protection for a very narrow range of conditions—often only one disease (e.g., polio).

By the early 1950s, commercial health insurers introduced the major medical concept, characterized by a comprehensive range of coverage with high dollar limits after some initial deductible and, usually, a coinsurance or percentage participation clause. Originally designed primarily as supplements to one or more of the basic coverages described previously, these policies soon emerged in yet another form, so-called comprehensive major medical plans, which actually eliminated the need for any separate basic policies.

With the exception of a few special areas, such as dental insurance, most of the changes in medical expense reimbursement coverages since the late 1950s have merely been refinements reflecting pressure for broader coverage brought on as a result of some combination of the rapid escalation of health care costs, changes in medical technology, or consumer demand. Other obvious exceptions have resulted from federal or state policy actions, such as the emergence of so-called Medigap policies after the enactment of Medicare and state-mandated benefits that have been added to policies, as required, in a number of jurisdictions.

One other type of hospital insurance has acquired fairly wide acceptance. It is the so-called hospital indemnity policy. Patterned somewhat after disability income policies, these are not really indemnity policies at all. They could more appropriately be called "status" policies. They pay stated dollar amounts on either a daily, weekly, or monthly basis for people confined in a hospital (in some cases, skilled nursing facilities also are covered). They pay the predetermined amount without regard to actual charges incurred or income lost and, perhaps more important to many buyers, without regard to any other insurance holdings. Some of the popularity of these policies undoubtedly can be attributed to consumers' fears about the rapid escalation of health care costs; they see these policies as providing an added buffer, in case their medical expense reimbursement coverages should fall short.

EXTENT OF HOSPITAL INSURANCE

In part because it was the earliest form of health insurance and in part because the hospital continues to be the most costly setting in which to be treated, hospital insurance remains the most widely held form of health insurance protection in the country. The *Source Book of Health Insurance Data (1981–82)*, published by the Health Insurance Institute (HII), reports that over 186 million persons were covered by this form of insurance at the end of 1980. Unfortunately, this figure lumps hospital expense insurance and hospital indemnity coverage together for the general population, although they are segregated for policyholders over 65.

According to the *Source Book*, roughly 14.5 million persons over age 65 purchased private hospital insurance in addition to Medicare in 1980. Commercial health insurers served 6.5 million of these, with 3.3 million of these—over half—carrying hospital indemnity protection and 3.2 million holding so-called Medigap policies designed to supplement Medicare Part A. The Blue Cross and Blue Shield associations claimed approximately 8.8

million over age 65 persons (6.4 million were nongroup subscribers) with
Medicare supplement coverage as of mid-1981 and it was estimated that
another 2.0 million elderly also were covered under "other" Medicare
supplement plans, e.g. through HMOs.[1] Since the Blues and other plans do
not offer hospital indemnity policies, their numbers reflect only hospital
expense benefits. Obviously, the estimate of 14.5 million for the total
number of covered persons allows for a good deal of duplication of coverage; no precise figures are available on this, but it is known many of the
elderly purchase several Medigap policies out of fear and ignorance, while
others cannot afford coverage, do not want extra protection, or mistakenly
believe that Medicare coverage is complete.

For policyholders under 65, it seems reasonable to believe a much larger
proportion of those covered by commercial insurers hold hospital expense
protection or carry hospital indemnity coverage in addition to it. In any
case, hospital indemnity coverage is insignificant as an employee benefit,
being sold most often to individuals or through so-called association groups,
such as alumni or professional associations. When employee benefits are
involved, specific daily, weekly, or monthly allowances of this type typically
are associated with disability income insurance or found in sick leave
programs, where the amounts of benefit are related to earnings.

Health Insurance Institute data show group hospital expense policies—
typically part of an employee benefit plan—cover roughly three times as
many persons as do individual and family policies. A substantial number of
persons are covered by both types, though exact figures are unavailable. It
is worth noting that benefits under group policies tend to be more generous
than those under individual policies (e.g., fewer or no restrictions on
preexisting conditions).

Although hospital expense insurance is the most widely held form of
health insurance, it is trailed closely by surgical and medical benefits.
Various types of supplementary or comprehensive major medical insurance
also are widespread now, with over 154 million persons covered.

CHANGING MARKET FORCES

In its latest published data on *New Group Health Insurance (1981)*, the
HII reported that only 23.1 percent of the employers covered by new
group policies issued in early 1981 (groups of 25 to 499 employees)
obtained hospital expense protection.[2] The focus was on groups in this
category of size to avoid "distortions that could result if any one survey

---

[1] Telephone conversation with Planning, Research, and Evaluation Department on May 24,
1982.

[2] Health Insurance Institute of America, *New Group Health Insurance (1981)*, (New York,
1981), p. 1.

period included either too many small cases or one or two extremely large cases." During the same period, 76.1 percent of the newly covered employees obtained either supplementary or comprehensive major medical coverage. Indeed, the pressure for comprehensive coverage under group health insurance programs is so strong it is somewhat unusual for a hospital expense policy to be sold except in combination with surgical and, frequently, medical expense benefits. (Surgical and medical benefit plans are discussed in detail in Chapter 12, while supplementary and comprehensive major medical plans are covered in Chapter 13.)

In certain parts of the country, notably the Northeast, sale of basic group hospital expense benefits has been virtually abandoned to Blue Cross by commercial insurers, who now compete largely in the arena of so-called wrap-around (supplementary) major medical on top of basic Blue Cross programs. This rather strange phenomenon is explained in terms of the often enormous disparity that exists between costs and charges in the delivery of hospital services.

In regions where Blue Cross market penetration is substantial, where Blue Cross has negotiated cost-reimbursement or other discount contracts with its member hospitals, and where a large elderly population is covered under another cost-based program, Medicare, commercially insured patients and self-paying patients must bear the brunt of attempts by hospitals to remain fiscally viable. Charges billed to these patients may be as much as 15 to 20 or more percent higher than the charges to Blue Cross and Medicare patients receiving identical services.

In New York City, for example, the disparity can be over $100 per day for basic hospital room and board. When added to another competitive advantage, the exemption from premium tax, which is afforded to Blue Cross in many states, it is not surprising commercial insurers sometimes find it difficult to compete. The impact of the premium-tax exemption becomes even greater as costs rise, since it is a flat percentage tax.

Insurers, especially in areas where their market share is modest, find their premiums to group subscribers must rise even more sharply than the already disproportionate increase in the medical price index. As hospitals try to shift their losses arising from narrowly defined cost definitions issued by the government under Medicare and negotiated by Blue Cross from its dominant market position, "the paying customers" with commercial insurance get caught in the middle. Some state legislatures have indicated their concern with this situation. While several have considered legislation that would alleviate the problem, either by prohibiting or limiting a hospital's right to charge third parties differently for the same services, only Wyoming has enacted such a bill to date. Barring some form of legislative relief under the circumstances described above, commercial health insurers may continue to suffer a decline in their market share of basic group hospital expense benefits.

SCOPE OF HOSPITAL EXPENSE BENEFITS

Ever since first introduced, hospital expense benefits encompassed two major categories of benefits: basic room and board, plus a range of additional hospital expense benefits, variously described as "miscellaneous," "additionals," or "hospital extras." The scope of these extras has broadened over the years. A general demand for more comprehensive benefits as well as cost-containment features in the face of escalating medical care costs and changing medical technology have spurred the changes. Some of the extras now afforded coverage under basic hospital expense plans were formerly available only under major medical policies, while some (e.g., ambulance service to and from the hospital) were not covered under any insurance programs.

Room and Board

Room and board benefits typically are defined in one of two ways. Early commercial insurance policies provided reimbursement for actual room and board charges up to a specified maximum amount per day, with a second limit on the number of days for which benefits would be paid for each hospital confinement. This form of benefit design still exists, though it is by no means as prevalent as the alternative, which is a service-type benefit patterned after the Blue Cross model.

For example, a typical insuring clause in a Blue Cross contract would describe benefits in a Blue Cross plan member hospital as:

> Bed and board in semiprivate accommodations; or an allowance toward the cost of a private room equal to the hospital's most prevalent daily charge for semi-private accommodations. Full cost of a private room will be allowed when your condition requires isolation for your own health or that of other patients if ordered and certified by attending physician prior to the time you are placed in a private room. (Taken from Comprehensive Hospital Plan, Blue Cross of Greater Philadelphia, 1981.)

The contract, of course, also would specify the number of days for which the benefit would be available. In both Blue Cross and commercial health insurance contracts, the bed and board coverage includes general nursing service and all other regular daily services and supplies furnished by the hospital.

If, under the Blue Cross plan described above, a subscriber were confined in a nonmember hospital of any Blue Cross plan, the bed and board benefit would be reduced sharply to a credit "up to $100 for the first day of your hospital stay and up to $50 per day for the remaining days of your benefit period." Furthermore, no coverage would exist for admissions that were primarily for diagnostic study unless performed or done in a member hospital.

In the Health Insurance Institute study of new group health insurance in 1981, cited earlier, 88 percent of the employees covered by new hospital insurance plans (among groups from 25 to 499 in size) had the benefit defined in terms of "payments equal to a hospital's average semiprivate room and board charge." In a similar study in 1976, 48 percent of the newly covered employees obtained this service benefit type of protection. Among all new groups in 1981, regardless of size, 81 percent had coverage for full semiprivate accommodations.

Even in those plans (25–499 in size) which still offer reimbursement for actual charges, a dramatic increase has occurred in the level of benefits in the last five years. In 1976, 88 percent of the employees without service benefits had daily room and board benefits of $50 per day or more. By 1981, nearly 98 percent had such coverage. Normally, these benefits are offered in any dollar amount in $5 multiples. By 1981, most were for $100 per day or more.

Though they have no need to distinguish between member and non-member hospitals as does Blue Cross, commercial insurers almost always include a precise definition of a hospital in the general provisions of their contracts. Though some variation exists, it is customary for the definition to cover facilities accredited as a hospital under the Hospital Accreditation Program of the Joint Commission on the Accreditation of Hospitals, as well as under other appropriately licensed institutions. Normally, they must be under the supervision of a staff of physicians, have 24-hour-a-day nursing service, and be engaged primarily in providing general inpatient medical care. Standard exclusions include facilities used principally as a convalescent, rest, or nursing facility, a facility for the aged, those providing primarily domiciliary or custodial care, and those operated primarily as a school.

Duration of benefits also can vary widely. In the Blue Cross plan referred to above, a sliding scale of 50 to 120 days per benefit period is provided, depending on the age of the plan. For example, 50 days first year, 60 days second year, 80 days third year, 100 days fourth year, 120 days fifth year and each year of continuous membership thereafter. The specifics, of course, may vary between different Blue Cross organizations as well as among different plans offered by the same local Blue Cross.

Similar variations in duration exist among commercial insurers. One major underwriter, for example, offers a standard plan with a fixed 70-day duration of coverage. In addition, it offers an alternate plan under which the insured can select options of 31, 70, 120, 180, or 365 days of protection. The HII study also notes that, in 1981, 73 percent of the employees were covered for 120 or more days, up from only 40 percent in 1976. Forty-two percent had 190 or more days of protection in 1981.

It is still commonplace, though not universal, to find special restrictions on room and board benefits for psychiatric patients. Most Blue Cross plans and many commercial insurers follow this practice. The limitation may be a shorter allowance of days per confinement or a fixed lifetime limit, such as 365 days, or both.

Naturally, it is possible to include some form of deductible with a basic hospital insurance plan. The Blue Cross plan cited, for example, is available with either a $5 or $10 deductible, which would last for the first 10 days of hospital confinement. After 10 days, the contract provides full-service benefits until the coverage is exhausted. Similar options are offered by virtually all insurers. All policies contain some statement of the conditions under which their benefits are payable. Usually, these statements are simple, such as when confinement is: (1) caused by sickness or injury and ordered by a physician, (2) commences while the person is a covered individual, and (3) is one for which room and board charges are actually made by the hospital to the employee. Some policies also define a minimum period of confinement (e.g., 18 hours) before an insured may be covered for inpatient services, though they often waive the minimum for accidents and where surgery is involved. This time standard, once common, is seldom encountered today. The more important question is, was the patient billed as an inpatient (e.g., room and board charge, and the like) or as an outpatient?

ADDITIONAL HOSPITAL EXPENSE BENEFITS

Though variously referred to as "hospital extras," "miscellaneous," or "additional hospital expense benefits," all basic hospital expense policies provide for a wide range of benefits beyond room and board and general nursing services. As might be expected, such benefits typically are enumerated and provided on a full-service basis by Blue Cross plans. Among commercial insurers, the dominant approach from a historical viewpoint was to enumerate the type of benefits covered and define the amount of benefit in terms of a flat-dollar amount. The latter frequently was stated in terms of a multiple of the daily room and board allowance. As has been true for room and board, however, a distinct trend exists toward the provision of unlimited or full-service benefits. Of all the new groups surveyed by HII in early 1981, for example, 88 percent provided unlimited coverage for these benefits, and another 9 percent allowed expenses of $500 or more. One major group underwriter, for example, offers a range of limits for "additionals" from $500 to $3,000 in multiples of $100 in its standard plan. In its popular alternate plan, coverage is unlimited.

The precise scope of the additional hospital expense benefits covered, predictably, can vary substantially among insurers and even among different groups covered by the same insurer. Once again, the trend has been to expand the definition in recent years. An example of a fairly simple, but inclusive, definition is: Additional benefits are payable for the following services and supplies ordered by a physician in connection with a person's hospital confinement:

1. Services and supplies furnished by the hospital for medical care therein, other than professional services.
2. An anesthetic and its administration, when given in the hospital and charged for by a physician.
3. Ambulance service for local travel in transporting the person to and from the hospital.

The "services and supplies" referred to in 1 above would routinely include, among other things, special dietary service; use of operating, delivery, recovery, and other special treatment rooms and related equipment and supplies; splints, casts, and surgical dressings; drugs and medications in general use, including intravenous injections and solutions; oxygen and oxygen therapy; laboratory examinations; X-ray examinations; administration of a variety of tests, such as electrocardiograms, electroencephalograms, and basal metabolism tests; and the administration of blood and blood plasma, including the processing of blood, though usually not the cost of the blood itself.

The list, of course, may be either more or less inclusive (ambulance service, for example, often is excluded), and a variety of internal limits or maximum allowable charges can be imposed on specific services. Conditions for these additional benefits typically are the same as for room and board, except when ambulance service is covered, it may be limited to use within 48 hours after an accidental injury and only for emergency treatment. X-ray and laboratory examinations may be covered for outpatients only if made within 10 days (or some other designated period) prior to a subsequent hospital confinement for which room and board charges are made for the sickness or injury requiring the subsequent confinement.

Many hospitals now have highly specialized intensive care units that utilize sophisticated and expensive equipment and personnel. Care in those units ordinarily is covered under the broad scope of additional benefits; but some insurers break it out as a separate item, identifying a specific limit stated in dollars or as a multiple of the daily room and board allowance. In many instances, a separate limit exists on the maximum number of days of intensive care provided.

Increasingly, as the high costs of inpatient hospital care become ever more oppressive, insureds and insurers have been seeking ways to broaden available outpatient and other alternative coverage under hospital expense policies. Emergency room treatment, of course, has long been standard. Now, however, it is not uncommon to provide benefits for ambulatory provision of such services as radiation therapy, certain forms of chemotherapy, physical and inhalation therapy following an inpatient stay, and a variety of diagnostic services.

An increasing number of group hospital expense contracts provide regular benefits for so-called ambulatory surgical procedures, whether provided through a special short procedure unit in a regular hospital or through an approved, free-standing surgi-center.

Following a pattern adopted by Medicare, most hospitalization policies automatically cover confinement in an extended care facility (skilled nursing facility) where such confinement is deemed necessary for continued treatment of an illness or injury that required hospitalization. Usually, at least 3 days in a regular hospital is a prerequisite, and admission to the skilled nursing facility (SNF) must be within 14 days following the discharge from the hospital. As with the regular hospital coverage, benefits in an SNF usually are specified either in days and dollars (e.g., 60 days at up to $20 per day) or in terms of days and level of service (e.g., 60 days in semiprivate accommodations). As with hospitals, "other services" usually provided and billed for by the facility also are covered. No attempt is made here to document all the various ways of defining SNF benefits, but some examples may be helpful. Frequently, they are provided on a two-for-one exchange for inpatient hospital coverage. In some cases, coinsurance provisions are adopted (e.g., giving 100 percent coverage for the first 60 days and 90 percent coverage for days 60 to 180). Some forms include a lifetime maximum, such as 365 days.

Some hospital insurance policies also provide for home health services, especially when prescribed by a physician as a followup to a period of hospital confinement. Such benefits are defined carefully and limited in terms of their nature, cost and duration.

As the foregoing illustrates, a wide range of benefits can be and has been made part of basic hospitalization insurance programs. Some of the benefits are of relatively recent origin as new modalities of treatment have emerged. Others have previously been available, if at all, either as separate, individual coverages or only as part of comprehensive major medical benefits. The degree to which benefits are included in a basic hospital plan is a function of insurer policy and buyer demand. Many of the extensions of coverage, clearly, have been added because they are seen as potentially lower-cost alternatives to more traditional inpatient hospital treatment.

Some benefits, or modifications of benefits, have been responses to either federally mandated coverages or legislative requirements at the state level. One major group underwriter, "to minimize the need for state-specific benefits and to accommodate current legislative trends," automatically includes the following:

1. Same benefits for complications of pregnancy as for any injury or sickness.
2. If pregnancy benefits are available for normal pregnancy, they will apply to all dependents (married or not).

3. Child care benefits from birth for all except well-baby care in the first 14 days.
4. An inpatient rehabilitation institute benefit, plus a broad definition of expanded outpatient psychiatric services, to meet mandated minimum benefits for alcohol and drug abuse and mental and nervous disorders.
5. Ambulatory care benefits as alternatives to hospitalization.
6. Regarding providers, broadly defined as any practitioner of the healing arts providing services within the scope of his or her license and for which benefits are required by law when provided by such a practitioner.
7. Full extended benefits for employees and dependents.

The same company notes that when dual choice is afforded employees under provisions of the federal HMO law, mandatory annual open enrollment periods also must be granted to insureds under Blue Cross or commercial insurance plans. Not all companies sell this blanket approach, using instead individual clauses or riders as necessary.

EXCLUSIONS

Fairly standard exclusions exist under most hospital expense policies. Among them are: occupational illness or injury eligible for benefits under workers' compensation laws; professional services of a physician, surgeon, private duty nurse, or technician not employed by the hospital; convalescent or rest cures, custodial or domiciliary care; services not ordered by a physician or not reasonable and necessary for diagnosis or treatment; procurement or use of special appliances or equipment; services a patient is entitled to receive under the laws or regulations of any government or its agencies; war or service connected injuries or diseases. These examples are not exhaustive, and the specific list of exclusions, of course, must be checked in the case of each individual policy.

GENERAL PROVISIONS

All group insurance contracts contain a range of general provisions, many of which are almost universal, whether by law or custom. Examples include the 31-day grace period for payment of premiums, a clause on incontestability, an entire contract clause, which also specifies how valid changes can be accomplished, and a provision to adjust benefits automatically whenever and wherever they conflict with statutes. Another whole set of uniform provisions has to do with claims submission and payment procedures. These provisions often apply equally to a whole set of employee benefits, from life insurance to health insurance.

Provisions specific to hospital insurance that deserve mention are those dealing with the definition of a benefit period of confinement and coordination of benefits. The latter is a cost-containment mechanism to prevent duplication of benefits, and is discussed in more detail in Chapters 19 and 20. A single benefit period under hospitalization insurance typically is considered to be any one or more periods of confinement of the insured, unless separated by a return to full-time employment for at least one week, or unless subsequent confinement is due entirely to causes unrelated to the previous confinement. For dependents, unless the causes are unrelated, a subsequent confinement in less than three months generally is considered a continuation of the prior hospital stay. Some insurers apply the harsher three-month rule to primary employee/insureds as well.

An important provision to check is the definition of "dependent." The term normally encompasses the spouse and all unmarried children, including those who may have been legally adopted, until age 19. An extension of coverage usually is granted until age 24 or 25 for children who are students. Naturally, the specific ages may vary by company policy.

SUMMARY

Group hospital expense insurance, as the earliest of the health-oriented employee benefits, is the most widely held in the United States today. Over the years, it has undergone many changes in response to competitive pressures, changes in technology, regulatory constraints, and changing consumer demands. Many of the early differences between Blue Cross plans and commercial insurance plans have been blurred by these evolutionary changes. More recently, the intense search for means to control costs has reshaped the coverage to reduce the focus on inpatient services, in the belief that equally effective and less-costly care may be available in less traditional settings. This evolutionary process is likely to continue in the foreseeable future, with the added likelihood that consumers will be increasingly interested in nonhospital benefits as they come to recognize their medical and economic viability.

CHAPTER 12

Surgical and Medical Expense Benefits

ZELDA LIPTON

INTRODUCTION

Since 1955, the rise in the medical care component of the consumer price index has almost consistently outpaced the rise in prices for all consumer goods and services combined. It has been driven primarily by hospital costs—the largest single item in the delivery of medical care. Although hospital costs therefore offer the greatest opportunity for cost control, design of the remaining benefits in a health insurance plan can influence significantly the utilization of the entire package. Physicians' fees alone represented $35.3 billion dollars or 18.3 percent of the total health care dollar spent in 1978. Even more significant, however, physicians themselves are key to the most effective use of the health care system and therefore very directly influence the cost of medical care.

Plans to cover the cost of physicians' services were first introduced in 1920 by county medical societies. Blue Shield plans, which didn't begin until 1939 with the California Medical Association Plan, however, were at the forefront of plan development. They attempted to follow the same full-service philosophy as Blue Cross did for hospital expenses. Physicians contracted with Blue Shield, which paid an agreed-upon level as full payment for services provided to subscribers. However, physicians had long been accustomed to charging patients based on their incomes. As a result, Blue Shield modified its approach to allow a physician to charge patients, with incomes above a stated level, the difference between the Blue Shield reimbursement and the physician's usual fee.

At the same time, private insurance companies were developing indemnity contracts, which reimburse the insured person for services provided by a physician up to the agreed amount in the contract. Physicians would look to the patient, rather than the insurer, for payment. Otherwise patterned after Blue Shield plans, the insurance plans pay first-dollar coverage for a limited number of medical services. Together with hospital benefits, these came to be known as basic benefits. Many insurers have since developed procedures for reimbursing the provider directly, should the buyer prefer that approach.

SURGICAL EXPENSE BENEFITS

The earliest of these basic benefits for physicians' charges covered surgical expenses, because those represented comparatively large expenditures and were believed to be more easily defined and controlled. Surgical expense benefits provide coverage for the cost of surgical procedures required as a result of accident or sickness wherever the surgery is performed.

Surgeons' Fees

Plans are designed to cover surgeons' fees on either a scheduled or reasonable and customary basis.

Dollar-Fee Schedules. Typical early surgical schedules still in use today list about 100 procedures in such major categories as abdomen, heart and blood vessels, chest, mouth, and obstetrics.

For each procedure, a specific maximum-dollar payment is allowed. Each maximum depends on the value of that procedure, compared to others, and the overall maximum for multiple procedures by which the schedule is usually identified. The level of overall maximums available ranges from as low as $200 to $1,000 and more. Payment to the insured is the charge made by the surgeon, up to the maximum payment allowed in the schedule for the procedure performed, subject to the multiple procedure provision explained later. For an unlisted procedure, reimbursement is based on its relative difficulty, compared to those listed.

If an employer desires to avoid encouraging escalation of charges, schedules may be set to reimburse at a level below the usual charges in an area. Such scheduled plans can contribute toward control of the cost of a plan, since, regardless of inflation, reimbursement for any procedure remains constant. Furthermore, since the patient is directly responsible for the difference between the plan payment and the charge, it is possible fees will not escalate as rapidly. However, the plan very quickly can become outdated in the current environment and result in large out-of-pocket expenses for the insured.

The following are sample allowances in a typical schedule with a $900 overall maximum:

Procedures	Maximum Payment
Valvotomy	$900
Extraction of lens for cataract	600
Hysterectomy	540
Cesarean section	450
Appendectomy	330
Herniotomy, single	330
Tonsillectomy	120

Relative Value Schedules. These schedules were developed in the 1950s, with California Medical Services leading the way. The first California Relative Value Schedule was designed in 1956 and has been revised twice, in 1969 and 1974. It served as a model for many insurance plans. Relative value schedules attach a unit value to a large number of surgical procedures. The relationship of the unit values to each other typically is a function of the relative difficulty of the procedures. The maximum amount payable for a procedure is its unit value multiplied by a dollar amount purchased by the employer; it commonly is referred to as a conversion factor. Payment is subject to the overall schedule maximum and typical multiple procedures provision explained later. A wide range of conversion factors is available; but, as for dollar-fee schedules, the conversion factor should be selected to produce no more than the usual charges in an area.

A relative value schedule permits greater flexibility, particularly for employers with more than one location. Appropriate conversion factors can be applied to the schedule to produce the level of reimbursement reflecting regional differences in cost. Schedules can be kept current by adjusting the conversion factor as costs change.

The following is a sample from a typical relative value schedule. The last column has been added to illustrate the maximum amount payable, subject to the overall maximum and multiple procedure provisions. It assumes a $15 conversion factor had been purchased.

Procedure	Unit Value	Maximum Payment with $15 Conversion Factor
Valvotomy	140	$2,100
Extraction of lens	80	1,200
Hysterectomy	60	900
Cesarean section	50	750
Appendectomy	40	600
Herniotomy	35	525
Tonsillectomy	20	300

Since the 1974 revision of the California Relative Value Schedule, the Federal Trade Commission has ruled it to be a form of fee setting. As a result, the California Medical Association no longer updates or uses it. Insurance plans continue to include relative value schedules based on each insurer's own nationwide charge data.

Reasonable and Customary Fees. Alternatively, a surgical plan may be designed to reimburse for a surgeon's fee up to the reasonable and customary charge for the procedure performed, without any identified schedule. "Reasonable and customary" is based on both the charge usually made by the physician for the procedure and the range of charges made by physicians for that same procedure in the locality where performed. Typically, it is set to cover the full charge of 85 or 90 percent of all physicians in a geographical area. Differences arise because of different charge data bases and area designations.

Reasonable and customary surgical plans have the advantage of automatically adjusting to inflation without plan change. For the same reason, they build inflation into the cost of a medical care plan and are accused of encouraging continually increasing charges by surgeons.

Multiple Procedures. Scheduled surgical benefit plans usually limit reimbursement for multiple procedures. The following is one such provision:

> If two or more procedures are performed at the same time in the same operative field, the benefit payable is the largest amount specified for any one of the procedures, and in some plans 50 percent of the others as well.

> If two or more procedures are performed at the same time in different operative fields, payment will be made for each, up to the overall schedule maximum.

> If two or more procedures are performed as a result of the same or related causes, but not during the course of a single operation, payment will be made for each procedure, but the total amount payable for all such procedures will not exceed the overall schedule maximum, unless they are separated by (1) a return to active, full-time employment in the case of an employee, or (2) typically three or six months in the case of a dependent.

Although reasonable and customary plans often do not include similar language, they may apply similar rationale in evaluating the reasonable charge for multiple procedures.

Associated Benefits

Regardless of the approach to reimbursement of the surgeon, surgical expense benefits plans may cover other physicians' charges associated with surgery.

Assistant Surgeon. Charges for an assistant surgeon sometimes are reimbursed on a scheduled basis. In that case, a dollar amount is identified for each procedure. However, it usually is determined as a percent of the maximum payment provided for the surgeon's fee for the same procedure. Therefore, whether the allowance is expressed as a specific dollar amount or as, in some plans, simply as a percent (e.g., 20 percent) of the surgical allowance, the result is the same. Most relative value plans exclude any assistant surgeon benefit for a surgical procedure with less than 35 units, since such surgery should not require an assistant.

Anesthesiologists. The charge for an anesthetic generally is included in the hospital or outpatient facility charges in connection with a surgical procedure. It is considered part of necessary services and supplies.

However, charges for the administration of anesthetics may be reimbursable in different ways. Some plans consider them part of the hospital benefit, regardless of whether they are billed by a hospital or by a provider who works independently. A more common approach offers coverage for administration of an anesthetic by a physician who is not a salaried employee of a hospital under the surgical benefit. In that case, charges may be reimbursed as a percent, such as 20 percent, of the surgical allowance, as a specified unit value that may include a time factor as well or on a reasonable and customary basis.

Pregnancy

Historically, pregnancy expense benefits have been provided, excluded, or limited at the option of the policyholder, because at least normal pregnancies were considered budgetable but represented a relatively high-cost portion of the total health care package. Through the years, several states have mandated coverage for at least complications of pregnancy in all insurance policies.

Complications have been variously defined. A typical definition includes expenses incurred as a result of an extra-uterine pregnancy, a pregnancy which terminates by cesarean section or miscarriage, or expenses incurred as a result of sickness caused or contributed to by pregnancy. Some plans use what appears to be broader language, although the intent is the same. They may define complications of pregnancy as pregnancy complicated by concurrent disease or as abnormal conditions significantly affecting usual medical management.

Federal legislation, effective October 31, 1978, changed much of that. It required that, by May 1, 1979, employers with 15 or more employees engaged in interstate commerce (i.e., employers who are, or become, subject to Title VII of the Civil Rights Act of 1964) must provide the same benefits for pregnancy as for any other sickness. The law does not require an employer to provide benefits for abortions "except where the life of the mother would be endangered if the fetus were carried to term or except where medical complications have arisen from an abortion." The burden of compliance rests with the employer and need not be insured even if other benefits are. However, most employers now include equal coverage for pregnancy in their health care insurance plans.

This approach changed the historical treatment of most insured pregnancy benefits. It eliminated the extension of pregnancy coverage for a pregnancy that began while insured and was therefore covered, even if the individual was no longer insured under the plan when the pregnancy terminated. Today, to match the treatment of any other sickness, an insured must be totally disabled as a result of the pregnancy when coverage terminates or the pregnancy is not covered under the extension provisions.

The equal treatment for pregnancy requirement also affects the benefit amount provided to the obstetrician in the surgical schedule of a health insurance plan; it must follow the relativity of the schedule for other procedures. Thus, if surgery is covered on a reasonable and customary basis, pregnancy also must be covered on a similar basis.

Although the law itself left the status of pregnancy benefits for dependents unclear, there has been a court decision interpreting dependent pregnancy not to be included in the requirements. Still, most consider it impractical in today's environment to provide different pregnancy benefits for employees and dependents. Any potential cost saving is likely to be offset by dissatisfaction among male employees with dependents, and the final interpretation has yet to be made.

Employers with fewer than 15 employees, or those with 15 or more employees who are not subject to Title VII of the Civil Rights Act of 1964, may continue to exclude or limit pregnancy benefits subject to state law. However, since individual state legislation is increasingly following the federal approach, this also may be short-lived.

Special Features

Second Surgical Opinion Programs. Past studies have questioned the necessity for the growing number of surgical procedures being performed throughout the country. As a result, whenever nonemergency surgery is recommended, an individual may wish to obtain a second and even a third opinion to verify the need for the procedure. Many in-force major medical plans consider second surgical opinions as a covered medical expense, and reimburse such charges on a reasonable and customary basis subject to any deductible and coinsurance provisions.

However, to encourage the seeking of a second opinion, insurance plans increasingly are covering the cost of these consultations without any additional cost to the patient. One way is through a predetermined fee payable to consulting surgeons who have agreed to accept the fee as payment in full. Another approach pays 100 percent of reasonable and customary charges of a consulting surgeon, regardless of the rest of the plan design. Sometimes an overall dollar limit is included. In any case, charges for any additional necessary X-rays, laboratory tests, and other diagnostic studies also are covered.

Most plans leave the decision to seek a second opinion up to the insured. Some, however, require a second opinion for elective surgery, or payment for the surgery either will be reduced or eliminated. Although results to date are inconclusive, indications are that savings are greater with a mandatory program.

Surgi-Centers. Surgical plans always have covered surgery wherever it was performed, and continue to do so. Recently, however, in the interest of further discouraging hospital confinement and its associated high cost, insurance plans have covered the charges for use of a relatively new type of facility. It is variously referred to as a surgi-center, freestanding or ambulatory surgical facility, or one-day surgical facility. It provides an appropriate setting for certain types of comparatively simple surgical procedures that don't normally require overnight confinement and may or may not be part of a hospital. In either case, the charges for use of the surgi-center generally are covered under the plan's hospital benefits.

To assure quality care, the following are typical requirements that must be met. The facility must:

1. Comply with all legal requirements in the jurisdiction in which located.
2. Be mainly engaged in surgery on its premises, which include operating room(s), recovery room(s), and equipment for emergency care.
3. Have a medical staff, including physicians and graduate registered nurses.
4. Have an agreement with a hospital for immediate acceptance of patients requiring hospital care on an inpatient basis.

Limitations and Exclusions

Normally, surgical expense benefits will not cover the cost of cosmetic surgery. With the growth of separate dental insurance, surgical schedules in a medical care plan also commonly exclude dental surgery unless it is the result of an accident.

PHYSICIANS' VISITS EXPENSE BENEFITS

It was a logical next step, after surgical benefits were added to insurance plans, to address coverage for physicians' charges for other medical services. Thus, physicians' visits coverage was developed and, together with other nonsurgical benefits, often is referred to as basic medical expense insurance. It has remained a comparatively limited first-dollar benefit.

Two types of first-dollar physicians' visits plans commonly offered provide benefits, (1) in the hospital only, or (2) in either the hospital, home, or office.

In-Hospital Visits Only

Following the early direction of medical insurance, physicians' expense benefits plans at first were designed to cover only fees for visits made while the patient is confined in the hospital. Benefits are subject to a specified maximum-dollar amount for each period of hospital confinement and often subject to a maximum per day. The daily amount may vary, depending on the day of confinement on which the visit is made; if so, it is most often higher on the first day, to reflect the greater involvement of the physician at that time.

The benefit period normally coincides with the benefit period for hospital expense benefits. For example, under a 120-day hospital expense insurance plan, with a $20 daily in-hospital physicians' visits benefit, the maximum payment for physicians' visits would be $2,400 (120 × $20). Frequently, too, plans limit payment to the charge for only one visit in any one day.

Hospital, Office, and Home Visits

It wasn't long before plans were expanded to cover physicians' visits in the office or home, as well as in the hospital, but total disability often is required. Such plans, for example, may provide $10 for an office visit, $15 for a home visit, and $15 for a hospital visit. In addition, an overall maximum, such as $600, is established. This limit may be applied to all visits for the care and treatment of any one injury or sickness, or in the case of sickness, all visits in either a calendar year or in 12 consecutive months.

When purchasing a plan to cover physicians' fees in and out of the hospital, the policyholder selects the visit when benefit payments begin, usually any visit from the first to the fourth. If hospital confinement is required, a provision often is added to begin payment with the first visit in the hospital, regardless of when it otherwise would have started. Benefits normally are restricted to only one visit per day.

Compared with hospital-only coverage for physicians' charges, this broader benefit has not been as commonly included on a first-dollar basis. It can result in many small claims, which some believe are covered more appropriately under major medical coverage on a shared basis.

Limitations and Exclusions

Neither of the two types of plans described for physicians' visits expense benefits normally covers charges for a visit after surgery if it is made by a physician connected with the surgical procedure, since a surgeon's charge usually includes post-operative care. Similarly, physicians' visits for pregnancy are not separately covered, because they normally are included in the obstetrician's charge for managing the total pregnancy. In addition, physicians' visits made for dental treatment commonly are excluded from this part of a plan, as are examinations for the prescription or fitting of eyeglasses or hearing aids.

Special Features

Well-Baby Care. The question of whether expenses for normal, healthy babies should be covered from birth under an insurance plan has been debated through the years on much the same grounds as has normal pregnancy. It became even a bigger issue as the pregnancy laws changed and the costs for care of the healthy baby escalated. As coverage for newborns developed, they first were covered only for accident or sickness after 14 days of age. Soon, however, this was extended to include children with specific abnormal conditions at birth. The latter remains true in many plans today. However, it is increasingly common to also cover a defined number of days of nursery charges for the normal child. Before the recent pregnancy legislation, some plans did this only to the extent the mother did not otherwise use her entire pregnancy allowance. With pregnancy no longer specially limited, nursery charges usually are limited to a maximum number of days, if covered at all.

Other charges for a healthy baby, such as a pediatrician's visits, whether the first, usually in the hospital, or subsequently in the office, are under discussion but more commonly are addressed in a preventive care benefit.

Preventive Care.   Preventive care has become a buzz word in this era of increasing interest in how it might improve the health of the nation and decrease the cost of medical care for all. In the course of its development, its definition has begun to move from annual physical examinations for everyone to more sophisticated approaches. New concepts address the cost effectiveness of the procedures recommended, the intervals at which they are performed, and even more basically, methods for changing lifestyles that contribute toward illness. Many approaches are being tried and evaluated.

> Health maintenance organizations, which by their nature include more preventive care than most current insurance plans, are studying the effect on health and costs and adjusting their practices to reflect results.

> Employers are providing in-house exercise facilities, considering health risk evaluations, and beginning to sponsor programs to foster better health by changing lifestyles, such as smoke-ender and stress-control courses.

> Coverage in insurance plans varies greatly. Those that include preventive care at all, typically cover charges for periodic physical examinations up to a maximum-dollar amount, such as $75, for the examination and for any required diagnostic procedures. Other plans are providing routine immunizations and educational materials to insureds to raise awareness of the value of prevention.

The jury is still out, but in the meantime, medical benefit plan designers are involved heavily in how best to provide preventive benefits.

DIAGNOSTIC X-RAY AND LABORATORY EXPENSE BENEFITS

This coverage is designed to compliment other first-dollar medical expense benefits already discussed. Without it, X-ray and laboratory analyses normally would be covered as hospital services and supplies, but only if the services are performed when the insured is hospital confined. This benefit, though, provides reimbursement for diagnostic X-ray and laboratory examinations made in a doctor's office, in an independent laboratory, or in an outpatient department of a hospital on an ambulatory basis. As with surgical plans, benefits may be covered on a scheduled or nonscheduled basis.

Scheduled

A scheduled plan is a more controlled approach to first-dollar coverage of diagnostic X-ray and laboratory expenses typical of early designs for each new benefit as it developed. Plans of this type itemize the maximum allowance for each examination—as a dollar amount or as a unit value to be multiplied by a conversion factor. Benefits are provided up to an overall schedule maximum, such as $200 or $250, either for all examinations for any one accident or sickness or for all accidents or sicknesses during any one year. In the past, a two-part schedule sometimes was used. The first part provided coverage for diagnostic X-ray and radioisotope studies, and sometimes was written as a separate coverage. The second part provided payment for diagnostic laboratory services, and generally was written only in conjunction with the first part of the schedule.

Nonscheduled

A nonscheduled plan is more common today and has been for some time. It is a less-restrictive approach since it eliminates maximums for each service. Instead, a nonscheduled plan provides reimbursement for the actual fee charged for each service, subject to the reasonable and customary test.

As for scheduled plans, overall maximums are set, for example, at $100 or $200, either for all examinations for any one accident or sickness, or for all accidents or sicknesses during any one calendar year. These first-dollar maximums have remained comparatively low because major medical covers expenses that exceed them.

Limitations and Exclusions

Early plans did not cover diagnostic X-ray and laboratory examinations for pregnancy. Since the 1979 Federal Maternity legislation, however, this is no longer true; but the benefit continues to exclude costs for fitting of eyeglasses or of hearing aids or for dental treatment, unless the examination is made to diagnose an injury caused by an accident.

RADIOTHERAPY EXPENSE BENEFITS

Coverage for radiotherapy as a first-dollar benefit developed as the treatment became more prevalent and the cost more significant. However, charges continued to escalate and the first-dollar portion became an ever-smaller part of the total cost. Like diagnostic benefits, the balance was covered under major medical. Many plans, however, have eliminated the first-dollar radiotherapy benefit as it became less meaningful and, instead, cover the cost only under major medical.

If a first-dollar plan is included, it frequently is done through the use of a schedule that assigns a maximum-dollar amount or a unit value to identified services. The cost of covered radiological treatment (e.g., radium or cobalt therapy) usually includes: (1) administration of the treatment, (2) materials and their preparation, and (3) the use of facilities. The maximum payment for all treatments received during any one day often is limited to the largest payment provided in the schedule for any one of the treatments.

Whether a dollar-amount or unit value schedule is used, the total amount payable for all treatments for the same or related injury or sickness is the overall schedule maximum. Maximums are available that range from as low as $200 on a dollar-amount schedule to $1,500 or more on a unit value schedule. In some plans this approach is modified to apply the maximum to all treatments for the same or related injury or sickness in a calendar year. The benefit is intended to cover treatment and, therefore, excludes diagnosis.

SUPPLEMENTAL ACCIDENT EXPENSE BENEFITS

This coverage also is variously referred to as additional accident or special accident expense benefits. The concept was first developed to provide an extra limited amount of first-dollar coverage for medical expenses resulting from an accident. Although that was long before the current concern with cost containment, the benefit does address that issue somewhat; it avoids the penalty of the major medical deductible and coinsurance, because treatment for a minor accident is received in a doctor's office and not in a hospital outpatient department.

The coverage usually provides payment toward the cost of the following services as a result of an accidental injury: (1) treatment by a physician, (2) hospital care, (3) registered graduate nursing care (RN), and (4) X-ray and laboratory examinations. Benefits are payable for covered medical expenses that exceed the amount the insured otherwise is entitled to under the rest of the basic medical care plan, up to a maximum for any one accident. The most common maximums are $300 and $500. Most plans require the costs be incurred within 90 days of an accident that happened while the individual was insured.

EXTENSION OF BENEFITS

A key provision of basic benefits from the beginning, which adds significantly to their value to the insured, is the extension of benefits provision. Under its terms, if an individual's insurance terminates, for whatever reason, payment is made for covered services received within three months of termination. But the service must be for an injury or sickness that caused the individual to be totally and continuously disabled from the day his or her insurance terminated until the day the service is rendered. Thus, disabled persons are not left without coverage for an existing disability because their insurance ended.

CONVERSION PRIVILEGE

Similarly, the conversion privilege offers a way to fill what might otherwise be a gap in coverage for terminating employees. The provision allows an individual whose insurance under the employer's medical care plan terminates after being insured for at least three months to convert to a personal medical care policy without evidence of insurability. Some states require this provision, and even specify the levels of coverage that must be available. Many insurers, however, include it in all plans. The converted policy usually provides more restrictive benefits than those under the terminating group coverage, and experience proves individuals most likely to use the plan take advantage of it. The privilege is not generally available to individuals who terminate coverage for failure to pay premiums, are eligible for Medicare, or become insured under another group medical plan within 31 days of termination.

SUMMARY

The development of basic benefits started with hospital coverage—since it represented the greatest cost of an illness. Additional benefits were developed as other costs increased and as health care plans expanded to satisfy the buyer.

A variety of such benefits have evolved through the years from the continuing demand for fuller coverage. Some, such as the prescription drug benefit, have developed along somewhat different lines, because special administrative issues made the use of participating providers and of a third-party administrator cost-effective. Interest in the vision care benefit is growing, and plans have been written on either a scheduled or participating provider basis. Other benefits, such as home health care and skilled nursing facilities, offer alternatives to hospital confinement and may be covered as either basic or major medical benefits. All are discussed in detail elsewhere in this text.

Furthermore, several limitations not yet mentioned do often apply to basic benefits. These are designed to avoid payment for custodial care, duplicate coverage, illegal or unnecessary charges, and the like. Because many also affect major medical benefits, they are treated in the next chapter.

CHAPTER 13

Supplemental Major Medical and Comprehensive Plans

ZELDA LIPTON

INTRODUCTION

Although the scope of basic medical care benefits has been expanded through the years, most plans remain primarily hospital-oriented and geared toward acute care. Benefits usually are first-dollar, but limited both in the services and charges covered. As medical technology advanced and costs increased, the need for additional coverage for a variety of expenses not covered under the so-called basic benefits and for protection against the financial catastrophe of serious and prolonged illness became increasingly apparent.

In response to that need, major medical insurance plans were introduced in 1949. They grew rapidly, covering over 32 million people by the end of 1960. That number increased steadily to over 154 million persons with major medical coverage in some form by the end of 1980.

Major medical provides broad coverage and substantial protection from large, unpredictable, and therefore unbudgetable medical care expenses. As might be expected, with hundreds of companies involved in the development of benefits, many variations in design have appeared. Difficult as it is to call anything typical, patterns have emerged. From the start, most plans covered a wide range of medical care charges with few internal limits and what was then considered a high per person overall maximum benefit, such as $10,000. Both the range of charges covered and the maximums have increased steadily through the years, but the early requirement that the insured participate to some extent in the cost of care through deductibles and coinsurance remains a conviction for most designers. Although born as a supplement to basic medical care plans, that too has changed—so now two approaches exist to major medical: (1) supplemental major medical over some form of basic benefits, and (2) the stand-alone package, referred to as a comprehensive plan.

163

APPROACHES DEFINED

Supplemental Major Medical

A supplemental major medical plan pays benefits when the basic benefits are exhausted. The claimant is reimbursed first for any charges covered by specific formulas in the basic plan. Major medical covered expenses not reimbursed under the basic plan are covered under the supplemental major medical, subject to a deductible, payable by the claimant. After satisfaction of this deductible amount, a percentage of the remaining covered expenses are paid up to the supplemental major medical maximum. A more recent, but now commonly included, provision caps the claimant's costs by paying 100 percent of major medical covered expenses after the insured has incurred the plan's out-of-pocket maximum.

Depending upon the basic benefits over which it is written, a supplemental major medical, or the plan of which it is a part, has come to be designated in several different ways:

1. With the insurer's own basic hospital, surgical, medical benefits, the package is called a base-plus major medical plan.
2. Over another basic plan, such as Blue Cross or Blue Shield, the supplemental major medical more commonly is referred to as superimposed major medical.
3. Over Blue Cross only, the supplemental major medical is known as a wraparound. But even a wraparound can use different design concepts. Traditionally, a wraparound was written to include basic surgical and medical benefits supplemented by major medical. This is much like a base-plus major medical plan except that Blue Cross provides the basic hospital benefits. However, another wraparound design is beginning to gain favor for its added simplicity and potential for cost control. It covers all benefits not covered by Blue Cross as part of the major medical subject to a deductible and coinsurance; the Blue Cross hospital benefits are the only basic benefits.

Coverage under the major medical portion of all these approaches differs only to the extent that it must adjust to the basic benefits over which it is written. Whatever its form, the two-part basic and major medical coverage persists for several reasons. It usually reflects the history of the development of medical insurance, in general, as well as the history of the particular plan—and sometimes the collective bargaining that gave rise to that plan. Over the Blues, the basic Blue Cross plan may have cost advantages in a particular geographical area, because of cost-reimbursement contracts with hospitals, making competition for basic hospital benefits difficult. As a result, the basic Blue Cross plans cover a substantial part of the market in such states as New York, New Jersey, Pennsylvania, Ohio, and Michigan. More attention is being paid to the equity of different hospital charges based on the source of funding, but for now this remains a factor in some locations. Although most Blue Cross/Blue Shield plans working together also offer an extended medical care or master medical plan, patterned after the private insurance industry's supplemental major medical, basic Blues plans with private supplemental major medical continue to be written.

Whatever its form or the reason for using it, a two-part medical care plan with two carriers has some disadvantages. Administration becomes more difficult, since premiums and claims must be submitted to both carriers and benefits must be coordinated. Duplication may exist; however, there may be gaps in coverage caused by such inconsistencies as different definitions, reasonable and customary levels, and preexisting conditions limitations. Furthermore, when two carriers are involved, if the basic plan changes, the liability of the major medical carrier does also. Clear communication between carriers and with the insured is essential. Typical base-plus major medical, superimposed, and wraparound plans are illustrated in Figure 13-1.

Comprehensive

The next step in the logical development of medical care plans was a single integrated program covering both basic and catastrophic costs—a comprehensive plan. The earliest of these were written in 1954. Their growth was slower than supplemental major medical plans at first, but by 1978 almost 37 million of those persons with major medical coverage in some form were covered by comprehensive plans, and the trend toward the comprehensive approach seems to be growing.

A comprehensive plan is simpler to understand and easier to communicate. By applying one overall reimbursement formula to the total covered expenses, without attempting to distinguish between those that would have been eligible for basic or major medical benefits, it avoids the hazards of both the duplicate coverage and the gaps discussed earlier. Furthermore, since most comprehensive plans have few of the inside limits of a basic plan, the frequency of plan revisions is reduced.

The earliest and simplest form of comprehensive plan, a pure comprehensive, provides for reimbursement of a percent of all combined covered expenses in a calendar year after the deductible is met, up to an overall lifetime maximum. This design achieves the main purposes of the comprehensive approach; but its acceptance was at first limited because of the appeal of the first-dollar, full-pay coverages buyers had become accustomed to in basic plans. As a result, a variety of modified comprehensive designs were developed and are discussed later in this chapter. Typical comprehensive plans are illustrated in Figure 13-2.

Supplemental major medical and comprehensive plans have many common provisions. Their differences can perhaps best be identified by considering the supplemental features in detail, and then how some of those vary because of the comprehensive design.

Figure 13-1
Typical Supplemental Major Medical Plan Designs

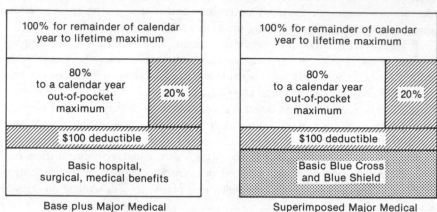

Base plus Major Medical   Superimposed Major Medical

Wrap-arounds

Key: [ ] Plan pays
        [////] Insured pays
        [::::] BC and/or BS pays

FEATURES OF SUPPLEMENTAL MAJOR MEDICAL PLANS

Covered Expenses

Supplemental major medical plans cover reasonable and customary charges incurred for a wide variety of necessary medical services and supplies prescribed or performed by a physician. Reasonable and customary

Figure 13–2
Typical Comprehensive Plan Designs

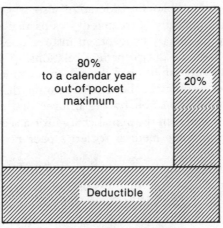

Pure Comprehensive

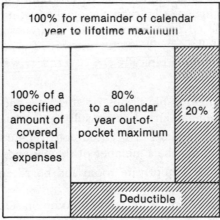

Modified Comprehensive

Key: ☐ Plan pays
    ▨ Insured pays

charges may be interpreted differently by different carriers. Generally, however, they are the lesser of those charges normally made by a provider for the service rendered or an amount large enough to cover the charges made by a percent of the providers in a given geographical area for a similar service. The percent is set by each insurance carrier and applied to the best data available. A carrier with a large enough data bank of its own to be valid will use it. Otherwise, industry-compiled charge data often is used, since its size makes it more credible. Consideration also is given to the special circumstances and complexity of treatment in a particular case. In applying the reasonable and customary concept, an insurer does not try to set fee levels or interfere with the doctor/patient relationship. Rather, the insurer establishes a contractual liability and the patient assumes the obligation to pay any charges exceeding the benefit maximum that results. Disputes arising out of the determination by the insurer that the reasonable and customary charge is less than the actual charge for a service frequently are referred to the appropriate medical society's peer review committee for settlement.

From the beginning, supplemental major medical plans included some out-of-hospital benefits; in fact, that was part of the reason for their development. Continuing advances in medical technology have resulted in new and sophisticated outpatient procedures to deal with many conditions that formerly required hospitalization. At the same time, although all medical care costs have continued to escalate faster than the consumer price index, hospital costs remain the worst offender. As a result, the trend in recent years has put even greater emphasis on coverage for outpatient services in the hope of containing costs by reducing or eliminating hospital stays.

Although specific covered expenses and their descriptions vary from plan to plan, the following illustrates the broad scope of services and facilities for which charges typically are covered as well as some of their limitations and rationale.

Professional services of physicians or surgeons and other recognized medical practitioners, including consulting physicians.

Services of registered nurses or licensed practical nurses for private duty nursing. Neither may be a member of the patient's immediate family.

Hospital charges for semiprivate room and board and other necessary services and supplies.

Private room charges usually at the most common semiprivate room rate to discourage use except if medically necessary, but an extra allowance may be provided. Confinement in an intensive care unit may be at two or three times the most common semiprivate room rate or even the actual charge.

Preadmission testing prior to a scheduled hospital confinement.

Ambulatory surgical facilities to encourage one-day surgery when medically advisable.

Mental illness or alcohol and drug abuse treatment centers for a limited number of days, such as 30 or 60, either per confinement or per calendar year. This is based on the concept that short-term therapy in such facilities is beneficial, but long-term treatment often is custodial in nature and not intended to be covered.

Skilled nursing facilities that meet prescribed requirements. This is limited to a specified number of days, such as 30, per confinement or per calendar year, and usually must follow a hospital stay of at least 3 consecutive days. The intent is to provide for the person who no longer needs acute care in a hospital but does need intermediate care and monitoring. Longer confinement is likely to be custodial.

Home health care for a defined number of visits per calendar year, such as 40 or 80, by physicians, nurses, and home health aides. Care must be under a plan supervised by a home health agency and generally must follow confinement in either a hospital or skilled nursing facility. Home care in lieu of confinement may be covered if services required can be provided more comfortably and less expensively at home.

Anesthetics and their administration.

X-rays and other diagnostic laboratory procedures wherever performed.

X-ray or radium treatments.

Oxygen and other gases and their administration.

Blood transfusions, including the cost of blood if charged.

Prescription drugs.

Professional ambulance service to or from the nearest hospital where care can be provided.

Rental of equipment required for therapeutic use.

Casts, splints, and initial prosthetic appliances, trusses, braces, and crutches.

As explained in the previous chapter, federal legislation now requires certain defined employers to provide the same benefits for pregnancy as for any other illness. The pregnancy benefits need not be insured even if other benefits are. But, if normal pregnancy or only complications are included in the insurance plan, covered expenses described above apply equally to services for the covered pregnancy as to any other illness.

Deductible

The deductible is the amount of covered major medical expenses that must be incurred by the insured before supplemental major medical benefits become payable by the insurer. Its basic purpose is to lower costs by reducing unnecessary utilization and by eliminating small claims and the expense of handling them. It attempts to accomplish this by giving the insured some interest in the up-front cost of medical care.

Levels. Through the years and still today, the most common individual deductibles have been $50 and $100. Recently, however, some employers have opted for higher deductible amounts, such as $200, $500, $1,000, even $2,000. Some of this reflects an effort toward further control of utilization and, therefore, of premium during a period of rapid inflation.

There are employers, though, who choose to self-insure the very high deductibles. For them, some insurance carriers administer all claims and inform the policyholder of the obligation between the insured's $100 and the high $2,000 deductible, for example. The insurance company assumes the risk over and above the $2,000. This approach allows the employer some of the advantages of self-insurance on a small scale with limited risk. It does at the same time, though, defeat the purposes of a high deductible in terms of utilization control.

Some consideration also has been given to relating an insured's deductible amount to income, either as a percent of earnings or by identifying a different deductible amount for various earnings ranges. The premise is that a higher-paid employee can afford to cover a larger part of medical expenses and, unless the deductible is significant enough, it will have little effect on utilization. Earnings related deductibles could become more prevalent in the future in spite of the difficulties with administration of many individual deductible levels on each account which also could change every year.

Type. There are two types of supplemental major medical deductibles: (1) corridor and (2) integrated. The former is by far the more common today.

Corridor. This type of deductible is so named because it serves as a corridor between the basic benefits and the supplemental major medical plan. It is applied to covered major medical expenses that exceed amounts covered under the basic plan. Benefits payable under the basic plan are not counted toward satisfaction of the corridor deductible.

Although in wraparound plans the deductible is expressed as benefits paid or payable under the Blue Cross plan plus a specific dollar amount, such as $100, the $100 remains a corridor deductible. This contractual approach is used to allow elimination of any obligation under the major medical portion for expenses which are covered under the basic Blue Cross plan, or would have been except that the insured was for some reason not covered under the Blue Cross portion.

Integrated. An integrated deductible was an early approach to the application of the deductible in a supplemental major medical plan. It is rarely used today. The deductible is the greater of (1) a fairly high amount, such as $1,000, or (2) the basic plan benefits. For example, if the basic plan paid $1,250, a $1,000 deductible would be satisfied and supplemental major medical benefits would be payable for the remaining covered expenses with no further deductible. However, if the basic plan only paid $800, the balance of $200 that is needed to satisfy the deductible would have to be assumed by the insured before supplemental major medical benefits would be payable.

Basis for Application. In conjunction with the deductible, an accumulation period feature is included in one form or another. The accumulation period is that time during which covered medical expenses sufficient to satisfy the deductible must be incurred. It was designed originally as a device to further insure that only relatively substantial claims would be covered. In addition to the length of the accumulation period, the basis for application of the deductible and the benefit period to which it applies vary according to the needs of the policyholder and the underwriting requirements of the insurer.

The following are the two common deductible bases and illustrate how the above features can be combined in a variety of ways.

All-Cause Deductible. Under the all-cause approach, all expenses incurred by an insured, regardless of the number of illnesses or accidents giving rise to the expenses, are considered for purposes of satisfaction of the deductible. Although it is possible to combine the all-cause deductible with various accumulation periods and benefits periods, the calendar year is almost universally used for both (e.g., a $100 deductible applies to each calendar year benefit period and must be satisfied between January 1 and December 31). As a result, this all-cause deductible approach often is referred to as a calendar year deductible.

Its most important advantage is it is simple to administer, and is considered the easiest for the insured to understand. Benefits are paid, following the satisfaction of the calendar year deductible, for expenses incurred during the remainder of that calendar year. To reduce the seeming inequity between insureds who incur expenses early in the year and those who do so late in the year, a carry-over provision normally is included. This permits expenses incurred in October, November, or December, which are applied toward satisfaction of the deductible for that year, to be used toward satisfying the deductible for the next calendar year.

A policy year or a running 12 months may be substituted for a calendar year. The former is a period beginning with the date each year on which the policy was effective; it is sometimes referred to as the plan year. The latter is any period of 12 months, beginning with the date the first charge is made, counting toward an individual's deductible. This approach is no longer commonly used because of the difficulty of administering a different period for each individual under the plan.

Most plans also have a special deductible modification known as the common-accident provision. It provides that only one deductible will be applied to the total covered expenses incurred when two or more insured persons of the same family sustain injuries in a single accident.

In addition, to reduce the financial effect of the deductible on large families if several members have major expenses in one year, a "family deductible" provision usually is added with an all-cause deductible. This provision can operate in several different ways. The deductible may be waived for any further family members after either any two or any three of them have individually satisfied their deductibles in the same year.

Another approach waives any further deductible for the year when any combination of family members has satisfied a total of two or three times the individual deductible amount. The latter may be modified by requiring that at least one family member satisfies the individual deductible.

Per-Cause Deductible. Under the per-cause approach, all expenses incurred by an insured because of the same or related causes are considered for purposes of satisfaction of the deductible. An accumulation period most often is included, in which case the deductible for each cause must be satisfied within a specified period, typically 60 or 90 days, from the date the first expense is incurred.

In such a plan, the benefit period for each cause starts with the first expense used to satisfy the deductible, and normally ends one or two years after the date it starts or two years from the date the deductible was satisfied. When benefit periods longer than one year are provided, it is common to include an alternate cutoff date that terminates the benefit period. This might be the end of a period of 60 or 90 days, during which less than a certain amount of expenses (such as the deductible amount) is incurred. Once a benefit period ends, the deductible must be satisfied again to start a new one.

The chief advantage of the per-cause approach is that claims for minor, unrelated illnesses can be eliminated. However, an individual may have to satisfy two or more deductibles in any 12-month period. This approach is more difficult to understand and can cause administrative problems since, especially with advancing age, it often is difficult to distinguish among causes of diseases. The per-cause deductible was common in early major medical plans but is not very popular today.

Coinsurance

Coinsurance provides further participation by the insured in part of the cost of medical care. By reimbursing for less than 100 percent of ongoing expenses over the deductible, coinsurance reinforces the objective of retaining the insured's financial interest in the cost of medical services. Thus, it is one more tool in keeping plan costs down.

Levels. By far the largest majority of plans use 80 percent for most reimbursements, but 75 percent to 100 percent are available. However, since even with 80 percent reimbursement the cost of a catastrophic illness can cause financial disaster, many plans eliminate coinsurance and reimburse at 100 percent after a certain dollar amount is reached. This amount has come to be most often expressed as the out-of-pocket maximum (e.g., $1,000) paid by an insured as a result of deductible and coinsurance provisions. Some plans begin to reimburse at 100 percent after an identified amount of covered expenses are incurred. The purpose is the same. In either case, the 100 percent usually applies to the same period used for application of the deductible, most often the remainder of the calendar year. In some plans, however, it applies to the following year as well. For even further protection, a family out-of-pocket maximum equal to two or three times the individual amount often is included.

Mental Illness and Alcohol or Drug Abuse. Although reimbursement for charges for treatment of inpatient mental and nervous disorders or alcohol and drug dependency is at the same coinsurance level as for other inpatient charges, an overwhelming number of plans require greater participation by the insured in the cost of these services on an outpatient basis. They are not only still considered somewhat discretionary but also open-ended as far as control is concerned. A variety of coverage designs and levels are available, but coinsurance for outpatient care is most often set at 50 percent subject to a maximum payment under the plan each calendar year, such as $1,000. This may apply separately to (1) mental illness and to (2) alcohol and drug dependency, or to all combined.

It also is still common, for mental illness and nervous disorders, to limit outpatient coverage to a specific maximum number of visits per year (e.g., 50) and a maximum covered charge per visit (e.g., $50) for even further control. Neither inpatient nor outpatient charges generally are included in out-of-pocket maximums, and they are rarely if ever payable at 100 percent.

Maximum Benefit

Except for specifically identified coverage limitations, reasonable and customary charges for all eligible expenses are covered by the plan provisions up to the overall maximum benefit of the plan. In the 1960s, a $10,000 maximum was common; today $1 million is not uncommon, and many plans are written as unlimited. Consistent with the application of the deductible, the overall maximum benefit may be written as either (1) lifetime (all-cause), or (2) per-cause.

Lifetime. Under the lifetime approach, the overall maximum benefit applies to all covered expenses during the entire period of coverage. However, major medical plans, from their beginning, typically included a reinstatement provision to avoid penalizing insureds who have either partially or wholly exhausted their benefits, but who have recovered to the extent of again being acceptable insurance risks. This provision might provide that after a minimum amount of benefits (e.g., $1,000) is used, the maximum may be reinstated to its original level by submitting evidence of insurability satisfactory to the insurance company. In addition, it is common to provide some form of "automatic" reinstatement. For example, benefits paid in a calendar year may be reinstated automatically as of January 1 of the following year for amounts from $1,000 to as much as $25,000. Some plans allow continued reinstatement each January 1 until the full amount is restored.

For further control, it is not unusual to include a separate lifetime, nonreinstatable maximum for all mental and nervous disorders, such as $25,000 or $50,000 lifetime. This is in addition to the coinsurance, per-visit and maximum-dollar amount or duration limits discussed earlier.

Per-Cause. Under the per-cause approach, the overall maximum benefit applies to each cause. Thus, if an insured individual is receiving benefits under a per-cause plan for the treatment of both diabetes and a heart condition, a separate overall maximum benefit would be applicable to each illness, as would a separate deductible amount. A typical per-cause reinstatement provision states that, when a covered person has received benefits for any one accidental injury or any one sickness equal to the overall maximum benefit, major medical benefits for that injury or sickness terminate and can only be reinstated if satisfactory evidence of insurability is submitted to the insurance company. Another approach reinstates some or all of the maximum if the insured does not incur medical expenses for the injury or sickness of more than a specified amount, such as $500, during a given period, such as six months.

With the very high maximums being written today, especially on lifetime all-cause plan designs, the maximum benefit reinstatement provisions no longer have the significance they did in the past. Nevertheless, they typically continue to be included unless the maximum benefit is unlimited.

Limitations and Exclusions

The following describes the charges and services most commonly limited or excluded from medical insurance coverages today, with a brief explanation of the reason for each. Those which apply to major medical only are so identified. In addition, such coverages as vision and hearing care are listed, although they are well on their way to being included in the future.

Preexisting Conditions. Because of the potential for selection against the plan, it is common practice to pay major medical benefits for preexisting conditions only after certain requirements are met. A typical preexisting conditions limitation might read:

> A preexisting condition is defined as a condition resulting from an injury or sickness for which expenses were incurred during the three months prior to the effective date of insurance. For such a condition, benefits will be payable only (1) after the completion of a period of three consecutive months ending after insurance becomes effective, and during which the individual received no care or treatment for the condition, or (2) after the individual has been covered for major medical benefits for a period of one year.

Some plans also may cover a preexisting condition of an employee insured for major medical benefits for six months without any interruption in full-time active work. The preexisting conditions provision may be waived either for the group insured on the effective date of the plan only or for all future insureds as well. When this is done, the active service requirements continue to apply, but once an individual is insured under the plan its benefits will be paid for a preexisting condition as for any other condition.

In the case of a plan transferring from one carrier to another, however, many plans universally apply a "no loss—no gain" or "hardship" provision required in some states. It usually provides that an insured will be reimbursed under the new plan at the lesser of the amount which would have been payable under the terminated or the new plan regardless of any preexisting conditions limitations or active service requirements of the new plan.

Duplicate Coverage. In many households today, more than one family member is employed. As a result, a person may be covered under more than one group medical care insurance plan and could profit financially from an illness. Thus, in the interest of cost control for all concerned, a coordination of benefits (COB) provision routinely is included to avoid overinsurance. It follows the guidelines recommended by a health insurance task force and adopted by the National Association of Insurance Commissioners (NAIC) in 1971. The NAIC Model Group COB Provisions and Guidelines establish the order in which carriers are responsible for reimbursement. The provisions allow a claimant to recover as much of his or her medical care expenses as coverage under each plan permits, up to 100 percent of charges for expenses allowable under any of the plans. When a plan provides benefits in the form of services rather than cash payments, the reasonable cash value of the services is considered both an "allowable charge" and a benefit paid. To the extent any plan, therefore, does not need to pay its full liability, benefit credits are accumulated and available if they should be needed to cover expenses later in the benefit period. Examples are included on Figure 13-3.

Medical care plans coordinate benefits not only with other group medical insurance plans and health maintenance organizations, but also may do so with at least the mandatory benefits under state no-fault automobile laws and Medicare, which until recently has always been primary.[1] Particularly in the case of Medicare, another approach often is used in place of coordination of benefits to avoid duplicate coverage. Normal liability under the insured plan is determined and directly reduced by the amount paid by Medicare for the same expenses. This is commonly referred to as carve-out. It attempts to provide the individual eligible for Medicare with the same reimbursement under the insured plan and Medicare together as any other insured would receive under the group medical care insurance plan itself. This same approach also may be applied to "no-fault" benefits.

Other variations have been developed to coordinate benefits for the same charges under several plans. For example, in some cases, a plan is

---

[1] Although many questions remain as of this writing, it is clear that as a result of the Tax Equity and Fiscal Responsibility Act of 1982, Medicare is no longer automatically primary under most employer plans for active employees age 65 to 69. The employee may choose for Medicare to be either primary or secondary. Details of coordination under the new law will be determined as soon as final federal regulations are issued.

All the methods described above remain available to avoid duplication for employees not subject to the new legislation.

Figure 13–3
Use of Benefit Credits with Coordination of Benefits

Example 1:

A benefit credit (unused liability) that remains after payment of benefits as secondary carrier may be stored and used at a later date to pay allowable expenses that otherwise would not be paid. For example, the primary carrier may consider certain charges covered under its plan, such as nursing home care, and pay up to its limits. Even though the charges are not covered under the secondary plan, they become allowable expenses under the secondary plan and can be paid with previously accumulated benefit credits (assume $1,500).

Billed for nursing care	$5,000
Carrier #1 payment at 80 percent	4,000
Carrier #2 normal liability	0
Carrier #2 payment from benefit credits	1,000 to pay 100% of charges
Balance due	0
(Remaining balance in benefit credits $500)	

Example 2:

Carrier #1 has not paid a $20 charge for an office visit since the insured's $100 deductible has not been met.

Carrier #2 has a $50 deductible which has been met previously and some benefit credits have been accumulated from an earlier claim.

Billed	$20
Carrier #1 payment	0
Balance due	20
Carrier #2 liability paid at 80 percent	16
Carrier #2 payment from benefit credits	4 to pay 100% of charges
Balance	0

designed to specifically fill the gaps in coverage under the primary plan. This has been a common way to supplement Medicare but is more difficult to keep current. Whatever the variation, all such approaches have the same objective—cost-control by elimination of overinsurance.

Other Limitations and Exclusions

Care Received in Federal or State Hospitals. Experience revealed many of these hospitals furnish free service except when a patient has insurance coverage, in which case some make a charge for services rendered. Since the existence of insurance coverage should not affect the way a hospital's charges are billed, it is the practice of insurers to honor such claims only when an unconditional requirement exists for a person to pay for the services provided, without regard to the existence of insurance. This type of exclusion is very common, although most government hospitals no longer base their charges on the existence of insurance.

Cosmetic Surgery.   This is only covered if it is necessary to correct injuries caused by an accident that occurred while insured, or to correct a congenital anomaly in an insured newborn infant. Elective cosmetic surgery is excluded.

Custodial Care.   Since the purpose of health insurance is to provide benefits for the treatment of an injury or sickness, various exclusions and limitations are included to terminate benefits when institutionalization of the patient becomes custodial in nature (i.e., there is no longer any medical care being provided).

Dental Care and Treatment.   Care or treatment of teeth and gums is usually excluded, except for treatment required because of accidental injury to natural teeth and charges for hospital confinement for dental treatment. With the rapid growth of group dental expense insurance, care must be taken to avoid duplicate coverage.

Elective Items.   There are many services, such as television, telephone charges, air conditioners, swimming pools, bath massagers, and trips to different climates, that a patient can elect to use, which can relate to the illness or injury being treated, but which do not contribute materially to the cure of a patient. Charges for many of these might be billed by a medical care provider, such as a hospital or a physician, or secured with a prescription. Because of the questionable relationship of many of these expenses to medical treatment, they usually are excluded.

Routine Health Examinations.   Since there is no illness, these budgetable expenses generally have been expected to be paid by the covered person. However, a trend is developing toward the inclusion of preventive care benefits, such as these, either as part of the basic coverage as described or under the major medical plan.

Occupational Accidents and Sicknesses.   No benefits are payable for any medical care expenses resulting from an occupational accident, or from sickness covered by any workers' compensation law or similar legislation. Workers' compensation benefits cover the medical care expenses of a worker for job-related accidents and sicknesses. However, in some jurisdictions, owners and partners are not covered for workers' compensation benefits because, by its definition, they are not considered employees. In these cases, insurers may waive this exclusion for owners and partners provided they meet the definition of employee in the insurance plan.

Purchase or Fitting of Eyeglasses or Hearing Aids and Examinations for Them.   These services are considered routine care not expected to result in significant expense to the individual, and are not usually reimbursable. No illness in the usual sense is involved in the majority of cases. Nevertheless, in response to demand, plans have been developed covering these services either as basic or major medical benefits.

War.   Injuries or illness because of war, whether declared or undeclared, are excluded from coverage because a substantial catastrophic risk is created that is beyond the scope of group health insurance.

Extension of Benefits

As with basic benefits, major medical benefits will be continued after insurance terminates for an injury or sickness that causes the insured to be totally disabled from the date of termination. However, unless the individual is or becomes covered under another group plan for the same injury or sickness, major medical benefits will be extended for one year rather than the three months provided by basic plans. This extension terminates when the individual is no longer totally disabled by the injury or sickness, if that is earlier than one year from termination.

Survivor Coverage

Although not a standard coverage included in all plans, this provision often is available and adds considerably to the value of a medical expense benefit plan. It provides that the medical care insurance in effect for dependents on the date of an employee's death remains in force, usually without payment of premium, for some specified period ranging from six months to two years from the date of the employee's death. Coverage is terminated before the end of that period only if the surviving spouse remarries, in which case the coverage for all dependents terminates, or if any dependent becomes insured under another group insurance plan, becomes eligible for Medicare, or no longer qualifies as a dependent according to the terms of the contract. Alternatively, some carriers allow an employer to maintain coverage on dependents of a deceased employee by continuing to pay the required premium.

Handicapped Children Provision

As early as 1965, states began to require continuation of coverage on handicapped children beyond the age limit provided by the contract. Today, 40 states have such mandates and most insurers provide the benefits on all plans nationwide. The child must be unmarried, incapable of self-support because of mental or physical handicap, and primarily dependent upon the employee for support. This provision provides a vehicle for coverage of a group of individuals otherwise likely to be uninsurable.

Conversion Privilege

When insurance terminates under previously described circumstances, the right to convert to a personal medical care policy without evidence of insurability generally is available and mandated by some states. Until recently, only limited hospital, surgical, and medical benefits were required to be included in the converted policy. Since 1973, however, a few states have legislated the availability of major medical benefits as well. Insurers are providing the coverage where required, and investigating alternatives to filling the need for broader coverage under converted policies in the most cost-effective way.

COMPREHENSIVE PLAN VARIATIONS AND DIFFERENCES FROM SUPPLEMENTAL MAJOR MEDICAL

Single Formula

As described earlier, a comprehensive plan, in its simplest form, is a medical care benefit design that covers under one formula those expenses earlier considered basic benefits as well as those included in supplemental major medical benefits. In a pure comprehensive, that formula is applied to reasonable and customary charges without the inside limits of basic benefits, such as maximum hospital days or surgical schedules. Although a comprehensive plan can be written on a per-cause or policy year basis, the all-cause calendar year approach is used almost exclusively. The features described as applying to that type of supplemental major medical plan also apply to a calendar year comprehensive plan or their differences are discussed below.

Deductible and Coinsurance

Unlike supplemental major medical, a comprehensive deductible generally is referred to as an "initial" deductible rather than integrated or corridor, since at least in the pure comprehensive, the insured must bear expenses up to the deductible amount before the insurance carrier begins to reimburse for any charges. Further participation by the insured through coinsurance until the out-of-pocket maximum is reached applies in a pure comprehensive just as it does in a supplemental major medical plan.

However, to satisfy the market need for a single easy-to-understand design, but with some first-dollar benefits, many other modifications have been made in comprehensive plans concerning the application of the deductible and of coinsurance. The following are some of the variations available, either individually or in combination, depending on the products and underwriting practices of the insurer.

1. The deductible may be waived on all or on some portion of covered hospital expenses, such as the first $2,000, but applied to hospital expenses above that.
2. Coinsurance may be waived for the hospital expenses described above.

Together with waiver of the deductible, this creates the commonly called "full-pay hospital" area.

3. The deductible may be waived on surgeons' fees.
4. Surgeons' fees may be payable according to a schedule, plus coinsurance for reasonable and customary fees in excess of the schedule with or without a deductible between.
5. The deductible and coinsurance may be waived in other areas—such as $300 of supplemental accident expenses, physicians' hospital visits, or diagnostic tests—to further match the base-plus major medical concept.
6. The deductible may be waived on certain outpatient services—such as ambulatory surgical facilities, preadmission tests, and second surgical opinions—to encourage their use and to avoid high cost hospital confinements if not necessary.
7. The coinsurance percent reimbursement level may be higher than the coinsurance level for the rest of the plan, increased even to 100 percent for some outpatient services to further encourage their use.

Clearly, as some first-dollar (no deductible) and full-pay (no coinsurance) benefits are built into a comprehensive plan, it becomes more like a base-plus major medical and loses some of its simplicity. Its potential for cost containment may be either diminished or increased depending upon the variation and its utilization.

Maximum Benefit

The overall maximum benefit and its reinstatement provisions apply to the entire comprehensive plan, since there is no separate major medical portion. With the rapid escalation of medical care costs, such earlier maximums as $100,000 or $250,000 typically have been increased to $1 million. Many plans even have an unlimited lifetime maximum.

Preexisting Conditions

The preexisting conditions limitation in supplemental major medical plans, from the beginning, has only applied to the major medical portion of the total plan, because benefits under the basic portion were relatively limited. This allowed some reimbursement for a preexisting condition, but up to controlled maximums. Although basic benefits have become so liberal that large amounts can now be paid under that part of the plan for such a condition, the limitation continues to apply only to the major medical.

Application of the same limitation to a comprehensive plan would be much more restrictive, since it would apply to all benefits. A variation on the theme, therefore, has been developed. It defines a preexisting condition in the same way as for a supplemental major medical plan and covers it from the effective date of insurance, but applies a dollar limit, such as $1,000, for the first year of coverage.

Extension of Benefits

The supplemental major medical one-year extension of benefits after termination for a totally disabling injury or sickness applies to the entire comprehensive plan. The confusion of 3 months for basic benefits and 12 for major medical is eliminated.

SUMMARY

The number of persons covered under some form of major medical insurance continues to grow. To the extent paid for with employer funds, the cost of additional services demanded is felt only very indirectly by the insured; but the pressure driving medical costs upward grows relentlessly. As a result of continued cost escalation, renewed interest exists in medical care plan designs aimed at maintaining the insured's concern with the cost of care by requiring that he or she share in it. The comprehensive plan design fits that bill, but the flexibility in plan design available in the marketplace can be used best to serve each policyholder's particular interests.

CHAPTER 14

Dental Plan Design

RONALD L. HULING AND
JOHN T. LYNCH

INTRODUCTION

In recent years, dental plans have been one of the nation's fastest growing employee benefits. From 1965 to 1979, dental plan participation grew from 3 million individuals to over 70 million. By 1985, enrollment is expected to exceed 100 million.

It is not surprising that dental plans have become so popular, because dental disease in the United States is almost universal. Approximately 95 percent of the population is affected by tooth decay. It is estimated that half of the children in the U.S. experience tooth decay by age two, and over 40 percent of all young adults have some form of gum disease. It is estimated that one fifth of the population has lost all their natural teeth and that, even today, there are over one billion unfilled cavities. Probably less than half of the population is receiving proper treatment, and it is fair to say that millions of manhours are lost annually in business because of dental disease.

The Difference between Medicine and Dentistry

Medicine and dentistry have many differences, and sound dental plan design recognizes these. Two of the more important differences relate to the location and nature of care.

Location. The practice of the typical physician is hospital oriented, while dentists practice almost exclusively in an office setting. Partly because of these practice differences, physicians tend to associate with other physicians with greater frequency than dentists with other dentists. This isolation, along with the inherent differences in the nature of medical and dental care, tends to produce a greater variety of dental care patterns than is the case in medicine. In addition, practicing in isolation does not afford the same opportunities for peer review and general quality control.

Nature of Care. Perhaps contributing more significantly to the differences in medicine and dentistry are the important differences between the nature of medical and dental care. Medical care usually is mandatory, while dental care is often elective. In medicine, the patient typically visits a physician with certain symptoms—often pain or discomfort—and seeks relief. Whether real or imagined, the patient's perception is that delay can mean more pain and, under certain circumstances, even death. Under these circumstances, the physician's charge for treatment traditionally has not been an issue, perhaps from fear of alienating the individual whom the patient has entrusted with his care or perhaps in gratitude for the treatment.

Dental treatment, on the other hand, often is elective. Again, unless there is pain or trauma, dental care often is postponed. The patient recognizes that life is not at risk and as a result has few reservations about postponing treatment. In fact, postponement may be preferable to the patient—perhaps because of an aversion to visiting the dentist, which was rooted many years in the past when dental technology was less well developed.

As a result, dentists' charges for major courses of treatment are often discussed in advance of the treatment where there is no pain or trauma and, like any number of other consumer decisions, the patient may opt to defer the treatment to a later time and spend the money elsewhere.

A second difference in the nature of care is that, while medical care is rarely cosmetic, dental care often is requested for cosmetic purposes. A crown, for example, may be necessary to save a tooth, but it also may be used to correct only minor decay because it improves the patient's appearance. Many people place orthodontia into the same category—although evidence exists that failure to obtain needed orthodontic care may result in major gum problems in later life.

A third major difference between the nature of medical and dental care is that dentistry often offers alternate procedures for treating disease and restoring teeth, many of which are equally effective. For example, a molar cavity might be treated by a two-surface gold inlay, which may cost nine times as much as a simple amalgam filling. Another condition might indicate the need for partial removable dentures, which cost one fifth as much as fixed bridgework. In these instances, the choice of the appropriate procedure is influenced by a number of factors including the cost of the alternatives, the condition of the affected tooth and the teeth surrounding it, and the likelihood that a particular approach will be successful.

There are other significant differences in medical care and dentistry that will have an effect on plan design. These include frequency of treatment, the cost of the typical treatment, and the emphasis on prevention.

When dental and medical plans cover the same or similar groups, there will be significantly higher utilization of the dental plan than of the medical plan. In one year, for example, 60 percent of a covered group may use a dental plan, whereas only 12 to 14 percent may use the medical program. One major company had seven times as many dental claims each year as medical. Of course, for any one company, the relative number of claims between the two plans will be heavily influenced by plan design, particularly the deductible provisions.

Another significant difference is that dental expenses generally are lower, more predictable, and budgetable. The average dental claim check is only about $100. Medical claims, on the average, are much higher.

The last difference of significance is the emphasis on prevention. The advantages of preventive dentistry are clearly documented. While certain medical diseases and injuries are self-healing, dental disease, once started, almost always gets progressively worse. Therefore, preventive care probably is more productive in dentistry than medicine.

Providers of Dental Benefits

Providers of dental benefits generally can be separated into four categories: insurance companies; Blue Cross and Blue Shield organizations; state dental association plans (e.g., Delta plans); and others, including self-insured, self-administered plans, and group practice or HMO-type plans. Insurance companies cover, by far, the largest share of the population (about 60 percent of those eligible for dental benefits in 1978). Dental service corporations, sponsored largely by the various state dental associations, enroll about 25 percent, and Blue Cross/Blue Shield plans another 10 percent. The balance (about 5 percent) participate in other types of plans.

Insurance company-administered dental benefits and most self-insured, self-administered plan benefits are provided on an "indemnity" or reimbursement basis. Expenses incurred by eligible individuals are submitted to the administrator, typically an insurer, for payment; and, if the expense is covered, the appropriate payment is calculated according to the provisions of the plan. Payment generally is made directly to the covered employee, unless assigned by the employee to the provider. When benefits are provided on this basis, the plan sponsor normally has substantial latitude in determining who and what is to be covered and at what level.

The dental benefits of both the dental service corporations and the Blue Cross/Blue Shield plans generally are provided on a "service" basis. The major differences between indemnity and service benefits relate to the roles of the provider and the covered individual. Service benefits are payable directly to the provider, generally according to a contract, which fixes the reimbursement level between the dentist and the plan. In some instances, this payment may actually be lower than what would be charged to a direct-pay or indemnity patient. Despite the differences between the indemnity and service approaches, plan design plays an equally important role in both.

Under the group practice or HMO-type arrangement, a prescribed range of dental services is provided to eligible participants, generally in return for a prepaid, fixed, and uniform payment. Services are provided by dentists practicing in group practice clinics, or in individual practice but affiliated for purposes of providing plan benefits to eligible participants. Many of the individuals eligible under these arrangements are covered through collectively bargained self-insurance benefit trusts. In these instances, trust fund payments are used either to reimburse dentists operating in group practice clinics or to pay the prescribed fixed per capita fee. Group practice or HMO-type arrangements generally offer little latitude in plan design. As a result, the balance of this chapter, since it is largely devoted to the issue of plan design, may have limited application to these types of arrangements.

Covered Dental Expenses

Virtually all dental problems fall into eight professional treatment categories:

Diagnostic. Examination to determine the existence of dental disease or to evaluate the condition of the mouth. Included in this category would be such procedures as X-rays and routine oral examinations.

Preventive. Procedures to preserve and maintain dental health. Included in this category are topical cleaning, space maintainers, and the like.

Restorative. Procedures for the repair and reconstruction of natural teeth, including removal of dental decay and installation of fillings and crowns.

Endodontics. Treatment of dental-pulp disease and therapy within existing teeth. Root canal therapy is an example of this type of procedure.

Periodontics. Treatment of the gums and other supporting structures of the teeth, primarily for maintenance or improvement of the gums. Quadrant scraping is an example of a periodontic procedure.

Oral Surgery. Tooth extractions and other surgery of the mouth and jaw.

Prosthodontics. Replacement of missing teeth and the construction, replacement, and repair of artificial teeth and similar devices. Preparation of bridges and dentures is included in this category.

Orthodontics. Correction of malocclusion and abnormal tooth position through repositioning of natural teeth.

In addition to the recognition of treatment or services in these eight areas, the typical dental plan also includes provision for palliative treatment (i.e. procedures to minimize pain, including anesthesia), emergency care, and consultation.

These eight different types of procedures usually are categorized into three or four general groupings for purposes of plan design. The first classification often includes both preventive and diagnostic expenses. The second general grouping includes all minor restorative procedures. Charges in the restorative, endodontic, periodontic, and oral surgery areas are included in this classification. The third broad grouping, often combined with the second, includes major restorative work (e.g., prosthodontics). The fourth separate classification covers orthodontic expenses. Later in this chapter, plan design is examined in greater detail, with specific differences evaluated in traditional plan design applicable to each of these three or four general groupings.

Types of Plans

Dental plans covering the vast majority of all employees can be divided broadly into two types: scheduled and nonscheduled. Other approaches discussed below are essentially variations of these two basic plan types.

Scheduled plans. These are characterized by a listing of fixed allowances by procedure. For example, the plan might pay $5 for an oral exam and $75 for root canal therapy. In addition, the scheduled plan may include deductibles and coinsurance (i.e., percentage cost-sharing provisions). Where deductibles are included in scheduled plans, amounts usually are small or, in some cases, required on a lifetime basis only.

Coinsurance provisions are extremely rare in scheduled plans, since the benefits of coinsurance can be achieved through the construction of the schedule (i.e., the level of reimbursement for each procedure in the schedule can be set for specific reimbursement objectives). For example, if it is preferable to reimburse a higher percentage of the cost of preventive procedures than of other procedures, the schedule can be constructed to accomplish this goal.

There are three major advantages to scheduled plans:

Cost Control.   Benefit levels are fixed and, therefore, less susceptible to inflationary increases.

Uniform Payments.   In certain instances, it may be important to provide the same benefit regardless of regional cost differences. Collectively bargained plans occasionally may take this approach to ensure the "equal treatment" of all members.

Easy to Understand.   It is clear to both the plan participant and the dentist how much is to be paid for each procedure.

In addition, scheduled plans sometimes are favored for employee-relations reasons. As the schedule is updated, improvements can be communicated to employees. If the updating occurs on a regular basis, this will be a periodic reminder to employees of the plan and its merits.

There also are disadvantages to scheduled plans. First, benefit levels, as well as internal relationships, must be examined periodically and changed when necessary to maintain reimbursement objectives. Second, where participants are dispersed geographically, plan reimbursement levels will vary according to the cost of dental care in a particular area, unless multiple schedules are utilized. Third, if scheduled benefits are established at levels that are near the maximum of the reasonable and customary range, dentists who normally charge at below prevailing levels may be influenced to adjust their charges.

Nonscheduled plans.   Sometimes referred to as comprehensive plans, these are written to cover some percentage of the "reasonable and customary" charges, or the charges most commonly made by dentists in the community. For any single procedure, the usual and customary charge typically is set at the 90th percentile. This means that the usual and customary charge level will cover the full cost of the procedure for 90 percent of the claims submitted in that geographical area.

Nonscheduled plans generally include a deductible, typically a calendar year deductible of $25 or $50, and reimburse at different levels for different classes of procedures. Preventive and diagnostic expenses typically are covered either in full or at very high reimbursement levels. Reimbursement levels for other procedures usually are then scaled down from the preventive and diagnostic level, based on design objectives of the employer.

There are two major advantages to nonscheduled plans:

Uniform Reimbursement Level.   While the dollar payment may vary by area and dentists, the percent of the total cost reimbursed by the plan is uniform.

Automatically Adjusts for Change.   The nonscheduled plan adjusts automatically, not only for inflation but also for variations in the relative value of specific procedures.

This approach also has disadvantages. First, because benefit levels adjust automatically for increases in the cost of care, in periods of rapidly escalating prices, cost control can be a problem. Second, once a plan is installed on this basis, the opportunities for modest benefit improvements, made primarily for employee relations purposes, are limited, at least relative to the scheduled approach. Third, except for claims for which predetermination of benefits is appropriate, it rarely is clear in advance what the specific payment for a particular service will be, either to patient or dentist.

Other approaches are, for the most part, merely variations of the two basic plans. Included in this list are combination plans, incentive plans, and dental combined with major medical plans.

Combination Plan.   This is simply a plan in which certain procedures are reimbursed on a scheduled basis, while others are reimbursed on a nonscheduled basis. In other words, it is a hybrid. While many variations exist, a common design in combination plans is to provide preventive and diagnostic coverage on a nonscheduled basis (i.e., a percentage of usual and customary, normally without a deductible). Other procedures than preventive and diagnostic are provided on a scheduled basis.

The principal advantage of a combination plan is that it provides a balance between (1) the need to emphasize preventive care, and (2) cost control. Procedures that are traditionally the most expensive are covered on a scheduled basis, and, except where benefit levels are established by a collective bargaining agreement, the timing of schedule improvements is at the employer's discretion. Preventive and diagnostic expenses, however, adjust automatically so the incentive for preventive care does not lose its effectiveness as dental care costs increase.

The combination approach shares many of the same disadvantages as the scheduled and unscheduled plans, at least for certain types of expenses. Benefit levels—for other than preventive and diagnostic expenses—must be evaluated periodically. Scheduled payments do not reimburse at uniform levels for geographically dispersed participants. And dentists may be influenced by the schedule allowances to adjust their charges. Also, actual plan payments for preventive and diagnostic expenses rarely are identified in advance. Finally, it can be said that the combination approach is more complex than either the scheduled or unscheduled alternatives.

Incentive Plan. This type, a second variation, promotes sound dental hygiene through increasing reimbursement levels. Incentive coinsurance provisions generally apply only to preventive and maintenance (i.e., minor restorative) procedures, with other procedures covered on either a scheduled or nonscheduled basis. Incentive plans are designed to encourage individuals to visit the dentist regularly, without the plan sponsor having to absorb the cost of any accumulated neglect. Such plans generally reimburse at one level during the first year, with coinsurance levels typically increasing from year to year only for those who obtained needed treatment in prior years. For example, the initial coinsurance level for preventive and maintenance expenses might be 60 percent, increasing to 70 percent, 80 percent, and, finally, 90 percent on an annual basis as long as needed care is obtained. If, in any one year, there is a failure to obtain the required level of care, the coinsurance percentage reverts back to its original level.

The incentive portion of an incentive plan may or may not be characterized by deductibles. When deductibles are included in these plans, it is not unusual for them to apply on a lifetime basis.

The incentive concept, on the one hand, has two major advantages. In theory, the design of the plan encourages regular dental care and reduces the incidence of more serious dental problems in the future. Also, these plans generally have lower first-year costs than most nonscheduled plans.

On the other hand, there are major disadvantages. First, an incentive plan can be complicated to explain and even more complicated to administer. Second, even in parts of the country where this design is more prevalent, little evidence exists to suggest that the incentive approach is effective in promoting sound dental hygiene. Finally, this particular plan is vulnerable to misunderstanding. For example, what happens if the participant's dentist postpones the required treatment until the beginning of the next plan year?

Plans Providing Both Medical and Dental Coverage. The last of the variations is the plan that provides both medical and dental coverage. During the infancy of dental benefits, such plans were quite popular.

These plans generally are characterized by a "common" deductible amount that applies to the sum of both medical and dental expenses. Coinsurance levels may be identical, and, sometimes, the maximum applies to the combination of medical and dental expenses. However, recent design of these plans has made a distinction between dental and medical expenses so each may have its own coinsurance provisions and maximums.

The advantages of this approach are the same as for the nonscheduled plan (i.e., uniform reimbursement level, automatically adjusts to change, and relatively easy to understand). But this approach fails to recognize the difference between medicine and dentistry, unless special provisions are made for dental benefits. It must be written with a major medical carrier, whether this carrier is competent or not to handle dental protection; it makes it extremely difficult to separate and evaluate dental experience; and it shares the same disadvantages as the nonscheduled approach.

Orthodontic Expenses

With possibly a few exceptions, orthodontic benefits never are written without other dental coverage. Nonetheless, orthodontic benefits present a number of design peculiarities which suggest this subject should be treated separately.

Orthodontic services, unlike nonorthodontic procedures, generally are rendered only once in an individual's lifetime; orthodontic problems are highly unlikely to recur. Orthodontic maximums, therefore, typically are expressed on a lifetime basis. Deductibles, which are applicable only to orthodontic services, also are often expressed on a lifetime basis. However, it is quite common for orthodontic benefits to be provided without deductibles, since a major purpose of the deductible—to eliminate small, nuisance-type claims—is of no consequence.

Because adult orthodontia generally is cosmetic, and also because the best time for orthodontic work is during adolescence, many plans limit orthodontic coverage to persons under age 19. However, an increasing number of plans are including adult orthodontia as well, and many participants are taking advantage of this feature.

The coinsurance level for orthodontic expenses is typically 50 percent, but it varies widely depending on the reimbursement levels under other parts of the plan. It is common for the orthodontic reimbursement level to be the same as what applies for major restorative procedures.

Reflecting the nature of orthodontic work—and unlike virtually any other benefit—orthodontic benefits often are paid in installments, instead of at the conclusion of the course of treatment. Because the program of treatment frequently extends over several years, it would be unreasonable to reimburse for the entire course of treatment at the end of the extended time.

Factors Affecting the Cost of the Dental Plan

A number of factors including design of the plan, characteristics of the covered group, and employer's approach to plan implementation affect the cost of the dental plan.

Plan Design. Many issues must be addressed before determining a particular design that is sound and reflects the needs of the plan sponsor. Included in this list are the type of plan, deductibles, coinsurance, plan maximums, treatment of preexisting conditions, whether covered services should be limited, and orthodontic coverage.

An employer's choice between scheduled and nonscheduled benefits requires a look at the employer's objectives. The advantages and disadvantages of scheduled versus nonscheduled, of combination plans, and of others have been described earlier in this chapter. In addition, at least one major insurer suggests that a scheduled plan, where scheduled benefit levels approximate prevailing charges, may prove to be more expensive than a comparable nonscheduled plan. The carrier's explanation is tied to the nature of the practice of dentistry. A wide range of charges exists within the dental profession for any particular procedure. Where benefits are scheduled and the schedule approximates prevailing levels, dentists who normally charge at the lower end of the range may have a tendency to increase their charges. Nonscheduled plans do not afford the dentists this kind of information.

Deductibles may or may not be included as an integral part of the design of the plan. Deductibles usually are written on a lifetime or calendar-year basis, with the calendar-year approach by far the more common.

Numerous dental procedures involve very little expense. Therefore, the deductible eliminates frequent payments for small claims that can be readily budgeted. For example, a $25 deductible can eliminate as much as 20 percent of the number of adult claims and 30 percent of the claims on children. A $50 deductible can reduce the number of claims by as much as 45 percent for adults and 55 percent for children. Clearly, a deductible can effectively control the cost of claim administration.

However, evidence exists that early detection and treatment of dental problems will produce a lower level of claims over the long term. Most insurers feel the best way to promote early detection is to pay virtually all the cost of preventive and diagnostic services. Therefore, these services often are not subject to a deductible.

Several insurance companies are advocates of a lifetime deductible, designed to lessen the impact of accumulated dental neglect. It is particularly effective where the employer is confronted with a choice of (1) not covering preexisting conditions at all; (2) covering these conditions, but forced otherwise to cut back on the design of the plan; or (3) offering a lifetime deductible, the theory being, "If you'll spend X dollars to get your mouth into shape once and for all, we'll take care of a large part of your future dental needs."

Opponents of the lifetime deductible concept claim the following disadvantages:

A lifetime deductible promotes early overutilization by those anxious to take advantage of the benefits of the plan.

Once satisfied, lifetime deductibles are of no further value for the presently covered group.

The lifetime deductible introduces employee turnover as an important cost consideration of the plan.

If established at a level that will have a significant impact on claim costs and premium rates, a lifetime deductible may result in adverse employee reaction to the plan.

More and more dental plans are being designed, either through construction of the schedule or the use of coinsurance, so that the patient pays a portion of the costs for all but preventive and diagnostic services. The intent is to reduce spending on optional dental care and to promote cost-effective dental practice. Preventive and diagnostic expenses generally are reimbursed at 80 to 100 percent of the usual and customary charges. Full reimbursement is quite common.

The reimbursement level for restorative and replacement procedures generally is lower than that for preventive and diagnostic procedures. Restorations, and in some cases replacements, may be reimbursed at 70 to 85 percent. In other cases, the reimbursement level for replacements is lower than for restorative treatment.

Orthodontics, and occasionally major replacements, have the lowest reimbursement levels of all. In most instances, the plans reimburse no more than 50 to 60 percent of the usual and customary charges for these procedures.

Most dental plans include a plan maximum, written on a calendar year basis, which is applicable to nonorthodontic expenses. Orthodontic expenses generally are subject to a separate lifetime maximum. Also, in some instances, a separate lifetime maximum may apply to nonorthodontic expenses.

Unless established at a fairly low level, a lifetime maximum will have little or no impact on claim liability and only serves to further complicate design of the plan. Calendar year maximums, though, encourage participants to seek less costly care and may help to spread out the impact of accumulated dental neglect over the early years of the plan. The typical calendar year maximum is somewhere between $750 and $1,500.

To put things in perspective: in 1977, only about 9 percent of people visiting a dentist spent from $300 to $999 annually, including insurance company payments, and just 2 percent spent over $1,000 or more, including insurance company payments. Most claims are small (42 percent spent $50 or less) and, therefore, the maximum's impact on plan costs is minor.

Another major consideration is the treatment of preexisting conditions. The major concern is the expense associated with the replacement of teeth extracted prior to the date of coverage. Preexisting conditions are treated in a number of ways:

They may be excluded.

They may be treated as any other condition.

They may be covered on a limited basis (perhaps one half of the normal reimbursement level) or subject to a lifetime deductible.

If treated as any other condition, the cost of the plan in the early years (nonorthodontic only) will be increased by about 12 to 15 percent.

Another plan design consideration is the range of procedures to be covered. In addition to orthodontics, other procedures occasionally excluded are surgical periodontics. Although rare, some plans cover only preventive and maintenance expenses.

Orthodontic expenses, as noted, may be excluded. However, where these are covered, the plan design may include a separate deductible to discourage "shoppers." The cost of orthodontic diagnosis and models is about $50, whether or not treatment is undertaken. The inclusion of a separate orthodontic deductible eliminates reimbursement for these expenses. Also, orthodontic plan design typically includes both heavy coinsurance and limited maximums to guarantee patient involvement.

An indication of the sensitivity of dental plan costs to some of the plan design features discussed can be seen in the following illustration. Assume a nonscheduled base model plan, which has a $25 calendar-year deductible applicable to all expenses other than orthodontics. The reimbursement, or employer coinsurance, levels are:

100% for diagnostic and preventive services (Type I).

75% for basic services (Type II), including anesthesia, basic restoration, oral surgery, endodontics, and periodontics.

50% for major restoration and prosthodontic (Type III).

50% for orthodontics (Type IV).

There also is an annual benefit maximum of $750 for Types I, II, and III services, and a lifetime maximum of $750 for orthodontics. Based on this base model plan, Table 14–1 shows the approximate premium sensitivity to changes in plan design. If two or more of the design changes shown in this table are considered together, an approximation of the resulting value may be obtained by multiplying the relative values of the respective changes.

The change in deductibles has a significant impact on cost, as much as a 20 percent reduction in cost to increase the deductible from $25 to $100. The change in benefit maximums has some impact, but it is minor. Coinsurance has a definite effect, especially changes for restoration, replacement, and orthodontic portions of the plan, all of which represent about 80 to 85 percent of the typical claim costs. Finally, the inclusion of orthodontics in the base plan is another item of fairly high cost.

Characteristics of the Covered Group. A second factor affecting the cost of the dental plan is the characteristics of the covered group. Important considerations include, but are not limited to, the following:

Table 14-1
Model Dental Plan

	Relative Value (in percent)
Base model plan	100%
Design changes:	
Deductible:	
Remove $25 deductible	113
Raise to $50	91
Raise to $100	80
Benefit maximum (annual):	
Lower from $750 to $500	97
Raise to $1,500	105
Coinsurance:	
Liberalize percent to: 100-80-60-60*	108
Tighten percent to: 80-70-50-50*	92
Orthodontics:	
Exclude	89

* For Types I, II, III and IV services, respectively.

Age.

Sex.

Location.

Presence of fluoride in the water supply.

Income level of the participants.

Occupation.

The increased incidence of high-cost dental procedures at older ages generally makes coverage of older groups more expensive. Average charges usually increase from about age 30 up to age 55 or so and then decline. One possible explanation for the decline from age 55 to 65 is the existence of prosthetic devices at that point and the generally poor dental habits of the current older generation.

Sex is another consideration. Females tend to have higher utilization rates than males. One study showed that females average 1.8 visits to dentists per year compared with 1.6 for males. These differences probably are attributable to better dental awareness by females rather than to a higher need.

Charge levels, practice patterns, and the availability of dentists vary considerably by locale. Charge levels range anywhere from 85 to 125 percent of the national average, and differences exist in the frequency of use for certain procedures as well. There is evidence, for example, that more expensive procedures are performed relatively more often in Los Angeles than, say, in Philadelphia.

Interestingly, the presence of fluoride and the time it has been in the water supply also are important. Plan costs can vary up to 40 percent between areas with natural fluoride and those without.

Another consideration is income. A recent study shows that total family expenditures for dental care (for those undergoing dental treatment) are more than twice as high for families whose income is $28,000 or more than for those with incomes of $10,000 to $13,000. In addition, 95.5 percent of all families in the $28,000-plus bracket use the plan compared to only about 69.2 percent of the $10,000 to $13,000 families.

Essentially four reasons may account for income being a key factor. First, the higher the income level, the greater the likelihood the individual already has an established program of dental hygiene. Second, in many areas there is greater accessibility to dental care in the high-income neighborhoods. Third, a greater tendency exists on the part of higher-income individuals to elect higher-cost procedures. Last, high-income people tend to use more expensive dentists.

Another important consideration is the occupation of the covered group. While difficult to explain, evidence suggests considerable variation between blue-collar plans and plans covering salaried or mixed groups. One possible explanation is higher awareness and income-level differences. One insurer estimates that blue-collar employees are 20 to 30 percent less expensive to insure than white-collar employees.

Sponsor's Approach to Implementation. The last of the factors affecting plan costs is the sponsor's approach to implementation. Dental work, unlike medical care, lends itself to "sandbagging" (i.e., deferral of needed treatment until after the plan's effective date). Everything else being equal, plans announced well in advance of the effective date, tend to have poorer first-year experience than plans announced only shortly before the effective date. Advance knowledge of the deferred effective date easily can increase first-year costs from 25 to 30 percent or even more.

Employee contributions are another consideration. Dental plans, if offered on a contributory basis, may be prone to adverse selection. While there is evidence that the adverse selection is not as great as was once anticipated, most insurers continue to discourage contributory plans. Many insurance companies will still underwrite dental benefits on a contributory basis, provided there are appropriate safeguards. Typical safeguards include:

Combining dental plan participation and contributions with medical plan participation.

Limiting enrollment to a single offering, thus preventing subsequent sign-ups or dropouts.

Requiring dental examinations before joining the plan and limiting or excluding treatment for conditions identified in the exam.

The last item to be addressed, which is dealt with in several chapters later in this book, is claims administration. The nature of dentistry and dental plan design suggests that claims administration is very important. While several years may lapse before an insured has occasion to file a medical claim, rarely does the year pass during which a family will not visit the dentist at least once. Therefore, claims administration capability is an extremely important consideration in selecting a plan carrier—and might very well be the most important consideration.

One key element of claims administration is "predetermination of benefits." This common plan feature requires the dentist to prepare a treatment plan that shows the work and cost before any services begin. This treatment plan generally is required only for nonemergency services and only if the cost is expected to exceed some specified level, such as $200. The carrier processes this information to determine exactly how much the dental plan will pay. Also, selected claims are referred to the carrier's dental consultants to assess the appropriateness of the recommended treatment. If there are any questions, the dental consultant discusses the treatment plan with the dentist prior to performing the services.

Predetermination is very important both in promoting better quality care and in reducing costs. These benefits are accomplished by spotting unnecessary expenses, treatments that cannot be expected to last, instances of coverage duplication, and charges higher than usual and customary before extensive and expensive work begins. One major insurance company indicates that predetermination of benefits can be effective in reducing claim costs by as much as 15 percent. Predetermination also advises the covered individual of the exact amount of reimbursement under the plan prior to commencement of treatment.

CHAPTER 15

Vision Care Benefits

ROBERT M. NEISWANGER

INTRODUCTION

The vision care benefits described in this chapter present some of the same actuarial and administrative problems inherent in other benefits that cover high-frequency occurrences for which there is a comparatively low charge per occurrence. Prescription drug benefits and, to some degree, dental plans present similar problems. Developing a successful vision care program is further complicated because covered services include a product—lenses and frames—the latter usually selected by the individual for aesthetic value, rather than primarily for utility.

Furthermore, unlike other health insurance covered services, providers of glasses offer their product in a highly competitive marketplace. At a time when the concept of introducing competition into the health care delivery system is being discussed, the importance of an existing competitive delivery system should not be disregarded, nor should insurance plans be developed that discourage the individual's interest in the cost of care.

Finally, the services to be covered under a vision care program involve eye examinations and glasses. Traditional group health programs already cover surgical and medical treatment of the eye necessitated by disease or injury. Some plans also cover eye examination and glasses if required because of accidental injury or the removal of cataracts. Of course, vision care covered services should not duplicate those services already covered by existing health sublines.

Group benefits for vision care are not new. Plans that reimburse on a schedule basis and that are similar in other respects to traditional plan design have been in force for many years. Recently, there has been some interest, stimulated by collective bargaining, in nonschedule plans that would enable the individual to obtain an examination and glasses by paying a relatively small deductible. To develop that type of benefit it is important to have some understanding about the providers of care: how services are delivered, what factors influence the individual's choice of product, and how these factors can be reflected in fees and utilization.

PROVIDERS OF CARE

Vision care services are provided by ophthalmologists, optometrists, and opticians whose functions generally are as follows:

Ophthalmologists

An ophthalmologist is a doctor of medicine or osteopathy. Basic graduate education is that of a physician or an osteopath with subsequent specialization and training in defects and diseases of the eye. The ophthalmologist may perform surgery and provides medical care and treatment in addition to prescribing corrective lenses.

Some ophthalmologists also dispense glasses, but the majority give the patient a written prescription and the patient then visits an optician for the preparation of the glasses.

In general, ophthalmologists are located in metropolitan areas because, as physicians who perform eye surgery as well as other vision care services, the ophthalmologist is on the staff of a hospital and his or her practice generally is located within the same geographical area as other physicians who use that hospital.

Optometrist

A doctor of optometry also is trained to perform a variety of ocular diagnostic procedures. The extent to which an optometrist may use pharmaceuticals varies, depending on state licensing requirements. Almost all optometrists dispense glasses in addition to their other professional duties.

There are approximately 20,000 optometrists currently practicing in the United States. While the majority of optometrists are in individual or small group practices, a number of large retail outlets are emerging in shopping centers and other areas where the location of the business is selected to be most attractive to the consumer.

Optician

An optician does not perform eye examinations or diagnose problems of the eye. The optician grinds or molds lenses in accordance with a prescription written by an ophthalmologist or optometrist. The lenses then are fitted into the frame and adjusted to fit the face. In general, the independent optician relies on ophthalmologists for patients.

COVERED SERVICES

As mentioned previously, vision care plans cover both a health service—an eye examination—and a product—lenses and frames.

Eye Examination

The plan covers an eye examination that may be performed by an ophthalmologist or optometrist and involves a case history and a series of tests. Most insurance plans limit covered examinations to one every year or, alternatively, one every two years. The length of the examination varies, depending on many factors, including the extent and nature of tests performed by the examiner. In addition to evaluating the structure of the eye and the possible need for corrective lenses, the examination attempts to detect certain eye diseases, such as glaucoma and cataracts, as well as systemic diseases, such as diabetes and hypertension.

Materials

Lenses. A variety of lenses are available and are prepared from a prescription written by an ophthalmologist or an optometrist. It is not the purpose of this chapter to describe the technical preparation of lenses and frames. Many dispensers order total fabrication, including lenses and frames, from a full-service laboratory. Some dispensers of glasses, however, also may perform certain laboratory services.

While lenses perform an essential corrective function, they may be selected by the individual for aesthetic reasons. For example, many individuals prefer contact lenses even though they are not medically necessary. Others want photosensitive lenses or oversized lenses, and these optional selections increase the price of the product. To control the potential cost of the program, some vision care plans provide limitations on certain types of lenses.

Frames. Frames usually are selected more for appearance than utility. There are over 200 foreign and domestic frame manufacturers and thousands of frame styles to choose from. Most dispensers display several hundred frames and change their display to conform with changes in fashion. Charges for frames vary significantly, particularly for "designer" frames and those endorsed by famous personalities. This range in price, and the highly personalized nature of the individual's frame selection, present certain problems in the design of a vision care plan that pays on a nonschedule basis.

FACTORS AFFECTING FEES

In general, the charges for an eye examination do not vary significantly among similar providers within a geographic area, provided the tests and length of the examination are similar.

However, a wide range in prices for glasses, including contact lenses, can exist in large metropolitan areas. Such factors as the number of providers, availability of large chain or retail outlets, and the extent of advertising

influence local retail prices. Furthermore, competition exists among manufacturers and laboratories, and that type of price and service competition
indirectly affects the retail price of the product.

The competitive price of glasses, plus the wide variety of styles in lenses
and frames, makes it virtually impossible to develop precise data on all
combinations of products. Unlike other health care services, fees in urban
areas may be less than in suburban areas.

MARKET POTENTIAL

Scheduled vision care benefits have been available for many years without generating any significant sales market. Within the past few years,
certain large unions have bargained for nonscheduled vision care programs,
and details of some bargaining agreements require the establishment of
participating provider plans (discussed later in this chapter).

The extent to which an underwriter may wish to develop a variety of
standard vision care products that can be offered to small- and medium-size
employers depends on an evaluation of the potential sales market. Programs, such as a participating provider plan, generate considerable start-up
costs and require claim and computer functions different from other lines of
insurance. The commitment of resources and the ability to amortize administrative costs also are a function of market potential. Therefore, some
providers may prefer to offer only schedule plans to programs of small and
medium size, and to retain the option of tailor-making plans for large
employers.

A perceived need by employees for the benefit is only one reason an
employer may purchase a vision care plan. Nevertheless, those who wear
glasses know their price and generally respond favorably to this addition to
the firm's benefit package. While the number of people with vision deficiencies tends to increase with age, a typical employee group is likely to
include between 40 and 60 percent with vision defects.

Addition of a vision care plan also may produce positive results that are
difficult to measure. For example, improved worker productivity and a
reduction in the number of accidents may occur. Many people do not wear
glasses because of lethargy, vanity, or cost, and the availability of a vision
care benefit not only defrays part of the cost but gives publicity to the
importance of eye care and prompts some people to place a higher priority
on this important health service.

Many reasons exist why employers and unions seek group programs to
protect employees. Certainly, one important reason is to create an employee satisfaction with the place of employment so as to attract new
employees and diminish turnover. Some feel this objective is best achieved
by providing programs that reimburse for high-frequency services such as
dental care, prescription drugs, and vision care. These programs provide
reimbursement to many employees and their families who might not other-

wise use the benefit program, thereby making them more aware of the advantages of working for an employer who has such a plan. In addition, the majority of group programs do not include benefits of this nature, and so individuals may perceive their program is superior to that of other companies.

Market potential also is limited because the predictable and elective nature of the service may require the underwriter to establish stringent underwriting rules to avoid adverse selection, and these rules preclude quotations on certain prospects. Employees often are aware of their need for eye examinations and glasses and the approximate cost. Thus, individuals can determine whether any required payroll deduction is likely to exceed the expected charge for the service. Also, those who know that they do not need glasses would be unlikely to enroll in a contributory plan. Therefore, some underwriters may not offer vision care without other lines of coverage unless no employee contributions are contemplated and all employees are to be covered.

BENEFIT DESIGN

There are three basic approaches to designing benefits for a vision care plan. These approaches are the schedule plan, the participating provider plan, and reasonable and customary charge plan. Each approach has advantages and disadvantages and, to date, no one pattern has emerged to dominate the marketplace.

Schedule Plans

These plans list the covered vision services and pay the charges of the provider, but not more than the amount listed for the services in the schedule. Figure 15-1 shows an example of a typical schedule plan.

Advantages. This type of basic approach for vision care has four advantages.

1. A schedule plan is likely to encourage economies on the part of individuals in selecting providers and products. In general, a delivery system that maintains the interest of the individual in "price" is likely to be less expensive for the employer than a program which may encourage more expensive products.

2. Schedule plans provide greater premium stability for employees because benefit payments do not change with inflation.

3. The schedule plans produce lower claim administrative costs because the plans are simpler to administer.

4. Schedule plans are less confusing to employees because the maximum benefit for each item is known in advance. Nonschedule plans do not cover certain items (these options are discussed later in the chapter) and so the individual who selects an option does not know what will be paid.

Figure 15-1
A Typical Schedule Plan

Procedure	Maximum Amount
Eye examination	$ 30
Lenses (pair)*	
Single vision	25
Bifocal	40
Trifocal	50
Lenticular	75
Frames	20
Contact lenses (pair)*	
1. If visual acuity is not correctable to 20/70 in the better eye, except by the use of contact lenses.	150
2. If the patient is being treated for a condition, such as keratoconus or anisometropia, and contact lenses are customarily used as part of the treatment.	150
3. If required following cataract surgery.	150
4. All other contact lenses.	45

* The maximum amount for a single lens is 50 percent of the amount shown for a pair of lenses.

Disadvantages. There are three:

1. Some employees interpret schedule amounts to represent the amount that should be charged by the provider. Such an interpretation may lead to ill feelings between employees and providers, particularly if scheduled amounts purposely are designed to be modest.

2. Schedule plans can be designed to bear some relationship to average charges. However, inflation can quickly destroy that relationship and may prompt employee pressures to increase the schedule.

3. Several schedules may be necessary to achieve benefit equity in situations where employees are located in different states.

Participating Provider Plans

Participating provider programs for vision care were developed on the premise that they would be successful because (1) that concept was widely used with prescription drugs, and (2) both programs cover not only a "service" but a product that has an acquisition cost and mark-up by the provider.

The vision care insurer or administrator offers all providers in the area a contract that fixes payment to the participating providers, and stipulates that the provider will not charge insured individuals more than the deductible for covered vision care services and products. Those who agree to this contract are called "participating providers."

Payment for covered services is made directly to the participating provider by the insurance company or administrator. Payments under schedule or under reasonable and customary programs may be made to the individual unless an assignment of benefits has been made to the provider. The formula for determining payment to the provider includes two items: first, the acquisition cost of the lenses and frames (material, laboratory charges and the like); second, the formula includes a dispensing fee (this amount may vary by single vision, bifocals, or trifocals, or there may be a single dispensing fee for all conventional glasses). This formula may vary slightly for medically necessary contact lenses. Reimbursement for contact lenses not medically necessary is expressed as a dollar amount, and that amount is known to the individual. Most plans also reimburse for any sales tax and include requirements concerning the quality of lenses and frames.

The participating provider contract and the fixed payment apply to all of the underwriter's policyholders who purchase plans on a participating provider basis and whose employees receive covered services in the area. However, the amount of the deductible, usually $5, $7, or $10, may vary. Some plans provide that the deductible may be satisfied by all covered services, but other programs use a deductible only for lenses and frames. Such items as the frequency when payment is made for examinations and glasses (some plans reimburse once every 12 months, other plans provide benefits once every 24 months) and the specifications on the "covered" lenses and frames also may vary among programs.

The insured individual also may obtain an examination and glasses from providers that do not elect to participate in the plan. In this situation, benefits are paid to the employee, not to the provider. The amount of benefit is based on the determination of reasonable and customary charges and, of course, the employee does not know that amount before the expenses for lenses and frames are incurred.

Advantages.   There are three for a participating provider plan:

1.   Employees know in advance the exact amount (i.e., the deductible amount) they must pay to obtain covered services from a participating provider. Since that amount is minimal, compared to the full retail charge, individuals are encouraged to have regular examinations and correct lenses.

2.   Participating provider agreements include quality assurance requirements. For example, the plan specifies minimum standards for lenses and frames. The participating contract may be cancelled if the provider abuses the plan or does not conform to the stipulated quality standards.

3.   The vision care provider may increase the dispensing fee for all participating providers, but the ability to control the timing of that increase provides some of the premium stability of a scheduled plan. Of course, part of the payment formula includes "acquisition cost" of the materials; there-

fore, increases in material and laboratory costs are passed automatically through to the vision care plan.

Disadvantages.   There are five:

1.   Individuals who select "options" not covered by the plan may lose the advantage of knowing what they must pay before agreeing to the service. Furthermore, unless the participating provider contract specifies what the provider charges for options, the plan may provide incentives for the provider to sell "options" to secure full retail price.

To evaluate this potential disadvantage, it is helpful to understand what material is covered by the plan. Participating provider contracts specify the plan covers all frames under a specific wholesale price. The participating provider is required to display these frames and, while the selection is broad, some individuals prefer frames with a higher wholesale cost than those covered by the plan. The plan also does not cover all types of lenses. For example, it may not cover prescription sunglasses, tinted lenses, or lenses over a certain size.

Obviously, the provider would prefer to charge full retail for these option items. However, some plans limit the charge to acquisition cost, plus a dispensing fee, because the option does not always generate additional expense for the provider. However, in some cases, options may necessitate counseling by the provider, and some participating provider plans recognize a slightly higher dispensing fee if options are selected.

The question of "option" items that are not considered under prescription drug plans is minimal, because such plans cover all drugs requiring a prescription (except for contraceptives and supplies over a certain quantity). Also, drugs are therapeutic and the patient expects only the item prescribed by the physician. However, glasses are selected primarily for appearance, with the patient choosing from a variety of styles.

2.   Participating providers need specific employee information before providing services for an individual. For example, if the plan limits glasses to once each two years, the participating provider needs to know that the individual is now eligible for another pair of glasses. This information should be available before the glasses are ordered so the provider may discuss the charge with the individual: deductible, if the glasses are covered, or full retail, if the individual is not eligible. Also, the participating provider needs to know the amounts of the deductible, exclusions, and options.

This information is furnished in various ways, but any method increases the administrative costs of the plan. Furthermore, if the employee is involved in furnishing advance certification, the procedure employees must follow is different and more complicated than for other health insurance benefits.

3.   All providers in the area will not enroll as participating providers. Thus, employees may be dissatisfied because their longstanding provider did not join or because it may be necessary to travel an inconvenient distance to locate a participating provider.

4. Monitoring the quality assurance provisions of a participating provider contract are difficult and expensive. Thus, this feature may not be
implemented to reduce plan administrative costs.

5. Participating providers cannot afford to accept a payment that produces a significantly lower profit margin than for noninsured patients.
Therefore, either dispensing fees will have to be raised periodically, increasing the cost of the plan, or a decrease in the number of participating
providers will result.

Reasonable and Customary Charge Plans

The basis for determining benefit payments under this type of plan is the
same as used under traditional health lines for nonscheduled benefits. The
payment is specified as a percentage—usually 80 percent—of the provider's charge, but not more than an amount established by the underwriter
as the maximum for the procedure. The maximum for each procedure is
revised periodically. In general, the maximum allowable covers the charge
made by almost all providers in the area.

Advantages. The third basic approach to designing benefits for a
vision care plan—reasonable and customary charge—has three advantages:

1. This plan provides benefit equity because, regardless of geographic
location, all individuals receive the same percentage benefit.

2. Employees share in inflation. That is the case because, as retail
charges increase, the dollar coinsurance amount paid by the individual also
increases.

3. The benefit may be similar to all other health benefits provided by
the employer. In other words, if other medical expenses are reimbursed
based on a percentage of charges, some employers may prefer to continue
that method rather than introducing a more complicated certification system, as would be the case with a participating provider plan.

Disadvantages. There are four:

1. Employees have little incentive to price shop.

2. Claim payments increase with inflation. Thus, policyholder budgeting may necessitate covering past losses, because premium levels may have
been inadequate.

3. The wide variation in charges because of product differences, and
the low level of charges compared to the amount charged by a physician for
a surgical procedure, mean it is difficult to establish maximum charge
guidelines for use by claim processors. Guidelines set too low generate
excessive administrative expenses and create employee dissatisfaction. For
example, if on the one hand the guideline is $40 and the provider charges
$45, the reduction of $5 may be more than offset by claim administrative
expenses. On the other hand, guidelines set too high do nothing to contain
costs.

4. It is difficult to provide a different reimbursement level for "options" and this plan could pay considerably more for items, such as designer frames, than either the schedule or the participating provider plan.

EXCLUSIONS AND LIMITATIONS

Vision care programs usually limit the frequency for eye examinations and glasses. For example, the individual may not have a covered exam and glasses until 24 months have elapsed from the time the last exam or glasses or both, were covered by the plan.

Plans do not provide the same reimbursement for medically necessary contact lenses as for contact lenses primarily for aesthetic purposes. The schedule plan illustrates the manner in which "medically necessary" contact lenses may be defined. In general, even under participating provider or reasonable and customary plans, cosmetic contacts are paid at a specified dollar amount.

Nonschedule plans also provide that certain services are optional and not subject to the full provisions of the plan. For example, if the individual wishes oversized lenses, plan reimbursement is intended to be at the same level as would have been provided for standard-size lenses.

Of course, vision care programs exclude eye services covered under the traditional health program. A sample list of other exclusions follows:

1. Lenses that can be obtained without prescription.
2. Orthoptics, vision training or subnormal vision aids.
3. Any service or supply not listed as a covered service or supply.
4. Benefits provided under workers' compensation.

TYPES OF VISION CARE PROVIDERS

Many types of underwriters can make available vision care benefit plans. Two of the more common providers are insurance companies and Blue Cross/Blue Shield organizations. These traditional mechanisms, with experienced claim, underwriting, and legal staffs offer distinct advantages to buyers who already have their group benefits with the insurance company or Blue plan. However, other mechanisms, in a given situation, may offer an attractive program to the employer. This is particularly true in situations involving a service-type, participating provider plan, similar to that described earlier in this chapter. That type of plan not only requires the establishment and maintenance of a network of participating providers but a claim payment system designed to work effectively and efficiently with this specialized benefit.

Some insurance companies and Blues have networks of providers and dedicated claim payment systems, but these may have been established in specific areas and for very large group buyers and so may not be available everywhere for all sizes of groups.

Alternative mechanisms that administer vision care programs are:

1.   Local providers may band together to offer the group purchaser a "closed panel" type of delivery mechanism. These groups may be reimbursed on the traditional fee-for-service, or by acquisition cost plus dispensing fee or capitation system.

2.   The employer may contract directly with the same organization that provides safety glasses for plant employees. Employees may obtain lenses and frames and other services either at no cost or at a discount.

3.   Specialty companies also have been established that are not closely related to the providers of vision care services. These companies are similar to the specialty organizations that administer prescription drug programs and sell their administrative services. They have recognized there is currently a limited market for service-type participating provider vision care, but that market requires a specialized product and administration. All the traditional insuring and administrative mechanisms may not establish these programs because of start-up and administrative costs. Thus, the specialty company markets its networks and administrative skills to others who may wish to establish vision care programs.

Employer/buyers of group vision care programs should consider more than the traditional competitive factors (rates, retention, service, and the like) in selecting a mechanism for a participating provider program. If reimbursement is to be based on acquisition cost plus dispensing fee, the employer should know who will establish the amount of dispensing fee and how often that fee is to be redetermined. While the dispensing fee must be sufficient to attract a reasonable number of participating providers, it should not be so high as to unnecessarily increase claim payments. It is also important for the employer to know the extent of participating provider networks. Some employers prefer relatively few participating providers, but others want a broad network, including all provider specialties. Furthermore, buyers should be certain the type of lenses and frames covered by the participating agreement offer both quality and style that is pleasing to most employees.

CONCLUSION

Vision care benefits are another example of the expansion of employee benefits to cover high-frequency, low-cost medical services, as opposed to the more traditional concept of insurance as a means of protecting the individual from major financial loss.

It is clear employees are receptive to programs that reimburse for such items as dental expenses, prescription drugs, and glasses. While taken as a single expense, any one of these items is affordable for most people in the employed population; nevertheless, these expenses often are incurred in combination and their total, particularly for individuals with families, can represent a large financial commitment for the employee.

Finally, it is important that claim procedures be as efficient and accurate as possible so the presence of a benefit does not greatly increase the "cost" of the medical service by the addition of significant claim administration costs. In fact, most programs have been successful in that objective.

CHAPTER 16

An Overview of Group Disability Income Insurance

DONALD J. DOUDNA

Losing the ability to work can be devastating to a family's emotional and financial well-being. Yet, the exposure of disability often is neglected by families in their financial planning and not dealt with sufficiently by employee benefit plans. After a brief analysis of the disability exposure, this chapter focuses on issues in providing disability income coverage for employee groups and the various products available for this purpose.

POSSIBILITY OF DISABILITY

The possibility of losing earnings due to an accident or illness is significant. Approximately 17 percent of the 128 million persons age 18 to 64 in the United States are limited in their ability to work because of a chronic illness or impairment. Of these 21.8 million persons, approximately half cannot work at all or do not work regularly.[1] It is estimated that one out of four adults between ages 55 and 64 is severely disabled, that is, cannot work regularly if at all. Table 16–1 indicates the probability of a disability lasting three months or longer for various age groups.

Although results vary among employee groups, it is evident the possibility of disability is an exposure that should be considered thoroughly. This chapter provides some historical perspective on disability insurance, an overview of available disability coverages, an analysis of issues in plan design, and a discussion of administration and cost-saving procedures of the plans. Chapter 18 provides greater detail on specific insured and self-insured plans for short- and long-term disability income.

---

[1] *Work Disability in the United States: A Chartbook* (Washington, D.C.: U.S. Department of Health and Human Services SSA Publication, No. 13–11978, December 1980).

Table 16-1

Group Long-Term Disability Insurance Crude Rates of Disablement per 1,000 Lives Exposed (three-month elimination period; calendar year of issue excluded; calendar years of experience 1973-77)

Attained Age	Life Years Exposed	Number of Claims	Rate of Disablement per 1,000 Lives
All Experience: Males, Females, and Sex Unknown			
Under 40	480,881	887	1.84
40-44	93,547	389	4.16
45-49	88,377	556	6.29
50-54	77,055	668	8.67
55-59	57,292	873	15.24
60-64	35,856	743	20.72
All ages	833,008	4,116	4.94

Source: *Transactions, Society of Actuaries, 1979 Reports of Mortality and Morbidity Experiences*, 1980, p. 363.

GROUP COVERAGES AVAILABLE

Historical Perspective

Following the adverse claims experience of the 1930s, insurers were reluctant to provide disability income coverages again until about two decades ago. Some of the adverse claims experience in the early years of disability insurance, of course, can be attributed to the Great Depression. Even if the economy had been stable, however, the probability of negative disability income insurance results was high for several reasons. First, the definitions of disability in the early contracts were extremely liberal, and thus an inordinately high number of cases received benefits. Second, insurers in the disability income market used a flat rate structure. Prices were charged per unit of income replaced, with the same premium sometimes being applied to all ages. Third, insurers neglected to use underwriting safeguards, such as a maximum cutoff age for benefits, and some disability income benefits that should have been terminated earlier continued for life. These reasons accompanied by the economic pressures caused by the Depression encouraged overfiling, and insurers in the 1930s found themselves with inadequate reserves and experienced several years of substantial losses.

Although hospital indemnity policies were revived and became profitable in the early 1950s, disability income protection was not readily available until the 1960s when it became available from two primary sources. The Social Security program initiated a disability income program for disabled workers over the age of 50, and by 1960 an amendment had been passed to provide this protection to workers of all ages. The Social Security disability income program was characterized by a very strict definition of disability and a six-month waiting period. To be eligible for benefits, a claimant had to be incapable of performing any substantial gainful employment, and many persons though ill or injured could not meet the "definition-of-disability" or "waiting-period" requirements of this program. When collective bargaining units across the country became aware their disabled members might not be able to collect governmental benefits, they encouraged insurers to make coverage available for the varying needs of their members. Therefore, products were designed to cover a worker who could not perform his or her *own occupation* with benefits that could start after a waiting period of as little as one day and could continue until retirement. Thus began the emergence of short- and long-term disability income coverages as we know them today. The following section describes short- and long-term coverages available today through private insurers or by self-insuring.

Short-Term Disability

Short-term disability income insurance applies to cases in which the injured or ill worker is unable to perform the duties of his or her current position. Benefits may be paid for as short a period as one week or may continue for as long as 26 weeks. Although some short-term plans provide income beyond 26 weeks, (some for as long as 52 weeks), 26 weeks normally is considered the break point between short-term and long-term plans. Benefit duration often is dependent upon the length of time an employee has served the employer. Income replacement for short-term disability is available from four major sources: (1) self-insured sick leave plans; (2) insured income replacement plans; (3) state-mandated plans (found in California, Hawaii, New York, New Jersey, Rhode Island, and Puerto Rico); and (4) workers' compensation. The first two of these sources are discussed briefly below; the last two are discussed in Chapter 18.

For short periods of disability, say between 1 and 10 days, the employer may continue the worker's entire salary as though the worker had been on the job. This arrangement, called a sick leave plan, normally is self-funded. It is common in such a plan to allow an employee to carry unused benefit days from one year to the next (usually up to some maximum number of days), thereby enabling an employee to "bank" or "save" days to be used in the event of an extended illness or disability. Some sick leave plans provide additional days of sick leave as the length of service with the employer increases. For example, an employer might provide 10 sick leave days the first year and an additional 10 days for each year of service up to a maximum of 180 sick leave days. Unused sick leave days could be carried forward to arrive at the maximum more quickly. Sick leave plans are common for salaried personnel and often are combined with insured long-term disability plans.

A common plan for employees paid on an hourly basis is a group insured income replacement plan. To qualify for short-term disability benefits under an insured group plan, an employee must be unable to work and be off the job, usually for a minimum of five working days because of illness, or one day because of accident. Waiting periods vary, but the general intent is to discourage staying off the job. An attempt is made to assure that the benefit program is not abused because it provides too much income replacement. Income replacement in the insured plans is stated in terms of hundreds of dollars per week or, more commonly, as a percentage of salary. A common benefit agreement replaces 50 to 66.6 percent of gross salary for up to 26 weeks. Newer plans may give a benefit based upon take-home pay or spendable income.

Long-Term Disability (LTD) Insurance

Long-term disability insurance is characterized by a program that provides income replacement on an insured or formalized self-insured program for a period starting after six months and lasting for the duration of the disability (or until normal retirement age). The definition of disability under the long-term plans usually is broken into two parts. During the first two years of disablement, employees must be disabled to the extent they cannot perform the duties of their own occupations. To quote from a standard contract, "Total disability for the purposes of this policy means the complete inability of the person due to accidental bodily injury or sickness or both during the first 24 months of such disability to perform any and every duty pertaining to his or her own occupation." If the person remains disabled after 24 months, the second part of the definition applies: "Benefits will continue during any continuation of such disability following the first 24 months of disability if the person is unable to engage in any work or occupation for which he or she is reasonably fitted by education, training, or experience."

Most long-term disability programs have either a three-month, six-month or one-year waiting period. The most common waiting period historically has been six months, but a tendency exists to move toward the three-month period.[2] After the waiting period, long-term disability insurance provides benefits to injured or ill employees until the point they are able to return to work. However, benefit payments for long-term disability usually

---

[2] Because of changes in Social Security, many plans now will start paying benefits after a five-month waiting period.

end at retirement age and cease earlier if the disabled participant should die. Because of the 1978 amendments to the Age Discrimination in Employment Act (ADEA), coverage for active employees cannot be terminated prior to age 70.

The amount of income replaced by LTD benefits usually is based upon gross salary, with some monthly limitation or maximum. In long-term plans, income is often replaced at a rate of 50–66.6 percent, but can be as much as 75–80 percent of gross income.

ISSUES IN DESIGN

Eligible Groups

Whether a group of employees or labor union members can obtain disability coverage depends upon a number of factors. Key factors in eligibility are group size, sex, age, occupation, and income.

Group Size. Many long-term disability carriers restrict their group disability policies to groups with a minimum of 25 participants. If smaller groups desire coverage, individual underwriting applies, and other lines of coverage often must be purchased to obtain long-term disability for small groups. Although smaller groups may require individual underwriting, claims experience indicates "jumbo" groups with over 5,000 participants also may produce a high incidence of disability. As the group becomes extremely large, there may be a loss of employer control or interest, or both. Thus, groups at both ends of the spectrum may produce a higher incidence of disability and cost the employer more.

Gender. Discussion has arisen over the reason for rate variation based upon the number of females in a group. Table 16–2 demonstrates the statistical difference in incidence of disability for males and females.

As can be seen from Table 16–2, females have a higher incidence of disability than men at younger ages, but a lower incidence at older ages, and their overall morbidity factor is approximately 10 percent greater than for men. Thus, in some organizations with a high percentage of young female workers, disability rates may increase by as much as 25 percent.

Some insurers are concerned about the movement toward the unisex mortality and morbidity table. There may be valid reasons for using this table in long-term disability insurance, but these reasons probably do not apply for short-term. Maternity and related illnesses increase group rates for groups that have short waiting periods, but group plans with at least a six-week waiting period are not affected as much by this morbidity factor.

Disability plans that have a long waiting period may consider changing to a unisex table because of shifting roles in society and the resultant changes in incidence of disability. As women enter more professions and acquire training for numerous occupations, their incidence and continuation of disability may decrease. That is because the definition of disability is based

Table 16–2
Group Long-Term Disability Insurance Rate of
Disablement by Gender per 1,000 Lives Exposed
(calendar years of experience 1973–77)

Six-Month Elimination Period	Male Experience	Female Experience
Under 40	0.88	1.14
40–44	1.79	3.34
45–49	3.65	4.60
50–54	6.64	6.87
55–59	11.74	10.59
60–64	16.00	12.24
All ages	3.74	3.33

Three-Month Elimination Period	Male Experience	Female Experience
Under 40	1.76	2.26
40–44	3.76	6.69
45–49	5.91	8.39
50–54	8.34	9.80
55 59	16.53	15.37
60–64	23.29	18.26
All ages	5.15	5.37

Source: *Transactions, Society of Actuaries, 1979 Reports on Mortality and Morbidity*, 1980, pp. 344 63.

on the ability to perform any occupation for which the insured is suited by education, training, or experience. Disabled women will have greater opportunities to be rehabilitated and placed back in active employment. Thus, disability rates for men and women may converge.

Age. Age is a key factor in the eligibility of a group for both short- and long-term disability coverage, and is even more important in determining the rate to be paid than are group size and gender. The Society of Actuaries *Reports on Mortality and Morbidity Experiences*, show that disabled rates vary significantly from the younger to older ages. See Table 16–3.

The ages of participants in a group affect the number of claims that will occur over the years. Young workers (between ages 20 and 40) have a small probability of disablement and a great capacity for retraining. Young workers have significant incentive to regain their capacity and, therefore, little moral hazard of malingering exists. In most cases, the cost of insuring groups of young employees should be reasonable. However, a large claim reserve may be required to cover the possibility of a young worker becoming seriously disabled.

Older age groups present a cost problem to insurance claim departments. The probability of sustaining a disability is much greater at older ages, and between 80 and 90 percent of disabilities in older people are caused by

Table 16-3
Group Long-Term Disability Insurance Crude Rates Of Disablement per
1,000 Lives Exposed (six-month elimination period; calendar years of
experience 1973-77)

Attained Age	Life Years Exposed	Number of Claims	Rate of Disablement per 1,000 Lives
	All Experience: Males, Females, and Sex Unknown		
Under 40	2,014,998	1,917	0.95
40-44	450,156	978	2.17
45-49	454,819	1,762	3.87
50-54	404,461	2,708	6.70
55-59	307,479	3,508	11.41
60-64	187,855	2,757	14.68
All ages	3,819,768	13,630	3.57

Source: *Transactions, Society of Actuaries, 1979 Reports of Mortality and Morbidity Experiences*, 1980, p. 344.

sickness or disease and not by accidental injury. Therefore, if the mean age of the insurance group is high, the probability of disablement caused by sickness is high. Among other reasons, claims tend to last longer among older workers, because of low educational levels and inability to be trained for other positions.

While the increase in retirement age and the passage of the 1978 amendments to the Age Discrimination in Employment Act (ADEA) could have a significant impact upon disablement rates, it is too early to know what the exact impact will be. As more workers continue in their jobs after age 65, the likelihood of disablement and therefore increased claims may be greater. The ADEA, as amended, prohibits forced retirement prior to age 70; but in benefit programs it is still possible to provide for shorter benefit durations without discriminating against an older person. For example, if a working person at age 69 became disabled, the benefits could still be cut off at retirement at age 70. Therefore, the reserve and the cost for that disabling condition would be minimal. If disability occurred between the ages of 62 and 65, a stated number of months of disability income might be provided. Under some plans, if the person becomes disabled prior to age 62, benefits under the disability program are limited to 60 months. In another example, if the person becomes disabled after reaching age 62, the amount of benefit will be based on a sliding schedule as demonstrated in Table 16-4.

Table 16-4
ADEA Option for Benefits

Employee Attained Age at Disablement	Maximum Months of Income Replacement
62	42
63	36
64	30
65	24
66	21
67	18
68	15
69	12

Source: Group Contract, The Banker's Life Insurance Company, Des Moines, Iowa.

In summary, if the group has a high percentage of persons over the age of 60, the potentiality for an increase in disability incidence is present. However, the duration of that disability is limited by the benefit cutoff age.

Occupation. Claim frequencies vary from one occupation to another, and each class of occupation demonstrates a distinctive accident and sickness frequency. That is, working with steel is more hazardous than working with a computer and thus produces more disabilities. Although workers' compensation provides benefits for occupational injuries, group disability plans may still be affected. In some jurisdictions, workers' compensation income replacement does not begin until after a three to seven day waiting period, and thus claims could be paid out of a short-term sick leave plan. Additionally, some workers' compensation benefits are inadequate, and the group plan would be needed to supplement income replacement. A long-term disability program may be affected further because of the susceptability of certain occupations to various chronic conditions. For instance, people employed in mining or chemical industries may develop serious heart or lung conditions, and these ailments may or may not be ruled to have resulted from occupational hazards. If workers' compensation benefits are not awarded, group disability benefits probably will be paid.

Job classification of the employee also may affect disability plans. Historically, hourly paid and lower-paid workers either were declined or rated very heavily. This rating may be attributable to overinsurance problems, discussed later in this chapter. Whether a group is insurable may depend on the percentage of workers in hourly paid or lower-paid positions and the type of job performed. Each insurer has a different underwriting standard, but it is not uncommon, for example, to decline groups involved in agriculture, fishing, chemicals, entertainment, or construction.

Income eligibility. Certain employees may be considered ineligible for coverage because of their age or occupational status. It is common to exclude seasonal or part-time employees from disability plans, as well as persons who have been working for the firm a short time, even if they are employed on a full-time basis. If qualification procedures have been met, there generally is a waiting period before disability income benefits begin. As mentioned previously, waiting periods for short-term disability range from 1 day because of accident, and 7 days because of illness, to 7 days because of accident, and 14 days because of illness. In long-term plans, waiting periods range from one month to one year.

Disability income benefits continue as long as the definition of disability is met and are paid according to the contractual provision until one of several things occurs. First, disability contracts require that the participant be under the care of a physician and that statements to that effect be made on a regular basis, and payments terminate when the participant stops receiving this care. Death of the participant, of course, will terminate disability benefits. In short-term plans, most disability benefits are terminated when the employee has returned to work or has been paid for the maximum number of weeks, and in long-term plans, benefits are terminated when the definition of disability can no longer be met. Because of the two-stage definition of disability discussed earlier, it is normal for an individual to go off benefit status at the end of the 24-month *"own* occupation" definition of disability. If such person continued to be disabled under the *"any* occupation" definition, disability benefits could continue to age 65 or 70 depending on how the benefit package is coordinated with any pension plan that may be in effect. If the pension plan is so set up that retirement income can begin at age 65, disability income stops at that point. If there is no pension plan, disability income should continue until age 70 or until contractual provisions are met. Proper drafting of a disability and pension plan should include some provision for accrual of pension benefits during disablement.

Amount of Benefits

Two perspectives on the amount of income to be replaced by disability income benefits may be valid. Some benefit managers believe disability income should be high enough to allow disabled persons to continue in their normal lifestyle, while others believe disability benefits should be closer to a subsistence level, thereby encouraging employees to return to work. In either case, the goal is to control overall income in a way that discourages malingering. Historically, some firms did not consider that income might be available to participants from several sources, and that participants might collect from various other plans as well as from the employer-provided disability plan. Today, target replacement is in the range of 60 to 70 percent of gross salary, with an offset for benefits received from other sources. Even at this level, overinsurance may result if the disabled party is collecting from several sources. For example, an employee might have an 80 percent replacement of spendable income under workers' compensation and a minimum payment from a disability income plan. This might provide more real income after disability than before. Contributory disability plans should be analyzed carefully, because benefits received as a result of participant premiums are received income-tax free. Thus, the benefit manager faces the task of determining an income replacement level that allows the disabled party to live in a reasonable fashion, but not to the extent that the worker will have so much income that no incentive exists to return to work. The problem is particularly acute for young hourly paid and lower-paid workers because of the amount of income potentially available from Social Security. A high-income replacement percentage from Social Security, combined with a benefit from a disability income plan, may cause an overinsurance problem.

Probably, the most common benefit level in disability income plans today is a replacement of 60 percent of gross pay. This 60 percent could consist of income from Social Security, workers' compensation, group life insurance, group long-term disability income benefits, and disability benefits under pension plans. If the entire 60 percent of income is replaced by public disability or other group benefits, the group disability insurer pays a minimum benefit or no benefit at all. The increase in cost attributable to the overinsurance problem is not easily quantified. Insurers agree, however, that overinsurance increases both frequency and duration or continuation of claims. Some figures are available concerning cost consequences of increasing the aggregate income level from a 50 percent benefit to a 60 or 70 percent benefit. In a typical group, an increase from 50 to 60 percent of gross income might increase premiums by as much as 50 percent. An increase from 50 to 70 percent could increase premiums by as much as 90 percent. This change of premium reflects an increase in both annuity value and in claims frequency. Careful analysis should be made to assure all offsets are known, and managers need to explicitly state offsets for primary and family Social Security benefits, workers' compensation benefits, and pension and other group insurance benefits. All salary continuation benefits or sick leave plans also should be taken into consideration.

A topic related to the percentage of monthly income to be replaced is the maximum amount of such income to be replaced. In older plans it was common to replace a maximum of $2,000 to $3,000 per month, while newer plans are shifting to $5,000 and $10,000 monthly limits. It is desirable to provide a higher level of income because of inflation, but a reasonable maximum should still be selected. For highly compensated employees, particularly if a plan is contributory, $10,000 per month may cause a problem. On the other hand, if a person were earning $7,000 a month prior to disability, a $2,500 maximum benefit could cause a severe economic strain on the person's family. In cases of highly compensated employees, individual insurance with a higher limit may be purchased or self-insurance may be used to supplement the group plan.

Limitations and Exclusions

Group disability plans have some limitations and exclusions. Some plans have a preexisting clause. That clause could say, "We the insurance company will not pay for disabling conditions that commence within 12 months after the effective date of the person's insurance if the person received treatment or service for such disability during the 3-month period preceding the effective date of his or her insurance." The time periods may vary, but the concept is the same. If a person has been receiving treatment or has been off work because of disabling conditions, or both, he or she may not have group coverage benefits available until the coverage has been in effect for a minimum of 12 months. In addition, a limitation for disability because of intentional or self-inflicted injury is found in most contracts. It also is common to have a limitation or exclusion for disability because of war or any act of war, declared or undeclared.

In the past, disability contracts had limitations for alcoholism, drug addiction, and mental and nervous disorders; but such limitations are being used less frequently now, and in many accident and sickness policies, alcoholism is treated as any other illness. As stated in other chapters of this book, however, it is common to have some limitations for dollar indemnity for psychiatric wards or the cost of being in a nonconfined rehabilitative program. In any event, mental disorders may keep a person from performing his or her own job. A prime example of a circumstance in which rehabilitation may be very effective is drug addiction. A person who has a drug-related problem may well be a nonproductive employee, and income replaced while such an individual is off the job being rehabilitated may be considered dollars well spent to encourage return to productive work.

ADMINISTRATIVE AND FINANCIAL ISSUES

Cost Sharing—Contributory versus Noncontributory

As with other employee benefits, it is important to consider whether disability benefits should be paid for on a contributory or noncontributory basis prior to the installation of the plan. The amount of cost sharing affects benefit levels and the taxability of benefits received under disability plans. Benefits attributable to an employee's contributions are received tax free without limit. Therefore, if an employer is asking an employee to contribute a significant portion of the disability insurance premium, the percentage of income replaced must be decreased to take into consideration the tax-free status of benefits received or an overinsurance problem can result.

Disability benefits attributable to an employer's contribution fall under Section 105 of the Internal Revenue Code, and amounts received by an employee on disability income may be excluded from gross income up to $100 per week. The Tax Reform Act of 1976 replaced the more lenient prior definition of disability for this purpose, and to obtain this exclusion now, the employee must be unable to engage in any substantial gainful employment by reason of any medically determinable physical or mental impairment which can be expected to result in death or which has lasted or can be expected to last for a continuous period of not less than 12 months. This is the same definition used by the Social Security disability income program. Therefore, to receive tax benefits under a disability program, a person must be severely disabled and meet the stringent definition of disability. In addition, the Tax Reform Act of 1976 instituted a phase-out provision whereby, if the disabled participant has annual earnings in excess of $15,000, there will be a dollar-for-dollar reduction in the amount that can be received income-tax free. Thus, if a disabled employee has an adjusted gross income (including income from all disability payments) of $20,200 or more, no "disability pay exclusion" is available to him or her in that year. When the employer is providing the entire cost of the disability program, the possibility of overinsurance caused by tax exclusions usually is not a problem. Less than 50 percent of the disability claimants qualify for the exclusion, and the amount of the exclusion is small. If a large proportion of participants earn less than $15,000 per year, the percentage of income replaced should be analyzed for tax ramifications that might lead to overinsurance.

An additional issue in contributory versus noncontributory plans is the minimum benefit. If an employee is required to contribute, should a minimum benefit be paid from the disability plan even though overinsurance problems might result? In many plans, whether contributory or not, a minimum benefit of $50 per month is provided. As the contribution level rises, employees could reasonably request a higher minimum payout from the plan.

Claims Administration

Claims administration in the group disability area can have a very large impact upon the cost of the program. A variety of claims administration techniques exist, and each technique and form has advantages and disadvantages. The three main types of administration can be characterized as regional, centralized, and combined.

Regionalized Administration. Some large insurers have totally decentralized claims administration and control, in which the claims investigation and claims decision and monitoring take place at a local or regional level. Claims examiners in each state or sales region of the country handle all claims administration for disability in that area. In some cases, when disability income insurance volume is too small to make it efficient to have a claims examiner who specializes in disability claims, a claims examiner may deal in a number of different types of coverages, including disability. It is the responsibility of the claims examiner in the specific region to collect medical data and make a decision on the qualification of a claimant for disability benefits. The claims examiner must have a working knowledge of the various group contract provisions and be able to interpret medical and personal data.

Centralized Administration. The second type of claims administration is the centrally located claims department. In this type, claims work and investigation are performed from a central office. The group policyholder files claims applications directly with the home office. Backup investigations may be performed by independent claims adjusters or by credit bureaus. However, most information about the claim is gained by mail or telephone directly from the policyholder and physicians involved; there usually is no personal interview with the claimant. Generally, the claimant fills out the entire claim form, and payment usually is made directly from the home office, but in some instances it is made by the employer in the interest of better employee relations. Continued monitoring of the data is performed at the central location.

Combined Administration. To obtain the advantages of both the claims contact of regional administration and the cost savings of central administration, certain large insurers have claims systems that use regional claims people but keep the decision process in the home office. Local claims people are used for investigative purposes and to contact the claimant and his or her employer. Employees make claims to the home office, but regional personnel deal with the policyholder. The regional claims people bring together all pertinent claims information and make a personal call on the claimant if it is considered necessary. Compilation of a claims file takes place at the regional outlet. Regional office personnel may make a recommendation on the claim, but approval or denial comes from the central office.

The employee benefit manager must decide what type of claims administration is appropriate for its organization. Because of the delicate nature of disability claims, whether short- or long-term, it seems desirable in most cases that claims administration be handled by a third party and that the third party have a centralized or combined system for adjudicating claims. Claims services may be procured from insurers or specialty firms that monitor and control claims. Then, in the event an employee is dissatisfied, the dissatisfaction is aimed not at the employer but at another entity. In any event, it is important to have quick processing of claims and to have claim investigations started immediately.

Not only should proper claims processing be started for the private coverage, but a system to encourage disabled employees to file for Social Security disability income benefits should be in place. The number of people who receive Social Security disability benefits has changed drastically in the last decade. In the period between 1957 and 1969, it was not uncommon for the percentage of disability claims approved by Social Security to be above 50 percent, and in some years the percentage of claims approved by Social Security for disability benefits was above 60 percent. Because of massive changes in the economy, the percentage of persons who apply for and receive Social Security awards dropped drastically in the

1970s. In the period 1970 to 1974, the percentage of applicants approved was less than 50 percent, usually between 40 and 50 percent. In the 1980s, the approval rate for Social Security disability claims has dropped into the 30 percent range. It is important to understand that the increased cost to integrated plans resulting from a lower percentage of Social Security disability claim approvals must be borne by the group policyholder. Thus, for potential cost savings, claims should be followed to their completion. Careful application and possibly reapplication should be made under Social Security if it seems at all possible the claimant could qualify for Social Security disability benefits.

Rehabilitation. An important part of the employee benefit manager's responsibility in the disability area is to make sure the rehabilitation process gets started as soon as reasonably practicable. Rehabilitation services may be provided on a local basis or may be provided by an insurance company. To be most effective, rehabilitation should begin as soon as possible for claims in which a loss of use of a bodily member occurs. The employee benefit manager should aid the insurance company or private rehabilitation firm. Benefit managers sometimes can identify employees who could benefit from rehabilitation and motivate these employees to seek rehabilitative services. Several disability insurers now have trained rehabilitation specialists who will help locate services at the local level. Rehabilitation programs first seek to put the person back in the job he or she was performing prior to the disabling condition. This may be accomplished by restructuring that job or by moving the employee into a slightly different work environment. If restructuring does not work, the next step is retraining for a position in the same company. In each case, early help is most important in getting people back into the production process. The best rehabilitation programs stress existing skills. If it is not possible to go back to the existing workplace, the insurance company involves the claimant in vocational rehabilitation. This is required if a claimant is to receive Social Security benefits. In addition, specific workshops and other education and training can be considered. The employer and the benefit manager must compare the cost of rehabilitation with the cost of keeping the person on the disability rolls. If the insurance carrier is not providing rehabilitation services for people on disability, services should be sought independently. Rehabilitation is a cost-effective device—both in human terms and in dollar terms—and should be part of the plan design.

SUMMARY

This brief overview of the types of coverages available for short- and long-term disability provides background for the more detailed information that follows in Chapter 18. Proper underwriting and claims administration help assure the employee benefit manager that the firm's employees are well protected at an acceptable cost.

CHAPTER 17

Social Security and Other Governmental Disability Benefit Plans

ROBERT J. MYERS

Economic security for disabled workers in the United States is provided, in the vast majority of cases, through the multiple means of Social Security, other governmental plans, sick leave, private retirement plans, and individual savings. This is sometimes referred to as a "three-legged stool" or the three "pillars" of economic security protection. Still others look upon the situation as Social Security providing the floor of protection, with private-sector activities building on top of it, and with public assistance programs, such as Supplemental Security Income, providing a net of protection for those whose total income does not attain certain levels or meet minimum subsistence needs.

Some people believe the Social Security program should provide complete protection for disabled workers and their families. However, over the years, it generally has been agreed that Social Security should be only a floor of protection. It is desirable, for a number of reasons, that people should supplement it through the efforts of their employers and themselves jointly and through their own individual efforts. It does not seem desirable that people should be wholly dependent on the government for their economic security, because this would be debilitating to the national character and thus very likely to national productivity. Individuals properly take a sense of pride in what they do for themselves in supplementing Social Security.

Furthermore, private planning for economic security in the event of disability can often adapt to special needs, such as very short periods of disability or types of disability that are not of such a severe nature as Social Security requires to be qualifying, but which prevent the individuals from doing their usual work. In addition, the capital needs of industry for development funds are well served by the accumulation of assets under private plans, whereas Social Security operates on a largely unfunded basis, with any investments being in government obligations.

As described elsewhere in this book, private pension and insurance plans to a significant extent have been developed to supplement Social Security. This is done in a number of ways, directly and indirectly.

This chapter discusses the disability benefit provisions of the Social Security program, not only their historical development and present structure but also possible changes in the future. Following this, various other governmental programs in this area are described. Then, the public assistance programs supplementing, when necessary, other forms of disability income, are outlined. Finally, the relationship is considered of the Social Security program with governmental benefit plans that cover other risks, such as work-connected accidents.

The discussion of the Social Security program in this chapter deals only with the disability benefit provisions applicable equally to active and retired insured workers. Actually, the program is a closely coordinated one, also covering the risks of death of the worker and retirement of the worker (which are dealt with in Chapters 5 and 28, respectively).

The term *Social Security* as used here is the meaning generally accepted in the United States—the cash benefits provisions of the Old-Age, Survivors, and Disability Insurance program (OASDI). International usage of the term *social security* is much broader and includes all other types of programs protecting individuals against the economic risks of a modern industrial society (e.g., unemployment, short-term sickness, work-connected accidents and diseases, and medical care costs).

OLD-AGE, SURVIVORS, AND DISABILITY INSURANCE PROGRAM

Historical Development of Disability Provisions

When what is now the OASDI program was developed in 1934-35, it was confined entirely to retirement benefits (plus lump-sum refund payments to represent the difference, if any, between employee taxes paid, plus an allowance for interest, and retirement benefits received). It was not until the 1956 act that monthly disability benefits were added, although the "disability-freeze" provision (in essence, a waiver-of-premium provision), described later, was added in the 1952 Act.[1]

The monthly benefits initially were available only at ages 50 and over, that is, deferred to that age for those disabled earlier, with no auxiliary benefits for the spouse and dependent children. These limitations were quickly removed, by the 1958 and 1960 acts.

---

[1] Actually, it was so written in that legislation as to be inoperative, but then was reenacted in 1954 to be on a permanent, ongoing basis.

Persons Covered

OASDI coverage, for both taxes and earnings credits toward benefit rights, currently applies to somewhat more than 90 percent of the total workforce of the United States.

Eligibility Conditions

To be eligible for OASDI disability benefits, individuals must have a certain amount of covered employment. Eligibility depends upon having a certain number of "quarters of coverage" (QC) and being both fully insured and disability insured.[2] Disability status requires 20 QC earned in the 40-quarter period ending with the quarter of disability, except that persons disabled before age 31 also can qualify if they have QC in half of the quarters after age 21.[3]

Beneficiary Categories

In addition to the disabled worker, two general categories of dependents can receive monthly benefits. In all cases, the benefits are based on the primary insurance amount (PIA), computed in the same manner as retirement benefits (see Chapter 28), except that fewer dropout years than five are allowed in the computation of the averaged indexed monthly earnings (AIME) for persons disabled before age 47. The disabled worker receives a benefit equal to 100 percent of the PIA.

Spouses aged 62 or over are eligible for benefits in the same manner as those of retired workers. Similarly eligible are children under age 18, or at any age if disabled before age 22, and children aged 18 who are full-time students in elementary or secondary educational institutions,[4] and the spouse when such children are under age 16 or disabled.

The aged spouse receives a benefit at the rate of 37.5 percent of the PIA if the claim is first made at age 62, and then in gradually larger amounts for older ages, up to 50 percent at age 65. Spouses regardless of age who are caring for an eligible child (under age 16 or disabled) have a benefit of 50 percent of the PIA. Divorced spouses, when the marriage had lasted at least 10 years, are eligible for benefits under the same conditions as undivorced spouses. Eligible children receive benefits at a rate of 50 percent of the PIA.

An overall maximum on total family benefits is applicable, which is lower

---

[2] Blind persons need be only fully insured. The details of the terms—quarter of coverage, as well as currently and fully insured status—are described in detail in Chapter 28.

[3] For those disabled before age 24, the requirement is six QC in the last 12 quarters.

[4] Post-secondary student benefits (up to age 22) were available before legislation in 1981. For those previously qualifying (before May 1982), these benefits are still available, but on a gradually phased-out basis on benefit amount, until being eliminated after April 1985.

than that for survivor and retirement benefits, as discussed in Chapter 28. If a person is eligible for more than one type of benefit (e.g., both as a worker and as a surviving spouse), in essence only the largest benefit is payable.

Benefit Computation Procedures and Indexing

As indicated in the previous section, all OASDI benefits are based on the PIA.[5]

Eligibility Test and Other Restrictions on Benefits

From the inception of the OASDI program some form of restriction has existed on the payment of benefits to persons who have substantial earnings from employment. This provision is referred to as the earnings or retirement test. It does not apply to nonearned income, such as from investments or pensions. The test applies to the auxiliary beneficiaries of disabled workers (see Chapter 28 for details as to the test), but *not* to the disabled-worker beneficiary. However, the earnings of one beneficiary (e.g., the spouse of the disabled worker) do not affect the benefits of the other beneficiaries in the family (e.g., the disabled worker or the children). The test does not apply to disabled-worker beneficiaries, because any earnings are considered in connection with whether recovery has occurred, except those during trial work periods (which may possibly lead to recovery later).

Financing

The disability benefits (including auxiliary benefits) are financed by a payroll tax that is part of the combined OASDI tax rate.

Possible Future Developments

Possible future changes concerning the disability benefits under the OASDI program are discussed in detail in Chapter 28, along with possible future changes in the retirement benefit portion of the program. Changes that would apply only to the disability benefits portion include:

1.   Tightening up the definition of disability, such as by using "medical only" factors (and not vocational ones, such as age, education, and previous experience) or by lengthening the 12-month prognosis period on the disability being of long-extended duration; or conversely, liberalizing the definition so that, for example, it would be on an occupational basis at ages 50 and over.

---

[5] The method of computing the PIA is described in detail in Chapter 28.

2. Lengthening the five month waiting period; or, conversely, shortening it.

3. Imposing more stringent eligibility conditions, such as requiring currently insured status, in addition to the other two insured-status requirements.

RAILROAD RETIREMENT (RR) PROGRAM

The OASDI system covers virtually all nongovernment wage employment except for railroad employees, who are covered by the Railroad Retirement system. This separate system is coordinated closely with OASDI, and its general structure is similar. The disability benefit amounts, however, are significantly higher.

Eligibility Conditions

The eligibility conditions for disability benefits require at least 120 months of railroad service. Benefits for permanent and total disability, corresponding closely to the OASDI definition, are available after such 10 years of service have been completed. Also, occupational disability benefits are available after 20 years of service, or at ages 60–64, for persons who have 12 months of service in the 30-month period preceding disability. Unlike OASDI, there is no waiting period for disability benefits.

The RR disability benefit amounts are the same as what the retirement benefit would be, namely, what the OASDI one would be on the same earnings record, even though it might not actually be payable because of the nature of the disability, plus an amount based on the Tier-II retirement benefit, as described in Chapter 28. The automatic-adjustment provisions for changes in the consumer price index (CPI) apply in the same manner as under OASDI, as far as the OASDI portion of the benefit is concerned, but an increase of only 32.5 percent of the CPI rise is applicable to the Tier-II portion.

Financing

The RR disability benefits are financed as an integral part of the financing of the entire RR program.

GOVERNMENT EMPLOYEE PLANS

Governmental employee retirement plans initially provided only retirement benefits, but disability benefits often were made available later. Many of these plans have provided disability benefits by becoming coordinated with OASDI, as is common in the private sector, but others did so by merely adding OASDI on top (e.g., the military plan).

Civil Service Retirement (CSR) System

The basic nature and coverage of CSR is described in Chapter 28. Disability benefits are payable under a very liberal occupational definition, with no waiting period after sick leave and vacation leave have been used up.

The benefit amount is determined in the same manner as for the retirement benefits, except a minimum benefit of 40 percent of high-three-year average salary is provided (and except this percentage cannot exceed the percentage that would be applicable for retirement benefits if service had continued to age 62). Survivor benefit protection after disability retirement can be obtained in the same manner as for age retirements, namely, by a small reduction in the pension (at far less than the actuarial cost).

Automatic cost-of-living adjustments for CSR pensions are made annually, based on the percentage increase in the CPI over a 12-month period (except that, for 1983, 1984, and 1985, the increases are made at 13-month intervals, instead of annually).

The cost of the CSR disability benefits is included within the overall cost of the program.

Retirement Systems for Other Federal Civilian Groups

Both the Tennessee Valley Authority and the Board of Governors of the Federal Reserve Bank have established pension plans for their employees. In both instances, OASDI coverage (with the accompanying disability benefit protection) is applicable. The supplementary pension plans are quite similar to those of private employers.

Employees of the State Department and certain related agencies that are in the Foreign Service have a separate retirement system, which resembles CSR, but is significantly more liberal.

Supreme Court justices and other federal judges have a noncontributory retirement system, with disability benefits being included.

Military Retirement System

In addition to OASDI, members of the military services are covered by a noncontributory pension plan. This plan provides disability benefits regardless of length of service. The disability retired pay is the larger of 2.5 percent of final basic pay times years of service, or the percentage of disability times basic pay, with a maximum of 75 percent of basic pay in either case. However, veterans compensation (payable by the Veterans

Administration) is available for service-connected disabilities in lieu of the military disability retired pay; the former often is larger, especially for those in the lower pay grades.

Retirement Systems for State and Local Government Employees

Many separate retirement systems exist for employees of state and local governments. A wide divergence exists among the various state and local systems depending on whether they have elected OASDI coverage, which would provide some disability benefit protection.

These state and local plans are quite diverse about how they provide disability benefit protection. Generally, the definition of disability used is quite liberal, and often the benefit amounts are higher for service-connected disabilities than for other types.

PUBLIC ASSISTANCE PROGRAMS

Public assistance programs provide a financial backstop for disabled persons if OASDI and other governmental benefits, plus private-sector benefits, are insufficient. This is accomplished through the Supplemental Security Income (SSI) program in the same manner as for aged persons (see Chapter 28). Two separate categories are involved—the blind and other disabled persons. The eligibility conditions and certain benefit conditions are more liberal for the blind.

RELATIONSHIP OF OASDI PROGRAM WITH OTHER GOVERNMENTAL PROGRAMS

The disability benefits payable under the OASDI program parallel those available under other governmental programs. OASDI benefits are coordinated directly with those under the Railroad Retirement program as a result of the combining of the earnings records under the two systems for purposes of benefit computations.

OASDI benefits also are coordinated with disability benefits payable under other governmental programs (including those of state and local governments), except for needs-tested ones, benefits payable by the Veterans Administration, and government-employee plans coordinated with OASDI. The most important of such coordinations is with workers' compensation (WC) programs, whose benefits are taken into account in determining the amount of the OASDI disability benefit (except for a few states that provide for their WC benefits to be reduced when OASDI disability benefits are payable—possible only for states that did this before February 19, 1981). The total of the OASDI disability benefit (including any auxiliary benefits payable) and the other disability benefit recognized cannot exceed 80 percent of "average current earnings" (generally based on the highest year of earnings in covered employment in the last six years, but indexed for changes in wage levels following the worker's disablement).

There is coordination, in a sense, of OASDI benefits with SSI payments, because the latter take into account all other income, including OASDI benefits.

CHAPTER 18

Group Disability
Income Insurance

MORTON D. MILLER

Income maintenance systems in the United States today cover the major areas of retirement, unemployment compensation, survivor death benefits, and disability benefits.

Disability programs constitute a significant part of the overall system with total cash disability benefits (including government payments at the federal, state, and local levels and private payments) estimated to have been about $34 billion in 1975. This is nearly 25 percent of the $147 billion total cash income benefit payments made to retired, unemployed, and disabled persons (and dependent survivors). In addition to income replacement benefits, disability programs often provide medical payments and offer other direct, principally rehabilitation, services.

As can be seen in Table 18-1, whether viewed in absolute terms or as a portion of the gross national product (GNP), disability income payments are large and rapidly growing. Such payments increased from $10 billion, 1.4 percent of GNP, in 1965 to $42 billion, 2.2 percent of GNP in 1977, with the federal share of the total growing from a low during this period of 54 percent in 1970 to 62 percent in 1977.

The high percentage of federal government involvement from 1950 to 1960 came about by reason of the initiation of several new programs, the first of which was the addition of the disability component of public assistance begun in 1950 and later to become Supplemental Security Income (SSI). This was followed in 1956 by the adoption of the Disability Income (DI) program as a part of Social Security and the enactment of the Black Lung Disease Law in 1969. The more recent rise in federal expenditures for disability can be attributed to liberalizations in the DI and SSI programs and to an increase in the number of beneficiaries.

HISTORICAL BACKGROUND

The origins of disability insurance can be found in Europe during the late 19th century, when the economies of the European countries were gradu-

Table 18-1
Cash Disability Income Payments ($ millions)

	1950	1955	1960	1965	1970	1975	1977
Total payments	$3,094	$4,672	$6,603	$9,729	$17,140	$33,865	$42,230
Total as percent of GNP	1.1%	1.2%	1.3%	1.4%	1.7%	2.2%	2.2%
Composition of total:							
Percent federal	65%	60%	56%	55%	54%	64%	62%
Percent state and local	18	20	22	23	22	16	19
Percent government	83	80	78	78	76	80	81
Percent private	17	20	22	22	24	20	19

Note: In making the estimates of the extent of cash disability income payments shown in Table 18-1, work-caused disabilities, workplace-based programs, and nonworkplace-based public assistance-type programs were considered. Payments under individual insurance and private savings were not included. The magnitude of such payments was on the order of $9 billion in 1977.

Source: Jonathan Sunshine, *Disability*, OMB Staff Technical Paper, 1979, and updates thereto, page 29.

ally changing from agrarian to industrial and as European workers sought protection for their earnings against loss by reason of illness or injury through the formation of guilds or fraternal societies.

In America, small cash payments in the event of sickness or accident were made through "establishment funds," which developed in the 1800s. The first public programs to deal with disability were Civil War era provisions for military personnel.

Further developments did not take place until the end of the 19th century when increasing concern for injured employees led to the strengthening of the employer liability laws and caused many employers to turn to insurance companies for protection against adverse judgments in accident cases. It was for this purpose that workers' collective insurance was introduced around 1896 in the form of a rider to employers' liability policies. Such riders covered accidents, sometimes both occupational and nonoccupational, but did not deal with the problem of disability of a worker through illness.

It wasn't until 1911 that negotiations of the Montgomery Ward Company on behalf of its employees led to the emergence of group life insurance, in which the problem of disability caused by illness was faced. Montgomery Ward made an arrangement with a casualty insurance company for the provision of a more comprehensive workers' collective policy providing benefits for sickness as well as accidents. Many industrial firms followed Montgomery Ward's pioneering effort, and shortly thereafter, in about 1915, a number of insurance companies began to experiment with a

Table 18–2
Number of Persons in the United States with Disability Income Insurance by Type
of Program (000s)

		Insurance Companies				
End of Year	All Programs	All Insurance Companies	Group Policies	Individual Policies	Formal Paid Sick Leave Plans	Other
1946	26,229	14,369	7,135	8,684	8,400	3,460
1950	37,793	25,993	15,104	13,067	8,900	2,900
1955	39,513	29,813	19,171	13,642	8,500	1,200
1960	42,436	31,836	20,970	14,298	9,500	1,100
1961	43,055	32,055	21,186	14,301	9,900	1,100
1962	45,002	33,602	22,313	14,854	10,200	1,200
		Short-Term Disability Income Protection				
1963	44,246	31,946	20,865	12,902	10,900	1,400
1964	45,092	32,692	21,267	13,964	10,900	1,500
1965	46,927	33,527	22,409	11,937	11,700	1,700
1966	49,931	35,631	23,765	13,919	12,500	1,800
1967	51,975	36,675	24,805	13,188	13,300	2,000
1968	55,636	39,736	26,868	15,648	13,800	2,100
1969	57,770	39,970	27,373	15,446	15,500	2,300
1970	58,089	39,789	27,876	14,901	15,900	2,400
1971	59,280	40,180	28,408	13,866	16,500	2,600
1972	61,548	41,208	29,151	14,527	17,640	2,700
1973	64,168	43,298	29,279	16,890	18,170	2,700
1974	65,282	43,672	29,320	17,291	18,910	2,700
1975	62,971	41,071	28,607	15,024	19,400	2,500
1976	62,250	38,940	27,534	13,742	20,610	2,700
1977	64,627	40,047	28,176	14,302	21,880	2,700†
1978	68,307	43,289	28,676	17,606	22,318	2,700†
1979	65,808	40,208	27,005	15,907	22,900†	2,700†

group policy approach to provide disability benefits; these led to the emergence of group disability income insurance much as we know it today. By
1919, group disability income insurance was widely available from a number of insurance companies, and thereafter, the market for workers' compensation gained momentum as the group-writing companies promoted
group disability insurance.

The decade beginning in 1910 also saw the establishment of workers'
compensation statutes in all but six states. Legislation establishing these new
systems came in response to a changing legal climate in which workers were
winning more frequent and larger settlements under long-standing common
law principles that employers were required to provide safe working conditions and could be sued for damages if they negligently failed to do so.

Workers' compensation set up a no-fault system of defined benefits
under which work-related injuries were compensable through employer-

Table 18-2 (concluded)

End of Year	All Programs	Insurance Companies			Formal Paid Sick Leave Plans	Other
		All Insurance Companies	Group Policies	Individual Policies		
		Long-Term Disability Income Protection				
1963	3,029	3,029	749	2,280	—	—
1964	3,363	3,363	1,240	2,123	—	—
1965	4,514	4,514	1,864	2,650	—	—
1966	5,068	5,068	2,321	2,747	—	—
1967	6,778	6,778	3,722	3,056	—	—
1968	7,836	7,836	4,574	3,262	—	—
1969	9,282	9,282	5,544	3,738	—	—
1970	10,966	10,966	6,954	4,012	—	—
1971	12,284	12,284	7,951	4,333	—	—
1972	14,538	14,538	9,471	5,067	—	—
1973	17,011	17,011	10,595	6,416	—	—
1974	17,799	17,799	11,116	6,683	—	—
1975	18,396	18,396	11,526	6,870	—	—
1976	17,779	17,779	11,516	6,263	—	—
1977	19,364	19,364	12,481	6,883	—	—
1978	19,100	19,100	12,635	6,465	—	—
1979	19,920	19,920	13,409	6,511	—	—

†Preliminary estimate.

Note: For 1975 and later, data include the number of persons covered in Puerto Rico and other U.S. territories and possessions. Data in the category "Insurance companies" refers to the net total of people protected (i.e., duplication among persons who are covered by both group and individual policies has been eliminated). Any duplication resulting from the combination of numbers covered for short-term and long-term protection has not been eliminated. This category excludes Administrative Service Only Agreements and Minimum Premium Plans, except for those companies who include them in their regular reporting. The category "Formal Paid Sick Leave Plans" refers to people with formal paid sick leave plans but without insurance company coverage. The category "Other" includes union-administered plans and the Federal Mutual Benefit Association.

Sources: Health Insurance Association of America and U.S. Department of Health and Human Services.

paid insurance. This system was intended as a compromise beneficial to both workers and employers: workers would gain compensation for work-related injuries, regardless of who was at fault and without the need to resort to a lawsuit, and employers would gain a system in which damage awards were not open-ended but limited in amount.

A further new development of the period was the provision of disability retirement benefits for federal civilian employees initiated in 1920.

By the mid-1930s, group disability insurance was well established. Unfortunately, records of its growth prior to that time are not available. Table 18-2 sets forth the growth in both group and individual coverage from 1946 to 1979.

At the end of 1979, some 66 million people in the United States were covered by short-term protection through insurance company plans or other formal arrangements, and 20 million were covered by long-term policies of insurance companies. More than 2 million persons covered by long-term plans also had short-term coverage. In total, then, apart from Social Security, 85 million people in the United States had some form of disability coverage in 1979. This amounts to nearly 9 out of every 10 civilian workers.

It is appropriate to add that the strong growth in group plans in the 1940s was stimulated in good measure by the wage and salary controls imposed during World War II and thereafter. Employee benefit plans were exempted from these controls so that both employees, through their unions, and employers turned to the adoption of such plans as a means of improving total employee compensation.

STATE PLANS

Another factor was the adoption of statutory disability income plans in six states. Rhode Island was the first state to adopt a statutory disability income plan; it became effective in 1942. The state disability fund is the sole provider of benefits, and the law provides specified weekly benefits in case of nonoccupational disability for the employees of all employers subject to the law, with funding provided by a payroll tax on employees.

California was next, with its law adopted in 1946. Similar to the Rhode Island law, the California law differs in an important respect by permitting employers to establish private insurance or self-insurance plans as an alternative to coverage under the state fund. For a private plan to be accepted, however, it must provide benefits more liberal in some respect than those of the state fund, be acceptable to a majority of the employees, and not result in a substantial selection of risks adverse to the state fund. When tests involving distributions of employees by age, sex, and earnings were imposed in 1963, the effect of the adverse selection requirement resulted in the virtual elimination of private plans.

The New Jersey law, which became effective January 1, 1949, is similar to the California law, with an important innovation. The state fund sets its charge for each group on the basis of its own experience, avoiding the need for a protective "adverse selection" provision and permitting competition with private plans. Approximately 40 percent of New Jersey employees are covered by private plans.

The laws of Rhode Island, California, and New Jersey are part of the unemployment compensation statutes, and their funds, therefore, use a tax on wages as a source of revenue. Rhode Island and California levy the tax on employees only. New Jersey taxes both employees and employers and accomplishes its experience rating by varying the employer's tax rate according to the experience rating as evidenced by the amount of benefits paid to its employees.

The New York law, which became effective in 1950, is part of the Workers' Compensation Statute and has a different approach. Weekly benefits of a certain level are required, and subject employers must take positive action to either self-insure or to insure the required benefits with an insurance company or with the state fund. The state fund operates as an insurance company, determining and charging premiums and paying taxes on its premiums.

A period of 20 years elapsed after the passage of the New York law before similar laws were adopted by Puerto Rico, in July 1969, and Hawaii, in January 1970.

As in California and in New Jersey, the Puerto Rico law provides benefits through a state fund but permits the establishment of private plans. Benefits provided by the state fund are financed by a payroll tax shared by employees and employers. Since premium rates for private plans recognize the effect on claims of factors, such as age, sex, and wage composition, it was reasonable to expect that in the absence of any controls, the low-risk, low-cost group would choose to be insured under a private plan. To minimize such adverse selection against the state fund, assessments are made against private plans deemed to be "select groups" as determined by the age, sex, and wage composition of the group.

The Hawaii law differs from those in the other states in that it permits no competing plan. Subject employers can comply only by insuring the benefits with an authorized insurer or by self-insurance. To assure that coverage will be available for all employees, the law requires that each authorized insurer participate in a "pool" for the purpose of spreading among all insurers the risk attendant in insuring employer applicants who must comply with the law but who cannot secure insurance through ordinary means.

In establishing a group plan under one of these laws, it is necessary to conform to legal specifications on benefits and policy provisions, and to comply with regulations concerning special reports and filing requirements. Special benefit provisions, as well as policy and reporting forms, are needed for this purpose.

OTHER FACTORS

A further influence on the increase in the number of persons insured for group disability income benefits has been the gradual decrease in the minimum size of a group that insurers consider acceptable. Over the last ten years, group insurance marketing has broadened its outreach to the point where groups with as few as two or three employees are considered eligible.

Table 18-3 shows the growth in insurance company premiums earned for disability income protection. The increase in premiums reflects not only the larger number of persons covered but also the rise in wage levels, since an employee's benefit amount usually is dependent on his or her earnings. The larger role of long-term plans is another factor influencing the number of persons insured.

Table 18–3
Loss of Income Premiums Earned by Insurance Companies in the United
States ($ millions)

Year	Total Premiums	Percent Increase	Group Policies	Percent Increase	Individual and Family Policies	Percent Increase
1935	$ 26		$ 26		N.A.	
1940	48		48		N.A.	
1945	125		125		N.A.	
1950	652		291		$ 361	
1955	1,107		553		554	
1960	1,521		777		744	
1965	1,897		1,050		847	
1966	2,069	9.1	1,183	12.7	886	4.6%
1967	2,218	7.2	1,270	7.4	948	7.0
1968	2,491	12.3	1,473	16.0	1,018	7.4
1969	2,855	14.6	1,724	17.0	1,131	11.1
1970	3,072	7.6	1,968	14.2	1,104	−2.4
1971	3,343	8.8	2,189	11.2	1,154	4.5
1972	3,429	2.6	2,332	6.5	1,097	−4.9
1973	3,718	8.4	2,414	3.5	1,304	18.9
1974	4,048	8.9	2,603	7.8	1,445	11.8
1975	4,635	14.5	2,828**	8.6	1,807	25.1
1976	4,998	7.8	3,144**	11.2	1,854	2.6
1977	5,402	8.1	3,543**	12.7	1,859	.3
1978	6,529	20.9	4,539**	28.1	1,990	7.0
1979	6,855	5.0	4,759**	4.9	2,096	5.3

N.A.: Not available.
**Insurance company premiums for 1975 and later include administrative service only agreements and minimum premium plans. Aggregates in prior years contain only a portion of these data.
Note: Data are revised for 1975 and later data include premiums paid in Puerto Rico and other U.S. territories and possessions. Data prior to 1972 refer to written premiums (which, for group policies, include minor adjustments to reflect premiums of the particular year) and include accidental death and dismemberment premiums in the loss-of-income categories. Data for 1972 and later refer to earned premiums and are revised to exclude premiums for accidental death and dismemberment and other such limited coverages.
Source: Health Insurance Association of America.

DISABILITY INCOME PROTECTION

Accident and health policies provide disability income benefits for the partial replacement of income lost by employed men and women as a result of accident or illness. The amounts of such benefits vary, depending on whether the disability is total or partial and on the length of time the benefits are paid, which usually depends on whether the loss is the result of an accident or an illness.

There are two basic types of disability income coverage—short-term and long-term. Short-term policies provide benefits for periods from 13 weeks to 2 years, whereas long-term plans provide benefits for durations such as 5 years, 10 years, or to age 65 and sometimes beyond.

While this chapter is intended to deal primarily with *group* disability income insurance, it is worth mentioning that individual policies sometimes are used by employers in a similar way, mainly to purchase individual disability income coverage for highly paid employees and key people who are included in their executive compensation programs.

Definition of Disability

A typical definition of disability for a short-term income policy might be:

> Upon receipt of due proof that an employee, while insured under this policy, shall have become wholly and continuously disabled as a result of (*a*) nonoccupational accidental bodily injuries, or (*b*) nonoccupational illness, and thereby be prevented from performing any and every duty pertaining to his employment, the Insurer will, subject to the limitations and provisions of the policy, pay to such employee for the period set forth in the provision hereof entitled "Period of Benefits" payments at the rate determined in accordance with the provision hereof entitled "Amount of Insurance."

The following is typical of a long-term disability income policy:

> Upon receipt of due proof that any employee while insured under this policy became totally disabled (as defined below) as a result of nonoccupational bodily injury or nonoccupational sickness and remained continuously so disabled during a qualifying period hereinafter set forth, the Insurer, subject to the provisions, conditions, and limitations of this policy, will pay monthly benefits to such employees at a rate determined in accordance with the provision entitled "Amount of Insurance" except that in no event shall benefits be payable:
>
> 1. On or after the date (*a*) the employee ceases to be totally disabled or (*b*) the employee fails to furnish due proof of the continuance of total disability, nor
> 2. After the expiration of 120 months of total disability following the completion of the qualifying period, with any one period of disability, nor after the expiration of a combined total of 120 months of total disability following the completion of the necessary qualifying period, with respect to two or more periods of disability arising from the same or related causes, (120-month limitations are generally not adhered to) nor
> 3. After the date the employee attains the 65th anniversary of his or her date of birth.
>
> For purposes of this policy,
>
>   (a) An employee shall be considered totally disabled if he or she is wholly and continuously unable
>
> 1. During the first two years of any one period of disability, to perform any and every duty pertaining to his or her employment, and
> 2. During the remainder of such period of disability, to engage in any occupation or perform any work for compensation or profit for which he or she is or may become reasonably fitted by education, training, or experience.

Limitations

For both short- and long-term policies, limitations are likely to exclude disability during a period in which the employee is not under the direct care of a physician, during disability caused by self-inflicted injuries, and during disability caused by accidental bodily injuries arising out of, or in the course of, employment by an employer to which benefits are payable under workers' compensation, occupational disease, or similar laws.

With the passage of Federal Public Law 95-555 in 1978, employers are required to provide the same benefits for disabilities resulting from pregnancy as for disabilities resulting from other causes. Most short- and long-term disability policies now cover disabilities caused by pregnancy in the same way they do disabilities caused by any other illness.

Under the benefit administration of one major company, pregnancy is accepted as a cause of disability after completion of the eighth month, and continued disability will be presumed for four weeks following normal delivery and six weeks after a cesarean section. In the case of abortion, disability is assumed to last two weeks after the procedure is performed.

Objective medical proof of disability is claimed prior to the completion of the eighth month of pregnancy or after four weeks following normal delivery, six weeks in the case of a cesarean delivery, and two weeks in the case of abortion.

Elimination Period

An elimination or waiting period of 3, 4, 5, 7, or as long as 14 or 30 days prior to the commencement of benefits may be included in short-term plans in the case of sickness. The purpose of a waiting period, by delaying financial support, is to discourage malingering, to reduce the administrative work load by eliminating claims for short-term episodes of disability, which are the more frequent, and to let individuals bear the relatively small losses, permitting the collective resources to be spent on the large losses that individuals cannot afford.

Accident coverage under short-term plans has the same waiting period as sickness, or it may have no waiting period because accidents, which account for about one eighth of all disabilities, are seldom within the control of the employee to the extent they may be for sickness.

The elimination period for long-term policies generally is longer, being on the order of three months, six months, or a year, and the period usually is chosen to mesh appropriately with the benefits provisions of any accompanying short-term plan.

The significance of the waiting period can be seen from the data in Table 18-4. The table sets forth the frequency of disability among 1,000 male employees in a given year and the extent of disability among them in one year of exposure.

Table 18-4
Annual Disability Experience (per 1,000 male employees)

Duration of Disability t (in days)	1 Number Disabled at Beginning of Duration t	2 Number of Days of Disability on and after Duration t
1	196	6,476
2	193	6,279
3	189	6,086
4	183	5,898
5	176	5,715
6	168	5,539
7	159	5,371
8	150	5,212
14	97	4,457
15	92	4,360
21	67	3,876
22	65	3,809
28	51	3,458
29	49	3,407
35	41	3,134

Source: Morton D. Miller, "Group Weekly Indemnity Study," *Transactions of Society of Actuaries* 3 (1951), pp. 31-67.

Column 1 shows the annual frequency per thousand of those who become disabled for *t* days or more, and column 2 shows the total number of days of disability after *t* day to to be expected from those remaining disabled for longer than *t* days.

Among a group of 1,000 male employees, 196 disabilities, which will result in a total of 6,476 days of disability, can be expected over a one-year period. According to the table, 46 (196 minus 150), or about 23 percent of the disabilities, do not last as long as eight days and would be eliminated by a seven-day waiting period.

Correspondingly, 1,264 days of disability (6,476 minus 5,212), or approximately 20 percent of the total days, would be eliminated. A waiting period of 21 days would eliminate 131 (about 67 percent) from receiving benefits for the disabilities, and 2,667 (41 percent) of the disability days would be eliminated.

Thus, because they eliminate claims for a great many trivial disabilities for which earnings loss is small and omit payment for only a few days in the case of longer disabilities, waiting periods can serve the useful function of reducing costs for employers who wish to utilize them. As mentioned previously, in addition to saving claim dollars, waiting periods eliminate the disproportionate expense of handling many small claims and minimize the tendency for the plan to encourage unwarranted absence from work.

Amount of Benefits

In deciding on the amount of benefits to be provided, it is important that overinsurance be avoided. The failure to do so would furnish a strong incentive to both claim disability and to continue disabled once receiving benefits. Consequently, the benefit amounts should relate to take-home pay rather than to gross income. Overtime bonuses and other special compensation should not be taken into account when arriving at benefit amounts.

Disability benefits are always exempt from Social Security payroll taxes and generally are exempt from federal and state income taxes. This comes about because there is a $100 per week sick pay exemption for lower-paid employees, so taxable short-term disability benefits are usually modest.

The result is that a disabled person's predisability take-home pay can usually be replaced by a benefit that is 75 to 85 percent of predisability gross income. The percentage needed to replace predisability take-home pay varies by income and may be 70 percent or less for high-income individuals. However, this takes into account only the effect of taxes, so additional factors need to be considered.

Certain work-related expenses are not needed during a period of disability. Taking these into account would further reduce the required percentage of predisability income to 65 to 75 percent of gross pay to reach the same level of spendable income for the average individual. With this level of income, the individual will not suffer financially from the disability unless the individual's out-of-pocket medical expenses are high.

The amount of benefit is sometimes expressed in terms of a schedule, such as the following:

Normal Weekly Earnings	Weekly Benefit
Less than $210	$125
$210 and less than $270	$166
$270 and less than $330	$200
$330 and less than $390	$240
$390 and less than $450	$280
$450 and less than $510	$320
$510 and less than $570	$360

The above table is intended to be illustrative only. In today's inflationary economy, maximum benefits are often considerably higher.

Occasionally, the benefit amount may be determined by the title or occupational classification of the employee. If so, it is hard to maintain a proper relationship between the benefit and normal earnings. Furthermore, it is difficult to arrive at suitable occupational groupings that are precise, definite, and properly differentiated.

Also, when plan specifications are established by union bargaining, the benefit level may be the same for all persons covered. Where wage rates are fairly homogeneous this may be satisfactory, but steps should be taken to be sure that the benefit amount bears an appropriate relationship to the extremes of pay reported by the group. A special clause usually is included, stating that the benefit payable may not exceed some percentage, such as 66.6 percent of the employee's normal earnings.

Change of Classification

When an employee's insurance classification or level of compensation changes, it is usual to stipulate that the amount of insurance will change automatically. Should the employee not be actively at work at the time of change, however, any increase in the insurance would not become effective until his or her return to work.

Incentive to Return to Work

To encourage a return to work as soon as the individual is physically able, an economic incentive usually is desirable. Such an incentive could be provided by limiting benefits to a level somewhat below that described above. A benefit of 55 to 65 percent of predisability gross income generally serves this purpose.

This should be supplemented by a strong rehabilitation program designed to help the individual return to work. The individual who is just recovering and is facing the decision of whether or when to return to work should be encouraged to make the attempt, rather than remain on disability. Those disabled persons who have no potential for returning to work would still have an income sufficient to provide the necessities of life at a level close to that enjoyed before disablement.

The problem of determining what constitutes adequate incentive to return to work becomes difficult because the very existence of disability is often highly subjective. Most people are motivated to remain in the active work force and will return as soon as possible. This is readily apparent in the case of the many severely handicapped individuals who lead active, productive lives. Some, however, will remain disabled beyond the time they are physically able to return to work and pursue other activities—to avoid returning to an unpleasant work atmosphere or because they are apprehensive about their ability to perform. An economic incentive to return to work tends to minimize these problems.

Overlapping Benefits

There are a significant number of programs, both public and private, which undertake to provide benefits for individuals who become disabled, and for the most part they operate independently of one another and have no means for effective integration. It is apparent that ways must be found to coordinate the various systems more effectively so the carefully designed incentives built into a given program are not made inoperative by the overlapping benefits of other programs.

An indication of the impact of overinsurance may be obtained by reviewing the periodic studies made by the Society of Actuaries of experience under employer-sponsored long-term disability plans. Experience for the period 1971 to 1975, published in 1978, indicates that claims were 91 percent of the average when benefits were 50 percent of gross pay or less; 100 percent for benefits from 51 to 60 percent; 106 percent for benefits from 61 to 70 percent; and 119 percent for benefits in excess of 70 percent. Similar studies have been done covering different periods and, while the percentages vary, one can clearly identify a direct relationship between the level of benefits and claim utilization.

The above data relate to overinsurance without regard to the source of benefits or to the overlapping of two or more programs. The same Society of Actuaries studies also provide data which show the effect on programs of overlapping benefits. The studies found that, if group long-term disability benefits were reduced by total Social Security benefits, the rate of claims grew to 101 percent of the average, and with no integration it became 112 percent. If this degree of unfavorable experience develops where duplication of benefits is moderate, it is likely that the experience is far worse where duplication is greater.

The multiplicity of programs providing disability benefits, the impact of taxes, the absence of work-related expenses, and the need for some financial incentive to return to work all complicate the overinsurance issue. However, there is evidence that the general public has a basic understanding of the concept. A report on public opinion published by the Health Insurance Institute reveals that 93 percent of those surveyed support the provision of disability benefits at a level no greater than take-home pay. This tends to agree with the view of many experts who contend that few people set out to abuse or defraud the system, but once they become disabled and are receiving benefits at a level above that needed to maintain their prior standard of living, the financial incentive to remain on disability takes hold and they stay on the disability rolls longer than necessary.

Considerable care should be taken in designing plans for employers in unstable industries and for those where employment is erratic or seasonal and accompanied by periodic unemployment or shutdowns. In the latter category are school teaching and such seasonal industries as food canning, summer amusement, and resort operations. Whenever significant layoffs or interruptions in employment are to be expected, experience has shown that the insurance may be used as a kind of unemployment benefit.

Feigned or imaginary illnesses, or those which the employee disregards when regular employment is available, become the causes of lengthy claims when unemployment is prevalent. Malingering is always a hazard and is exaggerated when those insured lose their source of livelihood. For seasonal industries, it is sometimes provided that protection ceases—and even benefit payments for those disabled cease—when the period of regular employment ends and are resumed when the period of regular employment starts again.

A longer waiting period for sickness may help to bring about satisfactory results. Also, in irregular and unstable employment, it is important to limit the coverage to those who are employed for a substantial minimum period, such as six months, to exclude the seasonal and temporary employees.

For plans with long maximum benefit periods, disability benefits from other sources should be taken into account. Social Security is the principal source of such other income, but workers' compensation, veterans' pensions, disability income provisions under employer pension and group life plans, and individual disability income policies constitute other sources of income. The different benefits should be so integrated that the total payment from all sources is not too attractive when related to normal earnings.

Cost Control

Cooperation by the employer policyholder is a most important element of cost control throughout, particularly in claims administration for group disability income insurance. While the establishment and continuation of a claim depend upon the physician's certification of the disability, it has been demonstrated conclusively over the years that the employer's attitude toward absences significantly influences the frequency and duration of claim payments. Lax employment practices and the lack of employer followup of employees with minor disabilities can seriously impair the control of group disability income costs.

The need for employer cooperation extends well beyond the income program. There is a growing awareness among employers that the cost of effective preventive programs, which bring to light and place potential disability claimants under early treatment, may be more than offset by the resultant savings under their disability plans. This is particularly true for those with alcoholic tendencies or with mental and nervous conditions. Also, the trend to longer and more extended benefit periods under short-term plans emphasizes the importance of rehabilitative programs.

Inflation

Inflation has a complex influence on disability income systems. It diminishes the purchasing power of benefits for programs that are not adjusted for inflation, thus providing an increasing incentive for a return to work. Yet, today, many private and most governmental programs adjust for inflation after disablement. The development of programs that adjust for inflation places greater importance on the overinsurance problem. Claims are prolonged beyond their normal or proper duration, and claims are submitted for conditions that normally would not be disabling or for spurious or exaggerated causes.

Termination of Coverage

Most short- and long-term group disability policies permit the insurer to terminate the policy on any anniversary date, though this provision is seldom employed. Of course, the benefits being paid to an already disabled person are unaffected by the termination of the master policy.

In addition, it usually is stipulated that the insurance company may terminate the policy on any premium due date, generally once a month, when the number of employees covered drops below some stated minimum or percentage (usually 75 percent) of those eligible. The employer can terminate the policy on any premium due date and, except as provided in the 31-day grace provision for payment of premium, the policy will terminate on default in payment of the premium.

The nature of the insurance is reflected in the policy provision dealing with the termination of the insurance of individuals when they cease work. Protection generally is not continued following termination of active work, and certainly not for any extended time. This is consistent with the basic purpose of the insurance. When wages have ceased because of termination of employment, there can be no income loss resulting from a subsequent disability. Experience has shown that disability insurance, if continued during periods of layoff, leaves of absence, or following terminations of the employment relationship, is likely to be used as a form of unemployment compensation.

Plan Design and Administration

As can be seen from the foregoing discussion, disability income insurance is a highly complex form of coverage. Success with a particular plan depends in large measure on what is the employer's philosophy about employee benefits and on the objectives in establishing a disability income plan for his or her employees.

Fortunately, a great deal of flexibility in plan design is possible, which permits an employer to tailor the plan to meet both his or her objectives and the requirements of the employees. Among the considerations which the employer must resolve are the following.

1. Is eligibility to be confined to full-time employees? Should there be a waiting period before employees can join the plan? The latter question is a matter of particular importance where employee turnover is high.

2. Is the plan to cover short-term or long-term disabilities alone, or to include both short and long-term disabilities?

3.   Is there to be an elimination period, such as four or seven days, for sickness under a short-term plan, and what should the longer period be, such as 3, 6, or 12 months, under a long-term plan?

4.   Is the plan to be contributory? If so, to what extent?

5.   What is to be the schedule of benefits that should relate to the level of take-home pay? To avoid overinsurance, are Social Security benefits to be offset against the plan benefits? If so, should the offset be on the primary insured amount or on family benefits? The trend appears to be toward the former. Are there workers' compensation, pension-oriented, or other benefits that also should be offset?

6.   Are the benefits to be adjusted for inflation, which has the effect over time of diminishing the value of the benefits? Most government programs adjust the benefits for inflation and some private plans do also.

7.   The plan must meet the requirements of: the state plans, if the employer has employees in any of the six states, of the Employee Retirement Income Security Act of 1974 (ERISA) and also of the Age-Discrimination in Employment Act (ADEA) provisions. The act provides that benefits be provided to age 65 for disabilities commencing after age 60, and to the first to occur of five years or attainment of age 70 for disabilities commencing at age 60 and above.

8.   From the standpoint of administration, is the employer prepared to support rehabilitative measures designed to help disabled individuals to return to work?

The passage of ERISA and its preemption of state laws' provision that reads ". . . neither an employee benefit plan nor any trust established under such a plan shall be deemed to be an insurance company or other insurer . . . or to be engaged in the business of insurance . . . for purposes of any law of any state purporting to regulate insurance companies . . ." have made possible other options involving various degrees of self-insurance that may appeal to employers with 200 or more employees.

In considering self-insurance for the larger employers, the following should be kept in mind:

1.   The employer retains the use of funds that otherwise would have been established as reserves for other liabilities by the insurer under an insured plan.

2.   Virtually all states have eliminated premium taxes on self-funded plans. There is no payment of the insurance company's risk charge. And there are reduced retention charges.

3.   Under the Administrative Services Only (ASO) approach, the employer contracts with an insurer solely for the purpose of paying the claims totally and directly out of employer funds. Any risk of any loss remains with the employer.

4.   Under the minimum premium approach claims also are paid directly from employer funds. To retain the existence of an insurance contract, however, the employer pays the insurer a small premium, which represents

the insurer's expenses, risk charges, and, if the insurer is holding the claim reserve, the amount required to fund the increase in the insurer's claim reserve during the given year.

5. The so-called split funding approach is really a form of what was referred to in item 4 as minimum premium. Split funding normally involves a monthly limit on the amount of claim liability that an employer can incur under the plan. Under split funding there may be an option for the employer rather than the insurer to hold the claim reserve.

Under minimum premium or split funding, it has become increasingly common for the insurer to accept a "hold harmless" letter or agreement from the employer representing the employer's assumption of liability for claims. This is used by the insurer as an asset when setting up a claim reserve liability on the balance sheet.

6. While self-funding has many advantages, it is not without some potential problems. One that has been pointed out is the lack of predictability of cash-flow requirements, particularly in years of fluctuating claims. Another relates to the need to establish appropriate administrative arrangements, which should receive periodic review and updating where necessary.

The self-insuring employers differ from one another so much that there is no standard way to agree on administrative arrangements. Four general areas of administration are deserving of some general comments:

Banking Arrangements. It is important to distinguish between uninsured plans under which the insurer has terminal liability for unreported or in-process claims and extended benefits and arrangements under which the employer assumes these liabilities. If the plan is ASO, with the insurer having no liability for outstanding claims in the event of termination, there is good reason to consider having benefit payments drawn on a bank account established, maintained, and controlled by the employer or by the trust, if there is one, with payment identified as by the employer or through trust payment instruments.

In this way the payment instruments reflect the fact that the insurer is merely acting as agent of the employer or trust in the administration of the plan, which may be of special significance in the case of a long-term disability plan, where benefit payments may extend over many years. If the payment instruments are to be handled in this way, it is important from the beginning that the insurer and the employer have a clear understanding about the information and data that are to be made available for monitoring activity of the benefit account and handling reconciliation.

Drafts issued or Drafts Cleared. Drafts cleared would appear to be the most appropriate basis for securing funds from uninsured plans to cover benefit payments, because funds are not actually needed until the drafts clear. This also is the way charges are routinely made against group policyholders' accounts under conventional plans.

Premium Accounting and Statistics. The same type of statistical information is provided for minimum premium and split-funded plans as would be available if the plans were fully insured.

Terminal Liability Provisions. Under a minimum premium plan, coverage is provided during the continuance of the agreement for claims in excess of the aggregate or stop-loss limit, and upon termination, for claims incurred while the agreement was in effect but unreported or in the process of payment at termination. The minimum premium agreement includes a terminal retrospective premium provision to cover possible reserve deficiency.

GROUP CREDITOR DISABILITY INSURANCE

Credit insurance is a specialized form of group disability coverage written in connection with loan or credit transactions. It was developed after World War II and initially sold on an individual policy basis. In the early 1960s, insurers began writing these benefits under group policies, which is now the predominant basis.

Group credit disability income insurance usually is written as an addition to group credit life insurance, and generally is available to institutions lending money to be repaid on an installment basis or providing for the financing of goods or services to be paid for in installments. Few creditors provide disability coverage alone, although some may offer it in connection with home mortgage loans.

Data concerning group credit disability income insurance are available only since 1967. Table 18–5 shows the growth of this coverage since then in terms of premiums earned.

Unlike other forms of group disability insurance, group creditor disability insurance provides for the payment of benefits to a creditor rather than to the person covered. Benefits are payable for disabilities that begin while the debtor is insured, provided he or she remains continuously disabled for a specified period. The specified period, sometimes referred to as the qualification period, usually is 14 or 30 days. Benefits may be retroactive to the first day of disability (the first day of the qualification period), or, when not retroactive, are payable only for continuous disability after the qualification period.

Table 18–5
Premiums for Group Credit Disability Insurance in the
United States ($ millions)

Year	Premiums	Percent Increase	Year	Premiums	Percent Increase
1967	$100,600		1974	$ 495,641	3.8%
1968	118,000	17.3%	1975	547,158	10.4
1969	126,500	7.2	1976	592,193	8.2
1970	153,700	21.5	1977	742,867	25.4
1971	175,215	14.0	1978	847,523	14.1
1972	362,505	106.9	1979	1050,575	24.0
1973	477,707	31.8			

Source: the Health Insurance Institute and the Argus Charts.

The 30-day nonretroactive waiting period is more common in plans written for banks and sales finance companies. These institutions generally make credit transactions for larger amounts to persons whose income levels can be expected to absorb monthly installment repayments despite a disability. Companies licensed under a small loan or similar act prefer a 14-day qualification period with retroactive benefits.

Determination and Duration of Benefits

Benefits are determined on the due date of the debtor's monthly installment by one of two methods. The first, referred to as the monthly installment method, pays benefits equal to the debtor's full monthly payment if he or she completes the qualification period and continues to be totally disabled to the monthly premium due date. Since nothing is paid under this method unless the debtor is disabled on the installment due date, the second approach, the pro rata payment method, is preferred despite necessitating some additional administrative detail.

Under the pro rata method, if the debtor qualifies and is disabled, thereafter, one 30th of the monthly installment is paid for each day of continuous disability. Thus, so long as the debtor qualifies, some benefit is paid whether or not he or she is disabled on the payment due date.

Disability benefits continue under either method while the insured debtor remains totally disabled, but not beyond the scheduled maturity of the indebtedness. The maximum period of indebtedness covered normally is five years, but recently longer coverage has been offered in recognition of the longer installment period common to home-improvement loans and loans made for the purchase of mobile homes. The usual periods of coverage for these plans are 84 and 96 months, but some extend for 10 years or longer. Insurers who offer plans for longer than five years do so cautiously, however, because of the uncertainties present in underwriting a plan which, in effect, provides long-term disability income and is coupled with the short qualification period typical of group credit.

Exclusions and Limitations

A credit disability income policy contains a preexisting conditions clause to control possible adverse selection by individual borrowers. Benefits are excluded for disability resulting from a condition that manifested itself within a stated period, normally six months, immediately preceding the date the debtor became insured. As a result, this exclusion is modified to allow benefits for such preexisting disabilities due to the condition six months after the debtor has become insured. Hence, the exclusion is often called the "six and six" provision. Some policies provide for a 12-months exclusion. Periods as short as three months have been tried, but with a "three and three" provision a person with a chronic illness could obtain disability coverage by refraining from treatment for just a few months. Such a short time has been opposed by some as likely to be ineffective and to prove quite costly especially when the benefits under the plan are payable for an extended period.

While credit disability policies may require that the debtor be actively at work at the time his or her loan is taken out, this provision is not frequently used. It is felt that the creditor ordinarily will insist upon the debtor being gainfully employed before credit is extended.

Since Social Security and other forms of retirement income are not interrupted by periods of disability, the same need for disability coverage does not exist among those age 65 and over. Hence, it is common practice to limit coverage of credit disability income to debtors who have not yet attained age 65.

Two methods are used to achieve this age limitation. The first and more frequently used is to restrict eligibility to those who have not attained age 65 at the time debt is incurred. The second is to require that the debt mature before the debtor attains age 66.

Disabilities resulting from acts of war are excluded from benefit payment. Some states will not permit group creditor disability insurance on those whose incomes will not be interrupted by disability. The main impact of this restriction is to exclude members of the armed forces. Unlike short-term disability income benefits, group creditor disability benefits are payable for both occupational and nonoccupational disabilities, since installment payments must continue in either event.

Indemnity Amount

The amount of the monthly disability indemnity is determined by the amount and number of repayment installments to be made by the borrower. The credit disability policy usually stipulates that the monthly disability benefit shall not exceed a maximum amount.

The policy also limits the aggregate of the disability payments that may become payable in respect to a disabled debtor's original indebtedness. The maximum insurance on an individual loan typically depends upon the ultimate loan volume to be expected from the case as a whole. It is reasonable to anticipate that the loan volume, depending upon the size of the lending institution and the amount of business it anticipates from its installment loan activities, will level off eventually.

The maximum insured amount would not necessarily restrict a vendor or a lender in making loans for a larger amount. However, the insurer's liability would be limited to the maximum amount in the event the debtor became disabled. In such a case, the amount of the monthly insured payment would be determined in one of two ways, depending upon how premiums were charged. If, on the one hand, under the terms of the group policy, the coverage was paid for by means of a single premium that was due at the time the indebtedness was incurred and was calculated to be sufficient to cover the loan in its entirety, the monthly disability indemnity would be prorated. On the other hand, if premiums were payable monthly on the outstanding balance of the loan, the insurer would indemnify the full monthly installment during the disability until the maximum insured amount was reached.

For example, a $10,000 loan that is insured for half the amount, and was to be repaid in monthly installments of $200, would be indemnified at the rate of $100 per month extending over the full duration of the loan when the single-premium basis is used. If, instead, premiums relate to monthly outstanding balances, disability indemnity would be at the rate of $200 a month but would cease when payments totaled $5,000. In the latter circumstances, premiums would continue to be due and payable during the disability.

Participation

As with other group insurance contracts, participation must be maintained at such a level that significant adverse selection is avoided. Thus, some plans are written to include all eligible debtors for coverage. In such instances, there would be no specific extra charge above the financing charges made by the creditor for the insurance. Where the cost of insurance is borne by the debtor, the coverage is optional and participation by eligible debtors must be maintained at a 75 percent level. In the event participation falls below 75 percent, the insurer reserves the right to require evidence of insurability and to accept or reject an individual debtor.

CHAPTER 19

Health Care Cost-Containment Techniques

WILLIAM G. WILLIAMS

INTRODUCTION

It is hard to pick up a copy of any general or trade publication these days without seeing some reference to health care cost-containment. The unprecedented rise in the cost of providing health care is a problem in which we are all both victims and culprits. It is obvious that so intricate a problem is not going to yield to a single, sweeping solution. Frankly, the dilemma is the result of living in a complex society with many conflicting objectives. For example, we want everyone to have the best medical care, *and we want cost-containment*. We want everyone to have the freedom to choose who will provide them with health care, and to go to that provider as often as they want, *and we want cost-containment*. We want every community, neighborhood, and religious group to have their own hospital, *and we want cost-containment*. We want every hospital, nursing home, and doctor's office to be equipped in the most modern fashion, *and we want cost-containment*. We want every citizen to have access to care without money being a barrier to receiving that care, *and we want cost-containment*.

Anyone who has ever served on a health systems agency (HSA) or a hospital board or worked with a cost-containment coalition is aware of these conflicting objectives and of the difficulties involved in resolving them. Problems are easy to identify; workable solutions are not. Nevertheless, growing concern with the substantial increase in the money spent for health care has focused the attention of employers, the public, government, and the providers of medical care services on finding ways to solve the cost problem.

Health care cost-containment techniques involve a set of interrelated components that produce cost savings for the employer. Included among the components are benefit plan design ideas, claims review, external cost control systems, and health education and promotion. It is unlikely that any one health care cost-containment technique will produce large savings for a

251

plan. However, when a number of these techniques are put into effect together, then meaningful cost reductions can be achieved.

BENEFIT PLAN DESIGN IDEAS

Today, changes in health insurance plans are taking place because of legislative mandates, changes in medical care institutions, emergence of new types of providers, development of new methods of medical care and treatment, and continuing health care cost increases. These changes affect the overall costs of health insurance plans, and if the changes cannot be controlled, plans must be designed to minimize their effect. Such benefit plan design ideas as deductibles, coinsurance, coordination of benefits, preadmission testing, skilled nursing care, home health care, preventive care, and second surgical opinions serve this function.

Deductibles

A deductible, which is the cost of medical care expenses an insured person must incur and pay before medical care benefits become payable under a plan, may be expressed as a dollar amount ($100, $200, $1,000), a percentage of the insured employee's income (1 percent), or both. Traditionally, they have been expressed in fixed-dollar amounts; however, there recently has developed a tendency to adopt or to consider income-related deductibles, because such deductibles adjust automatically to inflationary trends and may serve as a health care cost-containment technique.

Deductibles eliminate the high costs of investigating and paying for small claims; they lower employer costs for a medical care expense plan and employee costs for a contributory plan; and they contribute to controlling misuse of medical care, because the user's financial involvement encourages questioning the amount and type of treatment received. However, the use of deductibles may pose a financial impediment to treatment, and the costs of care may increase if treatment is postponed. Employees may be dissatisfied with insurance plans including deductibles and opt for alternative plans, such as health maintenance organizations, that do not use the deductible approach. The combination of a deductible and other cost-sharing features (such as coinsurance, copayment, or inside limits) also may impose a financial hardship on insured persons. Modifications of the deductible principle that have evolved in response to these concerns include benefit designs that involve separate deductibles, maximum family deductibles, common accident deductible provisions, and deductible carry-over provisions.

Ultimately, the impact of deductibles applied to inpatient care is likely limited to discouraging frivolous admissions. When applied to outpatient care, however, this technique may discourage prompt diagnosis and treatment of legitimate illnesses, with a result that the higher cost of later treatment may outweigh the savings accrued through the intended avoidance of nuisance claims.

Coinsurance

Another way to assure the insured person participates in sharing a risk is to require that his or her participation in the payment of covered expenses be a continuing one. A coinsurance provision typically indicates the insurance plan will pay a specified percentage (usually 80 percent) of all or of certain covered medical care expenses in excess of any applicable deductible. The remaining percentage (20 percent) is borne by the insured. In many plans today, a coinsurance limit or "cap" eliminates the coinsurance factor for the balance of the calendar year, after the insured has paid a fixed amount in expenses (e.g., $1,000, $1,500, $2,500).

Variable coinsurance percentages are found in many major medical expense insurance plans. In one plan, for example, inpatient and outpatient benefits are payable at 80 percent of all covered medical care expenses incurred during any one calendar year, in excess of any deductible, until the out-of-pocket maximum is reached; thereafter, 100 percent of all additional covered expenses for the balance of the year are paid. These features (where permissible) do not apply to the expenses incurred for outpatient treatment of alcoholism, drug addiction, and mental and nervous disorders, which are payable at 50 percent of the charges incurred and limited to a total maximum amount each calendar year (e.g., $1,000).

To entice employees to obtain care outside of a hospital, a plan could reimburse only 90 percent of semiprivate hospitalization expenses as opposed to 100 percent for ambulatory surgery. Also, to focus on the uselessness and wastefulness of Friday and Saturday hospital admissions, only 80 percent of such expenses would be covered except for emergencies.

Coinsurance, more than any deductible, gives insured persons a financial stake in the medical care services they use and a financial incentive to help control their use. Coinsurance also lowers plan costs for the employer and for the employees in a contributory plan. The arguments against coinsurance are identical to those against deductibles, and the response of many insurers has been to place caps on the coinsurance provisions.

The use of deductibles and coinsurance as disincentives to overutilization and unnecessary care will probably increase, resulting in an immediate containment of premium costs. However, there does not seem to be any optimum deductible amount or coinsurance rate in which excessive utilization is reduced but people are not discouraged from getting necessary care. Whatever the amount or percentage, there must always be some trade-off in the efforts to balance the two competing objectives of coverage adequacy and cost control.

Coordination of Benefits (COB)

Very simply defined, coordination of benefits (COB) is:

A process by which two or more insurers, insuring the same person for the same or similar group health insurance benefits, limit the aggregate benefits he or she receives to an amount not exceeding the actual amount of loss, that is, not more than 100 percent of allowable expenses.

Coordination of benefits was developed as a health care cost-containment technique because of the rapid growth of overinsurance. Overinsurance occurs when a person is insured under two or more insurance policies and is eligible to collect an aggregate of benefits that exceeds his or her actual loss. The main sources of overinsurance are:

1. Both husband and wife employed and eligible for group health insurance benefits.
2. Persons employed in two jobs, both of which provide group health insurance benefits.
3. Association group plans, especially among salaried and professional people who usually already have group health insurance benefits through their employers.

Since COB is an arrangement among several group insurance plans to predetermine responsibility for coverage so the total of all "coordinated" benefits paid will not exceed 100 percent of allowable expenses, it is necessary to determine which insurer is to pay any claim first. If only one group insurance plan has a COB provision, the group insurance plan without the COB provision pays its benefits first and the group insurance plan with a COB provision pays second, that is, it coordinates its benefits based on the benefits paid by the primary group insurance plan. However, when both group insurance plans have a COB provision, both have the right to reduce their benefits based on the benefits paid by the other group insurance plan. To prevent the possibility of an insured being caught in the middle of a dispute between two insurers, and to provide a consistent and simple order of benefit determination (i.e., who pays first), the COB provisions set out the following system:

1. The plan covering the patient as an employee pays before the plan covering the patient as a dependent.
2. The plan covering the patient as a dependent of a male person pays before the plan covering the patient as a dependent of a female person.
3. Where the order of payment cannot be determined by these rules, the first plan to make payment will be the one that has covered the insured for the longer period of time.

The following claim example illustrates what occurs in the absence, and the presence, of a COB provision:

> Mrs. Jones has filed a claim for $600 with both company A and company B. Company A insures Mrs. Jones as a female employee under a plan covering 80 percent of eligible expenses after a $25 deductible is satisfied. Company B insures her as a dependent spouse under a plan providing 75 percent of eligible expenses after a $100 deductible is met. In the absence of COB both companies would have to pay Mrs. Jones as follows:

Company A:		Company B:	
Allowable expenses	$600	Allowable expenses	$600
Less deductible	25	Less deductible	100
	$575		$500
× 80% coinsurance	.80	× 75% coinsurance	.75
Benefit payable	$460	Benefit payable	$375

In the absence of a COB provision, both insurers would pay the full benefits payable under the plans which in this example totals $835. In this case the insured, Mrs. Jones, would have made money to the extent of $235 as a result of her medical care expenses.

Using our example again, here is how the payments would be calculated with the presence of a COB provision in both plans:

Company A:		Company B:	
Allowable expenses	$600	Allowable expenses	$600
Less deductible	25	Less Company "A"'s benefit	460
	$575	Company B pays	$140
× 80% coinsurance	.80		
Company A pays	$460		

Thus under COB, company B paid only $140, producing a benefit saving of $235. This amount is credited to Mrs. Jones, to be applied to any future claims she might have against company B during the claim determination period, generally a calendar year. This credit can be used to provide benefits that would not have otherwise been paid. If, for example, the policy with company B provides psychiatric outpatient benefits, but only to a maximum of $500 in a claim determination period, and Mrs. Jones incurs $750 of psychiatric outpatient expenses in that same claim determination period, then the $235 credit could be used to extend benefits beyond the $500 maximum. The effect of COB in Mrs. Jones's case, then, is that, between the two insurers, she received reimbursement of the full $600 of expenses and has a $235 credit with company B.

Coordination of benefits is a necessary health care cost-containment technique used to minimize duplicate payments for covered services and thereby limit the potential of a net financial gain to the person seeking medical care. It is estimated the use of COB saves approximately 4 to 8 percent in claim payments that would otherwise have been made.

Preadmission Testing (PAT)

The purpose of preadmission testing is to help contain hospital costs by reducing the number of in-hospital patient days through having the necessary X-rays, laboratory tests, and examinations conducted on an outpatient basis, prior to a scheduled hospital admission, and reimbursed as if on an inpatient basis. It is important to note PAT is not an outpatient diagnostic benefit program, but is offered as an inpatient reimbursement alternative to a longer hospital confinement or, in some cases, to an unnecessary hospital confinement.

Advantages to Patients.   The advantage for the patient who is being admitted for medical care is that treatment can begin immediately. This is far better than admitting the patient a day or two ahead of time to have tests run and then waiting for the results before treatment is begun.

It reduces the possibility of patients being admitted on weekends for routine or elective surgery and necessary tests scheduled for the following week. It allows the patient to become familiar with the hospital before admission, and means an alleviation of anxiety as well as less time away from home and job.

Advantages to Physicians.   Getting test results early—especially in cases where there is a history of heart disease, diabetes, and the like—is a great advantage to the patient's physician. It helps the provider get a jump on planning the course of treatment. Should there be negative test results, the admission can be canceled before the patient comes to the hospital.

The physician who is able to confirm a diagnosis and develop a plan of treatment before the patient is admitted is also able to begin treatment promptly upon the patient's arrival. Once the test results are available and the physician is sure of the admission, all the admitting department has to do is type the bed assignment and date of admission on the admission form and wait for the patient to show up. Because all the paperwork can be prepared in advance, the admissions process is effectuated promptly and smoothly.

The tests also are available for the anesthesiologist's evaluation prior to the patient's arrival for surgery. This enables the anesthesiologist to determine the proper type and amount of anesthesia in an unharried atmosphere.

How PAT Works.   In general, this is how preadmission testing works:

1. After the diagnosis has been established, the procedure scheduled and the patient's room reserved by the hospital, the attending physician orders those tests and examinations which he or she considers to be necessary before the procedure can be performed.
2. The patient is instructed to report at a scheduled time and specified place in the hospital where the tests are to be completed. The results of the tests are reported to the attending physician and are made a part of the patient's hospital chart at the time of admission.
3. Charges for the tests are billed by the hospital to the insurer as a part of the bill for in-hospital care, according to the benefit provisions of the patient's insurance plan.

4. The time period prior to admission, during which the tests and examinations are to be made, is determined by the medical judgment of the attending physician. Most tests will be made as close to the admission date as practicable so the test results may be completely dependable and acceptable.

5. When the admission must be cancelled or postponed for any reason outside the patient's control, the insurer will still make payment for the tests, and when the admission is rescheduled will make the same benefits available again.

6. The above procedures apply to elective surgical admissions and medical confinements.

How Is PAT's Cost-Containment Potential Compromised? It is compromised in the following ways:

1. By the pattern of medical practice in the community. For example, providers in a fee-for-service setting lack the financial incentive to use PAT. In addition, some providers admit their patients several days prior to surgery to allow for their adjustment to hospitalization.

2. By the often-mistaken assumptions of the patient, doctor, or hospital that the patient's insurer provides more comprehensive coverage for inpatient care.

3. By the desire of hospitals to keep their beds filled. Hospitals with low occupancy, on the one hand, have strong financial incentives to fill beds and to render all possible services on an inpatient basis. On the other hand, hospitals with high occupancy have strong incentives to reduce the length of hospital stays and make beds available.

4. By the physician's time involvement in the scheduling of tests.

5. By the matter of convenience to both physician and patient. For example, some patients find it difficult to go back and forth to the hospital on an outpatient basis; other patients are very sick or elderly and cannot go back and forth to the hospital.

6. By the mistaken notion of the patient that testing on an inpatient basis is more thorough.

7. By the lack of coordination in the scheduling of tests and the availability of beds and operating rooms. Inefficient scheduling of all elements in this process leads to delays, which offset any PAT savings.

8. By the reluctance of hospitals and physicians to participate because of the spectre of malpractice suits. This attitude is probably the result of concern about any testing done in facilities outside the hospital, such as an ambulatory care center, independent clinical laboratory, or physician's office. In addition, in many cases hospital-based laboratories are contracted out to a physician or group of physicians. Since their reimbursement formula often is dependent upon utilization, it would not be in their interest to encourage the use of "outside" facilities.

Conclusions. PAT benefit programs, which are relatively easy to add to existing benefit plans, are provided at no additional cost to employers or employees. Effectively utilized, they can generate cost savings. PAT programs alone can help to reduce hospital lengths of stay. When combined with a hospital utilization review program evaluating the necessity of a hospital admission, the quality of care, and the length of stay for a given diagnosis, PAT has considerable potential to encourage hospitals to improve their admission and presurgical testing procedures. Ultimately, it usually is the physician who decides whether to use PAT, but his or her decision can be influenced by the patient concerned about the escalating cost of medical care who asks, "Can't my presurgical tests be done on an outpatient basis?"

PAT programs offer the potential for reducing both the cost per hospital admission and the time lost from work. At the same time, PAT can help reduce the need for more hospital bed construction.

Skilled Nursing Care

The shift in emphasis today to out-of-hospital care (i.e., insurers providing less costly alternatives to hospitalization without sacrificing the quality of the care) has resulted in development of a concept sometimes referred to as progrsssive care. In this environment, a patient proceeds through various levels of care, as dictated by his or her health condition, not necessarily beginning with a hospital confinement. For example, these levels could include intensive care, normal acute inpatient hospital care, confinement in a skilled nursing facility requiring limited medical attention, and home health care.

It is well recognized that the latter days of a hospital confinement require a lesser level of care than that provided in a general acute care hospital. Accordingly, if a plan includes skilled nursing care and home health care, the patient with the concurrence of the attending physician could be prevailed upon to transfer to a lesser level of care. The obvious cost savings relative to these levels of care is the greatly reduced per diem charge, compared to a hospital's room and board charge.

Home Health Care

Like skilled nursing care (care in an extended care facility, nursing home, or convalescent home), home health care is an alternative to costly inpatient hospital care. A comprehensive range of health care services (e.g., part-time or intermittent nursing care provided under the supervision of a registered nurse, physical therapy, occupational therapy, medications and laboratory services, and part-time or intermittent services of a home health aide) can be provided to a patient at home. Decisions to use home health care benefits are based on such factors as family capabilities and patient desires.

Home health care programs are appropriate for chronically ill or disabled persons as well as for patients who require only monitoring during rehabilitation or maintenance care.

Home health care provides supportive care at costs considerably less than hospital confinement, and in an atmosphere often far more restful to the patient.

Preventive Care

Traditionally, medical care has focused on treatment rather than on prevention of illness. However, many health experts today believe the incidence and/or severity of illnesses, such as heart disease, stroke, and cancer, can be greatly reduced through proper preventive care and early diagnosis.

Preventive care can take many forms, some of them being periodic physical examinations to minimize complications through early detection, well-baby care (under two years; including immunizations), well-child care (2–15 years; including immunizations), and patient counseling by physicians for non-illnesses (e.g., smoking cessation, weight control, diet counseling, physical fitness, nutrition). Insurers are increasingly involved in examining the value of all of these forms to determine which preventive measures are health and cost effective. For example, some differences of opinion exist, even within the medical profession itself, concerning the value of annual physical examinations versus cost and the most effective use of physicians' time. Those who approve the concept of preventive physical examinations lean toward providing specific tests periodically, the frequency being based on age and sex. Ultimately, say the experts, preventive care may reduce a company's health care costs, though results are difficult to measure.

Second Surgical Opinions

"Second opinion" has been defined as a prospective screening process that relies on a consulting physician's or surgeon's evaluation of the need for surgery that another surgeon has recommended. Thus, anyone for whom elective, nonemergency surgery is recommended is well advised to obtain a second opinion before proceeding. For example, while one doctor may recommend surgery, another may recommend medication or postponing an operation. A second opinion encourages doctors to review the necessity and advisability of surgery, instills patient confidence by reducing anxieties, and discloses alternatives that may avoid or postpone surgery. The decision whether to accept surgery or alternative treatment is still the patient's.

What Kinds of Surgery Are Suitable for Second Opinions? The following are typical procedures often suitable for a second surgical opinion:

Dilatation and curettage (D and C).

Surgery of the thyroid, tonsils, or adenoids.

Surgery of the back, hip, or knee joint.

Surgery of the colon, duodenum, or stomach.

Surgery of the gallbladder or prostate.

Surgery for hernia.

Hysterectomy.

Surgery of the breast.

Surgery for hemorrhoids.

Surgery of the heart, veins, or arteries.

This is a partial list, because many observers say that almost 90 percent of all surgery can be categorized as elective and nonemergency. It is important to remember second surgical opinion programs do not cover second opinions for the following:

Normal pregnancies.

Elective abortions.

Occupational accidents or diseases.

Surgery involving local infiltration anesthesia.

Second opinions rendered while confined in hospital.

Surgery that may be performed in a doctor's office, such as incision and
    drainage of an abscess.

Cosmetic surgery.

Dental surgery.

Sterilizations.

How Are Second Opinions Reimbursed? In specifically designed second surgical opinion programs, the manner of reimbursement may be as follows:

1. One hundred percent of the first $100 of such charges and eighty percent of the balance of such charges are payable. No cash deductible applies.
2. A fixed fee (e.g., $50) is payable to the consulting surgeon if he or she agrees to accept the fee as payment in full. Charges for necessary X-rays and laboratory tests, up to a fixed limit (e.g., $75) will be reimbursed in addition to the fixed fee payable to the consulting surgeon. No deductible or coinsurance provisions are applicable to this benefit.
3. One hundred percent of usual, customary and reasonable charges incurred in seeking a second (and third) opinion from a consulting surgeon, prior to being hospitalized for the proposed elective surgery. This surgical consultation benefit also includes any charges for addi-

tional necessary X-rays, laboratory tests, and other diagnostic studies. No deductible or coinsurance provisions are applicable to this benefit.

4. No cost to the patient for expenses related to second opinions.

Voluntary versus Mandatory Second Surgical Opinion Programs. A second surgical opinion program is instituted either on a voluntary or a mandatory basis. The major problem with the voluntary program is under-utilization. Indeed, many employees do not understand the second surgical opinion option. The degree to which voluntary programs are used often hinges directly on the enthusiasm of management in promoting the concept and the inclusion of an incentive. For example, surgery without a second opinion is reimbursed at 80 percent, whereas surgery following a second, or even a third opinion, is reimbursed at 100 percent.

Mandatory programs, which require patients to seek a second opinion before insurance will pay for the surgery, have been subject to many objections. They concern the denial of payment if second opinions are not obtained; payment of a reduced benefit if the claimant has surgery without getting a second opinion or after receiving a nonconfirming second opinion; regimentation that takes away the patient's right of free choice; and, possible adverse effects on the physician/patient relationship. Enforcement is a problem for mandatory programs, as well as denial of payment, which can cause employee dissatisfaction. Despite the objections and concerns, mandatory second surgical opinion programs show promise as an effective cost-containment technique.

Under either type of program, and regardless of the consulting surgeon's opinion, the final decision whether to go ahead with the operation lies with the patient. The potential for cost savings in a second surgical opinion program lie primarily in the following areas:

Surgeries not confirmed and not performed.

Surgeries performed on an ambulatory rather than an inpatient basis, as initially recommended.

General reduction in surgical claims because of physician awareness of the program. This is known as the "sentinel" effect.

CHAPTER 20

Health Care
Cost-Containment
Techniques
(Continued)

WILLIAM G. WILLIAMS

CLAIMS REVIEW

Hospital Utilization Review

Hospital utilization review (UR) is designed to reduce the incidence of unnecessary or inappropriate hospitalization. The procedure, used for both cost and quality control, involves the use of locally determined criteria to establish guidelines for appropriate admissions, hospital lengths of stay, and course of treatment. These criteria are based on age, sex, and diagnosis. The actual review process is performed by professional review organizations (PROs) or foundations for medical care (FMCs).

Hospital utilization can be reviewed on a prospective, concurrent, or retrospective basis. A combination of these approaches comprises the most effective UR program, but concurrent review is the most prevalent.

Prospective Review. A prospective review program involves preadmission screening, by physicians, to limit hospital admissions to those "medically necessary;" to second surgical opinions prior to elective surgery; and to predetermination of dental benefits. Physicians in HMOs often use prospective URs to control hospital utilization.

While prospective review provides an effective front-line defense against unnecessary hospitalization, its usefulness is limited because control is lost once a patient is admitted and the physician is then free to order any number of tests and keep the patient hospitalized as long as he or she would like. When coupled with concurrent and retrospective review, prospective review can be effective.

Concurrent Review. A concurrent review program involves determining whether treatment and continued inpatient care during a patient's hospitalization are necessary and appropriate. Because it can lead to a shortened length of stay, this procedure has definite potential to produce cost-savings.

262

Retrospective Review.   A retrospective review program determines the appropriateness of the care that has been provided and the extent to which hospitalization costs should be reimbursed. This mechanism can create substantial economic incentive for changing patterns of care.

This type of claims review allows an employer to establish a utilization profile to use in monitoring trends. Included in such a profile would be diagnoses, the kinds and prices of medical services purchased by each employee, where they were provided, and the portion paid by the company. Appropriate action could then be taken in excessively high-cost areas.

A hospital utilization review program may be delegated or nondelegated, binding or nonbinding, and involve all-patient review or focussed review.

Delegated or Nondelegated Review.   Delegated review refers to the authorization granted by a qualified review program to a hospital to conduct one or more review functions (i.e., a hospital is either fully or partially delegated and utilizes its own nurse coordinators and physician advisors). Many employers prefer nondelegated review (i.e., the qualified UR program places its own nurse coordinators and physician advisors in hospitals) because of the "fox guarding the henhouse" analogy, which questions the wisdom or appropriateness of asking a hospital's professional personnel to police themselves.

Binding or Nonbinding Review.   Under binding review, the UR program directs the type or level of payment, including payment "denials," by the appropriate payor. Health insurance companies participate in nonbinding review programs because the UR decisions are not binding on the payors and because the decisions whether and to what extent health benefits should be paid are the sole and independent judgments of the payors.

All-Patient Review or Focussed Review.   Most UR programs start out doing all-patient review and, after developing credible data relative to physician treatment patterns by diagnoses, opt for focussed review, which is more relevant and less costly. Focussed review involves the exemption from detailed review of certain groups of patients or common diagnoses where credible data indicate it is reasonable to do so. It is an application of sampling techniques.

A basic objective of any UR program is to assure the patient is not located in a care setting that exceeds medical necessity. Far too many hospital beds are filled with people who should be in a nursing facility, outpatient department, or at home. Achievement of this objective would result in great cost savings. An important result of an effective UR program is the reduction of "defensive medicine," where physicians tend to overutilize medical services for fear of malpractice suits, and also overutilization for other reasons. Accepted utilization criteria define the necessary tests and services for common diagnoses.

An effective hospital utilization review program most probably will shorten hospital stays and reduce hospital utilization. However, in areas where hospital beds are not in excess, shorter stays and more appropriate hospital utilization will increase hospital revenues through increased usage of ancillary services. In areas that have an excess of hospital beds, effective hospital utilization review can negatively affect hospitals' financial positions. But, employers can offer assistance to these hospitals in developing new or expanded services when review has highlighted specific needs.

Employer interest in UR (i.e., to scrutinize claims to determine the appropriateness of the care and services rendered, and to determine the costs eligible for coverage) is being expressed individually and through employer coalitions. The potential for implementation of such programs continues to be contingent on the density of insureds in a given geographic area, and on the contractural commitment of an area's hospitals to participate in a private-sector utilization review program. Ultimately, it is the individual physicians who control the resources of a hospital. If any UR system is to have an impact, the behavior of the physicians who have demonstrated consistent patterns of high utilization and excessive lengths of stay by diagnosis must be changed.

Hospital Audit Programs

Hospital audit programs exist because insurers have long been aware that good medicine and good accounting do not necessarily go hand in hand. To deal with this problem, insurers use independent or internal (sometimes both) auditors to conduct a continuing series of audits for hospital claims most likely to be in error, such as bills exceeding $10,000 or bills submitted by hospitals with a history of billing errors. Some of the most prevalent errors are in pharmacy, laboratory, radiology, inhalation therapy, and oc-cupational therapy. For example, auditors check the doctors' orders, the nurses' notes, pharmacy records, the total charges for therapy divided by the recorded number of hours spent by the therapist, radiology and labora-tory records, as well as the room-and-board charges and length of stay for a ,iven diagnosis. Insurers have found that every dollar spent on hospital audit programs saves almost two dollars in overcharges.

EXTERNAL COST CONTROL SYSTEMS

External cost control systems include alternative delivery systems, such as ambulatory surgery centers, or HMOs, as well as involvement in health planning, or support of hospital budget review.

Ambulatory Surgery Centers

Recognition that many surgeries could be performed on a same-day, outpatient basis (e.g., cataract removal, tonsillectomies, simple hernias, removal of noncancerous cysts, minor gynecological procedures, and biop-sies of various kinds) led to the development of ambulatory surgery centers.

The concept was fostered by the development of new surgical techniques and by the discovery of faster-acting anesthetics that wear off sooner and leave fewer aftereffects.

Two types of ambulatory surgery centers are in operation today: those independent and separate from any hospital—commonly referred to as freestanding ambulatory surgical centers (FASCs) and often called "surgicenters"—and those operating under the auspices of a hospital and known as short-procedure units. In any case, the purpose of these facilities is the performance of surgical procedures considered too demanding for a doctor's office but not serious enough to warrant an inpatient hospital stay. However, the benefits for ambulatory surgery usually are treated as an extension of inpatient hospital benefits with the same level of coverage as if the surgery had been performed on an inpatient basis.

What Are the Savings in the Ambulatory Surgical Concept? It is estimated the percentage savings for procedures performed under this concept can range from 15 to 40 percent. Incidentally, the proponents of freestanding (i.e., not hospital-based) surgical facilities point to two reasons for such savings. First, they state they operate more efficiently than do hospitals and thus can handle more patients at lower average cost. Second, they need not provide extensive ancillary and support services, nor 24-hour staffing, and thus are not obliged to redistribute costs for expensive procedures and services to the minor surgical patients.

The counterargument of hospitals is certain services must be provided to the community (e.g., emergency room, open heart, burn treatment, intensive care) and the revenues to fully support these and other expensive services must be obtained by distributing the costs throughout the spectrum of hospital charges. The development of competing, low-cost freestanding surgical facilities therefore is indicated as contributing to higher community costs. Furthermore, some hospital officials assert independent freestanding day surgery services further worsen hospital finances by neglecting to handle a proportionate number of medically indigent patients.

It also should be noted in this "savings debate" that some nonsurgical procedures are appropriate in a day surgery setting. For example, among the most frequently performed procedures are chemotherapy and extensive radiological examinations. Finally, it is estimated between 20 and 40 percent of all surgical procedures could be performed on an outpatient basis.

What Are Some of the Advantages of the Ambulatory Surgical Center Concept?

1. Lower cost than inpatient surgery as a patient foregoes a two-to-three day hospitalization by having surgery performed on an outpatient basis.
2. Less time away from home and work, because this type of surgery is less disruptive and permits a patient to return to a regular schedule more quickly.
3. Frees hospital beds for more acutely ill patients.

4. Scheduling is quick and relatively easy, as opposed to the process of securing a hospital bed for inpatient surgery, which may require a wait.
5. Offers great convenience to physicians and patients.
6. The environment is conducive to high patient morale and faster recovery.
7. May obviate the need for the expansion of hospital beds.

By eliminating overnight (or longer) confinement, the cost of a surgical procedure is reduced drastically, while the traumatic effect of hospital confinement on a patient is minimized. Thus, coverage of ambulatory surgery serves to lower a company's health care expenditures in the short-term. However, unless community hospitals respond to the decreased patient load by reducing beds, labor, and assets, hospital rates undoubtedly will rise and effectively negate any savings.

Health Maintenance Organizations (HMOs)

The most publicized form of alternative health care delivery system is the health maintenance organization, which refers to any public or private organization providing a full range of health services to an enrolled population (i.e., generally through employer-sponsored plans) within a defined geographic area in return for a fixed, prepaid premium for all services provided. The two major types of HMOs are distinguished by the manner in which their physicians are organized and are called individual practice associations (IPAs) and prepaid group practices (PGPs).

Individual Practice Associations. An IPA is composed of a central administrative component (e.g., a foundation sponsored by a medical society, a county medical society, an insurer, or a hospital) and a group of physicians in a community. The participating physicians continue to practice in their own offices and are reimbursed on a fee-for-service basis according to agreed-upon fee schedules. The HMO, however, receives a prepaid premium from its enrollees, and it is thus "at risk" financially for providing the stipulated health care services to its subscribers. The individual physicians are also "at risk" in the sense their fees from the plan may be reduced in the event of poor overall plan experience. Conversely, they may share in any plan profits.

The IPA's greatest strength, physicians practicing in their own offices, is also its greatest weakness because it lacks the peer interaction and physician selection that facilitates control of utilization and costs. IPAs usually do succeed in lowering inpatient hospital utilization rates, but they seldom attain the levels associated with effective prepaid group practices.

Prepaid Group Practices. A PGP may be a medical group model, in which the plan contracts with an existing or forming group practice, or a staff model, in which physicians are hired by the plan and paid a salary. The participating physicians represent the various medical specialties and practice as a team. Primary patient care is provided in multispecialty clinics usually associated with the HMO's own hospital or with participating hospitals. The HMO receives a prepaid premium from its enrollees and is "at risk" for the costs of the covered health care services because it must provide them for the predetermined premiums as well as meet their financial obligations to their closed panel of physicians.

Advantages and Disadvantages of HMOs to Employers. An employer normally wants to provide adequate health care benefits to its employees and their dependents in an effective and economical manner. Thus, many of the advantages and disadvantages for employers also relate directly to employees. However, there are differences in their perspectives.

Advantages.

1. Broader coverage.
2. Greater preventive care.
3. Less administrative work.
4. Coordinated services at one location.
5. Lower hospitalization rates (i.e., hospital days per 1,000 insureds).
6. Cost-effective, because they offer an incentive to the primary care physicians to constrain health care expenditures.

Disadvantages.

1. Loss of freedom of choice as to doctors and hospitals.
2. Increased cost of health care coverage.
3. Geographically limited.
4. Employee misunderstandings (communication problems).
5. Out-of-plan area coverage problems.
6. Loss of physician/patient relationship.
7. Increased administrative work load/cost.
8. Location of HMO facilities (transportation problems).
9. Concern about fiscal condition of many HMOs.

HMOs offer a potential solution to severe problems found in traditional health care plans. First, the difficulty some people have in finding satisfactory medical care services—an HMO provides access to a team of doctors of all specialties available at most times. Second, the fragmentation of services (e.g., services are at various locations and communication is poor)—an HMO team works together at a single location, where patient records and histories are readily available (true for PGPs but not IPAs). A third problem is the high cost of services. Rich inpatient benefits encourage the use of high-cost hospital facilities. The monies saved by an HMO in limiting hospital confinements, in theory, go to provide preventive care and comprehensive outpatient benefits.

The HMO field in most areas is very volatile. Continued overall enrollment growth is predicted, but many HMOs have too low an enrollment and, with time, probably will merge, expand, or go bankrupt.

Health Planning

Health planning, whether the activity occurs in the public or private sector, is a continuous process requiring the participation of both providers (e.g., physicians, hospitals, nurses, skilled nursing facilities, home health care agencies, dentists, and the like) and consumers (i.e., individual purchasers of health care) of health care services to identify needs, inventory resources, establish priorities, and recommend courses of action.

In the public sector, health planning involves the process created by the National Health Planning and Resources Development Act of 1974 (Public Law 93-641). Under this act, health planning is carried out at the local community level by health systems agencies (HSAs), at the state level by the State Health Planning and Development Agency (SHPDA) which is advised by the Statewide Health Coordinating Council (SHCC), and all is overseen at the national level by the National Council on Health Planning and Development, an advisory body to the Secretary of Health and Human Services (HHS). The council develops national health planning guidelines and national health planning goals, and monitors the implementation of the law.

In the private sector, health planning activities are carried out voluntarily by providers, consumers, and third-party payers (e.g., health insurance companies, Blue Cross/Blue Shield plans, HMOs) through various organizations that study health care issues and make recommendations for improvements (at the national, state, and local levels) and through boards of trustees and planning departments (at the institutional level).

Why Is a Health Planning Program Needed? Two key reasons exist to fight for the retention of a health planning program. First, health planning programs are an important means to address the availability, accessibility, delivery, and cost of health care services. Second, opponents of health planning programs have argued that competition is a better way to allocate health care resources. However, competition advocates admit that competitive health care environments will take at least 10 to 15 years to develop. Even then, what will be required, as it is now, is a balance between the incentives of a competitive environment tempered by an appropriate regulatory framework designed to assure that both public and private responsibilities are met. Thus, even if the theorists are correct, current health planning programs should not be abandoned during the "black hole" period when competitive health care environments may be developing.

Effective health care planning is a major step toward stemming the tide of rising health care costs. Moreover, it invites and needs the participation of employers. Members of the business community are in a key position to enter that health care arena called "planning" because of their influence in the community and the business expertise they can offer. While health planning cannot by itself solve the problem of rising health care costs, it is a significant part of an overall strategy to contain costs. Undertaken as part of an overall comprehensive health care strategy, health planning activities have the potential to help contain company health care costs by controlling costs in the community's health care industry. Perhaps even more important, they have the potential to improve the health care system's performance for the benefit of all.

Hospital Budget Review

In very general terms, a hospital budget review program requires a hospital to submit its budget to a government agency for approval in advance of setting rates to be charged in the coming fiscal year. In this regard, a number of states have established hospital budget review programs. For example, such states as Connecticut, Maryland, Massachusetts, New Jersey, and Washington have mandated that controls be placed on certain hospital costs. While no two state agencies work exactly alike, the basic procedure is for the state agency to review the budget of each hospital in that state and to determine whether:

1. The hospital's total costs are reasonably related to the total services rendered.
2. The hospital's rates are reasonably related to its costs.
3. Rates are set equitably among all purchasers and classes of purchasers.

Then, no hospital may change its rates without the approval of the state agency. Of the 15 states with hospital budget review laws, Connecticut and Maryland stand out. These states have agencies that are independent commissions and not part of any existing state bureaucracy. Most observers attribute the success of the Connecticut and Maryland programs to the following:

1. The budget review commissions in these two states have *the legal authority to require hospitals to justify increases on a prospective basis.*
2. The commissions set rates for *all private-sector patients.*
3. The commissions *coordinate their actions with the health system agencies* set up under the Health Planning Act.

Each hospital budget review is unique, using such techniques as disclosure and review of all hospital budgets in an area or state; review of individual budgets by exception; application of a formula that sets target rates; or negotiation of budgets for individual hospitals or groups of hospitals. In addition, the rates established may apply to the services provided for all payment sources (i.e., Medicare, Medicaid, Blue Cross, health insurance companies, self-insureds, HMOs, and self-paying) or only certain named payment sources. While no single hospital budget review program has been judged universally acceptable, several issues relative to this cost containment technique have become clear, specifically:

1. No real influence can be exerted unless controls are applied equally, regardless of the source of funds. Reduction in payments for hospital care under government programs, for example, merely transfers even greater increases to the private-sector patient since the overall cost of operating the hospital still must be covered.
2. Cost control is inextricably tied to planning for the most efficient use of facilities; this may result in closing or converting surplus beds, or in abandoning services duplicated elsewhere in the community.
3. Review must consider total revenue of the hospitals, as opposed to the price of individual services, since increased utilization can more than make up the savings that controlled charges might realize.

Indications are that, in states with mandatory hospital budget review programs, there has been a slowdown in the rate of increase in patient revenue to hospitals, which is the amount of money hospitals receive from insurance carriers, government, and other payment sources. If the rate of increase can be slowed down, compared with the national average, then real cost savings are being achieved. A coalition of all concerned groups, as in Maryland, can be the catalyst that helps to implement a hospital budget review program.

HEALTH EDUCATION AND PROMOTION

The past decade has witnessed a renaissance of interest in health education, disease prevention, and health promotion. The public has become increasingly cognizant of the impact of lifestyle—smoking or excessive drinking, uncontrolled hypertension, poor diet, lack of exercise, and the like—on the incidence of disease and injury. Individuals have begun to assume more responsibility for their own health, with the understanding that changes in lifestyle can significantly reduce risk factors associated with premature death and disability.

A new philosophy also has emerged regarding the role of the employer in promoting well-being or wellness. There is growing opinion among at least major employers that they have a distinct responsibility to help improve the quality of health of their employees, and company-sponsored programs in health education/promotion offer a promising means to carry out that responsibility.

Health education includes a combination of learning experiences (both informational and educational) that help people to make informed and voluntary decisions about their health and safety, and about the health resources available to them. It provides individuals and families with the knowledge for making their own choices and pursuing their own actions about what is important for health and prepares them to accept the consequences of their decisions just as they would in any form of endeavor.

A health promotion program uses a variety of educational/behavioral strategies (e.g., health risk appraisal, one or more risk-reduction components, health education) to foster changes in daily life habits that could lead to better health. It attempts to integrate the concepts of disease prevention and lifestyle modification with the more traditional practice of treating diseases after they occur. The expectation is that such a program will benefit not only employees and their families but the employer as well by effecting reduced absenteeism and turnover, improved employee morale and productivity and savings on insurance and other employee benefit costs—important objectives of any employer. The program costs might be considered an investment in a company's human resources. The following examples of health promotion programs vary in difficulty to start, in the effort, equipment, and dollars required, and in their benefit:

Smoking cessation.

Hypertension recognition and control.

Stress management.

Weight control.

Employee assistance programs.

Exercise fitness.

Alcohol/drug abuse control.

Cancer risk reduction.

CPR training.

Accident risk reduction.

Self-care.

Emergency medicine.

Glaucoma screening.

Wise utilization of medical care benefits.

Retirement.

This new philosophy is consistent with the mounting intensity of interest in and expectations for health promotion activities. It also coincides with efforts to more effectively contain the escalation in the direct and indirect health, economic, and social costs associated with accidents and illness.

Is There Evidence that Health Education/Promotion Programs Reduce Health Costs? In all fairness, it is difficult, at this time, to obtain hard data on cost savings, because of the short time these programs have existed. To see the effects of risk factor intervention on morbidity and mortality will take years. However, common sense alone suggests that prevention is preferable to curing, that staying healthy is less expensive than being sick, and that improved lifestyles should improve a person's health and longevity.

One cannot be certain of the effect of these programs over many years in strictly economic terms. For example, the United States has an aging population and more people living longer could mean higher costs to deal with the chronic problems of old age. Nevertheless, most experts are convinced that while health education/promotion programs will save money, their greatest value lies in improvement of employee health and well-being, which must increase productivity.

CONCLUSION

No small set of health care cost-containment techniques can be offered as a unique answer to the problem of ever-increasing health care costs. Each technique interacts with others, and employers must strive to maintain medical care expense plans that are well-integrated, consistent with other employee benefits, and appropriate to overall corporate objectives. It is unlikely any one health care cost-containment technique will produce large savings for an employer. However, when a number of these techniques are put into effect together, meaningful cost reductions can be achieved.

PART FOUR

Designing Employee Benefit Plans— Additional Benefits and Services

Part Four consists of six chapters dealing with the design of various employee benefit plans and several service-type plans.

Chapter 21 presents a brief review of property and liability insurance as an employee benefit, and deals with such issues as the types of coverages offered, the kinds of programs under which they are made available, advantages and disadvantages to the employee, the role of the employer, and regulatory issues.

Legal service plans are covered in Chapter 22, and the need for this type of plan and its increasing popularity as an employee benefit plan are discussed.

The next three chapters deal with programs that provide services directly to employees in the form of counseling or other help with various aspects of their private lives. The three forms of this type of employee benefit covered in Part Four are financial counseling in Chapter 23, employee assistance programs in Chapter 24, and retirement preparation in Chapter 25.

The concept of flexible or "cafeteria" benefits is one that has gained much attention recently, and this topic is covered in detail in Chapter 26.

CHAPTER 21

Property and Liability Insurance as an Employee Benefit

BERNARD L. WEBB

INTRODUCTION

While forms of property and liability insurance have been provided as employee benefits for many years, the practice was very limited until the late 1960s. There were reports of automobile insurance benefit plans as early as 1925, but few details are available. Because of the hostility of agent associations and insurance regulatory authorities, the plans were not discussed in public and were sold and serviced in an almost clandestine manner.

The practice received considerable attention at the 1926 meeting of the National Convention of Insurance Commissioners, the predecessor organization of the National Association of Insurance Commissioners.[1] Many commissioners issued regulations at that time prohibiting the practice of insuring employee-owned cars under fleet policies covering company-owned cars. One such ruling was challenged in the courts, but the commissioner's authority to issue it was upheld.[2] Little more was heard of property-liability employee benefit plans for 20 years, though it is clear a few such plans persisted.

Such plans apparently began to spread in the middle 1950s, though progress was slow and not well publicized. The major public manifestation of their growth was the activity of agents' associations in promoting administrative and legislative rules prohibiting the plans.

The first open promotion of property-liability employee benefit plans began in 1965, when the Continental National American Group (CNA) insurance companies announced their entry into the field. Other insurers followed, and plans proliferated until the middle 1970s. Severe underwriting losses at that time caused CNA and a number of other insurers to

---

[1] National Convention of Insurance Commissioners, *Proceedings* (Chicago: National Convention of Insurance Commissioners, 1926), pp. 117–20, 272–76.

[2] *Flat Top Insurance Agency* v. *Sims,* 178 S.E. 518, (W.Va., 1935).

discontinue such plans. As this is written (1982) several insurers are actively selling property-liability employee benefit plans, primarily automobile insurance.

KINDS OF BENEFITS

Virtually all kinds of property-liability insurance for individuals and families have been offered as employee benefits at some time. However, automobile and homeowners insurance (especially the former) have been most common.

Automobile Insurance

Automobile insurance has been the major property-liability insurance employee benefit for two reasons. First, it is compulsory (or virtually compulsory) for car owners in many states. Second, it is the largest single insurance purchase, in terms of premium, for most families.

In most cases, all automobile insurance coverages are offered, including liability, collision, comprehensive, medical payments, towing-cost coverage, and, in the states where applicable, no-fault benefits. The coverages offered under employee benefit plans usually are identical to those offered under policies sold to individuals. In a few cases, the medical payments coverage is modified to coordinate benefits with the employer's medical expense benefit plans. Also, where permitted by state law, a substantial deductible may be provided in the no-fault benefits, applicable only to the employee and family, to coordinate benefits with the employer's medical and income-loss plans.

Employees usually are permitted to select any reasonable limits of liability coverage, and are not restricted to predetermined limits as under group life and health coverage. The same right of selection usually is available for medical payments and no-fault coverage. Physical damage coverages (collision and comprehensive) usually are written for the actual cash value of the vehicle, and employees usually are permitted a selection of deductibles.

In most automobile insurance plans, coverage is provided under individual policies issued to the employees. Some insurers issue master policies to employers with certificates to employees, but the practice is not widespread and is prohibited by law in some states.

Homeowners Insurance

The second most important property-liability insurance employee benefit is homeowners insurance, including tenants coverage for those who do not own a home. It has proved less popular than automobile insurance for two reasons. First, the annual premium for homeowners is likely to be less than automobile insurance premiums for most families. Consequently, the potential savings are smaller. Also, many mortgage lenders require borrowers to pay the premium for homeowners coverage through monthly deposits to an escrow account. This requirement complicates the handling of homeowners policies through employee benefit plans.

Another complication in using homeowners insurance as an employee benefit is the wide variation in the coverages needed, even among families in the same income class. Some families own their homes, while others do not. Some families may need coverage for musical instruments, photographic equipment, golf or other sports equipment, stamp or coin collections, and a wide variety of other special personal property items, while others do not.

Personal Umbrella Liability Coverage

Several insurers offer personal umbrella liability policies under employee benefit programs. These policies offer high limits of liability coverage (usually in multiples of $1 million). The umbrella policy is excess over automobile liability and the liability coverage of the homeowners policy, and does not begin to pay until the limits of those policies have been exhausted.

Personal umbrella policies are especially popular among professional employees, executives, and other highly paid persons. Little variation exists in coverage needs from one person to another, so the administrative burden is much lighter for personal umbrella coverage than for automobile insurance and homeowners policies.

Other Coverages

Several other property-liability coverages have been offered as employee benefits. Boat insurance has been offered by several employers, and at least one airline offers insurance for the personal aircraft owned by its employees. Many employers provide coverage for employees' liability for their on-the-job activities.

KINDS OF PROGRAMS

All the coverages mentioned may be provided under three different kinds of programs. They are distinguished primarily by the relative cost and the amount of underwriting discretion retained by the insurer.

Franchise Plans

The earliest plans were franchise plans, in which the insurer charged the same rates it charged for its individual policies and retained its normal underwriting prerogatives. The principal advantage to the employee was the convenience of installment payment of premiums through payroll deduction. Insurers frequently did not charge interest for the installment payment privilege. In a few cases, the employer paid some or all of the premium, especially for sales personnel or other employees who used their cars for business purposes. Beginning in the late 1960s, franchise plans began to lose ground to mass merchandising plans.

Mass Merchandising Plans

Franchise plans and mass merchandising plans are similar in that the insurer retains the right to underwrite individual employees under both. However, they differ in one important respect because there is a price reduction (in comparison with policies issued individually) under the mass merchandising plans but not under franchise plans.

The extent of the price reduction varies among insurers. It also may vary according to the number of participants in the plan. The amount of expense saving in a particular plan also may affect pricing. The expense savings result primarily from reduction of the agent's commission, but the expense of premium collection and bad debts also may be reduced. Some have suggested better accident prevention measures made possible by mass merchandising may reduce losses, providing another source of premium reduction. However, no statistical evidence of such savings has been made public.

Mass merchandising plans first appeared in substantial numbers around 1970. They still are the dominant form of property-liability employee benefit insurance, but the number of true group plans is increasing.

True Group Plans

Unlike franchise and mass merchandising plans, the insurer under a true group plan agrees to provide coverage for all eligible employees, without the right of individual underwriting. Of course, such an agreement would leave the insurer open to adverse selection in the absence of some method for compelling or enticing low-risk employees to participate in the program.

To avoid adverse selection, insurers that write group property-liability insurance require the employer to pay a part of the premium, a practice not common in franchise or mass merchandising plans. The amount of employer payment required varies among insurers. One insurer requires the employer to pay three or four dollars per week for each employee. Others require the employer to pay at least a specified percentage of the employees' premium, usually from 40 to 60 percent.

For automobile insurance, the insurer may require the employer pay a part of the premium for only one car for each employee. Employees who own more than one car would pay the full premium for the additional vehicles. Without some employer premium payment, the low-risk employees might be able to find insurance outside the plan at a cost equal to or less than the cost within the plan, since the rates within the plan are increased somewhat by the requirement that the insurer provide coverage for all eligible employees. The loss of low-risk employees to competitors, of course, would result in even higher rates for the remaining participants.

ADVANTAGES FOR EMPLOYEES

The advantages realized by the employees vary according to the kind of plan. Quite obviously, a true group plan offers more advantages than a franchise plan.

Lower Cost of Insurance

Both mass merchandising and true group plans offer the advantage of lower cost of insurance to the employee. The difference is especially noticeable under true group plans because the employer usually pays a part of the premium as a requirement of the plan. The magnitude of the premium reduction may vary from a negligible amount to 15 percent or more, not considering any premium payment by the employer. By definition, franchise plans do not offer any reduction in premium.

Greater Availability of Insurance

True group plans make insurance available to some employees who might otherwise be uninsurable. Under franchise and mass merchandising programs, the insurer retains the right to refuse insurance to employees who do not meet its underwriting requirements. However, it appears insurers are more lenient in underwriting individuals under such plans than they are for persons who apply otherwise. Consequently, even franchise and mass merchandising plans probably provide insurance for some people who would find it difficult to obtain in the absence of such plans.

Payroll Deduction

All the plans mentioned usually provide the advantage of installment payment of premium through payroll deduction. In many cases, the insurer does not charge interest or a service fee for the installment payment privilege.

DISADVANTAGES FOR EMPLOYEES

The disadvantages for employees appear to be small. The insurance may terminate when the employment terminates, though some insurers provide some form of conversion privilege. Also, the employees may not have the same flexibility in the selection of coverages that they would have if they purchased their insurance independently. Finally, some employees have expressed concern that their employers may obtain sensitive personal information through the processing of insurance claims or underwriting forms.

ROLE OF EMPLOYER

The role of the employer may vary from plan to plan. In some cases, the employer pays a part of the premium. The employer also may provide advice to employees on the kinds and amounts of insurance they should purchase. However, it is more common for the insurer or agent to provide such advice. It may be illegal in some states for any other person than a licensed insurance agent to provide such advice or to solicit applications for insurance.

In any case, the employer needs to give insurer or agency personnel access to employees for the explanation of the program and the negotiation of applications. The administration of property-liability insurance plans is substantially more complex than the administration of group life and health plans because of (1) the greater variation in the coverage provided, (2) greater frequency of changes, and (3) the complexity of handling claims, especially liability claims. For that reason, most employers prefer not to become involved in the detailed administration of the plan. The details of administration usually are delegated to the insurer or its representatives. Claims administration is seldom if ever performed by the employer, not only because of the complexity of the task but also because many employees would prefer their employer not have access to such detailed information about their off-the-job habits and activities.

In most property-liability insurance plans, the employer's role is limited to (1) selection of the insurer, (2) payment of the premiums from the employer's own funds, through payroll deduction or a combination of the two, (3) mediation of disputes between the insurer and employees. The employer may be involved in notifying the insurer of needed changes in employees' coverage, such as changes of cars or increasing homeowners limits to reflect inflation. However, it is more likely the employees will handle such changes directly with the insurer or its representatives.

FEDERAL INCOME-TAX CONSEQUENCES

Property-liability insurance plans do not enjoy the tax advantages that have been granted for pension plans, group life and health insurance, and prepaid legal insurance plans. This lack of tax incentive is a major reason for the slow growth of property-liability insurance plans.

Any property-liability insurance premiums paid by the employer on behalf of an employee are considered taxable income to the employee. It must be reported as income by the employee and the appropriate tax must be paid. Such payments by the employer are deductible expenses for the employer. Several bills have been introduced in Congress to grant property-liability plans the same tax advantage as other employee benefit plans, but none has been passed.

U.S. LABOR CODE

The U.S. Labor Code contains two provisions that may relate to property-liability insurance benefit plans. The first provision prohibits any employer from giving anything of value to any labor organization or an officer or employer thereof if such labor organization represents or could represent the employer's employees.[3] There is a specific exemption for payments into a fund to provide pensions, life insurance, or health benefits for employees. Payments into a fund to provide property-liability insurance for employees are not exempt, and would be illegal. Consequently, such plans could not be administered by labor unions if the employer pays any of the premium.

The second applicable provision of the labor code specifies the factors related to the employment concerning which the employer can be compelled to bargain in good faith with the union. Property-liability insurance plans are not specifically included among the bargainable items, but employers can be required to bargain about ". . . rates of pay, wages, hours of employment, or other conditions of employment."[4]

The National Labor Relations Board (NLRB) held in the *Inland Steel* case that: "The term 'wages' as used in Section 9(a) must be construed to include emoluments of value, like pension and insurance benefits, which may accrue to employees out of their employment relationship."[5] The NLRB's view has been supported by the U.S. courts in at least two circuits.[6] The interpretation adopted by the NLRB and the courts would seem to be sufficiently broad to include property-liability insurance. Consequently, it seems likely an employer can be compelled to bargain for such benefit plans.

STATE REGULATION

The primary responsibility for insurance regulation rests with the states. Historically, state regulation has been hostile to the use of property-liability insurance as an employee benefit. In many cases, regulatory prohibitions

---

[3] 29 U.S.C. 186.

[4] 29 U.S.C. 158(a), 159(a).

[5] 77 NLRB 4 (1948).

[6] See *United Steel Workers* v. *N.L.R.B.*, 170 F.2d 247 (1948) and *W. W. Cross Co., Inc.* v. *N.L.R.B.*, 174 F.2d 875 (1949).

have been based on statutory provisions prohibiting unfair discrimination in insurance rating. In some cases, specific statutory prohibitions have been enacted.

Fictitious Group Regulations

Beginning in the 1950s, the insurance commissioners of 17 states adopted fictitious group regulations. The regulations differ somewhat from state to state, but the Florida regulation is reasonably typical:

> The Insurance laws of Florida require that any rate, rating plans or form of fire, casualty or surety insurance covering risks in this state shall not be unfairly discriminatory. Therefore, no insurer, admitted or non-admitted, shall make available through any rating plan or form, fire, casualty or surety insurance to any firm, corporation, or association of individuals, any preferred rate or premium based upon any fictitious grouping of such firm, corporation, or association of individuals, which fictitious grouping is hereby defined and declared to be any grouping by way of membership, license, franchise, contract, agreement, or any other method or means; provided, however, that the foregoing shall not apply to accident and health insurance.[7]

Unfair discrimination would seem to be a weak basis for such rulings. Group life and health insurance has been accepted as not unfairly discriminatory in all states for many years. No apparent reason exists to treat property-liability insurance differently.

Fictitious Group Statutes

In 1957, Florida replaced its fictitious group regulation with a fictitious group statute. The statute provided:

> (1) No insurer or any person on behalf of any insurer shall make, offer to make, or permit any preference or distinction in property, marine, casualty, or surety insurance as to form of policy, certificate, premium, rate, benefits, or conditions of insurance, based upon membership, nonmembership, employment, of any person or persons by or in any particular group, association, corporation, or organization, and shall not make the foregoing preference or distinction available in any event based upon any fictitious grouping of persons as defined in this code, such fictitious grouping being hereby defined and declared to be any grouping by way of membership, nonmembership, license, franchise, employment, contract, agreement or any other method or means.
> (2) The restrictions and limitations of this section shall not extend to life and disability insurance.[8]

---

[7] Fla. Ins. Dept., Bulletin No. 211 (1957).
[8] Fla. Stat., Sec. 626.973 (1972).

Effectiveness of Rulings and Statutes

The fictitious group rulings and statutes seemed to be effective for several years after their adoption. However, by the late 1960s, several insurance commissioners had approved filings for franchise and mass merchandising programs in spite of the seeming regulatory and statutory prohibitions. Their actions were challenged in the courts by agent associations, but were generally upheld.[9] Although most of the fictitious group regulations and statutes remained on the books, they became increasingly less effective in controlling property-liability insurance plans for employees.

Enabling Legislation

Beginning in 1969, several states enacted legislation designed specifically to authorize the use of property-liability insurance for employee benefit plans. Minnesota was the first state to adopt such a statute. It reads as follows:

> One rate is unfairly discriminatory in relation to another if it clearly fails to reflect equitably the differences in expected losses, expenses and the degree of risk. Rates are not unfairly discriminatory because different premiums result for policyholders with like loss exposures but different expense factors or like expense factors but different loss exposures, so long as the rates reflect the differences with reasonable accuracy. Rates are not unfairly discriminatory if they attempt to spread risk broadly among persons insured under a group, franchise or blanket policy.[10]

The Minnesota statute was the model for several other states, but Hawaii took a slightly different route. It enacted a rather detailed enabling law specifically for automobile insurance.[11]

Present Status

It appears property-liability insurance can be used as employee benefit plans in all states. However, policy forms, rates, and rating plans must be filed with the insurance commissioner in virtually all states and must be approved before use in over half of the states. In early 1981, one insurer was offering its true group automobile insurance plan to employers in nine states and was seeking approval in additional states. Its plan provided for

---

[9] See for example, *Georgia Ass'n of Independent Ins. Agents* v. *Travelers Indem. Co.,* 313 F. Supp. 841 (N.D. Ga. 1970); *Independent Ins. Agents* v. *Bolton,* 235 N.E. 2d 273 (Illinois, 1968); and *Independent Ins. Agents* v. *Herrmann,* 486 P. 2d 1068 (Washington, 1971).

[10] Minn. Stat. Ann., Sec. 70A.04(4), (1981).

[11] 24 Hawaii Rev. Stat., Sec. 431-751 et. seq.

experience rating of each group, a feature that might complicate approval in some states.[12]

SUMMARY AND CONCLUSIONS

Only a small percentage, probably less than one percent, of personal property-liability insurance is now sold through employee benefit plans. The practice is growing, though at the slow pace that would be expected of an experimental marketing technique.

State regulation, which historically has been hostile to the use of property-liability insurance as an employee benefit, now seems less hostile. However, few states have specific enabling legislation.

Provisions of the federal Internal Revenue Code and the Labor Code place group property-liability insurance at a competitive disadvantage, relative to group life and health insurance and pension plans. Use of property-liability insurance in employee benefit plans is likely to grow slowly unless these federal laws are changed.

---

[12] Russ Banham, "Prudential Has 2 Plans in Force In California," *Journal of Commerce,* March 3, 1981, p. 7.

CHAPTER 22

Legal Service Plans

CLAUDE C. LILLY III

ENVIRONMENT

Legal service plans are really not a new development; they have been in effect since the early 1900s. In fact, insurance contracts providing legal benefits were available by 1907. However, legal benefit plans were relegated to a secondary role until the 1970s.

As an employee benefit, legal service plans made substantial gains in the 1970s and early 1980s. While legal plans are not as widespread as many of the more traditional benefits, the rate of growth has been increasing and should increase more rapidly as insurers become involved in offering group plans. Four factors, however, have been primarily responsible for providing an environment conducive to the growth of legal service plans: (1) a change in the public's attitude about using lawyers, (2) a change in federal laws, (3) a change in the attitude of the bar associations, and (4) a change in state laws.

PUBLIC'S LEGAL NEEDS

The public always has had a need for lawyers, even if it has not always sought legal help. A study done for the Association of American Law Schools in 1938 found in a sample of 412 families that 315 legal matters arose. However, legal advice was sought for only 35.2 percent of the 315 legal matters.[1] While comparable data are not available today, it is probably safe to assume that the legal needs of Americans have increased. The United States seems caught up in a litigious arena that seems to affect every strata of society. For example, expenditures for legal services grew more rapidly than the national income account during the 1970s. Even in non-

---

[1] Charles E. Clark and Emma Corstvet, "The Lawyer and the Public: An A.A.L.S. Survey," 47 *Yale Law Journal* 1276 (1938).

litigious areas of legal practices (e.g., wills, real estate sales, and taxation), consumers are finding the services of a lawyer are needed more frequently.

FEDERAL LAWS

Three changes in federal laws have affected the growth of legal service plans. First, in 1973, Senators Williams and Javitz introduced S.1423. The bill modified the Labor Management Relations Act of 1947. The bill stated:

> . . . section 302(c) of the Labor Management Relations Act, 1947 is amended . . . by adding immediately before the period . . . or (8) with respect to money or any other thing of value paid by any employer to a trust fund established by such representative for the purpose of defraying the cost of legal services for employees, their families, and dependents.[2]

S.1423 was amended prior to enactment, but the basic provision cited above was not changed. The impact of S.1423 was to introduce prepaid legal service benefits into the area of collective bargaining.

The second federal change was initiated in 1974 by the passage of the Employee Retirement Income Security Act (ERISA). Since prepaid legal plans provided on a group basis are subject to ERISA, state insurance regulation over these plans is limited. Specifically:

> Neither an employee benefit plan described in section 4(a), which is not exempt under 4(b) (other than a plan established primarily for the purpose of providing death benefits), nor any trust established under such a plan, shall be deemed an insurance company or other insurer.[3]

This allowed prepaid legal plans offered on a group basis (and subject to ERISA) to avoid state insurance regulations unless the group plan is offered by an insurance company.

The third, and perhaps the most important, federal legislation was passed in 1976. Section 120 of the Internal Revenue Code was so modified that:

> . . . Gross income of an employee, his spouse, or his dependents, does not include—
> (1) Amounts contributed by an employer on behalf of an employee, his spouse, or his dependents under a qualified group legal services plan (as defined in subsection (b)), or
> (2) The value of legal services, under a qualified group legal services plan (as defined in subsection (b)) to, or with respect to, an employee, his spouse, or his dependents.[4]

Section 120(b) defines a qualified legal service plan as:

---

[2] U.S. Congress, Senate, Subcommittee on Labor, "Joint Labor-Management Trust Funds for Legal Services, 1973: Hearings on S.1423" 93rd Congress, 1st session, 10, 11, and 16 April 1973, pp. 2, 3.

[3] Public Law 93-406, Section 514(b)(2)B.

[4] *Internal Revenue Code,* Chapter 26, Section 120.

. . . a separate written plan of an employer for the exclusive benefit of his employees or their spouses or dependents to provide such employees, spouses, or dependents with specified benefits through prepayment of, or provision in advance for, legal fees in whole or in part by the employer.[5]

The law further stipulates that contributions can be made only to insurance companies, to qualified trusts, or to legal service providers.

THE AMERICAN BAR ASSOCIATION AND STATE BAR ASSOCIATIONS

Until the 1970s, the bar worked vigorously to block the development of legal service plans. The bar contended legal service plans interfered with the lawyer-client relationship. The American Bar Association Canons of Professional Ethics, under which most lawyers functioned until 1969, specifically set forth that lawyers could provide service to associations or groups but not to the individual members of a group or association.[6] The canons also prohibited a lawyer from letting his or her name or professional services be used to allow the unauthorized practice of law; group plans constituted the unauthorized practice of law.[7] The content of these canons formed the primary weapons for attacking banks, hospital collection agencies, unions, and real estate services when any type of legal activity was involved.

The bar's attack on the provision of legal services can be documented easily. As early as 1919, the bar attacked legal service plans offered to retail merchants by merchants' protective associations. Generally, these associations concentrated on collecting overdue accounts.[8] The services offered by these associations were attacked successfully in the courts by the bar as being the unauthorized practice of law.

Automobile clubs in the 1930s offered, as one of their benefits, to provide legal advice and to defend members against legal problems relating to the operation of automobiles. These plans were also attacked successfully by the bar as being the unauthorized practice of law.[9]

---

[5] Ibid.

[6] Special Committee on Evaluation of Ethical Standards, American Bar Association, "Code of Professional Responsibility," preliminary draft, Canon 35 (Chicago: American Bar Association, 1969), pp. 124, 125.

[7] Ibid., Canon 47, p. 127.

[8] See *State ex rel Lundin* v. *Merchants' Protective Corporation,* 177 P.694 (1919); *People ex rel Lawyers' Institute of San Diego* v. *Merchants' Protective Corporation,* 189 Cal. 531 (1922); and *People ex rel Los Angeles Bar Association* v. *California Protective Corporation* 76 Cal. App. 354 (1926).

[9] See, *People ex rel Chicago Bar Association* v. *Motorists' Association of Illinois,* 854 Ill. 595 (1933); *People ex rel Chicago Bar Association* v. *Chicago Motor Club,* 199 N.E. 1 (1935); *Seawell* v. *Caroline Motor Club, Inc., et al,* 209 N.C. 624 (1936); *Rhode Island Bar Association* v. *Automobile Service Association,* 100 A.L.R 226 (1935); *in re Maclub of America Inc.,* 3 N.E. 2d 272 (1936); and *Automobile Club* v. *Hoffmeister,* 338 S.W. 2d 348 (1960).

The 1930s saw the development of a legal aid department by the Brotherhood of Railroad Trainmen (BRT). The union plan was the first major plan to survive bar attacks. The BRT aided members in settling major injury claims workers had against the railroads. Generally, a member paid no fee for legal advice about how a claim should be handled. If a claim involved litigation, the member was given a list of approved lawyers that could be utilized in fighting a claim. The agreement between a member and a listed lawyer was approved by the BRT, and the contingency fee was established by the BRT with the approved lawyer. The approved lawyers were required to pay a percentage of their contingency fee to the union to continue the operation of the legal program. This system was slowly modified. By 1959, the contingency fee was no longer fixed, and the union stopped receiving any payments from the lawyers.

The bar attacked the BRT plan for many years.[10] But, the attacks were never reviewed by the United States Supreme Court until 1964. Then a case involving the BRT reached the Supreme Court.[11] It ruled the BRT plan was permitted under the First and Fourteenth Amendments to the United States Constitution.

The bar had lost another fight eight months prior to the BRT decision by the Supreme Court. The Virginia legislature had amended the Virginia Code in 1956 to expand the definition of a runner (a person who sought out legal cases) to include "an agent for an individual or organization which retains a lawyer in connection with an action to which it is not a party and in which it has no pecuniary right. . . ."[12] The National Association for the Advancement of Colored People (NAACP) in Virginia challenged the law because it blocked the Virginia State Conference of NAACP from pursuing school desegregation litigation with the use of the conference's staff lawyers. The U.S. Supreme Court ruled the Virginia Code violated the First and Fourteenth Amendments.

The BRT and NAACP cases were reinforced in 1967. The United Mine Workers (UMW) Union in Illinois was accused of the unauthorized practice of law because it maintained a staff lawyer who helped members settle workers' compensation claims. The Supreme Court reiterated that vital rights could not be denied and sided with the union.[13]

In spite of the BRT, NAACP, and UMW cases, the American Bar Association maintained its opposition to legal service plans when it developed the Code of Professional Responsibility in 1969 to replace the Canons of Professional Ethics. The new code afforded substantial barriers to legal

---

[10] See, *Ryan* v. *Pennsylvania R.R. Co.*, 268 Ill. App. 372 (1932); *In re O'Neill*, S.F. Supp. 465 (1933); *Hildebrand et al.*, v. *State Bar of California*, 225 P.2d 509, 510 (1950); *Atchison, Topeka, and Santa Fe Railway Company* v. *Jackson*, 235F. 2d 392 (1956); and *In re Heinrich*, 140 N.E. 2d 835.

[11] *Brotherhood of Railroad Trainmen* v. *Virginia ex rel Virginia State Bar*, 377 U.S. 1 (1964).

[12] *National Association for the Advancement of Colored People* v. *Button*, 371 U.S. 422 (1963).

[13] *United Mine Workers* v. *Illinois Bar Association*, 389 U.S. 219 (1967).

service plans. The code stipulated specifically that nonprofit legal service plans should be offered only if they met these criteria:

> DR2-103(D) (5) Any other nonprofit organization that recommends, furnishes, or pays for legal services to its members or beneficiaries, but only in those instances and to the extent that controlling constitutional interpretation at the time of the rendition of the services requires the allowance of such legal service activities, and only if the following conditions unless prohibited by such interpretation, are met:
>
> (a)   The primary purpose of such organizations does not include the rendition of legal services.
> (b)   The recommending, furnishing, or paying for legal services to its members is incidental and reasonably related to the primary purposes of such organization.
> (c)   Such organization does not derive a financial benefit from the rendition of legal services by the lawyer.
> (d)   The member or beneficiary for whom the legal services are rendered, and not such organization, is recognized as the client of the lawyer in that matter.[14]

While innocuous in appearance, this section, in conjunction with other provisions of the code, was used to block the provision of free legal advice by unions.

The code was attacked in 1971 in the *United Transportation Union* case.[15] The Supreme Court again ruled that unions had the right to group legal services. The court stated:

> . . . the principle here involved cannot be limited to the facts of this case. At issue is the basic right to group legal action, a right first asserted in this Court by an association of Negroes seeking the protection of freedoms guaranteed by the Constitution. The common thread running through our decision in *NAACP* v. *Button*, *Trainmen*, and *United Mine Workers* is that collective activity undertaken to obtain meaningful access to the courts is a fundamental right.[16]

The American Bar Association has since so modified the code that group legal service plans can be provided. In fact, some bar associations have become involved in the development of legal service plans. However, all of the state supreme courts, which are responsible solely or in conjunction with the state bar associations for establishing the rules of conduct for lawyers, have not developed a code of professional responsibility similar to the American Bar Association Code. Technically, some states still have codes of professional responsibility that could impede group legal service plan growth. But, because of the existing case law, it seems unlikely any

---

[14] American Bar Association, "Code of Professional Responsibility and Canons of Judicial Ethics," Disciplinary Rule 2-103 (D) (X), p. 8.

[15] *United Transportation Union* v. *State Bar of Michigan*, 401 U.S. 585 (1971).

[16] Ibid., p. 585.

state code is actually a barrier to the development of group legal service plans.

STATE REGULATION

Until the 1970s, state regulation of legal service plans was minimal. Most regulation was handled through the courts and aimed at obtaining jurisdiction over legal service plans. The first efforts by states to control legal service plans took place during the early 1900s. During this period, the Physician's Defense Company offered legal and defense coverage to doctors. For an annual premium of $15, a doctor could purchase a policy that had an annual aggregate limit of $10,000 and a per case limit of $5,000. Insurance commissioners in some states sought to regulate the company, but the company resisted. Several suits ensued, and the commissioners were generally successful in gaining jurisdiction over the company.[17] As a result, the company finally quit selling its policies. Following these cases, state regulation of legal service plans was fairly dormant until the *United Transportation Union* case in 1971. Following this decision, the states became more interested in legal service plans.

Since 1971, insurance departments have had to deal with several problem areas associated with legal insurance plans. These include:

1. The language to be used (especially in view of the easy-to-read policy movement).
2. The difficulty in ascertaining if rates are appropriate.
3. Possible conflicts with fictitious group laws (this would not apply in all states).
4. Agent's licensing procedures.
5. Premium tax collections.
6. A determination of whether legal insurance plans are life or property and casualty contracts.
7. A determination of whether individual contracts should be written.

The National Association of Insurance Commissioners (NAIC) appointed a subcommittee to examine these and other legal insurance questions. The subcommittee met in 1973 and developed a model act designed to serve as a guideline for the states. Most states that have enacted legal insurance plan statutes have followed the NAIC lead.

The problems cited above were covered in the model legislation; however, some areas were only examined superficially. For example, agent's licensing procedures were glossed over; the model bill stated a commissioner should establish rules and regulations for licensing.

One aspect of the law seems incongruous in view of the regulatory

---

[17] See *Physicians' Defense Co.* v. *O'Brien*, 111 N.W. 396 (1907) and *Physicians' Defense Co.* v. *Cooper* 199 F. 576 (1912).

environment. The model bill provides a commissioner has a responsibility to approve the compensation paid to lawyers and to determine if the rate of compensation is fair. The bill sets what a commissioner should consider in determining if a rate is fair:

(a) The usual and customary fees charged by lawyers, generally in the area where the services are performed.
(b) The services to be provided.
(c) The extent to which participation in the plan guarantees lawyers a steady flow of employment and income.
(d) Any agreement by which a lawyer assumes a part of the risk of operation.[18]

Since commissioners do not approve the fees charged by doctors and hospitals under health contracts, it seems discriminatory that they should approve the fees charged by lawyers.

Legal insurance plans, as of 1980, (1) cannot be written in 6 states, (2) are permitted in 10 states by statute or interpretation as a casualty line, (3) are permitted as life or property and casualty contracts in 10 states, and (4) probably could be offered in 25 states as a miscellaneous casualty line.[19]

While the regulatory environment at times has been hostile toward the development of legal service plans, the regulatory environment since 1976 has been sufficiently receptive to permit the growth of legal service plans. The growth rate of these plans has been increasing steadily, but not spectacularly.

PLANS AND BENEFITS

To understand the types of plans currently being offered, it is necessary to understand the general types of plans and benefits available. The material that follows presents a brief discussion of the types of plans and benefits that have been developed.

Types of Plans

Legal Service Plans. Legal service plans refer to any plans designed to offer legal services. They can vary from a very informal plan where a company in-house counsel offers advice to elaborate plans with a wide range of scheduled benefits.

Prepaid Plans. Legal service plans can be provided either on a funded basis (i.e., prepaid) or on a current funding basis where the cost of a plan is

---

[18] NIARS Corporation, *Official N.A.I.C. Model Laws Regulations and Guidelines* (Minneapolis: NIARS Corporation, 1977), vol. 2, pp. 680–86.

[19] Sandy Dement, "Legal Insurance in the Decade of the 1980s, Part II," *National Underwriter–Life/Health* (December 13, 1980), p. 13.

handled out of current income. Generally, only employer or union sponsored plans are available on a current basis.

Legal insurance contracts, some labor union plans, and some bar association plans can be classified as prepaid legal plans. One important distinction exists under a trustee plan (e.g., a union or a bar association plan)—benefits may not be guaranteed. If the legal costs exceed the funds in the trust, benefits may be terminated. An insured plan is backed by the surplus of the insurance carrier and, therefore, could offer additional security to those purchasing legal service benefits.

Group versus Individual Plans.   Legal service plans may be provided on either a group or an individual basis. (The NAIC model legislation stipulates that coverage can be written on a group or individual basis. However, as mentioned earlier, group legal insurance violates the fictitious group statutes in some states.) Most coverage has been written on a group basis. There are several reasons. First, it is easier to obtain a spread of risk within a group. Second, administrative costs are held to a minimum. Third, and perhaps most important, the major impetus for legal service plans has come from labor unions for the benefit of their members. Many group plans require a minimum number of participants in each plan or a minimum participation percentage.

Closed versus Open Panel Plans.   Union legal service plans, especially in the early stages of their development, have tended to be closed panel plans. Under a closed panel arrangement, a group of lawyers and paralegal personnel is hired by the unit providing the legal services. The individuals are paid salaries and are responsible for handling all legal matters set forth in the plan.

Funds are provided by employer contributions or by the union's membership through dues. The funds are invested by the union, and the funds plus the interest earned are used to defray the cost of legal services. This approach not only can provide quality control but also provides cost control. Under closed panel plans, the spectre of having the legal cost exceed the available funds may be offset since the lawyers are paid salaries. Thus, costs are fixed. (Even if expenses exceed the funds available, the employer or union often is responsible for any deficit.) However, the demands on the closed panel lawyer can become excessive; as a result, in some plans, members may not be provided prompt service.

Another weakness of a closed panel plan is that it may not provide the expertise necessary to handle all of the legal problems that arise. This can be overcome by hiring outside help as needed. The external counsel is paid from the closed panel's funds. When this approach is used, the plan is called a "modified closed panel plan." (The term *modified closed panel plan* has been given at least two definitions. In addition to the one just presented, a modified closed panel plan has been defined as a panel where participants can choose between panel attorneys and external attorneys. If participants use an external lawyer, they are reimbursed for their expenses. To illustrate, a plan may sign up half of the attorneys in a city who agree to provide services for set fees. These are called "enrolled lawyers." If a participant does not want to use these enrolled lawyers, he or she can use another attorney. The benefits, however, are reduced if a nonenrolled attorney is selected.)

Another method is available to handle the problem of not having adequate expertise. Instead of having an in-house closed panel plan, an external closed panel plan can be developed. In this situation, a group of lawyers is retained by a plan. The lawyers agree to work for a flat fee per hour or per case as long as the funds are available. They bill the plan directly for their services. If the funds are not adequate to meet all legal costs, the lawyers still provide services. The lawyers, therefore, become risk bearers; they guarantee services even if they have to work for free. Some lawyers find risk retention unacceptable. So, some plans have formed an external closed panel plan, which provides guaranteed rates; but the lawyers are not required to provide services if the funds are not sufficient to cover the service demands.

Legal service benefits also can be provided under an open panel plan. Under this approach, plan participants are permitted to select any lawyer they wish. The plan pays a schedule of benefits regardless of the cost of a lawyer's services. Benefits may be paid to plan participants or directly to the lawyers. Frequently, these types of plans provide participants with a list of lawyers that provide services for a fixed rate.

Legal Insurance Plans.   Contracts affording legal service benefits sold by insurers have several names. The terms most often used are *legal insurance, group legal insurance, prepaid legal insurance,* and *legal expense insurance.* The term used in this chapter to refer to insurance plans is *legal insurance.*

TYPES OF BENEFITS

Schedule of Legal Services

Benefit packages vary significantly. Nearly all plans provide a schedule listing the covered legal areas. For example, a list of covered legal areas might include:

Bankruptcy.
Divorce.
Wills.
Adoption.
Traffic violations.
Felony representation.
Misdemeanors.
Juvenile delinquency actions.

Condemnation.

Real estate.

Debt collection.

Property damage.

Small claims proceedings.

Workers' compensation.

Representation before governmental or administrative boards.

Coverage for Legal Services

Establishing what legal areas are covered is the first step in evaluating benefits. The next step is to ascertain the extent of the benefits in each category. A legal service plan may only provide advice. There may or may not be a charge to the plan participant for each visit or for each occurrence. These are called "limited plans." They often provide a referral service, which will recommend lawyers who provide services for fixed fees or hourly rates. In addition to advice, some plans afford services: a will may be drawn up, adoption papers may be processed, or defense advice on civil or criminal charges may be provided. Those plans that provide advice and a group of services (e.g., will preparation, adoptions, and the like) are called "basic plans." The amount of the benefit will vary.

Plans that provide a broad range of benefits, including advice, basic services, and legal defense are called "major plans." Closed panel plans have the ability to offer full coverage for the legal service areas for which benefits are provided, but full coverage is rarely used.

Most open panel plans and some closed panel plans require a plan participant to share in the payment of legal costs, or the plans limit the maximum amount of benefits available in each legal service area. Sharing can be accomplished by:

1. A flat dollar deductible per year—open. (Open or closed indicates the type of plan that normally would use this limitation.)
2. A coinsurance provision—open. (Normally, the plan pays 80 percent; this generally would not apply to closed panel plans unless outside legal talent had to be obtained.)
3. A maximum number of hours of legal service per year or per occurrence—open or closed. (An occurrence could be a visit or a sequence of visits resulting from the same legal problem.)
4. A maximum amount paid for each hour of legal service—open.
5. A maximum number of occurrences per year—open or closed.

Some plans provide legal checkups in addition to the benefits that have been described. Theoretically, these serve the same purpose an annual physical examination does under health insurance contracts. It may be more difficult to detect potential legal problems than existing health problems.

Exclusions

Most plans exclude some types of legal services. Possible exclusions include:

Criminal charges.

Business ventures.

Collection suits (as a plaintiff).

Charges not made except for existence of a legal service plan.

Class actions.

Tax return preparation.

Contingency for cases.

Divorce (limited to one spouse per family).

Unreasonable charges.

When fees are paid by another source.

Appeals.

Fines and penalties.

Controversies with the plan.

While still included in many plans, the exclusion for criminal charges is slowly being eliminated. It has been found for many groups that the criminal coverage does not encourage criminal activities, as some early plan administrators had feared it might.

NONINSURANCE PLANS

Union Plans

As indicated earlier, unions have been in the forefront of the legal services plan movement. While the Brotherhood of Railroad Trainmen is important because of its initial efforts, the first modern-day plan to gain national attention was the Shreveport Bar Association plan.

In 1969, Southwestern Administrators, Inc., (SA), agreed to operate a legal service plan for the Shreveport Legal Services Corporation (SLSC). SLSC was formed by the Shreveport Bar Association. The plan developed by SA afforded benefits for:

1. Advice and consultation.
2. Conferences and negotiations.
3. Investigation and research.
4. Document preparation.
5. Litigation costs.
6. Major legal expense benefits.
7. Domestic relations benefits.

SLSC contracted with the Western Louisiana Council of Laborers, AFL-CIO, and one of its members, Local No. 229 of Shreveport, to enter into an open panel prepaid group legal service plan. The plan started operation in 1971.

The purpose of the plan was to gather data. Its results were valuable. The data indicated that contrary to preconceived ideas, low-income individuals did not abuse a legal service plan through excess utilization. The data also showed that an open panel plan was feasible. The plan is still operating.

Many unions established plans following the success of the Shreveport program. The Amalgamated Clothing Workers of America instituted a plan in 1972 that provided benefits for consumer transactions, domestic relations, adoptions, landlord/tenant problems, real estate transactions, and wills.[20] In 1973, District Council 37 of the American Federation of State, County, and Municipal Employees entered into a program that was proposed jointly by the Columbia University School of Law, the Columbia University School of Social Work, and itself. Prior to entering into the pilot plan, the council had a closed panel plan designed to handle only employment rights cases. The council's membership was and is comprised of civil service workers in New York. When the plan was initiated, the membership was (1) 30 percent clerical and administrative, (2) 22 percent technical and professional, (3) 15 percent hospital workers, (4) 18 percent social aides, and (5) 15 percent blue-collar workers. The salaries of the employees ranged from $5,800 to $16,000 (1973 dollars).[21] The program has grown. Today, covering 140,000 active and retired New York City workers, it is one of the largest plans in operation. It is funded by the City of New York and is self-insured and self-administered.[22] The United Auto Workers and Chrysler have a major program that covers approximately 125,000 active and retired workers.[23] Other programs for laborers locals, firemen, teamsters, and teachers have been started.

Bar Association Plans

Following the BRT decision described earlier, some bar associations started or attempted to start legal service plans. For example, the Los Angeles County Bar Association attempted to start a plan in 1970 and 1971

---

[20] Amalgamated Clothing Workers of America, Chicago Joint Board, Prepaid Group Legal Service Plan, initiated in Chicago on April 1, 1972.

[21] District Council 37, American Federation of State, County and Municipal Employees, Columbia University School of Law, Columbia University School of Social Work, "Proposal for Pilot Study of a Legal Services Program for a Working Class Population," mimeographed, 1973, pp. 4, 5.

[22] Sandy Dement, "Legal Insurance in the Decade of the 1980s, Part I," *National Underwriter–Life/Health* (November 29, 1980), pp. 16, 17.

[23] Ibid, p. 17.

with the California Teachers Association, but it was not successful.[24] The Monroe County Bar Association proposed a plan for Rochester, New York.[25] The New Mexico State Bar formed a prepaid group legal services corporation in 1973 to provide legal services.[26] As stated earlier, the Shreveport Bar Association formed the Shreveport Legal Services Corporation. In 1972, the State Bar Association of Texas formed the Texas Legal Protection Plan, Inc. The goal of this nonprofit corporation when it was incorporated was to help the citizens of Texas obtain legal services.[27] The Arizona Bar Association formed Arizona Legal Services (ALS), which offers what ALS terms a tri-open plan. Under this approach, members of the Arizona Bar Association can provide services for ALS for the amounts set forth in the fee schedule. A plan participant selects a lawyer. If the lawyer operates as a member of ALS, he or she will provide legal services for the fee agreed to in the plan schedule. If a plan participant elects to use the service of a lawyer who is not enrolled, the benefit payments are less than those for a participating lawyer.[28]

Bar association plans have not grown as rapidly as their union counterparts. The lack of growth is due, in part, to the lack of a captive market and, in part, to a lack of enthusiasm. This lack of success has not daunted bar associations, however. The Florida Bar Association recently embarked on a program to establish legal service plans.

Other Plans

Legal service plans have been developed or sold by other organizations. Benefits have been offered to credit-card customers. Some universities offer legal services to students, and some plans operate through the mail. Most of these plans have not had a major impact in the more complex areas of legal services. Most of their success has been in offering limited programs.

INSURANCE PLANS

A review of legal insurance plans proposed in the early 1970s indicates the insurance industry planned to become deeply involved in the legal

---

[24] Marshall A. Caskey, Director of Information, Los Angeles County Bar Association, letter, December 4, 1973.

[25] Edwin L. Gasperini and Max Schorr, "Prepaid Group Legal Services—Where We Are," 45 N.Y.S.B. *Journal* 76 (1973).

[26] Claude C. Lilly, *Legal Services for the Middle Market* (Cincinnati: National Underwriter Company, 1974), p. 97.

[27] Bylaws of Texas Legal Protection Plan, Inc. Article X, pp. 15, 16.

[28] H. Lee Pickering, "Prepaid Legal Insurance—'Justice for All'," *Management World*, 7:10 (1978), p. 18.

services movement. A tremendous gap existed between the initial insurance industry interest and the actual involvement. By 1973, CUMIS Insurance Society, Inc., Federated Insurers of Nashville, Inc., Fireman's Fund Insurance Company, Financial Indemnity Company, Insurance Company of North America, St. Paul Companies, Stonewall Insurance Company, Stuyvesant Insurance Company, and Midwest Mutual Company had designed legal insurance policies or plans, or both. Only Midwest Mutual and CUMIS ever took an active role in offering legal insurance policies.

The reasons for the reduction in the insurance industry's interest can be attributed to several factors. First, loss data were not available. Estimates of plan utilization ranged from 20 to 100 percent. So, insurers who had developed policies were unable to determine an appropriate rate, and were unwilling to gamble.

Second, prepaid legal exposures do not meet all the criteria established by the industry in deciding what is an insurable risk. A loss may not be fortuitous in nature, and it can be difficult to verify. Payments for investigation, research, and trust preparation are examples. Obtaining a large number of homogenous risks also is difficult.

The industry also lacked the ready access to markets that was available to unions. This problem was compounded by the economic decline in the middle of the 1970s and the concomitant high inflation. Employees wanted increased pay, not legal service benefits.

Fourth, the industry encountered opposition from insurance regulators. As indicated earlier, group legal insurance plans probably cannot be written in some states because of the fictitious group statutes. In addition, a few regulators did not seem sure who should sell legal insurance, life companies or property and casualty companies.

Finally, insurers were not sure whether they should offer indemnity plans or service contracts. The latter would have required establishing panels of lawyers to work with the insurers; the former would have limited the degree of cost control.

Currently, many of these obstacles have been eliminated or reduced. Some rating data are now available, and it appears utilization per year will be between 20 and 30 percent. The state regulatory environment has been partially cleared. Employees seem to be more interested in legal services as an employee benefit, and a hybrid between indemnification and service is developing.

Insurance Companies

As mentioned above, CUMIS Insurance Society and Midwest Mutual Insurance Company (Midwest) have been involved in the legal insurance areas since the early 1970s. CUMIS is part of a financial holding company, which specializes in offering coverage to members of credit unions. CUMIS serves as the servicing and funding mechanism.

Midwest has developed one of the largest pools of insureds for legal insurance. Currently, it has more than 20,000 insureds in 17 states. Coverage is provided in group policies, and individual certificates are issued to the group members. The basic coverage offered by Midwest includes legal advice, legal representation, and major trial coverage. It should be noted that the Midwest plan includes maximum-dollar amounts per hour, as well as aggregate-dollar maximums.

Midwest attempts to enroll all the lawyers in the states in which it operates. The success rate ranges from 30 to 70 percent. A plan participant is encouraged to use enrolled lawyers because these lawyers have agreed to work for the rate set forth in the contract. For example, if a divorce action is being handled by an enrolled lawyer, he or she agrees not to charge more than the hourly rate or more than the aggregates found in the policies. If a plan participant uses a nonenrolled lawyer, the contract shifts from a service contract to one of indemnification. The plan participant is paid directly; however, the benefit levels for nonenrolled lawyers are less than those paid to enrolled lawyers. So, a strong incentive exists for plan participants to use an enrolled lawyer.

Prudential Property and Casualty Insurance Company has initiated a group legal insurance plan in California entitled Prudential Plus. The program utilizes a closed panel plan to handle advice and other preventive services. Major legal problems are handled on an indemnification basis. The preventive services in California are provided by the Law Store Group, Inc. (Law Store), of Santa Monica, California. According to the vice president of the Law Store, 80 to 85 percent of plan participant problems can be handled without having to hire a lawyer.[29] Travelers also has entered into an agreement with the Law Store in which it would handle preventive legal services, but Travelers has not actively entered the marketplace, yet.[30]

Nonprofit Organizations

Blue Cross and Blue Shield (BC and BS) plans (most of which are nonprofit) have been very active in the legal insurance areas. Because BC and BS associations usually are operated on a service basis, they are logical organizations to provide legal insurance on a service basis.

At least 17 BC and BS associations offer coverage or have initiated research into the legal service area.[31] In Minnesota, Blue Cross and Blue Shield have formed Minnesota Indemnity, Inc. The company markets coverage to the teachers union in Minnesota. Two plans are available to teachers. One provides limited benefits, bar advice, consultation, office

---

[29] Al Haggerty, "Prudential Group Legal Plan A Plus," *National Underwriter–Life/Health* (October 18, 1980), p. 6.

[30] Ibid.

[31] Sandy Dement, "A New Bargaining Focus on Legal Services," *AFL-CIO American Federationist,* 85:5 (1980), p. 9.

work, and defense; one provides broad coverage for the same categories.[32] Blue Cross of Indiana also is forming a new plan.[33] Blue Cross of Western Pennsylvania offers coverage to groups of ten or more through its wholly owned subsidiary, Consumer Service Casualty Insurance Company.[34]

THE FUTURE OF LEGAL SERVICES
AS A FRINGE BENEFIT

> Prepaid legal insurance has now developed to the same point where group health was 50 years ago.[35]

While this quote may be slightly understating the current position of legal services as an employee benefit, it is reasonably accurate. However, the future of these plans appears excellent. The future of legal services as an employee benefit will be tied both to demand/pull and supply/push.

Demand/Pull

Demand for legal services will be affected by (1) demographic changes, (2) increasing litigation, (3) union pressures, and (4) the economic environment. If the current demographic trends continue, the need for personal legal services will expand. As more women move into the work force in the 1980s, there will be more legal problems.

The litigious nature of our society has been discussed in numerous articles. It is sufficient to state the existing attitude of the public can only mean the rate of growth of suits will increase.

More than 300 legal service plans currently are being operated by or in conjunction with unions. (Most of these plans are not insured.) This is a small number of plans relative to the potential union membership market. Many unions have brought legal service plans to the bargaining table but have not pushed the plans because other fringe benefits were more important or because their membership was more interested in monetary increases. If inflation can be controlled and less emphasis placed on monetary increases by unions, the environment for legal service benefits should be excellent in the 1980s.

Supply/Push

Supply will be affected by the demand for legal services. However, any growth in legal services as a fringe benefit will be provided some impetus if the insurance industry makes a commitment to become involved in the legal

---

[32] Personnel Research Associates, *Group Legal Service Plans* (Verona, N.J.: Personnel Research Associates, 1980), p. 16.

[33] Sandy Dement, "A New Bargaining Focus on Legal Services," p. 9.

[34] Personnel Research Associates, p. 20.

[35] H. Lee Pickering, p. 17.

insurance area. As stated earlier, most union plans are not insured. There are, however, many unions that would be interested in a plan run by an insurer which placed no responsibility on the union to handle funding or to provide legal services. Insurer involvement will increase during the 1980s, but the extent of the involvement is impossible to predict.

Also, of course, the supply of lawyers should be considered. If lawyers per capita increase, they may be looking for new methods for marketing their services. This also would increase the likelihood of additional legal service plans being started.

As an employee benefit, legal service plans should flourish in the next ten years. The environment for their growth is good and should get even better.

CHAPTER 23

Financial Counseling

CHARLES E. HUGHES AND
ROBERT T. LECLAIR

INTRODUCTION

Personal financial management is concerned with acquiring and employing funds in a manner consistent with established financial objectives. Since money represents a limited resource that can be spent in an endless variety of ways with widely different results, financial planning plays a critical role in the satisfactory achievement of objectives.

Individuals or families experience problems with debt, current income and expenditures, protection, savings, investments, conflicting objectives, and haphazard or impulsive decisions. Perhaps most important, the individual or family may fail to meet needs and objectives in an economical and satisfactory way. Therefore, advice or consultation on the management of funds becomes a valuable service to those persons.

At one time a common belief existed that only the very wealthy needed to be concerned with personal financial planning. This is no longer the case. Inflation, increased income levels, taxation, sophisticated financial markets and instruments, and the generally higher standard of living have all added to the complexity of managing finances. The growth and change of our economy and social structure have contributed to the widespread acceptance of the need for planning.

The need for and applicability of financial planning is much broader in our society today than most individuals realize. Many people look only at their bank accounts or investment portfolios in determining the extent of their wealth. They fail to consider other assets, including such items as equity in a home, automobiles, furniture, paintings, cash value of life insurance, pension and profit-sharing programs, Social Security benefits, and other hidden assets as part of their financial position. Finally, an individual concentrating on the demands of a career simply doesn't have time to explore all the possibilities for putting money to work and may fail to consider the consequences that can occur if financial planning is neglected.

FINANCIAL COUNSELING DEFINED

The management of financial affairs has been changing through the years. There was a time when setting a budget for household expenditures was considered to be adequate financial planning. If it was difficult adhering to that budget, or impossible to carry out that plan, an individual might have sought the advice of a counselor. Such a planner would have reviewed the client's income and expenditures and devised a spending plan that made efficient use of the available income.

As income levels increased, larger amounts of surplus disposable income became available. Individuals and families sought ways of making money work harder for them. Various investments looked interesting, but the complexities of the securities markets appeared to be overwhelming. At this point, the financial planner also was asked to take on the role of an investment adviser. However, investment opportunities were much broader than just securities. The adviser also was expected to be knowledgeable concerning real estate, tax-advantaged investments, and even such "hard" assets as gold or diamonds.

Add to this the client's need for an accountant to prepare tax returns, a lawyer to draft wills and other documents, and an insurance agent to assist in the protection, preservation, and distribution of an estate. Today, the financial planner has become someone who counsels clients in all of these areas, and who serves as an intermediary in all of these functions. From the growing needs of consumers has emerged a new professional, the financial counselor.

The role of the financial counselor is that of providing total financial management for individuals or families to enable these persons to realize the maximum enjoyment of their finances in an efficient and economic manner. The best means of accomplishing the financial objectives of a client is to develop specific plans to direct and control financial activity and progress. The financial counselor must assess the client's current financial position, assist in establishing his or her objectives, consider all constraints and variables that bear on those objectives, and develop realistic projections and plans based on these factors. Financial counseling, then, is an ongoing series of interrelated activities. It is a *process.*

COUNSELING AS AN EMPLOYEE BENEFIT

The array of programs, plans, and services that have been added to an employee's benefit package has expanded greatly over the past few years. Most benefits, by design, are selected or offered as part of the package for all employees; some are offered only to specific employees or groups of employees.

Financial counseling is one benefit that has been limited to key executives or other highly compensated employees. This results partly from the belief that aspects of the program dealing with estate planning apply only to those individuals who will accumulate sufficient wealth to be subject to significant estate taxes.[1] Also, since programs recommended by financial counselors may include forms of tax shelters that contain considerable risk, employees other than top executives might not have sufficient assets or income to justify the amount of risk involved. Finally, from the point of view of the employer, the full financial counseling process generally is expensive and this inhibits extension to large numbers of lower-income employees.

Services Provided

Because of the relatively high cost many firms have opted for a partial financial counseling service rather than the full process. These separate services include:

1. Estate planning—disposition at death, insurance arrangements, minimization of taxes, estate liquidity.
2. Tax preparation—federal, state, and local returns; estate and gift tax returns.
3. Investment management—short- and long-term investment programs, tax shelters.
4. Compensation planning—analysis of options available, explanation of benefits.
5. Preparation of wills.

Some of these services may be provided by employees of the firm, while others are contracted for and performed by outside specialists knowledgeable in a particular area. As the number of individual services available expands, the need for full financial counseling becomes more apparent. Many companies are now providing financial counseling benefits to their top executives, and some have expanded it to middle managers as well.

Advantages

The major advantages of financial counseling as an employee benefit are:

1. Many executives do not have sufficient time to devote to their own financial affairs. Financial counseling as a benefit relieves them of having to spend time in financial planning and permits them to concentrate on business matters.
2. By reducing the likelihood a poor decision will be made on his or her own finances, the executive has greater personal peace of mind.
3. The employer is probably better able to screen and select financial

---

[1] The Economic Recovery Tax Act of 1981 made major changes in the law relating to federal estate taxes. The size of estates not subject to tax will increase to $600,000 by 1987.

counselors. Thus, the executive is less likely to receive poor advice from unqualified planners.

4. Salaries offered may appear more attractive and competitive since such compensation is being used more efficiently to reach each executive's goals.

Disadvantages

Although financial counseling as an employee benefit would appear to be attractive to both employer and employee, there are several reasons for not providing such services:

1. Financial counseling might be construed as meddling in an employee's personal affairs.
2. There is a feeling the company might be held responsible for bad advice, since it has endorsed the services and employed the counselor.
3. Although the counseling service is considered helpful to highly compensated employees, many companies are reluctant to provide benefits that are restricted to select groups of employees.
4. The cost of financial counseling.

Cost

The cost of financial counseling varies, based on the range of services to be provided and the type of individuals employed to provide them. A financial counselor or counseling firm may operate on a fee-only basis or on a commissioned, product-oriented basis. The latter approach may be further subdivided into commission-only operations and those that receive a combination of commissions and fees.

Other Factors

The existence of commissions, which may eliminate or greatly reduce costs to the employer, can be a strong incentive for companies to seek product-oriented purveyors of financial counseling services. It should be understood, however, that insurance or investment advice given to employees could be heavily weighted in favor of products available from the counseling firm. Companies should be very careful about hiring counselors who may advise employees to purchase a product which they sell.

The following guidelines should help assure that the counseling advice is both expert and independent:

1. Where feasible, employ knowledgeable, experienced counselors who do not work for firms from which products can be purchased.
2. Wherever possible, pay counselors' fees based on time and services provided, rather than commissions on products sold to employees.

3. If a fee-only service is not available, seek those firms that offer a wide range of financial products and services.

A financial counseling firm's work often is extremely detailed and complicated. Costs of $3,000 to $6,000 per executive are common for a complete counseling program. Another approach used by some counseling firms involves seminars where the counseling process and available services are explained to groups of eligible employees.

Some firms charge a separate fee of $1,000 to $3,500 for the initial data-gathering or fact-finding visit with the employee. In addition, if legal documents or certified financial statements are required, there may be additional legal and accounting fees. Finally, after the initial year of the program, the annual fees for maintaining and updating the program are based on required time and effort, generally averaging $1,000 to $2,000 per employee.

The relatively high cost of financial counseling as an employee benefit has undoubtedly contributed to its limited availability to only highly compensated executives or perhaps to its adoption at all. The cost of financial counseling to the firm can be reduced by offering the benefit to employees on a contributory basis.

The fees paid for financial counseling generally are deductible by the corporation for tax purposes if the total compensation to the employee, including the counseling fee, is not considered unreasonable compensation by the IRS.[2] When this benefit is offered to highly compensated executives, the fee generally would be small, compared to the executive's total compensation, and it is unlikely that total compensation would be considered unreasonable.

The amount the employer pays to the counseling firm for services performed for an employee is considered taxable income to the employee and is subject to withholding tax.[3] However, an offsetting tax benefit may be available to the employee since deductions are allowed for services directed to tax matters or allocable to investment advice.[4] Therefore, it could be possible for the employee to contribute the cost associated with those services allowed as deductions. The counseling firm should indicate clearly the charge for these services as a separate item on its billing.

In addition to the tax aspects, when supplemental legal or accounting fees are necessary, these expenses should be borne by the employee. Overall, contributions by employees could reduce the cost to the employer and make it possible for the firm to offer financial counseling as an employee benefit.

---

[2] I.R.C. Section 106.

[3] I.R.C. Section 61.

[4] I.R.C. Section 212.

THE FINANCIAL COUNSELING PROCESS

It is most important to understand the concept of financial planning not as a product, or as a service, but as a process. Many persons claiming to engage in planning are really selling products and nothing more. A "good plan" is simply one that requires extensive use of their product whatever it may be. Similarly, a view of financial planning as a service provided at one point in time is also inadequate. This concept does not provide for the continuing needs of an individual or family for information, analysis, and review of its program.

Financial counseling should be thought of as a series of interrelated activities a person participates in on a continuing basis. It is not something that is completed, even successfully, and then put away or forgotten. This is similar to the modern view of education that embraces learning not only through formal schooling but also throughout one's lifetime. In the same way, financial planning must be done regularly to take account of changes in an individual's circumstances, the availability of new products, and varying financial market conditions.

Good examples of ways in which conditions can change are six-month savings certificates and money market mutual funds. Both of these relatively new devices have altered drastically the way people and businesses handle money, as well as the rates of return earned on liquid funds. As new products appear and market conditions change, even the best prepared financial plan will tend to become obsolete. Changes in an individual's personal situation also may require adjustments in the overall plan. Births, deaths, marriage, divorce, or a new business venture can have a great impact on financial as well as personal planning.

The following activities in the process of financial planning must be carried out regularly and, when necessary, should involve qualified, professional advisers:

1. Gather background information.
2. Establish objectives.
3. Develop financial plans.
4. Control and execute plans.
5. Measure performance.

The flowchart shown in Figure 23–1 provides a summary of the individual activities involved in the process and shows the relationships among them.

Background Analysis

Financial planning requires comprehensive data on everyone participating in the program. Such information includes a record of income and expenditures as well as the current financial position of the individual or

Figure 23-1
The Financial Counseling Process

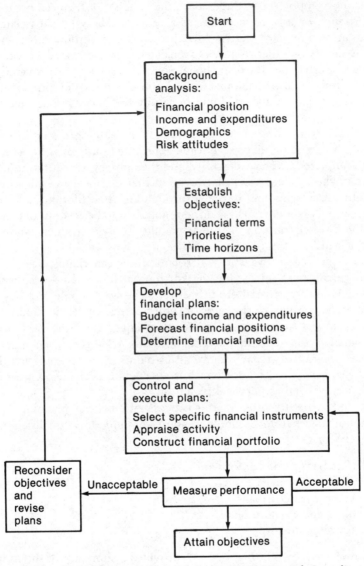

Source: "Introduction to Financial Counseling," *Financial Counseling*
(Bryn Mawr: The American College, 1982), p. 133.

family. Prior to determining objectives, the counselor needs information regarding the sex, health, age, lifestyle, tastes, and preferences of individual family members. Much of this information is subjective, and attitudes may shift considerably over the years. Such changes make it important that the financial counselor maintain frequent contact with the client to be aware of important changes in these personal and family characteristics.

Another important area of background analysis is the client's attitude toward the degree of risk in the overall financial plan. Feelings about investment risk, personal financial security, and independence are just as important as the client's income statement or net worth. An awareness of risk attitudes permits realistic, acceptable objectives to be established with the individual or family. By ignoring these feelings, the counselor runs the risk of developing a "good plan" that is simply out of touch with the client's personality. Such plans are not likely to be accepted or implemented, and a great deal of time and effort will have been wasted.

Unfortunately, for a number of reasons, attitudes toward risk are very difficult to measure or to judge. First, defining the nature of "risk" is highly subjective and varies considerably from one person to another. Second, attitudes about risk are likely to change dramatically over an individual's or family's life cycle. What seemed perfectly reasonable to the 25-year-old bachelor may be totally unacceptable to the 40-year-old father of four children. Finally, risk attitudes are a function of many personal, psychological factors that may be difficult for the financial manager to deal with. Yet, the counselor should try through discussions and interviews with clients to determine their feelings about risk and to be alert to significant changes which may occur in this area.

Setting Financial Objectives

Stating worthwhile financial objectives in a meaningful way is a difficult but necessary part of the planning process. One reason why many plans fail is that financial goals are not described in operational terms. Objectives often are presented in vague language that is difficult to translate into action.

Each objective statement should have the following characteristics. First, it should be *well-defined* and clearly understood by all participants, including members of the financial planning team. Unless individuals really know and understand what they are trying to accomplish, it is not likely they will succeed. Writing down objectives is one way of working toward a set of clear and useful statements. Such comments as "I want a safe and secure retirement income" do not provide much guidance for financial planners. They merely express an emotion that may be very real to the speaker but one that is hard to translate into effective terms and plans.

Second, good financial objectives generally are stated in *quantitative terms*. Only by attaching numbers to our plans can we know when the objective has been accomplished. This is a particularly important factor for long-term objectives, such as those concerning educational funding or retirement. It is desirable to measure progress toward these goals at various points along the way.

The goal of having a particular sum for retirement in 20 years can be reviewed annually to see if the necessary progress has been made. If earnings have been lower than anticipated, larger contributions may have to be made in succeeding years. If a higher rate of return actually has been realized, future contributions can be reduced. Such fine-tuning is impossible unless numbers are associated with plan objectives. Adding numbers to objectives also helps to make them more understandable to all members of the planning team as well as to participants in the plan.

Finally, each goal or objective should have a *time dimension* attached to it. When will a particular goal be accomplished? How much progress has been made since the last review? How much time remains until the goal is to be accomplished? These questions and similar ones can be answered only if a schedule has been established with objectives listed at particular points in time.

Some aspects of the plan, such as retirement objectives, will have very long timelines associated with them. Others, such as an adjustment to savings, may be accomplished in a few months or a year. Whether long-term or short-term in nature, the timing feature of objective statements is very important. Even long-term goals can be broken down into subperiods that can coincide with an annual review of the plan.

After the objectives have been stated, they must be put in *priority order.* This ranking process is necessary since different objectives normally compete for limited resources. It is unlikely that a planner will be able to satisfy all of the client's objectives at the same time. Some goals are more important, more urgent, than others. Critical short-term needs may have to be satisfied ahead of longer-range plans.

Once certain goals have been reached, funds may be channeled to other areas. An example would be the funding of children's education. After this goal has been met, resources previously spent on education costs may be allocated to building a retirement fund or some other long-range objective. Unless these and other goals have been assigned specific priorities, it is impossible to organize and carry out an effective plan. Conversely, a set of well-integrated financial objectives can make the actual planning process a relatively easy task.

Individuals and families should have workable objectives in each of the following areas:

1. **Standard of Living.** Maintaining a particular "lifestyle" normally takes the majority of an individual's financial resources. Setting an objective in this area calls for an analysis of required expenditures, such as food and shelter, as well as discretionary spending on such items as travel, vacations, and entertainment. If almost all income is being spent in this area, it is virtually impossible to accomplish any other objectives.

One widely used rule of thumb states that no more than 80 percent of income should be spent on maintaining a given standard of living. The remaining 20 percent of disposable income should be allocated among the other financial objectives. Obviously, this guideline varies from one person or family to another. But, unless a significant portion of income can be channeled toward the remaining objectives, those goals are not likely to be reached.

2. Savings. Almost everyone recognizes the need for funds that can be used to meet an emergency or other special needs. However, determining the ideal level of savings can be a complex problem. It is influenced by the nature of income received, individual risk attitudes, stability of employment, and other factors, such as the type of health and dental insurance coverage.

It is recommended that savings balances should be equal to at least three months' disposable income. These funds should be maintained in a safe and highly liquid form where rate of return is a secondary consideration. Today, the typical money market mutual fund offers an excellent vehicle for maintaining savings balances. These funds offer a high degree of safety, ready access through the use of checks or telephone redemption of shares, and an excellent rate of return.

3. Protection. This objective incorporates property, liability, disability, life, and medical insurance coverage. It should be designed to provide protection against insurable risks and related losses. Objectives in this area should take account of coverage provided through public programs, such as Social Security, as well as group insurance offered as an employee benefit.

4. Accumulation (Investment). This is possibly the most complex objective in a number of ways. It relates to the buildup of capital for significant financial needs. These needs can be as diverse as a child's college education, a daughter's wedding, or the purchase of a vacation home. The sheer number and variety of such goals makes it difficult to define this objective and to set priorities.

Adding to the difficult nature of this area is the generally long time-horizon for planning that may encompass 20 years or more. Finally, the wide variety of possible investment vehicles that can be used in the planning process adds to the overall complexity. Regardless of the reason for building capital, the critical ingredients in this objective are the ability to quantify the needed amount and to state a target date for its accumulation.

5. Financial Independence. This objective may be thought of as a particularly important subset of the accumulation objective. It concerns the accumulation of assets over a relatively long time in most cases. Such independence may be desired at a particular age and may or may not actually correspond with retirement from employment. Many persons may wish to have complete financial security and independence while continuing to work at a favored occupation or profession.

Since the planning-horizon is such a lengthy one, this objective should be broken down into subgoals that can be evaluated, analyzed, and reworked over the years. More than most others, this area is affected by changes in government programs, such as Social Security, and in benefits paid by employers.

6. Estate Planning. Objectives in this area typically are concerned with the preservation and distribution of wealth after the estate owner's death. However, accomplishing such goals may call for a number of actions to be taken well before that time. Writing a will probably is the most fundamental estate planning objective, and yet thousands of persons die each year without having done so. These people die "intestate" and leave the distribution of their assets to state laws and the courts.

For larger estates, avoidance or minimization of estate taxes is an important consideration. These objectives can be accomplished, but call for careful planning and implementation prior to the owner's death. The use of various trust instruments, distribution of assets through gifts, and proper titling of property all can result in a smaller taxable estate. Carrying out such a program, however, takes time and should be considered as various assets are being acquired. This also is an area where professional guidance generally is necessary. If the financial counselor is not an attorney, one should be consulted in drafting a will or in preparing a trust document.

Developing Financial Plans

Once a realistic, well-defined set of objectives has been established, the financial counselor can begin to develop actual plans. This planning stage includes the budgeting of income and expenditures for the near term, along with a forecast of future activity. A projection of the client's financial position for the next several years also should be made.

These plans should identify the financial instruments that will be included in programs to meet specific objectives. For example, specific savings media should be recommended for those who need more in the way of emergency funds. Should a family increase its regular savings accounts, purchase money market certificates, or buy shares in a money market fund? If an investment program is called for in the plan, recommendations should be made as to the appropriate *types* of investments, such as securities, real estate, or tax shelters.

Executing and Controlling Plans

The next stage of the model calls for the financial counselor to assist in setting the plan in motion. This may involve the purchase or sale of various assets, changes in life insurance protection, additional liability coverage, and other changes. All these activities should be monitored closely and appraised to see that they are effective in accomplishing the stated objectives. The outcome of some actions will be quickly apparent, while others may take a long time to produce results that can be evaluated.

Measuring Performance

The financial counselor is responsible for gathering data on the plan's operations that are used to evaluate his or her performance and the actions of other professionals who may be involved. Such persons may include a banker, an attorney, a life insurance consultant, and an accountant.

This important step determines progress made toward the attainment of objectives. If performance to date is acceptable, no particular corrective action need be taken until the next scheduled review. However, if it is discovered progress to date is unacceptable, several actions may need to be taken. These would include a review of the plans to see if they are still valid, and analysis of the market environment to take note of unanticipated changes.

It also may be necessary to review and alter the original objectives if they are no longer realistic and desirable. When this occurs, the entire plan may have to be recycled through each of the stages described above. This model of financial planning is a dynamic one that is continually repeated as personal, financial, and environmental factors change.

WHO PROVIDES FINANCIAL COUNSELING?

Financial counseling services are provided by numerous individuals and firms, including banks, insurance companies and agents, investment brokers, benefit consultants, lawyers, accountants, and others. The major firms specializing in financial planning services generally have a staff of professionals who are experts in investments, insurance, tax shelters, and so on, and who work as a team to provide the counseling service. Smaller organizations may concentrate on one area and hire consultants to complete the planning team.

The selection of a counseling firm requires care. It is important that the objectives of the employer are satisfied, and, from the employee's standpoint, that their individual confidences be protected and the advice be in their best interests. Some employers have attempted to provide financial planning services through in-house personnel. This is most effective when the benefit is limited to a single service, such as tax advice. However, problems occur because many executives are hesitant to discuss details of their personal financial affairs with fellow employees.

Although it was indicated earlier that, wherever possible and feasible, fee-basis independent counselors should be employed, the objectives of the firm may warrant consideration of product-oriented counselors. For example, if the objective of the counseling benefit is limited to advice on life insurance planning, a competent life insurance agent may be able to satisfy the need. It would be difficult for any single individual to give professional advice in all areas included in a comprehensive plan. However, banks, brokerage firms, and life insurance companies are forming financial counseling divisions that provide support services for their personnel.

Individual professionals are beginning to call themselves financial counselors, financial planners, financial consultants, or financial advisers. Most of these persons still depend upon commissions for their income. However, as this trend continues, more of them will join together to form firms rich in experience, professionally qualified in all aspects of financial counseling, and compensated through fees for their services.

There exist today several quality firms that provide financial counseling on a fee-only basis. These are the leaders of the field and should be given first priority by the larger firms seeking financial counseling services for their employees. Perhaps the most important ingredient, however, is to seek the individual or firm that understands financial counseling as a process, one that can have important beneficial results for employers and employees alike.

Fiduciary Responsibility

As financial counselors take on a wider range of responsibilities for their clients, a special fiduciary relationship develops between them. This arrangement arises whenever one person places confidence and trust in the integrity and fidelity of another. A fiduciary relationship is characterized by faith and reliance on the part of the client and by a condition of superiority and influence on the part of the counselor.

The existence of a fiduciary responsibility does not depend upon the establishment of any particular legal relationship. Nonlegal relationships can be fiduciary in nature, especially where one person entrusts his or her business affairs to another.

When a fiduciary relationship exists, the fiduciary (counselor) has a duty to act in good faith and in the interests of the other person. A fiduciary is not permitted to use the relationship to benefit his or her own personal interest. Transactions between the client and counselor are subject to close scrutiny by the courts. Especially sensitive are transactions in which the fiduciary profits at the expense of the client. Fiduciaries must subordinate their individual interests to their duty of care, trust, and loyalty to the client.

The Investment Advisers Act of 1940 is particularly important in defining the nature of a fiduciary relationship. One objective of the act is to expose and eliminate all conflicts of interest that could influence an adviser to be other than disinterested. Congress thus empowered the courts to require full and fair disclosure of all material facts surrounding the fiduciary relationship. The adviser must disclose in a meaningful way all material facts that give rise to potential or actual conflicts of interest. For example, an adviser who receives commissions on products sold to clients, such as securities or life insurance, should disclose the amount of sales compensation received on recommended transactions.[5]

CONCLUSION

Financial counseling will become an increasingly important employee benefit. This will occur as more firms offer such services and as more

---

[5] Robert T. Fasic, "Standards and Disclosure Problems for the Money Manager Marketing Financial Services," *Financial Planning Today* 3, no. 2 (May 1979).

employees qualify for eligibility. Another factor contributing to this growth will be the maturity of the financial planning industry itself. While the costs associated with offering financial counseling services as a benefit are not insignificant, clear advantages exist for both the employer and the employee. There also are areas of concern, however, and firms should carefully analyze the nature of their employees and the qualifications of those offering to provide financial counseling services for them.

Employee Assistance Programs[1]

CHARLES A. WEAVER

OVERVIEW

The problem of employees with alcohol or other personal problems has reached alarming proportions in our society. The economic losses to industry associated with such problems are estimated in the billions of dollars annually. The social costs are beyond estimation.

In response to the need to deal with this problem in business and industry, a few companies developed occupational programs in the early 1940s. These early programs, which operated in a vacuum of information and experience, concentrated on alcoholism alone. The result was a program designed to identify the alcoholic in the workplace. Incorporated were traditional attitudes toward alcoholism as a self-inflicted disease denoting moral weakness. These attitudes meant that one was not considered an alcoholic until the final stages of the illness were reached and when stereotypical symptoms like bloodshot eyes, trembling hands, alcohol breath, and lack of cleanliness and personal grooming appeared.

THE CONCEPT

During the 1960s, it was discovered that employees who were not performing their work tasks satisfactorily were much easier to identify than were employees with alcoholic problems. An approach evolved reflecting this observation—the employee assistance program (EAP). The concept of EAPs was simple. That is, a predictable number of employees will have declining job performance because of personal problems.

Analysis and follow-up of employees identified because of job performance problems like absenteeism, erratic performance, decreasing productiv-

---

[1] To establish continuity and develop the content of an Employee Assistance Program (EAP) the reader may wish to peruse the list of definitions and the statistics listed under "Who Benefits" at the end of the chapter before beginning the main text of the chapter itself.

ity, tardiness, poor judgment, and excessive material spoilage indicates that 11.5 percent of any employee population will have personal problems serious enough to affect job performance. Forty-five percent of this total will experience a primary problem with alcohol abuse. Fifty-five percent will experience other problems. Employees whose job performance is affected by alcohol abuse or other problems will be absent from work more often than will employees without job performance problems or employees whose job performance is related to a lack of training or other supervisory deficiencies.

Major causes appear with statistical regularity, as indicated in the following table:

Table 24-1

Job Performance Problem Source	Percent of Employee Population	Percent of "Troubled" Employee Population	Absenteeism Rate
Alcohol abuse	5.2%	45%	4 × greater
Emotional problems	2.9	25	5 × greater
Family problems	1.5	13	5.7 × greater
Drug abuse	.8	7	5 × greater
Miscellaneous "other"	1.1	10	2 × greater
Total problem employees	11.5 percent of work force.		

Source: From a study of seventeen selected industries by the author, 1978.

These employees are not "troublemakers." They are "troubled employees," and they often are among the best and hardest working employees an employer has when they work free from the burdens of their personal problems. Troubled employees appear at any level, from the executive suite to the assembly line.

Employee assistance programs should be designed to meet the needs of the individual organization. Personnel policies and management philosophies differ from organization to organization, but EAPs must be an integral part of the organizational structure.

Responsibility for identifying troubled employees in the workplace is a function of supervisors at all levels. It is not the responsibility of supervisors to *diagnose* or to *counsel* employees, only to deal with poor performance.

A process for supervisors making an EAP recommendation to employees might be as set forth in Figures 24-1 through 24-4.

Before supervisors can confront an employee with a job performance problem, several steps must be taken. These early steps to correcting inappropriate job performance do not mention the EAP as a possible solution. During this phase of problem solving, supervisors are just getting a handle on the scope, magnitude, and changes needed to bring job performance back into line. However, supervisors, as well as the EAP coordi-

Figure 24-1
Step 1 in Supervisor's Process of Making EAP Recommendation to Employees

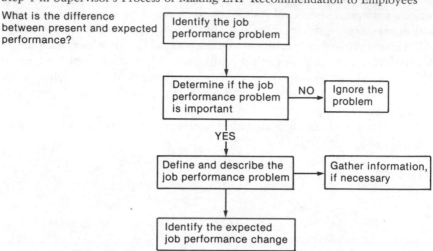

nator, should take every opportunity to make EAP information available to employees. EAP information should be given on a continuing basis, but it is not part of solving job performance problems at this point.

The second part of changing job performance is determining how the job performance problem will be resolved. After supervisors have determined what changes are expected, they should decide when this is to occur. Do they expect an employee to change immediately? If absenteeism is a problem, how many days will a supervisor allow an employee to be absent and within what time frame? After they have made some decisions on this and decided that the employee can do the job as expected, supervisors should develop a plan of action to achieve the job performance change. During this process, supervisors should make the employee aware of the problem, what

Figure 24-2
Step 2 in Supervisor's Process of Making EAP Recommendation to Employees

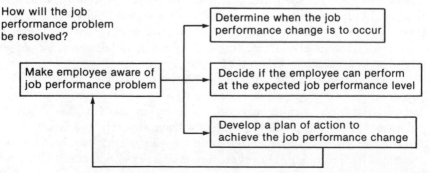

Figure 24-3
Step 3 in Supervisor's Process of Making EAP Recommendation to
Employees

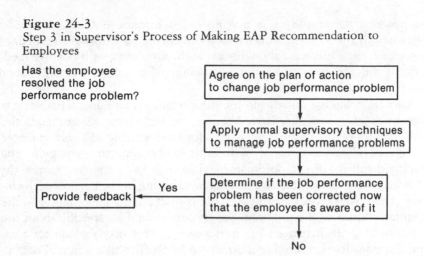

is expected, and when it is expected. It may be best to jointly develop a plan
of action with the employee.

At this point, supervisors are still using normal supervisory techniques,
that is, they are doing the same things they have and would be doing
without an EAP. Also note that the EAP has not been mentioned. At this
point, however, supervisors may want to mention the existence of the EAP
and provide the employee with additional information on the procedures,
what to expect if he or she decides to try the EAP, particularly stressing
confidentiality and the voluntary nature of the program.

Once the supervisor and employee have agreed upon a plan of action and
are carrying out that plan, the supervisors will want to periodically review

Figure 24-4
Step 4 in Supervisor's Process of Making EAP Recommendation to
Employees

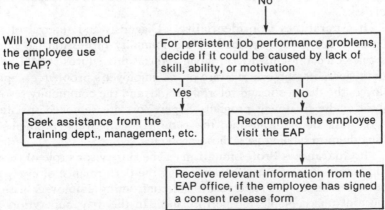

the progress the employee is making and determine if further action is warranted. If the job performance has been corrected within the guidelines developed, the supervisor should provide the employee with positive feedback. If the job performance is not being corrected satisfactorily, then supervisors move to step four.

After this plan has failed, and job performance is still unacceptable, it is time to check a few alternatives before the supervisor recommends the EAP. Are there any other explanations for unacceptable job performance? If the supervisor has covered all areas, it is now time to recommend the employee call the EAP coordinator and to urge the employee to use the EAP to resolve any problems that may be affecting his or her job performance. Again, supervisors should spell out confidentiality guidelines, and the voluntary nature of the program. Supervisors should be specific about the consequences of unchanged job performance. This may include termination. Supervisors also should report to the EAP office that a formal recommendation has been made.

The EAP provides supervisors with an additional option to solving job performance problems. It helps employees resolve any personal problem that may be interfering with job performance, and it often prevents termination. The earlier that job performance problems are identified, the sooner problems can be resolved, either through normal supervisory techniques or through the assistance of an EAP. Employees also may want to use the EAP for personal problems not yet affecting their job performance. In this case, supervisors and employees will be ahead of the game. Moving the employee from unacceptable job performance through the EAP system can be graphically seen in Figure 24-5.

An employee assistance program is a general term for a subsystem of interdependent components of the overall organizational system. It is a program for solving or reducing problems that affect the employee's acceptable job performance through the process of linking the employee with resources located within the community.

The systems approach embodied in the EAP model accomplishes four major tasks:

1. **It Guarantees Confidentiality.** Diagnosis and referral of troubled employees is accomplished by a community professional bound by strict rules of confidentiality. Program referral procedures should be designed to guarantee no one is aware of the employee's problem except the employee, the diagnostic and referral person, and the community resource involved in the treatment program. Supervisors are removed specifically from the task of inquiring into the nature of employees' problems and assisting them in dealing with those problems.

2. **It Guarantees Professionalism.** The supervisor's role of supervision includes responsibility for monitoring the performance of every individual under his or her supervision and confronting employees with any evidence of unacceptable job performance. In this way, supervisors per-

Figure 24–5
Organizational Employee Assistance Program

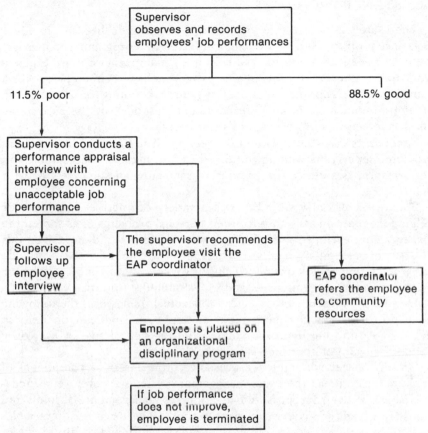

form job-oriented tasks: they supervise. If assistance is needed, the supervisor is not involved in rendering such assistance. Rather, trained professionals from the community are utilized to assure proper, efficient, and professional treatment.

3. **It Promotes Efficiency.** Early intervention is a key to efficient problem solving. Delays in intervention allow problems to grow and intensify. A program that focuses on indicators of problems, while the problems are still relatively minor, promotes efficiency in terms of individual problem solving. In economic terms, it promotes production as a result of a larger work force of nontroubled employees.

4. **It Helps Assure Utilization by Avoiding Stigmas.** Employee assistance programs offer assistance for all problems. A particular employee's problem is not identified by participation in a specific program, such as an alcohol program. As a result, many of the negative implications of participating in a particular program are avoided.

INTEGRATING COMPONENTS OF EMPLOYEE ASSISTANCE PROGRAMS

There are undoubtedly as many ways to conceptualize an employee assistance program as there are people affected by a program. Top management may see it as a way to save money by maintaining a more efficient work force, as a way of providing an extra benefit to help employees live happier lives with no concrete monetary benefits resulting for management, or simply as one more problem management must deal with because someone has forced them to provide this service.

Supervisors may view it with mixed feelings. The EAP may be viewed as providing supervisors with an additional tool to manage unacceptable job performance, as a device for graciously terminating an employee, or with indifference.

Employees also may view EAPs in a variety of ways: as a method for helping them obtain assistance for their personal problems or as something management developed to further control and intimidate them. Given this diversity of perceptions, it appears vital that an attempt be made to provide integrating components around which some consensus might be formed for the organization, the employee, and the community resources.

Despite the present lack of a clear conceptual framework, the following discussion of integrative concepts is an attempt to add a degree of clarity to the area. Again, the discussion stems from the perspective of a broadly defined program of assistance for all problem areas.

Broadly conceived, employee assistance programs are a component of organizational human resources management systems. Therefore, a fundamental integrative concept is human resources management. Business and industrial organizations exist to make a profit. The three major variables that can be manipulated are direct cost, indirect cost, and overhead. Thus, the management of human resources is a vital area of business and of industrial productivity, efficiency, and profit. Employee assistance programs must be a part of that broad picture and be incorporated into the overall goals of the organization whether it be for profit or nonprofit. Such a human resources management system would include many components in addition to an employee assistance program (e.g., recruiting, training, promotion, wages, benefits, safety, supervisory practices, and so on). However, an EAP might be vital to that system in several ways involving additional integrative concepts.

First, an employee assistance program can reduce losses and inefficiency related to distressed and dysfunctional employees. Ample evidence exists from the behavioral sciences to demonstrate people suffering from emotional distress are less able to concentrate and work efficiently than those who are relaxed and dealing with stress effectively. In the work setting, distress may be manifested by such things as high absenteeism, low productivity, unsatisfactory workmanship, and disruptive interpersonal behavior.

To reduce those losses at a cost less than the losses themselves saves an organization money. Cost/benefit, then, is another key to the integrative concept. This concept involves the identification of such employee problems and providing treatment which reduces or eliminates the cause of the dysfunctional behavior.

A second way an EAP might be vital to a human resources management system is in its potential as a problem-prevention tool. Preventive occupational mental health is, therefore, another integrative concept. Employees may be unconcerned with saving their employer's money; therefore, the risk management, cost/benefit model that appeals to employers cannot be presumed to motivate employees to support and participate in an EAP program. However, it generally is accepted that human beings are motivated to reduce painful distress in their lives when they have the means available. The system provided by an employee assistance program supports mental health education and entry into community resources (i.e., community mental health centers, hospitals, and the like), making it easier for employees to gain assistance on a *voluntary* basis. Data indicate a majority of the employees using the system have done so on a voluntary basis, rather than as a result of a supervisor's recommendation related to poor job performance. However, voluntary participation also may lead to savings for the employer and meet the needs of the employee. This savings may be more difficult to measure, especially if large numbers of employees use the system *before* work-dysfunctional behaviors appear, but it would appear to be the ideal result of an effective employee assistance program.

Those concepts previously discussed (i.e., human resources management, cost/benefit, and preventive occupational mental health) are concepts of considerable breadth, under which other key concepts may be subsumed. The most basic of those are briefly discussed below.

1. *Systems* theory is implied in developing employee assistance programs. Systems theory assumes an agency or other social organization consists of an interdependent set of activities composed of subsystems that function within the larger set of parent institution and community. The step-by-step approach to EAP development (e.g., beginning with assessing management commitment and proceeding through implementation to evaluation) represents a systems approach. Each component affects the other components and the overall program affects the organization. The organization, in turn, affects the community. Careful analysis of the key factors affecting the system is essential to employee assistance program development.

2. Gaining stronger commitment and broader-based support within an organization is enhanced by participative management through an employee assistance program advisory committee formed at the outset of the program. *Participation management* is another key concept inherent in the model EAP development. It generally is an accepted organizational development principle that people more strongly support what they help create.

Thus, committee involvement in setting policy, establishing goals, planning for employee education, and evaluating program effectiveness is viewed as a vital component of a successful EAP system. To enhance their effectiveness, goal setting and group development skills training should be provided the advisory committee. The committee, as well as the coordinator, must be the driving and organizing forces for the EAP to succeed.

3. *Human relations training for supervisors* is another integral concept in program development models. Supervisors are key members of the problem identification and referral process. Vital to their facilitating worker problem resolution is their ability to listen to troubled employees with a nonjudgmental attitude, convey a sense of compassionate understanding, and, yet, remain sufficiently detached to firmly confront them with job performance inadequacies. These are skills for which many supervisors need training beyond what an organization normally provides. However, skills in human relations are vital to motivating workers to seek assistance rather than avoiding their problems and suffering serious consequences.

4. *Early detection based on job performance* has remained an integrative concept since the inception of EAPs.

5. *Utilization of existing community resources* also has remained an integrative concept and remains central to EAP philosophy. The use of existing community resources is viewed as an alternative far superior to creating internally based programs that duplicate existing resources. The former is both more efficient and cost/beneficial. Effective linkages to a community-based diagnostic/referral source often means bringing accountability to mental health systems and assistance in providing access to those services through the reduction of stigmas.

6. *Integration with personnel management systems.* For the EAP to survive and succeed it must be linked with the way job performance is evaluated, rewards or incentives are provided, health benefits are administered, and labor relations are managed. This is not to say that personnel managers should administer all aspects of EAPs, but that EAPs must be an integral part of all system elements that serve to interact with the organization's human resources. Many organizations may not be able to visualize or adopt EAP concepts because of the limited scope of their human resource management system.

7. *Use of self-help groups.* Although many individuals receive assistance through formal performance management/supervisor referral systems, other organizations that respond to persons in distress out of strictly altruistic motives should not be ignored. Alcoholics Anonymous (A.A.), Alanon, Gamblers Anonymous, and other self-help groups are examples of information-giving nonprofessional means of intervening in crisis situations and of providing emotional support for personal changes. Self-help organizations need to be recognized and legitimized as a means of developing more voluntary modes of participation in EAPs. Self-help organizations should

not replace professional diagnosis and treatment, but they are an important ingredient in creating the impetus for an individual to decide to seek help.

THE EAP COORDINATOR

Most EAPs depend on a small staff or a single person to implement the program. The success of the EAP often depends on the capabilities and support of the coordinator. Current literature on EAPs often provides a rather narrow or limited description of the role of the coordinator and the involvement in program planning. The coordinator's role seems to be deemphasized if the program focuses on alcoholism or substance abuse and has limited commitment from management.

The role of the coordinator includes serving as a point of contact for troubled employees, discussing documentation and ways of handling unacceptable job performance with supervisors, maintaining confidential employee records for evaluation and follow-up purposes, and planning and implementing training programs for supervisors, education programs for employees, and orientation programs for advisory committees.

As part of the program planning process, the number of personnel assigned to the EAP, the amount of staff time allocated to the EAP (i.e., full-time or part-time staff), and whether the EAP is an internally based or externally based program must be determined. These factors, in turn, affect the efficiency of program operation.

The problem is not with specific functions of the EAP coordinator's office but with the perspective of the organization concerning its understanding of the program, its commitment to the concept, and the economic return on invested dollars.

The author supports an externally based program that defines the coordinator's roles as administrator and as referral center to operate from either inside or outside of an organization. While change can occur from inside the organization, an autonomous EAP, such as the consortium model, also can induce change from outside an organization.

The coordinator's role involves stressing the need for change as applied to a particular group (i.e., employees with unacceptable job performance). One of the basic functions of the EAP coordinator is to supply the organization with information to make decisions. In this capacity the coordinator is acting as a catalyst for change. This means demonstrating the need for an EAP in terms of its ability to improve production, reduce absenteeism, protect company assets, and, in general, produce a financial return on money invested in the program. Management also may be sensitive to the humanitarian aspects of EAPs as a secondary concern.

The impact of relevant information may not be immediate. Careful attention to detail and to development seem appropriate for effective program planning. Overnight implementation often meets immediate needs but later undermines the continuing success of an EAP. It is suggested that hurried implementation solves immediate problems but leads to "paper" programs later. Overzealous coordinators should give way to long-term planning that will result in an operating program 5, 10, or 15 years from now. Hence, alliances, timing, and coordinated efforts are important considerations.

The EAP coordinator may induce change by providing the best answer to a problem. In other words, the coordinator can provide part of the solution to job performance problems at the appropriate time (i.e., during the development of an EAP). However, resistance can be generated by attempting to force a solution on reluctant, uninformed management or on community treatment resources. Furthermore, the demands of the coordinator's role often necessitate a full-time person with support staff. However, in many situations the coordinator's role is secondary to his or her other responsibilities, such as personnel director, education director, and so on. While certain circumstances may dictate the EAP coordinator perform several functions within the organization, the primary emphasis of the role is of great importance. The success of the program may depend on whether the EAP coordinator is education director first and coordinator second or coordinator first and education director second. Ideally, the EAP coordinator's role is a full-time position with support staff, but a practical solution might be that the position is filled with someone whose primary duties are the EAP with secondary responsibilities.

The establishment of the EAP coordinator as a component of program planning is only part of the development process. The EAP coordinator can assume various role models. For example, a change agent is anyone who seeks to alter or modify the way organizations and people function. Ronald G. Havelock (1973) described four methods of being a change agent. He indicated a change agent may act as a catalyst to initiate change, provide solutions at timely moments, serve as a process helper in problem solving, and link resources with needs.

The roles of a change agent are not mutually exclusive. The EAP coordinator must choose the appropriate emphasis for different circumstances that arise in the development of an EAP. The coordinator will act as a catalyst in starting an employee education program while linking and developing community resources to meet the needs of the EAP, for example. The difficulty lies in the coordinator's ability to select and execute the proper role. A coordinator acting as a change agent can influence a management that does not view employee problems and job performance problems in the same light. To minimize resistance to EAPs as part of the solution to job performance problems, guidelines can be established.

The coordinator's role is a demanding one in terms of the skills required and the level of involvement. According to Havelock (1973) process helpers involve working with the system to recognize and define needs, establish goals and objectives, search for relevent resources, select, create, and match resources with objectives and needs, implement the EAP model, and evaluate the model.

For the program coordinator, process helping skills are necessary to work with the advisory committee, community resources, management structures, and union officials, if applicable. The EAP coordinator should have group facilitation skills to perform this role. A model training program for committees promotes shared leadership, rather than dominance or manipulation by the coordinator.

A key in the process helping role is effective interaction among relevant groups, individuals, and the coordinator. Effective interaction may be viewed as part of the process helping role, while management of information is part of the role of providing solutions. Switching from the providing solutions to the process helper role should occur after corporate commitment has been obtained. As the EAP coordinator becomes a process helper, he or she should develop support for the program, facilitate involvement, and create joint ownership and leadership in the EAP.

For example, the needs and concerns of the organization should be determined prior to offering a solution. The EAP, as part of the solution, must be appropriate for the problem. This may mean determining if absenteeism or production problems are present in the organization, and then determining whether the EAP can assist in solving those problems. The EAP coordinator can assist management in establishing criteria for measuring the effectiveness of the EAP as part of the solution to job performance problems. Management, therefore, can determine if an EAP solves part or all of its job performance problems. The EAP coordinator should build a relationship with management based on trust to discuss problems, manage the adoption process, and promote sharing of knowledge. The coordinator should help establish the EAP in such a manner that the decision makers in the organization have ownership of the solution.

An issue for EAP coordinators is how to utilize their skills and ideas. The EAP coordinator should become a *resource* person for the system, while the advisory committee should discuss, evaluate, and adopt solutions for referral procedures, policy statements, supervisory training, employee education, and the like.

Finally, the EAP coordinator can act in the capacity of linking resources with the needs of the EAP by providing access to community resources for employees. The EAP coordinator should arrange and monitor linkages for employees to community resources. Services available in the community should not be duplicated; however, nonexistent resources should be developed. Often employees do not know that resources exist or how to utilize them; therefore, the coordinator is assuming the role of linking the employee with community resources. This role involves the process of building relationships in which two-way communication is essential.

THE ADVISORY COMMITTEE

The advisory committee operates to give direction and guidance to other components of the EAP. While most advisory committees do not have decision-making authority, the committee can be influential in helping management.

The advisory committee can be given responsibilities that will increase its influence and provide the groundwork for management/labor ownership of the EAP. It is suggested the inclusion of the advisory committee in the planning process increases the probability of a successful EAP. The advisory committee can be assigned to assist in writing policy and procedure statements, for example. Other areas for the advisory committee to provide input include the goals and objectives for the EAP, strategies for implementing the EAP, reviews of proposed supervisory training and employee education programs, development of a strategy for publicizing the program within the organization and community, and monitoring the implementation and evaluation of the program. From the list of tasks given the group, it should be evident the advisory committee is a vital component in the program planning process, and that a committee satisfied with only marginal responsibilities will not be in the best interests of the EAP.

For an EAP to provide long-term benefits for employees, the committee must be committed and have a thorough understanding of its role and responsibilities in the system. Issues and concepts must be discussed, and shared leadership is crucial to its growth. If one element (i.e., labor, management, or program coordinator) dominates the committee, its ability is diminished. Again, the committee should be representative of the major employee groups within the organization. A training program for advisory committee members in effective group decision making is recommended to insure shared leadership and a committee that remains vital.

Although many EAPs have advisory committees, few of them function in an effective manner. The author supports a training program for advisory committees designed to develop group concensus decision-making skills and to provide impetus for continued growth.

The goals of the advisory committee training program are:

1. To provide an understanding of the EAP concept.
2. To develop commitment to the EAP through shared program planning.
3. To teach group concensus decision-making skills.
4. To provide an ongoing group planning structure for future meetings; and
5. To complete important EAP planning tasks (i.e., establish program goals, policies, and procedures).

The design of the advisory committee training should assist participants in becoming effective group members. The design makes use of the *Par-*

ticipation Training concepts developed by Dr. John McKinley from Indiana University.[2] The advisory committee learns through the processes of:

1. Volunteering for group roles (i.e., recorder, leader, observer).
2. Determining a topic, goal, and outline for a series of discussion sessions.
3. Obtaining feedback from trained group leaders.
4. Practicing task functions and maintenance roles.
5. Sharing in the evaluating process.
6. Using the group's resources, ideas, and experiences.
7. Developing trust through open communication and responsible risk-taking.

The advisory committee training balances process with content in that the participants discuss issues and solve problems while improving their awareness of group decision-making processes.

The trainer's role is to insure participation remains voluntary, to provide process information and group feedback, to serve as a resource person, and to provide guidance for group cohesiveness. Part of the task to be accomplished during the advisory committee training is to develop a policy statement for the EAP congruent with organizational policy statements.

One element found in EAPs is the program policy and procedures statements. Many programs have little depth beyond the policy and procedure statements and can be identified as "paper programs." While the policy and procedure statements do not insure the existence of a program, they are essential to effective programs. Well-designed, publicized statements of policy and procedures can provide momentum for EAPs. The policy statement should outline:

1. The recognized need for the program.
2. Support for the program from both management and labor.
3. The willingness of the organization to commit time and resources to the EAP.
4. Accessible points of contacts for employee assistance and procedures to follow.
5. An acceptable attitude about mental illness, alcoholism, and family/marital problems.
6. A concern by the organization for its employees.
7. The scope of problems to be covered by the EAP.
8. The target group for the EAP.
9. Job security and promotional opportunities of those participating in the program.
10. Confidentiality of records.

---

[2] John McKinley, *Participant's Manual for Participation Training Institute* (Indianapolis, Ind.: CHR, Inc., 1978).

11. Job performance as the basis for supervisory recommendations.
12. The voluntary nature of the program.
13. Sick leave and insurance benefits.
14. The relationship to other personnel and administrative policies.

The explicitness, scope, and tone of the policy must be given careful consideration.

ESTABLISHING LINKAGES WITH COMMUNITY RESOURCES

When EAPs initiate linkages with community resources tension is likely to exist because of uncertainties over roles and expectations. The following are some guidelines for developing productive linkages with community resources which will help overcome tensions caused by distrust, conflict, and inefficiency in the referral system. The guidelines are not absolute but provide direction for both the EAP and the community resource.

1. Understand and know your own organization. Try to clearly identify your organization's goals, values orientation, and contributions to the linkages. Both groups should be able to articulate these elements.
2. Develop a joint agreement on the general purposes of the linkage. Write a broad statement oriented toward the common goals of each organization.
3. Deal openly with issues about power, boundaries, and responsibilities. For the linkage to be effective, all these elements must be negotiated. Shared credit for the formation of the linkage is essential.
4. Establish direct confidential communication systems between the community resources and the EAP office. This communication system will be a key component of the EAP model.
5. Identify facilitators that may assist with the community resource linkages. These persons must not be leaders of the EAP or the community resource. They may be counselors, volunteers, board members, union leaders, A.A. members, or ministers. As linkage facilitators, they should help to prevent an organization from being dependent on one individual.
6. Identify persons with a variety of skills in such areas as planning, change processes, negotiation, interpersonal communications, and group processes. These persons may include and assist in facilitating understanding between community resources and the EAP. Persons with expertise in specific areas may or may not be outside both systems. Similarly, not all occupational program consultants have these skills.
7. Learning aspects of the linkages should be emphasized. The linkage should create new knowledge, ideas, models, and innovations needed to make the linkage effective.

8. Emphasize program accountability and responsible management of employees flowing into and out of the EAP system. Good record-keeping is essential, and agreement on referral procedures is necessary.
9. Carry out and use evaluation in the decision-making process. Evaluation models should fit the objectives. The future of an EAP may depend on how well the referral and the diagnosis, treatment, and client progress are documented.
10. Publicize newsworthy and successful activities of the EAP. This may encourage other community resources to participate in the system. Build on successes rather than dwelling on failures. Continually review and revise the system to meet employee needs and correct inadequacies.

The EAP–Community Resource Agreement

This section discusses specific items that may be part of an agreement between the community resources and an EAP. The word agreement is used, rather than contract, since it denotes a more flexible and less authoritarian relationship. An agreement is a vehicle to develop a clear understanding of what each agency expects from the other. The process of negotiating agreements should be done in a pleasant nonthreatening atmosphere where solutions can surface that will allow both participants to have their needs met. Prior to developing agreements, both partners should have their individual needs focused and be able to accurately communicate them to each other. Below are some areas for possible inclusion in an agreement:

1. Specific services offered to the EAP by the community resources.
2. Professional qualifications and roles of individuals to be involved in providing services.
3. Referral procedures to be utilized by the EAP coordinator and employees.
4. Operating schedule and location of the services.
5. Fees for assessment and ongoing treatment.
6. Procedures for handling third-party payments.
7. Procedures for flow of information between the EAP coordinator and community resources and for maintenance of client confidentiality.
8. Follow-up procedures and plans for ongoing support of employees.
9. Treatment modalities to be used.
10. Procedures and criteria for making referrals to other community resources.
11. Plans for evaluating treatment processes.

A key in the EAP model is to establish a clearly focused set of expected behaviors for the EAP and the community resources when referring employees. These expectations should be communicated to all the employees in a general manner and explicitly when an employee seeks assistance through the EAP.

The Referral Process

Referral is a common denominator in many EAPs since few of them can handle all aspects of an employee's problem (i.e., identification, assessment, diagnosis, and treatment). Therefore, referral to community resources is an essential element for EAPs not promoting an internally based program.

A recommendation to the EAP coordinator by the supervisor may be misused unless supportive job performance data are the basis for recommendations. Referral is the process by which the EAP links an employee with the appropriate community resource, as opposed to the recommendation made by the supervisor to visit the EAP coordinator. The linkage resulting from the referral of an employee by the EAP coordinator may include assessment, diagnosis, information, and treatment. Referrals are reserved for persons who have some expertise in determining the cause of problems and in choosing the appropriate community resource for handling the problem. If an EAP coordinator does not have this expertise, he or she would make a recommendation that an employee visit a centralized agency handling all assessments and making the appropriate referrals. Supervisors should *not* make a referral to the EAP, but rather should *recommend* the employee take advantage of the EAP. EAPs are voluntary programs and the supervisor's role should be focused on the job performance of the employee. Referrals should be made by the EAP coordinator or the person performing the assessment or diagnostic function.

When an employee with a problem contacts the EAP coordinator or the person assigned to be the entry point into the community resource system, a number of actions take place. The employee should be clearly told about the EAP's policy and procedures, especially as they relate to pending disciplinary action. It should be made clear at the onset, that the EAP is a means for employees to seek and to receive assistance for problems affecting job performance and that it is not a shelter from disciplinary action. Making sure that the employee is made responsible for the consequences of his or her job performance actions is an essential element throughout the referral process, both for the EAP and the community resource system. Additionally, it must be clear that utilization of the EAP will in no way affect future job security or advancement. The process of diagnosis, company insurance, and costs should be explained to the employee. Consent forms for authorizing release of information to the EAP coordinator should be available. Protection of confidentiality is essential in all elements of the referral process. Referral to a community resource should be made only after the EAP coordinator or the diagnostic agent has carefully explained the treatment options available to the employee.

To restate, the following should be discussed with the employee at the time of referral:

1. The company's insurance coverage for expenses incurred for services rendered by the treatment resource.
2. The assurance that the employee's promotion opportunities will not be hindered by the use of the EAP or any community resources.
3. Continued employment, pay raises, promotions, or disciplinary action will be based on job performance and not clinical progress.
4. Any type of communication about employee progress in a treatment program will be governed by confidentiality statutes that allow release of certain information only with the consent of the employee.
5. Receiving treatment during working hours will be handled according to the organization's general policy on absences for health reasons or statements on EAP procedures.
6. The process of making the appointment should be outlined. Having a specific person to contact is very helpful to the employee.

Motivating an employee to accept a referral may remain an ongoing problem. An even greater problem is created when the employee denies that a problem exists, even though job performance clearly indicates something is wrong and action required. Dealing with these conditions requires a skilled interviewer who can:

1. Clearly identify with the employee what the consequences will be if behavior is not changed.
2. Identify and help resolve any preconceived barriers to accepting services.
3. Preserve the employee's self-esteem. It is the job performance actions that are unacceptable, not the employee's personality or being.
4. Avoid attaching labels such as psychotic, alcoholic, and so on to employees.
5. Assure the employee that the least restrictive alternative will be used.

Services to Be Provided by Community Resources

One of the first things the EAP coordinator, with the aid of the advisory committee, must do to establish linkages with community resources is to locate them. Many large cities have community service councils or other bodies for coordinating human resources. These organizations frequently publish directories of community resources or have available information. Other excellent sources of information are crisis counseling centers, ministerial associations, police departments, and chambers of commerce. Other EAP or occupational program coordinators may have identified and compiled lists of community resources and should be consulted for advice and sharing of relevant information. Finally, state departments of mental health may offer assistance. They often have directories of public and private facilities.

At least four basic categories of services should be identified.

1. **Crisis Intervention.** Included in this category are:

    a. Twenty-four hour "hotlines" and telephone counseling services.
    b. Drop-in centers for immediate service without an appointment.
    c. Self-help groups, such as Alcoholics Anonymous.

2. **Outpatient Services.** These may include assessment, diagnosis, information, education, and ongoing treatment for a variety of problems, such as:

    a. Child abuse.
    b. Child/adolescent problems.
    c. Mental health counseling.
    d. Marital counseling.
    e. Family counseling.
    f. Alcohol/drug dependency.
    g. Debt management.
    h. Career counseling.
    i. Legal counseling.
    j. Grief counseling.
    k. Family planning/sex education.

Outpatient services may be in the day or evening but are usually focused around a specific problem. Outpatient services will be able to handle many employee problems.

3. **Inpatient Services.** These services provide intensive care for employees with severe, chronic, and life-threatening problems. A continuum of inpatient services exist, ranging from hospital care to residential treatment. A number of intermediate services, such as half-way houses and day treatment centers, are also available.

4. **Self-Help Groups.** These groups focus on a specific problem and are operated by persons who have faced and overcome similar situations. The groups are effective in providing aftercare support, education, and crisis assistance. Self-help groups exist in such problem areas as:

    a. Alcoholism (A.A. and Alanon).
    b. Overeating.
    c. Child abuse (Parents Anonymous).
    d. Death or dying.
    e. Divorce.
    f. Single parenting.
    g. Gambling and other addictions.
    h. Chronic credit management.

Self-help groups are effective for ongoing support. However, they are not a substitute for professional diagnosis and treatment.

Evaluating Community Resources

The emphasis on accountability has spread to all aspects of society, including community resources. The reasons for evaluating community resources are to provide information for making decisions on program operation and to provide the best possible assistance to employees. An evaluation begins with the development of a system to gather data on the flow of employees into and out of community resources. However, there is additional information that should be gathered.

Community resource evaluation should be based on a set of standards, criteria, or principles against which to compare the data gathered. Listed below are some suggested criteria by which to evaluate community resources.

1. The principle of the least-restrictive alternative is followed. For the EAP, this means an emphasis on outpatient care whenever possible, unless it can be demonstrated that inpatient care is essential.
2. Services designed to meet client needs, not agency needs, are incorporated in the community resource principles.
3. A concern for quality of life and a holistic approach for the client is demonstrated.
4. Opportunities for the continuation and integration of normal life experiences are provided.
5. Necessary services are provided to maintain the maximum amount of client stabilization.
6. Overlapping or duplicated services are minimized and program gaps are eliminated.
7. Responsive, timely coordination and referral procedures exist among the community resources.
8. Knowledge and innovations are sought to upgrade the quality of services.
9. Citizen/client participation in planning, implementation, and evaluation of services is present. This is especially crucial for EAP linkages.
10. Regular and thorough evaluations are performed with data being used to improve services.
11. Prevention should be emphasized. Many community resources are willing and able to initiate educational programs for employees on various topics.
12. The needs of special groups should be given attention. These group needs may include the problems of women, minorities, occupational groups such as isolated workers and executives, etc.
13. Client dignity and confidentiality are never compromised.

14. Effective liaison with all types of community resources is maintained whether they are degreed or nondegreed, professional or para-professional, paid or volunteer.
15. Fees are clearly stated and related to well-defined services and the client's ability to pay.

Criteria for determining effectiveness of community resources might include the opinions of certain individuals.[3] For example:

1. Direct users of the community resource both present and past.
2. Indirect users of the community resource, such as:
   a. Families of the user.
   b. Community planning groups.
   c. Interest groups (mental health associations, counselors associations, and the like).
   d. Other community resources.
3. Administrators, board members, and staff of the community agencies.
4. State planning and regulatory agencies (mental health, public health, welfare, education, licensing agencies).

As a general rule, an EAP coordinator should have access to information that does not violate client confidentiality or employee privacy, such as personnel records if the community resource receives public money from the local, state, or federal government. Private community resources are not obligated to disclose information. However, private resources may provide data, since the information will help referral sources make decisions on the use of services.

To summarize, evaluation is a process to be used for judging decision-making alternatives. The evaluation of community resources, therefore, has to be based on clearly stated needs and objectives articulated by the EAP coordinator and the employee. Community resource performance can be measured against the established criteria. Evaluation is not isolated from the community resources, linkages, and referral process but is a key to making good decisions on the appropriate use of community resources for the benefit of the employee.

SUPERVISORY TRAINING

This section is in response to a much-needed conceptualization of the education and training function present in employee assistance programs. The author views EAPs as a major human resource preservation tool, with important implications for mental health, alcoholism, social work, and other human service professions. Many pioneering efforts have gone on in hun-

---

[3] Val D. MacMurray, *Citizen Evaluation of Mental Health Services* (New York: Human Services Press, 1976).

dreds of settings around the country to advance EAPs through the training function. Unfortunately, few of these efforts have been evaluated, so their impact is not known. The training and adult education professions have conspicuously ignored this whole area. Many organizational development books or journals leave the impression that all performance problems with workers are caused by the job or the organization.

Practically all proponents of EAPs recognize that supervisors need training to effectively implement a program. A number of programs expend some effort in educating their employees on the uses of EAPs and mental health/alcoholism concepts.

The notion of a systems approach to training and education is important because of the interlocking nature of our social structures presented by individuals, the company, families, and treatment resources. EAPs make the most sense when they are mainstreamed into the daily functions of the individual and his world. Any approach to personal interventions must consider the entire system affecting the individual.

Another way of viewing education/trainer functions is as a change agent. The EAP cannot exist as a separate entity. The trainer or EAP coordinator, in designing education/training programs may at various times serve as a: (1) catalyst, to energize the system into legitimizing needed changes; (2) solution-giver, to provide timely, pertinent information; (3) process-helper, to facilitate planning and create positive interaction among the system elements; and (4) resource-linker, to bring people, resources, and tasks together.

The task of the agent of change is to (1) diagnose the needs of the organization, (2) select an approach, and (3) evaluate the result. The key is using the right approach at the right time. Effective long-term training approaches result from the change agent utilizing appropriate strategies.

Systems approaches also recognize that learning is a natural activity that goes on constantly, whether planned or unplanned. Education is the process of intervening to efficiently direct that activity toward chosen goals. Conversely, it is possible for education activities to take place without any learning (at least not the kind intended). Education at its best prepares people to be independent, life-long, deliberate learners.

With those thoughts in mind, certain major areas of concern become apparent with the way education/training functions are currently managed.

Some flaws in current occupational educational programming practices seem to be:

1. Participative planning is seldom used to design programs.
2. Programs are seldom based on clear and specific, indications of need.
3. Instructional objectives, when present at all, are often determined with no factual basis and frequently do not allow for accountability.
4. Educational programs may be a collection of unrelated or trendy theories.

5. Film and lectures (methods that often allow little participation) form the basis of most programs.
6. Evaluation designs of programs often are absent.
7. Programs seldom are a part of long-term planning but merely reflect discontinuous, short-term objectives.
8. Supervisors are given confusing information about their role as an intervener with the problem employee.
9. Alcoholism/mental health information is given to supervisors during training sessions when it should be reserved for employee education programs.

Characteristics of the Adult Learner

Experienced trainers recognize that programs for adults have to take into account their unique characteristics. Adults' needs are different from children's in learning situations.

Learning Is an Activity. Receiving information is not the same as learning. Learning implies the ability to do something. As such, the focus always should be on involving the learner in an active way.

Learning Must Be Related to the Learner's Needs. Everybody is motivated. It often is the direction of the motivation that causes the conflict. It is the trainer's role to assess the direction and the force of the learner's motivation. The result is educational relevance.

Learning Involves Emotions. Adults are complex beings who have a variety of needs, some rational, some not. All have fears about being accepted, doubts about self-worth, and a desire for stability and look for opportunities to be unique and independent.

Learning Is Dependent upon the Environment. The trainer is responsible for the climate in which the learning is conducted. Physical arrangements are important, but the psychological elements are even more critical. It is important for the trainer to establish norms and model behavior that establish a climate whereby the learners feel accepted and free to participate, find the content personally relevant, and are encouraged to be increasingly more responsible for their own continuing learning.

Learning Must Balance Individual and Group Needs. The trainer must be alert to group norms and pressures to insure full participation in the activity. Task and maintenance roles must be brought to the attention of the group. Voluntary participation and individual autonomy are important aspects of the training experience that need to be preserved. Cooperative, rather than competitive, interactions maximize the likelihood that the instructional goal will be met. Full use of the adult learners' experiences and skills should be brought to bear in the learning activities.

Learning Activities Should Be Able to Be Evaluated. Both the delivery and the outcomes of the training sessions should be measured. Adult learners must be free to decide whether the expertise of the trainer is relevant to their situation, and be able to disengage themselves from the activity if their perceived needs are not being met. Clearly defined objectives should be made available to the learner. Feedback should be directed to both learner and instructor. Evaluation should provide a means for the learner to look at future or continuing needs that logically follow from the learning experience.

Learning Requires Practice and Reinforcement. One of the prime ingredients of any training program that hopes to produce a tangible result is the use of practice in a meaningful way. Meaning is acquired if positively reinforced.

Malcolm Knowles presented his view of the "androgogical process of program development," which represents one comprehensive perspective on the trainer's role.[4] The androgogical process described by Knowles involves making full use of the learners' experiences and resources. Knowles's list of the steps involved in program development are:

1. Establish a climate conducive to effective adult learning.
2. Create an organizational structure for participative planning.
3. Diagnose the learning needs.
4. Formulate the directions for learning (objectives) based on the learning needs.
5. Design appropriate learning activities.
6. Implement the activities.
7. Rediagnose the needs for learning (evaluation).

A variety of methods should be used to implement the training program and accomplish the selected objectives. These should be selected on the basis of ability to complete the learning transaction. Every attempt should be made to take advantage of the participants' experiences, rather than use hypothetical cases. The sessions should be flexible and oriented around the learners. Open discussion of significant current problems should be encouraged. The emphasis should be on developing effective supervisory skills and the use of company resources, especially the EAP.

It is important to stress that learning should be looked upon as a continuous process that takes place over a lifetime. This perspective means that a single educational program may not suffice to teach a particular skill or to insure adequate implementation of the EAP.

PLANNING AND IMPLEMENTING EFFECTIVE TRAINING PROGRAMS

Planning an effective program involves more than finding a good film and then getting people to attend a showing of it. Poorly done training

---

[4] Malcolm Knowles, *The Adult Learners: A Neglected Species* (Houston: Gulf Publishing, 1973).

actually may inhibit a program. Since credibility and accountability are major issues for most EAPs, having well-designed training can be the vehicle to help accomplish both. Outlined here is a process that will likely produce results for the employee assistance program.

The Program Development Process

1. **Gather Information about the Needs of Your Target Group.** Needs may be defined in terms of the motivational orientation of an individual, and are not the same as wants. This step will help you to define the kind of activity that should be performed. The needs may take the form of either gaps between what individuals are doing and what they should be doing; or they may take the form of determining what skills or knowledge an individual should have to accomplish goals. Include essential knowledge, such as the policies and procedures of the EAP.

It is important that some kind of standard be applied to evaluate the data on individual needs. Most often, a representative sample of the target group is sufficient to serve as the source of needs data. Several methods should be employed in gathering the data to insure its reliability. The data should be reviewed by the program's advisory committee for comparison with the EAP's goals and objectives.

2. **Form Learning Objectives from the Needs Assessment Data.** Objectives should be clear, concise, specific statements that use action verbs. The objectives should specify the desired outcome sought as a result of the training. They should be realistic, honest, and attainable.

3. **Assess the Resources Needed.** A wide variety of resources should be considered. (Consider the demand on your, or staff time and capabilities.) Include the cost of such resources as facilities, supplies, and learner man-hours required.

4. **Obtain Legitimization for the Training Proposal.** Many programs fall by the wayside because a broad base of support for the training effort has not been obtained. The first three steps should form the basis for the proposal to be submitted to both formal and informal sources of authority. This should include union leaders, top management, other key opinion leaders in the work force, the training department, and, of course, the advisory committee. The proposal should be tentative and flexible—spread ownership of the proposal so a feeling of legitimate participation is generated.

5. **Design the Program of Learning Activities.** Translate objectives into an action plan. The plan should include a number of alternative instructional activities. Some of the best plans on paper sometimes do not work with certain groups. The trainer should be able to adjust the plan if the desired responses are not being obtained. Time and the nature of learning objectives are the primary factors in selecting the kind and se-

quence of instructional activities. Affective domain learning (i.e., attitudes, feeling, and values) requires intense group interaction. Cognitive domain (i.e., knowledge, comprehension) learning may be handled with more didactic methods. In any event, the design should maximize the participation of learners and make full use of their knowledge and experience. The design should include topics or major points to be stressed, physical arrangements, the instructional techniques in sequence with alternatives, and the amount of time to be devoted to each section. Each section should be related to a specific learning objective. Also, include the method of evaluating the training. Evaluate both the delivery of the instruction as well as the content.

Implementing the Training Program

The implementation of the training program must utilize individuals or technology (multi-media), or both, competent to deliver the content and facilitate the learning experience. Pilot test the training design to work out any flaws or rough spots.

A major step should be to prepare the learners for the activities. This involves informing the learners of the objectives of the program and of their involvement. This should be done in both written and oral forms. An open-ended inquiry into the expectations and concerns of the learners early in the training program also is recommended. Valuable data on composition of the group and its specific needs can be obtained in this manner. Feedback from the learners should be sought at various points in each session.

Give attention to facilities that are comfortable, flexible, and appropriate. Preplanning and management support often can help obtain better facilities than would otherwise be possible.

Care should be given to the mixture of the learners and their motivations for attending the program. The presence of senior management with front-line supervisors can have a deadening effect on any discussion. The scheduling of the program should provide the learners with choices that will allow them to minimize disruption of daily work schedules. An anxious, hostile supervisor is not likely to be a receptive learner.

Modular type programs that ask the supervisor to choose elements of a program most immediately beneficial to him or her should be seriously considered.

Handouts are desirable in most learning situations when they: (1) are relevent to the situation; (2) can be integrated with the class activity; (3) offer long-term, out-of-class utility; and (4) are brief and practical.

A brief comment about the use of training films: avoid showing any films you have not previewed. Films should have a practical task.

Consider using parts of films or stop-action techniques. Fifteen-minutes is the maximum time that film segments should be used. Information overflow is a real possibility if the film is too long. Role-playing, discussions, and other group activities interspersed with the film can be highly reinforcing.

This section concludes with a few tips on handling several common instructional problems.

When a learner becomes disruptive, try to ignore him and confront him privately. Avoid putting down disruptors publicly; rather, keep pushing ahead with your task in a positive but assertive manner. Make sure you have the group's consent if you run over the planned time. When a divisive issue arises between you and the class, spend time listening, clarifying, and checking out their assumptions. Avoid win/lose situations. You can't force your opinion on the learner. Be honest enough to admit it when the class has made a valid point.

A final point to remember is the importance of modeling the kind of behavior you expect from the learners. This means showing respect for them as people, communicating accurately, listening emphatically, and demonstrating responsible, open behavior.

Evaluating the Training Program

The end result of a training program for supervisors is to change their behavior. Evaluation should be seen not only as a tool for accountability but as a process of making better decisions on future learning activities.

Two kinds of evaluation are possible. The first is a learning process evaluation, which seeks to assess the adequacy of the instructor and the design to make necessary design revisions based upon the evaluation data.

A second type of evaluation seeks to measure the results or outcome attributable to the program. This type of evaluation is used to determine how well the objectives have been met.

In planning for evaluation, several questions need to be asked:

1. What information do we need to know?
2. Who has that information? Where and when is it available?
3. What procedures are needed to obtain it?
4. How do we want to use the information, and who needs to act on it?

A variety of techniques should be considered in collecting the data. Some of the techniques include interviews, pre- and post-testing, the use of standardized instruments, job performance records, organizational statistics, products of the training, trainer evaluation, and appropriate use of the EAP. You may consider consulting with a research professional on the application of statistical techniques in processing the data. Computer analysis should be considered for any kind of substantial effort.

Another factor in evaluating the impact of the training is the ability to control variables; inability may make it difficult to demonstrate a relationship between the training program and behavior changes in the learner, and it may affect both internal and external validity. One way to control some of the threats to internal validity, and to show a relationship between training and changes in supervisor behavior, is to include a control group in the evaluation. The validity of an evaluation may be affected by:

1. Built-in bias (slanting a question to give positive responses).
2. Pretesting effects (cueing the learner how to respond).
3. Effect of concurrent interaction with learner (other training, promotion to new position, changes in work climate, and the like).
4. Maturation (some people change and improve regardless of the training).
5. Biased selection process (the group evaluated may not be representative of the entire target group).

This is, by no means, an exhaustive list of the problems that can confound the interpretation of evaluation results. Do not be put off, though. With careful planning, most of these variables can be controlled. Most training programs have problems receiving support because they cannot show decision makers that the program has actually changed anybody's behavior.

Attention should be given to the dissemination of the evaluation data. The advisory committee of the EAP should be given a concise, understandable report. Include recommendations for revisions of the design and future training needed.

THE ROLE OF THE SUPERVISOR REVISITED

The supervisor's role in employee assistance programs has been the subject of a considerable amount of written material. These materials usually encourage the supervisor to follow several basic steps in productively managing the troubled employee. The first step involves documentation of unacceptable levels of performance: to include incidents, behavior patterns, and attendance. A second step is to conduct an interview or series of interviews to confront the employee with the documented performance deficiencies. The employee then is referred to the employee assistance program for help in solving any problems causing the performance deficiencies. The supervisor was not to become involved in solving the employee's personal problems or even attempting a diagnosis. The supervisor's role was to offer the employee a tool for improving his job performance.

The matter of supervising a troubled employee is, however, considerably more complex. Three types of barriers provide special problems to the supervisor in working with a troubled employee.

One of the most basic problems for supervisors is the absence of specific production goals or well-defined tasks to be performed by employees. EAPs are founded on the notion that the supervisor should not diagnose the employee's problems but should stick solely to working with job performance. When performance standards are vague or even nonexistant, the supervisor is put in a compromised position. The program must recognize those deficiencies and design training programs to assist the supervisor. *Close coordination is essential with other organizational training efforts.*

Another problem area is that of job stress related to role conflicts, work addiction, job obsolescence, or other work-climate aggravations. The supervisor needs to learn how to sort out the factors that make work unrewarding. Training in diagnosing the presence of those factors may be necessary in some work settings.

A third area that requires attention is the kind of social sanctions and expectations placed upon the employee about drinking on the job. Many organizations place employees in a role that seems to require drinking on the job or in related social settings. The supervisor needs to be able to recognize those situations where the risks of problem drinking are encouraged by the organization. This is especially difficult for the supervisor. Training in this area may help the supervisor identify organizational roles and expectations that may contribute to performance problems for employees.

Another perspective on the role of the supervisor is that, once a performance problem has been identified, the supervisor must determine whether the problem is caused by inadequate training of the employee or by the lack of potential to perform the job. If the supervisor determines the employee is able to do the job, then another reason must be sought. These "other" reasons assume that the employee could do the job if he or she wished.

The supervisor should check three organizational factors as possible reasons for the performance deficiency:

1. Is the desired performance punishing?
2. Is nonperformance rewarding?
3. Does performing really matter?

If none of those factors is present, then other external variables, such as family, mental health, and alcoholism problems, are likely causes. It is possible that organizational variables and personal/emotional variables are interrelated. When organizational and training factors can be eliminated, an offer of assistance from the employee assistance program is indicated.

Another way of looking at supervisory roles and responses is to deal with the emotional aspects of the supervisor's behavior in managing the troubled employee. The supervisor's behavior can portray a pattern of interaction that parallels that of the spouse of the alcoholic. The pattern typically includes a process of ignoring the problem and hoping for a "miracle," heart-to-heart talks, or reasoning; begging or pleading; and finally bleeding (transfer, fire, retire). The supervisor, in this pattern, feels anger, guilt, fear, and strong ego involvement with the successes and failures of the employee. The supervisor often is unwilling to recognize deviant behavior he is not prepared to handle.

What this suggests is that the traditional training done to teach supervisors to identify, confront, motivate, and refer employees is not enough. In traditional training programs, supervisors are given information they will not use in the near future. However, the supervisor needs to develop a connection between the employee's behavior, feelings, and resultant behavior. With such a model, the supervisor is taught to seek out the EAP coordinator at the earliest sign of problems with an employee. Specific procedures are then taught by the EAP coordinator. Excellent interpersonal skills are required of the program coordinator in this model.

The literature on leadership and supervision does not provide many answers to the problem of how to respond to the troubled employee. Leadership is usually defined as a social-influence process. Research has failed to identify any common characteristics shared by leaders across all situations, nor has one style of leadership been shown to produce a desired set of results in all situations.

The question of task-oriented versus person-oriented behavior is one that is situation bound also. The nature of the task, the amount of structure involved, and the kind and amount of power of the leader—and the quality of leader/employee relations—appear to be the most prominent factors involved in determining what supervisory behavior is appropriate.

There is a decision-making process to help supervisors decide what type of leadership style to exercise. Among the questions for the supervisor to ask are: (1) does the problem possess a quality requirement? (2) does he or she (the supervisor) have sufficient information to make a high-quality decision? (3) is the problem structured? (4) is acceptance of the decision by subordinates important for effective implementation? (5) if I were to make the decision by myself, am I reasonably certain that it would be accepted by my subordinates? (6) do subordinates share the organizational goals to be obtained in solving this problem? and (7) is conflict among subordinates likely in preferred solutions? The supervisor in managing the troubled employee may have to ask himself or herself many of these and related questions.

The implications for supervisory training are:

1. Supervisors need to be taught how and what to observe about the employee's behavior.
2. Developing clear standards of performance and behavioral expectations of the employee is a skill that must be taught to supervisors.
3. The supervisor should be taught how to utilize the program coordinator, especially in procedural and problem-solving situations. The supervisor should *not* be taught to "turn the employee over" to the coordinator but to work cooperatively with the coordinator in creat-

ing a joint plan of action. Early involvement with the coordinator is needed.

4. Learning to diagnose organizational stressors that make work unsatisfying or performance unrewarding is an area of primary concern for the supervisor.

5. Training should help supervisors to link their behavior and emotions so they can avoid being manipulated by the troubled employee. They should learn to seek help at the earliest possible moment, both for themselves and the employees.

6. Supervisors should be taught to use systematic decision-making, problem-solving processes to work with troubled employees.

7. Supervisors should be taught communication and conflict management skills to be able to effectively intervene with troubled employees.

8. Supervisors need to be able to contract with employees to change job behaviors.

9. In skill-building sessions, where interaction with other participants is usually necessary, the groups of supervisors should be as homogeneous as possible.

10. Any supervisory training conducted should be integrated with other organizational training efforts to avoid confusion, overlap, and wasting of resources.

EMPLOYEE EDUCATION

For people to commit themselves to any course of action, they must have some cognizance of alternatives available to them, plus a basis for believing that a particular course of action is better for them than others. Otherwise they act blindly or not at all. The aims of education are behavior change and to enable individuals to gain increased awareness and understanding of alternatives, which, in turn, enable them to make better decisions about those things affecting the quality of their lives.

The educational task inherent in implementing and evaluating effective employee assistance programs is formidable, especially at this early stage of development of the field. All of the institutions of society have long been affected by their members who exhibit dysfunctional behavior. However, mental health service delivery systems have lagged far behind our recognition of the problems. A key component in creating such systems must be education.

The educational process in developing an employee assistance program for an organization begins when initial contact with management personnel is made. Many people in management and the work force have not even heard of the term *employee assistance program;* of those, only a few have a good concept of the process or possible outcomes involved in such a program. However, assuming one can successfully educate management to the value of a program, what must be done to inform and educate the work force in order to bring about appropriate program utilization?

There appear to be two general areas of education and information of importance. The first is the structure and mechanics of the program's operation. All workers should be informed of the purposes of the program, who is responsible for its operation, how they can utilize it, the protection offered by confidentiality, the costs they might incur in using it, and so on. This information should be made available to all workers and their families at the outset. Such vehicles as the company and union newsletters, direct mailing, and informational posters are obvious means of communication. In addition, well-trained and informed supervisors can help.

A second dimension of the educational program is the more complex task of providing ongoing employee education aimed at increasing awareness of mental health issues affecting their lives and familiarizing the employees with helping resources and processes. Ignorance and fear remain formidable obstacles to people in our society who should be utilizing mental health services. Though neither can be eliminated, a systematic approach to increasing awareness and acceptance of mental health services should be made.

There are many alternatives to topics covered, media used, time spent, money allocated, and so on, in a solid educational program. However, educational programs should be related to the goals of the organization. The most obvious goals are:

1. Increased employee awareness of the EAP program and how it operates.
2. Increased employee awareness of mental health issues affecting their own lives.
3. Increased employee understanding of treatment alternatives available to them.
4. Increased utilization of the program.

All of these factors could be measured to determine the effect of the educational program.

The strategy for implementing the educational program includes the following steps:

1. Assess current levels of understanding and need for additional information.
2. Share the results with the advisory committee and assist it in developing an educational program for a given time—perhaps one year.
3. Assess the results of the program to determine the extent to which the goals were met.
4. Modify the educational program based on the results and changing needs.

Program content should be based on a needs assessment. However, it could include such things as the mechanics of utilizing the program, and specific content areas such as family problems, stress management, marital relationships, parenting, alcohol problems, dealing with depression, how therapy works, financial planning and management, and sexuality.

Any number of media and methods—including literature racks, movies, lectures, discussions, pay envelope enclosures, the organization's newsletters, posters, radio coverage, and new employee orientation—could be utilized.

A sound, systematic educational program is clearly a vital component in an effective employee assistance program. The company must be willing to commit sufficient resources, time, and money, to see that the objectives of the educational program are realized. Reducing or eliminating this component of the program would severely diminish the potential impact of the EAP.

Examples of employee education programs include:

1. A 30-to-45 minute mobile education program presented by the coordinator in the work area on the EAP and how to use it.
2. Posters placed around the plant that stress the use of the EAP and human relations. Bumper stickers or buttons also might be used.
3. Regular articles by the EAP coordinator in the company newspaper and local media.
4. Short messages with the paychecks.
5. Guest speakers to address various in-plant groups.
6. Reading room(s) with material on alcoholism and mental health.
7. Film festivals between shifts and during meal breaks, showing continuously to employees who want to attend. Pamphlets available.
8. An EAP pamphlet mailed to all employees' homes.
9. Luncheon discussion groups around various topics. Invite community resource personnel.
10. Workshops in churches or other community facilities on the weekends.
11. A published list of local education programs and community resources.
12. Visual displays rotating into various areas of the company.

A COST/BENEFIT ANALYSIS OF AN EMPLOYEE ASSISTANCE PROGRAM

Employee assistance programs have been based on the premise that an employee's job performance can be influenced by alcoholism, drug abuse, emotional, family/marital, and financial problems, and by a family member's problem. Whenever the magnitude of a personal problem becomes great enough, it has the potential to influence work behavior to the extent that the employee is a "troubled employee."

The author directed a cost/benefit analysis of an employee assistance program during its first year. The study focused on supervisory training to make recommendations; the coordination, referral, and counseling of troubled employees; and the cost/benefit comparison of an employee assistance program in one plant with another plant not having a program.

The population for this study consisted of 1,900 employees in one plant and 1,200 employees in the second. Sites were selected on the basis of similarities in size, age, production, community demographics, and demographics of the work forces. Community populations were similar with regard to males/females, race, death rates, income, unemployment, education, and voting preference. Similarities in the communities, plant production, and plant history make it likely that the second plant was an adequate choice for a comparison group.

The study considered three groups: a treatment group of only troubled employees; a randomly selected comparison group of troubled and nontroubled employees in the same plant; and a randomly selected comparison group of troubled and nontroubled employees in a second plant.

The treatment group of troubled employees was identified as entrants into the employee assistance program. During the one-year study, 59 employees were identified as having substandard job performance by their supervisors, or referred themselves to the EAP, resulting in a penetration rate of 3.1 percent of the total population.

Data collection consisted of training costs, absenteeism, accidents, grievances, spoilage, insurance costs, achievements, and suggestions for employees. Company records were obtained for two previous years to establish trends that may have been attributable to other programs (e.g., safety programs). Information was collected for all troubled employees and the comparison groups. Standard accounting procedures were used to determine total and standard costs for each variable. This provided baseline information against which the cost or benefit, or both, of the employee assistance program could be determined.

Data revealed that troubled employees were about two years younger but had about the same education as comparison groups. Fewer troubled employees were single, more were divorced, and more were separated from the job than comparison groups. Troubled employees had fewer years of employment, spent less time in training for their jobs, and received a lower rate of pay per hour than comparison groups.

Total savings of the EAP to the company was $94,214 and total cost to the company was $57,964. This results in a savings of $36,250 to the company from the program. In other words, for every $1 spent, $1.63 was saved.

Absenteeism, accidents, achievements, and disciplinary actions decreased for troubled employees after the employee assistance program began. However, insurance, grievances, suggestions, and spoilage increased for troubled employees. Relatively few incidents were reported for disciplinary actions, grievances, spoilage, and training while absenteeism, insurance, accidents, achievements, and suggestions occurred with greater frequency.

Two of the most costly items for the company also were indicators of troubled employees; absenteeism and insurance. Absenteeism seems to be the best discriminator of troubled employees prior to an employee assistance program. Insurance seems to be the best discriminator of troubled employees after implementation of a program. Absenteeism was approximately two and one-half times greater for troubled employees than for other employees.

EMPLOYEE ASSISTANCE PROGRAMS: WHO BENEFITS— AN OVERVIEW OF ONE COMPANY

Troubled Employees

- The mean age for troubled employees in one company was 38.1 years.
- Of the troubled employees, 6.7 percent were single, 81.7 percent were married, and 11.7 percent were divorced, in comparison to 16.3 percent single, 79.9 percent married, and 3.8 percent divorced in the entire work force.
- Of the troubled employees, 21.7 percent were female and 78.3 percent were male. This was similar to the ratio for the work force.
- Ten percent of the troubled employees had a high school diploma, 71.7 percent were high school graduates, 11.7 percent had attended college but had not received a degree, and 6.7 percent had a college degree. This was compatible to the rest of the work force.
- Of the troubled employees, 13.3 percent were separated from employment and 86.7 percent were still employed at the completion of the study, in comparison to 7.7 percent separated and 92.3 percent employed in the work force.
- Troubled employees had been employed, on the average, 15.2 years.
- It required, on the average, 7.9 months to train an employee who later became troubled.
- Of the troubled employees, 83.3 percent received wages and 16.7 percent were salaried, while 79.5 percent of the entire work force received wages and 20.5 percent were salaried.
- On the average, troubled employees received $7.90 per hour.
- Of the entire work force, 3.1 percent was identified during the first year of EAP operation as troubled employees.
- Between 8.6 and 11.5 percent of the work force at any given time are potential troubled employees.
- It costs on the average $17,206 to replace a troubled employee. This indicates that they are valuable assets to the company.

The Company

- It cost the company $174.28 a day when a troubled employee was absent. This included wages, replacement costs, insurance, processing, and the like.
- The EAP saved the company 463 days in absenteeism (i.e., $80,698.47) during the first year of operation.
- During the first year of operation, absenteeism was reduced from 12.83 days absence per employee to 10.91 days per employee. That was a reduction of 15 percent in absenteeism for troubled employees and a 2.42 percent reduction in absenteeism for the entire plant.
- There was an increase in the number of accidents for troubled employees during the study; however, the severity of the accidents was greatly reduced and was reflected in the cost of the accident.
- Accident cost for troubled employees was reduced from $585.37 before the EAP to $122.36 after the EAP was implemented. That was a reduction of 79.10 percent, and the savings to the company was $6,483.40 during the first year.
- However, accident cost for the rest of the work force tended to increase. Before the EAP, all other employees were costing the company $149.35 per accident; after the EAP, the cost had risen to $237.75 per accident.
- Increased productivity returned $1.63 for each $1 invested.
- The study showed the EAP saved $614 per troubled employee per year—3.1 percent of the 1,910 work force were troubled employees.
- The EAP saved $94,214 during the first year and cost $57,967, which was a net savings of $36,250. It was projected that the EAP will save approximately $74,000 each year thereafter.

The Supervisor

- The supervisor benefits by having an additional resource available to handle job performance problems. The EAP may prevent termination of a valuable employee while supporting supervisors to do something about the problem and keep them from labeling an employee, or diagnosing and counseling problems.

The Family

- The EAP gives the family a means for handling personal problems that indirectly are affecting the employee's job performance, and helps the family handle problems of the employee.

The Community

- The EAP provides a positive image for the company in the community. It also helps the community handle problems before they become chronic, as well as providing a network of services and better communication.

A GLOSSARY OF TERMS

(1) *Acceptable job performance:* the standards of job performance determined by the organization as appropriate behavior for performing specified tasks.

(2) *Advisory committee:* an organizational committee, made up of employees who represent the entire work force, which gives direction and guidance to an EAP.

(3) *Assessment:* the process by which the EAP coordinator determines the situation causing employee problems. Identification of the problem may or may not be made during the assessment, which usually leads to a referral.

(4) *Assistance:* the term refers to the resources provided by the organization, supervisor, EAP coordinator, and community resources to resolve or solve the employee's personal problem.

(5) *Community linkage:* is the *process* of connecting the EAP and community resources so the employee may be referred in an efficient and effective manner.

(6) *Community resource:* any agency, professional organization, hospital, private practice, clergy, and the like, that provides assistance to employees. Community resources may be divided into two groups: primary and secondary community resources. *Primary* community resources are those resources within the identified community. *Secondary* community resources are those resources that are not within the identified community boundaries.

(7) *Consultation:* one of the roles of an EAP coordinator is to provide information, education, and coordination of the EAP program for employees, supervisors, the organization, and community resources. In this capacity, the EAP coordinator acts as a consultant.

(8) *Cost/benefit evaluation:* is implemented to determine the cost and savings of a program to the company. The total net value or net cost of the program is determined in a cost/benefit evaluation.

(9) *Cost effectiveness evaluations:* are utilized to determine the impact of the program on the employee in nonmonetary terms and the total cost of the program.

(10) *Diagnosis:* the process by which a qualified professional identifies the cause of an employee's problem or problems.

(11) *EAP:* an employee assistance program (EAP) refers to a program established in an organization to provide employees with help in resolving or solving any personal problem that may or may not affect their job performance. Employee problems may include but not be limited to financial problems, family/marital problems, emotional problems, and substance abuse.

(12) *EAP coordinator:* the person designated to make assessments and referrals of employees with problems, to coordinate the functions of the EAP office with community resources, and to act as director and administrator of the EAP program.

(13) *EAP model:* the employee assistance program developed from organizational commitment, supervisor training, employee education, assessment, and referral of employees to community resources, as advocated in this chapter.

(14) *EAP policy:* a statement identifying and describing the EAP that is not intended to alter or supersede the normal employment rules, policies, regulations, and disciplinary processes of an organization.

(15) *EAP procedure:* a guideline for actions of an EAP that is not intended to alter or supersede the normal employment rules, policies, regulations, and disciplinary processes of an organization.

(16) *Employee education:* information that employees may utilize to acquire access to the EAP system, to better understand and destigmatize problems, and to assist employees in resolving or solving their problems.

(17) *Employee problem:* any problem that may or may not affect job performance. These may include but are not limited to financial problems, family/marital problems, emotional problems, drug abuse, and alcohol abuse.

(18) *Evaluation:* information with which to judge the worth of any endeavor. Stufflebeam defines evaluation as "the process of delineating, obtaining, and providing useful information for judging decision alternatives."[5]

(19) *Externally based programs:* assistance programs where the diagnosis and treatment of employee problems are conducted by a professional, qualified organization within the community.

(20) *Internally based programs:* assistance programs that conduct the diagnosis and treatment of employee problems within the confines of the organization or under the auspices of a professional, qualified person in the organization.

(21) *Management commitment:* the management must be committed to the EAP through a thorough understanding of the concept, and the management's and organization's role and responsibilities. Management must participate in the actualization of the EAP through commitment of time and resources.

(22) *Needs assessment:* evaluating the difference between what exists and what is necessary to function. A needs assessment may refer to the organization's need for an EAP, the training needs of supervisors, the education needs of employees, the need for additional or different community resources, and so on.

(23) *Penetration rate:* the number of identified troubled employees divided by the total number of troubled employees in any organization for a given time.

(24) *Performance appraisal interview:* a discussion between the employee and supervisor or employee and EAP coordinator who reviews the job performance of the employee.

(25) *Performance management:* the management of personnel to perform tasks of the organization, and part of which is the employee assistance program.

(26) *Referral:* the process by which the EAP coordinator makes an appoint-

---

[5] Daniel T. Stufflebeam et al., *Educational Evaluation and Decision Making* (Itasca, Ill.: F. E. Peacock Publishers, 1971).

ment for the employee with the appropriate community resource to seek assistance in resolving or solving the employee's personal problem.

(27) *Research:* often is confined to laboratory situations in which the researcher has control over the outcome. The situation under the auspices of research is controlled more by the researcher, whereas in evaluation the problem is controlled by the situation.

(28) *Self-referral:* any employee who seeks assistance for a personal problem from the EAP office or community resources on his or her own. The employee may or may not have acceptable job performance.

(29) *Supervisory recommendation:* during the performance appraisal interview, the supervisor may recommend that the employee seek assistance from the EAP office.

(30) *Supervisor training:* the training provided supervisors to properly and efficiently use the employee assistance program, including an understanding of EAP policy, procedures, and conducting a performance appraisal interview with a supervisor recommendation.

(31) *Systems approach:* Miller and Rice define a system of activities as ". . . that complex of activities which is required to complete the process of transforming an intake into an output.[6] A system has component activities which are interdependent on other activities within the system, and a system or subsystem is in part identifiable as being independent of other systems or subsystems. In this context the EAP subsystem will be identified as part of the organizational system. Secondarily, the EAP can be viewed as an independent subsystem with several interdependent components.

(32) *Troubled employee:* (a) any employee identified as having unacceptable job performance, whose supervisor then recommends the employee visit the EAP office and the EAP coordinator makes an assessment or referral, or both; (b) any employee who has a problem and seeks assistance from the EAP office or the community resources, or both, as a self-referral.

---

[6] E. J. Miller and A. K. Rice, *Systems of Organization* (New York: Tavestock Publications, 1973), pp. 6–7.

CHAPTER 25

Retirement Preparation

EDMUND W.
FITZPATRICK

INTRODUCTION

After decades of slow growth, the number and scope of retirement preparation programs began to increase dramatically in the mid-1970s.[1] Some of the reasons for this phenomenon are:

The advent of double-digit inflation and its expected impact on retirement patterns.

Federal legislation affecting private pensions and raising the age at which retirement can be mandatory.

Improved pension systems that enable more people to retire early.

Recognition that the population and work force are aging, and the political, economic, and employment implications of this.

Each of these factors represents a long-term trend likely to continue. Since this suggests continued growth of retirement preparation programs, a brief review of the trends seems warranted.

FACTORS AFFECTING GROWTH OF RETIREMENT PREPARATION PROGRAMS

An Aging Population

In 1980, the population age 55 and over was about 45 million and represented about 20 percent of the population (see Table 25–1). By the year 2030, this group is expected to number 83 million and, barring a new baby boom, will constitute about 31 percent of the population.

Indeed, unless there is a new baby boom the population age 65 and over in the year 2030 will represent about one in five persons (see Table 25–2).

---

[1] Retirement preparation goes by many names, such as retirement education, retirement counseling, preretirement planning, and life planning.

Table 25-1
Projection of
Population Age 55
and Over

Year	Persons Age 55 and Over (millions)
1980	45
1990	49
2000	54
2010	66
2020	79
2030	83

Source: U.S. Bureau
of the Census.

Table 25-2
Growth in the "Over
65" Population

	Persons Age 65 and Over
1900	1 in 25
Today	1 in 10
2030	1 in 5

Source: U.S. Bureau
of the Census.

This age shift of the population has enormous implications for business and industry.

Increased Life Expectancy

Contributing to the aging of the population are significant increases in life expectancy. In fact, the fastest growing segment of the population is the age 75 and over segment. Longer life expectancies, of course, mean spending more years in retirement. If a man 62 and his wife 59 retire this year, he will likely live another 17 years, until about age 79, and she will likely live another 23 years, until about age 82. In reality, chances are that both will live even longer, since traditionally we have underestimated average life expectancies and must continuously revise them upward.

Early Retirement

The trend toward early retirement began decades ago and is continuing. In 1981, almost three of four employees (70 percent) were retiring early—

that is, before age 65—and the great majority of this group retired at age 62 or before. Since this generally coincides with benefit eligibility under private and public pension systems (most notably Social Security), it reinforces the notion that the great majority of employees will retire as soon as they think they can afford it.

Uncertain National Economy

A 10 percent inflation rate will reduce the purchasing power of a fixed pension by 50 percent in 7 years and by 75 percent in about 14 years. Despite this fact, the effect of double-digit inflation on retirement patterns is not clear. There have been pauses in the early retirement trend, but they were only temporary. It is too early to know whether a high inflation rate, if it continues long enough, will put a lasting halt to early retirement or cause more employees to stay on past "normal" retirement at age 65. Reductions in the levels of Social Security benefits payable at age 62 or 65, which are among the alternatives being considered to bolster Social Security financing, could have a greater impact on retirement patterns than high inflation rates.

ONE RATIONALE FOR RETIREMENT PREPARATION PROGRAMS

A national survey found that 81 percent of current employees and 84 percent of retirees feel their standard of living during retirement should be about the same as before retirement.[2] The reality today is that the average income of persons over 65 is about one half the national average.[3] An important advantage of a retirement preparation program is it can encourage and show employees how to save and invest for their retirement and how to counter the effects of inflation on fixed retirement income. Thus, they could provide the "third leg" of the "three-legged stool" of retirement income—Social Security, private pension, and personal savings.

HOW PERSONNEL DIRECTORS SEE IT

Personnel directors and other human resource professionals generally believe a need exists for retirement preparation programs and that companies will be paying more attention to this matter in the future. In a survey conducted at an annual conference of the American Society of Personnel

---

[2] Louis Harris and Associates, *1979 Study of American Attitudes Toward Pensions and Retirement,* commissioned by Johnson & Higgins (New York: Louis Harris and Associates, 1979), p. iv.

[3] Herman B. Brotman, "The Aging of America: A Demographic Profile," *The Economics of Aging* (Washington, D.C.: National Journal, 1978), p. 37.

Table 25-3
Developments in Retirement Planning Expected by
Fortune 1,000 Personnel Directors (December 1979)

	Frequency (percent)
Companies will be more committed to retirement planning	92
More emphasis on retirement planning	87
Retirement planning will be started earlier in career	79

Source: *Retirement Preparation: Growing Corporate Involvement* (New York: Research & Forecasts, 1979), p. 21.

Administrators, 92 percent of the 1,500 survey respondents agreed that "preretirement counseling programs will receive increased emphasis" in the next five years.[4] Later in the same year, a survey of *Fortune* 1,000 company personnel directors obtained identical results (Table 25-3).

INDEPENDENT PLANNING BY EMPLOYEES

Employees apparently do relatively little advanced retirement planning of their own. This does not mean employees do not want to plan or are unaware of the need to plan. A survey of employees over age 40 from seven large companies found the following:[5]

That 6 in 10 had made no plans for retirement and only 1 in 10 had made any definite plans.

Of the employees, 70 percent said they wanted to attend a retirement counseling program; 15 percent said they did not want to; and 15 percent refused to answer.

Over two thirds expect to run into money problems in retirement, while only one in four expects to have a health problem.

Retirement preparation programs, they said, should be conducted in the early evening (56 percent), on weekends (13 percent), or late evening (7 percent). Only one in four (24 percent) said they should be conducted during the day, which coincided with work hours.

EXTENT OF PROGRAM USAGE

Generally, two factors are present before a company is likely to have its own retirement preparation program: (1) an "adequate" pension plan, and

[4] Harold L. Schneider, "Personnel Managers Look to the '80's," *The Personnel Administrator,* November 1979, p. 48.

[5] Edmund W. Fitzpatrick, "An Industry Consortium Approach to Retirement Planning—A New Program," *Aging and Work* 1, no. 3 (Summer 1978), pp. 184–88.

(2) enough employees retiring each year to justify a program. Consequently, in-house retirement preparation programs tend to be concentrated among large companies with good retirement benefits.

A survey of *Fortune* 1,000 companies in late 1979 found that two thirds of the companies responding either had a retirement preparation program or were "working on one."[6] A little more than one third had a program in place, and 85 percent of such programs had five or more topics. In a study conducted three years earlier, only one sixth of the large companies responding had a retirement preparation program in place, and only 48 percent of such programs had five or more topics.[7]

An organization may not have an in-house retirement preparation program but, instead, may make arrangements to send its employees to a program offered by an outside source, such as a community college. The extent that small, medium, and large organizations are using such outside programs is not known. However, the proliferation of outside sources suggests that the number of companies using them is growing.

CHARACTERISTICS OF PROGRAMS

Corporate Goals

Essentially, a retirement preparation program is a method of helping employees and their families plan for retirement. However, the main corporate goals of retirement preparation programs, according to personnel directors, are to improve employee relations, morale, and productivity (see Table 25-4).

Reflecting the strength of their commitment, a growing number of large corporations have created a new position of "manager of retirement and retiree relations." This person, who may report to a vice president, has corporate-wide responsibility for the quality of retirement preparation and for retiree communications programs and the extent to which such programs are contributing to realizing corporate goals. His or her functions may include acquainting divisions with new developments and helping them to design, implement, and improve their retirement preparation and retiree communications programs.

Target Groups for Programs

Many companies face a backlog of employees when they begin to offer a retirement preparation program. Although an employer may invite all

---

[6] *Retirement Preparation: Growing Corporate Involvement* (New York: Research & Forecasts, 1980), p. 20.

[7] J. Roger O'Meara, *Retirement: Reward or Rejection?* (New York: The Conference Board, 1977), p. 37.

Table 25-4
Corporate Goals for Retirement Preparation Programs, as Cited
by Personnel Directors

	Frequency Selected by Personnel Directors (percent)
Improve relations with employees	91*
Reinforce morale/productivity	83
Fulfill social responsibilities	68
Enhance corporate image	53
Recruit and retain dependable employees	39
Induce early retirement among nonproductive employees	31
Protect funds in pension plans	29
Keep pace with competitors	22
Improve relations with unions	12
Comply with ERISA	8

* Many gave more than one goal.
Source: *Retirement Preparation: Growing Corporate Involvement,* p. 16.

employees over age 50 or 55 to attend, the great majority of those accepted
may be employees who have announced the date of their retirement or who
are close to or past the average age of retirement in the company. When the
backlog is reduced, all employees who have reached the eligibility age will
be given a more equal opportunity to attend.

Employees generally are encouraged to have their spouses attend the
program with them. The extent of spouse participation will vary, depending
on the efforts made by the employer to encourage their attendance, the
convenience of the time and location of the program, and the nature of the
program.

Content Coverage

Retirement preparation programs may be classified as narrow, medium,
or comprehensive in terms of topic coverage. A *narrow program* may concern only the financial and legal aspects of retirement. A *medium program* is
likely to include three or four topics, such as finances, legal aspects, health,
and leisure. A *comprehensive program* often will include seven to nine topics—the four just mentioned plus new careers, interpersonal relations,
living arrangements, and lifestyle planning.

Among large companies with retirement preparation programs, about 85
percent of the programs fall into the medium or comprehensive categories.
Indeed, the trend is toward comprehensive programs.[8]

Of course, how well a topic actually is covered can vary immensely from
program to program. Financial planning, for example, may be dealt with in

---

[8] *Retirement Preparation: Growing Corporate Involvement,* p. 32.

two hours in one program and in nine hours in another. In one program, a topic may be dealt with superficially, while in another it may be treated in some depth.

Here are some typical topics for retirement preparation programs:

Lifestyle planning.

Psychological adjustments.

Company and union benefits.

Financial planning.

Social Security.

Leisure time.

Interpersonal relations.

New careers.

Living arrangements.

Staying healthy.

Community services.

Who Conducts the Program

An organization's retirement preparation program may be conducted by (a) its own staff, (b) outside consultants, or (c) a combination of the two.

Large organizations generally prefer to use in-house staff to conduct their programs, though they may use outside experts in specific subject areas if they are not available within the organization. One major new "packaged" retirement preparation program is designed to be used without subject-matter experts; the expertise is built into the materials.

A not uncommon approach is for a firm to hire a consultant to serve as "program coordinator." This person generally has experience in organizing and presenting retirement preparation programs that rely on a speaker or resource person for each subject covered. The difficulty frequently encountered is finding knowledgeable, up-to-date experts who also are good communicators, will stick to the objectives of the program, and will be there as scheduled. Some firms hire a consultant to provide the materials and to personally conduct the complete program, except for the presentation and discussion of company benefits.

College- and university-based retirement preparation programs may draw upon experts from among their own faculties, which may include gerontologists, psychologists, legal and medical specialists, and others. Additionally, they may draw their experts from the local community, much as the "program coordinator" does.

Number and Length of Sessions

The time devoted to a retirement preparation topic in a group program may vary from one hour to three hours or more. Two hours per topic probably is typical, except for the financial topic(s), which may be allocated more time. In general, the total length of a program in terms of hours usually is related to the number of topics covered.

Scheduling Sessions

Several formats for scheduling program sessions are being used. Some of the most common are discussed below.

One Session per Week. One two-hour session per week for six to eight weeks is most common. Typically, one topic is dealt with each session, except that financial planning might be allotted two or even three sessions.

Back-to-Back Topics. The one topic per week format is practical when there are large concentrations of employees and few commuting problems. If employees are at a number of locations in the city, topics may be presented in back-to-back sessions to reduce the number of meetings and the travel required. For example, two two-hour sessions may be combined to form a four-hour meeting, which may be held on Tuesdays and Thursdays for two weeks.

All-Day Programs. All-day programs of one, two, or three days may be used when employees are dispersed over a wide area and are brought in to attend a group program. Other companies simply prefer the full-day format over other formats.

In the case of dispersed employees, they and their spouses may be transported to a hotel, where the company will conduct the program. A company without dispersed employees may run its program either entirely on work time or on part work time and part personal time, such as on a Friday and a Saturday, or from 3:00 in the afternoon until 9:00 in the evening on two weekdays.

Inviting Employees

It generally is agreed that all employees of a given age within a region, plant, or division should be invited at the same time. Even a hint of selective invitations will generate suspicion regarding management's purpose in offering the program. Attendance should not be made compulsory. If employees don't wish to attend, it is better to learn why and to correct the problem. Surveys show that up to 85 percent of employees over age 40 want to attend such programs.[9]

In some cases, an initial reluctance exists among employees to attend, since they harbor concern that attendance could somehow jeopardize promotions and better job assignments. One way to combat these concerns is by giving much publicity to the program and its pilot presentations. Notices

---

[9] Fitzpatrick, "An Industry Consortium's Approach to Retirement Planning," p. 187.

on bulletin boards, articles in company publications, and supportive statements by top management are helpful.

Some organizations enlist the aid of employees who enjoy much trust among their peers. These employees are encouraged to attend the pilot programs and to ask associates to join them. Also, publicizing the fact that specific supervisory and management personnel will attend the programs can help to dispel fears employees have about attending.

Employees are invited by notices on bulletin boards, articles in company publications, and by personal letters that go to the home. Letters to the home should be addressed to Mr. and Mrs. if the employee is married. In any case, the employee often is encouraged to bring any other person with whom he or she plans to retire. This is particularly important for single persons, who may retire (and share expenses) with a sister, brother, other relative, or friend. The chances are the single person will not bring another person, but much good will is generated by the sincere offer from the company. For the targeted employees (e.g., age 50 or 55 and over), a series of several invitational letters should be considered to ensure that a large percentage of these employees attend.

ESTABLISHING A PROGRAM

Basic Planning Questions

In establishing a retirement preparation program, a number of questions need to be answered:

1. What are the objectives of the program, and how will its success be measured?
2. Is top management committed to the program?
3. How much money can be devoted to the program? Over what time?
4. How many employees can be expected to attend the program? Who are they and where are they located? How many spouses will probably attend?
5. Are the company's retirement benefits adequate? Above average?
6. Are competitors offering retirement preparation programs? If so, what are the programs like?
7. What is the state of employee relations? Is there a problem that needs resolution before offering the program?
8. How concentrated or dispersed are the employees, and how will the program be made available to them?
9. Is the public relations value of the program important locally or nationally?
10. Is there a need to promote better understanding of company benefits, especially retirement benefits, among employees?

Program Design Considerations

The design of a retirement preparation program determines its effectiveness. There are four considerations.

1. In view of company characteristics, objectives, and the distribution of employees, what type of program or programs are feasible and will achieve the objectives? What trade-offs are necessary? What will be the measures of success?

2. Who should conduct the program? Central or division staffs? Consultants? Should there be a "traveling team" that conducts the program? Should employees be sent to programs conducted by community colleges or other organizations? Are subject-matter experts available (assuming they are needed) at proposed program locations?

3. Should the company purchase a commercially available package or develop its own? If purchased, should it be customized and by how much? (The development of professional quality retirement counseling materials involves a commitment of time, money, and specialized expertise that most companies do not have, or which is often more profitably focused on the company's main business. Consequently, the tendency is for companies to purchase packaged programs and then to customize them).

4. What should be the nature of program follow-up activities? Should there be periodic updates through written communications and through refresher meetings? Should there be encouragement for the formation of employee planning or investment clubs? What about postretirement communications? Should there be a formal postretirement program?

Selecting Program Materials

Materials employed in a retirement counseling program should be designed to maximize the probability of success. Here are some aspects to consider:

1. Are the materials compatible with company philosophy and with the basic values of the employees who will attend the program?

2. Do the materials support the specific objectives for the program in each area? The personal finances area? Health area? Other areas?

3. Is the content presented efficiently and at the appropriate level, given the target employees? Or is it shallow and vague with too much jargon, or too technical?

4. What is the visual impact of the materials? Impressive in appearance to imply importance? Easy to read and use? Is the print large enough?

5. With regard to audiovisual materials, are the visuals (photographs and artwork) pleasant, and do the people look somewhat younger than the target employees (this is important)? Is the narrator's style, tone, and pronunciation suitable for the employees? How easily can the audiovisual materials be used? What equipment is required? Who will set up and operate it?

6. Are skill-building exercises provided for employees? Checklists for planning? Games, simulations, small group exercises, individual exercises, other aids? Are they merely entertaining or do they have a clearly identifiable objective?

7. How is the seminar or workshop designed? What will participants actually *do* in it—be active or passive? Is there a balance among lectures, audiovisual materials, small group activities, group discussion, and individual work? What qualifications or training are required of the seminar/workshop leaders?

Conducting the Pilot Program

An important objective of a pilot program is to give other people in the organization an opportunity to make recommendations and take part in making the final decision on the program. A pilot program generally will become the final program because the organization already has tooled up to present it and has gained experience in doing so. If a manager skips the pilot and makes the final decision independently, those who did not have an opportunity to make recommendations could be a source of continuing criticism, which ultimately dooms the program.

Even though an organization may plan to have its own staff regularly conduct its retirement counseling programs, it may decide to involve an experienced outside consultant to co-conduct the pilot and thereby maximize the likelihood that the pilot will be successful.

The location of the pilot is important. It should be convenient to those expected to attend. Room size and shape must be appropriate for the number attending and for the desired seating arrangements; effective room temperature control is necessary; dimming the lights and covering the windows must be possible if audiovisual presentations are to be used; and it should be free from outside noises; and have adequate electrical outlets. It may be important to have eating and sleeping accommodations close by.

Prior to conducting the pilot, there should be a detailed plan for its evaluation, complete with forms and procedures for how the data will be captured and analyzed and how the results will be used. Care must be exercised in how and when data are obtained from employees participating in the pilot program. Employees need to wear the "participant" hat and not the "evaluator" hat. In the program, they must concentrate on being a participant—and on their retirement concerns, needs, and objectives, or the evaluation will not have validity.

Postretirement Programs

Postretirement programs also are increasing in number and variety. Generally, they are aimed at updating former employees on benefits changes that may affect them, keeping them informed about company activities, and providing other information that may be of interest or help.

A company may accomplish this through a special newsletter to retirees or by sending retirees the regular employee publication, which may include a section about and for retirees. Some companies hold annual affairs in large cities to which all retirees in the area are invited. Others send a person on tour from area to area to hold "update" meetings with groups of retirees. And some companies purchase subscriptions for all their retirees to a retirement-oriented newsletter or magazine.

BENEFITS OF RETIREMENT PREPARATION PROGRAMS

Benefits for the Employee

A well-designed retirement preparation program can have important benefits for employees and their spouses. Here are some of the major ones:[10]

1. Recognition that they have the responsibility for ensuring their own financial security and happiness in retirement (i.e., the company and union may help, but the ultimate responsibility is the employee's).
2. Better realization of the degree of control and options they have regarding future finances, health, personal relationships, and the like.
3. Knowing when retirement is financially possible for them—or what they must do to make it so.
4. Opportunity to articulate and discuss fears they and others may harbor about retirement.
5. Opportunity to specifically define one or more lifestyles they would find enjoyable and affordable, so they can look forward to concrete and positive alternatives.
6. Identification of problems that could arise during their own retirement, which they have an opportunity to solve before retirement.

Benefits for the Employer

The employer that provides an effective retirement preparation program for employees also benefits. In fact, the employer may find the returns are considerably greater than the investment. Here are the major benefits the employer may enjoy:[11]

1. General performance levels of employees may improve; when employees believe their employer cares about them, they in return care more about the quality of their work.

---

[10] Edmund W. Fitzpatrick, "Retirement Counseling: A Necessity for the 1980's," *Textbook for Employee Benefit Plan Trustees, Administrators, and Advisors,* Proceedings of the 1979 Annual Educational Conference, vol. 21 (Brookfield, Wis.: International Foundation of Employee Benefit Plans, 1980), pp. 295–301.

[11] Ibid.

2. The productivity of specific employees may improve, since they will be able to make an informed retirement decision, rather than be afflicted by indecision and perhaps hang on beyond the time when they wish to retire.

3. Employees gain a better appreciation of the value of the employee benefits provided.

4. Employers can fulfill a social responsibility to loyal employees who helped the company prosper over the years.

5. It can help the employer maintain a leadership role in the employee benefits area.

6. It can result in positive feedback from retirees to present employees.

7. It can help to build and maintain a positive image in the community.

Postretirement Benefits

While the "preretirement" benefits of retirement preparation programs seem clear, the "postretirement" benefits require further research. Longitudinal studies examining the postretirement benefits either have been flawed or have pointed to weaknesses in the retirement preparation programs that were used. One study concluded that ". . . no retirement preparation program that involves a small, one-shot investment in time and effort is likely to have a long-term effect on personal adjustment and life satisfaction."[12] This argues for intensive and comprehensive programs, with periodic refreshers or updates and postretirement communications.

Some of the most intensive and comprehensive retirement preparation programs are very new. When employees who have attended these programs reach retirement, the postretirement effects may be significant in several areas, including the area of retirement finances.

PROGRAM EVALUATION

In general, retirement preparation programs are not being subjected to formal evaluations based on measurable objectives. Most rely upon asking participants if they like the speakers, the content, the method of conducting, and so on. These findings are important—but concern the process not the results. Employees typically are so grateful for retirement preparation programs that almost any program, regardless of quality, will be given a high rating using such an evaluation approach.

One hindrance to the use of more scientific evaluation procedures is the newness of the programs and the fact they are still evolving. It is not practical to invest in longitudinal studies, which may involve years, before

---

[12] Francis D. Glamser, "The Impact of Preretirement Programs on the Retirement Experience," *Journal of Gerontology* 36, no. 2 (March 1981), p. 249.

an organization is satisfied that it has arrived at the "best" feasible program and has standardized the use of it.

Most existing longitudinal studies are seriously flawed, so caution must be exercised in considering their conclusions.[13] However, as more organizations get their programs in place and "fine-tune" them, there are likely to be a growing number of useful longitudinal studies based on experimental design methodology.

Another appropriate evaluation methodology is based on defining measurable human performance objectives.[14] This assumes that the basic rationale for a retirement preparation program is to cause people to plan and thereby prevent certain problems or unfulfilled expectations when they retire. If human performance objectives are prepared for each topic or module in the program, effectiveness can be determined by measuring the degree to which participants achieve those objectives at the conclusion of the program. A human performance objective, as used in this approach, needs to be both measurable and observable—as an example, "the participant will be able to identify his tax bracket and compute aftertax earnings from a given investment." "Pre-post" assessments may be used to determine not only achievement but also the "learning gain" produced by the program.

The measurable objectives evaluation approach makes possible evaluation/revision cycles capable of producing successively more powerful versions of a module or complete program. A program development activity employing this evaluation approach can produce a statistically validated program—one that can be expected to produce similar results each time it is used.

Figure 25–1 illustrates the use of this approach for evaluating a retirement financial planning workshop in which the human performance objectives took the form of 14 measurable and observable financial planning tasks. The effectiveness of the workshop was determined by (*a*) the percent of the participants who actually performed each of the tasks by the end of the workshop, and (*b*) the *gain* in the percent performing each task, based on a comparison of preworkshop achievement with post-workshop achievement.

A retirement preparation program is a vehicle for communicating information and influencing human behavior. Whether its objectives are achieved depends on the skill with which the vehicle is used. A person lacking musical talent and training may blow sour notes on a trumpet, but it is the fault of the player, not the horn. As with retirement preparation programs, the quality of the output depends upon the quality of the input.

---

[13] Glamser, pp. 244–50.

[14] Edmund W. Fitzpatrick, "Evaluating a New Retirement Planning Program—Results with Hourly Workers." *Aging and Work,* Spring 1979, (Washington, D.C.: National Council on the Aging), pp. 87–94.

Figure 25-1

Short-Range Effect of Personal Financial Planning Module: Change in Percentage of White-Collar Clerical Employees Taking Specified Financial Planning Actions as a Result of Workshop

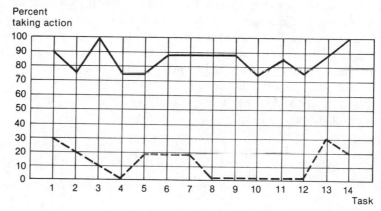

— Percent who had taken action by end of work shop.

— Percent who had taken action prior to work shop.

Financial Planning Tasks

1. Gathered and listed your important financial papers.
2. Discussed retirement finances in detail with your spouse or someone else.
3. Developed an estimate of your retirement expenses.
4. Developed a realistic, fact-based estimate of your future retirement income.
5. Determined what survivor's benefits you or your spouse (or other person) would get if either one of you died.
6. Figured the approximate amount of the nest egg you will have or will need at the time of your retirement.
7. Identified your own major financial assets and projected how they will grow in value between now and retirement.
8. Determined how much purchasing power your pension will lose in your retirement if inflation continues.
9. Figured how much money you would need in a fund to protect your pension from the effects of inflation.
10. Drawn your own Retirement Income Profile.
11. Obtained useful information for you to get more out of your savings and investments.
12. Used basic measures (e.g. growth versus income, risk versus return) in evaluating savings and investment alternatives.
13. Selected one or more investments for further investigation.
14. Made a plan to improve your own approach to saving and investing.

Source: Edmund W. Fitzpatrick, *Aministrator's Guide: A Component of the Industry Consortium Retirement Planning Program* (Washington, D.C.: NCOA, 1980), p. 12.

The talent and monetary and physical resources being devoted to these programs are improving, compared to past years, and we can expect improved results.

CONCLUSION

Basic trends in our society suggest that retirement preparation programs will continue to grow. Because of pressures on public and private pension systems, there may be more encouragement for employees to save now to help finance their own retirement. Retirement preparation programs can communicate this need to employees and identify fruitful savings and investment alternatives.

A realization exists that a satisfying retirement depends on more than financial security. "Free time" can be a blessing or a curse, depending on what is done with it. Retirement preparation programs, by helping individuals and couples explore aspects of life that may have been long ignored, can open new doors to life enrichment and happiness in the later years. Perhaps the greatest ultimate impact of these programs will be in these more personal areas. And this is important to a society with a large older-person population.[15]

---

[15] For an annotated bibliography on retirement planning, see John N. Migliaccio and Peter C. Cairo, "Preparation for Retirement: A Selective Bibliography, 1974–1980," *Aging and Work* 4, no. 1 (Winter 1980), pp. 31–33.

CHAPTER 26

Cafeteria Approaches to Benefit Planning

ROBERT W. COOPER AND
BURTON T. BEAM, JR.

INTRODUCTION

Employee benefit plans that provide employees with some choice about the types and amounts of benefits they receive have become quite common. In most cases, the cost of the optional or supplemental benefits made available under these plans must be borne by the employee on an aftertax, payroll-deduction basis. Recently, however, a small but growing number of employers have established benefit programs in which all or a large segment of the employees are permitted to design their own benefit packages by using a prespecified number of employer dollars to purchase their benefits from among a number of available options. While all employee benefit plans offering employee options might be viewed broadly as being cafeteria (or flexible) approaches to benefit planning, this chapter focuses more narrowly on those cafeteria compensation plans giving employees some choice in selecting the types and levels of benefits that are provided with employer contributions.

The employee benefit program in effect since 1974 at Educational Testing Services (ETS) provides an example of the cafeteria approach to benefit planning. As is typically the case, the ETS program, referred to as a flexible benefit program, consists of two portions—a minimum level of benefits, called "basic" or "core" benefits, that is automatically received by all employees, and a second layer of optional benefits, called flexible benefits, that permits an employee to choose which benefits he or she will add to the basic benefits. The basic benefits provided to all employees include term life insurance equal to $1\frac{1}{2}$ times salary, travel accident insurance (when on ETS business), medical expense insurance for the employee and dependents, and disability income insurance. Employees also are provided with "flexible credits" equal to from 3 percent to 6 percent of salary, depending on length of service. Each year, an employee is permitted to use his or her flexible credits to purchase benefits from among several options, including additional life insurance equal to one times salary, accidental death insurance when the basic travel accident insurance does not apply, term life insurance on dependents, dental insurance for the employee and dependents, an annual physical examination for the employee, and up to two weeks of additional vacation time. If an employee's flexible credits are insufficient to purchase the desired flexible benefits, additional amounts may be contributed on a payroll-deduction basis.

The approach used by ETS can be used by firms wishing to improve their benefit programs by spending more dollars as well as by firms only wishing to try a new approach to benefit planning. In the former case, the existing employee benefit plan may be treated as the basic benefits under the cafeteria compensation plan, and the employer may provide additional contributions to be used by the employees to purchase optional benefits. In the latter case, an employer might reduce the types and amounts of benefits available in the existing employee benefit plan to establish the basic layer of benefits under the cafeteria compensation plan. Employer contributions made available because of this reduction may be used by employees to purchase optional benefits.

An alternative approach allows employees some flexibility in the basic benefits provided. Employees may be given the opportunity to select options that are less comprehensive than certain standard basic benefits. For example, this might include the option of selecting a medical expense plan with a larger deductible. The choice of less-comprehensive benefits frees employer contributions, which can be used by the employee to increase other basic benefits or to purchase optional benefits.

REASONS FOR EMPLOYER INTEREST

Although the number of cafeteria compensation plans currently is small, many employers have expressed an interest in the concept, and an increasing number of employers currently are exploring the feasibility of adopting this type of employee benefit plan. This growing interest on the part of employers can be traced to a number of factors. Many employers are concerned that employees often do not appreciate the value of the benefits provided under conventional plans. They feel that, by giving an employee a specified total number of dollars to use for purchasing benefits and a list of available benefits with their associated costs, the employee will better perceive not only the total value of the benefits being provided by the employer but also the nature and relative costs of the individual benefits themselves.

The inflexible benefit structure of conventional employee benefit plans does not adequately meet the varying benefit needs of different employees and often leads to employee dissatisfaction. For example, single employees or older employees whose children are grown may see little value in substantial life insurance benefits. Employers view the cafeteria approach to benefit planning as not only a means of more effectively meeting the benefit needs of different employees at a particular time but also as a way of enabling an individual employee to better meet his or her needs as they change over time. Closely related is the feeling among employers that cafeteria compensation plans are viewed as being less paternalistic than conventional employee benefit programs.

Employers also see the cafeteria approach to benefit planning as providing opportunities to control the escalating benefit levels and costs associated not only with inflation but also with the increasing need to comply with the requirements of newly enacted federal and state legislation. Since a cafeteria compensation plan is essentially a defined contribution plan, rather than a defined benefit plan, it provides a number of opportunities for controlling increases in benefit levels and costs. For example, it may encourage employees to choose medical expense options with larger deductibles to more efficiently use the fixed number of dollars allotted to them under the plan. It also may enable the employer to pass on to the employees any increased benefit costs arising out of compliance with legislation prohibiting age and sex discrimination or mandating additional benefits. In addition, since increases in employer contributions for optional benefits are not tied directly to increases in benefit costs, the employer has the opportunity to grant percentage increases in the flexible credits below the actual overall increase in employee benefit costs.

POTENTIAL BARRIERS

While many employers have shown considerable interest in the cafeteria approach to benefit planning, the failure of most of these employers to actually establish a cafeteria compensation plan stems from the variety of obstacles that must be overcome before a plan can be successfully implemented. These potential barriers to the establishment of cafeteria compensation plans have included, among other things: (1) an unsettled federal income-tax environment; (2) potential problems associated with unwise benefit selection by employees; (3) negative attitudes on the part of employees, insurers, and unions; (4) regulatory restraints on individual benefit selection; and (5) increased implementation and administration costs. Despite the fact that the Revenue Act of 1978 went a long way in clarifying the confused federal income-tax picture, many remaining obstacles continue to make the implementation of a cafeteria compensation plan a rather complex, costly, and time-consuming project.

Taxation

Prior to the passage of the Revenue Act of 1978, a federal income-tax picture clouded by the issue of constructive receipt probably was the principal barrier to the establishment of cafeteria compensation plans.

The Issue of Constructive Receipt. Basically, the doctrine of constructive receipt holds that, if money or property is made available to an employee without significant restriction, it is treated as having been received by him or her for federal income-tax purposes even though he or she does not actually receive it. Since the taxable benefits in a cafeteria compensation plan containing both taxable (e.g., group term life insurance in excess of $50,000) and nontaxable (e.g., group medical expense insurance) benefit options are made freely available to the employee, the employee presumably would be held to be in constructive receipt of the employer's contribution to the extent that it could be used to purchase taxable benefits, regardless of the actual benefit choices made.

Prior to the enactment of ERISA in 1974, several private letter rulings were sought from the IRS for plans that were specially designed to include provisions aimed at blocking constructive receipt. While a few favorable private letter rulings were issued, the IRS ruling position on cafeteria compensation plans was never made totally clear; uncertainty resulted.

With the passage of ERISA in 1974, the development of cafeteria compensation plans substantially was halted. Section 2006 of ERISA forbid the Treasury from issuing new regulations on cafeteria compensation plans before January 1, 1977 (later extended until 1980), to give Congress time to enact appropriate legislation pertaining to these plans. The IRS interpreted this section of ERISA as a mandate for refusing to issue private letter rulings on new cafeteria plans. In addition, in interpreting another unclear portion of Section 2006 of ERISA, the IRS apparently took the position that under any cafeteria compensation plan established after June 27, 1974, employer contributions would be includable in the employee's gross income to the extent the employee could have elected to apply the contribution to a taxable benefit. As a practical matter, Section 2006 effectively halted the development of new cafeteria compensation plans containing both taxable and nontaxable benefit options. While the American Can Company established its cafeteria compensation plan after the passage of ERISA, the plan was designed carefully to contain no benefits that might result in current taxation to any employees.

Section 125. The Revenue Act of 1978 added Section 125, dealing with cafeteria plans to the Internal Revenue Code. This section defines the term *cafeteria plan* as a written plan under which all participants are employees and under which the participants may choose from among two or more benefits that may consist of nontaxable benefits, or cash, property, or other taxable benefits. The Internal Revenue Code also states that the term cafeteria plan does not include any plan which provides for deferred compensation.

Section 125 provides that a participant in a cafeteria plan will not be taxed on employer contributions solely because the participant may choose among the benefits of the plan. This makes it possible to design a cafeteria compensation plan containing both taxable and nontaxable benefits without suffering the adverse tax consequences associated with the constructive receipt doctrine. Section 125, however, also includes certain standards designed to prevent cafeteria plans from discriminating in favor of highly compensated participants. A "highly compensated participant" under Section 125 includes any employee who is an officer, a shareholder owning more than 5 percent of the voting power or value of all classes of stock of the employer, a highly compensated employee, or a spouse or dependent of such an individual. If a cafeteria plan violates the Section 125 nondiscrimination standards, employer contributions to the plan will be included in the gross income of highly compensated employees to the extent that such individuals could have elected taxable benefits. However, other employees are not penalized.

If a cafeteria plan is to avoid a loss of tax benefits to highly compensated employees, the plan must satisfy certain nondiscrimination standards regarding coverage, eligibility, and contributions or benefits. A cafeteria plan will satisfy the coverage standards if it benefits a classification of employees that the Secretary of the Treasury determines does not discriminate in favor of highly compensated employees. Moreover, a cafeteria plan will meet the eligibility standards contained in Section 125 if it (1) does not require an employee to complete more than three consecutive years of employment to become eligible to participate, and (2) allows an employee who is otherwise eligible to participate to enter the plan as a participant not later than the first day of the first plan year beginning after the date the employee completes three consecutive years of employment.

Different standards exist regarding contributions or benefits depending on whether a cafeteria plan provides health insurance benefits. A cafeteria plan that does not provide health benefits is considered to be nondiscriminatory if the total benefits and the nontaxable benefits (or the employer contributions for both types of benefits), each measured as a percentage of compensation, are not significantly greater for highly compensated employees than for other employees. If a cafeteria plan provides health benefits, the following special set of nondiscrimination requirements must be satisfied:

- (a) contributions under the plan on behalf of each participant include an amount which:
    - (i) equals 100 percent of the cost of the health benefit coverage under the plan of the majority of the highly compensated participants similarly situated; or
    - (ii) equals or exceeds 75 percent of the cost of the health benefit coverage of the participant (similarly situated) having the highest cost health benefit coverage under the plan; and
- (b) contributions or benefits under the plan in excess of those described in . . . (a) bear a uniform relationship to compensation.

Collectively bargained cafeteria plans are accorded special treatment in Section 125. A cafeteria plan is considered to meet all the nondiscrimination tests if it is maintained under an agreement that the Secretary of the Treasury determines is a collective bargaining agreement between employee representatives and one or more employers.

Remaining Issues. While the Revenue Act of 1978 reflected a major effort on the part of Congress to deal with the legal issues and the uncertainty surrounding the taxation of cafeteria plans, a number of pertinent issues were not settled and several new issues of statutory interpretation have arisen. While Section 125 contains a rather rigorous set of nondiscrimination requirements that must be satisfied to avoid adverse tax consequences with a cafeteria plan providing both taxable and nontaxable options, including health benefits, the Internal Revenue Code, as is typically the case, does not specifically indicate how to design a nondiscriminatory plan. Given the difficulties that undoubtedly will arise in attempting to design cafeteria plans that will comply literally with the requirements of Section 125, future regulations probably will be required to clarify the various problems of interpretation that arise. Also, despite the special set of nondiscrimination requirements for cafeteria plans providing health benefits, Section 125 can apparently impose no adverse tax consequences on discriminatory cafeteria compensation plans that contain only nontaxable benefits, because the doctrine of constructive receipt would not ordinarily cause the availability of such a choice to result in taxable income to any participants. Thus, for example, if an employer were to establish a cafeteria compensation plan that provided the employees with a choice between several alternative medical insurance coverages, Section 125 apparently could not effectively require such a plan to be offered on a nondiscriminatory basis, or require that the medical benefits be nondiscriminatory.

In defining a cafeteria plan for purposes of the Internal Revenue Code, Section 125 states, "The term cafeteria plan does not include any plan which provides for deferred compensation." A literal interpretation of this statutory language would suggest an employee benefit plan that permits a choice between two or more benefits, one of which is deferred compensation, would not be a cafeteria plan within the scope of Section 125 and thus not subject to its provisions. However, the Congressional committee reports relating to the 1978 legislation implied that if deferred compensation is included as an optional benefit in a cafeteria plan, it would simply not be treated as a nontaxable benefit. The issue concerning the treatment of deferred compensation plans was partially settled by the Miscellaneous Revenue Act of 1980, which provides that cafeteria plans are permitted to provide deferred compensation under the rules applicable to cash or deferred profit-sharing and stock-bonus plans. Unfortunately, the situation still remains unclear on other types of deferred compensation plans.

Unwise Employee Benefit Selection

Often employers are concerned that many employees may not have the expertise to select the proper benefits from among the alternatives offered under a cafeteria compensation plan. Among other things, unwise employee benefit selection may result in inadequate employee protection following a catastrophic loss, in employee dissatisfaction with the plan, and in an increased potential for liability suits against the employer. To avoid, or at least minimize, these problems, employers establishing cafeteria compensation plans must establish effective ongoing communication programs aimed at educating (and perhaps even counseling) employees about the full implications of various benefit choices available to them. However, despite the employer's best efforts, there remains a risk that the communication of incomplete or incorrect information may give rise to increased corporate liability. Moreover, in some cases, a strong conviction on the part of an employer that the organization has a moral obligation to prevent employees from financial injury through faulty decisions may itself be a major barrier to the establishment of a cafeteria compensation plan.

Negative Attitudes

Negative attitudes on the part of employees, insurers, and unions also may serve as obstacles to the institution of a cafeteria compensation plan.

Employees. Negative reactions on the part of employees to an announced proposal to convert from a conventional fixed benefit plan to a cafeteria approach can arise from a variety of sources, such as suspicion concerning the employer's motivation in making the change, a fear that some important long-standing benefits may be lost, and an apprehension about now having to make choices among benefits of which the individual employee has little knowledge. Since employee support is critical if a cafeteria compensation plan is to be truly successful, the employer must be willing to commit the time and resources necessary to combat these negative attitudes through adequately informing the employees about the reasons for the proposed program, its advantages and disadvantages, and its future implications for them. Moreover, by soliciting the opinions of employees on their perceived benefit needs and incorporating those findings into the decision-making process, the employer will not only help to allay initial employee concerns but also minimize negative employee attitudes once the cafeteria compensation plan has been instituted.

Insurers. The growth of the cafeteria approach to benefit planning also has been inhibited by the reluctance or inability of some insurance companies to underwrite the optional benefits an employer may wish to include in a cafeteria compensation plan, or to provide meaningful assistance in connection with the implementation and administration of such a plan. While a few insurers seem unwilling to experiment with almost any new concept, most are concerned with the problem of adverse selection because of employee choice. Although the potential for adverse selection is a real problem, which must be faced in underwriting a cafeteria compensation plan, insurers are finding it is possible to control the problem at an acceptable level by incorporating certain safeguards in plan design. As a result, the number of insurers willing to underwrite cafeteria compensation plans and provide administrative services for such plans is growing.

Unions. Unions generally have had a negative attitude toward employee benefit plans that contain optional benefits. Union management often feels that bargaining over optional benefits is contrary to the practice of bargaining for the best benefit program for all employees. As a result, few cafeteria compensation plans apply to union employees.

Regulatory Restraints

Because cafeteria compensation plans permit individual employees to choose the types and amounts of benefits they receive, they violate, in a literal sense, the group life insurance laws of many states. More specifically, these plans are in conflict with the section of the law defining a legal group, which often provides that amounts of coverage be based on some plan precluding individual selection. This does not mean, however, that cafeteria compensation plans cannot be written in those states, but rather that a favorable ruling should be sought from state insurance authorities prior to the establishment of such a plan.

Costs

Cafeteria compensation plans involve a number of additional developmental, administrative, and benefit costs over and above those associated with conventional employee benefit programs. Because of the greater complexity associated with employee choice, employers establishing cafeteria compensation plans encounter higher initial and continuing administrative costs associated with, among other things, the need for additional employees to administer the program, additional computer time to process employee choices, and a more comprehensive communication program.

In addition to adverse selection, other factors are associated with cafeteria compensation plans that might lead to increased benefit costs. For example, if an employee elected to divert a portion of the employer's contribution from a deferred compensation benefit (such as a profit-sharing plan) to an option involving current benefit payments (such as health insurance), the employer would lose the opportunity to recapture that contribution if the employee were to leave the company before becoming fully vested. Also, the establishment of a cafeteria compensation plan may involve what one benefit consulting firm terms "buy-in" costs for the employer. While conventional employee benefit plans generally require employees to contribute at a uniform rate for group life insurance, cafeteria compensation plans usually charge employees at rates that vary according to age. Since a shift from a conventional benefit plan to a cafeteria compensation plan would increase substantially the cost of group life insurance for older employees, the employer may be required to subsidize that group.

CONSIDERATIONS IN PLAN DESIGN AND ADMINISTRATION

Before committing itself to the establishment of a cafeteria compensation program, an employer must be sure a valid reason exists for converting the company's traditional benefit program to a cafeteria approach. For example, if there is strong employee dissatisfaction with the current benefit program, the solution may lie in clearly identifying the sources of dissatisfaction and making appropriate adjustments in the existing benefit program, rather than making a radical shift to a cafeteria compensation plan. However, if employee dissatisfaction arises from widely differing benefit needs on the part of the employees, conversion to a cafeteria compensation plan may be quite appropriate. Beyond having a clearly defined purpose for converting from a traditional benefit program to a cafeteria compensation program and being willing to bear the additional administrative costs associated with a cafeteria approach, a number of considerations must be faced by the employer in designing the plan itself and the system for its administration.

Plan Design

Numerous questions arise that must be answered before a cafeteria compensation plan can be designed properly. What benefits should be included in the plan? How should benefits be distributed between the basic and optional portions of the plan? How should an employee's flexible credits be calculated? To what extent should employees be allowed to change their benefit selections?

Benefits to Be Included. Probably the most fundamental decision that must be made in designing a cafeteria compensation plan is determining what benefits should be included. If an employer wants the plan to be viewed as meeting the differing needs of employees, it is important that the employer receive employee inputs concerning the types of benefits perceived as being most desirable. An open dialogue with employees undoubtedly will lead to suggestions that every possible employee benefit be made available. The enthusiasm of many employees for a cafeteria compensation plan will then be dampened when the employer rejects some, and possibly many, of these suggestions for cost, administrative, or psychological reasons. Consequently, it is important that certain ground rules be established regarding the benefits that are acceptable to the employer.

The employer must decide whether the plan should be limited to the types of benefits provided through traditional group insurance arrangements or be expanded to include other welfare benefits, retirement benefits and, possibly, cash. At a minimum, it is important to ensure that an overall employee benefit program provide employees with protection against all major areas of personal risks. This suggests that a benefit program make at least some provision for life insurance, disability income protection, medical expense protection, and retirement benefits. However, it is not necessary that these benefits be included in a cafeteria plan. For example, some employers have a retirement plan separate from their cafeteria plan; other employers make a certain type of retirement benefit one of the available options. Where retirement benefits are included, employees are provided with basic retirement benefits, which can be supplemented on an optional basis.

Probably the most controversial issue among employers who have adopted cafeteria compensation plans is whether cash should be an available option. Arguments in favor of a cash option often are based on the rationale that employees should not be forced to purchase optional benefits if they have no need or desire for them. In addition, cash may better fulfill the needs of many employees. For example, a young employee's greatest need may be the necessary down payment for a home, and an older worker's greatest need may be the resources to pay college tuition for children. Some employers may believe the purpose of a cafeteria compensation plan is to provide employee benefits only and not current income. If cash is available, employees will view the plan as a source of increasing their wages or salary rather than as an employee benefit. In plans where cash is an option, the amount that may be withdrawn is sometimes limited. Also, experience has shown that most employees will elect nontaxable benefits in lieu of cash.

In some respects a cafeteria compensation plan may be an ideal vehicle for providing less traditional types of benefits. Two examples are extra vacation time and use of day-care centers. Some plans allow an employee to use flexible credits to purchase additional days of vacation. When available, this has proven a popular benefit, particularly among single employees. A problem may arise, however, if the work of vacationing employees must be assumed by nonvacationing employees in addition to their own regularly assigned work. Those not electing extra vacation time may feel resentful of doing the work of someone else who is away longer than the normal vacation period.

In recent years, there has been increasing pressure on employers to provide day-care centers for the children of employees. These represent an additional cost if added to a traditional existing benefit program. By including them in a cafeteria compensation plan, those employees using them pay the cost from their flexible credits.

An important consideration is the number of benefits to be included in a cafeteria compensation plan. The greater the number of benefits, particularly optional benefits, the greater the administrative costs. A wide array of options also may prove to be confusing to many employees and require the need for extra personnel to counsel employees or to answer their questions.

A final concern is the problem of adverse selection. Few difficulties have arisen with respect to life insurance and medical expense insurance, even when these benefits are optional. Problems have arisen, however, for dental expense insurance, but it appears the difficulties are similar to those arising under optional dental expense plans in general and not peculiar to cafeteria compensation plans. As in separate plans, adverse selection can be controlled somewhat by benefit limitations and, possibly, restrictions on obtaining coverage at a date later than initial eligibility.

Basic versus Optional Benefits. As mentioned earlier, cafeteria compensation plans generally consist of two portions—a minimum level of basic benefits received by all employees, and a second layer of optional benefits that may be purchased by each employee with flexible credits provided by the employer. Once a list of benefits to be included in a cafeteria plan has been determined, it is necessary to decide what benefits should be included as basic benefits and what should be included as optional benefits. At a minimum, the basic benefits should provide a reasonable level of protection against the major sources of personal risk. This suggests that basic benefits should include at least some life insurance, disability income benefits, medical expense benefits, and retirement benefits (unless these are included under a separate retirement plan). Some employers with established cafeteria compensation plans have included additional but less-critical benefits, such as travel accident insurance or dependent life insurance in the basic portion of the plan.

The optional layer of the plan may include additional types of benefits not included in the basic plan. It also may include additional amounts of coverage for some of the same types of benefits included in the basic plan, such as additional amounts of life insurance on the employee. In addition, the employee may have the option of electing alternative benefits to some or all of the benefits provided in the basic plan. For example, for an additional cost an employee may elect a medical expense plan with a smaller deductible.

Because of the current provisions of Section 125 of the Internal Revenue Code, cafeteria plans that include both taxable and nontaxable benefits should not include other deferred compensation plans than those involving cash or deferred profit-sharing or stock-bonus options in the optional benefit layer if the issue of constructive receipt is to be avoided. Also, the plan will be more meaningful to employees if it is so structured that all or most employees will be able to purchase at least some of the optional benefits.

Level of Employer Contributions. An employer has considerable latitude in determining the amount of flexible credits that will be made available to employees to purchase optional benefits under a cafeteria compensation plan. These may be a function of one or more of the following factors: salary, age, family status, and length of service.

The major difficulty arises in those situations where the installation of a cafeteria compensation plan is not accompanied by an overall increase in the amount of the employer's contributions to the employee benefit plan. It generally is felt each employee should be provided with enough flexible credits so he or she can purchase optional benefits, which, together with basic benefits, are at least equivalent to the benefits provided by the old plan. This probably will lead an employer to determining the amount of flexible credits on some basis so each employee is provided with an amount of flexible credits comparable to the difference in value between the benefits under the old plan for that employee and the basic benefits under the new cafeteria compensation plan.

Employees' Ability to Change Benefits.   Because the needs of employees change over time, a provision regarding the employees' ability to change their benefit options must be incorporated into a cafeteria compensation plan. Since the changing of options results in administrative costs and may result in adverse selection, employees probably should not be permitted to change their benefit selections more frequently than once a year.

Two situations may arise to complicate the issue of the frequency with which benefits may be changed. First, the charges to employees for optional benefits must be adjusted periodically to reflect experience under the plan. If the charges for benefits rise between dates on which employees may change benefit selections, the employer must either absorb these charges or pass them to the employees, probably through increased payroll deductions. Consequently, most cafeteria compensation plans have annual dates on which benefit changes may be made that are the same as the dates when charges for benefits are recalculated. This also usually coincides with the date on which any insurance contracts providing benefits under the plan are renewed.

The second situation arises when the amount of the employees' flexible credits are based on their compensation. If an employee receives a pay increase between selection periods, should the employee be granted additional flexible credits to purchase additional benefits at that time? Under most cafeteria compensation plans, the flexible credits available to all employees are calculated only once a year, usually at a date prior to the date by which any annual benefit changes must be made. Any changes in the employee's status during the year will have no effect on an employee's flexible credits until the following year on the date on which a recalculation is made.

Communication

The complexity of a cafeteria compensation plan, compared to a traditional employee benefit plan, requires additional communication between the employer and the employees. Since the concept is new, employees will have many questions. It is doubtful if all these questions can be answered through written information. Group meetings and individual meetings between employees and representatives of the employer probably will be required to explain the operation of the plan. Obviously, the need for these meetings will be greatest when a cafeteria compensation plan is first installed, and for newly hired employees.

Many employees unaccustomed to making choices regarding employee benefits also will seek advice concerning their benefit selections. An employer must make the decision whether to require employees to make their selections with little guidance or to provide extensive counseling services. Either alternative may have legal as well as moral implications. When counseling is provided, it is imperative it be provided by a qualified and competent staff.

Updating the Plan

Any employee benefit plan will need periodic updating. However, some unique situations exist for cafeteria compensation plans. Since such plans are advertised as better meeting the needs of individual employees, the employer must continually monitor the changing needs and desires of employees. As employee interest increases for benefits not included in the plan, they should be considered for inclusion. If little interest is shown in certain benefits already made available, a decision must be made regarding their continued availability. However, if certain optional benefits are selected by most employees, perhaps they should be incorporated into the basic benefit plan.

The employer is faced with a dilemma if employee benefit costs rise more rapidly than the increases in flexible credits made available to the employees. For example, if the amount of flexible credits are a function of an employee's salary, which is usually the case, an increase of 10 percent in salary results in an increase of 10 percent in flexible credits. However, at the same time, the employee may be faced with an increased cost of 20 percent to retain the optional benefits currently selected under the plan. The employee must either reduce benefits or pay for a portion of the increased cost through additional payroll deductions. Obviously, neither situation is appealing to the employee. In deciding whether to increase flexible credits further, so the employee can choose the same benefits as previously selected, the employer is faced with the difficult task of balancing employee satisfaction with benefit cost control.

PART FIVE

Designing Employee Benefit Plans— Retirement and Capital Accumulation Plans

This part begins with an overview of the design of retirement plans in Chapter 27, which discusses defined benefit and defined contribution plans. Chapter 28 covers Social Security—often considered the floor of protection on which private plans build and with which they often are integrated—and other governmental retirement plans. Following this, Chapter 29 covers the basic features of retirement plans.

Chapter 30 is the first of two chapters dealing with profit-sharing plans, and these chapters are followed by a discussion of thrift and savings plans in Chapter 32. The current emphasis on cash or deferred arrangements is covered in Chapter 33.

Chapters 34 and 35 are an in-depth look at the various types of employee stock ownership plans.

Chapter 36 deals with retirement plans for the self-employed, concentrating on Keogh (H.R.-10) plans, while Chapter 37 discusses individual retirement accounts (IRAs), which have been receiving so much attention of late, and simplified employee pension plans (SEPs).

Chapters 38 and 39 cover tax-deferred annuities and executive retirement benefit plans, respectively.

CHAPTER 27

Retirement Plan Design

PRESTON C. BASSETT

INTRODUCTION

The primary purpose of a retirement plan is to provide employees with pensions following their retirement. Secondary purposes include retirement benefits to employees who terminate employment after several years of service but before reaching retirement age, pensions to surviving spouses, and often pensions in event of disability before retirement, and death benefits in event of death before or after retirement. In designing a pension plan, factors considered include who are to get the benefits, when they are to be paid, and how much is to be provided. For example, consideration must be given to employees who do not have a full working career of participation under the plan. Generally, a pension plan is designed to provide adequate benefits for the career workers, but many employees work for an employer for less than a full career. Provision must be made for partial pensions to short-service employees. As is discussed in more detail later, federal law requires that pension plans provide some credit for pensions for any employee who has ten years of credited service (or less, in some circumstances). Another consideration is benefits for dependents of workers. What benefits should be provided to survivors of the participants who die either before retirement or after retirement? Also, many pension plans provide for disability benefits in the event the participant becomes disabled before retirement. Thus, while the primary purpose of a pension plan is to provide pension benefits, other areas also are considered in the design of a pension plan.

Employers considering the adoption of a retirement plan may put emphasis on other factors, such as the employees sharing in the profits of the company. Such a company would adopt a profit-sharing plan under which a percentage of the profits would be set aside annually to be used in lieu of or as a supplement to a conventional retirement plan. Profit-sharing plans are not discussed in this chapter but are covered in later chapters, specifically in Chapters 30 and 31. Also, this chapter does not cover plans for the self-

387

employed or the thrift and savings plans, also covered in subsequent chapters, which also may be used as a substitute or a supplement to a conventional retirement plan.

This chapter discusses two types of conventional benefit plans: defined benefit plans and defined contribution plans. Precise definitions of defined benefit plans and defined contribution plans are set forth in the Employee Retirement Income Security Act of 1974 (ERISA).[1] A defined benefit plan is a pension plan in which benefits payable to the participants are defined by the terms of the plan, and the contributions to the plan are variable, being based on an actuarial determination of the amount of money estimated to be necessary to provide the defined benefits. Alternatively, a defined contribution plan is a plan under which the contributions to the plan are defined by the terms of the plan, and the benefits are variable, depending on the funds available at the time a participant retires or becomes eligible for the benefits.

DEFINED BENEFIT PLANS

Level of Retirement Benefits

One of the first steps in establishing a defined benefit retirement plan is the determination of the level of the retirement benefits to be provided to the employees. Generally, the objective of the private plan is to provide a reasonable pension for career employees, taking Social Security benefits into account. For example, if the objective is to provide a gross retirement income sufficient to maintain the preretirement standard of living, the retirement income for low-paid employees might be 80 percent of their final pay. For the high-paid employees, the ratio to maintain the standard of living might be 50 percent. These replacement ratios decline as pay increases because a smaller pension, as a percentage of pay, is needed to maintain the standard of living after retirement. For higher-paid employees, generally, a larger proportion of their income goes for federal, state, and local taxes and into personal savings prior to retirement; thus, a lower percentage of the gross income is used to provide for their standard of living. A study prepared by the President's Commission on Pension Policy developed replacement ratios of 79 percent to 51 percent for single persons and 86 percent to 55 percent for married couples (see Tables 27–1 and 27–2).[2]

The retirement income provided by these replacement ratios includes income from Social Security benefits, private pension plan benefits, and personal savings. Table 27–3, also from the President's Commission on

---

[1] ERISA, Title I, Sec. 3, (34) and (35).

[2] President's Commission on Pension Policy, February 1981, Final Report Tables 19 and 20.

Table 27-1
Retirement Income to Maintain Prereriement Standard of Living: Single Persons Retiring in 1980, for Selected Income Levels

Gross Preretirement Income	Preretirement Taxes		Disposable Income	Reduction in Expenses at Retirement			Net Preretirement Income	Post-retirement Taxes		Equivalent Retirement Income	
	Federal Income[1]	State, Local[2]		Work-Related Expenses[3]	Savings	Investments		Federal Income	State, Local[2]	Dollars	Ratio
$ 6,500	$ 906	$ 97	$ 5,497	$ 330	0%	$ 0	$ 5,167	$ 0	$ 0	$ 5,167	.79
10,000	1,785	223	7,992	480	3	240	7,272	0	0	7,272	.73
15,000	3,259	444	11,297	678	6	678	9,941	0	0	9,941	.66
20,000	5,055	728	14,217	853	9	1,280	12,084	166	32	12,282	.61
30,000	8,926	1,429	19,645	1,179	12	2,357	16,109	1,077	205	17,391	.58
50,000	18,921	3,328	27,751	1,665	15	4,163	21,923	3,153	599	25,675	.51

[1] Federal income and Social Security (OASDHI) taxes.
[2] Based on state and local 1978 income-tax receipts, which were 19 percent of federal income tax receipts. Does not include property taxes.
[3] Estimated as 6 percent of disposable income.
[4] Postretirement taxes are on income in excess of Social Security benefits, which are nontaxable. Retirees without Social Security benefits would need higher replacement ratios.
Source: Preston C. Bassett, consulting actuary, President's Commission on Pension Policy, 1980.

Table 27-2
Retirement Income to Maintain Preretirement Standard of Living: Married Couples Retiring in 1980, for Selected Income Levels

| Gross Preretirement Income | Preretirement Taxes | | Disposable Income | Reduction in Expenses at Retirement | | | Net Preretirement Income | Postretirement Taxes | | Equivalent Retirement Income | |
	Federal Income[1]	State, Local[2]		Work-Related Expenses[3]	Savings	Investments		Federal Income	State, Local[2]	Dollars	Ratio
$ 6,500	$ 549	$ 29	$ 5,922	$ 355	0%	$ 0	$ 5,567	$ 0	$ 0	$ 5,567	.86
10,000	1,311	133	8,556	513	3	257	7,786	0	0	7,786	.78
15,000	2,550	310	12,140	728	6	728	10,684	0	0	10,684	.71
20,000	3,968	520	15,512	931	9	1,396	13,185	0	0	13,185	.66
30,000	6,986	1,061	21,950	1,317	12	2,634	17,999	53	10	18,062	.60
50,000	15,202	2,622	32,176	1,931	15	4,826	25,419	1,651	314	27,384	.55

[1] Federal income and Social Security (OASDHI) taxes.

[2] Based on state and local 1978 income-tax receipts, which were 19 percent of federal income-tax receipts. Does not include property tax.

[3] Estimated as 6 percent of disposable income.

[4] Postretirement taxes are on income in excess of Social Security benefits, which are nontaxable. Retirees without Social Security benefits would need higher replacement ratios.

Source: Preston C. Bassett, consulting actuary, President's Commission on Pension Policy, 1980.

Table 27-3
Hypothetical Social Security Replacement Ratios

Gross Earnings	Goal[1]	Social Security[2]	Remainder for Idealized Workers and Couples
Single:			
$6,500	.79	.57	.22
10,000	.73	.49	.24
15,000	.66	.42	.24
20,000	.61	.34	.27
30,000	.58	.23	.35
50,000	.51	.14	.37
Married—equal earners:			
$6,500	.86	.82	.04
10,000	.78	.63	.15
15,000	.71	.54	.15
20,000	.66	.49	.17
30,000	.59	.42	.17
50,000	.50	.27	.23
Married—one earner:			
$6,500	.86	.85	.01
10,000	.78	.73	.05
15,000	.71	.64	.07
20,000	.66	.51	.15
30,000	.60	.34	.26
50,000	.55	.21	.34

[1] See Tables 27-1 and 27-2.
[2] Based on a continuously employed worker retiring at age 65 in 1980 and, if married, a spouse of age 65. Prior earnings were assumed to increase at 6 percent per year.
Source: Preston C. Bassett, consulting actuary, President's Commission on Pension Policy, 1980.

Pension Policy, builds on Tables 27-1 and 27-2 by estimating the replacement ratios that might be provided by Social Security and shows the difference or additional amount needed to meet these particular goals.[3]

These replacement ratios can only be taken as rough guides for the makeup to be provided by the private pension and personal savings. These particular ratios are based upon specific assumptions concerning current and prior earnings, years of employment, taxes, savings, and many other factors that vary from individual to individual. The benefits provided by a private pension plan generally are less than the amount to maintain the preretirement standard of living. Plans costs and other factors must be considered.

[3] President's Commission on Pension Policy, November 1980, an Interim Report, Table 12.

Coordination with Social Security Benefits

For a pension plan to qualify for favorable tax treatment, certain requirements of the Internal Revenue Service must be met. One of these requirements is that the benefits may not discriminate in favor of employees who are officers, shareholders, or highly compensated.[4] Thus, the pension as a percentage of pay may not be higher for high-paid employees than it is for low-paid employees. However, in testing for discrimination, Social Security benefits may be taken into account. Thus, the Internal Revenue Code maintains a private pension plan is not considered discriminatory solely because it takes Social Security benefits into account in determining the benefits provided under the plan. Discrimination in the private plan benefits can be made in favor of the shareholders, officers, and highly compensated employees to this extent.[5]

Integration of private plan benefits with Social Security applies to retirement benefits, to survivor's benefits, and to disability benefits for the plan to be qualified. In Revenue Ruling 71-446, the total value of all Social Security benefits, pension benefits, survivor's benefits, death benefits, and all other ancillary benefits is stated to equal approximately 162 percent of the primary Social Security benefit. The employer is paying half the Social Security costs and, therefore, the employer is entitled to take credit for half the Social Security benefits, which is 81 percent of the primary benefit. The IRS has increased the limit to 83.3 percent. Thus, the maximum credit that can be taken by the employer under a retirement plan is 83.3 percent of the primary Social Security benefit. This can be done only if no other ancillary benefits are being provided by the plan. There can be no integrated death or disability benefits, and the benefits cannot be provided prior to age 65 unless reduced.

Three ways exist for private pension plans to be integrated with Social Security benefits. These are known as (1) offset, (2) exclusion, and (3) step-rate.

With the offset approach, the private pension plan benefits are defined as a percent of pay less a certain percent of the Social Security benefit. The typical offset pension plan might provide a career employee with a pension of 50 percent of his or her final average pay less half the primary Social Security benefit. The maximum that could be deducted would be 83.3 percent of the Social Security benefit payable to the employee at retirement. However, most offset plans in the United States today offset half the Social Security benefit.

With the exclusion method, the earnings subject to the Social Security tax are excluded from the benefit formula. Thus, the plan would provide a benefit of, say, 30 percent of pay in excess of the pay that is taxed to provide

---

[4] ERISA, Title II, Section 410(b).

[5] Section 1.40-3(e) of Income Tax Regulations, TP 7134, IRB 1971-34, 15, RR 71-446.

Social Security benefits. The maximum benefit percentages on pay in excess of the Social Security tax base is 37.5 percent. However, there are restrictions on this percentage, and it is different if another base than the Social Security tax base is used in the formula. The more typical pension plan provides for a percent of pay for each year of service. A plan might provide for a benefit of 1.4 percent of pay in excess of the Social Security tax base for each year of service with a retirement age of 65. If the benefit percentage is applied to average pay of the final highest five consecutive years, then the annual accrual cannot exceed 1 percent of average final pay in excess of "covered compensation."[6] Very few pure excess plans are in existence today. The more usual approach is step-rate.

The step-rate plan is, in effect, the combination of two plans: (1) an exclusion or excess plan, as defined above, and (2) a plan that provides the same benefits for all employees. For example, a typical plan might provide a benefit of 1 percent of pay up to the Social Security tax base, plus 1.5 percent of pay in excess of the Social Security tax base for each year of service. The differential between the percentage on excess pay and the percentage on pay subject to Social Security tax for a pension plan based on career earnings can be as much as 1 4 percent per year for a career pay plan, and for a pension plan based on final average pay, 1 percent per year of covered compensation.

Only the primary insurance amount can be taken into account in the Social Security offset. Also, the amount of the Social Security offset must be frozen at the time of termination of employment. Social Security increases that occur subsequent to termination of employment, either with a vested benefit or at retirement, cannot be taken into account to reduce the private plan benefits.

The limits stated above must be adjusted if certain other conditions prevail under the plan. If the normal retirement age is lower than 65, or if the early retirement benefits are greater than the actuarial equivalent, the limits must be reduced. Also, the limits must be reduced if the form of benefit is other than a life annuity. If the annuity is a joint and survivor annuity, or a refund or certain period plus a life annuity, the percentages are reduced. Also the limits are reduced if there are preretirement disability benefits or death benefits. The limits may be increased if employees contribute to the plan.[7]

Many of the major pension plans in the United States use the offset method. There are several advantages to this method. It is easy for the employees to understand how the benefits are determined. The adjustments to changes in Social Security benefits are automatic, in that as soon as the Social Security benefit changes, the adjustment is made in the private

---

[6] "Covered compensation" is the average Social Security wage at time of retirement upon which Social Security benefits are based (Revenue Ruling 71-446).

[7] Revenue Rulings 71-446 and 78-92.

retirement plan. When Social Security benefits are increased, there is a decrease in the private plan benefit for active employees—to which many employees object. Employees object, saying that the employer is getting the advantages of the increases in Social Security benefits since future plan benefits and costs are reduced. However, only 50 percent of the amount of the increase usually is applied. Another disadvantage: the amount of the pension to be provided by the plan is uncertain until actual time of retirement, because the level of Social Security benefits is unknown.

A popular variation to the offset type is a provision in plans to have a "cap" on the total benefits from Social Security and the private plan. Plans may contain a normal benefit formula, but, in addition, they state that in no event will the total benefit from this plan and Social Security exceed 100 percent (or some other percent) of the final pay of the employee. The basic formula may be nonintegrated or integrated in some manner, but the final test is whether Social Security plus the plan benefit exceed some stated limit.[8]

Types of Benefit Formulas

Three basic or fundamental types of benefit formulas are in common usage today. These generally are called: (1) unit benefit formulas, (2) career-pay formulas, and (3) final-pay formulas.

Unit benefit formulas are most common in union-negotiated pension plans. These plans provide, for example, $12 per month for each year of credited service payable at normal retirement age. An employee with 30 years of service would be entitled to $360 a month in retirement. These plans are not integrated with Social Security. Because the dollar amount of the pension is fixed by the terms of the plan, these benefits soon become inadequate under inflationary conditions. Thus, every three years or so the union and company negotiate an increase in the dollars of benefits. These plans are more suitable under conditions where the covered employees all are earning somewhere near the same level of pay, because the pension is independent of pay. Higher-paid employees would receive inadequate benefits, if only adequate benefits are provided, for lower-paid and middle-paid employees. Some dollar-per-month plans have had different levels of benefits for different levels of pay at time of retirement. However, the more popular approach is to provide a fixed-dollar amount and to renegotiate every three years or so.

Under the typical career-pay formula, a benefit is credited each year, based on the pay of the employee in that specific year. For example, the pension benefit might be defined as 1.5 percent of pay each year. These plans frequently are integrated with Social Security benefits by providing

---

[8] While this provision has not been disallowed by the Internal Revenue Service, it appears to conflict with current revenue rulings.

one level or percentage on earnings up to some specified amount, and a higher percentage on earnings in excess of that amount. These plans were particularly popular when wages remained fairly stable over a worker's career. However, under inflationary conditions, benefits credited many years in the past become inadequate by the time of retirement. To retain the viability of career-pay formulas with rapid pay increases, it becomes necessary to update periodically the career-pay formulas. A common way of accomplishing this is to restate the benefits for service prior to the amendment date by assuming current pay was in effect for all prior years. A lower percentage often is used for these past benefits. Thus, for example, a benefit formula might state that the plan will provide a benefit for 1 percent of 1981 pay for all years of service prior to January 1, 1982, and 1.25 percent of pay for each year of service thereafter.

Final-pay formulas may overcome the objection to inadequate benefits or to the need to update a career-pay formula. Final-pay formulas base the pension on the salary of the participant when close to time of retirement. For integrated pension plans, the IRS requires the use of at least five consecutive years of pay for the maximum limit. If the average of four consecutive years' pay is used, only 95 percent of the normal limit can be applied, and for three consecutive years, only 90 percent. Most plans typically provide for averaging pay over the 5 consecutive years of highest pay, perhaps over the last 10 years. Overtime, shift differentials, bonuses, and the like, may be excluded or included as long as no discrimination exists in favor of the highly compensated group. These final-pay plans may be integrated with Social Security either by step-rate or offset.

Often a pension plan provides for minimum pensions, under certain circumstances. Minimum pensions may be provided to avoid very small pensions that could result from the operation of the basic formula. Thus, a plan would provide that in no event will the monthly pension be less than $25.

Another form of frequently used minimum pension occurs when a company has a negotiated plan that is in effect for bargaining employees and a second plan that is in effect for salaried or nonbargaining employees. The latter plan will provide a minimum pension equal to the pension provided under the negotiated plan.

A third form of minimum occurs with unit benefit or career-pay plans. An employer frequently adds a final-pay formula as a minimum to protect participants who receive significant pay increases late in their working careers.

In addition to the Internal Revenue Service requirement of non-discrimination, there are requirements under ERISA concerning benefit formulas. One of the main concerns leading up to the passage of ERISA was to provide benefits to plan participants who, after several years of service, terminate employment prior to becoming eligible for a pension. One of the features in this protection is to provide that the vested benefits are not overly disproportionate during a working career. ERISA prohibits plans from providing for significantly higher benefits for later years of service or after a certain date than in prior years. There are three basic rules for qualifying the levels of benefits under ERISA.[9] These rules are known as the 3 percent rule, 133.3 percent rule, and the proportion rule. The first requires the accrual at any time cannot be less than 3 percent times the years of service to date, times the prospective benefit that would be payable under the plan assuming the employee continues to earn the same pay as he or she was currently earning at age 65 or at the normal retirement date under the plan, if earlier. The 133.3 percent rule states that the benefit in any future year cannot exceed by more than 33.3 percent the benefit in any prior year. Finally, the proportion rule states that the benefit accrued to date must be the same proportion of the benefit payable at retirement, assuming current pay continues, as credited service to date is to total expected service. A plan must satisfy at least one of these rules.

Eligibility for Retirement Benefits

Eligibility for retirement benefits is now pretty much determined by the requirements of ERISA. Eligibility covers such issues as who should participate in the plan, what constitutes credited service, when benefits vest, and when employees must be eligible to retire.

ERISA requires that participation in the plan begin no later than age 25 and one year of service. There is an exception, in that a plan can use three years of service for participation if there is 100 percent immediate vesting. Under a defined benefit plan, all employees who are hired up to within five years of retirement must be included in the plan. However, most plans provide that employees will participate in the plan from date of hire and that all service counts.

ERISA requires that all participants working more than 1,000 hours in a 12-month period must be credited with a year of service. Those working less than 500 hours can be excluded.[10]

All pension plans must provide that employees will have vested rights in their accrued benefits after certain minimum requirements have been met. All employee contributions, or the benefits provided by them, must vest immediately. ERISA sets three standards for vesting of the employer-provided benefits of pension plans.[11] These are:

1. Vesting at 100 percent of all employer-provided benefits after 10 years of service.
2. Graded vesting over 5 to 15 years of service. This provision calls for 25

[9] ERISA, Title II, Section 202.

[10] ERISA, Section 202.

[11] ERISA, Section 411.

percent vesting after 5 years of service, grading up to 50 percent after 10, and 100 percent after 15 years of service.

3. Graded vesting after 5 years of service and when the sum of the number of years of credited service and the age of the employee reaches 45. At that point or after 10 years of service, if earlier, the vesting must be 50 percent, which is then graded up to 100 percent over the next 5 years. In any case, benefits must be 50 percent vested after 10 years of service, with 10 percent additional vesting for each year thereafter.

The Internal Revenue Service reserves the right to require earlier vesting if it believes the plan may be discriminatory in its operations. Generally, the more restrictive provision is for 40 percent vesting after 4 years of service, grading up to 100 percent after 11 years of service.

For determining credited service for vesting purposes, service prior to age 22 can be excluded and any service performed before the plan was in effect can be excluded. Any years in which the employee declines to contribute to a plan that requires employee contributions can be excluded.[12] If a participant works fewer than 500 hours in a 12-month period, this constitutes a break in service. For an employee who has a one-year break in service, years of service prior to the break need not be reinstated until the employee has completed a year of service after returning to work. Employees without vested benefits who have breaks in service do not lose their prior credited service until their breaks in service exceed their years of credited service.[13]

The normal retirement age of a pension plan must be the earlier of the age set forth in the plan or the later of age 65 or ten years participation in the plan. This does not prohibit a plan from providing a full benefit at an age earlier than 65. However, the early retirement benefits generally are reduced because of the longer period over which these benefits are expected to be paid. The maximum reduction is the actuarially equivalent benefit. That is, the current value of the pension accrued to early retirement date, but payable at normal retirement date, is equated to the current value of the reduced pension starting immediately upon early retirement. Most plans provide for a percentage reduction, such as 5 percent a year for each year of early retirement benefits, the participant must meet stated age and service requirements, such as age 55 and 10 years of service. Most plans also provide an employee may postpone his or her retirement beyond normal retirement age. The general practice is not to increase the benefit for service beyond normal retirement age but to pay the same benefit that would have been payable at normal retirement. It should be noted the 1978 amendments to the federal Age Discrimination in Employment Act prohib-

---

[12] ERISA, Section 203.

[13] ERISA, Section 202.

its compulsory retirement for most employees prior to age 70. At present, it is not necessary to provide additional accruals of pensions beyond age 65.

Other Benefits

ERISA requires the normal form of the pension under the plan be a joint and survivor benefit, which, in the event of death of the employee, provides that 50 percent of the pension will be continued to a surviving spouse. Moreover, the benefit payable under this provision is the actuarial equivalent of the lifetime benefit payable under the plan's provisions. Therefore, the cost of providing this death benefit to a surviving spouse may be borne by the plan participant and his or her beneficiary. Also, prior to retirement, the plan must provide that the employee can elect within 10 years of retirement to provide that, if he or she should die before retirement, 50 percent of the actuarial equivalent of the credited benefit at time of death will be payable to a surviving spouse. Again, the cost of this provision can be passed on to the employee and spouse. Other death benefits may be provided under a pension plan, but the IRS requires that any death benefits be ancillary to the primary purpose of providing retirement benefits. Further discussion of this topic appears in a later chapter.

Frequently, pension plans also provide for disability benefits, which are covered in Part Three of this book. The development of disability benefits is quite similar to that of developing retirement benefits. There will be certain eligibility requirements, which usually include both an age requirement and a service requirement. Also, it is necessary to define carefully what constitutes disability. Generally, the pension plan covers long-term disability benefits and not short-term. Customarily, the plan provides for a waiting period of six months before disability benefits commence. Frequently, disability benefits payable under the plan also are subject to qualifying for Social Security disability benefits. The plan also provides for periodic reviews of the status of the disability. Often, the disability benefits are integrated with any disability benefits payable under Social Security, and also may take other income into account.

Other Plan Features

A few plans provide that employees, to participate, must make contributions to the plan. Because of the lack of tax deductibility of mandatory employee contributions, contributory plans are not popular in the United States.

ERISA placed limits on the amount of the annual benefit that can be paid under a qualified plan. Section 415 of ERISA stated that the maximum annual pension under a qualified plan is $75,000 or, if less, 100 percent of the participant's average compensation for his or her highest consecutive three-year period. However, the $75,000 is increased in accordance with any increase in the cost-of-living adjustment. The $75,000 has been increased to $136,425 in 1982. If an employee is covered by both a defined benefit plan and a defined contribution plan, the combined limit was 140 percent. The Tax Equity and Fiscal Responsibility Act of 1982 (TEFRA) rolled back these limits beginning in 1983. The limit is now $90,000 for a defined benefit plan, and if there are both a defined benefit plan and a defined contribution plan, the combined limit is now 125 percent. Companies that want to provide benefits greater than these amounts can install "excess benefit plans." There are no special tax incentives for the benefits in excess of the stated limits. The excess benefits are not prefunded, but would be paid to the qualifying employees out-of-pocket, and a tax deduction would be taken by the employer at the time the payment is made to the employee.

Most government plans, such as for the U.S. Civil Service, military, and others, provide that pension benefits will be increased automatically in proportion to changes in the cost of living. Such a provision is highly unusual for a private pension plan. Some plans do provide for cost-of-living increases, but always with a ceiling on the amount of the annual increase—usually 3 to 5 percent. The more common practice during these inflationary times has been for companies to grant ad hoc increases to employees currently retired. Generally, the ad hoc increases are paid through the pension plan by an amendment to the plan. However, it is not unusual for them to be paid out-of-pocket with no effect on the pension plan. Often the ad hoc increases are a percentage increase in the current benefits, depending on the number of years in retirement or since the last benefit increase. Usually, the increase is somewhat less than the actual cost-of-living increase over the same period.

Finally, the provisions of the plan must cover such items as the establishment of a funding agency, how the plan will be funded, under what conditions the plan can be amended or terminated, and what the rights of the participants will be in the event of the plan termination.

Cost of the Plan

The annual cost to fund the pension plan is not directly part of the design of the plan. Yet, indirectly, the cost may have a significant impact on the design. If the estimated cost is too high, consideration will be given to lowering the level of the benefits, or to adding employee contributions, or to dropping some of the ancillary benefits. Conversely, if the estimated costs are low, additional features may be considered.

Multi-Employer Plans

Many unions have established multi-employer pension plans, under which several companies with employees in the same union establish one pension plan covering all employees within the union. These are particularly popular in the transportation and trade fields. For example, a carpenter might work for several different employers during his or her career; but, as long as he or she stayed in the union, would receive benefits from this multi-employer pension plan. The various employers participating in the plan contribute an agreed-upon number of cents per hour worked by the participants (or some other measure) to a central fund, which is administered jointly by the employers and the union. Basic features of the multi-employer plan are similar to those described above for a defined benefit pension plan. The distinction, however, is that, periodically, the union and the employers negotiate the amount to be contributed to the fund and, on the basis of the contributions, an actuarial determination is made of the defined benefits to be paid to the plan participants.

DEFINED CONTRIBUTION PLANS

With a defined contribution plan, the employer and, perhaps, the employees as well, contribute a specified amount, usually a percentage of pay, to a fund that is invested and becomes available to the employee when he or she retires. The objective of the plan may be to provide a pension at retirement or a single lump-sum payment. Many plans give an employee a choice. If the purpose is to provide a lifetime pension, extra care must be taken in the selection of the percentage of pay to be contributed each year. Examples are needed to illustrate the levels of pensions that may result from various levels of contributions and from under various patterns of pay, service, retirement ages, and investment experience. The plan provision will state the amount to be contributed each year by the employer and the employees. The pension at retirement is not known in advance, since it depends on the size of the retiree's fund at time of retirement, as well as the employee's age and sex.[14] Individual accounts are maintained for each employee and are expected to increase each year by the contributions and the investment earnings from the fund.

These plans may be integrated with Social Security. Contributions on pay not subject to Social Security tax are 7 percent greater than the contributions on pay subject to Social Security tax. TEFRA reduces this percentage to 5.4 percent for 1984, 5.7 percent for 1985–89, and 6.2 percent for 1990 and thereafter. The maximum tax deductible annual amount that can be contributed on behalf of any one employee is the lesser of $25,000 or 25 percent of the participant's compensation. The $25,000 is adjusted annually by the changes in the cost of living. By 1982 the $25,000 maximum was increased to $45,475, and TEFRA has rolled back this amount to $30,000 beginning in 1983.

---

[14] Benefits differing by sex have been ruled illegal by some courts' interpretation of the Equal Employment Opportunities Act.

Generally, the ERISA requirements for participation, credited service, vesting, and retirement age are the same as described above for a defined benefit pension plan. One minor difference is that, under defined benefit pension plans, employees within five years of normal retirement age can be excluded from participation. This exclusion is not permitted under a defined contribution plan. The general practice is to provide more liberal vesting in defined contribution plans than in defined benefit plans.

The investments of the funds under defined contribution plans usually are quite different than under defined benefit plans, because the return on the investments is allocated directly to the employees participating in the plans. Often plans provide the employees with a limited choice about how they would like their account balances invested. For example, there might be a fund invested solely in the employer's stock that would be available to the employees. There might be a fund invested in government obligations, or in a bond fund, or in an equity fund, and so on. The employees would decide in which funds to participate and would have some flexibility in moving their account balances from one fund to another. The choices usually are limited, and many plans have no employee choices.

Death benefits generally are provided under defined contribution plans equal to the amount accumulated in the employee's account at the time of the death of the employee. Also, disability benefits generally are provided equal to the amount that can be provided by the employee's account.

The Equal Employment Opportunity Commission has ruled that if the employee continues employment beyond normal retirement age to age 70, contributions under defined contribution plans must continue until actual retirement if the plan is supplemental. This is different from defined benefit plans, where benefit accruals may cease at normal retirement age.

Finally, a defined contribution plan must have provisions similar to a defined benefit plan for investment responsibilities, under what conditions the plan can be amended or terminated, and the rights of the plan participants.

TAX EQUITY AND FISCAL RESPONSIBILITY ACT OF 1982 (TEFRA)

The enactment of TEFRA may affect the design of retirement plans. In addition to changing the deduction limits for defined benefit and defined contribution plans described earlier, the act introduces a new concept—the "top heavy" plan that could face important restrictions on plans that fall into this category. Additional administrative complexities may also have to be faced by employers because of the necessity to withhold taxes from retirement plan payments. These and other TEFRA changes and the implications for retirement plans are discussed in Chapter 58 of the *Handbook*.

CHAPTER 28

Social Security and Other Governmental Retirement Benefit Plans

ROBERT J. MYERS

Economic security for retired workers in the United States is, in the vast majority of cases, provided through the multiple means of Social Security, private pensions, and individual savings. This is sometimes referred to as a "three-legged stool" or the three "pillars" of economic security protection. Still others look upon the situation as Social Security providing the floor of protection, with private sector activities building on top of it and public assistance programs, such as Supplemental Security Income (SSI) providing a net of protection for those whose total retirement income does not attain certain levels or meet minimum subsistence needs.

Although some people may view the Social Security program as one that should provide complete retirement protection, over the years it generally has been agreed that it should only be a floor of protection.

As described elsewhere in this book, private pension plans have, to a significant extent, been developed to supplement Social Security. This is done in a number of ways, both directly and indirectly. The net result, however, is a broad network of retirement protection.

This chapter discusses in detail the retirement provisions of the Social Security program, not only their historical development and present structure but also possible future changes.[1] Following this, other governmental retirement programs, such as the separate one for railroad workers and the numerous plans for governmental employees, are described. Then, the public assistance programs that are present to supplement other forms of retirement income, when necessary, are dealt with. Finally, the relationship of the Social Security program with governmental benefit plans which cover other risks, such as work-connected accidents, unemployment, and short-term sickness, is analyzed.

The consideration of the Social Security program in this chapter deals

---

[1] The implications of the Social Security Act Amendments of 1983 are summarized in Appendix A of this *Handbook*.

only with the retirement provisions applicable to living insured workers. Actually, the program is a closely coordinated one, also covering the risks of long-term disability and death of the breadwinner or retired worker (which are dealt with in Chapters 17 and 5, respectively).

The term *Social Security* as used here is the meaning generally accepted in the United States, namely, the cash benefits provisions of the Old-Age, Survivors, and Disability Insurance program (OASDI). International usage of the term *social security* is much broader than this and includes all other types of programs protecting individuals against the economic risks of a modern industrial system, such as unemployment, short-term sickness, work-connected accidents and diseases, and medical care costs.

OLD-AGE, SURVIVORS, AND DISABILITY INSURANCE PROGRAM

Historical Development of Retirement Provisions

When what is now the OASDI program was developed in 1934–35, it was confined entirely to retirement benefits plus lump-sum refund payments to represent the difference, if any, between employee taxes paid, plus an allowance for interest, and retirement benefits received. It was not until the 1939 act that auxiliary (or dependents) and survivors benefits were added, and not until the 1956 act that disability benefits were made available. It is likely that only retirement benefits were instituted initially because such type of protection was the most familiar to the general public, especially in light of the relatively few private pension plans then in existence.

The normal retirement age was established at 65. This figure was selected in a purely empirical manner, because it was a middle figure. Age 70 seemed too high, because of the common belief that relatively so few people reached that age, while age 60 seemed too low, because of the large costs that would be involved if that age had been selected. Many of the existing private pension plans at that time had a retirement age of 65, although some in the railroad industry used age 70. Furthermore, labor-force participation data showed that a relatively high proportion of workers continued in employment after age 60. A widely quoted reason why age 65 was selected is that Bismarck chose this age when he established the German national pension program in the 1880s; this, however is not so, because the age actually used originally in Germany was 70.

The original program applied only to workers in commerce and industry. It was not until the 1950s that coverage was extended to additional categories of workers. Now, almost all are covered, including the self-employed.

The initial legislation passed by the House of Representatives did not require eligible persons to retire when age 65 or over to receive benefits, although it was recognized that this would be essential to include in the final legislation. The Senate inserted a requirement of a general nature that benefits would be payable only upon retirement, and this was included in the final legislation. Over the years, this retirement test, or work clause, has been the subject of much controversy, and it has been considerably liberalized and made more flexible over the years.

Beginning in the 1950s, pressure developed to provide early-retirement benefits, first for spouses and then for insured workers themselves. The minimum early-retirement age was set at 62, again a pragmatic political compromise, rather than being based on any completely logical reason. The three-year differential, however, did represent about the average difference in age between men and their wives but, of course, as with any averages, the difference actually is larger in many cases. The benefit amounts are reduced when claimed before age 65, and are increased, although to not as great an extent, for delaying retirement beyond age 65.

Persons Covered

OASDI coverage—for both taxes and earnings credits toward benefit rights—currently applies to somewhat more than 90 percent of the total work force of the United States. About half of those not covered have protection through a special employee retirement system, while the remaining half are either very low-paid intermittent workers or unpaid family workers.

The vast majority of persons covered under OASDI are so affected on a mandatory, or compulsory, basis. Several categories, however, have optional or semi-optional coverage. It is important to note that OASDI coverage applies not only to employees, both salaried and wage earner, but also to self-employed persons. Some individuals who are essentially employees are nonetheless classified as self-employed for the sake of convenience in applying coverage.

Compulsory coverage is applicable to all employees in commerce and industry, interpreting these classifications very broadly, except railroad workers, who are covered under a separate program, discussed in the following section. Actually, however, financial and other coordinating provisions exist between these two programs, so that, in reality, railroad workers are really covered under OASDI. Compulsory coverage also applies to American citizens who work abroad for American corporations. Self-employed persons of all types (except ministers) also are covered compulsorily unless their earnings are minimal (i.e., less than $400 a year). From a geographical standpoint, OASDI applies not only in the 50 states and the District of Columbia but also in all outlying areas (American Samoa, Guam, Puerto Rico, and the Virgin Islands).

Elective coverage applies to a number of categories. Employees of state and local governments can have coverage at the option of the employing entity, and, in the case where a retirement system exists at the time of election, only when the current employees vote in favor of coverage.

Somewhat similar provisions apply for lay employees of churches and nonprofit charitable and educational institutions. In any event, when these organizations elect coverage, all new employees must be covered. Similar provisions are available for American employees of foreign subsidiaries of American corporations, the latter having the right to opt for coverage. In all the foregoing cases, the election of coverage can be terminated after a period of years, and currently there is some such action being taken. Approximately 75 percent of state and local government employees are now covered as a result of this election basis, while the corresponding figure for nonprofit organizations is somewhat over 85 percent.

Because of the principle of separation of church and state, ministers are covered on the self-employed basis, regardless of their actual status. Furthermore, they have the right to opt out of the system within a limited time on grounds of religious principles or conscience. Americans employed in the United States by a foreign government or by an international organization are covered compulsorily on the self-employed basis.

Eligibility Conditions

To be eligible for OASDI retirement benefits, individuals must have a certain amount of covered employment. In general, these conditions were designed to be relatively easy to meet in the early years of operation, thus bringing the program into effectiveness quickly. Eligibility for retirement benefits—termed *fully insured status*—depends upon having a certain number of "quarters of coverage" (QC), varying with the year of birth or, expressed in another manner, depending upon the year of an individual's attainment of age 62.

Before 1978, a QC was defined simply as a calendar quarter, during which the individual was paid $50 or more in wages from covered employment; the self-employed ordinarily received four QCs for each year of coverage at $400 or more of earnings. Beginning in 1978, the number of QCs acquired for each year depends upon the total earnings in the year. For 1978, each full unit of $250 of earnings produced a QC, up to a maximum of four QCs for the year. In subsequent years the requirement has increased, and will continue to increase in the future, in accordance with changes in the general wage level; for 1983, it is $370.

The number of QCs required for fully insured status is determined from the number of years in the period beginning in 1951, or with the year of attainment of age 22, if later, and the year before the year of attainment of age 62, with a minimum requirement of six. As a result, an individual who attained age 62 before 1958 needed only six QCs to be fully insured. A person attaining age 62 in 1983 has a requirement of 32 QCs, while a person attaining age 65 in 1983 needs 29 QCs. The maximum number of QCs that will ever be required for fully insured status is 40, applicable to persons attaining age 62 after 1990. It is important to note that, although the requirement for the number of QCs is determined from 1951, or attainment of age 22, and before attainment of age 62, the QCs to meet the requirement can be obtained at any time (e.g., before 1951, before age 22, and after age 61).

Beneficiary Categories

Insured workers can receive unreduced retirement benefits in the amount of the primary insurance amount, or PIA, beginning at age 65, or actuarially reduced benefits beginning at ages 62–64. For retirement at age 62, the benefit is 80 percent of the PIA.

Retired workers also can receive supplementary payments for spouses and eligible children. The spouse receives a benefit at the rate of 50 percent of the PIA if claim is first made at age 65 or over, and at a reduced rate if claimed at ages 62–64 (a 25 percent reduction at age 62—i.e., to 37.5 percent of the PIA). However, if a child under age 16 or a child aged 16 or over who was disabled before age 22 is present, the spouse receives benefits regardless of age, in an unreduced amount. Divorced spouses, when the marriage had lasted at least 10 years, are eligible for benefits under the same conditions as undivorced spouses. Children under age 18 (and children aged 18 or over and disabled before age 22, plus children attending high school full-time at age 18 also are eligible for benefits, at a rate of 50 percent of the PIA; prior to legislation in 1981, post-secondary school students aged 18–21 were eligible for benefits, and spouses with children in their care could receive benefits as long as a child under age 18 was present. An overall maximum on total family benefits is applicable as is discussed later. If a person is eligible for more than one type of benefit (e.g., both as a worker and as a spouse), in essence only the largest benefit is payable.

Benefit Computation Procedures and Indexing

As indicated in the previous section, OASDI benefits are based on the PIA. The method of computing the PIA is quite complicated, especially because several different methods are available. The only method dealt with here in any detail is that generally applicable to people who reach age 65 after 1981.

Persons who attained age 65 before 1982 use a method based on the average monthly wage (AMW). This is based essentially on a career average, involving the consideration of all earnings back through 1951. To take into account the general inflation in earnings that has occurred in the last three decades, automatic-adjustment procedures are involved in the benefit computations. However, these turned out to be faulty, because they did not—and would not in the future—produce stable benefit results when comparing initial benefits with final earnings. Accordingly, in the 1977 amendments, a new procedure applicable to those attaining age 62 after 1978 was adopted, but the old procedure was retained for earlier attainments of age

62. The result has been to give unusually and inequitably large benefits to those who attained age 62 before 1979, thus creating a "notch" situation.

Persons who attain age 62 in 1979–83 can use an alternative method somewhat similar to the AMW method, but with it having certain restrictions, if this produces a larger PIA than the new, permanent method. In actual practice, however, this modified-AMW method generally produces more favorable results only for persons attaining age 62 in 1979–81 and not continuing in employment after that age.

A still different method is available for all individuals if they have earnings before 1951. In the vast majority of such cases, however, the new-start methods based on earnings after 1950 produce more favorable results.

The first step in the ongoing permanent method of computing the PIA applicable to persons attaining age 65 in 1982 or after, is to calculate the average indexed monthly earnings (AIME). The AIME is a career-average earnings formula, but it is determined in such a manner as to closely approximate a final average formula. In a national social insurance plan, it would be inadvisable to use solely an average of the last few years of employment, because that could involve serious manipulation through the cooperation of both the employee and the employer, whereas in a private pension plan, the employer has a close financial interest not to do so. Furthermore, as described later, OASDI benefit computation is not proportionate to years of coverage or proportion of worklife in covered employment, as is the case for private pension plans generally.

The first step in computing the AIME is to determine the number of years over which it must be computed. On the whole, such number depends solely on the year in which the individual attains age 62. The general rule is that the computation period equals the number of years beginning with 1951, or the year of attaining age 22, if later, up through the year before attainment of age 62, minus the so-called five dropout years. The latter is provided so the very lowest five years of earnings can be eliminated.

As an example, persons attaining age 62 in 1983 have a computation period of 27 years (the 32 years in 1951–82, minus 5). The maximum period will be 35 years for those attaining age 62 after 1990. For the infrequent case of an individual who had qualified for disability benefits under OASDI (see Chapter 17) and who recovered from the disability, the number of computation years for the AIME for retirement benefits is reduced by the number of full years after age 21 and before age 62 during which the person was under a disability.

The AIME is not computed from the actual covered earnings, but after indexing them, to make them more current at the time of retirement. Specifically, covered earnings for each year before attainment of age 60 are indexed to that age, while all subsequent covered earnings are used in their actual amount. No earnings before 1951 can be utilized, but all earnings subsequently, either before age 22 or after age 61, are considered.

The indexing of the earnings record is accomplished by multiplying the actual earnings of each year before the year that age 60 was attained by the increase in earnings from the particular year to the age-60 year. For example, for persons attaining age 62 in 1983 (i.e., age 60 in 1981), any earnings in 1951 would be converted to indexed earnings by multiplying them by 4.920, which is the ratio of the nationwide average wage in 1981 to that in 1951. Similarly, the multiplying factor for 1952 earnings is 4.632, and so on. Once the earnings record for each year in the past has been indexed, the earnings for the number of years required to be averaged are selected to include the highest ones possible; if there are not sufficient years with earnings, then zeroes must be used. Then, the AIME is obtained by dividing the total indexed earnings for such years by 12 times such number of years.

Now, having obtained the AIME, the PIA is computed from a benefit formula. There is a different formula for each annual cohort of persons attaining age 62. For example, for those who reached age 62 in 1979, the formula was 90 percent of the first $180 of AIME, plus 32 percent of the next $905 of AIME, plus 15 percent of the AIME in excess of $1,085. For the 1980 cohort, the corresponding dollar bands are $194, $977, and $1,171, while those for the 1981 cohort are $211, $1,063, and $1,274, those for the 1982 cohort are $230, $1,158, and $1,388, and those for the 1983 cohort are $254, $1,274, and $1,528. These bands are adjusted automatically according to changes in nationwide average wages.

Prior to legislation in 1981, if the PIA benefit formula produced a smaller amount than $122 in the initial benefit computation, then this amount was nonetheless payable. However, for persons first becoming eligible after 1981, no such minimum is applicable.

A special minimum applies to the PIA for individuals who have a long period of covered work, but with low earnings. As of June 1982, this minimum is $17.26 times the "years of coverage" in excess of 10, but not in excess of 30; thus, for 30 or more years of coverage, the minimum benefit is $345.10. A "year of coverage" is defined as a year in which earnings are at least 25 percent of the maximum taxable earnings base; for 1979 and after, this base is taken to be what would have prevailed if the ad hoc increases in the base provided by the 1977 act had not been applicable, and, instead, the automatic increases had occurred. Thus, for this purpose, the 1983 base is taken as $26,700, instead of the actual one of $35,700.

The resulting PIAs then are increased for any automatic adjustments applicable because of increases in the consumer price index (CPI) that occur in or after the year of attaining age 62, even though actual retirement is much later. These automatic adjustments are made for benefits for each June, if the average CPI for the first quarter of the year increases by at least 3 percent over such average for the previous year, or for the latest previous base year, if the increase had been less than 3 percent. Such CPI increases in the recent past have been 9.9 percent for 1979, 14.3 percent for 1980, 11.2 percent for 1981, and 7.4 percent for 1982.

The resulting PIA then is reduced, in the manner described previously, for those who first claim benefits before age 65. Conversely, retired workers who do not receive benefits for any months after they attain age 65, essentially because of the earnings test, which will be described later, receive increases that are termed *delayed-retirement credits.* Such credits are at the rate of 3 percent per year of delay (actually, .25 percent per month) for the period between ages 65 and 72. For those who attained age 65 before 1982, such credit is at a rate of only 1 percent per year. The credit applies only to the worker's benefit and not to that for spouses or children. A maximum family benefit (MFB) is applicable when there are more than two beneficiaries receiving benefits on the same earnings record (i.e., the retired worker and two or more auxiliary beneficiaries). Not considered within the limit established by the MFB are the additional benefits arising from delayed-retirement credits and the benefits payable to divorced spouses. The MFB is determined prior to any reductions, because of claiming benefits before age 65, but after the effect of the earnings test as it applies to any auxiliary beneficiary (e.g., if the spouse has high earnings, any potential benefit payable to her or him would not be considered for purposes of the MFB of the other spouse).

The MFB is determined from the PIA by a complex formula. This formula varies for each cohort of persons attaining age 62 in a year. The resulting MFB is adjusted for increases in the CPI in the future (in the same manner as is the PIA). For the 1983 cohort, the MFB formula is: 150 percent of the first $324 of PIA, plus 272 percent of the next $144 of PIA, plus 134 percent of the next $142 of PIA, plus 175 percent of PIA in excess of $610. For future cohorts, the dollar figures are changed according to changes in nationwide average wages. The result of this formula is to produce MFBs that are 150 percent of the PIA for the lowest PIAs, with this proportion rising to a peak of 188 percent for middle-range PIAs and then falling off to 175 percent—and levelling there—for higher PIAs.

Earnings Test and Other Restrictions on Benefits

From the inception of the OASDI program, there has been some form of restriction on the payment of benefits to persons who have substantial earnings from employment. This provision is referred to as the "earnings or retirement test." It does not apply to nonearned income, such as from investments or pensions. The general underlying principle of this test is that retirement benefits should be paid only to persons who are substantially retired.

The basic features of the earnings test is that an annual exempt amount applies, so that full benefits are paid if earnings, including those from both covered and noncovered employment, are not in excess thereof. Then, for each $2 of excess earnings, $1 in benefits is withheld. For persons aged 65 or over (at any time in the year), the annual exempt amount is $6,600 for 1983, with the amounts for subsequent years being automatically determined by the increases in nationwide wages. Beginning with the month of attainment of age 70 (age 72 prior to 1983), the test no longer applies. For persons under age 65, the exempt amount is $4,920 for 1983, with automatic adjustment thereafter.

An alternative test applies for the initial year of retirement, or claim, if it results in more benefits being payable. Under this, full benefits are payable for all months in which the individual did not have substantial services in self-employment and had wages of $1/12$ of the annual exempt amount or less. This provision properly takes care of the situation where an individual fully retires during a year, but had sizable earnings in the first part of the year, and thus would have most or all of the benefits withheld if only the annual test had been applicable.

Earnings of the "retired" worker affect, under the earnings test, the total family benefits payable. However, if an auxiliary beneficiary (spouse or child) has earnings, and these are sizable enough to affect the earnings test, any reduction in benefits is applicable only to such individual's benefits.

If an individual receives a pension from service under a government-employee pension plan under which the members were not covered under OASDI on the last day of her or his employment, the OASDI spouse benefit is reduced by the amount of such pension. This provision, however, is not applicable to women—or to men who are dependent on their wives—who become eligible for such a pension before December 1982, while for December 1982 through June 1983, the provision applies only to those (both men and women) who cannot prove dependency on their spouse. This general provision results in the same treatment as occurs when both spouses have OASDI benefits based on their own earnings records; and then each receives such benefit, plus the excess, if any, of the spouse's benefit arising from the other spouse's earnings over the benefit based on their own earnings, rather than the full amount of the spouse's benefit.

Financing

Ever since its inception, the OASDI program has been financed entirely by payroll taxes, with only minor exceptions, such as the special benefits at a subminimum level for certain persons without insured status who attained age 72 before 1972. Thus, on a permanent ongoing basis, no payments from general revenues are available to the OASDI system; the payments for covered federal civilian employees and members of the armed forces are properly considered as "employer" taxes.

The payroll taxes for the retirement and survivor benefits go into the OASI trust fund, and all benefit payments and administrative expenses for these provisions are paid therefrom. The balances in the trust fund are invested in federal government obligations of various types, with interest rates at the current market values. The federal government does not guarantee the payments of benefits. If the trust fund were to be depleted, it could not obtain grants, or even loans, from the general treasury. However, a temporary provision (effective only in 1982) permitted the OASI trust fund to borrow, repayable with interest, from the DI and HI trust funds; a total of $17.5 billion was borrowed ($12.4 billion from HI).

Payroll taxes are levied on earnings up to only a certain annual limit, which is termed the *earnings base*. This base is applicable to the earnings of an individual from each employer in the year, but the person can obtain a refund (on the income-tax form) for all employee taxes paid in excess of those on the earnings base. The self-employed pay taxes on their self-employment income on no more than the excess of the earnings base over any wages which they may have had.

Since 1975, the earnings base has been determined by the automatic-adjustment procedure, on the basis of increases in the nationwide average wage. However, for 1979–81, ad hoc increases of a higher amount were legislated; the 1981 base was established at $29,700. The 1982 and 1983 bases of $32,400 and $35,700 were determined under the automatic-adjustment provision.

The payroll tax rate is a combined one for OASI, disability insurance (DI), and hospital insurance (HI), but it is allocated among the three trust funds. The employer and employee rates are the same, but the self-employed pay approximately 1.5 times the employee rates for OASI and DI, but the same as the employee rate for HI.

The employer and employee rates were 1 percent each in 1937–49, but have gradually increased over the years, until being 6.65 percent in 1981 and 6.70 percent in 1982–84 (the latter subdivided 4.575 percent for OASI, 0.825 percent for DI, and 1.3 percent for HI). These rates are scheduled to increase to 7.05 percent in 1985, 7.15 percent in 1986, and 7.65 percent in 1990 (and after), the latter being subdivided 5.1 percent for OASI, 1.1 percent for DI, and 1.45 percent for HI. The ultimate (1990 and after) rate for the self-employed is 10.75 percent.

In the mid-1970s, the OASI trust fund (and the DI trust fund as well) were projected to have serious financing problems over both the long range and the short range. This was thought to be remedied as to the short range by the 1977 act, which raised taxes (both the rates and the bases). At the same time, the long-range problem was partially solved by phased-in significant benefit reductions, by lowering the general benefit level, by freezing the minimum benefit, and by the "spouse government pension" offset, although an estimated deficit situation was still present for the period beginning after about 30 years.

As experience turned out, the short-range problem was not really solved. The actuarial cost estimates assumed that earnings would rise at a somewhat more rapid rate than prices in the short range, but the reverse occurred— and to a significant extent—in 1979–81. Because increases in tax income depend on earnings and because increases in benefit outgo depend on prices, the financial result for the OASI trust fund was catastrophic; and it would have been exhausted in late 1982 if it had not been for legislation enacted in 1981. The DI trust fund did not have this problem, because the disability experience, which had worsened significantly in 1970–76, turned around and became relatively favorable—more than offsetting the unfavorable economic experience.

The 1981 legislation significantly reduced benefit outgo in the short range by the following actions:

1. The regular minimum benefit (an initial PIA of $122) was eliminated for all new eligibles after 1981, except covered members of religious orders under a vow of poverty.
2. Child school-attendance benefits at ages 18–21 were eliminated by a gradual phase-out, except for high school students aged 18.
3. Mother's and father's benefits with respect to nondisabled children terminate when the youngest child is age 16 (formerly age 18).
4. Lump-sum death payments were eliminated, except when a surviving spouse who was living with the deceased worker is present, or when a spouse or child is eligible for immediate monthly benefits.
5. Sick pay in the first six months of illness is considered to be covered wages.
6. Lowering of the exempt age under the earnings test to age 70 in 1982 was delayed until 1983.
7. Workers' compensation offset against disability benefits was extended to several other types of governmental disability benefits.
8. Interfund borrowing among the OASI, DI, and HI trust funds is permitted, but only until December 31, 1982, and then no more than sufficient to allow payments of OASI benefits through June 1983.

Possible Future Developments

The 1981 amendments, described above, did not take action in certain broad areas that will now be discussed.

Advisory groups have, over the years, urged that there should be so-called universal coverage. Nothing was done in the 1981 legislation about covering the few employee categories not now covered—namely, permanent federal employees, some state and local government employees, and some employees of nonprofit organizations. However, further steps were taken to reduce the windfall benefits that persons who are primarily in such employment can receive from OASDI.

Also, there has been growing support for increasing the minimum retirement age at which unreduced benefits are payable from the present 65 to, say, 68. This would be done in recognition of the significant increase in life expectancy that has occurred in the last 40 years, as well as the likely future increases. This change would, at the same time, reduce the long-range future cost of the program (although it would still be higher than the cost at present).

The earnings test has always been subject to criticism by many persons, who argue that it is a disincentive to continued employment and that "the benefits have been bought and paid for, and therefore should be available at age 65." The Reagan administration recommended that this test be eliminated after age 65, but the 1981 amendments did not do this, but rather moved slightly in the other direction—by postponing for one year the moving of the exempt age down from 72 to 70.

The general benefit level was significantly increased in 1969–72 (by about 23 percent in real terms), but financial problems caused this to be partially reversed in subsequent legislation (1974 and 1977). Nonetheless, there will be efforts by many persons to reverse the situation and expand the benefit level.

Over the years, the composition of the OASDI benefit structure— between individual-equity aspects and social-adequacy ones—tended to shift more toward social adequacy. The 1981 amendments, however, moved in the other direction (e.g., by phasing out student benefits and the minimum-benefit provision). There may well be efforts in the future to inject more social adequacy into the program—or, conversely, more individual equity.

It frequently has been advocated that people should be allowed to opt out of the OASDI system and provide their own economic security through private-sector mechanisms, using both their own taxes and those of their employer. Although this approach has certain appealing aspects, it has some significant drawbacks. First, it is not possible to duplicate to any close extent the various features of OASDI, most importantly the automatic adjustment of benefits for increases in the CPI.

Second, because the low-cost individuals (young, high-earnings ones) would be the most likely to opt out, there is the question of where the resulting financing shortfalls of the OASDI program would come from, with respect to the high-cost persons remaining in it. Those who make such proposals (or even the more extreme ones, which involve terminating OASDI for all except those currently covered) do not answer this question. The only source of financing would be from general revenues, and this means more general taxes, which would be paid to a considerable extent by those who have opted out!

Many proposals have been made in the past that part of the cost of OASDI should be met from general revenues. At times, this has been advocated to be done in an indirect manner, such as by moving part of the HI tax rate to OASDI and then partially financing HI from general revenues. The difficulty of this procedure is that there are no available general-revenues monies; but instead, the general fund of the Treasury has large deficits. In turn, this would mean either that additional taxes of other types would have to be raised or that the budget deficit would become larger, and inflation would be fueled. Those opposed to general-revenues financing of OASDI, and of HI as well, believe that the financing, instead, should be entirely from direct, visible payroll taxes. Nonetheless, it is likely that there will continue to be pressure for general-revenues financing of OASDI.

RAILROAD RETIREMENT (RR) PROGRAM

The OASDI system covers virtually all nongovernment wage employment except for railroad employees, who are covered by the Railroad Retirement system. This separate system is coordinated closely with OASDI, and its general structure is similar. The retirement benefits are significantly higher and the retirement conditions are more liberal. RR is a social insurance program, although it has certain characteristics of large multi-employer, private pension plans.

Eligibility Conditions

The eligibility conditions for all types of benefits require 120 months of railroad service. If a person does not meet the eligibility condition, then the earnings record is transferred to OASDI for whatever benefit rights it will produce.

Monthly Beneficiary Categories and Rates

Retirement benefits are available on a full-rate basis at age 65 or, with 30 years of service, at age 60. Benefits are also available at ages 62–64 for those with fewer than 30 years of service, but on a reduced-rate basis using the same factors as OASDI.

The benefits are payable only if the individual ceases work for a railroad or the last nonrailroad employer. Tier-1 consists essentially of a benefit amount equivalent to the OASDI benefit based on combined RR–OASDI earnings. Benefits under Tier-2 are not payable for any month when the individual works for a railroad, or the last nonrailroad employer, but they are payable regardless of other employment.

Full-rate spouse benefits are payable to retirement beneficiaries (1) if the spouse is age 60 or over and the worker had at least 30 years of service, (2) if the spouse is age 62 or over, or (3) if the spouse is caring for a child under age 16 or disabled, and the worker is age 62 or over. If the spouse cannot meet the foregoing conditions but is age 62–64, reduced benefits are available.

RR does not pay benefits to all the categories that OASDI does (e.g., child's benefits for retired beneficiaries). This difference, however, is recognized, and compensated for in some cases, by the Social Security minimum guarantee (to be discussed later).

Benefit Amounts

The formula used to determine retirement benefit amounts was complex for employees who were covered before 1975 and who retired in the past, but it is much simpler for later entrants. For new entrants, the components in the monthly benefit are:

1. OASDI benefit based on RR-OASDI earnings.
2. The factor 0.7 percent, times years of service, times average compensation in highest 60 months.
3. For 25 years of service and a current connection with RR, a supplemental annuity of $23 for 25 years of service, increasing to $43 for 30 or more years (applicable only for employees hired before November 1981).

Credited RR wages have differed from those under OASDI because the maximum earnings bases were not usually identical. The RR bases have been monthly, whereas under OASDI they have been annual. Also, the RR bases were generally higher, although the same during 1966–78.

After 1978, RR will have two bases for benefit purposes—the OASDI or Tier-1 base for item (1) above and what the OASDI base would have been if the ad hoc increases in 1979–81 had not been legislated, but rather the automatic-adjustment provisions had applied, for item (3) above, part of Tier-2. The resulting figures for Tier-2 for 1983 are $2,975 and $2,225.

The OASDI benefit component is increased for changes in the CPI in the same manner as OASDI benefits. The second component is increased after retirement by 32.5 percent of the CPI increase. The third component is not subject to CPI adjustments.

Beneficiaries at the end of 1974 continued to receive the same benefit amount as previously. However, their benefit was divided into (1) an OASDI component (after considering any OASDI benefit from OASDI earnings), (2) a windfall dual benefit (derived from the advantage gained from having a separate OASDI benefit when having covered employment under both systems), and (3) the residual. The first will be increased in the future for changes in the CPI just as OASDI benefits; the third will be increased by the 32.5 percent procedure.

The Social Security minimum-guarantee provision is that the total family benefit will not be less than the OASDI benefit, based on the same wage record. This provision had little effect in the recent past and will have even less in the future. It is only through it that child's benefits, as under OASDI, are recognized.

Spouse Benefit Amounts

Spouse's annuities are 50 percent of the Tier-1 component, plus 45 percent of the Tier-2 component of the employee's annuity, except for the supplemental annuity, but subject to reductions for being under age 65 when benefits are initially claimed or, as to the OASDI or Tier-1 component, for OASDI benefits on the spouse's own earnings record. Frozen windfall dual spouse's benefits also are provided.

The CPI adjustments for spouse's annuities are made in the same way as for employee annuities, except that the entire Tier-2 benefit is so adjusted.

Financing

RR has always been financed on a self-supporting basis from payroll taxes on employers and employees. In 1974, a government subsidy was introduced to pay for the windfall dual benefits. A financial interchange provision with OASDI results in payments from OASDI to RR to compensate for the fact that the RR group is a high-cost one (largely because of its age composition); the theory of this provision is that OASDI neither gains nor loses financially because railroad workers are not covered by it.

The RR taxes are deposited in the RR account; the benefit payments and administrative expenses are disbursed from it. The payments under the financial interchange with OASDI and HI likewise are made to (or from) the account. The assets are invested in government bonds, just as is done for the OASDI trust funds, except that more favorable treatment is given to RR.

The RR tax rate for employees is the rate under OASDI-HI, plus 2 percent. The employer rate is the sum of (1) the employer OASDI-HI rate, and (2) 11.75 percent of taxable payroll. The employee OASDI-HI rate and the matching employer rate are payable on the Tier-1 base, and the additional 2 percent employee rate and the 11.75 percent employer rate applies to the Tier-2 base.

In addition, the employers pay the cost of the supplemental annuities (item 3, as previously listed). This is financed by a tax determined quarterly by the RR Board in terms of cents per hour worked; the rate was 18.5 cents in early 1983.

GOVERNMENT EMPLOYEE PLANS

The first governmental retirement plans in the United States were for military personnel and veterans of military service. Then came plans for civilian employees of the federal government and of various state and local entities. Many of these plans are coordinated with OASDI, as is common in the private sector, but others merely added OASDI on top (e.g., the military plan). Yet other plans are the sole retirement protection (e.g., the plan for general civilian employees of the federal government).

Civil Service Retirement (CSR) System

CSR is completely independent of OASDI, although it could readily be integrated with it. The logic always has been for coordination by providing coverage under the latter and adjusting the former. Federal employees have opposed OASDI coverage and coordination of CSR with OASDI. This opposition arose because career employees have an advantage by having CSR separate (although this is not true for short-term employees). About 80 percent of career employees qualify for dual benefits and thus have the windfall arising from the heavily weighted OASDI benefits for short periods of coverage and low covered earnings.

Virtually all federal civilian employees are under CSR. The only exceptions are those who are covered under certain small special systems, and temporary employees who are covered under OASDI. Members of Congress and their employees are covered under CSR on a voluntary basis and have special benefit conditions.

The retirement benefits are payable under several combinations of age and service—namely, age 55 with 30 years of service, age 60 with 20 years of service, and age 62 with 5 years of service. Special provisions apply for involuntary separation without cause—namely, any age with 25 years of service, and age 50 with 20 years of service, with a reduction of 2 percent for each year below age 55.

The basic pension is determined from the years of service and the average salary during the highest three consecutive years. The formula for general employees is 1.5 percent per year for the first five years of service, 1.75 percent per year for the next five years, and 2.0 percent per year thereafter to a maximum of 80.0 percent.

Higher benefit factors apply for certain special groups. For example, members of Congress and Congressional employees have a 2.5 percent benefit rate for all years of service.

Individuals withdrawing from service who are not eligible for an immediate pension may elect a deferred pension at age 62 if they have at least five years of service. In lieu of a deferred pension, and in all cases of less than five years of service, the withdrawing employee can receive a lump-sum refund of the CSR contributions. No interest is paid, except when there is at least one year of service, but fewer than five years.

If survivor benefits for the spouse are desired after retirement, a reduction in the basic pension is made (see Chapter 5).

Automatic cost-of-living adjustments for CSR pensions are made annually based on the percentage increase in the CPI over a 12-month period (except that, for 1983, 1984, and 1985, the payments are made at 13-month intervals, although still based on 12-month CPI increases).

The CSR employee contribution rate is 7.0 percent, although it is 7.5 percent for congressional employees and 8.0 percent for members of Congress—in *partial* recognition of their more liberal benefits. The remainder of the cost is borne by the federal government, about 33 percent of payroll, although not quite met on a current basis, but nearly so.

Retirement Systems for Other Federal Civilian Groups

Both the Tennessee Valley Authority and the Board of Governors of the Federal Reserve Bank have established pension plans for their employees. In both instances, OASDI coverage is applicable, and the supplementary pension plans are quite similar to those of private employers.

Employees of the State Department and certain related agencies who are in the Foreign Service have a separate retirement system which resembles CSR but has significantly more liberal provisions. The pension rate is 2 percent for all years of service, and the normal retirement age is 50 with 20 years of service. The employees contribute 7 percent, as under CSR, and the government meets the balance of the cost, which averages about 60 percent of payroll.

Supreme Court justices and other federal judges have a noncontributory system, with retirement at age 70 after 10 years of service, at age 65 with 15 years of service, or for disability. Their salary continues for life, and the retired pay increases just as does the salary of active judges.

Military Retirement System

In addition to OASDI, members of the military services are covered by a noncontributory pension plan, which is operated on a completely pay-as-you-go basis from current appropriations. Retirement is after 20 years of service. Retirement before 20 years is possible only for disability (and even then the pension may not be payable, because a larger benefit would often be available from the Veterans Administration, as described subsequently).

The retired pay is 2.5 percent of final pay for each year of service, up to 30 years. Such pay includes only the basic pay, plus increments for service, and does not include the various allowances. There are no vesting provisions for those with an insufficient number of years to qualify for immediate retirement. A small reduction is made to provide survivor protection after retirement (see Chapter 5).

The pensions are subject to automatic adjustment for changes in the cost of living in about the same manner as under CSR.

Retirement Systems for State and Local Government Employees

There are many separate retirement systems for employees of state and local governments. The general pattern is that the state has two separate systems for its employees: one for school teachers and the other for general employees. The state law-enforcement officers have either a separate system or more liberal provisions within the general program.

Local governments often have separate retirement systems, although in some cases their employees are covered by a state program. Almost invariably, local governments have separate retirement systems for police and firemen with very liberal benefits and usually with very early retirement provisions.

A wide divergence exists among the various state and local systems about whether they have elected OASDI coverage. In some instances, OASDI was merely added on top of the previous plan, whereas in other cases there was coordination with OASDI, as is generally done in private plans.

In general, the benefit level, including the effect of OASDI, where present, is relatively high. Like CSR, liberal early retirement is possible with full benefits.

Most state and local retirement systems, other than plans for police and firemen, are on a contributory basis. Employee contributions are usually at a level of 5 to 7 percent. The cost met by the government entity is usually at least twice as large as the employee share. In police and firemen plans, the employer cost often exceeds 50 percent of payroll. Many state and local retirement systems are financed on an actuarial funding basis, but many others are inadequately funded.

SUPPLEMENTAL SECURITY INCOME (SSI) PROGRAM

The SSI program replaced the federal/state public assistance programs of aid to the aged, blind, and disabled, except in Guam, Puerto Rico, and the Virgin Islands. Persons must be at least age 65 to qualify for the SSI payments for the aged (see Chapter 17 for discussion of the blind and disabled categories).

The basic payment amount, before reduction for other income, for July 1982 through June 1983 is $284.30 per month for one recipient and 50 percent more for an eligible couple. An automatic-adjustment provision closely paralleling that used under OASDI is applicable.

A number of "income disregards" are present. The most important is the disregard of $20 of income per month per family from such sources as OASDI, other pensions, earnings, and investments. The first $65 per month of earned income is disregarded, plus 50 percent of the remainder.

SSI has certain resource exemptions. In order to receive SSI, resources cannot exceed $1,500 for an individual and $2,250 for a couple. However, in determining resources, certain items are excluded—the home, household goods, personal effects, an automobile, and property needed for self-support—if these are found to be reasonable. Also, if life insurance policies have a face amount of $1,500 or less for an individual, their cash values are not counted as assets.

Some states pay supplements to SSI.

RELATIONSHIP OF OASDI PROGRAM WITH OTHER GOVERNMENTAL PROGRAMS

The retirement benefits payable under the OASDI program parallel those available under other governmental programs. The preceding sections have described how the OASDI benefits are coordinated or not coordinated, as the case may be, with those under the Railroad Retirement program, government-employee retirement plans, and the Supplemental Security Income program. Finally, the relationship of OASDI retirement benefits with governmental programs covering various other social risks is discussed.

Workers' Compensation (WC)

The payment of both cash and medical-care benefits under the various state and federal workers' compensation programs (for work-connected accidents and diseases) will often overlap with OASDI and Medicare benefits. However, there will generally be little overlap with OASDI retirement benefits, although there will be considerable overlap with the OASDI disability and survivor benefits and the Medicare benefits (these situations are discussed in Chapters 17, 5, and 9, respectively).

An individual can receive both OASDI retirement benefits (note that OASDI disability benefits are automatically converted to retirement benefits at age 65) and WC benefits for an event which occurred before age 65, or even after then, without any reduction in the full amount of either benefit. A few state WC systems, however, do reduce their benefits when OASDI benefits are paid. In some cases, this may mean that the combined benefit income exceeds the previous net take-home pay of the individual. This could possibly be justified on the grounds that the "excess" income is an indemnification for the loss of physical faculties due to the work-connected cause, and that any resulting disincentives to return to work are not important with respect to persons aged 65 or over.

Unemployment Insurance (UI)

Benefits under state unemployment insurance programs are usually paid for, at most, 39 weeks for a given spell of unemployment. Thus, there can be some overlap with OASDI retirement benefits for a short period. This will often occur at retirement, and the separation is (or can be made to seem) compensable under UI. However, federal legislation prevents this by requiring that state UI laws provide for the offset of OASDI retirement benefits against any UI benefits payable.

Temporary Disability Insurance (TDI)

Five states and Puerto Rico have established temporary disability insurance, or cash sickness benefits, programs. There is little likelihood of overlap between OASDI retirement benefits and TDI benefits. This would only occur in the case where retirement occurs because of illness. Under such circumstances, the maximum duration of TDI benefits would generally be only 26 weeks. There is, however, the danger that persons may retire under normal conditions and feign sickness, in whole or in part, to qualify for TDI benefits.

CHAPTER 29

Pension Plans— Basic Features

NORMA NIELSON

A pension plan should be beneficial to the employees, affordable by the employer, and provide the desired tax advantages to both parties. This chapter examines the various aspects of the plan that must be considered to assure these objectives are achieved and introduces some of the alternatives available in pension plan design.

WHO IS INVOLVED

The parties involved in a pension plan are the sponsors, the participants, and the governmental regulators. The purpose of this chapter is to describe the roles of each of these parties in the decision making relative to the design of a pension plan.

The Role of the Sponsor

The sponsor is the employer—a person or corporation—that makes the decision to offer retirement benefits and that bears a substantial portion of the cost of the plan. In the absence of collective bargaining, it controls all the elements of the plan's design. It establishes the requirements for employee eligibility and participation, sets the terms and benefits of the plan based on cost estimates, and chooses the insurance company or trust company to administer the plan.

Eligibility Requirements. Pension plans generally are established to meet the sponsor's actual or perceived obligation to long-term employees of the firm. The sponsor may feel that those employees with the longest terms of service should have highest priority, and the eligibility requirements for pension benefits frequently are more restrictive than for other employee benefits provided by the firm. The specific provisions are discussed later in this chapter.

Benefits and Cost Estimates. After the sponsor has determined which employees are to be covered under the pension plan, a specific benefit structure must be designed. The employer must decide:

1. What percentage of salary the pension plan will replace for employees with a given amount of service.
2. Whether the benefit amount will be specified in the plan or determined solely by contributions made to the plan and investment results.
3. Whether the benefit will be based on the career earnings of the employee or on average earnings for some shorter period such as the five years preceding retirement.
4. Whether benefits will be integrated with Social Security and, if so, what type of integration formula to use.
5. The amount of benefits to which the employee will be entitled if he or she leaves employment before retirement.
6. Whether any death or disability benefits are to be included.

The sponsor must begin with a tentative plan design that meets the income objectives established for the plan. This preliminary design is then submitted to either the insurance company's pension department or to the sponsor's consulting actuary. Actuarial methods using extensive demographic data on the age, sex, dependent status, employment history, and so on of the employees provide estimates of the direct costs of the plan. Indirect costs involved with implementing the plan also should be recognized. At the very least, the sponsor is expected to make any needed payroll deductions, make the contribution payments, and submit completed applications for benefits. The sponsor may agree to perform some additional administrative functions, such as disbursement of monthly benefit checks or extensive employee educational programs, in return for a further reduction in plan costs. Estimates of total costs for the various years may influence the sponsor to redesign some elements of the plan, such as eligibility or benefits, or to redistribute administrative responsibility to keep costs within acceptable limits.

Insured versus Trust Fund Plan.   Pension plans can be established either through an insurance company or a trust fund. In traditional insured plans, the insurance company makes an estimate of the mortality experience expected under a plan and also estimates the expected investment return on the contributions to the plan. These estimates are used to price the contract(s) needed to fulfill the promises of the pension plan. The plan may provide one or more insurance company contracts for each covered employee. These individual policy plans generally are used for groups with fewer than 10 participants. They may be convenient for some larger groups but are seldom used for groups as large as 50 participants because the administration of the plan becomes very burdensome. The type of contract used in individual policy plans varies depending upon the type of death benefit, if any, provided by the retirement plan. Some type of cash value life insurance is used if death benefits are to be provided; single premium or installment premium annuity contracts are more appropriate if no death benefits are provided. Individual policy plans are one example of allocated funding instruments (i.e., each dollar of sponsor contribution is assigned to a particular employee).

For larger employee groups, it is impractical to have separate contracts for each individual employee, and pension plan participants are covered under a single contract. Group pension contracts first developed as group permanent and group deferred annuities. These group contracts are direct counterparts of the individual contracts, in that they are also allocated funding instruments. The group permanent contract provides death benefits and policy values corresponding to an individual whole life policy. The group deferred annuity provides a buildup of funds to be used to provide monthly retirement benefits; no death benefits are provided, except a return of any employee contributions, usually with interest.

In most insured plans, the bulk of the expenses are paid by the insurance company out of margins in their premium rates. Margins for expenses and contingencies range from 5 percent or less for a large group deferred annuity contract to as high as 20 percent of the gross premium for individual insurance and annuity contracts.

Unallocated contracts also are available from insurers. Under this arrangement, all employer contributions are held in an undivided account and credited with the interest rate specified in the contract. Under one form of unallocated contract, a deposit administration contract, withdrawals are made from the deposit account to purchase the appropriate life annuity for a retiring participant. Under smaller plans, the insurer deducts an annual contract charge from the deposit account to cover expenses. In larger plans, the insurer usually recovers its expenses by earning a higher rate of return on invested assets than is credited to the contract and, therefore, may not impose a direct contract charge.

Over the last 25 years, the high rates of investment return available from noninsured plans have resulted in growing competition and forced the development of more innovative insured pension contracts. Immediate participation guarantee (IPG) contracts, which allow the insurer to credit actual rates of investment return, mortality, and expense experience to plan sponsors or plan participants, or both, were the first to be developed. Under another type of arrangement, the insurer and sponsor mutually agree to have the plan assets maintained in a separate account. This allows the sponsor a great deal of investment flexibility and control. One of the more recent contracts introduced is the "investment only" contract, where the sponsor does not purchase the usual administrative services, payment services, or minimum guarantees. These newer unallocated funding contracts enable the plan sponsor to purchase only needed services from the insurance company.

The primary alternative to insured pension plans is the trust fund plan. The trust is administered by a trust company, the trust department of a bank, or by any other corporation that has the ability to manage the funds, make the benefit payments, and is willing to assume the fiduciary responsibility for the pension's assets. Under such plans the sponsor's pension contribution is deposited either on an allocated or unallocated basis, together with any employee contributions, into the trust. At retirement, the accumulated assets are used to pay benefits directly or to purchase group single premium annuities if the sponsor does not wish to assume the responsibility for the mortality experience during the retirement years.

A trust fund plan usually is charged two types of fees. An investment fee is assessed annually or quarterly, and generally is a percentage of the market value of the trust fund. The percentage decreases as the size of the fund increases, and may be adjusted to reflect the trustee's degree of responsibility. A small remittance fee also is assessed for each benefit check the trustee prepares and mails. The sponsor may pay these fees and any reimbursable expenses directly or may authorize the trustee to charge them against the assets of the fund.

Often, plan eligibility and benefits influence—or even dictate—the funding instrument to be used; the funding instrument should never dictate the benefit provisions. The sponsor's own specific circumstances and objectives must be analyzed carefully before a decision is made on the funding instrument to be used. The need or desire for investment and contribution flexibility is an important consideration, as are the sponsor's tax objectives. The most important tax consideration is, of course, whether to establish a qualified plan. Beyond this, a plan that provides contribution flexibility also provides an increased ability to manage future tax liability. An existing bargaining agreement could influence the choice of a funding instrument as well.

The sponsor's size is of considerable significance when weighing the costs of the various funding instruments. The cost estimates themselves should not be the sole variable used in selecting a funding instrument, however. Estimating the cost of a pension plan is very complex, and many funding instruments permit a wide choice of actuarial cost methods and assumptions. The cost method used does not influence the ultimate cost of the plan, except to the extent investment income will be affected by the incidence of contributions. The specific cost estimates received by a plan sponsor, therefore, should have little or no bearing on the final selection of a funding instrument or funding agency. The flexibility of a particular funding instrument in permitting a wide choice of actuarial cost methods and assumptions, though, may appropriately influence the choice.

The Participants in the Plan

To qualify for the substantial tax advantages of offering a pension plan, an employer's eligibility requirements must not discriminate in favor of officers, shareholders, or highly paid employees. Initial eligibility for the pension plan usually includes requirements for: (1) minimum age or length of service, or both, and (2) employment for at least 1,000 hours during a 12-month period. Minimum service requirements may be some fixed time, usually one year. Early, or even immediate, participation in the plan may be allowed with restrictions on the amount of benefits that can be received by short-term employees.[1] The Employee Retirement Income Security Act of 1974 (ERISA) prohibits a qualified plan from requiring employees age 25 or more to meet a service requirement exceeding one year. It also prohibits maximum age limitations, except in certain cases, such as on employees of a defined benefit plan within five years of normal retirement age when first employed.

The 1,000-hour requirement is designed to permit exclusion of some part-time employees from the plan. The 12-month computation period is measured from the date the employee first enters the service of the employer. He or she legally may be required to start over toward meeting the 1,000-hour requirement if such has not been reached by the first anniversary of employment and if the person is still employed.

To meet ERISA's nondiscrimination standards, at least 70 percent of all employees must be eligible, and at least 80 percent of the eligible group must participate in the plan if the plan is contributory. The 80 percent requirement is superimposed to prevent a plan from requiring employee contributions so high that only high-salaried employees could afford to participate despite liberal eligibility requirements. Before applying the percentages, the sponsor may exclude part-time and seasonal workers (i.e., those employed for fewer than 1,000 hours per year) and employees who have not yet met the plan's age and service requirements, as well as employees who have bargained in good faith for a pension plan. Plans failing to meet these percentage requirements still can qualify with any classification system found to be nondiscriminatory by the IRS commissioner.

Role of Regulators

The requirements of ERISA are the primary regulatory concern of pension administrators. ERISA is administered jointly by the Department of the Treasury and the Department of Labor, with each department having its own filing requirements on some matters.

AMOUNT OF BENEFITS

Income Objectives

The sponsor first should establish income goals or objectives for the plan. Many sponsors believe a career employee's income after retirement, including Social Security benefits, should be 50 to 55 percent of gross

---

[1] Potential abuse of this practice, referred to as "back loading," led Congress to impose limitations on its use. These limitations are incorporated in ERISA's vesting standards, described later in this chapter.

earnings just prior to retirement for higher-paid employees and graduating up to 70 to 80 percent for lower-paid employees. For employees considered to be less than career employees (e.g., those with fewer than 25 or 30 years of service), the percentages would be proportionately smaller. Of these percentages, the private (employer) plan needs to provide a larger share of the total income for higher-paid than for lower-paid employees to meet the specified objectives.

The differences between the higher-paid and lower-paid groups can be substantially explained (as indicated in Chapters 27 and 28) by the nature of the Social Security benefit structure and by the tax treatment of Social Security benefits. The Social Security System generally replaces a larger percentage of income for lower-paid workers than for higher-paid workers. In addition, a portion of Social Security benefits are not subject to federal income tax. The effect of combining these facts is that, stated as a percentage, different income replacement objectives for pretax income result in approximately the same aftertax replacement rate for the higher- and lower-paid employees, and lower-income workers need less supplement from the private plan to meet the stated objectives.

Type of Formula to Be Used

The sponsor considers two basic types of benefit formulas. The first is called a "defined contribution," or "money purchase," formula because the contribution rates are fixed. A participant's benefit varies with the amount of the contributions made, plus the investment earnings on plan assets, and with the participant's age at plan entry, sex, and age at retirement. The second type is called a "defined benefit" formula. Under this type of formula, a definite benefit is established for each participant, and contributions are whatever is necessary to provide the promised benefit.

Defined Contribution Formulas.   The contribution under this type of formula usually is expressed as a percentage of the employee's base earnings, and often is contingent upon an employee's contribution. In most cases, the sponsor's contribution either matches or is a multiple of the employee's contribution. For example, the plan could call for the employer and employee each to contribute 5 percent of the employee's compensation; or the employee's contribution could be set at 3 percent of compensation, with the employer contributing 6 percent.

Accumulated funds are used to provide whatever pension benefits can be purchased. The amount of benefit varies with the age at which it is being purchased, the age at which benefit payments are to begin, and, in most cases, the sex of the employee. The benefit for any employee depends upon these individual characteristics, upon plan characteristics, such as contribution levels and investment income, and upon the annuity rates available at retirement. The use of the sex of the participant as a factor in determining the level of benefits (i.e., the annuity rates) is attempted only with great caution, because the Supreme Court ruled in 1978 that pension plans could not require different contribution levels from men and women.[2] Although this case directly affected only a portion of U.S. pension plans, several subsequent cases reinforce the view that differentiation between workers on the basis of sex may soon be a thing of the past.

A defined contribution plan is, in effect, a career average plan; however, unlike career average defined benefit plans, relatively few employers "update" the benefits accrued under a defined contribution plan. High inflation can cause the benefits of a defined contribution plan to be painfully inadequate. Those contributions invested for the longest time are based on the participant's earliest salaries. Rising salaries in later years would, in turn, produce higher contributions. But these higher contributions will not be in the plan as long as the earlier lower contributions. Even the current higher investment returns available may not completely offset the diminishing purchasing power of benefits caused by inflation.

Contributions to a defined contribution plan are applied differently, depending on the funding instrument used in the plan. In fully insured individual policy plans, contributions are applied as a level premium to purchase the amount of insurance available based on the employee's current age, sex, and expected retirement age. Where a group deferred annuity contract is used, contributions purchase a unit of paid-up deferred annuity each year at the insurer's current annuity rates. In plans using other funding instruments, the contributions usually are combined with investment earnings at retirement to purchase an annuity at then-prevailing annuity rates. With many types of funding instruments, the employee's benefit under a defined contribution formula can only be estimated. The benefit varies with salary level and investment return. This uncertainty about benefits, while not a major problem, can cause employee relations problems for the plan.

A defined contribution formula has other limitations, as well. For example, a participant who joins the plan at an older age will have only a short time to accumulate funds. If he or she has no vested benefit credits from previous employment, the benefits available at retirement might be unacceptably low. Variations in benefit levels among different employees make it difficult, if not impossible, to uniformly meet income objectives the sponsor has set for the plan. A defined contribution plan will seldom be implemented, therefore, if the owners of a business are advanced in years, and more favorable results can be obtained for those individuals by using a defined benefit formula.

Despite these limitations, the popularity of the defined contribution plan has increased in recent years. In fact, over 80 percent of all new plans installed since the 1974 passage of ERISA have been of the defined contribution type of plan.[3] A defined contribution plan provides the sponsor of the plan a higher degree of accuracy than a defined benefit plan when

---

[2] *City of Los Angeles, Department of Water and Power* v. *Marie Manhart et al.*, April 25, 1978.

[3] Everett T. Allen, Jr., Joseph J. Melone, and Jerry S. Rosenbloom, *Pension Planning*, 4th ed. (Homewood, Ill.: Richard D. Irwin, 1981), p. 66.

projecting the cost of the plan into future years. Defined contribution plans comply more readily with the court rulings to date concerning sex differentiation among employees because annuity rates do not enter the contribution formula. ERISA's minimum funding requirements are much simpler than for defined benefit plans, and a defined contribution plan avoids the employer contingent liability imposed for plan termination insurance.

Regardless of the type of benefit formula chosen, only basic compensation normally is considered for benefit purposes. Bonuses, overtime, and other forms of extraordinary compensation are not included. To do so could be expensive and could attract special attention from the Internal Revenue Service if considered to discriminate in favor of the prohibited group.

Defined Benefit Formulas. The four basic defined benefit formulas are: (1) a flat amount formula, which provides a flat benefit unrelated to an employee's earnings or service; (2) a flat percentage of earnings formula, which provides a benefit related to the employee's earnings, but which does not reflect service; (3) a flat amount per year of service formula, which reflects an employee's service but not earnings; and (4) a percentage of earnings per year of service formula, which reflects both an employee's earnings and service.

As indicated above, the flat amount formula provides a flat benefit for all eligible employees, regardless of their service, age, or earnings. For example, the benefit might be $250 a month for any employee meeting the minimum service requirement. The flat amount formula seldom is used alone, but it is occasionally combined with some other type of formula. For example, a plan may provide a flat benefit plus a percentage of earnings.

The flat percentage of earnings formula specifies a percentage, usually from 25 to 50 percent, which is then applied to the employee's earnings. The sponsor may base plan benefits on the average earnings paid over the entire period an employee participated in the plan, or on average earnings during some shorter time near retirement. The first type of formula is called a "career average" benefit and the latter is called a "final average" formula.

A typical final average formula would average earnings over the last three or five years of employment or over the highest three or five consecutive years in the ten-year period preceding retirement. It relates benefits to the employee's earnings just prior to retirement. This type of plan is more likely to satisfy the sponsor's income replacement objectives than is a career average plan, because the employee's initial benefit takes into account preretirement inflationary trends.

The price of these advantages is that the final-pay plan is usually more expensive than a career average type of plan. Also, if the amount or cost of benefits for an employee changes dramatically shortly before retirement and the plan is an individual contract plan, the additional benefits must be purchased over a brief period. Rather than to accept these costs, some employers prefer to use a career average earnings formula and to make periodic ad hoc adjustments in the benefit formula to recognize inflation.

Table 29-1
Excerpt from a
30 Percent Earnings
Bracket Schedule

Earnings	Monthly Pension
$584–$616	$180
617– 649	190
650– 683	200
684– 716	210
717– 749	220

To simplify the administration of the flat percentage of earnings formula, an "earnings bracket" schedule sometimes is used. Table 29-1 shows a portion of a 30 percent earnings bracket schedule. It applies the chosen percentage of earnings to the midpoint of each earnings bracket.

The flat amount per year of service formula provides a flat dollar amount for each year of service accumulated by the employee. The dollar amount varies from plan to plan, but a benefit of $10 to $15 a month for each year of service is common. Thus, in a plan that provides a benefit of $12 a month for each year of service, an employee with 25 years of employment would receive a pension of $300 per month. This type of formula often is found in negotiated plans.

The percentage of earnings per year of service approach, in its simplest form, provides a retirement benefit equal to some fixed percentage times the number of years of credited service. For example, a plan might provide 1.5 percent of final pay for each year of service. Again, either career-average or final-average pay could be used.

Two types of adjustment to the benefit formula may be applied when a plan is first implemented. First, an employee is not always credited with the total number of years worked prior to plan adoption. The time required to become eligible for participation may be deducted or a cap may be placed on the maximum number of years of past service credit that can be granted, or both. Second, a lower percentage may apply to past service credits than to service after the retirement plan was implemented. The past service percentage usually is applied to the employee's earnings at the time the plan is adopted. Both of these measures are used to limit the cost of the plan. A typical plan might provide 0.7 percent of earnings per year of past service and 1.2 percent of earnings per year of service after plan adoption. An employee who had 12 years of past service and earnings of $600 per month at the time a plan was started would receive $600 × 12 × .007 = $50.40 in monthly benefits as a result of past service. An employee retiring 25 years after the plan was adopted, with average earnings of $1,500, would receive a benefit for those 25 years of $1,500 × 25 × .012 = $450. The employee's total benefit for 37 years of service would be $50.40 + $450.00 = $500.40 per month.

Integration with Social Security. The plan sponsor may wish to adjust the amount of covered compensation or otherwise recognize that it bears a part of the cost of Socal Security benefits. One way to do this is to exclude employees whose earnings are less than the Social Security taxable wage base. A more prevalent approach is to provide a higher level of benefits for earnings above the taxable wage base than is provided for earnings below this amount. Such a benefit formula is said to be integrated with Social Security. The IRS requirements for integration are designed to prevent discrimination in favor of the prohibited group. Though the benefit formula under a qualified plan may legally favor the higher-paid employees, the combined Social Security and private plan benefits must produce a total retirement income that is a relatively equal percentage of compensation for all employees. Integration formulas are discussed in Chapter 27, along with other requirements for a qualified plan.

WHEN BENEFITS CAN BE RECEIVED

Benefit eligibility requirements include one or more of the following: a normal retirement age, provisions for early retirement, minimum service requirements, and provisions for delayed retirement. The amount and conditions of payment to employees who terminate employment prior to retirement also must be provided.

Normal Retirement Age

Normal retirement age is the earliest age an employee can retire with full benefits without the consent of the employer under the plan's formula.[4] Age 65 is the most common age for normal retirement, primarily because that is the age when workers can collect full Social Security benefits. Since the Age Discrimination in Employment Act (ADEA), as amended, generally prohibits employers from forcing employees to retire prior to age 70, why should a pension specify a normal retirement age lower than 70? The main reasons are financial and administrative. A normal retirement age serves as a base for making reasonable actuarial cost estimates and adjustments under a defined benefit formula. It also offers security to employees; workers understand what their benefits will be at the normal retirement age and that adjustment may be necessary if retirement actually occurs earlier or later than that age.

The normal retirement age need not be the same for all employees. Age 65 might be used for some occupations and a lower age used for others. A normal retirement age higher than 65 may be a possibility in the future, because of the recent changes in Social Security. (See Appendix A.)

---

[4] Sometimes a minimum service requirement is superimposed on the age requirement. Benefits payable to employees with only a few years of service would provide only a small amount of benefit and would be costly because of the short time available to fund the benefit.

Early Retirement

Many plans permit employees who meet certain conditions, such as reaching age 55 and completing 10 years of service, to retire early.[5] Early retirement privileges can be expensive to the plan, so some reduction in benefits for early retirees is used in most plans to help control costs. The benefit is scaled down from the normal retirement amount to reflect the difference in the actuarial cost of early retirement. For example, a life income of $700 per month at age 65 might be reduced to $575 per month if it were to begin at age 60.

An early retirement benefit is the lowest amount to which an employee will ever become entitled. Any salary reductions that occur after an employee first becomes eligible for early retirement cannot under federal law reduce the retirement benefit below the amount the employee would have received if he or she had opted for the early retirement. This is a distinct complication, particularly in a final-pay plan.

Employers occasionally use liberalized early retirement benefits to soften the impact of general economic downturns. When a recession hits a company hard, the management of that firm may decide to "sweeten" the early retirement package to induce eligible workers to retire early. The resulting reduction or elimination of the number of layoffs the company must make avoids the labor problems and the higher unemployment insurance costs of firing larger numbers of employees. For example, when New Jersey's Public Service Electric & Gas Company (PSE&G) received an inadequate rate increase in 1980, a special early retirement program was one cost-cutting measure developed. Some 2,120 employees age 55 and over became eligible for an unreduced early retirement benefit, plus a pension supplement payable until age 65. The amount of the supplement was $500 per month initially and is guaranteed to increase by $50 per month every three years. Within 10 days after the plan was announced, twice the number of PSE&G employees who would have been expected to retire in an entire year applied for early retirement. Overall, more than 1,200 employees, with an average age of 59, retired under the special early retirement program.[6]

Deferred Retirement

Most plans permit employees to work beyond normal retirement age and must, under ADEA, permit a worker to delay retirement to age 70. Most plans do not increase benefits to those who defer retirement, however, even though benefits of employees electing early retirement are reduced.

---

[5] Additionally, early retirement may be based on the employee's physical condition or on the employer's consent, as well as the employee's age and service. Some plans require the employee to be totally disabled to qualify for early retirement, and, while employer consent may be required, that consent is seldom difficult to obtain.

[6] "Early Retirement Incentives Used to Cut Costs," *Employee Benefit Plan Review*, November 1980, pp. 44, 92.

The sponsors prefer to use the resulting cost savings to pay some of the costs of early retirement benefits or to reduce the overall costs of the plan.

A few employers do wish to encourage late retirements, and will pay higher benefits to those who retire later than normal. The higher benefit results from (1) an actuarial adjustment for the shorter life expectancy remaining at the later retirement age, (2) the additional benefit credits accumulated during the years of service after normal retirement age, or (3) an increase in the average compensation base. The only guarantee for an employee is ADEA's mandate that he or she will not be forced to retire prior to age 70; neither ADEA nor ERISA requires continued benefit accrual or increases in the benefit amount for retirement beyond normal retirement age.

Benefits if Employment Terminates

The mobility of modern society makes it highly unlikely an individual will remain in a single job for his or her entire working lifetime. Many workers become disabled or die before reaching the normal retirement age, and many more change employers. The pension plan's benefit structure must allow for these contingencies and spell out what benefits, if any, will be payable in these events.

The Internal Revenue Code requires that an employee retain full rights at all times to the benefit attributable to his or her own contributions. This does not mean the employee is necessarily entitled to the amount he or she has contributed. For example, investment losses may result in a value less than the amount actually contributed to a defined contribution plan. In such a situation, the employee would be entitled to the value of his or her contributions after investment losses are taken into account.

An employee also may be entitled to plan benefits attributable to the sponsor's contributions to the plan if he or she terminates employment prior to retirement. Such benefits are said to be "vested" under a pension plan. Accrued benefits attributable to sponsor contributions must vest when the employee reaches normal retirement age. Upon termination of employment prior to normal retirement age, ERISA requires vesting according to one of three rules:

1. The 10-Year Rule provides that an employee must be 100 percent vested after 10 years of service.
2. The 5- to 15-Year Rule provides graduated vesting beginning with 25 percent after 5 years, increasing 5 percent a year for the next 5 years, and 10 percent for the next 5 years. This produces a 50 percent vested interest after 10 years of service, and a 100 percent vested interest after 15 years of service.
3. The Rule of 45 provides that an employee has a 50 percent interest after the earlier of 10 years of service or when the combination of service (minimum of 5 years) and the employee's age total 45; thereafter, the employee's vested interest increases 10 percent per year for the next 5 years.

These rules are the minimum acceptable vesting schedules under current law. The Internal Revenue Service has the authority to impose stricter vesting requirements if such action is deemed necessary to prevent discrimination. Of course, more liberal vesting schedules are acceptable.

Disability Benefits. An employee frequently is eligible for more liberal vesting provisions if termination occurs as a result of disability. Plans funded with individual policies frequently provide full vesting if an employee becomes totally and permanently disabled. The plan also may provide for continued contributions to the pension during the period of disablement.

In addition to these types of provisions, some group pension and trust fund plans, particularly those which are union negotiated, provide for a separate and distinct cash benefit in the event of total and permanent disability. The benefit provided under such plans may be a specified dollar amount, a specified percentage of earnings, or an amount equal to the employee's accrued or projected pension credits (with or without actuarial reduction). Generally, an employee must have attained some minimum age (such as 50) or must have completed some minimum period of service or participation (such as 10 years) to qualify for the disability benefit. The benefits generally are paid directly from plan assets and immediately increase the cost of the plan for the years benefits are paid.

Often, the disability benefit provided by the plan is integrated with benefits available under government plans, such as worker's compensation or Social Security. Some plans treat a disability as an early retirement if the employee has completed some minimum period of service and has attained some minimum age. Other plans provide that the disability benefit terminates when the employee reaches normal retirement age, at which time he or she will be entitled to the accrued normal pension benefit.

Death Benefits. Death benefits are optional under a pension plan and usually take one of two forms. Some form of individual or group life insurance contract issued by an insurer may be provided, or cash distributions of plan assets may occur. Death benefits must be "incidental" to a retirement plan for the plan to be qualified. The IRS has ruled that a lump-sum death benefit is incidental if it does not exceed the greater of (1) 100 times the expected monthly pension, or (2) the reserve of the pension benefit. Death benefits may be payable in the event of death before or after retirement, or both.

TAX EQUITY AND FISCAL RESPONSIBILITY ACT OF 1982 (TEFRA)

The changes introduced by TEFRA must be considered in the design of any retirement plan. Changes and implications of TEFRA for employers and employees are discussed in Chapter 58 of the *Handbook*.

CHAPTER 30

Profit-Sharing Plans

BRUCE A. PALMER

INTRODUCTION

Programs providing retirement income have been the recipients of great attention in recent years. Reasons for this attention are many and varied but most of them relate fundamentally to inflation, other economic problems, and the inability of individuals to provide for their own economic security during their retirement years without assistance from some formal group savings or social program. With the increasing concern expressed about the future viability of the Social Security program and its ability to provide significant benefit levels to most retirees, substantial additional attention has been focused on private employer-sponsored retirement programs.

This chapter continues the discussion of retirement plans that began in Chapter 27 and will extend throughout Part Five of the *Handbook*. Specifically, the chapter focuses on profit-sharing plans as defined in Section 401(a) of the Internal Revenue Code (IRC). Collectively, these plans constitute a major component of the overall retirement benefit structure existing in the private sector.

DEFINITION OF PROFIT SHARING

A profit-sharing plan, as the name implies, is a plan or program for sharing company profits with the firm's employees. The contributions to a qualified deferred profit-sharing plan are accumulated in a tax-sheltered account for the primary purpose of providing income to employees during their retirement years. While the accumulation of income for retirement purposes is their main objective, deferred profit-sharing plans often provide for the distribution of monies on other prescribed occasions to employees or their beneficiaries.

It is important to examine the definition of a profit-sharing plan, as described in federal income-tax regulations:

A profit-sharing plan is a plan established and maintained by an employer to provide for the participation in his profits by his employees or their beneficiaries. The plan must provide a definite predetermined formula for allocating the contributions made to the plan among the participants and for distributing the funds accumulated under the plan after a fixed number of years, the attainment of a stated age, or upon the prior occurrence of some event such as layoff, illness, disability, retirement, death, or severance of employment.[1]

Under the Employee Retirement Income Security Act of 1974 (ERISA) and the Internal Revenue Code (IRC), profit-sharing plans are treated as defined contribution or individual account plans. Thus, as is true for all defined contribution plans, the employer's financial commitment under a profit-sharing plan relates to the payment of (annual) contributions to the plan. The employer is under no financial obligation to provide a specific dollar amount of retirement benefit in these plans. Further, the employer contributions to defined contribution plans are allocated to individual accounts set up for each plan participant.[2] The contribution amounts in the individual accounts are augmented by each employee's share of any investment earnings on the plan assets and, possibly, in the case of profit-sharing plans, further by the proceeds of any forfeitures of accounts created by nonvested (or partially vested) participants who have terminated employment with the firm. As a defined contribution type of plan, the amount of benefit available to the participant at retirement will be solely a function of the amount in the individual account at that time and the level of monthly income which that accumulated amount will purchase. The larger the individual account balance, the greater the amount of monthly income that can be purchased.

For purposes of qualifying a plan with the Internal Revenue Service, certain other types of defined contribution or individual account plans generally may be treated the same as, or similar to, profit-sharing plans. These plans include thrift or savings plans (when employer contributions are made from "current or accumulated profits"), stock-bonus plans, and employee stock-ownership plans (ESOPs). However, since thrift and savings plans (Chapter 32), stock-bonus plans and ESOPs (Chapters 34 and 35) are covered elsewhere in the *Handbook*, these plans will not be described here. Further, while many Keogh (HR-10) plans also involve a profit-sharing-type formula, the discussion presented in this chapter focuses on corporate profit-sharing plans. Profit-sharing plans in a Keogh (HR-10) environment are described in Chapter 36.

The concept of profit sharing, in its broadest sense, encompasses any program under which the firm's profits are shared with its employees. Thus, this concept includes both cash plans and deferred distribution plans. Un-

---

[1] Reg. 1.401-1(b)(1)(ii).

[2] Federal regulations require that individual accounts be maintained for each plan participant in defined contribution plans.

der cash profit-sharing plans, the share of the profits to be paid to the employees is distributed to them currently as a bonus or a wage/salary supplement (either in the form of cash or employer stock). As a result, these distributions are included in the employees' income in the year of distribution and taxed on top of their other wages, salaries, and other income.[3] Deferred distribution profit-sharing plans are programs in which the profits to be distributed are credited to employee accounts (held under trust) and accumulated for later distribution (e.g., upon retirement, or some other specified event, such as death, disability, or severance of employment, or according to the terms of any plan withdrawal provisions).

In actuality, there are three basic approaches to profit sharing since it is possible for a firm to have a combination cash and deferred profit-sharing plan covering essentially the same group(s) of employees. Under this arrangement, a portion of the profit-sharing allocation is distributed currently to the participant with the remainder deferred. A combination plan can be designed in one of two ways: (1) there may be two separate plans—one cash and the other deferred, or (2) there may be only one plan that possesses both current and deferred features. This latter type of combination plan often is referred to as a cash *or* deferred profit-sharing plan. Many employers have shown a renewed interest in this type of plan since the passage of the Revenue Act of 1978.[4]

While ERISA, under a "grandfather" provision, permitted existing (on June 27, 1974) cash or deferred profit-sharing plans to remain in effect, the act provided no authority for the creation of new plans. The Revenue Act of 1978 added two IRC Sections, 401(k) and 402(a)(8), which together create a basis for the establishment of new qualified cash or deferred plans. IRC Section 401(k) established special additional qualification rules for cash or deferred profit-sharing plans.[5] These rules became effective for plan years

---

[3] Since payments under cash profit-sharing plans may be made as soon as the respective participants' allocations are determined, the structure of these plans is much simpler than that of deferred plans, in that there is no trust fund, no assets to be invested, and so on. Of course, their major disadvantage lies in their tax treatment.

[4] Robert C. Wender, "Renewed Life for Cash or Deferred Profit Sharing Plans," *CLU Journal* 35, no. 4 (October 1981), pp. 18–21.

[5] Prior to the proposed regulations in November 1981 (see Chapter 33), these additional qualification rules included, but were not limited to, the following:

(1) Deferred amounts held in trust made pursuant to the participant's election (i.e., amounts not automatically deferred under the plan provisions) may not be distributed to plan participants or their beneficiaries prior to termination of employment, death, disability, retirement, attainment of age 59½, or the determination of "hardship." (This qualification rule is substantially more restrictive than what generally applies to profit-sharing plans in that deferred-only profit-sharing plans usually are permitted to make distributions to active employees at the completion of a stated period of plan participation or at the expiration of a fixed period of years. As such, the typical qualified deferred-only profit-sharing plan is not limited by the requirement that distributions be made only on the account of "employment separation, death, disability, retirement, hardship, or the attainment of age 59½").

beginning after December 31, 1979. IRC Section 402(a)(8) relates to the tax treatment accorded these plans. IRC Section 402(a)(8) is particularly important to the future viability of cash or deferred profit-sharing plans, because under these plans the participant has the right to elect what portion of the total distribution will be received in the current year (and therefore taxed currently) and the remaining portion that will be deferred. Under this section of the code, the plan participant can elect annually to receive all or part of the yearly profit-sharing allocation in cash. The portion of each year's allocation that is not received in cash would be contributed to the individual participant's account under the deferred portion of the plan, held in trust, and invested until distribution at a later time. The key tax advantage associated with these plans is that, to the extent that the qualification requirements of IRC Section 401(k) are met, the participant's right to elect cash will not trigger the application of the doctrine of constructive receipt to that portion of the profit-sharing distribution that is actually deferred, thereby preserving its tax-deferred status. If the deferred portions of the allocations do not meet the requirements of IRC Section 401(k), all employer contributions (over which the employee held an option to elect) will be considered to have been distributed or made available and, consequently, would be currently taxable to the employee.

When discussing profit-sharing plans in the context of qualified deferred compensation programs (as determined under IRC Section 401), the concept of profit sharing refers to the deferred distribution form or the combination cash/deferred profit-sharing plan. In the subsequent discussion of profit sharing in this chapter, the term *profit-sharing plan* refers to the deferred distribution type of plan, rather than cash profit-sharing, unless otherwise noted. Further, even though combination cash/deferred profit-sharing plans may be qualified with the IRS, future discussion concentrates primarily on the features of the deferred component of these plans. Al-

---

(2) Amounts subject to the deferred election that are held in trust must be nonforfeitable (fully vested). (This nonforfeitability rule is not applicable to any amounts that are not subject to the cash/deferred election. The usual vesting rules under IRC Section 411 may be applied to those amounts automatically deferred.)

(3) Either of two statutory antidiscrimination standards must be satisfied: *(a)* the actual deferral percentage for the highly compensated group (defined as the highest-paid one third of total eligibles) is not more than the actual deferral percentage of all other eligible employees (the lowest-paid two thirds) multiplied by 1.5; or *(b)* the excess of the actual deferral percentage for the group of "highly compensated" over that of all other eligible employees is not more than three percentage points, and the actual deferral percentage of the "highly compensated" is not more than the actual deferral percentage of all other eligible employees multiplied by 2.5.

For an additional treatment of these requirements, see Robert C. Wender, "Renewed Life for Cash or Deferred Profit Sharing Plans," *CLU Journal* 35, no. 4 (October 1981), pp. 18–21; "IRC Sec. 401(k) of Revenue Act of 1978 Liberalizes Qualification of Cash Profit-Sharing Plans," *Employee Benefit Plan Review*, March 1977, pp. 18, 90; "New Rules for Qualified Cash or Deferred Plans," *Employee Benefit Plan Review*, April 1980, pp. 81–82; and Francis X. Roche, "Cash or Deferred Profit Sharing Plans after the Act of '78," *Journal of Pension Planning and Compliance* 6, no. 1 (January 1980), pp. 17–22.

though cash distributions of profits are a relatively popular device for sharing profits, this chapter is more concerned with the aspects of plan design, the legal requirements, and the tax aspects surrounding deferred distributions from profit-sharing plans.[6]

Many profit-sharing plans provide for the payment of supplementary contributions (usually voluntary) by the covered employees. However, this chapter does not focus on any distinctive features that might be attributed to contributory profit-sharing plans nor, as stated earlier, will it focus on thrift or savings plans.[7]

While later sections in this chapter describe, in detail, employer contributions to a profit-sharing plan and the qualification requirements applicable to a profit-sharing plan, it is worthwhile to make three further observations. First, since employer contributions are keyed to the existence of profits, profit-sharing plans provide maximum contribution flexibility to the employer, because in a low, zero, or negative profit year it is possible the firm does not have to make any contributions at all. There is no fixed minimum level of contribution required by the Internal Revenue Code, as is the case for money purchase and defined benefit pension plans. It also is possible for the firm to provide that no contribution will be made to the plan in any year unless profits exceed a specified level or a predetermined rate of return on stockholder equity. As a result, employer contributions to profit-sharing plans may even be characterized as "voluntary;" however, contributions must be "substantial and recurring" to meet the qualification requirement of plan permanency. Second, Section 404(a)(3) of the IRC permits deductible contributions to a qualified profit-sharing plan to be made out of either current or accumulated profits of the firm. Thus, if a firm has accumulated profits from previous years of operations, it is possible for the firm to make deductible contributions to the profit-sharing plan that

---

[6] Although enjoying significant popularity as an employee benefit, cash (or current distribution) profit-sharing plans are at a considerable disadvantage in terms of their tax treatment when compared with the tax advantages possessed by qualified deferred profit-sharing plans. Further, since these plans provide for a current distribution of profits (and thus are simply a method of providing for the payment of bonuses to all covered employees), they do not constitute retirement plans. This chapter is concerned essentially with profit-sharing plans as a vehicle for providing cash accumulation or retirement income, or both.

[7] Although many thrift and savings plans qualify with the IRS under the profit-sharing rules (since the IRS does not have a separation or division of requirements addressing only thrift plans) and hence would be deemed to be profit-sharing plans, the purist would argue that there still exists a fundamental difference between a contributory profit-sharing plan and a thrift or savings plan. In the latter case, employer contributions to the plan are usually fixed at some predetermined percentage "match" (e.g., 25, 50, or 100 percent) of the employee contributions for the purpose of encouraging thrift on the part of the employee. Thus, employer contributions to a thrift plan are dependent primarily on the "level of employee thrift." In contrast, employer contributions to a contributory profit-sharing plan are primarily a function of the "level of profits." Further, in the case of contributory profit-sharing plans where the employee contributions are voluntary, employer contributions to a participant's account often are not made contingent on the payment of contributions by the participant.

exceed the firm's profit for that year.[8] Finally, when there exist multiple corporations belonging to an "affiliated group" (e.g., a chain of corporations controlled by a common parent) that jointly maintain a profit-sharing plan, IRC Section 404(a)(3)(B) permits those members of the affiliated group that have profits to contribute (and receive a deduction) on behalf of those members that do not have profits.

IMPORTANCE OF PROFIT-SHARING PLANS

While several notable profit-sharing plans had been in existence prior to 1939, that year seems to signal the beginning of the major growth experienced in profit-sharing plans. In 1939 the U.S. Senate's endorsement of the profit-sharing concept, together with subsequent favorable tax legislation, provided the stimulus for the establishment of profit-sharing plans. In the 25 years preceding the enactment of ERISA, the number of deferred profit-sharing plans doubled approximately every 5 years. However, the passage of ERISA, with its reforms and the uncertainties created by its enactment, had a major deterrent effect on the establishment of all types of qualified plans, initially even including profit-sharing plans. (Today, it is believed that ERISA is a major factor contributing to the current popularity enjoyed by profit-sharing plans.) The numbers of new profit-sharing plans qualified during 1974 (the year of enactment of ERISA) and during each of the three following years are presented below:[9]

Year	Number
1974	24,779
1975	11,162
1976	6,439
1977	9,523

The year 1978 became a record-setter—the number of profit-sharing plan approvals exceeded 25,000. Profit-sharing plans continue to remain extremely important in terms of the number of annual new plan approvals.

As indicated above, ERISA had a dramatic reduction effect on the number of new profit-sharing plan approvals for the three years immediately following the year of ERISA's passage. However, the reduction percentage in the number of new pension plan approvals (particularly in the case of defined benefit plans) was even more dramatic.[10] The major reason

---

[8] Although in practice this event is probably rare, under certain circumstances (presumably related to tax planning), a firm might decide to contribute amounts to the plan which are greater than the firm's profits in a given year.

[9] These figures were obtained from the *Employee Benefit Plan Review Research Reports* (Chicago: Charles D. Spencer & Associates).

[10] Ibid.

why deferred profit-sharing plans (and defined contribution plans, in general) have assumed a greater role in retirement income planning since the enactment of ERISA in 1974 is that these plans are subject to fewer of ERISA's requirements than are defined benefit pension plans, particularly in the areas of minimum funding and the plan termination insurance and contingent employer liability requirements (pertaining to plan terminations) of the Pension Benefit Guaranty Corporation (PBGC).[11] The growing popularity of profit-sharing plans also may be due to the increasing recognition of their possible importance as contributors to improved corporate performance. A major study of the 38 largest profit-sharing plans concluded that they seem to have a positive correlation with superior corporate performance.[12] This study further concluded that profit-sharing companies, on average, tend to outperform their competitors who do not have profit-sharing plans, and that a significant reason for the difference in performance is caused by the existence of a profit-sharing plan. The results of this study indicate that the profit-sharing companies outperformed the *Fortune* 500 companies both in terms of the return on sales and the return on equity for the years 1973–76.

The importance of profit-sharing plans is further underscored by the dual purpose that they serve in the overall structure of retirement income planning. Profit-sharing plans often exist as the sole type of retirement income plan in many firms, particularly in firms of small-to-medium size, where the employers may feel unable to assume the financial commitment associated with a money purchase or defined benefit pension plan.[13] In addition, profit-sharing plans many times are formed as a supplement to a pension plan. There are several advantages of this combination approach. Most important, in addition to providing for the possibility of greater total benefits, the pension plan can provide employees with protection against the down-side risk that corporate profits will be low, leading to low levels of

---

[11] Approximately 80 percent of all new plans since the enactment of ERISA are of the defined contribution type (including deferred profit-sharing, stock-bonus, and money purchase pensions). Further, approximately 50 percent of the new plan approvals (post-ERISA) have been profit-sharing plans (including stock-bonus plans); this figure is 5 or 6 percentage points higher than what profit-sharing plans constituted as a percentage of the total universe of pension and profit-sharing plans existing pre-ERISA. The corresponding pre-ERISA percentage for all defined contribution plans combined was 72 percent. For tables containing these various percentages, see *Employee Benefit Plan Review Research Reports* (Chicago: Charles D. Spencer & Associates). The statistics presented in the *EBPR Research Reports* were based on calculations made by the Profit Sharing Research Foundation, Evanston, Ill.

[12] *Profit Sharing in 38 Large Companies* (Evanston, Ill.: Profit Sharing Research Foundation, 1978). Collectively, these 38 companies provided coverage to more than 1 million participants.

[13] Profit-sharing plans have become especially popular in those corporations where the ownership is closely held. As with all forms of qualified retirement plans, the profit-sharing plan has the capability to convert a significant portion of the profits that would likely otherwise be paid either in corporate or personal income taxes into a tax-sheltered account where the monies compound with tax-sheltered investment income.

contributions to the profit-sharing plan and, ultimately, to the payment of inadequate profit-sharing plan benefits.

The 24th annual survey of profit-sharing experience of member firms of the Profit Sharing Council of America disclosed certain important statistics in regard to employer contributions to profit-sharing plans.[14] This survey, conducted by Hewitt Associates in cooperation with the Profit Sharing Council of America, is based on the 1980 experience of 559 companies out of a total of approximately 1,400 firms that are members of the trade association. The survey results indicate that employer contributions to profit-sharing plans averaged 9.5 percent of payroll during 1980, and over the past five years employer contributions have remained at a relatively constant level at between 9 percent and 10 percent of pay. The 1980 experience also shows that the average employer contributions, as a percentage of net profits, was 23.2 percent.[15]

It is anticipated that the features of profit-sharing plans will continue to be attractive in the future to firms considering the establishment of new qualified retirement plans covering their employees. Upon review of their retirement income programs, many companies recently have strengthened their profit-sharing plans in lieu of establishing supplemental defined benefit plans.[16]

EMPLOYER OBJECTIVES IN ESTABLISHING A DEFERRED PROFIT-SHARING PLAN

An employer normally has a number of specific objectives in electing to establish a qualified deferred profit-sharing plan. Certainly, the one objective that comes immediately to mind is that of providing a means or a vehicle, on behalf of covered employees, for the accumulation on a tax-favored basis of substantial amounts of assets that, in turn, would constitute a primary source of income to be distributed at retirement or at other specified occasions. As part of the overall objectives in establishing a qualified plan of any type, the employer is seeking the various tax advantages associated with such a plan. These include the deductibility (within

---

[14] *1981 Profit Sharing Survey (1980 Experience)* (Chicago: Profit Sharing Council of America, 1981).

[15] These percentages are for all types of profit-sharing plans, including cash plans, deferred plans, and combination cash and deferred plans. In general, the combination profit-sharing plans tend to have a higher contribution level than deferred-only or cash-only plans. For deferred-only plans, the 1980 employer contribution rate was 8.9 percent of pay. Further, approximately 30 percent of the firms surveyed also have pension plans. Although certainly not true in all cases, firms that did not have a pension plan in addition to a deferred or combination profit-sharing plan tended to make slightly higher contributions to the profit-sharing plan.

[16] It must be pointed out, however, that due to lower levels of profits in recent years, other employers have been faced with substantial employee pressure to establish a defined benefit plan.

limits) to the firm of employer contributions, the tax-free accumulation of monies held in trust under the plan, the current nontaxability to the employee of employer contributions and investment earnings on plan assets, and special income-tax treatment accorded qualifying lump-sum distributions. In addition to these, however, employers typically have one or more other important objectives in establishing a profit-sharing plan covering the firm's employees.

As an employee benefit, profit-sharing plans constitute a significant method of compensating employees and of achieving various employer compensation objectives. As such, a profit-sharing plan may be viewed as a compensation device that constitutes a major component of the total compensation approach of those employers who have adopted such plans.

Employers might also desire to establish profit-sharing plans in the hope of improving the productivity and efficiency of the firm.[17] Finding ways to increase productivity has become a major concern of many U.S. firms today. For many firms, although sales have been increasing over recent years, costs have increased more rapidly and thus have resulted in declining profits. The establishment of new profit-sharing plans might constitute a partial solution to the productivity problem in the United States. Increased productivity might result in one or more of several ways. The establishment of a profit-sharing plan may lead to improved employee morale, and provide a source of motivation to employees to perform in a more productive and efficient manner.[18] Since employer contributions to the plan (and consequently the ultimate level of benefits received by the employee) are tied to the firm's profits, a profit-sharing plan provides the employee with a direct incentive to become more efficient, more productive, resulting in lower costs and higher profits to the firm.[19] To the extent that these anticipated results actually are attained, employees, management, and stockholders alike should all benefit from the establishment of a profit-sharing plan. Also, improved productivity might result in other ways, such as through a reduction in employee turnover rates,[20] through a decrease in the absenteeism rate of employees, through an improved ability of the firm

---

[17] For an extensive treatment of profit sharing and its effect on productivity, see *Increasing Productivity Through Profit Sharing* (Evanston, Ill.: Profit Sharing Research Foundation, 1981).

[18] See Bert L. Metzger, "How to Motivate With Profit Sharing," *Pension World,* February 1978, pp. 24–28, 32–33.

[19] Major arguments also are presented against this line of reasoning. For example, it is argued that profit-sharing plans reward poor performance equally as well as good performance, thereby questioning whether profit-sharing plans are truly motivational. Further, there is the question about how many employees in a firm can really influence profitability. In summary, the relationships between motivation, increased productivity, and the establishment of deferred profit-sharing plans are still strongly debated issues.

[20] Since the employee is likely aware (*a*) that the vested portion of the funds in his or her individual account will increase with time, and (*b*) that his or her account balance will be further augmented by reallocated forfeitures of other terminating participants who were less than fully vested, an incentive is created for this employee to remain with the firm.

to attract higher caliber individuals, and through stimulation of employees to make suggestions for improvement in the "way things are done." All these have the potential to result in a dramatic increase in the productivity and profits of those firms establishing profit-sharing plans. Some firms, in fact, have experienced increased productivity levels of 30 to 40 percent or more after the establishment of a profit-sharing plan. As further support, an important study comparing the profit records of a large number of companies throughout six major industries during the period 1958–77 showed that companies with profit-sharing plans outperformed those companies without such plans by substantial margins.[21] It might be argued that the establishment of a pension plan (either money purchase or defined benefit) also might result in improved productivity to the firm; however, in theory one would have to argue that there certainly exists a more direct relationship between the establishment of a profit-sharing plan and increased productivity than is true for the establishment of a pension plan.

Although both profit-sharing plans and pension plans constitute major approaches to providing asset accumulation and economic security for the covered employees and their dependents (whether the income be made available during retirement years, termination of employment, death, disability, or on the occasion of other special events with special income needs), these two approaches provide the employer with substantially different levels of funding flexibility. Under a money purchase or a defined benefit pension plan, the employer has a fixed commitment (not contingent on profit levels) to contribute amounts each year that meet certain ERISA-prescribed minimum requirements.[22] In most instances, these requirements will result in the employer having to make contributions to the plan during each and every year. Under a profit-sharing plan, of course, it is possible for the firm to not make any contributions to the plan for a given year (or years). This results in substantially greater contribution flexibility to the employer under the profit-sharing approach than under either the money purchase or defined benefit pension plan approach. Further, the profit-sharing plan creates no financial strain on the firm in maintaining the plan's existence. The lack of a fixed obligation to make definite contributions each year is an extremely significant advantage of profit-sharing plans over pension plans; this is especially true for small businesses and for new firms that may be unable to assume the fixed costs required of pension plans. In years of no profits, or when profits fall below a predetermined level, no employer contributions need be made. In contrast, in years of high profits,

---

[21] *A Study of the Financial Significance of Profit Sharing–1958 to 1977* (Chicago: Profit Sharing Council of America, 1980).

[22] For money purchase plans, this entails the payment of a fixed rate of contribution; for defined benefit plans, it requires the payment of contributions at a level necessary to fund the promised benefits. In both cases, it means a specific contribution commitment without regard to the profit levels of the firm.

larger than average contributions might be made to the profit-sharing plan. In summary, profit-sharing plans possess maximum flexibility with regard to employer contributions.

In establishing any new employee benefit program, most employers will want to take employee desires into account. From the standpoint of the individual employee, in terms of choosing between a profit-sharing plan (or for that matter, any defined contribution plan) and a defined benefit pension plan, the younger and middle-aged employees might prefer the individual account approach inherent in the profit-sharing arrangement over a promised definite level of benefits to be payable many years later at retirement. The defined contribution approach often provides the opportunity to accumulate much greater sums on behalf of younger employees than is true in the case of defined benefit plans. Conversely, older employees generally tend to prefer a defined benefit plan (with its predetermined level of benefits payable in the near future) to either a profit-sharing or a money purchase pension plan. The reason for this preference on the part of older employees is that a profit-sharing or money purchase plan generally will not provide a sufficiently large accumulation of monies to provide adequate retirement benefits for those employees near retirement at the time the plan is established. In choosing between the two approaches, profit-sharing (or money purchase) and defined benefit, the employer should consider the age distribution and the distribution by position within the firm of the employee group covered by the plan. These distributions may be such that the employer may decide to have a combination profit-sharing and defined benefit plan to appeal to both young and older workers alike.

The employer may be influenced by other objectives in deciding to adopt a profit-sharing plan. For example, as an individual account plan, the employee is provided with the opportunity to share in favorable investment results, which potentially could lead to much higher levels of benefits that can be purchased at retirement.[23] Under defined benefit plans, favorable investment earnings accrue to the benefit of the employer. In addition, in a profit-sharing plan, forfeitures of nonvested (and partially vested) terminating participants may be allocated among the remaining participants, thus providing the possibility of even greater benefits to those employees who remain with the firm for long periods. To the extent the employer desires for the employees to share in favorable investment earnings and also share in forfeitures, the profit-sharing approach may be preferred.

Further, the employer may prefer certain other features that may be

---

[23] However, the employee also is exposed to the downside risk of low or otherwise unfavorable investment results. This may be a potential source of employee (and possibly employer) dissatisfaction with the plan and, in addition, generates a greater sensitivity on the part of the employer to fiduciary obligations associated with the investment of plan assets. This exposure to potentially increased fiduciary liabilities constitutes an important disadvantage associated with the adoption of defined contribution plans.

incorporated into the design of a profit-sharing plan whose incorporation into pension plans is either prohibited or substantially restricted. Specifically, the employer may want to provide the covered employees with the option to make loans or withdrawals from their individual accounts while still actively employed, or the employer may desire that the funds held in the profit-sharing trust be invested in employer stock or other employer securities to a greater extent than permitted under a pension plan. To the extent that assets in a profit-sharing plan are invested in employer securities, the employees have the opportunity to participate to an even greater extent in the success of the company.

Finally, the employer may have an objective in establishing a profit-sharing plan of avoiding certain requirements imposed on defined benefit pension plans. These include satisfying specific funding requirements and compliance with the associated minimum funding standards, the payment of plan termination insurance premiums to the Pension Benefit Guaranty Corporation (PBGC) (the premium rate currently is $2.60 per plan participant per year for single-employer defined benefit plans), and the exposure to contingent employer liability (up to 30 percent of net worth) and the attendent impact on the firm's accounting and financial reports. Further, under profit-sharing plans there should be fewer requirements in the aggregate that must be complied with, less paperwork, and the absence (or substantial reduction) of actuarial cost calculations.

In spite of the many important advantages associated with profit-sharing plans, this discussion would not be complete without identifying some of the important disadvantages associated with the operation of profit-sharing plans (in comparison with pension plans), especially since many of these disadvantages are quite significant. One relative disadvantage of profit-sharing plans relates to the difficulty of providing employees with adequate credit for any periods of past service (service prior to plan inception). Past service credits can be incorporated with relative ease in most pension plans. Second, the ultimate benefits payable at retirement under a profit-sharing plan (and for that matter under any defined contribution plan) may be inadequate for those employees near retirement at the time of plan inception. Third, the profit-sharing amounts contributed to the plan in any year usually are allocated among the individual employee accounts on the basis of the employee's annual compensation. Thus, years of service together with age generally are ignored in the profit-sharing allocation formula. Additional disadvantages of profit sharing as a retirement plan relate to the employee's assumption of the inflation risk, the investment risk (see footnote 23), and the risk of little or no profits to the firm which, collectively, could result in inadequate benefits to the employees. Finally, in comparison to defined benefit pension plans, there is an inefficient ability on the part of profit-sharing plans to integrate with the benefits payable under Social Security.

QUALIFICATION REQUIREMENTS APPLICABLE TO DEFERRED PROFIT-SHARING PLANS

For the most part, the same or similar qualification requirements as those applicable to pension plans apply to deferred profit-sharing plans. These requirements relate to (1) the plan provisions being contained in a written document (ensuring a formal, enforceable plan), (2) plan permanency, (3) communication of plan provisions to the employees, (4) the plan being established and operated for the exclusive benefit of plan participants or their beneficiaries, (5) minimum participation (eligibility) standards, (6) nondiscrimination in coverage and contributions/benefits, (7) minimum vesting standards, and so forth. Because of the similarity of treatment between pension plans and profit-sharing plans, the discussion of the general legal requirements for plan qualification will be minimized here.

There are, however, a few ways in which profit-sharing plans are treated differently from pension plans for qualification purposes. Additionally, although pension and profit-sharing plans alike are subject to essentially the same eligibility and vesting rules, the eligibility and vesting requirements found in many profit-sharing plans often tend to be more liberal than these same plan design features when applied to pension plans.

Probably the most notable difference in the treatment of pension and profit-sharing plans for qualification purposes relates to the "definitely determinable benefits" requirement that applies to money purchase and defined benefit pension plans. This qualification requirement does not apply to deferred profit-sharing plans, and the lack of this requirement is the primary feature that distinguishes a profit-sharing plan from a pension plan. A defined benefit pension plan meets the "definitely determinable benefits" requirement through the promise of a specific benefit payable at retirement (the amount of retirement income is the determinable benefit); a money purchase pension plan also meets this requirement through specifying a formula stating a fixed rate (or level) of employer contribution, usually expressed as a percentage of pay, where such contribution is not contingent on profits of the firm (the benefit that can be actuarially determined from the known level of contribution is a determinable benefit).[24] In contrast, a deferred profit-sharing plan, even though a type of defined contribution plan, does not meet the "definitely determinable benefits" requirement since any employer contributions to the plan are contingent on the existence of profits. If there are no profits, the employer is under no obligation to make any contributions to the plan. Thus, under a deferred profit-sharing arrangement the employer does not have the fixed contribution commitment found in money purchase plans, and therefore it is impossible to actuarially determine, in advance of retirement (or other occasion), the specific amount of benefits that will be provided to the plan participants.

---

[24] Reg. 1.401-1(b)(1)(i).

The major effect of the application of the "definitely determinable benefits" requirement to money purchase and defined benefit pension plans relates to the permissible treatment of forfeitures created by the termination of one or more plan participants whose benefits/contributions are less than fully vested. Under a pension plan (both money purchase and defined benefit), any such forfeitures must be used to reduce future employer contributions to the plan. Deferred profit-sharing plans are not restricted in this way, however. Rather, in profit-sharing plans, forfeitures resulting from terminations may be used either to reduce future employer contributions or (as is the usual case) they may be allocated among the remaining participants in the plan, thereby increasing the amounts in their individual accounts.[25]

A second major way in which the qualification requirements differ between pension plans and profit-sharing plans relates to the investment of plan assets in employer securities. Pension plans (including both defined benefit and money purchase plans) are restricted in terms of their ability to invest plan assets in employer stock. These plans are subject to the ERISA requirement that no more than 10 percent of the fair market value of plan assets can be invested in qualifying employer securities and employer real property. This 10 percent limitation becomes fully effective after December 31, 1984.[26] ERISA Section 404 limitations do not apply to profit-sharing plans. As a result, profit-sharing plans may invest plan assets in qualifying employer securities and employer real property without restriction on any percentage limitation.[27]

Many employers believe that investment of a portion of profit-sharing plan assets in employer stock provides the employees with additional incentive to improve their performance in job-related activities. The extent to which companies with profit-sharing plans invest a portion of the plan assets in employer stock is likely to be related to several factors, including company size, overall profitability of the firm (including future prospects as regards profitability), marketability of the stock, and others. The Profit Sharing Research Foundation's study on the largest profit-sharing plans in the United States, cited earlier,[28] showed that the investment of profit-sharing plan assets in employer stock is substantially more prevalent among larger companies than among medium-sized firms, and also is more prevalent among companies whose ownership is closely held. The study under-

---

[25] From the standpoint of the plan participant, the advantage inherent in profit-sharing plans that accrues from reallocation of forfeitures is somewhat mitigated by the presence of more rapid vesting typically found in profit-sharing plans. See *infra.*

[26] From the covered employee's standpoint, this limitation may not be as important under a defined benefit plan as it is under a money purchase plan, since any appreciation in the employer's stock under the defined benefit plan would serve to reduce future employer contributions, thus resulting in no direct benefit to the employee.

[27] Of course, investment of profit-sharing plan assets in employer stock (along with other investment media) must meet the prudent expert standard of ERISA.

[28] *Profit Sharing in 38 Large Companies.*

taken on behalf of the Profit Sharing Council of America[29] examined a much larger sample of plans and observed that 22 percent of the surveyed plans invested in employer stock. In 84 percent of those plans, the amount of employer stock held by the profit-sharing trust represented less than 50 percent of total plan assets. Aside from the issue of whether a company's stock is a sound investment for profit-sharing monies, there is a significant income-tax advantage that accrues to a plan participant upon a lump-sum distribution of plan assets consisting of employer stock.[30]

As mentioned earlier, profit-sharing plans are not subject to certain provisions of ERISA affecting qualified defined benefit pension plans. These primarily relate to the minimum funding standards and the various plan termination insurance requirements.

In addition to those qualification requirements that are distinctive of profit-sharing plans, as described above, other requirements imposed on qualified profit-sharing plans that are the same as or very similar to those applied to pension plans are still of importance to this section. This is because of their specific application to profit-sharing plans and the way in which these requirements are met (and superseded) in actual plan design. The following discussion will focus on two areas: (1) eligibility (participation) requirements, and (2) vesting requirements.

In regard to permissible eligibility requirements, ERISA establishes age 25 as the highest minimum age requirement and one year of service as the longest minimum period of service that may be imposed. (A three-year service requirement is permitted, together with age 25, if the plan provides for full and immediate vesting upon satisfying the plan's eligibility requirements.) These eligibility requirements apply to both profit-sharing and pension plans alike. In addition, the basic coverage rules—the so-called objective rule (70 percent/80 percent test) and the subjective rule (facts and circumstances test)—contained in IRC Section 401(b)(1)(A and B) apply to both profit-sharing and pension plans. However, for many deferred profit-sharing plans in existence today, the eligibility requirements tend to be more liberal than what is required as a minimum standard for qualification purposes.[31] The eligibility requirements used in profit-sharing plans also tend to be more liberal than those commonly employed in pension plans.

Most profit-sharing plans provide broad coverage of employees although the plans often exclude seasonal and part-time employees (e.g., those who work fewer than 1,000 hours per year). A minimum compensation requirement (for the purpose of integrating the plan with Social Security) is seldom applied in determining eligibility for participation;[32] however, the plan may

---

[29] *1981 Profit Sharing Survey*, p. 29.

[30] This tax treatment is described in Chapter 31.

Since there are several advantages and disadvantages surrounding the investment of plan assets in employer stock, great care should be exercised in making this decision.

[31] See *Profit Sharing in 38 Large Companies.*

[32] As will be described in Chapter 31, few profit-sharing plans are integrated with Social Security benefits as a result of the limitations imposed on such plans under federal tax law.

restrict coverage to salaried-only employees provided the plan does not result in the prohibited discrimination. Some plans make employees eligible on the date of hire. Many others use a minimum service requirement of less than one year. It appears, however, that the majority of plans impose a one-year service requirement. Further, there is probably only a limited number of plans that require more than one year of service, in which event the plan must provide full (100 percent) and immediate vesting. Certainly, the use of a maximum age limitation (e.g., age 60) at date of hire is not permitted in profit-sharing plans since these plans are of the defined contribution type. Most profit-sharing plans do not even use a minimum age requirement, despite being permitted to do so under ERISA. In summary, as regards eligibility and participation, most deferred profit-sharing plans impose only a service eligibility requirement along with the requirement that employees meet a minimum employment test (generally 1,000 hours per year).

As regards vesting in profit-sharing plans, IRC Section 411(a) specifies three alternative minimum statutory vesting standards, of which at least one must be complied with under both profit-sharing and pension plans. These three rules are commonly referred to as the "10-Year Rule," the "5-to-15 Year Rule," and the "Rule of 45."[33] In addition, the IRS often applies a "4-40 vesting standard" to new plans seeking qualification and in those instances where the IRS feels that discrimination may occur.[34] There are two important exceptions to these four minimum vesting standards that apply to profit-sharing plans. These two exceptions are the "class year plan rule" under IRC Section 411(d)(4),[35] and the special "cash or deferred plan rule." The latter rule requires that IRC Section 401(k) cash or deferred plans provide full and immediate vesting, upon plan participation, in regard to those amounts subject to the cash/deferred election.[36] Under class year vesting, the employer contributions become 100 percent vested after lapsation of a specified time, measured from the date that each set of contribu-

---

[33] Each of these three vesting rules, together with the "4-40 rule" (see *infra*), is described in detail in Chapter 27 of the *Handbook*.

[34] Because of forfeiture allocation procedures in profit-sharing plans, the IRS, in some instances, may require more rapid vesting (e.g., 4-40) than the ERISA-specified minimum standards. This might occur where deemed necessary to prevent discrimination in favor of the "prohibited group" (consisting of the officers, shareholder-employees, and the highly paid) resulting from the allocation of nonvested forfeitures among the group of remaining participants who, in turn, might be comprised primarily of members of the "prohibited group."

In addition, for years beginning after 1983, plans that are classified as "top-heavy" plans must comply with additional vesting requirements imposed under the Tax Equity and Fiscal Responsibility Act of 1982 (TEFRA). Specifically, if a plan is "top-heavy," its vesting schedule must comply with either one of two rules: (*a*) "three-year vesting," or (*b*) "six-year graded vesting."

[35] The class year plan vesting rule also may be applied to stock bonus and money purchase plans.

[36] Hence, if 40 percent of the distribution may be received in cash or deferred with the other 60 percent required to be deferred, then IRC Section 411 requires nonforfeitability only for the 40 percent subject to the cash/deferred election; vesting for the other 60 percent may be delayed subject to the other minimum vesting standards (e.g., 10-year rule, and the like).

tions was made; that is, each year's contributions vest separately from the vesting of contributions for all other plan years. The IRC Section 411(d)(4) class year plan vesting rule requires that the employee's right with respect to employer contributions for any plan year must become nonforfeitable no later than at the end of the fifth plan year following the plan year for which each specific set of contributions is made.

While the vast majority of defined benefit pension plans provide for 100 percent vesting after 10 years of service (10-year "cliff" vesting; see *infra*), the substantial majority of profit-sharing plans provide for more liberal vesting than prescribed under any of the three IRC Section 411(a) alternative minimum standards. The trend in recent years is that an increasing number of deferred profit-sharing plans require fewer years of service in order to become 100 percent vested. Today, while a significant percentage of profit-sharing plans provide full and immediate vesting upon plan participation and others provide "cliff" vesting (no vesting until the end of a specified period of plan participation—such as five or ten years—at which time benefits become 100 percent vested), the substantial majority of plans use some type of graduated (graded) vesting schedule. The most common type of graduated vesting arrangement provides an additional 10 percent per year of service (beginning after the first year of service), thereby resulting in 100 percent vesting in the employee's individual account after 10 years of service.[37] In a small percentage of plans, a class year vesting system is used. In addition to these vesting schedules, some companies provide for full vesting to all plan participants reaching a specified age (e.g., 55) regardless of length of service. Other firms provide full vesting if a participant's employment is terminated "through no fault of the employee;" this might occur, for example, at the closing of a plant, department, or smaller organizational unit. Finally, while the law requires that full vesting occur at retirement and upon plan termination, nearly all deferred profit-sharing plans also provide full vesting in the event of the participant's death or total and permanent disability.

The liberal eligibility and vesting requirements typically found in most profit-sharing plans are consistent with an overall employer objective (as regards the establishment of a profit-sharing plan) of providing employees with an incentive to work more efficiently, which, it is hoped, will lead to increased profits for the firm.[38] This objective can be maximized in

---

[37] Under both "cliff" vesting and graduated vesting, once the plan participant becomes 100 percent vested, all future employer contributions vest fully and immediately at the time they are made. This is in direct contrast to the situation existing under class year vesting.

[38] It also should be noted that the employer's contributions (costs) to a profit-sharing plan are not increased or otherwise affected either by a larger number of participants (through more liberal eligibility requirements) or through more rapid vesting; assuming, of course, that nonvested forfeitures are reallocated among the remaining participants (the typical case) rather than used to reduce future employer contributions. (While this statement is generally true, it is not applicable to those profit-sharing plans that base their contribution on a percentage of compensation subject to a maximum contribution based on profit.) This is in direct contrast to

a deferred profit-sharing plan only through broad participation, through the imposition of few eligibility restrictions, and the providing of liberal vesting.

In conclusion, the employer's reason(s) for establishing a deferred profit-sharing plan, in all likelihood, should have a direct bearing on the specific eligibility and vesting requirements adopted by the plan. That is, an objective of providing employee incentives would indicate short periods for vesting and minimum or no eligibility requirements. Other objectives, such as maximizing the retirement income that may be provided to long-service employees from a specified amount of employer contribution, might indicate longer vesting periods and more stringent eligibility requirements as long as ERISA's minimum standards are complied with.

---

the situation that results in either a money purchase or a defined benefit pension plan. Pension plans that are designed with more liberal eligibility and vesting rules should result in higher costs to the employer. Thus, to reduce total plan costs, pension plans tend to impose more restrictive eligibility rules and less liberal vesting requirements than those used in deferred profit-sharing plans. It is important to note, however, that under profit-sharing plans, the *allocation* of both contributions (profits) and forfeitures among plan participants would be affected, of course, by the plan's eligibility and vesting requirements.

CHAPTER 31

Profit-Sharing Plans (continued)

BRUCE A. PALMER

CONTRIBUTIONS TO DEFERRED PROFIT-SHARING PLANS

The subject matter pertaining to profit-sharing contributions constitutes a most important topic in regard to the overall design of deferred profit-sharing plans. It is these contribution amounts, together with investment earnings and forfeiture reallocations, that ultimately determine the magnitude of the funds available for distribution to plan participants at retirement or upon other prescribed occasions.

The discussion of profit-sharing contributions is divided into three major subsections. These subsections describe, respectively, the various methods of ascertaining contribution amounts to deferred profit-sharing plans, alternative formulas for allocating the profit-sharing contributions among the plan participants, and the maximum limits imposed under federal tax law on contributions and allocations.

Methods of Determining Profit-Sharing Contributions

A most important concern of profit-sharing plans centers on the question, "How much of the profits should be shared with the employees?" In regard to a specific employer, the portion or percentage of profits that should be contributed is likely to depend on several factors, including (1) the amount and stability of the firm's annual profits; (2) the capital requirements of the firm (e.g., needs for working capital, reserves, and expansion); (3) the level of return to be provided stockholders on their investment in the firm; (4) the presence (or absence) of other capital accumulation or retirement income programs sponsored by the firm; (5) the portion of profits that is to be used in upgrading the (cash) payroll levels of the employees; (6) the maximum limitations under federal tax law applying to annual contributions, deductions, and allocations to participants' accounts; and, of course, (7) the objectives of the plan, particularly the extent to which management believes that the profit-sharing plan serves as a motivator to the covered employees and the extent to which employee behavior can affect, in a significant way, the profit levels of the particular firm in question.[1]

A second area of interest relating to profit-sharing contributions concerns how profits are to be defined. Employers have considerable flexibility in defining "profits" for purposes of their deferred profit-sharing plans, since this term is not defined in great detail under the federal tax laws governing profit-sharing plans. While traditionally profits as used in the context of profit-sharing plans relate to current year profits, it is legally permissible for deferred profit-sharing plans to base their profit-sharing contributions on both current profits and profits accumulated from prior years. If desired, the definition also may include capital gains and losses. Further, profits can be defined either in terms of "before-tax profits" or "aftertax profits," with the majority of companies basing their profit-sharing contributions on before-tax profits.[2] Additionally, a significant number of plans provide that only profits in excess of some stipulated minimum dollar amount, or of minimum return on invested capital, are available for profit sharing.[3] Conditions such as these are commonly referred to as "prior reservations for capital," or simply "prior reservations." Their purpose is to protect the financial interests of the company's shareholders. Employers that incorporate a prior reservation in regard to their profit-sharing contributions commonly share a greater percentage of profits, once the reservation has been satisfied, than plans that do not include a prior reservation. The rationale for smaller profit-sharing percentages (often between 5 percent and 10 percent of before-tax profits) in companies not stipulating a prior reservation is that these percentages are applied to all profits, not just those amounts in excess of some stipulated level, as is the case with employers that specify a prior reservation. Prior reservations may be stated in a number of ways including, for example, (1) placing a minimum dollar limitation (e.g., $25,000) on profits, (2) requiring a specified minimum

---

[1] One fairly basic concept in this regard is to split profits equally into three shares: (*a*) one third to employees in the form of profit-sharing contributions, (*b*) one third to stockholders in the form of dividends, and (*c*) one third to customers, either through price reductions or expenditures for product improvement. In some instances, element (*c*) is eliminated, with that share going into company surplus and being available for reinvestment in the company's operations. It is important to note that when companies provide as much as a one-third share of profits to employees, it may very well be the case that not all of these monies will flow into a deferred profit-sharing arrangement, because of limitations on tax deductions and allocations (and possibly for other reasons). Rather, a substantial portion of these profit-sharing monies might be distributed immediately to the employees.

[2] It should be noted that employers are permitted to determine "profits" in accordance with generally accepted accounting principles, rather than in accordance with federal income-tax laws to the extent that these definitions may differ.

[3] Even when a specific provision for a minimum return on capital is not included in a profit-sharing formula, the concept generally is taken into consideration in the profit-sharing deliberations, even though in an indirect way.

return (e.g., 5 percent) on net worth, or (3) stating a minimum amount (e.g., 30 cents per share) for stockholder dividends before any profit-sharing distributions will be made to the employees.

Another aspect relating to methods of determining profit-sharing contributions centers on the issue of whether to share profits on the basis of a fixed formula, with its terms and conditions communicated in advance to the plan participants, or to permit the company's board of directors annually to determine in a discretionary manner the percentage of profits to be shared. As stated in Chapter 30, qualified deferred profit-sharing plans are not subject to the requirement applicable to pension plans that the benefits (or the contributions) be "definitely determinable." As a result, employers possess considerably greater flexibility in regard to the timing and amount(s) of contributions to profit-sharing plans than they possess in regard to money purchase or defined benefit pension plans. In fact, sponsors of profit-sharing plans are not even required to incorporate in the plan provisions a definite predetermined contribution formula, since they are not required to contribute "the same amount or contribute in accordance with the same ratio every year."[4] Rather, the company's board of directors is permitted to annually ascertain and determine, on a discretionary basis, the amount of profits to be shared with the plan participants. In any event, whether employer contributions to the plan are discretionary or based on a predetermined formula, the employer does not have to consider such actuarial factors as investment experience, age distribution of employees, and employee turnover in determining the periodic contributions to the plan.

Although the use of a predetermined or fixed-contribution formula is not required under the law (and, consequently, no specific minimum level or rate of contribution is required), profit-sharing contributions must meet two other legal requirements. Specifically, the contributions must be "substantial and recurring"[5] to lend support to the qualification requirement pertaining to plan permanency, and these contributions cannot be applied in any manner (either in amount or time) that would result in discrimination in favor of the prohibited group of employees. As long as these general restrictions are complied with, an employer may establish any method or formula for determining the profit-sharing amounts that are to be contributed to the plan.

The major advantage of the discretionary approach, of course, is its tremendous contribution flexibility in the annual determination of contributions. Under this approach, the board of directors has the opportunity of viewing past experience and the firm's current financial position and capital requirements before making the decision on how much or what portion of profits are to be shared in the current year. Contribution rates may be

---

[4] Reg. 1.401-1(b)(2).

[5] Reg. 1.401-1(b)(2).

adjusted upward or downward from previous years' rates based on any number of factors, including the current financial picture of the firm. Under the predetermined formula approach, the plan itself would have to be amended in order to accommodate an employer's desire to adjust the profit-sharing contribution rate. Use of the discretionary method also provides the employer with the assurance that the firm will not have to make contributions to the deferred profit-sharing plan in amounts that might exceed the maximums that may be deducted currently for federal income-tax purposes or that these contribution amounts, when taken together with forfeiture reallocations, might violate the "annual additions limit" applicable to additions to the individual participants' accounts.[6] When the discretionary method is used, the plan often stipulates minimum and maximum percentages of profits to be distributed (e.g., 10 percent to 30 percent of profits, or whatever predetermined range that is desired by the employer). These limitations therefore create a more narrow range within which the board of directors may exercise discretionary authority in regard to contributions to the profit-sharing plan. Other illustrations of discretionary arrangements include "discretionary, but not to be less than 10 percent of before-tax profits," and "discretionary, but approximately 20 percent of before-tax profits." The purpose of such arrangements is to provide some guidelines or constraints to the board of directors as it exercises its discretionary authority. Again, any of these guidelines also could include some form of a prior reservation for capital.

When a firm uses the discretionary method, the general procedure is for the board of directors to make the determination of the dollar amount of profits to be shared shortly before the end of the corporation's taxable year. This is in accordance with the basic rule that, to be deductible, the tax liability must be established prior to the end of the taxable year. With a fixed-formula approach, the formula establishes the liability, and thus the amount of profits to be shared does not have to be ascertained in dollar terms until after the end of the tax year for those corporations whose tax is figured on an accrual basis.

At one time, the Internal Revenue Service, for qualification purposes, required that deferred profit-sharing plans include a fixed-contribution formula. However, as a result of several court decisions to the contrary, the IRS rules were liberalized to permit employers to determine the profit-sharing amounts (or percentages) without a predetermined formula. Despite the fact that the discretionary approach currently has the approval, albeit given reluctantly, of the Internal Revenue Service, this method is not without its disadvantages. One of these disadvantages relates to the pres-

---

[6] While these are legitimate concerns when using fixed-contribution formulas, satisfactory results may be obtained through including conditions in the plan specifying that contributions not be in excess of the maximum deductible amount, and that they not be in violation of the "annual additions limit." As a result, these concerns should not be viewed as a deterrent to the use of predetermined or fixed-contribution formulas.

sures that the board of directors must face in making the decisions pertaining to profit-sharing amounts. If flexibility is a major employer goal, then the firm probably will find the discretionary approach more advantageous; but, at the same time, some type of formula method takes many of the burdens and pressures off the board of directors in making decisions on profit-sharing amounts during periods of economic instability (e.g., when the firm has experienced high profit levels for the current year but the forecast is for a severe economic downturn next year; or, conversely, there are low profits in the current year with much brighter prospects for next year). Previously established guidelines would be helpful to the board of directors when these circumstances occur.

A second potential disadvantage associated with the discretionary method relates to the morale of the employees and their sense of financial security. Without a fixed formula, employees may experience feelings of uncertainty about the extent they can count on sharing in the profits that they have helped produce. In this context, the argument for using a fixed formula for determining profit-sharing amounts is that the "ground rules" are established in advance. At the beginning of the year the employees have the knowledge that their share of the profits will be determined in accordance with the terms contained in the formula.

A third potential disadvantage is that the Wage-Hour Division of the Department of Labor requires that a company use a definite formula if the firm desires to exclude the profit-sharing contributions from regular pay rates in calculating overtime pay. There are exceptions to this requirement, however. If the profit-sharing contributions are allocated to the participants on a basis that includes overtime pay or the plan provides for full and immediate vesting, contributions determined on a discretionary basis do not have to be included in pay when computing overtime rates.

Finally, the use of the discretionary method may expose the contributions to the potential risk that they will come under any wage (and price) guidelines in effect at the time the contributions are made to the deferred profit-sharing plan. For example, in 1979 the President's Council on Wage and Price Stability released its decision on the treatment of profit-sharing plans. Contributions to profit-sharing plans using a discretionary approach were to be treated as incentive pay and, therefore, come within the wage guidelines. Under the decision, qualified deferred profit-sharing plans that apply a fixed (definite) formula were not to come under the wage guideline calculations to the extent that the formula is not changed.

The aforementioned disadvantages associated with the discretionary approach, despite its flexibility, are major reasons why many large employers have decided to use a definite predetermined formula. Thirty-six of the 38 companies surveyed in *Profit Sharing in 38 Large Companies* used a predetermined formula for determining annual profit-sharing contributions. Smaller companies (up to 1,000 plan participants) have a greater tendency to determine profit-sharing contributions on a discretionary basis, since they appear to be more concerned with contribution and financing flexibility.

In essence, there is an unlimited variety of fixed formulas that an employer may choose from as long as the contributions are made out of profits (current or accumulated). Most definite predetermined formulas specify fixed percentages or sliding scales (either ascending or descending) of percentages based on before-tax or aftertax profits and with or without prior reservations. Examples of predetermined formulas using a fixed percentage are "10 percent of before-tax profits" and "25 percent of before-tax profits but no more than the amount that is available as a current tax deduction." An illustration of a formula involving a sliding scale (ascending) of percentages used by one large company is: "3.5 percent on the first $100 million of before-tax profits, 5.0 percent on the next $50 million, and 6.0 percent on before-tax profits in excess of $150 million." Because of its obvious drawbacks, primarily relating to employee motivation, a formula providing for a scale of decreasing percentages rarely is used. An example of a fixed formula with a prior reservation is "20 percent of before-tax profits in excess of 5 percent of net worth." Certainly, many other examples of predetermined formulas exist.

It also is possible that a formula prescribing a percentage of compensation (of covered employees) could be used, but only if the plan imposes conditions pertaining to the availability of profits (current or accumulated).[7] Otherwise, without such conditions, plans using a percentage of compensation formula likely would be classified by the IRS as a money purchase pension plan (or, possibly, a funded nonqualified deferred compensation plan with adverse tax consequences). A sample compensation-based profit-sharing formula appears in Table 31-1.

Table 31-1
A Sample Compensation-Based Profit-Sharing Formula

Level of Profits	Profit-Sharing Contribution as a Percent of Covered Compensation
Below $50,000	None
$50,000–$199,999	3%
200,000–349,999	5
350,000–499,999	7
500,000 and over	9

In addition to its relative inflexibility, from an employee relations standpoint a possible disadvantage of a definite predetermined formula is that the

---

[7] To use a percentage of compensation formula, it would be necessary for the plan to define "compensation" (e.g., base compensation only, base compensation plus bonuses or overtime, and the like) in addition to defining "profits."

amending of the formula may be difficult to accomplish in the event that the amended formula clearly produces a lesser share of profits for the employees. Thus, careful consideration should be given to the initial decision on the profit-sharing percentage(s) that will be included in the formula. To take advantage of the desirable features of both discretionary and fixed formulas, some employers, especially employers of smaller size, use a combination method whereby the plan uses a definite formula providing a minimum fixed-contribution rate applied to profits and supplements these amounts with additional profit-sharing distributions determined, on a discretionary basis, by the board of directors. The specific approach adopted, whether discretionary, predetermined formula, or combination of these, and the precise details of the method chosen will be reflective of the employer's goals and objectives for the plan and the perceived impact of the plan and its profit-sharing method upon the employee group.

Methods of Allocating Employer Contributions among Plan Participants

Once the amount of profit-sharing contributions has been determined for the year, these monies, in turn, must be allocated to the individual participants' accounts. While qualified deferred profit-sharing plans are not required to use a fixed (or predetermined) formula for determining the level of contributions to the plan, the law does require that a predetermined formula for allocating profit-sharing contributions among employee accounts be specified in the plan. The purpose underlying this requirement is to ensure that the contribution allocation does not discriminate in favor of employees who are officers, shareholders, or highly compensated (i.e., the "prohibited group").[8] In other words, to ascertain whether a plan meets the qualification requirements, the IRS must be able to examine the allocation formula to determine that allocations will be made in a nondiscriminatory manner.

The employer has a wide range of alternative methods for allocating profit-sharing contributions among individual employee accounts, depending on the nature of the plan and the employer objectives that are sought. The most commonly used approach is based on compensation (with age and years of service ignored); that is, the amounts are allocated based on the ratio of each individual employee's compensation to the total compensation of all covered participants for the year. There generally is no discrimination problem when profit-sharing amounts are allocated on the basis of compensation. To illustrate this method, assume employee A has compensation of $20,000 during the year. If the total covered compensation for the plan participants is $400,000 for the year, employee A would be entitled to 5 percent ($20,000 divided by $400,000) of the total profit-sharing alloca-

---

[8] IRC Section 401(a)(4).

tion. If the aggregate profit-sharing contributions amount to $50,000 for the year, employee A's share would be $2,500 (5 percent of $50,000). When using a contribution allocation formula based on compensation, the plan sponsor also must specify the amounts that are to be included in determining compensation. For example, compensation for an individual participant may include all compensation paid the employee during the plan year, even though this individual was a plan participant for only part of the year; or compensation may be defined to include only the amounts earned by the employee for that portion of the year that he or she also was a participant in the plan. Further, compensation must be defined in terms of whether it includes base (or regular) pay only or if it also includes bonuses, overtime, commissions, or other forms of cash compensation.[9] However compensation is defined, it must be determined and allocations based on compensation must be accomplished in a nondiscriminatory manner.

Another type of contribution allocation formula bases the allocation on both compensation and length (years) of service. Formulas incorporating both compensation and service typically allocate profit-sharing contributions on the basis of each participant's number of "points" awarded for the current year in proportion to total credited points of all plan participants for the year. Commonly, one point might be awarded for each $100 of compensation. An additional point, for example, might be given the employee for each of his or her years of service.[10] To illustrate, an employee whose compensation (as defined in the plan) is $25,000 and who has 15 years of service with the employer would be credited with 265 points [($25,000/$100 = 250) + 15] for the current year. The contribution allocation to this employee's account for the current year would be determined first by computing the ratio of his or her number of points, 265, divided by the total number of points credited to all plan participants during the year. This ratio (percentage) would then be applied to the current year's profit-sharing contribution to derive the share that is to be allocated to this employee's individual account.

Relatively few deferred profit-sharing plans base their contribution allocations on length of service only. As evidenced by previous rulings, it should be anticipated that the IRS will closely scrutinize any contribution allocation formula based on length of service (either service-only formulas or compensation-and-service formulas) for the purpose of ascertaining

---

[9] If the profit-sharing plan does not contain a fixed predetermined contribution formula (i.e., the plan uses a discretionary method), the plan is required under federal labor law (1) to provide for full and immediate vesting, or (2) to include overtime earnings in any definition of compensation on which the allocation of contributions is based; otherwise, the profit-sharing allocations themselves must be added to base pay rates in computing overtime pay. See *supra*.

[10] It is possible that more than one point would be credited to each year of service. Further, units other than $100 might be used in determining the number of points to be awarded for a specific amount of compensation. Considerable flexibility exists in specifying the exact way in which the points are to be awarded, conditioned on the point system not being found by the IRS to be discriminatory.

whether the "prohibited discrimination" exists. The underlying rationale on why the IRS might express a concern regarding service-based formulas is that employees who are members of the prohibited group often have long periods of service in comparison with other employees.

In summary, the plan's contribution allocation formula is used in determining the participant's share for accounting or other recordkeeping purposes. These monies are then allocated to individual employee accounts. However, this does not imply that the contribution dollars are segregated for investment purposes. While the profit-sharing trust may permit each participant's account to be invested in "earmarked" assets (an insurance contract, for example), profit-sharing contributions often are received, administered, and invested by the trustee as commingled assets. In the latter case, the balance in each participant's account at a specific time simply represents his or her current share of the assets (commingled) of the trust. Further, the concept of individual employee accounts does not require that the participant be entitled currently to all or any part of the funds credited to his or her individual account. Rather, this entitlement would depend on the plan's provisions regarding vesting, withdrawals and loans, and automatic distributions.

Maximum Limits

A number of maximum limits, each of substantial importance, apply to deferred profit-sharing plans. Several of these relate to maximums placed on the amount of profit-sharing contributions that may be deducted, for federal income-tax purposes, by an employer in any one tax year. Other limits, such as the "annual additions limit" and the "1.4 (140 percent) rule," relate to maximums imposed on employer-provided contributions/benefits under qualified plans. Collectively, these limits place important constraints on what the employers can do for their covered employees through deferred profit-sharing arrangements. All of these limits will be described here.

An overriding consideration in this area is that profit-sharing contributions, when added to all other compensation paid an employee for the year, must be "reasonable" for the services performed by the employee and, in addition, be shown to be an "ordinary and necessary expense" of doing business.[11] If this is not the case, the IRS may deny the tax deduction to the employer for any part or all of the profit-sharing contributions (and, possibly, other compensation amounts as well) made on behalf of the employee.[12]

---

[11] This statement is not restricted to profit-sharing contributions but is equally true for all forms of compensation.

[12] In most large publicly held firms the question of "unreasonable compensation" arises only on an infrequent basis. When this question is raised, it tends to be in those businesses whose ownership is closely held by a small number of individuals.

In the context of specific maximums, probably the single most important limit affecting deferred profit-sharing plans is the IRS limit on the maximum amount of contributions that may be deducted by the employer in any one tax year. This limit, together with other important provisions which provide an element of contribution flexibility to the employer, is set forth in IRC Section 404. In deferred profit-sharing plans, the basic limit on the deductibility of employer contributions is that annual deductible contributions may not exceed "15 percent of compensation otherwise paid or accrued during the taxable year to all employees under the plan."[13] The 15 percent limitation on deductions applies regardless of the manner in which employer contributions are determined (i.e., discretionary versus formula, or type of formula); however, the limit applies only to employer contributions to a deferred profit-sharing arrangement. Thus, employers who provide for both cash and deferred profit sharing, either through an IRC Section 401(k) cash or deferred plan or through separate cash and deferred plans, are affected by the 15 percent limit on employer deductions only for contributions to the deferred portion of the profit-sharing arrangement. Thus, if an employer's profit-sharing arrangement calls for the sharing of 30 percent of the before-tax profits, and if 40 percent of this amount is to be distributed in cash (with the balance deferred), then the limit of IRC Section 404(a)(3) applies only to the 18 percent [30% − (30%)×(40%)] of before-tax profits that is contributed to the deferred plan. Furthermore, the 18 percent of before-tax profits (or a portion thereof) will be deductible as a contribution to the deferred profit-sharing plan to the extent that this amount does not exceed 15 percent of the total compensation of the plan participants.

If the 15 percent limitation were the only provision of IRC Section 404(a)(3) affecting employer deductions for contributions to deferred profit-sharing plans, the employer's contribution flexibility and his or her ability to utilize the full 15 percent deduction, each and every year, would be seriously curtailed. This is attributable to the very nature of profit-sharing contributions, in that employer contributions are based on the existence and levels of profits. Since a firm's profits fluctuate over time, the only way that the employer's deductible contributions could "average" 15 percent over a long period is for the employer to contribute (and deduct) monies equaling 15 percent of compensation *each* and *every* year. Given the variable nature of profits, this is not likely to be achieved without some form of regulatory relief. To provide the employer with both greater contribution flexibility and a reasonable opportunity of achieving the 15 percent maximum deduction (if desired) over the long-run, IRC Section 404 also permits the use of credit and contribution carry-overs.[14]

---

[13] IRC Section 404(a)(3).

[14] Of course, it may be that the employer does not desire to contribute the maximum amount.

A credit carry-over results whenever the employer's contribution for the year is less than the maximum allowable deduction of 15 percent of covered compensation for the year. This credit is carried forward and may be used by the employer in any subsequent tax year in which contributions exceed 15 percent of covered compensation, thereby enabling the employer to take a deduction in a later tax year for an amount in excess of 15 percent of the then-current covered compensation.[15] Two additional comments are of importance here. First, while there is no limitation on the amount(s) of credit carry-over that may be accumulated for use in subsequent years, the maximum overall deduction including credit carry-overs cannot exceed the IRC established limit of 25 percent of covered compensation for any given tax year.[16] Second, the credit carry-over amounts are expressed in dollars, not in terms of percentages [e.g., when the employer makes contributions equaling 10 percent of $600,000 of covered compensation, the credit carry-over is $30,000 ($600,000 multiplied by 5 percent); the credit carry-over is not equal to 5 percent (15 percent minus 10 percent) of a subsequent year's covered compensation—an amount that may be either greater or less than $600,000]. Both of these points are illustrated in Table 31-2.

A contribution carry-over is created whenever the employer's annual contributions are in excess of the maximum allowable deduction for the year. The maximum allowable deduction is 15 percent of covered compensation (as stated above) unless credit carry-overs are available, in which case the maximum allowable deduction is the lesser of (a) 25 percent of compensation or (b) 15 percent of compensation plus the credit carry-overs. As is true for credit carry-overs, contribution carry-overs may be accumulated without limit into the future. In turn, they may be deducted in any subsequent year (or years) in which the employer's contribution that year is less

---

[15] A profit-sharing formula that limits contributions to the amount deductible under IRC Section 404(a)(3) will not preclude the availability or operation of the credit carry-over feature. However, if a company uses a fixed formula that limits profit-sharing contributions to 15 percent of the participants' compensation, it will be impossible for the company to take advantage of the credit carry-over feature.

[16] On occasion, this "25 percent limitation" can be confusing because ERISA also established a 25 percent (of covered compensation) aggregate limit on employer deductions when the employer has both a profit-sharing plan and a money purchase pension plan that cover a common group of employees [IRC Section 404(a)(7)]. In the case of a combination profit-sharing plan and defined benefit pension plan, the maximum annual deductible contribution to the combined plans is limited to 25 percent of covered compensation or, if larger, the amount necessary to meet the minimum funding requirements of the defined benefit plan alone. If circumstances are such that the minimum funding rules require the employer to contribute amounts to the defined benefit plan during a year that, by themselves, are in excess of 25 percent of covered compensation, the employer, in effect, is precluded from making a deductible contribution to the profit-sharing plan that year; however, the employer will be eligible for a credit carry-over that is available for use in subsequent years. The separate limit on the deductibility of employer contributions to the profit-sharing plan still applies in combination pension and profit-sharing plans. Another factor that increases the potential for confusion in this area is the "25 percent annual additions limit," which restricts the amount of certain types of additions that may be made to defined contribution plans, including both deferred profit-sharing and money purchase pension plans.

Table 31-2
Annual Allowable Tax Deductions for Contributions to a Deferred Profit-Sharing Plan: A Hypothetical Example

(1) Year	(2) Profit Before Taxes	(3) Contributions (fixed formula of 20 percent of before-tax profits)	(4) Covered Compensation	(5) 15 Percent of (4)	(6) 25 Percent of (4)	(7) Allowable Deduction	(8) Carry-over Contribution	(8) Carry-over Credit
N	$ 300,000	$ 60,000	$ 600,000	$ 90,000	$ 150,000	60,000 [lesser of $60,000, $90,000, or $150,000]	$ 0	$30,000
N + 1	500,000	100,000	700,000	105,000	175,000	100,000 [lesser of $100,000, ($105,000 + $30,000 = $135,000), or $175,000]	0	35,000
N + 2	200,000	40,000	700,000	105,000	175,000	40,000 [lesser of $40,000, ($105,000 + $35,000 = $140,000), or $175,000]	0	100,000
N + 3	1,200,000	240,000	800,000	120,000	200,000	200,000 [lesser of $240,000, ($120,000 + $100,000 = $220,000), or $200,000]	40,000	20,000
N + 4	750,000	150,000	800,000	120,000	200,000	140,000 [lesser of ($150,000 + $40,000 = $190,000), ($120,000 + $20,000 = $140,000), or $200,000]	50,000	0
N + 5	350,000	70,000	800,000	120,000	200,000	120,000 [lesser of ($70,000 + $50,000 = $120,000), $120,000, or $200,000]	0	0
Totals	$3,300,000	$660,000	$4,400,000	$660,000	$1,100,000	$660,000	$ 0	$ 0

than the otherwise maximum allowable deduction. Of course, unless credit carry-overs are available the maximum allowable deduction for any year, including contribution carry-overs, cannot exceed 15 percent of the then covered compensation amount.

Table 31–2 illustrates the application of contribution and credit carry-overs for a hypothetical deferred profit-sharing plan. As exemplified in the table, it is possible under certain circumstances (namely, when the 25 percent aggregate limit on employer deductions is reached) for a plan to have both contribution and credit carry-overs existing in the same year. In the illustrated table, this occurs in year N+3.

Since the hypothetical example depicted in Table 31–2 is quite complicated, its intricacies should be studied in detail to obtain a full understanding of the importance of the 15 percent (annual) deduction limit, the 25 percent aggregate (annual) deduction limit, and contribution and credit carry-overs. However, in spite of its complexity, it is easy to see in Table 31–2 the role that carry-overs play in increasing the contribution flexibility to the employer and, simultaneously, in permitting larger *average* annual deductions than what would result if carry-overs were not allowed in profit-sharing plans. Since the contribution and credit carry-overs are both equal to zero at the end of year N+5, the employer has been able to achieve an average annual tax deduction of 15 percent of covered compensation ($660,000 divided by $4,400,000 equals 15 percent) over the six-year period, even though profit levels and contributions, together with compensation, have fluctuated over this period. Without the availability of carry-overs, the employer would have received total deductions of only $510,000 ($60,000 + $100,000 + $40,000 + $120,000 + $120,000 + $70,000 = $510,000),[17] which equals 11.6 percent of the total covered compensation amount of $4,400,000. Thus, the employer would not have been able to achieve (if desired) an average 15 percent annual deduction without the permitted use of carry-overs.

Contributions, together with forfeiture reallocations, in deferred profit-sharing plans are subject to the "annual additions limit" of IRC Section 415(c). This section of the code prescribes limitations on the amounts of monies that can be added, on an annual basis, to individual participants' accounts under defined contribution plans. Thus, IRC Section 415 applies to both deferred profit-sharing plans and money purchase pension plans. Contributions in excess of the IRC Section 415 limits will result in dis-

---

[17] These amounts were derived as follows:

Year	Deduction
N	Lesser of $60,000 or (.15 × $600,000 = $90,000)
N + 1	Lesser of $100,000 or (.15 × $700,000 = $105,000)
N + 2	Lesser of $40,000 or (.15 × $700,000 = $105,000)
N + 3	Lesser of $240,000 or (.15 × $800,000 = $120,000)
N + 4	Lesser of $150,000 or (.15 × $800,000 = $120,000)
N + 5	Lesser of $70,000 or (.15 × $800,000 = $120,000)

qualification of the plan. Thus, the employer must make sure that these limits are complied with. Conceivably, the annual additions limit could reduce the contribution that an employer might otherwise make to the account of an individual participant in a given year.

The term *annual additions* includes (a) employer contributions, (b) forfeiture reallocations, and (c) under some circumstances, a portion of the employee's own contributions.[18] For purposes of the annual additions limit, investment earnings allocated to employee's account balances, rollover contributions, and loan repayments are not part of annual additions. Since this chapter is concerned primarily with deferred profit-sharing plans that are funded exclusively with employer contributions, component (c) of the annual additions limit is of little importance here and therefore will be ignored.

Under the defined contribution plan limits of IRC Section 415, a qualified plan may not provide an annual addition, in any year, to any participant's account which exceeds the lesser of 25 percent of compensation (for that year) or a stipulated dollar amount ($30,000 for 1983). To illustrate how the annual additions limit might impose a constraint in the context of a deferred profit-sharing plan, let us consider two simple examples. First, assume that employer contributions to the profit-sharing plan for the year are equal to the maximum deductible amount (no credit carry-over) of 15 percent of covered compensation. To the extent that forfeitures exist and are reallocated to participants' accounts, the amount of such reallocated forfeitures cannot exceed 10 percent of compensation (applied individually). If, in a second example, the current year's profit-sharing contributions (assuming sufficient credit carry-overs) constitute 20 percent of covered employee compensation, any forfeiture reallocations must be restricted to no more than 5 percent of compensation, applied individually. It should be observed that the possibility exists that for higher-income employees the stipulated dollar maximum (e.g., $30,000) may act as a constraint, thereby possibly resulting in the situation where the annual additions, as a percentage of compensation, for these higher-income employees will be smaller than the annual additions percentage for those employees whose compensation is at such a level (lower) that they are unaffected by the dollar maximum on annual additions. Employers often include specific plan provisions that are designed to avoid this result.

Many employers have combination pension and profit-sharing arrangements that are designed to provide significant amounts of retirement in-

---

[18] Employee contributions not exceeding 6 percent of pay do not have to be included in the annual additions limit. To the extent that employee contributions exceed 6 percent, only the lesser of (a) employee contribution amounts exceeding 6 percent of pay, or (b) 50 percent of the total employee contributions will be included as annual additions. Further, deductible employee contributions that are deemed "qualified voluntary employee contributions" as provided for by the Economic Recovery Tax Act of 1981 are not included as annual additions for purposes of applying the IRC Section 415 limit (see *infra*).

come from the pension plan (a plan that is often integrated with Social Security) and to provide for asset or capital accumulation through the establishment of the required individual accounts under the profit-sharing plan. Recently, a number of companies have elected to supplement an existing pension plan through the establishment of a deferred profit-sharing plan. Other companies in recent years have established pension plans to supplement existing profit-sharing arrangements. It is anticipated that this trend will continue, whereby more companies will establish both pension and deferred profit-sharing programs to work in tandem in providing employees with greater retirement income security.

In essence, there are two basic ways in which to have a combination plan that includes a deferred profit-sharing arrangement: (1) combination of a money purchase pension plan and a profit-sharing plan; and (2) combination of a defined benefit pension plan and a profit-sharing plan. In the first arrangement, since both plans are of the defined contribution variety and assuming the plans cover the same group of employees, the combined plans must comply with the annual additions limit of the lesser of 25 percent of pay or a stated dollar maximum ($30,000 in 1983). (In addition, assuming no credit carry-overs, the usual 15 percent annual maximum on the deductibility of employer contributions, in effect, would act as an "internal" limit with regard to the portion of the 25 percent that might be accounted for by the employer contributions to the deferred profit-sharing program.) To illustrate, if in a particular year, 15 percent of covered compensation is contributed by the employer to the deferred profit-sharing plan, then the contribution formula in the money purchase pension plan cannot specify a contribution rate in excess of 10 percent applied to covered compensation.[19] Similarly, if the money purchase plan specifies a formula with a 20 percent contribution rate, no more than 5 percent of covered compensation can be contributed annually by the employer to the deferred profit-sharing plan. The maximum percentage that could be contributed to the profit-sharing program would be further reduced by any forfeiture reallocations.[20]

When a defined benefit pension plan is combined with a deferred profit-sharing plan covering the same employees, the 1.4 (140 percent) rule of IRC Section 415(e) applies. It should be noted that the Tax Equity and Fiscal Responsibility Act of 1982 (TEFRA) revised this rule and also revised the method for calculating defined benefit plan and defined contribution

---

[19] This assumes there are no forfeiture reallocations that year. If there are forfeiture reallocations, the percentage amount contributed to the profit-sharing plan would have to be reduced to comply with the annual additions limit, since the money purchase plan specifies a fixed-contribution commitment that must be met by the employer each year (or a partial or total plan termination will likely result, with possible adverse consequences).

[20] See footnote 19. Further, both these illustrations assume that 25 percent of covered compensation does not exceed the then-current stipulated dollar limitation ($30,000 in 1983).

plan fractions.[21] In essence, the revised plan fractions effectively provide an aggregate limit equal to the lesser of 1.25 (as applied to the dollar limits) or 1.4 (as applied to the percentage-of-pay limits). (See Chapter 58).

ALLOCATION OF INVESTMENT EARNINGS AND FORFEITURES

In addition to specifying a predetermined contribution allocation formula, deferred profit-sharing plans also must prescribe the methods for allocating investment earnings and forfeitures among the participants' accounts. These latter allocation methods, depending upon the circumstances, may differ from the method applied in allocating employer contributions to participants' accounts under the plan.

Allocation of Investment Earnings

Unless the profit-sharing assets allocated to the participants' individual accounts are "earmarked" for investment purposes (e.g., when life insurance contracts are purchased), these assets will be pooled and invested in a composite manner typically by the plan's trustee. As a result, the investment earnings generated from these commingled funds, in turn, must be allocated to the participant's accounts. The most equitable approach in accomplishing this is to allocate investment earnings on the basis of the respective sizes of the individual account balances. Presumably, this is because the funds theoretically assigned to each participant's account contribute in a pro rata fashion to the total investment earnings of the plan, and, therefore, each account should share on a pro rata basis in these earnings. Thus, if a participant's account balance comprises 10 percent of the total of all account balances, that participant's account should be credited with 10 percent of the total investment earnings. Since investment earnings invariably are allocated on the basis of individual account balances, the plan will be applying procedures that will differ between the allocation of investment earnings and the allocation of employer contributions.

Investment earnings on assets held under the profit-sharing trust are measured on a "total return" basis. That is, investment earnings for a given year are defined to include interest and dividends, as well as adjustments in the market value (both realized and unrealized capital gains and losses) of the underlying assets during the year of measurement. The net result of all

---

[21] It is assumed here that the reader is familiar with the workings of this rule and the IRC Section 415 defined benefit limitations (the lesser of 100 percent of compensation averaged over the highest three consecutive years or a stated dollar amount —1983 limit of $90,000).

this is that the assets of the profit-sharing plan must be valued periodically to determine their market value.[22] In fact, the IRS requires that the accounts of all plan participants be valued in a uniform and consistent manner at least once each year.[23] Many large employers, however, provide for more frequent valuation. It would not be uncommon to find monthly valuations in these plans. Arguments favoring frequent market valuation of plan assets are that the sponsor is provided with greater flexibility in plan administration and that the plan participants are treated more equitably. This latter point is particularly important in the accounting and in the general overall treatment of plan transactions (primarily withdrawals) that occur between valuation dates. Total withdrawals of the participants' shares (represented by their individual account balances) might occur when the employment relationship with the sponsoring firm is terminated or when membership in the plan is terminated due to some other reason(s). Partial withdrawals by active plan participants also might occur if permitted by, and according to, the provisions of the profit-sharing plan document. The issue facing the plan on the occasion of withdrawals, whether partial or total, relates to the values to be placed on the account balances and, consequently, the dollar amounts that are available for distribution. More frequent asset valuations will assist in achieving a more equitable result (a) between individuals making withdrawals and those who do not, and (b) among individuals making withdrawals at different points in time. This issue also relates to the policy question of whether investment earnings are to be credited to the individual account balances for the period between the last valuation date and the date the funds are withdrawn. If interest is not credited for this period, the amounts (interest) lost to the participants making withdrawals could be substantial unless relatively frequent valuations (e.g., monthly or every two months) are made.

Allocation of Forfeitures

Forfeitures arise under profit-sharing plans when a participant terminates employment and the funds credited to his or her account are less than fully vested. As described earlier, the qualification requirements applicable to deferred profit-sharing plans permit the periodic reallocation of forfeitures

---

[22] This does not apply when the entire assets of the plan are invested with a life insurance company through its "general asset account." Rather, in this event, transactions with plan participants (e.g., withdrawals) occur on a book value basis, and interest earnings are credited to participants' account balances according to the life insurance company's own accounting procedures. See Dan M. McGill, *Fundamentals of Private Pensions*, 4th ed. (Homewood, Ill.: Richard D. Irwin, 1979), p. 534, footnote 5.

[23] There are a limited number of exceptions to this. For example, an annual valuation is not required when all of the plan assets are invested, immediately, in individual annuity or retirement contracts meeting certain requirements. See Revenue Ruling 73-435, 1973-2 C.B. 126.

among the remaining plan participants. While profit-sharing plans are also permitted to use the forfeitures to reduce future employer contributions, seldom is this the case. The advantage of being able to allocate forfeitures among remaining plan participants is somewhat lessened by the more rapid vesting typically found in profit-sharing plans (in comparison with pension plans) which, in turn, reduces the amounts of forfeitures that otherwise are available for reallocation. Further, any amounts of forfeiture reallocations, together with employer contributions for the year, must comply with the "annual additions limit" contained in IRC Section 415. For example, if in a given year the employer makes profit-sharing contributions to each participant's account amounting to 15 percent of the participant's compensation, forfeitures may be reallocated only to the extent (in regard to any individual) that they do not exceed 10 percent of compensation, or that employer contributions together with reallocated forfeitures do not exceed the stipulated dollar maximum ($30,000 in 1983), whichever is less. To further illustrate this concept, if the employer contributes and deducts amounts equaling 20 percent of compensation (utilizing a credit carry-over), forfeitures may be reallocated during the year only to the extent that they do not exceed 5 percent of compensation for any one individual, again subject to the stipulated dollar maximum.

All methods of forfeiture reallocation are subject to the principal requirement that they not discriminate in favor of the prohibited group (officers, shareholders, and the highly paid). This is of particular concern when forfeitures are reallocated on the basis of account balances. The underlying rationale here centers on the premise that officers, shareholder-employees, and highly compensated employees are more likely to have longer periods of service with the firm and, consequently, that they will have much larger account balances than other plan participants. Thus, if account balances constitute the basis for allocating forfeitures, employees in the prohibited group may be entitled to substantially larger shares of forfeitures than other employees. The IRS may find this practice to be discriminatory. The IRS does not hold that it is "inherently discriminatory," or that the plan will automatically fail to qualify, simply because the plan allocates forfeitures on the basis of account balances.[24] However, the IRS requires that the allocation (based on account balances) be tested annually to determine whether the plan, in fact, is discriminatory. This is accomplished through a submission of all pertinent plan data to the IRS for its determination. Because of the fear of a potential charge of discrimination

---

[24] See Revenue Ruling 71–4 and Revenue Ruling 81–10. Revenue Ruling 81–10 basically restates the position of the IRS contained in Revenue Ruling 71–4, but it also provides a permissive formula that can be applied in determining whether forfeiture reallocations based on account balances produce the prohibited discrimination. See also the discussion of this topic in Carmine V. Scudere, "Is It too Risky to Allocate Forfeitures under a P/S Plan on the Basis of Account Balances?" *Journal of Pension Planning and Compliance*, July 1981, pp. 288–93.

(and possible loss of the plan's qualified status), "account balances" is seldom used as a base in allocating forfeitures. This is particularly true in small plans.

Most commonly, forfeitures are reallocated among the accounts of the remaining participants on the basis of each participant's compensation.[25] Under normal circumstances, a compensation-based method will be considered to result in an equitable allocation among plan participants.

WITHDRAWAL AND LOAN PROVISIONS

While the primary objective of many deferred profit-sharing plans is to provide covered employees with the opportunity to accumulate substantial sums of monies to be available at retirement, a number of these plans also provide employees with access to these funds on earlier prescribed occasions. This is accomplished by designing the profit-sharing plan to include withdrawal or loan provisions, or both.

Loan Provisions

A substantial number of profit-sharing plans contain loan provisions. These provisions allow participants to borrow up to a specified percentage (e.g., 50 percent) of the vested amounts in their individual accounts. While profit-sharing plans are not legally obligated to include a loan provision, certain regulatory requirements will apply when such a provision is incorporated into the plan design.[26] One such requirement is that loans must be made available to all plan participants on a reasonably equivalent basis. Further, loans cannot be made available to officers, shareholder-employees, and highly compensated employees (the prohibited group) on a basis that is more favorable than that available to other employees. It also is required that the loan be repaid in accordance with a predetermined repayment schedule, and that it bear a reasonable rate of interest. As regards any loans not repaid, the Internal Revenue Service may view them as withdrawals, in which case they must meet the conditions described below. As long as the

---

[25] Thus, it is common to find many deferred profit-sharing plans using the same method in allocating both forfeitures and employer contributions.

[26] With the passage of TEFRA in 1982, it is possible that certain loans will be treated as plan distributions and, therefore, subject to current income taxation. Generally, loans will be treated as plan distributions (and subject to taxation) unless two conditions are met:

(1) The employee's total outstanding loan amount does not exceed the *greater* of (*a*) $10,000 or (*b*) one half of the present value of the employee's nonforfeitable benefit. In any event, however, the outstanding loan amount cannot exceed $50,000.

(2) The loan (according to its terms and conditions) must be repaid within five years; however, the five-year repayment rule is waived for loans used to acquire, construct, reconstruct, or substantially rehabilitate a dwelling used as a principal residence of the employee (or a member of his or her family).

specified terms under the loan provision are properly drawn and prudent, the loans will be exempted from the prohibited transaction provisions under ERISA, and also should comply with ERISA's fiduciary standards.

Withdrawal Provisions

Some deferred profit-sharing plans provide for automatic distributions of plan assets to employees (during active employment) after the completion of a stated period of participation or after the lapse of a fixed period of years.[27] Other plans provide employees with the option to withdraw portions of the monies in their individual accounts on "the attainment of a stated age, or upon the prior occurrence of some event such as layoff, illness, disability, retirement, death, or severance of employment." Distributions to participants on these prescribed occasions are permitted under Reg. 1.401–1(b)(1)(ii). Distributions of profit-sharing funds made sooner than the happening of any one of the aforementioned events may lead to the disqualification of the plan.

Obviously, an employee's right to withdraw funds from a deferred profit-sharing plan is dependent on the actual provisions of the plan itself. The plan is under no regulatory obligation to permit distributions on the occurrence of all the events described above. In fact, some plans do not permit withdrawals prior to the participant's termination of employment. In addition, only vested amounts are available to be withdrawn (together with employee contributions, if the plan is contributory). When a profit-sharing plan provides for automatic distributions (or permits voluntary withdrawals) after a fixed number of years, IRS regulations require in these situations that only funds that have been deposited for at least two years may be distributed. Thus, if employer contributions have been credited to the participant's account for three years, only amounts equal to the first year's contribution, together with investment income credited that year, are eligible to be withdrawn, but only to the extent the plan permits such withdrawals.[28] Of course, distributions of funds held less than two years may be made in the event of " . . . disability, retirement, death . . ." without affecting qualification. Further, distributions of monies held less than two years also may be made upon the showing of "hardship," if this term is sufficiently defined and consistently applied under the plan. In any event, the actual amounts withdrawn (exclusive of any amounts representing the employee's

---

[27] The inclusion of such provisions is prohibited in IRC Section 401(k) cash or deferred profit-sharing plans.

[28] After completion of five years of participation in the plan, an employee is legally permitted to withdraw all employer contributions credited to his or her account (assuming the plan so permits), including monies contributed during the two years preceding the date of withdrawal. The completion of five years of participation is an "event" within the meaning of Reg. 1.401–1(b)(1)(ii). As a result, the two-year rule is made inapplicable.

own contributions) must be included as taxable income, subject to ordinary income-tax rates, by the participant in the year in which the distribution is received.

Relative Advantages and Disadvantages of Withdrawals and Loans

Plan provisions permitting loans or withdrawals, or both, prior to termination of employment provide participants with much added flexibility. Employees may be able to use these funds for down payments on homes, for children's college education expenses, or for other financial needs. An important disadvantage is that these provisions (particularly withdrawal provisions) may prevent the plan from accumulating sufficient funds at retirement.

Loan provisions have certain inherent advantages over withdrawal provisions. Specifically, funds made available through a loan do not create taxable income to the borrowing employee, but the employee may deduct the interest paid on the loan. In addition, since loans are likely to be repaid, the retirement income objective of the profit-sharing plan is protected. Some potential disadvantages of loan provisions are:

1. The administrative expense associated with processing loans.
2. An employee objection to being charged interest on his or her "own money."
3. The lower overall investment earnings rate on the total asset portfolio when the loan interest rate is below the earnings rate at which the trustee could otherwise invest the borrowed funds.[29]

Previously, profit-sharing plans containing withdrawal provisions had to be concerned with the "constructive receipt doctrine." The question arose whether the right to withdraw *any* monies from a participant's individual account, whether or not exercised, constituted constructive receipt of *all* (withdrawable) monies allocated to the account. If the constructive receipt doctrine applied, all such amounts that were permitted to be withdrawn would be taxable currently to the participant, even though the monies are not actually withdrawn. To avoid application of the constructive receipt doctrine to amounts not withdrawn, plans usually assessed a substantial penalty (e.g., denying participation rights for six months) on employees who made withdrawals.[30] Of course, the constructive receipt problem also could have been avoided by substituting a loan privilege for the withdrawal provision. Today, however, the constructive receipt doctrine is no longer a

---

[29] This last disadvantage exists only to the extent that the plan treats participant loans as loans from the entire assets of the trust, rather than treating them as loans from the participants' own individual accounts.

[30] For a discussion of the types of penalties imposed, see McGill, *Fundamentals of Private Pensions*, p. 540.

problem issue in deferred profit-sharing plans. The Economic Recovery Tax Act of 1981 (ERTA) amended IRC Section 402(a)(1) of the Internal Revenue Code, which deals with the taxation of benefits from a qualified retirement plan. Under the amended provision, distributions from qualified plans are taxed only when actually received by the participant, not when simply made available to him or her. Thus, the basis for the constructive receipt doctrine has been removed from IRC Section 402(a)(1). This affects the tax treatment of all qualified plans, including profit-sharing plans, and it applies both to distributions at termination of employment and to withdrawals made by active employees. The amended provision became effective for taxable years beginning after December 31, 1981. Profit-sharing plans containing withdrawal provisions should be reviewed for the purpose of identifying penalties or restrictions that have constructive receipt origins. Plan sponsors then should determine whether, and to what extent, these penalties and restrictions should be modified or eliminated in order to meet plan objectives and to control administrative costs.

ADDITIONAL FEATURES OF DEFERRED PROFIT-SHARING PLANS

Certain additional features pertaining to deferred profit-sharing plans are worthy of mention. These plan design features relate to voluntary employee contributions, the inclusion of life insurance benefits, and integration of the plan with Social Security benefits.

Employee Contributions

Historically, while many plans (qualified under the Internal Revenue Code as profit-sharing plans) have required employee contributions in order to share in employer profits or have permitted voluntary contributions, from a technical standpoint a majority of these plans are more properly known as thrift or savings plans (see Chapter 32 of the *Handbook*). However, there are a number of deferred profit-sharing plans, properly classified as such, that in the past have provided for employee contributions without requiring employees to make such contributions in order to receive profit-sharing allocations and without any specific employer "matching" of any employee monies voluntarily contributed to the plan. Under these circumstances, any attractiveness to the employee of making voluntary contributions has been related to (1) the investment facilities available in the plan, which may provide an opportunity for a higher return than what an employee individually could earn on his or her own and still with possibly less risk if the investments are well-diversified; and (2) the tax-sheltering of the income earned on the invested contributions. Primarily as a result of the passage of the Economic Recovery Tax Act of 1981 (ERTA), it is anticipated that employee contributions will become a more popular feature and that a number of deferred profit-sharing plans will be amended to permit voluntary employee contributions. This is because ERTA contains a provision whereby employers may amend a qualified plan (as of January 1, 1982) to accept annual amounts up to the lesser of 100 percent of pay or $2,000 from any employee under age 70½ as tax deductible IRC Section 219(e) "qualified voluntary employee contributions" (QVECs). If an employee elects to make deductible voluntary contributions to an employer-sponsored plan (conditioned on the plan accepting such QVECs), these contributions must be in lieu of tax-deductible contributions that the employee otherwise would be permitted to make to an Individual Retirement Account (IRA) established with a bank, a savings and loan, a mutual fund, a life insurance company, or any other financial service institution. As a result, QVECs are treated, for the most part, in a manner similar to IRAs. QVECs experience the same tax treatment when the contributions are made to the employer-sponsored qualified plan, as occurs with contributions to IRAs; that is, both QVECs and contributions to IRAs are made from current aftertax income but then are deductible on the employee's personal income-tax return, irrespective of whether the standard deduction is taken or the employee itemizes deductions. Distributions from QVEC accounts also are taxed in the same manner as distributions from IRAs, in that all monies are taxed as ordinary income, with the additional stipulation that any distributions made prior to age 59½, except in the event of the employee's death or disability, will incur a tax penalty of 10 percent on the amount distributed. Since the tax treatment accorded QVECs, both on monies going in and coming out, differs considerably from the tax treatment surrounding employer-provided monies in the profit-sharing plan, a separate accounting and reporting of QVECs will be necessary.

Life Insurance Benefits

There are two important ways in which life insurance benefits might be incorporated into the design of qualified deferred profit-sharing plans.[31] First, life insurance coverage on key personnel in the firm might be purchased by the trust as an investment. The underlying rationale here is that the profit-sharing trust has an insurable interest in the lives of certain employees who are "key" to the successful operation of the firm. These key employees may include officers, stockholder-employees, and certain other employees of the company. Since contributions to the profit-sharing trust are dependent on the continued success and profitability of the firm, and if the future profitability is contingent on the performance of these key employees, then the profit-sharing trust is likely to suffer a substantial

---

[31] Only a limited discussion is provided here on life insurance in qualified profit-sharing plans. For a more extensive treatment of this topic, see Allen, Melone, and Rosenbloom, *Pension Planning*, 4th ed. (Homewood, Ill.: Richard D. Irwin, 1981), pp. 290–95; and McGill, *Fundamentals of Private Pensions*, pp. 541–46.

reduction in future contribution levels upon the death of one or more of the key employees. This may be particularly true in the case of small-to-medium-size corporations. Under these circumstances, if permitted by the trust agreement, the trustee may desire to protect the profit-sharing trust against potential adverse consequences by purchasing insurance on the lives of the key employees. In such cases, the life insurance contracts are purchased and owned by the trust, with the necessary premiums paid for out of trust assets. While the trust is designated as the beneficiary under such contracts, upon the death of an insured the insurance proceeds are allocated among the individual accounts of the plan participants, typically on the basis of the respective sizes of their account balances.[32]

Second, while deferred profit-sharing plans primarily are plans providing deferred compensation, most plans also provide a benefit payable upon the death of a plan participant. Most profit-sharing plans, at a minimum, pay a death benefit equal to the participant's individual account balance. In addition, however, under Reg. 1.401-1(b)(1)(ii) amounts allocated to participants' accounts may be used to purchase incidental amounts of life insurance coverage. There are several reasons why a participant might desire to have explicit life insurance benefits provided under the profit-sharing plan, including (1) the relatively small accumulation (and, consequently, available death benefits) in the participant's account during the early years of participation, and (2) inadequate amounts of coverage provided under the employer-sponsored group life insurance program.

To the extent that employer contributions to the profit-sharing plan are used to purchase life insurance on plan participants, these contributions must meet certain limitations; however, the limitations are sufficiently liberal that, in many cases, it is possible for plan participants (if desired) to acquire substantial amounts of life insurance coverage. Specifically, if the participant's funds used to pay the life insurance premiums have been accumulated in the participant's account for at least two years, or if the funds are used to purchase either an endowment or a retirement income contract, there are no IRS limits on the amount of life insurance that can be purchased (or the portion of the account balance that may be used to pay premiums). If neither of these requirements is met, the aggregate amount of funds used to pay life insurance premiums must be less than one half of the total contributions and forfeitures allocated to the participant's account to avoid risking disqualification of the plan. Additional restrictions pertain-

---

[32] In contrast to the situation where life insurance is purchased on plan participants (see *infra*), the purchase of life insurance on key employees, for the collective benefit of the trust as a whole, does not create any current income-tax liability for the participants. Furthermore, the tests requiring that purchases of life insurance be incidental in amount do not apply to the types of life insurance purchases described above. However, as a practical matter, the trust is not likely to invest a substantial portion of its assets in such life insurance purchases. Also, under ERISA's fiduciary provisions, the trustee will be under the obligation to show that the purchase of life insurance on key personnel is a prudent investment and in the best interests, collectively, of the plan participants.

ing to the inclusion of life insurance (on plan participants) in profit-sharing plans are: (1) that the plan must require the trustee to convert the entire value of the life insurance contract at or prior to retirement either to cash or to provide periodic income (in order that no portion of such value is available to continue life insurance protection into the retirement years), or to distribute the insurance contract to the participant; and (2) that the participant must treat the value (P.S. 58 cost) of the pure life insurance protection as taxable income each year.[33]

To maintain its qualified status, a plan must meet the requirements of Reg. 1.401-1(b)(1)(ii); however, life insurance need not be purchased on *all* plan participants to maintain qualification. Rather, the purchase of life insurance can be the decision of individual participants (with some electing the coverage and others not) as long as all participants are offered the same opportunity. To accomplish this, the trust agreement should specifically allow each participant, individually, to direct the trustee to purchase specific investments (e.g., insurance contracts) and "earmark" them for the participant's account. Normally, the trustee is the applicant and the owner of any life insurance contracts purchased on the lives of the plan participants. In addition, the trustee pays the premiums on the policies, although these amounts are then charged directly to the individual accounts of those participants electing insurance coverage. Typically, the insured participants designate their own personal beneficiaries, in which case the proceeds payable upon the death of a participant are paid by the insurer directly to the named beneficiary. If the trustee has been named as beneficiary under the insurance contract, the death proceeds are paid to the trustee who, in turn, credits the proceeds to the deceased participant's account.

Integration with Social Security

Deferred profit-sharing plans are seldom integrated with the benefits payable under Social Security (OASDHI). A major reason is that any employee incentive factor sought by the employer in establishing a profit-sharing plan would tend to be defeated by a plan design that either excludes employees earning less than a specified minimum or calls for contributions at a lower rate on their behalf. A second reason relates to the more

---

[33] The reason that a current tax liability exists in this event is that the premium for the pure insurance protection is deemed by the IRS to be a current distribution from the trust and therefore currently taxable to the plan participant. The amount that must be included in the participant's gross income each year is determined as follows: [(face amount minus cash value) × (Table P.S. 58 attained age term insurance rate)]. With each succeeding year, the first factor in this formula decreases, providing the face amount is held constant, while the second factor increases. The portion of the premium that is applied to the buildup of the cash value component of the life insurance contract is considered to be an investment of the profit-sharing trust and, consequently, is not treated as a current distribution and, therefore, does not result in any current tax liability.

restrictive requirements imposed by the Internal Revenue Service on profit-sharing plans that are integrated. These requirements are described below.

Because of the defined contribution nature of profit-sharing plans, plans that are integrated with Social Security are done so on some type of an excess earnings basis, rather than under an offset approach in which plan benefits are reduced by a specified percentage of the employee's primary retirement benefit payable from Social Security.[34] There are two possible approaches to integrating profit-sharing plans on an excess basis: the excess-only plan and the step-rate excess plan. In both plans it is necessary to establish an earnings level (known as the integration level) which defines a dollar amount whereby the employer contribution rate differs between earnings above and earnings below this level. Specifically, the employer contribution rate is greater on compensation in excess of the integration level. While lesser dollar amounts are permissible, the integration level often is defined as the current Social Security maximum taxable wage base.

An *excess-only plan* is a plan whereby profit-sharing contributions are allocated on the basis of compensation amounts that are in excess of the plan's integration level. Stated differently, the employer contribution rate on earnings below the integration level is zero percent. As a result, only those employees whose earnings are in excess of the integration level are eligible to participate in the profit-sharing plan. Under an excess-only plan, the maximum annual amount (including both employer contributions and forfeiture reallocations, but exclusive of investment earnings) that may be allocated to each participant's account is limited to 5.4 percent of the participant's compensation in excess of the integration level.[35] In contrast, under nonintegrated profit-sharing plans, employers are permitted an annual deductible contribution up to 15 percent of total covered compensation. Further, under nonintegrated plans, forfeitures may be reallocated without reducing the 15 percent annual deduction limit (subject to the annual additions limit, of course). In an excess-only integrated plan forfeiture reallocations, together with employer contributions, must not exceed 5.4 percent of *excess* compensation amounts. Any remaining forfeitures must be applied to reduce future employer contributions. Another limiting factor is that contribution and credit carry-over provisions, otherwise available in deferred profit-sharing plans, are not permitted when the plan is integrated with Social Security on an excess-only basis. As a result, allocations (consisting of contributions and forfeitures) to participants' accounts,

---

[34] For a discussion of integration approaches in pension plans, see Chapter 27 of the *Handbook*.

[35] This 5.4 percent limitation also applies to money purchase pension plans that are integrated with Social Security. Of course, in these plans the limitation applies strictly to employer contributions, since allocation of forfeitures among remaining plan participants is prohibited.

on average, might not even amount to 5.4 percent of excess compensation. These special requirements constitute serious drawbacks to the establishment of an integrated profit-sharing plan on an excess-only basis. Finally, in a number of firms the employer has established both a pension plan and a deferred profit-sharing plan covering (at least to some extent) the same employees. If both of these plans are integrated, the regulations will not permit the combined integration under both plans to exceed 100 percent of the integration capability of a single plan. (When the employer sponsors two plans covering the same group of employees, and when maximum integration is desired, the simplest approach to integration is to fully integrate one plan and not integrate the other plan at all. Other combinations are permissible, however.) If both plans were permitted to be fully integrated, the employer would be allowed to take double recognition for the portion of Social Security benefits bought with the corporation's contributions; this would likely result in discrimination in favor of those employees comprising the prohibited group.

It is possible to increase the employer contribution rate on excess compensation to an amount above the otherwise allowable 5.4 percent limitation if employer contributions also are allocated on compensation below the integration level. This is, in fact, the approach taken under *step-rate excess plans*. Specifically, if contributions are set equal to "X" percent of compensation on earnings up to the permissible integration level, then "X + 5.4" percent may be contributed on compensation amounts in excess of the integration level. In essence, the procedures applied under the step-rate excess approach are equivalent to applying a basic "X" percent contribution rate to total compensation (including compensation both below and above the integration level) and up to a 5.4 percent contribution rate to compensation in excess of the integration level. The various restrictions that apply to excess-only plans affect step-rate excess plans to a much lesser extent. As described above, it is possible for the employer contribution rate on compensation amounts over the integration level to exceed 5.4 percent. Also, forfeitures may be reallocated under a step-rate plan, without being charged against the permitted 5.4 percent differential, to the extent that they are reallocated on the basis of total compensation. In addition, the carry-over (contribution and credit) provisions are available on the same basis as for a nonintegrated plan, thereby providing the employer with increased contribution flexibility.

DISTRIBUTIONS

Earlier sections described specific events or occasions leading to distributions under profit-sharing plans. The discussion here is limited to aspects relating to the form and taxation of distributions from qualified deferred profit-sharing plans.

Form

Distributions from profit-sharing plans may take several forms, including lump-sum, installment payments, or a paid-up annuity. Distributions in the form of withdrawals during active employment or distributions to employees who have terminated employment (for reasons other than death, disability, or retirement) generally are made in the form of a lump-sum payment. At death or disability of the plan participant, distributions usually are in the form of a lump-sum payment or installment payments. Finally, at retirement, distributions typically are payable to the participant either as a lump sum, on an installment-payment basis, or as a life annuity provided through an insurance company. To the extent that the plan permits an annuity payout form, the plan must satisfy ERISA's rules relating to qualified joint-and-survivor annuities.

Taxation

In general, the tax treatment of distributions from qualified profit-sharing plans is identical to the tax treatment accorded distributions from qualified pension plans except for the fact that there is one potential favorable tax aspect regarding distributions from profit sharing plans that should be mentioned. This aspect relates to the taxation of distributions consisting of employer securities. This is extremely important to profit-sharing plans, since they are not subject to ERISA's 10 percent limitation on the investment of plan assets in employer securities, and, as a result, profit-sharing plans tend to invest more heavily in securities of the employer. When employer securities are distributed as part of a lump-sum distribution under such conditions that otherwise qualify the distribution for favorable tax treatment, IRC Section 402(e)(4)(J) permits the entire net unrealized appreciation on the securities (excess of fair market value over cost basis of securities to trust) to escape taxation at the time of the distribution. In effect, the only portion taxed to the participant at the time of distribution is the amount of the original employer contributions (i.e., the trust's cost basis). The tax on any unrealized appreciation at date of distribution is deferred until the participant sells the securities at a later date. Further, if the participant holds the securities for more than one year from the date of distribution, upon the sale of the securities he or she is entitled to long-term capital gains treatment on the entire appreciation (both before and after the distribution).

Thrift and
Savings Plans

HENRY BRIGHT AND
HARRY McBRIERTY

INTRODUCTION

A thrift plan is the trade name given to an employee benefit plan that promotes savings and thrift among employees by requiring each participant to make periodic contributions to the plan to be credited with an employer contribution on his or her behalf. The amount of the employer contribution usually relates, in whole or in part, to the amount the participant contributes. These plans also are referred to as savings plans, thrift incentive plans, savings and investment plans, and by a variety of other names that generally denote an employee savings feature.

Most thrift plans are established by employers as secondary plans, and are not the primary source of providing retirement income for their employees. These plans provide employees with an incentive to save. Furthermore, they provide a convenient mechanism to accumulate funds to supplement the retirement income from the employer's regular pension plan or other sources. In addition, many employers design their thrift plans so the accumulated savings may be used by their employees before retirement.

From the employer's viewpoint, a thrift plan is a part of the firm's retirement program that provides significant benefits, which are financed to a great extent (depending upon the ratio of the employees' contributions to its own) by the contributions of its employees. From the employees' viewpoint, a thrift plan provides an opportunity to realize an immediate and substantial return on their own contributions, with the added opportunity of accumulating investment earnings on a deferred tax basis and receiving benefits on a favorable tax basis upon retirement or termination.

With a few exceptions, all thrift plans have been established within the last 30 years. Their prevalance among employers of all sizes has grown continuously. The rapid growth of these plans is due, no doubt, largely to their relatively low cost to the employer, and to their enthusiastic acceptance by most employees.

The influence on the prevalence and design of thrift plans, of the Economic Recovery Tax Act of 1981 (ERTA), of the Tax Equity and Fiscal Responsibility Act of 1982 (TEFRA), and of the provisions of Section 401(k) of the Internal Revenue Code (IRC) are not yet fully apparent on the date of this writing. This chapter takes into account the applicable changes in the law, resulting from ERTA and TEFRA, but it has not taken any account of Section 401(k) of the code or the proposed regulations thereunder. The provisions of Section 401(k) are outlined briefly at the end of this chapter and are discussed in detail in Chapter 33.

QUALIFIED STATUS UNDER INTERNAL REVENUE CODE

The Internal Revenue Code includes no specific provisions relating to thrift plans as such. A thrift plan is simply a term used in the industry to describe a contributory defined contribution plan which provides for an individual account for each participant with benefits based solely on: (1) the amounts contributed to the participant's account; (2) any income, expenses, gains, and losses; and (3) any forfeitures of accounts of others that may be allocated to the participant's account. This description is the same as that of a profit-sharing plan and of a money purchase pension plan, because thrift plans are qualified under Section 401(a) of the Internal Revenue Code as either profit-sharing plans or money purchase pension plans.

If the employer's contribution is required to be made from either current or accumulated net profits, the thrift plan must be qualified as a profit-sharing plan. If the employer's contribution is required, regardless of whether it has any current or accumulated profits, the thrift plan must be qualified as a money purchase pension plan. Technically, a thrift plan could alternatively be qualified as a stock-bonus plan if it has all of the attributes of a stock-bonus plan.

The provisions of the IRC that govern profit-sharing plans are different in many respects from those that govern money purchase pension plans. Accordingly, corresponding differences exist in the provisions and in the operations of a thrift plan, according to whether it is qualified as a profit-sharing plan or as a money purchase pension plan.

Features common to both types of thrift plan include: (a) the plan must provide a definite predetermined formula for allocating contributions among the participants in the plan, and (b) the plan must provide for valuation of plan assets at least once a year.

Table 32–1 lists some of the principal differences between the two types of thrift plans. These differences are important in deciding which type of plan to establish. In particular, if the thrift plan is to be a supplement to an existing pension or profit-sharing plan, the difference in limitations on the amount of the combined contributions and the difference in tax treatment of lump-sum distributions can be decisive factors in making the choice.

Table 32–1
Principal Differences between Two Types of Thrift Plans

Feature	Plan Qualified as a Profit-Sharing Plan	Plan Qualified as a Money Purchase Pension Plan
1. Amount of employer contributions	No definite formula required. Usually expressed as a percentage of employee's contributions.	There must be a fixed formula to determine the amount of employer contributions.
2. Source of employer contributions	Can only be made out of current or accumulated profits.	Are required to be made even if there are no current or accumulated profits.
3. Allocation of forfeitures	May be allocated in addition to employer's contributions or used to reduce employer's contributions.	Must be used to reduce employer's contributions.
4. Employer contributions in excess of normal formula	Plan may provide for such excess contributions to be made at the employer's option.	No excess contributions may be made.
5. Withdrawal of employer contributions prior to severance of employment	May be permitted (contributions must have accumulated for at least two years).	No withdrawal of employer contributions is permitted except upon severance (or attainment of normal retirement age).

PLAN PROVISIONS

Most provisions of thrift plans are similar to those of other employee benefit plans qualified under Section 401(a) of the IRC. The plan must be so structured that, in addition to satisfying the objectives of the employer, it conforms to the requirements of the Internal Revenue Code, the Employee Retirement Income Security Act (ERISA), and other applicable governmental rules and regulations.

Eligibility Requirements

Employees must be eligible to participate upon reaching age 25 or upon completing one year of service, whichever is later. However, if the plan

Table 32-1 *(continued)*

Feature	Plan Qualified as a Profit-Sharing Plan	Plan Qualified as a Money Purchase Pension Plan
6. Limit on tax deductions for employer contributions to thrift plan		
a. No other plan maintained	15 percent of covered compensation.	None, but note that Section 415 of the IRC effectively imposes a maximum on contributions of 25 percent of covered compensation.
b. Separate profit-sharing plan maintained	Combined limit of 15 percent of covered compensation.	Combined limit of 25 percent of covered compensation.
c. Separate defined benefit pension plan maintained	Combined limit of 25 percent of covered compensation.	None, but note that Section 415 effectively imposes a maximum of 25 per cent of covered compensation on the thrift plan contributions.
7. Favorable tax treatment for lump-sum distributions on termination or retirement	Available, provided there is no other profit-sharing plan benefit, or, if there is, provided a lump sum also is received thereunder. Usually, these conditions would be met.	Available, provided there is no other pension plan benefit, or if there is, provided a lump sum also is received thereunder. Usually, these conditions would not be met.

provides immediate 100 percent vesting, the plan may require as much as three years of service before the employee is eligible. An employee cannot be excluded from participation under a thrift plan because of attainment of a specified maximum age. In practice, most thrift plans permit participation after a year or less.

As with other qualified plans, a thrift plan either must cover a sufficient number of employees, to satisfy the percentage coverage requirements of Section 410(b) of the Internal Revenue Code, or must cover a non-discriminatory classification of employees. The Section 410(b) requirements are met if 70 percent of all employees are covered (after certain exclusions), or if 70 percent of all employees are eligible and 80 percent of those eligible are covered. Since thrift plans require employee contributions and participation is normally not mandatory, the prescribed percentage coverage requirements are sometimes difficult to satisfy, and those plans that cannot meet the percentage tests need to make sure that a fair cross-section of employees is covered under the plan if the plan is to achieve and retain a qualified status.

Employee Contributions

The requirement for employee contributions is a distinguishing characteristic of all thrift plans. This is because the amount of the employer's contributions and the predetermined formula for allocating those contributions among the participants are almost always based upon the amount that each participant contributes.

All thrift plans require one type of employee contributions, and some thrift plans permit a second type. The first type is that which determines the employee's share of the employer's contribution. The second type is an employee contribution in excess of the maximum employee contribution of the first type. Employee contributions of the second type have no effect whatsoever upon the amount of the employer's contribution or upon the employee's allocated share of the employer's contribution. For convenience, these types of employee contributions are referred to in this chapter as "basic employee contributions" and as "voluntary employee contributions," respectively.

Basic Employee Contributions. It is not necessary for a thrift plan to require or permit all participants to contribute at the same rate. Most plans permit employees to choose the amount to be contributed, up to the maximum permissible, and some plans have different maximums for different classifications of employees. For example, a plan may permit employees with fewer than a certain number of years of service or participation to contribute within a specified range, while this range may be increased for employees with more years of service or participation. In addition, many plans specify that a minimum contribution, expressed either as a dollar amount or as a percentage of pay, is required. The minimum requirement usually is included for administrative purposes; but, in the past, this minimum was believed to affect the amount of voluntary employee contributions that a plan might permit.

Basic employee contribution requirements must not result in discrimination in favor of highly compensated employees. Such discrimination could arise either because the contributions are burdensome; resulting in inadequate plan coverage for lower-paid employees, or because the rates of contribution and benefits are less for lower-paid employees under a plan that provides for optional rates of contribution. In comparing benefits for lower-paid and higher-paid employees, allowance may be made for integration with Social Security benefits, unless the employee also is covered by a separate, fully integrated plan.

The IRS ruled in 1972 that if the maximum rate of basic employee contributions is 6 percent or less, there typically would not be a discrimination problem. As a result, 6 percent is the maximum limit for basic employee contributions used in most thrift plans. However, a 1980 ruling appears to state that a 6 percent maximum rate is not a "safe harbor," so an employer should be concerned about the problem of discrimination regardless of the level of basic contribution permitted.

Voluntary Employee Contributions. A provision for voluntary employee contributions is an optional feature included in some thrift plans. This provision enables participants to take advantage of the favorable tax treatment afforded the earnings on such contributions. Voluntary employee contributions need to be accounted for separately and may be permitted up to 10 percent of the employee's compensation.

In the past, the maximum total employee contribution to a thrift plan (basic and voluntary combined) was considered to be 10 percent of the employee's compensation plus the minimum basic employee contribution. However, Revenue Ruling 81-234 makes it clear that a voluntary contribution may be as much as 10 percent of compensation and is not affected by either the minimum or the actual basic contribution.

Beginning January 1, 1982, if the plan so provides, voluntary employee contributions to a thrift plan (or other qualified plan) may be taken as a tax deduction, up to $2,000 a year. A plan could permit these contributions as part of, or in addition to, the voluntary contributions described above. Separate accounting would be needed for the deductible employee contributions, and some special rules apply to these contributions. Notably, a 10 percent penalty tax is imposed if they are distributed prior to age 59½ (except for death or disability), and the proceeds are always taxed as ordinary income when received.

Employer Contributions

The employer's contribution generally is defined in a thrift plan as a fixed percentage of basic employee contributions, although this is not a requirement for a plan qualified as a profit-sharing plan. That percentage also may vary for different classifications of employees as long as the classifications are nondiscriminatory. Some thrift plans qualified as profit-sharing plans provide that the employer, at its discretion, may make contributions in excess of the defined amount of contribution. Thrift plans qualified as money purchase pension plans cannot provide for such additional contributions, since the benefits would no longer be definitely determinable.

The employer's contribution is most often allocated among the participants in direct proportion to the basic employee contribution of each participant. However, other methods of allocation (e.g., a varying percentage based on years of service or participation) may be used, provided such other methods are not discriminatory.

Forfeitures

When a plan participant incurs a break in service, his or her nonvested benefits may be forfeited and, thereby, become available for other uses. Forfeitures under a thrift plan may be included as part of the employer's contribution (or, stated in another way, used to reduce the amount of the employer's contribution), or, if the thrift plan is qualified as a profit-sharing plan, may be allocated among the participants in addition to the employer's contribution. If the plan is qualified as a money purchase pension plan, the forfeitures must be included as part of the employer's contribution.

When forfeitures are included as part of the employer's contribution, they are allocated, of course, to the accounts of the participants in the same manner as the rest of the employer's contribution. If the forfeitures are allocated in addition to the employer's regular contribution, they generally are allocated among the participants in the same manner as the employer's contribution, but they may be allocated under other methods. However, if some other method is used, it may be necessary to demonstrate to the IRS that such other method does not discriminate in favor of officers, shareholders, or highly compensated employees. After forfeitures have been allocated to the accounts of the participants, they generally are treated as though they were employer contributions.

Limits on Contributions to Employees' Accounts Each Year

Section 415 of the Internal Revenue Code places a limit on the total amount of employer contributions, forfeitures, and employee contributions in excess of 6 percent of pay (exclusive of deductible employee contributions) that can be credited to the accounts of any participant during a specified year.

This limit, which applies to the aggregate of all defined contribution plans of the employer, requires that the sum of the employer's contributions and forfeitures allocated to the employees' accounts plus one half of total employee contributions (or if less, the portion of the total employee contributions that are in excess of 6 percent of his or her pay) not be greater in any year than the smaller of: (a) 25 percent of his or her pay; or (b) a specified dollar amount that is subject to increase to take into account cost-of-living adjustments (this dollar amount was originally $25,000 in 1974, was increased to $45,475 on January 1, 1982, but was reset by TEFRA at $30,000 on January 1, 1983).

If the employee also is a participant in a defined benefit plan of the employer, an overall limitation exists on the amount of his or her benefits under both types of plans. Consequently, the above limit on the defined contribution plan benefit may have to be reduced, if the required reduction is not made under the defined benefit plan, so that the total benefit from both the defined contribution and defined benefit plans of the employer does not exceed the overall limitation.

The overall limitation is tested by adding the percentage of the maximum limitation computed separately for each type of plan that is being provided for an employee. The resulting sum must not exceed 125 percent for the dollar limitations, or, if less, 140 percent for the percentage limitations.

The overall limitation could be met by reducing benefits under either plan. It usually is preferable to make the reduction in the defined benefit plan, because the precise amount of reduction required cannot be determined until the employee retires, and because the reduction in a defined benefit plan does not become effective until retirement. However, other considerations may make it preferable to reduce the defined contribution plan. A choice should be made and incorporated in the plan document.

Investment of Contributions

Most thrift plans provide for more than one investment fund or type of investment. The participant may specify the percentage of his or her own contributions to be invested each year in each fund. A similar choice may or may not be available to the participant concerning the investment of employer contributions allocated on his or her behalf. Plans that permit the participant to choose investment funds typically provide the participant may change the specified percentages and may transfer funds credited to his or her account from one investment fund to another on a periodic basis.

Other thrift plans, primarily because of the accounting complexities caused by a multitude of investment options, restrict the options available to employees. Some of those plans, nevertheless, permit participants nearing retirement age to make a one-time election to transfer funds from an equity type investment fund to either a fixed-income or guaranteed-income fund, so fluctuations in value may be minimized as participants near retirement.

Among the more common investment funds are employer stock, fixed-income funds invested in government bonds or notes, guaranteed-return contracts offered by insurance companies, common stock funds, and money market funds, not necessarily in that order. The relative popularity of different investment funds can vary widely at different times; a tendency exists for one or the other type of investment to become extremely popular at certain times, often for very good reasons.

In any case, because both the financial markets and the plan's needs and objectives change over the course of time, it is sound policy to review the available choice of investment funds at regular intervals and to make changes when necessary or appropriate. The plan's wording should be designed to facilitate the making of such changes.

Vesting

Because of their nature and purpose, and as an incentive to encourage broad participation, thrift plans commonly provide for fairly rapid vesting, usually on a graded basis.

There are two broad types of plan, which are distinguished principally by the difference in their vesting provisions. They are referred to as "class year" thrift plans and as "regular" thrift plans, respectively.

Table 32–2 gives a comparative summary of the vesting and distribution arrangements typical of the two types of plan.

From the employee's viewpoint, the class year plan has greater flexibility since, after the initial period of three to five years, there is an automatic distribution each year unless the participant elects otherwise. However, this may make it more difficult to adhere to a program of systematic savings.

From the employer's viewpoint, the class year approach is significantly more complicated to administer, but its popularity and high visibility among employees may compensate for that drawback. The class year approach also has the characteristic that an employee who leaves before retirement always forfeits the most recent years of employer contributions, regardless of length of service, while there is no forfeiture under the regular plan approach if the employee has the service required for full vesting.

Prior to the passage of ERTA, class year plans had to be written carefully to avoid having benefits taxed when becoming available, even though not withdrawn; but this constructive receipt doctrine no longer applies to qualified plans.

Minimum Vesting Requirements

For class year plans, the minimum vesting requirements call for full vesting of the employer's contribution for each class year, and earnings thereon, by the end of the fifth year following the end of the class year in which they were allocated to his or her account.

For regular plans, minimum vesting requirements are the same as for all other qualified pension and profit-sharing plans. In brief, all employer contributions, and funds attributable thereto, must vest at least as rapidly as under one of the following alternatives:

1. After 10 years of service, 100 percent vesting.
2. After 5 years of service, 25 percent vesting, plus an additional 5 percent for each of the next 5 years (50 percent after 10 years of service) plus an

Table 32–2
Comparision of Typical Vesting Arrangements under Class Year
and Regular Thrift Plans

Characteristic	Class Year Plan	Regular Plan
1. Employees own contributions, and earnings thereon	Always fully vested.	Always fully vested.
2. Separation of employer contributions in employee's account	Each year's contributions, and earnings thereon, are accounted for separately until fully vested.	All employer contributions, and earnings thereon, are commingled as one account.
3. Vesting of employer contributions	Each year's employer contributions and earnings thereon become fully vested two to five years after the contribution is made.	All employer contributions, and earnings thereon, become vested after 5 to 10 years of participation, usually on a graded basis.
4. Vesting at retirement, attainment of normal retirement age, death or disability	Generally 100 percent.	Generally 100 percent.
5. Distribution to employees while still employed	Employer's contributions, and earnings thereon, are payable to employee when they become vested, unless he or she elects at that time to defer receipt until retirement. In addition, there may be provisions for loans or withdrawals from the aggregated "matured classes."	No provision for distribution except in case of a specific need for funds.

additional 10 percent for each of the next 5 years (100 percent after 15 years of service); or

3. After 10 years of service or when age plus service (minimum of 5 years) first equals or exceeds 45 years, 50 percent vesting, plus an additional 10 percent for each of the next 5 years of service.

In accordance with Revenue Procedure 75–49, the IRS might require even more rapid vesting (the "4/40" rule, which requires vesting at 40 percent after 4 years of service, increasing at 5 percent a year for the next 2 years, and then at 10 percent a year, reaching 100 percent after 11 years).

Of course, an employee must always be 100 percent vested in funds attributable to his or her own contributions and be 100 percent vested in the total account upon reaching normal retirement age under the plan, or if earlier, upon reaching age 65 and the 10th anniversary of participation in the plan.

Withdrawals while in Service

The withdrawal provisions included in a thrift plan generally are dependent upon the objective of the employer in establishing the plan. For the great majority, when the objective of the plan is to provide a means by which the participants can accumulate funds that may be used to meet their financial needs before (as well as after) retirement, the withdrawal provisions are very liberal. However, if the objective of the plan is solely or primarily to provide a source of income after retirement, the withdrawal provisions, if any, will not be as liberal.

Withdrawal of Employee Contributions

The withdrawal of all or a portion of an employee's own contributions and interest earned thereon is permitted under many thrift plans. Such a provision must not be such that it can be reasonably expected to result in manipulation of the employer's contribution. Prior to the passage of ERTA, plans that permitted withdrawal of interest on employees' contributions often provided for restrictions or penalties designed to avoid constructive receipt. While no longer needed for that purpose, many such restrictions may be retained to further discourage manipulation and to encourage savings for retirement.

The potential for the manipulation of employer's contributions arises if the employee is permitted to withdraw all or a portion of basic employee contributions (the employee contributions to which the employer's contribution is geared) without penalty so he or she could effectively use the same contributions year after year and thereby manipulate the formula allocating the employer's contribution under the plan. The IRS has ruled that plans permitting such manipulations without penalty will not be qualified under Section 401(a) of the Internal Revenue Code. This problem is avoided by providing an appropriate penalty, which is typically the suspension of participation for a specified period, such as six months.

The withdrawal of voluntary employee contributions does not present any problems concerning the manipulation of the employer's contributions. Of course, voluntary contributions made on a tax-deductible basis would be subject to a 10 percent penalty tax if withdrawn before age 59½, unless they are "rolled over" into an individual retirement account (IRA).

Withdrawal of Employer Contributions

The withdrawal of all or a portion of the employer's contributions in which the participant has a vested interest is permitted in many thrift plans qualified as profit-sharing plans. Such withdrawals are not permissible under thrift plans that are qualified as money purchase pension plans. The amounts withdrawn normally have to be accumulated in the trust fund for at least two years, although amounts that have not been accumulated for at least two years may be withdrawn by employees with at least five years of participation.

Prior to the enactment of ERTA, some form of penalty was required for withdrawal of employer contributions to avoid constructive receipt. This might take the form of a penalty of 6 percent of the withdrawal, imposed by reducing future allocations of employer contributions, or by suspending the employee's participation for a specified time. While no longer required, such penalties may be retained, and some controls are still required to avoid the possibility of manipulation by employees.

Some thrift plans permit withdrawal of the total account balance when an employee reaches normal retirement age even if still employed. A thrift plan qualified as a profit-sharing plan may permit such a withdrawal any time after the employee reaches age 59½.

If the thrift plan is qualified as a money purchase pension plan, it cannot incorporate this type of provision, because it is the position of the IRS that pension plans may not provide for any distributions prior to retirement or termination of service. However, a withdrawal can be made from such a plan after the employee attains normal retirement age even though he or she does not separate from service.

Loans

Loans to plan participants are permissible under thrift plans if such loans are expressly allowed by the plan on a nondiscriminatory basis, are adequately secured, bear a reasonable rate of interest, and provide for repayment within a specified period not greater than 5 years. TEFRA limits the amount of a loan to the lesser of $50,000 or 50 percent of the participant's vested interest, but this 50 percent limit does not apply if the loan is for $10,000 or less. Also, the loan may be for a period longer than 5 years, if the purpose of the loan is to acquire or construct a principal residence for the participant or a member of the family.

To provide that loans will not affect the investment performance that could be expected if loans were not permitted, some plans provide that loans will be treated as a directed investment by the participant of the proportion of the account represented by the loan. The investment yield credited to such directed investment then is based solely on the interest payments made in the repayment of the loan.

Distributions upon Retirement or Termination

Benefits upon the retirement or termination of service of a participant under a thrift plan normally are distributed in a lump-sum payment, by a series of installment payments, or through the purchase of an annuity contract from an insurance company. Lump-sum payments are the most common form of distribution.

Many plans have eliminated the purchase of an annuity as a method of distribution to avoid the complications associated with qualified joint-and-survivor annuities. Participants who wish to have a life annuity purchased on their behalf may roll over that portion of the distribution exclusive of their own contributions to an individual retirement account (IRA) sponsored by an insurance company within 60 days after the date they receive their distribution from the thrift plan and use such amount to purchase an annuity. However, the employee's own contributions (other than tax-deductible voluntary contributions) cannot be transferred to an individual retirement account. The plan itself could pay the proceeds, including employee contributions, in installments over a fixed period, such as 10 or 15 years.

A thrift plan is required to commence the payment of benefits to a participant not later than the 60th day after the close of the plan year in which the latest of the following events occurs: (1) attaining age 65, or attaining any earlier normal retirement age specified under the plan; (2) 10 years have elapsed from the time participation in the plan commenced; or (3) service with the employer is terminated.

The payment of benefits to the participant may be deferred to a date later than the dates specified above if (a) the plan permits such a deferral and the participant submits to the plan administrator a signed written statement which describes his or her benefit and the date on which the participant elects to have it commence, and (b) the deferral of such payment will not cause the benefits payable upon death to be more than "incidental" (which means, essentially, that the participant should be expected under normal life expectancies to receive more than 50 percent of the benefit before his or her death). For example a participant who retires at age 65 might elect to defer receipt of any benefits until age 70, and then take a percentage of the fund (such as 10 percent) each year thereafter. In practice, benefit payments under a thrift plan typically begin shortly after the date of termination of the participant's service, although some plans provide that payments will not begin until the participant has been gone long enough to incur a forfeiture that is not required to be restored in the event of his or her reemployment.

Top-Heavy Provisions of TEFRA

TEFRA imposes severe restrictions on plans that are "top-heavy." A plan is top-heavy if 60 percent or more of the total of all account balances are for key employees (officers and significant owners).

The principal requirements for top-heavy plans are: (1) vesting at 20 percent after 2 years' service, grading up to 100 percent after 6 years, or 100 percent vesting after 3 years' service; (2) an employer contribution for each non-key participant of at least 3 percent of compensation; (3) no more than $200,000 of compensation counted for plan purposes; and (4) if the participant is also covered by a defined benefit plan, the overall dollar limitation is based on 100 percent, rather than 125 percent, of the separate dollar limitations, unless additional conditions are met.

Distributions to a key employee from a top-heavy plan before age 59½ are subject to a 10-percent penalty tax. Distributions must begin by age 70½ for such a key employee, even if he is still employed.

TAX ASPECTS OF CONTRIBUTIONS TO THRIFT PLANS

Contributions to qualified thrift plans are afforded the same tax treatment and considerations afforded contributions to other qualified pension, profit-sharing, and stock-bonus plans. Briefly, these include:

1. The employer can take a current deduction for its contributions to the plan (provided the contributions are not in excess of the prescribed deductible limits), and such contributions are not taxable to the employee or his or her beneficiary until actually distributed.
2. Employee basic contributions may not be claimed as a tax deduction.
3. Employee voluntary contributions may be deductible up to a maximum of $2,000 a year, if the plan so provides. Other voluntary contributions are not deductible.
4. The contributions of both the employer and employees are allowed to earn and compound income on a tax-free basis (to the extent that such income is not deemed to be unrelated business income of the trust), and such earnings are not taxable to the employee or his or her beneficiary until they are actually received.

TAX ASPECTS OF DISTRIBUTIONS FROM THRIFT PLANS

The taxation of distributions from thrift plans varies, of course, in different circumstances. Distributions and withdrawals from qualified thrift plans are taxed in the same manner as distributions and withdrawals from other qualified pension, profit-sharing, and stock-bonus plans. It is not the purpose of this chapter to discuss in detail the taxability of distributions from qualified plans, but some general tax features include:

1. Employee contributions that have been made from aftertax dollars are
    not subject to federal income tax when distributed or withdrawn.
2. Employer contributions and investment earnings on both the employer
    and employee contributions are taxable as ordinary income when dis-
    tributed or withdrawn except to the extent provided otherwise below.
3. Employee contributions that have been taken as a tax deduction, and
    the investment earnings thereon, are taxable as ordinary income when
    distributed, and in addition, a 10-percent penalty is imposed if the
    withdrawal is made before age 59½. No special tax treatment is avail-
    able for these amounts, but a participant may roll them over into an
    IRA on a tax-free basis and thereby defer all taxes until the proceeds
    are withdrawn from the IRA.
4. Special tax treatment is available for qualified lump-sum distributions
    due to the employee's separation from service, or death, or, under a
    profit-sharing thrift plan, after he has attained age 59½, (even if he
    remains in service). Under this special tax treatment, the portion at-
    tributable to service before 1974 is subject to capital gains treatment,
    and the portion attributable to service after 1973 is subject to special
    10-year averaging treatment. Alternatively, the recipient may elect to
    use 10-year averaging treatment for the entire distribution.
5. Alternatively, a qualified lump-sum distribution may be rolled over
    into an IRA on a tax-free basis.
6. The unrealized appreciation in the value of stock of the employer
    during the period that it is held in the trust fund is not taxable at the
    time that it is distributed on behalf of the participant if such stock is
    distributed as part of a qualified lump-sum distribution or if such stock
    is attributable to the employee's own contributions.
7. The first $5,000 of any otherwise taxable distribution from the trust
    fund due to the employee's death is excluded from federal income tax if
    such death benefit is paid in a lump sum, or if it is forfeitable and paid in
    installments. All qualified plans of the employer must be combined in
    applying this exclusion.

In general, the options on form and timing of payment that can be made
available under thrift plans are valuable, because they allow for flexibility in
an employee's overall tax planning.

ADMINISTRATIVE CONSIDERATIONS

A primary consideration in the design and operation of any thrift plan is
the administrative and recordkeeping capabilities available to the employer.
A thrift plan is required to allocate the contributions to the plan each year
among the participants, and must provide for an annual valuation of the
trust investments, on a specified date each year, to allocate the investment
gains or losses (both realized and unrealized) among the accounts of the
participants. While such allocations are required to be performed only once
a year, many employers (primarily those with sophisticated recordkeeping

capabilities) choose to perform either or both allocations more frequently, often on a monthly or quarterly basis.

It also is necessary under a thrift plan to be able to determine the benefits to which a participant is entitled. To make such a determination, it is necessary to be able to ascertain the amount of the employee's own contributions (both basic and voluntary), and the funds attributable thereto, and the amount of the employer contributions and forfeitures that have been credited to the participant's account and the funds attributable thereto. In addition, if employer stock is distributed to the participant, it is necessary, for tax purposes, to ascertain the time of acquisition and the cost to the trust fund of each share of stock distributed to the employee.

Other tasks involved in the administration of a thrift plan include: communicating to each participant the amount of his or her accrued benefits (normally done at least once a year); enrolling the eligible employees as participants in the plan; and obtaining their authorizations for the deduction of the desired employee contributions, their investment fund designations, and their beneficiary designations (and subsequent changes in such authorizations and designations).

While the general operation of a thrift plan is fairly simple and easy to understand, the accounting methods and recordkeeping system required to maintain the accounts and to determine the benefits of the participants can be quite complex, depending upon the variety of options available to the participants.

SECTION 401(K) OF THE INTERNAL REVENUE CODE

This chapter has taken no account of the provisions of Section 401(k) of the IRC; however, these provisions are summarized very briefly below, and are dealt with more thoroughly in Chapter 33 of the *Handbook*. Section 401(k) would permit qualified profit-sharing plans, including thrift plans, to give employees the option of cash or a tax-deferred contribution to the plan. The required funds might be generated by a salary reduction arrangement. Specific quantitative discrimination tests are provided, to ensure that the average deferrals for the highly compensated employees are not unreasonable in relation to those for lower-paid employees. Only those deferrals that are fully vested can be taken into account. Distributions can only be made at termination or for hardship.

The key feature of Section 401(k) is that it might enable employees to make what, in effect, are tax-deductible contributions, but which would have more favorable treatment on withdrawal than is accorded to contributions, to a qualified plan or to an IRA, that are deductible under the provisions of ERTA.

A major disadvantage of Section 401(k) is that, to meet the special discrimination tests prescribed, the amount of tax-deferred contribution that can be made for higher-paid employees may be much less than would be desirable.

CHAPTER 33

Cash or Deferred Arrangements

JACK L. VANDERHEI

INTRODUCTION

The recent "discovery" of Sections 401(k) and 402(a)(8)—added to the Internal Revenue Code (IRC) by the Revenue Act of 1978—offers another technique which should be considered in employee benefit planning. IRC Section 401(k) permits qualified profit-sharing and stock-bonus plans to include cash or deferred arrangements (CODAs) under which plan participants are allowed to elect certain payments, either in the form of current salary or as employer contributions to the qualified plan. IRC Section 402(a)(8) allows income deferrals under a CODA to be treated as employer contributions; amounts deferred under these arrangements will be excluded from the employee's taxable income.

Proposed regulations under IRC Sections 401(k) and 402(a)(8) were published on November 10, 1981. In addition to specifically authorizing the use of salary-reduction arrangements in the case of a qualified CODA,[1] the proposed regulations apparently provided the guidance that many employers had been waiting for. Surveys conducted by the major consulting firms only a few months after the publication of the proposed regulations indicated that a majority of the companies contacted were seriously considering a CODA.[2]

---

[1] In contrast to a *cash-option* CODA in which the employee defers his or her share of a profit-sharing bonus, a *salary-reduction* CODA allows an employee to defer a portion of his or her regular compensation. See Theodore E. Rhodes and Harry J. Conaway, "Cash or Deferred Arrangements," *40th NYU Institute on Federal Taxation* (Supplement 1982), p. 2.

[2] The surveys and responses varied among consulting firms. Nearly three quarters of the more than 300 companies responding to a survey conducted by Towers, Perrin, Forster & Crosby's Employee Benefit Information Center in February 1982 had either already decided to adopt a CODA, were actively studying the possibility, or planned to do so very soon. A random sample of the top 1,000 U.S. corporations by Hazlehurst & Associates, Inc., in 1982 showed that 93 percent of the top 500 companies and 78 percent of the second 500 companies were currently evaluating salary-reduction plans. A questionnaire sent by Buck Consultants to a broad cross-section of companies in the second quarter of 1982 revealed that 71 percent of the 287 respondents were favorably considering a CODA. See "Substantial Interest in 401(k)

Given the historical propensity of many employers to avoid rushing into the latest fad in employee benefits (especially in the absence of final tax regulations) how can this sudden interest in CODAs be explained? This chapter will attempt to answer the question by first reviewing the legislative history of the provisions affecting CODAs and then explaining the current requirements to qualify such a plan. Illustrations of some of the most common types of CODAs will be provided, and the advantages and limitations of CODAs will be summarized from the perspectives of both the employer and the plan participant. Finally, several technical issues which were not resolved by the proposed regulations will be analyzed.

Although this chapter is limited to a discussion of the most prevalent CODA formats, the reader should note that this type of program can be combined with IRC Section 125 "cafeteria" plans (Chapter 26) to create additional flexibility for the employee.[3]

HISTORY OF CODA LEGISLATION

Although there appears to be a widespread belief that the Revenue Act of 1978 marked the genesis of retirement and capital accumulation programs that permitted employee contributions on a pretax basis, in fact, these arrangements were extremely popular in certain industries in the 1950s and 1960s. This section reviews the evolution of the tax treatment for these arrangements from the situation existing before the 1972 proposed regulations to the imposition of social security and federal unemployment taxes on CODA deferrals by the Social Security Amendments Act of 1983.

Pre-1972

Before 1972, the IRS provided guidelines for qualifying cash-option CODAs in Revenue Rulings 56-497, 63-180, and 68-89. In essence, more than one half of the total participation in the plan had to be from the lowest-paid two thirds of all eligible employees for a cash-option CODA to be qualified and therefore avoid the consequences of the constructive-receipt doctrine (that is, employees would not be taxed on the contributions in the

---

Plans, Survey Shows," *Employee Benefit Plan Review*, September 1982, p. 18; Philip M. Alden, Jr., "Where Less Means More—Sec. 401(k) Plans," *Pension World*, April 1982, p. 43; "Corporate Attitudes and Approaches to Cash or Deferred Arrangements," (New York: Buck Consultants, Inc., 1982).

[3] For an excellent discussion of this concept, including an example of integrating IRC Sections 401(k), 125, and 105(h) (medical reimbursement plans), see James E. Martin, "Salary Reduction/Flex—Second Generation Cafeteria Plans," *Journal of Pension Planning and Compliance*, April 1983, pp. 107-13. Detailed examples of flexible benefit plans that use salary reduction are presented in "Benefits Revolution Picks Up Steam As More Firms Combine Flexible Benefits with Salary Reduction," *Employee Benefit Plan Review*, May 1983, p. 9.

year they were made). Salary-reduction plans satisfying these coverage requirements were eligible for the same favorable tax treatment.[4]

1972 Proposed Regulations

In December 1972, the IRS issued proposed regulations which stated that any compensation which an employee could receive as cash would be subject to current taxation even if it was deferred as a contribution to the employer's qualified retirement plan. The proposals were withdrawn, without having been finalized, in July 1978.

It has been suggested that the 1972 proposed regulations were issued in response to a feeling on behalf of the IRS that the discrimination standards were not being followed by cash-option and salary-reduction CODAs. Apparently, it was assumed that once the tax advantage was eliminated, the CODAs and the consequent discrimination problems would soon terminate.[5]

The Employee Retirement Income Security Act of 1974

As the gestation period for the Employee Retirement Income Security Act of 1974 (ERISA) was coming to an end, Congress became increasingly aware of the need to devote additional time to study the CODA concept. Therefore, ERISA Section 2006 provided that the existing tax status for CODAs was to be frozen until the end of 1976. As a result, the three revenue rulings mentioned above would continue to apply to all plans in existence on or before June 27, 1974. However, contributions to CODAs established after that date would be treated as employee contributions and, therefore, currently taxable.

Unable to meet its self-imposed deadline, Congress extended the moratorium on CODAs twice, the second time extending the deadline until the end of 1979.

The Revenue Act of 1978

Prior to its third deadline, Congress used the Revenue Act of 1978 to enact permanent provisions governing CODAs by adding Sections 401(k) and 402(a)(8) to the IRC. For plan years beginning after December 31, 1979, two rules were provided relating to amounts that employees elect to defer under qualified CODAs:

---

[4] See Richard Bassuk, "Salary Reduction Plans and Individual Retirement Plans Examined," *C.L.U. Journal*, April 1973, pp. 47–54, for a description of tax-qualified salary-reduction plans during this time period.

[5] See Gary C. Quintiere, "Tax-Sheltered Contributory Retirement Plans: Which One to Choose?" *Employee Benefits Journal*, December 1982, p. 7.

1. If certain nonforfeitability and withdrawal requirements (described in the next section) are met, then contributions made by an employer on behalf of an employee "shall not be treated as distributed or made available to the employee nor as contributions made to the trust by the employee merely because the arrangement includes provisions under which the employee has an election whether the contribution will be made to the trust or received by the employee in cash."[6]

2. Mechanical antidiscrimination rules for CODAs (described in the next section) were provided. Although these rules have been perceived by many commentators as a substantial impediment to establishing qualified CODAs, IRC Section 401(k) does not require that these *special* rules be satisfied—they are merely alternatives to the *general* coverage and nondiscrimination requirements.[7]

1981 Proposed Regulations

As mentioned previously, the proposed regulations issued under IRC Sections 401(k) and 402(a)(8) in late 1981 specifically recognized that a qualified CODA may be in the form of a salary-reduction agreement. In addition, the proposed regulations incorporate a special rule which recognizes the need for a mechanism that will assure compliance with the antidiscrimination requirements applied to qualified CODAs.[8]

The IRS has stated that the proposed regulations can be relied on for plan qualification until final regulations are published.[9] Accordingly, the material in this chapter is based on the proposed regulations.

The Social Security Act Amendments of 1983

The Social Security Act Amendments of 1983 made several major changes in the types of deferred compensation subject to Social Security and federal unemployment taxes. With regard to CODA deferrals, the act subjects elective amounts available under a CODA to Social Security and federal unemployment taxes, regardless of whether the participant defers the amount.[10] However, the Conference Committee Report on the bill

---

[6] IRC Sec. 402(a)(8).

[7] IRC Secs. 401(a)(4) and 410(b)(1). In practice, however, it may well be that most plans that include a CODA will find it necessary to apply the special coverage and nondiscrimination rules. For an excellent description of the problems most CODAs would have satisfying the general rules, see Rhodes and Conaway, "Cash or Deferred Arrangements," pp. 18–19.

[8] See the discussion of fail-safe devices in the next section.

[9] IRS Notice 82–1.

[10] For an interesting analysis of the issues leading to the adoption of the proposal to subject CODA deferrals to Social Security taxation, see Alan P. Cleveland, "The Proposal of the National Commission on Social Security Reform Bearing on 401(k) Plans," *Newsbriefs*, May/June 1983, pp. 8–11.

makes it clear that these taxes will not be imposed on employee elections under Section 125 cafeteria plans *other than* the CODA election. Although Social Security taxes are imposed on compensation paid after December 31, 1983, and federal unemployment taxes after December 31, 1984, a transition rule may defer those effective dates for employer contributions attributable to earlier service.[11]

It is difficult to determine the impact of this event on a plan sponsor's decision to adopt a CODA; however, before Congress enacted the bill in March 1983, many commentators were suggesting that employers could use the savings of payroll-based Social Security and federal unemployment taxes to cover the entire cost of plan administration in salary-reduction plans. A related, albeit minor, advantage that may still exist for employers establishing salary-reduction plans is that with a lower gross payroll, the insurance premium for workers' compensation coverage might be lower.

TECHNICAL REQUIREMENTS

IRC Section 401(k) states that a qualified CODA is any arrangement which:

1. Is a part of a profit-sharing or stock-bonus plan that meets the requirements of IRC Section 401(a).
2. Allows covered employees to elect to have the employer make contributions to a trust under the plan on behalf of the employees, or directly to the employees in cash.
3. Subjects amounts held by the trust that are attributable to employer contributions made pursuant to an employee's election to certain specified withdrawal limitations.
4. Provides that accrued benefits derived from employer contributions made to the trust pursuant to an employee's election are nonforfeitable.[12]

This section will describe and analyze the impact on plan design of each of these requirements. In addition, the amplifications and restrictions introduced by the proposed regulations will be explained.[13]

Part of a Profit-Sharing or Stock-Bonus Plan

Given that a qualified CODA must be part of a profit-sharing or stock-bonus plan, the employer has the following choice when designing the plan:

---

[11] See FICA–FUTA Taxes on 401(k) Elective Amounts," *Employee Benefit Plan Review*, May 1983, p. 19.

[12] IRC Sec. 401(k)(2).

[13] For an excellent review of the actual implementation process for a company—from management's original approval through the first payroll run—see Ronald J. Rakowski, "Ninety Days to a 401(k)—It Can Be Done," *Pension World*, March 1982, pp. 29–30.

Either the elective contribution must be made out of profits, or the plan would have to offer participants the right to elect that their distribution be in employer securities.[14] Regardless of which alternative is chosen, the employer must still consider the deduction limitation in IRC Section 404(a)(3).[15] Since employers will rarely desire to contribute any more than the maximum deductible amount, the deduction limit of 15 percent of includable compensation (25 percent in the case of credit carryovers) may seriously restrict the opportunity of some plans to shelter additional salary. This caveat will be particularly relevant for an employer with an existing profit-sharing plan.

The profit-sharing/stock-bonus requirement has an additional implication worth noting. Not all of the plans grandfathered by ERISA Section 2006 were profit-sharing or stock-bonus plans. Salary-reduction plans that were in existence as a part of a defined benefit pension plan or a defined contribution money purchase pension plan on June 27, 1974, lost their favorable tax status at the end of 1979.[16]

Withdrawal Limitations

The withdrawal limitations for qualified CODAs in IRC Section 401(k) go beyond simply imposing the distribution limitations applicable to profit-sharing plans.[17] CODA amounts attributable to elective contributions may not be distributed to participants or other beneficiaries earlier than retirement, death, disability, separation from service, hardship, or the attainment of age 59½. The proposed regulations made two modifications to these withdrawal limitations. First, any *nonelective* employer contributions which are used to satisfy the mechanical antidiscrimination sales (described later in this section) must satisfy the withdrawal limitations applied to elective

---

[14] This should present no problem if the CODA is a cash-option plan; however, salary-reduction CODAs may have difficulty proving that the cash or deferred portion of regular compensation is directly attributable to profits of the employer. Suggestions for dealing with this problem are given in Rhodes and Conaway, "Cash or Deferred Arrangements," p. 12.

It has been noted elsewhere that the IRS has issued determination letters to new profit-sharing CODAs even though a profit limitation was not imposed on employer contributions made to fund employee deferrals. See Ethan Lipsig and Jeffrey Quinn, "Tax-Sheltered Savings for Employees through Cash or Deferred Plans," *Employee Benefits Journal*, September 1982, p. 18.

[15] For a complete discussion of the deduction limits for profit-sharing and stock-bonus plans, see Chapter 30.

[16] Some commentators have argued that salary reduction should be applicable in the case of a defined benefit pension plan or a defined contribution pension plan. For a summary of the relevant issues, see John E. Lanz, Jr., and Jeffrey D. Mamorksy, "Cash or Deferred Plans and Salary Reduction: Alternatives to IRAs," *Pension World*, January 1982, p. 52.

[17] The distribution limitations for profit-sharing plans are described in Chapter 30. Note that unlike a traditional profit-sharing plan, a CODA cannot distribute employer contributions merely by reason of completion of a stated period of plan participation or by the lapse of a fixed period of time.

contributions. Second, guidance was provided with respect to whether a withdrawal would qualify as a *hardship distribution*.

The proposed regulation specified that a withdrawal would be considered a hardship distribution if:

1. The withdrawal is necessary in light of immediate and heavy financial needs of the employee.
2. The withdrawal does not exceed the amount required to meet the immediate financial need created by the hardship and not reasonably available from other resources of the employee.
3. The determination of the financial need and the amount of money necessary to meet it must be made in accordance with "uniform and nondiscriminatory standards set forth in the plan."[18]

As an illustration of the types of hardship distributions permitted by employers, Savannah Foods & Industries provides withdrawals in the case of medical emergencies, purchase of a primary residence, and family educational needs. The withdrawal must be approved by a company retirement committee, and employees are required to certify that the money is not available from other sources.[19]

Nonforfeitability Requirement

Qualified CODAs must provide that the employee's rights to accrued benefits attributable to elective contributions are nonforfeitable.[20] This requirement will also apply to any nonelective contributions used to satisfy the mechanical antidiscrimination rules; however, different vesting rules can apply to any other employer contributions to the plan.

Coverage and Discrimination Requirements

A qualified CODA must meet the usual profit-sharing or stock-bonus plan qualification rules, including the nondiscrimination requirements of IRC Section 401(a)(4) and the coverage requirements of IRC Section 410(b)(1). To satisfy the *nondiscrimination* requirements, a qualified plan must provide either contributions or benefits which do not discriminate in favor of employees who are officers, shareholders, or highly compensated. The *coverage* test may be satisfied by a qualified plan in either of two ways:

---

[18] Prop. Reg. Sec. 1.401(k)-1(d)(2).

[19] See "401(k) Plan Has a 'Start-Up Account,' 100% Match," *Employee Benefit Plan Review*, September 1982, p. 18.

[20] Specifically, Prop. Reg. Sec. 1.401(k)-1(c)(1)(i) requires that the employee's rights must be nonforfeitable within the meaning of IRC Section 411, without regard to IRC Section 411(a)(3) (i.e., forfeiture on account of death and suspension of benefits upon reemployment of retiree).

the percentage test or the fair cross-section test.[21] In many cases however, once a CODA is introduced into an otherwise qualified plan it would appear that continued qualification of the plan under the *general* coverage and nondiscrimination requirements would be unlikely. The reason for this, of course, is the greater propensity for the highly compensated employees to defer a portion of their salary or profit-sharing bonus. Therefore, *special* antidiscrimination rules for CODAs were introduced in IRC Section 401(k).

Before describing these special rules, it may be helpful to clarify exactly which situations they may be used in. A plan which consists only of elective contributions will satisfy the coverage and nondiscrimination requirements if it satisfies either the general rules or the special rules. A combined plan, defined as one that consists of both elective and nonelective contributions, will satisfy the coverage and nondiscrimination requirements if:

1. The combined elective and nonelective portions of the plan satisfy the general rules;
2. The nonelective portion of the plan satisfies the general rules, and the elective portion satisfies the special rules; or
3. The nonelective portion of the plan satisfies the general rules, and the combined elective and nonelective portions of the plan satisfy the special rules. Note that for purposes of this option, only the portion of the nonelective contributions which satisfy the CODA withdrawal limitations and nonforfeitability requirements can be considered in applying the special rules.[22]

A plan will satisfy the special CODA nondiscrimination rules if:

1. The eligible employees satisfy one of the two basic coverage tests.[23]
2. The contributions satisfy the actual deferral percentage (ADP) test described below.

The ADP test involves several steps. First, any employee who is more

---

[21] For more detail on the coverage tests see Chapter 27. In testing whether the coverage requirements are met under the general CODA noindiscrimination rules, the employees benefiting from the plan may be either the eligible employees (those who are eligible for employer contributions under the plan) or the covered employees (those whose accounts are credited with a contribution under the plan). However, the chosen designation must also be used in testing for discrimination under IRC Section 401(a)(4).

[22] Prop. Reg. Sec. 1. 401(k)-1(b).

This presents an obvious advantage of satisfying the general nondiscrimination rules without passing the special tests. For examples of plan designs which may satisfy IRC Section 401(a)(4) without regard to the special test, see Leonard S. Hirsh, "Qualified Cash or Deferred Arrangements Offer Unusual Tax Benefits and Flexibility," *Journal of Taxation*, March 1982, p. 144.

[23] In testing whether the coverage requirements are met under the special CODA nondiscrimination rules, all eligible employees are considered to benefit from the plan. Eligible employees are defined in footnote 21.

highly compensated than two thirds of all eligible employees must be identified. After all eligible employees are classified into one of two groups (the "top one third" or the "lower two thirds"), the ADP for each group must be calculated. This percentage is obtained by simply computing the following ratio for each employee:

$$\frac{\text{Employer contribution paid under the plan on behalf of the employee}}{\text{The employee's compensation}}$$

and then averaging the ratios for each group.[24]

For example, employees A, B, and C are the eligible employees and their entire compensation is used by the employer to determine contributions to a profit-sharing plan under a qualified CODA. Their compensation and elected contributions for the plan year are given below:

Employee	Compensation	Elected Contribution	$\frac{\text{Elected Contribution}}{\text{Compensation}} \times 100\%$
A	$30,000	$1,500	5 %
B	20,000	900	4.5
C	10,000	0	0

Therefore, the ADP for the top one third (ADP_T) is 5 percent, while the ADP for the lower two thirds (ADP_L) is:

$$\frac{4.5\% + 0\%}{2} = 2.25\%$$

Note that the deferral for employee C must be considered even though it was 0 percent. This is due to the fact that the special tests apply to the *eligible* employees not the *covered* employees.[25] Also note that an ADP is not a weighted average: It would not be proper to calculate ADP_L by summing the total elected contributions ($900) for the lower two thirds and dividing by the total compensation for the lower two thirds ($30,000) to obtain a value of 3 percent.

Next, to assure that the deferrals for the highly compensated employees are reasonable in comparison to the deferrals for the other employees, the test shown in Table 33–1 must be met.

---

[24] An employee's compensation is defined as the amount taken into account under the plan prior to calculating the contribution made on behalf of the employee under the deferred election.

Employer Social Security contributions cannot be considered in the calculation of an ADP. However, it appears that they may be considered under the general nondiscrimination rules. For an example of an integrated CODA, see Hirsh, "Qualified Cash or Deferred Arrangements," p. 146.

[25] These terms are defined in footnote 21.

Table 33-1
Actual Deferral Percentage Test

If ADP_L Is	Then ADP_T Can Be No Larger than
0–2%	$ADP_L \times 2.5$
2–6%	$ADP_L + 3\%$
over 6%	$ADP_L \times 1.5$

Note: ADP_T is the actual deferral percentage for the eligible highly compensated employees (top one third), ADP_L is the actual deferral percentage for the other eligible employees (lower two thirds).

This test would be satisfied in the example above since the value of ADP_L was 2.25 percent and the value of ADP_T did not exceed 2.25 percent + 3 percent = 5.25 percent.

The ADP test in Table 33-1 determines a maximum value for the *average* actual deferral percentage for the top one third; it does not necessarily indicate the maximum deferral percentage for an *individual* in the top one third. In other words, as long as the average deferral for the top one third was less than or equal to the maximum allowable value determined from Table 33-1, then it would be permissible for an individual in the top one third to defer an amount in excess of that limitation.

Fail-Safe Devices

Neither IRC Section 401(k) nor the proposed regulations issued thereunder require a qualified CODA to contain a fail-safe device. However by allowing nonelective employer contributions that are subject to the CODA withdrawal and nonforfeitability requirements to be used in satisfying the ADP test, the proposed regulations provide a means by which an employer can automatically satisfy the special nondiscrimination requirements through proper plan design. As an illustration of this concept, the proposed regulations give an example in which an employer contributes 5 percent of each eligible employee's compensation to the plan and the employees can elect to defer all or a part of an additional 2.5 percent of compensation. Assuming that the CODA nonforfeiture and withdrawal requirements are met, the plan will automatically pass the special nondiscrimination tests. The validity of this statement can be tested by assuming the worst possible scenario for actual deferrals during the plan year. This occurs if the high one third elect to defer the maximum amount permitted and the low two thirds elect to defer nothing. In that case, the actual deferral percentages (after accounting for the nonelective contributions) will be 5.0 percent for ADP_L and 7.5 percent for ADP_T. This situation will pass the ADP test in Table 33-1, since with an ADP_L of 5 percent the value of ADP_T could be as large as 8 percent.

The proposed regulations also allow a plan to provide more flexibility for the higher-compensated employees if the *total* amount subject to deferral is nondiscriminatory. For example, a CODA could provide that the top one third may elect to have all or a portion of 15 percent of their compensation paid in cash or deferred. The plan would also provide that the lower two thirds will have 10 percent of their compensation contributed without being subject to election and that an additional 5 percent will be subject to the cash or deferred election. If the nonelective contributions satisfy the CODA withdrawal and nonforfeiture requirements, the plan will satisfy the nondiscrimination tests, since, as can be seen from Table 33–1, the minimum possible value of ADP_L (10 percent) would allow the value of ADP_T to be as large as 15 percent.

Although the IRS has not formally recognized other fail-safe devices, various mechanisms designed to ensure compliance with the CODA requirements have been suggested in the literature. These alternative mechanisms can be categorized as pre-plan-year mechanisms, post-plan-year mechanisms, and concomitant mechanisms.[26]

The pre-plan-year mechanism is an extension of the concept illustrated in the proposed regulation example above. A system is designed in which the employees select deferral percentages before the plan year commences and any necessary adjustments for IRC Sections 404 (employer deduction limits) and 415 are made.[27] The expected values of ADP_L and ADP_T are then calculated from the employee's (adjusted) selections. If the ADP_T value exceeds the maximum allowable value (determined from Table 33–1), the deferrals for the top one third would be reduced. When the ADP_T value has been reduced to an acceptable level, the (adjusted) employee elections are set as "base deferral percentages" for the entire plan year. At this time, the employer may either require the elections to be irrevocable or permit the lower two thirds to increase their deferrals and the top one third to decrease their deferrals as desired throughout the plan year.

The post-plan-year mechanism consists of a system in which the employer makes nonelective contributions on behalf of the lower two thirds at the end of the plan year if the ADP test in Table 33–1 is not satisfied. For example, if at the end of the plan year the value of ADP_T was 12 percent and ADP_L was 5 percent, the ADP test would be satisfied if the employer made a contribution of 3 percent for the lower two thirds.

---

[26] The pre-plan-year and post-plan-year mechanisms were articulated in Rhodes and Conaway, "Cash or Deferred Arrangements," pp. 45–51.

[27] No maximum contribution limitations are found in IRC Section 401(k); however, the annual limits on defined contribution plans found in IRC Section 415(c) would apply. These limits were changed by the Tax Equity and Fiscal Responsibility Act of 1982 (TEFRA). Starting in 1983, annual additions to accounts of participants must be limited to the lesser of $30,000 or 25 percent of compensation. Note, however, that in calculating these limitations compensation would be the amount after any salary reduction. In fact, the limitation would be 20 percent of compensation before salary reduction.

The concomitant mechanism involves the use of a monitoring system to ensure that the ADP test is being satisfied throughout the plan year. An example of this concept is the FMC CODA plan which uses a computer program to continuously monitor applications from the 18,000 eligible employees.[28] Concurrent adjustments are made if the lower two thirds elect to receive too much cash by cutting back the deferrals for the top one third.

Failure to Satisfy Requirements

The proposed regulations under IRC Section 401(k) state that the consequences of not satisfying the requirements for a CODA "include the present inclusion of employer contributions deferred at the employee's election under the cash or deferred arrangement in the income of the employee." The proposed regulations further provide that "the special nondiscrimination rules may not be used if the other new requirements are not satisfied."

This was a major area of concern among many employers since an inadvertent violation of the ADP test by a CODA could be interpreted as a disqualification of the entire plan if the plan was unable to qualify under IRC Section 401(a). However, during hearings held by the IRS to discuss the proposed regulations, the actuarial division director of the IRS Office of the Assistant Commissioner for Employee Plans and Exempt Organizations stated that in this situation, any excess money would only be includible in an employee's income, and that the plan would not be disqualified.[29]

Time When Contributions Credited

For purposes of applying either the general or special CODA discrimination rules, the proposed regulations require that any elective contributions for a plan year actually be made no later than 30 days after the end of the plan year. Nonelective contributions, however, may be made until the due date (including extensions) for the filing of the employer's tax return for the taxable year within which the plan year ends.

---

[28] See "FMC Amends Thrift-Stock Plans into 401(k) Plan," *Employee Benefit Plan Review*, March 1982, p. 6.

Burlington Northern has combined a concomitant mechanism with an automatic enrollment procedure to help meet the nondiscrimination test. See "Burlington Northern Cash-or-Deferred Plan Uses 3% Minimum Contribution, Automatic Enrollment," *Employee Benefit Plan Review*, May 1983, p. 30.

[29] See "IRS Hears Constructive Criticism for 401(k) Plans," *Employee Benefit Plan Review*, June 1982, p. 48.

Many practitioners originally thought that CODA contributions in excess of the permissible limits could be recharacterized or withdrawn. However, the IRS has subsequently stated that the proposed regulations do not permit this treatment. See Howard V. Sontag, "CODAs: Better than IRAs?" *Compensation Review*, Third Quarter 1982, p. 17.

Separate Accounting

The proposed regulations state that *all* amounts held by a plan that has a CODA will be subject to the CODA nonforfeitability and withdrawal requirements *unless* a separate account is maintained for benefits specifically subject to these CODA requirements.[30] This will include amounts contributed for plan years before 1980, contributions not subject to a deferral election, and contributions made for years when the CODA is not qualified.

EXAMPLES OF CODAs

This section illustrates the three principal types of CODAs established under IRC Section 401(k): cash-option profit-sharing plans, salary-reduction plans (without matching employer contributions), and pretax thrift plans.[31]

Cash-Option Profit-Sharing Plan

This type of CODA will appeal primarily to employers with a profit-sharing plan already in existence. The introduction of a CODA to this type of plan will placate employees who prefer cash to deferred compensation. A cash-option profit-sharing plan should also be the easiest type of CODA to administer since employee contributions are not involved.

Each year the employer will determine the contribution to the profit-sharing plan and this amount will be allocated to the individual participants. The employees will then be given some flexibility in determining what proportion of their share will be received in cash. If the employer contributions meet the CODA nonforfeitability and withdrawal requirements, either the pre-plan-year mechanism or the concomitant mechanism would be feasible for fail-safe devices.

As an illustration of this approach, Eastman Kodak Company has had a cash option CODA since 1960.[32] The board of directors declares a "wage dividend" each November based on both the cash dividends paid to stock-

---

[30] Prop. Reg. Sec. 1.401(k)-1(e).

[31] For an excellent summary of the comparative characteristics of these types of CODAs, see Thomas C. Graves and Gary W. Richards, "Employee Benefit Planning Opportunities under Section 401(k) of the Internal Revenue Code," *Journal of Pension Planning and Compliance*, July 1982, pp. 294–98.

Another possible application of the cash or deferred concept would be a deferred-stock purchase plan. See Ethan Lipsig, "Cash and Deferred Plans," *National Law Journal*, April 5, 1982, p. 26.

It has also been suggested that the concepts of salary reduction and floor plans can be combined to produce a contributory pension plan to which employees can make pretax contributions. See Thomas S. Terry, "Benefit Floor Plans: An Idea Whose Time Has Come . . . Again," *Business Insurance*, July 5, 1982, pp. 17–18.

[32] See "Kodak Details Experience with Cash or Deferred Profit-Sharing," *EBPR Research Reports* (Chicago, Ill.: Charles D. Spencer & Associates), p. 206.1–.15.

holders and the payroll costs (the most recent wage dividend was approximately 12 percent of payroll). Individual allocations are based on an employee's wages relative to that of all participants.

Participants may elect to defer the anticipated dividend in any of the following percentages: 5, 10, 25, 50, 75, or 100 percent. The difference is paid in cash the following March after any across-the-board reduction in deferral percentages required to satisfy the nondiscrimination tests are made.

Salary Reduction Plan

A conventional salary reduction plan (that is, a plan without matching employer contributions) should definitely be investigated by an employer considering a payroll-deduction Individual Retirement Arrangement (IRA).[33] This type of CODA may offer employees a plan which compares quite favorably with an IRA on an aftertax basis (the tax advantages of CODA's are described in the next section) without requiring the employer contributions implicit in a thrift plan.[34] Similar to the cash-option profit-sharing plans, either the pre-plan-year mechanism or the concomitant mechanism could be utilized as fail-safe devices if the employer contributions meet the CODA nonforfeitability and withdrawal requirements.

The new retirement savings plan established by Honeywell Corporation in 1982 is an example of how this concept may be applied.[35] Although a company-sponsored pension plan already existed, there was no profit-sharing or thrift plan and the company chose to establish a salary-reduction CODA which would give employees a choice of how they could defer taxes and save for retirement. The salary-reduction option permits employees to defer a maximum of 4 percent of their pretax earnings each year. Of the 55,000 nonunion employees eligible to participate, 48 percent elected the salary-reduction option. Much like the FMC plan mentioned earlier, Honeywell will monitor contributions from the lower two thirds monthly, suspending contributions by the top one third if the ADP test is in danger of being violated.

Pretax Thrift Plans

Surprisingly, a major reason for the adoption of the third type of CODA may be as a response to certain unintended effects of the Economic Recovery Tax Act of 1981 (ERTA). When ERTA extended IRA coverage to employees already participating in qualified retirement plans, many em-

---

[33] See Chapter 37 for details on payroll-deduction IRAs.

[34] See Chapter 32 for details on thrift plans.

[35] See James C. Lawson, "Honeywell Plan Packs One-Two Punch," *Business Insurance*, March 1, 1982, p. 24.

ployees were faced with an alternative to their nondeductible contributions to a thrift plan. Of course there is no requirement that an employee choose between a contribution to an IRA or a thrift plan, but it would be unlikely that many of the lower-paid employees would be able to make both the maximum contribution to the IRA and a contribution to the thrift plan. Since the advantage of a current tax deduction (regardless of the loss of the matching employer contribution and the eventual tax treatment at the time of distribution) may induce the lower-paid employees to choose the IRA contribution over the nondeductible thrift-plan contribution, participation rates among this group may be expected to diminish in conventional thrift plans. This would increase the likelihood that contributions and/or coverage would be deemed to be discriminatory. As a result, many employers have converted their conventional thrift plans to CODAs which will allow employee contributions to be made on a pretax basis.

There appears to be a great deal of uncertainty regarding the proper application of the coverage and nondiscrimination tests when a conventional thrift plan is converted into a pretax thrift plan. Thrift plans have traditionally been considered to be nondiscriminatory if the rate of mandatory *employee* contributions (those contributions matched by the employer) was not more than 6 percent of compensation. Under IRC Section 402(a)(8), however, CODA contributions will be treated as *employer* contributions. Given that the highly compensated employees demonstrate a tendency to contribute a higher percentage of their compensation to thrift plans than the lower-paid employees, certain features in the existing thrift plan may have to be redesigned.[36]

One possibility for a design change would be an increase in the employer match, but a decrease in the rate of mandatory employee contributions. For example, when *The Washington Post* converted their thrift plan to a CODA, the employer-matching provisions were changed from 50 percent on the first 5 percent of compensation to 100 percent of the first 2.5 percent of compensation.[37] The logic behind this change is that the new provisions will obviously make plan participation more attractive to the lower-paid employees. Other provisions of the *Post*'s plan demonstrate the flexibility of a pretax plan. Employees are permitted to contribute up to an additional 10 percent of compensation in supplemental contributions, 4.5 percent of which can be tax deferred. Supplemental contributions which are not tax deferred can be withdrawn as often as once per quarter while tax-deferred employee contributions and company contributions may be withdrawn only for serious financial need.

---

[36] For complete details, see Louis T. Mazawey, "Need for Certainty and Flexibility in Cash or Deferred Arrangements—Comments on Proposed Regulations under Sec. 401(k)," *Journal of Pension Planning and Compliance*, March 1982, pp. 93–94.

[37] See Michael S. Stolbach, "Converting a Thrift Plan to Take Advantage of Tax Deferral Regulations," *IF Digest*, April 1983, p. 3.

ADVANTAGES OF CODAs

From the perspective of the employee, the primary advantage of any type of CODA is obviously the favorable tax treatment. At the time elective contributions are deferred they will be deemed employer contributions and consequently excludable from the employee's income for federal and most state tax purposes.[38] In the case of a thrift-plan conversion, take-home pay will increase as a result of the tax deferral.

After the contributions are deferred, but before they are eventually distributed, the employee will have the advantage of tax-sheltered earnings accumulation on the deferred amounts. The possibility of taking a participant loan is another advantage for the employee during this period, but in the aftermath of TEFRA this transaction may cause a portion of the loan to be taxed as ordinary income.[39] Although funds in an IRA could be withdrawn at this time, in most cases amounts distributed before age 59½ will be subject to two taxes: ordinary income tax and a nondeductible 10-percent penalty tax.

When elective contributions are finally distributed from the CODA, they may be eligible for rollover and lump-sum distribution treatment. Lump-sum distributions are eligible for 10-year forward averaging, an advantage not extended to IRA distributions.[40] CODA distributions may qualify for 10-year forward averaging if they become payable:

1. On account of the employee's death;
2. After the employee attains age 59½;
3. On account of the employee's separation from service after 5 years of plan participation; or
4. After the employee has become disabled.

Even if the CODA distributions are taken in installments and not as a lump sum, the funds will be taxed as ordinary income when withdrawn—probably at a time when the employee is in a lower tax bracket.

From a tax standpoint, it can be seen that employees should clearly prefer a salary-reduction CODA to an IRA. However, a comparison of a

---

[38] As of May 1983, at least four states (Alabama, New Jersey, Oklahoma, and Pennsylvania) and three major cities (Cleveland, Denver, and Philadelphia) taxed employee contributions to salary-reduction plans. See "Some Tax 401(k) Donations," *Business Insurance*, May 2, 1983, p. 49.

It has been noted elsewhere that elective contributions to CODAs may be exempt from state income taxes in some cases in which identical IRA contributions are taxable. See Lipsig and Quinn, "Tax Sheltered Savings," p. 30.

[39] The tax treatment of policy loans is described in Chapter 31.

[40] The 10-year forward averaging rule is explained in Chapter 27. For a numerical illustration of the advantage of 10-year forward averaging on a distribution from a CODA, see Keith Swenson, "Oft-Asked Questions about Cash or Deferred Plans," *Pension World*, May 1982, p. 63.

IRA distributions may qualify for standard 5-year averaging, however. See Chapter 37.

pretax thrift plan with a traditional thrift plan may yield ambiguous results. Although an employee's aftertax investment is lower in the pretax-thrift-plan situation, the entire account balance will be subject to tax at the time of distribution; under a traditional plan the employee's contributions are paid out of aftertax income and are not subject to tax again. Although there are numerous ways to analyze the impact of these countervailing influences,[41] in most cases it would appear that participation in a pretax thrift plan would be preferred to the traditional alternative. From the employee's perspective, another advantage of a CODA relative to many other employer-sponsored retirement-income or capital-accumulation programs is that benefits attributable to any employee contributions or employer contributions which were used to satisfy the ADP test will be immediately vested. This will be particularly attractive to a transient work force which experiences high turnover.

From the perspective of the employer, the relative advantages of a CODA depend largely on the type of plan chosen, and these aspects were mentioned in the previous section. Regardless of the type of CODA selected, however, the employees will definitely have increased flexibility to set their own retirement-benefit levels by supplementing an existing retirement plan. This may reduce pressures on the employer to increase the benefit levels under the existing plan. It has been suggested that this device would be particularly useful in those industries where profits have not kept pace with escalating benefit costs.[42]

LIMITATIONS OF CODAs

From the employee's perspective, the only major disadvantage of participating in a CODA is the limitation on withdrawals.[43] This may result in an unfavorable comparison with IRAs which impose no limitation on the participants' ability to withdraw funds. Even though CODA withdrawals avoid any premature penalty if distributed before age 59½, lower-paid employees may be hesitant to contribute to an arrangement in which they have only limited access to their account balances until they terminate

---

[41] For examples of the types of quantitative methods which may be used to analyze the relative financial benefits of these alternatives, see Graves and Richards, "Employee Benefit Planning Opportunities," p. 199; and Alden, "Where Less Means More," p. 44.

A simpler analysis can be used in the case of salary-reduction plans (without matching employer contributions). See James E. Martin, "Considerations in Establishing Salary-Reduction Plans", IF Digest, August 1982, p. 3.

[42] See Francis X. Roche and James M. Ballard, "The Reemergence of Cash or Deferred Plans, Journal of Pension Planning and Compliance, January 1982, p. 10.

[43] The impact of this requirement may be more imagined than real. For example, prior to The Washington Post's decision to switch their thrift plan to a CODA, employees were polled for their feelings about how the more stringent withdrawal rules would affect their participation: Few felt that there was a disadvantage. See Stolback, "Converting a Thrift Plan," p. 3.

employment or retire. However, this impediment may be eased with proper plan design.

Four specific solutions have been suggested to mitigate the CODA restrictions on withdrawals:[44]

1. Establish a hardship withdrawal rule.
2. Allow amounts other than those contributed through elective employee contributions to be withdrawn.
3. Allow employees to make contributions on an aftertax basis.
4. Allow employees to borrow from the plan.

The disadvantage of the first approach is that a liberal plan definition of "hardship" (discussed in the next section) may disqualify the CODA while a definition which is too rigid would be useless to most employees. The second approach could be used in the case of a pretax thrift plan by permitting matching employer contributions to be withdrawn after they are vested. However, the amount subject to withdrawal may be less than the employee's total contributions—a situation that is not likely to go unnoticed. The third approach would not only be difficult to administer, but it increases the likelihood that the CODA will be disqualified if the aftertax option appeals to too many lower-paid employees.

The fourth suggestion, that of allowing for participant loans, would appear to be the optimal solution.[45] Although neither IRC Section 401(k) nor the proposed regulations issued thereunder expressly permit participant loans under a CODA, an attorney for the Office of Tax Legislative Council, U.S. Treasury, expressed an opinion at the Employers Council on Flexible Compensation seminar on CODAs that "the proposed regulations' silence about participant loans could be taken to mean that such loans are permitted."[46]

If a CODA does provide for participant loans, the general requirements applying to loans from profit-sharing plans must be satisfied.[47] In addition, two situations which apply specifically to CODAs must be considered. First, the consequences of a CODA loan violating the new TEFRA loan provisions have not been definitely resolved. Although a portion of the loan will certainly be *taxed* as a distribution, will this be considered as a violation of the CODA distribution limitations, thereby jeopardizing the qualified sta-

---

[44] These were articulated in Lipsig and Quinn, "Tax Sheltered Savings," p. 18.

[45] It has been noted elsewhere that plans which permit loans have experienced better participation even though they have experienced very few loan requests, usually for small amounts. See "Hardship Withdrawal Rules in Cash-or-Deferred Plans Must Be Strict, Says Sollee," *Employee Benefit Plan Review*, January 1983, p. 22.

[46] See "IRS Coy About Regs," *Employee Benefit Plan Review*, June 1982, p. 20.

[47] Basically, the loan provisions must be in writing, be uniformly nondiscriminatory, provide for adequate security, provide a definite repayment schedule, and require a reasonable rate of interest. See Chapter 31 for more detail.

tus of the plan? Informed practitioners doubt that this will be the interpretation used by the IRS.

The second situation deals with the use of account balances as security
for the participant loans. Although this practice may be permitted in plans
not subject to the CODA withdrawal provisions, these amounts may not be
used to satisfy CODA loan defaults prior to those events specifically delineated in the CODA withdrawal requirements. As an alternative, an employer
may want to require repayment by payroll deduction.

From the employer's perspective, many of the limitations of the CODA
concept deal directly with the increased administrative burden of complying
with IRC Section 401(k). Three essentials for a successful CODA, all of
which can be translated into additional administrative expense, are:[48]

1. Adequate communication to employees.
2. A computer system capable of handling the extra recordkeeping.
3. Enough time to install the plan.

A related expense is the administrative cost of ensuring that the CODA
nondiscrimination tests are met. Employers may find that a payroll-based
employee stock-ownership plan (PAYSOP)[49] is at least a partial solution to
this problem. Although the PAYSOP was readily dismissed by many practitioners as providing a benefit too small to be meaningful, when this concept
is combined with a CODA on a per-capita basis rather than as a percentage
of pay, it can leverage the amounts deferrable under the CODA for higher-
paid employees. In addition, the PAYSOP rules grant tax credits for certain
start-up and administrative expenses.[50]

Implementing the CODA withdrawal limitations described earlier may
be another source of aggravation to employers even though some may
privately be thankful for the opportunity to restrict the scope of thrift-plan
distributions to those more suitable for a retirement income plan. Several
employers who commented at the IRS hearings on the proposed regulations under IRC Section 401(k) said that they did not want to know the
details of their employees' financial circumstances and that such scrutiny
might be regarded as an invasion of privacy.[51]

Two additional employer concerns involve the CODA nonforfeitability
requirement and the requirement that elective contributions be made to the
plan no later than 30 days after the end of the plan year. The significance of

---

[48] See "Advantages, Disadvantages in Salary Reduction," *Employee Benefit Plan Review*,
June 1982, p. 27.

[49] See "Using PAYSOPs to Meet Discrimination Test in 401(k) Plans," *Employee Benefit
Plan Review*," December 1982, p. 30.

[50] Ibid.

[51] At least one company is offering an independent service to process and evaluate
employee withdrawal requests, thereby avoiding disclosures of personal financial data to the
sponsor's administrative committee. See "Third Party Service to Process 401(k) Hardship
Withdrawal Requests," *Employee Benefit Plan Review*, November 1982, p. 110.

the nonforfeitability requirement for the employer will undoubtedly depend on the plan design. The employer would not care if elective contributions were subject to this restriction because these amounts would presumably be paid to the employees in cash if the CODA did not exist. However, if nonelective amounts are used to satisfy the ADP test they will also be subject to the restriction.

The 30-day requirement will be a problem for employers who are unable to determine their profits for the plan year within that time period. This is an essential part of the administration process because in a profit-sharing plan, a profit must exist before the employer can make the elective contributions requested by the employees.[52]

UNRESOLVED ISSUES

Before a company adopts a CODA, it may want to consider a number of unresolved technical issues. Presumably, some of these uncertainties will be resolved when the final regulations under IRC Section 401(k) are issued. Although a number of companies have established CODAs under the guidance provided by the proposed regulations, it appears that many are waiting for the final regulations. This section summarizes the important technical issues that remain to be resolved.

The Effect of CODA Deferrals on Pension Plan Benefits

It was originally thought by most practitioners in this field that employers could base pay-related benefits on the level of an employee's salary before a CODA deferral. Amendments were required in some cases to change the definition of salary in the plans, but apparently no major difficulties were encountered. At least this was the case until the first half of 1982 when two IRS general information letters suggested that "prohibited discrimination may result if elective deferrals under a 401(k) plan are counted as compensation for purposes of determining employees' benefits under a pension plan also maintained by the employer."[53]

It is not necessary that the IRS formally adopt the position reflected by the information letters. But if it does, the incentive for employees to elect CODA deferrals will be diminished, since these contributions will reduce the pension benefit provided by the employer.

---

[52] See "N.Y. State Bar's Comments on Deferred or Cash Plans," *Journal of Pension Planning and Compliance*, March 1982, p. 146.

[53] Mark D. Wincek and William J. Vesley, Jr., "The 401(k) Controversy: Will Deferrals Reduce Pension Plan Benefits?" *Journal of Pension Planning and Compliance*, November 1982, p. 424. This article includes an excellent description of the authorities for the IRS position and suggestions for planning in light of the information letters.

Definition of Hardship Distribution

Since the proposed regulations do not define exactly what constitutes a "hardship," many commentators have looked for guidance in other sections of the IRC. Based on these interpretations, one author observes that while the purchase of a second car or a vacation home would not qualify as a hardship distribution, it appears that uninsured medical expenses and extended work layoffs would qualify.[54]

Other unresolved questions dealing with hardship distribution include:[55]

1. May a hardship distribution be made if the employee could have borrowed the necessary funds, but only at substantial borrowing costs?
2. Do eligible financial needs of the employee include those of members of the immediate family and dependents?
3. Must the financial need be unexpected?
4. What is a reasonably available resource? Would an employee be expected to sell relatively illiquid assets before a hardship distribution could be made?
5. Will the resources of other members of the employee's family be considered in the determination of the employee's hardship status?

Miscellaneous Considerations

Other CODA issues which will need to be clarified include:[56]

1. How late may the cash or deferred election be made?
2. What constitutes disability for CODA withdrawal provisions?
3. Would a premature distribution affect only the participant involved, or would the entire CODA be disqualified? In the latter case, would the disqualification apply on a prospective or retroactive basis?
4. When does a defaulted participant loan become a withdrawal?

(Author's Note: Subsequent to the time this chapter was written, the IRS resolved the uncertainty concerning the effect of CODA deferrals on pension plan benefits. Revenue Ruling 83-89 holds that the inclusion (or exclusion) of *elective* contributions under a qualified CODA as compensation in a defined benefit pension plan "does not cause the pension plan to be discriminatory within the meaning of Section 401(a)(4) of the Code." However, *nonelective* contributions will still be subject to the discrimination standards.)

---

[54] See Kenneth M. Cymbal, "Qualified Cash or Deferred Profit Sharing Plans under Code Sec. 401(k)," *C.L.U. Journal*, January 1983, p. 46. Cymbal refers to Rev. Rul. 71-224, in which a plan permitted accelerated distributions in "circumstances of sufficient severity that a participant is confronted by present or impending financial ruin or his family is clearly endangered by present or impending want or privation." Reference was also made to Prop. Reg. Sec. 1.457-2(h)(4) (subsequently finalized) in which the need for sending a child to college or the desire to purchase a home were interpreted not to be hardships.

[55] See "N.Y. State Bar's Comments," p. 148.

[56] Ibid., pp. 147–49.

CHAPTER 34

ESOPs & TRASOPs:
Their Nature and
Purpose

ROBERT W. SMILEY, JR.*

INTRODUCTION AND OVERVIEW

Employee Stock-Ownership Plans (ESOPs)

Kelsoism, Two-Factor Economics, and the Results. Louis Kelso started a movement almost 25 years ago which has, through his own efforts and the efforts of many other capable people, resulted in millions of Americans owning part or all of the companies they work for—"a piece of the action." His concept is "universal capitalism," and its thrust is to spread the benefits of capital ownership to all Americans, not just to a few. Simply put, Kelso divides the economic sphere into two factors: labor (the human factor), and capital (the nonhuman factor). Hence the name two-factor economics. He originally proposed that the ownership of productive assets would be represented by shares of stock in corporations that make capital expenditures. These shares would be owned by new capitalists, the employees of the companies making these capital expenditures. This shift to new capitalists was to be accomplished through the use of corporate credit and reinvestment into the capital necessary to repay any indebtedness arising from the use of such credit. What Kelso proposed was to have every company set up a tax-qualified employee stock-ownership plan and its attendant trust. The trustee would then go to the financial community and borrow money to buy stock in the company the employees work for. The loan would be repaid out of the profits produced by the new plant and equipment that would be purchased with the proceeds of the stock sale. Ultimately, the employees or their beneficiaries at death, upon disability, retirement, or other termination of service would receive their shares, and "would live happily ever after" on the dividends. There are now well in

* The author gratefully acknowledges the help of Ronald L. Ludwig, Esq., of San Francisco, whose review and comments were invaluable; as well as those of Richard M. Acheson, Jr., CPA, Esq., of Los Angeles, Anthony I. Mathews and James F. Geld of Benefit Systems, Inc., and Ronald S. Rizzo, Esq., all of Los Angeles.

517

excess of 6,000 such plans across the country, and more being adopted every day.

Background and Description. The first stock-bonus plans were granted tax-exempt status under the Revenue Act of 1921. In 1953, the Internal Revenue Service (IRS) first recognized the use of a qualified employees' plan for debt financing the purchase of employer stock when it published Revenue Ruling 46. In recent years, Congress has encouraged the use of the ESOP financing technique in 14 different pieces of legislation.

Employee stock-ownership plans (ESOPs) generally can be described as defined contribution, individual account plans similar to stock-bonus plans and profit-sharing plans. By relating ESOPs to these familiar employee benefit plans, a base may be established from which these plans may be analyzed and reviewed. As a form of stock-bonus plan, ESOPs differ from profit-sharing plans in that an ESOP need not base company contributions on company profits, and it must make distributions in employer stock, although cash can be distributed—provided the employee is given the option to demand his distribution in employer securities. It is the ESOP's ability to borrow on the credit of the company that allows the ESOP to be used as a technique of corporate finance. An ESOP is essentially a stock-bonus plan that uses funds that are borrowed to finance the purchase of a company's stock for the firm's employees. The ESOP is a tax-sheltered employee benefit plan on one hand, and a bona fide technique of corporate finance on the other.

The following example will illustrate the simplest and most basic use of an ESOP:

An Example. Assume that a company in a 50 percent combined federal and state income-tax bracket has pretax earnings of $150,000, a covered payroll of $600,000, and makes a $90,000 (15 percent of $600,000) contribution to the plan, which then buys stock from the company.

Compare this situation with a profit-sharing plan to which the company contributes the same amount. Table 34–1 shows the effect of different plans.

Leveraged ESOPs. An ESOP also may leverage its investments to acquire employer stock, something that a normal pension or profit-sharing plan (except under very limited circumstances) is not permitted to do. This feature makes an ESOP very useful in debt financing. For example, assume the ESOP borrows $500,000 for 10 years at an annual interest rate of 12 percent. (The lender relies on the solvency of the company.) The ESOP then buys $500,000 worth of stock from the company, and the company can use this money as additional working capital in any way it wishes. The company then contributes to the ESOP approximately $90,000 each year, which is used to pay the principal and interest on the $500,000 loan. The company gets a tax deduction for the entire $90,000, even though part of it is used to pay the principal.

Assuming a 50 percent corporate tax rate, the company has reduced its

Table 34-1
Comparing Plans

	No Qualified Plan	Profit-Sharing Plan	ESOP
Pretax income	$150,000	$150,000	$150,000
Less contribution	0	90,000	90,000
Net taxable income	150,000	60,000	60,000
Income tax (federal and state)	75,000	30,000	30,000
Net aftertax income	75,000	30,000	30,000
Company cash flow	75,000	30,000	120,000*

* The $90,000 contribution goes to work inside the corporation, as additional equity capital.

ultimate tax bill by $250,000, and the cash flow of the company has been increased by $250,000, the amount of the tax reduction. At the same time, the employees have become beneficial stockholders of the company and, presumably, now have a greater interest in making the company more profitable and in generating the profits necessary to repay the loan.

The Economic Recovery Tax Act of 1981 (ERTA) altered the funding limits applicable to leveraged ESOPs. Whereas prior to ERTA, the combination of limits on deductible contributions and maximum allowable annual additions created a practical limit to the size of an ESOP loan, ERTA greatly expanded that limit. After ERTA a plan sponsor may contribute on a deductible basis an amount up to 25 percent of covered payroll to be used for principal reduction on an ESOP loan. In addition, the sponsor may contribute on a deductible basis an unlimited amount to service interest on the loan. Equivalent adjustments were made to code Section 415 to allow for the allocation of all released shares (i.e., forfeited and reallocated loan shares need not be considered "annual additions" for purposes of the limitations). Obviously, this allows a much larger block of stock to be purchased than could have been under pre-ERTA law.

For purposes of this chapter, an ESOP means a qualified stock-bonus plan, or a combination stock-bonus and money purchase pension plan that meets certain requirements under the Employee Retirement Income Security Act of 1974 (ERISA), and under the Internal Revenue Code (IRC), which allow the plan to borrow from, or on the credit of, the company or the shareholders, for the purpose of investing in the company's securities. The trust gives the lender its note for the money borrowed, which may or may not be secured by a pledge of the stock. The company, shareholders, or both, guarantee the loan. Usually there is an agreement with the lender that the company will make contributions to the trust in sufficient amounts to repay the loan, including interest. As the plan contributions are used to repay the loan, a number of shares are released to be allocated to the employees' individual accounts. As in other qualified plans, benefits usually are paid after employees die, retire, or leave the corporation.

Alternatives to an ESOP. Compliance with the requirements of the definition of an ESOP is necessary only if the trust forming part of the plan is to be a borrower for the purpose of acquiring stock. If stock is to be acquired without this "debt financing," any plan of the eligible individual account variety can be used to accomplish essentially the same purpose. Such plans include profit-sharing plans, stock-bonus plans, savings plans, and thrift plans, as well as ESOPs. It may well be that the most attractive stock ownership alternative will prove to be a payroll TRASOP whereby benefits can be funded entirely with what would otherwise be tax dollars. Even though benefits under a payroll TRASOP are very small, on an individual participant basis, the fact that they result in a tax credit (as opposed to a deduction) to the company can effectively double their value from a corporate point of view.

Plans other than an ESOP can aid the company in its financing and also provide employees with the benefits of stock ownership. The most common alternative is a profit-sharing plan. While trust borrowing with corporate or shareholder guarantees is prohibited, most if not all of the benefits of an ESOP are available to the company and to the employees through a well-designed profit-sharing plan. Tax-deductible contributions can be made from either current or accumulated earnings and profits, thus allowing a contribution to be made in a year in which there is an operating loss. Distributions may be made to participants in either cash or stock. Contributions may be made in cash or stock; and cash, once contributed, may be used to purchase company stock from the company or the shareholders, as long as the rules are followed.

The next most common alternative is a stock-bonus plan, which is similar to a profit-sharing plan, except that benefits are normally distributable in stock of the employer and contributions are not necessarily dependent upon profits. IRC Section 401(a)(23) now permits a stock-bonus plan to distribute cash in lieu of stock, provided the employee has the right to have his or her distribution in employer securities. The primary purpose of a stock bonus plan is " . . . to give employee-participants an interest in the ownership and growth of the employer's business. . . ."[1] This distinction in purpose from pension plans and profit-sharing plans is important in interpreting the fiduciary responsibility provisions of ERISA.

Thrift plans and savings plans[2] were not previously defined in federal income-tax law but would encompass the whole gamut of very successful plans that match employee contributions on some basis. Under many thrift and savings plans, especially the larger plans, a very high percentage of the investments end up in company stock.

As for these plans being a technique of corporate finance, the same amount usually can be borrowed by the company directly, and then contri-

---

[1] Rev. Rul. 69-65, 1969-1 C.B. 114.
[2] ERISA Sec. 407(d)(3).

butions to the ESOP can be made in company stock having a value equal to the amount of the amortization payments on the debt. If the stock goes up in value, from the point of view of company costs, it will be less costly for the company to incur the debt than the trust. The reason is that less stock will be contributed, thereby reducing the repurchase liability for closely held companies.[3] Additional stock will not have to be contributed to the ESOP to pay the interest, because the interest already is deductible as an expense by the company.

As discussed earlier, after ERTA a leveraged ESOP can be structured to provide contributions in excess of 15 percent of covered payroll.

If a contribution of more than 15 percent of payroll is desired without using a leveraged ESOP, certain pension plans, combined with a profit-sharing plan, may be in order. The pension plan could be a savings plan, and since savings plans generally require the employee to contribute, some assurance of employee contributions can be made by establishing an attractive matching rate, usually 3-to-1 or better. The two plans combined then would permit a deductible contribution of up to 25 percent of covered payroll.

ESOP as a Financing Vehicle. This subject is covered in greater detail in the discussion later in this chapter: Corporate Objectives in Establishing ESOPs or TRASOPs.

Tax Reduction Act Stock-Ownership Plans (TRASOPs)

Background and Description. When Congress was working on the Tax Reduction Act of 1975, there was strong support to increase the investment tax credit from 7 to 10 percent to spur a lagging economy. Senator Russell B. Long of Louisiana supported the increase, but added a unique twist—the TRASOP. TRASOP stands for tax reduction act stock-ownership plan.[4] This provision allowed businesses to take an extra 1 percent investment tax credit if the total additional 1 percent is put into a TRASOP. Let's suppose a company had spent $20 million on new capital outlays in 1980. That corporation would be entitled to $2 million of investment tax credit (usually a direct offset to taxes currently due) under the regular 10 percent investment tax credit. If that company had established a TRASOP, it would have been eligible for another credit of 1 percent of the $20 million ($200,000). The company would get the additional credit by issuing $200,000 worth of stock (or $200,000 in cash to buy stock) to the plan. The Tax Reform Act of 1976 sweetened the pot by extending the provisions for TRASOPs to 1980 (later extended by the

---

[3] Robert W. Smiley, Jr. "How to Fund for an ESOP's Repurchase Liability," Prentice-Hall's *Pension and Profit Sharing Service*, April 3, 1980, pp. 1431–40.

[4] Renamed Tax Credit Employee Stock Ownership Plan, Technical Corrections Act of 1979.

Revenue Act of 1978 through the end of 1983 and finally phased out by ERTA at the end of 1982) and by adding an extra ½ percent investment credit contribution by the employer bringing the total in the example above to 1½ percent ($300,000). However, another ½ percent ($100,000) had to be contributed to the plan by the employees as a "matching contribution." The TRASOP provisions permitted a company to elect to take an additional investment credit for acquisition, construction, and other qualifying expenditures made after January 21, 1975, and before January 1, 1983.

As amended by ERTA, the TRASOP credit after December 31, 1982, is available not based on a company's existing investment tax credit, but instead on its covered payroll. After that date, a tax credit is available for contributions equal to .5 percent of payroll for contributions equal to .5 percent of payroll for calendar years 1983 and 1984 and .75 percent for 1985, 1986, and 1987. The TRASOP provisions currently in effect are scheduled to expire in 1988. For a company with a $20 million covered payroll in 1983, the additional tax credit available to that company through a TRASOP for 1983 is $100,000.

After the enactment of the Revenue Act of 1978, all TRASOPs are effectively required to be qualified plans under IRC Sections 401 and 409A. The TRASOP may be a new plan, or an existing plan amended to satisfy the TRASOP requirements. With respect to qualified investments made in taxable years beginning prior to January 1, 1979, the plan must be a profit-sharing plan, a stock-bonus plan, or a stock-bonus and a money purchase pension plan in combination. For taxable years after December 31, 1978, the TRASOP need only be a defined contribution plan. Accordingly, a money purchase pension plan may alone satisfy the requirements— provided the plan can qualify as a thrift or a savings plan to qualify for the eligible individual account plan exemption under ERISA.

In addition, the TRASOP must meet certain rules regarding eligibility, participation, vesting, allocation of employer contributions, benefit and contribution limits, and the kinds of stock that can be held in trust, as discussed later. Several references to current material also are noted in the bibliography at the end of the next chapter.

CORPORATE OBJECTIVES IN ESTABLISHING ESOPs/TRASOPs

ESOP/TRASOP as an Employee/Employer Benefit Plan

Advantages of an ESOP to Employer.   The principal reasons for the gradual rise in interest in ESOPs are the number of potential advantages of the use of such plans by the employer. ESOPs are advertised as being able to solve corporate financial worries by the following methods:

1.   Finance future growth with pretax dollars.

2. Motivate employees to regard the company through the eyes of an owner by letting them share in a "piece of the action."
3. Minimize—or eliminate—the negative impact of union activity.
4. Create a financial tool for estate planning which will help maintain stock values in an estate.
5. Remain private, while providing an in-house, liquid market for stock.
6. Enable majority private shareholder(s) to sell all or part of their holdings at fair market value without the expense and uncertainty of public underwriting.
7. Create a friendly base of stockholders (employees) as opposed to disinterested speculators in the public marketplace.
8. Divest an incompatible subsidiary without the publicity, expense, and uncertainty of finding an outside buyer.
9. Increase cash flow without increasing sales or revenues.
10. Acquire another company with pretax dollars.
11. Convert present employee benefit plans from pure expense items and liabilities to vehicles that increase working capital and net worth.
12. Refinance existing debt, repaying both principal and interest with pretax dollars.
13. Provide significant retirement benefits without the increased expense and potential corporate/personal liability established under pension reform legislation (ERISA).
14. Provide for the potential recapture of the prior three years' federal income taxes.
15. Defend against a takeover raid.
16. Encourage employee ownership of closely held company stock without relinquishing voting control.
17. Increase available tax credit.
18. Create a tool to help attract and retain high-quality management and supervisory personnel while cutting down on employee turnover.

Disadvantages of an ESOP to Employer. As with almost all things, ESOPs have some disadvantages.

The value of the company's stock may be independent of company performance. If the company's stock experiences a market decline, or a decline based on appraised values, a substantial risk of employee dissatisfaction may occur. This dissatisfaction may be accentuated if there is leveraging in the ESOP. In most cases, however, the direct link between company performance and trust fund performance will only be a disadvantage if the company stock performs poorly.

Further, since an ESOP may have to make distributions in stock, and since the employee may owe taxes, the company must be certain that the employee has sufficient cash to pay taxes. Otherwise, the stock must be sold to pay taxes, thereby creating a morale problem. A put option provision may alleviate this problem.

Dilution is a key disadvantage. When new stock is contributed to the trust, or purchased from the company, the earnings per share on each remaining share may be reduced. A careful analysis must be made to determine whether this potential disadvantage is offset by the increase in working capital and the increased cash flow from the tax savings.

The emerging repurchase liability is another problem that must be dealt with. Again, a careful analysis and the series of solutions available here have to be worked through, scheduled, and acted upon.[5]

Voting control may become an issue, unless the ESOP is monitored with considerable forethought. Sometimes, this is what is desired; and if it is not, safeguards should be established that tend to avoid a loss of control.

The degree of risk is another factor. The ESOP invests primarily in employer securities and may subject the trust funds to capital financing risks. The value of the benefit to both the employer and the employee depends upon the performance of company stock and the timing of capital financing.

Advantages of an ESOP to Employees. The advantages of an ESOP to employees are obvious: they receive stock in the company by which they are employed without any cash outlay or financial liability, and without any income-tax liability until they receive the stock.

Since employees may receive company stock in a lump-sum distribution, they can escape current taxation of the unrealized appreciation in the company stock until when they sell the stock. They are required to pay tax only on the trust's basis (or fair market value, whichever is lower), in the year a lump-sum distribution is made. This can be quite a benefit if the stock has done well, and the employees hold the stock until the tax year that appears most advantageous. In smaller companies, the stock usually is sold immediately, either to the trust or to the company.

Other advantages to employees include:

1. Employees are not currently taxed on their interests in the trust. Tax liability occurs only when a distribution is made available by the trust.
2. The participant may claim favorable tax treatment on a lump-sum distribution under code Section 402(e)(4) or may roll over such distribution under code Section 402(a)(5).
3. If a lump-sum distribution is made, the participant is not immediately taxed on the unrealized appreciation on the employer's securities.
4. The participant may qualify for the $100,000 estate tax exemption under code Section 2039(c) on the account balance attributable to employer contributions.

Disadvantages of an ESOP to Employees. The major potential drawback is the "eggs-all-in-one-basket" problem: the lack of diversification. If the employer company has financial difficulties, the employee can suffer a double loss: he or she can lose both the ESOP benefits and the job.

---

[5] Smiley, "How to Fund for an ESOP's Repurchase Liability," pp. 1431–40.

Having to sell a block of stock in a closely held corporation can be very difficult. With the "put" option requirements mandated by recent legislation, the problem is easier; but an employee could let his put expire, and be faced with this problem well into retirement.

Since most distributions are in company stock, ESOPs will place the employees in the position of having to sell the stock they receive, because they usually will not have the cash to pay the taxes. An individual retirement account rollover may eliminate this need for cash to pay taxes at the time of the distribution.

Employees also must face the problem of a "liquidity crisis" if the employer (or ESOP) does not have sufficient cash on hand to purchase distributed shares. Proper planning can almost eliminate this problem; however, it must be considered.

"Leverage" to purchase employer securities is never a disadvantage to the employees if the employer is assuming the risk of the loan.

Advantages and Disadvantages of TRASOPs to Employer/Employees.

Reasons for Adopting a TRASOP:

1. No direct cost to employer in making contributions.
2. Competitive reasons.
3. Employee morale hurt if employer passes up government-funded benefit plan, and may replace other existing plans or contemplated plans.[6]
4. Allows employees a piece of the action.

Reasons for not Adopting a TRASOP:

1. Pass through of voting rights on employer securities.
2. Large administrative cost versus benefits to employees.
3. Employer contributions may not be large enough to be meaningful.

Applications of the ESOP Technique to Corporate Finance

1. **Capital Formation.** The basic ESOP model provides for financing new capital formation and corporate growth, with pretax dollars being used to repay debt. While conventional loans require repayment of principal with aftertax dollars, ESOP financing enhances the ability of the employer company to meet debt service requirements with pretax dollars. (See Table 34–1.)

2. **Transfers of Ownership.** Existing shareholders may now dispose of all or a portion of their shares without the potential dividend treatment, which may apply to a corporate redemption under code Section 302. ESOP

---

[6] Please note, however, that the Senate Report to Tax Reduction Act of 1975, S. Rep. No. 94-361, 94th Cong., 1st Sess. 56 (1975) provides that additional investment credit is *not* to be used as a trade-off for other benefit plans or rights of employer.

financing permits the acquisition of stock from existing shareholders using pretax dollars, and the existing shareholders are selling capital assets that can be taxed as long-term capital gains. Normally for closely held companies, corporate stock redemptions are fraught with potential dividend treatment, and also require the use of aftertax dollars.

3. **Refinancing Existing Debt.** An ESOP may be used to refinance existing corporate debt and pay it with pretax dollars. The company would issue new shares of stock to the ESOP equal in value to the amount of debt assumed by the ESOP. Sophisticated lenders generally understand that they have greater security with an ESOP since they get their share, even before the tax collector.

4. **Alternative to Going Public.** The costs of a public stock offering, SEC registration, and the high expense of operating as a publicly owned company can be avoided through ESOP financing. The shares may be acquired by the ESOP from either the company or from existing shareholders, or for that matter, from both. Since employee shareholders are usually more loyal as shareholders than outsiders, and because an "in-house" market is usually more stable, the value of the stock may not be subject to the wild fluctuations often found in the public market.

5. **Financing of Acquisition and Divestiture.** ESOP financing provides a way for a company to "spin-off" a division or subsidiary to a new company owned by the employees in whole or in part through an ESOP. The new company earnings then would be available to pay off the purchase price, which may have been financed by an installment purchase from the divesting company—or through loans from outside lenders, venture capitalists, or investor/operators, expert in leveraged buyouts. The same technique in reverse may be used to finance the acquisition of other companies. The often-increased pretax earnings of the acquired company, as well as the generally increased employee payroll, are variables that may permit accelerated repayment of the debt incurred for financing the acquisition.

Estate Planning. An ESOP may provide a very ready market for the shares of a deceased shareholder. Acquisitions of employer stock from the estate can be debt financed and then repaid with pretax dollars. None of the redemption provisions under code Sections 302 and 303 apply. Further, the value of the company's stock for estate purposes may be established.

Problem Areas in ESOP Financing.

Acquisition of Stock. ESOPs may acquire stock from parties in interest if no more than "adequate consideration" is paid. If the purchase price exceeds fair market value, the acquisition would constitute a prohibited transaction subject to penalty taxes and corrective action under code Section 4975, and the fiduciaries would have liability for any resulting losses.

Care must be taken, if the stock is not publicly traded, to determine the value of the company stock. Use of an outside appraisal is more than just strongly recommended; it is almost mandatory. The Internal Revenue

Service and the Department of Labor are currently "closely scrutinizing" ESOP acquisitions of employer stock, especially with respect to fair market value.

Debt Financing. ERISA Section 408(b)(3) and IRC Section 4975(d)(3) allow a prohibited transaction exemption for an ESOP loan primarily for the benefit of participants. The collateral given for a party-in-interest loan by the ESOP must be limited to employer stock, and the loan must bear a reasonable rate of interest. However, if these conditions are not met, the entire loan will be subject to prohibited transaction penalty taxes, corrective action, and, of course, fiduciary liability.

Usually a loan will be primarily for the benefit of participants if the proceeds are used to acquire company stock on fair terms for the benefit of employees in connection with the financing of corporate capital requirements. Primary security for the loan should be corporate credit, and the company should make a commitment to pay sufficient dividends on the company stock or make sufficient contributions to pay off the debt, or both. Liability of the ESOP for repayment of the loan should be limited to payments received from the company, including dividends, and to any stock remaining in the ESOP that is still used as collateral. The loan, by its nature, should be nonrecourse on other ESOP assets.

The employer contributions required to service debt principal and interest must not exceed the allocation limitations under IRC Section 415, however, since forfeitures of loan shares are not considered "annual additions," actual allocations may exceed 25 percent of pay or the then in effect dollar limit.

Determination Letter. The usual Internal Revenue Service determination letter issued under code Section 401(a) offers little protection for the real concerns of ESOP financing. While the letter applies to the requirements for the tax exemption of the ESOP, it does not apply to issues of compliance with the prohibited transaction exemptions under ERISA Section 408(b)(3) and (e) and under code Section 4975(d)(3) and (13). It is now possible to request and to receive a determination letter that the ESOP is qualified under IRC Section 4975. Worse still, the ERISA Conference Report and the final ESOP Regulations direct the Internal Revenue Service and Department of Labor to give *all* aspects of ESOP financing special scrutiny—ostensibly to protect the interests of participants and to prevent abuses of the ESOP technique.

Existing Plan Conversions. If the prudence requirement (discussed in the next section) of ERISA can be satisfied, the assets of an existing plan may be used to acquire company stock either directly from the company or from existing shareholders by converting the existing plan into an ESOP. The conversion of an existing plan into an ESOP is accomplished by means of an amendment to the plan. This subject is covered in more detail in a later section of this chapter.

Which Type of ESOP Will Provide the Greatest Benefits?

Even though ESOPs are a technique of corporate finance, they are compensation programs. The company contributions to these plans involve real economic costs incurred in exchange for employee services. As a form of compensation, they have the advantage of making the employees owners of a company. This may, in fact, be their main advantage.

Not all ESOPs, however, are the same. Selecting the proper form depends upon the characteristics and goals of the sponsoring company and how the plan is to be used. Careful consideration must be given to how the plans differ. Often, the ESOP-leveraging characteristics are not desired and another type of plan may be in order.

Simplicity is a virtue in the benefit field. Stock-bonus plans have this major attribute. They are not subject to code Section 4975(e)(7) regulations. They can use nonvoting and nonconvertible stock, which may be an important consideration when voting control is a key issue. Stock-bonus plans, which do not meet the ESOP requirements, cannot be leveraged if the loan is guaranteed by the company, nor can the stock-bonus plan acquire company stock from a shareholder using the popular installment method. Stock-bonus plans may now distribute cash in lieu of employer securities, but the employee still has the option to require that his or her distribution be made in employer securities. A profit-sharing plan, which invests primarily in company stock, is not subject to this demand from employees to distribute company stock.

Previously, TRASOPs were most appealing to large capital-intensive companies. Following ERTA, they are most appealing to the more labor-intensive companies because of the payroll basis for the tax credit. While it is possible to combine a TRASOP with a stock-bonus plan or a leveraged ESOP, the distinct characteristics of these plans tend to discourage that approach. The TRASOP requirements—that the plan grant immediate 100 percent vesting and must retain contributed stock for seven years—are typical reasons for avoiding this combination. Further, the provisions of the law providing for a tax credit reimbursement of *some* of the costs of establishing and administering the plan are only available for a TRASOP. Other types of plans receive a tax *deduction*, rather than a tax credit, for the costs of establishing and administering a qualified plan.

Leveraged ESOPs make possible immediate transfers of the ownership of companies, subsidiaries, and divisions from the existing owners to the employees. They are, however, subject to the ESOP regulations, including the put option requirements and the "special scrutiny" mandates. The leveraged ESOP and TRASOP are required to invest primarily in common or convertible preferred stock of the employer. Finally, leveraged ESOPs cannot take advantage of the additional investment tax credit unless they incorporate a TRASOP feature.

Increase in Employee Productivity—Pros and Cons

Increased employee productivity often is cited as one advantage of ESOPs. Unfortunately, productivity is a term with a decidedly nonspecific meaning. There currently are no real scientific methods of measuring it. It can be expressed in terms of dollar output per hour of labor, but little, if any, agreement exists among experts on how to increase it—and how to break down the relative contributions of capital and labor. It is almost impossible to prove that giving millions of workers a piece of the action will motivate them to increase productivity. Peter Drucker, in *The Unseen Revolution*, points out that, during a working life of approximately 40 years, the average worker will see the stock of the company he or she works for perform erratically. Many such workers will see their company stock become worthless, and many will see it rise dramatically, far beyond their wildest dreams. Each company has a group of diverse employees with diverse temperaments, interests, goals, and objectives, and each group may react differently. Some employees are "long-term oriented": they think and talk years ahead. Other employees are much more "short-term oriented." Obviously, there are millions of employees in between. Each company has to analyze its own employee base, make careful and well-thought-out value judgments, and decide which kind of employees it has and wishes to attract.

There appears to be, at least in manufacturing companies, some correlation between the existence of ESOPs and increases in productivity.[7] The U.S. Senate Finance Committee did a survey of companies using ESOPs. More than 80 companies responded, with statistical results gained from 72, which included complete information. The results provided Senator Russell B. Long, then chairman of the Senate Finance Committee, with vital information to help him show Congress and the regulatory agencies that the pronounced success of ESOP and TRASOP companies is contributing to the economic welfare of the country. The following averages emerged from this important study: at the time of the ESOP installation, which took place three years ago, the typical company had been in business for 24 years. Over the past three years, an average of 7 percent of the ownership of the company was transferred each year—until the employee stock ownership plan now has 20.6 percent of the company stock. During those three years, from pre-ESOP to post-ESOP, annual sales increased from $19,596,000 to $33,780,000, a 72 percent rise. The number of employees increased from 438 to 602, representing an employment jump of 37 percent. The incentive provided by employee stock ownership may have had an effect in significantly raising the productivity from $44,700 sales per employee to

---

[7] Randy G. Swad, "ESOPs and Tax Policy: An Empirical Investigation of the Impact of ESOPs on Company Operating Performance." Unpublished dissertation, Louisiana State University, 1979.

$56,000—an increase of 25 percent. The annual profit generated before ESOP was $794,000, and soared (post-ESOP) to $2,039,000, an increase of 157 percent. In this profile, the company paid taxes, prior to ESOP, which averaged $312,000 per year. Now, that typical ESOP company paid an average of $780,000, an increase in revenue to the government of 150 percent. While the sample was fairly small, other ESOP companies can report similar results.

The author's own experience consisting of observations of several hundred ESOP companies would tend to confirm these results.

SPECIAL FIDUCIARY LIABILITY RULES UNDER ERISA FOR ESOPs

Introduction

The primary purpose of a stock-bonus plan (the ancestor and major building block of an employee stock ownership plan) is "to give employee-participants an interest in the ownership and growth of the employer's business . . ." (Revenue Ruling 69-65). This distinction is critical to interpreting the fiduciary responsibility provisions of ERISA. ERISA Section 404(a)(1) has fiduciaries serving for the "exclusive purpose of providing benefits to participants," and serving as a "prudent man acting in a like capacity . . . would . . . in the conduct of an enterprise of a *like character* and with *like aims*." The purpose of ESOP financing is the use of corporate credit to acquire ownership of employer stock for participants, and also to finance the capital requirements of the employer corporation. Revenue Ruling 79-122 properly recognizes the ESOP ". . . as a technique of corporate finance." The "prudent man" and "exclusive purpose" requirements of ERISA Section 404(a)(1) and the "exclusive benefit" rule of code Section 401(a) must be analyzed and interpreted with the understanding that the ESOP is a technique of corporate finance. As long as an ESOP prudently acquires and holds company stock as the benefit to be provided to employees, ERISA's Sections 404(a)(2) and 407(b)(1) (which specifically permit an ESOP to be wholly invested in employer stock) are satisfied. Also, under Revenue Ruling 69-494, the "exclusive benefit" rule generally is satisfied if the purchase price does not exceed the "fair market value" *and*, if the "prudent man" standard also is complied with. Section 803(h) of the Tax Reform Act of 1976 makes it clear that Congress intended for ESOPs to be used under ERISA as a technique of corporate finance. Code Section 4975(d)(3) and ERISA Section 408(b)(3) provide for prohibited transaction exemptions, which *only* are available to an ESOP and are not applicable to conventional stock-bonus or profit-sharing plans. No other qualified plans may incur debt to be used to finance corporate capital requirements, nor be used as a vehicle for debt financing transactions involving parties-in-interest.

Internal Revenue Code

The "Exclusive Benefit Rule." Treasury Regulation 1.401-1(b) provides: "No specific limitations are provided in code Section 401(a) with respect to investments which may be made by the trustees of a trust qualifying under code Section 401(a). Generally, the contributions may be used by the trustees to purchase any investments permitted by the trust agreement to the extent allowed by local law." This exclusive benefit rule allowed the IRS to permit the trustees of tax-qualified trusts to invest in the stock of the employer maintaining the plan with the proviso that:[8]

1. The investment had to be permissible under the trust agreement.
2. The investment had to be permissible under local law.
3. The investment had to be for the "primary purpose" of benefiting the employer's employees.
4. The trustee had to notify the district director of IRS of the investment so a determination could be made whether the requirements were met.

The third requirement, the "primary purpose" rule, was liberally construed to mean that the investment in company stock had to be for the primary purpose of benefiting employees. This meant that other people or groups, such as the employer maintaining the plan, or a key shareholder, also could derive a benefit. Revenue Ruling 69-494 also restated its requirements for compliance with the exclusive benefit rule when a qualified employees' trust invests funds in employer securities. The problem, of course, was that other people could derive a benefit only if the cost of the employer's stock or securities did not exceed its fair market value at the time of purchase. A fair return commensurate with the prevailing rate had to be provided, and sufficient liquidity was to be maintained to pay benefits in accord with the terms of the plan, and the safeguards and diversity a prudent investor would adhere to were to be present. A criterion was established for permissible investments based upon the purpose of the plan. Congress, while drafting ERISA, was aware of the position taken by the IRS, and this position is still a reference for post-ERISA interpretation. Notably, a fiduciary who meets the prudent-man rule contained in ERISA Section 404(a)(1) will be deemed to have satisfied the exclusive benefit rule contained in IRC Section 401(a).[9]

"The Prudent-Man Rule." Post-ERISA interpretations are less liberal. If the fiduciary rules outlined in ERISA Section 404(a) are complied with, then the exclusive benefit rule of IRC Section 401(a) is deemed to be satisfied. The prudent-man rule, as indicated above, has to be interpreted in light of the nature and purpose of the plan, and in particular, the characteristics of the plan as communicated to participating employees. However,

---

[8] Rev. Rul. 69-494, 1969-2 C.B. 88.
[9] See H. R. Rep. No. 93-1280, 93d Cong., 2d Sess., 302 (1974).

satisfaction of the conditions contained in Revenue Ruling 69–494 does *not* mean that the prudent-man rule has been satisfied. The prudent-man rule would appear to be controlling. Even though ERISA Section 3001(d) provides that the receipt of a favorable IRS determination letter is "prima facie" evidence of compliance with ERISA Section 404(a)(1), it will not be of much use in providing protection from liability from civil suits brought under ERISA Section 502. It will be some time before the courts have resolved exactly what the prudent-man rule means. The agencies appear to prefer to leave the resolution on a case-by-case basis.

The Department of Labor's final regulation pertaining to the investment of plan assets under ERISA's "prudence" requirement does not specifically address the issue of an ESOP's investments in company stock under the prudence rule. The final regulation, however, does refer to the role of a particular investment "in furthering the purposes of the plan." The Department of Labor (DOL) discussion of the regulation states that an ". . . investment reasonably designed . . . to further the purposes of the plan . . . should not be deemed to be imprudent merely because the investment, standing alone, would have, for example, a relatively high degree of risk. . . ." In addition, the DOL states, ". . . the prudence rule does not require that every plan investment produce current income under all circumstances. . . ." There appears to be an implicit recognition of the "special purposes" of an ESOP as an employee benefit plan and that proper investments in employer securities should comply with ERISA's prudence requirement.

Fiduciary Rules. The general fiduciary rules of ERISA are applicable to ESOPS. These rules are discussed in Chapter 46 of the *Handbook* and will not be discussed at length. However, neither ERISA nor its legislative history gives any indication about how the general fiduciary rules are to be applied to ESOPs. Although ESOPs are exempt from the diversification requirements, and specific transactions involving ESOPs are exempt from the prohibited transaction rules, the general fiduciary responsibility provisions of ERISA for trustees and other fiduciaries is to act prudently, in the sole interests of participants and beneficiaries, and for the exclusive purpose of providing them benefits and defraying reasonable administrative expenses. The ESOP must operate for the exclusive benefit of employees and their beneficiaries. These are important considerations in deciding whether an ESOP is appropriate as a tax-qualified "employee pension benefit plan" and not simply as a financing vehicle for a company.

Employee Pension Benefit Plan. ERISA Section 3(2) defines the key aspects of all employee pension benefit plans, including ESOPs. The key ingredients of the definition include "retirement income" and a "deferral of income." The nature, purpose, and characteristics of a particular plan are relevant; but so is the degree of risk Congress decided that employees could and should assume. ESOPs are recognized as different from other types of pension plans; but this recognized difference doesn't mean that the characteristics of an ESOP are appropriate in every case. It is important to note that ESOP administration and management are subject to both the provisions containing the fiduciary standards and the prohibited transaction restrictions. Each and every aspect of an ESOP transaction must be analyzed in terms of ERISA Section 404 and Sections 406 through 408. While a fiduciary must abide by the plan and the trust documents, these documents must be otherwise consistent with the duties of fiduciaries, and these duties override plan documents.

ERISA Fiduciary Rules

1. **"Exclusive Purpose Rule."** This rule has been discussed earlier in this section. It is contained in ERISA Section 404(a)(1)(A), and is directed at self-dealing and other conflicts of interest. It has a direct impact on ESOP loans and purchases and sales of employer securities. Such self-dealing is subject to special scrutiny by the regulatory agencies. ESOP fiduciaries are urged to "scrupulously exercise their discretion" in approving the nature, purpose, and the like of transactions with the ESOP.

2. **"Prudent-Man Rule."** ERISA Section 404(a)(1)(B) states the prudent-man rule. It is a comparative rule and is to be viewed with reference to the "special nature and purpose of employee benefit plans."[10] Further, the relative riskiness of a specific investment does not make such investment, per se, prudent or imprudent. Accordingly, it would appear that a prudent ESOP fiduciary, subject to fiduciary duties under ERISA Section 404(a)(1), is one who prudently acquires, holds, and distributes employer stock for the benefit of participants (and their beneficiaries), and who prudently uses debt financing where appropriate, in a manner consistent with the plan documents and the provisions of Title I of ERISA.

3. **"Diversification Rule."** ERISA Section 404(a)(1)(C) states the diversification rule and ERISA Section 404(a)(2) specifically provides that an eligible individual account plan is not subject to the general diversification requirements of 404(a)(1)(C), but only to the extent the plan invests in "qualifying" employer securities or employer real property.

One other important exception to this diversification rule: The diversification rule and related aspects of the prudent-man rule are not violated by the acquisition or retention of the employer's stock—provided the acquisition and retention is consistent with ERISA Section 407. ERISA Section 407 contains an exception from the normal 10 percent limitation with respect to employer securities, so long as the ESOP explicitly provides for such acquisition and holding. ERISA Section 404(a)(2) does not seem to permit the holding of employer securities, if such holding would *otherwise* be considered imprudent. And so we have a "facts and circumstances" test, and the agencies retain for themselves the advantage of the "hindsight

---

[10] See H. R. Rep. No. 93–1280, 93d Cong., 2d Sess., 302 (1974).

rule"—being able to look at a transaction or series of events with the clear piety of absolute knowledge and history. To the extent the ESOP does diversify its investment in assets to hold assets other than employer stock, it is subject to the ERISA investment diversification requirement.

4. **"Document Rule."** ERISA Section 404(a)(1)(D) states the "document rule." The significance of this rule is that it changes the pre-ERISA rules. Prior to ERISA, the trustee was required to carry out the intent of the trustor as specified in the trust agreement. With the advent of the "document rule," ERISA now is controlling the conduct of ESOP fiduciaries, and the plan document(s) now can only authorize conduct that is consistent with ERISA. An ESOP fiduciary is in the interesting position of having to disregard the plan and trust agreement if compliance with those documents would be inconsistent with ERISA.

5. **"Prohibited Transactions and Special Exemptions and Exceptions."** Fortunately for employers and shareholders, ERISA contains statutory exemptions from many of the restrictions that would otherwise prohibit ESOP transactions. ERISA's Sections 406 through 408 contain the prohibited transaction restrictions and the related exemptions. These restrictions apply independently of the fiduciary standards. Violation of any of the fiduciary standards or of the prohibited transaction restrictions by a fiduciary may result in personal liability. ERISA Section 409 provides that a fiduciary in breach will be personally responsible for any losses to the ESOP as a result of his breach, and profits have to be restored.

An ESOP is not subject to the prohibition on acquiring and retaining an investment in qualifying employer securities that exceeds 10 percent of the fair market value of its assets. ESOPs are exempt, with limitations, from the diversification requirement.

An ESOP also may purchase stock from (or sell stock to) the employer, a major shareholder, or any other party-in-interest without violating the prohibited transaction rules, provided the transaction is for adequate consideration and no commission is charged.

An ESOP may leverage its stock purchases, if the interest rate is reasonable, if the loan is primarily for the benefit of plan participants and their beneficiaries, and if certain other stringent requirements are met.[11] The only collateral acceptable for such loans is the stock purchased with the loan proceeds.

The ESOP loan documents must specifically provide that all the foregoing conditions be met, and that:

1. The loan will be repaid only from employer contributions made to enable the trustee to repay debt, earnings attributable to contributions, earnings on unallocated shares, and dividends on stock acquired with the loan proceeds or the proceeds of another exempt loan.

---

[11] Sec. 408(b)(3) of ERISA and Sec. 4975(d)(3) of the IRC Code.

2. The lender's recourse on the note against the trust must be limited to the stock used as collateral, and the contributions and other amounts described in (1) above.

3. Each year as the loan is repaid, the stock is allocated to the accounts of active participants as payments are made under the loan, according to the prescribed formulas.

Special Fiduciary Problems

Securities Exchange Act. The 1934 Securities Exchange Act relates to the rules regarding transactions in securities normally conducted on national securities exchanges and in the over-the-counter markets. It contains both registration and antifraud provisions. The act's registration and antifraud provisions are beyond the scope of this subsection. Since the rules in regard to all qualified plans (including employee stock ownership plans) are in a state of change, the currrent securities aspects should be carefully checked prior to engaging in transactions with the ESOP. For example, on February 19, 1981, the Securities and Exchange Commission (SEC) eliminated Rule 10B-6 for all employee benefit plans. Previously this rule on trading by persons interested in a distribution of securities required that ESOPs (and other employee benefit plans) stick to a strict set of criteria. In another example, the SEC exempted a qualified plan from the SEC requirement of the 5 percent beneficial owner disclosure rule in company proxy statements. The SEC reasoned that the true beneficial owners of the stock are the plan participants when there is full voting pass through, and when the plan documents and participants control the disposition of the stock.

National Bank Act. The Glass-Stegall Act relates to nationally or federally chartered banks and the activities engaged in by these entities. This act permits banks to act as trustees, and places the responsibility with this exercise of fiduciary responsibility squarely on the bank's board of directors. Assets held must be reviewed immediately, and then periodically. However, the SEC in its 1934 Securities Exchange Act has provided that "inside" information, which can be easily compiled by the commercial side of the bank, should not be used by the trust department to violate the 1934 act. The comptroller of the currency has specified that written policies and procedures must preclude the trust department from using any material inside information, of which it may become aware, to make recommendations or decisions to sell or purchase securities for the account of pension and welfare plans. Employers maintaining these plans should be aware of these policies and discuss them with their trustees to prevent any surprises.

Blue-Sky Laws. Various states have laws and rules relating to transactions of employer securities. These laws generally require disclosure of the transactions and can be extremely complicated. Normally, there are exemptions for transactions with an ESOP, but there are exceptions, and care should be exercised that the applicable state laws are complied with.

SUMMARY

Each of the series of laws mentioned earlier has some relevance to ESOPs. These laws highlight the importance of carefully considering the structure of an ESOP in terms of the relationships created and contemplated among the employer (and the officers and directors), the trustee, the shareholders, the public, and the participants. Responsibilities should be carefully discussed and allocated—at the outset. Once determined, careful monitoring and documentation of the ESOP's administration is mandatory for a smooth-running and trouble-free plan.

CHAPTER 35

ESOPS & TRASOPS
(continued)

ROBERT W. SMILEY, JR.*

PLAN DESIGN CONSIDERATIONS

Issues Inherent in All Qualified Plans as Applied to ESOPs[1]

Coverage. The requirements of Section 410 of the Internal Revenue Code (IRC), which impose the age and service conditions for eligibility to participate, are applicable to ESOPs. However, most ESOPs, in practice, are more liberal. This is partially because employers adopting ESOPs have expressed a desire to permit all employees to participate in a "piece of the action," and also to provide the maximum compensation base for purposes of assuring that contributions to the ESOP are sufficiently large to make the loan payments and are deductible under Section 404 of the code. Many ESOPs do not have minimum age requirements. They may provide for a single, retroactive entry date. However, certain individual limitations on these generally liberal plan provisions may be important.

The rules that apply to all qualified plans for the inclusion or exclusion of particular groups or classes of employees are applicable to ESOPs and are covered elsewhere in the *Handbook*. Two different ESOPs may be established for purposes of satisfying the antidiscrimination and coverage tests if the proportion of employer securities to the total plan assets is substantially the same in each ESOP, and, if either the securities held by each ESOP are the same class or the ratio of each class of employer securities to all classes of employer securities in each ESOP is substantially the same.[2]

---

* The author gratefully acknowledges the help of Ronald L. Ludwig, Esq., of San Francisco, whose review and comments were invaluable; as well as those of Richard M. Acheson, Jr., CPA., Esq., of Los Angeles, Anthony I. Mathews and James F. Geld, of Benefit Systems, Inc., and Ronald S. Rizzo, Esq., all of Los Angeles.

[1] See, generally, Ronald S. Rizzo, *Specific Drafting and Other Problems of ESOPs* (New York: Practicing Law Institute, 1979).

[2] Treasury Reg. Sec. 54.4975-11(e)(2).

The final regulations on ESOPs[3] specifically prohibit a plan designated as an ESOP after November 1, 1977, from being integrated, directly or indirectly, with contributions or benefits under Social Security. These final regulations are *excise* tax regulations; therefore, integrating the plan would not disqualify it. However, there would be a prohibited transaction if the plan engaged in a loan or another extension of credit to a disqualified person, and therefore an excise tax would be due.

Break-in-Service Rules. The two groups of break-in-service rules which are important for solving ESOP design and drafting problems are the eligibility break-in-service rules and the vesting break-in-service rules. Under these rules, an employee may have a one-year break in service if he or she fails to complete more than 500 hours of service in the defined computation period. These rules are identical for ESOPs as for other qualified plans.

An advantage of class year plans (where the vesting occurs separately for each year and not later than at the end of the fifth year following each year's contribution) permits a forfeiture to arise and be reallocated in the plan year of an employee's separation from service. This may be done without any concern for the reinstatement of the employee's account if the employee returns to employment in the following year but before incurring a one-year break in service.

Under the final regulations, if any portion of a participant's account is forfeited, employer securities that have been acquired with the proceeds of an exempt loan may be forfeited only after other assets have been forfeited. For example, if a participant's account reflects both company stock acquired with the proceeds of an exempt loan and other investments, the participant's forfeiture(s) first must come from the other investments—if the amount forfeited is greater than the other investments available, then some of the company stock may be forfeited. If the distribution is to be deferred, say, until some specified age and/or actual retirement, the ESOP must provide for separate accounts for pre-break and post-break service, until vesting in an account reaches 100 percent.

Most ESOPs do not have a "repayment" provision under the cashout and buy-back rules of ERISA. Any such repayment may be a problem under the Securities Act of 1933. The repaid amount is voluntary on the part of the employee, and, therefore, none of the exemptions discussed later would be available, since employee "contributions" are being used to acquire employer securities. The alternative is to establish a separate account vesting schedule or to provide that any repayments will not be used to purchase employer stock.[4]

Reemployment Problems. It is possible for a plan to require that a former participant, who is reemployed after a one-year break in service, meet the eligibility requirements of the plan again. However, once the

---

[3] Treasury Reg. Sec. 54.4975-11(a)(7)(ii).
[4] Treasury Reg. Sec. 1.411(a)-7(d)(5)(iii).

eligibility requirements are re-met, participation is retroactive at least to the reemployment date, and, if overlapping plan years are involved, allocations already may have been done and distributions made, making reallocation impossible.

Additionally, some care should be taken in utilizing the complex set of rules that relate to crediting and disregarding service for eligibility purposes.[5] When designing this section, and when designing the vesting computation period, several well-thought-out and well presented examples can go a long way in educating the plan sponsor on just what the provisions mean. ESOPs traditionally have been for larger companies, and larger companies rehire employees on a more regular basis than smaller companies.

Section 415 Considerations. As a condition of tax qualification, a defined contribution plan must provide that the "annual addition" to the account(s) of a participant for a limitation year may not exceed the lesser of a stated dollar amount or 25 percent of the participant's compensation. This annual addition includes both contributions and forfeitures, and, if participant contributions are permitted (or required), the participant's own contributions in excess of six percent of such compensation for the limitation year. However, no more than one half of the participant's total contributions for the year have to be included in the calculation.

A new code Section, 415(c)(6), increased the dollar amount of the annual addition to certain ESOPs. The limitation is increased to an amount equal to the sum of (1) the regular maximum dollar annual addition for the year, and (2) the lesser of the regular annual addition or the amount of employer securities contributed to the plan for the year. This special "doubling" is available only if no more than one third of the employer's contributions for a limitation year is allocated to the accounts of participants who are officers, 10-percent shareholders, or employees whose compensation for the year exceeds twice the regular annual addition for the year. Note the phrase, "employer securities contributed." This will include employer securities purchased within 30 days with employer contributions in cash.

When securities are released from the suspense account provided for the holding of the "unpaid-for securities," the contributions used by the ESOP to pay the loan are treated as annual additions to participants' accounts, not the value of the securities released from the suspense account which could conceivably be much greater.

Forfeitures, for purposes of the annual addition, are valued at fair market value on the date of reallocation. Several potential problems arise because of this requirement. First, accurate and timely valuations are critical. Second, in the event of an audit, if the employer securities that were forfeited and reallocated to participants' accounts in a plan year were undervalued, the plan could be disqualified if the additional value, as determined by the IRS, increased any participant's annual addition beyond the permissible

---

[5] Labor Reg. Sec. 2530.202-2(b)(2).

maximum amount. Third, since most loans require fixed-payment dates, timely valuations are necessary to know whether the plan is qualified by the time the employer's contribution is due, because of forfeitures being revalued. The forfeiture suspense accounts, which are permitted by the final code Section 415 Regulations, require limiting employer contributions first—so, with forfeitures high enough, an ESOP may end up in default on the loan, since large enough contributions can't be made on a timely enough basis to amortize the loan repayment on schedule.

The Economic Recovery Tax Act of 1981 (ERTA) resolved this to a certain extent by amendments to both Section 415 (the allocation limits) and Section 404 (the deductibility limits) of the code. After ERTA, an employer contributing to a leveraged ESOP may contribute and deduct an amount up to 25 percent of covered participants' compensation for purposes of principal reduction. Additional contributions used to service interest due on the ESOP loan are deductible in any amount.

At the same time the allocation limits (Section 415) were modified to eliminate from consideration as "annual additions," employer contributions used to make interest payments on an ESOP loan, and re-allocated forfeitures of ESOP stock originally purchased with an exempt loan.

These amendments partially resolved the obvious difficulty arising when three equally inflexible requirements (i.e., debt service, deduction limits, and allocation limits) are applied on different, sometimes unrelated bases to the same transaction. For a particular company, therefore, the deductible and allocable contribution will set the practical limit for the amount of an ESOP loan.

When designing the ESOP, the other plans of the employer have to be taken into account. The other plan(s) might be drafted to provide for a reduction in benefits under the other plans before reducing benefits under the ESOP. This would help to minimize the code Section 415 problems and, at the same time, maximize the allocations to the ESOP participants. The favorite order of priority appears to be to first refund participants' contributions under both plans to the extent they are included in the excess annual additions; if more of a reduction is required, then place the excess forfeitures in a forfeiture suspense account or reduce or reallocate them in the *other* defined contribution plan.

Reversion of Employer's Contributions. As a qualified plan, an ESOP must provide that it is impossible for any part of the plan's assets to be used or diverted to purposes other than for the exclusive benefit of participants. In an ESOP, there are unallocated shares and allocated shares (disregarding the forfeiture suspense account). The nonreversion provision applies both to the allocated and to the unallocated securities. If the unallocated employer securities are pledged as collateral for a loan upon which a default occurs, they may be taken out of the trust in a foreclosure, provided the value of the securities taken does not exceed the amount of the loan default.

Employer contributions may be returned if made under a good-faith mistake of fact or if deductions are disallowed and those contributions were conditioned on deductibility if that condition is specifically stated in the plan document.

In Revenue Ruling, 80-145, the IRS addressed the definition of "compensation" for computing the deduction limitation under code Section 404(a)(3) and 404(a)(7). The IRS held that the deduction limits are based upon total compensation, even in a situation where the plan defines compensation (for allocation purposes) as excluding certain items (such as limiting compensation to basic pay). Some ESOP companies may increase their deductible ESOP contributions by properly applying these guidelines. However, employer contributions can be conditioned only on initial qualification and not on continued plan qualification. Revenue Ruling 77-200 also made clear that a permissible reversion will not be treated as a forfeiture in violation of Section 411(a) of the code, even if an adjustment is made to participants' accounts that are partially or wholly nonforfeitable. If this is done, participants' accounts should be adjusted by first withdrawing assets other than employer securities. Also, leveraged ESOPs may not be able to take advantage of the reversion provisions conditioned on deductibility if they are subsequently determined to be nondeductible. It would be hard to establish that an employer, who is making a contribution subject to the requirements of a fixed payment loan, which satisfies the loan agreement, but exceeds the deductible limits under code Section 404, has made a "good-faith mistake" in determining the deductibility of the contributions.

Issues Unique to an ESOP

Leveraging. While leveraging has its positive aspects, some potential negatives exist that should be considered. Further, there will be an immediate dilution of existing shareholders' interests if the company issues new shares to the ESOP; this may, however, be offset by the other benefits, and a careful analysis should be done.

A leveraged ESOP also commits the employer to make contributions at least sufficient to amortize debt. This "commitment" disadvantage is offset in most cases by increased employee morale.

Dividends on a large block of stock purchased all at once can be a substantial cash drain over a long time. Further, a contraction in business conditions, and consequently fewer employees, could be construed as a termination or a partial termination of the plan. Shares then distributed would be subject to the "put option" requirements (to be discussed in subsequent sections) and would have to be purchased with nondeductible dollars, causing an additional and often untimely cash drain.

Allocation of Employer Securities, Income, Etc. An ESOP is required to contain specific provisions governing accounting for employer securities purchased with the proceeds of an exempt loan. The ESOP must provide for a suspense account, to which the securities acquired with the proceeds of an exempt loan must first be credited, even if the securities are not pledged as collateral for the loan. Also, all ESOPs must provide for the release of the securities and their allocation to participants' accounts as payments of principal, or payments of principal and interest are made with respect to the loan. Further, if the income from the securities is to be used to repay the loan, both the ESOP and the loan agreement must provide for that. By disregarding this rule, any income must be allocated to participants' accounts. The provisions relating to the release of the shares from the suspense account for allocation to employees' accounts should be contained in the loan documents.[6]

The release of shares from the suspense account may be done in two ways. Under the first method of release permitted by the final regulations, the number of securities released each year is equal to the number of securities held in the suspense account immediately before release—multiplied by a fraction, the numerator of which is the amount of principal and interest payments for the year, and the denominator of which is the sum of the numerator plus the amount of future principal and interest payments to be made during the remaining term of the loan, including the current year. The number of future years must be definite and cannot take into account any possible extensions or renewal periods. If the interest rate is variable, the interest is computed, for purposes of the fraction, by using the interest rate applicable at the end of the plan year in which the fraction is applied.

The second method is based on releasing securities based upon the payment of principal alone. When a loan is amortized over a period of years, the interest portion of the payment is higher in the early years than in the late years. Many lenders would prefer that the shares be released based *only* on principal payments so they stay secured. The final regulations only require that the securities be released from the suspense account of the ESOP in the same manner that the loan agreement provides. This second method gives some leeway for negotiation with lenders. The only other restrictions on this second method provide that the release, based solely on principal payments, must be part of a loan that cannot exceed 10 years (including extensions and renewals), and the annual payments of principal and interest under the loan may not be cumulatively less rapid than level annual payments of principal and interest. In computing amounts of principal under this method, interest is disregarded only to the extent it would be disregarded under standard loan amortization tables.[7] Apparently the agencies are concerned that the terms of the loan might provide greater interest payments during each year of the loan than would be permitted under standard loan amortization tables.

The unrealized appreciation or depreciation on the suspense account

---

[6] Treas. Reg. Secs. 54.4975-11(c), 54.4975-7(b)(8); Labor Reg. Sec. 2550.408b-3(h).
[7] Treas. Reg. Sec. 54.4975-7(b)(1)(ii); Labor Reg. Sec. 2550.408b-3(h)(2).

securities are not allocated to the participants' accounts. Shares are allocated; then the value is extended to show a dollar amount. Employees who become participants in an ESOP after securities have been purchased and credited to the suspense account, but prior to these securities being released, will share in the unrealized appreciation or depreciation that occurred prior to their participation and will realize that appreciation or depreciation upon distribution. The reverse is also true, in that employees who were participants when the shares were credited to the suspense account will not share in the unrealized gains or losses if they are not participants when the securities are released.

The forfeiture provisions must be so drafted as to require that a participant forfeit other plan assets before a forfeiture of employer securities may occur. When more than one class of employer securities has been allocated to the participant's account, forfeitures must reduce each class of security proportionately.[8]

Dividends from the securities purchased with the proceeds of an exempt loan, to the extent not utilized to repay the loan, would be allocated entirely to participants' accounts. Alternatively, the dividends may be currently distributed to participants. Allocations to each participant's account and to the suspense account would be made in proportion to the shares held in the respective accounts.

Allocation of Cost Basis of Shares.   Because of the suspense account requirement, code Section 415, and the requirement that employer securities that are acquired with the proceeds of an exempt loan be allocated to participants' accounts in nonmonetary terms,[9] most ESOP allocation sections contain two accounts for each participant. The first account is the "company stock" account, which contains employer securities; and the other is the "other investments" account, which is maintained to account for the participant's share of plan assets other than employer securities. The final regulations also provide that amounts contributed to an ESOP must be allocated as provided under Section 1.401-1(b)(1)(ii) and 1.401-1(b)(1)(iii) of the regulations. These sections relate to the requirement for a definite predetermined formula for allocating contributions among participants. Further, acquisition of employer stock must be accounted for, as provided under 1.402(a)-1(b)(2)(ii) of the regulations. This section refers to the determination of the cost basis of the securities of the employer and sets forth four methods to treat cost basis. Cost basis is used primarily to determine the "net unrealized appreciation" in employer securities on distribution. The plan document need *not* contain whichever cost basis rule is adopted.

Public Policy Problems.   The ESOP is clearly a long-range plan. This requires, of course, a healthy legislative environment. While plans that

---

[8] Treas. Reg. Sec. 54.4975-11(d)(4).

[9] Treas. Reg. Sec. 54.4975-11(d)(2).

permit and encourage employee ownership have been around for decades, the tax benefits are fairly recent, and a rather important consideration is in their ongoing effectiveness. While some practitioners are of the opinion that there are "tax expenditures," which means that any of the taxpayers' money not going to the government and which taxpayers get to keep, is a tax expenditure (since the government doesn't take it), this author is not of that school. However, it is important to realize that many purported policy makers have this view, and they ask questions like, "Who will pay the taxes saved or deferred by the establishment of ESOPs?" and "How is this claim on the federal treasury made by ESOPs to be reconciled with other claims?"

Other questions, however, are more pertinent and deserve thoughtful consideration. For example, "Do ESOPs result in employees having too many eggs in one basket?" When employees' retirement income and their salaries are both dependent upon the financial position of their employer, what will result over the long run? Care should be taken to examine when and if other plans should be implemented to help spread the retirement risk.

Voting Rights.   As an eligible individual account plan, an ESOP of a closely held company must provide that each participant is entitled to exercise any and all voting rights in the employer's securities allocated to his or her account, with respect to corporate matters that must, by law or charter, be decided by more than a majority vote of the common shares voting on the issue. An ESOP or TRASOP of an employer whose securities are of a type generally required to be registered under the Securities Exchange Act of 1934 must pass through voting rights on all matters for all allocated shares. These provisions would appear to apply only to shares of employer securities acquired after December 31, 1979. Since the block of securities held in the ESOP may constitute a controlling interest, how voting rights are to be handled is very important now and in the future! Further, it can be argued that passing through voting rights is strong evidence that the ESOP is being operated for the exclusive benefit of plan participants, absent other clear evidence. These passing through of voting rights requirements for closely held companies extend not only to ESOPs but to any eligible individual account plan that invests more than 10 percent of its assets in the plan sponsor's stock.

ERTA limited the voting pass-through requirement by adding the phrase "(other than a profit-sharing plan)" to code Section 401(a)(22). This gave birth to the "profit-sharing stock ownership plan" which is not required to pass through voting rights at all. The other problems associated with this type of plan, though, are distinct in many ways from employee stock ownership plans and will not be treated here.

Rights and Restrictions on Employer Securities.

1.   General Rule.   The general rule is that employer securities held by a qualified plan must have "unrestricted" marketability[10] and must make the

---

[10] Rev. Rul. 57-372 1957-2, C.B. 256, modified by Rev. Rul. 69-65 1969-1 C.B. 114.

issue one of plan qualification. This rule was further modified by TIR 1413's prohibition on a mandatory "call" option exercisable by the employer within a specified time. The final regulations provide that employer securities acquired with the proceeds of an exempt loan may not be subject to a "put, call, or other option, or buy-out, or similar arrangement," except that restrictions required under federal and state laws are permitted.[11] Since this applies only to securities purchased with the proceeds of an exempt loan, a violation of this provision will result in a prohibited transaction, not plan disqualification. However, since Revenue Ruling 57-372 continues to apply, a violation of this provision would also result in plan disqualification if the violation takes the form of a buy-sell, call option, or other market restricting arrangement.

2. *Rights of First Refusal.* The final regulations permit a limited right of first refusal to attach to certain securities. First, the securities must not be publicly traded at the time the right may be exercised. Second, the right of first refusal may be only in favor of the employer, the ESOP, or both, in any order. Third, the right must not be in favor of shareholders *other* than the ESOP. Last, the right of first refusal must lapse no later than 14 days after written notice of the offer to purchase has been given to the party holding the right.

Further, the payment terms and purchase price must not be less favorable to the seller than the *greater* of (1) the purchase price and other terms offered by the buyer (other than the sponsor or the ESOP, who has in good faith made an offer to purchase); or (2) the value of the security determined on the most recent valuation date under the ESOP.[12]

If the seller of employer securities is a disqualified person and the ESOP is buying, a special valuation date applies. The purchase price is determined on the date of the proposed transaction. A disqualified person is a person described in 4975(c)(2) of the code. The key difference between a party-in-interest and a "disqualified person" is that, while ERISA says all employees are parties-in-interest, the code limits disqualified persons to officers and employees earning 10 percent or more of the yearly wages of an employer. Therefore, most employees receiving in-service distributions will not be disqualified persons even though they are parties-in-interest. The following chart (Figure 35-1) and accompanying explanation illustrate the relationships prepared for properly identifying the parties.

3. *Buy-Sell Agreements.* An ESOP is not permitted to enter into agreements obligating it to acquire securities from a shareholder at an indefinite time in the future that is determined upon the happening of an event—including certain events like the death of a shareholder.[13]

An ESOP also is not permitted to be obligated under put option arrange-

---

[11] Treas. Reg. Sec. 54.4975-7(b)(4); Labor Reg. Sec. 2550.408(b)-3(d).

[12] Treas. Reg. Secs. 54.4975-7(b)9, 54.4975-11(d)(5); Labor Reg. Sec. 2550.408b-3(i).

[13] Treas. Reg. Sec. 54.4975-11(a)(4)(ii).

Figure 35-1

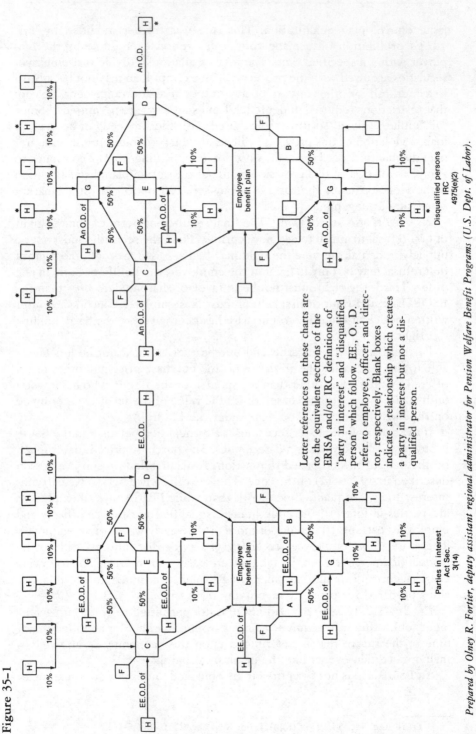

Letter references on these charts are to the equivalent sections of the ERISA and/or IRC definitions of "party in interest" and "disqualified person" which follow. EE., O., D. refer to employee, officer, and director, respectively. Blank boxes indicate a relationship which creates a party in interest but not a disqualified person.

Parties in interest
Act Sec.
3(14)

Disqualified persons
IRC
4975(e)(2)

Prepared by Olney R. Fortier, deputy assistant regional administrator for Pension Welfare Benefit Programs (U.S. Dept. of Labor).

*A highly compensated employee (earning 10 percent or more of the yearly wages of an employer).

The term *party in interest* means, to an employee benefit plan:

(A) Any fiduciary (including, but not limited to, any administrator, officer, trustee, or custodian, counsel, or employee of such benefit plan.

(B) A person providing services to such plan.

(C) An employer, any of whose employees are covered by such plan.

(D) An employee organization, any of whose members are covered by such plan.

(E) An owner, direct or indirect, of 50 percent or more of:
 (1) The combined voting power of all classes of stock entitled to vote, or the total value of shares of all classes of stock of a corporation,
 (2) The capital interest or the profits interest of a partnership,
 (3) The beneficial interest of a trust or unincorporated enterprise,

which is an employer or an employee organization described in subparagraph (C) or (D);

(F) A relative (as defined in paragraph (15)) of any individual described in subparagraph (A), (B), (C), or (E);

(G) A corporation, partnership, or trust or estate of which (or in which) 50 percent or more of:
 (1) The combined voting power of all classes of stock entitled to vote, or the total value of shares of all classes of stock of such corporation,
 (2) The capital interest or profits interest of such partnership,

Disqualified person—for purposes of this section, the term *disqualified person* means a person who is:

(A) A fiduciary.

(B) A person providing services to the plan.

(C) An employer any of whose employees are covered by the plan.

(D) An employee organization, any of whose members are covered by the plan.

(E) An owner, direct or indirect, of 50 percent or more of:
 (1) The combined voting power of all classes of stock entitled to vote or the total value of shares of all classes of stock of a corporation,
 (2) The capital interest or the profits interest of a partnership,
 (3) The beneficial interest of a trust or unincorporated enterprise,

which is an employer or an employee organization described in subparagraph (C) or (D).

(F) A member of the family (as defined in paragraph (6) of any individual described in subparagraph (A), (B), (C), or (E).

(G) A corporation, partnership, or trust or estate of which (or in which) 50 percent or more of:
 (1) The combined voting power of all classes of stock entitled to vote or the total value of shares of all classes of stock of such corporation,
 (2) The capital interest or profits interest of such partnership,

Figure 35-1 (*continued*)

Act Sec 3(14)	*IRC* 4975(e)(2)	*IRC* 267(C)
(3) The beneficial interest of such trust or estate, is owned directly or indirectly, or held by persons described in subparagraph (A), (B), (C), (D), or (E);	(3) The beneficial interest of such trust or estate, is owned directly or indirectly, or held by persons described in subparagraph (A), (B), (C), (D), or (E).	Constructive ownership of stock.—For purposes of determining, in applying subsection (b) a stockholder for purposes of 4975(e)(2)(E)(i) and (G)(i), the ownership of stock.
(H) An employee (EE.), officer (O.), director (D.) (or an individual having powers or responsibilities similar to those of officers or directors, or a 10 percent or more shareholder directly or indirectly, of a person described in subparagraph (B), (C), (D), (E), or (G), or of the employee benefit plan; or	(H) An officer, director (or an individual having powers or responsibilities similar to those of officers or directors), a 10 percent or more shareholder, or a highly compensated employee (earning 10 percent or more of the yearly wages of an employer) of a person described in subparagraph (C), (D), (E), or (G).	
(I) A 10 percent or more (directly or indirectly in capital or profits) partner or joint venturer of a person described in subparagraph (B), (C), (D), (E), or (G).	(I) A 10 percent or more (in capital or profits) partner or joint venturer of a person described in subparagraph (C), (D), (E), or (G).	
The secretary, after consultation and coordination with the Secretary of the Treasury, may by regulation prescribe a percentage lower than 50 percent for subparagraph (E) and (G) and lower than 10 percent for subparagraph (H) or (I). The secretary may prescribe regulations for determining the ownership (direct or indirect) of profits and beneficial interests, and the manner in which indirect stockholdings are taken into account.	The secretary, after consultation and coordination with the Secretary of Labor or his delegate, may by regulation prescribe a percentage lower than 50 percent for subparagraphs (E) and (G) and lower than 10 percent for subparagraphs (H) and (I).	

(1) Stock owned, directly or indirectly, by or for a corporation, partnership, estate, or trust shall be considered as being owned proportionately by or for its shareholders, partners, or beneficiaries;

(2) An individual shall be considered as owning the stock owned, directly or indirectly, by or for his family;

(3) An individual owning (otherwise than by the application of paragraph (2)) for purposes of 4975(e)(2)(E)(ii) and (iii), (G)(ii) and (iii) and (I);

(4) The family of an individual shall include only spouse, ancestor, lineal descendent, and any spouse of a lineal descendant; and

(5) Stock constructively owned by a person by reason of the application of paragraph (1) shall, for the purpose of applying paragraph (1), (2), or (3), be treated as actually owned by such person, but stock constructively owned by an individual by reason of the application of paragraph (2) or (3) shall not be treated as owned by him for the purpose of again applying either of such paragraphs in order to make another the constructive owner of such stock.

ments.[14] Ostensibly the purpose of these prohibitions is to eliminate the possibility that plan fiduciaries may be required to act imprudently in the future, at the time of purchase.

Even agreements spelling out that the transaction will take place at "fair market value" and for "adequate consideration" at the time the obligation becomes due will not be acceptable, since the purchase (for all of the reasons outlined in this chapter) may not be an acceptable transaction.

Option arrangements, however, are permissible. An ESOP may enter into an agreement that would provide the ESOP with an option to purchase employer securities from a shareholder at some definite or indefinite date in the future. This type of arrangement clearly is in the interest of both the ESOP and the participants, since it provides a place to purchase employer securities and gives the fiduciaries a chance to determine the prudence of the exercise of the option. Careful drafting would require that the ESOP trust provisions specifically authorize such agreements, but not require that they be entered into.

4. Put Options. One key question, which has always troubled nearly everyone concered with ESOPs, is "What good is stock without a market?" Part of the answer has been set forth in regulations[15] and modified by statute.[16]

The Revenue Act of 1978 provides that participants or beneficiaries receiving a distribution of employer stock from a leveraged ESOP (or TRASOP) generally must be given a put option for the stock, if the employer securities are not readily tradeable on an established market, and if a participant who is entitled to a distribution from the plan has a right to require that the employer repurchase employer securities under a fair valuation formula.

As finally codified by ERTA, the put option must give the following benefits:

1. The trustee of the participant's individual retirement account must be able to exercise the same option.
2. The participant must have at least 60 days, after receipt of the stock, to require that the employer repurchase the stock at its fair market value.[17]
3. The ESOP *may* elect to take the employer's role and repurchase the stock in lieu of the employer.
4. The participant must have an additional 60-day period in which to exercise the put option in the following plan year.[18]
5. At the option of the party buying back the stock, the stock may be bought back on an installment basis over a period not to exceed five

---

[14] Treas. Reg. Sec. 54.4975-7(b)(10); Labor Reg. Sec. 2550.408b-3(j).

[15] Treas. Reg. Sec. 54.4975-7(b)(10); Labor Reg. Sec. 2550.408b-3(j).

[16] Revenue Act of 1978, Sec. 17(n).

[17] Economic Recovery Tax Act, Section 336.

[18] Ibid.

years, provided the seller is given a promissory note, which will accelerate (all become due at once) if the buyer defaults on any installment
payment.

6. The installment period above may be extended to 10 years if the person
   (or party) receiving the distribution agrees and if adequate security is
   given, in addition, for the outstanding amount of the note.

A put option is always required on distributed stock that was acquired
with the proceeds of an exempt loan, and that is not publicly traded, even if
the plan is subsequently changed from an ESOP. After ERTA, this does not
apply in the case of a bank which is prohibited from purchasing its own
stock if participants are given the right to receive benefits in cash. Also, if it
is known at the time the exempt loan is made that honoring the put option
would cause the employer to violate federal or state law, the put option
must permit the securities to be put to a third party having substantial net
worth at the time the loan is made and whose net worth is reasonably
expected to remain substantial. Very few individuals would, or could,
accept the obligations of a perpetual putee. Also, the substituted putee rule
was clearly not intended to cover situations in which the employer may be
temporarily prevented from honoring the option, such as in the situation
when the employer sponsor has no retained earnings from which to purchase securities (a requirement of many states). Not even publicly traded
companies that are exempt from the rules can afford to ignore them.
Sometimes public companies are acquired and are no longer public. Sometimes trading is suspended in certain securities, or perhaps the company
goes "private," or fails to meet the continuing rules of the exchange(s) on
which it is traded.

Payments under put options also may not be restricted by loan agreements, other arrangements, or by the terms of the employer's bylaws or
articles of incorporation, except to the extent necessary to comply with
state laws.[19]

The ESOP will very likely lose its attractiveness as an employee benefit
plan if terminating employees and their beneficiaries are liable for taxes on
shares they have no market for. Also, this lack of marketability is a factor in
determining the value of the shares and, without a put option, there will be
a lower valuation of the securities. The company may wish to give "discretionary" put options, which do not have to conform in any respect to the
rules applicable to mandatory put options.[20] If the discretionary put options
are granted in a manner which is not uniform and nondiscriminatory,
prohibited plan discrimination may result. This can be eliminated if the
discretionary put options are for a fixed number of securities for each and
every party receiving a distribution.

5. *Valuation.* The final regulations require that a valuation be made in

---

[19] Treas. Reg. Sec. 54.4975-7(b)(12)(v); Labor Reg. Sec. 2550.408b-3(1)(5).
[20] Treas. Reg. Sec. 54.4975-11(a)(7)(i); Labor Reg. Sec. 2550.407d-6(a)(6).

good faith on the basis of *all* relevant factors affecting the value of securities.[21] While the final regulations do not require an annual independent appraisal of the employer securities, they do encourage them.[22]

Conversions and Mergers Involving ESOPs.

1. Conversions to an ESOP. The conversion of an existing plan's investments in general assets, which have been accumulated for the purpose of providing retirement benefits into an ESOP, should only be undertaken with extreme caution. Fiduciaries should document carefully why the conversion was prudent. Normally, it is only when the fortunes of the company and the value of the stock decline during the period following conversion that the fiduciaries are called upon to explain. The board of directors authorizing the conversion would be a fiduciary in connection with the adoption of the amendment.

Under proper circumstances, existing pension and profit-sharing plans may be converted (by amendment) into ESOPs. Once the requirement of prudence under ERISA can be satisfied, existing assets of such converted plans *may* be used to acquire employer securities. Almost all the rules discussed earlier in this chapter come into play; a review of that section, in conjunction with this subsection, is essential. The shares may be purchased from existing shareholders, the employer corporation or the public market, or both.

Further, credit carry-overs attributable to the existing plan under code Sections 404(a)(3)(A) are available for use under the ESOP, provided the ESOP is "similar" to the preexisting trust within the meaning of the second sentence of code Section 404(a)(3)(A), which means a stock-bonus or a profit-sharing plan. No credit carry-over is permissible if the profit-sharing or stock-bonus plan is converted into a money purchase pension plan, or vice versa.[23] Conversion of a money purchase pension plan into an ESOP may result in 100 percent vesting if the new ESOP does not constitute a comparable plan.

Conversion of a defined benefit pension plan into an ESOP is to be treated as a termination of the plan for purposes of Title IV of ERISA and therefore will require 100 percent vesting of participants' actuarially determined benefits. Other types of plans, such as thrift and savings plans, also may be converted.

For any conversion, the provisions of such plans with respect to permissible investments are indeed critical. Since vested employee accounts are being used to purchase qualifying employer securities, the plan provisions almost universally require substantial amendments. Prior plans may be converted to an ESOP just to preserve the old vesting schedules or the provisions that are "grandfathered."[24]

---

[21] Treas. Reg. Sec. 54.4975-11(d)(5).

[22] Treas. Reg. Sec. 54.4975-11(d)(5).

[23] Rev. Proc. 76-11 Sec. 4.

[24] T.I.R. 1413, para. T-9.

Potential fiduciary liability for plan conversions may exist. Further information is available by reading the following decisions. They are (1) *Usery* v. *Penn*, 426 F-Supp. 830 (W. D. Okla. 1976), Aff'd sub nom.; *Eaves* v. *Penn*, 587 F.2d 453 (10th Cir. 1978); (2) *Marshall* v. *Whatley*, Civ. No. 77-04-A (E.D. Va. April 18, 1977), and (3) *Baker* v. *Smith*, Civ. Action-Law, No. 80-3067 (E.D. Penn., August 6, 1980).

2. *Mergers into an ESOP.* Each qualified plan, as a condition of *qualification*, must provide that, in the case of merger or consolidation with or transfer of assets or liabilities to any other plan after September 2, 1974, each participant must receive a benefit immediately after the merger, consolidation, or transfer, determined as if the plan being transferred were then terminated, that is, no less than the benefit the participant would have been entitled to receive before the merger, consolidation, or transfer determined as if the plan into which the transfer occurs had then terminated.[25] This will be referred to as the "transfer rules." The rules are extremely complicated and generally beyond the scope of this chapter. However, a few of the more essential rules are stated below.

If two or more defined contribution plans are merged or consolidated, the transfer rules will be met if all of the following conditions are met:

1. The sum of the account balances in the plans equals the fair market value of the assets of the surviving plan on the date of the merger or consolidation.

2. The assets of each plan are combined to form the assets of the plan as merged.

3. The participants' balances in the plans that survive right after the merger are equal to the sum of the participants' account balances (individually determined) in the plans just before the merger.

A defined benefit plan being merged into an existing ESOP is considered as being, first, converted to a defined contribution plan, and then, once converted it is considered as merged.[26] The Pension Benefit Guaranty Corporation (PBGC) requires the plan administrator to allow each participant to elect in writing either to receive the value of the participants' accrued benefits in the form provided under the plan or to have plan assets equal in value transferred to an individual account under the ESOP.[27] This election probably constitutes a sale within the meaning of Section 2(3) of the Securities Act of 1933 and would require compliance unless some exception from registration is available.

3. *Conversions from an ESOP.* If the conversion out of an ESOP is accomplished by plan merger, consolidation, or transfer of assets, the "transfer rules" discussed earlier would apply and there would be no particular problems. If the plan merger, consolidation, or transfer of assets out of

---

[25] IRC Secs. 401(a)(12); 414(1).

[26] Treas. Reg. Sec. 1.414(1)–1(i).

[27] P.B.G.C. Opinion 76–30 (March 8, 1976); P.B.G.C. Opinion 76–12 (January 27, 1976).

an ESOP is into another type of defined contribution plan, it will not necessarily trigger a termination within the meaning of the vesting requirements of code Section 411(d)(3).

The conversion out of an ESOP also will not in itself relieve the employer from the put option requirements. However, the put option rule applies only when employer securities are distributed; and enough securities of the employer could be converted to other assets to permit distributions in other assets, or future contributions may supply enough cash for many years. Outstanding loans are a problem on the conversion out of an ESOP. If the balance of the loan cannot be repaid prior to conversion, ESOP fiduciaries have three options: (1) defer the conversion until the loan is paid off, (2) seek a specific exemption from the prohibited transaction rules of ERISA Section 408(a) and code Section 4975(c)(2), or (3) proceed with the conversion risk and incur the penalties imposed with respect to prohibited transactions. There is a further risk that plan fiduciaries may be held liable for any losses incurred by the plan as a result of their violation of the prohibited transaction provisions of ERISA Section 409(a), and they may be removed by a court. The same fiduciary considerations, applicable to converting *to* an ESOP are applicable in converting from one.

Last, converting to any other kind of plan but an eligible individual account plan gives rise to the 10 percent limitation of ERISA Section 407 on the holding of employer securities.

Types of Employer Securities. With the changes brought about by the Technical Corrections Act of 1979, the definition of "qualifying employer securities" in code Section 4975(e)(8) is now the same as the definition of employer securities which is applicable for code Section 415(c)(6) and code Section 409A(1). This definition includes only the following:

1. Common stock readily tradeable on an established securities market.
2. If there is no readily tradeable common stock, common stock having a combination of voting power and dividend rights at least equal to the classes of common stock having the greatest voting power and the greatest dividend rights.
3. Preferred stock convertible (at any time) into common stock meeting one of the above definitions.

This definition of employer securities is now applicable to stock acquired by a statutory ESOP after December 31, 1979, but may be limited to stock acquired pursuant to the "ESOP loan exemption." Please note that any kind of stock may be contributed or purchased on a nonleveraged basis.

Types of Distributions—Cash versus Stock.

General. Until the changes brought about by the Revenue Act of 1978, the Technical Corrections Act of 1979, and the Miscellaneous Revenue Act of 1980, the final regulations for ESOPs required that the portion of an ESOP consisting of a stock-bonus plan must provide for benefits to be distributable only in "stock" of the employer.[28] This provision restated the requirements applicable to stock bonus plans set forth in Treasury Regulations 1.401-1(a)(2)(iii) and 1.401-1(b)(1)(iii).

The Revenue Act of 1978 provided that a "leveraged employee stock ownership plan" could distribute cash in lieu of employer securities so long as the participant could demand that his or her distribution be made in employer securities.

The Technical Corrections Act of 1979 provided that the cash distribution option available to an ESOP under Code Section 4975(e)(7) and 409A(h) be made effective with respect to distributions of benefits after December 31, 1978.

The Miscellaneous Revenue Act of 1980 added code Section 401(a)(23), which permits any qualified stock-bonus plan, not just an ESOP or TRASOP, to make distributions of benefits in either cash or stock after December 31, 1980, so long as the participant or beneficiary has the right to demand distributions in the form of employer stock. ERTA further modified this to provide that mandatory cash distributions could occur if the articles or by-laws of the corporation restrict ownership of substantially all the company's stock to current employees as an employees' trust. Code Section 401(a)(23) cross-references IRC Section 409A(h), which outlines the distribution provisions for TRASOPs. This "put option" under 401(a)(23) will be required only if the stock-bonus plan (other than an ESOP or TRASOP) includes a cash-distribution option and will be the same as that required for ESOPs and TRASOPs under code Section 409A(h). Administratively, with the cost-basis accounting rules of Treasury Regulation Section 1.402(a)-1(b)(2) and the lump-sum distribution rules, it is sometimes appropriate to provide for a deferral of distributions and any forfeitures until the end of the plan year in which a break in service occurs, unless special circumstances require an earlier distribution.

Which Distribution Is Best?   A nearly universal participant question is, "Which distribution type is best—cash or stock?" The answer depends upon the tax picture of the employee, the interplay of the "lump-sum distribution" rules under the code, and code Sections 402(e)(4)(D) and its regulations, which provide that the taxable amount of a "lump-sum distribution" does not include "net unrealized appreciation" on the employer's securities distributed to a participant. Net unrealized appreciation is the excess of the fair market value of the employer securities at the time of distribution from a plan over the trust's adjusted basis in the securities. The net unrealized appreciation on the date of distribution is taxed as a long-term capital gain when the securities are subsequently disposed of. Any additional appreciation is either short- or long-term capital gain, depending on how long the stock is held.[29]

---

[28] Treas. Reg. Sec. 54.4975-11(f)(1).
[29] Rev. Rul. 81-122.

To determine which distribution is most advantageous, calculate the total tax from lump-sum treatment with each of the various possibilities. Surprisingly, in many large distributions, taking stock clearly results in a lower tax, both currently and subsequently.

Rollovers.   Rollovers are now very flexible for ESOPs. The stock may be distributed, then sold, and the proceeds contributed to an individual retirement account (IRA), provided the proceeds are contributed within the statutory 60-day period. Alternatively, partial rollovers are permitted, and of course, if the stock is acceptable to an IRA custodian or trustee, the stock can go right into the IRA. No tax is due by participants or beneficiaries if these special IRA rules are followed. The disadvantage of an IRA, however, is that the various options available by carefully calculating the tax effect of stock and cash in a lump-sum distribution are not available if the distribution stays in an IRA until distributions start. If a distribution is rolled over into an IRA, the benefit of the lump-sum and capital gains provisions of the code are not available. The distributions from the IRA are taxed at earned ordinary income-tax rates, and the special averaging and capital gains rates are lost forever. The only exception is when the amount rolled over is subsequently rolled over into another qualified plan.

Pass-Through of Income on Employer Securities.   The last sentence of Section 803(h) of the Tax Reform Act of 1976 reflects the intent of Congress to permit the employer to structure an ESOP "to distribute income on employer securities currently." The final regulations provide that an ESOP will not fail to meet[30] the qualification requirements of Code Section 401(a) merely because the ESOP provides for the current payment of income with respect to employer securities.

First the limitation of the pass-through is only on allocated securities, not on securities held by the suspense account. Income on the unallocated securities is either to be used to repay debt or it must be allocated to participants' accounts. However, additional shares are normally released by the dividends being used to pay off debt.

Second, income accumulated for a two-year period or longer by an ESOP (that is a stock-bonus plan) must be distributed in the form of the employer's stock, subject to the cash-distribution option that is available to stock-bonus plans.

Unfortunately, these rules are difficult to administer, and, in the opinion of the author, discourage dividend pass-through. An additional discouraging factor is that dividends are not deductible to employers, while compensation to employees is, and further those dividends are currently taxable to employees.

Stock Purchase by an ESOP.   When a taxpayer sells shares of stock, he or she recognizes gain to the extent of the excess over the taxpayer's adjusted

---

[30] Treas. Reg. Secs. 54.4975-11(a)(8)(iii); 54.4975-11(f)(3).

basis in the stock. When the stock is redeemed by the issuing corporation, the transaction is considered a distribution by the corporation, with respect to its stock, and will be taxable as a capital gain (or loss) only if the requirements of code Section 302(b) are satisfied. Otherwise, it is a dividend to the shareholder and taxed twice—once at the corporate level and then again at the shareholder level.

The ESOP is clearly a separate entity, and so under normal circumstances the sale by a shareholder to an ESOP would be taxed as a sale or exchange at capital gain rates, too. However, the IRS may view certain transactions as a redemption by the sponsoring employer and hence subject to dividend treatment.

Revenue Procedure 77-30 sets forth operating rules with respect to the issuance of an advance ruling of the IRS: that the proposed sale of the employer's stock by a shareholder to a related employee plan is a sale or exchange, rather than a corporate distribution taxable under code Section 301. The revenue procedure only provides a safe harbor, and to fail to meet its tests will not be an automatic application of code Section 301 to the sale of stock to a qualified plan. These guidelines do not, as a matter of law, precisely define the only situations in which the sale of stock to a plan will avoid treatment as a corporate distribution of property under code Section 301. In the absence of such a ruling, the tax ramifications of such a sale will be subject to examination upon audit.

A favorable ruling under Revenue Procedure 77-30 will be issued if three conditions are met:

1. The combined beneficial interests of the selling shareholder and all related persons in the plan on the date of the sale cannot exceed twenty percent (20%) of the total plan beneficial interests. This requirement will *not* be satisfied if *any* one of the following occurs:
    a. The combined covered compensation of the selling shareholder and related persons on the date of the sale exceeds 20 percent of the total compensation of all participants under the plan.
    b. The total account balances (vested and nonvested) of the selling shareholder and related persons under the plan on the date of the sale exceeds 20 percent of the account balances of all plan participants.
    c. The total interest (vested and nonvested) of the selling shareholder in any separately managed fund or account within the plan on the date of the sale exceeds 20 percent of the total net assets in that fund or account.
    In determining whether the interest of the selling shareholder and related persons in any fund exceeds 20 percent of the net assets of that fund, there may be excluded from consideration any separately managed fund or account of a plan that at no time may be invested in the

employer's securities.[31] For purposes of these tests, "related person(s)" includes the spouse, parents, grandparents, children, and grandchildren of the selling shareholder.

2. The second requirement for an advance determination letter is that the restrictions on the disposition of the employer's stock held and distributed by the employee plan can be no more onerous than the disposition restrictions on at least a majority of the shares of the employer's securities held by other shareholders. This was later modified by Revenue Procedure 78-18 to provide that certain rights-of-first refusal, which comply with the provisions of the ESOP regulations, are acceptable restrictions which can apply to employer securities held or distributed by an ESOP.

3. The third requirement is that there be no intention, plan, or understanding on the part of the employer to redeem from the plan any of the stock being purchased by the plan from the selling shareholder.

A private letter ruling should always be obtained in those situations in which doubt exists.

ADDITIONAL ESOP CONSIDERATIONS

SEC Aspects

1933 Securities Act. On February 1, 1980, the Securities and Exchange Commission issued Release No. 33-6188 on the application of the 1933 Securities Act to employee plans. The purpose of the release was to provide guidance to the public and to assist employers and plan participants in complying with the act. The release discusses circumstances under which interests in plans and related entities may be subject to the requirements of the act. The release also provides an analysis of the criteria to be used to determine when an offer or sale of a security will occur, discusses the various exemptions from the act's registration provisions, discusses the act's application to the various types of securities transactions in which plans may engage, as well as resales of securities participants acquire through the operation of the plan, and further describes the methods of registration of securities under the act.

The interests of employees in a plan are securities only when the employees voluntarily participate in and contribute to the plan. Employee interests in plans that are not both voluntary and contributory are not securities and are not subject to the 1933 act, according to the release. While the release is lengthy and is intended to provide guidance, the release does point out that it should not be viewed as an all-inclusive treatment of the subject and that the SEC staff will continue to provide interpretive advice and assistance upon request.

Another release (Release No. 33-6281), was issued January 22, 1981,

---

[31] Rev. Proc. 78-23, 1978 C.B., clarifying Rev. Proc. 77-30, 1977-2 C.B. 539.

and further clarifies the SEC's position on the application of the act to employee benefit plans, as well as describes developments under the act after the 1980 release was issued. Both releases are invaluable to an understanding of the issues involved.

1934 Securities Exchange Act. There are registration requirements that are applicable under certain circumstances. These requirements are beyond the scope of this chapter.

Other Reporting and Disclosure Rules. There are additional reporting and disclosure rules that should be looked at:

1. Section 15(d) provides that if a registration statement pursuant to the '33 act has to be filed with respect to certain stock-related qualified plans, then the registrant must file "such supplementary and periodic information documents and reports as may be required pursuant to Section 13 of this title."

2. Section 16(a) Reporting–Rule 16a-8(a)(2) provides that the "vested beneficial interests in a trust" must be reported by officers and directors and beneficial owners of more than 10 percent of any class of equity security, and they must report periodically on changes of ownership. The rules are exceedingly complex, and several exemptions may be available.

3. *Antifraud rules.* The '34 act's antifraud rules apply to both initial sales as well as to subsequent sales. Section 10 of the '34 act regulates the use of manipulative and deceptive devices in the trading of securities. Certain fraudulent and deceptive practices are a crime. Various other rules require an issuer and its affiliate(s) to follow certain procedures in the repurchase of its stock, which might include the ESOP's trustee. Another section provides that a person who relies on a false or misleading statement contained in a document filed with the SEC may recover for reliance on such a statement. Other rules require insiders to disgorge profits made under certain circumstances. There are many unanswered questions under these rules. For example, Does a company have a duty to disclose material nonpublic information regarding the company? Does the employer or the ESOP have a duty to disclose "complete" information to a participant if it is known that the participant will immediately resell the employer securities in the public market?

Accounting Considerations*

ESOPs must address some difficult accounting issues, both from the employer's point of view in preparing the financial statements, and in the trust accounting and participant accounting areas.

---

* This material, which originally appeared in Employee Stock Ownership Plans: Problems & Potentials, edited by Richard Reichler, was written by Norman N. Strauss. Copyright 1977, 1978, Law Journal Seminars-Press. Reprinted by permission of the publisher.

Employer Accounting Considerations. The American Institute of Certified Public Accountants (AICPA) has issued a statement of position on accounting issues relating to ESOPs.[32]

The Financial Accounting Standards Board (FASB) has not yet issued its opinion on accounting for ESOPs.

The AICPA has determined that "an obligation of an ESOP should be recorded as a liability in the financial statements of the employer, when the obligation is covered by either a guarantee of the employer or a commitment by the employer to make future contributions to the ESOP sufficient to meet the debt service requirements. The obligation is with the employer; the assets belong to the employees."[33]

With any liability goes an "offsetting debit of the liability . . . (which should be) . . . accounted for as a reduction in stockholders' equity."[34] This means that there is an immediate reduction in stockholders' equity in the amount of the guaranteed debt. As the loan is paid down on a debt that relates to newly issued shares of the employer, the increases in equity are recorded.

When the ESOP acquires shares already outstanding on a leveraged basis, the existing shareholders' equity in the employer is reduced, and increases in equity will be recorded as the debt is satisfied. A separate line item deduction in the stockholders' equity section is preferable.

As the ESOP makes its payments, the corresponding liability on the balance sheet should be reduced, and the stockholders' equity section also adjusted. The accounts should move symmetrically.[35]

There is a difference of opinion whether the full amount contributed to the ESOP and used to reduce the ESOP debt is a compensation expense or a combination of compensation expense and interest expense. In any event, a footnote on the interest rate and debt terms is critical.[36]

When reporting dividends per share, the dividends should be charged to retained earnings, just as dividends paid to any other shareholder. Dividends are *not* compensation expense, even if they are passed through to participants.

The earnings-per-share questions are not clearly resolved. The AICPA asserts "that all shares held by an ESOP should be treated as outstanding shares in the determination of earnings per share.[37]

A more conservative, less anti-ESOP approach has been considered, where shares held by a leveraged ESOP are not used in calculating earnings

---

[32] American Institute of Certified Public Accountants, Accounting Standards Division: "Statement of Position on Accounting Practices for Certain Employee Stock Ownership Plans," issued December 20, 1976.

[33] AICPA Statement of Position, para. 5.

[34] AICPA Statement of Position, para. 7.

[35] AICPA Statement of Position, para. 8.

[36] AICPA Statement of Position, para. 9.

[37] AICPA Statement of Position, para. 11.

per share until they have been released from the suspense account and allocated to employees' accounts.[38] Dividends then would be charged to retained earnings only to the extent the shares in the ESOP are unencumbered. The dividends on encumbered shares would be recorded as compensation expense.[39]

When an ESOP receives a contribution in excess of the allowable deduction limitation, such excess is usually treated as a timing difference by the employer in determining the provision for income tax, since excess contributions made in one year can generally be carried over to ensuing years.

The financial statement reclassification into interest expense and compensation expense will not affect the deduction of the contribution(s) for tax purposes. Also, the possible impact of the ESOP financial statement accounting techniques on a future business combination from being accounted for as a pooling of interests may be a consideration.

Any additional investment tax credit allowed for TRASOP contributions should be recorded as a reduction of the income tax expense in the year the contribution to the ESOP is charged as an expense. The recognition should conform to the general rule for any investment credit: that the credit will be utilized with reasonable certainty or is a reality.[40] This treatment applies regardless of the manner in which the employer normally accounts for investment tax credits in the financial statements (i.e. the "flow-through" or amortization method).

The footnotes should be as complete and descriptive as possible, and should at the barest minimum include a description of the plan, including the purpose, any formula for contributions, how the trust assets are held, its effective date, and how employer stock has been (or will be) purchased. The current qualified status of the plan, dates of determination letters from the IRS, and a complete description of the loan also should be listed.

ESOP Accounting Considerations. There are three generally accepted accounting principles for accounting for employer securities held by an ESOP. These are: (1) the lower of cost or market value, (2) market value, and (3) cost. The FASB in a recent exposure draft determined that investments should be valued at current value,[41] and is consistent with the ERISA requirements that plan assets and liabilities be valued at current value.[42]

The trust also must account for the cost basis of the shares of stock held by the trust for purposes of calculating the net unrealized appreciation in the accounts of participants receiving employer securities upon distribution.[43]

A determination must be made about which accounting method is most

---

[38] APB Opinions No. 8 (para. 27) and No. 15 (Interpretations 82 and 83).

[39] APB Opinion No. 25.

[40] APB Opinion No. 11.

[41] FASB Exposure Draft on Defined Benefit Plans, dated April 14, 1977.

[42] ERISA Act Sec. 103(b)(3).

[43] Treas. Reg. Sec. 1.401(a)(1)-(b)(2).

appropriate: cash, accrual, or modified accrual. Each has its distinct advantages and disadvantages. The cash basis is used by most corporate trustees because it's simple. Accrual accounting is preferred by most accountants because it's accurate. Modified accrual is a compromise and uses the cash basis for everything except the contribution (and dividends on employer securities), both of which are accrued.

The cost-basis accounting for shares is actually done by the participant recordkeeping system. Each year the trustee is informed about the cost basis of the shares distributed to participants and beneficiaries during the year, so the trust's cost basis can be adjusted in the shares yet held by the trustee.

ESOP Administration and Manuals for Recordkeeping Rules. It is strongly suggested that written manuals be adopted to provide continuity in administration in the event of personnel turnover and, perhaps more important, to document the many discretionary decisions of the sponsoring company to insure "uniform and nondiscriminatory" application. This latter function conceivably would forestall much potential litigation in the event of a participant's dissatisfaction with a particular policy. Manuals which would be advisable include: a brief plan interpretation, with examples covering the salient provisions; an accounting procedures manual, which specifies the various choices about methods discussed in this section; a distribution procedures manual, which reflects the company's policies on timing and method of distributions; and a general administration manual, designed to include all of the documentation required to be available to and for participants. Other manuals may be useful and should be designed for individual cases.

One disadvantage of these types of manuals is that a policy once formally documented becomes potentially enforceable. Briefly, whatever a manual documents must be what is done.

Repurchase Liability

The ESOP repurchase liability[44] has not been given much attention. Basically, it arises because the employer contributes cash or stock and the stock has to be bought back. And, the employer must buy it back—for cash. Since ESOPs are relatively new, the cash needed to repurchase company stock from departed employees and their beneficiaries has not yet created a problem for most companies. But it will, unless a company properly plans for it. It is this author's opinion that, potentially, this is the most serious difficulty the ESOP will experience.

Since the repurchase liability affects the value of company stock, the

---

[44] Robert W. Smiley, Jr., "How to Fund for an ESOP's Repurchase Liability," Prentice-Hall's *Pension and Profit Sharing Service*, par. 1107, New Ideas, pp. 1431–40 (Englewood Cliffs, N.J.: Prentice-Hall, 1980).

balance sheet and income statement, the number of shareholders, and employee morale, it should be calculated and planned for.

The first step in facing this potential problem is to develop a projection of future cash requirements. A computer model specifically suited for this purpose is particularly advantageous, since without one it is almost impossible to see how the plan operates under different operating assumptions. The final step is to analyze the various funding methods to determine which would work best in a particular situation. Studies show that each share owned by an ESOP will have to be repurchased once every 15 to 25 years and, by the time a typical company's ESOP is 25 years old, its entire contribution may have to be used to make repurchases. In some cases, it may be as often as every 10 to 15 years.

The repurchase liability is alleviated by varying distributions over time, varying the size of the contribution, varying the stock and cash-contributions mix, properly timing stock repurchases, and carefully planning for the proper use of dividends on employer securities and of the income on other assets. Other solutions include: going public, private placements, being acquired, or the creative use of corporate-owned life insurance.

Companies should not be discouraged from adopting or continuing an ESOP because of the "unknown" repurchase liability. Careful advance planning, ongoing review, good communications with stockholders, employees' increased productivity, and increased company profits should solve almost every problem created by the repurchase liability—but not without planning for it today.

TRASOP Considerations[45]

A TRASOP must be structured differently from an ESOP. This subsection will discuss many of the plan provisions necessary to satisfy the requirements for a plan and trust intended to qualify as a TRASOP. TRASOPs are subject to the same rules on coverage as any other qualified plan. A TRASOP, like any other qualified plan, need not cover all employees, nor is it required to cover the employees of the corporation who earned the credit. Under the Revenue Act of 1978, the definition of a controlled group of corporations was expanded to include a first-tier subsidiary and all 80-percent subsidiaries of such subsidiary, so long as the parent owns at least 50 percent of the voting and nonvoting stock of the first-tier subsidiary.[46] For qualified investments made in taxable years beginning after December 31, 1978, the TRASOP must be a tax-qualified defined contribution plan. One basic difference between a normal ESOP and a TRASOP, other than the difference in contribution basis, is that the

---

[45] While TRASOPs were at one time not required to be qualified, the nonqualified TRASOP is beyond the scope of this subsection.

[46] Code Sec. 409A(1)(4)(B).

plan and trust do not have to be in existence prior to the end of the fiscal year for a TRASOP. The plan and trust must be in existence, adopted, and executed prior to the time of the election of the additional investment credit for the first year in which the credit will be elected, and no funding is necessary until 30 days after the election. This means adoption is permissible at any time prior to the filing of the sponsor's tax return, including extensions. A plan that is dependent upon shareholder approval, or on any other condition subsequent, may jeopardize the timely election of the investment credit.[47] The TRASOP may be a new plan, or an existing plan can be amended. The TRASOP plan must be either a profit-sharing plan, a stock-bonus plan, or a combination stock-bonus and money purchase pension plan, or some other defined contribution plan, including a straight money purchase pension plan. In practice however, since the contributions vary from year to year, a profit-sharing or a stock-bonus plan is normally used.

In addition to the normal code Section 401 rules on qualification, there are several special rules regarding participation, vesting, allocations of employer and employee contributions, benefit and contribution limits, and the kind of employer securities to be held in the trust.

Basic Plan Provisions That Are Different from ESOPs. The TRASOP must be designed like an ESOP: to invest primarily in employer securities. The contribution must be in employer securities, or cash may be contributed and used to acquire employer securities. Like an ESOP, the plan year and the employer's tax year do not have to be identical.[48]

A TRASOP must provide for immediate vesting. Therefore, it may use the three-year waiting period of code Section 410(a)(b)(i). However, with the advent of the payroll basis for the tax credit under ERTA, the incentive for restricting participation is significantly reduced.

Allocations to all participants were at one time required whether they were employed at plan year-end or not. The Revenue Act of 1978 changed this rather "expensive" requirement, provided no prohibited discrimination results. It now is permissible to require employment at plan year-end to receive an allocation.

ERTA accelerated the phase out of the tax credit based TRASOP to December 31, 1982. After that date, the tax credit available for contributions to an employee stock ownership plan meeting the requirements of code Section 409A are based on covered payroll. For 1983 and 1984, a tax credit is available for a stock contribution (or a cash contribution which is then invested in stock) to a qualified employee stock ownership plan of up to .5 percent of covered payroll. For 1985 through 1987, the available contribution tax credit is .75 percent.

"Covered payroll" for purposes of calculating the available tax credit is

[47] Treas. Reg. Sec. 1.410(a)-2(c)(1).
[48] Treas. Reg. Sec. 1.46-8(d)(2).

limited only by code Section 415 regulations (which basically give the outer limits of what can be considered compensation for the maximum allocation limits). Allocations, however, cannot be based on more than $100,000 of compensation for any participant.

If the allocations on behalf of any participant would exceed the limitations of code Section 415(c)(6) or code Section 415(c)(1), or both, the excess gets allocated to the accounts of participants who are not limited under code Section 415(c), based upon a participant's proportionate share of the total compensation paid to participants who would be eligible to receive additional shares, until each participant's account exceeds the limit. Suspense accounts for the excess are appropriate, but are normally held-over (like contribution credit carry-overs) and allocated like a new contribution. No TRASOP may provide for a suspense account for the benefit of a participant who has gone over the limits of code Section 415.

The TRASOP may not be integrated with Social Security, directly or indirectly. Also, an excess-only plan for compensation over $100,000 won't work, either, since this would defeat the limits on compensation defined by statute.[49] It also is not possible, if the Senate Report to the Tax Reduction Act of 1975 is any precursor, to provide the additional investment credit as a trade-off for other existing benefit plans, or rights.[50] This requirement is not in the final regulations, however.

Since there are no forfeitures in a TRASOP, it is in some respects easier to draft the break-in-service rules for eligibility and vesting.

The TRASOP must provide that employer securities allocated in accordance with the rules governing TRASOPs may *not* be distributed prior to the end of the 84th month beginning after the month an amount is allocated to the participant's account except in the event of death, disability, or separation from service. The final regulations provide that the 84-month period begins on the date when the TRASOP securities are allocated.

Even if the TRASOP is terminated or is merged with another plan, the securities may not be distributed prior to the 84th month, except for a termination of service by a participant or, as added by ERTA, in the case of a divestiture by a company of a subsidiary (or division) which results in the severing of the employment relationship. All defined contribution TRASOPs, other than a money purchase pension, may distribute either the stock or earnings after the prerequisite period of years. Earnings distributions are subject to the same rules as discussed previously in this chapter. Money purchase pension plan TRASOPs may not distribute either stock or earnings until the plan is terminated, or until the participant has separated from service, died, or become disabled.[51]

---

[49] T.I.R. 1413, at R-8, (November 4, 1975).

[50] S. Rep. No. 94-36, 94th Cong., 1st Sess. 56 (1975).

[51] Treas. Reg. Sec. 1.46-8(d)(9).

Employer securities voting rights are the same as for leveraged ESOPs; the fiduciary may accumulate votes on fractional shares.

Unallocated securities do not have to be voted, as in a normal ESOP; however, the fiduciary cannot vote the allocated employer securities for which it receives no direction.[52] The rule on unexercised voting rights allows the solicitation and exercise of participants' voting rights by management (and others) under a proxy provision applicable to all securities holders, including participants.[53]

Unlike an ESOP, a TRASOP has statutory provisions and limitations for the reimbursement of some costs for the establishment of the plan, and for certain ongoing expenses.[54]

The contribution to a TRASOP must be made within 30 days after the time for filing the employer's tax return, plus extensions, except where the full amount of the additional credit is not allowed for a year because it is limited on the basis of the tax due for the year, the additional credit is to be contributed to the plan when it is allowed. There are fairly complex rules for credit carry-backs, and credit carry-forwards, and recaptures which have become quite a bit less problematic with the advent of the PAYSOP wherein the contribution and tax credit are more easily determinable. The final regulations provide detailed answers to many issues, as does the Revenue Act of 1978.

The put option rules with respect to ESOPs are all applicable to TRASOPs as well.

Once the contribution is made, it may not revert to the employer. There are some exceptions for taxable years beginning after December 31, 1974, and ending prior to December 31, 1979. As an alternative to recapture withdrawal, an employer is allowed to use the amount of the investment credit recaptured or redetermined as an offset against the contributions for other years or as a deduction subject to the limits of code Section 404.[55]

The one exception is that the employer is permitted to recover the contribution to a TRASOP if it is conditioned upon receiving a favorable approval from the IRS, and an application for determination is filed with the IRS not later than 90 days after the date on which the credit is allowed and the contribution is returned within one year after the date on which the IRS issues a notice that the plan is not qualified under the tax laws.

Matching Employee Contributions.   Starting with taxable years beginning after December 31, 1976, the code allows an additional investment tax credit of up to a maximum of 0.5 percent of the amount of the qualified investments that qualify for the investment credit, provided that matching employee contributions are collected. The employer must elect and qualify

---

52 Treas. Reg. Secs. 1.46–8(d)(8)(iv), 1.46–8(d)(8)(i).

53 Treas. Reg. Sec. 1.46–8(d)(8)(ii).

54 IRC Sec. 409A(i)(1).

55 IRC Sec. 48(n)(4).

for the 1 percent credit, as well as make a separate election for the 0.5 percent credit. This feature is eliminated for periods after December 31, 1982, by ERTA. However, employee pledges may be paid beyond that date if appropriate elections were made timely.

Each employee who participates in the 1 percent TRASOP must also be entitled to participate in the 0.5 percent plan. Employee contributions cannot be compulsory for participation, and must be earmarked as intended for employee matching. The contribution must be in cash and paid within two years following the end of the taxable year for which the credit is allowed. The employee's pledge to make the matching contribution has to be filed with the employer before the tax return is filed. To the extent matching contributions aren't collected, the employer loses that portion of the additional investment tax credit. Increases in the investment tax credit over what was projected by the employer can be made by employees to equal the excess even though the matching contributions would exceed the original pledge.

Valuation of Employer Stock Contributed to TRASOPs. Employer securities contributed to a TRASOP for the purpose of funding the additional investment tax credits will be valued, if listed on a national securities exchange, based upon the average closing prices for the 20 consecutive trading days immediately preceding the date on which the stock is contributed to the TRASOP.

COMPARISON OF ESOPs WITH OTHER TYPES OF EMPLOYEE STOCK-OWNERSHIP ARRANGEMENTS

General

Stock-ownership arrangements have been around for a long time. Sears has had a profit-sharing plan invested primarily in employer securities since July 1916. Procter & Gamble had a plan prior to 1900 where employees shared ownership. When the Revenue Act of 1921 was enacted, certain types of stock-bonus trusts and profit-sharing trusts were granted tax exemptions. Many of the qualified deferred compensation plans are currently permitted to invest and hold employer securities.

Other Defined Contribution Plans

Defined contribution plans generally can give the feeling of meaningful employee ownership. The account balances of the participants reflect, like a mutual fund, how much gain or loss there is for the year. The ESOP is unique among employee stock ownership arrangements. First, it generally involves a broad base of employees and is operated within the purview of qualified deferred compensation plans, giving it a lot of flexibility. Second, it permits financing acquisitions of employer securities, through borrowing, by using the credit of the employer. Third, the initial purchase of stock on a leveraged basis generally means the employer is permanently committed to an ESOP-type plan, at least for the period of the loan repayment. From the employee's point of view, it's very hard for an employer to "back out" of a plan once the stock has been acquired by the trust. Other qualified plans cannot leverage to acquire the employer's stock by using the credit of the employer.

However, sometimes a non-ESOP eligible individual account plan may serve many of the same purposes as an ESOP, without some of the obvious disadvantages such as put options, specific allocation of shares, required distributions in employer securities, and the like. The eligible individual account plan, however, can help an employer add to its capital by means of contributions in employer securities or by cash contributions that purchase newly issued (or treasury) stock. Employees also share in the economic benefits of corporate success in a visible way. All of these plans must face the repurchase liability problem eventually, however.

Other Stock Plans of an Employer

There are many other ways in which stock-ownership opportunities are granted to executives and other selected employees. These include stock-option plans under code Section 422, nonqualified stock-option plans, stock-appreciation rights plans, performance share plans, phantom stock plans, restricted stock plans, key employee stock plans, employee stock-purchase plans under code Section 423, stock *gifts* by the employer, stock sales to employees by the employer or by shareholders, and so on. Most of these are aimed at a limited group of employees, and since the context is so different, it is difficult to make comparisons. The qualified stock purchase plan under code Section 423, while directed to a broad-based group, is substantially different from an ESOP, in that the contribution required of the employee is a major part of the acquisition cost. An ESOP's stock-acquisition costs are, in most instances, borne solely by the employer!

CONCLUSIONS

Employee stock-ownership plans involve a complex array of business, legal, tax, accounting, and investment banking questions. These include the basic questions any employer asks such as, "Do I want it?" "What will it do to me and for me?" "How do I get out of it if something happens?" and "What do my employees get and when?"

The legal questions include all the qualification questions under code Section 401, the distribution, eligibility, vesting sections, the fiduciary and prohibited transaction questions under ERISA, the accounting and financial questions, securities and corporate law questions, alternative financing questions, and myriad more. Congress has continually sought to encourage employers to share the fruits of capital and labor through profit participation and a "piece of the action." The ESOP is the latest, most popular and by far the most practical, and in many ways, least-expensive approach to providing employees a piece of the company in which they work, on a tax-favored and creditor-proof basis.

BIBLIOGRAPHY

Bachelder, Joseph E., ed. *Employee Stock Ownership Plans*. New York: Practicing Law Institute, 1979.

Bonaccorso, Matthew J.; Sheridan M. Cranmer; David G. Greenhut; Daphne T. Hoffman; and Niel Isbrandtsen. "Survey of Employee Stock Ownership Plans: Analysis and Evaluation of Current Experience." Master's thesis, University of California at Los Angeles, 1977.

Bushman, Ronald M. "ESOPs: A Trustee's Perspective." *Trusts and Estates* 115 (June 1976).

Chow, Andrew; Thomas Cunningham; Michael Horstein; and Jerrald Zweibel. "Repurchase Liability for ESOPs and Other Employee Stock Ownership Plans." Master's thesis, University of California at Los Angeles, 1979.

Conte, Michael, and Arnold S. Tannenbaum. *Employee Ownership*. Report to the Economic Development Administration, United States Department of Commerce. University of Michigan, Institute for Social Research, June 15, 1977.

Drucker, Peter F. *The Unseen Revolution*. New York: Harper & Row, 1976.

Employee Stock Ownership Council of America. *Conference Proceedings* (Los Angeles, May 8–9, 1978). Los Angeles: Employee Stock Ownership Council of America, 1978.

_____. *Conference Proceedings* (Arlington, Va., May 7–8, 1979). Los Angeles: Employee Stock Ownership Council of America, 1979.

Epstein, Stanley A. "Employee Relations Considerations in Establishing ESOPs." *Employee Relations Law Journal* 3 (Autumn 1977), pp. 266–80.

ESOP Association of America. *National Employee Stock Ownership Conference Proceedings* (Washington, D.C., June 20–21, 1980). San Francisco: ESOP Association of America, 1980.

Hewitt Associates. *ESOPs: An Analytical Report*. Chicago: Profit Sharing Council of America, 1975.

Kelso, Louis O., and Mortimer J. Adler. *The Capitalist Manifesto*. New York: Random House, 1958; reprint ed., Westport, Conn.: Greenwood Press, 1975.

_____. *The New Capitalists*. New York: Random House, 1961, reprint ed., Westport, Conn.: Greenwood Press, 1975.

Kelso, Louis O., and Patricia Hetter. *Two-Factor Theory: The Economics of Reality*. New York: Random House, 1967.

Kurland, Norman G. "Beyond ESOP: Steps Toward Tax Justice. Part 1." *Tax Executive*, April 1977).

_____. "Beyond ESOP: Steps Toward Tax Justice. Part II." *Tax Executive*, July 1977).

Ludwig, Ronald L. "ESOPs—Compliance with the Fiduciary Rules of ERISA." *Executive Compensation Journal* 76-6 (June 1976).

————. "Employee Stock Ownership Plans After ERISA." *Employee Relations Law Journal* 1 (Winter 1976).

Ludwig, Ronald L., and Jeffrey R. Gates. "The Final ESOP Regulations—A Return to Certainty." Prentice Hall's *Pension and Profit Sharing Service,* March 23, 1978, pp. 1237-54.

Metzger, Bert L. "ESOPs Only Apply to Proper Situations." *Pensions and Investments,* September 15, 1975.

Metzger, Bert L., ed. *Pension, Profit Sharing, or Both?* Evanston, Ill.: Profit Sharing Research Foundation, 1975.

Metzger, Bert L., and Jerome A. Colleti. *Does Profit Sharing Pay?* Evanston, Ill.: Profit Sharing Research Foundation, 1971.

Metzger, Bert L., and Bernard A. Diekman, eds. *Profit Sharing: The Industrial Adrenalin.* Evanston, Ill.: Profit Sharing Research Foundation, 1975.

Miller, Marilyn V. "The Ins and Outs of ESOP Administration." *Financial Planner* 10 (January 1981), pp. 28, 30, 32.

Pavlock, Robert S., and Paul Lieberman. "The Taxation of ESOTs: Part I." *Tax Advisor* (February 1976).

————. "The Taxation of ESOTs: Part II." *Tax Advisor* 7 (March 1976).

————. "Employee Stock Ownership Trusts: The Final Regulations." *Tax Advisor* 9 (May 1978).

Practising Law Institute. *ESOPs: Employee Stock Ownership Plans.* New York: Practising Law Institute, 1976 (Course Handbook No. 99).

Practising Law Institute. *ESOPs and TRASOPs: Employee Stock Ownership Plans.* New York: Practising Law Institute, 1977 (Course Handbook No. 112).

Practising Law Institute. *ESOPs, TRASOPs, and Other Employee Stock Ownership Plans.* New York: Practising Law Institute, 1978 (Course Handbook No. 126).

Practising Law Institute. *ESOPs and TRASOPs.* New York: Practising Law Institute, 1979 (Course Handbook No. 140).

Practising Law Institute. *ERISA, Securities Laws and Banking Regulatory Effects on Empoyee Benefit Plans, Corporate Sponsors, and Investments Managers.* New York: Practising Law Institute, 1978 (Course Handbook No. 122).

Riechler, Richard, ed. *Employee Stock Ownership Plans: Problems and Potentials.* New York: Law Journal Press, 1978.

Savage, Michael D. "The Attack on Proposed ESOP Regulations: A Battle Won at the Expense of the War?" *American Bar Association Journal* 63 (May 1977).

Smiley, Robert W., Jr. "How to Fund for an ESOP's Repurchase Liability." Prentice Hall's *Pension and Profit Sharing Service,* April 3, 1980, pp. 1431-40.

Speiser, Stuart M. *A Piece of the Action.* New York: Van Nostrand Reinhold, 1977.

Stoeber, Edward A. "A Further Look at ESOPs: Advantages and Disadvantages." *Pension and Profit-Sharing Tax Journal* 2 (September 1976).

Taylor, Bradley J. "Challenges to Capital Gains Treatment for Stock Sales to an ESOP." *Journal of Pension Planning and Compliance* 5 (September 1977), pp. 378-97.

U.S. Congress. Joint Economic Committee. *Employee Stock Ownership Plans (ESOPs)*. Hearings before the Joint Economic Committee, 94th Congress, 1st session. Part 1, December 11, 1975; Part 2, December 12, 1975. Washington, D.C.: Government Printing Office, 1976.

Wassner, Neil A. "ESOPs: Can They Work for Your Corporation?" *Pension World*, June 1977.

Wells, Colin A. "The Role of Key-Man Life Insurance in an ESOP." *Financial Planner* 10 (January 1981), pp. 34, 36.

Zukin, James H. "Capital Stock Valuations for Employee Stock Ownership Plan (ESOP) Purposes," *Conference Proceedings*. Los Angeles: Employee Stock Ownership Council of America, 1978.

Retirement Plans for the Self-Employed

GARY K. STONE

Deferred compensation, including pension and profit-sharing plans, has become a typical method of compensating corporate employees. This type of benefit dramatically increased after World War II, brought about mainly by the favorable tax treatment allowed and by collective bargaining. Unfortunately, the self-employed were not provided the benefits available to corporate employees. Several bills were introduced to correct the inequity, and finally Congress passed the Self-Employed Individuals Tax Retirement Act of 1962. Pension plans set up under this act popularly became known as H.R. 10 or Keogh plans.[1]

The act proved disappointing because of the severe limitations imposed which negated potential advantages. Since 1962, adjustments have so liberalized the original legislation that the benefits have become more in line with corporate pension plans.[2] With the enactment of the Tax Equity and Fiscal Responsibility Act of 1982 (TEFRA), for all practical purposes, the distinction between self-employed and corporate pension plans was eliminated. The rules detailed in this chapter will be inapplicable, in many respects, for tax years beginning after December 31, 1983. The reader should be aware of the changes that have resulted from TEFRA.

The primary changes resulting from the law change are summarized below and are covered in more detail in Chapter 58.

1. The special deduction limits (lower of 15 percent of earned income or $15,000) have been eliminated.
2. The rule limiting defined benefit accruals has been eliminated.
3. The $200,000 limitation on the amount of compensation that may be

---

[1] H.R. 10 is the original House bill number and Eugene J. Keogh was the moving force in Congress that pushed for passage of the legislation.

[2] Primary modifications took place in 1966 (P.L. 89-809), in 1974 (P.L. 93-406), and in 1981 (P.L. 97-34).

taken into account under defined contribution plans and the $100,000 limit for defined benefit plans have been eliminated.

4. The current rule that defined benefit plans may not permit integration with Social Security has been repealed.

5. Current rules require plans that benefit an owner-employee to include all employees with three or more years of service. This rule has been repealed.

6. The new law repeals the restriction on excess contributions for an owner-employee. The current 6 percent excise tax on the excess contributions no longer will have any effect and has been repealed.

7. At present, an early withdrawal of an owner-employee means that no contributions can be made for five years after the withdrawal. This has now been repealed.

8. The 10 percent penalty on distributions to owner-employees has been dropped but it is now applicable to key employees in the so-called "top-heavy" plans. An exception to the new rule is distributions because of death or disability of the key employee.

9. The law dropped the provision which prevented the beneficiary of a self-employed from getting the $5,000 income exclusion for death benefits paid. The exclusion is now available to self-employed plans.

TEFRA includes a number of new qualifications for top-heavy pension plans. Basically, a top-heavy plan is one in which the present value of accrued benefits for key-employees in the plan exceeds 60 percent of total accrued benefits (defined benefit plan) or 60 percent of the sum of account balances of all employees (defined contribution plan). Key employees normally include officers, owners of more than 5 percent of the stock, one of the ten employees owning the largest interest in the firm, or owners of more than a 1 percent interest in the firm if one has an annual compensation of over $150,000. The following additional rules have been enacted for the top-heavy plans:

1. The maximum compensation that can be considered for benefit or contribution determination will be $200,000.

2. Every employee must be allocated minimum contributions or benefits and the plan must vest fully either within three years or on a graded scale over six years.

3. The minimum contribution for non-key employees will be 3 percent of the employees' earned income. The only exception is if the key-employee contribution rate is under 3 percent. In that case, the contribution rate for non-key employees can be equal to the greatest contribution rate among key employees.

4. As previously noted, the law imposes a 10 percent penalty tax on early withdrawals by key employees. The exception to this is if the withdrawal is the result of death or disability.

5. Finally, maximum limitations on benefits or contributions are imposed

for key employees that participate in both defined benefit and defined contribution plans.

In summary, self-employed plans and regular corporate plans will be treated in a similar manner. The maximum contribution to defined contribution plans will be $30,000 per year and the maximum annual benefits under defined benefit plans will be $90,000 per year. These limits will remain at this level until 1986. In 1986 a cost-of-living adjustment will be made on these levels to reflect inflation increases since 1984. Also, the plan limits in defined benefit plans will be reduced should benefits be paid before age 62. The law provides a transition period for plans to adapt to the new rules. For the most part, the new rules are effective after December 31, 1983[3] and should be considered in reading the following discussion of the situation that existed before that time.

One restriction imposed before the new rules is that the plan must include all employees in the firm if the owner is to be included. The law requires a self-employed individual to provide comparable and non-discriminatory coverage for all full-time employees. If the owner(s) set up a plan covering himself or herself, they in turn must cover all permanent (common law) employees who have three or more years of service. In the situation where an employer has been in business for fewer than three years, the requirement is lowered to correspond to the time actually in business. This feature prevents an employer from establishing a pension plan for himself or herself and not including employees who have worked fewer than three years. The plan, of course, may include the employees with fewer than three years service if the owner desires.

A technical distinction is made in the law between one who is self-employed and one who is an owner-employee. A self-employed is one who has earned income from operating a sole proprietorship or who performs personal services as a partner for a partnership during a tax year. An owner-employee is a sole proprietor or a partner who owns more than 10 percent of either the capital or the profit interest in a partnership. The provisions of H.R. 10 plans are more liberal for the self-employed who is not an owner-employee.

The requirements for plan qualification depend upon whether the retirement plan includes an owner-employee. A plan including self-employed but no owner-employees must meet the following general requirements:

1. The plan must be in writing.
2. The plan must not discriminate in favor of highly paid employees.
3. The plan must be funded.
4. The plan must be a pension, profit-sharing, annuity, or bond-purchase plan set up by the employer to benefit employees.

   Should it be desirable to include owner-employees, the rules for qualifi-

---

[3] P.L. 93-406 enacted September 2, 1974, was the enabling legislation for these accounts.

cation become stricter. The major rules include not only those previously mentioned but also the following:

1. Employees' rights or benefits from contributions must be nonforfeitable (immediate vesting).
2. All employees of all businesses controlled by owner-employees must be included, and the benefits or contributions must be at least as generous as those of the owner-employee.
3. Contributions for owner-employees can be based only upon earned income of the business for which the plan is established.
4. All employees with at least three years of service must be included (including those under age 25).
5. Payouts to owner-employees prior to age 59½ except for disability and death are not permitted.
6. Should the owner-employee have control over more than one firm, all firms must be combined in a single plan.
7. Owner-employee contributions are limited.
8. Transactions between the owner-insured and the retirement plan are prohibited.
9. A profit-sharing plan must have a definite formula for determining the contribution for nonowner-employees.
10. Special rules apply when the plan is integrated with Social Security.
11. The plan must not commence retirement distributions to the owner-employee later than age 70½.

TAXATION OF H.R. 10 PLANS

The tax advantages are the key to the success of these plans. Qualified pension plans, including H.R. 10 plans, have a number of tax benefits. Generally, they are:

1. Employer contributions are considered as a tax-deductible business expense.
2. Employer contributions are not currently taxable to the employee.
3. Earnings on contributions are not taxable during the preretirement period.
4. Employees can make voluntary contributions to the plan, and these contributions will generate nontaxable investment gains during the preretirement period.
5. Employees will be taxed during retirement on benefits recovered, but the lower tax brackets, age deductions, 10-year averaging, and the like, usually result in benefits on a tax-preferred basis.
6. Estate tax exclusions from the decedent's estate are possible.[4]

---

[4] James R. Howe, *Pension World,* "Tax Qualified Retirement Plans," November 1980, pp. 62–63.

Although taxation eventually will be incurred, the advantage comes from the tax deferral into the future.

The deductibility of contributions depends upon the type of H.R. 10 plan in force, the nature of the contributions, and whether the plan is to be integrated with Social Security. The taxation of benefits depends upon the type and nature of the payments. Each of these factors is reviewed in the sections that follow.

TYPE OF PLAN

The plans may be classified as either defined contribution or defined benefit. Defined contribution plans are those in which the contributions are predetermined, and the ultimate pension benefit is a function of the years to retirement, the investment results, and amount of the contributions. Defined benefit plans predetermine the benefit. The benefit is related to a formula based upon years of service or salary, or the benefit may be a stated flat benefit. The actual contribution each year in defined benefit plans would be the amount needed to fund the promised benefit level at retirement. Initially, the self-employed, because of restrictions in the IRS Code, could only set up a defined contribution plan; but with the passage of ERISA, defined benefit plans became practical to adopt.

Defined Contribution Plans

The defined contribution plan can be either a money purchase type of plan or a profit-sharing plan. The difference is that the contributions under a profit-sharing plan are contingent upon profits, whereas a money purchase plan requires contributions irrespective of profits.

The general rule is that the maximum deduction in a plan in which an owner-employee participates is 15 percent of gross earned income, with a maximum of $15,000.[5] A special rule exists for earned incomes below $15,000. In this case, a contribution and deduction of $750 or 100 percent of gross earned income, whichever is the lower figure, is permitted.

The maximum earned income that can be considered in applying the contribution rate is $200,000. Furthermore, the law requires that if compensation in excess of $100,000 is to be used in the calculation, the minimum employee contribution rate shall not be less than 7.5 percent. This protects employees of the owner-employee from discrimination in potential benefits for high-income owners. For example, consider an owner-employee with earned income of $300,000 and with one employee with a $30,000 salary. To obtain the maximum allowable contribution, the owner-employee could contribute 5 percent of earnings and obtain the $15,000 allowable contribution if it could be based upon the $300,000

---

[5] The original law allowed a maximum contribution of 10 percent with a dollar maximum of $2,500.

income. The contribution for the employee's benefit would be 5 percent and $1,500. With the $200,000 limit and the 7.5 percent contribution rate, the contribution for the employee would be $2,250 ($30,000 × .075).

The law imposes another requirement in those cases in which the owner-employee has ownership in more than one business. The combined deduction may not be more than $15,000 or 15 percent of earned income, whichever is the lower figure. Should the total of plan contributions exceed this level, a limit on contributions of each employer, is imposed. The deductible contribution for each employer is calculated as follows:

$$\text{Maximum amount deductible} \times \frac{\text{Earned income from employer}}{\text{Earned income from all businesses with plans}}$$

This rule prevents the establishment of several plans and allowing the owner-employee to have contributions in excess of the allowable amounts.

Defined Benefit Plans

The Employee Retirement Income Security Act of 1974 (ERISA) provided a practical method for the use of defined benefit plans in H.R. 10 plans. The $15,000 and 15 percent contribution allowance provided for a defined contribution plan was to be converted into an amount that would provide equality for a defined benefit plan.

The guidelines in the code provide that the annual deduction is limited to an amount needed to fund a specified retirement benefit.[6] The level of benefit is based upon one's compensation and the age when participation began in a plan. Table 36–1 provides the percentage maximum that can be applied to one's annual compensation (not in excess of $100,000) to determine deductibility.

Table 36–1

Age When Participation Began	Applicable Percentage
30 or under	6.5
35	5.4
40	4.4
45	3.6
50	3.0
55	2.5
60 or over	2.0

A first-year employee, age 40, with a salary of $15,000 would be able to have funded a life annuity of approximately $660. This would be calculated as $15,000 × .044 or $660. This would require a contribution of approximately $2,242 at age 40 to fund this benefit.[7] The permission to use a

---

[6] IRC Sec. 2001(J)(3).

[7] This contribution is based upon a typical rate of current pension plans.

defined benefit plan provided an incentive to adopt new H.R. 10 plans. The contribution allowances for these plans may well exceed those allowed for defined contribution plans. A savings and loan officer stated that in one month 200 new accounts were set up and within a six-month period $5,000,000 of new dollars flowed into the association. Another firm established 115 new accounts within a two-week period.[8] There is no doubt this has provided an increase in the number of firms adopting H.R. 10 plans.

Assume an employee began to participate in the pension plan and worked continuously until age 65. Also, the compensation was as follows:

Age	Compensation	Allowable Annual Retirement Benefit
45–54	$20,000	$.036 \times 10 \times \$20,000 = \$ 7,200$
55–64	25,000	$.036 \times 10 \times \$25,000 = \$ 9,000$
		$16,200

The allowable contribution would be an amount needed to fund a straight-life annuity of $16,200 at age 65.[9] The basic benefit is in the form of a straight-life annuity, beginning at the later of age 65 or the day five years after the day the participant's current period of participation began.[10] If a break in service should occur, the employee will be allowed to use only the percentage applicable at age of re-entry for the remaining years in the plan. An employee, age 40, is allowed a 4.4 percent allowance until retirement. Let us assume the 40-year-old employee terminates employment at age 45 and does not re-enter covered employment again until age 55. The applicable percentage for the years from age 55 until retirement would be limited to 2.5 percent. The following illustration may clarify the point:

Age	Compensation	Maximum Benefit
40–44	$25,000	$.044 \times \$25,000 \times 5 = \$ 5,500$
55–64	25,000	$.025 \times \$25,000 \times 10 = \$ 6,250$
	Maximum retirement benefit	$11,750

Voluntary and Excess Contributions

It may be desirable to permit plan participants to make voluntary non-deductible contributions to the plan. Although the contributions would not be deductible, they would result in investment returns over the years that

---

[8] *Savings and Loan News,* March 1978, p. 81.

[9] IRC Sec. 415(b) establishes general limitations on benefits payable under defined benefit plans. The annual benefit cannot exceed the lower of the participant's average compensation for his or her high three consecutive years of earnings or $136,425 in 1982. The three consecutive years must be while the participant was an active participant in the pension plan.

[10] IRC Sec. 2001.

would not be taxable until the point of distribution. The amount and conditions permitting voluntary contributions are restructured by the tax code.

Any plan that includes only owner-employees may not provide for any voluntary contributions. A plan with owner-employees plus others may make voluntary contributions of up to 10 percent of compensation subject to a maximum amount of $2,500. The contribution rate permitted for owner-employees may not be greater than the rate for nonowner-employees. Should voluntary contributions (or regular contributions) exceed the amounts provided in the law or the plan, then the excess will be considered as excess contributions and subject to a special tax.[11]

The tax code levies a 6 percent tax on the amount of the excess contributions that is determined at the close of the taxable year.[12] This tax is imposed each year and, unless a correcting distribution is made on the excess contributions, the tax will be incurred every year.

The term *excess contributions* needs to be clarified. It is the total of: (1) excess voluntary contributions of owner-employees, (2) excess contributions to defined benefit plans, and (3) excess contributions to defined contribution plans, less any correcting distributions.[13] Although voluntary contributions are not allowed under defined benefit plans, excess contributions still would be possible. They would amount to the contributions of the employer above the amount needed to fully fund the plan and the contributions that were not deductible in prior years. Excess contributions to defined contribution plans would be employer contributions that were not deductible this tax year or in a prior tax year.

As an illustration of excess contributions, assume an owner-employee has made voluntary contributions of $4,500. The plan permitted voluntary contributions of 10 percent of compensation, with $2,500 the maximum permitted. The owner-employee had earned income of $65,000, so the permissible voluntary contribution would be $2,500. The total taxable excess would be calculated as follows:

1.	Voluntary contributions for the taxable year	$4,500
2.	Less permitted voluntary contributions for the tax year	2,500
	Excess	$2,000
3.	Plus excess contributions in prior years	0
	Total excess contributions	$2,000

This $2,000 would be subject to the 6-percent tax.

---

[11] Excess contributions that are used to purchase life insurance, annuity, or endowment contracts are not subject to the tax.

[12] IRC Sec. 4972(a).

[13] IRC Sec. 4972(b).

Brief mention has been made of "correcting distributions." The excess contributions tax can be eliminated by distributing the excess contributions back to the proper party. The party would depend upon the type of plan.[14] Table 36–2 should help clarify the correcting contributions.

A final point to consider is the possibility of a carry-over of excess contributions from one year to the next. This is permitted. Therefore, an excess contribution one year can be offset in a future year by making a smaller contribution than permitted in the future year. For example, if the allowable contribution is $10,000 and the actual contribution is $8,000, a $2,000 excess from a prior year could be offset.

Integration with Social Security

The law permits self-employed individuals to consider contributions for retirement already being made by payment of Social Security taxes for employees. Social Security contributions are allowed to be deducted from H.R. 10 contributions or to be integrated with the plan. Integration is permitted, as long as the final net contributions do not discriminate unfairly towards the owner-employee. The only type of plan allowed to integrate is a defined contribution plan. Defined benefit plans may not integrate.

The test of whether a plan discriminates is based upon the relationship between final net contributions of all employees to those of the owner-employees. The rule is that the owner-employee contributions may not be more than one third of the total contributions after the integration. Table 36–3 illustrates the process.

Integration is permitted in the example, because the $7,141.80 is less than one third of the total of $22,981.80. In the above example, the owner-employee is allowed to reduce the contributions for the employees by

Table 36–2
Illustration of Correcting Contributions

Year	Plan Contributions	Allowable Contribution	Correcting Contributions	Cumulative Taxable Excess	Tax (6 percent)
1	$30,000	$20,000	$ 0	$10,000	$ 600
2	30,000	20,000	0	20,000	1,200
3	30,000	20,000	10,000	20,000	1,200
4	20,000	20,000	10,000	10,000	600
5	20,000	20,000	10,000	0	—

[14] IRC Sec. 4792(b)(5) allows the following distributions:

1. Defined benefit plans—distributed to employer.
2. Defined contribution plans—distributed to employer or employee, whichever made the contribution.
3. Excess voluntary contributions—distributed to owner-employees.

Table 36-3
Illustration of Contributions to a Defined Contribution Plan after Integration

Given: 1 owner-employee—earned income $65,000
       9 employees:
          4   —earned income $18,000 each
          4   —earned income $20,000 each
          1   —earned income $13,000

H.R. 10 provides a contribution of 15 percent of earned income, subject to legal maximums.

Individual	Earned Income	Employer Contribution	Social Security Tax Paid[1]	Net Contribution to H.R. 10 Plan
Owner-employee	$65,000	$ 9,750	$ 2,608.20	$ 7,141.80
4 Employees	72,000	10,800	3,999.00	6,912.00
4 Employees	80,000	12,000	4,320.00	7,680.00
1 Employee	13,000	1,950	702.00	1,248.00
		$34,500	$10,133.50	$22,981.80

[1] The Social Security rate for 1982 for the self-employed is 9.35 percent, and the employed rate is 6.70 percent of the first $32,400 of earned income. The hospital rate, which is included in the total percentage, is 1.3 percent. Therefore, the net contribution rate for the self-employed is 8.05 percent and for the employed is 5.40 percent.

$8,910 ($3,888 + 4,320 + 702). The owner's contribution also must be lowered by $2,608.20.

Benefits

The taxation of H.R. 10 plans takes place when the benefits are received or the plan makes what is called "a premature distribution." There are certain time restrictions about when benefits are payable without special tax penalties. The law requires that retirement benefits must begin no earlier than age 59½ and no later than age 70½. The purpose of an H.R. 10 plan is retirement benefits, and, consequently, a tax penalty is imposed upon a premature distribution.

Premature Distributions.   An owner-employee will incur a serious tax penalty should he or she receive a plan distribution prior to age 59½. There are several exceptions to the general rule:[15]

1. That a distribution will be allowed if it is a result of the owner-employee becoming disabled.[16]
2. That a distribution to an owner-employee will be allowed if it is in the form of a dividend from a life insurance contract or an annuity.

---

[15] IRC 72 (M)(5)(A)(i).

[16] The definition of disability is a long-term total disability. The disability must be such that the owner-employee is unable to engage in any substantial gainful activity.

3. That a distribution, representing amounts from contributions made
    while the recipient was not an owner-employee, is permitted.

The penalty for a premature distribution is 10 percent of the amount
received that is included in the income of the owner-employee. Furthermore, if the owner-employee does receive a premature distribution, he or
she will be prevented from participating in the plan for five years from the
date of distribution.[17]

Table 36–4 provides an example of the amounts subject to the premature tax penalty. The example assumes the plan participant was a self-
employed (owner-employee) for the years 1975 and 1976, and was a
nonowner-employee during the year 1977, 1978, and 1979. Furthermore,
the total plan was distributed at the end of 1979 to the participant.

Table 36–4
Amounts Subject to Premature Tax Penalty

Year	Voluntary Participants' Contribution	Increase in Value of	Company Contribution	Increase in Value of
1975	$ 2,000	$ 900	$ 2,500	$ 1,000
1976	2,000	800	7,500	4,500
1977	2,000	700	7,500	4,000
1978	2,000	600	7,500	3,000
1979	2,000	500	7,500	800
	$10,000	$3,500	$32,500	$13,300

The premature distribution portion subject to penalty is calculated as
follows:

1.	Company contributions while participant was an owner-employee	$10,000
2.	Increase in value of company contribution for 1975 and 1976	5,500
3.	Increase in value of participants' contributions for 1975 and 1976	$ 1,700
	Total premature distribution subject to penalty	$17,200

A question might arise about how one calculates the penalty if the plan
distribution is not total but partial. In such situations, the order of distribution is (1) excess contributions, (2) employee contributions, (3) employer

---

[17] The five-year restriction will not apply should the withdrawal be made, because the
H.R. 10 plan is terminated.

contributions not included in (1) and the increase in value from employer and employee contributions.[18]

Normal Retirement Distributions.   The form of income taxation depends upon the time period of the distribution and the investment of the participant into the plan. The distribution is either considered as a lump-sum distribution or an annuity.

Lump-Sum Distribution.   A lump-sum distribution is one in which the total balance in an account is distributed within a one-year period. The distribution will be considered as ordinary income and taxed accordingly. The taxable amount is the employer contributions and interest earnings on the total account. Any portion of the distribution attributable to pre-1974 contributions to the plan may be taxed as capital gains. Also, any voluntary contributions (nondeductible prior contributions) will not be subject to tax and, therefore, offset against the total contributions.

The tax law allows one to treat both post- and pre-1974 contributions as ordinary income, as opposed to separating into ordinary and capital gains amounts. The question immediately comes up: why would anyone want the total treated as ordinary income if a tax-preference capital gain was available? The answer is that the capital gains taxation may be subject to an alternative maximum tax and, consequently, result in a total tax higher than if the total were treated as ordinary income. This is especially true when one considers that the amount subject to ordinary income taxation could use the 10-year average concept.

The 10-year averaging concept, in many circumstances, may provide a lower overall tax than would be true even under capital gains treatment. The purpose of the rule is to lower the tax rate on the lump-sum distribution, so the income that is averaged falls under a separate income-tax procedure. To be eligible for the 10-year averaging, one must be at least 59½ years old (unless disabled or dead), be a pension plan participant for at least five years prior to the distribution, and agree to include in the averaging all amounts received during the year that qualify. Another point is that a self-employed individual also may use the regular five-year income-averaging technique in filing his or her annual income-tax form.[19]

It is possible that a lump-sum distribution does not involve a gain but a loss. This could easily happen should the investments backing the plan decline in value. If a loss should occur, the resulting loss can be taken as an itemized deduction on one's tax form.

Installment Distribution.   Retirement benefits often are paid in periodic installments, as opposed to a lump-sum distribution. The law provides a restriction on the length of time over which installments may be paid. This is required because a distribution over a long time would mean that little of

---

[18] *Tax Information on Self-Employed Retirement Plans,* Publication No. 560 (Washington, D.C.: Department of the Treasury, Internal Revenue Service), p. 10.

[19] *Pension Plan Guide* (Chicago: Commerce Clearing House, 1981), par. 9513.

the money would be provided for actual retirement benefits. Distribution in installments may be on a basis not extending beyond one of the following: (1) the employee's life, (2) the joint lives of the employee and spouse, (3) a period certain which is not longer than the employee's life expectancy, and (4) a period certain which is not longer than the joint life and survivor life expectancies of the employee and spouse.

The amount of each installment taxable as ordinary income depends upon the participant's investment or cost in the contract. The investment or cost for H.R. 10 plans would be the nondeductible (voluntary) contributions that have been made by the participant. The deductible amounts would not be considered as part of the cost. In short, the participant's cost portion of each installment is nontaxable, whereas the portion representing deductible contributions would be taxed as ordinary income. Two rules are used for determining taxability of the installments. One rule is the three-year rule and the other is the general rule.

The three-year rule is used when it is possible for the annuitant to receive his or her entire cost back within three years. Should this be possible, the entire installment is considered as nontaxable until the total cost or investment has been recovered. After that point, the entire installment would be fully taxable. Assume the following facts:

Annuitant's cost	$29,000
Annual annuity	$15,000 for three years
Retirement date	January 1, 1981

The 1981 annuity of $15,000 would not be subject to tax. For 1982, only $1,000 would be taxable. The entire annuity would be taxable for 1983.

When the cost will not be recovered within three years, the general rule is used. This amounts to taxing a specific proportion of each annuity payment. A ratio is developed using the participant's cost and the expected total return to the annuitant. The exclusion formula is:

$$\frac{\text{Investment in the contract}}{\text{Expected return}} \times \text{Annuity installment}$$

Assume a male age 65 will receive a single life annuity of $9,000 per year. Further assume these facts:

Participant's investment (cost)	$29,000
Expected return	$72,318[20]

$$\text{Exclusion} = \frac{\$29,000}{72,318} = 40.1\%$$

---

[20] The value of a single life annuity for a single male age 65 is 8.0353. See: *Pension and Annuity Income,* Publication No. 575 (Washington, D.C.: Department of the Treasury, Internal Revenue Service), p. 24.

Therefore, the nontaxable portion each year would be .401 × $9,000 or $3,609, and the taxable income would be $5,391 ($9,000 − $3,609).

Estate and Gift Tax Considerations

Decedents do not have to include in their gross estates the value of annuities payable to their beneficiaries from H.R. 10 plans. They can be excluded to the extent the benefits are attributable to past deductible contributions.

Should the distribution be paid in a lump-sum, the gross estate must include the value in the estate. The law provides some relief, however, to this rule. The gross estate can exclude the lump-sum, provided the beneficiary agrees to pay ordinary income tax on the lump sum and not use the 10-year income averaging rule. It also should be mentioned that a participant in an H.R. 10 plan can name a contingent beneficiary for proceeds without incurring a gift tax liability.

Prohibited Transactions

Certain transactions between the plan and the owner-employee are not allowed. The owner-employee may be in a fiduciary situation and, therefore, it is illegal to jeopardize the plan assets. The following transactions are not allowed.

1. The sale, exchange, or lease of any property between the plan and a disqualified person.
2. Providing a disqualified person with credit or lending him or her money from the plan.
3. Allowing a disqualified person the use of plan facilities or services.
4. Allowing a disqualified person to benefit from the assets or income of the plan.
5. Allowing a disqualified person who is a fiduciary to deal for his or her own account with plan income or assets.
6. Allowing a disqualified person who is a fiduciary the receipt of any consideration for dealing in the plan income or assets.[21]

The tax penalty is 5 percent of the amount involved in the transactions. This tax is to be paid by the owner-employee, or, in the case of more than one person being liable, the responsibility is joint. The disqualified person is allowed a specified period to correct the prohibited transaction. Failure to correct the situation will result in an additional tax of 100 percent of the value of the prohibited transaction.

---

[21] *Tax Information on Self-Employed Retirement Plans,* Publication No. 560, p. 12.

FUNDING MEDIA

The adoption of the self-employed retirement plan is tantamount to an investment decision, the merits of which are dependent upon the following variables:

1. The expectations regarding the income to be generated by the funding agency.
2. The flexibility of the investment fund regarding possible withdrawals and investment policy.
3. The timing and nature of tax deductions and payments to the participants.
4. The marginal tax rates of the self-employed individual during the contribution period and the retirement period.
5. The number of employees that must be included and the fact that their benefits are fully vested immediately.

An important consideration with respect to contributions is the requirement that retirement benefits be funded. The following are the major funding alternatives: (1) trusts, (2) life insurance companies, (3) mutual funds, and (4) government retirement bonds.

Trusts

Contributions are made to a trustee who invests the funds, accumulates the earnings of the trust, and pays benefits to eligible participants. The trustee must be a commercial or savings bank, a domestic savings and loan association, an insured credit union, or a trust company, unless all of the funds of the trust are invested in annuities, life insurance contracts, or endowment contracts issued by an insurance company.

The use of the trust as a funding alternative assures maximum investment flexibility. If desired, the funds may be allocated among fixed-dollar investments or to common stocks. Some trusts in the past invested in rare stamps, coins, precious jewels, and precious and strategic metals. The 1981 tax revision restricted the purchase of "collectibles," so their purchase is no longer practical in most cases. Furthermore, the current favorable capital gains taxation on "collectibles" may overshadow the tax advantages of a pension plan. In other words, these investments may be better suited for purchase outside of the pension plan.[22] The trustee acts as a fiduciary and is accountable for carrying out the expressed desires of the developers of the plan. The trust agreement sets forth the assets in which the trust would invest. Although the trustee has great flexibility, he or she is subject to strict fiduciary requirements.

---

[22] "Stashing Keogh, IRA Funds," *Forbes*, December 8, 1980, p. 167.

Life Insurance Companies

Life insurance companies are able to make guarantees on interest and principal and can assure participants a lifetime income. These plans, like trusts, are already established in prototype, so the complexities of plan formation for the self-employed individual are minimized.

The primary limitation of an insured plan is the unfavorable effect of inflation upon fixed-dollar annuities. The concept of a variable annuity has been an attempt by insurance companies to counter the adverse effects of inflation upon the value of retirement fund assets. Variable annuity plans invest in common stocks, instead of in bonds and other fixed-income securities. Variable annuity plans generally are now available to the self-employed as a funding investment type.

"Split-funding" is an alternative type of fund investment policy that has been devised. Premium funds are used to purchase a combination of variable annuities, mutual fund shares or other equities, and fixed-dollar securities. This type of investment policy offers the security of fixed minimum guarantees and the inflation hedge with the variable portion.

It is possible that life insurance might be an integral part of the plan. This is permissible as long as the life insurance portion of the contract is only "incidental" to the annuity itself. In a defined benefit plan funded with life insurance, the life insurance is considered incidental if it is no more than 100 times the monthly annuity. In defined contribution plans, the life insurance is considered incidental if no more than 25 percent of the employee's contribution is used to buy life insurance.

Mutual Funds

Mutual funds, like many other investment media, have developed prototype plans that facilitate qualification under the law. Mutual fund investment policies are diverse, with some investing only in common stock, some in fixed securities, and others including only securities from certain industries. Mutual fund advantages include flexibility of investment policy. The self-employed individual and employees may select a fund that best fits their investment propensities. Some individuals may wish to assume high levels of risk through growth company investments, while others prefer to invest in conservative mutual companies because of a preference for the security of final payment. Mutual funds also offer professional investment portfolio management services.

Government Retirement Bonds

Government retirement bonds should not be considered a funding agency but a type of funding instrument. The U.S. Treasury has a type of bond designed solely for pension plans. These bonds are issued by Federal

Reserve banks or branches, or by the Treasury itself, but commercial banks and trust companies may handle the applications for these bonds.

The bonds are similar to Series H bonds. They are issued in face amounts of $50, $100, $500, and $1,000. Interest accrues from the issue date until redemption at the current annual rate of 9 percent compounded semiannually. Redemption of these bonds may not be made before an employee reaches age 59½, except for total and permanent disability or death. The bonds are not transferable and cannot be sold, used as collateral for a loan, or as security for a debt.

Retirement bonds furnish a convenient funding source, in that employers do not have to develop a detailed plan instrument. This convenience or advantage is now somewhat offset by the prototype plan services that are provided by the insurance, mutual fund and trust media.

These bonds provide the least expensive way to establish a qualified pension plan, because the bond purchases are made through banks and no commission charges are made. Another convenient aspect is that they will be replaced if lost, stolen, or destroyed, and the owner has the right to change beneficiary designations with respect to death benefits. Disadvantages include: (1) a low interest rate on invested funds, and (2) inflexibility of investment policy. Only one type of fixed-investment security is offered, and may result in substantial purchasing power erosion prior to the retirement date. Government bond purchase plans should be discouraged for all self-employed individuals, except those who desire maximum security and low risk.

FACTORS INFLUENCING ADOPTION OF A QUALIFIED PENSION PLAN

Tax considerations exert a substantial influence upon the decision process. The attractiveness of all properly qualified pension plans is because of the following economic ramifications:

1. Employer contributions are immediately tax deductible, whereas the proceeds are not subject to tax until retirement years. Thus, the timing of tax cash flows becomes significant to the plan adoption decision. The time value of money is relevant. The present value of $1 of immediate tax write-offs is normally greater than the present value of future tax payments during retirement.
2. The earnings on the pension funds are not subject to taxation until the benefits are distributed.
3. Tax rates during retirement years for self-employed individuals are generally lower than during the productive working years. Tax incentives for the adoption of deferred compensation plans are obviously greater for those individuals in marginally high tax brackets.

Flexibility, security of benefits, and cost are the underlying decision considerations for the adoption of the plan and the choice of a funding medium. The attractiveness and relative importance of these factors vary, depending upon the objectives and the economic position of each participant. Cost attractiveness becomes highly relevant to a self-employed individual who is currently in a high tax bracket. Cost attractiveness also is related to the type of funding agency selected, and to the desired security of benefits and the corrolary willingness to assume given levels of risk on fund investments. The selection of a mutual fund, split-funding, or variable annuities offered by insurance companies may help to offset the effects of inflation. The risk, however, is increased, but such media might be selected by self-employed individuals willing to assume this element of risk. The lowest return and lowest risk are probably received by investing in government retirement bonds. As a general rule, one should assume that the higher the risk and volatility of the price of the investment, the less desirable it would be for an H.R. 10 plan. This is true if one assumes the plan is critical to one's retirement needs.

Security of pension benefits for the typical small employer depends to a large degree upon third-party guarantees. Life insurance companies guarantee minimum principal and interest payments in addition to providing a fixed life income if desired by the plan participant. Their guarantees usually are conservative and reflect a level of benefits that is low relative to historical average rates of return.

The third consideration is flexibility in funding. A trust generally provides the greatest flexibility. The trustee may invest in various types of investment securities, and the investment policy may be directed by the self-employed individual. For most small plans, life insurance companies provide relatively little flexibility. Little, if any, discretion is permitted the employer in specifying investments. In some larger plans, special unallocated funding is used when the benefits accumulate in a special fund. The mutual fund and the government retirement bond media also are fairly inflexible.

In recent years, certain trends have been noticed. Larger employers tend to place flexibility ahead of plan guarantees. They probably are able to assume greater risk. Small- or medium-sized firms prefer the added guarantees, with the related lower risk, and are willing to sacrifice flexibility in funding. Each funding agency is unique, however, and careful consideration should be given to the specific features available to the self-employed individual.

CHAPTER 37

Individual Retirement Accounts (IRAs) and Simplified Employee Pension Plans (SEPs)

WILLIAM H. RABEL AND
ERNEST L. MARTIN

At the beginning of the 1970s, substantial numbers of American workers were covered by private pension plans. One important sector of the labor force, however, still was not receiving the benefits of a federal income-tax policy that had fostered the growth of qualified plans. This sector, comprised of employees of companies without pension plans, was forced to rely on accumulated aftertax savings to provide for future retirement income. Furthermore, unlike those covered by qualified plans, individuals in this sector were required to pay income taxes on the annual earnings of their aftertax retirement savings.[1] Thus, such individuals found it doubly difficult to accumulate funds for their future retirement.

In 1974, Congress enacted the Employee Retirement Income Security Act (ERISA), which profoundly affected the pension field. This act, as modified by subsequent legislation,[2] provides in part that an individual can make an annual tax-deductible contribution of 100 percent of personal services compensation up to $2,000 to an individual retirement account (IRA) or to a qualified employer-sponsored plan. The funds in the account accumulate on a tax-free basis until the individual retires and begins to receive distributions. Provided distributions begin within the authorized age period, withdrawals are taxed as ordinary income in the year that they are received. Since 1979, employers have been allowed to set up simplified employee pension (SEP) plans for their employees. These plans use IRAs as a funding instrument and are subject to certain special requirements.

---

[1] Tax-exempt investments, of course, would be an exception to this rule.

[2] The Economic Recovery Tax Act of 1981 made many substantial changes in rules regarding IRAs.

ELIGIBILITY

Although IRAs initially were created for the employee who was not an active participant in a qualified employer-sponsored plan, the Economic Recovery Tax Act of 1981 (ERTA) broadened the eligibility to include qualified pension plan participants as well. After 1981, any individual under age 70½ receiving personal service compensation may set up an IRA or choose to make voluntary contributions to a qualified employer-sponsored plan.

CONTRIBUTIONS

Tax-deductible contributions of $2,000 or 100 percent of compensation, whichever is less, may be paid into an IRA each year. For the purpose of determining the maximum annual contribution an eligible individual can make to an IRA, compensation is held to include any payment received for rendering personal service, such as salaries, wages, commissions, tips, fees, and bonuses. Investment income and capital gains may not be included in the calculation of compensation for IRA contribution purposes. Moreover, although a community property state regards one half of a spouse's income as belonging to the other spouse, the nonworking spouse may not count this amount for purposes of determining compensation.

Employees may contribute to qualified employer plans in lieu of setting up their own IRAs. Plans established by federal, state, or local governmental bodies receive the same treatment as those of private employers. For contributions to be deductible, the following conditions must prevail: (1) the plan must permit such contributions, (2) they must not be mandatory, and (3) the employee must not stipulate that the voluntary contribution is not to be considered a deductible contribution.

Contributions may be attributed to a calendar year if they are made by April 15 of the subsequent year (or later if an extension for filing the federal income-tax return is granted). This provision prevents the taxpayer from having to guess what his or her earnings will be before the end of the tax year.

A working spouse with an IRA can set up a separate IRA for a nonworking spouse (called a spousal account or spousal IRA), with the maximum combined contribution to the two accounts being limited to the lesser of $2,250 or 100 percent of personal service compensation. To receive a deduction for the spousal contribution, the husband and wife must file a joint tax return. Prior to 1982, the law encouraged an equal division of contributions between the individual and spousal accounts, but this is no longer the case. Contributions may be split in any way as long as no more than $2,000 is paid into either account. If a nonworking spouse begins to work, the spousal account then becomes a regular account and the spouse may contribute to it 100 percent of compensation up to $2,000 for that year. Contributions to spousal accounts must cease whenever the elder spouse reaches age 70½. However, if the younger spouse continues to be eligible otherwise, he or she may establish a new IRA and contribute to it until reaching age 70½.

A divorced spouse with a spousal IRA (or one separated under a decree of separate maintenance) can continue to make deductible contributions to the spousal IRA. The contributions are limited to the lesser of $1,125 or the sum of the spouse's compensation and taxable alimony. Also, the spousal IRA must have been established for at least five years prior to the calendar year of the divorce, and the ex-spouse must have made contributions in at least three of the previous five years.

The tax penalty for contributions in excess of the allowable amount for a year is 6 percent of the excess. This tax penalty is cumulative from year to year, inasmuch as it applies not only to any excess that is not removed from the account, but also to income earned on the excess as well. The penalty is not tax deductible.

The penalty for excess contributions may be avoided under any one of three conditions. First, the amount of excess contributions and any earnings on them may be withdrawn before the individual's federal income-tax return is filed for the year when the excess contribution is made. Earnings on the excess contributions must be treated as taxable income for the year the contribution was made. Second, excess contributions made in a preceding year subsequently may be applied to years when an employee's contributions are less than the maximum permitted. Third, if the excess contribution is made based on erroneous information supplied by a financial institution, and accepted in good faith, the excess may be withdrawn at any time.

As discussed in greater detail below, IRAs may be funded through trust or custodial agreements, or through annuity and endowment contracts sold by life insurance companies. Since November 6, 1978, most life companies have sold only flexible premium annuities to fund IRAs. Prior to that time, both endowment and annuity contracts were sold. However, the IRS took the position that funding instruments must provide for flexible (variable) premium payments to provide for a reduction in earned income that could mandate a reduced IRA contribution. Traditionally, endowment contracts have had only fixed premiums, and therefore could not conform with IRS requirements. Those owners of fixed premium contracts issued prior to November 6, 1978, were permitted by the IRS to exchange them tax-free for flexible premium annuities prior to January 1, 1981. This option, however, did not govern the contractual relationships between the insured and insurer; it related to the tax issue only. Thus, in some cases a surrender of a fixed-premium policy might have resulted in the loss of valuable rights and in a substantial duplication of expenses. In recognition of this, some companies offered their policyowners the opportunity to exchange an endowment policy for an annuity without suffering any disadvantage.

The maximum annual premium that may be payable to an IRA funded by life insurance or annuity is $2,000. However, the entire premium is not deductible if the contract contains an element of preretirement life insurance protection. The insurance company must notify the policyowner of the premium allocation between protection and retirement savings, using costs calculated according to mortality rates in the P.S. 58 table published by the Treasury Department.[3] The policyowner may use an amount equal to the difference between the maximum annual contribution and the amount allocated by the insurer to retirement savings to purchase an IRA through some other funding mechanism. Any dividends paid on a policy must be allocated to reduce future contributions. Payments used to purchase disability waiver of premium benefits are deductible as contributions to the IRA.

ROLLOVERS

The law permits a tax-free transfer of assets from one IRA to another. These so-called rollovers also are permitted from the following types of plans into an IRA: (1) pension and profit-sharing plans qualifying under Section 401(a) of the Internal Revenue Code, (2) tax-deferred annuities meeting the requirements of Section 403(b), and (3) bond-purchase plans satisfying Section 405. Also, proceeds received as a distribution from a qualified plan, because of the death of a spouse, can be rolled over tax free into an IRA. Rollovers provide an element of flexibility that fosters investment, administrative, and other benefits arising from consolidation.

Every rollover must meet three requirements. First, it must be a lump-sum distribution of all the old plan's assets. Second, an individual is limited to only one tax-free rollover in any one year. (However, it is worth noting that it is possible to make a direct transfer of funds from one funding agency to another without effecting a rollover subject to the one-year restriction.) A third requirement calls for the rollover to take place within 60 days after the distribution is made.

In addition to the requirements cited above, distributions from a plan qualified under Section 401(a) must meet other tests. First, only employer contributions may be rolled over. If contributions attributable to an employee are rolled over, they shall be treated as excess contributions and subjected to the penalties discussed above. Second, the distribution of all funds must be made within one taxable year. Third, the distribution must be made because the employee is separated from service, has reached age 59½, or the plan has been terminated.

---

[3] Since the maximum premium equals the maximum contribution, and that part of a premium allocable to protection is not deductible, insured IRAs alone do not provide the degree of tax deductibility and maximum savings that are provided by IRAs funded through other mechanisms.

Assets rolled over into an IRA from a tax-sheltered annuity can be rerolled over into another tax-sheltered annuity. By the same token, when assets are rolled over from a qualified plan into an IRA, they may be rolled over again into the qualified plan of a subsequent employer; however, such a rollover is allowable only if it is permitted by the subsequent employer's plan and if the assets of the IRA consist solely of the assets from the first qualified plan and earnings on those assets. The individual should not contribute to an IRA that is set up as a conduit between two qualified plans. Rather, to keep from losing favorable tax treatment, he or she should set up a second IRA for his or her contributions.

FUNDING AGENCIES AND INVESTMENTS

Individuals have a large degree of freedom in the way they allocate their contributions in any particular year among the various financial institutions that offer IRAs. In addition, the amount allocated to any given institution need not remain fixed—the entire contribution may go to one plan in one year, and then be shifted to another plan the next year.

Among the financial institutions offering IRAs are commercial banks, savings and loan institutions, brokerage firms, mutual fund management companies, credit unions, life insurance companies, and companies that offer a broad variety of financial services. Accounts may be so arranged that the owner may make all investment decisions, or such decisions may be turned over completely to a financial institution.

Self-Directed Accounts

Where the individual decides to make all investment decisions, a self-directed retirement trust is set up. A corporate trustee is selected to take charge of all assets and to ensure that the activities of the account conform to the rules of the law. In some cases, the corporate trustee is directly connected with the financial institution through which the IRA is marketed. Alternatively, the services of a single independent trustee may be marketed by one or more brokerage or other financial services firms or both. These firms link up with a trustee in the belief they can serve their clientele more effectively by staying in their particular field, and by recommending another organization to provide services that clients need. Such an arrangement is not devoid of benefits for the firm recommending the trustee. Investments of the trust may bring to it brokerage or underwriting fees, or both. The trust also engenders a certain amount of good will, which may enhance other business relationships between the trustee and the firm that markets its services.

Normally, the trustee charges the grantor (contributor to the IRA) three types of fees. The first is an acceptance fee, a flat charge to cover the expense of setting up the trust. For example, such a fee might be $35 for the grantor and $5 for a spousal account. The second fee is an annual charge expressed as a percentage of the assets in the trust, subject to a minimum amount. For example, a fee might be .0015 of the first $100,000 and .0010 of any amount over that, subject to a minimum charge of $35 for the grantor's account and $5 for the spousal account. Finally, charges may be levied for services, such as certain processing activities, statements, returned checks, disbursements, terminations, and the like.

Self-directed trusts have provided great investment latitude since IRAs first were introduced, and, as a matter of practice, grantors have invested in all types of assets, including securities, commodities, debt instruments, real property, and personal property. However, after 1981, grantors have had less flexibility. Assets in an IRA may no longer be invested in collectibles, including works of art, rugs, antiques, metals, gems, stamps, coins, alcoholic beverages, or other items of tangible personal property specified by the IRS.

Single-Institution Trust or Custodial Accounts

Many persons setting up an IRA do not want to actively manage the assets in the account. Instead, they prefer to invest them with a particular financial institution, such as a bank, a broker, or a savings and loan institution. The customer chooses from among the investment options offered by the institution, such as various types of accounts, certificates of deposit, and investment funds, according to his or her belief on what will offer the greatest rate of return in the long run.

In response to the desire by customers for a single-institution approach, financial institutions of all types have developed trust or custodial accounts under which investments cannot be made outside the institution without rolling over the account. An exception to this rule (as explained in the section on rollovers) is that transfers directly from one funding agency to another are not regarded as rollovers.

While some technical distinctions exist between the trust and custodial approaches, from the purchaser's standpoint these differences are inconsequential in terms of cost or service.[4] For purposes of simplicity, and to help distinguish them from self-directed trusts, all such accounts will be called "custodial accounts." The institution with which funds are invested will be called the "custodian." However, this simplification of terms should not be construed as implying that all institutions are equally attractive—the customer should shop carefully for an IRA just as for any other product.

Just as there are a wide variety of financial institutions offering single-institution accounts, there are a wide variety of charges. Many deposit

---

[4] Institutions providing these accounts may adopt model forms provided by the Treasury Department (No. 5305 for trusts and No. 5305A for custodial accounts), or request a letter of opinion concerning the acceptability of their own prototype master form. Many institutions have chosen the latter approach.

institutions, such as banks and savings and loan institutions, do not assess a direct charge for setting up an IRA. They operate under the philosophy that this is a way to attract funds, and that costs will be covered by the margin between the rate of interest earned by the institution and what is credited to the IRA. Other institutions levy charges that are similar to those employed with self-directed trusts. Also, some investments, such as mutual funds (and, as discussed below, life insurance contracts and annuities) may contain a specific sales load, in addition to certain ongoing charges for managing the assets in the portfolio.

Insured Plans

Traditionally, premiums for endowment and annuity contracts were commingled with other funds accumulated over various periods. They were invested in the general account of the life insurance company, which guarantees a minimum rate of return and assumes the full investment risk. Because interest rates were comparatively stable for most of the 20th century, consumer savings were not considered "hot money," which moved rapidly among investment alternatives seeking the highest rate of return. Insurers made long-term investments and remained competitive in the market for savings as well as for protection.

The traditional practice of commingling funds received in different periods works very well in a stable financial environment. However, in a period of rising inflation, policies designed as savings vehicles find it difficult to compete favorably, because rates of return on new investments rise more rapidly than the rates of return on the entire portfolio. The reverse holds true in the case of deflation, of course, but savers throughout the world have grown cynical about the possibility prices will stabilize in the foreseeable future. Therefore, instead of settling for a long-run rate of return, they have demanded products reflecting current market rates of return, and financial institutions, including life insurance companies, have responded.

Life insurance and annuity products (both participating and nonparticipating), which were developed for the IRA market, offer a wide range of investment options and guarantees. Most still offer a minimum rate of return over the life of the contract, in which case the insurer must balance maturities in the portfolio to be able to meet guarantees and, at the same time, stay competitive with other financial institutions offering current market rates. A few annuity contracts (e.g., some of those invested in equities) offer no investment guarantees at all, thus shifting the investment risk to the policyowner. Premiums from such contracts are invested to gain a rate of return that is competitive in the market the insurer wishes to penetrate, and the policyowners may be offered a variety of investment portfolios from which to choose. Often the policy provides that new premiums and existing funds may be shifted from one portfolio to another. In effect, an annuity policy that does not guarantee a rate of return can be compared to a mutual fund that offers a guaranteed annuity option at a given date.

Typically, four types of charges are associated with insured IRAs. First are those that vary as a percentage of the premium. The most prominent of these is the sales charge, designed to cover the agent's commission. It is worth noting that many companies now market annuities having no sales load. A second charge, a fixed amount per anum, is designed to cover the expenses of putting the policy on the company's books and maintaining the policy. A third charge is associated with policies that contain life insurance protection. The policy must be underwritten to assess the mortality risk, and, to some degree, the amount of expense involved varies in proportion to the amount of insurance coverage under the policy. Thus, this third charge varies roughly with the amount of coverage. The final type of charge, which normally is applied only with annuities, is designed to cover the cost of investing funds. It is expressed as a percentage of the assets, subject to a minimum amount.

BENEFITS

The distribution of benefits from an IRA may begin no earlier than age 59½ (with the exception of death or disability, discussed below), nor later than age 70½, or else penalties are imposed. All distributions are taxable as ordinary income in the year they are received. The form the benefits take varies somewhat with the type of financial institution through which they are funded.

Trust or Custodial Accounts

The options for distributing benefits are identical for both self-directed and single-institution IRAs. The first approach is the single-sum distribution, whereby the account owner receives all contributions and the interest earned on them in one payment. However, a single-sum distribution may have unfavorable consequences for the individual's tax liability and post-retirement financial security. Because of the progressive nature of income-tax rates, a single distribution of any size could subject the depositor to a much higher tax bill than would result from a series of smaller distributions.

In most cases, it is advisable for the individual to at least begin with the second approach, the period certain option, which allows the distribution of benefits to be made in a series of equal payments. These disbursements are spread out over a period that may not exceed the life expectancy of the depositor, or the joint life expectancy of the depositor and the depositor's spouse. If the depositor chooses, the payments may be received over a shorter time. The limitation on the distribution period, when coupled with the requirement that the depositor begin to receive distributions not later than age 70½, in effect prevents a depositor from using an IRA as a mere tax shelter for investments, rather than as a means of providing for retirement income.

Typically, custodians make several payment intervals available for election by depositors—including monthly, quarterly, semiannually, or annually—thus accommodating the budgetary needs of most retired persons.

When the custodial account depositor selects the joint life expectancy of the depositor and spouse as the benefit period, payments continue to be made to the spouse on the same basis if the depositor dies. Conversely, when some other payment period is chosen and the depositor dies, the remainder in the account is paid to beneficiaries designated by the depositor. In fact, it is not unusual to have a class of primary beneficiaries (rather than an individual) whose interests in the account are succeeded at the death of the last class member by a class of secondary beneficiaries. However, all assets in the IRA must be distributed within five years after the death of the depositor and, where applicable, the spouse.

Usually, one associates retirement benefits with the concept of a lifelong pension. However, only a life insurance company can offer payments for a lifetime—through the mechanism of a life annuity contract. Such lifetime payments cannot be offered by a bank, a savings and loan institution, or any other thrift institution. Indeed, under the life expectancy distribution option of a custodial account, it would not be at all unusual for an individual to outlive the life expectancy established for an IRA account and thus to exhaust the funds. After all, life expectancy is only an average figure. To provide life income annuity options to their depositors, some custodians have established arrangements with one or more life insurance companies, under which immediate life annuities may be purchased by depositors at retirement, using custodial account funds. This arrangement allows a depositor to avoid tax complications by utilizing the rollover provisions described previously. While such an annuity purchase does not provide the depositor with a guarantee of annuity rates during the period when contributions to an IRA are being made, as an insured plan would have, this limitation may possibly be offset by the increased investment flexibility provided during the accumulation period by the noninsured IRA.

Insured Plans

The individual endowment and annuity contracts issued by insurers to fund IRAs provide that at retirement (normally between ages 59½ and 70½) a policyowner can select one of the settlement options guaranteed in the contract. No option need be selected prior to that time. Because of established minimum distribution requirements under the Internal Revenue Code (IRC), described above, policyowners may not select an interest-only option. However, both the period certain and the life income annuity options are made available.

As is the case with custodial IRAs, the maximum length of time over which a period certain benefit can be stretched is the life expectancy of the owner or the joint life expectancy of the owner and the owner's spouse. When a policyowner selects a period certain distribution, it is permissible to make early withdrawals. It is advisable for the depositor who selects a period certain guarantee to designate a beneficiary.

A life income annuity may be so designed that all payments cease at the death of one or more annuitants, or it may pay until death but guarantee a minimum number of payments. In practice, most persons who choose a life income option also elect at least a minimum period certain. The prospect of giving up the full purchase price of an annuity when death occurs immediately after payments begin is a risk that most annuitants are unwilling to take. Of course, the longer the minimum guarantee period of a life income annuity, the more expensive the annuity.

All assets in the IRA must be paid to the beneficiary within five years of the time the rights to them vest in the beneficiary.

No trustee or custodian is required for insured plans, since the policy is endorsed to conform with IRS requirements. Accordingly, the policy loan provision normally found in life insurance contracts is not available in insured IRA plans.

U.S. Retirement Bonds

Some individuals prefer to have their IRA funds invested in United States government securities over any other investment. To facilitate such IRA investment in government obligations, the Treasury created a special series of bonds issued in denominations of $50, $100, and $500. The interest on these bonds is compounded semiannually and the rate is determined by the Treasury. As of July 1982, the rate was 9 percent. Rates for outstanding IRA bonds do not change when the Treasury changes the rate for bonds being sold.

The bonds, which may be purchased from a Federal Reserve bank or an office of the Treasury, were designed to conform with the requirements and restrictions applicable to IRAs. The payment of interest stops when the holder reaches age 70½, and at this time the bond is considered to be redeemed for tax purposes even if redemption has not taken place. If a bond has been bought and redeemed within 12 months, no interest is paid and no tax deduction is allowable. At the same time, the withdrawal is not taxed.

TAXATION OF RETIREMENT BENEFITS

Providing the amount of the retirement benefit meets minimum requirements, it is taxed as ordinary income in the year received, irrespective of the funding mechanism. This taxation policy applies to sums received under life income options, as well as under periods certain. One rationale underlying the tax policy is that, since contributions are tax deductible when made, they are regarded as a deferred wage that therefore should be subject to taxation at some point.

Preretirement death benefits paid under life insurance provisions, however, are not taxed, since premiums allocated to life insurance coverage under an insured account are not tax deductible.

Distributions from IRAs are treated as ordinary income. As such, they qualify for general income averaging, although not for special 10-year averaging or capital gain treatment, or both, available with a qualifying lump-sum distribution under a qualified employer plan or a Keogh (H.R. 10) plan. This should be considered by employees before rolling over assets from a qualified plan into an IRA, because, depending on such factors as the date of retirement and pre- and post-retirement income, the financial advantage may lie with electing a qualified lump-sum distribution rather than rolling over the account and deferring the tax.

DISABILITY BENEFITS

A worker who becomes disabled before age 59½ may withdraw all or part of the funds in an IRA without incurring a penalty in the form of an excise tax. A person is considered to be disabled if "unable to engage in any substantial gainful activity by reason of any medically determinable physical or mental impairment which can be expected to result in death or to be of long or continued duration."

Distributions of contributions and investment income to a disabled person under age 59½ are taxed as they would be at normal retirement age under an IRA. However, disability benefits provided under an annuity or life insurance contract are received tax-free. It should be noted, some funding agencies charge a "back-end load" for premature withdrawals, even if the individual is disabled.

PENALTIES FOR PREMATURE WITHDRAWAL OR BORROWING

Unless the depositor is disabled, any withdrawal of funds prior to age 59½ results in a penalty tax of 10 percent of the amount withdrawn over and above the ordinary income tax on the funds. Thus, an individual age 45 who withdraws $4,000 from an IRA is subject to the ordinary income tax on the funds during the year received plus an additional $400 as penalty tax. If any portion of an IRA is pledged as collateral for a loan, that portion is treated as a distribution and is subject to both ordinary income tax and the tax penalty for the year in which the pledge was made.

A depositor who borrows from an IRA is considered to have received the entire interest in the account. Thus, the fair market value of the entire account is taxed as ordinary income and the account loses its tax-exempt status.

PENALTY FOR INSUFFICIENT WITHDRAWAL[5]

The depositor of an IRA incurs a penalty if distributions are not begun by age 70½, or if individual distributions are less than account assets would provide if distributed evenly over (1) the life expectancy of the depositor, or (2) the joint life expectancy of the depositor and the depositor's spouse. The minimum amount to be distributed in each year after age 70½ is calculated annually by dividing the amount in the account by the years of life expectancy at age 70½ less the number of years elapsed since then. The penalty is a tax of 50 percent on the difference between the amount that should have been distributed and the amount that was distributed. Thus, if the distribution for a year should have been $600 and was actually only $400, the penalty would be $100 (50 percent of $600 − $400).

THE SCOPE OF INDIVIDUAL RETIREMENT ACCOUNTS

Comprehensive information concerning the number of persons covered by IRAs and the dollar amounts represented by these accounts is unavailable. It is known, however, that at the end of 1979 the total amount in all IRAs, except those administered by commercial banks and brokerages, was $11.1 billion. By the end of 1979, just over 1 million persons had set up IRAs with life insurance companies, and reserves for these insured accounts amounted to $2.5 billion. Some notion of the degree of participation can be gained from Internal Revenue Service statistics for tax-year 1978, showing that 2,388,520 returns claimed deductions amounting to a total of $3 billion for contributions of IRAs. It is estimated that 49 million persons were enrolled in retirement plans other than Social Security at the end of 1979. Thus, to date IRAs account for a comparatively small segment of retirement plan participants, and it is fairly safe to assume that the amounts invested in IRAs constitute an equally minor proportion of all retirement funds.

However, individuals have been eligible to establish IRAs only since the beginning of 1975. The available figures of 1978 and 1979 show that the amounts in IRAs administered by life insurance companies, mutual funds, mutual savings banks, and savings and loan associations alone grew from $8 billion to $11.1 billion in one year—an increase of almost 39 percent. This kind of growth rate, even if limited to employees not covered by a qualified plan, would suggest that the amounts held in IRAs will increase substan-

---

[5] These penalties do not apply where an employee contributes to a qualified employer plan in lieu of an IRA.

tially in the future.[6] However, with the extension of IRAs to anyone receiving compensation after 1981, there is no question that the growth in these plans is assured.

SIMPLIFIED EMPLOYEE PENSION PLANS

A simplified employee pension plan (SEP) is an arrangement under which an employer sets up an IRA for each covered employee.[7] First authorized in 1979, SEPs simplify the administration and reduce the paperwork associated with many other types of pension plans; for this reason, they are especially attractive to smaller employers. In particular, SEPs reduce the paperwork normally required for H.R. 10 or corporate plans covering common-law employees.

For a SEP to qualify for favorable tax treatment, an employer must make contributions for all eligible employees. An employee who is at least 25 years of age, received compensation for service during the calendar year, and worked for the employer during three of the preceding five years must be eligible. These rules also may extend to employee groups controlled by the employer, even though such groups technically are employed by a separate firm (such as a wholly owned subsidiary), if exclusion of such group would result in discrimination in favor of the prohibited group. Two exceptions to these general rules are: (1) members of a collective bargaining unit, which engaged in good faith bargaining of retirement benefits, and (2) certain nonresident aliens.

Contributions on behalf of employees are deductible up to 15 percent of total employee compensation or $15,000, whichever is less. In addition, an employee covered by a SEP can set up an IRA and contribute the lower of $2,000 or 100 percent of employee compensation to it, notwithstanding the fact that the employer has contributed to the SEP on the employee's behalf. The employee can also contribute directly to the SEP without setting up a separate IRA.

Contributions to a SEP must be made for all eligible employees in a manner that does not discriminate in favor of certain "prohibited classes," which include officers, shareholders of more than 10 percent of the common stock, self-employed persons, or highly compensated employees. Discrimination is automatically deemed to exist if contributions do not represent a uniform percentage of each eligible employee's total compensation and favor the prohibited group. Only the first $200,000 of an employee's salary can be used to determine whether contributions are

---

[6] The source for available data on IRAs is *1980 Pension Facts,* published by the American Council of Life Insurance.

[7] Form 5305 SEP is being used widely as a prototype.

discriminatory. If income in excess of $100,000 is considered in setting an employee's contribution, the contribution rate of all covered employees must be at least 7.5 percent. An employer may choose to place a limit on the amount contributed on behalf of employees, so the contribution is lower than the statutory limit of $15,000. Such a limit could result in having contributions represent a higher percentage of salary for lower-paid employees than for those in higher salary brackets. However, discrimination in favor of lower-paid workers is not prohibited.

The following example illustrates the application of these rules. Assume that R. M. Company has two employees: X earns $20,000 per year and Y earns $250,000. If R. M. wanted to contribute the maximum permissible amount to Y, it would calculate its contributions as follows. Only $200,000 of Y's salary could be used to calculate benefits. Since $15,000 is 7.5 percent of $200,000, R. M. would establish a 7.5 percent plan (the minimum possible amount, since Y's earnings over $100,000 are considered). Thus, contributions would be $7,500 on behalf of Y, and $1,500 on behalf of X. It is possible that R. M. would like to favor lower-paid employees, and if so, the company could contribute up to 15 percent of salary, or $3,000 for X. Of course, contributions for Y would be limited to $15,000, an amount that represents only 6 percent of Y's salary (and 7.5 percent of Y's applicable salary), but the plan is permissible since it does not discriminate in favor of the prohibited group. In fact, R. M. could legally set a limit of $3,000 and still maintain its 15 percent plan, in which case contributions for both X and Y would be $3,000.

Benefits under a SEP may be integrated with Social Security to recognize that employers are contributing to both forms of retirement plans on behalf of employees. However, only one approach is available to a SEP, as contrasted with three for qualified plans. Furthermore, even this approach may not be used if Form 5305-SEP (the widely used prototype plan) is adopted. If a SEP is integrated with Social Security, amounts paid to Social Security are directly offset against the amounts allocable to the SEP. Thus, if the SEP calls for a contribution of $3,000 for an employee, and FICA (Social Security) taxes of $1,226 were paid during the year for the benefit of that employee, the employer contribution to the SEP would be $1,774 ($3,000 − $1,226).

Some of the requirements typically associated with pension plans also apply to SEPs. For example, the plan must be in writing, it must set forth the eligibility requirements, and it must specify the ways in which contributions are computed. However, SEPs are somewhat unusual in that all rights to contributions are 100 percent vested in the employee immediately, and an employee may freely withdraw funds, subject to the penalties described above for withdrawing funds from an IRA. Most employers would consider these vesting provisions to be a disadvantage. It is important to note that the existence of a SEP does not prohibit an employer from setting up an IRA.

IRAs AND SEPs—PANACEAS OR PARTIAL SOLUTIONS

Perhaps not since the roaring twenties has a financial services product been given such enthusiastic and, in some cases, misleading promotion as have IRAs. Throughout the United States, financial institutions have lured savers with the promise that they can retire rich. These claims are supported by projecting $2,000 contributions for 30 or 40 years at interest rates of 12 percent or more.

While it is true that a contribution of $2,000 per year for 40 years will accumulate to a sum of $1,534,182 when invested at a rate of 12 percent, it is highly unlikely the individual who saves this sum will be considered rich in terms of the purchasing power of the savings. If historic relationships between inflation and interest rates hold true, an interest rate of 12 percent implies that the inflation rate will be about 9 percent. Thus, our "millionaire" will pay $24.81 for a $.79 loaf of bread, and the official poverty level for a family of two will be $178,666.

Over the years, the real rate of interest (interest rate less inflation) has held reasonably constant at about 3 percent. Therefore, a fairly accurate picture of the future real purchasing power of savings (i.e., how much they buy in 1982 dollars) can be obtained by projecting them with three percent earnings. Table 37-1 shows the amount to which annual investments of $1,000 accumulates when invested at 3 percent over different periods. It also shows the amount of annual income in real dollars these savings provide at age 65, assuming payments are spread over the life expectancy of the contributor. To determine the maximum amount provided under an IRA, multiply the figures in Table 37-1 by 2, then multiply them by 15 to determine the maximum amount provided by a SEP.

Table 37-1
Accumulated Amount of $1,000 per Annum
at 3 Percent and the Annual Life Income It
Will Buy

		Annual Life Income at Age 65	
Year	Amount	Male*	Female†
10	$11,463.88	$ 764.25	$ 629.88
20	26,870.37	1,791.35	1,476.39
30	47,575.42	3,171.69	2,614.03
35	60,462.08	4,030.81	3,322.09
40	75,401.26	5,026.75	4,142.93
45	92,719.86	6,181.32	5,094.50

* Assumes a life expectancy of 15 years at age 65.
† Assumes a life expectancy of 18.2 years at age 65.

Clearly, the retiree who has paid into an IRA is far from rich. While the funds provided should represent an attractive component of a retirement plan, they alone are not sufficient to meet retirement needs. In planning for retirement, the individual still will have to rely on Social Security, on an employer-sponsored pension and profit-sharing plan (including SEPs), and other savings. Those who are lulled by the suggestion an IRA alone can make them rich may be bitterly disappointed by their purchasing power after retirement.

CHAPTER 38

Tax-Deferred Annuities

MARK R. GREENE

Tax-deferred annuities (TDAs) are annuities available to certain eligible groups of employees on such a basis that they provide special exemptions from current federal and usually state income taxes. TDAs offer a way to create or supplement retirement income on a basis whereby taxes on current savings by the employee (or by the employer on behalf of the employee) are deferred until such time as the annuity begins, presumably at retirement. TDAs had their origin in the 1942 tax code, which provided that charitable organizations could make contributions to an annuity for their employees without having the employee pay current income tax on the benefits. The 1958 revisions in the federal income-tax code (Section 403(b)) refined the provisions for these annuities and established a 20 percent limitation on the amounts that could be used for this purpose. TDAs frequently are referred to as "403(b)" annuities, although subsequent legislation in 1974 under the Employee Retirement Income Security Act (ERISA) made further changes so that, strictly speaking, the distributions from a 403(b) account need not be in the form of a life annuity, but may be in a lump sum or in installments of any size or duration.

HOW TDAs WORK

A typical procedure in establishing a TDA program is as follows: The eligible employer wishing to authorize a TDA program draws up an agreement with participating employees to reduce the employee's salary by the amount the employee wishes to contribute, subject to specified limits. (The employer also can make a contribution without a corresponding salary reduction.) The employer actually makes the purchase of the TDA through payroll deduction on behalf of the employee, who becomes the legal owner. The employee can name the beneficiary in case of death. The employer does not report the contribution to the U.S. Internal Revenue Service (IRS) and does not withhold taxes; the employee does not show the amount of the salary reduction as income for current federal income or Social Security tax purposes. Only when funds are distributed are they subject to federal income taxation.

The TDA is purchased from a custodian, such as a life insurer or a mutual fund authorized to set up TDA accounts. The most common investment media include fixed annuities, variable annuities, and mutual funds.

Requirements

Tax-deferred annuities must meet certain requirements:

1. The employee must be "eligible" and work for an eligible employer (see below).
2. The annuity must be nonforfeitable and be purchased by the employer.
3. The premium must not exceed certain limits (see below).
4. There may not be more than one salary reduction agreement per year (Reg. 1.403(b)-1(b)(3)).
5. The TDA must be "nontransferable." This means that the owner may not sell, assign, discount, or pledge it as collateral for a loan.
6. If the employee has more than one employer, a separate exclusion allowance is calculated for each employer.

Eligible Organizations

In general, organizations that are eligible include those mentioned in IRS Code 501(c)(3) or in a public school system. Eligible groups are those employees of religious, charitable, educational, scientific, and literary organizations, which are all chartered on a nonprofit basis. One must be an employee of such a group, not an independent contractor (Rev. Ruling 70-136 CB 1970-1, 12 and 73-607). Part-time employees are eligible, but the maximum allowable contribution is reduced in proportion to the time worked. A state, county, or city itself is not eligible; so, for example, a hospital operated directly by a city or county cannot qualify (Rev. Rul. 60-384), although a state university may qualify, as do public schools.

Advantages of Tax-Sheltered Savings

It generally is appreciated that saving under a program exempt from current income taxation can be advantageous to the saver. The extent to which more wealth may be accumulated under a tax shelter than with a taxable investment is greater than commonly realized. A major benefit of tax shelter is the interest earned on funds that would otherwise be payable in federal income taxes and state income taxes over a long period of years. In the example shown in Table 38-1, not only is the current amount saved exempt from income taxes but the interest and other investment returns on

Table 38-1
Illustrative Results of a Tax-Sheltered Savings Program versus a Program Subject
to Current Taxation

Assumptions:	Marginal tax rate	40%
	Average annual interest return, after management fees	8%
	Period of savings	20 years
	No current sales loading	

		Plan 1 (without tax shelter)	Plan 2 (with tax shelter)
(1)	Annual savings, before taxes	$ 1,000	$ 1,000
(2)	Current taxes	400	0
(3)	Available for savings	600	1,000
(4)	*(a)* Accumulation of $1 a year for 20 years at 8%	—	45.76
	(b) Accumulation* of $1 at 4.8%	32.38	—
(5)	Value of accumulation (3)×(4)	$19,428	$45,760
(6)	Ratio of retirement fund under Plan 2 to that of Plan 1	2.36	

* After taxes of 40 percent, an 8 percent yield is reduced to 4.8 percent.

this saving also are exempt until the time received. The example assumes a combined federal and state tax bracket of 40 percent[1] that would otherwise be levied on a savings program of $1,000 a year. It also is assumed that long-term interest return of 8 percent is achievable each year. As of 1982, 8 percent was a conservative figure to use as an estimate of an average available investment return over a period of years.

In reviewing Table 38-1, if one saves $1,000 a year for 20 years under tax shelter, the retirement fund is 2.36 times what would be available under an investment program fully taxable during the accumulation period. Even if the individual is in a higher tax bracket after retirement than before, the larger retirement income will make it extremely advantageous to have saved under tax shelter. In most cases, however, the taxpayer will be in a lower bracket after retirement than before. This is because much retirement income currently is exempt from income tax, such as Social Security income, and double personal exemptions are available after age 65. Other sources of income may cease, such as from employment, putting the individual in a lower tax bracket.

Conditions for Successful Use of TDAs

There are six conditions that should be considered if the TDA is to be used successfully. These are:

_____

[1] In 1980, a joint return showing over $29,900 of taxable income was taxed at 37 percent for federal taxes. In most states, state income tax of another 6 percent or higher would also be applied, bringing combined tax rates to over 40 percent in most areas.

1. The income tax bracket of the investor following retirement will be such that total taxes paid on the TDA will not be more than would have been the case had income taxes been paid on the funds saved during the accumulation period. As demonstrated by Table 38-1, the investor's tax bracket actually can be higher after retirement than before, and a benefit will still accrue because of the compounding of interest on the "tax-free loan" by the government of current income taxes that would otherwise have been due during the accumulation period.

For example, if the investor purchases a straight life annuity with the accumulation funds shown in Table 38-1, a monthly life income of approximately $175 might be obtained, of which about $148 could be received tax-free under the "annuity rule" of the IRS under Plan 1. A fully taxable $412 would be received under Plan 2.[2] Thus, if the investor's income is taxed less than 64 percent after retirement, the net income after income taxes in retirement would be greater under Plan 2 than under Plan 1. In 1982, the maximum income tax bracket was 50 percent. Thus, most individuals correctly assume they will gain a tax advantage by delaying the imposition of income taxes on funds earmarked for savings.

2. It is assumed that capital losses will not be incurred in the TDA media, and that total investment return will be as high or higher than would be the case in taxable media. Inasmuch as media used for both taxable and tax deferred savings plans are usually similar, this assumption is justified in most cases.

3. It is assumed that, in emergencies, permission can be received to withdraw funds set aside in TDAs, if necessary, before retirement age or age 59½, and that income taxes or any withdrawal charges or penalties which must be paid upon such withdrawals are not so high as to destroy the advantages of tax deferral up to that point. Ordinarily, funds invested in TDAs are available to the employer before reaching age 59½, in cases of financial hardship or in case of separation from the employer's service. Income taxes due upon such withdrawal can be minimized in some cases by using the five-year averaging rule which may be appropriate when the employee wishes to avoid a high income tax levied because a TDA payout has put the employee into an unusually high tax bracket in a single year.

4. It is assumed that the TDA will be sufficiently liquid to allow withdrawal of the funds, if necessary, as discussed in condition 3, above.

5. It is assumed that loading and management fees charged on TDAs

---

[2] Assumes an annuity paying monthly life income of $9 for each $1000 of available funds, for male age 65. Under the "annuity rule," that portion of an annuity representing return of principal (the taxpayer's cost) on which income taxes have been previously paid may be excluded from annuity income. The exclusion ratio is *Taxpayer's cost: Expected return*. In the current example, using 15 years as a life expectancy, the exclusion ratio would be:

$$\frac{19,428}{\$175 \times 12 \times 15} = \frac{19,428}{\$31,500} = 61.7\%$$

Thus, .617 × 175, or $108, may be received tax-free, and $67 is taxed. Assuming a 40 percent tax bracket, taxes amount to $27, leaving $148 as spendable income.

will not be so high as to destroy the economic advantages of the TDA compared to other investments (see discussion below).

6. It is assumed that savings made in TDAs will be regular and systematic, so as to gain the advantages of dollar cost averaging over a specified time.

Loading and Expense Charges

Costs of acquiring TDAs, and continuing expenses of maintaining them, should not be ignored in the decision to utilize TDAs. Two general types of charges are made: sales charges, or loading charges, applicable to each deposit made to purchase a TDA; and overhead or continuing fees levied on the assets comprising the TDA fund each year. For convenience, the first charge may be termed a *deposit charge* and the second an *asset charge*.

Deposit Charges. Sales charges for acquiring TDAs depend on the type of media utilized. Not all media make explicit charges for sales commissions, since in some cases, the issuers of TDAs do not employ sales personnel, preferring instead to distribute their products by other means. Any marketing expense is absorbed by the particular medium as a part of general management expense. When sales charges are made, the amount usually ranges from 3 percent to 8 percent of the deposits made, although in some cases a TDA funded by an individually sold life insurance contract or endowment may carry a sales commission amounting to 50 percent or more of the first year's premium. In cases where mutual funds are utilized for funding TDAs, the loading is either zero for "no-load" funds or 8.5 percent, graded downward as the size of the deposit or the size of the accumulating fund increases for "load" funds. Thus, if the saver deposits $100, a sales commission of say $8 may be deducted first, and $92 is the actual amount invested in the TDA fund.

Asset Charges. Asset charges are levied to cover the continuing expenses of managing the TDA account. The size of these charges varies from about 0.5 percent to 1.5 percent of assets each year, although they may exceed this amount in some cases. Asset charges are earmarked for three general purposes: general overhead, investment advisory service, and mortality or annuity guarantees. Investment advisory fees cover the costs of buying and selling securities in a managed portfolio comprising the fund in which the TDA accounts are invested. The mortality charge is for guaranteeing that future annuity rates will not exceed a given level, and that, in case of death, at least the minimum amount invested will be returned to the estate of the owner, even if the amount in the owner's account is less than the total invested, a situation which might occur if the TDA is invested in common stocks that have gone down in value subsequent to the time the deposits were made.

A typical breakdown for these types of charges might be 0.15 percent for general overhead and administration, 0.85 percent for annuity or mortality guarantees, and 0.5 percent for investment advisory services.

Not all types of TDAs contain annuity or mortality guarantees. For example, TDAs funded by mutual funds offer no such guarantees and make charges only for general management and investment advisory fees. TDAs issued by life insurers contain annuity or mortality guarantees.

Importance of deposit and asset charges. Loading and expense charges can amount to a sizeable sum, particularly over a period of years. For example, consider a case in which the saver in a TDA variable annuity is putting aside $100 a month on which a 6 percent deposit and a 1 percent asset charge are being made. First, consider the relative cost of the 6 percent loading. Assume that the interest return credited to the TDA is 7 percent annually. The TDA value stemming from the initial deposit will be $100.58 at the end of the first year: $(100 - \$6)1.07 = \$100.58$. At the end of the second year, the $100.58 will have grown to $107.62: $(100.58)1.07 = 107.62$. At the end of the third year, the $107.62 will have grown to $115.15, and so on. By the 10th year, the account value will have grown to $184.91, and by the 20th year to $363.74. The initial charge of $6 represents only about 3.2 percent of the savings fund of the 10th year and only 1.6 percent of the fund as of the 20th year. The longer one keeps the TDA, the lower the relative size of the deposit charge when compared to the original investment.

The asset charge made by TDA media is a much more significant item than the deposit charge. This is so because the percentage figure applied to the savings fund is cumulative in nature. For example, assume $100 is saved, to which a 1 percent asset charge is applied to cover the costs of investment service, administration, and annuity rate and mortality guarantees. Table 38–2 shows what these charges amount to:

Table 38–2
Asset Charges on TDAs

Year	Cumulative Value of $100 at 7 Percent	Asset Charge of 1 Percent
1	$107.00	$ 1.07
2	114.49	1.14
3	122.50	1.22
4	131.08	1.31
5	140.26	1.40
6	150.07	1.50
7	160.58	1.60
8	171.82	1.72
9	183.85	1.84
10	196.72	1.97
		$14.77

Total, as a percent
of original $100 = 14.77%
Percent of 10-year
value   = 7.51%

Note that the cumulative sum of all the asset charges for continuing expenses amounts to nearly 15 percent of the original amount saved, compared to 6 percent typically charged for the deposit charge. Thus, even a modest-appearing asset charge may amount to over 2½ times the initial typical deposit charge after 10 years.

Comparing charges. Frequently, the question is asked, "Don't all media charge about the same fees for TDAs?" The answer is, "Decidedly not." In one comparison of 26 insurers, a wide range of charges was discovered.[3] A way to compare the effect of the differences in charges may be described as follows:

Step 1. Calculate how much one would have in a simple savings account at some assumed rate of interest, say 7 percent, by saving $100 a month for periods up to 20 years.

Step 2. Calculate how much one would have in the account balance of a given TDA applying the insurer's stated deposit charges and asset charges, under the assumption that an identical amount, $100, is invested in the TDA for identical periods.

Step 3. Subtract the amount obtained in Step 2 from the amount obtained in Step 1. The difference represents the cost of dealing with the insurance company as compared to dealing with a medium not making explicit deposit or asset charges.

Step 4. Calculate the ratio of the amount determined in Step 3 by the amount determined in Step 2. This may be called the administrative cost ratio (ACR). The ACR can be expressed as a percentage. It reveals what it costs, as a percentage of one's TDA account balance, to deal with an insurer. One is then in a position to compare the "administrative costs," as defined, among several insurers.

To illustrate the above steps, assume that one saves $100 in a savings institution at 7 percent interest compounded annually. The account balance at the end of one year is $107 (Step 1). If one purchased a TDA from an insurer with a 6 percent deposit charge and a 1 percent asset charge, the account balance at the end of one year would be approximately $99.57, if the insurer also credits 7 percent to the account (Step 2). The difference between these amounts is $7.43 (Step 3). The $7.43 represents the cost of dealing with the insurer, when compared to the savings institution. The administrative cost ratio would be calculated at $7.43/$99.57, or about 7.46 percent.

The above method is illustrated as it applies to an actual case in Table 38–3. After this first year, the ACR is 6.1 percent, but it rises steadily to 24.7 percent after 20 years. In dollars, the total administrative charge amounted to $5,765.69 after 20 years, which was comprised of $1,200 in deposit charges and $4,565.96 in asset charges. Asset charges were 3.8

---

[3] Mark R. Greene and Paul Copeland, "Factors in Selecting Tax Sheltered Annuities," *CLU Journal,* October 1975, pp. 34–46.

Table 38-3
Calculation of Administrative Cost Ratio for a Variable Annuity

| Year | (1) Cumulative Deposit | (2) Compound Deposit[1] | (3) Deposit Charge[2] Cumulative | Asset Charge[3] | | | (7) Total Charges Cumulative | (8) Account Balance | (9) Administrative Cost Ratio[4] |
				(4) Admin. Charge Cumulative	(5) Guaranty Cumulative	(6) Advisory Cumulative			
1	$ 1,200	$ 1,239.72	$ 60	$ .94	$ 5.32	$ 2.76	$ 69.02	$ 1,168.51	.061
2	2,400	2,555.91	120	3.67	20.79	10.76	155.22	2,391.34	.069
3	3,600	3,953.28	180	8.27	46.87	24.26	259.40	3,671.02	.077
4	4,800	5,436.83	240	14.83	84.05	43.51	382.39	5,010.20	.085
5	6,000	7,011.89	300	23.45	132.85	68.77	525.08	6,411.63	.094
6	7,200	8,684.09	360	34.21	192.83	100.34	688.38	7,878.22	.102
7	8,400	10,459.43	420	47.21	267.54	138.49	873.24	9,412.98	.111
8	9,600	12,344.27	480	62.57	354.56	183.54	1,080.67	11,019.10	.120
9	10,800	14,345.36	540	80.39	455.52	235.80	1,311.71	12,699.89	.130
10	12,000	16,469.87	600	100.78	571.08	295.62	1,567.47	14,458.82	.139
11	13,200	18,725.42	660	123.86	701.90	363.33	1,849.10	16,299.52	.149
12	14,400	21,120.09	720	149.77	848.69	439.32	2,157.79	18,225.80	.159
13	15,600	23,662.46	780	178.63	1,012.21	523.97	2,494.80	20,241.63	.169
14	16,800	26,361.13	840	210.57	1,193.22	617.67	2,861.46	22,351.17	.179
15	18,000	29,227.28	900	245.74	1,392.54	720.85	3,259.13	24,558.79	.190
16	19,200	32,269.68	960	284.30	1,611.03	833.94	3,689.27	26,869.04	.201
17	20,400	35,499.73	1,020	326.39	1,849.56	957.42	4,153.38	29,286.69	.212
18	21,600	38,929.00	1,080	372.19	2,109.08	1,091.76	4,653.03	31,816.74	.224
19	22,800	45,569.78	1,140	421.86	2,390.56	1,237.47	5,189.89	34,464.42	.235
20	24,000	46,435.11	1,200	475.59	2,695.02	1,395.07	5,765.69	37,235.18	.247

[1] Compounded at the rate of 6 percent monthly, without charges.
[2] Equal to 5 percent of each deposit.
[3] Equal to 0.15, 0.85, and 0.44 percent, respectively, of the account balance applied monthly.
[4] Col 2 minus Col 8 divided by Col 8.

times the deposit charges, in this example. Note, if the saver had saved $100 monthly in an alternative income-tax-free plan, the accumulated sum of $46,735.11 (col. 2) would have been in the account balance, compared to $37,235.18 (col. 8) in the variable annuity plan.

How did the 26 insurers compare when the above four steps were applied to each company's TDA contracts, using amounts stated in the prospectus to represent deposit and asset charges? The following were the ranges of charges. Over a 10-year period: 11.1 percent to 28.1 percent. Over a 20-year period: 13.2 percent to 45.7 percent. These findings mean that for the highest cost insurer, over a 20-year period, the saver would have paid an amount for administration and other costs equal to 45.7 percent of the actual account balance in the TDA. The lowest cost insurer, over the same period, would have charged only 13.2 percent. Stated another way, the ACR represents a sum that could have been credited to the saver's account over 20 years in a bank or a savings and loan association had the saver not wanted to pay for the various services of the insurance company in connection with the TDA policy. Essentially, most insurers offer the same package of services, but the fees charged vary greatly.

In terms of dollars, the study results showed that, for the insurer with the lowest administrative cost ratio, the saver would have had an account balance of $41,031 at the end of 20 years. For the insurer with the highest administrative cost ratio, the saver's account balance would have been only $31,865, a difference of nearly $10,000. The difference is truly significant, particularly when one is receiving about the same package of services from these insurers.

Now, how can the average buyer of a TDA use these findings to make more effective purchases of a TDA? It usually is not practical for the buyer to repeat the study outlined above personally. However, the buyer armed with the above analytical findings can compare three or four TDA contracts. The buyer can ask many pertinent questions of each salesperson about the various costs of the TDA under consideration. The buyer can obtain some guidance in the matter from the following short table.

Annual Asset Charge*	Approximate 20-year Administrative Cost Ratio Associated with Asset Charge (assuming 6% interest compounded monthly)
0.5%	11.6%
1.0	21.8
1.5	30.3

* The numbers are rounded off from actual results of the author's study conducted in 1975, cited above.

By examining the above guidelines, one can make a better and more easily understood estimate of the importance of the costs charged by insurers for both deposit and asset charges. If the prospectus says there is an asset charge of 0.5 percent, for example, one knows that, over a 20-year period, the dollars in the savings fund will be reduced by about 11.6 percent by the insurer's fees. If the asset charge is 1.0 percent, the savings fund will be reduced by about 21.8 percent by these fees, and so on. In terms of dollars, the fees are approximately as follows, when applied to a savings program of $100 monthly for 20 years:

Annual Asset Charge	Dollars Saved at 6% without Insurer Fees	Approximate TDA Account Balance	Difference
0.5%	$46,435	$41,598	$ 4,837
1.0	46,435	38,109	8,326
1.5	46,435	35,630	10,805

Thus, if the insurer makes an asset charge of 1 percent, over a 20-year period the saver will be paying about $8,326 for insurer services in addition to deposit charges above what would be paid if one saved the same amount in a savings and loan association or a bank at 6 percent compound interest.

MEDIA FOR FUNDING TDAs

In general, three types of funding media are employed for TDAs: fixed and variable annuity contracts, and mutual fund shares. Only life insurers issue fixed and variable annuities; mutual fund shares are sold by investment companies, by life insurers affiliated with mutual funds, and by investment brokerage firms affiliated both with life insurers and investment companies. Life insurers, through "separate accounts," also offer TDAs invested in a diversified portfolio of common stocks, an arrangement very similar to a mutual fund, except that the separate account is controlled by the life insurer.

Insurer-Controlled Mutual Funds

At the end of 1979, 81 insurers or insurer groups had affiliation with 302 investment companies of one type or another. Assets controlled represented 21.7 percent of the total assets of all open-end investment companies. In addition, "separate accounts" of insurers contained another 2 percent or 3 percent of the assets. Some 64 insurers had directly organized 172 investment companies, mostly after 1957. The remainder were either acquired by insurers or were affiliated with them.[4]

---

[4] *Wiesenberger Investment Companies Service,* 1980 ed. (New York: Wiesenberger Financial Service, 1980), p. 520.

Fixed-Dollar Annuities

Fixed-dollar annuities provide participants with lifetime annuity payments, guaranteed in dollar amount. Contributions applied to fixed annuities accumulate at a guaranteed minimum rate of interest (usually 3.5 percent) with the possibility of higher actual rates being applied. At retirement, annuity payments are guaranteed each month for life, and each payment is a guaranteed fixed-dollar amount. The contract can be surrendered for its cash-surrender value at any time before the annuity begins. Funds are invested mainly in "fixed-dollar" securities, such as bonds, mortgages, and other investments permitted for life insurers under state law.

Variable Annuities

Variable annuities provide participants with lifetime annuity payments, the amounts of which are designed to reflect changes in the cost of living. Variable annuities were first offered in 1950 by the College Retirement Equities Fund (CREF).[5] Contributions applied to variable annuities are invested principally in a broad spectrum of carefully selected common stocks, in units similar to shares in a mutual fund. Following retirement, annuity payments will be made during the life of the participant; the amount of the payments, however, will vary with the investment performance of the fund. The principal investment objective is to maintain growth of capital sufficient to offset any decline in value of the dollar. Like the fixed annuity, the variable annuity (except for CREF) may be "cashed in" before retirement, subject to specific conditions discussed later.

Variable versus Fixed Annuities

Variable annuities may be contrasted with fixed annuities in the following way: in fixed annuities, the retiree receives a guaranteed retirement income for life in dollars, the value of which is expected to fluctuate with the changing value of the dollar. Most economists expect the value of the dollar to decline, in the long run, because of inflation. In variable annuities, however, the retiree receives a guaranteed number of annuity units for life (similar to mutual fund shares) the value of which will fluctuate according to the plan's underlying portfolio of investments. Most studies reveal a long-run correspondence between consumer prices and stock market prices, but the correlation is not perfect and there may be periods of several years (e.g., the 1970s) in which stock market prices and consumer prices move in opposite directions. Nevertheless, the conceptual framework of variable annuities is based on the assumption that whatever risk is taken by the annuitant will be rewarded by longer-term gains and by protection against

---

[5] The College Retirement Equities Fund is a companion organization to the Teachers Insurance and Annuity Association (TIAA), a life insurer organized to serve college personnel.

an ever-declining value of a fixed number of dollars, which characterize a fixed annuity.

In both fixed and variable annuities, the retiree is given some retirement income for life. Thus, even if the retiree outlives the normal life expectancy by many years, an income will be assured. Thus, these instruments protect the retiree from the longevity risk (i.e., the risk of outliving a retirement income).

It is sometimes stated that in variable annuities the retiree takes the investment risk, while in fixed annuities the insurer takes the investment risk. While it is true that with fixed annuities the retiree is guaranteed a fixed number of dollars, there is no assurance that these dollars will have sufficient purchasing power over a period of years. For example, an income of $10,000 annually for a male age 65 will decline over a 15-year normal longevity to about $2,400 in real purchasing power if the inflation rate is a constant 10 percent. Thus, the retiree must accept financial risk whether depending either on a fixed or variable annuity. One might even argue the risk is greater with a fixed annuity, since it is likely that inflation will continue to cause a certain loss to the fixed annuity recipient.

Mutual Funds

Many mutual funds have qualified as vehicles for Sec. 403(b) savings plans under which the TDA is issued. The saver simply designates a fund that is qualified for such a plan to be the media to receive the TDA contributions. The funds are accumulated in the mutual fund under tax shelter, and may be distributed either as a lump sum or in fixed installments, depending on the wishes of the retiree. If funds are kept in the mutual fund shares, no charges usually are made to cover mortality or annuity rate guarantees, inasmuch as there are no such guarantees as long as funds are kept in the mutual fund itself.

A mutual fund may have an arrangement with a life insurer, under which the funds also may be employed to purchase either a fixed or variable annuity at or before retirement. If funds are invested by the life insurer in a separate account, the arrangement essentially is that of a variable annuity, discussed above.

One advantage of utilizing mutual funds as investment vehicles for TDAs is the investment flexibility many of these plans afford to the saver. The mutual fund management arrangement may offer the saver a choice of several funds from which to choose during the accumulation period. The saver may switch investments among these funds, according to current economic conditions, without charge and without undue delay. For example, if the saver wishes to take advantage of currently high interest rates, the money could be switched into a "money market" fund. If the saver believes the stock market will rise, the money could be moved into a fund invested in the type of stock portfolio that is expected to rise in the future. In such arrangements, the saver bears all the investment risk. Investments may be allocated among several of the available funds at one time, subject only to a stated minimum dollar amount, such as $500, which can be transferred at any one time.

Load versus No-Load Funds. The TDA investor may choose between mutual funds which charge a "loading," usually between 3 percent and 8.5 percent of the amount deposited, and a "no-load," in which there is no deposit charge or other sales charge due when funds are invested. From some perspectives, a typical investor should prefer, other things being equal, a no-load mutual fund for long-term investment purposes. Unless the investor believes the investment potential of a load fund is superior to the potential of a no-load fund, the investor would prefer the no-load fund because in this way the full unreduced deposit will "go to work" for the investor. Various studies have been made of the relative performance of load versus no-load funds and, in general, little difference in average performance over a period of years has been observed. In any event, it is obvious that if a mutual fund has a similar portfolio of investments, the net investment performance for the investor will be superior in a no-load fund than in a load fund.

Group versus Individual Contracts. Some TDAs are issued only through master group contracts in a manner similar to the issuance of group life insurance to employees of a common employer. Other TDAs are sold individually on an individual contract basis and purchased through payroll deduction facilities of the employer. Although the technical arrangements for issuing both group and individual TDAs are similar, their contracts may differ somewhat in their terms and in the loading fees applicable. In general, group contracts are more favorable to the investor than individual contracts.

Investment Annuities. If the employee wishes to control the type of investment made, an investment annuity may be used, which gives the employee this power. Under this arrangement, the employee can select mutual funds, stocks, bonds, mortgages, or even savings accounts. However, the IRS has ruled that after March 9, 1977, all income earned on such annuities will be taxed to the policyholder in the year such income is received by the custodian. Investment annuities set up before this date are not affected by the IRS ruling (Rev. Rul. 77-85, IRB 1977-15) if no further contributions are made. It would appear that these annuities are no longer viable because of the adverse tax ruling.

LIFE INSURANCE

A life insurance element may be included in a TDA so long as the protection is "incidental" (i.e., if the amount does not exceed 100 times the monthly retirement benefit or cash accumulation), (Reg. 1.403(b)-(c)(3). However, the contract must not cover the employee's family or it will be disqualified (Rev. Rul. 69-146). If life insurance is included, its pure insurance value is subject to current taxation.

The Treasury has ruled that a modified endowment policy, which contained an annuity rider in which life insurance was incidental, could be considered an annuity contract for purposes of a TDA. A disability waiver-of-premium provision, or a disability income provision, are considered incidental insurance and subject to tax in the employee's gross income—it may not be excluded for purposes of a TDA.

MAXIMUM CONTRIBUTION LIMIT

Congress has placed certain maximum limits on contributions to TDAs. In general, the annual limit is 20 percent of "includible" compensation, which is defined as compensation left over after deducting the TDA contribution and other contributions to employer-paid, tax-deferred pension programs in all prior years. Thus, a new employee with a gross salary of $12,000 could contribute as much as $2,000 to a TDA if the employer had made no other tax-deferred contribution. In this case, includible compensation would be $10,000 ($12,000 − $2000). The $2,000 represents 20 per cent of includible compensation.

If the employer is also contributing (say $500 a year) to a tax-deferred pension plan on behalf of the new employee, this contribution must be taken into account in establishing the maximum TDA contribution of the employee. In the above case, the allowable TDA contribution by the employee would be reduced to $1,500 ($2,000 − 500 = $1,500).

Prior years of service with an employer and prior years of contributions by an employer to a tax-deferred pension plan must be considered in calculating the maximum TDA limit. Another consideration is a 1974 provision of the Employee Retirement Income Security Act (ERISA). Under ERISA, the limits are 25 percent of annual compensation after the reduction, or $25,000 (adjustable for changes in the cost of living after 1974—in 1982 the limit had reached $45,475). However, because of the enactment of the Tax Equity and Fiscal Responsibility Act of 1982 (TEFRA), the overall limit was changed to a maximum of $30,000. To illustrate, assume employee A has been with a current employer for five years. A's current salary is $14,000 a year, and the employer has been contributing $500 a year in a tax-qualified employer pension plan. For the current year, A wishes to start contributing $1,500 a year toward a TDA. Does this fall within the allowable limits? Yes. The calculations are:

1. Take 20 percent of estimated "includible" compensation:
$$(\$13,500 - 1,500) = \$2,400$$

2. Multiply the results in Step 1 by the number of years of prior service:
$$(\$2,400 \times 5) = \$12,000$$

3. Determine prior employer's contribution on behalf of A:

$$(\$500 \times 5) = \$2,500$$

4. Subtract (3) from (2):

$$(\$12,000 - \$2,500) = \$9,500$$

This is the final includible compensation.

5. Take 20 percent of Step 4:

$$(\$9,500 \times .20) = \$1,900$$

Since the $1,500 that employee A is contributing does not exceed Step 5, nor does it exceed (25 percent of $12,500 = $3,125), the ERISA limit, the full salary reduction exempt from taxation would be permitted.

EFFECT OF ERISA

Limits Imposed by ERISA

In addition to the exclusion allowance limitation discussed above, there are three "catch-up" exceptions to the limitation on contributions applicable to TDAs. These provisions permit greater than normal exclusions to allow eligible persons to make up for past years in which no contribution or small contributions were made, even though they could have been made under the law. The exceptions apply only to employees of hospitals, educational institutions, and home health service agencies (IRC Code Par. 415(C)(4)). Only one of the three catch-up exceptions may be elected in a given year, and the election is irrevocable for that year. Once an election is made, no alternative election may be made for any other limitation or taxable year.

First Catch-Up Exception. The first exception, which may be used only once, is that an employee may contribute an amount equal to *the smaller* of the following: *(a)* amounts that normally would have been contributed, but were not during the previous 10 years of service ending on the date of separation from service, or *(b)* $30,000 (TEFRA limitation) as of 1982 (this number is subject to adjustment for consumer price index changes). Under this catch-up provision, the employee would be permitted to contribute everything that he or she could have contributed under the normal exclusion allowance, times 10, but not to exceed $30,000.

Second Catch-Up Exception. Instead of the first exception, an employee could elect to use the following rule. Contribute in a given year the smaller of the following: (1) the exclusion allowance as calculated above, or (2) 25 percent of the includible compensation plus $4,000, or (3) $15,000. This catch-up exception may be employed during any one or more of the employee's taxable years. The defined contribution limit of $30,000 is not applicable, since obviously the maximum amount that can be contributed under this exception is $15,000.

Third Catch-Up Exception. Instead of the previous two exceptions, the employee simply elects to apply the regular defined contribution limit. This means that, in each year, the employee could elect to contribute the smaller of $30,000 (TEFRA limit) or 25 percent of his compensation in lieu of the regular exclusion allowance.

Procedure to Utilize. In utilizing one or more of the various catch-up rules, the employee need only file a statement of intention with the Internal Revenue Service. Intention could show the particular designation of which catch-up provision is being used, the year when it is being used, and the name and address and Social Security number of the employee. There is no special form for this purpose. Regulations provide that the catch-up exceptions may be elected starting with years after 1976 (Temporary Regulation Par. 11.415C).

Excludible Amounts under Defined Benefit Plans. When an employee is covered by a defined benefit plan, amounts contributed by the employer to the ultimate pension plan often are unknown to the employee. Thus, the Internal Revenue Code has provided a method by which the value of the employer's contribution may be estimated. This value must be subtracted from the amounts otherwise allowable to the employee in making TDA contributions. Formulas provided by the Internal Revenue Service specify a method to estimate this sum (Par. 1.403(b)-1(d)(4)). Details of this calculation will not be elaborated in this chapter.

Tax Status upon Distribution

An employee with a TDA not only is exempt from current federal income and Social Security taxes on contributions and corresponding investment returns on these contributions, but, in addition, obtains certain tax advantages upon death, disability, or retirement.

When Distributions May Be Taken. Distributions may be taken from a TDA upon death, disability, reaching age 59½, separation from the employer's service, or upon encountering financial hardship.[6] When these conditions are met, the proceeds are taxed according to the rules stated below. Thus, in case of lump-sum withdrawals, no penalty is levied other than that cash is reportable as ordinary income in the year it was received. Capital gains treatment is not available, but the taxpayer may use the rules of income averaging over five years, if desired. The TDA thus enjoys an advantage over Individual Retirement Account (IRA) or Keogh plans, which are subject to penalties for distributions taken prior to age 59½.

---

[6] This rule applies after December 31, 1978 (P.L. 95-600, Par. 154, IRC Code 413(b)(7)).

Taxation of Annuities. TDA income received under an insured annuity plan is taxed as ordinary income when received, if the TDA was purchased with funds on which the employee paid no prior tax. To the extent that the employer has contributed to the TDA with income subject to prior tax (such as for the cost of life insurance protection), no second tax is due.

Similarly, in case an annuity is settled as a lump sum, no capital gains tax treatment is available if the TDA has been purchased with funds on which no prior tax has been paid.

Taxation of Investment Company Distribution. If the TDA has been invested in mutual fund shares, the value of these shares is taxed as ordinary income when received. If paid in installments, the funds must be paid out over a period not exceeding the life expectancy of the employee (or joint life expectancy of the employee and spouse) or 30 years, whichever is less (Rev. Rul. 73-239 and 74-325).

Tax-Free Rollovers. Present law permits a tax-free rollover of a lump-sum distribution from an employer-qualified pension plan, from a 403(b) annuity, or a custodial account to another 403(b) TDA plan or to an IRA. Furthermore, a distribution from a 403(b) plan that is rolled over to an IRA may later be rolled over to another 403(b) plan. There is a prohibition, however, against distributing such funds later on, that is, rolling them over to an employer-qualified pension plan, even if it is first transferred to an IRA. Rolling over a TDA into an IRA may give certain investment flexibility that is not possible under a 403(b) plan.

Taxation of Death Benefits. In general, if an employee covered by a TDA dies, the beneficiary has the same income-tax status as the employee had the employee received the proceeds of the TDA as an income during retirement. However, if the TDA has been financed by a retirement income policy or by another type of an insured annuity with a pure life insurance element, that part of the proceeds representing a pure insurance element escapes income taxation to the beneficiary. Only the cash value portion of the payment would be taxed in the manner indicated above. In some cases, a $5,000 exclusion is available to the beneficiary, whether life insurance is involved or not.

Estate Taxation. In general, amounts attributable to employee contributions are subject to estate taxation. Amounts attributable to employer contributions, if any, are not subject to estate taxation. However, an exception to this rule exists for employees of certain "favored" institutions, such as a religious, educational, or charitable organization that comes within the definition of 501(c)(3). In these cases, amounts attributable to employer contributions that were excluded from employee gross income are not subject to federal estate taxation (IRC Par. 2039(c)(3)).

Gift Taxation. In all but favored institutions, such as state universities, irrevocable designation of a beneficiary amounts to a gift, which is subject to gift tax. Employees of favored institutions, however, escape such gift taxes, even if they make an irrevocable gift of their TDA to a beneficiary.

Effect of State Premium Taxes

As of 1981, seven states levied a state premium tax of amounts ranging from 0.5 percent to 2.25 percent on annuity considerations received by insurance companies. The tax may be imposed either at the time of purchase of the contract or at the annuity commencement date, when the fund balance is actually committed to the purchase of the annuity agreement. All states have a premium tax on insurance contracts, but most have eliminated the state premium tax as applied to annuity considerations. Obviously, if the TDA investor resides in a state with such a tax, the advantages of the tax shelter are somewhat reduced. For example, if a saver has accumulated, say, $50,000 in a mutual fund for the purchase of an annuity, and actually purchases this annuity from an insurer, a state premium tax ranging from $250 to $1,250 must be paid by the insurer at the time of purchase, thus reducing the amount available to provide annuity payments.[7] The amount of the annuity reduction would be proportional to the amount of the tax.

The existence of state premium taxes favors the use of mutual funds as TDA media in states where these taxes exist, inasmuch as premium taxes apply only to insurance premiums, not to mutual fund savings.

Comparisons of TDAs in the Marketplace

There are many bases on which the investor in a TDA may make comparisons among agencies offering TDAs. Among the more important selection factors are:

1. Investment returns earned by funding agencies on funds committed to them.
2. Annuity rates offered to the annuitant.
3. Expenses charged for management, mortality and annuity rate guarantees, and for investment advisory services, if any.
4. Flexibility of investment media among agencies—opportunity to move funds from one type of media to another without difficulty or undue expense.
5. Extent and quality of service to the annuitant.

It is obvious that agencies with the greatest investment returns, the lowest expenses, and the largest annuity rates will be in a position to offer the highest annuities to the investor. Reference to the importance of

---

[7] States requiring a tax on 403(b) annuities in 1980 were: Alabama, 1 percent; California, 0.5 percent; District of Columbia, 2 percent; Georgia, 2.25 percent (Georgia's tax is phased out and will no longer exist after 1982); Kentucky, 2 percent; Louisiana, 1.7 percent; and West Virginia, 1 percent.

expenses has been made earlier in this chapter. Studies of variations that occur in investment returns and annuity rates are discussed below. It should be noted that the ability of, and cost to, the investor to move funds from one type of investment to another may be a very important selection factor in the uncertain investment climate that characterizes the economy in any one period. As noted above, the superiority of agencies offering "families" of mutual funds with different investment objectives is apparent when it comes to judging this factor.

The extent and quality of service to the investor is difficult to compare in any quantitative sense, because of the subjective nature of this factor. It is undoubtedly a significant factor, however, because of the complexity of TDAs, the ever-changing nature of the tax regulations, and the need for continuous study of and contact with the investment scene. TDA buyers should consider the number of states in which the agency servicing the TDA is operating, the number and quality of sales or service personnel, and the quality of service available from the research department of the agency. The last factor is important, inasmuch as the knowledge disseminated to sales and service personnel will be only as good or as current as the knowledge produced by those supplying it to these personnel.

Two recent studies of the important factors of annuity rates, interest returns, and annuity rents have been made that will illustrate some of the variations occurring in the marketplace among TDAs.

These studies reveal substantial differences among various agencies offering TDAs in the marketplace. The general conclusion of these studies is that it will be worthwhile for the potential investor in a TDA to make careful comparisons among funding agencies and their products at the time a long-term savings program is started, giving due consideration to the selection factors of greatest concern to the investor.

Rosenbloom Study. Rosenbloom (see Bibliography at end of chapter) studied fixed-dollar TDA offerings among 24 large life insurers in 1976 with regard to annuity rates and benefits (both current rates and guaranteed). Insurers were ranked both for guaranteed benefits and current benefits, according to a composite analysis of the factors. The study also revealed these rankings separately, according to the three selection factors.

Some of the findings of the Rosenbloom study were: (1) insurers ranking high on some factors did not rank as high on others. For example, one insurer ranked first on offering the best annuity rates, but ranked 10th on expenses and 4th on current interest rates. (2) Insurers ranking high for short durations did not always rank as high on longer durations. For example, an insurer ranking second on accumulations of funds produced under current interest rates paid, ranked eighth on 30-year accumulations produced by its interest rate schedule. (3) However, it was fairly easy to pinpoint insurers that ranked fairly low on several of the selection factors and those that ranked fairly high on several selection factors. This finding suggests that the potential TDA investor would find it relatively easy to isolate the best four or five insurers for most of the important selection factors.

The following short table reveals the ranges and averages of three different selection factors for the 24 insurers in the Rosenbloom study:

	Monthly Life Annuity[1]	Annuity Rate[2]	Average Interest Rate[3]
Average	$423.78	$8.36	6.68%
Highest	500.57	9.10	7.78
Lowest	360.96	7.32	5.24
Ratio, highest to lowest	1.39	1.24	1.48

[1] Payable on a 10-year certain basis, male age 65, for a contribution of $100 monthly for 20 years, if the insurer continues to earn current interest rates.

[2] An average over seven years of the fixed-dollar current annuity rates payable to males and females as a monthly life income per $1,000 of cash investment, 10 years certain.

[3] Average current interest rates paid by the insurers over the period 1970–76.

From the above tabulation, it is easy to see that an annuitant would have obtained 39 percent greater monthly life income from the insurer that ranked highest in this factor than from the insurer that ranked lowest. Similarly, an average annuity rate from the highest-ranking insurer was 24 percent greater than from the insurer ranking lowest in this study. Average interest rates available from the top-ranking insurer were 48 percent greater than from the insurer ranking lowest in average interest rates paid.

Greene, Tenney, Neter Study. In a comparison of 42 life insurers and their TDA fixed annuities in 1975, Greene, Tenney, and Neter (see Bibliography at end of chapter) had findings similar to those of Rosenbloom. Wide variations existed concerning annuity rents and rates, both on a guaranteed as well as upon a current basis. Among the major findings were: (1) variability seemed to stem more from variations in investment performance of insurers than from variations in mortality or expense experience. (2) Large insurers generally did not offer, on the average, higher annuity rents than smaller insurers. (3) Stock insurers offered slightly higher rents than mutuals. (4) Insurers offering higher annuity rates also tended to offer above-average investment performance. (5) There was practically no correlation between guaranteed and current annuity rates (i.e., one should not expect an insurer with a high (low) guaranteed annuity rate necessarily to have a high (low) current annuity rate). (6) There appear to be profitable opportunities for "switching" (i.e., saving funds in one insurer with a relatively high current investment return, and then at retirement, switching on a tax-free basis the accumulated funds to an insurer with a relatively high annuity rate). The reason for this is the substantial variation that exists among insurers on annuity rates and investment returns, particularly over longer periods. The charges for withdrawing funds and reinvesting them elsewhere should be considered.

Variations in Mutual Funds. It is well known that large variations also occur in the performance of mutual funds invested in common stocks, particularly over a long period of years. When using these media as a device to fund the TDA plan, the investor should consider the investment objectives and past investment performance of the particular funds that offer 403(b) annuities. Fortunately, several readily available services (Wiesenberger, Standard & Poor's, Moody's, and the like) are available that make continuous comparisons of fund performance. Obviously, it is to the advantage of the saver to select those funds with the best performance and those offering opportunities for switching money among funds with differing investment objectives.

Market Acceptance of TDAs

Aggregate data are not available showing the extent to which TDAs are being utilized in the marketplace. However, a recent study by Mark Dorfman (see Bibliography) provides some evidence on the matter. Three thousand eligible faculty members of 13 different institutions of higher education in Ohio were surveyed, developing 1,753 usable replies—a response rate of 60 percent. It was discovered that about half of the respondents were currently purchasing TDAs. The use of TDAs varied directly with age and income. When nonusers of TDAs were asked reasons for their nonparticipation in the program, dominant reasons given were: "Could earn more on other investments" (31.2 percent), "Saw no tax advantage in program" (27.2 percent), "Program not sufficiently flexible" (22.1 percent), "Do not currently save" (22 percent), "Procrastination" (18.7 percent), and "Insufficient information to make decision" (18.2 percent). For participants in TDA programs, "reduction of current taxable income" was given as the most important reason by 60 percent of the respondents. Another 32.6 percent of the users gave as a reason that it provided an "automatic savings program."

Dorfman's study indicates the advantages of TDAs are not fully appreciated by all, and shows the need for further educational efforts to expand the use of this potentially valuable retirement media.

BIBLIOGRAPHY

Caplin, M. M. "Taxing Tax-Deferred Annuities: A Critique of 1978 Carter Proposal." *Taxes,* June 1978.

Colley, G. M. "Deferred Annuities as Tax Shelters." *CA Magazine: for Professional Accountants and Financial Managers,* October 1978, pp. 90–94.

Conant, Roger R. "Inflation and the Variable Annuity—Revisited." *CLU Journal,* October 1976, pp. 12–18.

Dorfman, Mark. "The Use and Nonuse of Tax Deferred Annuities." Paper given at the 1981 meeting of the Western Risk and Insurance Association, San Diego, Ca.

Greene, M. R., and J. Paul Copeland. "Factors in Selecting Tax-Deferred Annuities." *CLU Journal,* October 1975, pp. 34–46.

————; John Neter; and Lester I. Tenney. "Annuity Rents and Rates—Guaranteed vs. Current." *The Journal of Risk and Insurance,* September 1977, pp. 383–401.

————. "A Note on Loading Charges for Variable Annuities." *The Journal of Risk and Insurance,* September 1973, pp. 474–78.

Healy, Richard C., Jr. "An Economic Analysis of Tax-Sheltered Annuities for Employees of Non-Profit Institutions." *Journal of Insurance Issues and Practices,* January 1981, pp. 43–50.

Morehart, Thomas B., and Gary L. Trennepohl. "Evaluating the Tax-Sheltered Annuity vs. the Taxed Investment." *CLU Journal,* January 1979, pp. 23–31.

Pusker, H. C. "Tax Deferred Annuities since ERISA." *Taxes,* November 1978.

R. & R. Service of America, Inc. "Tax-deferred Annuity Plans," Sec. 17 235 17-253.

Rosenbloom, Jerry S. "Fixed Dollar Tax Deferred Annuities—An Evaluation." *The Journal of Risk and Insurance.* December 1978, pp. 611–33.

Snyder, Bernhart R. "Income Tax Treatment of Variable Annuities." *Trusts and Estates,* August 1973, pp. 582–83.

Stoeber, Edward A. "A Review of Tax Sheltered Annuity Plans." *CLU Journal,* April 1978, pp. 37–52.

Todd, Jerry D. "Reevaluation of Tax-Sheltered Annuity Cost and Performance Measurement Techniques." *The Journal of Risk and Insurance,* December 1978, pp. 575–92.

Wallach, Maximilian. "Variable Annuities: Profits, Loading, and Expenses." *Best's Review,* Life Edition, February 1971, pp. 11+.

Wood, Glenn L. and J. Finley Lee. "Mutual Funds and Variable Annuities: Consumer Purchase Decisions." *The Journal of the American Society of Chartered Life Underwriters,* January 1969, pp. 8–15.

CHAPTER 39

Executive Retirement Benefit Plans

DAVID L. HEWITT

WHY EXECUTIVE RETIREMENT BENEFITS

Special executive retirement benefits often are needed in addition to an organization's broadly based employee retirement plans. Many reasons exist for such arrangements. One is that executives themselves may have special needs. Another is that qualified plans must be nondiscriminatory, and a purpose of executive plans is to discriminate in favor of an executive or group of executives on a practical and economical basis. Also, the basic company plans often have built-in limits which prevent giving equal recognition to the highest pay levels.

The plans for executives are referred to as supplemental retirement plans or as deferred compensation agreements. This chapter reviews the background shared by these plans and then discusses the two types separately.

Special Needs of Executives

Executives, particularly top executives, differ from the remaining workforce of a company. They often have unique abilities and have an impact so great that extraordinary efforts are made to attract them and recognize their achievements. For an officer who joins the company in middle or late career, this may necessitate the promise of full career-equivalent retirement benefits. It also may necessitate the promise of benefits to replace those given up when leaving the prior employer.

For an executive being recruited, or one who is otherwise in a "high-risk" situation, it is often appropriate to provide pension guarantees in case he or she is terminated prematurely. Further, many executive jobs involve such pressure that "burn-out" can be a problem, and it may be mutually advantageous to the company and the individual to make available unreduced retirement benefits at a younger age than can be offered to the entire work force.

The compensation of top executives is high enough so they may seek to postpone the receipt and taxation of a part of current earnings. At the same time, the company may wish to postpone a part of their compensation and make it depend on their meeting stated conditions, such as continued employment, availability to consult after retirement, or noncompetition after retirement. Also, a significant part of an executive's compensation may be geared to the operating success of the company and be payable in addition to salary.

Limits of Basic Plans

The limits on recognizing the earnings of top executives in basic retirement plans include restrictions on: the *types of pay* counted (perhaps base pay only, excluding bonus or incentives); the *amounts of pay* counted; and the contributions or benefits which may be *provided* (including the ERISA limits[1]).

Social Security reflects income only up to the maximum wage base, and its benefit formula is weighted in favor of the lower-paid. As a result, it can provide only a small fraction of an executive's retirement income. Company-wide plans usually are integrated with Social Security to make up part of this difference. However, Social Security benefits are fully indexed for inflation, while plan benefits are only partly adjusted for inflation, if at all, and usually on an occasional ad hoc basis, at best. This means the combined pension from the plan and Social Security has better inflation-proofing for the lower-paid worker than for the top executive, because Social Security represents a higher percentage of the lower-paid worker's total retirement income.

LEGAL, ACCOUNTING, AND RELATED CONSIDERATIONS

The application of federal law to executive retirement plans, as contrasted to qualified plans, has an important impact on their design. These considerations are discussed below.

Prohibitive Conditions for Funding

If an executive retirement plan were formally funded, it would have to satisfy ERISA's benefit and fiduciary requirements—including those concerning reporting, disclosure, vesting, accrual, joint and survivor annuity,

---

[1] IRC Sections 415 and 416 state the ERISA limits on benefits or contributions for individuals under qualified plans. The benefit limit is $90,000 annually and the contribution limit is $30,000 annually, subject to cost-of-living adjustments starting in 1986. When prior accruals exceed the $90,000 limit, the prior accruals apply. There are also combined ceilings for participation in more than one type of plan.

other intricate benefit standards, merger and transfer rules, funding standards, fiduciary rules, prohibited transaction rules, and bonding.[2] But the plan would still not be tax-qualified—unless it was broadened to include nondiscriminatory benefits for rank-and-file employees, in which case it would no longer be an executive plan. The formal funding of executive retirement benefits is rarely a worthwhile option because of the twin burdens of ERISA requirements and nonqualified tax status. Formal funding means placing plan assets beyond the reach of the employer or its creditors, usually by means of a trust. (See the discussion below of the income-tax problems of nonqualified, funded benefits.)

Because executive benefits usually are unfunded, they depend on the future solvency of the company. This is a disadvantage to the executive; at the same time the availability of the assets for corporate uses can be an advantage to the company.

Other ERISA and Tax Law Distinctions

To be exempt from ERISA's benefit and fiduciary rules, an executive retirement plan must be maintained "primarily for . . . a select group of management or highly compensated employees"—as well as being unfunded.[3] It can then discriminate in benefits and coverage to whatever extent is needed to meet its specific objectives.

ERISA, along with its upper limits on qualified plans,[4] also defines a class of nonqualified "excess benefit plans," whose purpose is to pay benefits or contributions above those limits.[5] Excess benefit plans are particular examples of the executive retirement plans discussed in this chapter.

ERISA requires only minimal reporting and disclosure of unfunded executive retirement programs,[6] and none for those which are excess benefit plans.[7] Further, it omits such plans from its termination insurance program and from its federally imposed employer liability upon plan termination.[8]

Normal Taxation and Deductibility of Benefits

Unfunded deferred executive benefits are deducted as business costs by the employer when they are paid to the executive (or assets representing

---

[2] ERISA Title I, "Protection of Employee Benefit Rights," covers all retirement plans except as specifically exempted by Sections 4, 201, 301(a), and 401(a). The exemptions for executive plans are contingent on their unfunded status.

[3] ERISA Sections 201(2), 301(a)(3), and 401(a)(1).

[4] See footnote 1.

[5] ERISA Section 3(36).

[6] Department of Labor Regulations 2520.104-23.

[7] ERISA Section 4(b)(5).

[8] ERISA Section 4021(b)(6).

their value are transferred to his or her unrestricted ownership).[9] This is also true when the executive reports the benefits as income, with the following exception: if he or she is considered to have current access to the benefits, because the deferral is indefinite in duration or is subject to cancellation by him or her without substantial penalty, the benefits can be deemed "constructively received" and taxable at the time he or she first has such access.[10] (This differs from qualified plans, where the availability of unpaid benefits is no longer a taxable event.)

A principal goal of executive retirement planning is to give some assurance that benefits will be paid—often including informal earmarking of assets—but not so much assurance that the executive currently is taxed for the value of the amounts being deferred.

Reasonableness

Executive retirement benefits must represent reasonable rewards for service to be deductible by the employer as business expenses. (This also is true of qualified plans.)[11]

Taxation of Survivor Benefits

The value of survivor benefits under a nonqualified executive retirement plan generally is included in the executive's gross estate for federal tax purposes.[12] (Under qualified plans, on the other hand, there is an exclusion for the first $100,000.[13]) If the beneficiary is the executive's spouse, there is now an unlimited marital deduction regardless of whether the plan is qualified or nonqualified. Also, the sum of gifts and bequests to beneficiaries other than spouses is tax-free up to $275,000 in 1983, growing by annual steps to $600,000 in 1987 and later.[14] Such amounts also are subject to income tax (except to the extent they qualify for any part of the allowable exclusion—up to $5,000 in total—of employer-provided death benefits[15]). The estate tax attributed to survivor benefits is deductible in computing the income tax thereon.[16]

---

[9] Federal Tax Regulations 1.404a-12(b)(2).

[10] Federal Tax Regulations 1.451-2. Revenue Ruling 60-31.

[11] Federal Tax Regulations 1.162-7.

[12] IRC Section 2039.

[13] Tax Equity and Fiscal Responsibility Act of 1982, amending IRC Section 2039.

[14] Economic Recovery Tax Act of 1981, amending IRC Sections 2001, 2010, and 2056.

[15] IRC Section 101(b).

[16] IRC Section 691(c).

Taxation and Deductibility of
Nonqualified Funded Benefits

The income tax problems of a nonqualified, formally funded executive retirement plan have existed for many years. The executive is taxed on the plan's assets as soon as they become either nonforfeitable or transferable, even though *benefits* are deferred. The executive thus can be required to pay taxes on monies to which he or she does not yet have access.[17] The employer deducts its contributions when they become nonforfeitable to the executive, provided a separate account is maintained for each participant. Executive plans are seldom formally funded, because of these problems combined with the ERISA requirements.

The investment earnings of nonqualified trusts are taxable, subject to most of the same rules as apply to individuals.

Increased Accounting and SEC Disclosure

The accounting profession is clarifying its requirements about the recognition of executive retirement obligations in company financial statements. The costs of deferred benefits, net of estimated deferred tax deductions, must be recognized as current expenses over the executive's active employment—and the value of accumulated benefits to date, disclosed—subject to exceptions if the ultimate requirement to pay is uncertain. The same standards apply regardless of whether the benefits are formally funded.[18] The fact that such costs must be recognized as current expenses during the executive's service—even though the payments will not be made until a future time—must be considered at the outset, and can have an impact on the initial decision whether to adopt such a plan at all.

The Securities and Exchange Commission (SEC) also has clarified *its* requirements for disclosure of executive compensation and retirement arrangements. The possibility of obscuring or omitting deferred payment rights in SEC disclosures has largely disappeared.[19]

Aside from disclosure requirements, there appear to be no significant securities law issues in connection with the usual form of unfunded executive retirement benefits. However, unusual investment features, or the presence of employee contributions, could turn an interest in deferred compensation into a security.

---

[17] This derives from the idea of "economic benefit": the value of a deferred right to the assets on hand. IRC Section 83 and the regulations thereunder.

[18] Accounting Principles Board *Opinions Nos. 8* and *12*. Financial Accounting Standards Board (FASB) *Statements Nos. 35* and *36*. FASB Discussion Memorandum, February 19, 1981, on "Employers' Accounting for Pensions and Other Postemployment Benefits."

[19] SEC release December 4, 1978, on "Amendments to Disclosure Forms." SEC release December 3, 1981, on "Staff Interpretation on Management Remuneration Disclosure Requirements."

Shareholder-Employees in Closely Held Corporations

When the executives of a corporation also are its directors and principal shareholders, a deferred compensation agreement with them may lose some of its credibility. If the corporation has the financial ability to pay the deferred amounts currently, the IRS might assert the doctrine of constructive receipt applies. Where deferred compensation arrangements are provided, in addition to basic pay, for the shareholder-employees of a closely held corporation, the question of reasonableness is certain to receive closer IRS scrutiny.

However, situations exist when such a company would be justified in deferring a part of compensation and making it conditional on the long-run performance of the corporation. If the corporation then performed exceedingly well over a period of years, the ultimate payment of the deferred amounts might be justified as a reasonable reward for good management, even if payment of the same amounts on a current basis might have been found to be unreasonable.

Even then, however, the corporation might have interim problems in satisfying the IRS that any reserves being booked for payment of the deferred amounts should not be taxed as accumulated earnings.

Therefore, in a closely held corporation, the deferrals for a major shareholder are more easily handled through share accruals or expansion of ownership (with buy-back agreements if necessary).

TOTAL PLANNING CONTEXT

Executive retirement planning is part of a total picture, which also includes salary, short-term and long-term incentives, and other qualified and nonqualified benefits. These interact, and all should be planned at once to achieve an optimum result.

Therefore, several steps are appropriate in designing the executive retirement plan. First, consider the effects of any existing or contemplated long-term incentive arrangements or capital accumulation arrangements that may incidentally provide for the executive's retirement needs. These include for example, stock options, stock appreciation rights, phantom stock, stock bonuses, performance shares, restricted stock, and cash accumulation plans.

Second, take whatever reasonable steps are available to provide for the needs of the executive within the qualified plan. The tax and funding advantages of a qualified plan should be enjoyed to the maximum extent, within the framework of company policy for employees generally. Such measures include:

1. Recognizing the executive's service and earnings as fully as possible in computing plan benefits—for example, by removing upper limits on credited earnings and counting some or all of current bonus or incentive

payments. The extent to which this meets other objectives of the organization, of course, must be considered. Some organizations may prefer to base retirement income only on salary—and to regard bonuses and incentive payments as extras, on the basis of which executives should make their own provision for added retirement income. This also must coordinate with the organization's policies on the plan's recognition of bonuses, overtime, and the like for employees below the select executive level.

2. Integrating the qualified plan with Social Security to the fullest extent. This permits the plan to focus on the part of pay in excess of the Social Security wage base—to slant its formula in favor of the higher-paid—within allowable limits.

3. Introducing other design features into the qualified plan, which can provide for executive needs. Depending on the company, its population distribution among executives and other employees, and its objectives, such features might include: (a) unreduced retirement after age 60 and 30 years' service; or (b) a benefit formula that gives more than proportional credit for persons hired within, say, 20 years of the normal retirement age; or (c) provisions that permit optimum coordination of executive plan benefits with the qualified plan.

4. Advising or aiding the executive to make maximum use of deductible voluntary contributions (either through an IRA or a qualified plan) up to the limit of $2,000, plus an added $250 to an IRA if the executive has a nonworking spouse. Since such amounts are deductible when contributed, and since the investment earnings are also tax-exempt until drawn out as benefits, they can accumulate to much higher levels than if taxed at the outset and during each year of their income accumulation.

5. Incorporating a cash-or-deferred feature in an existing profit sharing or thrift plan, and structuring it so that executives can make maximum use of the salary reduction option. This allows individual retirement savings on a pretax basis. The percent of compensation which the high-paid may defer is limited by a rule which relates it to the percent which the low-paid actually defer.

SUPPLEMENTAL RETIREMENT PLANS

Supplemental retirement plans usually are adopted for one of the following reasons:

1. To restore to the executive any benefits lost under qualified plans because of maximum provisions.
2. To provide full benefits for short-service executives.
3. To provide more generous benefits for executives than for the rest of the work force.
4. To provide unreduced benefits at an earlier age.

They can cover either broad groups of executives—all above a stated level—or select groups, or specifically designated individuals. Supplemental plans, like qualified plans, take either the defined benefit or the defined contribution form.

Defined Benefit

If the benefit is defined, it may be a flat-dollar amount, an indexed-dollar amount, or a percent of some part of earnings with or without service weighting and with or without indexing. It may be offset by the basic pension plan, by the value of specified incentives, by the value of deferred compensation contracts, by Social Security, or by benefits retained from a previous employer. Payment may be for life or for a specified period.

A typical formula might provide 2 percent of final average earnings per year of service, including credit for predecessor company service, usually to a combined maximum of 25 or 30 years, less basic plan benefits from both the current and former company and primary Social Security. A variation might provide 4 percent per year, to a maximum of 15 years, less company plans. Other companies simply guarantee a stipulated percentage—usually 50 percent to 75 percent—less current and predecessor company benefits. The formula would apply to total compensation.

In addition, such guarantees would either reproduce the company's basic survivorship benefit formula or expand it to an automatic benefit, if it is not already automatic. The ancillary benefits are either similar to those of the company's basic plans or more generous. The plan also may include options to convert from one form of annuity (such as single-life) to another form (such as joint-life) or to earlier or later retirement. The basis of converting from one form of benefit to another may be actuarially equivalent or may be subsidized or penalized by the employer. The plan's obligations following retirement may be unconditional or be conditioned on the executive's meeting requirements for length of service, noncompetition after retirement, or availability to consult after retirement. Conversely, the obligation may be limited specifically to those cases where the executive is dismissed prematurely or becomes disabled. In other words, within the limits of reasonableness, the plan may be designed to meet whatever simple or complex objectives the parties seek.

When the purpose is to provide unreduced benefits at an age lower than the qualified plan's normal retirement age, the employer has the choice of (a) paying a lifetime supplement, which restores the basic plan's early retirement reduction, or (b) paying a temporary full benefit up to normal retirement age and deferring the executive's qualified plan benefit until the normal age. The latter choice may be more desirable—particularly if the deferral period can be deemed to be a leave of absence during which benefit credits accrue—but care should be taken to ensure the qualified plan maintains survivor benefit protection during the deferral.

Defined Contribution

If contributions are to be defined, the first step is to spell out how. They may be related to the individual's earnings, to his or her performance, to the company performance, and so on. They even can be stated-dollar amounts. The so-called contribution cannot be a transfer of assets to an entity insulated from the employer or its creditors. In fact, it is usually represented only by a bookkeeping entry. There is no typical pattern for such defined contribution: each plan is designed to meet its own set of objectives. Frequently, a dollar amount or percent of pay is stipulated.

The second step is to determine a basis of "investment" growth. One approach is to hold specified assets earmarked for the purpose of defining such growth and meeting the benefit obligation when due. Another approach is to make hypothetical investments to determine the growth. An alternative is to define the growth by reference to the employer's earnings, a specified fixed or variable interest rate, or a specified index of investment yield or asset fluctuation, or of wage or living cost fluctuation. Many companies use the prime rate or else the rate available to them for short-term borrowing.

As with defined benefit-type plans, other decisions include the commencement, timing, and duration of payments, the options to be offered, and the conditions for continuing payment. Lifetime payments to the executive or to specified dependents can be arranged by purchase of a life insurance or annuity contract (with the employer as beneficial owner). Unlike a qualified defined contribution plan, lifetime payments also can be offered with the plan (the employer) directly assuming the longevity risk.

A defined contribution arrangement can slide over into the defined benefit area, depending on what added promises are made, and how closely benefits are limited to the specific growth of the agreed "contributions."

Earmarked Assets

Even if assets are held and informally earmarked to provide the source of future benefits, the company receives no deduction for the "contribution." Furthermore, it must pay tax on any investment earnings (unless the investment is tax-exempt). However, if the earmarked assets consist of stock in other companies, 85 percent of the dividend income is exempt from tax[20] and any capital gains are taxed at the lesser of 28 percent or the corporation's regular tax rate.[21]

If an insurance or annuity contract is purchased on the life of the executive to back up the supplemental retirement plan, it must be carried as an asset of the corporation and be payable to the corporation. Premiums

---

[20] IRC Section 243.
[21] IRC Section 1201.

may not be deducted from the corporation's taxable income. However, the investment earnings of the contract are not currently taxable to the corporation (although the insurer may have to pay tax on them, and this may be reflected in the dividends or premiums); nor are policy dividends or death benefits taxable when received by the employer. However, if the policy matures other than by death, is cashed in, or produces annuity payments, the value in excess of the net premiums paid is taxed to the employer as ordinary income.[22]

Generally, if insurance has a place as an earmarked asset, it is for small companies with substantial survivorship promises or other needs for liquidity upon the executive's death. Larger companies, whose cash flow can support substantial payouts, usually can make better use of the assets by keeping them liquid in their own business activities. The inclusion of insurance in a plan may cause the adoption of death and disability benefits during its early years more generous than the corporation would otherwise have offered.

The use of insurance nevertheless is attractive to some companies because of the potential of gain if the executive should die so that tax-sheltered income results. Such companies may purchase even more insurance than needed for the individual's own benefits, in which case any added profit therefrom can offset other costs of the program.

Comparative Merits of Defined Benefit and Defined Contribution Approaches

The relative merits of defined benefits versus defined contributions are not the same for a single executive, a group of executives, or a qualified plan. For a single executive, or several executives having similar age and service characteristics, defined benefits and defined contributions are simply different approaches. The defined benefit may be a more direct way of achieving the goal of retirement security. The defined contribution may be a more appropriate way of gearing the level of retirement security to the events that determine the amount of contribution and the rate of accumulation. The main differences between the two approaches parallel those between *qualified* pension and profit-sharing plans—that is, the risk or reward of investment performance lies with the employer in defined benefit plans, and with the executive in defined contribution plans; and vesting tends to be more rapid under defined contribution plans.

For a group of executives with varied age and service characteristics, there is a further consideration. If the goal is to provide a given level of retirement security, the defined benefit approach may be the more convenient way of achieving it. If the goal is to reward group performance, the defined contribution approach, with contribution levels based on results,

---

[22] IRC Section 72.

may be best. Note, however, the level of contribution needed to produce the same deferred benefits increases dramatically with the age at which it is set aside. Therefore, if the goal is both retirement security and reward for group performance, a more suitable approach may be a defined contribution plan under which the total contribution reflects the business performance of the organization, but the allocation to each individual is actuarially weighted for current age and, perhaps, also adjusted for length of past service.[23]

DEFERRED COMPENSATION AGREEMENTS

A deferred compensation agreement focuses primarily on the aspect of earnings deferral, and secondarily on the aspect of retirement income. The emphasis is more on the idea of an individual arrangement than of a plan perhaps covering more than one executive (although deferral for individuals may be done under the umbrella of a master agreement). While supplemental retirement plans (discussed in the preceding section) provide clear added benefits, a deferred compensation agreement delays specific income and places it in some peril.

Tax Purposes of Deferral

Traditionally, the idea behind deferred compensation agreements was to postpone income and thereby achieve a lower tax bracket. Marginal income-tax rates were steeply graduated in the 1940s to 1960s relative to compensation levels, and interest earnings and inflation had not reached the high rates prevailing in the 1970s and on. It often was desirable for the executive to defer the receipt and taxation of a part of pay until retirement, when his or her total income would be lower, because this would frequently result in significantly lower tax rates.

However, events since the mid-1960s have changed this relationship. Interest earnings and inflation have reached such high levels that any deferral carries with it the problem of making up for inflationary and interest losses. More liberal income averaging for tax purposes[24] and a tax limit of 50 percent on earned income[25] were adopted in 1969. The 50 percent limit was extended in 1976 to include deferrals of more than a

---

[23] Note that such a combined approach is not permitted under a qualified profit-sharing plan (except in the unlikely circumstance that the allocations as a percent of individual earnings will be as favorable to the low-paid as to the high-paid employee). Revenue Ruling 57-77.

[24] Tax Reform Act of 1969 Section 311, amending IRC Sections 1301 and 1302.

[25] Tax Reform Act of 1969 Section 804, adding IRC Section 1348.

year[26] and further extended, starting in 1982, to apply to all income, not just earned income.[27]

Meantime, incomes have grown with inflation, and retirement benefits have increased as a percent of preretirement earnings. The result is that more of the executive's earned income, whether received before or after retirement, reaches the 50 percent tax maximum. From a tax planning viewpoint, therefore, it might be better to take the income when earned, pay the 50 percent tax, and invest the net amount in a way which affords inflation protection.

A different tax planning opportunity may be offered after 1984, when tax rates below 50 percent will be available for increased levels of income if inflation continues.[28] Depending on events, this could restore the idea that the executive will be in a lower tax bracket after retirement, again making deferral worthwhile from a tax standpoint.

Nontax Purposes of Deferral

While tax planning continues to be a prominent consideration, the other objectives for deferral have grown in relative importance. Such goals are: to postpone or spread out the receipt of income beyond the executive's prime working life; to even out the effect of bonuses; to bind the executive to the organization for an extended period, by making receipt of the agreed amounts conditional on loyalty, availability, and the like; or simply to provide retirement income by this means.

Substance of Agreement

Much of the earlier discussion of defined contribution supplemental retirement plans applies equally to deferred compensation agreements. This includes, first, the definition of what compensation will be deferred; and second, the rules determining appreciation and earnings on such sums. There may be circumstances where no provision is made for growth— where the obligation is simply to pay the stated amounts at specified future times. Usually, particularly if the deferral is voluntary, there will be a defined basis of earnings growth. Also applicable are the earlier comments on earmarked assets, and on the choices as to benefit options under supplemental retirement plans.

The degree to which the contract limits the executive's rights to the deferred benefits (making them conditional on his or her availability to

---

[26] Tax Reform Act of 1976 Section 302, amending IRC Section 1348.

[27] Economic Recovery Tax Act of 1981, amending IRC Section 1.

[28] Economic Recovery Tax Act of 1981, amending IRC Section 1.

consult, or on refraining from competition with the company), and the degree to which the employer adds to the executive's rights (through inflation guarantees, commitments to provide added payments to dependents, and so on) are matters of mutual accord between the parties.

Drafting the Agreement

A deferred compensation agreement should be embodied in a written contract, specifically authorized or ratified by the corporation's directors. Drawing it up is a work of infinite care. The document must be drafted to accomplish the various nontax objectives that are being sought, and also to anticipate other pertinent circumstances that may arise—death, sickness, business changes, and so on. At the same time, it should protect the executive from incurring any tax liability until the deferred amounts actually are received. Finally, the agreement should be so structured that the employer is entitled to a tax deduction when the payments are made.

If the deferral is elected by the employee in lieu of income that could be taken currently, the IRS has indicated the following measures will protect the employee from constructive receipt in advance of actual payment:[29] (a) the election to defer must be irrevocable, (b) the election should be made before the services for which the income is payable are performed, and (c) the period of deferral should be specific. Measures short of these standards may suffice but leave the taxpayer vulnerable to challenge by the IRS.

SOCIAL SECURITY TAXES AND EARNINGS TEST

Federal Insurance Contributions Act (FICA) Tax

The FICA tax status of executive retirement benefits was clarified by the Social Security Amendments of 1983. Starting January 1, 1984, benefits under executive plans are subject to FICA at the later of the time when (a) the services are performed, or (b) there is no longer a substantial risk of forfeiture.[30] Under prior law, nonqualified benefits often escaped taxation entirely, under one of several loosely-defined exemptions for payments made on account of retirement.

For deferred compensation payments that become nonforfeitable during active employment, this change will have little practical effect, since most executives earn more than the Social Security wage base. However, if nonqualified benefits become nonforfeitable at retirement, the consequences will vary. If the retired executive has no other income subject to FICA, his or her nonqualified plan payments will be taxed. On the other

---

[29] Revenue Ruling 60-31.
[30] Social Security Amendments of 1983, adding IRC Section 3121(v)(2).

hand, if there is earned income during retirement that is greater than the taxable wage base, the nonqualified plan payments will not produce any additional FICA liability.

FICA Self-Employment Tax

If the deferred benefits are tied too closely to the performance of future services—for example, a substantial consulting requirement—the executive instead may run the risk of being declared self-employed, and therefore liable for the FICA self-employment tax at the time the payments are received.[31]

Earnings Test

The Social Security earnings test for receipt of benefits does not apply to amounts earned by an employee before retirement, even though paid on a deferred basis after retirement. However, if the deferred benefits are tied too closely to the performance of postretirement services, some portion of the payments may count toward the earnings test. The result would be to cancel $1 of Social Security benefits for each $2 of earnings in excess of specified amounts paid before age 70. (Starting in 1990 the penalty will be reduced to $1 of Social Security benefit for every $3 of excess earnings for those age 65 through 69. The $1—for—$2 tradeoff will remain in effect for anyone less than 65. Starting in 2000 the foregoing references to age 65 will gradually rise, reaching 67 in 2027.[32]

SUMMARY

An executive retirement plan can add to the executive's benefits, bringing them up to or above those offered the general work force. It can provide unreduced early retirement, full pension after short periods of service, extra protection for dependents, deferral of current earnings, and guarantees of income beyond working life. Since it is free of the requirements for qualified plans, it can be drawn up to meet the particular needs of the individual executive or of a select group of executives. Aside from providing added benefits for the executive, it also can impose added obligations. Plan design is concerned with avoiding the tax pitfalls of nonqualified plans, rather than enjoying the tax advantages of qualified plans.

---

[31] FICA tax on self-employment income is levied under IRC Section 1401. To determine whether an individual is retired, or whether he or she has performed substantial services in self-employment, the Social Security Administration considers several factors, which are outlined in SSR 404.446.

[32] Social Security Amendments of 1983, amending Sections 203(f) and 216 of the Social Security Act.

PART SIX

Costing and Funding of Employee Benefit Plans

Part Six begins with two chapters devoted to the costing and funding of retirement benefits. The first, Chapter 40, discusses funding media, types of contracts used for funding purposes, actuarial costs, and cost methods. This is followed by an examination of minimum funding requirements under the Employee Retirement Income Security Act of 1974 (ERISA) in Chapter 41.

Chapter 42 on alternative insurance company arrangements describes these arrangements, why they are used and the advantages of each.

This part concludes with an overview of other approaches to funding employee benefits in Chapter 43.

Costing and Funding Retirement Benefits

DONALD S. GRUBBS, JR.

INTRODUCTION

Funding retirement benefits includes setting aside contributions, investing them in a funding medium, and making benefit payments from the amounts set aside. It involves administrative and accounting functions and important tax considerations.

This chapter discusses funding retirement programs that are qualified plans under the Internal Revenue Code. Special considerations, not discussed here, apply to plans covering employees of governments and of churches.

FUNDING MEDIA

The funding medium is the vehicle which contains the plan's assets and from which the benefits are paid. All pension plan assets must be held by one or more trusts, custodial accounts, annuity and insurance contracts, or federal retirement bonds.[1]

Trusts and Their Investments

Trusts are used as the investment medium for about two thirds of all pension assets. A trust is a legal entity under which a trustee holds assets for the benefit of another. Trusts are governed by state law. However, the Internal Revenue Service deems a trust to exist even before it has a corpus (assets), even though most state laws require a corpus for a trust to exist.[2] A trust agreement is entered into between the employer or other plan sponsor and the trustee.

---

[1] Employee Retirement Income Security Act of 1974 (ERISA) sec. 403; Internal Revenue Code of 1954 (I.R.C.) sec. 401(a),(f), 403(a), 404(a)(2), 405.

[2] Rev. Rul. 57-419, 1957-2 CB 264.

The trust instrument states the purpose of the trust and defines the authority and the responsibilities of the trustee. It includes provisions for terminating the trust or replacing the trustee. A trust must provide that plan assets be used for the exclusive benefit of participants and beneficiaries.[3]

Trustees.   Generally, trustees may be either individuals or institutions with trust powers, such as banks or trust companies. For an HR-10 plan which benefits any owner-employee (proprietor or more than 10 percent partner), however, the assets must be held by a bank or an institution that satisfies certain requirements or regulations. Regardless of whether the plan is an HR-10 plan, a bank usually is designated as trustee. Some large plans divide plan assets among two or more banks serving as trustees.

Some plans have a board of trustees consisting of a group of individuals. Collectively bargained multiemployer plans usually follow this approach. In such a case, the board of trustees usually enters a second trust agreement with a bank, delegating responsibility for holding and investing plan assets. Sometimes the trustee is a single individual, but many individuals hesitate to assume the fiduciary responsibilities of trustees.

The duties of trustees differ from plan to plan. In every case the trustee must hold the plan assets and account for them. Some trustees have complete responsibility for determining investment policy and making every investment decision. Under other trust agreements the trustee is required to follow investment decisions made by the employer or a separate investment manager. For many plans the trustee's authority lies between these two extremes; for example the trustee may make individual investments in accordance with investment policies or limitations established by the employer, an investment manager, or trust agreement.

Trustees usually pay the plan's benefits to participants and often assume other administrative responsibilities. Sometimes the trustee is designated plan administrator, with the full responsibility for administering the plan. The trustee is a fiduciary of the plan and subject to ERISA's fiduciary responsibilities.

Trust Investments.   Many banks maintain one or more collective trust funds to pool the assets of a number of plans for investment purposes. These commingled trusts are very similar to mutual funds. They may provide more diversification and better investment management and may reduce investment expense, particularly for small plans, compared to a trust investing in individual securities. Many banks have several separate commingled funds for particular types of investments; e.g., common stocks or bonds. For the same reasons some trusts invest in commingled funds, others invest in mutual funds as an intermediary. Most larger trusts acquire individual securities rather than use commingled funds or mutual funds.

Many trusts invest only in securities listed on a major stock exchange to assure marketability, avoid valuation problems, and reduce fiduciary prob-

---

[3] I.R.C. sec. 401(a)(2).

lems. Common stocks and corporate bonds are the most common investments. Trusts also often invest in preferred stocks, certificates of deposit, commercial or government notes, government bonds, mortgages, and real estate. Occasionally, they invest in art, precious metals, and other collectibles, but this is, in effect, prohibited if individuals direct the investment of their own accounts in a defined contribution plan.

A plan may invest in securities of the employer only if they are "qualifying employer securities." A qualifying employer security is a security of the employer which is either a stock or a marketable security which meets several criteria of ERISA. A defined benefit plan generally may not invest more than 10 percent of its assets in securities of the employer, but stock bonus plans, profit-sharing plans, and some money purchase pension plans are not so limited.

Insured Plans

Approximately one third of pension plan assets are held by insurance companies. Many different kinds of contracts are used. These include group contracts covering a group of participants and individual contracts for each participant.

Annuity contracts and insurance contracts are used, and both generally provide annuity income after retirement. Life insurance contracts generally guarantee to pay death benefits which exceed the reserve for the individual participant while annuity contracts generally do not. The extent to which the contracts guarantee the payment of benefits or the employer's costs varies greatly between contract types.

Deposit Administration (DA) Group Annuity Contract. A deposit administration (DA) contract has a deposit fund into which all contributions to the plan are deposited. For defined benefit plans the fund is not allocated among participants. The insurance company credits the fund with interest at a guaranteed rate and may assess the fund with a stipulated expense charge. When a participant becomes eligible for a pension, a withdrawal is made from the deposit fund to purchase an annuity. Sometimes lump-sum distributions, disability payments, or other benefits are paid directly from the deposit fund without the purchase of an annuity.

The DA contract specifies the guaranteed rate of interest to be credited to the deposit fund, the expense charge to be subtracted from the deposit fund, and the rates which will be used to purchase annuities when individuals retire. There generally is no expense charge for larger plans. The insurer guarantees payment of the pensions after annuities have been purchased but does not guarantee the deposit fund will be sufficient to purchase the annuities.

The guaranteed interest rates and annuity purchase rates generally are quite conservative. When actual experience is more favorable than the guaranteed assumptions, the difference may be recognized by adding dividends or experience credits to the deposit fund. Consulting, administrative, and actuarial services for the plan may be provided by the insurance company, independent consultants, or the employer.

If the contract is discontinued, it may allow the employer either to apply the balance of the deposit fund to purchase annuities or to transfer it to a trust or another insurance company. If the fund is transferred in a lump sum, the insurance company may deduct a surrender charge or a market value adjustment or alternatively, the insurer may require that the transfer be made in installments over a period of years.

The assets of the deposit fund represent a contractual obligation of the insurer, but do not represent any particular assets of the insurer. The insurer invests the monies received as part of the total assets of the insurance company, usually primarily in bonds and mortgages. The insurer usually reflects the investment earnings of its entire portfolio in determining the amount of interest to credit in determining dividends or experience credits. In determining the interest to credit, most insurers use the "investment year" or "new money" method, which determines the rate of investment earnings on investments made by the insurance company in each year that deposits were added to the deposit fund.

Many deposit administration contracts provide that part or all of the employer contributions to the plan may be invested in separate accounts rather than the deposit fund. Separate accounts operate similarly to mutual funds and are invested in common stocks or other forms of investment. The employer may direct transfers from the deposit account into the separate account. As in a mutual fund, deposits to the fund are converted to units by dividing by the current unit value of the separate account. The unit value equals the total market value of the fund divided by the number of units held by all of the contracts that invest in the separate account. Withdrawals also are based upon the current unit value. Many insurance companies maintain separate accounts for common stocks, bonds, mortgages, and other classes of investment.

Immediate Participation Guarantee (IPG) Contract. An immediate participation guarantee (IPG) contract, like a deposit administration contract, has a deposit account into which employer contributions are paid. The insurance company generally agrees to credit to the deposit account the actual rate of investment earnings it earns on its general portfolio using the investment-year method, and to deduct an allocation of expenses for the particular contract based upon accounting records for that contract. Pensions are paid from the deposit account monthly as they become due, rather than by purchasing an annuity. Thus the contract immediately participates in its actual experience for mortality, expenses, and investment income. Annuity purchase rates are guaranteed under the contract, but annuities are not usually purchased unless the contract is discontinued. Some companies use an accounting device which appears to purchase annuities, but ordinarily no annuities are actually purchased. Some insurers call such contracts "pension administration" or "investment only" contracts, rather than IPG contracts. Separate accounts generally are used with IPG contracts, just as they are used with DA contracts.

Guaranteed Investment Contract (GIC).   A guaranteed investment contract (GIC) guarantees the rate of interest to be credited to the deposit account for a limited period, usually 5 to 10 years. Most GICs guarantee that the full principal will be paid out with no surrender charge or adjustment at the end of that period. It may provide only for an initial deposit or may provide for continuing deposits during its lifetime. It may allow benefits to be paid from the deposit account during that period. These characteristics can be particularly valuable for a thrift plan or a regular profit-sharing plan where the entire fund balance is allocated to individual participants; many participants want a guarantee of principal and interest.

The GIC may include all the plan's assets, or it may be only one of several investments held by the plan's trust. At the end of the guarantee period, the entire balance of the GIC will be paid out to the trust or other funding medium of the plan, or it may be left on deposit and a new guarantee period established. The GIC may have annuity purchase options, but in practice annuities usually are not purchased.

Group Deferred Annuity Contracts.   A deferred annuity contract is one under which the insurance company promises to pay a monthly annuity beginning at a future date. Under a group deferred annuity contract, the employer purchases a deferred annuity for each participant each year to fund the amount of pension earned in that year. The insurance company guarantees payment of the pension purchased to date, beginning at the normal retirement date, or payment of a reduced pension beginning at an early retirement date.

For example, assume a pension plan provides a pension at age 65 equal to $10 monthly for each year of participation in the plan. Each year the employer pays a premium for each participant to purchase a deferred annuity of $10 monthly to begin at age 65. Premium rates are based on the participant's age and sex. Since a small deferred annuity is purchased and guaranteed each year, by the time a participant reaches age 65 his or her entire pension will be purchased.

Before deposit administration contracts became popular, group deferred annuities were the most common type of group annuity. In recent years, however, very few new deferred annuity contracts have been issued, except to purchase annuities under terminated plans. Most plans which formerly used deferred annuities have changed to other methods of funding pensions earned after the date of change, but large amounts of deferred annuities purchased before the change remain in force.

Individual Level Premium Annuities.   Under some plans, usually small plans, an individual level premium annuity contract is purchased to fund the projected pension of each participant. The insurance company deducts an expense charge from each premium and accumulates the balance at a guaranteed rate of interest. At retirement the balance of the account is converted into a monthly annuity, applying guaranteed purchase rates. The insurance company actually may use interest credits and annuity purchase rates more favorable than the conservative rates guaranteed in the contract.

The annual premium is the level annual amount determined so that the accumulation at normal retirement age is sufficient to purchase the promised pension. If the participant receives a salary increase which causes the originally projected pension to increase, a second level premium annuity is purchased to fund the increase. Further salary increases may require purchase of a third, fourth, etc.

Upon termination of employment before retirement, the accumulated balance (cash value) of each policy is available to provide a benefit for the employee if he or she is vested or a credit for the employer if the employee is not vested. Upon death before retirement, the death benefit usually equals the greater of the cash value or the sum of the premiums paid.

Individual Retirement Income Insurance Contracts. An individual retirement income insurance contract (sometimes called "income endowment") is similar to an individual level premium annuity, except the death benefit equals the greater of the cash value or 100 times the projected monthly pension. The retirement income contract also has level annual premiums, but these must be larger than under the level annual premium annuity to provide the larger death benefit.

Split-Funded Plans—Ordinary Life and an Auxiliary Fund. Many plans are funded by a combination of individual ordinary life ("whole life") insurance policies plus an auxiliary fund (often called "side fund"). In many defined benefit plans, the amount of life insurance equals 100 times the projected pension, as in the retirement income contracts. The life insurance contract builds up a cash value sufficient to provide part of the pension. Deposits are made to the auxiliary fund to provide the balance. The auxiliary fund may be held by the insurance company or may be in a trust.

At retirement, two alternatives are available to provide a pension. Some plans surrender the insurance contract at retirement, deposit the cash value in the trust, and pay pensions monthly out of the trust. Other plans make a transfer from the trust to the insurance company at the time of retirement; the amount transferred is the amount required, together with the policy cash value, to purchase an annuity from the insurer to guarantee payment of the pension.

Many plans originally funded with retirement income insurance contracts have been converted to a split-funded basis to reduce the cost of funding the plan and to allow part of the plan's assets to be invested in common stocks. In turn, many split-funded plans have been converted to fund the pensions with a trust or group annuity contract and to provide the death benefits outside the pension plan under group term insurance in order to reduce the employer's cost.

When death benefits are funded with individual insurance under a qualified plan, the employee has current taxable income equal to the cost of insurance (called "P.S. 58" cost). Instead, if insurance is funded with group term insurance, the cost of providing the first $50,000 of insurance paid by employer contributions is tax-free to the employee, and the cost of insurance on amounts over $50,000 is computed on a less expensive basis than under individual contracts. Thus, employees pay less income tax if death benefits are funded with group term insurance. But death benefits provided by insurance contracts under pension plans generally are excluded from estate tax, which may be an advantage for participants with large enough estates to pay estate tax.

Group Permanent Contracts. Group permanent retirement income insurance contracts are designed to preserve the characteristics of individual retirement income insurance contracts while achieving some of the economy of group insurance. All participants are covered under a single contract which has cash values, death benefits, and other characteristics similar to a collection of individual retirement income contracts. Because the group contract pays lower commissions and has lower administrative expense than individual contracts, the premiums are lower. Such contracts are termed "permanent" insurance to distinguish them from group term insurance.

U.S. Retirement Bonds

A qualified bond purchase plan must be funded by certain U.S. retirement bonds issued under the Second Liberty Bond Act.[4] The bonds pay interest only upon redemption. They may be purchased only in the name of an individual and are nontransferable. They may be redeemed before age 59½ only upon death or disability. Each bond ceases to bear interest not later than five years after the death of the individual in whose name it is purchased.

Such bonds may be purchased by qualified pension and profit-sharing plans, as well as by qualified bond purchase plans. In practice, few qualified bond purchase plans exist, and few such U.S. retirement bonds have been purchased by any plan.

Insurance Company Book Reserves

A plan sponsored by a life insurance company for its own employees or agents is exempt from the requirement that plan assets be held in a trust or custodial account or invested in annuity or insurance contracts. Such a plan may be funded by establishing an accounting reserve on the books of the insurance company.[5]

---

[4] I.R.C. sec. 405.
[5] I.R.C. sec. 805(d)(3).

FACTORS AFFECTING FUNDING

Many factors affect an employer's decision regarding how much to contribute to the pension plan. Different considerations affect different plans.

Type of Plan

The type of plan and its provisions often completely or partially determine the amount of employer contribution. A thrift plan may require the employer to match employee contributions up to 6 percent of pay. A profit-sharing plan may require the employer to contribute 20 percent of profits but not more than 15 percent of pay. A money purchase pension plan may require contributions of 10 percent of pay. Such plans leave no discretion in the amount of contribution. But most profit-sharing plans provide the employer complete discretion in determining what to contribute, if anything, and most defined benefit pension plans allow substantial discretion in determining how much to contribute each year.

Laws and Regulations

Minimum funding requirements under the Employee Retirement Income Security Act of 1974 (ERISA) set an absolute minimum on the contributions for most pension plans. These are described later.

If the employer is a taxpayer, it is subject to limits on the amount of pension contribution that may be claimed as a deduction for income tax purposes. Employers generally do not want to contribute more than can be deducted currently. An employer may want to contribute more in a year when it is in a higher tax bracket and less in a year when it is in a low tax bracket or has no taxable income at all.

Other governmental requirements affect the amount of contributions of some employers. Armed Services Procurement Regulations and regulations of the Cost Accounting Standards Board control pension costs assessed under defense contracts. The Department of Housing and Urban Development has rules applicable to reimbursement of pension costs for local housing authorities. Public utilities commissions regulate the amount of pension contributions which may be recognized for rate-making purposes by utilities.

Collective Bargaining

Collective bargaining agreements affect the funding of many plans. Some collective bargaining agreements set the amount of employer contributions specifically in cents per hour, as a percent of pay, or as, for example, cents per ton of coal produced. Many other collective bargaining agreements, however, specify what benefits the plan provides but do not specify the amount of employer contributions.

Funding Media

For a plan funded entirely by individual insurance or annuity contracts, or by a group deferred annuity contract, the required premiums usually completely control the amount of contribution, leaving no discretion.

Under most plans funded with group annuity contracts or with trusts, the funding medium does not usually limit the amount of contributions. Under a traditional deposit administration group annuity contract, the deposit fund must be sufficient to purchase annuities for individuals currently retiring. Usually, the deposit fund is far more than sufficient for this purpose, so this requirement has no impact. But occasionally the deposit fund is not sufficient, particularly if a number of employees with large pensions retire shortly after the plan is established; this may require additional employer contributions to purchase annuities. To solve this problem, deposit administration contracts often are modified to allow annuities to be purchased in installments after retirement.

Accounting

Generally accepted accounting principles (GAAP) establish minimum and maximum limits on the charge for pension expense in the employer's profit and loss statement. This does not directly control the amount actually contributed, but some employers prefer the amount contributed to equal the charge to expense.

Financial Considerations

An employer often considers its cash position in determining the amount of contribution to the plan. Cash shortages may stem from lack of profits or from a need to reinvest earnings in the business or to reduce indebtedness. Reducing pension contributions helps solve cash shortages. But an employer in a strong cash position may want to increase its pension contributions, since an additional dollar paid this year reduces the required contributions in future years and earns tax-free income in the pension trust. For an employer with lots of cash, larger pension contributions may help in avoiding the accumulated earnings tax on accumulated earnings in excess of the greater of $150,000 or the amount required for the reasonable needs of the business.[6] Larger contributions also reduce the cash available for dividends.

---

[6] I.R.C. sec. 531–537.

Interest rates often are considered. Increasing the pension contributions may require increased borrowing by the employer or may prevent reducing debts. The rate of interest on debt may be compared with the rate of investment earnings of the pension fund, but taxes also should be considered. Similarly, an employer with no indebtedness may consider how much could be earned by additional investments in the business, using amounts that would otherwise be contributed to the pension fund.

Employers may establish a funding policy based on many other considerations. Most employers want the plan to be soundly funded to assure the plan actually will be able to pay promised benefits. Some employers want pension costs to be stable as a percent of pay over future years. The employer may decide to fund the unfunded liabilities over a fixed period, such as 20 years. Future trends in pension costs may be projected, based upon projected increases or decreases in the number of future participants, changes in work pattern histories, investment earnings, future salary increases, anticipated plan amendments, or possible plan termination or merger.

Statutory Requirement for Funding Policy

ERISA requires every employee benefit plan to "provide a procedure for establishing and carrying out a funding policy and method."[7] Many plan documents merely state the employer will contribute to the trust each year the minimum amount required by ERISA's minimum funding standards and such additional amounts as the employer determines in its discretion. This retains the maximum discretion to change the funding policy without a plan amendment.

ACTUARIAL COSTS

Fundamental concepts of actuarial science are used in the costing of retirement benefits. The following illustrate the factors involved in the actuarial costing of such benefits.

Probability

When rolling an honest die, the probability of getting a 3 is 1/6 (or .16667). This statement does not tell us what the outcome of the next roll will be, but it does tell us something about the average experience that might be expected if many dice were rolled.

Mortality tables show the probability of dying at each particular age of life. This probability is determined by examining the experience of many thousands of lives. For example, according to one mortality table the

---

[7] ERISA sec. 402(b)(1).

probability of death at age 30 is .000991. This means if there were 1 million men age 30, it might be expected that 991 of them would die before reaching age 31. It does not tell us which ones might die and which ones might live, and hence tells us nothing about the expected lifetime of any one individual. But it does give us information about the average experiences to be expected in a large group of persons age 30.

Interest Discount

If someone deposits $100.00 in a savings account at 5 percent interest, one year later it will grow to $105.00 (1.05 × $100.00). If the individual leaves the funds on deposit for a second year they will grow to $110.25 (1.05 × 105.00). Thus, if an individual wants to obtain $110.25 two years from now (assuming 5 percent interest), $100.00 must be deposited today. The $100.00 is the "present value" of $110.25 payable two years from now.

Viewed another way, the present value of an amount payable two years from now is .907029 times that amount (determined by dividing $100.00 by $110.25). At 5 percent interest, .907029 is the present value factor, or interest discount factor, for two years. To know the present value of any amount due two years from now (assuming 5 percent interest), simply multiply it by .907029.

There is a discount factor for any number of years. Of course, these factors vary with the interest rate. Sample discount factors for zero years to five years are shown in Table 40-1 at 5 percent interest and 6 percent interest.

Present Value of Future Amounts

Suppose a person agreed that two years from now 600 dice would be rolled, and the person must pay $1.00 for each 3 that resulted. Further suppose that he or she wanted to know the present value, the amount that could be set aside in a savings account today, which would be expected to be sufficient, together with interest, to pay the amounts when they become

Table 40-1
Sample Discount Factors

Number of Years	Interest Discount Factor	
	5 Percent	6 Percent
0	1.000000	1.000000
1	.952381	.943396
2	.907029	.889996
3	.863838	.839619
4	.822702	.792094
5	.783526	.747258

due. The total expected payments are $100.00 (1/6 × 600 × $1.00). Assuming 5 percent interest, the present value of that is $90.70 (the 2-year discount factor or .907029 × $100.00). Thus, if a deposit of $90.70 is made today it would grow to $100.00 two years from now, which would be sufficient to make the expected payments if exactly one sixth of the 600 dice turned up a 3. Thus, $90.70 is called the present value of the expected future payments. Of course, it might turn out to be more or less than needed, if the account earned more or less than the 5 percent assumed or if more or less than exactly one sixth of the dice turned up a 3. The present value of any future event is the number of exposures (600 dice) times the probability of occurrence (1/6) times the amount of payment on each occurrence ($1.00) times the interest discount factor (.907029).

Suppose, in addition to the obligation related to the 600 dice to be rolled two years from now, the individual had an obligation to pay $3.00 for each head that results from flipping 1,000 coins five years from now. The present value of the coin-flipping could be determined similarly to that for the dice-throwing. Then the two present values for dice-rolling and coin-flipping could be added to get the total present value of both obligations combined. Similarly, total present value can be determined for the combination of many possible future events, each with its own exposure, probability of occurrence, amount of payment, and time of occurrence.

Actuarial Cost Methods

Underlying actuarial concepts of pension funding are the actuarial cost methods which establish the level of pension contributions needed to fund promised pension benefits.

When a pension plan is first established, it may give past service credit to provide benefits related to employment before the effective date. Employees then covered under the plan will work for various amounts of time in the future. When employees terminate employment, some of them will be eligible to receive benefits, either beginning immediately or deferred into the future. After pension benefits begin, they usually continue for the retiree's lifetime, and sometimes payments are made after death to beneficiaries.

Actuarial cost methods are merely methods for assigning the cost of the benefit payments to particular years. Ultimately, the cost of a pension plan equals the sum of all the benefits and expenses paid from the plan, less any employee contributions and less the plan's investment return. If the employer contributes an additional dollar in any year, that dollar together with the interest it earns reduces the amount the employer needs to contribute in future years. Actuarial cost methods do not affect these ultimate costs, except as indirectly they may influence the amount of investment income by influencing the size of the fund or the timing of contributions.

To the extent any insurance or annuity contracts guarantee the costs of the plan, the employer's cost equals the premiums paid to the insurance company reduced by any dividends or credits, rather than the plan's own experience of benefits and expenses paid and investment return.

Basic Categories of Actuarial Cost Methods

All actuarial cost methods for pensions fall into three categories: current disbursement, terminal funding, and advance funding. All are in current use, although the advance funding is more commonly used and is required for plans subject to ERISA's minimum funding requirements.

Under the current disbursement method, also called "pay-as-you-go," each year the employer contributes the current year's benefit payments. This is not really an actuarial cost method at all. However, actuarial techniques can be used to project payments in future years, which may assist those responsible for the plan's operation. If a plan is funded precisely under the current disbursement method, the plan will have no assets whatsoever available to pay future benefits; next month's benefits will depend on next month's contributions.

Under terminal funding, as under current disbursement, no cost is recognized for a participant while he or she continues employment. The entire cost of the participant's future benefits is recognized, however, at the moment the participant retires and benefits begin. If a participant terminates and is entitled to a deferred pension beginning at a later date, the cost of the pension may be recognized either at the time of termination of employment or at the time payments begin, under two variations of the terminal funding method. If a plan is funded on the terminal funding method, the assets are expected to be sufficient to pay all the future benefits for those already retired (and terminated vested, if they also have been funded); no assets would be available to provide benefits for those not yet retired.

An advance funding actuarial cost method is one that spreads the cost of a participant's pension over a working lifetime. It recognizes the cost of a worker's pension as a cost of employment. If all the costs attributable to the past have been funded, the plan assets usually are larger than under the terminal funding method and thus usually expected to be sufficient to provide all future benefits for those already retired and terminated and to have some additional assets available to provide benefits for those still employed. Advance funding usually results in more rapid funding than terminal funding, but that is not always the case.

Except as otherwise noted herein, all actuarial cost methods are assumed to be advance funding methods.

Present Value of Future Benefits

For any group of individuals, the present value of their future benefits is the amount expected to be sufficient to pay those future benefits. If the present value of the future benefits were invested in a fund today, it would be sufficient, together with the investment income, to pay all such future benefits as they become due; no additional contributions would be needed, but the fund would be exactly exhausted when the last individual dies.

A participant or beneficiary may become eligible to receive future benefits if he or she retires (before or after normal retirement date), becomes disabled, dies, or otherwise terminates employment. The present value of future benefits is determined by the same principles as described earlier.

Consider a new employee just hired at age 25 under a pension plan which provides normal retirement benefits at age 65, assuming all payments are made annually at the beginning of the year. The present value of the single payment the participant may receive at age 65 is determined by multiplying the number of exposures (one person) times the probability of occurrence (the probability he or she will not die or terminate employment before age 65 and will then retire) times the amount of payment (the annual pension) times the interest discount factor (for 40 years from age 25 to 65). The present value of the payments to be received at 66, and each later age, could be similarly calculated; in each case the probability would need to consider not only the employee's chance of receiving the first payment but of continuing to survive to receive subsequent payments, and the interest discount factor would be smaller as the years become more distant. By adding the present value of each future normal retirement payment, the present value of all normal retirement payments can be determined. By similar techniques the present value of the payments that may be paid for this worker in the event of early retirement, disability, death, or vested termination can be determined. Adding these all together, the present value of all future benefits which may become payable to the individual or his or her beneficiary is ascertained.

For this individual, the present value may be meaningless. He or she may quit before becoming vested and never receive a cent. Or the employee may collect a pension until age 99, with costs greater than anticipated. But if the plan has a large number of participants, the sum of their present values will accurately reflect the amount needed to pay all future benefits, *if* the assumptions are correct concerning the various probabilities, the interest rate, and the amount of each future payment that might become payable. This concept is key to all actuarial cost methods.

Components of Present Value of Future Benefits

Actuarial cost methods generally divide the present value of future benefits into two portions, the part attributable to the past and the part attributable to the future. The part attributable to the past is called the "accrued liability." It also has sometimes been called "past service liability," "prior service liability," "actuarial liability," "supplemental present value," etc. The part of the present value of future benefits attributable to the future is called the present value of future normal costs. This present value of future normal costs is the portion of the present value expected to be paid in the future by "normal costs," the cost attributable to each of the future years.

If the same assumptions are used, all actuarial cost methods have the same present value of future benefits (although under one of the methods it is not required to calculate the present value of future benefits). The methods differ in how they divide this present value between the accrued liability and the present value of future normal costs. Obviously, a method which produces a larger accrued liability has a smaller present value of future normal costs, and vice versa. Under some methods, when a plan is first established no accrued liability exists at all, even though benefits are actually credited for past service; in this case, the present value of future normal costs equals the entire present value of future benefits.

Except when a plan is first established, it usually will have assets equal to part of the accrued liability. Any excess of the total accrued liability over the assets is the "unfunded accrued liability" sometimes called the "unfunded past service liability."[8]

If the assets exactly equal the accrued liability, there is no unfunded accrued liability, and the plan is "fully funded." Under some actuarial cost methods, the assets always exactly equal the accrued liability and there never is an unfunded liability.

Each actuarial method determines the normal cost for the current year.[9] The normal cost usually is calculated for the year beginning on the valuation date, but under one method it is sometimes calculated for the year ending on the valuation date. The normal cost may be calculated in dollars or it may be calculated as a percent of payroll, cost per employee, per hour, per shift, etc. If not originally expressed in dollars, it is converted to dollars by multiplying by the actual or expected payroll, number of employees, hours, shifts, etc. The normal cost for the coming year is, of course, part of the present value of future normal costs.

Gain or Loss

As part of the actuarial valuation, the actuary can calculate what the present unfunded liability would have been expected to be currently, if the experience since the date of the last actuarial valuation had exactly followed the actuarial assumptions. This expected unfunded liability can then be compared with the actual unfunded liability calculated in the current valuation. The difference between the expected unfunded liability and the actual unfunded liability is the gain or loss since the last valuation. This gain or loss shows the extent to which the actual experience was better or worse than would have been expected by the actuarial assumptions.

---

[8] ERISA sec. 3(30), 302(b)(2)(B), I.R.C. sec. 412(b)(2)(B).
[9] ERISA sec. 3(28).

Under some actuarial cost methods, called "spread-gain" methods, the actual unfunded liability is assumed to equal the expected unfunded liability and thus there is no gain or loss. Under these methods deviations between expected and actual experience are spread over the future working lifetimes of participants as increases or decreases in the normal cost.

SUMMARY OF VALUATION RESULTS

Under every actuarial cost method, the valuation produces the following results:

1. Normal cost for the current year.
2. Accrued liability.
3. Assets.
4. Unfunded accrued liability (the accrued liability less the assets, assumed $0 under one method).
5. Gain or loss (assumed $0 under spread-gain methods).

ACTUARIAL COST METHODS

Statutory Requirements for Actuarial Cost Methods

ERISA states, "The term 'advance funding actuarial cost method' or 'actuarial cost method' means a recognized actuarial technique utilized for establishing the amount and incidence of the annual actuarial cost of pension plan benefits and expenses. Acceptable actuarial cost methods shall include the accrued benefit cost method (unit credit method), the entry age normal cost method, the individual level premium cost method, the aggregate cost method, the attained age normal cost method, and the frozen liability cost method. The terminal funding cost method and the current funding (pay-as-you-go) cost method are not acceptable actuarial cost methods. The Secretary of the Treasury shall issue regulations to further define acceptable actuarial cost methods."[10] Under the statute, the Internal Revenue Service may recognize other methods as "acceptable" for determining ERISA's minimum funding requirements. They have so far recognized one additional method, the shortfall method. The same actuarial cost method and the same assumptions must be used for determining deductible limits as are used for minimum funding purposes.[11] The actuarial cost method and actuarial assumptions must be reasonable in the aggregate and must offer the actuary's best estimate of anticipated experience under the plan.[12]

---

[10] ERISA sec. 3(31).
[11] I.R.C. sec. 404(a)(1)(A).
[12] ERISA sec. 302(c)(3), I.R.C. sec. 412(c)(3).

Classification of Actuarial Cost Methods

There are a variety of ways in which actuarial cost methods may be classified. Only advance funding methods are considered in the following classifications.

Methods may be divided between (a) those which allocate the *benefits* of the plan to particular plan years and then determine the actuarial present value associated with the benefits assigned, and (b) methods which allocate the actuarial present *value* of all future benefits to particular plan years without allocating the benefits themselves. Those methods that allocate the benefits to particular plan years may be further divided between those that allocate the benefits according to the plan's provisions describing the accrued benefit and those that allocate the projected benefits as a level benefit for each year of service, either level in dollars or level as a percentage of pay.

A second way of classifying actuarial cost methods is between accrued benefit methods and projected benefit methods. An accrued benefit method is based upon the amount of benefit earned to date, while a projected benefit method is instead based upon the projected amounts of benefits expected to be paid from the plan upon retirement or other termination of employment. This is similar to the first classification above, since all *accrued* benefit methods allocate the *benefits* to particular years while *projected* benefit methods generally allocate the actuarial present *value* to particular years.

A third way of classifying divides actuarial cost methods between those which directly determine the actuarial gain or loss and those which do not. Actuarial cost methods which do not directly determine the actuarial gain or loss have the effect of automatically spreading the gain or loss over the future working lifetimes of all active participants as part of the normal cost; such methods are called spread-gain methods.

A fourth way of classifying divides actuarial cost methods between individual methods and aggregate methods. Under an individual method, the normal cost and the accrued liability may be calculated for each individual participant; the normal cost and the accrued liability for the entire plan are the sums of these respective items for all of the participants. Under an aggregate method, the costs are determined for the group as a whole in such a way that they cannot be determined separately for individuals.

A fifth way of classifying is between methods which result in an initial accrued liability when the plan is established or amended (usually related to past service benefits or plan amendments which increase accrued benefits) and those which do not. If a method does not produce an initial accrued liability, the cost of all benefits (including past service benefits) must be funded through normal costs.

A sixth way of classifying is between methods which use an entry age basis and those which use an attained age basis. Under an attained age basis, the normal cost is determined on the basis of the participants' current attained ages, without reference to their ages at entry. Under an entry age basis, age at entry is a key element in determining normal cost.

A seventh way of classifying is between open group methods and closed group methods. A closed group method considers only the group of present plan participants, while an open group method considers employees expected to be hired in the future as well.[13] Except as otherwise specifically noted, this chapter only considers closed group methods. All six methods listed in ERISA are closed group methods.

The above classifications are each presented as dichotomies. Actually a number of methods exist which combine elements of the dichotomies.

Accrued Benefit Cost Method

The plan document usually defines the "accrued benefit," the annual amount of benefit earned to date which is payable at normal retirement age. If a participant is 100 percent vested, his vested benefit equals his accrued benefit.[14]

The accrued benefit cost method, also called "unit credit cost method," defines the accrued liability as the present value of the plan's accrued benefits. The normal cost equals the present value of the benefit accrued during the current year. If a plan is funded with a group deferred annuity contract, a small deferred annuity is purchased each year to fund the amount of benefit assumed for each participant in that year, automatically using the accrued benefit cost method.

The traditional accrued benefit cost method is based upon the accrued benefit defined in the plan. This does not recognize future salary increases. If a plan's benefits are based upon final average pay, salary increases will cause the benefit credited for past years to increase from year to year as salaries increase, causing liabilities to increase and creating actuarial losses. For this reason, the IRS will not allow a final average pay plan to use the traditional accrued benefit cost method. Some actuaries use a modified accrued benefit cost method for final average pay plans. Under this method, the projected benefit at normal retirement age is first calculated based upon projected service to normal retirement age and future salary increases. A modified accrued benefit is then calculated, equal to the projected benefit multiplied by the ratio of the participant's actual years of service to date to his or her projected years of service at normal retirement age. This modified accrued benefit cost method does not have the problems of increasing liabilities and actuarial losses because of salary increases which are part of the traditional method.

---

[13] For a discussion of an open group method, see Donald R. Fleischer, "The Forecast Valuation Method for Pension Plans," *Transactions* 27 (1975), pp. 93–154, Society of Actuaries.

[14] ERISA sec. 3(23), 204, I.R.C. Sec. 411(b).

Entry Age Normal Cost Method

The entry age normal cost method is a type of projected benefit cost method. This means the cost is based upon the projected amount of pension expected to be payable at retirement, rather than the accrued benefit earned to date.

The entry age normal cost equals the level annual amount of contribution (level in dollars or as a percent of pay) from an employee's date of hire (or other entry age) to retirement date calculated as sufficient to fund the projected benefit. The accrued liability equals the present value of all future benefits for present employees, less the portion of that value expected to be funded by future normal costs.

Under the entry age normal cost method, unlike the accrued benefit cost method, the normal cost of each individual is expected to remain level each year. For plans with benefits not related to pay, the normal cost is calculated to remain level in dollars, while for a plan with benefits expressed as a percentage of pay the normal cost is calculated to remain level as a percentage of pay. The average normal cost for the entire group can also usually be expected to remain fairly level per employee or as a percentage of pay, even if the average attained age increases, unless there is a change in the average *entry* age.

Under the entry age normal cost method, when the plan is first established an initial accrued liability exists that equals the accumulation of the normal costs for members for years prior to the effective date. Similarly, if an amendment increases benefits, there is an increase in the accrued liability which equals the accumulation of prior normal costs for the increase in projected benefits.

Individual Level Premium Cost Method

The individual level premium cost method determines the level annual cost to fund each participant's projected pension from the date participation begins to normal retirement date. When participation begins, the plan has no accrued liability, even if the participant has substantial benefits credited for past service. Plans funded exclusively with individual retirement income insurance contracts and/or individual level premium annuity contracts automatically use this method. Usually no salary increase assumption is used in projecting the benefit at retirement. If a participant's salary increases during a year, the projected benefit also increases. This increase in the projected benefit will be separately funded by an additional level annual cost from the participant's then attained age to normal retirement age. If the plan is amended increasing benefits, the increase in the projected benefit for each individual is funded by a level premium from his or her then attained age to retirement age, with no immediate increase in the accrued liability.

Under the individual level premium cost method, the accrued liability for each individual equals the present value of future benefits less the present value of future normal costs. The accrued liability for the entire plan, less the plan assets, equals the unfunded accrued liability.

An allowable variation of this method is sometimes called the "individual aggregate method." Under this variation, the normal cost for the first year is the same as previously described. To determine the normal cost in subsequent years, it is first necessary to allocate the plan's assets. The assets attributable to retired or terminated vested employees are assumed to equal the present value of their benefits; those assets attributable to retired and terminated employees are subtracted from the total actual assets to determine the portion of the actual assets attributable to active employees. Several methods are used to allocate assets among active employees. Each individual's allocated assets are subtracted from the present value of future benefits to obtain the remaining unfunded cost of his benefits. This unfunded cost is spread as a level premium (level in dollars or as a percentage of pay) from attained age to the participant's retirement age.

Aggregate Cost Method

The aggregate cost method is another projected benefit cost method. Under this method, there is no unfunded liability. The accrued liability is, in effect, assumed to equal the assets. Thus, all costs are funded through the future normal costs, determined as a level percent of pay (or level in dollars) during the future working lifetimes of all current employees from their current attained ages.

The excess of the present value of future benefits over the value of any plan assets is the portion of that present value which must be funded by normal costs in the future. This excess is the present value of future normal costs. The actuary then determines the present value of all future compensation for all employees. By dividing the present value of future normal costs by the present value of future compensation, the actuary determines the ratio of future normal costs to future compensation. The actuary multiplies this ratio by the current year's compensation to determine the current year's normal cost. A similar procedure is used to determine the normal cost per employee, rather than as a percent of compensation, if benefits are not related to compensation.

Costs are determined in the aggregate and cannot be determined individually. Thus, the normal cost is calculated as a percentage of the total payroll, or a cost per employee for the entire group. The aggregate cost method automatically spreads gains and losses through the future normal costs and has no separately identifiable gains or losses.

Attained Age Normal Cost Method

The attained age normal method is a combination of the unit credit cost method and either the aggregate cost method or the individual level premium cost method. The accrued liability at the plan's effective date is calculated using the accrued benefit cost method. The cost of the excess of the projected benefit over the accrued benefit on the effective date is funded by level costs over the future working lifetimes of participants, using either the individual level premium cost method or the aggregate cost method. Both individual and aggregate variations have long been recognized as the attained age normal cost method, but some use the name only to apply to one or the other variation.

If the individual variation is used, each individual's original past service benefit is valued every year using the unit credit cost method to determine the accrued liability. The difference between the employee's total projected benefit and this frozen past service benefit is valued as under the individual level premium cost method, without spreading gains. As under the individual level premium cost method, this method often has been used without a salary scale, funding any increase in projected benefits because of salary increases from the then attained age to retirement age.

If the aggregate variation is chosen after the first year, the frozen initial liability technique, described below, is used. In that event, gains and losses are spread over the future working lifetimes of employees.

Frozen Initial Liability Cost Method

ERISA lists the frozen initial liability method. Many actuaries do not regard this as an actuarial cost method at all but rather a method for spreading gains under other methods. This latter group might describe a method as "entry age normal cost method with frozen initial liability" or "attained age normal cost method with frozen liability." But this difference of viewpoint does not reflect an actual difference in how the method operates.

The frozen initial liability method is not a method for determining the plan's initial accrued liability. The entry age normal cost method usually is used to determine the initial accrued liability and the first year's normal cost, but sometimes the attained age normal cost method is used instead. In subsequent years the unfunded liability is "frozen" and does not reflect actuarial gains and losses. This method has no gain or loss. What would be a gain or loss is spread over the future working lifetimes of all participants through increases or decreases in future normal costs.

To accomplish this, the unfunded accrued liability on the valuation date is set equal to the expected unfunded liability; i.e., what the unfunded liability would be if the actuarial assumptions had been exactly realized during the prior year. This unfunded liability plus the plan assets equals the total accrued liability. The excess of the present value of all future benefits over the accrued liability is the portion of that present value which must be funded by future normal costs and is designated as the present value of future normal costs. From this present value of future normal costs, the current year's normal cost is determined in the same manner as for the aggregate cost method.

Shortfall Method

The shortfall method was created to solve a problem created by ERISA's minimum funding requirements. It applies only to collectively bargained plans. The shortfall method is not really an actuarial cost method but a way of adopting other actuarial methods to ERISA's funding requirements.[15]

Retired and Terminated Participants and Beneficiaries

Under the traditional accrued benefit cost method, the accrued liability equals the value of accrued benefits. This is true for retired participants, terminated participants with vested rights, and beneficiaries of deceased participants, as well as for active employees.

This same approach is used for retired and terminated members and beneficiaries under all actuarial cost methods which determine the accrued liability on an individual basis. Thus, the accrued liability for retired and terminated members and beneficiaries is the same under the entry age normal cost method as under the accrued benefit cost method.

For aggregate methods, this same value for retired and terminated members and beneficiaries is part of the present value of future benefits.

Table 40–2 summarizes the actuarial cost methods.

Actuarial Assumptions

Purpose of Assumptions. Determining the present value of future benefits is basic to all actuarial cost methods. The present value of any future benefit is the amount of the future benefit times the probability it will be paid, discounted to present value at interest. For example, a plan may provide a disability benefit equal to 50 percent of pay to workers who become disabled after 15 years of service. The amount of future benefits depends upon the probability each worker will survive in the group to become eligible; i.e., that he or she will not die, retire, become disabled, or otherwise terminate employment before becoming eligible for such benefits. The amount of future benefits also depends upon the probabilities of becoming disabled, as well as the period of disability before either death or recovery. It also depends on future salary increases. Actuarial assumptions are used to predict these matters.

The present value of future benefits is calculated using an interest discount. It may not be apparent why an assumption concerning the assets is used to determine the present value of future benefits. The present value of

---

[15] Treasury Reg. 1.412(c)(1)-2.

Table 40-2
Summary of Actuarial Cost Methods (excluding shortfall)

	Accrued Benefit or Projected Benefit	Calcu- lates Gain or Loss	Individual or Aggregate	Initial Accrued Liability	Age Used for Com- putation of Normal Cost
1. Accrued benefit cost	Accrued	Yes	Individual	Yes	Attained
2. Entry age normal cost					
a. Individual ages	Projected	Yes	Individual	Yes	Entry
b. Average entry age	Projected	Yes	Aggregate	Yes	Entry (average)
3. Individual level premium					
a. No-spread	Projected	Yes	Individual	No	Attained
b. Spread-gain	Projected	No	Individual	No	Attained
4. Aggregate cost	Projected	No	Aggregate	No	Attained
5. Attained age normal					
a. Individual	Mixed	Yes	Individual	Yes	Attained
b. Aggregate	Mixed	No	Aggregate	Yes	Attained
6. Frozen initial liability	Projected	No	Aggregate	Yes	Attained

Note: For a more detailed presentation of actuarial cost methods, see C. L. Trowbridge and C. E. Farr, *The Theory and Practice of Pension Funding* (Homewood, Ill.: Richard D. Irwin, 1976); and B. N. Berin, *Fundamentals of Pension Mathematics* (Chicago: Society of Actuaries, 1971).

a future benefit is the amount of assets which could be invested today, so that the assets plus the interest they would earn would be sufficient to provide the expected benefits in the future. The interest to be earned is key to deciding what amount of present assets are needed.

The actuarial valuation allocates the present value of benefits to various periods of the past and future. Frequently, that allocation is made in proportion to periods of employment or to compensation. For example, actuarial assumptions are used to estimate those periods of employment or amount of compensation. Thus, the selection of the assumptions affects the allocation of present values between periods of the past and future.

Long-Range Nature

For an employee now age 25, the actuarial assumptions are used to estimate whether he or she may become eligible for a pension 40 years in the future, what the employee's salary will be after 40 years, how long the employee will live to receive a pension, and what the fund will earn over the entire period.

Thus, the actuarial assumptions are extremely long-range in nature. The more distant any event is, the less likely it can be predicted correctly. Mortality rates for next year are fairly predictable (barring a war), but mortality rates 50 years hence depend upon events that cannot possibly be predicted such as remarkable medical discoveries or a disastrous deterioration of the environment. Assumptions other than mortality are even less predictable for long periods. The experience of last year, or expected experience of next year, is relevant to the process of establishing assumptions only to the extent that it may indicate long-term trends.

Most experts will not even conjecture for such long periods. When economists talk of long-range projections, they often mean five years. Yet such long-range assumptions are essential to actuarial valuations. The actuary, faced with this difficult task, usually assumes the future will be generally similar to the present, often with some element of conservatism (conservative in the direction of producing higher costs).

ERISA Requirements for Assumptions

ERISA requires the actuary to use "actuarial assumptions and methods which, in the aggregate, are reasonable expectations and which, in combination, offer the actuary's best estimate of anticipated experience under the plan."[16] The statutory language provides more questions than answers. What is the meaning of "reasonable"? How can the assumptions be reasonably related to the plan's experience when the large majority of plans are so small their experience is not statistically valid? Is the "best estimate" one that has a 50 percent chance of being on the high side and a 50 percent chance of being on the low side (in which case the "best estimate" requirement would tend to weaken the funding of pensions)? If not, what does "best estimate" mean? What should the probability be that the estimated costs are less than sufficient to fund the plan in the long run? Detailed discussion of the individual assumptions may be found in the actuarial literature.[17]

Asset Valuation Methods

Under some actuarial cost methods, the value of plan assets affects the unfunded liability, which must be funded by amortization payments. Under other actuarial cost methods, the value of plan assets affects the normal cost.

---

[16] ERISA sec. 302(c)(3). I.R.C. sec. 412(c)(3).

[17] Study notes of the Society of Actuaries and articles and discussions in numerous volumes of the *Transactions* and *Record* of the Society of Actuaries, and the *Proceedings* of the Conference of Actuaries in Public Practice.

Under either approach, the method used to determine the value of plan assets determines the required employer contributions for a particular year and the fluctuation in contributions from year to year.

Some plans use the market value of assets for the actuarial valuation. It is argued this is the real value of the plan's assets and therefore makes the valuation more realistic. The disadvantage of this method is that fluctuations in market value may result in substantial fluctuation in the required employer contributions from year to year, which is generally undesirable.

Some plans use cost or book value of assets for the actuarial valuation. This can avoid the problems of fluctuation in plan costs. However, if the asset value used differs substantially from market value, it may present an unrealistic picture of the true costs and liabilities.

A variety of actuarial methods of asset valuation are used to avoid these problems. Some plans use the cost or book value so long as it lies within a stated corridor around market value; e.g., not less than 80 percent or more than 120 percent of market value. Some plans use a formula or method to gradually recognize asset appreciation; e.g., five-year-average market value. A wide variety of methods are used to gradually recognize appreciation but avoid extreme asset value fluctuation. ERISA requires plans to use "any reasonable actuarial method of valuation which takes into account fair market value and which is permitted under regulations." Regulations require the asset value used either be between 80 percent and 120 percent of market value or between 85 percent and 115 percent of the average market value for a period of five years or less. A plan is permitted to elect to value bonds and other evidences of indebtedness separately using amortized cost, but few plans have done so.

CHAPTER 41

Costing and Funding Retirement Benefits (continued)

DONALD S. GRUBBS, JR.

MINIMUM FUNDING REQUIREMENTS

General Requirements

The Employee Retirement Income Security Act of 1974 (ERISA) established minimum funding requirements to provide greater assurance that pension plans will be able to pay the promised benefits.

Applicability

The minimum funding requirements appear twice in ERISA in duplicate language, in Title I and Title II.[1] The Internal Revenue Service issues regulations that apply to both Title I and Title II.

Under Title II the minimum funding requirements apply to almost all qualified pension plans (excluding profit-sharing and stock bonus plans) except governmental plans, church plans, and "insurance contract plans." An insurance contract plan is a plan funded exclusively by the purchase of individual level premium insurance and/or annuity contracts which guarantee the benefits payable at normal retirement age, under which all premiums have been paid, and under which there has been no policy loan or other security interest against any contract. A plan funded exclusively with level premium "group permanent" insurance and annuity contracts, which have the characteristics of individual level premium contracts, also is treated as an "insurance contract plan" exempt from the funding requirements. Thus, this exemption is limited to a class of plans which have their own requirements to assure sound funding.

Under Title I, the minimum funding requirements apply to nonqualified

---

[1] ERISA sec. 301-306, I.R.C. sec. 412.

plans as well as qualified plans. The exemptions described above for Title II also apply under Title I along with a few other exemptions. Plans exempt from the funding requirements include "a plan which is unfunded and is maintained by an employer primarily for the purpose of providing deferred compensation for a select group of management or highly compensated employees" and "excess benefit plans." The broad definition of "pension plan" under ERISA makes the funding requirements apply to many deferred compensation arrangements, previously unfunded plans, and other arrangements not previously thought of as pension plans.

Basic Requirements. Employers are required to contribute at least the normal cost plus amounts calculated to amortize any unfunded liabilities over a period of years. The required amortization period ranges from 15 years to 40 years depending on when it arose and its source. If contributions in any year exceed the minimum required, the excess reduces the minimum required in subsequent years.

Penalties and Enforcement. If contributions are less than required, the shortfall is an "accumulated funding deficiency." If an accumulated funding deficiency exists at the end of the plan year, a 5 percent excise tax is assessed on the deficiency. If the funding deficiency is not corrected within 90 days after IRS mails a notice of deficiency, an additional tax is imposed equal to 100 percent of any uncorrected deficiency. In addition to paying these nondeductible taxes, the employer must also correct the accumulated funding deficiency itself. These taxes apply only to qualified plans. Whether or not the plan is qualified, the Secretary of Labor, participants, beneficiaries, and fiduciaries may bring civil actions to enforce the minimum funding requirements.

Funding Standard Account. A "funding standard account" is an accounting device used to keep track of the funding requirements. Amounts which increase the funding obligation for the year are charges to the funding standard account. This includes the normal cost and annual payments needed to amortize any unfunded liabilities. Amounts that decrease the employer's obligation are credits to the funding standard account. This includes employer contributions and annual amounts that may be used to amortize any decrease in the unfunded liability.

If the credits exceed the charges for a year, the excess is carried over as a credit balance to decrease the contributions required for the following year. Similarly, if the credits are less than the charges, the resulting accumulated funding deficiency is carried forward to increase the contributions required in the following year.

Reporting. For defined benefit pension plans, the plan administrator must engage an enrolled actuary "on behalf of all plan participants." Satisfaction of the minimum funding requirements is demonstrated on Schedule B "Actuarial Information," which must be certified by an enrolled actuary and attached to Form 5500. For defined contribution pension plans, satisfaction of the requirements is shown on Form 5500 itself.

Timing of Contributions. To satisfy the funding requirements, employers may make contributions for the plan year up to 8½ months after the end of the plan year.

Full Funding Limitation

No employer is required to contribute more than the amount needed to fully fund the accrued liability. This full funding limitation may reduce or eliminate the minimum contribution otherwise required. If the plan uses the aggregate cost or frozen initial liability for funding, then for purposes of the full funding limitation it must calculate the accrued liability under the entry age normal cost method.

Alternative Minimum Funding Requirement

Some plans are allowed to use the alternative minimum funding standard to determine their minimum funding requirement. If a plan uses the alternative minimum funding standard, it must nonetheless also maintain records for the regular funding standard account. A plan may not use the alternative minimum funding standard unless it uses the entry age normal cost method under its regular funding standard account. If an alternative minimum funding standard account is maintained, it is charged with (1) the lesser of the normal cost under the actuarial cost method used under the plan or the normal cost determined under the unit credit cost method, (2) the excess, if any, of the present value of accrued benefits over the fair market value of assets, and (3) any credit balance in the account as of the beginning of the year. The alternative minimum funding standard account is credited with employer contributions for the year.

The alternative minimum funding requirement is based upon a plan discontinuance concept. It is not a sound basis for funding an ongoing plan. Very few plans use this alternative.

Extension of Amortization Period

Another form of relief from the minimum funding requirement is an extension of the amortization periods. The Secretary of Labor may extend the time required to amortize any unfunded liability by up to 10 years. Extending an amortization period reduces slightly the required employer contribution. No employer is known to have applied for such an extension.

Waiver

The Internal Revenue Service may grant a waiver of part or all of the minimum funding requirement. A waiver will be approved only if the employer faces "substantial business hardship" and if failure to approve the waiver would be "adverse to the interests of plan participants in the aggregate."

Multiemployer Plan Requirements

ERISA contained slightly different funding requirements for collectively bargained multiemployer plans than for other plans. The Multiemployer Pension Plans Amendment Act of 1980 (MEPPA) made further changes for multiemployer plans. The most significant difference is that an employer that withdraws from a multiemployer plan may be assessed "withdrawal liability," requiring significant contributions after the withdrawal.

TAX DEDUCTION OF EMPLOYER CONTRIBUTIONS

Purposes

Like most other business expenses, contributions to qualified pension plans must be deducted as ordinary and necessary business expenses. In addition, Section 404 of the Internal Revenue Code sets maximum limits on the amount that may be deducted in each year. Section 404 reflects two concerns of Congress.

First, Congress wanted to encourage employers to establish qualified plans for their employees. Congress also wanted to encourage employers to soundly fund the plans to assure promised benefits would be paid. Thus Congress wanted to allow tax deductions for the amounts needed to soundly fund the plans.

Second, Congress wanted to limit the deduction for a particular year to expense attributable to that year. This would prevent an employer from prepaying future expenses to evade taxes. But it is not clear how much of the payments for past service costs and actuarial gains and losses should be considered attributable to a particular year.

Timing of Deductible Contributions

To be deductible, contributions to pension and profit-sharing plans for a year must be paid no later than the tax filing date for the year, including extensions. No deduction may be claimed for the contribution of a promissory note of the employer, even if secured.

Maximum Deductible Limit for Pension Plans

Section 404 has three alternative ways to determine the maximum limit on deductible employer contributions. Usually, the maximum deductible limit equals the normal cost plus the amount needed to amortize any past service liability over 10 years. If a plan has no unfunded liability, its deductible limit does not include a past service amount.

The amount of past service cost to be amortized is called a "10-year amortization base." For a new plan, the 10-year amortization base equals the initial unfunded accrued liability base. If the unfunded accrued liability is changed by a plan amendment, change in the actuarial method or assumptions, or actuarial gains or losses, the amount of change in the unfunded accrued liability becomes an additional 10-year amortization base. The old base continues until it is fully amortized. Any event which increases the unfunded liability creates a new positive base. Any event which decreases the unfunded liability creates a new negative base. A plan may have many bases.

The amount required to amortize each 10-year amortization base over 10 years is the "limit adjustment." Each 10-year amortization base has its own limit adjustment. The limit adjustment is positive if its base is positive and negative if its base is negative. All of a plan's limit adjustments are added to determine the plan's maximum deductible limit for past service contributions. Detailed regulations provide rules for determining the amount of bases and limit adjustments.[2]

The second method of determining the maximum deductible limit is the individual aggregate method. The maximum deductible limit for each participant is the amount necessary to provide the remaining unfunded cost of the projected benefit distributed as a level amount, or a level percentage of compensation, over the participant's remaining future service. But if the remaining unfunded cost for any three individuals exceeds 50 percent of the unfunded cost for the entire plan, then the unfunded cost for each such individual must be distributed over at least five years.

The third alternative for determining the deductible limit equals the amount required to satisfy the plan's minimum funding requirement. The full funding limitation determined under the minimum funding requirements is an overriding maximum limit on the amount that may be deducted for a year. If the employer contributes more than the maximum deductible limit for any year, the excess may be carried over to be deducted in the following year.

Maximum Deductible Limits for Profit-Sharing and Stock Bonus Plans

The maximum deductible limit for a profit-sharing plan or stock bonus plan is 15 percent of the compensation paid or accrued for all participants during the tax year. The limitation is on the aggregate contributions for all

---

[2] Treasury Reg. sec. 1.404(a).

participants not the contribution for each. Thus, more than 15 percent may be contributed and deducted for a particular participant if the aggregate limit is not exceeded. If the employer contributes less than the maximum deductible limit in one year, the difference is carried forward to increase the deductible limit in the following year, but the following year's deductible limit, including the carry-forward, may not exceed 25 percent of the compensation for the year of deduction.

If the employer contributes more than the deductible limit for a year, the excess is carried over to be deducted in future years, subject to the 15 percent deductible limit in future years.

Maximum Deductible for Combined Plans

If an employer maintains more than one profit-sharing or stock bonus plan, they are treated as a single plan for purposes of determining the deductible limit. If an employer maintains both a pension plan and a profit-sharing or stock bonus plan, there is an additional limitation on deductible contributions. Deductible contributions to the combined plans are limited to 25 percent of compensation of all of the participants in either plan or, if greater, the pension plan contribution required by the minimum funding requirements. This is so even though an employer that has no profit-sharing plan may deduct more than 25 percent of pay under a pension plan. If contributions to combined pension and profit-sharing plans exceed the combined 25 percent limit, they may be carried over for deduction in a later year.

DEDUCTION OF EMPLOYEE CONTRIBUTIONS

Some plans require employees to contribute to the plan as a condition for participation or for receiving certain employer-provided benefits. Such mandatory employee contributions are not deductible by employees.

Some plans allow employees to make voluntary contributions to increase the benefits otherwise provided under the plan. The Internal Revenue Code does not classify contributions as voluntary if any benefit derived from employer contribution is linked to them. An employee may claim a deduction for voluntary contributions up to $2,000, but not more than 100 percent of compensation. This is a combined limit that applies to the sum of such voluntary employee contributions plus any contributions to an individual retirement account (IRA). Such deductible voluntary employee contributions are generally subject to the same tax rules as an IRA. An employee making voluntary employee contributions to a plan who does not want them treated as deductible contributions subject to the IRA tax rules may elect not to have them so treated if he or she is willing to forgo the deduction.

ACCOUNTING FOR PENSION PLAN LIABILITIES AND COSTS

There are two parts to pension plan accounting, accounting for the plan itself and accounting for the employer.

Accounting for the Plan

Form 5500 or a related form must be filed each year with the Internal Revenue Service. Form 5500 includes a statement of plan assets and liabilities, a statement of income and expenses, and certain other financial information. For plans with 100 or more participants the plan administrator is required to engage an independent qualified public accountant. A statement from the accountant, prepared in accordance with generally accepted accounting principles must be attached to Form 5500. *Statement of Financial Accounting Standards No. 35* of the Financial Accounting Standards Board (FASB) established generally accepted accounting principles for pension plans.

For defined benefit plans with 100 or more participants Schedule B of Form 5500 requires reporting the value of accrued benefits. This same item is required in accounting statements under *Statement No. 35*. It ordinarily bears no relation to the plan's funding, is misleading as an indication of funding for an ongoing plan, and does not purport to represent the plan's liabilities if the plan were discontinued.

Both Form 5500 and *Statement No. 35* also require a statement of assets and liabilities (other than actuarial liabilities), a statement of changes in fund balances, and additional information.

Accounting for the Employer

An employer's accounting for a defined contribution plan usually is simple. Contributions paid for the employer's fiscal year are treated as an expense. An employer's accounting for a defined benefit plan is more complex. It requires certain disclosures in addition to determining the charge to expense and possible balance sheet entries.

An employer's charge to expense for pension cost is the subject of *Opinion No. 8* of the Accounting Principles Board of the American Institute of Certified Public Accountants (AICPA). *Opinion No. 8* requires the profit and loss statement to include a charge for pension expense that represents the pension cost properly attributable to the current year, regardless of the amount contributed for the year. It contains minimum and maximum limits for the charge to expense, and requires the accounting method and actuarial cost method used be consistently applied from year to year. The minimum charge to expense equals the normal cost, plus interest on any unfunded accrued liability, plus, if the value of vested benefits exceeds the assets, a provision for vested benefits. This minimum provision for vested benefits is the amount calculated to reduce the unfunded value of vested benefits by 5 percent during the year, or if less, the amount calculated to amortize the total unfunded liability over 40 years. The maximum charge to expense under *Opinion No. 8* is the normal cost plus 10 percent of the past service cost. This maximum limit coincided with previous limits on maximum deductible contributions, and most accountants assumed the current maximum deductible limit is acceptable as a charge to expense. Actuarial gains and losses generally must be amortized over 10 to 20 years. The requirements of *Opinion No. 8* are currently being reviewed by the FASB.

Statement of Financial Accounting Standards No. 36 requires the notes to the employer's financial statement to include disclosures comparable to those required for the plan by *Statement No. 35*.

Relationship of Accounting and Funding

Accounting for the pension plan itself and accounting for the employer do not directly control the plan's funding. However, there may be an important indirect effect, since the manner in which accountants report funding influences some employers' decisions concerning funding.

CHAPTER 42

Alternative Insurance Company Arrangements

RICHARD L. TEWKSBURY, Jr.

The cost of employee group insurance plans has become an increasingly significant part of the corporate budget. Similarly, as these plans have grown in size, the claims experience of an employer's group insurance program has become more predictable. These factors have caused the conventional insurance arrangement to be considered as much a corporate financing vehicle as a direct transfer of the corporate personnel risk.

Responding to these influences, insurance companies have designed a number of alternative arrangements for insuring group insurance programs. This chapter highlights the development of alternative insurance company arrangements and describes each arrangement in detail.

CONVENTIONAL INSURANCE ARRANGEMENT

Alternative insurance arrangements provide an employer ways of potentially reducing the normal costs of a conventional insurance arrangement. It is important to first define a conventional insurance arrangement and its various cost factors so the purpose and advantages of alternative insurance arrangements become apparent.

Definition

In a conventional insurance arrangement, an employer purchases a group insurance contract and agrees to pay premiums to an insurance company. In return, the insurance company agrees to pay specific benefit amounts for such events as death or disability. The employer's annual premium cost is based on the previous financial experience of employers of similar size and characteristics and the actuarial statistics and administrative expenses of the insurance company.

The insurance company uses the premiums paid by all employers to pay all claims incurred under the group insurance plans. The employers whose actual claims costs are less than their premium payments subsidize the employer whose claims costs exceed their premium payments. In a conventional insurance arrangement, there is no reconciliation of an employer's premium payments to its actual claims costs. Instead, any adjustment of premium charges reflects the overall loss experience of all employers.

Premium Cost Factors

The insurance company considers a number of different factors as part of the total cost of insuring a risk.

Paid Claims

This is the total benefits paid to insured employees or their dependents during the policy period.

Reserves

This cost reflects the insurance company's liability to pay benefits in the future for a loss incurred during the policy year. The most common reserve is the incurred but unreported claim reserve established to pay losses incurred during the policy year but not reported for payment until after the policy year has ended. Reserves also are established for special benefit payment liabilities. The most common special reserves are the life insurance waiver of premium reserve and the reserve for future disability benefit payments.

Other Claim Charges

Several additional costs are assumed by the insurance company for providing special benefit coverages, such as extended liability coverage and conversion to an individual insurance policy when a participant terminates employment.

Administrative Charges

Although the terminology and allocation of administrative expenses vary by insurance company, there are six main cost categories:

1. **Commissions.**   This is the payment to a licensed insurance agent or broker for helping the employer obtain the insurance coverage and receive ongoing administrative services. The commission amount normally is determined as a percentage of the premium paid, with the percentage remaining either level or, more often, declining as premium increases.

2. **Premium Taxes.**   A state tax is levied on the premiums received by insurance companies in the resident states of insured employees. This tax expense is passed directly to the employer, normally as a percentage of

premium paid. The current tax rate averages about 2 percent of premium, but can vary depending on the state.

3. **Risk Charge.** Each insured employer contributes to the insurance company's contingency reserve for unexpected, catastrophic amounts of claims in a future period. The risk charge normally is determined by a formula based on the premium amount.

4. **Claims Administration Expenses.** These are the expenses incurred by the insurance company to investigate claims and calculate and pay the appropriate benefits. These expenses normally are fixed per claim, with the per claim cost varying by the type of benefits paid; e.g., life insurance benefits are relatively simple and quick to administer and have a low administrative cost per claim compared to disability and medical claims that often require medical review and more difficult benefit calculations.

5. **Other Administrative Expenses.** Charges for actuarial, legal, accounting and other such services, plus overhead expenses are shared by all contractholders. These expenses are determined either as a percentage of the premium amount, a fixed charge, or a variable charge based on the insurance company's actual services provided to the employer.

6. **Insurance Company Profit (Stock Company) or Contribution to Surplus (Mutual Company).**

ALTERNATIVE INSURANCE ARRANGEMENTS

Definition

An alternative insurance arrangement is a means of financing the transfer of risk that in some way *defers* or *reduces* the premium paid by the employer to the insurance company. Essentially, this is accomplished by varying the normal reserves, claim charges, and administrative costs of the insurance company.

The deferral or reduction of paid premium provides the employer *direct* and *indirect* savings. Direct savings result from the reduction or elimination of specific insurance company charges. Indirect savings are gained through the more efficient and profitable corporate use of money that normally would be held and invested by the insurance company.

The trade-off for these employer savings is the assumption by the employer of certain normal insurance company functions or risk. For example, the employer might assume all or part of the financial liability, i.e., benefit payments to employees, and therefore reduce the necessary premium paid to the insurance company to pay benefit claims. Similarly, the employer might agree to administer all or part of the plan to reduce the insurance company's administrative charges.

Reasons for Alternative Insurance Arrangements

Three main reasons exist for alternatives to the conventional insurance arrangement: the corporate effort to reduce premium charges, the increasing importance of corporate value of money, and the intense competition among insurance companies for the best insurable risks.

Reduce Premium Charges.   The employer's main reason for purchasing group insurance is to transfer a personnel risk that has unpredictable occurrence and potential financial loss significantly greater than the insurance company's premium charge. If a significant loss occurs, the insurance is a valuable investment to the employer. But if the losses over a period of time are less than the premium charges, employers begin to further analyze the insured risk and the financial value of the conventional insurance arrangement.

Employers with large insured employee groups have more predictable loss experience. These employers can reasonably project the expected claims costs of their employee groups over time and thereby determine the *expected* annual cost to provide the group insurance benefits. The conventional insurance arrangement then becomes most valuable to protect against the unexpected catastrophic losses.

Because large employers can reasonably project their future benefit costs, they can determine the financial advantages and trade-offs of participating in the financing and assumption of the risk. This participation reduces the premium paid to the insurer and potentially reduces the overall cost to the employer through lesser claim charges, premium tax, risk charge, and other administrative charges. These financial advantages have been the impetus to such alternative insurance arrangements as participating and experience-rated contracts and the many variations of self-insurance by employers.

Corporate Value of Money.   The influence of corporate value of money has become increasingly significant with rising premium costs and interest rates. Under the conventional insurance arrangement, the employer periodically pays premiums to the insurance company. To the extent the paid premium exceeds claims costs, the insurance company invests the excess premiums. Similarly, the insurance company earns income from the various claim reserves that it maintains for each group insurance plan. Some of this investment income is credited to the employer, but the total may not equal the rate of return actually earned by the insurance company.

Interest rates have increased to unexpected levels, causing employers to scrutinize the use of corporate money and assure earning the highest available rate of return. If the employer can earn more after taxes in its business than the interest rate credited by the insurance company on surplus premium and claim reserves, it is advantageous to minimize the transfer of funds to the insurer. This influence has encouraged the development of deferred premium arrangements, reduction or total return of accumulated reserves to the employer, and various self-insurance arrangements.

Competition.   The third reason for alternative insurance arrangements is the intense competition between insurance companies for insuring "good" risks. Under the conventional insurance arrangement, employers share equally in the financing of claims costs through similar premium charges, which means that employers with favorable loss experience, i.e., premiums in excess of plan costs, subsidize employers with unfavorable loss experience, i.e., plan costs in excess of premiums. Employers with favorable loss experience—the "good" risks—will look for alternatives that better reflect their actual costs. The financial advantages and administrative flexibility of alternative insurance arrangements often are the key factors in an employer selecting and continuing with an insurance company.

Also, many employers, especially those with favorable loss experience, have changed to or at least have considered self-insurance of all or part of their group insurance program which minimizes, or even eliminates, the need for an insurance company. For instance, a 1980 study found that 29 percent of surveyed employers self-insured their medical plans in some form in 1978, and by 1980, 50 percent of surveyed employers self-insured all or part of their medical plans.[1]

To attract and maintain insured group insurance plans and to stem the movement toward self-insurance, insurance companies have introduced alternative insurance arrangements that meet the employer's financial needs and offer essentially the same advantages as self-insurance.

BASIC ALTERNATIVE INSURANCE ARRANGEMENTS

Participating Arrangement

A *participating insurance arrangement* differs from the conventional insurance arrangement in that the employer participates in the favorable and unfavorable financial experience during the policy period. If the financial experience is favorable; i.e., the claims and administrative costs are less than the premium paid during the policy period, the employer receives the surplus premium from the insurance company at the end of the policy year. If the financial experience is unfavorable; i.e., the claims and administrative costs are greater than the premium paid during the policy period, the plan is considered to be in a deficit balance equal to the difference between total plan costs and paid premium. In most instances, this deficit balance is carried forward by the insurance company to be recovered in future years of favorable experience.

Therefore, in a participating insurance arrangement the true cost, or *net cost,* of the group insurance plans is the premium paid during the policy year adjusted for the balance remaining at year-end.

Underwriting Factors

Because the insurance company shares with each employer in the actual financial experience of the group insurance plans, there are several under-

---

[1] The 1980 Hay/Huggins Noncash Compensation Comparison.

writing factors included in a participating insurance arrangement that are unnecessary in a conventional insurance arrangement.

Employer Participation.   An insurance company will vary the *percentage of employer participation* in the actual financial experience depending on two key factors: the "spread" of risk and the predictability of losses.

Spread of risk refers to the ability of the employer's benefit plan to absorb a major, catastrophic loss relative to its paid premium base. The larger the employee group, the easier it becomes to incur a major loss without dramatically affecting the year-end actual financial experience of the plan. This is because the premium charge being paid per insured participant in the plan provides a fund large enough to pay the infrequent major losses as well as the normal benefit costs. Thus, the risk is effectively "spread" across the premium base of the insured employee group. Normally, employee groups of more than 100 employees are considered large enough for a participating insurance arrangement.

Predictability of losses is the second key factor in determining the percentage of participation. Essentially, the more predictable the total losses for each year, the greater the percentage of employer participation. Plans such as medical care, dental, and short-term disability cover risks in which losses normally occur frequently and at relatively low benefit costs per occurrence. The predictability of loss experience for these plans is much better than life insurance and long-term disability plans that cover risks with less frequent losses and normally much higher total benefit costs per loss. Similarly, participating insurance arrangements are more common in medical care, dental, and short-term disability plans.

To limit the employer's percentage of participation in the plan's actual financial experience, the insurance company sets *pooling points*. A pooling point is a dollar limit of annual benefit costs per individual that will be included in the actual financial experience of the participating insurance arrangement. Any individual benefit costs in excess of the pooling point will not be assessed against the plan's financial experience. Instead, this excess amount is included in the insurance company's "pool" of conventional insurance arrangements for the same risk. For example, a group life insurance plan could insure employees with potential benefits of $100,000 or more but have a pooling point of $50,000. This means an individual's benefit claim up to $50,000 is reflected in the plan's actual financial experience and any benefit amounts in excess of $50,000 are assumed by the insurance company.

The employer pays an additional premium charge, called a pooling charge, for the exclusion of benefits in excess of the pooling point. This charge is based on the "pool's" loss experience and reflects the type of risk and expected benefit costs over time that each employer will have in excess of the pooling point. For instance, a life insurance plan pooling charge normally equals the volume of life insurance in excess of the pooling point, multiplied by the insurance company's conventional arrangement premium charge. The medical care plan pooling charge normally is determined as a percentage of annual premium or paid claims.

Table 42–1 illustrates a typical schedule of pooling point levels for medical care and life insurance plans, which are the most common participating insurance arrangements requiring pooling points.

Table 42–1
Pooling Points

Life Insurance Plan

Volume of Insurance	Pooling Point
$ 1 million	$ 20,000
2.5 million	25,000
5 million	35,000
10 million	60,000
25 million	85,000
50 million	135,000

Medical Care Insurance Plan

Annual Premium (000s)	Annual Benefit Pooling Point
Less than $250	$ 20,000
$ 250– 500	30,000
500– 750	40,000
750–1,000	50,000
1,000–1,500	75,000
1,500–2,000	100,000
Over 2,000	None

Underwriting Margin. The premium paid under a participating insurance arrangement includes a charge for the possible fluctuation of actual costs in excess of the expected claims and administrative costs during the policy year. This charge commonly is called the insurance company's *underwriting margin.*

Underwriting margin reflects the normal range of deviation of the plan's actual loss experience in any year to the expected loss experience. The underwriting margin is determined from actuarial studies on the fluctuation of actual claims experience relative to insurance company norms for similar employee groups and types of insurance coverage. In general, the underwriting margin decreases as the predictability of the plan's expected claims experience increases.

The underwriting margin for a basic group life insurance plan varies between 10 percent and 40 percent of premium depending on the size of the employee group and volume of life insurance. Table 42–2 illustrates the typical level of underwriting margins for medical care plans.

Table 42–2
Medical Care Insurance Plan

Number of Covered Employees	Percent of Premium
Fewer than 1,000	10–15%
1,000 to 2,000	8–10
Over 2,000	5– 8

Determining the Year-End Balance

The key principle in a participating insurance arrangement is that the employer's final or net cost equals paid premiums adjusted for the year-end balance (surplus or deficit). The year-end balance is determined by the *actual* plan costs in relation to the paid premium.

Basic Formula. The determination of a surplus or deficit year-end balance for group insurance plans is rather straightforward:

Paid premium (−) Claims costs (−) Administrative costs = Balance

Paid premium refers to the employer's total payments to the insurance company during the plan year.

The *claims costs* factor is made up of various charges:

1. *Paid claims:* This total is the actual benefit payments during the policy year.
2. *Reserve charge:* This equals the establishment of or adjustment to claims reserves held for incurred but unreported claims and any other specific pending liabilities, such as waiver of premium life insurance claims and unsettled claims payments at year-end.
3. *Pooling charge:* This is the additional cost for having large individual claims "pooled" in excess of a specific pooling point.
4. *Other claim charges:* The most common charge included in this category is a penalty charge levied against the employer when a terminated employee converts from a group to an individual insurance policy.

The *administrative costs* essentially are the same six expense categories mentioned previously for a conventional insurance arrangement.

Surplus Balance. If the year-end balance is positive, there will be surplus premiums available to be returned to the employer. The following example illustrates how a surplus year-end balance is determined.

Example. During the policy year the employer pays $500,000 of group insurance premiums to the insurance company. Claims paid during the year are $375,000, reserve charges are $10,000, pooling charges are $20,000 and other claim charges $5,000, for a total of $410,000 in claims costs. Total administrative costs equal $60,000. These total costs related to the paid premium result in a year-end balance of $30,000 surplus premium.

Paid premium		$500,000
Less: Claims costs		$410,000
Paid claims	$375,000	
Reserve charges	10,000	
Pooling charges	20,000	
Other charges	5,000	
Less: Administrative costs		$ 60,000
Year-end balance		$ 30,000

Surplus premium that accumulates with the insurance company during the plan year normally is credited with interest earnings that are used to reduce the insurance company's administative costs. The interest rate credited is usually based on the investment performance of the insurance company's general assets.

The insurance company can return the surplus balance by issuing a *dividend* check equal to the surplus amount. This dividend reduces the year-end employer paid premium total that is tax-deductible as an ordinary business expense under Section 162 of the Internal Revenue Code.

Alternatively, the insurance company could deposit the surplus balance in a special reserve, normally called a *premium stabilization reserve*. The major advantages of a premium stabilization reserve are twofold:

- To avoid a reduction in the tax-deductible paid premium amount at year-end.
- To help stabilize the future budget and cash flow requirements of the plan by supplementing premium rate increases with funds from the special reserve.

A common disadvantage of a premium stabilization reserve is the lower investment earnings credited by the insurance company on the reserve amount compared to what the corporation could earn after tax by internally using the surplus premium. Also, an insurance company may be able to retain and use these funds to pay unexpected plan costs after contract termination.

Deficit Balance. A negative year-end balance, or *deficit* balance, means the employer's premium paid during the policy year is insufficient to pay the plan's total costs during the year. Such a situation is illustrated in the following example.

Example: The premium and plan costs are the same as the previous example, except paid claims during the year are $425,000 and the total administrative costs are $70,000. The total plan costs now result in a year-end deficit balance of ($30,000) premium.

Paid premium		$500,000
Less: Claims costs		$460,000
Paid claims	$425,000	
Reserve charges	10,000	
Pooling charges	20,000	
Other charges	5,000	
Less: Administrative costs		$ 70,000
Year-end balance		$ (30,000)

The deficit balance is offset during the policy year from the insurance company's corporate surplus to pay all claims and other immediate costs of the plan. In a sense, these insurance company funds act as a "loan" to the employer. In most instances, an employer's deficit balance will be carried forward to future policy years and be repaid through surplus premium balances that may result in future policy years. However, the employer normally is not *contractually* required to repay this insurance company "loan" and can switch insurance companies while a plan deficit is outstanding. This is a risk assumed by the insurance company and is reflected in the risk charge and the underwriting margins of the insurer. While a plan deficit exists, the outstanding balance is charged with an interest expense normally equal to the interest credited on surplus premiums of other policyholders.

Instead of repaying the deficit balance through future surplus premium, the employer could negotiate with the insurance company to repay the "loan" in lump sum or in installments over a specified period. However, the insurance company interest charge on the outstanding deficit balance normally is less than the interest charge if the employer were to borrow monies from another financial institution. In these instances, it is more cost-effective to repay the outstanding deficit balance through the possible surplus premiums of future policy years.

Employer Advantages. The potential advantage of a participating insurance arrangement is that the employer pays its "actual" insurance cost and is rewarded for favorable financial experience by the return of year-end surplus premium. During a policy year of favorable experience, cost savings can be gained in several additional ways:

1. *Premium tax* is reduced because it is based on the *net* premium received by an insurance company; i.e., the employer's premium paid during the policy year less the surplus balance returned at year-end.
2. *Administrative costs* are reduced by lower general overhead charges based on net premium paid and by interest income earned on the surplus premium during the policy year, which normally is credited to the plan by reducing the total administrative costs.

The financial trade-off to the employer of a participating insurance arrangement is a higher risk charge and underwriting margin assumed by the insurance company in comparison to a conventional insurance arrangement. Also, the carryover of deficit balances in policy years of unfavorable financial experience will increase the future years' plan costs due to interest charges on the outstanding deficit balance and possibly additional underwriting margins required by the insurance company.

Experience-Rating Arrangement

Whereas a participating insurance arrangement enables the employer to participate in the actual financial experience of each plan year through year-end surplus or deficit balances, an *experience-rating insurance arrangement* enables the actual financial experience of previous policy years to affect the employer's future premium charges. If the employer's actual financial experience has been favorable in the past, the future premium rates will be less than the conventional premium rate of other similar employers. Similarly, if the loss experience has been unfavorable, future premium rates will be increased more than the rates of conventionally insured employers to stabilize the financial condition of this employer's plan.

An experience-rating arrangement can be included with either a participating or a conventional, nonparticipating insurance arrangement. In either case, the actual previous financial experience of the employer's plan is the basis for determining the future plan year's premium rates.

Underwriting Factors

If an employer's actual loss experience has fluctuated significantly in the past, volatile changes can occur in the experience-rated premium charges from year to year. For example, a plan year with favorable loss experience could substantially reduce the next year's premium charges. If unfavorable experience actually occurred during that next year, subsequent premium charges likewise would increase substantially to reflect this unfavorable year. Such yearly swings in premium costs usually disturb employers and hinder their ability to budget future costs and control cash flow needs. Similarly, the insurance company usually finds it more difficult to maintain the loyalty and understanding of the employer when the required premium charges vary significantly from year to year.

To minimize this problem, the insurance company controls the degree of influence of an employer's actual loss experience in determining premium charges. This is done through underwriting factors based on the statistical credibility of the actual paid claims experience and the type of risk.

Statistical Credibility.   *Statistical credibility* refers to the validity of an employee group's actual paid claims experience representing the normal, expected loss experience of such a group. The greater the statistical credibility, the greater the signifigance given the plan's year-end financial results in determining future premium rates.

Statistical credibility is based on the applicability of the *law of large numbers*. The law of large numbers doctrine states that:

> The larger the number of separate risks of a like nature combined into one group, the less uncertainty there will be as to the relative amount of loss that will be incurred within a given period.[2]

Besides employee group size, statistical credibility also is determined by the number of years of actual paid claims experience that can be analyzed. The statistical credibility of cumulative years of actual experience for a smaller employee group will be similar to that of a much larger employee group for a one-year period. For example, the cumulative five-year life insurance experience of a 350 to 400 employee group has similar statistical credibility to the one-year experience of a 1,750 to 2,000 employee group.

The importance of the *type of risk* is similar to the underwriting of a participating insurance arrangement. Statistical credibility of actual loss experience is greater for risks that occur more frequently and have a lesser average cost per occurrence, such as medical care and short-term disability. Therefore, greater significance can be given to the actual paid claims experience for these types of risks. For instance, one to three years of loss experience normally is necessary to determine the experience-rated premium charges of medical care, dental, and short-term disability coverages.

On the other hand, the insurance company applies statistical credibility to the employer's life insurance and long-term disability loss experience only if three to five years of paid claims experience are available for review. This is due to the volatility of loss experience from year to year for these coverages. By analyzing three to five years' loss experience, individual years of unusually favorable or unfavorable loss experience are melded into a more common overall trend of claims costs.

Credibility Factors. There are several ways an insurance company can control the effect of year-to-year fluctuations of actual loss experience in an experience-rated insurance arrangement. The most common method is to use a weighted average of the employer's actual claims experience and the insurance company's normal loss factors for a similar conventional insurance arrangement. The percentage factor applied to the employer's actual paid claims experience is called the *credibility factor.* The greater the statistical credibility of the risk, the closer the credibility factor is to 100 percent, which implies the employer's prior loss experience is wholly representative of future loss experience.

Table 42–3 shows the common credibility factors applied to life insur-

---

[2] S. S. Huebner and K. Black, *Life Insurance,* 10th ed. (Englewood Cliffs, N.J.: Prentice-Hall, 1982), p. 3.

Table 42-3
Credibility Factors

Life Insurance Plan

Number of	Number of Years of Experience		
Covered Employees	1	3	5
250– 500	10%	25%	35%
500– 1,000	20	45	55
1,000– 2,500	30	55	65
2,500– 5,000	45	75	85
5,000–10,000	60	80	90
Over 10,000	75	100	100

Medical Care Insurance Plan

Number of Covered Employees	Credibility Factors
50–100	30–50%
100–200	50–75
200–500	75–97
Over 500	100

ance and medical care plans. The life insurance factors are determined by the number of covered employees and the number of available years of actual claims experience. The factors for a medical plan normally are based on the number of employees covered by the plan.

For example, if an employer's medical plan covers 200 employees and incurred $150,000 of paid claims last year, a 75 percent credibility factor would be applied to this loss experience. If the insurance company's expected losses for a similar size and type of employee group is $180,000, the expected paid claims for the next plan year would be $157,500.

$$\frac{\text{Employer's past year's actual claims}}{\$150,000} \times \frac{\text{Credibility factor}}{.75} = \$112,500$$

Plus

$$\frac{\text{Insurer's expected losses}}{\$180,000} \times \frac{\text{Noncredible factor}}{.25} = \$\ 45,000$$

Next year's expected claims $= \$157,500$

Pooling Points.   A second method of controlling the loss experience fluctuation on future premium rates is to establish *pooling points,* as described previously in the section on participating insurance arrangements. By placing dollar maximums on the individual and total plan claim costs that will be included in each plan year's actual financial experience, the volatility of losses in any year is substantially limited. For providing this limitation on the employer's "experience-rated" losses, the insurance company levies a fixed annual charge, or pooling charge.

With a life insurance plan, the pooling charge is added to the average of the prior years' experience-rated paid claims to determine the expected claims costs for the next policy year. For example, if the average experience-rated losses over the last five plan years are $100,000, the life insurance volume in excess of the pooling point is $2,500,000, and the monthly pooling charge is $.75 per $1,000 of life insurance, the expected claims costs for the next policy year are $122,500.

Pooling cost:		
Excess life insurance volume	$2,500,000	
Monthly premium charge	.00075	
Monthly cost	$ 1,875	
	× 12	
Annual pooling cost		$ 22,500
Experience-rated claims cost:		$100,000
Next year's expected claims cost		$122,500

The medical insurance pooling charge normally is stated as a percentage of annual premium or paid claims. For instance, if the paid premium is $150,000, the pooling point is $20,000 per individual, and the pooling charge is 5 percent of premium, a charge of $7,500 would be included in determining the necessary premium charges for the next year.

Premium Stabilization Reserve. Another alternative for controlling the effect of annual loss fluctuation on premium charges is a *premium stabilization reserve,* previously discussed in the section on participating insurance arrangements. If additional premium is required in the coming plan year to reflect previous years of unfavorable loss experience, a part or all of the necessary premium rate increase is supplemented by premium stabilization reserve funds. For example, assume a premium stabilization reserve of $45,000 exists and additional premium of $40,000 is necessary to equal expected losses for the coming plan year. All or part of this additional premium could come from the premium stabilization reserve.

Determining the Experience-Rated Premium

The exact method for determining the experience-rated premium charges varies by the type of insurance coverage and the insurance company. The explanation below describes the common principles for life insurance and medical care coverages.

Life Insurance. The life insurance premium charge is based on the expected paid claims, underwriting margin, reserve adjustment, pooling charge, and administrative costs.

Expected Paid Claims. Determining the next year's expected paid claims depends on the credibility factor given to the employer's previous actual loss experience. The credibility factor is applied to the average actual paid claims total for a three- to five-year period. This average actual paid claims total should reflect annual changes in the volume of life insurance to provide a meaningful comparison of year-to-year claims experience.

Reserve Adjustment. The incurred but unreported reserve initially is established as a percentage of premium or paid claims and is adjusted each year thereafter to reflect changes in these factors. An estimate of the next year's adjustment is included in the premium charge calculation based on expected paid claims or premium.

Underwriting Margin. This charge normally is stated as a percentage of expected paid claims and reserve adjustments or of total premium. If a participating insurance arrangement is included with the experience-rated arrangement, additional underwriting margin is added.

Pooling Charge. Annual charge based on the volume of "pooled" life insurance and premium rate for the employee group.

Administrative Costs. These normally are determined as a percentage of the experience-rated premium charges.

The sum of these factors cumulatively determines the experience-rated life insurance premium charge for the next policy year. An example of calculating a required premium rate is illustrated in Exhibit 42–1.

Exhibit 42–1
Life Insurance Experience-Rating Calculation

Assumptions:	Five-year average actual paid claims	$100,000
	Expected annual losses*	80,000
	Credibility factor	.60
	Underwriting margin	10% of incurred claims
	Reserve adjustment	2,000
	Pooling charges	6,600
	Administrative costs	10,000

Example:		
1.	Expected paid claims ($100,000 × .6) + ($80,000 × .4)	$ 92,000
2.	Reserve adjustment	2,000
3.	Incurred claims	94,000
4.	Margin: (10% of incurred claims)	9,400
5.	Pooling charges	6,600
6.	Administrative costs	10,000
	Required premium	$120,000

* Based on insurance company's acturial statistics.

Medical Insurance. The medical insurance premium charge is based on expected paid claims, inflation/utilization trend, underwriting margin, reserve adjustments, pooling charge, and administrative costs. These factors are determined in the same manner as the life insurance premium charges, *except* for the following.

Expected Paid Claims. Much greater credibility is given to the loss experience of the prior plan year, such that developing average loss history over several years normally is unnecessary.

Inflation/Utilization Trend. Rising medical costs (inflation) and plan utilization are distinct economic factors that will increase the next year's paid claims; therefore, the expected paid claims are increased by a trend factor projected for the next policy year.

Pooling Charge. This charge normally is a percentage of paid claims or premium.

The sum of these factors cumulatively determines the experience-rated medical premium charge, as illustrated in Exhibit 42–2.

Exhibit 42–2
Medical Care Experience-Rating Calculation

Assumptions:	Prior year's paid claims	$250,000
	Expected annual losses*	300,000
	Credibility factor	.85
	Pooling charge	5% of paid claims
	Inflation/utilization trend	14% of expected claims costs
	Underwriting margin	10% of trended losses
	Reserve adjustment	10,000
	Administrative costs	37,000

Calculation:

1.	Expected paid claims:			$257,500
	Actual experience factor	($250,000 × .85)	$212,500	
	Insurance company factor	($300,000 × .15)	45,000	
2.	Pooling charge			12,875
3.	Inflation/utilization trend: (1) + (2) × 14%			37,852
4.	Trended losses (1) + (2) + (3)			308,227
5.	Underwriting margin (4) × 10%			30,823
6.	Reserve adjustment			10,000
7.	Administrative costs			37,000
	Required premium: (4) + (5) + (6) + (7)			$386,050

* Based on insurance company's actuarial statistics.

Employer Advantage. An experience-rated insurance arrangement is much more a method for financing the employer's actual plan costs than a true insurance arrangement in which employers share in the loss experience and have a common premium rate. With the experience-rating arrangement, the primary insurance protection is against the unexpected catastrophic losses in one plan year that might severely affect the ongoing financial condition of the plan. To the employer with favorable and predictable claims experience, this arrangement is a very cost-effective way to share the plan's financial gains without assuming significant financial risks.

ADVANCED ALTERNATIVE INSURANCE ARRANGEMENTS

Advanced alternative insurance arrangements are variations of the basic alternative arrangements. They further increase the financial and administrative flexibility of employer-sponsored group insurance programs.

Realizing the initial savings gained through the basic alternative insurance arrangements, large employers have demanded even greater reliance on their own claims experience to gain potentially significant additional savings. Also, these large employers have become more aware of their own personnel risks and the predictability and severity of losses. With this increased understanding, the need for purchasing insurance has been considered through much the same cost-benefit analysis, based on the corporate value of money, as any other major corporate investment.

The employer's goal is to pay only the actual claims costs incurred during the plan year and reasonable administrative costs, without losing the budget stability of a maximum expected plan cost per policy year. To attain this goal, many of the insurance company's specific claim and administrative charges have been reduced or eliminated by the employers assuming the financial liability or administrative function. This reduction, or at least deferral, of premium payments to the insurance company has maximized the cash flow and direct cost savings to the corporation.

Financial Alternatives for the Total Plan

Deferred Premium Arrangement. One to three months' premium payments to the insurance company can be deferred and instead may be used more advantageously by the employer. If and when the insurance contract terminates, the deferred premium payments must be paid to the insurance company.

In essence, this arrangement allows the employer to retain an amount similar to the plan's incurred but unreported reserves until it is actually needed by the insurance company at contract termination. The necessary amount of reserve varies by the type of coverage, with life insurance plan reserves equaling one to two months' premium and disability and medical plan reserves being three to four months' premium. These reserves are part of the insurance company's total corporate assets and normally earn investment income credited against the employer's administrative charges or used to reduce the necessary reserve amount held by the insurer. The interest earned is related to the insurance company's aftertax investment return on its general assets and often is significantly less than an employer's aftertax rate of return earned from funds invested for its own use.

If such a situation exists, the deferred premium arrangement allows an employer to "borrow" the incurred but unreported reserves from the insurance company and invest the funds more effectively to enhance its cash flow and year-end earnings level.

To illustrate this advantage, assume an employer normally pays monthly premiums of $50,000 and has an aftertax corporate value of money of 14 percent. The insurance company currently credits 7 percent interest on incurred but unreported reserves. If the employer and insurer agree to a three-month deferred premium arrangement, the financial advantage would be the annual *additional* investment earnings the employer can earn on the three-month deferred premium amount. In the example below, the employer would earn an additional 7 percent return on each of the $50,000 monthly premium deferrals for the remainder of the policy year, which provides an annual cash flow advantage of $9,625. This is shown in Table 42-4.

Table 42-4
Example of Savings to Employer under a Three-Month
Deferred Premium Arrangement

Month	Deferred Premium	Additional Interest Credit	Duration of Policy Year	Savings
1	$50,000 ×	7%	× 1 year =	$3,500
2	50,000 ×	7%	× 11/12 year =	3,208
3	50,000 ×	7%	× 10/12 year =	2,917
			Total =	$9,625

The loss of the interest credits from the insurance company would be reflected by an increase in the annual administrative or reserve charges. However, these increases should be offset by the additional employer investment earnings.

Annual Retrospective Premium Arrangement

An annual retrospective premium arrangement reduces the employer's monthly premium payments by a specified percentage with the understanding this percentage of premium will be paid to the insurance company at year-end if the plan's actual claim and administrative costs exceed the paid premium to date. The specific percentage reduction of premium normally relates to the insurance company's underwriting margin. The employer gains a cash flow advantage through the corporate use of this premium amount during the plan year if the corporate value of money exceeds the insurance company's interest credit on surplus premium.

Underwriting margin provides the insurer with premium in excess of the expected premium necessary to pay claims and administrative charges, as illustrated below. During the plan year, any surplus premiums held by the insurance company are credited with interest based on the investment return of the insurance company's general corporate assets. In a participating insurance arrangement, this surplus premium is returned to the employer at the end of the plan year.

Total Premium Payable to Insurance Company	Underwriting Margin	Retrospective Premium
	Administrative Charges	Premium Paid During Plan Year
	Expected Claim Charges	

If the insurance company's interest credit is less than the corporate value of money, an annual retrospective premium arrangement is advantageous. By investing during the plan year the premium amount otherwise held by the insurer as underwriting margin, the employer can improve its current cash flow and its year-end earnings level through the additional investment income earned by the corporation.

For example, assume an employer's annual premium cost is $3 million, or $250,000 per month, and the plan's underwriting margin is 10 percent of premium. A 10 percent annual retrospective premium arrangement would reduce the premium payments to $2,700,000 per year and provide $300,000 premium to be invested by the employer during the plan year. The financial advantage is the *additional* investment earnings the employer can earn on the $300,000 reduced premium amount. If the corporate value of money is 14 percent and the insurance company interest credit is 7 percent, the additional investment income to the corporation is approximately $10,500. (This value assumes premiums are paid monthly and the additional investment earnings equal the monthly interest rate times the remaining months of the plan year.)

As part of the annual retrospective premium arrangement, the employer agrees to pay a part or all of the reduced premium amount to the insurance company at the end of the policy year if the actual claims and administrative charges exceed the actual premium paid during the plan year. The insurance company pays charges in excess of paid premium during the year from its capital or surplus accounts. An interest charge is applied to these excess charges which represent the insurance company's lost investment earnings on the funds provided to pay the excess plan costs.

Terminal Retrospective Premium Arrangement

With a terminal retrospective premium arrangement, the employer agrees to pay the outstanding deficit that may exist at the time the insurance contract is terminated with the insurance company. The agreement usually specifies a maximum percentage of premium or dollar amount up to which the employer will indemnify the insurance company at contract termination.

The employer's advantage is that the insurance company substantially reduces the annual risk charge and the underwriting margin factor used in determining the plan's required premium. Both these factors provide the insurance company with additional, contingency premium to be used in case of unexpected, catastrophic claim costs. The terminal retrospective premium arrangement transfers some of this catastrophic risk to the employer; therefore, these charges can be reduced. This reduction is reflected in lower monthly premium costs and gives the employer use of this reduced premium amount for potentially more profitable corporate uses.

Also, this arrangement offers more underwriting flexibility for insuring high benefit limits and special plan design features that pose a potentially greater financial risk to the insurance company. Because some of the risk of underestimating the losses from these special benefit arrangements is transferred to the employer, the insurance company is more apt to underwrite the coverage to satisfy the employer's needs.

Both an annual and terminal retrospective premium arrangement can be included to maximize the reduction of the risk charge and underwriting margin and the potential cash flow savings. However, a terminal retrospective premium arrangement is much less common than an annual arrangement. Insurance companies are less apt to offer a terminal retrospective premium arrangement because its long-term nature makes it difficult to determine a reasonable value to the insurer. Secondly, its attractiveness is limited to the very large employers willing to assume a potential long-term liability and considered a good, long-term credit risk by the insurance company. Therefore, the applicability and current use of this alternative insurance arrangement is rather incidental.

Extended Plan Year Accounting

Some insurance companies will extend the plan year's accounting of claims paid as a means of reducing or eliminating the necessary incurred but unreported claims reserves. These insurers will record the claims incurred before the end of the plan year but paid during the initial months after the plan year as actual paid claims during that plan year. This extended accounting period, which normally is an additional one- or two-month period, allows the actual incurred but unreported claims to be more accurately accounted to the appropriate plan year and substantially reduces or even eliminates the incurred but unreported claims reserves maintained by the insurance company.

For example, if the accounting period for a life insurance plan is extended an additional month, the incurred but unreported reserve, which normally is about 10 percent of premium, often is reduced to 2 to 3 percent of premium. Similarly, extending by two months the plan year accounting for a medical care plan may reduce the incurred but unreported reserve by 50 percent or more.

This financial alternative normally is available only to large employers with fairly consistent and predictable claims experience from month to month. For such employers, this arrangement provides an accurate accounting of incurred but unreported claims. To the extent these actual claims are less than the insurance company's normal reserve factors, the employer can gain a direct savings and cash flow advantage.

ADMINISTRATIVE ALTERNATIVES FOR THE TOTAL PLAN

Besides considering financial alternatives, many employers have implemented administrative options that can provide substantial savings for their group insurance plans. The common and varied uses of computers have made repetitive administrative functions of a group insurance plan relatively easy and inexpensive for an employer to assume. Also, the growing interest in self-insuring group insurance plans has prompted a new, peripheral market of plan administration firms, called third-party administrators. Such firms mainly offer computerized claims payment and data base services of varying sophistication. These services often can be adapted to the employer's needs and are offered at a cost significantly less than the normal administrative costs of a conventional or basic alternative insurance arrangement. In response to these influences, insurance companies offer several administrative alternatives to an employer.

Administrative Services Only Contract

If an employer self-insures all or part of its group insurance plans, the insurance company may provide only the administrative services for these plans through an administrative services only (ASO) contract. This contract is in direct response to the competition of third-party administrators and the employers' need for administering self-insured plans. No risk is assumed by the insurance company, and therefore, its administrative charges for this contract differ in several significant ways from an insured arrangement:

1. No premium tax liability is incurred by the insurance company on this type of contract; therefore, no premium taxes are transferred to it and paid by the employer.
2. There is no risk charge because the insurance company assumes no financial liability for the payment of benefits.
3. Normally there are no commission payments made through an ASO contract.
4. General administrative and underwriting activities normally are much

less in an ASO contract, which significantly reduces the costs for these activities in comparison to an insured arrangement.

An ASO contract is more effective for self-insured group insurance plans with high claim utilization and greater complexity in the payment of claims. Specifically, self-insured medical care, dental, and short-term disability plans are most often administered through an ASO contract.

There are a number of reasons why an employer might purchase an ASO contract instead of administering the plan itself:

1. The investment in and dedication of computer hardware and storage capacity is quite substantial.
2. Normally, the computer software for a claims payment system must be purchased because the details of such a system are complex and unfamiliar to the employer's computer programmers.
3. The hiring and training of employees to administer the plans can be costly and time-consuming to the employer.
4. There are economies of scale in standard operations performed by the insurance company that cannot be attained by the employer.
5. The insurance company is staffed with legal, medical, and other technical expertise necessary to administer the group insurance plans, especially the complex and unique claims situations that may be disputed, denied, or require extensive professional consultation.
6. The employer maintains a third-party "buffer" in disputing or denying benefit payments.

The insurance company administers the plan and determines the benefit payments under an ASO contract in the same manner as a conventional insurance arrangement. By performing these services, the insurance company accepts the fiduciary responsibilities and powers necessary to administer the plan. However, the insurance company assumes no financial responsibility under this contract. The benefit payment checks are drawn against the employer's cash balances, and the insurance company normally is not identified on these checks.

The services generally provided by the insurance company in an ASO contract are as follows:

Claims processing.

Financial and administrative reports.

Plan descriptions for employees.

Banking arrangements.

Government reporting requirements.

Underwriting services.

Individual conversion policies.

Legal, medical, and other professional services needed to administer the plans.

Selected Administrative Services Arrangement

Many large employers do not want to totally administer their plans but still are interested in assuming some of the group insurance plan administration to reduce an insurer's administrative charges as well as to gain more control over plan administration. Large employers also may be interested in maintaining a unique set of data about plan utilization and costs as a means of analyzing their specific financial trends and determining additional ways of controlling medical care and other plan costs. To meet these needs, some insurance companies are providing selected administrative services through their ASO contracts.

In most cases, the insurance company offers this arrangement only if some group insurance coverage, most often life insurance, is insured with the insurance company. If the employer-administered coverages also are insured, the insurance company normally requires it at least provide the underwriting services for these coverages.

This selected administrative services arrangement is rather new and just beginning to be provided to employers that specifically request it. However, as employers become increasingly involved in the financing and administration of their group insurance plans, this type of arrangement should become more common.

ALTERNATIVES FOR LIFE INSURANCE PLANS

Exclude Waiver of Premium Provision

The waiver of premium provision is common in a group life insurance program. It allows coverage to continue after an employee becomes totally and permanently disabled without continued premium payments by the employer for the employee's coverage. Although such a provision sounds attractive, the additional cost to include it in the life insurance plan often is greater than its actual value, especially for large employers.

It is common for the monthly premium costs to increase 10 to 15 percent because of the increase in incurred but unreported claims reserves and the additional risk of the waiver of premium provision. The additional monthly cost of this provision can be avoided in large part while still providing continued life insurance coverage to a totally disabled employee.

The employer can continue the life insurance coverage by merely continuing to pay monthly premiums for the disabled employees. In most cases, the total cost of these continued premium payments after the disability date will be substantially less than the additional 10 to 15 percent monthly premium charge for *all* employees that an insurance company requires to include the waiver of premium provision.

A disadvantage to excluding the waiver of premium provision potentially could exist if the employer changes insurance companies. There could be a problem in continuing life insurance coverage for previously disabled employees with the new insurer because most contracts only insure employees *actively at work* as of the effective date of the new life insurance coverage. Insurance companies often waive this actively at work provision for large employers but may be more hesitant for smaller employers if the inclusion of disabled employees' coverage could adversely distort the expected loss experience. Therefore, the exclusion of the waiver of premium provision often is suggested only for larger employers.

Claims-Plus Premium Arrangement

A claims-plus premium arrangement bases the employer's monthly life insurance premium on the *actual* loss experience of previous months, plus fixed monthly administrative and reserve charges. To the extent actual monthly loss experience is *less* than the level monthly premium payments normally paid during the plan year, this difference can remain with the employer as additional cash flow. If the employer's corporate value of money is greater than the insurer's interest credit on surplus premium, the employer gains additional investment income on this difference during the plan year.

To limit the risk of the employer having a cash flow loss under this arrangement by paying higher monthly payments than the level monthly premium amount, many insurance companies set the maximum monthly employer cost at the level monthly premium amount plus any "surplus" accumulated from prior months. Also, the maximum annual employer cost is limited to the annual premium cost based on the level monthly premium amount. In this way, the employer still is fully insured against unexpected or catastrophic loss experience that may occur during any policy year.

To illustrate how this claims-plus premium arrangement works, assume the employer's normal annual life insurance premium cost is $360,000, or a level monthly premium payment of $30,000. This $30,000 monthly premium payment is based on $27,000 of expected losses per month and a standard monthly administrative and reserve charge of $3,000. Table 42–5 shows the actual monthly premium costs under a claims-plus arrangement

Table 42–5
Life Insurance Claims—Plus Arrangement ($ thousands)

| | Months | | | | | | | | | | | | |
	1	2	3	4	5	6	7	8	9	10	11	12	Total
Normal premium	$30	$30	$30	$30	$30	$30	$30	$30	$30	$30	$30	$30	$360
Actual losses	20	0	20	50	10	0	0	70	20	50	30	20	290
Administrative/reserve	3	3	3	3	3	3	3	3	3	3	3	3	36
Actual monthly payment	30	23	3	23	53	13	3	3	73	23	53	26	326
Cumulative balance	—	7	34	41	18	35	62	89	46	53	30	34	34

given the above assumptions and assumed actual loss experience during the plan year.

The normal administration of the claims-plus arrangement is for the first month's premium payment to equal the level monthly premium payment amount and thereafter the premium payment to equal the actual loss experience of the previous month plus the standard administrative and reserve charge. In the example, the employer pays the normal monthly premium payment of $30,000 in month 1 and from then on pays the actual losses of the previous month plus the standard monthly administrative and reserve charge of $3,000. For instance, the premium payment for month 2 is $23,000, i.e., $20,000 of actual losses in month 1 plus the $3,000 administrative charge. The cumulative balance for month 2 and thereafter equals the cumulative difference between actual monthly payments and the normal monthly premium payments. In months 5, 9, and 11, the employer pays substantially more than the normal premium payment, reflecting the previous months' high actual losses. This can occur under this arrangement as long as any monthly premium amount does not exceed the normal premium payment plus the cumulative balance as of that date.

Insurance companies have various trade names for this arrangement, the most common being a "flexible funding" arrangement. Normally, such an arrangement is offered only to large employers that have substantial monthly life insurance premiums. Normally, for employers with less than a $6,000 to $8,000 monthly life insurance premium, this arrangement is not advantageous because of the increased internal administration and administrative costs, the volatile fluctuation in monthly claims, and limited potential financial gain.

ALTERNATIVES FOR LONG-TERM DISABILITY PLANS

Long-term disability insurance promises to pay a significant percentage of an employee's income for the duration of his or her total and permanent disability. The number of claims incurred by an employer normally are few, but the total cost per claim normally is quite large because of the expected duration of benefit payments. In the plan year a long-term disability claim is incurred, a reserve is charged to that year's financial experience equal to the expected cost of all future benefit payments. Often, the reserve charge is greater than the premium paid during that year. However, the limited number of claims over a three- to five-year period allows the insurance company to set the premium rate at the expected average annual cost for this time period, thereby keeping it relatively stable and affordable for the employer.

Partial Self-Insurance

The employer can partially self-insure its group long-term disability plan by assuming the financial liability for a specific duration of any claim and transferring the remaining liability to the insurance company. This arrangement reduces the monthly premium payments to the insurance company, provides potential cash flow savings through increased investment earnings on the premium difference, and still provides the employer significant insurance protection against a catastrophic claim situation. Two other financial advantages to a partially self-insured arrangement are (1) the incurred but unreported reserve requirement normally is reduced and (2) the premium tax liability is reduced.

There are two ways this arrangement can be designed. The more common method is for the insurer to assume the benefit payment liability for the first two to five years and the employer to continue benefit payments beyond this specific time period. The advantages of this plan design are several:

1. The average duration for a long-term disability claim is less than two years, so the long-term financial liability and administration assumed by the employer is limited.
2. The insurance company does not establish large reserves for future benefit payments in comparison to a fully insured arrangement, which reduces the required premium payment and offers cash flow savings to the employer.
3. Because an extended period exists before the employer assumes financial liability and begins periodic benefit payments, the employer normally prefunds its liability only from the time the disability actually occurs.

The second plan design option is for the employer to pay the long-term disability benefits for the initial two to five years and the insurance company to assume the risk thereafter. This type of plan design is less common. The main employer advantage is that premiums are substantially reduced because the employer is assuming the full liability of the majority of long-term disability claims.

As a general rule, this alternative insurance arrangement is offered only to employers with monthly premium charges of at least $8,000 to $10,000. For smaller plans, the claim occurrence is too volatile and the potential long-term financial liability normally too large for the employer to effectively self-insure the risk.

ALTERNATIVES FOR MEDICAL AND SHORT-TERM DISABILITY PLANS

Minimum Premium Arrangement

In a minimum premium arrangement, the employer pays the medical care and/or short-term disability benefits directly from a corporate cash account instead of transferring the money to pay benefits through premium payments to the insurance company. The employer essentially self-insures the payment of benefits up to the expected loss level for the plan year, with the insurance company assuming the financial liability for any claims costs in excess of the expected loss level. The only premium paid to the insurer is for the normal administrative, risk, and reserve charges.

A minimum premium arrangement in large part simulates and provides the advantages of a self-insured/ASO arrangement without the employer assuming the financial risk of benefit payments in excess of the annual expected loss level.

The primary advantages of this arrangement are twofold: reduced premium tax liability and potential cash flow savings. The payment of benefits from a corporate cash account is not considered an insurance arrangement in most states,[3] therefore, no premium tax liability is incurred. This offers a direct annual savings on the average equal to 2 percent of the normal premium amount used to pay benefits. Normally, a minimum premium arrangement is suggested only for employers with at least a $250,000 premium. At this minimum level of premium, approximately 85 percent of premium, or $212,500, is used to pay benefits. This implies the annual savings from reduced premium tax liability is approximately $4,250 (2 percent of $212,500). As the premium size increases, the percentage of premium used to pay benefits similarly increases, and the premium tax savings becomes more significant. For instance, an employer paying $5 million in annual medical premium may use 93 percent of the normal premium to pay benefits, or $4,650,000. At this level, the annual premium tax savings would be $93,000.

The second advantage is potential cash flow savings gained from the employer having the corporate use of "surplus" funds during the plan year. Minimum premium arrangements are generally designed so the employer pays benefit claims as they are incurred during the plan year up to the annual expected loss level determined by the insurance company. This limit often is called the employer maximum liability. The employer pays benefits periodically from a separate cash account[4] to meet the plan's claims liability. If the actual claims paid during the initial months of the plan year are less than the proportionate monthly level of expected claims costs, a "surplus" develops in the cash account. To the extent the investment return earned by the corporation on this "surplus" is greater than the insurance company's interest credit on surplus premium, the employer gains additional investment earnings and a cash flow advantage compared to a basic alternative insurance arrangement.

By paying benefit claims as they are reported during the plan year, the employer also could have a cash flow *loss* if claims in the initial months are greater than the proportionate level of expected claims costs. To avoid this possibility, a minimum premium arrangement can be designed so that the

---

[3] Connecticut and California assess a premium tax on minimum premium arrangements.

[4] This corporate cash account normally is a direct deposit account of a bank or savings institution, or a 501(c)(9) trust.

maximum monthly payment of claims from the cash account equals the proportionate monthly level of expected claims costs, plus any "surplus" funds accumulated during the plan year. If the actual claims costs in a month do exceed this limit, the insurance company pays all excess benefit claims from its funds. If "surplus" funds develop in future months, the insurer immediately uses these "surplus" funds to recoup its payment amount of prior months. The insurance company normally increases its administrative and risk charges to reflect the potential additional monthly liability it assumes in this specific case.

In a minimum premium arrangement, the insurance company administers all claims payments and assumes the risk of claims costs in excess of the annual expected loss level, just as in a conventional or basic alternative insurance arrangement. Exhibit 42-3 illustrates the flow of a benefit claim from its initial receipt, review, and benefit determination by the insurance company to the issuing and clearing of a corporate check through the corporate account.

The insurance company normally has similar administrative, risk, and reserve charges as in a basic alternative insurance arrangement. The employer pays a monthly premium to the insurer equal to the expected annual cost of these charges. Premium taxes must be paid by the employer on these monthly premium amounts. In the previous examples where 85 percent and 93 percent of normal premium are deposited into the corporate cash account, the remaining 15 percent and 7 percent of normal premium, respectively, reflect the monthly premium charge for administrative, risk, and reserve costs.

Minimum Premium—No Reserve Arrangement

A significant difference between a minimum premium and self-insured/ ASO arrangement is that in the minimum premium arrangement the insur-

Exhibit 42-3
Claim Flow of Minimum Premium Arrangement

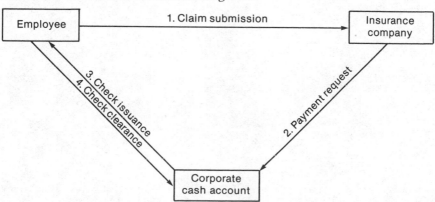

ance company still maintains a substantial reserve for incurred but unreported claims. As in other alternative insurance arrangements, the employer potentially can gain a cash flow savings by gaining the corporate use of the reserves. To meet this employer demand, the insurance companies offer a minimum premium—no reserve arrangement.

The employer gains the use of these reserves by the insurance company returning the incurred but unreported reserves it has been holding and reducing the future premium charges paid to the insurance company. This arrangement allows the corporation to use the reserve funds until they are required to pay incurred but unreported claims at the time of plan or contract termination. Because of state insurance regulations, it is generally agreed by insurance companies that they cannot fully release to the employer the financial liability for incurred but unreported claims at termination of its insurance contract with the employer. Therefore, the employer must either repay the reserve amount to the insurer at time of termination or specifically pay the incurred but unreported claims up to the insurer's normal reserve amount for a similar medical and/or short-term disability plan.

The minimum premium-no reserve arrangement essentially offers all the financial advantages of a self-insured/ASO arrangement, with the additional advantage of limiting the employer's liability for benefit payments in excess of the expected annual loss level. The liability for these possible unexpected costs still are assumed by the insurance company. A disadvantage to the minimum premium-no reserve arrangement is that administrative costs will be higher than a normal minimum premium arrangement because the interest credited by the insurance company on reserves, which is applied to reduce the administrative charges, no longer exists. However, the additional investment income gained through the corporate use of these funds significantly offsets this disadvantage.

CHAPTER 43

Noninsured Approaches to Funding Welfare Benefits*

CARLTON HARKER

This chapter reviews briefly some of the more significant aspects of the self-funding of welfare benefits by employers.[1] The most common welfare benefits currently being self-funded are medical, disability, and related benefits. Death and accidental death and dismemberment (AD&D) benefits generally are not self-funded because noninsured benefits of this type in excess of $5,000 are taxable to the beneficiary.[2] (Workers' compensation benefits are excluded because they are not ERISA-covered benefits[3] and also may not be funded by a tax-exempt trust.[4])

The term *employer*, as it is used in this chapter, includes both governmental employers and joint boards of trustees as defined by the Labor Management Relations Act of 1947 (Taft-Hartley Act).[5]

GENERAL BACKGROUND

Definition of Self-Funding

Self-funding, as used in this chapter, is limited to those arrangements where the total and ultimate responsibility for providing all plan benefits remains with the employer. Since this is the case with excess loss agreements, they are treated as part of self-funding. Partial self-funding arrangements, such as minimum premium, stop-loss, cost-plus, and retrospective

---

*Carlton Harker, *Self-Funding of Welfare Benefits* (Brookfield, Wis.: International Foundation of Employee Benefits Plans, 1981) treats self-funding of welfare benefits in a substantially expanded form. This chapter is a condensation of portions of that book.

[1] Employee Retirement Income Security Act of 1974, Section 3(1).

[2] Internal Revenue Code, Section 101. See also *Ross* v. *Odom,* 401 F. 2d 464 5th Cir. 1968) and Internal Revenue Service Technical Advice Memorandum, E.B.P.R. Research Reports, 341.3-21 (1979).

[3] Employee Retirement Income Security Act of 1974, Section 4(b)(3).

[4] Rev. Rul. 74-18, 1974-1 C.B. 139.

[5] Ibid., codified at 29 U.S.C., Section 141-187 (1976).

premium agreements, which modify conventional group insurance by amendatory agreements, are not considered. Traditional fully experience-rated group contracts are deemed to have no substantive element of self-funding because of the "upside limit" of risk to the employer and therefore are not covered here.

Extent of Self-Funding

Meaningful data on the nature and extent of self-funding is unavailable, but if we consider only the plans of the larger multistate and government employers and jointly administered (Taft-Hartley) trusts, a substantial percentage of welfare plans are self-funded. Because insurers offer "Administrative Services Only" (ASO) agreements and excess loss coverages to medium and smaller employers, there has been an increasing interest in self-funding among such employers.

Current Interest in Self-Funding

Among the reasons for the current interest in self-funding are:

Economic Considerations. The rapidly increasing cost of providing welfare benefits coupled with the current high interest rates have encouraged employers to consider self-funding in an attempt to control costs. Some employers wish to control, or reduce, reserves because of the current high value of money, and some believe cash flow is more easily managed with a self-funded program. In addition, certain expenses, such as insurer risk charges and state premium taxes, may be avoided with a self-funded program.

Avoidance of State Mandated Benefits. Since the Employee Retirement Income Security Act of 1974 (ERISA) exempts employee benefit plans from state regulation, the self-funding, multistate employer need not meet the requirements of state-mandated benefits or deal with the effects of the increasing aggressiveness of both the courts and regulators in applying these mandated benefits extraterritorially.

Accepted by Insurers. Many insurers facilitate self-funding by offering ASO agreements under which, as the name implies, the insurer provides only administrative services and does not assume any obligation for claims developing under the contract except at contract termination and for excess loss coverages under which an employer is covered for claims that exceed a specified amount.

Judicial Clarification. In *Farmer* v. *Monsanto* it was held that self-funding would not be construed as *doing an insurance business* if the self-funding was limited to the employees and dependents of the employer and affiliates and the profit motive was absent.[6]

---

[6] State ex. rel. *Farmer* v. *Monsanto Co.,* 517 SW. 2d 129 (Mo. Sup. Ct. 1974).

ERISA Preemption. State laws attempting to regulate employee benefit plans generally were preempted by ERISA.[7] This preemption clause of ERISA has been subject to much discussion and litigation and is discussed in more detail later in this chapter.

Elimination of the 85 Percent Income Restriction. The Tax Reform Act of 1969 eliminated the 85 percent income restriction which required that at least 85 percent of the income to a 501(c)(9) trust be made from employer or employee contributions and which had existed because the interest earnings on asset accumulations were not tax-exempt.

Increasing Popularity of Risk Management. The increase in the practice of risk management techniques by employers with other programs (e.g., state-required disability, workers' compensation) has contributed to employer interest in self-funding of welfare benefits and has facilitated the adoption of such programs.

Potential Limitations of Self-Funding

Many employers carefully consider self-funding and reject the option. There are several reasons why employers may not wish to self-fund. An employer may have a concern over the administrative and financial responsibilities involved, fear an unfavorable employee or union reaction, wish a third-party benefit buffer or wish the protection of the traditional arrangements, e.g., state insurance department protection, ease of providing conversion, or extended coverages. Then, too, some employers look to their insurers as a source of credit or as a carrier for their casualty policies.

When Is Self-Funding Appropriate?

A welfare plan may be fully insured, fully self-funded, or partially self-funded. When an employer has considered the advantages and disadvantages of each, he may decide to take a middle course and adopt partial self-funding in order to obtain some advantages of both extremes. In all cases, an employer's individual circumstances should be taken into consideration and a feasibility study done to determine the best approach for each employer.

Legal Issues

A number of legal issues relative to self-funding of welfare benefits should be reviewed. Most, but not all, of these issues are settled.

Doing an Insurance Business. As mentioned earlier, it was held in *Farmer* v. *Monsanto* that self-funding by an employer would not necessarily be deemed *doing an insurance business*. A survey of the 50 state insurance

---

[7] Employee Retirement Income Security Act of 1974, Section 514.

departments conducted by this writer indicated that no state, of the 29 which responded, would question the *Farmer* v. *Monsanto* decision.

ERISA Preemption. While Congress intended that ERISA would preempt those state laws attempting to regulate employee benefit plans, it worded the preemption very cautiously.[8] First, the preemption did not apply to insurance, banking, or securities laws.[9] Second, the Committee of Conference expected the Task Force provided by ERISA to consult closely with the states in its study and report to Congress.[10] Third, the preemption was limited to fiduciary and reporting and disclosure responsibilities.[11] Court decisions and law journal articles resulting from the preemption provisions are too numerous to be cited here, but some observations relating to the preemption provisions are:

1. The preemption issue is far from settled; there is a possibility of future clarifying ERISA amendments.
2. Preemption already has had an impact on several state laws; particularly significant is the preemption of self-funded plans by state laws mandating benefits.
3. Preemption does not apply to providers of health care or to insurers; the question of indirect state regulation of self-funded plans remained unanswered.
4. Significant state regulation of Taft-Hartley welfare funds has been preempted; this preemption may have been both an unanticipated and undesired result of the preemption provision.

State Mandated Benefits. Nearly one half of the states currently have some state-mandated benefits such as required coverage for physical therapy, convalescent home care, and surviving spouse medical expenses. The primary reason for the existence of such benefits is the political influence of special interest groups which is brought about in two ways. First, the groups lobby for special legislation, and second, the groups encourage the regulatory and judicial authorities to administer the laws extraterritorially. By self-funding, state-mandated benefits generally are preempted from state law.[12] Some observers have noted that state-mandated benefits will further encourage self-funding and weaken even more the states' ability to regulate.[13]

---

[8] ERISA, Section 514(a).

[9] ERISA, Section 514(b)(2)(A).

[10] ERISA, Section 3022(a)(4) and *II Legislative History of ERISA* (Washington, D.C.: U.S. Government Printing Office, 1974), p. 4650.

[11] See note 1, *supra*.

[12] ERISA, Section 514; *Wadsworth* v. *Whaland*, 562 F. 2d (1st Cir.) *cert. denied*, 435 U.S. 980 (1978).

[13] R. E. Younger, "Mandated Insurance Coverage—The Achilles Heel of State Regulation?", *Proceedings of the Association of Life Insurance Counsel*, 1978, p. 769.

Multiple Employer Trusts. Shortly after the enactment of ERISA, a number of Multiple Employer Trusts claimed status as employee benefit plans in order to achieve preemption from state regulation.

Several significant court decisions held that entrepreneur-sponsored Multiple Employer Trusts were not employee benefit plans and therefore were subject to regulation by the state.[14] The courts held that the trusts were not employee benefit plans in cases in which a commonality of employment was lacking and there existed a profit motive by the entrepreneur.

The Department of Labor, in various opinion letters, has ruled that a Multiple Employer Trust is not an employee benefit plan unless it is established and maintained by the employer.[15]

Discrimination Issues. The Revenue Act of 1978 and proposed regulations require that self-insured medical reimbursement plans must meet certain nondiscrimination standards in order for the prohibited group to receive favorable tax treatment.[16]

Self-Funding and a Trust. ERISA requires that "all assets of an employee benefit plan shall be held in trust by one or more trustees."[17] This provision would have eliminated all general asset plans which were contributory. However, the proposed regulations permit employee contributions to be held by the employer in a segregated account for up to three months with an employer *hold harmless* letter.[18]

Self-Funding and Collective Bargaining. Since the National Labor Relations Board ruled in 1973 that the selection of an insurer for welfare plans is a mandatory subject for collective bargaining, collective bargaining negotiations may have a significant impact on self-funding.[19]

FUNDING

So far as the funding of plan benefits is concerned, self-funded plans may be classified in one of the following ways:

1. *General Asset Plan:* This method uses no trust.
2. *Tax-exempt Trusteed Plan:* This method uses a tax-exempt trust that generally is qualified under Internal Revenue Code Section 501(c)(9).

---

[14] *Bell* v. *Employee Security Benefit Ass'n,* 437 F Supp. 382 (D. Ken. 1977). *Hamberlin* v. *VIP Ins. Trust,* 434 F. Supp. 1196 (D. Ariz. 1977). *Nat'l Bus. Conf.* v. *Anderson,* 451 Supp. 458 (S.D. Ia. 1977), *Wayne Chem. Inc.* v. *Columbus Ag'cy Serv. Corp.,* 426 F. Supp. 316 (N.D. Ind.), *aff'd as modified,* 567 F. 2d 692 (7th Cir. 1977).

[15] Dept. of Labor Op. Ltrs. 79-41A, June 29, 1979; 79-46A, July 19, 1979; 79-49A, July 31, 1979; 79-54A, Aug. 5, 1979 and 79-61A, August 29, 1979.

[16] Pub. L. No. 95-600, Section 366, *codified at* I.R.C., Section 105(h) and Treas. Reg., Section 1.105-7 (1981).

[17] ERISA, Section 403(a).

[18] Proposed Dept. of Labor Reg., Section 2550.403(b)01(3), 44 Fed Reg. 50.363 (1979).

[19] Connecticut Light & Power Co., 196 N.L.R.B. No. 149 (1972).

3. *Non-Tax-Exempt Trusteed Plan:* This method would use a non-tax-exempt trust and is rarely seen because of the lack of tax advantages.
4. *Captive Insurer:* By this method the employer uses its own insurer to fund the plan benefits.

General Asset Plan

With a general asset plan, any plan assets are commingled with the general assets of the employer. There usually are no plan assets other than withheld employee contributions because ERISA requires plan assets to be under a trust and contributions to general asset plan liabilities usually are not tax deductible by the employer.[20]

Several administrative advantages are gained with a general asset plan. Certain filing requirements are avoided (filing for the tax-exemption of a trust)[21] or simplified (a modified Form 5500 without financial statements or an independent auditor's opinion).[22] Furthermore, no fidelity bond is required, and plan restrictions from the Treasury regulations on the 501(c)(9) trust are avoided.[23]

501(a) Trust

An employer may self-fund medical benefits for certain retired lives as part of a qualified retirement plan.[24] In such circumstances, a pension or profit-sharing trust, qualified under the Internal Revenue Code Section 501(a) would be used. More commonly seen is a situation where the tax-exempt trust qualifies under Internal Revenue Code Section 501(c)(9).

501(c)(9) Trust

A special tax-exempt trust is provided by the Internal Revenue Code and Treasury Regulations for a voluntary employees' beneficiary association.[25] When used herein, a 501(c)(9) trust means a vehicle used for self-funding. A 501(c)(9) trust also may be used as a conduit into which employer contributions may flow and out of which insurance premiums may flow, but the term is not used in that sense in this chapter.

The regulations *(a)* set forth the conditions which a voluntary employees' beneficiary association must meet in order to be a qualifying organization, *(b)* specify the membership requirements, *(c)* enumerate the permitted

---

[20] See note 18 *supra;* Rev. Rul. 79-338, 1979-2 C.B. 212.
[21] I.R.S. Form 1024 (1980) and I.R.A. Form 990 (1980).
[22] Instructions to the Annual Return/Report, Form 5500.
[23] Treas. Reg. Section 1.501(c)(9) (1981).
[24] I.R.C. Section 401(h); Treas. Reg. Section 1.401-14 (1964).
[25] I.R.C. Section 501(c)(9); Treas. Reg. Section 1.501(c)(9) (1980).

benefits, *(d)* provide certain guidelines relative to discrimination, and *(e)* set forth other requirements relative to dissolution and record keeping.

Several significant Revenue Rulings have clarified the operation of the 501(c)(9) trust:

1. A 1958 Revenue Ruling determined that the plan and trust are interdependent agreements which together create a voluntary employees' beneficiary association within the contemplation of that term.[26]

2. A 1959 Revenue Ruling determined that membership in a 501(c)(9) trust would exclude such persons as individuals, proprietors, partners, self-employed persons, or trustees designated to administer the funds.[27] This position of the Internal Revenue Service was upheld by the court.[28]

3. A 1969 Revenue Ruling determined that a nonforfeitable contribution to a 501(c)(9) trust with retired lives benefits is deductible as an ordinary and necessary business expense and not as a contribution to a plan of deferred compensation.[29]

4. A 1973 Revenue Ruling determined that a contribution to a 501(c)(9) trust is deductible if it is actuarially determined and legal.[30]

5. A 1974 Revenue Ruling determined that workers' compensation benefits are not acceptable benefits for a 501(c)(9) program.[31]

Non-Tax-Exempt Trusteed Plan

While it is possible to meet the trust requirements of ERISA by using a non-tax-exempt trust, there are no tax advantages in doing so, and therefore such a trust would likely never be used.

Captive Insurer

A captive insurer is formed by a firm for the primary purpose of underwriting some or all of the sponsoring company's risk.[32] ERISA views insuring with a captive insurer as a form of self-dealing but provides an exemption if less than 5 percent of the insurer's premiums are those of the sponsor.[33] This statutory 5 percent limitation was increased to 50 percent by the Department of Labor in 1979.[34]

---

[26] Rev. Rul. 58-442, 1958-2 C.B. 194.

[27] Rev. Rul. 59-28, 1959-1 C.B. 120.

[28] *Milwaukee Sign Painters Welfare Fund* v. U.S., 17 A.F.T.R. 2d 264 (E.D. Wisc. 1965).

[29] Rev. Rul. 69-478, 1969-2 C.B. 29; I.R.C. Section 162; I.R.C. Section 404(a).

[30] Rev. Rul. 73-599, 1973-2 C.B. 40.

[31] Rev. Rul. 74-18, 1974 C.B. 139.

[32] See note 18 *supra*.

[33] ERISA Section 406; ERISA Section 408(b)(5).

[34] Prohibited Transaction Exemption 79-41, 44 Fed. Reg. 46,365 (1979).

ADMINISTRATION

When an employer self-funds, the administrative services to the plan may be provided by the employer, by a third-party administrator under a benefit services agreement, or by an insurer under an administrative services only (ASO) agreement. The three most important services from the viewpoint of the employer usually are administration, accounting, and actuarial ones.

Benefit Administration

Benefit administration probably is the single most important administrative consideration in a self-funding arrangement. Some aspects of benefit administration are:

1. Benefit complaint, denial, and litigation.
2. Benefit control activities, such as peer review.
3. Monitoring for duplicate coverage and abuse.
4. Statistical reports.
5. Coverage interpretation.
6. Determining and processing benefit payments.
7. Cash flow planning.

A third-party buffer to protect the employer from the potential of bad employee relations associated with benefit payment difficulties may be desirable in a self-funding arrangement.

ACCOUNTING

The three accounting considerations connected with a self-funded welfare plan are deduction accounting, plan accounting, and employer accounting.

Deduction Accounting

General Asset Plan. A basic theme supported by statutory, regulatory, and judicial law is that an employer payment to a self-funded reserve maintained in a general asset plan is deductible only when the events establishing the liability have all occurred and the liability is reasonably ascertainable.[35] Deduction for such reserve contribution has not been easily obtained.

---

[35] I.R.C. Section 461(a). Treas. Reg. Section 1.461-1 (1960); Rev. Rul. 79-338. 1979-2 C.B. 212; Rev. Rul. 70-262, 1970-1 C.B. 122; Rev. Rul. 69-512, 1969-2 C.B. 24; Rev. Rul. 57-165, 1957-2 C.B. 117. *Wien Consol. Airlines* v. *Comm'r of Int. Rev.,* 528 F. 2d 753 (9th Cir. 1976); *Crescent Wharf & Warehouse Co.* v. *Comm'r of Int. Rev.,* 518 F. 2d 772 (9th Cir. 1975); *Thriftmart, Inc.* v. *Comm'r of Int. Rev.,* 59 T.C. 598 (1973).

Trusteed Tax-Exempt Plan. Contributions to a 501(c)(9) trust generally are deductible as ordinary and necessary business expenses if they are irrevocable and reasonable and actuarially supportable.[36]

Plan Accounting

Plan accounting is the process by which the plan and trust are reflected in the required government reporting and disclosure forms. Table 43-1 summarizes the government reporting and disclosure requirements for self-funded plans.

The Internal Revenue Code requires that an annual return be filed for a tax-exempt trust.[37] ERISA requires that an annual return be filed for a welfare plan unless an exemption is provided.[38] A trust return is due 4½ months after the end of a trust year, and a plan return is due seven months after the end of a plan year.[39] A general asset welfare plan with fewer than 100 participants need not file an annual return.[40] A general asset welfare plan with 100 or more participants need only file a modified annual return that has no financial data and need not have an independent auditor's opinion.[41] Late filing penalties accrue with the trust return.[42]

Table 43-1
Government Reporting and Disclosure Regulations
for Self-Funded Plans

Method of Funding	Number of Participants	Annual Plan Return	Annual Trust Return
General asset	Fewer than 100	No	No
	100 or More	Yes; Mod. Form 5500	No
501(c)(9) trust	Fewer than 100	Yes; Form 5500-C	Yes; Form 990
	100 or More	Yes; Form 5500	Yes; Form 990

---

[36] I.R.C. Section 162(s)(i); Treas. Reg. Section 1.162-10 (1958). Rev. Rul. 56-102 1956-1 C.B. 90; Rev. Rul. 58-128, 1958-1 C.B. 89; Rev. Rul. 69-478, 1969-2 C.B. 29; Rev. Rul. 73-599, 1973-2 C.B. 41; Ltr. Rul. 7828030, April 12, 1978; Ltr. Rul. 7839040, June 28, 1978.

[37] I.R.C. Section 6033. Treas. Reg. Section 1.6033 (1972).

[38] ERISA Section 103.

[39] Instructions to Internal Revenue Service Form 990. Instructions to Annual Return/ Report Form 5500.

[40] 29 C.F.R. Section 2550.104-20 (1975).

[41] Id. Section 2550.104-44 (1975).

[42] I.R.C. Section 6033.

Employer Accounting

Employer accounting is the process by which the plan is reflected in the employer's accounts and in any footnote disclosure. There presently is a lack of clear authority in the employer accounting of self-funded welfare plans. The recent attention has been directed primarily to retirement plans. There is, however, a current study in progress of the employer accounting of self-funded welfare plans.

The most significant current accounting guides are the American Institute of Certified Public Accountants Audit Guide and the various guides provided by the federal government.[43]

Actuarial Considerations

Regardless of how the benefits are funded, there usually are certain matters to which actuarial attention is, or should be, directed. A feasibility study of self-funding should be made as should a cash-flow study. Levels of contributions and reserves should be reasonable and adequate, management benefit or control-type statistical reports should be prepared, and attachment points with related excess loss coverage should be reasonable.

---

[43] Audits of Employee Health and Welfare Funds (N.Y.: A.I.C.P.A., 1972). Medicare Provider Reimbursement Manual (1980); Armed Services Procurement Regulation, 32 C.F.R. Section X. Par. 502 (1976); Cost Accounting Standards Board Regulations, 4 C.F.R. Section 416.50 to 416.80 (1978).

PART SEVEN

Administration of Employee Benefit Plans

An overview of the principles of administration of employee benefit plans is presented in the first chapter of this part to set the stage for the chapters that follow.

Chapter 45 provides a look at the types of administrators of group welfare plans with special attention to administrators under the Taft-Hartley Act and the Employee Retirement Income Security Act of 1974 (ERISA). This latter subject is explored further in Chapter 46 which deals with the important issue of fiduciary responsibility under ERISA.

Administration of group life insurance plans under ERISA is covered in Chapter 47 with special emphasis on reporting requirements and the responsibility of administrators with regard to them.

Chapters 48 and 49 cover federal taxation of group life insurance and federal gift and estate taxation of group life insurance, respectively.

Chapter 50 deals with developing plan specifications after reevaluating a group insurance program. The steps in the process from determining whether a program should be rebid through the screening of new bidders is covered. The subject is continued in Chapter 51 where the analysis of group insurance bids and the selection of an appropriate insurance carrier and/or service organization are analyzed.

Implementing and reviewing employee benefit plans is discussed in Chapter 52 which covers obtaining top management approval, development of plan specifications for bidding (where appropriate) and analysis of proposals, legal document preparation; development of administrative procedures and manuals, and preparation and distribution of announcements and enrollment materials.

Chapter 53 covers the communication and disclosure procedures of employee benefit plans approaching the subject in terms of legal and management requirements.

Chapters 54 and 55 discuss qualified plans for small business taking into account the administrative considerations, problems, and other issues unique to this type of plan.

CHAPTER 44

Principles of
Administration

EDWARD E. MACK, JR.
AND
MARY A. CARROLL

To an average participant, the complex issues of plan design, costing, and funding seem mysterious and perhaps irrelevant—problems for the decision makers in the executive suite or on the board of trustees to ponder. The participant's questions are more practical. Am I covered? How do I file a claim? How much of my claim will be paid? How long will I have to wait for payment? Just what does this plan do for me? Answering these questions—and establishing systems to ensure these questions can be answered promptly, accurately, efficiently, and in ways that will help the participant to understand his or her benefits—is the central objective of benefit plan administration.

"Administration," as discussed in this chapter, is not necessarily the work of an "administrator" as defined by ERISA:

(i)   the person specifically so designated by the terms of the instrument under which the plan is operated;

(ii) if an administrator is not so designated, the plan sponsor; or

(iii) in the case of a plan for which an administrator is not designated and a plan sponsor cannot be identified, such other person as the Secretary may by regulation prescribe (Section 3, 353(16)(A)).

The administrator, under this definition, would typically hold discretionary authority and responsibility under the plan and serve in a fiduciary capacity. Throughout this chapter, however, "administration" is viewed as the implementation of decisions—on plan design, costing, funding, and any other discretionary issues—made by the plan sponsor or other plan fiduciaries.

Administration includes all the activities that translate elaborate proposals, complicated cash-flow analyses, and labyrinthine contract language into the daily operating reality which is the participants' only point of contact with the plan. In many cases, participants will evaluate their plan largely, if not entirely, on the basis of their satisfaction (or dissatisfaction) with its day-to-day administration. Thus, it is essential the plan sponsor pay at least as much attention to the administration of its benefit plan as to its structure and funding.

Administrative functions may be performed by employees of the plan sponsor (the personnel or benefits department of a corporation, for example, or the salaried administrator(s) of a jointly administered Taft-Hartley fund), or by firms which specialize in this field (contract or third-party administrators, benefit consultants, insurance brokers, or insurance companies). All administrative functions may be performed by a single entity, or there may be a number of groups involved.

No matter what structure is selected, those who manage the administration of a benefit plan must be prepared to perform certain basic functions: to determine participants' eligibility for coverage; communicate the nature and impact of plan provisions to participants and their families, plan advisers, and government agencies; adjudicate claims for benefits; and maintain the accounting and data processing systems which enable them to perform these functions.

DETERMINATION OF ELIGIBILITY

Determining who is eligible for the plan is the first requirement, and a number of plan provisions interact to affect eligibility. If the program does not require employee contributions, all employees within the eligible class(es) are covered; if employees contribute to the cost of coverage, their election of the benefit and payment of the required contribution must be verified. Health programs frequently delay the effective date of coverage until the employee is actively at work (or until a dependent ceases to be confined in a hospital or at home under the care of a doctor); if such a provision applies, eligibility cannot be verified without determining whether the individual has satisfied this requirement. Many employers impose an eligibility waiting period of 1 to 3 months (and may impose an even longer waiting period, such as 6 to 12 months, for certain benefits); the administrator must establish systems to ensure that new employees' protection becomes effective after the applicable waiting period. Special care must be taken when coverage terminates—for an employee, a dependent, a class of employees, or the entire covered group—since claims incurred before termination are a liability of the plan, while those incurred after the termination date should generally be denied. Many programs, however, extend protection for a period of time if termination occurs because of certain specified reasons, such as total disability or employee death. The details of the plan's provisions will govern eligibility in such cases. The plan administrator also generally is responsible for determining individuals' eligibility for special plan provisions, such as conversion privileges or waiver of premium. A pension or profit-sharing plan administrator generally is responsible for maintaining the records which permit determination of participants' years of service for vesting and benefit accrual purposes as well as the applicability of other plan provisions.

Special Problems

Employers frequently assign responsibility for eligibility verification to their personnel departments. Large firms with multiple locations may need one or more employees at each plant or office to maintain accurate eligibility records, together with a home office staff to coordinate the eligibility provisions of various plans and assist in resolving questions and disputes. Within a smaller company, eligibility determination may be only one of the several responsibilities of a personnel or administration department employee.

For most plans—and especially for multiple and multiemployer benefit plans—a second eligibility verification will be made by the insurance company or third-party administrator which handles claims for the plan. This function is particularly important in the administration of multiemployer plans in industries (like construction) where participants change employers frequently. If no single employer can certify an individual has worked enough hours, days, or weeks to earn eligibility for plan benefits, it is vital that the administrative office maintain comprehensive and accurate data on participants' service with all participating employers.

COMMUNICATIONS

Effective communication of plan benefits to participants and their families is essential if the plan is to achieve its objectives. In establishing a program of benefits, most employers hope to attract and retain productive employees and maintain good morale; if the program is poorly communicated, however, it is likely to be unappreciated and even ignored until a claim arises and may lower, rather than improve, employee morale when a claim must be denied or reduced. This internal need for benefit communication is matched by an external mandate: under the Employee Retirement Income Security Act of 1974 (ERISA), all benefit plans subject to this legislation must be communicated "in language calculated to be understood by the average plan participant." The passage of ERISA has stimulated a major investment in improved communication techniques by large employers, benefit consultants, brokers, and insurers; since 1974, benefit communications has been a "growth industry."

Communicating with Participants and Their Families

ERISA established minimum standards for benefit plan communications with participants in specific documents like the summary plan description and summary annual report. Larger companies frequently supplement these plan documents with employee meetings, multimedia presentations, and other printed material designed to gain for benefit plans the visibility that their place in the expense budget demands; they feel employee understanding is essential to the plan's effective operation. These formal modes of communication, however, are probably less important to plan participants than their direct contact—on the telephone and through correspondence— with those who administer the plan. The administrative office answers participants' questions about their eligibility and the plan's benefits, assists them in filing claims and appealing claim denials, and explains how specific payments were calculated. The skill and empathy of the administrator's staff in handling these communications may have more impact on participants' sense of security and satisfaction with their benefits than glossy brochures and films and slide-shows.

Communicating with Providers

In underwriting coverage and processing claims, an administrator often needs to communicate directly with hospitals and other providers. The most frequent contact of this type is undoubtedly verification of benefits calls or letters from hospitals, which seek to ascertain what portion of the participant's charges will be paid by the plan. Accuracy in confirming benefits is particularly vital in certain parts of the country where carrier- provider agreements may require a plan to pay provider charges when coverage is erroneously confirmed. In addition to benefit confirmations, an administrator's communications with providers frequently include requests for additional information about participants' medical histories and about specific charges, audits of large or complicated claims, and direct payment of assigned benefits. In all these areas, an administrative staff which under- stands providers' operations and concerns is likely to provide more effec- tive service to plan participants.

Communicating with Other Plan Advisers and Government Agencies

The administrator's control of plan data establishes an important infor- mation flow from the administrative office to the various professionals who provide services to the plan, as well as to the plan sponsor. Actuaries, brokers, and consultants need detailed information on participation, losses, expenses, and trends to evaluate the plan's status from time to time. As a surrogate for both the plan sponsor and, in insured plans, the insurance company, the administrator must provide sponsor and carrier with frequent reports comprehensive enough to convince these entities that the functions they have delegated are being performed properly. The administrator must provide the plan's (or company's) attorney with details of any situation which may produce legal action against the plan or its sponsor, and fre- quently works with counsel in analyzing the impact of federal and state legislation. Auditors, too, must depend upon the cooperation of the admin- istrator in performing their examination of the plan's financial condition.

Finally, most benefit plans are required to file reports with a variety of government agencies; compiling the information needed to develop these reports often is the responsibility of the administrator, with the assistance of other plan advisers. Although most of the administrator's communications with the plan sponsor, professional advisers, and government agencies are invisible to participants, they are essential to effective functioning of the plan, and an important part of the administrator's overall responsibilities.

Special Problems

Large employers can take advantage of economies of scale and centralization in developing sophisticated benefit communication programs; jointly administered plans frequently supplement required plan documents with articles in union publications and presentations at union meetings. Effective communications may be most difficult for multiple employer plans: association-sponsored programs and multiple employer trusts with minimal communications budgets and covering primarily small employers. For such plans particularly, the quality of participants' day-to-day contact with the administrative office is likely to be central to their satisfaction with the plan. And at the heart of that contact are participants' claims for benefits.

PROCESSING OF CLAIMS

Some types of employee benefit plans—for example, group term life insurance or a retirement program covering younger workers—can operate successfully for years without ever paying a claim: their value lies in their promise to pay, and participants understand that there may be no current claims activity. Most employees judge their benefit program, however, by those portions which pay rather than promise to pay: by their program's handling of the medical, dental, and disability claims they submit from time to time. However effective an administrator's functioning in other areas may be, its claims processing must satisfy participants' expectations if the program is to achieve the sponsor's objectives.

In reviewing claims, the administrator has obligations to many masters. The demands of the plan sponsor, insurer, provider, and participant compete for the administrator's attention and may produce different treatment of specific claims. In general, the administrator must rely on the plan document (and the insurance contract, if the plan is insured), together with any deviations adopted by the plan sponsor (and agreed upon with the carrier, where appropriate) in resolving doubtful situations. At the same time, the administrative staff must be diplomatic and empathetic in working with participants and providers. The administrator is a "middleman," balancing the desire of participants and providers for speedy, complete payment against the plan's requirement—of vital interest to the sponsor (and insurer)—that claims be investigated carefully and adjudicated in accordance with all relevant plan provisions. In the conflict between speed and accuracy, the administrative office must opt for accuracy, working hard meanwhile to help participants understand why investigative delay is necessary. An administrator able to handle these multiple demands on its claims operation effectively has a head start toward success in other areas of administration as well.

Retirement Plans

In pension plans, once the administrator has reviewed the participant's eligibility for benefits and determined the benefit payable based on work history and plan provisions, payments are generally issued automatically. Even here, however, it is essential the administrative office establish checking procedures to prevent issuance of benefit payments to deceased or ineligible individuals.

Health Protection

Medical claims are probably the most difficult to adjudicate because of the number of factors involved in determining the availability and amount of benefits for submitted charges. The administrative staff must examine whether the claimant is a covered individual, what benefits are in force, when the claimant's coverage became effective, and whether any special restrictions or exclusions apply. It must analyze the availability of other coverage—under government programs, including Medicare, workers' compensation, or occupational disability laws, or other insurance programs—and the effect, if any, of such duplicate coverage on the plan's liability for the charges submitted. In reviewing specific charges, the administrator's claim specialists must make sure that the expenses themselves are eligible for payment under the plan and that they were incurred at a time when the relevant coverage was in force for the individual. The plan document must be reviewed for any exclusions or limitations which may apply; "preexisting condition" provisions require special care at this point in claim adjudication. Proper investigation of medical claims is complex and often time-consuming: the examiner must carefully compare the claim submitted to eligibility records and to the plan document and may seek additional required information from other administrative records, from providers, and from the claimant before a single calculation can be made. This attention to detail is essential, however, to make sure only legitimate claims are paid under the plan.

Once an examiner has verified that the submitted expenses are *eligible* for benefits under the plan, he or she must apply all relevant plan provisions to determine the amount which should be paid. Unless first-dollar benefits are available for these charges, the file must be checked for possible satisfaction of the plan's deductible and coinsurance provisions. If the plan includes "first-dollar" coverage or internal limits for particular types of treatment, the applicability of these provisions to the submitted charges must be reviewed. If the plan's benefits are provided on a "usual, reasonable, and customary" basis, the administrative office must compare the charges submitted with the appropriate statistical data. Whether benefits are scheduled or unscheduled, the examiner should analyze each claim to be sure that the claimant's treatment, including the duration of any hospital confinement, is consistent with the diagnosis indicated, perhaps recommending an audit of the provider's billing if there appear to be serious discrepancies.

Life and Accidental Death and Dismemberment (AD&D) Coverage

In some respects, death claims would seem to be the least complicated claims to adjust, since the occurrence of the covered event can be easily verified by reviewing certified death certificates, newspaper obituaries, and other documents. Although life and accidental death plan provisions may affect the availability of benefits for a particular claimant and the deceased participant's file must be reviewed to ascertain the proper beneficiary, most death claims can be processed straightforwardly. It is this area of claim administration, however, which insurance companies have been most reluctant to delegate, generally insisting that, even if an outside administrator reviews the submission and file and prepares the payment authorization, the draft itself must be issued by the carrier. The relatively large dollar amounts payable for death claims, the complexity of probate law, and the special legal problems involved in adjusting AD&D claims are the major reasons offered in support of maintaining insurer control of these claim payments.

Loss of Income Protection

Disability income claims also are frequently a source of concern for the plan sponsor and/or insurer. The loss itself is difficult to prove (or disprove), the plan's potential liability may be quite large, and the combined disability benefits available under employment-related, Social Security, and other plans may be sufficient to discourage claimants from returning to work. Therefore, careful investigation is essential when a claim is first submitted, recertification of disability by the claimant's physician is frequently required, and carriers providing long-term disability benefits often review claims on a regular schedule, using service bureau investigators or their own employees to confirm the continued qualification of the claimant for plan benefits.

Special Problems

Self-administration of employee benefit plans may be attractive to large employers because it appears to give the corporate staff more direct control over plan costs and services; however, many companies prefer to retain an outside administrator (or to have claims processed by insurance company employees) to direct employee dissatisfaction with claim denials away from the company and toward a third party. Multiemployer plans frequently employ a staff of salaried administrators, including experienced claim examiners; other jointly-administered plans delegate claim administration to a third-party administrator or an insurance carrier. In both corporate and Taft-Hartley plans, claim administration may sometimes be subject to internal pressures (from a key manager in a corporate plan or a trustee in a jointly administered plan) to handle some claims more favorably than would be justified by the plan's provisions. While the plan sponsor may intend for some provisions to be enforced less rigidly than others, the administrator must use extreme care in making exceptions to these provisions.

A significant problem in processing claims for multiple employer plans (whose participants are, for the most part, employees of smaller employers) is that, with no one on the employer's staff who is really qualified to assist employees, many claims are incomplete or otherwise unacceptable when first submitted. Claim examiners for these plans must be especially patient in explaining to participants the reasons for various requirements. A similar problem may exist in the administration of some industrywide Taft-Hartley funds; here, too, participants may not have ready access to advice in submitting claims (although union trustees and business agents may be able to provide some assistance).

ACCOUNTING FOR PLAN FUNDS

In essence, an employee benefit plan is simply a flow of funds: dollars flow in from the employer (and the employees if the plan is contributory) and out to reimburse employees, pay providers' charges, and cover the plan's expenses. To control this flow, the administrator must establish accounting systems adequate to ensure the plan's monies are being used properly. Larger plans, particularly those which are funded through a trust, generally maintain accounting systems parallel to those of other economic entities: the plan sponsor and/or trustee(s) regularly review financial statements for the plan; the administrative office must maintain the general and subsidiary ledgers which are the basis for these statements, must control accounts payable and receivable and cash receipts and disbursements, and may be involved in tax reporting for the plan, its participants, and providers to whom benefits have been paid. If the plan is insured, premium reporting frequently requires detailed information from the administrator, who is sometimes also involved in claims-accounting functions and in commission accounting on plans marketed through a network of insurance agents or brokers.

Special Problems

In some respects, administrative accounting systems for large corporate benefit plans are fairly simple, since plan funds generally come from a single source. Even here, however, benefit expenses are likely to be charged to the corporation's profit centers on some equitable basis, and accounting systems must be established to handle this allocation. More complicated systems may be required to control the billing and collection process for the hundreds of smaller firms which participate in multiple employer or multi-employer plans.

DATA PROCESSING

There are few areas of plan administration which cannot benefit from the application of flexible, thoughtfully designed data processing systems. While a very small benefit plan can perhaps be handled effectively with manual systems, most larger life, health, and disability plans can provide faster, more efficient service to participants and more accurate information for the plan sponsor, advisers, and insurers if the administrative office can rely on an appropriate level of computer support.

In designing data processing systems for benefit plan administration, administrative managers and systems analysts often work together to establish the system's parameters, define the data base and reporting requirements and backup and retention criteria, and analyze methods of developing or converting data to build the system's master files. This approach has the advantage of matching the administrator's knowledge of the details of the plan's benefit provisions and limitations, rate structure, and other variables with the systems analyst's expertise in solving information-handling problems through computer hardware and software.

Special Problems

The objectives of the plan sponsor generally determine which aspects of the administrative operation are most likely to be automated. In an industry-wide Taft-Hartley welfare or pension plan, eligibility record-keeping may be high on the list because of the errors and expense which result from manual tracking of participants' relatively transient work records. Large employers may be most interested in establishing a data base which permits effective cost control and analysis of health care cost trends. Insurance carriers also are likely to be vitally concerned with information of this type. Because of the number of firms involved, multiple employer plans generally require substantial computer support in the billing and collection process. The volume of paper generated in processing claims—and the impact of normal human error on benefit calculation—encourages administrators of all types of plans to develop or purchase software to allow computer adjudication of many types of claims. For most employee benefit plans, more information and more efficient systems are almost always better; the only significant restriction on the value of more sophisticated reports and analyses and more automated operations is the investment required to produce them.

SUMMARY

Though employee benefit plans existed before World War II, they have had a significant impact on the American economy and the American public only during the past 40 years. Their administration, like their benefit structure, funding, and other areas, has changed substantially during this period, and this pattern seems likely to accelerate in the coming decade. However much benefit plans may change, however, it seems clear that cost-efficient administration which meets employee needs and achieves the objectives of the employer will continue to be a vital element of effective plans.

CHAPTER 45

Types of Administrators

CARLTON R. SHERMAN

ERISA TITLE VS. WORKING TITLE

The word *administrator* is one of those job titles that serve as an "umbrella" word—it is popularly used to describe persons working at many different levels of authority and autonomy and performing many different functions.

For employee benefit plans, the Employee Retirement Income Security Act (ERISA) makes very clear the distinction between "administrative" functions and "executive" functions but adds to the confusion surrounding the definition of administrator by naming the people who exercise executive functions "administrator." ERISA applies the name "administrator" to the Board of Trustees (in the case of Taft-Hartley Funds) and corporate entities (in the case of corporate plans) but specifically reserves for them all policy determination authority. In reality, these governing bodies are not administrators as the word generally is understood. They do not perform the day-to-day tasks which, in their totality, add up to administration. Those governing groups ERISA calls administrators really function as policymakers not administrators.

Before discussing the types of administrators operating in the employee benefits field, a differentiation must be made between Administrator, with a big letter *A* to describe those who bear this title by reason of ERISA and not by the work they do, and administrator with a small letter *a* to describe those persons and groups who do perform the actual job of "administration." Some writers have chosen to refer to the administrator (small letter a) as "administrative agent." I believe this makes sense and aptly describes the status of the people in this chapter. Indeed, they are agents of the "Administrator" named by ERISA. So the name for those who actually perform the varied tasks of operating an employee benefit plan is administrative agent.

THE FIRST GENERATION

It is a fair statement, in the author's opinion, to call the present administrative agents the first generation. It was the passage of the Taft-Hartley

729

Act in 1947 which spread the seed for the breeding of the Taft-Hartley Trust Funds for the operation of many multiemployer plans and corporate benefit plans. It was ERISA, passed in 1974, which made new, more complex technical demands in this field. From a life-span view, those presently in the field have lived through the most important developments to affect their work.

This "first generation" comes from varied backgrounds. Accountants, group insurance salesmen, union researchers, corporate personnel and finance people—all of these disciplines have contributed some practitioners to the field of employee benefit administration.

The importance of this point is that most of the early administrative agents were forced to hastily educate themselves since a formal training curriculum for the administration of employee benefit plans had not been created.

It is a tribute to the entrepreneurial imagination of many of these first generation people that there exist the varied types of administrative arrangements discussed in this chapter.

IMPACT OF TAFT/HARTLEY AND ERISA

Before examining the different types of administrative agents now operating, it might be useful to briefly look at the legislative catalysts which so markedly affected this field.

The Taft-Hartley Act (the popular name for the Labor-Management Relations Act of 1947) fundamentally changed the business of funding and administration of employee benefit plans. Taft-Hartley made it illegal for unions to receive and for employers to pay into health care or pension funds operated by the union. This had been a common practice.

Unions and employers were forced to adopt one of two structural plans for providing benefits. One method was to negotiate levels and kinds of benefits and give the employer the general responsibility of providing and administering the negotiated benefits. This course of action led to the establishment of large corporate employee benefits functions requiring employment of personnel skilled in both administration and, to some extent, labor relations. Of course, employers have always faced the necessity of providing such services for nonunion employees.

The alternative offered by the Taft-Hartley Act was to establish special purpose trusts set up specifically to provide and administer benefit plans. These trusts are, by law, operated by equal numbers of union and employer trustees and generally found in situations where the same union negotiates with a number of employers, usually in the same or related business, in a narrow geographical area, and joined together in a trade association.

In these situations, the union negotiates the level of employer contributions to the trust. The trustees decide on the level and kinds of benefits to be provided as well as the type of administration to use.

TAFT-HARTLEY TRUSTS

Generally, Taft-Hartley trusts have chosen to have administration performed by either contract administrators or salaried administrators. Contract administrators are independent businesses set up for the specific purpose of performing the administrative functions required for the proper operation of employee benefit plans under ERISA and Internal Revenue Code (IRC) regulations. These services are provided under the terms of a contract between the trustees and the administrative firm—hence, the working title of "contract" administrator.

The contract administrator serves a number of clients, including other Taft-Hartley employee benefit funds. Thus, the fund itself has no employees, does not maintain its own office, and relies completely on the contract administrator to perform all necessary administrative functions.

Fees charged by contract administrators generally are set either on a capitation arrangement where the charge is a set amount per participant or, as an alternative, a flat monthly fee. Both methods of payment usually are not only based on the number of participants but also contain adjustments for the complexity of the plan of benefits (particularly if the administrator pays claims), number of employers to be billed, and other characteristics of the plan which affect the administrative function.

Salaried administrators are employees of the trustees and usually devote their full time and energies performing the administrative functions for the one fund that employs them. In this situation, the fund operates an office complete with staff and office equipment as may be required to properly perform the administrative duties required.

Some banks and insurance companies offer administrative services to Taft-Hartley funds but are utilized to a much lesser extent by trustees of such funds. Many insurance companies, in an effort to compete with the fast growth of self-funding, offer so-called administrative services only (ASO) contracts. These contracts provide certain administrative services but generally are limited to claims processing and claims accounting and do not provide the full range of services, such as billing for and receipting employer contributions and maintaining eligibility lists.

Which is the best system for a particular employee benefit plan? The following are some selected quotes from practitioners.

Contract Administrator

First, the contract administrator can bring his know how, his professional competence to bear on a small trust which obviously cannot afford to hire its own administrator . . . By combining several trusts in one administrative office, skilled help may be spread across all at a reasonable cost.

Second, the contract administrator by putting many trusts together in one office (or through a number of offices) can match the salaried administrator in his use of sophisticated office equipment and data processing systems even though no single trust could afford anything but a hand system.

Third, by administering several trusts whose trustees may have diverse opinions—in fact they usually do—the contract administrator probably has knowledge of problems and solutions under more varying circumstances than does the salaried administrator. He is dealing with diverse unions and members who are in different occupations and employed by different employers who elect trustees who are different.

Fourth, a savings in administrative costs can be achieved by using a contract administrator who can spread the expenses of office space, furniture, fixtures, equipment, and personnel.

Fifth is the incentive for overall efficiency of operation in the contract administrative operation. A contract administrator is in business to make a profit. The profit motive still guides American business, and it is questionable whether any other motive can provide an equivalent stimulus to the search for overall efficiency.

Last and probably the most important advantage of the contract administrator over the salaried administrator is the limiting of trustee liability. Trustee responsibility and liability is sufficiently onerous and burdensome without shouldering the additional responsibility and problems in running their own administrative office. The direct legal responsibility is enough.[1]

Salaried Administrator

Because the salaried administrator is concerned with the administration of a single fund, he has time to render personal service to his members . . . Thus, a major consideration in choosing a salaried administrator over a contract administrator is the personal service rendered by a salaried administrator. Another important consideration is the cost factor.

The operational costs of a fund office with a salaried administrator can be controlled by expanding or contracting as circumstances warrant.

The rigid fees contained in the contract of a professional are based not on the operations of any single fund but on a proportionate percentage of the total operating costs of the many funds he administers. In this way the trustees of any single fund have no control over operating costs, and a single small fund may very well be paying a highly disproportionate share of the professional administrator's office.[2]

Bank Representative

In the field of administration, a bank occupies a unique position in that it is the only vehicle that is able to offer complete and full services for any one, or any combination of, the following types of trusts: health and welfare, pensions,

---

[1] Charles W. Earhart, "Why Contract Administration on Your Plan?" 1967 Conference Proceedings of the National Foundation of Health, Welfare, and Pension Plans, pp. 146-48.

[2] James V. O'Sullivan, "The Profile of a Salaried Administrator," 1967 Conference Proceedings of the National Foundation of Health, Welfare, and Pension Plans, pp. 139-41.

vacation, supplemental unemployment benefits, promotional and advertising, apprenticeship and training.

It should be pointed out that the type of bank services we are discussing are not offered by banks in every section of the United States; but in most areas represented here today, banks are available that do provide these particular services.

The banking industry was one of the first industries to recognize the desirability and necessity of adopting standardized procedures to fully utilize electronic data processing equipment. In order to achieve maximum usage of electronic word processing devices, various committees have been set up to develop standards of uniformity. Standardized reporting forms applicable to all variations of contribution requirements for all types of plans and industries have been formulated. Because a bank is required to maintain records covering every conceivable type or business transaction, its programmers, its equipment, its programs as well as the know-how, must be available on the staff of a bank.

The same personnel are available and the same equipment is adaptable to provide the type of records necessary for the complete administration of employee benefit plans. Since these services can be provided without any major capital expenditures, and since the cost of machinery and programming can be spread over all accounts, these savings are passed on to the fund in the form of reduced charges.

Costs and services available are two elements trustees must judge in deciding who shall administer. Bank costs are competitive and realistic. It would appear impractical and somewhat extravagant for a fund to provide office space, telephone facilities, disbursing agents, and claim services when all these and other necessary functions are available from a qualified bank at a minimum cost.[3]

Insurance Company Representative

I am not saying that in every situation administration by an insurance company is the best arrangement—or even a desirable one. In a given situation though, and depending upon the circumstances, an insurance company may be the best answer. I want to take nothing away from the salaried administrator, the professional administration company, or administration by a bank. Each of us has his place in the scheme of things.

In my judgment, an insurance company is suitable to function as administrator in the smaller- and medium-sized funds. I would consider up to 1,000 lives as appropriate.

Administrative costs have to be a prime concern to trustees. The importance of this has been acknowledged by the sessions on the control of administrative workshops over the last several years. There must be a constant awareness and control of costs in order that the interests of the beneficiaries be best served.

---

[3] Joseph L. Healy, "Why a Bank?" 1967 Conference Proceedings of the National Foundation of Health, Welfare, and Pension Plans, pp. 149–51.

From the standpoint of cost, an insurance company is particularly well suited to administer a fund. We have the experience, we have the electronic data processing equipment, and we have the depth of talent—and the cost of maintaining the people and the equipment is spread among many customers not borne by one alone.[4]

Corporate Plans

Employee benefit plans sponsored and administered by single employers generally are called corporate plans. When union employees are involved, these plans are the result of the parties choosing the "negotiated benefits" option under the provisions of the Taft-Hartley Act as discussed above.

However, even in this situation, some corporations have chosen to set up special purpose trusts for certain tax advantages, primarily; investment income earned by the trust is not taxed. These trusteed plans generally are referred to as single-employer trusts. In any event, the administrative functions required basically are the same as those required from a Taft-Hartley multiemployer Trust.

The structural organization of the administration varies widely in corporate plans depending on the size of the participant population, geographical distribution of the population, complexity of the benefit plan, and policy of the corporation. In many smaller groups, the administration of benefit plans is assigned to the personnel department, and the personnel manager carries the responsibility of supervising the operation of the program.

In the case of large corporations, the administration of the employee benefit plans is performed by a separate department whose manager usually is responsible to a corporate financial vice president or comptroller. In most cases, large corporations separate investment functions, particularly for pension plans, from the administrative functions. Frequently the corporate officer in charge of other investment activity is responsible for pension fund investments. This does not necessarily mean that this person makes specific investment decisions; rather he or she is active in setting investment policy and monitoring the performance of outside "money-managers" or investment advisers.

Corporations, perhaps more than the usual Taft-Hartley multiemployer trusts, tend to differentiate the various elements in the total administrative process and to use more outside expertise in the operation of their employee benefit programs.

SPECIALIZED ADMINISTRATION

Regardless of the kind of benefits provided by a plan (health care, pension, legal services, etc.) there are at least six basic administrative functions that must be performed. They are:

---

[4] R. David Carter, "Benchmarks of Administration," 1967 Conference Proceedings of the National Foundation of Health, Welfare, and Pension Plans, p. 143.

1. Collection or allocation of money to fund the plan.
2. Accounting.
3. Communications.
4. Claims processing and payment.
5. Claims controls.
6. Investment of surplus funds.

In recent years, aided by the use of newer computers which permit high-speed and very sophisticated output, many contract administrators (also called "third-party" administrators in the health insurance field) have offered specialized services which provide, for example, only claims processing and payment. As a result, many corporations and some Taft-Hartley multiemployer plans, have farmed out this function to these agents. In fact, claims payment has become a substantial part of the operations of some contract administrators. In addition, a number of large national insurance brokerage companies have set up claims payment subsidiaries. This enables them to market self-funded hospital and medical care plans and earn commissions on the "stop-loss" and life coverages plus administrative and consulting fees.

Many contract or "third-party" administrators are vigorously marketing multiple employer trusts (METS) and single employer self-funded or partially self-funded welfare plans. A number of insurance companies are working closely with these administration firms by providing both "stop-loss" coverage as well as "front-end deductible" plans. These plans are based on a large front-end deductible which is self-funded by the employer. These plans are especially attractive to small- and medium-sized employers.

For pension plans, in addition to contract and salaried administrators, banks and insurance companies offer administrative services—to varying degrees.

For example, many banks now offer Master Trust services. Usually, this provides investment accounting and measurement of the performance of the plan's money managers. Such Master Trusts, if so desired, also pay benefits upon written authorization of the plan sponsor. One of the important features of most Master Trust arrangements is the "fail-float" service which simply means in case an investment fails to be consummated by the required date, the bank automatically invests the funds in money market instruments thus keeping the plan assets fully invested at all times.

Master Trusts offer advantages to very large corporate plans. For example, a very large multibillion-dollar international corporation has 18 different pension plans for salaried personnel and over 100 plans for hourly paid employees. Through the use of a Master Trust with a large Chicago bank, all the plans' money managers draw on accounts set up in their names at the bank. This enables the bank to furnish the company individual plan investment accounting by an individual money manager as well as consolidated reporting. This means the company is able to get an overall view of investment activity.

Insurance companies offer pension fund services somewhat similar in scope, including paying participant pensions and investment accounting. Neither banks nor insurance companies, however, usually perform all the administrative services required. For example, in the case of a Taft-Hartley multiemployer trust, these organizations usually do not bill contributing employers. So it may still be necessary to have certain administrative functions performed in-house or by a contract administrator.

GRAY AREAS OF ADMINISTRATION

With such a variety of administrative agencies operating in the employee benefit plan arena, it is not surprising there are overlapping services or gray areas. For example, some contract administrators offer consultation services in addition to the basic administrative services required to properly manage such plans. This consultation may include performing underwriting (measuring risk and setting contribution rates) for health care plans as well as actuarial services for pension plans. However, as a general rule, the largest and most successful consulting firms do not provide the full range of administrative services.

It can be seen from this discussion that administrative services to employee benefit plans come in many varieties, both in scope and type.

There are a number of changes taking place in terms of how these services are structured.

In addition to the salaried, or in-house, administrator and the individual entrepreneurial contract administrator, insurance companies set up subsidiary companies offering full range ERISA services. There are a few contract administration firms which are owned by large conglomerate corporations with other businesses in totally unrelated fields.

The development of "specialty" shops also has grown where only part of required administration is performed, such as making claim payments as well as the increasing participation of banks and insurance companies in the administrative process.

Employee benefit plan sponsors, whether trustees of Taft-Hartley multiemployer plans or corporate plans, have at their disposal almost any combination of administration services they may desire. Finally, it is a truism that one cannot evaluate these differing administration agencies in a vacuum. Each plan must seek out it's best fit to achieve its objectives.

CHAPTER 46

Fiduciary Responsibility under the Employee Retirement Income Security Act of 1974

JAMES D. HUTCHINSON
AND
PAUL J. ONDRASIK, JR.

INTRODUCTION

In 1974, Congress enacted the Employee Retirement Income Security Act (ERISA).[1] This statute, covering virtually all private sector employee pension plans and welfare benefit plans,[2] displaced state regulation of the employee benefit plan field and erected in its place a comprehensive federal regulatory scheme.[3] As a result, ERISA and companion provisions of the Internal Revenue Code are now the preeminent reference points for questions concerning the administration, management and operation of private employee pension and welfare benefit plans.

Included within the regulatory framework established by ERISA is a code of conduct for individuals, known as "fiduciaries," who administer and control employee benefit plans.[4] This code is, in certain respects, derived from, and thus similar to, the duties imposed upon the trustees of trusts at common law.[5] However, its coverage extends far beyond traditional trust-

---

[1] 29 U.S.C. §§ 1001, *et seq.*

[2] *See* ERISA § 4, 29 U.S.C. § 1003.

[3] *E.g.,* Alessi v. Raybestos-Manhattan, Inc., 451 U.S. 504 (1981); Delta Airlines Inc. v. Kramarsky, 666 F. 2d 21 (2d Cir. 1981); ERISA Section 514, 29 U.S.C. § 1144; H. Rep. No. 93–1280, 93d Cong., 2d Sess. 383 (1974) (hereinafter "Conference Report"). *See generally* Hutchinson & Ifshin, *Federal Preemption of State Law Under the Employee Retirement Income Security Act of 1974,* 46 Chic. L. Rev. 23 (1978).

[4] ERISA Sections 3(21)(A), 401–414, 29 U.S.C. §§ 1002(21)(A), 1101–1114.

[5] *See, e.g.,* Donovan v. Bierwirth, 680 F. 2d 263, 271, 272 n.8 (2d Cir. 182), *aff'g as modified,* 538 F. Supp. 463 (E.D.N.Y. 1981), *cert. denied,* 103 S. Ct. 488 (1982); Eaves v. Penn, 587 F. 2d 453 (10th Cir. 1978), *aff'g in part and remanding,* 426 F. Supp. 830 (W.D. Okla. 1976); Bueneman v. Central States, Southeast and Southwest Areas Pension Fund, 572 F. 2d 1208 (1978); Morrissey v. Curran, 567 F. 2d 546 (2d Cir. 1977); Donovan v. Mazzola, 2 EBC 2115 (N.D. Cal., Nov. 17, 1981); Preamble, Final Regulation, Rules and Regulations for Fiduciary Responsibility—Investment of Plan Assets Under the "Prudence Rule [hereinafter cited as "Prudence Regulation"] 44 Fed. Reg. 37221, 37222 (June 26, 1979).

ees.[6] Moreover, reference to common law principles may be misleading because ERISA's code has been refined carefully with "the special nature and purpose of employee benefit plans" in mind.[7] This code of conduct is the focal point of this chapter.

FIDUCIARIES AND PARTIES IN INTEREST

Fiduciaries: Who Are They?

The term *fiduciary* for purposes of ERISA is defined in § 3(21)(A) of the Act:[8]

> [A] person is a fiduciary with respect to a plan to the extent (i) he exercises any discretionary authority or discretionary control respecting management of such plan or exercises any authority or control respecting management or disposition of its assets, (ii) he renders investment advice for a fee or other compensation, direct or indirect, with respect to any moneys or other property of such plan, or has any authority or responsibility to do so, or (iii) he has any discretionary authority or discretionary responsibility in the administration of such plan.

As is evident from a reading of § 3(21)(A), the statute eschews a definition based upon titles or labels. Rather, it establishes a functional definition which focuses on an individual's discretionary authority or control with respect to any aspect of a plan's affairs. Thus, a person's duties and responsibilities, rather than title, determine whether he or she is a fiduciary with respect to a plan.

This functional definition obviously encompasses individuals charged with the day-to-day management of an employee benefit plan who would be considered fiduciaries under traditional standards. For example, under ERISA, the documents pursuant to which a plan is maintained must specify one or more "named fiduciaries" who "have authority to control and manage the operation and administration of the plan."[9] Clearly, the broad responsibilities possessed by such individuals would render them "fiduciaries" under Section 3(21)(A) regardless of their title.

Similarly, the trustees of the trust in which the plan's assets are held would constitute fiduciaries. Under § 403(a) of ERISA,[10] the assets of an employee benefit plan are to be held in trust by "one or more trustees" either named in the trust instrument or by the named fiduciary. Subject to

---

[6] See discussion *infra* beginning at p. 742.

[7] Conference Report at 302. *See also* Donovan v. Mazzola, 2 EBC at 2133; Marshall v. Glass/Metal Ass'n & Glaziers & Glassworkers Pension Plan, 507 F. Supp. 378, 383 (D. Hawaii 1980); Marshall v. Kelly, 465 F. Supp. 341 (W.D. Okla. 1978); Marshall v. Teamsters Local 282 Pension Trust Fund, 458 F. Supp. 986 (E.D.N.Y. 1978).

[8] 29 U.S.C. § 1002(21)(A).

[9] ERISA Section 402(a)(1), 29 U.S.C. § 1002(a)(1).

[10] 29 U.S.C. § 1103(a).

certain exceptions, such trustees are to "have exclusive authority and discretion to manage and control the assets of the plan."[11] Once again, these duties would render these trustees "fiduciaries" just as they were at common law.

The statute's functional definition, however, encompasses far more than such obvious fiduciaries. As Section 3(21)(A) makes clear, investment advisers constitute fiduciaries to those plans which they serve for a fee. Regulations promulgated by the Department of Labor have interpreted this aspect of § 3(21)(A) to include not only those investment advisers who possess actual investment discretion over a plan's assets, but also those who render advice to a plan on a regular basis with the understanding the party with investment authority will utilize such advice as a primary source of guidance in making investments.[12]

Moreover, any party exercising discretionary responsibilities with respect to a plan would come within § 3(21)(A)'s scope. For example, an employer who has no role in a plan's operation other than to select the plan's fiduciaries would, nonetheless, constitute a fiduciary in making such selections.[13] Similarly, a plan's "benefit supervisor" would be a fiduciary if he or she possesses "final authority to authorize or disallow benefit payments in cases where a dispute arises as to the interpretation of plan provisions relating to eligibility for benefits."[14] Indeed, while the professional or ministerial services they perform for plans generally will not render them fiduciaries,[15] attorneys, accountants, consultants, or other providers of services may, in appropriate circumstances, constitute fiduciaries if in the rendition of services they, in effect, exercise discretionary authority or control over some aspect of the plan's affairs.[16]

At the same time it expands the definition of fiduciary, Section

---

[11] ERISA Section 403(a), 29 U.S.C. § 1103(a).

[12] 29 C.F.R. § 2510.3-21(c).

[13] See Eaves v. Penn, 587 F. 2d 453 (10th Cir. 1978); Freund v. Marshall & Ilsley Bank, 485 F. Supp. 629 (W.D. Wis. 1979); 29 C.F.R. § 2509.75-8, D-4; see also Donovan v. Williams, 4 EBC 1237 (N.D. Ohio, Feb. 2, 1983) (union official who had power to appoint and remove plan trustees is a fiduciary); Connors v. Drivers, Chauffeurs & Helpers Local Union No. 639, (iv. Act. No. 82-1840 (D.D.C. Nov. 11, 1982) (same); cf., United States Steel Corp. v. Pennsylvania Human Relations Comm'n, 669 F. 2d 124 (3d Cir., 1982).

[14] 29 C.F.R. § 2509.75-8; see also Schulist v. Blue Cross of Iowa, 4 EBC 1193 (N.D. Ill., Dec. 15, 1982); Brink v. DaLesio, 496 F. Supp. 1350 (D. Md. 1980), aff'd in part and remanded, 667 F. 2d 420 (4th Cir. 1981); Eaton v. D'Amato, 3 EBC 1003 (D.D.C. May 1, 1980).

[15] 29 C.F.R. § 2509.75-5, D-1; see also O'Toole v. Arlington Trust Co., 681 F. 2d 94 (1st Cir. 1982) 29 C.F.R. § 2509.75-8, D-2; 29 C.F.R. § 2510.3-21(d)(1); cf. Austin v. General American Life Ins. Co., 498 F. Supp. 844 (N.D. Ala. 1980).

[16] Conference Report at 323; 29 C.F.R. § 2509.75-5, D-1; see also Donovan v. Nellis, 2 EBC 2209 (N.D. Fla., Dec. 16, 1981) (attorney representing pension fund in foreclosure proceedings may be fund fiduciary). The Department of Labor has taken the position that labor arbitrators may constitute plan fiduciaries under certain circumstances. DOL Adv. Opins. Nos. 79-66A, 78-14; see also UAW v. Greyhound Lines, Inc. 4 EBC 1105 (6th Cir., March 11, 1983) (agreeing that arbitrators may be fiduciaries but extending them arbitral immunity from civil suit).

3(21)(A)'s focus on an individual's discretionary authority and control also serves as a limitation on that definition. Implicit in the fact that a person is a fiduciary "to the extent" that he or she possesses discretionary powers of the type enumerated in § 3(21)(A) is the notion that, as a general matter, he or she is a fiduciary *only* "to the extent" of those powers.[17] As a result, a person may be a fiduciary for some purposes and not for others. For example, the employer described earlier who played no part in the plan's operation other than in the selection of the plan's fiduciaries would be a fiduciary only to the extent of that discretionary power; for all other purposes, the employer would not be a fiduciary.[18] Similarly, an investment adviser given investment authority over a portion of a plan's portfolio would be a fiduciary only for those plan assets; the adviser would not be a fiduciary and thus would have no fiduciary responsibilities with respect to the investment of the other assets of the plan.[19] The chief consequence of this limitation is that, as a general matter, a fiduciary faces potential liability only for his or her own breaches of fiduciary duty and not for breaches committed by other fiduciaries outside of his or her area of responsibility and control.[20]

In sum, under ERISA § 3(21)(A), virtually any party who exercises discretion in the administration or management of a plan or its assets constitutes a "fiduciary." However, as a general rule, such person is a fiduciary only to the extent of his or her discretionary authority. Thus, as a practical matter, the functional definition established by § 3(21)(A) serves both to expand and limit the scope of fiduciary responsibility under ERISA.

Parties in Interest

In addition to fiduciaries, ERISA establishes a second category of individuals closely related to employee benefit plans—parties in interest.[21] As

---

[17] Brandt v. Grounds, 3 EBC 1780 (7th Cir., July 6, 1982). 29 C.F.R. § 2509.75-8, FR-16; 29 C.F.R. § 29 C.F.R. § 2510.3-21(c)(2), (d)(2); DOL Adv. Opin., WSB No. 79-11 (savings and loan associations offering investment accounts to employee benefit plans are not fiduciaries where an independent service corporation administers the plan and is responsible for investment decisions); DOL Adv. Opin. No. 77-68A (investment manager's evaluation of plan's current asset management staff will not render it a fiduciary since "it will not exercise any discretionary authority or responsibility in the administration of the plan").

[18] *See* 29 C.F.R. § 2509.75-8, D-4, FR-16; DOL Adv. Opin. Nos. 77-69, 70 A (named fiduciary who is responsible for the appointment of independent investment managers is a fiduciary only when executing this appointment responsibility).

[19] 29 C.F.R. § 2510.3-21(c)(2), (d)(2); DOL Adv. Opin. Nos. 77-69, 70 A (each independent investment manager having exclusive authority to manage certain allocated plan assets is a fiduciary only with respect to those specifically allocated assets); DOL Adv. Opin. No. 76-76 (a bank acting as the custodial agent to a fund would be a fiduciary to the extent it had any discretion in plan investment transactions).

[20] Brandt v. Grounds, 3 EBC at 1782-84. However, he may be liable for such actions under ERISA's co-fiduciary liability provisions, see discussion *infra* at p. 754.

[21] ERISA Section 3(14), 29 U.S.C. § 1002(14).

such, parties in interest are not subject to ERISA's fiduciary responsibility provisions. Nonetheless, their identity is important to plan fiduciaries because of ERISA's prohibited transaction rules. Those rules, discussed *infra,*[22] generally prohibit a fiduciary from causing a plan to engage in any transaction, either direct or indirect, involving a party in interest to that plan.

The term *party in interest* is defined in ERISA § 3(14),[23] a broad and complex provision establishing nine separate categories of parties in interest. These nine categories can be divided roughly into two types of parties in interest. The first, defined in Sections 3(14)(A), (B), (C), and (D), encompasses individuals or entities that have a direct relationship to the plan. These "direct" parties in interest include the plan's fiduciaries, counsel, and employees (§ 3(14)(A)); providers of services to the plan (§ 3(14)(B)); employers of employees covered by the plan (§ 3(14)(C)); and employee organizations whose members are covered by the plan (§ 3(14)(D)).

The second category encompasses individuals that have no direct relationship to the plan but instead have certain specified relationships to existing parties in interest. These "indirect" parties in interest are defined in a series of complex attribution rules set forth in Sections 3(14)(E), (F), (G), (H), and (I). Under § 3(14)(E), any party with a 50 percent or more ownership or other beneficial interest in an employer or employee organization that constitutes a direct party in interest is a party in interest as well. Likewise, any relative of a direct party in interest or a party described in § 3(14)(E) is deemed a party in interest (§ 3(14)(F)). Section 3(14)(G), on the other hand, encompasses any "corporation, partnership, or trust or estate" in which a direct party in interest or a party described in § 3(14)(E) has a 50 percent or greater ownership or other beneficial interest. Similarly, under § 3(14)(H), employees, officers, directors, or 10 percent or greater shareholders of any direct party in interest (other than a fiduciary), any party described in § 3(14)(E), any corporation, partnership or trust described in § 3(14)(G) and the employee benefit plan itself are deemed parties in interest. Finally, § 3(14)(I) reaches any 10 percent or greater partner or joint venturer of a direct party in interest (other than a fiduciary), any party described in § 3(14)(E) or any corporation, partnership, or trust described in § 3(14)(G).

As is thus evident, § 3(14) renders a large number of individuals and entities parties in interest, including numerous parties with no direct relationship to the plan. Accordingly, § 3(14) requires a plan fiduciary to monitor carefully the parties to any transaction in which the plan engages to insure compliance with ERISA's prohibited transaction provisions.

---

[22] See discussion *infra* at p. 757.
[23] 29 U.S.C. § 1002(14).

FIDUCIARY DUTIES: IN GENERAL

The specific duties imposed upon plan fiduciaries in carrying out their plan responsibilities are set forth in ERISA § 404(a)(1).[24] That section provides:

> [A] fiduciary shall discharge his duties with respect to a plan solely in the interest of the participants and beneficiaries and—
>
> (A)   for the exclusive purpose of:
>
>   (i)   providing benefits to participants and their beneficiaries; and
>
>   (ii)   defraying reasonable expenses of administering the plan;
>
> (B)   with the care, skill, prudence, and diligence under the circumstances then prevailing that a prudent man acting in a like capacity and familiar with such matters would use in the conduct of an enterprise of a like character and with like aims;
>
> (C)   by diversifying the investments of the plan so as to minimize the risk of large losses, unless under the circumstances it is clearly prudent not to do so; and
>
> (D)   in accordance with the documents and instruments governing the plan insofar as such documents and instruments are consistent with the provisions of this title.

With the exception of the diversification requirement, these basic obligations apply to all ERISA fiduciaries in carrying out their plan responsibilities. The diversification requirement, of course, applies only to those fiduciaries responsible for the investment of plan assets.

Solely in the Interest Standard

As a threshold requirement, Section 404 requires plan fiduciaries to discharge their duties to the plan "solely in the interest" of the plan's participants and beneficiaries. In effect, this requirement imposes on a fiduciary, the duty of undivided loyalty applicable to trustees at common law in performing their trust responsibilities.[25] Thus, as at common law, not only must a fiduciary's loyalty to his plan be "primary," it is "the *only* loyalty which may affect his judgment" when acting on the plan's behalf.[26]

This general obligation is given some specific content by reference to the common law and ERISA's prohibited transaction provisions. At common law, a trustee's duty of loyalty precluded him from purchasing or selling

---

[24] 29 U.S.C. § 1104(a)(1).

[25] NLRB v. Amax Coal Co., 453 U.S. 322 (1981); Donovan v. Bierwirth, 538 F. Supp. 463, 468–69 (E.D.N.Y. 1981), *aff'd as modified* 680 F. 2d 263 (2d Cir. 1982), *cert. denied*, 103 S. Ct. 988 (1982).

[26] Donovan v. Bierwirth, 538 F. Supp. at 468 (emphasis in original). *Accord,* NLRB v. Amax Coal Co., *supra;* Herman v. Painting Indus. Ins. Fund, 2 EBC 2438 (S.D.N.Y., Sept. 30, 1981) (trustees, who also acted as officers of either a participating union or employer, satisfied their duties under section 404(a)(1) when they abstained from participation in matters connected with the union or employer).

property to his trust,[27] from competing with the trust,[28] or from accepting compensation from parties dealing with the trust for his own account.[29] These common law prohibitions are carried forward in ERISA's prohibited transaction rules which prohibit a fiduciary from engaging in any direct or indirect transaction with the plan,[30] from dealing "with the assets of the plan in his own interest or for his own account,"[31] from representing or otherwise acting on behalf of a third party in any plan transaction,[32] and from receiving "any consideration for his own personal account from any party dealing with" the plan.[33]

Further specific content for the "solely in the interest" standard may be derived from judicial constructions of that provision and advisory opinions and information letters issued by the Department of Labor. Those interpretations have made clear that an ERISA fiduciary may not take actions at the expense of the plan's participants or beneficiaries which tend to favor himself or the employer or employee organization maintaining the plan. For example, a fiduciary has been found to have violated § 404(a)(1) where he caused the plan to pay salaries to employees who were engaged primarily in union, rather than plan, business or where he voted himself benefits that were not authorized under the plan.[34] Likewise, an employer's amendment of a plan to make eligibility standards more rigorous at the same time he was planning to lay off employees who would otherwise qualify for benefits has been held to violate § 404(a)(1).[35] A violation also has been found where a fiduciary purchased employer securities for an employee stock ownership plan, not in consideration of the participants' best interests, but to finance his acquisition of the employer.[36] Similarly, trustees of a corporate plan who were also officers of the employer plan sponsor were found to have violated the "solely in the interest" standard when they used plan assets to fend off a hostile takeover bid directed at the employer.[37]

---

[27] Restatement (Second) of Trusts § 170, Comments b, c (1959).

[28] Restatement (Second) of Trusts § 170, Comment p (1959).

[29] Restatement (Second) of Trusts § 170, Comment o (1959).

[30] ERISA Section 406(a), 29 U.S.C. § 1106(a).

[31] ERISA Section 406(b)(1), 29 U.S.C. § 1106(b)(1).

[32] ERISA Section 406(b)(2), 29 U.S.C. § 1106(b)(2).

[33] ERISA Section 406(b)(3), 29 U.S.C. § 1106(b)(3).

[34] Marshall v. Snyder, 430 F. Supp. 1224 (E.D.N.Y. 1977), aff'd, 572 F. 2d 894 (2d Cir. 1978) (salaries to employees primarily engaged in union business); Donovan v. Daugherty, 3 EBC 2096 (S.D. Ala., (Sept. 30, 1982) (unauthorized benefits).

[35] Dependahl v. Falstaff Brewing Corp., 491 F. Supp. 1188 (E.D. Mo. 1979), aff'd in part and remanded, 653 F. 2d 1208 (8th Cir. 1981), cert. denied 102 S. Ct. 512 (1981).

[36] Eaves v. Penn, 426 F. Supp. 830 (W.D. Okla. 1976), aff'd in part and remanded, 587 F. 2d 453 (10th Cir. 1978).

[37] Donovan v. Bierwirth, 680 F. 2d at 271. See also DOL Inf. Ltr., WSB No. 80-83 (cautioning plan fiduciaries presented with an offer to purchase the plan's employer securities in the course of a takeover bid to assess the offer "solely in the interests of plan participants and beneficiaries," and not in the interest of themselves or the employer).

These same principles have led the Department of Labor to condemn or view as inherently suspect under § 404(a)(1) certain conflict-of-interest situations that are particularly rife with potential for abuse, even in the absence of evidence of wrongdoing.[38] In this regard, the department has suggested that a bank may violate § 404(a)(1) by serving as trustee of a plan which held significant amounts of employer securities, while, at the same time, constituting a substantial secured creditor of the employer.[39] The department also has questioned the ability of plan fiduciaries to avoid § 404(a)(1) violations in the event their plan made an equity and second mortgage investment in a real estate development in which the fiduciaries held a significant equity interest.[40]

Finally, these broad principles have been fashioned not only into specific prohibitions but also affirmative notice and disclosure duties beyond those expressly imposed by ERISA. These additional disclosure duties have been held to arise when a fiduciary has knowledge of events that will jeopardize or terminate a participant's right to benefits but whose consequences can be avoided or rectified by action on the participant's part. Thus, plan trustees were found to have violated § 404(a)(1) where they failed to give a participant prior notice of a plan amendment that extinguished the right to early retirement benefits that he possessed but had not exercised prior to the amendment.[41] Likewise, a violation of § 404(a)(1) was found where the trustees of an individual account plan failed to notify participants in advance, and at a time when they could have withdrawn their monies from the plan as the trustees had done, of the full details of a sale of the plan's sponsoring employer which ensured the plan's financial demise.[42] Similarly, the Third Circuit Court of Appeals has held recently that "[a]t minimum, the fiduciary obligations of a pension fund trustee require he notify the pensioner of his employer's failure to contribute to the fund as required by the pension agreement."[43]

In short, the "solely in the interest" standard has been given a rather

---

[38] Indeed, the Department of Labor recently took the position that it was *per se* unlawful under ERISA § 404(a)(1) for officers and directors of an employer who also served as trustees of the employer's pension plan to make any decisions concerning the plan's employer's securities subsequent to a hostile tender offer directed at the employer. Donovan v. Bierwirth, 538 F. Supp. at 467–69. The court rejected this *per se* theory in light of ERISA § 408(c)(3), 29 U.S.C. § 1108(c)(3) which explicitly permits representatives of a party in interest to serve as fiduciaries despite the inherent conflict of interest present. *Id.*

[39] DOL Adv. Opin. No. 76-32.

[40] DOL Inf. Ltr., WSB No. 80-76.

[41] McCoy v. Mesta Machine Co., 213 BNA Pens. Reptr. D-1 (W.D. Pa.), *judgment vacated,* 260 BNA Pens. Reptr. D-1 (W.D. Pa. 1979). *See also* Burroughs v. Board of Trustees of Pension Trust, 542 F. 2d 1128, 1131 (9th Cir. 1976), *cert. denied,* 429 U.S. 1096 (1977); Pizzirusso v. Graziano, 125 BNA Pens. Reptr. D-7 (E.D.N.Y. 1978). *Cf.* Winpisinger v. Aurora Corp., 456 F. Supp. 559 (N.D. Ohio 1978).

[42] Freund v. Marshall & Ilsley Bank, 485 F. Supp. at 640.

[43] Rosen v. Hotel & Restaurant Employees and Bartenders Union, 637 (3d Cir. F. 2d 592 1981).

literal construction to date by both the courts and the Department of Labor. It imposes upon plan fiduciaries a duty of "undivided loyalty," and thereby prohibits a fiduciary from engaging in any self-dealing and, indeed, any activity that is not designed primarily to advance the interests of participants and beneficiaries.[44] Moreover, it imposes upon fiduciaries certain affirmative duties, at least in the notice and disclosure area, where the fiduciary's failure to act would be fundamentally unfair to the plan's participants and beneficiaries.

The "Exclusive Purpose" Rule

Section 404(a)(1)(A) requires a fiduciary to discharge his duties "for the exclusive purpose of: (i) providing benefits to participants and their beneficiaries; and (ii) defraying reasonable expenses of administering the plan." On its face, this requirement would appear to constitute no more than one aspect of the broader duty of undivided loyalty imposed under § 404(a)(1). However, since it would be contrary to normal rules of statutory construction to give this provision no independent significance, the courts and the Department of Labor most likely will construe the requirement as imposing some additional, and more specific, limitation on a fiduciary's activities.[45]

The ultimate scope of this requirement is difficult to predict. The provision's legislative history seems to treat it as a subcategory of the duty of undivided loyalty, with specific focus on the proper expenditure and use of plan assets.[46] Likewise, the interpretations rendered to date by the courts and the Department of Labor have focused primarily on this context. For example, these authorities indicate that violations have, or would, take place where a fiduciary caused a plan to pay excessive administrative fees or unnecessary expenses;[47] to compensate individuals who were prohibited by

---

[44] The "solely in the interest" standard, however, is not violated by actions which incidentally benefit a fiduciary or a party in interest so long as the action was taken solely with the interests of the plan's participants and beneficiaries in mind. As the Second Circuit had recent occasion to note:

Although officers of a corporation who are trustees of its pension plan do not violate their duties as trustees by taking action which, after careful and impartial investigation, they reasonably conclude best to promote the interests of participants and beneficiaries simply because it incidentally benefits the corporation, or, indeed, themselves, their decisions must be made with an eye single to the interests of the participants and beneficiaries.

Donovan v. Bierwirth, 680 F. 2d at 271. Nonetheless, fiduciaries who engage in such activities can expect their action to be scrutinized strictly. *See* Donovan v. Bierwirth, 680 F. 2d at 271-276.

[45] *See* 2A J. Sutherland, Statutes and Statutory Construction § 46.06 (4th ed. 1973).

[46] Conference Report at 303.

[47] Donovan v. Mazzola, 2 EBC at 2136-37; Gilliam v. Edwards, 492 F. Supp. 1255 (D.N.J. 1980) Marshall v. Snyder, *supra*; Marshall v. Wilson, No. 3-76.373 (E.D. Tenn., Consent Order filed June 6, 1977); *see also* Weisler v. Metal Polishers Union, 3 EBC 2339 (S.D.N.Y., Feb. 3, 1982).

law from employment with the plan;[48] to pay the salaries of individuals rendering services primarily to a union;[49] to reimburse trustees for legal fees incurred in a proceeding in which they were found to have violated their fiduciary obligations;[50] to provide benefits to himself that were both unauthorized and made available on a basis more favorable than for participants;[51] and to pay excessive fees for the construction of a plan-owned building.[52]

Despite its rather limited application to date, the "exclusive purpose" rule, by its express term, applies to *all* duties discharged by a fiduciary and not simply those pertaining to the expenditure of plan assets. Not surprisingly then, several recent cases have applied it to find fiduciary violations in the investment context. In one case, the trustees of a jointly trusteed, multiemployer pension plan were found to have violated the exclusive purpose rule in connection with a series of loans to a related, financially troubled convalescent fund that they also trusteed. The court found that the loans were made to benefit the convalescent fund and thus were not for the exclusive benefit of the pension plan's participants and beneficiaries.[53] In a second case, a plan fiduciary's investment of plan assets in a group annuity contract and bank deposit accounts under circumstances designed to benefit both himself and entities in which he had an interest were held to violate the exclusive purpose standard.[54] In still another, a plan's acquisition of employer securities as part of an alleged attempt to maintain control of a corporation was viewed as violative of the exclusive purpose rule.[55] The extension of the exclusive purpose rule in this fashion suggests that it yet may serve as a significant, additional limitation upon a fiduciary's actions. A prime example would be in the area of "social investing." Since "social investments" are designed to further goals other than the provision of benefits to participants and beneficiaries, an argument could be advanced that they violate the exclusive purpose rule even if they otherwise satisfy the "solely in the interest" standard, are "prudent," and do not entail a

---

[48] DOL Advisory Opin. No. 75-90.

[49] Marshall v. Snyder, *supra;* Marshall v. Wilson, *supra.*

[50] Donovan v. Mazzola, 2 EBC at 2137-38; DOL Advisory Opin. No. 78-29; *cf.* Eaves v. Penn, 587 F. 2d at 464-65; Freund v. Marshall & Ilsley Bank, 485 F. Supp. at 643-44.

[51] Donovan v. Daugherty, 3 EBC at 2095-96.

[52] Marshall v. Kelley, *supra.*

[53] Donovan v. Mazzola, 2 EBC at 2133-34. *See also* Marshall v. Davis 2 EBC 1721 (W.D. Mich., June 30, 1981) (vacation fund trustees who, on a monthly basis, segregated and did not invest union dues assessments even though disbursements were made to participants only on an annual basis violated exclusive purpose rule.) *Cf.* Baker v. Smith, 2 EBC 1380 (E.D. Pa., Feb. 24, 1981) (trustees, who invested plan assets in an ESOP of a company which went bankrupt, may have violated exclusive purpose and prudence standards).

[54] Marshall v. Carroll, 2 EBC 2491 (N.D. Cal., April 18, 1980).

[55] Dimond v. Retirement Plan, 4 EBC 1457 (W.D. Pa., Mar. 7, 1983).

"prohibited transaction."[56] In light of such potential impact, the evolution of this provision must be scrutinized closely.

The Prudent Man Rule

The "prudent man" rule, the most significant of the duties imposed on an ERISA fiduciary, is set forth in § 404(a)(1)(B). It requires a fiduciary to discharge his duties

> with the care, skill, prudence, and diligence under the circumstances then prevailing that a prudent man acting in a like capacity and familiar with such matters would use in the conduct of an enterprise of a like character and with like aims.

This rule, of course, has its genesis in the common law duty of a trustee to administer his trust with the skill that a man of ordinary prudence would exercise in managing his own affairs.[57] However, there are significant differences between the common law obligation and that imposed by ERISA, which stem primarily from the different purposes served by employee benefit plans and traditional trusts.[58] As a result, common law authorities can serve as but a starting point in determining the scope of the obligation imposed by ERISA.

As a threshold matter, it is important to recognize that ERISA's "prudent man" standard is far more flexible than that applicable at common law. At common law, a trustee's actions were analyzed rigidly against that conduct which a man of ordinary skill and prudence would employ in his own affairs.[59] The fact that an employee benefit plan was involved, the unique characteristics of that plan, and the relative skill and experience of the particular trustee,[60] would be largely irrelevant to the inquiry.

In sharp contrast, ERISA's prudent man rule takes these factors into

---

[56] *See* Hutchinson & Cole, *Legal Standards Governing Investment of Pension Assets For Social and Political Goals,* 128 U. Pa. L. Rev. 1340, 1369-71 (1980).

[57] *E.g.,* Harvard College v. Amory, 26 Mass. (9 Pick.) 446, 461 (1830); Restatement (Second) of Trusts § 174 (1959); 3 A.W. Scott, The Law of Trusts § 227 (3d ed. 1967); G. Bogert, The Law of Trusts & Trustees § 671-679 (rev. 2d ed. 1982).

[58] For example, in the employee benefit plan context, the tension between the interests of current income beneficiaries and remainderman, which formed the basis for a number of common law prudence principles, is completely absent. Similarly, unlike the traditional trust which is formed with a one-time infusion of capital, employee benefit plans typically have contributions made to them on a regular and on going basis. *See* Note, *Fiduciary Standards and the Prudent Man Rule Under the Employment* [*sic*] *Retirement Income Security Act of 1974,* 88 Harv. L. Rev. 960 (1975).

[59] *See generally* 3 A. W. Scott, The Law of Trusts § 227 (3d ed. 1967); G. Bogert, The Law of Trusts & Trustees §§ 671-679 (rev. 2d ed. 1982).

[60] *But see* Restatement (Second) of Trusts § 174 (1959) which holds the professional trustee to a higher standard of skill and care.

consideration. As its legislative history makes clear, Congress intended ERISA's prudent man standard to be interpreted "bearing in mind the special nature and purpose of employee benefit plans."[61] Thus, the universe of employee benefit plans, rather than of trusts in general, is the proper area of focus. Moreover, the statutory standard recognizes the wide variations within that universe. This view is reflected in the statutory language itself which establishes the conduct which a prudent man "would use in the conduct of enterprise of like character and with like aims" as the appropriate benchmark.[62] It is further evidenced by the standard's shift of focus from the ordinary prudent man, to one "acting in a like capacity, and familiar with such matters."[63] The result is a comparative standard of performance under which the gratuitous trustee of a small plan with an overriding need for liquidity should be held to a different standard of accountability than the professional trustee managing a plan holding millions of dollars in assets.[64] Thus, ERISA's prudent man rule is designed not only with the distinctive nature of employee benefit plans in mind, but also with sufficient flexibility to permit sensible application across the wide spectra of such plans.

Moreover, the broad scope of ERISA's prudent man rule cannot be overlooked. While prudence issues typically arise in connection with a fiduciary's management and investment of plan assets, ERISA's prudent man standard explicitly governs *all* of a fiduciary's plan responsibilities and, indeed, constitutes his most basic obligation. Accordingly, an ERISA fiduciary must satisfy this duty not only in connection with his investments but also in connection with such diverse matters as the delegation of any plan responsibilities, including the selection, appointment, and monitoring of an investment manager,[65] the selection of service providers,[66] the collection of delinquent contributions,[67] and even recordkeeping.[68]

---

[61] Conference Report at 302. *Accord* Donovan v. Mazzola, 2 EBC at 2133; Marshall v. Glass/Metal Ass'n & Glaziers & Glassworkers Pension Plan, 507 F. Supp. at 383; Marshall v. Kelly, 465 F. Supp. at 349-50; Marshall v. Teamsters Local 282 Pension Trust Fund, 458 F. Supp. at 990; Prudence Regulation Preamble, 44 Fed. Reg. at 37222.

[62] ERISA Section 404(a)(1)(B), 29 U.S.C. § 1104(a)(1)(B).

[63] *Id.*

[64] *See* Hutchinson, *The Federal Prudent Man Rule Under ERISA,* 22 V.11. L. Rev. 15, 42 (1976–77).

[65] 29 C.F.R. § 2509.75-8, FR-11. *See also,* Freund v. Marshall & Ilsley Bank., *supra. Cf.,* ERISA Section 405(c)(2), 29 U.S.C. § 1105(c)(2).

[66] Donovan v. Mazzola, 2 EBC at 2136-37.

[67] *See* PBGC v. Greene, 4 EBC 1169 (W.D. Pa., Mar. 16 1983); Central States Pension Fund v. Central Transport, Inc., 3 EBC 1844, 1899-1850 (E.D. Mich., Sept. 19, 1981), Marshall v. Wilson, *supra; cf. In re* J. L. Thomson Rivet Corp., 3 EBC 1582, 1586-87 (Bank Ct., D. Mass., Apr. 12, 1982).

[68] *See* Nichols v. Trustees of Asbestos Workers Pension Plan, 3 EBC 1726, 1731-32 (D.D.C. July 19, 1982); Corley v. The Hecht Company, 2 EBC 2397, 2404-05 (D.D.C. Jan. 18, 1982); Marshall v. Wilson, *supra.*

Nonetheless, like its common law counterpart, ERISA's prudent man rule is of primary importance in the investment area. With respect to certain specific investment matters, general guidelines can be derived for the ERISA fiduciary from the common law. For example, a common law trustee was under a duty to make trust property productive,[69] to preserve trust property,[70] and to evaluate the soundness of both the acquisition of plan investments and their retention.[71] Without question, an ERISA fiduciary charged with responsibility for a plan's investments faces these same obligations as a general matter.[72] However, even standards such as these cannot be applied with the same rigidity as at common law; as the Department of Labor has stated, "the common law of trusts . . . should . . . not be mechanically applied to employee benefit plans."[73] Rather, the prudence of any particular action must be determined on a comparative, case-by-case basis with reference to the needs and objectives of the plan in issue. Moreover, certain clear differences do exist, one of the most notable being ERISA's rejection of the common law's investment-by-investment prudence analysis[74] in favor of one which analyzes an investment's prudence within the context of a plan's entire investment portfolio.[75]

Because of the uncertainties in this key area of fiduciary responsibility, the Department of Labor promulgated a regulation, effective July 23, 1979, relating to the investment of plan assets under the prudence standard.[76] The regulation put to rest several matters of hot debate. First, the regulation's preamble made clear that for purposes of ERISA's prudence standard, no specific investment or investment course of action was *per se* prudent or imprudent based on its relative riskiness alone.[77] Rather, the prudence of any investment decision is to be determined on the basis of an analysis of all the pertinent facts and circumstances, including the needs and characteristics of the plan, the role the investment or investment strategy is to play in

---

[69] *See, e.g.,* Blankenship v. Boyle, 329 F. Supp. 1089 (D.D.C. 1971).

[70] *See* Restatement (Second) of Trusts § 176 (1959).

[71] *See* Restatement (Second) of Trusts §§ 230, 231 (1959).

[72] *See, e.g.,* Morrissey v. Curran, *supra* (duty to review portfolio and dispose of improper investments); Marshall v. Craft, 463 F. Supp. 493 (N.D. Ga. 1978) (to same effect as Morrissey); Marshall v. Wilson, *supra* (purchase of stock in financially unstable company imprudent).

[73] Prudence Regulation Preamble, 44 Fed. Reg. at 37222.

[74] *See* In re Bank of New York, 35 N.Y. 2d 512, 323 N.E. 2d 700 (1974). *See generally* 3 A. W. Scott, The Law of Trusts § 213 (3d ed. 1967); G. Bogert, The Law of Trusts & Trustees § 708 (rev. ed. 1982).

[75] Prudence Regulation Preamble, 44 Fed. Reg. at 37222. *See also* Conference Report at 304-05; DOL Advisory Opin. No. 75-83; Report, *ERISA and the Investment Management and Brokerage Industries: Five Years Later,* 35 Bus. Law. 189, 239 (1979).

[76] 44 Fed. Reg. 37221 (June 26, 1979), codified at 29 C.F.R. § 2550.404a-1.

[77] Prudence Regulation Preamble, 44 Fed. Reg. at 37222, 37225.

the plan's portfolio,[78] and, as several recent cases have suggested, the availability of alternative investments to meet the plan's goals.[79] Accordingly, the Department of Labor refused to establish a "legal list" of investments[80] and made clear that the universe of "prudent" investments was not limited to those permitted at common law.[81] Secondly, and closely related to the first point, the regulation rejects outright the common law approach of analyzing an investment's prudence on an individual basis, apart from the portfolio as a whole. Instead, an investment's (or investment strategy's) prudence is to be judged within the context of its role "within the overall plan portfolio."[82]

Against this background, the regulation sets forth a suggested course of action for the prudent fiduciary to follow in making investment decisions. As the regulation makes clear, a fiduciary will be deemed to have satisfied ERISA's prudence standard if he complies with this course of decision making.[83] However, the regulation's preamble further specifies that the regulation is in the nature of a "safe harbor" only.[84] Thus, while compliance with the regulation's terms will be deemed to satisfy § 404(a)(1)(B)'s requirements, such compliance is not the exclusive method of satisfying the prudence standard.

Under the terms of the regulation, the requirements of § 404(a)(1)(B) will be deemed satisfied with respect to a particular investment or investment course of action if the fiduciary:

> (A) has given appropriate consideration to those facts and circumstances that, given the scope of such fiduciary's investment duties, the fiduciary knows or should know are relevant to the particular investment or investment course of action involved, including the role the investment or investment course of

---

[78] Prudence Regulation Preamble, 44 Fed. Reg. at 37222. The preamble underscores this point by explicitly stating that "an investment reasonably designed—as part of the portfolio—to further the purposes of the plan, and that is made upon appropriate consideration of the surrounding facts and circumstances, should not be deemed to be imprudent merely because the investment, standing alone, would have, for example, a relatively high degree of risk. *Id.* Fed. Reg. at 37244.

[79] Donovan v. Bierwirth, 538 F. Supp. at 473. *See also* Donovan v. Mazzola, 2 EBC at 2126; Marshall v. Glass/Metal Ass'n & Glaziers & Glassworkers Pension Plan, 507 F. Supp. at 384; Baker v. Smith, 2 EBC at 1382.

[80] Prudence Regulation Preamble, 44 Fed. Reg. at 37225.

[81] *Id.*

[82] *Id.* at 37222. As the preamble states, "the prudence of an investment decision should not be determined without regard to the role that the proposed investment or investment course of action plays within the overall plan portfolio." *Id.* The Department's adoption of the "whole portfolio" approach, however, does not imply that a fiduciary may ignore material attributes of the contemplated investment, such as risk, merely because the return on the plan's other investments insures a favorable return on the portfolio as a whole. Rather, as the preamble makes clear, "appropriate consideration of an investment . . . must include consideration of the characteristics of the investment itself." *Id.* at 37224.

[83] Prudence Regulation Preamble, 44 Fed. Reg. at 37222.

[84] *Id.*

action plays in that portion of the plan's investment portfolio with respect to which the fiduciary has investment duties; and (B) has acted accordingly.[85]

For purposes of the regulation "appropriate consideration" is defined to include:

> a determination by the fiduciary that the particular investment or investment course of action is reasonably designed, as part of the portfolio . . . , to further the purposes of the plan, taking into consideration the risk of loss and opportunity for gain (or other return) associated with the investment or investment course of action, . . .[86]

In making that determination, the fiduciary is directed to consider:

> (i) The composition of the portfolio with regard to diversification;
>
> (ii) The liquidity and current return of the portfolio relative to the anticipated cash flow requirements of the plan; and
>
> (iii) The projected return of the portfolio relative to the funding objectives of the plan.[87]

Thus, the regulation, by its express terms, requires a fiduciary to analyze the investment or investment strategy thoroughly, both in terms of its own characteristics and within the context of the plan's entire portfolio, and then determine whether the investment or strategy is designed reasonably to serve the plan's overall needs and objectives.

As is thus evident, the regulation establishes a "procedural" prudence standard which focuses on the thoroughness of the fiduciary's analysis in reaching an investment decision and *not* on investment results. Without specific reference to the prudence regulation, this procedural approach has received judicial endorsement in several recent decisions. In those cases, the courts judged the fiduciary's prudence on the basis of his " 'independent inquiry into the merits of a particular investment' decision,"[88] with particular emphasis on his consideration of the factors that other knowledgeable investors would have evaluated in reaching the investment decision as well as the availability of alternative investments to meet the plan's goals and needs.[89] Thus, as both these decisions and the prudence regulation clearly indicate, the prudence of any investment decision is to be determined as of the time of decision. As one court has stated: "The standard to be applied is

---

[85] 29 C.F.R. § 2550.404a-1(b)(1).

[86] *Id.* at § 2550.404a-1(b)(2).

[87] *Id.*

[88] Donovan v. Bierwirth, 538 F. Supp. at 470. *See also* Dimond v. Retirement Plan, *supra.*

[89] Donovan v. Bierwirth, 680 F. 2d at 271; Donovan v. Mazzola, 2 EBC at 2133-2135; Marshall v. Glass/Metal Ass'n & Glaziers & Glassworkers Pension Plan, 507 F. Supp. at 384-85. *See also* Brink v. DaLesio, *supra;* DOL Inf. Ltr., WSB No. 80-26. *See generally* DOL Adv. Opin. No. 80-8A (setting forth factors to be considered when plan contemplates the purchase of goods and the making of loans to parties in interest).

that of conduct, tested at the time of the investment decision, rather than performance, judged from the vantage of hindsight."[90]

Diversification Duty

Under § 404(a)(1)(C), a fiduciary is obligated to "diversify[. . .] the investments of the plan so as to minimize the risk of large losses, unless under the circumstances it is clearly prudent not to do so." While generally recognized as a component of the prudent man rule at common law,[91] this diversification duty is stated separately to emphasize that "the basic policy [of ERISA] is to require diversification."[92] Moreover, just as in the case of the other obligations set forth in § 404, ERISA's diversification require- ment differs from its common law counterpart in several key respects.

First, unlike the common law, ERISA's diversification requirement can- not be overridden by contrary language in the plan instruments.[93] Rather, except in areas where statutory exceptions apply,[94] the diversification duty can be avoided only by a clear demonstration that prudence permits otherwise.[95]

Second, § 404(a)(1)(C)'s requirement that diversification must obtain except when "clearly prudent" not to diversify establishes a procedural departure from common law. As the Conference Report makes clear, the term "clearly prudent" was used, not to establish a rule of extreme pru- dence, but to require a fiduciary to establish the prudence of his actions once a failure to diversify was established. Thus, unlike the common law which required a plaintiff to demonstrate both a lack of diversification and the imprudence of that course of action, ERISA requires a plaintiff to establish only the former; once he has done so, the burden shifts to the fiduciary to establish the prudence of his decision not to diversify.[96]

Despite the emphasis placed upon diversification by ERISA, the statute does not establish any specific diversification standards for the ERISA fiduciary. Nor does the act's legislative history offer any guidance on this matter beyond the general admonitions that a "fiduciary usually should not

---

[90] American Communications Ass'n v. Retirement Plan for Employees of RCA Corp., 488 F. Supp. 479, 483 (S.D.N.Y. 1980), aff'd, 646 F. 2d 559 (2d Cir. 1980). Accord, Donovan v. Mazzola, 2 EBC at 2134; Marshall v. Glass/Metal Ass'n & Glaziers & Glassworkers Pension Plan, 507 F. Supp. at 384.

[91] See Restatement (Second) of Trusts § 228 (1959); 3 A. W. Scott, The Law of Trusts § 228 (3d ed. 1967); G. Bogert, The Law of Trusts & Trustees § 612 (rev. 2d ed. 1980).

[92] Conference Report at 304.

[93] Compare Restatement (Second) of Trust § 228 (1959) with ERISA Section 404(a)(1)(D), 29 U.S.C. § 1104(a)(1)(D).

[94] T..e diversification rule does not apply to certain individual account plans that are designed to hold employer stock. ERISA Section 404(a)(2), 29 U.S.C. § 1104(a)(2).

[95] See ERISA Section 404(a)(1)(C); see also Marshall v. Teamsters Local 282 Pension Trust Fund, 458 F. Supp. at 990-91.

[96] Conference Report at 304. Accord Freund v. Marshall & Ilsley Bank, 485 F. Supp. at 636.

invest the whole or an unreasonably large proportion of the trust property in a single security[,] . . . in one type of security or in various types of securities dependent upon the success of one enterprise or upon conditions in one locality. . . ."[97] Rather, the legislative history indicates that satisfaction of the diversification standard, like the prudence standard from which it is derived, turns on an analysis of the facts and circumstances of each particular case.[98] Several factors pertinent to this inquiry are enumerated for the prudent fiduciary to consider in determining the proper diversification of the plan's investments:

> (1) the purposes of the plan; (2) the amount of the plan assets; (3) financial and industrial conditions; (4) the type of investment, whether mortgages, bonds or shares of stock or otherwise; (5) distribution as to geographical location; (6) distribution as to industries; (7) the dates of maturity.[99]

Recent cases indicate that alternative investments available to satisfy the plan's diversification needs also should be considered.[100] Thus, like the prudence standard, ERISA's diversification requirement rejects a mechanistic approach in favor of a flexible analysis which focuses upon the investment needs of the particular plan committed to the fiduciary's care.[101]

Adherence to Plan Documents

The final duty imposed upon plan fiduciaries by § 404(a) is the obligation to discharge his plan responsibilities "in accordance with the documents and instruments governing the plan, insofar as such documents and instruments are consistent with the provisions of [Title I of ERISA]." This duty is largely self-explanatory. It carries forward the common law obligation of a trustee to adhere to the terms of the trust in carrying out his trust responsibilities[102] with one significant caveat. Unlike the common law which made the terms of the trust preeminent, this provision requires an ERISA fiduciary to disregard the plan documents or instruments where compliance with their

---

[97] Conference Report at 304.

[98] *Id.* The courts have endorsed this facts and circumstances analysis. *See* Donovan v. Mazzola, 2 EBC at 2135-36; Marshall v. Glass/Metal Ass'n & Glaziers & Glassworkers Pension Plan, 507 F. Supp. at 383.

[99] Conference Report at 304.

[100] *See* Donovan v. Mazzola, 2 EBC at 2135-36; Marshall v. Glass/Metal Ass'n & Glaziers & Glassworkers Pension Plan, 507 F. Supp. at 383-84; Brink v. DaLesio, *supra;* DOL Inf. Ltr., WSB No. 80-26.

[101] The flexibility of this standard is underscored by the fact that a plan's investment of all of its assets in such vehicles as a mutual fund or insurance or annuity contracts would not violate the diversification requirement if the underlying assets of those vehicles were diversified sufficiently. Conference Report at 305; DOL Adv. Opin. No. 75-79 (insurance or annuity contracts); DOL Adv. Opin. No. 75-93 (mutual fund). *See also* DOL Adv. Opin., WSB No. 78-37 (proper diversification of plan assets invested in real estate investment trust ["REIT"] determined by reference to REIT's assets).

[102] *See* Restatement (Second) of Trusts §§ 165-167, 227(c) (1959).

terms would be inconsistent with Title I of ERISA, including the act's fiduciary standards.[103] Consequently, in contrast to his common law counterpart, an ERISA fiduciary cannot deviate from his fiduciary obligations on the basis of plan language authorizing or even directing him to do so. Beyond this departure from the common law, ERISA's adherence to the plan documents requirement does little more than impose upon plan fiduciaries the familiar duties: *(a)* of complying with the terms of the plan documents and instruments; and *(b)* of refraining from activities not authorized thereby.[104]

CO-FIDUCIARY LIABILITY UNDER ERISA

As noted earlier, an ERISA fiduciary generally is liable only for his own breaches of fiduciary duty. However, Section 405 of ERISA[105] does hold a fiduciary accountable for the misdeeds of his co-fiduciary under three specified circumstances:

(a) where a fiduciary knowingly participates in or conceals his co-fiduciary's breach of duty (ERISA § 405(a)(1));

(b) where a fiduciary's own breach of fiduciary responsibility permitted his co-fiduciary's breach to occur (ERISA § 405(a)(2)); and

(c) where the fiduciary has knowledge of his co-fiduciary's breach and fails to take reasonable steps to correct it (ERISA § 405 (a)(3)).

For liability to attach under this provision, the co-fiduciary's breach need not have occurred within the fiduciary's area of responsibility.[106] Thus, a fiduciary faces potential liability for *any* breach of fiduciary duty committed by a co-fiduciary, regardless of any limitations on the scope of his own plan responsibilities.

The liability imposed upon a fiduciary for his co-fiduciary's misdeeds in the first two circumstances noted above cannot be termed vicarious in the true sense; in each instance, the fiduciary himself is guilty of wrongdoing that has contributed to the loss sustained by the plan, either by participating in or concealing his co-fiduciary's misconduct or by breaching his own

---

[103] ERISA Section 404(a)(1)(1). *See also* Marshall v. Craft, 463 F. Supp. at 497; H.R. Rep. No. 93-533, 93d Cong., 1st Sess. 12 (1973).

[104] *See, e.g.,* Iron Workers Local 272 v. Bowen, 4 EBC 1015, 1016 (11th Cir., Jan. 14, 1983) (suggesting that failure to adhere to plan documents constitutes an "automatic" breach of fiduciary duty); Connors v. Drivers, Chauffeurs & Helpers Local Union No. 639, *supra* (defendants' attempt to remove trustee prior to expiration of four year term conferred by trust agreement violates §404(a)(1)(D)); Donovan v. Daugherty, *supra* (trustees violated §404(a)(1)(D) when they authorized payment of benefits to themselves despite the fact that they were not eligible to participate in plan under plan documents). Marshall v. Teamsters Local 282 Pension Trust Fund, 458 F. Supp. at 991 (plan limitation on trustees' authority to invest plan assets binding on trustees); Marshall v. Wilson, *supra* (payment of benefits to ineligible parties violates § 404(a)(1)(D)).

[105] 29 U.S.C. § 1105.

[106] 29 C.F.R. § 2509.75-8, FR-13, FR-14, FR-16.

fiduciary responsibilities in a manner permitting his co-fiduciary's breach to occur. The third circumstance, however, does impose liability upon a fiduciary even where he himself has committed no wrong. In effect, it places an additional fiduciary responsibility upon him—a duty to make reasonable efforts to remedy a breach upon the breach's discovery.[107] The "reasonable efforts" that would satisfy this obligation are not entirely clear, although the Department of Labor has indicated that such efforts include notification of the plan sponsor or the Department of Labor and the institution of legal proceedings.[108] However, one fact is certain—a mere resignation in protest over the alleged breach will not satisfy the fiduciary's responsibilities.[109] Consequently, in order to avoid liability after discovering a breach of fiduciary responsibility, it is incumbent upon the fiduciary to take affirmative action to remedy the situation.

ALLOCATION AND DELEGATION OF FIDUCIARY DUTIES

As noted earlier, ERISA requires the documents establishing a plan to provide for one or more "named fiduciaries" who have the authority to control and manage the plan's administration and operation.[110] Pursuant to Section 405(c) of ERISA,[111] these named fiduciaries may allocate among themselves, or delegate to third parties, nearly all of their fiduciary responsibilities under the plan. The sole exception is the named fiduciary's "trustee responsibility" which is defined as "any responsibility . . . to manage or control the assets of the plan, other than a power . . . to appoint an investment manager in accordance with [ERISA] section 402(c)(3)."[112] Except in accordance with Sections 405(c) and 402(c)(3),[113] however, no allocation or delegation of fiduciary responsibilities can be made.

Under Section 405(c), named fiduciaries can allocate among themselves, or delegate to third parties, all but their "trustee responsibility," provided

---

[107] See Morrissey v. Curran, *supra;* Marshall v. Craft, *supra;* DOL Inf. Ltr., WSB No. 80-83; *see also* Donovan v. Crytzer, Civ. No. 81-2270 (W.D. Pa., filed Dec. 21, 1981) (one plan trustee not involved directly in approving questionable plan loans alleged to be liable for breaches of his co-fiduciaries because he knew of their actions and failed to "make reasonable remedial efforts.")

[108] 29 C.F.R. § 2509.75-5, FR-10. *See also* Weisler v. Metal Polishers Union, *supra;* Conference Report at 299-300.

[109] Freund v. Marshall & Ilsley Bank, 485 F. Supp. at 641; 29 C.F.R. § 2509.75-5, FR-10; Conference Report at 299-300. Indeed, a trustee may not resign if his resignation would impair the plan's operation. *See* PBGC v. Greene, 4 EBC at 1181; Freund v. Marshall & Ilsley Bank, 485 F. Supp. at 635.

[110] *See* discussion *supra* at p. 738.

[111] 29 U.S.C. § 1105(c).

[112] *Id.*

[113] 29 U.S.C. § 1102(c)(3).

that the plan documents contain procedures permitting such allocation or delegation.[114] In the case of responsibility to manage or control the plan's assets, the requirements of Section 402(c)(3) also must be satisfied. That provision permits the allocation or delegation of such responsibility only if:

(a) the plan authorizes the named fiduciary to appoint an investment manager;

(b) the party appointed is a registered investment adviser under the Investment Advisers Act of 1940, a bank as defined in that statute, or an insurance company qualified to manage, acquire, or dispose of assets under the laws of more than one state; and

(c) the party appointed acknowledges in writing that he is a fiduciary with respect to the plan.[115]

In the event that an allocation or delegation of fiduciary responsibility is made in accordance with these provisions, the liability of the named fiduciary for the activities of the party to whom his responsibilities have been allocated or delegated is strictly limited.[116] Under Section 405(c)(2),[117] he would be liable for such activities only if he violated his own fiduciary obligations in making the allocation or delegation, in establishing or implementing the procedures under which the allocation or delegation was made, or in permitting the allocation or delegation of such authority to continue.[118] In addition, he could be held liable under the co-fiduciary liability provisions of Section 405(a).[119] Otherwise, he would have no liability for the acts or omissions of the party to whom his responsibilities were transferred. Conversely, if a named fiduciary attempted to make an allocation or delegation of authority that did not comply with the requirements of Sections 405(c) and 405(c)(2), the allocation or delegation would be ineffective and he would remain fully liable for the activities of the allocatee or delegatee as if they were his own.[120]

The proper appointment of an investment manager pursuant to Section 402(c)(3) has additional consequences for the plan trustee that otherwise would be responsible for managing the plan's assets. In the event of such an appointment, the trustee would have no responsibility to invest or otherwise manage any assets committed to the investment manager's care.[121] Nor would he have any liability for the acts or omissions of the investment manager unless he knowingly participated in or concealed a breach of

---

[114] 29 C.F.R. § 2509.75-8, FR-12; Conf. Report at 302.

[115] *See* Marshall v. The Unicorn Group, No. 79 Civ. 1658 (S.D. N.Y., Jan. 7, 1981); ERISA Section 3(38), 29 U.S.C. § 1002(38); 29 C.F.R. § 2509.75-8, FR-14, FR-15.

[116] 29 C.F.R. § 2509.75-8, D-4.

[117] 29 U.S.C. § 1102(c)(2).

[118] 29 C.F.R. § 2509.75-8, FR-13, FR-14.

[119] *See* discussion *supra* at p. 754.

[120] *Cf.* Freund v. Marshall & Ilsley Bank, 485 F. Supp. at 640-41.

[121] Marshall v. The Unicorn Group, *supra;* ERISA Section 405(d)(1), 29 U.S.C. § 1105(d)(1).

fiduciary duty by that party.[122] The investment manager's appointment, however, will not relieve the trustee of any liability for his own actions.[123]

PROHIBITED TRANSACTIONS

As noted earlier, ERISA's fiduciary obligation provisions expressly prohibit plan fiduciaries from causing employee benefit plans to engage in certain transactions. These "prohibited transactions," which are set forth in ERISA § 406,[124] fall into two general categories. The first type, described in § 406(a)(1), are transactions which, either directly or indirectly, involve a plan and a party in interest to the plan. The second type, described in § 406(b), are transactions in which the fiduciary is guilty of self-dealing. In analyzing these prohibited transaction provisions, it is important to recognize that they establish absolute structural bars to the transactions in question.[125] Thus, in the absence of an exemption, the enumerated transactions are prohibited no matter how "fair" or "reasonable" the transaction otherwise might be from the plan's perspective.[126]

Transactions Involving Parties in Interest

ERISA § 406(a)(1) generally prohibits any direct or indirect transaction involving a plan and a party in interest. Specifically, the following transactions are prohibited:

1. The sale, exchange or leasing of any property.
2. The lending of money or other extension of credit.
3. The furnishing of goods, services or facilities.
4. The transfer to, or use by or for the benefit of, a party in interest, of any plan assets.
5. A plan's acquisition or retention of any employer security or employer property in violation of ERISA § 407(a).

As noted earlier, these transactions are interdicted absolutely in the absence of an exemption.

The transactions noted above, of course, are prohibited *only* when a party in interest is involved in the transaction. Indeed, in view of the breadth of the transactions covered, the presence or absence of a party in interest provides the only meaningful limitation on the scope of this category of prohibited transactions. Unfortunately, as noted earlier, ERISA's definition

---

[122] *Id.*

[123] ERISA Section 405(d)(2), 29 U.S.C. § 1105(d)(2).

[124] 29 U.S.C. § 1106.

[125] Cutaiar v. Marshall, 590 F. 2d 523 (3d Cir. 1979); Donovan v. Mazzola, 2 EBC at 2136; M & R Investment Co., Inc. v. Fitzsimmons, 484 F. Supp. 1041 (D. Nev. 1980) *aff'd*, 685 F. 2d 283 (9th Cir. 1982); Freund v. Marshall & Ilsley Bank, 485 F. Supp. at 637.

[126] *Id.*

of "party in interest" is both broad and complex, encompassing not only entities with a direct relationship to the plan, but also numerous parties related not to the plan, but to such "direct" parties in interest. Accordingly, to avoid problems with these prohibited transaction provisions, a fiduciary should identify all parties in interest to his plan and carefully monitor any transaction in advance for their presence.[127]

Since virtually all transactions involving a plan and a party in interest fall within this category of prohibited transactions, any attempt to describe every transaction subject to these provisions would be both futile and beyond the scope of this chapter. However, the following examples are illustrative of the types of problems a plan can encounter in this area. As noted above, any sale, exchange, or lease of property between a plan and a party in interest is prohibited. This prohibition includes not only such obvious transactions as a plan's acquisition of a piece of land from a party in interest such as an employer, but also an employer's purchase of its common stock from a plan in the course of a public tender offer.[128] Similarly, the prohibition on loans and extensions of credit is broad enough to encompass a plan's failure to collect delinquent contributions from an employer,[129] a plan's guarantee of a loan to a party in interest,[130] and an employer's contribution to the plan of its own debt instrument,[131] as well as direct loan arrangements.

The interdiction against furnishing goods, services and facilities is equally broad. It precludes a plan from not only furnishing goods, services or facilities, but also receiving them from a party in interest. Consequently, in the absence of an exemption, a plan cannot engage a party in interest, such as an employer or the union, to provide the plan with facilities or services that could be necessary or useful to the plan's operation, such as office space or administrative services.[132] Moreover, it poses particular problems in the "multiple service" area, i.e., where a plan seeks to engage an existing service provider, such as the bank serving as custodian of the plan assets, to provide the plan with additional services that are different in kind from those already provided by the party in interest.[133] Since this prohibition can impede a plan's efficient operation, statutory and admin-

---

[127] Indeed, the failure to conduct a reasonable investigation may constitute a violation of ERISA's prudence standard. Marshall v. Kelly, 465 F. Supp. at 351; Conference Report at 307.

[128] DOL Adv. Opin. No. 77-48.

[129] See Prohibited Transaction Class Exemption No. 76-1, 41 Fed. Reg. 12740 (March 26, 1976).

[130] Conference Report at 308.

[131] Id.

[132] See Conference Report at 308, 312; see also Prohibited Transaction Class Exemption No. 76-1, supra.

[133] See, e.g., Prohibited Transaction Class Exemption No. 79-1, 44 Fed. Reg. 5963 (Jan. 30, 1979); Prohibited Transaction Class Exemption No. 75-1, 40 Fed. Reg. 50845 (Oct. 31, 1975); see also 29 C.F.R. § 2550.408b-2.

istrative exemptions, discussed *infra,* have been crafted to mitigate the prohibition's impact.[134]

Moreover, these provisions prohibit not only direct but also indirect transactions involving a party in interest as best demonstrated by Section 406(a)(1)(D). By its express terms, Section 406(a)(1)(D) prohibits any "transfer to, or use by or *for the benefit of,* a party in interest, of any assets of the plan." (Emphasis added.) Thus, any transfer of plan assets to a nonparty in interest under circumstances designed to benefit an existing party in interest is forbidden.[135] Such a situation could arise, for example, where a multiemployer plan lends money to a property owner to make improvements to his property on the understanding that the property owner will contract with a participating employer to make the improvements.[136] Similarly, a corporate plan's acquisition of employer stock to fend off a hostile tender offer could run afoul of this provision.[137]

Finally, the prohibition on acquiring or holding employer securities or real property places express limitations on a plan's ability to hold employer stock or real property in its investment portfolio.[138] Under these provisions, employer securities or real property cannot be acquired or held unless they constitute "qualifying" securities or real property as defined in the statute.[139] Furthermore, the amount of a plan's portfolio which can be invested in such "qualifying" employer securities or real property is limited generally to 10 percent.[140]

---

[134] *See* discussion *infra* beginning at p. 761.

[135] *See* DOL Adv. Opin., WSB No. 79–63; DOL Adv. Opin. No. 75–103; *cf.* McDougall v. Donovan, 3 EBC 2385 (N.D. Ill., Nov. 23, 1982) (indirect transaction violates ERISA § 404(d)(1)(A)).

[136] *See* Prohibited Transaction Class Exemption No. 76-1, *supra.*

[137] *Cf.* Donovan v. Bierwirth, *supra;* DOL Inf. Ltr. No. 80-83.

[138] ERISA Sections 406(a)(1)(E), 406(a)(2), 407, 29 U.S.C. §§ 1106(a)(1)(E), 1106(a)(2), 1107.

[139] ERISA Section 407(a)(1), 29 U.S.C. § 1107(a)(1). ERISA defines a "qualifying employer security" as "an employer security which is stock or a marketable obligation." ERISA Section 407(d)(5), 29 U.S.C. § 1107(d)(5). "Qualifying employer real property" is defined in ERISA Section 407(d)(4) as: parcels of employer real property—

(A) if a substantial number of the parcels are disbursed geographically;

(B) if each parcel of real property and the improvements thereon are suitable (or adaptable without excessive cost) for more than one use;

(C) even if all of such real property is leased to one lessee (which may be an employer, or an affiliate of an employer): and

(D) if the acquisition and retention of such property comply with the provisions of this part (other than section 404(a)(1)(B) to the extent it requires diversification, and sections 404(a)(1)(C), 406, and subsection (a) of this section).

29 U.S.C. § 1107(d)(4).

[140] ERISA Section 407(a)(2), (a)(3), 29 U.S.C. § 1107 (a)(2), (a)(3). The ten percent limitation does not apply to "eligible individual account plans," which are defined in ERISA Section 407(d)(3), 29 U.S.C. § 1107(d)(3). ERISA Section 407(b)(1), 29 U.S.C. § 1107(b)(1); *see also* Conference Report at 317.

FIDUCIARY SELF-DEALING

In contrast to Section 406(a) which looks to the parties to a transaction, Section 406(b) focuses on a fiduciary's conduct in a transaction involving the plan. Specifically, it prohibits a fiduciary from:

(a) dealing with the plan's assets in his own interest or for his own account;

(b) acting in any transaction involving the plan in his individual or any other capacity on behalf of a party whose interests are adverse to the interests of the plan or the plan's participants or beneficiaries; or

(c) receiving any consideration for his own personal account from any party dealing with the plan in connection with a transaction involving the plan's assets.[141]

Generally speaking, these specific prohibitions are designed to insure that a fiduciary does not engage in any self-dealing with the plan's assets or exercise his discretionary authority in situations where he has a conflict of interest.[142] Consequently, they go "hand-in-glove" with ERISA's general fiduciary responsibility provisions, most notably, the duty of undivided loyalty, and are designed to control the same potential abuses.

Since Section 406(b)'s prohibitions are directed primarily at fiduciary self-dealing, their application in most contexts is self-evident—they prohibit a fiduciary from causing a plan to engage in any transaction from which he stands to profit personally.[143] However, it is important to recognize that their application is not limited to situations involving fiduciary self-gain. Section 406(b)(2) prohibits a fiduciary from acting in any transaction on behalf of a party whose interests are adverse to a plan. Both the Department of Labor and the courts have construed this provision as a *per se* prohibition against transactions between two related plans which have identical trustees but no complete identity of participants and beneficiaries, even where the trustees do not benefit personally from the transaction and the transaction itself is fair and reasonable to both plans.[144] In the view of the Department of Labor and the courts, the fact that the trustees stand on both sides of such a transaction and thus have divided loyalties constitutes a technical violation of Section 406(b)(2).[145] Similarly, the Department of Labor has interpreted Section 406(b) generally to prohibit a fiduciary from causing a plan to engage in any transaction in which he has an interest that could affect his best fiduciary judgment.[146] Thus, even if a fiduciary himself will derive no

---

[141] ERISA Sections 406(b)(1), (b)(2), (b)(3), 29 U.S.C. § 1106(b)(1), (b)(2), (b)(3).

[142] *See* Cutaiar v. Marshall, *supra;* Donovan v. Mazzola, *supra; see also* 29 C.F.R. § 2550.408b-2(e)(1), (f).

[143] *See, e.g.* Donovan v. Daugherty, *supra;* DOL, WSB No. 79-20; *see generally* 29 C.F.R. § 2550.408b-2(e)(1), (e)(2), (f).

[144] Cutaiar v. Marshall, *supra;* Donovan v. Mazzola, *supra.*

[145] *Id.*

[146] 29 C.F.R. § 2550.408-b2(e)(1), (e)(2), (f).

gain, he can take no part in a transaction that will benefit a relative or some other party in whom he has an interest that could affect his judgment.[147]

Exemptions

Statutory Exemptions. In light of the harsh impact of ERISA's prohibited transaction rules, the statute itself contains exemptions for a number of more routine plan transactions which do not present great opportunity for abuse. These statutory exemptions are set forth in ERISA Section 408.[148] It is important to recognize that these provisions establish exemptions only to Section 406 of ERISA; they do *not* relieve a fiduciary from complying with the other fiduciary obligations imposed upon him by ERISA in connection with the transaction.[149]

Briefly stated, Section 408 exempts the following transactions from Section 406 upon satisfaction of certain express conditions:

(a) plan loans to participants or beneficiaries;[150]

(b) contracts or reasonable arrangements with a party in interest for office space, or legal, accounting, or other services necessary for the establishment or operation of the plan, so long as no more than reasonable compensation is paid therefor;[151]

(c) a loan by a party in interest to an employee stock ownership plan;[152]

(d) the investment of plan assets in deposits of a bank or similar financial institution which is a fiduciary to the plan;[153]

(e) insurance or annuity contracts with an insurer who is the employer maintaining the plan or a party in interest;[154]

(f) the provision of ancillary services by a bank or similar financial institution which is a fiduciary to the plan;[155]

(g) the exercise of a privilege to convert securities;[156]

(h) transactions between a plan and (1) a common or collective trust fund maintained by a party in interest bank or trust company; or (2) a pooled investment fund of an insurance company;[157]

---

[147] *Id.*

[148] 29 U.S.C. § 1108.

[149] *See* Eaves v. Penn, supra; ERISA Sections 408(a), (b), 29 U.S.C. § 1108(a), (b); Conference Report at 310-11.

[150] ERISA Section 408(b)(1), 29 U.S.C. § 1108(b)(1).

[151] ERISA Section 408(b)(2), 29 U.S.C. § 1108(b)(2); *see also* 29 C.F.R. § 2550.408b-2.

[152] ERISA Section 408(b)(3), 29 U.S.C. § 1108(b)(3); *see also* 29 C.F.R. § 2550.408b-3.

[153] ERISA Section 408(b)(4), 29 U.S.C. § 1108(b)(4); *see also* 29 C.F.R. § 2550.408b-4.

[154] ERISA Section 408(b)(5), 29 U.S.C. § 1108b-5.

[155] ERISA Section 408(b)(6), 29 U.S.C. § 1108b-6; *see also* 29 C.F.R. § 2550.408b-6.

[156] ERISA Section 408(b)(7), 29 U.S.C. § 1108b-7.

[157] ERISA Section 408(b)(8), 29 U.S.C. § 1108b-8.

(i) a fiduciary's distribution of plan assets in accordance with the plan's terms;[158] and

(j) a plan's acquisition or sale of qualifying employer securities and acquisition, sale or lease of qualifying employer real property, provided that the acquisition, sale or lease is for adequate security, no commission is charged on the transaction, and either the plan is an eligible individual account plan or the transaction does not violate ERISA Section 407(a).[159]

As noted above, each of these exemptions is subject to certain express conditions set forth in the statute. Those conditions, which are designed to protect the interests of the plan, must be satisfied before the exemption is effective.

Of the transactional exemptions noted above, probably the most significant to the day-to-day operations of a plan is that which permits a party in interest to provide office space or services to a plan.[160] Although the statute suggests that the exemption is available only for "necessary" services, regulations issued by the Department of Labor have interpreted it to apply to any service that is "appropriate and helpful . . . in carrying out the purposes for which the plan is established or maintained."[161] Thus, the exemption permits parties in interest to provide a broad range of services as well as office space to a plan. In order to qualify for the exemption, the office space or services must be furnished pursuant to a "reasonable" contract or arrangement.[162] While the Department of Labor has not defined what is "reasonable" for these purposes, it has indicated that a contract or arrangement that does not permit a plan to terminate on reasonably short notice and without penalty is "unreasonable."[163] Finally, the plan must pay no more than "reasonable compensation" for the office space or services.[164] Whether the compensation paid by the plan is, in fact, reasonable depends on the particular facts and circumstances of each case.[165]

While this exemption generally permits a plan to engage a party in interest to furnish it with office space or services, there are two important limitations on its scope. First, despite statutory language seemingly to the contrary, the Department of Labor has taken the position that this exemption does not apply to the fiduciary self-dealing provisions of Section 406(b).[166] Consequently, a fiduciary generally may not cause a plan to

---

[158] ERISA Section 408(b)(9), 29 U.S.C. § 1108b-9.

[159] ERISA Section 408(e), 29 U.S.C. § 1108(e).

[160] ERISA Section 408(b)(2), 29 U.S.C. § 1108(b)(2); *see also* 29 C.F.R. 2550.408b-2.

[161] 29 C.F.R. § 2550.408b-2(b).

[162] ERISA Section 408(b)(2), 29 U.S.C. § 1108(b)(2).

[163] 29 C.F.R. § 2550.408b-2(c).

[164] ERISA Section 408(b)(2), 29 U.S.C. § 1108(b)(2).

[165] 29 C.F.R. § 2550.408b-2(d), 2550.408c-2.

[166] 29 C.F.R. § 2550.408b-2(a). This interpretation has received judicial endorsement. Marshall v. Kelly, 465 F. Supp. at 353-54.

engage himself or a person in which he has interest to provide the plan with services or office space.[167] However, if the fiduciary does not use his fiduciary authority to cause the plan to do so, i.e., if he absents himself from any and all consideration of the transaction, no violation of Section 406(b) will occur.[168] Moreover, he may provide services or office space to the plan so long as he does so without compensation or other consideration from the plan other than reimbursement of the direct expenses which he actually incurs.[169] Secondly, the exemption does *not* permit a plan to furnish office space or services to a party in interest.[170] It only exempts the provision of services and office space to the plan.

In addition to the transactional exemptions described earlier, Section 408 contains a number of provisions which relieve fiduciaries from the consequences of certain technical violations of the prohibited transaction rules that could arise in their administration of the plan. Section 408(c)(1) makes clear that a fiduciary is not prohibited from receiving benefits as a plan participant or beneficiary so long as the benefits are computed and paid on a basis consistent with the terms of the plan as applied to other participants and beneficiaries.[171] Section 408(c)(2) permits a fiduciary to receive reasonable compensation for his services, unless he is a full-time employee of an employer, employer association, or employee association whose employees or members are participants in the plan.[172] In addition, it allows fiduciaries to be reimbursed by the plan for the expenses which they properly and actually incur in the performance of their plan duties.[173] Finally, Section 408(c)(3) specifically authorizes a person who is an officer, employee, agent, or representative of a party in interest to the plan to serve as a plan fiduciary.[174]

Administrative Exemptions. Section 408 of ERISA also authorizes the Secretary of Labor[175] to grant administrative exemptions to the statute's

---

[167] 29 C.F.R. § 2550.408b-2(e)(1).

[168] 29 C.F.R. § 2550.408b-2(e)(1), (f)(7); see also DOL Adv. Opin., WSB No. 79-41.

[169] 29 C.F.R. § 2550.408b-2(e)(3).

[170] See Prohibited Transaction Class Exemption No. 76-1, *supra;* Prohibited Transaction Class Exemption No. 77-10, 42 Fed. Reg. 33918 (July 1, 1977). However, administrative class exemptions have been crafted which permit multiemployer plans to lease space or provide administrative services to a participating employee organization, participating employer, participating employer association, or another multiemployer plan under certain specified circumstances. *Id.*

[171] 29 U.S.C. § 1108(c)(1).

[172] 29 U.S.C. § 1108(c)(2). Of course, if the fiduciary is receiving full-time pay from the union or the employer, he may not receive compensation from the plan for his services. Donovan v. Daugherty, *supra*.

[173] *Id.*

[174] 29 U.S.C. § 1108(c)(3); see also Flinchbaugh v. Chicago Pneumatic Tool Co., 3 EBC 1195, 1198 (W.D. Pa., Jan. 28, 1982); Donovan v. Bierwirth, 538 F. Supp. at 467-70.

[175] In granting exemptions, the Secretary of Labor is directed to consult and coordinate with the Secretary of the Treasury. ERISA Section 408(a), 29 U.S.C. § 1108(a). Under Presidential Reorganization Plan No. 4 of 1978, 43 Fed. Reg. 47713 (1978), primary jurisdiction for processing administrative exemptions was consolidated in the Department of Labor.

prohibited transaction rules and directs him to establish an exemption procedure.[176] Such exemptions, which may be conditional or unconditional and may apply to a single transaction or a class of transactions, may be granted only upon a determination by the Secretary that the exemption is administratively feasible, in the interests of the plan and the plan's participants, and protective of the rights of the plan's participants and beneficiaries.[177] As a further safeguard, Section 408 requires that before an exemption may be granted, notice of the proposed exemption must be published in the *Federal Register,* adequate notice must be afforded interested persons, and interested parties must be provided an opportunity to present their views.[178] In addition, no exemption from the prohibitions upon fiduciary self-dealing may be issued unless a hearing has been held.[179] Finally, as in the case of statutory exemptions, these exemptions apply only to the prohibitions found in ERISA Section 406; they have no application to the fiduciary obligations set forth elsewhere in the statute.

In response to Section 408's directive, the Secretary of Labor has established a procedure for processing administrative exemption applications.[180] Pursuant to this procedure, both single transaction exemptions as well as class exemptions, i.e., exemptions which apply to a general category of transactions, have been granted. Thus, the exemption procedure provides a potential avenue of relief for the fiduciary considering a transaction which he believes to be in the plan's best interests, but which otherwise would violate ERISA's prohibited transaction provisions. Moreover, the class exemptions granted establish a body of law which supplements the exemptions set forth in the statute and may exempt a contemplated transaction without further administrative action. Accordingly, the existing class exemptions as well as the availability of the exemption procedure should be considered by plan fiduciaries whenever faced with a transaction arguably prohibited by the Act.

To date, the Department of Labor has issued approximately 25 class exemptions. Like the statutory exemptions, these exemptions exempt rather commonplace plan transactions involving parties in interest and fiduciaries that generally are beneficial to plans and do not present great opportunity for abuse. They are all subject to specific conditions which, in large part, are designed to insure that the terms of the transaction are as favorable to plans as those which could be obtained in arm's-length dealing. While a full discussion of these exemptions is beyond the scope of this chapter, some of the more significant class exemptions are those which apply to:

---

[176] ERISA Section 408(a), 29 U.S.C. § 1108(a).

[177] *Id.*

[178] *Id.*

[179] *Id.*

[180] ERISA Proc. 75-1, 40 Fed. Reg. 18471 (1975).

(a)   certain types of securities transactions involving plans and broker-dealers, reporting dealers, and banks;[181]

(b)   security transactions effected by plan fiduciaries on behalf of a plan through entities affiliated with the plan fiduciary;[182]

(c)   certain types of transactions involving employee benefit plans and insurance agents and brokers, pension consultants, insurance companies, investment companies, and investment company principal underwriters;[183]

(d)   a plan's purchase of mutual fund shares when a plan fiduciary is also investment manager to the mutual fund;[184] and

(e)   certain transactions in which multiemployer and multiple employer plans are involved.[185]

The Department of Labor has indicated that it will make increased use of the class exemption process in the future to further mitigate the impact of ERISA's prohibited transaction provisions.[186]

Transitional Rules

Although ERISA's fiduciary responsibility provisions generally became effective on January 1, 1975, the statute does contain a number of transitional provisions which ease the impact of the prohibited transaction rules on certain preexisting transactions. These provisions defer the effective date of the prohibited transaction rules to permit plans a period of time to extricate themselves from certain transactions that became invalid with ERISA's enactment.[187] As the end of this deferral period approaches, these provisions have become of diminished significance.[188]

The transitional provisions are found in ERISA § 414(c).[189] Under Sections 414(c)(1) and (c)(2), ERISA's prohibited transaction rules do not apply until June 30, 1984, to a loan or extension of credit between a plan and a party in interest, or to a lease or joint use of property involving a plan and a party in interest, provided that: *(a)* the loan, extension of credit, lease or joint use is pursuant to a binding contract in effect on July 1, 1974 (or

---

[181] Prohibited Transaction Class Exemption No. 75-1, *supra.*

[182] Prohibited Transaction Class Exemption No. 79-1, 44 Fed. Reg. 5963 (Jan. 30, 1979).

[183] Prohibited Transaction Class Exemption No. 77-9, 42 Fed. Reg. 32395 (June 24, 1977).

[184] Prohibited Transaction Class Exemption No. 77-4, 42 Fed. Reg. 18732 (Apr. 8, 1977).

[185] Prohibited Transaction Class Exemption No. 76-1, *supra;* Prohibited Transaction Class Exemption No. 77-10, *supra.*

[186] *See* Statement of Secretary of Labor Raymond J. Donovan before the Senate Subcommittee on Labor on S.1541, the "Retirement Income Incentives and Administrative Simplification Act," January 26, 1981, *reprinted in* 9 BNA Pens. Reptr. 163, 165 (Feb. 1, 1982).

[187] ERISA Section 408(a), 29 U.S.C. § 1108(a).

[188] Indeed, the transitional rule dealing with the provision of services between a plan and party in interest already has expired. ERISA Section 414(c)(4), 29 U.S.C. § 1114(c)(4).

[189] 29 U.S.C. § 1114(c).

renewals thereof); *(b)* the transaction "remains at least as favorable to the plan as an arm's-length transaction with an unrelated party would be"; and *(c)* the transaction was not a prohibited transaction when entered into by the parties.[190] Section 414(c)(3) permits the sale, exchange or other disposition of leased or jointly used property between a plan and a party in interest until June 30, 1984, so long as the plan receives at least the fair market value of the property in the case of a disposition, or pays no more than the property's fair market value in the case of an acquisition.[191] Finally, Section 414(c)(5) permits a plan to dispose of property which it owned on June 30, 1974, in order to comply with the limitations on holding employer securities or real property without violating ERISA's prohibited transaction rules if it receives adequate consideration for the property involved.[192]

Penalties for Violating ERISA's Prohibited Transaction Rules

Any party in interest who engages in a prohibited transaction is subject either to a civil penalty assessed by the Secretary of Labor if the plan involved is not tax-qualified under the Internal Revenue Code,[193] or an excise tax under the Internal Revenue Code if the plan is tax-qualified.[194] The civil penalty assessed by the Secretary of Labor may not exceed 5 percent of the "amount involved"[195] in the prohibited transaction.[196] However, if the prohibited transaction is not corrected within 90 days after the Secretary of Labor's notice of a violation, this civil penalty may be raised to 100 percent of the amount involved in the transaction.[197]

The excise tax imposed by the Internal Revenue Code in the case of tax-qualified plans is quite similar. Section 4975 imposes a tax equal to 5 percent of the amount involved in the prohibited transaction for each tax year that the prohibited transaction is in existence.[198] Once this initial tax is imposed, the failure to correct the prohibited transaction within the taxable period results in an additional excise tax equal to 100 percent of the amount

---

[190] 29 U.S.C. §§ 414(c)(1), (c)(2). *See also* 29 C.F.R. § 2550.414c-1, 2550.414c-2.

[191] 29 U.S.C. § 414(c)(3). *See also* 29 C.F.R. § 2550.414c-3.

[192] 29 U.S.C. § 1114(c)(5).

[193] ERISA Section 502(i), 29 U.S.C. § 1132(i). Plans not subject to civil penalties assessed by the Secretary of Labor are plans described in Section 401(a) of the Internal Revenue Code ("IRC") (certain stock bonus, pension, and profit-sharing plans), IRC Section 403(a) (qualified annuity plans), and IRC 405(a) (qualified bond purchase plans) that are tax-exempt under IRC Section 501(a), individual retirement account or annuity plans described in IRC Section 408, and retirement bond plans described in IRC Section 409. IRC Section 4975(e).

[194] IRC Section 4975.

[195] The term "amount involved" is to be defined in accordance with IRC Section 4975(f)(4).

[196] ERISA Section 502(i), 29 U.S.C. § 1132(i).

[197] *Id.*

[198] IRC Section 4975(a).

involved in the transaction. The principal distinctions between this excise tax and the civil penalty assessed by the Secretary of Labor are that the imposition of the excise tax is mandatory rather than discretionary; the amount of the tax is fixed at 5 percent or 100 percent of the amount involved in the prohibited transaction, rather than at an amount which may not exceed those figures; and the taxes may be assessed for each year that the prohibited transaction is in existence or remains uncorrected rather than simply once.[199]

In addition to the civil penalties and excise taxes noted above, the violation of ERISA's prohibited transaction rules can also lead to liability under ERISA Section 409,[200] the general fiduciary remedy provision. This provision is considered *infra* at p. 768.

Prohibited Transactions Checklist

In light of the complexity of ERISA's prohibited transaction provisions, fiduciaries should establish a procedure for monitoring transactions in order to insure compliance with the statute. The following is a suggested mode of analysis to assist fiduciaries in carrying out their responsibilities in this regard:

1. *How significant is the transaction; i.e., what is the amount involved?* Fiduciaries should make a threshold determination of the significance of the transaction. Obviously, a plan's acquisition of a box of pencils does not require the same degree of scrutiny as the acquisition of a piece of land.
2. *Who are the parties to the transaction?* Fiduciaries should identify the parties to the transaction as soon as possible to determine whether a party in interest is involved. An up-to-date list of parties in interest to the plan is useful in carrying out this examination.
3. *Is the transaction prohibited?* If a party in interest is identified in the transaction, the fiduciary should determine whether the transaction is prohibited in the absence of an exemption. Consultation with plan counsel is appropriate at this stage of the inquiry.
4. *Does an exemption apply or can one be obtained?* If the transaction is prohibited otherwise, plan counsel should be consulted to determine whether a statutory or class exemption applies or, if not, whether an administrative exemption can be obtained. If a statutory or class exemption applies, the plan might request an opinion of counsel before the transaction goes forward. If no such exemption applies, an administrative exemption will have to be secured before the transaction is consummated.

---

[199] IRC Section 4975(b).
[200] 29 U.S.C. § 1109; *see* Donovan v. Mazzola, 2 EBC at 2136.

5. *Is the transaction consistent with the fiduciary's other fiduciary obligations?*
    Even if the transaction is not prohibited, or, if prohibited, authorized
    by an exemption, the fiduciary should conduct a final analysis of the
    transaction to insure that it does not entail a violation of any of his other
    fiduciary responsibilities.

LIABILITY FOR BREACH OF FIDUCIARY DUTY

Criminal Penalties

ERISA does not establish any criminal penalties for violations of its
fiduciary responsibility provisions. Rather, it imposes criminal liability[201]
only for willful violations of the reporting and disclosure requirements
contained in Title I, Subtitle B, Part 1 of the statute.[202] Consequently, so
long as the reporting and disclosure requirements of the statute are satisfied, the ERISA fiduciary does not face the threat of criminal prosecution
under ERISA for his plan activities.[203]

Civil Penalties

Although ERISA does not establish criminal penalties for violations of
its fiduciary responsibility provisions, it does impose significant civil penalties upon the fiduciary who breaches his obligations under the statute.
These civil penalties are supplemented by statutory provisions extending
the Department of Labor broad investigative powers,[204] and granting participants, beneficiaries, fiduciaries and the Department of Labor liberal
access to the federal courts to redress fiduciary misconduct.[205] Consequently, the threat of civil liability to the errant fiduciary is real indeed.

The penalties for breach of fiduciary duty are set forth in Section 409 of
the act.[206] That provision provides that a fiduciary who breaches any of his
duties, responsibilities or obligations under the statute:

(a) shall be liable personally to the plan for any plan losses resulting from his
     breach of duty;
(b) shall be liable personally to restore to the plan any profits which he has
     obtained through his use of plan assets; and

---

[201] ERISA Section 501, 29 U.S.C. 1131.

[202] ERISA Section 101-111, 29 U.S.C. § 1021-1031.

[203] He, however, could face criminal prosecution for violations of any federal criminal law
or state criminal laws of general application committed in connection with his plan duties.
Section 514(b)(4) of ERISA, 29 U.S.C. § 1144(b)(4) specifically exempts state criminal laws of
general application from the scope of ERISA preemption. *See* Commonwealth v. Federico, 2
EBC 2382 (Mass. Sup. Jud. Ct., Apr. 28, 1981).

[204] ERISA Section 504, 29 U.S.C. § 1134.

[205] ERISA Section 502, 29 U.S.C. § 1132.

[206] 29 U.S.C. § 1109.

(c) shall be subject to such other equitable or remedial relief that a court may deem appropriate, including removal.

The federal courts have not been hesitant to enforce the liabilities imposed by this section. Fiduciaries have been held personally liable for plan losses occasioned by a breach of fiduciary duty, such as, for example, their failure to invest the assets of the plan prudently.[207] Likewise, they have been forced to disgorge profits obtained personally through their misuse of plan assets.[208] Finally, the courts have construed their authority to grant appropriate equitable and remedial relief as a broad mandate to fashion remedies for fiduciary breach. Such remedies have not been limited to the removal of fiduciaries[209] but also have included the appointment of independent investment managers to invest the plan's assets,[210] injunctions against, and the rescission of transactions violative of the statute,[211] and prohibitions against future transactions between employee benefit plans and fiduciaries found guilty of misconduct.[212]

Exculpatory Clauses and Insurance

Not only does ERISA impose personal liability upon plan fiduciaries for the consequences of their breach of trust, it contains provisions that insure that fiduciaries bear such responsibility and do not pass off such liability to their plans. Section 410(a) of ERISA[213] declares void as against public policy any exculpatory provision which purports to relieve a fiduciary from responsibility or liability for any duty, obligation, or responsibility imposed by the act's fiduciary provisions. Thus, plan provisions exculpating a fiduciary from responsibility for his breach of trust, valid prior to ERISA in certain jurisdictions,[214] are invalid and of no effect.[215] Moreover, while Section 410(b) permits a plan to purchase insurance for itself or its fiduciaries which covers liability or losses occurring by reason of a fiduciary's acts or omissions, such insurance cannot relieve a fiduciary of liability for his breach of fiduciary responsibility; it must permit recourse by the insurer against the fiduciary in the case of a breach of fiduciary obligation.[216] Rather, if insurance is obtained against losses resulting from fiduciary

---

[207] E.g., Eaves v. Penn, supra; Brink v. DaLesio, supra; Donovan v. Mazzola, supra; Marshall v. Carroll, supra.

[208] E.g., Brink v. DaLesio, supra; Marshall v. Carroll, supra; Gilliam v. Edwards, supra.

[209] E.g., Marshall v. Snyder, supra; Marshall v. Wilson, supra.

[210] E.g., Donovan v. Mazzola, supra.

[211] Eaves v. Penn, supra; Gilliam v. Edwards, supra.

[212] Marshall v. Carroll, supra; Marshall v. Wilson, supra.

[213] 29 U.S.C. § 1110(a).

[214] See 3 A. Scott, The Law of Trusts § 222 (3d ed. 1967).

[215] See Marshall v. Craft, supra; Conference Report at 320.

[216] 29 U.S.C. § 1110(b); Conference Report at 320-21.

breach, its cost must be borne by the fiduciary, an employer, or an employee organization, and *not* by the plan.[217]

Attorney's Fees

As part of its liberalization of access to the federal courts, ERISA contains a provision which authorizes an award of attorneys' fees and costs in any action brought by a plan participant, beneficiary, or fiduciary.[218] While the circumstances under which an award of fees is appropriate have not yet been defined fully, several courts of appeals have enunciated standards to guide the district courts in their exercise of discretion in this area. Those guidelines are:

(1) the degree of a party's culpability or bad faith;

(2) the ability of a party to satisfy an award of fees;

(3) whether an award of fees would deter others from acting in similar circumstances;

(4) whether the party requesting fees sought to benefit all participants or beneficiaries or to resolve a significant ERISA issue; and

(5) the relative merits of the parties' positions.[219]

The courts' emphasis upon culpability and deterrence, as well as the fact that the attorneys' fees provision clearly seems designed to encourage private enforcement actions, strongly suggest that fees will be awarded rather liberally to successful plaintiffs in actions charging fiduciary breach, at least where serious breaches of duty are involved.[220]

Although the law governing when an award of fees should be made remains unsettled, the courts have made clear that where an award of fees is appropriate, such fees should be borne by the offending fiduciary, and not by the plan. As one court has stated:

> By enacting a statutory authorization for award of attorneys fees, we believe Congress intended that the offending party bear the costs of the award, rather than non-culpable, non-party plan participants.[221]

Moreover, both the courts and the Department of Labor have taken the position that a plan's payment of the attorney's fees which the errant

---

[217] *Id.*

[218] ERISA Section 502(g)(1), 29 U.S.C. § 1132(g)(1).

[219] Marquardt v. North American Car Corp., 652 F. 2d 715 (7th Cir. 1981); Hummel v. S. E. Rykoff & Co., 634 F. 2d 446, 452 (9th Cir. 1980); Iron Workers Local No. 272 v. Bowen, 624 F. 2d 1255, 1266 (5th Cir. 1980). See also, Eaves v. Penn, 587 F. 2d 453, 465 (10th Cir. 1978) (such factors to be used in determining whether to award fees against fiduciary or common fund created in litigation); Ford v. New York Teamsters Pension Fund, 642 F. 2d 664 (2d Cir. 1981).

[220] *See* Eaves v. Penn, *supra;* Freund v. Marshall & Ilsley Bank, 485 F. Supp. at 643-44.

[221] Eaves v. Penn, 587 F. 2d at 465. *Accord* Donovan v. Mazzola, 2 EBC at 2138; Freund v. Marshall & Ilsley Bank, 485 F. Supp. at 643-44.

fiduciary incurs in the action may be an impermissible use of plan assets under ERISA Section 404(a)(1)(A) on the ground that such expenditure would not defray a "reasonable expense of administering the plan."[222] Thus, the fiduciary who is found to have breached his fiduciary duties faces the perspective of paying both his own attorneys' fees and those of the successful plaintiff as well.

---

[222] Donovan v. Mazzola, 2 EBC at 2138; DOL Adv. Opin. No. 78-29.

CHAPTER 47

Administration of Group Life Insurance Plans under the Employee Retirement Income Security Act of 1974 (ERISA)

JAMES E. ROBERTS
AND RONALD T. MARTIN

ERISA GENERAL REQUIREMENTS

The reporting and disclosure requirements and the fiduciary standards of the Employee Retirement Income Security Act ("the Act") by their terms are directly applicable to "employee welfare benefit plans." The Act defines an employee welfare benefit plan and "welfare plan" in Section 3(1) as "any plan, fund, or program which was heretofore or is hereafter established or maintained by an employer or by an employee organization, or by both, to the extent that such plan, fund, or program was established or is maintained for the purpose of providing for its participants or their beneficiaries, through the purchase of insurance or otherwise, . . . benefits in the event of . . . death . . . ." By this definition, it is clear a group life insurance plan, including a plan with a retired lives reserve provision, is an employee welfare benefit plan.[1]

Pursuant to Section 402(a)(1) of the Act, every employee benefit plan, including an employee welfare benefit plan, must be established and maintained pursuant to a written instrument. A written plan is required so that employees can, upon examination of plan documents, determine precisely

---

[1] Certain group insurance programs have been eliminated from the welfare plan definition. A group life insurance plan is not a welfare plan if (i) it is a "group" or "group-type" insurance program offered by an insurer to employees or members of an employee organization; (ii) no contributions are made by an employer or employee organization; (iii) participation in the program is completely voluntary; (iv) the sole functions of the employer or employee organization are, without endorsing the program, to permit the insurer to publicize the program to employees or members, to collect premiums through payroll deductions or dues checkoffs, and to remit them to the insurer; and (v) the employer or employee organization receives no consideration in the form of cash or otherwise in connection with the program, other than reasonable compensation, excluding any profit, for administrative services actually rendered in connection with the payroll deductions or dues checkoffs. Labor Reg. §2510.3-1(g). Plans designed to qualify under Section 79 of the Internal Revenue Code, since at least partly funded by employer contributions, cannot fall within this exclusion.

their rights and obligations under the plan.[2] In addition, the Act requires the instrument provide for one or more "named fiduciaries" who jointly or severally have authority to control and manage the operation and administration of the plan.[3] In this way, employees can ascertain who is responsible for operating the plan.[4] Also, every welfare plan must provide a procedure for establishing and carrying out a "funding policy" and funding method consistent with the objectives of the plan and the requirements of the Act.[5] This procedure is required to enable the plan fiduciary to determine the plan's short- and long-run financial needs and communicate these needs to the appropriate person.[6] It is difficult to see how the funding policy requirement could apply to an unfunded welfare plan such as a group life insurance plan in which no benefits under the plan are prefunded. Indeed, the Department of Labor has recognized that "in situations in which a plan is unfunded and Title I of the Act does not require the plan to be funded," the plan need not provide a procedure for establishing and carrying out a funding policy since such a procedure would not be "consistent with the objectives of the plan."[7] In the case of a group life insurance plan containing a retired lives reserve, however, the funding policy requirement would have to be met. It would appear that the requirement, if expressed in the plan, that contributions to the retired lives reserve fund be actuarially determined and made on a level basis,[8] would constitute the requisite funding policy.

Every employee benefit plan must also contain the following:

1. A description of any procedure under the plan for allocating responsibilities for the operation and administration of the plan;[9]
2. A procedure for amending the plan and for identifying who has authority to amend the plan;[10]
3. The basis on which payments are to be made to and from the plan.[11]

Finally, the Act requires, with some exceptions, that all the assets of an employee benefit plan be held in trust by one or more trustees, either named in the trust or in the plan instrument, or appointed by a named fiduciary. However, the requirement for placing the plan's assets in trust is not applicable to any assets which consist of insurance contracts or to any

---

[2] H. Conf. Rept. No. 93-1280, 93rd Cong. 2d Sess. 297.
[3] ERISA § 402(a)(1).
[4] H. Conf. Rept. No. 93-1280, 93rd Cong. 2d Sess. 297.
[5] ERISA § 402(b)(1).
[6] H. Conf. Rept. No. 93-1280, 93rd Cong. 2d Sess. 297.
[7] ERISA IB 75-5, question F-5.
[8] Rev. Rul. 73-599, 1973-2 CB 40, modified by Rev. Rul. 77-92, 1977-1 CB 41.
[9] ERISA § 402(b)(2)
[10] ERISA § 402(b)(3).
[11] ERISA § 402(b)(4).

assets of a plan which are held by an insurance company.[12] Even though insurance contracts or assets held by an insurance company need not be in trust, the person who holds such contracts or assets is a fiduciary. Thus, the person holding such contracts or assets must prudently take and keep exclusive control of the contracts and use prudent care and skill to preserve this property.[13] From the above, it is apparent that since the assets of most group life insurance plans consist only of insurance contracts, such assets need not be held in trust. Moreover, since the assets of most group life insurance plans containing a retired lives reserve consist of insurance contracts and monies held by a life insurance company in a retired lives reserve fund, the assets of most of these plans need not be held in trust.[14]

ADMINISTRATIVE REQUIREMENTS

The administrator of a welfare plan is required to file various reports and documents with the Internal Revenue Service and the Department of Labor. These requirements are discussed, in broad outline, below.

Reports to the Internal Revenue Service

Generally, welfare plans are not required to file with the Internal Revenue Service the annual reports and annual registration statements required to be filed by retirement plans.[15] However, for plan years beginning in 1977 and thereafter, welfare plans file the annual report (Form 5500 or 5500-C) with the Internal Revenue Service. Effective for plan years beginning on or after January 1, 1980, Form 5500-C, for use with plans which have fewer than 100 participants, is filed only once every three years (according to the last digit of the sponsor's employer identification number). In each of the intervening two years Form 5500-R is filed. However, the Internal Revenue Service will permit Form 5500-C to be filed for any year in which Form 5500-R would be filed. The Internal Revenue Service will forward a copy of the annual report to the Department of Labor.

Reports to the Department of Labor

Except for certain excluded plans[16] and exempt plans, to the extent they are exempt (see discussion infra), the plan administrator of every welfare

---

[12] ERISA §§ 403(b)(1) and (2).

[13] Conf. Rept. 93-1280, 93rd Cong., 1st Sess. 298 (1974).

[14] If the monies in the retired lives reserve fund are not held by an insurance company, they will be held in a nonexempt or exempt trust and the requirements of ERISA §403 will be satisfied. See discussion of alternative funding vehicles in text at notes 27 through 41 in Chapter 7.

[15] I.R.C. §§ 6057 and 6058.

[16] ERISA § 4(b).

plan must file with the Department of Labor each of the documents described below:

Plan Description and Updated Plan Description. A complete description of the plan must be filed with the Department of Labor by the plan administrator.[17] Generally, the plan description must be filed within 120 days after the plan is established.[18] An updated plan description must be filed not more frequently than once every five years, as prescribed by the Secretary of Labor.[19] The plan description and updated plan description reporting requirements are satisfied by filing with the Department of Labor a summary plan description and an updated summary plan description, respectively.[20]

Material Modifications and Changes. Any material modifications in the plan and/or changes in the information included in the plan description must be filed with the Department of Labor.[21] This requirement is satisfied by filing with the Department of Labor a summary of any such material modification or change not later than 210 days after the close of the plan year in which such modification or change was adopted.[22] A plan administrator is not required to file a summary of any material modification or change which is already incorporated in (i) a summary plan description or supplement, (ii) an initial plan description, or (iii) an updated plan description.[23]

Annual Report. An annual report must be provided to the Department of Labor. Generally, the annual report must include various statements, including financial statements and insurance statements. For 1977 plan years and thereafter, Form 5500 or 5500-C is filed with the Internal Revenue Service within seven months of the close of the plan year. Effective for plan years beginning on or after January 1, 1980, Form 5500-C, for use with plans having fewer than 100 participants, is filed only once every three years (according to the last digit of the sponsor's employer identification number) and in each of the intervening two years Form 5500-R is filed. Form 5500-C may be filed for any year in which Form 5500-R would be filed. The Internal Revenue Service will forward the appropriate information to the Department of Labor.

Summary Plan Description. A copy of the summary plan descriptions, which must be furnished to participants and beneficiaries (see infra), must also be filed with the Department of Labor on or before the last date on which it may be furnished to the participants and beneficiaries.[24]

---

[17] ERISA § 102.

[18] Labor Reg. § 2520.104a-2.

[19] Ibid.

[20] Labor Reg. § 2520.104a-2(b)(1).

[21] Labor Reg. § 2520.104a-4.

[22] Labor Reg. § 2520.104a-4(b)(1).

[23] Labor Reg. § 2520.104a-4(b)(2).

[24] ERISA § 104(a)(1)(c).

Terminal Reports. The Secretary of Labor may by regulation require that the administrator of any welfare plan that is winding up its affairs file a terminal report.[25] The Secretary may similarly require that a supplementary or terminal report be filed with the annual report in the year in which the plan is terminated.[26]

Certain Documents. The plan administrator must furnish to the Department of Labor upon request copies of any documents relating to the plan, including but not limited to the bargaining agreement, trust agreement, contract, or other instrument under which the plan is established or operated.[27]

Records. Every person subject to a requirement to file any description or report, or to certify any information therefor, or who would be so subject, absent an exemption or simplified reporting requirement, must maintain records on the matters with respect to which disclosure is required.[28] Such records must provide in sufficient detail the necessary basic information and data from which the required documents may be verified, explained, or clarified.[29] Such records must include vouchers, worksheets, receipts, and applicable resolutions, and must be maintained for a period of not less than six years after the filing date of the relevant document,[30] or six years after the document would have been filed but for an exemption or simplified reporting requirement.

Except for certain excluded plans[31] and exempt plans to the extent they are exempt (see discussion infra), the plan administrator of every welfare plan must furnish to plan participants and beneficiaries each of the documents described in broad outline below.

Reports to Participants and Beneficiaries

Summary Plan Description and Updated Summary Plan Description. Each participant and each beneficiary receiving benefits must be furnished with a copy of the summary plan description.[32] Generally, summary plan descriptions must be distributed within 120 days following the date upon which the plan became subject to the reporting and disclosure requirements of the Act, although certain rules provide extensions of time for initial distribution under specific circumstances.[33] Following initial dis-

---

[25] ERISA § 101(c)(2).
[26] ERISA § 101(c)(3).
[27] ERISA § 104(a).
[28] ERISA § 107.
[29] Ibid.
[30] Ibid.
[31] ERISA § 4(b).
[32] ERISA § 104(b)(1).
[33] Labor Reg. § 2520.104b-2.

tribution, each new participant or beneficiary must be furnished with a copy of the summary plan description within 90 days following the date upon which he became a participant or first received benefits.[34]

The format and content of the summary plan description are prescribed in detail by regulations.[35] Generally, the summary plan description must contain a statement of the rights of participants and beneficiaries under the Act, must be written in a manner calculated to be understood by the average participant, and must be sufficiently comprehensive and accurate to reasonably apprise participants and beneficiaries of their rights and obligations under the plan. Every fifth year an updated summary plan description must be prepared and distributed, unless the plan has not been amended during such period. In any event, an updated summary plan description must be prepared and furnished at least every tenth year.[36]

Material Modifications and Changes. A summary description of any material modification in the plan and/or change in the information required in the summary plan description, written in a manner calculated to be understood by the average plan participant, must be furnished to each participant and each beneficiary receiving benefits within 210 days following the end of the plan year in which such modification or change is adopted.[37] However, if the change is explained in a timely summary plan description, then no summary of material modifications or changes need be separately submitted.[38]

Summary Annual Report. Each participant and each beneficiary receiving benefits must be furnished a summary annual report.[39] Applicable regulations require that such report must generally be furnished within nine months after the close of the plan year.[40] Effective July 23, 1982, the summary annual report rules applicable to employee benefit plans with fewer than 100 participants have been modified to provide two alternative methods for such plans to satisfy their obligation to furnish a summary annual report to participants for the two years when Form 5500-R is filed under the triennial reporting system. In lieu of furnishing a summary annual report for the years in which Form 5500-R is filed, the plan administrator shall either furnish a Form 5500-R directly to each participant, or shall notify each participant that he or she is entitled to receive a copy of Form 5500-R upon request. The style, format, and content of the summary

---

[34] Ibid.

[35] Labor Reg. § 2520.102-3.

[36] For specifics regarding the five and ten year distribution requirements, see Labor Reg. § 2520.104b-2(b), added on January 14, 1983.

[37] ERISA § 104(b)(1).

[38] Labor Reg. § 2520.104b-3(b).

[39] Labor Reg. § 2520.104b-10(a).

[40] Labor Reg. § 2520.104b-10(b).

annual report and of the alternative methods of compliance applicable to small plans have been prescribed by regulations.[41]

Denial of Claims.   Each participant or beneficiary must, within a reasonable time following denial of any claim for benefits, be provided with a notice explaining why the claim has been denied, and he must be provided with a reasonable opportunity for a full and fair review of any claim denial.[42] More particularly, each plan must include a claims procedure which meets the detailed requirements of the applicable regulations.[43]

Certain Documents (Copies upon Request).   Each participant or beneficiary must, within 30 days following receipt of his written request, be furnished with a copy of the latest updated summary plan description, the plan description, the latest annual report, any terminal report, and the bargaining agreement, trust agreement, contract, or other instruments under which the plan is established or operated.[44] The plan administrator may make a reasonable charge to cover the cost of furnishing such copies.[45] Regulations dictate that costs are reasonable if they are equal to the least expensive means of acceptable reproduction, not to exceed 25 cents per page.[46]

Certain Documents (Available for Inspection).   The plan administrator shall make copies of the plan description and the latest annual report and the bargaining agreement, trust agreement, contract, or other instruments under which the plan is established or operated available for examination by any participant or beneficiary in the principal office of the administrator and in such other places as may be necessary to make all pertinent information available to all participants.[47]

Exemptions for Welfare Plans

Each of the types of plans described in the following sections is exempted from part or all of the reporting and disclosure requirements as indicated separately in each section.

Certain Small Welfare Plans.   (a) Department of Labor Regulations[48] provide a limited exemption for welfare plans:

(1) which have fewer than 100 participants at the beginning of the plan year;

(2) for which benefits are (i) paid as needed solely from the general assets

---

[41] Labor Reg. § 2520.104b-10(c).

[42] ERISA § 503.

[43] Labor Reg. § 2560.503-1.

[44] ERISA § 104(b).

[45] Ibid.

[46] Labor Reg. § 2520.104b-30.

[47] ERISA § 104(b)(2); Labor Reg. § 2520.104b-1(b)(3).

[48] Labor Reg. § 2520.104-20.

of the employer or employee organization maintaining the plan, or (ii) provided exclusively through insurance contracts or policies issued by an insurance company or similar organization which is qualified to do business in any state, or through a qualified health maintenance organization, as defined in section 1310(d) of the Public Health Service Act, as amended,[49] the premiums for which are paid directly by the employer or employee organization from its general assets or partly from its general assets and partly from contributions by its employees or members, provided that contributions by participants are forwarded by the employer or employee organization within three months of receipt, or (iii) both; and

(3) for which, in the case of an insured plan, (i) refunds to which contributing participants are entitled are returned to them within three months of receipt by the employer or employee organization, and (ii) contributing participants are informed upon entry into the plan of the provisions of the plan concerning the allocation of refunds.

(b) The plan administrator of any plan which meets the requirements of subsection (a), above, is exempted from filing each of the following documents with the Department of Labor:[50]

(1) plan description;

(2) copy of the summary plan description;

(3) description of a material modification in the terms of the plan or change in the information required to be included in the plan description;

(4) annual report; and,

(5) terminal report.

(c) The plan administrator of any plan which meets the requirements of subsection (a), above, is not required to:[51]

(1) furnish financial statements and summary annual reports to participants and beneficiaries receiving benefits;

(2) furnish upon written request of any participant or beneficiary a copy of the plan description, annual report, and any terminal report; or

(3) make copies of the plan description and annual report available for inspection by any participant or beneficiary in its principal office and in such other places as may be necessary.

(d) Except as otherwise indicated in subsections (b) and (c), above, plans described in subsection (a), above, must comply with the reporting and disclosure requirements discussed supra. Thus, administrators of such plans must furnish plan documents to the Secretary of Labor upon request and must keep plan records. In addition, administrators of such plans must furnish participants and beneficiaries summary plan descriptions, summary descriptions of material modifications to the plan, and upon request, copies

---

[49] 42 U.S.C. § 300e-9(d).

[50] Labor Reg. § 2520.104-20.

[51] Ibid.

of the latest summary plan description and plan documents. Such plans must include reasonable claims procedures, and the plan documents for such plans must be available for inspection by both participants and beneficiaries.

Certain Group Insurance Arrangements. (a) Department of Labor Regulations[52] provide a limited exemption for welfare plans:

(1) which have fewer than 100 participants at the beginning of the plan year;

(2) which are part of a group insurance arrangement, (i) which provides benefits to the employees of two or more unaffiliated employers but not in connection with a multiemployer plan as defined in Section 3(37) of the Act and any regulations thereunder (generally, a plan to which more than one employer contributes pursuant to a collective bargaining agreement between an employee organization and more than one employer), and (ii) which fully insures one or more welfare plans of each participating employer through insurance contracts purchased solely by the employers or purchased partly by the employers and partly by their participating employees, with all benefit payments made by the insurance company, provided, that contributions by participating employees are forwarded by the employers within three months of receipt, that refunds to which contributing participants are entitled are returned to them within three months of receipt, and that contributing participants are informed upon entry into the plan of the provisions of the plan concerning the allocation of refunds; and,

(3) which use a trust or other entity such as a trade association as the holder of the insurance contracts and the conduit for payment of premiums to the insurance company.

(b) The plan administrator of a plan that meets the requirements of subsection (a), above, is exempt from filing each of the following documents with the Department of Labor:[53]

(1) plan description;

(2) copy of the summary plan description;

(3) description of a material modification in the terms of the plan or change in the information required to be included in the plan description; and,

(4) terminal report.

(c) The plan administrator of any plan which meets the requirements of subsection (a), above, is not required to:[54]

(1) furnish upon written request of any participant or beneficiary a copy of the plan description and any terminal report; or,

---

[52] Labor Reg. § 2520.104-21.

[53] Ibid.

[54] Ibid.

(2) make copies of the plan description available for examination by any participant or beneficiary in its principal office and in such other places as may be necessary.

(d) Except as otherwise indicated in subsections (b) and (c), above, plans described in subsection (a), above, must comply with the reporting and disclosure requirements discussed supra. Thus, administrators of such plans must file annual reports with the Department of Labor, must furnish plan documents to the Department of Labor upon request, and must keep plan records. In addition, administrators of such plans must furnish summary plan descriptions, must furnish summary descriptions of material modifications, must furnish summary annual reports, must provide reasonable claims procedures, and must furnish upon request and/or make available for inspection the documents described in the text at notes 44 through 47, other than the plan description or terminal report.

Certain Plans for Selected Employees.

(a) Department of Labor Regulations[55] provide a limited exemption for welfare plans:

(1) which are maintained by an employer primarily for the purpose of providing benefits for a select group of management or highly compensated employees; and,

(2) for which benefits (i) are paid as needed solely from the employer's general assets, (ii) are provided exclusively through insurance contracts or policies, the premiums for which are paid directly by the employer from its general assets, issued by an insurance company which is qualified to do business in any state, or (iii) both (i) and (ii).

(b) Plans which meet the requirements of subsection (a), above, are exempted from all of the reporting and disclosure requirements, except for the requirement to provide plan documents to the Secretary of Labor upon request.[56]

Other Exemptions. Department of Labor Regulations also provide limited exemptions for the following types of welfare plans:

(1) plans which provide solely apprenticeship training benefits;[57]

(2) day care centers;[58]

(3) plans maintained by an employee organization and paid for out of the organization's assets, which assets are derived wholly or partly from membership dues, and which cover organization members and their beneficiaries.[59]

---

[55] Labor Reg. § 2520.104-24.

[56] Ibid.

[57] Labor Reg. § 2520.104-22.

[58] Labor Reg. § 2520.104-25.

[59] Labor Reg. § 2520.104-26.

Exemptions That May Be Applicable to a Group Insurance Plan (Including a Retired Lives Reserve Plan)

Certain Small Welfare Plans. Assuming that a group insurance plan, including a retired lives reserve plan, has fewer than 100 participants and is noncontributory (or, if contributory, satisfies the requirements discussed in the text at notes 48 through 50 regarding contributory plans), the question to be answered in determining whether the plan qualifies for the exemption for certain small welfare plans is whether the employer pays the premiums "directly." The Labor Regulations do not define "directly." In addition, there are no reported cases or pronouncements by the Department of Labor as to the meaning of "directly." However, if the employer's contributions are paid to a trust that serves as a conduit for the payment of premiums to the insurance company, the employer does not pay premiums directly to the insurance company, if this requirement is interpreted literally.

Certain Group Insurance Arrangements. An employer's plan, including a plan with a retired lives reserve provision, with fewer than 100 participants that is noncontributory (or, if contributory, satisfies the requirements discussed in the text at notes 52 and 53), will qualify for the exemption for welfare plans maintained under certain group insurance arrangements if the plan is part of a group insurance arrangement that provides benefits to the employees of two or more unaffiliated employers, and a multiple employer trust will be the legal owner of the group policies and will serve as a conduit for the payment of premiums.

Certain Plans for Selected Employees. This exemption will not apply to a group insurance plan, including a retired lives reserve plan, that is superimposed[60] upon another group insurance plan providing benefits to rank and file employees. This is because, under such circumstances, the two plans will be considered as a single plan[61] and the plan will not be considered to be maintained primarily for the purpose of providing benefits to a select group of management or highly compensated employees. Also, as indicated above, if the employer's contributions are paid to a trust that serves as a conduit for the payment of premiums to the insurance company, the employer probably will not be deemed to be paying premiums "directly" to the insurance company.

Annual Reports

Section 103 of the Act requires that the plan administrator of each welfare plan that is not excluded[62] or exempt[63] file an annual report. As

---

[60] See discussion of superimposing in Chapter 59.
[61] Ibid.
[62] ERISA § 4(b).
[63] See discussion in text at notes 47 through 58 supra.

indicated above,[64] the annual report is filed with the Internal Revenue Service within seven months of the close of the plan year. Effective for plan years beginning on or after January 1, 1980, plans with fewer than 100 participants are required to file a Form 5500-C once every three years. In the intervening two years a brief registration statement, Form 5500-R, is filed. However, the Internal Revenue Service will permit Form 5500-C to be filed for any year in which Form 5500-R would be filed. The Internal Revenue Service will forward the appropriate information to the Department of Labor.[65] Section 103 specifies certain information that must be contained in the annual report of each welfare plan. However, pursuant to authority granted by statute,[66] the Secretary of Labor has issued regulations which elaborate upon and/or modify the statutory annual report requirements, including the grant of various alternative methods and partial exemptions from the statutory requirements.[67]

---

[64] See discussion in text at note 15.

[65] Ibid.

[66] ERISA § 104(a)(3).

[67] Labor Reg. §§ 2520.103-1(a)(2), 2520.103-1(c), 2520.104-45, 2520.104-46, 2520.104-43, 2520.103-2, 2520.104-44, 2520.103-3, 2520.103-4, and 2520.103-9.

CHAPTER 48

Developing Plan Specifications

DAVID R. KLOCK

Every few years, an organization may wish to reevaluate its group insurance program and to test the marketplace by obtaining bids on its benefit program. This reevaluation process typically consists of the following steps:

1. Determine if the program should be rebid.
2. Review plan design.
3. Select appropriate financing techniques.
4. Draft specifications for either negotiated placement or competitive bid.
5. Undertake prebid screening.
6. Analyze bids and select insurer or other carrier.
7. Complete final negotiations with selected carrier.
8. Implement new program.

Before proceeding, one very important caveat should be emphasized. The entire selection process should be conducted at the highest professional level. Too frequently, group insurers perceive the selection process as very political, with apparent advantage going to friends and relations. As one publication recently reported,

> Insurance companies should never be selected based on the basis of friendship, old school ties, or other subjective means. In these days, the insurance broker represents an important business relationship. Treat him as a professional and expect and demand that he act like one.[1]

Many excellent insurers will not submit bids if nonprofessional conditions exist between them and the client.

This chapter focuses on the first five steps in the reevaluation process. Steps six and seven are covered in the next chapter. Plan implementation is covered in Chapter 50.

---

[1] Bernard M. Brown and Charles F. Moody, Jr., "Insurance Bidding and Specifications," *Risk Management Reports,* Vol. 5, no. 5, p. 14.

WHY REBID?

Some employers (especially government units) believe that frequent bidding of their group insurance plans results in the lowest possible cost outlay. This contention generally is a misconception. Organizations that too often enter the employee benefits marketplace face the risk of being considered unstable or capricious consumers who frequently seek bids and/or change carriers. Insurers, knowing an account is unlikely to prove profitable unless it remains with the insurer for several years and thus allows the insurer to recover certain front-end costs associated with the installation of a group insurance plan, may shy away from an organization with this reputation. The organization soon discovers that the number of cost competitive insurers or other service organizations willing to bid for its business declines dramatically.

This does not imply that the rebidding of an employee benefits package is seldom advisable. There are several excellent reasons why organizations may wish to enter the reevaluation process. The following discussion covers the most important considerations in this decision.

Irreconcilable Management Dissatisfaction

The executives of a firm occasionally become disenchanted or frustrated with their insurance agent/broker/consultant and/or with their insurance company. A thorough investigation of the reasons for the dissatisfaction should be conducted prior to any decision to rebid the coverage. Corrective actions and/or repair of poor communication lines may be a viable alternative. If, however, the credibility of the current insurer or advisor is beyond repair, rebidding will undoubtedly prove necessary.

Legal Requirements

Many government entities are required by law or by administrative resolution to rebid their insurance programs periodically. However, many experts believe a change in the regulations may be appropriate if rebidding is required more frequently than once every five to seven years. Brown and Moody summarize this viewpoint when they state:

> In our opinion, this situation [frequent rebidding] has created a belief among underwriters that municipalities tend to look only at short-term cost considerations and will move to another underwriter or broker without the slightest hesitation. Of course, the cost of coverage is very important and is a major factor in selecting an insurance program; but equally important is scope of coverage, service, and availability of acceptable markets. This practice of frequent rebidding has undoubtedly diminished the general market capacity available to municipalities. In our opinion, municipalities and other governmental entities, as a general rule, should not rebid more frequently than once every six years. This might be shortened, under certain circum-

stances. . . . However, the general principle remains that governmental entities should take a much longer term view of the implications of their insurance program decisions than they have in the past.[2]

The same guidelines apply to nongovernmental employers. Frequent rebidding should be avoided.

Underwriting Cycle

Many insurance markets undergo underwriting cycles, with periods of very restrained markets and conservative pricing/underwriting decisions followed by more aggressive and very competitive pricing/underwriting decisions. Employee benefit managers or risk managers occasionally try to take advantage of a perceived period of lower costs and/or expanded underwriting capacity by rebidding their insurance programs.

Advisor Recommendations

The agent/broker/consultant is responsible for maintaining a high level of knowledge regarding the availability and relative competitiveness of alternative insurance carriers. When an organization has confidence in its advisor, his or her advice should be given serious consideration. If this confidence is lacking, a reevaluation of the relationship with the advisor is in order. The employer should, however, be both skeptical of and interested in the advice of commissioned advisors not currently handling the account. These advisors obviously have a vested financial interest in rebidding the coverage.

Substantial Change in the Organization

Mergers, acquisitions, or rapid growth may mean that the nature of the organization has changed dramatically since the current group coverage was obtained. Such changes often result in a need for changes in plan design and can necessitate a level of service or expertise unavailable from the current insurer or service organization. This problem will be especially evident if the employer has developed significant foreign operations with many overseas employees because international employee benefits management often requires unique skills and products.

Nonrenewal or Significant Change in Conditions or Cost

An organization clearly has no choice but to rebid if its current plan is cancelled. Alternatively, rebidding may be needed if the current insurer has

---

[2] Ibid., p. 8.

given notice that renewed coverage will be altered significantly so that a serious diminution of benefits will occur. A renewal price increase that the employer perceives to greatly exceed general market costs likewise triggers a rebidding of the program.

Inadequate Service

The most important reason for changing insurance carriers (or advisors) is proof of an inadequate level of service. The key areas of service can be divided into the following categories: timeliness, quality and expertise in cost reduction analysis, review of all financing alternatives (e.g., self-funding), and claims handling.

Significant Time since Last Market Test

A periodic market test of the relative competitiveness of the current insurance program is recommended regardless of current service levels. Experts seem to hold that an appropriate rebidding cycle is once every five to seven years.

REVIEWING PLAN DESIGN

Prior to writing bid specifications, the organization and its agent/broker/consultant should review carefully the current plan design. Benefit programs often evolve in a piecemeal and haphazard fashion, with little or no consistent input for personnel goals, long-term cash flow constraints, and employee equity. The bidding process provides an excellent opportunity to seriously evaluate plan design in light of other critical and evolving corporate goals. A set of suggested questions to be answered would include:

1. What is the employer's attitude toward group insurance? For example, are group insurance benefits viewed as traditional compensation for work provided, an incentive to increase employee productivity, and/or a benevolent reward?
2. How should the responsibility for economic security be shared by the employer and individual employees?
3. What effect should seniority, salary, or position have on the level of benefits?
4. What is the firm's present cash flow available for employee benefits, and what are the probabilities of future cash flows at various levels?
5. How important is "income leveling?"
6. What are the quantity and quality of the corporate staff who will be responsible for handling the details of a group insurance program?
7. Should an agent, broker, or consultant be used?
8. Does the firm have subsidiaries with unique benefit planning problems?

9. Is company management concerned enough about unionization or about attracting key employees to affect employee benefit design by type of employee?
10. How should changes (increases) in employee benefits be ranked with other changes (increases) in the total employee compensation package?
11. Should flexibility be built into the program to recognize the differences in needs and desires among employees?
12. How much attention should be given to the attitudes of employees when making changes?
13. Is the proposed plan design consistent with cost control standards concerning plan objectives, eligibility, preexisting conditions, utilization of outpatient and home health care, second opinions on surgery, out-of-pocket and co-pay provisions, and preventive care in lieu of larger claims stemming from neglect?
14. How will the contributions of the employee benefit plan to the employer's benefit plan objectives be measured? How often?[3]

In addition to addressing these questions, the benefit planners will also wish to carefully review experience data to detect any areas where changes in the current benefits package might result in significant cost reductions and/or benefit improvements with little or no additional premium outlay or compromise in personnel goals. This in-depth statistical analysis of plan experience may lead, for example, to changes in the existing plan deductibles and/or the addition of new deductibles. Effective use of deductibles may reduce excessive utilization of certain medical services by creating a financial disincentive. Redesign of plan deductibles based on actual plan experience could help create one source of funds to be used for the expansion of benefits in more critical areas of potential catastrophic loss.

The effectiveness of the foregoing plan design analysis is dependent on both the quality of the loss data provided in periodic claims reports and the level of technical service provided by the outside advisor or by the insurer. If a satisfactory level of data or statistical assistance is not currently provided, this poor service emphasizes the need to rebid the coverage. New bid specifications should clearly communicate a request for periodic loss data analysis.

FINANCING TECHNIQUES

During the past several decades, numerous alternatives to the traditional methods of financing group employee benefits have been developed. These alternatives to a pure insurance arrangement include experienced-rated

---

[3] For further discussion of this topic, see David R. Klock and Bruce Palmer, "Group Insurance and the Role of the Professional Life Underwriter," *CLU Journal,* Vol. 33, no. 3 (July, 1979), pp. 44–53.

plans, monthly experience arrangements, retrospective premium agreements, minimum premium plans, administrative services only (ASO) programs, and various types of self-administered and/or self-funded plans. Other chapters of this handbook have covered these alternatives in considerable detail.

Prior to developing its bidding strategy, the organization (with help from its agent/broker/consultant) must decide on the financing or cash flow method most compatible with its circumstances. With today's high interest rates, the selection of the appropriate funding or financing technique has taken on heightened interest. The selection of certain financing alternatives will significantly influence the type of information solicited from bidders.

SPECIFICATIONS: NEGOTIATED PLACEMENT OR COMPETITIVE BID

There are at least three methods of entry into the employee benefits marketplace:

1. Negotiated placement with a single insurer or service organization.
2. Competitive bidding, with a public announcement that all qualified insurance companies may obtain bid specifications and submit proposals.
3. Closed bidding, with only invited insurers allowed to submit bids.

Negotiated placement is appropriate if the employer, upon advice from a qualified advisor, is convinced it has identified an insurer that is very competitive in the class of group business to be purchased. By developing and maintaining strong rapport and communication with a few highly competitive insurers in each line of group coverage, a firm can often obtain underwriting or pricing concessions that may not be possible in a more open bid process. Personal contacts and commitment can be very important in periods when the underwriting cycle is to the employer's disadvantage. However, it is often possible to obtain many of these financial gains through a multistaged bidding process that eliminates "nonqualified" bidders. The bidding process does not preclude personal contact and negotiations.

Open competitive bidding typically is used only when required by law. For example, many government entities advertise the bidding of group insurance. In theory, an open competitive bid system creates the widest possible market survey. It can, however, significantly increase the cost of the bidding process as a result of the added cost associated with reviewing very weak or poorly presented proposals. Without some prescreening, the employer or its consultant may be forced to analyze numerous noncompetitive bids.

With a closed or limited bidding process, the employer and/or the agent/broker/consultant will prescreen potential bidders. Only "qualified" bidders will be allowed to obtain detailed bid specifications and to submit a proposal. Since bids will be received from only a limited number of insurers, the employer retains the flexibility to negotiate the final contract. If a change of coverage or of financing techniques is desired by the employer, this can be accomplished in the final negotiation stage rather than in an expensive rebidding process. Most corporate employers and a growing number of public employers use some form of closed negotiated bidding.

Negotiated Placement

The negotiated placement method of purchasing group coverage is also referred to as the "interview method" because it consists of a series of preliminary interviews during which the list of several potential service organizations is narrowed to the one which will be provided with detailed census information and will be the only insurer or other service organization to submit a price quotation.

Negotiated placement typically consists of several steps. First, after informing the current insurer of a decision to consider a plan change, the employer or its agent/broker/consultant prescreens several insurers (including the current one). These insurers should be recommended by the advisor and/or by such reliable sources of information as other risk managers or employee benefit managers. Prescreening considerations include the financial solvency of the insurer, its service facilities, its reputation regarding cost, and the quality of its sales, administrative, and claims staff. Prescreening is described in more detail in a later section of this chapter.

Second, the decision makers will select a few insurers or service organizations (perhaps four to six) from those which have been prescreened and provide these organizations general information about the employer, its current group insurance program, and any changes it would like to see in the new plan. Each of these companies should be requested to prepare a brief report on the general approach, philosophy, and structure of its proposed group insurance program. The purpose of this step is to determine if the risk management philosophy of the proposed insurer or other service organization is compatible with that of the employer and if the organization has the expertise and capacity to handle the employer's unique needs.

Third, the suggestions of the alternative insurers will be evaluated to select the one company with which the final details of the group insurance plan will be negotiated. This company alone will be provided with detailed loss, financial, and employee data. Furthermore, only this one insurer or service organization will submit a detailed bid on the desired group plan.

Finally, after receiving this bid, the employer will negotiate any necessary changes with the help of the agent/broker/consultant. Success at this point depends heavily on the competence of the advisor. If an organization wishes to use the negotiated placement method but lacks confidence in the technical skills of its advisor, an obvious preliminary step would be the selection of a new advisor. This process is similar to that for selecting an insurer. Should an organization believe it will be incapable of selecting a highly qualified advisor, the organization will have an additional reason to prefer the bidding procedure for selecting an insurer or service organization.

BID SPECIFICATIONS

Assuming an organization wishes to use a multiple-insurer bidding process (either open or closed) rather than a negotiated placement with one insurer or other service organization, specifications must be designed and distributed to all qualified bidders. The specifications must deal with the role of any advisor, the coverage desired, and the financing method to be used. Bid specifications must also provide detailed underwriting data (e.g., employee census and paid losses).

The organization could provide several insurers with broad guidelines as to the type of coverage and then request proposals from these insurers. In fact, this is frequently what happens. The requests are often made verbally, and the specifications are so broad that different insurers propose significantly different benefit designs. The resulting proposals seldom furnish detailed information on the fixed and variable retention charges and interest credits. *The solution to the potential problem of incomparable proposals is to write clear specifications and to include a format for the itemization of all cost factors.*

Specifications should consist of the following parts:

1. Cover letter.
2. Plan experience data.
3. Description of desired coverage.
4. Census data.
5. Questionnaire and bid forms.

Cover Letter

A cover letter, which serves as an invitation to bid, should accompany the specifications. A primary purpose of this letter is to motivate the competitive insurers to bid. Responding to a bid request requires time and expenditure by an insurer. Each insurer needs some assurance that the process will be fair and that the corporation requesting the bid is a desirable client. The major elements of the cover letter include:

1. Name.
2. A description of the employer's principal operations.
3. If the organization has operations in more than one location, a complete listing of all locations should be provided.
4. Collective bargaining status. Indication should be made if any groups of employees will not be covered under the proposed plan.
5. Name of the employee or consultant to whom the proposal should be

submitted. This person should be capable of answering technical and nontechnical questions. If a consultant has been retained and is available to answer questions, this fact should be indicated in the cover letter or the bid specifications.

6. Date and place for proposal submission. Insurers should be given at least 30 days to prepare their proposals.
7. Anticipated effective date of the new plan.

Plan Experience

Most competitive insurers are unlikely to prepare a bid unless a reasonable amount of information for at least the last three (preferably five) years is provided.

The following types of historical information should be furnished:

1. *A complete description of the benefits in effect during each period for which claims data are furnished.* This description is essential in helping the actuaries detect if changes in rates or claims resulted from a change in the benefit plan or from adverse experience. If copies of the plan document are unavailable, any booklets containing descriptions of pertinent benefits and plan provisions will usually be adequate.

2. *A breakdown of monthly premium rates.* Rates per employee unit and per dependent unit should be supplied for each line of coverage: life insurance, disability income insurance, medical benefits, dental coverage, and for any other parts of the benefit package.

3. *Detailed information on premiums paid, all claims, and expenses.* If the firm does not maintain its own computerized database on premiums and losses, an alternative source of information on total premiums, claims experience, and expenses charged to the account may be the insurer's year-end financial accounting reports to the group. This report should contain a breakdown of both paid claims and changes in claim reserves. Data on the following deductions from premiums are also desirable: *(a)* changes in reserves other than those for incurred-but-not-paid claims, *(b)* any losses carried forward from prior years, *(c)* pooling charges, *(d)* conversion charges on death benefit coverage, *(e)* charges for waiver of premium claims, *(f)* retention charges for commissions, risk, and other expenses, and *(g)* balances in the various reserve accounts as of the end of the policy year. Any interest credited on the various categories of reserves and refunds should be clearly depicted.

4. *Pooling levels should be provided in the specifications.* If insurers use different pooling levels, the bids will not be strictly comparable. A breakdown of claims experience between employee and dependent claims is also desirable. While this report is not always furnished as a part of the insurer's annual financial statement, most carriers will make it available when requested by the group.

5. *Average number of persons insured during each period.* Premium statements for most insurers show the number of persons insured for the

premium payment period. If the average number of persons insured cannot be obtained in this way, the information can be documented from employment records.

The organization is likely to have some unique characteristics that should be explained to the bidding insurers. For example, large claims that heavily influenced the claims experience for a particular year should be documented. A listing of each large claim (over $10,000 or $25,000) with a brief description of the nature of the claim should be provided in the loss data section of the bid specifications. A special rate stabilization reserve will allow an existing insurer to offer a lower premium for the next premium paying period than is true for new insurers. The balance in this reserve should be obtained and furnished to all bidders. Currently disabled employees and other facts that might influence the rates quoted by an insurer should be furnished to all insurers.

Description of Desired Coverages

As noted earlier, specifications for desired coverages should be drawn up only after a very careful design of a plan which will meet the objectives of the group. The design should reflect a compromise among employer needs, employee desires, and the need for cost controls.

Detailed descriptions of all desired coverages should be provided to each insurer from whom bids are requested. If any "special" benefits are desired, they should be requested as "alternatives" so that they will not discourage insurers from bidding.

Sample specifications for group insurance coverages appear in Appendix A to this chapter.

Census Data

To prepare their bids, insurers need underwriting data about the people to be insured. This information typically is called an employee census report and includes distributions of employees by age, sex, geographical location, salary bracket, and dependent status. A listing by occupational class also may be helpful if many widely diverse occupations are represented.

Census data ideally should be supplied in a grid format. While a printout of personnel data is acceptable to most insurers, its use does not encourage bidding because of the extra time the insurer will have to spend in organizing the personnel data.

Questionnaire and Bid Forms

Bids will be easier to compare if the responding insurers are required to use the same format. The bid form should be designed to provide both an itemization of rates by type of coverage (life, employee health, dependent health, dental coverage, and any other benefits) and an exhibit detailing all the fixed and variable costs of the proposed retentions. The bid form also is an excellent tool to solicit insurer responses to questions about claims payment, services facilities locations, interest rates on reserves, and similar concerns. These questions can be valuable if later disagreements arise between the insurer and group since they provide a written record of the promises of the insurer.

A sample bid form appears in Appendix B to this chapter. Note that the questions in this appendix are only illustrative. Questions to be included in actual specifications vary with each situation.

PRESCREEN BIDDERS

To preclude the need to analyze proposals from insurers or other service organizations not qualified to serve the specific needs of an employer, a prescreening procedure often is advisable. This can be accomplished through the use of a pre-bid questionnaire and/or in a pre-bid conference.

Pre-Bid Questionnaire

Appendix C to this chapter contains two sample questionnaires that could be used to evaluate the qualifications of either an agent/broker/consultant or an insurer. The use of a prescreening device of this kind allows an employer to gain the advantages of both an open and a closed bidding process. A notice to bid insurance can be provided to all interested purveyors of group insurance products. A government entity might even go one step further and issue a press release giving notice of a desire to rebid an insurance program. Any letter or public notice would indicate that all respondents would be provided not with bid specifications but with a pre-bid application or questionnaire. Only those purveyors who "pass" this initial evaluation would be provided with the detailed bid specifications and invited either to proceed directly with bid preparation or to first attend a pre-bid conference.

Pre-Bid Conference

The pre-bid conference is designed to accomplish three important goals: (a) clarify any uncertainties about the specifications and the bidding forms, (b) motivate the selected insurance companies to submit bids, and (c) encourage creativity in bids.

Too frequently employers forget that in the bidding process they are marketing risks. Unless the insurance company representatives are convinced the potential new client will be profitable, they may decide not to bid. Thus, one goal of the pre-bid conference is to stimulate the enthusiasm of the agent/broker/consultant and insurer for the employer. The conference must be conducted in a very positive manner. As one expert says, "Present the package, 'warts' and all, in as appealing a manner as possible, but consistent with the facts."

Finally, it is important to encourage all bidders to be imaginative and creative because an advisor or insurer can conceivably make suggestions that would significantly improve the quality of the group plan. Many group insurance purveyors have decades of experience that can be used to the employer's advantage. All "creative" alternative bids should be submitted in addition to the bid requested in the detailed specifications.

Sample Group Insurance Specifications: Life and Health Insurance Benefits

THE PRESENT PLAN OF GROUP LIFE AND HEALTH INSURANCE

The employer has had its group life and health insurance plan underwritten by ABC Insurance Company under Group Policy 1234-A since January 1, 1975. Employees are provided $10,000 of life insurance and $10,000 of accidental death and dismemberment insurance. The health insurance consists of a comprehensive major medical plan. The principal provisions of the plan are set forth in detail in a group insurance certificate related to Group Policy 1234-A, issued by ABC Insurance Company.

The principal features of the plan are summarized in tabular form below.

POOLING LEVEL

Please pool all life and health claims at the level of $10,000 per claim per year.

OPTIONAL GROUP LIFE INSURANCE AND ACCIDENTAL DEATH AND DISMEMBERMENT INSURANCE

The employer will also consider an arrangement under which employees may obtain an additional $10,000 of group life insurance and $10,000 of group accidental death and dismemberment insurance. Premiums will be borne entirely by employees who choose this additional insurance.

Brief Summary of Existing Group Life and Health Plan

Life insurance	$10,000
Accidental death and dismemberment	$10,000

Comprehensive major medical:

Maximum benefit	Unlimited*
Deductible	$200 per person; $600 per family
Co-pay provisions	80%–20% of first $4,000; 100% thereafter
Hospital expenses	Paid according to normal co-pay provisions; based on average semiprivate room charge
Surgical expenses	Paid according to normal co-pay provisions; based on usual and customary fees
Supplementary accident benefit	100% of first $100 of covered expenses; balance paid according to normal co-pay provisions
Maternity	Covered as any other illness (for female employees and dependent wives only)
Premium arrangements	Premiums for insurance for employees are fully paid by the employer. Premiums for insurance for dependents are deducted from the paychecks of the employees. Premium classifications for dependents include: (a) children only, (b) spouse only, and (c) spouse and children.

* If your company does not write maximum benefits without limit, a $1 million maximum, or higher, will be considered.

Questionnaire and Bid Forms

Please complete this questionnaire and return it with your proposal. If you answer the questions on a separate sheet, please include the questions together with your answers.

Company   _____

Address _____

            _____

Company Service
  Representative _____

Address   _____

            _____

Telephone   _____

Nearest Claims Paying Office which will Supervise the Payment of Claims:

            _____

Manager   _____

Address   _____

            _____

Telephone   _____

Questions Related to Life Insurance, Accidental Death and Dismemberment Insurance, and Health Insurance

1. Please explain the services the employer may expect from the insurance agent who will receive a commission on this business (if there is an agent who will receive a commission; if none, so state).
2. To what licensed agent do you propose to pay a commission on this business?

   Name:
   Address:

   Telephone:
3. All items quoted shall be in compliance with these specifications. If you are taking exception, indicate those exceptions on company letterhead and attach to this proposal.

Questions Related to Group Health Insurance

4. For what period of time will the premium rates you quote be guaranteed?
5. Please briefly describe the basis on which your company determines health insurance reserves.
6. In the event of termination of the contract with the employer, either on or off the anniversary date, are all unused reserves returned to the policyholder? If so, when are they returned? If not, explain how these reserves are treated.
7. If incurred claims plus your retention and any other charges result in a deficit at the end of a policy year, how would this deficit be treated in the following year?
8. What rate of interest will be credited on reserves that are held for incurred-but-unpaid claims?
9. What would be the approximate dollar change in your retention:
   a. If the ratio of incurred claims to premiums increased by 10 percent?
   b. If the ratio of incurred claims to premium decreased by 10 percent?
10. Do the figures for paid claims or incurred claims in your retention exhibit include any allowance for administrative expense, actuarial expense, overhead expense, or other expense? If so, please explain.
11. Will your contract provide unlimited indemnity under the major medical coverage? If not, please state your maximum limit.
12. Will your company provide financial experience data in the same format as that indicated in the retention exhibits? If not, please

attach a form illustrating the type of report of financial results you propose to make each year.

13. What information will you provide to the employer related to health losses paid under the contract?

14. Please explain how a change from the present insurer will be made without depriving any employees of benefits.

15. Please describe, as you think appropriate, your method of handling claims.

16. If your claims handling procedure does not require the employer to participate in verification of claims and in additional processing of claims, please explain how these matters are handled.

17. Please describe the administrative and accounting procedures the employer must adopt to administer the plan if your company is selected as the carrier.

18. With respect to the anniversary date, when does renewal underwriting take place? When do rate changes (if any) become effective? How much advance notice is given?

Questions Related to Group Life Insurance and Group Accidental Death and Dismemberment Insurance

19. Please describe briefly the basis on which your company determines group life insurance reserves.

20. Please describe briefly the basis on which your company determines group accidental death and dismemberment insurance reserves.

21. In the event of termination of the contract, either on or off the anniversary date, are all unused reserves returned to the policyholder? If so, when are they returned? If not, explain how these reserves are treated.

22. If incurred claims plus your retention and any other charges result in a deficit at the end of a policy year, how would this deficit be treated in the following year?

23. What rate of interest will be credited on any group life insurance reserves and group accidental death and dismemberment insurance reserves that are held by the carrier?

24. Do the figures for paid claims or incurred claims in your retention exhibit include any allowance for administrative expense, actuarial expense, overhead expense, or other expense? If so, please explain.

25. Will your company provide financial experience data in the same format as that indicated in the retention exhibits? If not, please attach a form illustrating the type of report of financial results you propose to make each year.

26. What information will you provide to the employer related to

life insurance losses and to accidental death and dismemberment insurance losses paid under the contract?

27. Please explain how a change from the present carrier will be made without depriving any employees of benefits.

28. Please answer the following questions with regard to the optional life insurance and accidental death and dismemberment insurance.

   a. What would be the monthly premium rates in the following age and sex classifications for the optional group life insurance and accidental death and dismemberment insurance? (If you prefer not to quote rates at this time, please indicate how the rates would be determined.)

Age	Male	Female
30 and under	_____	_____
31–35	_____	_____
36–40	_____	_____
41–45	_____	_____
46–50	_____	_____
51–55	_____	_____
56–60	_____	_____
61–65	_____	_____
66–70	_____	_____

   b. What percentage participation do you require to put the optional insurance into effect?

   c. What other conditions, if any, would you require before placing the optional insurance into effect?

29. With respect to the anniversary date, when does renewal underwriting take place? When do rate changes (if any) become effective? How much advance notice is given?

INSTRUCTIONS FOR COMPLETING RETENTION EXHIBITS*

Retention exhibits are to be completed on the following basis:

1. The number and the amount of paid claims for each of the three years following a change in the contract or the carrier are to be shown on the retention exhibits.

2. Your figures for paid claims and for incurred claims on the retention exhibits should not include any allowance for administrative costs, actuarial costs, or any costs other than the claims. These costs should be included in Item 9 (Expense charges).

3. The entire amount your company plans to pay licensed agents, other than your company's regular employees, should be shown in Item 9.

---

* For illustrative purposes only one exhibit has been included.

Summary of Monthly Premiums—Present Plan (Life and AD&D at $10,000)

Name of Proposing Carrier: _____

	Number of Employees (as of 6/1/81)	Volume	Quoted (per person) Monthly Premium	Monthly Premium
Life insurance	962	_____	_____	_____
AD&D	959	_____	_____	_____
Employee health insurance	954	_____	_____	_____
Spouse only health insurance	76	_____	_____	_____
Child(ren) health insurance	111	_____	_____	_____
Spouse and child(ren) health insurance	101	_____	_____	_____
Employee medicare	16	_____	_____	_____
Dependent medicare	9	_____	_____	_____

Total Monthly premium _____

Total Annual Premium _____

Retention Exhibit—Based on Present Health Insurance Benefits

	First Year	Second Year	Third Year
1. Paid premiums	$600,000**	$750,000	$750,000
2. Pooled premiums			
3. Paid claims	1,600**	2,100	2,100
4. Number of paid claims			
5. Pooled claims			
6. Claim reserve, beginning			
7. Claim reserve, ending			
8. Incurred claims: (3) − (5) − (6) + (7)			
9. Expense charges			
a. Agents' commissions			
b. State premium taxes			
c. Other charges			
d. Credit for interest on reserves*			
Total: (a) + (b) + (c) − (d)			
10. Total of Item 9 (Expense charges) as percentage of Item 1 (Paid premiums)			
11. Credit (or debit) carried over from previous year			
12. Credit (or debit) carried over to following year: (1) − (2) − (8) − (9) ± (11)			

* Include interest on credit carried over from previous year (item 11).
** ABC Insurance Company, the present carrier, will be asked to assume that 2,100 claims will be paid amounting to $750,000 in the first year, since it will be responsible for claims incurred before a change in the contract is made.

Sample Pre-Bid Questionnaires

Insurance Agent/Brokerage House/Consultant Qualifying Questionnaire

Date _____

A. Name of Firm   _____
    Address   _____
                    _____ Zip _____ Phone _____
    Date Established _____

Name and residence address of principals, their experience, and professional qualifications. Attach a detailed resume which should as a minimum include the following information:

    Number of employee benefit accounts and premium levels
    Approximate percentage of accounts by type of insurance

Number of licensed agents _____

Premium volume: _____ Under $500,000
                 _____ $501,000–$1,000,000
                 _____ $1,001,000–$1,500,000
                 _____ $1,501,000–$2,500,000
                 _____ Over $2,500,000

Companies licensed by agent and brokerage houses utilized:

	Group Life	*As Agent*	*As Broker*
1.	_____	_____	_____
2.	_____	_____	_____
3.	_____	_____	_____
	Group Health		
1.	_____	_____	_____
2.	_____	_____	_____
3.	_____	_____	_____
	Group Disability		
1.	_____	_____	_____
2.	_____	_____	_____
3.	_____	_____	_____

Other

1. _____ _____ _____

2. _____ _____ _____

3. _____ _____ _____

Special services available (e.g., loss analysis, claims service, etc.)

In House   *Company or Outside*

_____   _____

_____   _____

_____   _____

_____   _____

If your firm is selected to handle part or all of the group insurance program, who would be responsible for account?

Principal _____

Alternate _____

Clients—Name and approximate annual premium of two (2) largest accounts most similar in each category:

_____

_____

B. Would you be willing to handle part or all of our program on a fee basis, rather than for a commission? On this basis, the services to be performed would be outlined for the particular category of insurance such as:

_____

_____

Company writing errors and omission coverage for you:

_____

Limits: _____ Deductible: _____

Insurance Company Qualifying Questionnaire

PLEASE NOTE: It is the intention of XYZ Company to rebid this group insurance program no sooner than five (5) years. In the past, we have remained with an insurance company for an average of eight (8) years. Our goal is to establish and maintain a long-term professional relationship.

Date _____

A. Name of Insurance Company _____
    Address   _____
               _____ Zip _____Phone _____

B. Please provide copies of the following:
    1. Best's financial rating report for last three years.
    2. Offices that will handle the group claims.
    3. Name of the individual in your company who will be responsible for the account in the event your firm is selected to handle the group insurance program.

C. Briefly describe the annual services you can provide in the following areas:
    1. Claims reporting and analysis.
    2. Cost control.
    3. Evaluation of financing alternatives (e.g., ASO).
    4. Evaluation of plan specifications.

D. With regard to your current operations, briefly summarize your premium volume and number of accounts in group life, health, and disability insurance.
    What percentage of this business is in the same state as XYZ Company?
    (Optional) Provide a list of at least two (2) of your current clients who are in the same size class as XYZ Company.

E. Would you be willing to allow a qualified representative of XYZ Company to negotiate directly with the internal underwriter assigned to this case?

F. Provide any other information relative to the firm which might be pertinent to selection:

    _____

    _____

    _____

    _____

    _____

    _____

    _____

    _____

    _____

G. (Optional) References qualified to judge your ability to provide service and insurance expertise:

_____

_____

_____

_____

_____

CHAPTER 49

An Analytical Framework for the Review of Insurance Bids

DAVID R. KLOCK,
PHYLLIS A. KLOCK,
AND JOSEPH CASEY

In the previous chapter, the process of preparing bid specifications was reviewed. In this chapter, the analysis of group insurance bids and the selection of an appropriate insurance carrier and/or service organization is analyzed. This critical process consists of the following steps:

1. Confirm that all bidders meet minimum requirements and eliminate any nonqualifiers.
2. Evaluate the financial implications of each bid (quantitative factors).
3. Review the policy specifications, claims handling procedures, and loss control services provided by each bidding organization (qualitative factors).
4. Select the best purveyor(s) and negotiate the final details of the group insurance plan.
5. Present your findings and recommendations to the appropriate decision-making body (generally superior officers, executive committee, or board of directors).

MINIMUM REQUIREMENTS

Employers seeking group insurance coverage often require that all bidders meet important minimum requirements, with no exceptions made for nonqualifiers. For example, the employer may require that bidding insurance companies have at least an "A" rating from Bests. Other minimum requirements may be that a qualified local agent or salaried representative is available on a regular basis at all employer locations to service the group and/or that the insurer maintain a full-time claims staff within a specified distance from the employer. Specified minimum requirements typically depend on the size and nature of the employer. For example, a very large corporate employer with a full-time risk management and/or employee benefits professional staff may not perceive the need for a local servicing agent, whereas a local or regional government employer may require all bidders to be domestic insurers and all servicing agents to maintain offices in the same community as the government seat.

FINANCIAL IMPLICATIONS

Assuming that bidders comply with the plan specifications, financial or cash flow implications typically will be the critical variable in selecting among proposed carriers. This analysis often is the subject of considerable confusion because employers do not understand the mathematics and resulting cash flow implications of group insurance proposals and because not all insurers use consistent terminology and methodology in presenting their proposed financial bids.

The confusion may easily result in the selection of an inappropriate bid by an employer who lacks a professional staff capable of fully understanding the financial implications of each bid. Accordingly, an employer without the appropriate internal staff is generally well advised to retain an experienced broker/consultant to review the financial implications of the bids.

Financial analysis of proposed group insurance programs is often considerably more complex than one might initially suspect. If, for example, the proposal under review contemplates an experienced or retrospective rated program, an analyst would be misled by a simple comparison of the standard premium paid at the beginning of the plan year (or monthly). Numerous other critical variables affect the ultimate cash flow cost of such a plan.

The true cost of a group plan can be depicted as follows:

$$\text{Cost} = \text{Claims} + \text{Retention} - \text{Interest return}$$

A thorough analysis of the retention exhibit should allow the risk manager/employee benefits manager or the broker/consultant to determine which bidders have presented the best financial proposal for the employer.

ANALYSIS OF RETENTION

Proposed retention factors are the major financial criteria that should be used to distinguish among bids. The term *retention* refers to that portion of the insurance premium kept by the insurer to cover expenses, pooling charges, risk charges, and/or profit. The part of the retention factor designed to realize a profit for the insurer is typically not an identifiable factor in the retention exhibit but is built into many of the other factors, especially the risk charge. Mutual insurance companies will not have a profit factor as such but will include a contribution to surplus in their risk charge.

Careful analysis of the retention exhibit requires a comparison of the dollars which alternative insurance companies seek to "retain" for their own use through their various charges and those funds which they will credit to the employer in the form of reserves, refunds, and/or investment returns on any premiums paid in advance.

In reviewing alternative retention exhibits, the risk manager/employee benefits manager or the broker/consultant should determine if any inconsistencies are present in the claims expense factors. If all insurers used the assumed claims provided in the bid specifications, the claims expense factor in the various proposals should be comparable. If, on the other hand, insurers were left on their own to estimate incurred claims and claims adjustment costs, significant variations could be expected. Comparable retention illustrations demand that claims assumptions be as close as possible to the specified level, but experience has proven that some bidders use different claims assumptions than those provided in the bid specifications. If such is the case, the "nonconforming" bids must first be adjusted to a claims level consistent with all other bids. If this adjustment is not feasible, the employer may wish to return the bid to the insurer with a request to make the necessary adjustments or to reject the bid from further consideration.

The risk manager/employee benefits manager or the broker/consultant should determine that all bidders have complied with specifications regarding premium quotations. Some insurers will quote abnormally high premiums to produce unusually high dividends or refunds which can then be credited with interest. Such a practice can result in an understatement of the insurer's retention because interest credited to a dividend or refund remains with the insurer and is used to reduce retentions. If this potential distortion is suspected, the bidding insurer should be requested to separately specify the interest credited to dividends.

Bids must be checked to assure insurers have consistently included expenses associated with claims processing in their retentions. Accounting practices relative to the treatment of claims payment expenses vary among insurers. Some insurers add these expenses to paid or incurred claims, while others combine claims payment expenses with the administrative expenses in the retention. The bid of an insurer that has assumed claims payment expenses to be part of the specified incurred claims will understate their retention. If such a problem is detected, the employer should request the insurer to provide the specific claims payment expense figures in order to adjust the retention illustration.

The manner in which bidding insurers have treated pooling charges should likewise be checked for consistency. Pooling charges are essentially a retention item because none of the pooling charges will be returned to the employer in the form of either dividends or retrospective rate credits. If the request for bids did not specify that pooling charges be itemized, some bidding insurance companies might have included these charges as a part of paid or incurred claims. The retentions of such a carrier would thus be significantly understated.

Premium taxes are another item which should be illustrated on a common basis. Unless specific instructions were included in the request for bids, some insurers might have depicted premium taxes on the basis of gross premiums, while other underwriters could have illustrated them as premiums minus anticipated dividends or other rate credits. These potential sources of retention exhibit distortion require adjustments on a case-by-case basis.

In summary, consistent retention illustrations can form the basis for determining the premium dollars that will be returned to the organization and the amount that will remain with the insurance company. This analysis must review not simply the absolute dollar amounts but the timing of the cash flows as well.

BID COST MATRIX

Table 49-1 provides an illustration of a quantitative analysis of group insurance bids. This type of analysis is commonly referred to as a bid-cost matrix. Section I of the matrix summarizes the basic assumptions the companies were requested to use in preparing their bids. Assumed claims levels have been provided in the bid specifications in order to increase the likelihood that the cost figures provided by the various insurance companies will be determined on a consistent basis.

Section II outlines the monthly rates quoted by each of five bidders. Premium bids for each line of coverage are separated into pooled and nonpooled premiums. This information is needed to provide details for the stop-loss provision. Section III provides both the retention factors quoted by each insurance company and the basis or method used by these bidders in calculating this factor.

Section IV gives the variable cost and the fixed cost for each bid based on the assumed claims and premium data appearing in Sections II and III. Most importantly, this section provides the critical "claims/cost ratio." Typically, the higher this ratio, the better the bid. On this basis, bids 1 and 5 appear to be the most attractive.

Section V responds to a question often asked by the ultimate decision body (CEO, board of directors, etc.): "What if assumed claims varied from the levels assumed in Section I?" Based on claims ranging from 70 percent to 130 percent of those used in Section I, total costs are calculated for each bid. In addition to summarizing the range of possible costs, Section V also provides the risk manager/employee benefits manager with the maximum costs for each bid and the level of claims where the maximum cost is obtained. If feasible, the risk manager/employee benefits manager is well advised to include this data in the cost matrix provided to executive management.

Table 49–1
ABC & Associates Group Insurance Bid Comparison Annual Cost

SECTION I

Life insurance in force	$37,500,000	Employee health claims	$390,000
AD&D insurance in force	37,500,000	Dependent health claims	350,000
Monthly covered payroll	2,083,333	Employee life claims	10,000
Covered employees[a]	800	Total claims	$750,000
Covered dependent units[a]	650		

SECTION II

Quote No.	1	2	3	4	5
Company	Longwood Life	Orlando Life	Sanford Life	Deland Life	Oviedo Life

Monthly rates (as quoted by purveyors):

	Longwood Life	Orlando Life	Sanford Life	Deland Life	Oviedo Life
Pooled Premium					
Life rate[c]	$ .275	$ .56	$ .322	$ .28	$ .1995
AD&D rate[c]	.055	.062	.06	.0598	.07
LTD[d]	.325	.581	.434	.55	.495
Employee health[e]	1.40	1.00	1.10	1.10	1.92
Dependent health[e]	2.05	2.00	1.95	1.65	1.92
Nonpooled premium (aggregate stop loss):					
Life rate	$ .28	$ 0[b]	$ .44	$ .40	$ .39
Employee health	36.25	40.00	50.00	42.27	35.00
Dependent health	52.37	51.50	72.25	52.65	39.50

SECTION III

Retention based on:	Longwood Life	Orlando Life	Sanford Life	Deland Life	Oviedo Life
Claims		6.00	.055	.07	5.25
Employees					
Aggregate	.065				

SECTION IV

Cost:

Pooled Premium					
Life	$123,750	$252,000	$144,900	$126,000	$89,775
AD&D	24,750	2,900	27,000	26,910	31,500
LTD	81,250	145,250	108,500	137,500	123,750
Employee health	13,440	9,600	10,560	10,560	18,432
Dependent health	15,990	15,600	15,210	12,870	14,976
Total fixed cost	$259,180	$450,350	$306,170	$313,840	$278,433
Claims cost	$750,000	$740,000[b]	$750,000	$750,000	$750,000
Retention	57,362	57,600	41,250	52,500	50,400
Total variable cost	$807,362	$797,600	$791,250	$802,500	$800,400
Total cost	$1,066,542	$1,247,950	$1,097,420	$1,116,340	$1,078,833
Claims/cost ratio	0.70	0.59	0.68	0.67	0.70

SECTION V

Cost at other claims levels:

70%	$841,542	$1,025,950	$872,420	$891,340	$853,833
80%	916,542	1,099,950	947,420	966,340	928,833
90%	991,542	1,175,950	1,022,420	1,041,340	1,003,833
110%	1,141,542	1,236,050	1,172,420	1,191,340	1,098,033
120%	1,141,666	1,236,050	1,247,420	1,266,340	1,098,033
130%	1,141,666	1,236,050	1,322,420	1,310,302	1,098,033
Maximum Cost	1,141,666	1,236,050	1,547,720	1,310,302	1,098,033

[a] Employee and dependent units eligible for Medicare supplements are excluded from consideration.
[b] Included in pooled premium.
[c] Life and AD&D rates are quoted per $1,000 face amount.
[d] LTD rates are quoted per $100 of monthly benefit.
[e] Employee and dependent health rates are quoted per unit.

QUALITATIVE FACTORS

In the previous section, the detailed financial or cash flow aspects of the premium bids provided by each insurance company were reviewed. While this analysis is extremely important, several reasons exist why a satisfactory analysis of bids must include far more than a consideration of financial aspects. Premiums and retention factors are guaranteed for only a short period of time (usually 12 to 18 months at best). Furthermore, as discussed in Chapter 48, a change of companies after only one or two years is generally undesirable although not always unconscionable. The employer and its broker/consultant must carefully consider the most important qualitative factors associated with the alternative bids and choose an insurer that has a verified reputation for the desired quality of service. The selection of an insurer with a questionable service capability or contract specifications typically is a mistake. Minor differences in retention charges do not justify acceptance if day-to-day difficulties concerning administration and claims service are to be expected.

The first step in analyzing the qualitative aspects of the bids is to verify that all proposals have complied with the minimum coverage provisions outlined in the bid specifications. A valid bid comparison is possible only if all proposals are consistent for both the type of program proposed (e.g., a comprehensive major medical plan or a basic hospital-surgical plan with a supplementary major medical) and such basic coverage elements as limits on the maximum lifetime benefits, deductible levels, co-pay provisions, maximum employee out-of-pocket amounts, and scheduled versus "reasonable and customary" coverage of medical expenses.

When applicable, the question of the length of any rate guarantees must be addressed. Differences among the bids often arise on the issue of both initial and renewal guarantees of premiums and retention factors.

The risk manager/employee benefits manager or the broker/consultant should carefully review any descriptive literature provided with the bids. Listings of definitions, covered expenses, exclusions, and limitations may reveal significant benefit differences. Variations sometimes exist, for example, in the definitions of the terms *hospital* and *physician*. Some plans may include coverage for second surgical opinions, home health care, ambulatory surgical facilities, nursing home care, hospitalization in a "progressive care unit," well-baby care, treatment of mental illness, and/or treatment of alcoholism and drug-related illnesses. Other plans may provide exceptional rehabilitation benefits. A review of the conversion provisions and of the provisions of any Medicare supplement included in the programs is also in order. For example, the analyst should know if a "carve-out" or a "coordination" approach is being utilized in the Medicare supplement.

In reviewing the qualitative areas of plan coverage, the risk manager/employee benefits manager should attempt to minimize the aggregate inconvenience for employees and should be conscious that the demographics and financial needs of the employee group will be important to the acceptance of any change in the group insurance plan. For example, if many of the employees reside in rural areas and receive their primary care from medical professionals other than M.D.s (e.g., D.O.s, chiropractors, and/or nurse practitioners), any restrictions on benefits for services provided by these medical professionals would be likely to create significant employee discontent. The best analytical decisions concerning the cost of alternative bids can be in error if the decision process fails to consider the cost of extensive employee dissatisfaction with a proposed change. Employee representatives should therefore participate in the group insurance reevaluation process from its beginning. As these representatives become aware of the cost/benefit relationship of various alternative plans, they may foster active employee approval of any proposed plan changes.

The risk manager/employee benefits manager or the broker/consultant should attempt to predict whether the various insurance companies will render a satisfactory level of claims and administrative service. Some questions which might be asked here include:

1. What is the average projected turnaround time for claims payments?
2. Are local claims facilities available? If not, will the insurer provide a toll-free telephone number or accept collect calls on claims inquiries?
3. What will be the extent of employer involvement in the verification or other processing of claims? Will this require the employer to hire or train additional staff?
4. What administrative and/or accounting procedures must the employer adopt to facilitate such matters as premium collections, enrollments, and terminations?
5. How satisfied with programs underwritten by the carrier in question are other employers with similar demographic characteristics?

Finally, the risk manager/employee benefits manager or the broker/consultant will want to evaluate the potential flexibility with which the alternative insurers could respond to major changes in the employer organization and/or to employer desires to consider alternative financial arrangements at some point in the future. This analysis is particularly relevant if, for example, the employer's five-year goals include acquisitions, mergers, or a major plant relocation. Alternatively, the employer might have determined that an ASO contract or a self-insurance arrangement did not suit its current needs but may wish to consider these alternatives in two to three years. The employer may place a high value on an ability to effectively respond to changes such as these without undergoing the potential disruption of a change in insurance carrier.

NEGOTIATING WITH CARRIER

Based on the analysis of the financial and qualitative implications of alternative bids, the company manager charged with responsibility for group insurance will select that carrier most compatible to the needs of employer and employees alike. In many situations, this company manager draws solely upon his or her own skills and experience in making the selection, and guidance from outside the company is not sought. In other situations, the decision is aided by technical advice from a qualified broker/ consultant. Regardless of the manner in which this preliminary selection is reached, two final steps usually are required: (1) detailed negotiation with the selected underwriter and (2) presentation of the recommendations to the appropriate decision-making body, be it the CEO, an executive committee, or the board of directors (as is common in many smaller- or medium-sized companies). The sequence of these steps may vary. Some risk managers/employee benefits managers prefer to obtain a consensus on the selection of a particular insurance company prior to initiating final negotiations with the underwriter; others attempt to wrest all available concessions from the carrier before presenting their findings for a final decision.

This section deals with the final negotiation process, and the final discussion considers the critical ingredients of an effective presentation to the ultimate decision makers. The importance of the final negotiation process rests on two assumptions. First, the cost and provisions of a group insurance program are in fact negotiable. Armed with knowledge of the very complex technical aspects of a group program, a competent broker/consultant or risk manager/employee benefits manager can win concessions from the insurance company that will benefit the corporation and its employees. Second, specific areas in the bid of the selected insurer may not be as competitive as those found in other bids. If these discrepancies are pointed out to the underwriter, he or she may be willing to reevaluate and improve this particular portion of the bid. This process takes on added importance if the insurance company with the "lowest" bid is not that selected by the risk manager/employee benefits manager and the broker/consultant. The "lowest" bidder may not be chosen for a variety of reasons relating to service considerations or to long-term costs not immediately evident in the bids. If this selection is going to "pass muster" with the CEO, the executive committee, or the board, all possible cost and coverage concessions must be obtained from this carrier.

The first step in the negotiating process is to select the proper "players." The decision as to whether the risk manager/employee benefits manager or the broker/consultant will handle direct negotiations with the underwriter is often a difficult one. Allowing the broker/consultant to take the lead in this area often proves more efficient. The broker/consultant is usually more familiar with the behavioral aspects of negotiations with specific underwriters; he or she may also have more leverage with the carrier. Should a decision be reached that the broker/consultant will primarily handle the negotiations, the risk manager/employee benefits manager should clearly understand the areas to be negotiated and should be prepared to use his or her influence with the insurer when and if called upon by the broker/ consultant.

Whomever is chosen, the negotiator must be familiar with the terminology used by the particular insurance company. Most home office underwriters converse in terms that may be unique to their company. In fact, many of the common group insurance terms (like *retro*) have different meanings depending on the insurer in question. An ability to speak the appropriate lingo is crucial if one is seeking financial concessions from an insurer. This simple but important step can reduce significant confusion.

The negotiator(s) for the employer must develop a strategy for quickly directing the attention of home office underwriters to the items where profit and/or excess interest may be hidden and thus where concessions may be obtained. This strategy often involves a list of very probing questions that go beyond the routine areas such as reducing premium margins, releasing incurred but not reported reserves, or negotiating commission levels.

Peter B. O'Brien, President of Johnson & Higgins of Colorado, has provided an excellent list of 10 very specific questions to use as the basis for final negotiations with a group insurance underwriter.[1]

1. Why should a C&R charge (conservation and review) be levied against our account when we have a 10-year service plaque hanging on the wall?

2. Why is your computer programmed to "load" our triangle chart when the results are supposed to represent our actual claims runout?

3. Why can't our "risk charge" be scaled based on our loss ratio rather than on a flat percentage of our premium?

4. Why, after years of consistency in policy language for disability payments, is there a wide inconsistency in percentage of face value claim charges?

5. Why can't we be presented with our state premium tax bill and eliminate the tax escrow account?

6. Why have you been lenient with customers whose premiums are delinquent by a few months while we are charged prevailing interest rates when late by only one month?

7. Why can't our pooling "point" and "factor" be adjusted to reflect our class of business and experience, rather than using overall company tables and rates that haven't been updated in years?

8. We hear lots of talk about severely escalating health care trend factors, but where is the offsetting, advance credit, life deflation factor?

9. Why does a financial accounting have to occur every 12 months? Can't we have custom rates and retention factors to coincide with our collective bargaining periods?

10. Can't we define paid claims as money that has actually been withdrawn from your account rather than amounts on claims forms?

---

[1] Peter B. O'Brien, "Negotiating Lower Costs for Group Insurance Plans," *Risk Management,* December 1978, pp. 34–38.

The foregoing questions are illustrative only. Some of these questions obviously may not be relevant in certain cases, while other questions of similar detail and nature may be more appropriate for other groups. The point is that the use of very specific questions significantly enhances the ability of negotiators for the employer to obtain all valid concessions. The underwriter should be allowed sufficient time (usually several weeks) to evaluate the case and to either agree to the requests or to propose alternative adjustments. The impact of the underwriter's decisions must, of course, be evaluated prior to a presentation to the appropriate decision makers.

PRESENTATION TO DECISION MAKERS

The risk manager/employee benefits manager typically will be required to make a presentation on the group insurance reevaluation process to a top management decision maker or committee. This presentation has taken on increased importance in recent years as high level executives have become more attentive to cost savings that may be realized in the employee benefits area. Rapid escalation of the costs of employee benefits (and especially of group insurance) means group insurance decisions no longer constitute a relatively minor decision. This phenomenon is compounded by a rapid rise of the cost of money. Faced with continuing high prime interest rates, executives have become very conscious of the need to optimize the management of scarce and very costly cash flows. CEOs and other high-level executives have decided to periodically review and influence group insurance decisions in the hopes of more effectively managing required cash flows.

The following outline suggests the critical items that should be communicated during the presentation to top management:

1. State the objectives that dictated and influenced the decision to re-market the group insurance program. What financial and/or employee benefit goals were to be achieved by the rebidding process?
2. Identify any weaknesses in the current group insurance contract or carrier and specify the steps in the bidding process that are aimed at avoiding these same weaknesses in any new program or insurance company.
3. Identify any restrictions imposed by top management on the use of certain alternative financial arrangements with an insurance company (e.g., self-insurance was or was not to be considered) and on the use of specific carriers, agents, or broker/consultants.
4. Identify the markets (insurance companies or self-funding service organizations) that have been approached, the responses received, and the bids that were considered qualified and responsive to the needs of the employer. The decision makers will want to know that a thorough market test was conducted and that all qualified and competitive insur-

ers had an opportunity to provide bids. If the decision makers perceive that the market test was less than complete, they may require a reexamination of other alternative purveyors.

5. Present the bid matrix (see Table 49–1), and outline the strengths and weaknesses of the individual bids.

6. Present the specific recommendation and the supporting logic.

7. Try to anticipate potential questions and deal with them in the presentation. For example, it was noted earlier that the decision makers are likely to ask why the bid specifications stipulated a specific level of claims be assumed in the preparation of the bids and how alternative loss assumptions would have affected the bid matrix.

CHAPTER 50

Implementing and Reviewing Employee Benefit Plans

JOSEPH D. YOUNG

THE IMPLEMENTING PROCESS

The process of implementing new benefits and amendments to existing employee benefit plans contains five essential steps, which are: (1) approval of top management (including board of directors); (2) development of plan specifications for bidding (where appropriate) and analysis of proposals; (3) legal document preparation, including government filing requirements; (4) preparation and distribution of announcement and enrollment materials; (5) development of administration procedures and manuals. The order in which these steps are taken may vary depending upon each organization's makeup and style. No matter what the order, each of these steps needs to be addressed during the implementation process.

Approval of Top Management

Once the organization's employee benefit reviewer(s) have adopted recommendations for new plans and amendments, final approval by top management, (unless the committee reviewer has been given the authority to move ahead) is necessary. In many companies today (since ERISA), a committee appointed by the board of directors is charged with the responsibility of ensuring that all benefit plans and proposals comply with ERISA. In some cases, the committee is named Plan Administrator as defined by ERISA—in other cases such committees merely serve to oversee the benefits function on behalf of the board to assure ERISA compliance. When such committee(s) exist, new plans and amendments should, of course, be presented to them as part of the implementation process. This may not be a distinctly separate step, depending on the organization—in some cases all levels of management may be parties to the review process so that when alternatives are adopted the next step in the implementation process can be taken. This may be the point at which board resolutions are prepared for adoption. The drafting of such resolutions is, of course, a task assigned to legal counsel and may not be done until all plan documents are drafted.

Development of Plan Specifications

In a situation where the new benefits are to be put out for bid by insurance carriers or other providers of services, it is critical that very precise plan specifications be drafted. This is an area where competent, impartial consulting help is invaluable. This is also the point at which the benefit manager must be assured that the consultant has "no stake" in the choice of carriers or providers. This is sometimes difficult to assess if the consultant's firm is one which accepts commissions from carriers as a part of its compensation. In such cases, even though a consultant is objective, the question always seems to be in the back of one's mind as to "how objective?" Of course, there are many excellent consulting firms which work strictly on a fee basis. This approach, at least, eliminates the question of financial motivation in the selection process.

Contract and underwriting provisions for insured plans including group insurance and pension plans can vary subtly from carrier to carrier   so too can the reserving and rating techniques used. Thus, the specifications drafted and presented to the various bidders should be as inclusive of all items of contractual concern as possible. This approach also helps to ensure that all bidders respond to the same questions—those which you the buyer deem to be important and not only those which they the sellers wish to emphasize.

Once specifications are completed and the bidders are selected, they should all be sent the same data, mailed at the same time, and with the same deadline for reply. To assure that none of the bidders is placed at a disadvantage, it is wise to contact them beforehand to (1) determine that they are truly interested in submitting a bid; (2) ascertain exactly who in their company should be the recipient of the specifications; and (3) be sure that they know and understand your "ground rules." To avoid giving one or more bidders an unfair advantage, it should be clearly stated and adhered to that the bids received after the deadline will not be considered.

Analysis of the proposals once received also is a critical point. It can be as complex and as interesting as the preparation of the specifications. It is important to make certain you verify for yourself the promises made in proposals. For example, one company decided to change from a conventional group insurance arrangement to self-funding, and also sought to enter into an administrative services only (ASO) contract with one of the bidding carriers. More than a half-dozen carriers including two of the prepaid medical provider organizations were asked to submit proposals. Since the employer company already had decided to self-fund the medical program, the real issues were quality and cost of administrative and claims services. Each carrier was allowed to present its proposal in writing and to also meet face to face with the benefit staff, the consultant, and other internal decision makers. Subsequent to these meetings but before a final decision was made, the benefit manager and selected staff members also visited the site of each carrier's claims processing unit. These visits were key in establishing the priority of choices based on the claims service to be provided. It can be very revealing to visit the site where the work will be done, to see and talk to the people and to see the equipment used and the atmosphere in which your company's claims work will be handled. In this case, after the visit, one of the carriers withdrew its bid because it felt the disorganized atmosphere viewed during the tour of its claims facility simply refuted the position it took in its proposal in promising quality claims service. The point is when you are buying a service, you should see first-hand how the service commitments will be met. This is especially critical because employees' perceptions about benefit plans can be affected by the quality of claims service they receive.

Because the relationship with a group insurance carrier (whether fully insured or an administrative services only arrangement) is so much a part of the very framework of personnel relationships, the design and implementations of these benefits is concerned with a myriad of human relationships. Hence, the atmosphere created by the carrier's staff of personnel who deals with the employer's plan is very important. There must be a commitment and a spirit of true service to the employer and its employees. The old line of a dogmatic and legalistic approach by carriers and others who administer employee benefits is simply not acceptable, and during this phase of implementation these concerns must be addressed by the employer. It has been proven that a benefit plan with lesser benefit levels but quality-level, employee-oriented claims service receives higher regard by employees than does one which pays higher levels of benefits with poor service, long delays, and incorrect benefit determinations.

Legal Document Preparation

When the time arrives to prepare legal documents, the early involvement of legal counsel as a member of the review committee is essential. Even if the company uses outside counsel for drafting these documents, the time spent in the review process by the inside legal counsel should make the document preparation go much smoother. Working with a clear set of benefit objectives should be most helpful to legal counsel in preparing plan instruments, trust agreements, and enrollment forms as necessary to implement new plans or provisions.

Pension Plans. If a group insurance or pension contract is involved, the insurance company prepares the plan document; even so, the employer's legal counsel should review the provisions of the instrument. Even though the insurance company has plan documents preprinted with the provisions having been predetermined, the employer's attorney(s) must review these forms and determine how appropriate they are for the plan design intended.

In a situation where the new plan or provisions do not involve an insurance carrier, the employer's attorney may have the assignment of drafting the plan documents alone. While the attorney has the drafting responsibility, the remaining professionals on the employer's team (i.e., the consultant and the actuary) should also provide input and review of the documents before they are finally adopted. This approach helps to ensure that the many administrative complexities imposed by ERISA and other regulations are addressed prior to full implementation.

Other legal documents may include (1) board and/or stockholders' resolutions, (2) trust agreements, and (3) employee enrollment forms. In the case of enrollment forms, even though they must meet legal requirements and so on, their design should be coordinated with other announcements and communications styles.

Self-Funded Health and Welfare Plans. The review process may very well result in a commitment to self-fund all or a portion of a welfare plan. While this decision can be a design and a funding issue, it also is an administration and an implementation issue.

Implementing a self-funded plan requires that the employer perform many responsibilities which might otherwise be done by a carrier. These include but are not limited to:

1. Drafting the plan, including a claims review process.
2. Drafting the trust document and related trust operational procedures.
3. Drafting employees' enrollment and informational and procedural forms, manuals, and documents.
4. Establishing a separate checking account from which claims will be paid.
5. Arranging for stop-loss protection (if appropriate).
6. Developing Summary Plan Descriptions.

Much of the new-found employer responsibility is legal in nature—thus the involvement of legal staff representatives in the review process pays dividends at the time of implementation.

Filing with Government Agencies. The regulatory environment of employee benefit plans was discussed in Chapter 3. There are, however, certain aspects of these regulatory requirements which must be addressed during the implementation phase to ensure timely compliance. The areas to be addressed are (1) obtaining an advance determination letter from the IRS for pension plan changes; (2) filing of a Summary of Material Modification in cases where an existing plan is being changed significantly; (3) in the case of certain capital accumulation plans adopted by public corporations, the Securities and Exchange Commission (SEC) has certain requirements regarding registration which should be addressed in the implementation process. The major portion of the regulatory reporting requirements dictate timing which substantially follows the implementation step. Even so, benefit planners and their legal counsel must be aware of those requirements which must be met early in the implementation phase.

Announcement and Enrollment Materials

An important step in the implementation of new benefit plans or changes is the preparation of (1) announcement pieces or letters to employees and managers; (2) administrative guidelines and manuals for supervisors and managers; (3) the enrollment materials and procedure. The actual design of these items and a plan for disseminating them are projects for which help should be obtained from communications specialists (especially in large organizations); but getting it done is an item for the implementation phase.

In most organizations, new benefit plans are announced in a letter from either the president or the top personnel executive. Regardless of who signs the letter, the organization should recognize that as the first news to employees of the new plan or improvements the letter must be drafted carefully. This is the stage where the best communications experts the organization has should be used to obtain the proper mileage out of this announcement.

It often is advisable to prepare and send confidential advance notification to managers and supervisors about what is coming. This gives them the opportunity to be "in the know" about these matters and also gives them time to prepare for the initial questions employees will ask after receiving the announcement letter.

If supervisors and managers are to be involved in the enrollment process, the confidential advance notice is more critical, and also clearly defined procedures should be provided to them in advance of the enrollment date.

Enrollment materials (i.e., descriptive literature and cards which include payroll deduction authorizations) are necessary, and good design calls for a plan that ties all of these items together to look like a "family" of literature. In addition to the need for enrollment materials to be well designed from an aesthetic point of view, there must be a view towards their use in the administration of the plan once implemented. Thus, the enrollment materials design should be done in conjunction with representatives from the staff of day-to-day administrators. This includes the payroll and accounting departments since they must also provide some administrative services once the plan is installed. It is amazing how much more effectively new plans can be implemented and later administered if all interested parties are given the opportunity to be a part of the planning and design of forms, procedures and manuals, etc., during the implementation phase. When all concerned are included early on, it becomes "our plan or program" and all have a stake in it.

Record-Keeping and Reporting

The subject of record-keeping and reporting is discussed in Chapter 44 on administration. It is important that implementation is done with an eye and concern toward record-keeping and reporting requirements. Consideration must be given to the electronic data processing requirements such as (1) the data base needed; (2) the system's input requirements; and (3) the reports to be generated. Many of these concerns and the related elements may already be a part of the current data processing system, and at this point the need may be only to ensure that necessary reports can be formatted and reviewed when needed. Facing these issues during the implementation process will make the subsequent administration and reporting processes much simpler. It also should assist in developing the information needed to perform future reviews of the benefit package.

REVIEWING EMPLOYEE BENEFIT PLANS

Establishing Objectives

An organization's overall philosophy about employee benefits and where they fit in the total compensation program should be established as an initial step before new benefit plans or changes in plans are implemented. An effective benefits package is part of the total compensation program which should be designed to meet specified objectives of the employer and also help to meet the needs and desires of employees. These objectives are not always as compatible as would be desired; hence, a need exists for the company's management to step back from the present benefit plans, rethink existing policy, and establish a posture for the future. Through this approach, a benefit program can emerge that implements the company's philosophy or objectives, rather than one that is a hodge-podge because it is merely a reaction to recommendations which come either from inside or outside the organization.

Management Review Committee

From the organization's viewpoint, one very effective way to review benefit plans, develop philosophy, and establish objectives is to appoint a committee of senior managers with the benefits manager as the lead person or chairperson. The size of the committee is optional but should include representatives from various areas of the organization. An example of one such committee would include (1) the controller, (2) the personnel executive, (3) the marketing executive, (4) the manufacturing executive, (5) the legal counsel, and (6) the benefits manager. Essentially, the committee makeup should be representative of the total organization without making it too cumbersome. The objective is to obtain individuals who have broad backgrounds and responsibilities so that a diversity of attitudes can be represented. This committee should be able to perform an in-depth study of the current program and develop a company philosophy themselves or to present it to top management for adoption.

If the company uses an outside benefits consultant, this process usually is more effective if the consultant is included in the meetings and used as a resource for the committee. The consultant can be helpful in supplying an outside perspective along with knowledge of what is being done by other organizations and generally what can be done. The consultant also can provide data on current trends in benefits, the status of legislation and proposed regulations, etc. Considering the proliferation of regulations and legislation in this area, it can be vital to the process.

Review Considerations

In its discussion of benefit goals and objectives, the committee should give consideration to some of the following issues and questions:

1. The organization's attitude toward its employees—its role as an employer. Are there social responsibilities to be considered?
2. What should be the relationship of benefits to direct compensation?
3. The organization's attitudes regarding retirement, survivor benefits, health care protection, etc.
4. Attitudes regarding forms and levels of survivor and retirement benefits.
5. To what extent is retirement security the responsibility of the company? The government? The individual employee?
6. In establishing benefit levels, should recognition be given to:
   a. Variations in length of service?
   b. Variations in pay level?
   c. Variations in levels of responsibility?
7. Which of the following is to be considered in determining the level of retirement income? Base salary? Bonuses? Overtime? Sales incentive? Other?
8. How important is competitive practice? In the industry? In the geographic location? In other industries?
9. Generally, how comprehensive should the benefits program be?

Certainly there are other issues and questions which the committee should address in this process. The idea is to achieve consensus on the issues addressed from which written benefit objectives can be prepared.

Analyzing Current Plans

Once the management review committee has completed the organization's statement of benefit objectives and it is adopted by top management, the committee should begin to determine to what extent the existing plans meet these objectives.

Some of the useful tools available to use in the analysis include:

1. Surveys conducted by the benefits staff, the consulting firm, and other organizations, such as The Conference Board, Chamber of Commerce of the United States, and others.
2. Comparative analysis (available from your group insurance carrier) of claims versus charges made for medical plans—also, the carrier(s) can and should provide analysis of how your plan benefits compare to the usual customary and reasonable (UCR) charges by geographic location, and essentially show the effectiveness of the current health care package.
3. Many benefit consulting firms today have their own very sophisticated benefits measurement tools which are helpful in this process. Some popular benefits measurement programs are:
    a. Benefits Index.
    b. Benefit Value Comparison.
    c. Benval.
4. Projected pension benefits payable from the current pension and capital accumulation plans.

Employee Sensing

During the review process, modern day management committees and benefit managers like to include in their consideration the views and perceptions employees have about their benefits. These views are best obtained by means of employee sensing. The sensing process has considerable value to the organization when its communications program is being developed; hence, internal communications specialists should be helpful in developing the sensing format. The sensing can be done formally with professionally drafted questionnaires, using third-party interviewers or by conducting meetings with employee groups or individuals in open guided discussions. It also can be achieved on a much less formal basis by asking employees to return postcards with indications of their benefit concerns and views. If formal sensing is to be done, consideration should be given to including spouses in the process. Retirement and survivor benefits affect spouses directly, and their input can be important. Also, the health care plans often are utilized more frequently by dependents than by employees, so that their views and perceptions should be significant when it comes to plan design or amendments.

The sensing must be done in such a way that employees understand management wants their views but that final decisions regarding benefits must necessarily be made by management. A key point in the sensing process is to avoid raising employees' expectations that some new benefit or changes are forthcoming.

Having measured the effectiveness of current plans compared to stated objectives, and having received input from employees and spouses, the review process should now be giving shape and direction to what needs to be done in the future. Moreover, the committee or benefits reviewer(s) should be able to establish priorities for benefit changes; i.e., immediate versus intermediate and long-term needs.

During the sensing process it may be discovered that employee's perceptions and management's benefit objectives are not totally compatible. If this is the case, the benefit planners need to address how to achieve compatibility. This may require that management's objectives be adjusted, or it may indicate a need to improve the communications process to better educate and inform employees.

Developing Alternative Plans or Amendments

Assuming that portions of the company's current benefit program are not consistent with its newly develoved objectives, the next step in the review process is to develop detailed descriptions of suggested revisions or of new plans and the pros and cons of each. This is a point where the professionals (i.e., consultant, actuary, and attorney) will be helpful in developing alternatives by reflecting on prior experience, what other employers are doing and the latest trends, and by acting as a sounding board regarding the choices. The actuary (who may also be the consultant) can provide cost information and also act as a sounding board regarding cost/ benefit trade-offs of the choices. The attorney simply provides legal direction, keeping in mind the many laws and regulations which affect employee benefits, and thus keeps the design choices on legally "safe" grounds. Together the professionals should perform not as decision makers but as a team to provide as much knowledge and information as possible so that the most intelligent and appropriate decisions can be made for the organization and its employees.

The final product of the committee or benefits reviewer(s) is a list of recommended alternative plans or amendments to existing plans with suggested time frames for implementation and related costs of each change. There may also be recommendations on the benefits communication process for the future. At this point the committee has developed a program of objectives and specific plans and amendments to be considered for adoption to meet those objectives. The next step is to implement these plans and objectives.

CHAPTER 51

Communication and Disclosure of Employee Benefit Plans

THOMAS MARTINEZ
AND ROBERT V. NALLY

REASONS FOR THE COMMUNICATION OF EMPLOYEE BENEFITS

The communication and disclosure of employee benefits to plan participants and their beneficiaries, in addition to fulfilling the reporting requirements of the federal law, is essential to the efficient operation of any benefit plan. The reasons for this can be categorized into two broad groupings: the legal requirements and the managerial requirements.

Legal Requirements

The Internal Revenue Code (IRC) has required from the very beginning of qualified pension or profit-sharing plans that such plans be in writing and communicated by appropriate means to covered individuals. Thus, for such retirement plans to receive the desired favorable tax treatment, communication is essential. Moreover, the Employee Retirement Income Security Act (ERISA) includes specific reporting and disclosure requirements covering private employee pension and welfare plans. All types of qualified pension and profit-sharing plans are subject to the disclosure requirements of ERISA regardless of the number of participants in the plan. Some nonqualified retirement plans also are subject to the reporting and disclosure requirements. Additionally, certain welfare plans providing such benefits as life insurance, medical expense, disability income, and other employee benefits are subject to the ERISA reporting and disclosure requirements.

The ERISA reporting and disclosure regulations provide for three categories of information. First, certain documents must be filed with the appropriate government agencies at required times and made available to employees. Second, certain information must be distributed automatically to plan participants under each plan and to beneficiaries receiving benefits under each plan. Third, certain specified information must be given to plan participants upon written request and/or made available for examination at the principal office of the plan administrator and at other locations convenient for participants. These three categories of information cover five general groups of activities: (1) annual plan maintenance, (2) ongoing plan maintenance, (3) the installation of a new plan, (4) revisions in an existing plan, and (5) the termination of a plan.

The annual plan maintenance activities that must be reported and/or disclosed include reporting the financial activity of a plan for the current year and payment of plan termination insurance premiums to the federal government. They also cover providing employees with a summary of the financial activities of the plan for the year and providing terminated vested employees with a status report on their individual benefits under a pension plan. The reporting and disclosure requirements concerning these activities are set forth in Exhibit 51-1.

The ongoing maintenance activities subject to the reporting and disclosure requirements basically cover situations and activities related to individual participants and employee requests for information. The federal government generally need not be notified of these matters. The only ongoing maintenance activity requiring notification of the federal government is when there is a reportable event; that is, a change in a plan or its activities that might lead to a termination of the plan by the Pension Benefit Guaranty Corporation (PBGC). The array of activities within this grouping and the applicable reporting and disclosure requirements are set forth in Exhibit 51-2.

New plan activities involve three major tasks. All participants must be furnished with a summary description of the plan. Application must be made to the Internal Revenue Service (IRS) for favorable tax qualification of a plan. Also, participants must be notified in advance of qualification that application has been made for such status. The specific activities within this group together with the accompanying reporting and disclosure requirements are set forth in Exhibit 51-3.

Revised plan activities cover cases of the merger, consolidation, or transfer of the assets of an existing plan. These actions require the filing of a new application for tax-qualified status and notification of participants in advance of the application. Any material modification that occurs in a plan also is classified as a revised plan activity. Moreover, any reportable event that might lead to termination of a plan under revision is treated as a revision activity too. The details of the reporting and disclosure requirements for plan revision activities are set forth in Exhibit 51-4.

Plan termination activities must be supported by notice to the PBGC of the intention to terminate a plan, advance notice to the participants of this intention, and an application to the IRS for determination of the matter. A terminal report also is required. The reporting and disclosure requirements concerning these activities are set forth in Exhibit 51-5.

Exhibit 51-1
Annual Plan Maintenance Activities

	Required for Covered:			To Participants:		To Following Government Agency	Due Date
	Pension Plans		Welfare Plans	Automatically	On Request		
	Defined Contribution	Defined Benefit					
1. Annual Report (Form 5500)	Yes	Yes	Yes	No	Yes	IRS	Last day of 7th month after end of plan year[1]
2. PBGC Annual Premium Filing (Form PBGC-1)	No	Yes	No	No	No	PBGC	Last day of 7th month after end of plan year
3. Summary Annual Report of Benefits	Yes	Yes	Yes	Yes	No	None	Last day of 9th month after end of plan year (or 2 months after extended Form 5500 due date, if later)
4. Statement of Benefits to Terminated Vested Participants	Yes	Yes	No	Yes	No	None	By time for filing Form 5500[2]

[1] Extension available up to:

9½ months after end of plan year if extension for filing granted by IRS in response to filing of Form 5558, *or*

8½ months after end of tax year (but not later than extended tax return due date) if plan year and tax year coincide and employer obtains extension for filing tax return to later date.

A copy of the IRS extension must be attached to annual report form (Form 5500 Series).

[2] Special rules apply: for single employer plans, statement must be distributed to participants and information must be included on Schedule SSA for plan year *following* plan year in which participant separates from service. For multiple employer plans (even those of a controlled group of corporations), deadline is Form 5500 due date for plan year within which participant completes second of two consecutive one-year breaks in service (IRS Reg. §301.6057-1).

Source: Towers, Perrin, Forster & Crosby (TPF&C).

Exhibit 51-2
Ongoing Plan Maintenance Activities

| | Required for Covered: | | | To Participants: | | To Following Government Agency | Due Date |
| | Pension Plans | | Welfare Plans | | | | |
	Defined Contribution	Defined Benefit		Automatically	On Request		
1. Preretirement Joint & Survivor Notice	No[1]	Yes[2]	No	Yes	No	None	Normally 180 days before a participant's "qualified early retirement age," plus any waiting period
2. Postretirement Joint & Survivor Notice	Yes[3]	Yes	No	Yes	No	None	180 days before a participant's qualified early retirement age if preretirement joint and survivor benefits are elective, otherwise 9 months before such age[4]
3. Statement of Benefit Rights on Request	Yes	Yes	No	No	Yes	None	30 days after receipt of written request
4. Statement of Benefit Rights upon Termination of Service	Yes	Yes	No	Yes	No	None	210 days after the end of the plan year in which a participant "separates from service," i.e., incurs a "break in service"
5. Statement of Benefit Rights after Incurring a One-Year Break in Service	Yes	Yes	No	Yes	No	None	By 180 days after end of plan year of one-year break in service

#							
6.	Inspection of Plan Documents	Yes	Yes	No	Yes	None	Within 10 days after request
7.	Copies of Plan Documents	Yes	Yes	No	Yes	None	Within 30 days after request
8.	Summary Plan Description for New Employees	Yes	Yes	Yes	Yes	None	90 days after person becomes participant or beneficiary
9.	Update of Summary Plan Description	Yes	Yes	Yes	Yes	None	If amendments made to plan, every 5 years, if no amendments to plan, every 10 years
10.	Statement of Reasons for Claim Denial	Yes	Yes	Yes	No	None	Within 90 days after denial of participant's claim for benefits (or within 180 days of such denial in special cases)
11.	Statement of Reasons for Decision to Deny Appeal of Claim	Yes	Yes	Yes	No	None	Within 60 days after receipt of request for review of a denied claim (or within 120 days of such receipt in special cases)
12.	Notification of Reportable Event (Form 5500 for some)	No	No	No	No	PBGC	Within 30 days after plan administrator knows event has occurred for some events: on Form 5500 for others

[1] Unless the plan provides a survivor's benefit less than the vested portion of the participant's account balance.

[2] Required only if plan has elective pre-retirement joint and survivor coverage.

[3] Required only if plan provides benefits in the form of a life annuity.

[4] Nine months before a participant's normal retirement age for plans with no early retirement benefits.

Source: Towers, Perrin, Forster & Crosby (TPF&C).

Exhibit 51–3
New Plan Activities

		Required for Covered:		
		Pension Plans		
		Defined Contribution	*Defined Benefit*	*Welfare Plans*
1.	Summary Plan Description	Yes	Yes	Yes
2.	Notification to Interested Parties	Yes	Yes	No
3.	Application for Determination of Qualified Status (Form 5300 Series)			
	a. For Defined Benefit Plan (Form 5300)	No	Yes	No
	b. For Defined Contribution Plan (Form 5301)	Yes	No	No
	c. Employee Census (Form 5302)—Attachment to Form 5300 or 5301	Yes	Yes	No
	d. For Collectively Bargained Plan (Form 5303)	Yes	Yes	No

Source: Towers, Perrin, Forster & Crosby (TPF&C).

A failure to comply with the qualification requirements including the communication requirement can result in the loss of qualified status for a pension or profit-sharing plan. The disclosure requirements are enforceable against noncomplying individuals by injunctive civil action. Violations also are subject to fine and/or imprisonment. Failure to comply with the qualification requirements can result in the loss of qualified status for a plan. Thus, communication of employee benefits is essential for an employer to retain the favorable federal income tax status of such plans and avoid legal penalties.

MANAGERIAL REQUIREMENTS

Even if plans did not receive favorable tax treatment upon meeting disclosure and other criteria, the basic managerial reasons for the communication of employee benefits still would exist. Modern management thinking fosters the use of employee benefits as an effective means of competing

To Participants:		To Following Government Agency	Due Date
Automatically	On Request		
Yes	Yes	DOL	Within 120 days after plan becomes covered (or 90 days after person becomes participant or beneficiary, if later)
Yes	No	None	Not less than 7 or more than 21 days prior to application if notice by posting or in person; not less than 10 or more than 24 days if by mail
			By date tax return is filed for year for which requested, in order to extend "remedial amendment period" until IRS determination received and/or amendments are made
No	Yes	IRS	
No	Yes	IRS	
No	No	IRS	
No	Yes	IRS	

in labor markets for the attraction and retention of qualified personnel. Benefit plans also are viewed as tools for building and maintaining high morale within a work force and for meeting the social and ethical responsibilities of employers within the employment relationship. These managerial reasons for instituting employee benefit plans can be met only if the relevant people are made aware of their existence. Benefit plans must be communicated and administered in a manner consistent with and supportive of the personnel policy goals that the benefits are designed to help accomplish. Benefit plans cannot motivate a person if the individual does not know of the existence of the plans or how they affect him or her individually. An employee cannot be influenced to remain with a specific employer, to be more productive, or to view an employer in a favorable light by the presence of benefits which have not been communicated properly. Moreover, an employee cannot use a benefit plan as it is fully intended (e.g., cost containment features in a medical plan or the use of a capital accumulation plan) if he or she is not acquainted with the nature and

Exhibit 51-4
Revised Plan Activities

	Required for Covered:			To Participants:		To Following Government Agency	Due Date
	Pension Plans		Welfare Plans	Automatically	On Request		
	Defined Contribution	Defined Benefit					
1. Report in Case of Merger, Consolidation, or Transfer of Assets (Form 5310)	Yes	Yes	No	No	No	IRS	At least 30 days before merger, transfer, or consolidation of plan assets
2. Notification to Interested Parties	Yes	Yes	No	Yes	No	None	See Exhibit 51–3, Item 2
3. Application for Determination of Qualified Status (Form 5300 Series or Short Form 6406)	Yes	Yes	No	No	Yes	IRS	See Exhibit 51–3, Item 3
4. Summary of Material Modifications (SMM)	Yes	Yes	Yes	Yes	Yes	DOL	Within 210 days after end of plan year in which modifications or changes occur
5. Notification of Reportable Event	No	Yes	No	No	No	PBGC	See Exhibit 51–2, Item 12

Source: Towers, Perrin, Forster & Crosby (TPF&C).

Exhibit 51-5
Terminated Plan Activities

	Required for Covered:			To Participants:		To Following Government Agency	Due Date
	Pension Plans		Welfare Plans	Automatically	On Request		
	Defined Contribution	Defined Benefit					
1. Notice of Intent to Terminate	No	Yes	No	Yes	No	PBGC	At least 10 days before proposed termination date
2. Notification to Interested Parties	Yes	Yes	No	Yes	No	None	See Exhibit 51-3, Item 2
3. Application for Determination Upon Plan Termination (Form 5310)	Yes	Yes	No	No	Yes	IRS	By date tax return is filed for year for which determination is requested, in order to extend "remedial amendment period" until IRS determination is received and/or amendments are made
4. Notification of Reportable Event	No	Yes	No	No	No	PBGC	See Exhibit 51-2, Item 12
5. Terminal Report	Yes	Yes	Yes	No	No	DOL & PBGC	At a time to be prescribed by regulations

Source: Towers, Perrin, Forster & Crosby (TPF&C).

purposes of such plan provisions. When viewed in this context, the communication of employee benefits is an essential factor in the whole array of activities commonly termed "good management practice."

RESPONSIBILITY FOR COMMUNICATING EMPLOYEE BENEFITS

Realistically, the responsibility for communicating employee benefits is shared throughout the management hierarchy of an organization. Top management, the employee benefits manager, and line managers all have roles to play.

Top Management

Top management ultimately is responsible for employee benefit communications since it has the basic authority for setting all organizational policies and plans. The term *top management* has different connotations depending on the size of an organization. In small organizations, there is usually little or no differentiation of top, middle, and first-line management people. There is just one level of management. However, as organizations grow in size, they tend to acquire several middle and upper levels of management, each with varying degrees and types of authority and responsibility. Moreover, the management positions are structured to function in a coordinated manner with each contributing to the fulfillment of the total management process.

In large corporate organizations, the responsibility for recommending policies and establishing and implementing plans and procedures is typically delegated to upper-level division and department heads. In addition, all line and staff managers of an organization are expected to administer their departments in a manner that is consistent and supportive of overall organizational policymaking and planning. For example, a vice president of marketing should run his or her division in a manner that accomplishes the marketing objectives of the firm and also includes appropriate consideration of the financial, production, personnel, and employee benefits policies established by top management. For employee benefits matters, the described planning and implementation responsibilities typically are placed with the person who serves as the vice president of personnel or as the employee benefits manager.

Employee Benefits Manager

An employee benefits manager engages in many activities in recommending and implementing employee benefits policies. The basic organizational responsibility for the communication of employee benefits to participants and their beneficiaries typically is vested in the individual who has this role or title in a firm. This situation exists regardless of whether a plan is self-funded and/or administered, insurance-funded and/or administered, or trusteed or structured under some other type of arrangement. Supporting services, including communications support activities and materials, usually are provided to the sponsoring employer by a third-party administrator of a plan. However, the overall responsibilities of an employee benefits manager may not be diminished under such arrangements. Indeed, the presence of an insured or trusteed plan could increase the workload of the employee benefits manager because the efforts of the third-party administrator must be monitored, evaluated, and coordinated with the firm's employee benefit program.

One of the employee benefits manager's major concerns is to make certain that the employees understand the coverages, operation, and value of the benefits package. Although many easily comprehend the nature of the benefits extended, there may be employees who need to have these matters explained with greater care.

Attractive and readable posters, standard forms, pamphlets, brochures, and other written materials should be prepared. Perhaps the development of audio and visual materials might be necessary. The planning and conducting of meetings with groups of employees also may be required. Additionally, staff and line personnel must be trained to conduct meetings and deal with employees individually about employee benefits matters. The actual communication of employee benefits information to employees and others occurs in many ways at both specified and unspecified times. The efforts of the employee benefits manager, other personnel department people, and line people all are involved.

Line Management

Contemporary management theory emphasizes that the process of personnel management is spread throughout an organization. All managers are viewed as personnel managers because they are vitally connected with directing and motivating human resources. Their job effectiveness is dependent on the quality of the performance of the employees over whom they exercise authority.

Line managers of sales, manufacturing, and other departments usually play a substantial role in recruiting, selecting, evaluating, training, developing, and disciplining employees. Because of their close daily contact line, managers often are initially approached by employees with personal and employment-related problems and questions. In carrying out these activities, all managers can be viewed as employee benefits managers as well as personnel managers. Each of these activities involves a real or potential employee benefit communication event. Line managers must be equipped to give accurate employee benefit information. At a minimum, a line supervisor should be able to direct an inquiring employee to the office within the firm where assistance or advice can be obtained. Also, when a line manager makes a decision or takes any action involving an employee, the implications concerning a change in the benefits status of an employee should be considered. Disciplinary transfers, suspensions, layoffs, and terminations all typically involve employee changes with respect to the entitlement or loss of benefits. Any such actions taken imprudently could be counterproductive.

Employee Benefit Communication Events

Many occasions exist in the working career of each employee that can be classified as employee benefit communications events. There are incidents in the life span of an organization that also involve such events. Several of these bear particular mention.

As part of the recruitment process, it is advisable to notify potential and active job applicants of the general nature of the total employee benefit package of the firm. Competition among employers for qualified people is an ever-present economic factor, and prospective employees usually are quite aware of the important role of employee benefits in the total compensation package of a firm. The presence of a fine benefits program could be the ultimate factor in attracting superior job applicants and maintaining their interest in the firm. At the selection and placement stages more specific employee benefit information should be given to employment candidates. This will reinforce the commitment of the employer and help to increase positive attitudes in the candidates. The recruitment, selection and placement processes typically are conducted through the interaction of personnel department staff and line people. Thus both should be advised concerning their benefit communication functions and supplied with supporting brochures and other materials through the employee benefits office.

In the orientation process, new employees usually receive a tremendous quantity of information about their jobs, the products or services produced by the firm, and the organization itself. The employee benefits manager and his or her staff typically play the primary role in the orientation process of explaining the employee benefits program of the organization. Effective communications are essential at this point to aid in establishing lasting positive attitudes and keeping productive and mobile employees in the organization. In such a case, employees should understand the program fully from the very earliest point in their employment relationship.

An organization also should schedule employee benefits communication events rather than merely react to or deal with them as they occur. It is necessary to keep established employees informed of their benefits as a matter of legal and managerial responsibility. This can be accomplished by the employee benefits manager through the use of a continuous schedule for contacting employees at definitely set time intervals. Attractive and creative written communications can be sent to employees directly, placed in their pay envelopes, or displayed on bulletin boards. Meetings and seminars with groups of employees involving written and oral messages integrated with audio and visual materials often are useful.

Most employee communications events are generated by employees themselves. Whenever an employee has some question or misunderstanding regarding benefit entitlements, has a claim processed, or meets some difficulty in the administration of a claim, this requires an immediate managerial response. The lines of communication between the employee benefits department and employees should be kept open continuously. This is essential to give proper attention to any benefits questions or problems that employees may have.

It has been noted that employee status changes. Events such as suspensions and layoffs have benefit effects that should be considered before making any decisions in these areas. As a corollary to this policy, the formal communications network of a firm should be geared to generate an awareness among employees of any loss, decrease or freeze of benefits that accompany a layoff, demotion, suspension, leave of absence, or termination. Likewise, increases or adjustments in benefits that take place in conjunction with transfers and promotions should be understood. When an event involving a change in the employment status of an individual takes place, the person should be counseled specifically about the benefit aspects as an additional measure of insurance. In connection with this, financial counseling programs and preretirement counseling sessions can play significant roles.

The general operating posture of a firm may be revised periodically. For example, product lines are changed or broadened, geographic relocations or expansions occur, and other types of return on investment-oriented decisions take place. These actions sometimes are facilitated through modifications of the existing structure of a firm. This could mean a change in the basic method of departmentalization, an increased emphasis on centralization, the entire sale of a firm as a subsidiary to a competitor or a conglomerate, a merger arrangement, or a consolidation. These types of incidents typically cause concern among employees regarding their employment status and existing employee benefit programs. A firm should take steps at the time of such events to acquaint its employees with the nature and purpose of the organizational realignment and its impact on them personally. Whenever a merger or consolidation is carried out, some revisions of existing employee benefit plans invariably are necessary to dovetail existing plans with those of the new partner firm. Aside from the legal disclosure requirements that might apply in such circumstances, there is a need to acquaint employees with any benefit adjustments made. Moreover, sound management practice requires that existing benefits programs should seldom be downgraded or reduced at these times.

THE COMMUNICATION PROCESS

The communication process includes a sequence of several steps, regardless of whether the form of communication is the spoken or written word or some other method. It begins with the formation of an idea and its placement into a message form. The message then is transmitted and received by the person or persons for whom it is intended. Understanding the content of the message and appropriate action by the receiver then follows. The final step consists of the transmission of feedback by the receiver to the sender of the message.

Steps of the Communication Process

A complete sequence of the steps in the communication process is set forth below. Each of the steps—Idea, Message Formation, Transmission, Receipt, Understanding, Action, and Feedback is discussed separately.

Idea. This step provides the content of a specific communication or message when the sender creates an idea or chooses a fact to communicate. An individual must have some fact, feeling, or concept to convey before the communication process moves forward. The first step is crucial because further steps are superfluous without a solid content message. Moreover, a poor message cannot be improved by trimmings such as glossy paper or a bigger loudspeaker.

Message Formation. The sender organizes an idea into a series of symbols that transmit the idea to those with whom communication is desired. The selected symbols may be words, gestures, pictures, scientific formulas, graphs, etc. After the message is organized for rationality and coherence, the appropriate media to be used are selected. Therefore this step is related to the media used as well as to intended receivers. For example, a letter usually is worded differently from a brochure, and both are different from a face-to-face conversation. Moreover, the media selected must be capable of transmitting a message to the intended receivers. Thus, the written word usually is used for employee benefit messages because of their nature and content. However, in other situations this would be totally inefficient. For example, hand signals are used to communicate with a crane operator because the spoken word or other media are inappropriate due to distance, noise, and other physical factors.

Transmission. The message is transmitted over or through the medium selected in the preceding step. A specific channel is chosen to perform this step, and appropriate timing also is important. For example, a channel may be used to bypass a particular group, or a message may be delayed because the sender feels this is not the best time for it to be sent. The sender also tries to keep the communication channel free of interferences so that the message can reach the receiver and hold his or her attention. For example, in interviewing a beneficiary regarding a complex claim, distraction is undesirable.

Receipt. In this step, the initiative in the communication process shifts to the receiver. He or she must be ready and capable of receiving the message. If it is oral, the receiver must be a good listener; if written, the receiver must be a good reader; if in some symbolic language, the receiver must be knowledgeable and observant in the appropriate area. If the receiver does not function well, the message is lost.

Understanding. The receiver takes meaning from the symbols used by the sender. An effective and cooperative receiver tries diligently to capture the meaning intended in the message by the sender. Nevertheless, the meaning the receiver takes will not be exactly the same as the one sent. This happens because the perceptions of the sender and receiver invariably differ to some extent. Thus, the sender of a message should be aware that some degree of distortion or lack of comprehension by the receiver usually is inevitable. This can be ultimately overcome by devoting careful attention to the formation of the message and through the use of repetition and message follow-up techniques.

Action. On the basis of the message, the receiver acts or responds in some way. For example, he or she may verbally respond to the sender by writing a memo to the sender requesting further information; the receiver may store the information contained in the message for the future or may engage in other activities in response to a request or command, such as forming a group to openly discuss the proposals at issue.

Feedback. It is desirable to give feedback to the sender to establish two-way communication. One-way communication processes unfortunately do not include this step. The purpose of feedback is to provide the sender with information about his or her message that clarifies whether it was understood or put into effect. In some cases the action step of the process includes the element of feedback. For example, when the beneficiaries of an employee benefit plan are sent notices of claims procedure changes, their degree of compliance in response to the message is an action step which can be observed as a form of feedback.

EFFECTIVE AND INEFFECTIVE COMMUNICATIONS

An effective communication takes place when a common understanding exists between the sender and receiver of a message. However, as indicated, this goal is not always achieved because of one or more of several interrelated factors. Sometimes individuals unintentionally send out messages, barriers can exist within the communications process itself, and all messages do not fully reflect the thoughts of the senders. In addition, the receiver can be an impediment to an effective communication because of a low level of literacy, a suspicious nature regarding management-sponsored benefits programs, or general indifference.

Many unintended messages are transmitted for innumerable reasons. For example, the receiver of a message may delay in responding to a request for information because of a heavy workload. The sender of the request, who does not know of the circumstances, interprets the delay as disinterest or hostility. Thus, a message has been communicated by each person, but only one was intended. The same result can occur because of body language or voice inflections unconsciously used by the sender.

The communication process does not always function in a complimentary environment. When this is the case, the existing barrier makes effective communications difficult. Noise usually is the most annoying barrier to effective communications because of its distracting characteristic. Organizational distance, another barrier, occurs when a message must be transmitted through several people before ultimately reaching the receiver. The presence of message competition also operates as a barrier to effective communication. This exists when the receiver is bombarded by many related messages at the same time. If there is little indication of the relative importance of each message, the receiver may become confused.

A message should be constructed carefully to reflect the thoughts of the sender. The language selected must be understood by the receiver. For example, employee benefits-oriented terms such as *coinsurance, deductible,* or *third-party payee* are not universally understood, and thus great care must be exercised in using them. The language of a message also should be geared not to antagonize the receiver. Words such as *minorities, unisex,* or *welfare* can produce negative feelings that impede understanding. Slang, jargon, and buzzwords can be effective. However, such terms tend to be fashionable for brief periods of time and thus should be avoided in written communications that are intended for use over an extended period.

Messages often can be too long or too brief. Excessively long messages lose reader interest and comprehension. Conversely, the receiver may make abstractions or inferences not intended by the sender if the message is too brief.

The sender and receiver of a message must be in tune for effective communications to take place. Unfortunately, the receiver sometimes presents a problem because his or her perceptions may differ from the sender's. Thus, when the sender refers to holding down costs, the receiver may interpret this as a directive to deny benefit claims accepted in the past. Also, the status of the sender can be important to the receiver. Communications from the employee benefits manager of a large organization may carry greater impact than those of the support staff in the benefits department. As another example, any message that involves a change of existing conditions may be met with resistance by the receiver. This includes such matters as changes in existing benefit policies, programs, or operating procedures.

FORMS OF COMMUNICATION

Communications typically are classified as written, oral, or action messages. Written communications consist of many types, from handbooks, booklets, bulletins, memos, letters, and standard forms to posters, cartoons, films, prepared tapes, and pictures. Oral communications, on the other hand, generally consist of the spoken word in a speech, an order, a comment, or a discussion. Actions also are recognized as communication forms, regardless of whether the action exists independently or occurs in consort with a written or oral communication. Thus such things as laughter, a smile, a handshake, silence and personal mannerisms have communicative significance.

Written Communications

The primary focus in this chapter is on the written form of communication because federal laws concerning employee benefits require the use of such communications in specific instances. Moreover, the basic principles of effective writing also apply to the development and transmission of oral messages.

Written communications have the characteristic of permanence with a record of the message transmitted as an inherent factor. Accordingly, written messages usually are constructed with greater care and have a higher degree of formality than oral messages. A written message can be read carefully and reread by the receiver to gain a fuller understanding of the content. Thus, when a message is lengthy or detailed, the written form often is used because oral communication would not be as effective. In addition, when a message must be transmitted through several people to the ultimate receiver, the written form is selected to avoid change or dilution of its content.

The federal regulations concerning the written communication of employee benefit matters provide that required information must be written in a manner calculated to be understood by the average plan participant. Also, it must be sufficiently accurate and comprehensive to inform participants and beneficiaries of their rights and obligations under a plan. Generally, plan sponsors do not encounter any great difficulty in complying with these broadly stated legal guidelines. However, to obtain the improved morale and productivity that can flow from an effective employee benefits communication system, preparers of written communications must understand the nature and steps of the writing process and some basic writing principles.

The Writing Process. The first consideration in developing written materials is the nature of the readership. The technical, educational, and literacy levels of anyone who will receive the message must be ascertained along with the language, social, and economic background of the reader. In writing, this is called knowing the audience. As one should not write down to or patronize an audience, one should always consider how an idea can be best expressed in writing to all who will read the message. Clarity, the precision of the words chosen, is of paramount importance for readers to understand a communication's major facets. Once this is accepted, the writing process can begin with its three fundamental steps, namely, prewriting, writing, and revising.

Prewriting. Before writing the first word of the first draft, there are preliminary considerations. A writer must gather the necessary data, review it, and order it in a fashion that will be clear and logical to the readers. The writer must shape the focus, reconsider the audience at hand, and finally pinpoint the general length of the treatise. At this time the writer should reflect on what will be written and for whom it will be written.

Writing. The next step is to compose the initial or rough draft. A writer need not be troubled with general correctness at this juncture because the central function is to elucidate the position being taken, express the ideas, and unravel what may seem to be ambiguous, sophisticated material. After this runthrough to test the length of the communication, the accuracy of its concepts, and their clarity, the writer may return to the draft to check for its stylistic flow. This is the time to work on those principles of style that add a sense of unity and fluidity to the thought. The basic reason for multiple drafts is to avoid rushing through the total composition process at one sitting. It is advisable to allow a first draft to rest, to age, as it were, so that ideas have time to reassemble, solidify in time, and perhaps be reshuffled to include fresh points of view, more solid information, and clarifying concepts not previously incorporated.

Revising. The process of revising is highly important because by this time writers have completed their thought processes, included all purposeful detail, and arrived at useful conclusions. From this point forward the writer must assess how his or her ideas have been expressed, how sentences have been structured, how paragraphs have been organized, and how well words have been chosen. The "fixing" of spelling, the "ironing out" of the style, the "correcting" of punctuation and other mechanical gremlins, and the "elimination" of infelicitous phrasing occurs during this process which then leads to what can be loosely called the final draft. However, in truth there may not be such a thing as a final draft because one can always find a better word than that which has been previously chosen. One can delete wordiness that has crept in seemingly from nowhere and change a sentence that has careened out of control.

Thus the writer can begin to relax when he or she becomes familiar with the composing process as a continuous one, rather than as a process that stops completely with the distribution of the written communication. What has been overlooked or ungracefully expressed can be improved in the future. Also, the revising process allows writers the luxury of time to evaluate and correct the real or imagined imperfections in their current drafts.

Overall Approach and Tone

Writers should take the middle road between high formality and low informality. An overly formal approach may be read as too pompous and officious while an informal presentation may appear too casual, hurried, and ill-formed. Both extremes produce negative responses from readers. The predominant impression sought should be one of careful, honest thoroughness to allow readers to judge the reasonableness of a communication's proposition.

Some Writing Principles. Additions to the steps outlined in the writing process undoubtedly will lead to more effective communications. Also, some specific guides should be followed to improve the efficiency of written communications. Among these are the "10-20-30 formula" for paragraphs, sentences, and word choice, and the "U-shaped curve" concept. Simply stated, the 10-20-30 formula is a rule of thumb which aids a writer to sustain reader interest. When the writer limits paragraphs to an average of 10 sentences, sentence length to 20 words, and the number of polysyllabic words to 30 percent of the total words in the entire composition, reader interest does not diminish, and more effective written communication takes place.

It is most important not to lose the interest of readers or receivers of messages. Initially, within the first paragraph of a written communication, the reader's attention is high. It is at the top or the peak of a U-shaped curve. Unfortunately, this interest wavers as one reads other paragraphs, and it drops to the bottom part of the U—the "valley of disinterest." Toward the conclusion of a communication, the typical pattern of attention moves upward to a second peak of the U, although this second peak is not as high as the initial peak. Thus, it seems to follow that when written communications are received, readers are compelled to read the first paragraph. The reader is highly motivated at first, particularly when the message may have singular significance for him or her. Nevertheless, disinterest tends to result as the message continues, especially when the receiver finds the message so common that it can be filed away for another day. However, curiosity could move that reader to push ahead to the concluding paragraphs to see if there may be some content more personally pertinent than that contained in earlier paragraphs. Thus, a writer should mold a written communication so that the full body of the message is contained in the early paragraphs. The meat of the message must be presented early and in a manner sufficiently viable to hold the reader's interest and not be casually dismissed.

There also is an "effort-reward ratio" theory associated with the effectiveness of written communication. The reader typically asks, "How much reward is there for the effort I expend over this reading?" More selfishly stated, the reader asks: "What will this memo do for me?" or "What will it not do for me?" If the first paragraph does not elicit interest for the overall message, the reader quickly dips into the valley of disinterest by skimming over the rest of the material. The earlier a written message can relay a sense of importance to the reader, the longer it will be read and the less disinterest there will be. A writer must strive to keep readers as constantly at the peak of interest as possible or else ineffective communication may result.

To the 10-20-30 formula can be added the "three S's." Writing should be Short, Simple, and Sincere. Brevity induces recipients to read the message totally. Simplicity and clarity enable readers to understand the transmitted ideas, and sincerity is the intangible that might convince them to accept the content of a message. Too little information may lead the reader to feel that the company is merely paying lip service to the idea of benefits, a point that can undermine the sincerity of effort behind the company's intentions.

Most people quickly tire of reading long, drawn-out communications. Conversely, they fully appreciate deriving the most information from the fewest words. Brevity is more than "the soul of wit;" it is the investment that pays ample dividends. A reader more frequently reads through something short and specific rather than something wordy and tedious.

A writing can be made visually appealing and immediately informative by headlining significant sections. This provides the reader with an opportunity to read a skeletal outline of a proposal and then return to each segment separately. Readers do not have to pore over each paragraph to find the topic thought. Instead, they can scan the entire report, look for substantive matter, and be directed to what catches their interest. Too much in a paragraph tends to bore, confuse, or turn readers against the topic at hand.

Samples of Effective Benefits Communications. Several samples and accompanying explanations are included to show applications of the preceding thoughts. The numbers in parentheses after each sentence in each figure represent, *first,* the number of words in the sentence, and *second,* the number of polysyllabic words used in the sentence to see how they both correspond to the 10-20-30 formula.

The first example consists of an introductory section of a memorandum regarding an employee benefit package:

TO: Current and Future Employees of XYZ Company

FROM: Employee Benefits Management Committee

SUBJECT: Employee Benefits Package

The management committee in charge of the Employee Benefit Package is presenting its plan to everyone currently employed and to all prospective employees [23 words, 11 polysyllabic words]. The introductory outline of the full package and the breakdown of each item should serve to acquaint you with the general provisions of each benefit [25,8]. If you have any questions about the following, Mr. B_____ from the Personnel Office will gladly discuss specific areas of the plan with you [24,7].

The memo clearly introduces its purpose. The approach is solicitous; the beginning suggests that there was a group meeting to discuss the welfare of the employees, the second sentence guides the reader to what the memo includes, and the last sentence opens the door for oral, personal communication if for some reason the written message is misunderstood. As for attention span, there would seem to be no time for disinterest, because by the time the reader might possibly begin to stray, the introductory pleasantries stop and the actual package is presented.

The second example consists of an outline of the benefits package made available by an employer. The outline is taken from the employee handbook of the sponsoring employer:

EMPLOYEE BENEFITS PACKAGE

Every employee with the XYZ Company at least six months is eligible for the benefits listed below [16,6].
A. Major Medical Insurance Coverage.
B. Accident Insurance Coverage.
C. Life Insurance Coverage.
D. Disability Income.
E. Supplemental Unemployment Benefits.
F. Scholarship Services.
G. Prepaid Legal Services.
Each of the above benefits is explained briefly in the following sections [12,5].

Visually, the above captures the reader because there is no word clutter. If the reader was turned off by the earlier introductory material, he or she can be brought to another peak of interest by looking through the seven offerings and selecting as many benefits as are appealing: two, three, five, or one. Therefore, the memo automatically directs the reader to a high peak of interest and sustains that level as he or she locates the areas to investigate further. If sections A through G above are kept relatively short, there should be no time to allow for a fall into that valley of disinterest. Note that the number of words per sentence and the number of polysyllabic words corresponds neatly to the 10-20-30 formula.

The third example consists of a section in the employee handbook explaining the nature of one of the employee benefits provided:

MAJOR MEDICAL INSURANCE COVERAGE ELIGIBILITY

All employees with the company at least six months are eligible for medical benefits as outlined by the participating program the employee chooses [23,10]. The company offers a choice of the following plans [9,3]:
A. Blue Cross/Blue Shield, Plan B.
B. Great River Valley Health Plan.
C. The Priority Health Maintenance Plan.
Each of the above is described in separate brochures available from the Personnel Office [14,7].

Cost

The company will underwrite the cost of whatever plan an employee chooses, provided that employee meets the requirements of the plan [21,8]. Dependent coverage is also available, but that cost must be paid by the employee [14,4]. Although the costs of some plans may vary, the company will pay the employee's fee regardless of the differential [19,6].

Exclusions

The only exclusions in medical coverage for employees and their families will be those imposed by the medical plan itself [20,9]. The company will not exclude any one of its employees from choosing one of its medical plans [17,5].

The above example demonstrates the principles outlined previously, and it shows the flexibility it gives management in citing its medical offerings. Under Eligibility, management may choose to introduce a brief summary of each plan or merely list the three. Each succinct paragraph forces readers to cover main points as they glance quickly at the benefits that interest them most.

The longest section is the first with its three sentences and list of three plans, but the spacing serves a good purpose because readers can easily follow what is being offered. Since everything is spelled out clearly, there are no traps. The eight sentences average 17 words each, well within the 10-20-30 prescribed formula; although approximately 35 percent of the words are polysyllabic, any layman can understand the language without resorting to a dictionary.

The sample is *short* and *simple,* but there is a note of erudition; nothing in the sample talks down or up to the reader. The tone is easy, direct, neither supercilious nor superior. It promotes its benefits honestly and adds *sincerity* by listing a number of alternatives, by informing an employee where specific material is available, and by insisting that the company excludes no one from its medical plans.

Oral Communications

Oral communications take place in many different ways. They involve face-to-face discussions or verbal orders between two or more people, the use of telephones, speeches, meetings, the employment of public address systems, and other uses of the spoken word. Generally, oral communications are transmitted faster than written communications. Also, under some circumstances, oral communication can provide a greater basis for achieving common understanding by the participants than that allowable through written communication. This ability to gain a higher degree of common understanding varies with the form of oral communication used. For example, face-to-face communications between two people or within small groups typically have this quality to a greater extent than telephone conversations and speeches. Face-to-face communication gives each participant the immediate opportunity to observe the body language of the other, ask questions, and eliminate misunderstanding.

The seven-step communication process—Idea, Message Formation, Transmission, Receipt, Understanding, Action, and Feedback—applies to oral as well as written communications. Thus, the sender of an oral message should know him or herself and the audience, understand the potential barriers to an effective communication, formulate the message in a thoughtful and articulate manner as well as select and use an appropriate medium to transmit the message. The action and feedback steps then can be used to appraise the receipt and understanding of the message by the receiver or audience.

Oral communications also are subject to the same guides or principles as written communications. That is, oral messages should be constructed in accordance with the 10-20-30 formula, the U-shaped curve or valley of disinterest concept, the effect-reward ratio theory, and the admonition of the three S's to keep messages short, simple, and sincere.

There are some additional factors concerning oral communication that should be noted. Oral communications are more effective when there is verbal interaction between the participants. A speaker can use gestures, facial expressions, and other types of body language to enhance the process. The level of the speaker's voice, the use of pauses, the rate of speaking, enunciation, and other vocal characteristics play an important role in speech communication. Moreover, as is the case with written communications, visual materials, such as pamphlets, graphs, charts, diagrams, posters, and slides can improve the quality of oral communications immensely.

CHAPTER 52

Qualified Retirement Plans for Small Business: Choice of Plan

HARRY V. LAMON, Jr.

INTRODUCTION

Adoption of a qualified retirement plan is one of the major tax benefits which may be obtained by a small business organization. Such a plan permits current income tax deductions by the small business, a deferral of income tax until receipt (actual or constructive) by the participants, tax-exempt earnings during the existence of the trust, exemption of the trust from the claims of most creditors of both the participants and the small business, and the availability of favorable treatment under the income and estate tax rules upon the payment of benefits from the plan. Although most of these tax advantages may be obtained by the *unincorporated* business under what is commonly referred to as an H.R. 10 plan, several distinctions remain between corporate plans and H.R. 10 plans despite Congress' attempt in the Tax Equity and Fiscal Responsibility Act of 1982 (TEFRA) to achieve parity between corporate and H.R. 10 plans.

First, this chapter will review the various types of qualified plans which are available to, and generally used by, small businesses and describe those factors which aid in choosing a particular type of qualified retirement plan. Second, the discussion will focus on the *top-heavy plan* concept which was inaugurated in TEFRA and the concept's effect on plan choice. Finally, Section 401(k) *cash or deferred plans* will be discussed separately because of their large potential for use by small businesses. The specific TEFRA changes which effect approximate parity between corporate plans and H.R. 10 plans are discussed in Chapter 53.

GENERAL CONSIDERATIONS IN PLAN CHOICE— TYPES OF PLAN

Once the decision to establish a qualified retirement plan is made by the small business, care should be taken to assure that the plan is designed to meet the goals of the small business. The decision regarding the type and design of the qualified retirement plan to be established is almost as crucial as the decision to adopt any plan at all.

Of course, a portion of the income received from any small business must be used to pay overhead (including rent, staff salaries, etc.), another portion must be used to provide direct compensation to the employees, and only the remainder may be used to provide fringe benefits and qualified retirement plan benefits. Thus, probably the most important aspect of choosing the appropriate qualified retirement plan is determining the amount of contributions that can be made on an annual, recurring basis to the plan. If the income of the small business is entirely exhausted with the payment of overhead expenses and the payment of direct compensation to the employees, funds will obviously not be available to make contributions to any plan. On the other hand, if the employer elects to reduce the amount of direct compensation, funds will be available for the plan.

The choice of qualified retirement plans is probably easiest in a small business with one shareholder and probably most difficult in a small business with fewer than ten shareholders, particularly where there is wide divergence in the ages of the various shareholders. The author's experience is that generally the older shareholders have seen the "writing on the wall" and desire to create as many retirement benefits as their incomes will allow, while the younger shareholders prefer to defer little or nothing. The establishment of a qualified retirement plan should not proceed without seeking the advice of attorneys and accountants. Even if the shareholders desire to adopt one of the many available master plans, the assistance of an attorney and accountant should be sought prior to the adoption of the plan. Only by reviewing the various needs and desires of the small business, in conjunction with the legal ramifications of the plan, can the most appropriate plan for the small business be chosen.

The following discussion is not intended to provide exhaustive treatment of all aspects of qualified retirement plans; rather, the discussion merely reviews those aspects which are particularly applicable to small business so that the owners of the small business and their advisors will not overlook them in designing the qualified retirement plan.

Regular Profit-Sharing Plans

A profit-sharing plan is normally the first type of qualified retirement plan which an employer should consider adopting. Profit-sharing plans are among the many types of defined contribution plans. The common characteristic of all defined contribution plans is that they provide individual accounts for each participant, although all plan assets are normally commingled for investment purposes. A participant's benefit under a defined contribution plan is based solely on the amount in the participant's account.[1] This arrangement provides a certain measure of security for the

---

[1] I.R.C. § 414(i).

employer maintaining the plan because, unlike a defined benefit plan, a defined contribution plan does not promise any specific level of benefits; therefore, if the plan suffers poor investment experience, the employer will not be called upon to underwrite the unanticipated shortfall in funds necessary to provide benefits. A necessary corollary is that participants in a defined contribution plan bear the burden of poor investment experience and reap the benefit of favorable investment experience.

Under a profit-sharing plan, contributions may be made only out of the current or accumulated profits of the small business. Contributions may be totally discretionary on the part of the board of directors, partners, or proprietor, or they may be made mandatory in the event sufficient profits exist. For example, a plan providing mandatory contributions could require contributions equal to 5 percent of compensation but not in excess of current profits. For purposes of determining the amount of current or accumulated profits out of which contributions may be made, the plan may define profits consistent with generally accepted accounting principles. If a small business has profits as determined under generally accepted accounting principles, contributions may be made even if there are no current or accumulated profits from a tax standpoint.[2] Amounts which are contributed to a profit-sharing plan are allocated to each participant based upon the percentage of the entire compensation of all participants which his or her individual compensation represents. However, if the profit-sharing plan is integrated with Social Security, as discussed below, then a participant's compensation that is not in excess of the Social Security wage base is disregarded in allocating employer contributions to the participant's individual account.

Amounts which are allocated to participant accounts are held by the trustee of the plan, and the earnings and losses arising from plan investments are allocated on an annual basis to the accounts of the participants. As noted, no guaranteed retirement benefit exists under a profit-sharing plan because a retiring participant is entitled to receive only the amount in his or her account, which may be more or less than the total of the contributions actually made to the account depending upon the investments made by the trustee.

A participant's account balance also may change due to forfeitures. A forfeiture is the unvested portion of a participant's account, said portion being forfeited by the participant upon early termination of employment and subsequently being reallocated among the remaining participants. Forfeitures, thus, increase the accounts of those participants who continue employment with the small business.

The allocation of forfeitures usually is based on the current compensation of the remaining participants in the year in which the forfeiture occurs. Allocation of forfeitures may be based on other factors, such as the account balances of all remaining participants; however, if this results in officers,

---

[2] Rev. Rul. 80-252, 1980-2 C.B. 130; Rev. Rul. 66-174, 1966-1 C.B. 81.

shareholders, or highly compensated participants receiving forfeitures that are a larger percentage of current compensation than is the case with rank-and-file employees, then the plan will lose its qualified status.[3] To prevent possible disqualification, forfeitures in profit-sharing plans should not be allocated on any basis other than current compensation.

Section 404(a)(3) of the Code limits deductible contributions to a profit-sharing plan to 15 percent of the compensation of all plan participants. However, if a contribution of less than 15 percent is contributed during a given year, then the amount of the shortfall may be carried over to a subsequent year, although total contributions to a profit-sharing plan for a given year may not exceed 25 percent of the compensation of all plan participants for the given year notwithstanding carryover amounts.

In addition to this annual aggregate contribution limitation, Section 415(c) of the Code limits annual additions to the account of each participant, a concept discussed further below.

The author feels that profit-sharing plans at least should be *considered* by any small business, primarily because profit-sharing plans allow the amount of contributions to depend entirely upon the profitability of the business. For example, profit-sharing plans may be very useful for new small businesses that desire to implement some type of qualified retirement plan but are unsure of exactly how successful the small business will be or for small businesses that experience wide fluctuations in income on an annual basis. Although the contributions to a profit-sharing plan may be discretionary, employers should be aware that plan contributions must be substantial and recurring.[4] In order to meet this test, the general opinion is that contributions must be made at least once every three years. In any event, however, the failure to make contributions because of insufficient profits will not disqualify the plan.[5]

The allocation of unintegrated profit-sharing plan contributions for a small business with four employees where the contribution equals 15 percent of compensation is illustrated in the following chart:

Participant	Compensation	Contribution Allocation
Shareholder	$175,900.00	$26,385.00
Staff employee	12,000.00	1,800.00
Staff employee	10,000.00	1,500.00
Staff employee	8,000.00	1,200.00
Total	$205,900.00	$30,885.00

As the chart illustrates, although the shareholder receives the largest contribution, the contribution is based on the same percentage of compen-

---

[3] Rev. Rul. 81–10, 1981–1 C.B. 172.

[4] Treas. Regs. § 1.401–1(b)(2).

[5] See *Sherwood Swan & Co.*, 42 T.C. 299 (1964); Rev. Rul. 80–146, 1980–1 C.B. 90.

sation (15 percent) as that granted to the staff employees. As explained below, however, TEFRA limits the flexible allocation of contributions in all defined contribution plans such that a minimum contribution must be made on behalf of non-key employees (generally nonowners and nonexecutive employees) equal to 3 percent of their compensation or, if lesser, the highest percentage contribution made on behalf of any key employee (generally an owner-employee, executive employee or officer).

An employer may alter this pro rata allocation by integrating its contributions to a profit-sharing plan with the Social Security taxes which the corporation must pay. Generally, if a profit-sharing plan is integrated with Social Security benefits, contributions will be allocated in the following manner: first, to those participants whose compensation is in excess of the Social Security wage base, in an amount equal to 7 percent of such excess, and second, to all participants as their compensation relates to total compensation. If the profit-sharing plan discussed above were integrated with Social Security benefits using the 1980 Social Security wage base and the same $30,885 contribution were made, then the allocations would be as follows:

Participant	Contribution Allocation
Shareholder @ $175,900	$27,914.87
Staff employee @ $12,000	1,188.05
Staff employee @ $10,000	990.04
Staff employee @ $8,000	792.04
Total	$30,885.00

Obviously, an integrated profit-sharing plan provides a larger allocation for the shareholder. However, an important factor that should be considered before integrating a profit-sharing plan is that an integrated profit-sharing plan may not permit distributions of accounts prior to retirement, death or other separation from service.[6] In contrast, a nonintegrated profit-sharing plan may provide for distributions to participants during their employment after a period of deferral of as little as two years, the attainment of a stated age, or the prior occurrence of some event demonstrating financial need. Finally, as discussed below, TEFRA severely restricts the integration of top-heavy profit-sharing plans, top-heavy plans being those plans in which a disproportionate amount of contributions are made on behalf of officers, owners and executive employees.

Profit-Sharing Thrift Plans

Mandatory or voluntary employee contributions may be a feature of any profit-sharing plan. As a general rule, aggregate voluntary employee contri-

---

[6] Rev. Rul. 71–446, § 15.03, 1971–2 C.B. 187.

butions may not exceed 10 percent of the compensation paid to an employee during his participation in the plan.[7] As a general rule, for any year, mandatory employee contributions (the minimum contribution required as a prerequisite for participation or as a condition for increased employer contributions) may not exceed 6 percent of the amount of compensation paid to the employee for the year in question; however, the Service refuses to treat the 6 percent rule as a "safe harbor" from a possible challenge of discrimination in operation.[8]

Where employee contributions to a profit-sharing plan are permitted, such a plan often is called a *contributory plan*. Where employer contributions are based on the amount or rate of employee contributions, such a plan normally is called a *thrift* or *savings plan*.

Thrift plans have several attractive features. First, employee contributions are normally made through payroll deductions and an employee receives no company contributions unless he has authorized payroll deductions. Second, the company contribution is not tied to current profits; rather, the company usually contributes a fixed dollar amount for each dollar contributed by the employee. Finally, such a plan usually provides *"class-year" vesting* and permits the participant to withdraw the employer contributions after they have become vested.

Thrift plans generally receive an enthusiastic employee response, which is somewhat unusual since a regular profit-sharing plan normally provides the same type of benefits without the requirement of employee contributions. Probably, the class-year vesting concept generates employee enthusiasm since, in effect, it turns the profit-sharing thrift plan into a short-term savings account-type plan.

As a general rule, thrift plans offer the same benefits as profit-sharing plans to a small business. However, thrift plans serve an additional need in those small businesses in which shareholders have divergent retirement desires since the amount which is deferred is directly related to each shareholders' own voluntary contributions and may be adjusted annually. As a *caveat*, however, if a thrift plan is adopted and the compensation of those employees who do not contribute to the thrift plan is adjusted upward by the employer, then the plan may be a *de facto* cash or deferred plan which is discussed below and which is only qualified if certain additional requirements are met.

A disadvantage of thrift plans is that employee contributions that are matched by employer contributions are not eligible for treatment as deductible employee contributions.[9] One alternative that may be used to allow employees to make before-tax thrift contributions would be to convert a thrift plan into a cash or deferred arrangement with the employer matching

---

[7] Rev. Rul. 80–350, 1980–2 C.B. 133.

[8] Rev. Rul. 80–307, 1980–2 C.B. 136.

[9] I.R.C. § 219(e)(2)(B).

the amounts that employees elect to contribute to the plan under the cash or deferred provision.

Pension Plans

Pension plans, as opposed to profit-sharing plans, must provide for definitely determinable benefits. Further, under pension plans, contributions are mandatory, irrespective of corporate profits, in an amount necessary to fund the benefits provided by the plan. Further, forfeitures created in pension plans do not increase the benefits of the individual participants but merely reduce the annual contributions required by the employer.[10]

Defined Benefit Pension Plans. As a general rule, defined benefit pension plans provide greater benefits for older employees than for younger employees.[11] This result occurs because the defined benefit plan rules fix the amount of the retirement benefit, not the amount of the annual contribution which will produce the benefit. The amount of annual contributions required to fund the benefit of the older employee is larger than the annual amount required to fund the benefit of the younger employee because the employer has fewer years in which to contribute the assets necessary to produce the older employee's benefit level. In contrast, the defined contribution plan rules fix the maximum amount of the annual *contribution* on behalf of each employee but do not limit the amount of the ultimate benefit. Thus, employers may produce a larger retirement benefit for younger employees than for older employees in a defined contribution plan because younger employees have more contributable years before retirement. Thus, defined benefit pension plans are often very useful in a small business where older employees desire to defer a substantial amount of current income until retirement.

If an employee has not been employed by the employer who maintains the plan for at least 10 years as of his date of retirement, then the maximum pension benefit must be reduced by 10 percent for each year of employment less than 10. A technique that is often available to increase the size of the maximum deductible pension plan contribution, particularly for senior employees, is to use a benefit formula that gives credit for service with the employer prior to the effective date of the plan; however, a limitation exists on the rate at which past service costs may be funded. If the unfunded cost of past and current service benefits attributable to any three individuals is

---

[10] See Treas. Regs. § 1.401–1(a)(2)(i) and § 1.401(b)(1)(i).

[11] In Rev. Rul 74–142, 1974–1 C.B. 95, a professional corporation established a pension plan providing a retirement benefit of 60 percent of average compensation for each participant. There were only two participants under the plan, a 60-year-old professional and a 52-year-old staff employee. Because of the differences in ages and compensation, 90 percent of the contributions were applied to fund the benefits for the older professional. Yet, the Service ruled that the plan qualified and did not discriminate in favor of the older professional. See also *Ryan School Retirement Trust*, 24 T.C. 127 (1955).

more than 50 percent of the unfunded cost of past and current service benefits of all participants covered by the pension plan, then the cost attributable to such three individuals may not be funded over fewer than five years.[12]

Although the ability to defer large amounts of compensation through deductible contributions to defined benefit pension plans may work well in some small businesses, it may create problems in others. For example, once the older employee has retired, the younger employees will be required to continue funding under the existing plan or to terminate the plan. A problem inherently exists if an older employee in a small business was credited with a significant amount of past service at the time the plan was established, and this past service credit is not fully funded by the date on which the older employee retires. In this case, the remaining younger employees will find their corporation making contributions to fund the pension of a person who no longer performs services for the corporation, and the temptation to terminate the plan will be overwhelming. Since a majority of the contributions of the employer to a defined benefit plan fund the retirement benefits of those employees closest to retirement, defined benefit pension plans work well in larger corporations where a sufficient number of employees exists at various age levels such that a level method of funding benefits over a number of years also exists. On the other hand, in a small corporation with one younger employee and one older employee, the majority of the employer contributions will be used to fund the benefit of the older employee, thus leaving the younger employee after the retirement of the older employee with a virtually unfunded benefit. As long as these aspects of defined benefit pension plans are understood, such plans may prove useful in a small business setting.

The annual contributions required under a defined benefit pension plan must be determined actuarially and based upon factors such as the ages of the participants, the earnings of the trust fund, and inflation. Consequently, the administration of a defined benefit pension plan is normally more costly than that of a profit-sharing plan or a money purchase pension plan.

Further, except for those defined benefit plans which at no time cover more than 25 active professional participants and which are maintained by employers whose principal businesses are providing services, defined benefit plans generally are subject to the pension benefit guaranty provisions of Title IV of the Employee Retirement Income Security Act (ERISA). The Pension Benefit Guaranty Corporation (PBGC) which administers these provisions of Title IV acts as an insurer of the pension plan benefits of plans which are not excepted from its protection.

One commonly used exception, the professional service provider exception, specifically includes employers whose principal business is the per-

---

[12] Section 404(a)(1)(A)(ii) of the Code. More rapid funding may be allowed under the minimum funding standard of Code Section 404(a)(1)(A)(i).

formance of professional services and who are owned or controlled by physicians, dentists, chiropractors, osteopaths, optometrists, other licensed practitioners of the healing arts, attorneys, public accountants, public engineers, architects, draftsmen, actuaries, psychologists, social or physical scientists and performing artists.[13]

The PBGC in a series of recent opinion letters has taken the position that the professional service provider exception does not apply to opticians, food brokers, artists, designers, real estate brokers, individuals in advertising and public relations, foresters, and river boat pilots.[14] The rationale of the PBGC in these opinion letters is that these occupational groups are outside the scope of the exception because the occupations involved do not require a prolonged course of specialized intellectual instruction and are not predominantly intellectual in character.

The exception is valuable to the employer because pension plans that are subject to Title IV must pay annual premiums to the PBGC of $2.60 per participant per year. For this purpose, the term *participant* includes all actual participants plus former participants or their beneficiaries who are currently receiving or who have a future right to receive plan benefits. Also, if a plan subject to Title IV of ERISA is terminated and has insufficient assets to pay benefits guaranteed by the PBGC, the employer becomes liable to the PBGC in an amount equal to the lesser of 30 percent of the employer's net worth or the value of the unfunded "guaranteed benefits" under the plan.

There also are other important restrictions, for example, the so-called 5717 limitations. The 5717 limitations, which are contained in Treasury Regulations Section 1.401-4(c) restrict the benefits which may be paid to the 25 highest paid employees at the time the plan is established or at the time that plan benefits are increased substantially. The 5717 limitations may have a substantial impact on pension plans of a small business since they generally are effective if a lump sum distribtuion is payable with respect to a participant within 10 years after the plan either is established or amended to increase benefits substantially or if the plan either is terminated within its first 10 years or within 10 years of an amendment that substantially increases benefits. Further, if the plan is underfunded within the first 10 years, these limitations may apply beyond 10 years. Several types of defined benefit plans exist and are described below.

Fixed Benefit Plans. Fixed benefit plans generally define a participant's ultimate retirement benefit in terms of a specified percentage of a participant's average monthly compensation for the 3 or 5 highest-paid consecutive years of service out of the last 10 years of service. However, the participant's entitlement to the benefit generally is phased in over a period

---

[13] Employee Retirement Income Security Act of 1974, Pub. L. No. 93–406, § 4021(c)(2)(B), 818 stat. 829 (1974) [hereinafter cited as ERISA].

[14] PBGC Opinion Letters 80–9 through 80–15.

of time. For example, if a participant has completed 15 or more years of service at his or her normal retirement age, then the participant might be entitled at normal retirement age to an annuity for his or her life equal to 25 percent of his or her average monthly compensation for the highest 5 consecutive years of service out of his or her last 10 years of service. If the participant has completed less than 15 years of service at his or her normal retirement age, the annuity determined under the immediately preceding sentence might be reduced by one-fifteenth for each year of service less than 15 which the participant has then completed. As a *caveat*, however, to the extent that a plan is top-heavy, as discussed below, the non-key employees (nonowners and nonexecutives) must accrue a benefit at least equal to 2 percent of their compensation for each year of service.[15] Thus, top-heavy fixed benefit plans may be unable to offer this advantageous phase-in period.

A fixed benefit plan also may be especially advantageous in a small business where a limited number of employees are in their mid-to late-forties or early-fifties and intend to work at least 10 more years. For example, assume that a company has the following employees:

Employee	Age	Years of Service	Salary
Older shareholder	55	20	$100,000
Younger shareholder	30	5	$ 30,000
Staff employee	30	5	$ 10,000

Assume further that the normal retirement benefit formula is 25 percent of a participant's average monthly compensation for the highest 5 consecutive years of service out of the last 10 years of service. Finally, ignoring interest considerations and salary increases, assume that a total of $500,000 will be needed to fund the older shareholder's benefit at age 65, $150,000 will be needed to fund the younger shareholder's benefit at age 65, and $50,000 ultimately will be needed to fund the staff employee's benefit at age 65. Based on these assumptions, $500,000 must be funded over 10 years for the older shareholder; hence, the contribution on his behalf must be $50,000 or 50 percent of his annual compensation. In contrast, $50,000 must be funded over 35 years for the staff employee, producing an annual contribution of under $1,500 or less than 15 percent of the staff employee's annual compensation.

If an interest assumption had been added to this example, the disparity in the percentage of compensation required to fund the older versus the

---

[15] I.R.C. § 416(c)(1).

younger shareholder's benefit would be even more pronounced since the contributions made on behalf of the younger shareholder will have a much longer period of time to compound interest; hence, even smaller contributions would be needed to fund the younger shareholder's benefit. To illustrate, a dollar invested at an 8 percent return for 10 years will be worth $2.16, while a dollar invested at an 8 percent return for 35 years will be worth $14.79. Admittedly, this example does not conform to accepted actuarial practice; however, it illustrates that a disproportionate percentage of the employer contributions in a fixed benefit plan will be allocated to the older shareholder.

Unit Benefit Plans. Unit benefit plans usually define a participant's pension amount by reference to an annual adjusted formula which takes into account both years of service and compensation. As before, top-heavy plans subject to the minimum benefit rules for non-key employees will face greater restrictions than the discussion below indicates.

1. Career Average Unit Benefit Plans. Under this type of plan, each participant is credited with a benefit for each year of service based on the participant's compensation for that particular year of service. For example, assume that a participant who is age 55 when first employed is entitled to a benefit equal to 1 percent of his or her compensation for each year of service. If such participant earns the compensation shown in the first column below, his or her annual benefit accrual and annual pension benefit will be as listed in the second column.

Year	Compensation	Benefit
1	$ 50,000	$ 500
2	55,000	550
3	60,000	600
4	65,000	650
5	70,000	700
6	80,000	800
7	85,000	850
8	90,000	900
9	95,000	950
10	100,000	1,000
	Annual pension equals:	$7,500

2. Final Average Unit Benefit Plans. Under this type of plan, each participant is credited with benefits for each year of service, and these benefits are based on a participant's average compensation for a particular period of time, generally the highest five consecutive years out of the last ten years. For example, assume a benefit formula of 1 percent for each year of service multiplied by the participant's highest five consecutive years of service out of the last 10 years. Assume further that the participant was age 55 when initially employed and worked ten years and that his or her compensation is as shown in the career average unit benefit plan example

above. The average compensation for the highest 5 consecutive years of service out of the last 10 years of service is $90,000. Since he or she has completed 10 years of service, he or she will be entitled to an annual pension of 10 percent of $90,000, or $9,000.

A unit benefit plan will principally be advantageous when the shareholders either have, or are expected to have, many years of service. A career average unit benefit plan, as opposed to a final average unit benefit plan, will serve to avoid both a large unfunded liability and accelerated funding during later years in the event of substantial salary increases, since benefits under a career coverage plan are determined each year based on each year's income. Of course, as a result, the benefits under a career average unit benefit plan are not likely to keep pace with inflation.

3. Flat Benefit Plans. Benefits under a flat benefit plan are not dependent upon a participant's compensation. Under a pure flat benefit plan, the participant will be entitled to a flat monthly pension at normal retirement, such as $200, irrespective of his or her length of service or compensation. Alternatively, the monthly pension at normal retirement may be defined in terms of a specified dollar amount per year of service, for example, $20 multiplied by the participant's years of service. Flat benefit plans usually are adopted only in collectively bargained plans between labor and management.

4. Choosing betweeen Defined Benefit Pension Plans. In the small-business setting, a fixed benefit final average earnings plan usually will provide the most appropriate type of defined benefit plan. Normally, after careful consideration of personal savings, investments, and anticipated Social Security benefits, an employer will be able to determine the percentage of the employees' income which must be continued after retirement by qualified plan benefits in order to provide adequate retirement security. Since the objective of the small business employer is the continuation during retirement of that standard of living attained by him or her immediately prior to retirement, a final average pay formula usually will be selected. Thereafter, the plan's actuary will make assumptions regarding the anticipated impact of inflation on salaries and, using these assumptions, calculate the amount of funding necessary to provide a benefit that compensates for inflation. Of course, if several shareholders or owners are involved, a collective decision must be made regarding the income continuation percentage.

Usually a flat benefit plan approach is completely out of the question for a small business employer since it fails to take compensation into account. A unit benefit plan is a plausible alternative; however, in many cases the owners or controlling shareholders will be uncertain as to how long they will remain in service with the small business, and, in many cases, age differences among the shareholders will result in a wide divergence of benefits based on a percentage of salary if this approach is used.

As previously discussed, defined benefit plans and, in particular, fixed benefit plans that require only a 10 or 15 year minimum period of service for full benefits create a greater funding obligation for the older participants. Acknowledging this fact, the compensation package of older and younger employees may be adjusted equitably after adoption of the qualified pension plan so that the current compensation of younger employees will be reduced as a result of the plan to a lesser extent than the compensation of the older employees. This kind of adjustment often responds to the financial realities and the desires of the employees since the younger employees generally want almost all their compensation paid currently while older employees are more cognizant of their retirement needs and, therefore, are more willing to relinquish current compensation to provide for retirement security. In addition, the younger employees often are faced with those personal expenses of starting a home and family that the older employees have already experienced. If the younger employees desire to shelter more current compensation than required to fund their defined benefits, adopting a defined contribution plan in addition to the defined benefit plan should be considered. Furthermore, the defined contribution plan may be drafted in such a manner that the older employees are excluded from participation.[16]

Target Benefit Pension Plans. Under a target benefit plan, benefits are defined by using formulae similar to those formulae used for defined benefit plans. However, employer contributions, earnings, and losses are allocated actuarially to the individual accounts of the plan participants, and actual pensions are based on the amounts in the respective individual accounts. Thus, a target benefit plan is simply a pension plan which sets as its goal a pension funded by the amount in the individual account. The employer only has an obligation to make the contribution required by the plan formula; the employer has no obligation to make sufficient contributions to produce the actual benefit targeted. A target benefit plan is, consequently, a hybrid arrangement combining some characteristics of a defined benefit plan with some characteristics of a defined contribution plan. The targeted benefit provided under the plan is not an actual promise to the participant of a fixed benefit since the actual benefit which will be paid will be based upon what is actually in the participant's account. The target benefit plan closely resembles a money purchase pension plan, which is discussed below.[17]

Four factors should be considered before a small employer adopts a target benefit plan: (1) the PBGC provisions of Title IV of ERISA do not apply to target benefit plans, (2) the 5717 limitations do not apply to target benefit plans, (3) determining whether a target benefit plan discriminates in favor of the highly-paid employees is sometimes difficult and the resulting need for actuarial allocations may prove quite costly, and (4) the annual

---

[16] See *James E. Thompson, Jr.,* 74 T.C. 873 (1980).

[17] Rev. Rul. 76-464, 1976-2 C.B. 115.

addition limitations which apply to target benefit plans are those which apply to defined contribution plans, a significant consideration since the dollar amount limitations have been reduced drastically by TEFRA as noted below.

Money Purchase Pension Plans. Money purchase pension plans are also hybrid plans. Money purchase pension plans contain a formula that determines the amount of employer contributions to the plan. The amount of contributions is not subject to the employer's discretion and is not based on profits. Amounts contributed to the plan are allocated to participant accounts and no guaranteed benefits exist. Consequently, upon retirement, the participant will be entitled only to the benefit that can be purchased with the "money" in his account, hence, the term *money purchase.*

Money purchase pension plans typically provide for a contribution based upon a stated percentage of a participant's annual compensation, and such plans may be integrated with Social Security benefits, subject, of course, to the new top-heavy limitations if applicable. Under the integration formula generally adopted in money purchase pension plans, a 7 percent differential may exist as to contributions on wages below and above the Social Security wage base. For example, the employer may contribute 0 percent of compensation below the wage base and 7 percent of compensation above the wage base, or 3 percent of compensation below the wage base and 10 percent of compensation above the wage base. The following table illustrates a fully integrated money purchase pension plan which has a contribution formula of 3 percent of compensation up to the Social Security wage base of $25,900 for 1980 plus 10 percent of all compensation in excess of that wage base. This table should be compared with the table illustrating the integrated profit-sharing plan which is presented above.

Participant	Contribution Allocation
Shareholder @ $175,900	$15,777.00
Staff employee @ $12,000	360.00
Staff employee @ $10,000	300.00
Staff employee @ $8,000	240.00
	$16,677.00

The comparison reveals that the shareholder who is more highly compensated receives 90.3 percent of the total contribution to the integrated profit-sharing plan, yet he receives 94.6 percent of the total contribution to the integrated money purchase plan. The staff employee having the least amount of compensation, on the other hand, receives 2.56 percent of the total contribution to the integrated profit-sharing plan, yet only 1.4 percent of the total contribution to the integrated money purchase plan. The amount of the differential is not inherent in the comparison of the two types of plans; however, the example illustrates the existence of a significant differential in a situation that is not atypical. A small business employer should not ignore the impact of the example's admittedly small differential over the working lives of plan participants.

In considering the adoption of a money purchase pension plan, the employer should note four facts. First, contributions to a money purchase plan are mandatory and are in proportion to compensation. The allocation is similar to the allocation under a profit-sharing plan and stands in contrast to the possibility of disproportionately higher contributions on behalf of higher-paid employees under fixed rate plans, unit benefit plans, and target benefit plans. Second, neither the PBGC provisions of Title IV of ERISA nor the 5717 limitations apply.[18] Third, a money purchase pension plan is a defined contribution plan for purposes of the annual addition limitation under Section 415 of the Code. Finally, unlike profit sharing plans, forfeitures in a money purchase plan, as with a pension plan, must be applied so as to reduce future employer contributions.

Combinations of Plans

Defined Contribution Plans. As noted, target benefit plans, money purchase pension plans, and profit-sharing plans all are classified as *defined contribution plans* because benefits are determined by the participant's individual account balance. Under Section 415 of the Code, the annual additions which are made to all such plans maintained by one employer on behalf of any participant must be aggregated. The aggregate maximum annual addition must not exceed the lesser of (a) 25 percent of the participant's compensation for the year or (b) $30,000 as adjusted annually for cost-of-living increases after 1986.

A combination of defined contribution plans, each requiring contributions of less than the Section 415 limit, often provides an excellent method of maximizing benefits while maximizing flexibility. For example, if only a profit-sharing plan is maintained, the maximum deductible contribution is limited to 15 percent of compensation paid during the year. Therefore, while the profit-sharing plan provides flexibility, the compensation ceiling under Code Section 415 cannot be fully utilized. On the other hand, an employer could adopt only a money purchase plan having a contribution formula that itself requires the maximum contribution allowed by Section 415; however, the full contribution to the plan will always be required, even in "lean" years, since money purchase plan contributions are mandatory. If, in a given year, the small business experiences cash flow problems and is unable to make the required contribution, a nondeductible excise tax equal to 5 percent of the deficiency may be imposed under Section 4971 of the Code. Moreover, if a timely correction of the deficiency is not made, an additional nondeductible excise tax equal to 100 percent of the deficiency may be imposed.

---

[18] ERISA,. supra n.12, § 4021(b)(1).

To escape these restrictions on single plans, a small business may adopt a money purchase plan requiring the contribution of that part of the total benefit which the employer feels reasonably certain could be paid even in cash-lean years, in tandem with a totally discretionary profit-sharing plan. This combination ameliorates the inflexible funding requirement created by exclusive use of a money purchase plan, yet it avoids the bar on making a full "25 percent of compensation" employer contribution which is created by exclusive use of a profit-sharing plan. Also, in this scheme, the money purchase plan may be fully integrated so that the employer always will receive the full benefit of integration even in those years when substantial contributions are not made to the profit-sharing plan.

Defined Benefit and Defined Contribution Plans. If a small business employer wants to defer more than the 25 percent of compensation or the $30,000 limit applicable to defined contribution plans, then the only alternative is to adopt either a defined benefit plan or a combination of plans that includes both a defined benefit and a defined contribution plan.

Any combination of defined benefit and defined contribution plans is subject to a complex mathematical limitation imposed by Code Section 415(e). Basically, an employer is prevented by this subsection from adopting *both* (1) a defined contribution plan or plans providing the *maximum contribution*, that is, 25 percent of compensation or $30,000 and (2) a defined benefit plan or plans providing the *maximum benefit*, that is, $90,000 or 100 percent of the participant's average compensation for his high three years.[19] Instead, as the percentage of the defined contribution maximum which is provided by the defind contribution plans increases, the percentage of the defined benefit maximum which may be provided by the defined benefit plans decreases. Prior to TEFRA, this limitation was embodied in the so-called 1.4 Rule; after TEFRA, the limitation is embodied in a "1.0 Rule."[20]

The calculation of these rules is complex; however the following example illustrates the old 1.4 Rule and the new 1.0 Rule.

Step 1: Assume Employee A is in his first year of service. He earns $60,000; participates in defined benefit and defined contribution plans; prefers to defer $7,500 of income, or 12.5 percent of his compensation, using the defined contribution plan; and wants to defer the maximum amount allowed under a defined benefit plan.

Step 2: Under the Old 1.4 Rule. The old and new rules are based on defined benefit and defined contribution fractions. One of the two fractions is computed first, using certain assumptions about the amount of contributions to that type of plan; thereafter, application of the appropriate "rule" produces the other fraction, from which the permitted amount of contribu-

---

[19] I.R.C. § 415(b), § 415(c).

[20] I.R.C. § 415(e), § 416(h).

tion to the other type of plan may be calculated. Given the assumptions above, the defined contribution fraction in this case equals

$$\frac{7{,}500 \text{ (amount of contributions to defined contribution plan)}}{15{,}000 \text{ (maximum according to § 415(c)(1) as amended)}} = .50$$

The 1.4 test: $1.4 - .5 = .90$
The defined benefit fraction can equal 0.9.
The calculation of the fraction is:

$$\frac{X \text{ (anticipated benefit which employee may fund)}}{\$60{,}000 \text{ (maximum anticipated benefit if employer}} = .90$$
$$\text{maintains only a defined benefit plan)}$$

$$X = \$60{,}000 \times .9 = \$54{,}000.$$

Step 3: Conclusion under 1.4 Rule. The employee can fund an anticipated benefit of $54,000 per year using the defined benefit plan.

Step 4: Under the New 1.0 Rule. The defined contribution fraction denominator is the lesser of:

A. 1.25 (assuming the plan is not a top-heavy plan as discussed below) multiplied by $30,000 (the § 415(c)(1)(A) limitation for the year) *or* $37,500; or
B. 1.4 multiplied by $15,000 (the § 415(c)(1)(B) limitation) *or* $21,000.

The fraction is thus:

$$\frac{\$ 7{,}500 \text{ (amount of contribution to plan)}}{\$21{,}000 \text{ (the maximum amount according}} = .357$$
$$\text{to new section 415(c))}$$

The 1.0 test: $1.0 - .357 = .643$
The defined benefit fraction can equal .643.
The defined benefit fraction denominator is the lesser of:

A. 1.25 (since not a top-heavy plan) multiplied by $90,000 (the dollar limitation in effect for the year for defined benefit plans) *or* $112,500; or
B. 1.4 multiplied by $60,000 (the § 415(b)(1)(B) limitation) *or* $84,000.

The calculation of the fraction is thus:

$$\frac{X \text{ (anticipated benefit which employee may fund)}}{\$84{,}000 \text{ (maximum anticipated benefit if only a}} = .643$$
$$\text{defined benefit plan)}$$

$$X = .643 \times \$84{,}000 = \$54{,}000$$

Step 5: Conclusion under New 1.0 Rule: The employee can fund an antici-pated benefit of $54,000 per year using the defined benefit plan.

Clearly, the new 1.0 Rule imposed by TEFRA produces no change from the old 1.4 Rule in the amount of compensation which an employee who earns $60,000 per year may defer. However, the small business owner's income may be far in excess of $60,000 in which case a substantial difference exists between the old 1.4 Rule and the new 1.0 Rule. Algebraic examination reveals that the new rule severely restricts the ability of an employee or owner/employee earning more than $80,357.14 to defer income using a combination of defined benefit and defined contribution plans. Moreover, as explained below, certain top-heavy plans are subject to a more restrictive version of the 1.0 Rule and employees and owner/employees who participate in those plans will be adversely affected if they individually earn more than $64,285.71.

Notwithstanding the 1.0 Rule, if a combination involves a defined benefit plan and a profit-sharing plan, a further limitation exists. The deductible contributions under the combined plans may not exceed the greater of 25 percent of the compensation paid to the plan participants during the year or the employer contributions required to satisfy certain minimum funding standards which are only applicable to defined benefit plans, target plans, and money purchase pension plans. Hence, if a defined benefit plan and a profit-sharing plan maintained by the same employer cover the same employees, and if the contributions under the defined benefit plan equal 20 percent of the compensation paid to such participants during the year, the deductible contribution to the profit-sharing plan will be limited to only 5 percent of the compensation paid to the participants during the year.

Therefore, where the objective is to defer as much compensation as is possible consistent with the 1.0 Rule limitation, the defined contribution plan selected should be a plan that is subject to the minimum funding standards, that is, a target benefit or money purchase plan, and not a profit-sharing plan. Of course, the minimum funding standards themselves are problematic since plans to which they apply *must* be funded at the minimum funding level specified in Section 412 of the Code, and failure to so fund the plans each year will result in imposition of nondeductible excise taxes under Section 4971 of the Code. Hence, the advantage of maximum deductibility available with target benefit and money purchase plans which are maintained with defined benefit plans carries with it a price tag of loss of funding flexibility available only with profit-sharing plans which are maintained with defined benefit plans.

Simplified Pension Plans

The Revenue Act of 1978 established the Simplified Employee Pension (SEP) for years beginning after 1978. Effectively, a SEP is not a qualified plan; rather, it is a plan for contributing to a group of individual retirement accounts (SEP–IRAs).[21]

---

[21] I.R.C. § 408(k).

The principal drawback of a SEP is that contributions on behalf of a given individual currently are limited to $17,000.[22] A SEP generally must cover every employee who is at least age 25 and has performed any service for the employer maintaining the plan during at least three of the immediately preceding 5 calendar years. Contributions must be fully vested when made. Only the first $200,000 of a given employee's compensation may be taken into account under the plan, and employer contributions to the SEP-IRAs must bear a uniform relationship to the total compensation of each participant, disregarding compensation over $200,000. Given these limitations, a SEP generally is not a desirable alternative for a small business employer.

SPECIFIC QUALIFICATION ASPECTS RELEVANT TO SMALL BUSINESS EMPLOYERS

Eligibility and Minimum Participation Standards

Section 410 of the Code sets forth the minimum participation standards imposed upon all qualified retirement plans. In order to obtain qualified status, a plan may not, as a condition of participation, require that an employee complete a period of service extending beyond the later of reaching age 25 or completing one year of service. Part-time employees working fewer than 1,000 hours during any given year may be indefinitely excluded, even if they are older than 25. Also, participation may be withheld until the completion of three years of service, but only if the plan provides for full vesting after three years of service.

A plan must provide that an employee who has satisfied the age and service requirements will participate in the plan no later than the earlier of (1) the first day of the first plan year beginning after the date on which the employee satisfied the requirements, or (2) the date six months after the date on which the employee satisfied the requirements.[23]

In the interest of simplicity, qualified retirement plans adopted by a small business should provide that participation begins after the completion of one year of service and attainment of age 25 and that participation is retroactive to the first day of the first plan year in which the latter of these two requirements is met.

A plan generally may not exclude from participation employees who are beyond a specified age. However, a defined benefit plan or a target benefit plan may exclude employees who are within five years of normal retirement age when they begin employment.[24]

---

[22] 1982 Technical Corrections Act, P.L. 97–448, § 103(D)(1)(B).

[23] I.R.C. § 410(a)(4).

[24] I.R.C. § 401(a)(3), § 410(a)(2); Treas. Regs. § 1.410(a)–4(a)(1).

The impact of the Age Discrimination in Employment Act (ADEA) on participation in qualified retirement plans is unclear. ADEA, which is applicable to all employers who have 20 or more employees, broadly prohibits discrimination based on age in the terms, conditions, and benefits of employment and protects privately employed individuals in the age group of 40 to 70. Section 4(f)(2) of ADEA generally permits employers to observe the terms of bona fide employee benefit plans such as retirement or pension plans; however, the regulations interpreting ADEA state that "[n]o employee hired prior to normal retirement age may be excluded from a defined contribution plan," and they restrict exclusion of those employees from defined benefit plans.[25]

Code Section 410(b) specifies minimum eligibility standards for qualified plans. To be qualified, a plan must benefit 70 percent or more of all employees or 80 percent or more of the employees who are eligible to benefit if 70 percent or more of all employees are eligible to benefit. The plan may qualify if fewer employees are included as long as the eligibility classifications established by the employer are found by the Secretary of the Treasury to be nondiscriminatory. Normally the classification test requires the plan to cover a reasonable cross-section of employees in all compensation ranges.[26]

The minimum eligibility requirements usually do not present a problem for a small business unless groups of related or affiliated small businesses are involved. If there are several such small businesses involved, then an insufficient number of employees may be eligible to participate in each business' plan or plans since Code Sections 414(b), 414(c), and 414(m) provide that all employees of all corporations and partnerships which are members of a controlled or affiliated group are treated as if employed by a single employer.

The major problem in the controlled group context is the definition of a brother-sister controlled group of corporations which is contained in Code Section 1563. Section 414 incorporates this definition for certain qualified plan purposes. The term *brother-sister controlled group of corporations* generally means two or more organizations conducting trades or businesses: (a) if the same five or fewer persons own, singularly or in combination, a controlling interest in each organization and (b) if, taking into account the ownership of each such person only to the extent such ownership is identical with respect to each such organization, such persons are in effective control of each corporation. The term *controlling interest* means ownership of 80 percent of the total combined voting power of all classes of stock entitled to

---

[25] 29 C.F.R. § 860.120(f)(1)(iv)(A).

[26] *Federal Land Bank Association of Asheville, North Carolina,* 74 T.C. 1106 (1980) (in which a thrift plan in which only 2 of 23 employees participated was held to cover a nondiscriminatory classification).

vote or at least 80 percent of the total value of shares of all classes of stock. The term *effective control* means ownership of stock possessing more than 50 percent of the total combined voting power of all classes of stock entitled to vote or 50 percent of the total value of shares of all classes of stock of such corporation.

In *U.S.* v. *Vogel Fertilizer Co.* [U.S., 70 L. Ed. 2d 792, 102 S Ct (1982)], the U.S. Supreme Court held that for purposes of computing the 80 percent controlling interest, only persons who owned an interest in each tested corporation should be taken into account—a holding which vastly restricts the Service's ability to amalgamate employees of several corporate employers for eligibility test purposes. The following two examples illustrate the interaction of the 50 percent test and the 80 percent test and the restrictive effect of *Vogel*.

Example One. Mr. A owns 90 percent of Corporation X and 55 percent of Corporation Y. Mr. B, who is unrelated to Mr. A, owns 10 percent of Corporation X and 45 percent of Corporation Y.

	80% Controlling Interest Test		50% Identical Ownership Test	
	Corp. X	*Corp. Y*	*Corp. X*	*Corp. Y*
Mr. A	90	55	55	55
Mr. B	10	45	10	10
	100	100	65	65

In example one, Mr. A and Mr. B together own 100 percent of both corporations; therefore, the 80 percent controlling interest test is satisfied. Mr. A's identical ownership interest in Corporations X and Y is 55 percent since Mr. A owns at least 55 percent of each Corporation. Mr. B's identical ownership of Corporations X and Y is 10 percent since Mr. B owns at least 10 percent of each Corporation. Since the sum of the identical ownership of Mr. A and Mr. B exceeds 50 percent, the 50 percent identical ownership test is met. Since both tests are met Corporations X and Y are brother-sister controlled corporations.

Example Two: Assume the same facts as in example one except that Mr. A owns 100 percent of Corporation X.

	80% Controlling Interest Test		50% Identical Ownership Test	
	Corp. X	*Corp. Y*	*Corp. X*	*Corp. Y*
Mr. A	100	55	55	55
Mr. B	0	45	0	45
	100	100	55	100

At first blush it might appear that both the 80 percent controlling interest test and the 50 percent identical ownership test are satisfied; however, under *Vogel*, Mr. B cannot be taken into account for purposes of applying the 80 percent controlling interest test, because Mr. B does not have an interest in each corporation that is being tested under the 80 percent test. As a result, the 80 percent controlling interest test is not satisfied in example two and the two corporations are not part of a brother-sister controlled group.

If two or more entities constitute either a controlled group of corporations or trades or businesses under common control as defined in Code Section 414(b) and (c), respectively, then the rules of Section 401 (qualification standards), Section 410 (participation), Section 411 (vesting), and Section 415 (limitations on benefits and contributions) are applied to all members of the controlled group as if all of the employees worked for the employer adopting the plan. The rules under Section 404 (deductions) and Section 412 (funding) generally are applied only with respect to members of the controlled group who adopt the same plan.

As noted, special rules exists under Section 414(m) of the Code which relates to affiliated groups of service corporations; however, these are discussed in Chapter 53.

Vesting and Benefit Accrual

Subject to Section 416 of the Code, which as discussed below establishes special rules for so-called top-heavy plans, Section 411 of ERISA provides the minimum vesting standards and permits the adoption of three types of vesting schedules, two of which are commonly used. The first is so-called cliff vesting. A cliff vesting schedule requires full vesting for a participant with at least 10 years of service, but no vesting for a participant with fewer than 10 years of service. The second common statutory vesting schedule is the so-called 5-15 vesting schedule. A 5-15 vesting schedule calls for at least 25 percent vesting after 5 years of service, and annual vesting increases every year thereafter so that the participant will be 100 percent vested after 15 years of service.

Notwithstanding these statutory vesting schedules, the Service has recently required that professional corporations use the so-called 4-40 vesting schedule unless it can be shown that the turnover rate of highly paid employees is not appreciably lower than the turnover rate among the rank-and-file employees.[27] The 4-40 vesting schedule calls for vesting as described below:

---

[27] See Rev. Proc. 75-49, 1975-2 C.B. 584, as modified by Rev. Proc. 76-11, 1976-1 C.B. 550.

	Nonforfeitable
Years of Service	*Percentage*
1	0
2	0
3	0
4	40
5	45
6	50
7	60
8	70
9	80
10	90
11	100

Of course, a longer permissible vesting schedule has advantages. The vesting schedule is obviously an inducement to employees to continue employment until they are fully vested. Moreover, if a participant's employment is terminated before he or she is fully vested, benefits which are forfeited either will be distributed to the advantage of the other participants under the plan or will serve to reduce employer contributions. Forfeitures may be substantial if the employee turnover rate is high.

During 1980, the Service made a concerted attempt to enforce vesting schedules which are significantly more restrictive than the 4–40 schedule. Specifically, they tried to enforce a three-year vesting schedule for closely held and professional corporations where the owners typically do not terminate their employment. There is, however, specific authority in the legislative history of ERISA that vesting at a rate more rapid than the 4–40 rate is not required, notwithstanding a substantial turnover rate among staff employees, unless there is actual misuse in operation of vesting to deny its participants' accrued benefits.[28] Assuming the faster vesting schedules applicable to top-heavy plans are not required, the author feels that the 4–40 vesting schedule is appropriate and should be adopted for most small businesses, unless a shorter vesting schedule is desired. The 4–40 schedule should provide a sufficient deferral period during the first three years of employment to eliminate short-term employees from the vesting rules, and the schedule should provide vesting which will induce employees to remain with the corporation during later years of employment.

Past Service

Past service with former employers may be used for determining eligibility to participate in a qualified retirement plan, accrual, and vesting of benefits. At one time, the Service maintained that past service as a self-

---

[28] House Comm. on Ways and Means, Brief Summary of the Provisions of H.R. 12481, 93 Cong., 2d Sess. 3 (February 5, 1974).

employed individual (partner or sole proprietor) could not be counted for purposes of a plan adopted by a corporate successor of the partnership. The Service was unsuccessful with this position in litigation,[29] and it now acknowledges that a corporate qualified plan may include service with a prior partnership or as a sole proprietor for purposes of participation, vesting, and benefit accrual.[30]

Until recently, the Service maintained that, if past service credit was given for purposes of benefit accrual in a defined benefit plan, then the plan provisions giving past service credit had to prohibit "duplication of benefits," the crediting of benefits under two plans simultaneously.[31] In Rev. Rul. 80-349[32], the Service reversed its position on prevention of "duplication of benefits"; however, the ruling implied that where duplication of benefits does exist it may result in discrimination, thereby disqualifying the plan.

The Service also takes the position that the use of prior service for purposes of eligibility, vesting, and benefit accrual is subject to the nondiscrimination rules. Using prior service may disqualify a plan where no staff employees received past service credit for their service with a former employer, or possibly where none of the existing staff employees were employed with the former employer.[33] Consequently, the author generally does not recommend that past service credit be granted for service with predecessor employers unless there are also staff employees who were employed by the predecessor organization.

Integration with Social Security Benefits

In computing contributions to a qualified retirement plan, the Service generally permits an employer in a nontop-heavy plan to take into consideration its contributions to the Social Security system. For example, in 1982 an employer paid a Social Security tax equal to 6.70 percent of the first $32,400 of compensation paid for each employee. Since social security taxes theoretically are used to fund an employee's retirement benefit, a somewhat lower qualified plan employee contribution or benefit is permitted with respect to compensation below the Social Security wage base. This concept of taking into account Social Security taxes when computing contributions or benefits under a qualified plan is known as "integration." Although the Service has, in the last several years, discussed the possibility of attempting to eliminate integration, the author feels that small business

[29] *Farley Funeral Home,* 62 T.C. 150 (1974).
[30] Tech. Advice Memo. 7742003.
[31] *See* Rev. Rul. 62-139, 1962-2 C.B. 123, Rev. Rul. 72-531, 1972-2 C.B. 221.
[32] 1980-2 C.B. 132.
[33] *See* Rev. Rul. 69-409, 1969-2 C.B. 98.

should definitely review the possibility of adopting integrated plans and should not hesitate to adopt those plans if they so desire.[34]

The present state of the law governing Social Security integration is based on Treasury Regulations Section 1.401–3(e) and Revenue Ruling 71–446.[35] Profit-sharing plans and money purchase pension plans are generally integrated with the Social Security wage base using a 7 percent integration factor. Thus, in both a money purchase pension plan and in a profit-sharing plan, the account of each participant may be credited with a contribution equal to 7 percent of the compensation earned by the participant during the plan year that was in excess of the Social Security wage base. Any contribution in excess of the amount allocated under the preceding sentence is then allocated to the accounts of all participants in an amount equal to a uniform percentage of all compensation earned.

A defined benefit pension plan is validly integrated with Social Security if the benefeits provided by the plan, when added to the benefits provided by the employer financed portion of Social Security, result in a combined benefit that is a uniform percentage of the compensation paid by the employer to each participant in the plan. Basically, there are three types of integrated defined benefit plans: excess plans, step-rate plans and offset plans.

Excess Plans. An excess plan pays a benefit based solely upon an employee's compensation in excess of a certain amount which is referred to as the plan's integration level. The plan provides proportionately greater benefits to higher-paid participants since a greater proportion of their compensation will exceed the integration level. For example, if Participant A's compensation is $10,000 and Participant B's compensation is $20,000, a nonintegrated defined benefit plan could provide a benefit to B that is no greater than twice the benefit provided to A. However, if the plan is integrated at an integration level of $8,000, then only $2,000 of A's compensation and $12,000 of B's compensation is taken into account in computing the benefits, and therefore, the plan can provide B a benefit that is 6 times greater than the benefit provided to A. In this example, if A's compensation had been less than the $8,000 integration level, A would not accrue any benefit.

The maximum *integration level* for an individual is determined by averaging the Social Security wage bases in effect during the individual's working career. Since the Social Security wage base has increased over the years, and will no doubt continue to increase in the future, a plan's integration level may be drafted to automatically increase with respect to active participants along with the Social Security wage base. Once a permissible integration *level* has been determined, the second critical variable to be determined is

---

[34] For a complete discussion of integration, see ¶ 19.056 et. seq. of Prentice-Hall *Federal Taxes*.

[35] Rev. Rul. 72–276, 1972–1 C.B. 111.

the integration *rate*. The integration rate is the retirement benefit provided by the plan expressed as a percentage of compensation in excess of the integration level. The range of permissible integration rates will depend upon whether the plan is a fixed benefit plan or a unit benefit plan.

In an integrated fixed benefit plan, the benefit is normally expressed as a fixed percentage of the excess of the final average compensation over the integration level. For example, assume that a plan provided a defined benefit equal to (1) the excess of average compensation for the last five years of participation over $8,000 (2) multiplied by 25 percent. This integrated benefit represents an *integration level* of $8,000 and an integration rate of 25 percent. The greatest integration *rate* permitted for a fixed benefit plan that provides no benefit other than a life annuity at age 65 is 37½ percent. If a participant has fewer than 15 years of service with the employer maintaining the plan, this 37½ percent rate may be phased in no more rapidly than 2½ percent per year. Thus, for example, if a participant retires with only 8 years of service with the employer, the greatest integration rate that may be used for the participant will be 8 times 2½ percent or 20 percent.

A participant's compensation with respect to which a fixed benefit plan's integrated benefit is determined normally must be averaged over a period of at least 5 consecutive years. This is to prevent the creation of a large integrated benefit based on only one or two years' compensation. An average over three or four years is permitted, however, the maximum permissible integration rate is reduced.[36]

As noted, a unit benefit plan provides a unit of benefit for each year of service. An integrated unit benefit excess plan provides a unit of benefit equal to the excess of compensation over the plan's integration level multiplied by the plan's integration rate. Thus, for example, if the benefit equaled (1) the average compensation in the last five years of service in excess of $8,000 (2) multiplied by ½ percent (3) multiplied by the years of service, then the integration level would be $8,000 and the integration rate would be ½ percent. The maximum permissible integration rate is 1.0 percent for final average unit benefit plans providing solely a straight life annuity at age 65. Such a plan may use an integration level determined in the same manner as for fixed benefit plans. The maximum permissible integration rate for a career average unit benefit plan is 1.4 percent and the integration level for such a plan may not exceed the Social Security wage base in each year for which benefits are accrued. This is, for *each* year of service a participant may earn a benefit equal to 1.4 percent of the excess of compensation earned in that year over the Social Security wage base in effect for that year.

If a plan provides benefits other than a straight life annuity beginning at age 65, then the integration rate for either fixed benefit or unit benefit

---

[36] Rev. Rul. 72-276, 1972-1 C.B. 111.

plans must be reduced. This reduction will be required, for example, if there is a preretirement death benefit, if early retirement before age 65 is permitted, or if the retirement benefit is other than a single life annuity. These adjustments are rather tedious and complex; however, the important fact for an individual contemplating adoption of an integrated plan to bear in mind is that, in order to add benefits other than an annuity for life beginning at age 65, the maximum permitted amount of integrated retirement benefits will normally decrease.

Step-Rate Plans.   A fixed benefit or unit benefit plan that provides an *integrated* benefit based on compensation in excess of the plan's integration level may, *in addition*, provide a nonintegrated benefit for compensation above *or* below the integration level. Such plans are referred to as step-rate plans, and can be thought of as a combination of an integrated excess plan and a nonintegrated plan. For example, a fixed benefit plan could provide, as a sole benefit, a straight life annuity beginning at age 65 of 30 percent of participant's final 5 years average pay up to $8,000 plus 67½ percent of his final 5 years average pay in excess of $8,000. This formula is acceptable since it provides the same benefit as an integrated excess plan paying 37½ percent of compensation in excess of $8,000 plus a nonintegrated plan paying 30 percent of compensation.

Offset Plans.   An offset plan establishes a defined benefit under which no participant and no part of a participant's compensation is excluded because of a minimum compensation level. However, the benefit so determined is then reduced or "offset" by a percentage of the participant's Social Security benefit. For example, a fixed benefit offset plan could provide a benefit equal to (1) 25 percent of participant's final five years average pay (2) minus one half of the participant's Social Security old age pension. The maximum permitted percentage offset for a plan that provides only a straight life annuity at age 65 is an offset of 83⅓ percent of the participant's Social Security benefit. As with excess plans, when the offset plan benefits provided are other than a straight life annuity beginning at age 65, the maximum permissible percentage offset must be reduced.

Payment of Benefits

Benefits normally become payable under qualified retirement plans upon retirement, the termination of employment prior to retirement, disability, or death. The vesting schedule established under the plan generally will apply only to benefits payable upon termination of employment prior to the normal retirement dates. Upon death, disability, or attainment of normal retirement age, participants generally will be fully vested. In drafting qualified retirement plans for a small business, questions often arise with regard to when benefits should be paid to employees who terminate employment prior to reaching normal retirement age. Some retirement plans provide, and some advisors recommend, that qualified retirement plans actually be *retirement* plans and that benefits should be postponed until actual retirement. Under this arrangement, an employee who terminates participation at age 30 must wait until either the normal or early retirement date established under the plan before benefits are received. Those who support this approach also state that it will prohibit employees who leave the business from receiving their benefits and using those benefits to fund a competing business.

Although providing retirement benefits for participants and prohibiting competition by departing employees are important, the author feels that benefit payments usually should be made to terminating participants as soon after termination as possible. If the benefits of terminated employees are withheld until retirement, such employees will remain participants under the plan and must be furnished with annual reports and other documents required under the reporting and disclosure regulations. Providing current benefits to terminated participants also should eliminate the proliferation of partially vested participants which will occur over the years as employees constantly leave a small business.

With the advent of ERISA, various rules were enacted with regard to providing annuities to participants under qualified retirement plans. In general, if a life annuity is available to the participant, he must also have available to him a joint and survivor annuity. A life annuity means an annuity which requires the survival of the participant or his spouse as one of the conditions for payment. For example, an annuity for the participant's life, and an annuity of 10 payments or until the participant's death whichever first occurs, would both constitute life annuities and would invoke the joint and survivor requirements. However, an annuity for a period of 30 years certain is not a life annuity and would not cause the joint and survivor provisions to apply to the plan.[37]

While the joint and survivor annuity rules do provide protection to employees, they also are unduly burdensome on plan administrators. Since, in practice, the author has found most small businesses have overlooked the notice and other requirements of the joint and survivor annuity regulations, the author generally recommends that the defined contribution qualified retirement plans of small business do not provide a life annuity option. While following the recommendation avoids the joint and survivor annuity regulations, the author feels that employees will not have been prejudiced since they should be in a position to obtain an annuity, if one is desired, through rolling over a lump sum distribution of their account into an individual retirement account or an individual retirement annuity as permitted under Section 402(a)(5) of the Code. If a rollover is made, the participant will not be taxed on the initial distribution of funds from the plan prior to the rollover, but he or she will be taxed upon subsequent distributions from the individual retirement account or annuity.

---

[37] Section 401(a)(11) of the Code and Treas. Regs. § 1.401(a)–11.

TOP-HEAVY RULES

One of the most radical changes effected by TEFRA is the creation of the top-heavy plan concept. TEFRA Section 240 adds Section 416 to the Code, effective for years beginning after December 31, 1983. Code Section 416(a) states that a trust is not a qualified trust if it is a part of a top-heavy plan unless the plan meets certain additional requirements. The top-heavy plan rules seem to be the Service's attempt to redeem its position of 1980 as discussed above, that is, its failed attempt to force professional corporations to use the three-year vesting method instead of the 4–40 vesting schedule. As discussed below, one consequence of application of the top-heavy plan rules is that six-year graded vesting *or three-year cliff vesting* is required.[38] Moreover, the establishment of parity between Keogh and corporate plans was accomplished in part by substituting parallel top-heavy plan restrictions for the former restrictions on Keogh plans.[39] For example, the requirements that distributions to key employees begin before age 70½ replaces the parallel former restriction on owner-employees, a Keogh plan concept.[40] Several new terms exist which are applicable to top-heavy plans.

Key Employee

Key employee means a plan participant who at any time during the plan year *or the last four plan years was:* an officer, one of the ten employees who owned the largest interest in the employer, a 5 percent owner of the employer, or a 1 percent owner of the employer who earned annually more than $150,000 from the employer.[41] The $150,000 compensation figure for 1 percent owners is not adjusted for cost-of-living increases.[42] The proposed regulations recently issued on Section 416 also provide that, for example, if twenty people have equal ownership of all of a corporation's stock, then all twenty are holders of the "largest interest in the employer."[43]

Employees

Not surprisingly, self-employed individuals, as defined in Code Section 401(c)(1), are treated as employees—an implicit "price" for the establishment of parity between corporate and noncorporate plans—and the earned income of self-employed individuals constitutes their "compensation" for

---

[38] I.R.C. § 416(b).

[39] *E.g.*, Tax Equity and Fiscal Responsibility Act of 1982, Pub. L. No. 97–248, § 242(a)(b), 96 Stat. 324, 521 [hereinafter cited as TEFRA].

[40] Id.

[41] I.R.C. § 416(i)(1)(A).

[42] Id.

[43] Prop. Reg. § 1.416–1, T–12.

purposes of computing their status as key employees.[44] Moreover, the terms *employee* and *key employee* include the beneficiaries of such persons.[45]

Officers

The number of employees who are treated as officers is limited to the lesser of: (1) 50 or (2) the greater of 3 or 10 percent of all employees.[46] The report of the conference committee on TEFRA states that if an employer has more officers than are required to be counted as key employees, then only those officers with the highest compensation are to be considered in applying the top-heavy rules.[47] The conference report relies on prior authority to define *officer*.[48] Thus, although all of the facts and circumstances are to be considered in determining whether a particular employee is an officer, several key facts which must be considered are: the source of the employee's authority, the term of service, the nature and extent of his or her duties, and whether the employee is characterized fairly as an administrative executive engaged in regular and continued service.[49] Noncorporate business organizations do not have officers according to the proposed regulations.[50]

Ownership

Ownership, for purposes of Code Section 416, is defined specifically and in a complex fashion. If the employer is a corporation, ownership, for purposes of the 1 percent owner and 5 percent owner rules, means (1) ownership of either 1 percent or 5 percent of the stock of the corporation or (2) ownership of stock possessing more than 1 percent or 5 percent of the total combined voting power of all stock of the corporation.[51] If the employer is not a corporation, ownership means possession of 1 percent or 5 percent of the capital or profit interest of the employer.[52] The constructive ownership rules of Code Section 318 generally apply in determining the ownership percentage of corporate employees. The "from entity" rules of Section 318 are altered, however, in that, if 5 percent of a corporation's stock is owned by a potential key employee (instead of 50 percent as usual) then the proportionate share of the corporation's holdings of the plan

---

[44] I.R.C. § 416(i)(3).

[45] I.R.C. § 416(i)(3); Prop. Reg. § 1.416–1, T–8.

[46] I.R.C. § 416(i)(1).

[47] S. REP. NO. 530, 97th Cong. 2d Sess. 626 (1982). See Prop. Reg. § 1.416–1, T–10.

[48] S. REP. NO. 530, 97th Cong., 2d Sess. 626, n. 1 (1982) (Citing Rev. Rul. 80–314, 1980–2 C.B. 152).

[49] Prop. Reg. § 1.416–1, T–9.

[50] Prop. Reg. § 1.416–1, T–11.

[51] I.R.C. § 416(i)(1)(B)(i),(ii).

[52] I.R.C. § 416(i)(1)(B)(i)(II), (ii).

employer's stock is attributed to the employee.[53] The conference report and code require the secretary to issue regulations which define *constructive ownership* as it pertains to *noncorporate employers*, and which are based on principles similar to the Code Section 318 regulations.[54] While Code Section 318 rules are used in determining ownership by employees, the Section 414 aggregation rules are not used in calculating ownership.[55]

Determination Date

Determination Date means the last day of the preceding plan year or the last day of the first plan year.[56]

What Is a Top-Heavy Plan?

A defined benefit plan is a top-heavy plan if "the present value of the cumulative accrued benefits under the plan for key employees exceeds 60 percent of the present value of the cumulative accrued benefits under the plan for all employees" on the determination date.[57] The "present value" aspect of the calculation means that the benefits are treated as if they were accrued in a defined contribution plan.[58] A defined contribution plan is a top-heavy plan if "the aggregate of the accounts of key employees under the plan exceeds 60 percent of the aggregate of the accounts of all employees under such plan" on the determination date.[59] The proposed regulations state that only accrued benefits attributable to deductible employee contributions are excluded from the computation of accrued benefits.[60]

A plan is also top-heavy if it is part of a top-heavy group. First, the proper grouping of plans must be determined. Two type of plans *must* be aggregated: plans in which any of the employer's key employees participate and plans which are grouped by the employer to meet the coverage and discrimination tests of Code Sections 401(a)(4) and 410(b).[61] The conference report states that the top-heavy group rule applies to affiliated service groups, a concept discussed in Chapter 53 and the other Section 414 groups of related employees which were discussed earlier.[62]

---

[53] I.R.C. § 416(i)(1)(B)(iii)(I).

[54] I.R.C. § 416(i)(1)(B)(iii)(II); S. REP. NO. 530, 97th Cong., 2d Sess. 626 (1982).

[55] I.R.C. § 416(i)(1)(C).

[56] I.R.C. § 416(g)(4)(C).

[57] I.R.C. § 416(g)(1)(A)(i).

[58] *See* Prop. Reg. § 1.416–1, T–18 for a discussion of how the present value of accrued benefits is determined for a defined benefit plan.

[59] I.R.C. § 416(g)(1)(A)(ii). See Prop. Reg. § 1.416–1, T–17, for a discussion of how the present value of accrued benefits is determined for a defined contribution plan.

[60] Prop. Reg. § 1.416–1, T–21.

[61] I.R.C. § 416(g)(2)(A)(i); Prop. Reg. § 1.416–1, T–3, T–5.

[62] S. REP. NO. 530, 97th Cong., 2nd Sess. 625 (1982).

The employer *also may* aggregate plans with a top-heavy group in an attempt to destroy the top-heavy group classification as long as the new aggregated group satisfies the coverage and discrimination requirements.[63] A group of plans is a top-heavy group if the sum of "the present value of the cumulative accrued benefits for key employees under all defined benefit plans included in such group" and "the aggregate of the accounts of key employees under all defined contribution plans included in such group" exceeds 60 percent of the same sum computed for all employees.[64]

Impact of Top-Heavy Rules

The consequences of being a top-heavy plan are severe. Aside from the 1.0 Rule discussed earlier, several restrictions exist on top-heavy rules.

First, only $200,000 of an employee's annual compensation during top-heavy years may be considered in computing plan benefits or contributions. The $200,000 limit is subject to a cost-of-living adjustment beginning in 1986.[65]

Second, a top-heavy plan must vest accrued benefits derived from employer contributions according to one of two vesting schedules:[66]

1. Three year cliff vesting, in which the benefits of an employee who has three years of service are 100 percent vested.
2. Six-year graded vesting according to the following chart:

Years of Service	Nonforfeitable Percent
2	20
3	40
4	60
5	80
6 or more	100

Third, a top-heavy defined benefit plan must pay an annual retirement benefit derived from employer contributions to non-key employees which at least equals the lesser of (1) two percent of the participant's average compensation per year of service or (2) 20 percent, multiplied by the employee's average annual compensation during his or her highest consecutive five years.[67] Social Security benefits originating from an employer's contribution to the Social Security system *cannot* be integrated to reduce the minimum benefit.[68]

---

[63] I.R.C § 416(g)(2)(A)(ii); S. REP. NO. 530, 97th Cong., 2nd Sess. 625 (1982); Prop. Reg. § 1.416-1, T-4, T-6.

[64] I.R.C. § 416(g)(2)(B).

[65] I.R.C. § 416(d).

[66] *See* I.R.C. § 416(b).

[67] I.R.C. § 416(c)(1); Prop. Reg. § 1.416-1, M-2 through M-5.

[68] I.R.C. § 416(e); Prop. Reg. § 1.416-1, M-9.

For defined contribution plans, the employer must contribute on behalf of non-key employees at least the smaller of 3 percent of the employee's compensation or the highest percentage contribution made on behalf of any key employee.[69] All percentage calculations must be based on the first $200,000 of any key employee's compensation.[70] As before, Social Security benefits arising from employer contributions to the Social Security system *cannot* be used to reduce the minimum contribution.[71]

The rule which allows minimum contributions on behalf of non-key employees merely to equal the highest percentage contribution on behalf of any key employee (instead of requiring such contribution to equal at least 3 percent) obviously creates the potential for abuse in the case of employers sponsoring two or more plans. To prevent this abuse, Code Section 416 requires use of the 3 percent rule if the defined contribution plan enables a defined benefit plan which is required to be included in a top-heavy group to meet the coverage and antidiscrimination rules of Code Sections 401(a)(4) and 410. Moreover, all defined contribution plans which are required to be included in a top-heavy group are treated as one plan.[72]

If an employer provides both a defined benefit and defined contribution plan to an employee, then the employee is not entitled to both minimum benefits.[73]

Fourth, as noted earlier, if a small business maintains a defined contribution plan and a defined benefit plan and the new 1.0 Rule is applicable, the required mathematical changes in the 1.0 Rule formula generally mean that the maximum contribution and benefits for employees earning over $64,285,71 will be severely reduced.

Finally, effective for plan years beginning after December 31, 1983, a top-heavy plan must provide that a key employee's distributions will commence not later than the taxable year in which the key employee attains age 70½. Non-key employees and employees in nontop-heavy plans may receive their interest at retirement even if they retire after age 70½. In either case, distributions before death must be made over the life of the employee, the lives of the employee and his spouse, the life expectancy of the employee, or the life expectancy of the employee and his spouse. The secretary is directed to issue regulations in this area.[74] Moreover, a 10 percent penalty is imposed on the amount of any distribution to a key employee made before he or she attains the age of 59½ unless the distribution is made on account of death or disability.[75]

---

[69] I.R.C. § 416(c)(2); Prop. Reg. § 1.416–1, M–6 through M–8.

[70] I.R.C. § 416(c)(2)(ii).

[71] I.R.C. § 416(e); Prop. Reg. § 1.416–1, M–9.

[72] I.R.C. § 416(c)(2)(B)(iii).

[73] S. REP. NO. 530, 97th Cong., 2nd Sess. 629 (1982).

[74] I.R.C. § 401(a)(9)(A); TEFRA, *supra* note 39, § 242(a); S REP. NO. 530, 97th Cong., 2nd Sess. 631 (1982).

[75] S. REP. NO. 530, 97th Cong. 2nd Sess. 631 (1982).

Obviously, the new top-heavy rules are exceptionally complex. Depending upon the circumstances, the consequences of having a plan characterized as top-heavy may be harsh and quite expensive. Accordingly, care must be taken to avoid top-heavy status whenever possible and, when not possible, to react in the most advantageous manner. One alternative that at least minimizes the effect of the maximum contribution rule is a cash-deferred/salary reduction plan since Code Section 416(c)(2)(C) provides that "employer contributions attributable to a salary reduction or similar arrangement" are not taken into account.

SECTION 401(k) CASH-DEFERRED/SALARY REDUCTION PLANS OUTLINE

In a recent survey of major U.S. companies, two-thirds of the 150 companies surveyed stated that they intended to provide, probably would provide, or favored providing a cash-deferred/salary reduction plan for the benefit of their employees.[76] These plans are sanctioned by Section 401(k) of the Internal Revenue Code as interpreted by several regulations. Any employer who is considering adopting a Section 401(k) plan should understand the basic elements of such a plan and the restrictions on employer and employee contributions to such a plan.

Basic Elements of a Cash-Deferred/Salary Reduction Plan

A Section 401(k) plan is distinguished by a cash or deferred option. The recently issued proposed regulations allow two types of cash or deferred options.[77]

Salary Reduction Agreement Plans.   The proposed regulations specifically allow a Section 401(k) plan to be in the form of a salary reduction agreement between an eligible employee and the employer. Under a salary reduction agreement plan, a contribution is made by the employer to the employee's account only if the employee elects to reduce his or her compensation or to forego an increase in his or her compensation equal to the contribution.[78] A salary reduction agreement plan may provide for contributions by the employer and the employee other than those subject to the salary reduction agreement.

Election Plans.   The proposed regulations also authorize a plan under which an eligible employee elects either to have his or her employer contribute an amount to the plan or to have the employer pay that amount to the employee in cash.[79] Again, the plan may provide for contributions by

---

[76] 390 Pens. Rep. (BNA) 621 (1982).

[77] Prop. Reg. § 1.401(k)–1(a).

[78] Prop. Reg. § 1.401(k)–1(a)(1).

[79] Id.

both the employer and the employee other than those subject to the election.

The proposed regulations limit the cash or deferred option to profit-sharing or stock bonus plans.[80] Of course, the plan and the trust which implements the plan must meet the general requirements of the Code for tax-favored treatment under Sections 401(a) and 501(a) of the Code.

Discrimination Restrictions on Contributions to Cash-Deferred/Salary Reduction Plans

The Code generally discourages discrimination between lower paid employees and other employees by imposing several coverage and discrimination requirement on *all* qualified retirement plans. If a cash-deferred plan consists only of elective contributions, then the plan satisfies the coverage and discrimination requirements imposed by the Code if the plan either satisfies the general discrimination requirements imposed by Code Section 410(b)(1) and Code Section 401(a)(4) *or* satisfies the special cash or deferred determination rules discussed below. Salary reduction agreement contributions are elective contributions. If a plan consists of both elective contributions and nonelective contributions, then the plan may satisfy the coverage and discrimination requirement if the nonelective portion of the plan satisfies the general requirements of Code Section 410(b)(1) and Code Section 401(b)(4) and if the combined elective and nonelective portions of the plan satisfy the special cash or deferred discrimination rules discussed below.[81] Such a plan may qualify in other ways, too.

The General Coverage Requirement of Section 401(b)(1). As noted earlier, this Section provides that a plan will qualify for favorable tax treatment only if one of two tests is met: (1) the plan benefits 70 percent of all employees or the plan benefits 80 percent of eligible employees as long as 70 percent of the employees are eligible for benefits under the plan, or (2) the plan benefits qualifying employees under a classification set up by the employer and found by the Secretary not to discriminate in favor of officers, shareholders, or highly compensated individuals.

Section 401(a)(1). This Section states that a retirement plan will qualify for favorable tax treatment only if the contributions or benefits provided under the plan do not discriminate in favor of officers, shareholders, or highly compensated individuals.

Special Cash or Deferred Discrimination Rules. In a cash-deferred/salary reduction plan, special discrimination rules apply.

In order to understand the special discrimination rules which apply to cash-deferred/salary reduction plans, the following terms must be explained.

---

[80] Id.

[81] Prop. Reg.. § 1.401(k)–1(b)(2)(iii).

Actual Deferral Percentage.   The actual deferral percentage of any employee is the amount of employer contributions paid under the plan on behalf of that employee for the plan year divided by the employee's compensation for the plan year. The actual deferral percentage for either the lower paid or highly compensated group of employees is the average of those separately determined ratios.[82]

Highly Compensated Employee.   A highly compensated employee is an eligible employee who receives more compensation during the plan year than two thirds of all eligible employees. The two-thirds fraction is calculated by rounding to the nearest integer.[83] A cash-deferred/salary reduction plan is not discriminatory if either of the following tests is satisfied.

The 1.5 Test.   The actual deferral percentage for eligible highly compensated employees is not more than the actual deferral percentage for all other eligible employees (the lower two thirds) multiplied by 1.5.[84]

The 2.5 Test.   The actual deferral percentage of eligible highly compensated employees is not more than the actual deferral percentage for all other eligible employees (the lower two thirds) multiplied by 2.5, as long as the excess of the actual deferral percentage for the highly compensated employees over the actual deferral percentage for the other eligible employees (the lower two thirds) is not more than three percentage points.[85]

An Example of a Cash Deferred/Salary Reduction Plan Which Satisfies the Special Cash or Deferred Discrimination Rules.   Assume that X Corporation has six employees who are all eligible to participate in the X Corporation Cash-Deferred/Salary Reduction Plan. The employees earn the following compensation:

Employee	Compensation
A	$100,000
B	100,000
C	50,000
D	50,000
E	50,000
F	50,000

Clearly, Employees A and B are highly compensated employees (the upper one third) and Employees C, D, E, and F are "all other eligible employees" (the lower two thirds). Assume further that X Corporation, *as a nonelective employer contribution*, contributes 2 percent of each employee's compensation to the plan. That is, each employee receives the following nonelective employer contributions:

---

[82] Prop. Reg. § 1.401(k)–1(b)(8)(v).

[83] Id.

[84] Prop. Reg. § 1.04(k)–1(b)(8)(vii).

[85] Prop. Reg. § 1.4501(k)–1(b)(5)(ii).

Employee	Compensation	Nonelective Employer Contribution	Percentage of Compensation
Upper 1/3:			
A	$100,000	$2,000	2%
B	100,000	2,000	2
Lower 2/3:			
C	50,000	1,000	2
D	50,000	1,000	2
E	50,000	1,000	2
F	50,000	1,000	2

Now assume that Employee C enters into a salary reduction agreement with X Corporation by which he elects to contribute $1,000 to the plan from his compensation. Employee D also chooses to reduce his salary by $1,000 and makes a $1,000 contribution to the plan. As to the lower-paid two thirds of X Corporation's employees, the chart below illustrates the actual deferred percentage for the group of lower-paid employees. As noted, the actual deferral percentage for the group of lower-paid employees is the average of the ratios, calculated separately for each employee in such group, of the amount of employer contributions paid under the plan on behalf of each such employee, to the employee's compensation for such plan year. Prop. Reg. § 1.401(k)-1(b)(8)(v).

Lower-Paid Employees	Compensation	Nonelective Employer Contribution	Elective Contribution	Percentage of Compensation
C	$50,000	$1,000	$1,000	4%
D	50,000	1,000	1,000	4
E	50,000	1,000	-0-	2
F	50,000	1,000	-0-	2
Average of all lower-paid employees' deferral percentages	—	—	—	3%

In this example, the average actual deferral percentage for lower-paid employees equals 3 percent. As noted above, the 1.5 Test allows the highly compensated employees as a group to defer 150 percent of the actual deferral percentage of the lower two thirds of employees. Under this test, Employees A and B as a group can defer 4.5 percent of their compensation. Under the 2.5 Test, Employees A and B may defer 250 percent of the average actual deferral percentage for the lower-paid employees as long as the difference is no more than three percentage points. In this example, therefore, the highly compensated employees may defer 6 percent of their compensation since 3 percent times 2.5 is 7.5 percent and 6 percent is within three percentage points of 3 percent.

Finally, assume that Employee B does not wish to make an elective contribution to the plan by way of a salary reduction agreement. Employee A, on the other hand, wishes to make the maximum elective contribution. As the following chart reveals, Employee A can defer 8 percent of his salary as an elective contribution in addition to the 2 percent nonelective employer contribution.

Higher-Paid Employees	Compensation	Nonelective Employer Contribution	Elective Contribution	Deferral Compensation
A	$100,000	$2,000 (2%)	$8,000 (8%)	10%
B	100,000	2,000	–0–	2
Average of all highly compensated employees' deferral percentage	—	—	—	6%

A final factor which does not appear in the above example but which limits contributions to a cash-deferred plan is the general limitation on employer contributions to profit-sharing plans imposed by Code Section 404. As noted, that section provides that an employer may not deduct employer contributions to a stock bonus or profit-sharing plan which are in excess of 15 percent of the employee's compensation. Obviously, few employers will allow employees to direct employer contributions to profit-sharing plans which the employers cannot deduct.

Cash-deferred/salary reduction plans offer an attractive alternative for those employers who are considering adoption of new retirement plans or revision of existing profit sharing and stock bonus plans. At the same time, all cash or deferred arrangements are restricted by Code Section 401(k) and the proposed regulations; therefore, a cash or deferred arrangement should only be adopted after careful thought and study.[86]

---

[86] Prop. Reg. § 1.4501(k)–1(b)(5)(iii).

CHAPTER 53

Qualified Retirement Plans for Small Business: Administrative and Other Issues

HARRY V. LAMON, Jr.

GENERAL ADMINISTRATION OF THE PLAN

Employers are often too busy to handle their own personal financial affairs and, as a result, the administrative aspects of the qualified retirement plans adopted by small businesses are often overlooked. It is important that qualified retirement plans be administered properly because, if they are not, it is possible that such plans may become "discriminatory in operation" and be disqualified by the Service.

Once a qualified retirement plan is established, someone should be assigned the responsibility of dealing with the attorney, the accountant, the trustee, and the investment manager (if all of these exist). Also, in establishing the plan, some consideration should be given to who will perform the technical administrative functions of the plan, such as filing annual reports and making annual allocations. Under defined benefit pension plans, these functions are almost always performed by the actuary, since an actuarial analysis is necessary to compute the benefit annually. The normal fees for actuaries for most small businesses' defined benefit plans range from $500 to $2,000 per annum, depending upon the number of employees and the complexity of the plan.

Most problems arise, however, under defined contribution plans where it is not necessary to have an actuary. In many such plans, the trustee of the plans is a local bank, and normally the bank will offer administrative services. However, not all banks seek out small businesses' plans because they are usually smaller plans given the scope of the bank's overall employee benefit area. Moreover, not all employees desire to have banks act as trustee and invest plan funds generally due to the conservative nature of most banks. Many brokerage houses and retirement plan consulting firms offer administrative services for defined contribution plans. Further, some accounting firms will assist a small business in its annual administrative function; but most accounting firms will do so only if there are fewer than

10 employees due to the complexity of the allocations when more than 10 employees are involved. The administrative services for defined contribution plans should normally run between $500 and $1,500 per year per plan depending on the number of participants and the activity in the plan.

The fees for administering qualified retirement plans on an annual basis may be paid either by the trust or by the business. The author generally recommends that such fees be paid by the business as they are deductible by the corporation. Further, payment of such fees by the plans would reduce the funds which will eventually be available to pay retirement benefits.

The author also generally recommends that the corporation, and not one of the employees, be designated as the plan administrator. To designate an individual as the plan administrator requires obtaining a separate employer identification number for the individual and changing plan administrators if the individual leaves the corporation. In addition, the individual would be subject to suits by disgruntled participants.

REPORTING AND DISCLOSURE REQUIREMENTS OF ERISA

The following are the reporting and disclosure requirements for qualified retirement plans.[1]

Summary Plan Description

A summary plan description, prepared in a manner calculated to be understood by the average plan participant, must be provided to participants and beneficiaries within 120 days after the plan is adopted. A copy must also be filed with the Department of Labor within that 120-day period. Further, a summary description of material modifications must be furnished to participants and beneficiaries within 210 days after the end of the plan year in which such modifications occur. The summary plan description must be provided to new employees within 90 days after they become participants.

The required contents of the summary plan description are described in Labor Regulations §2520.102-3 and include a general statement of the benefits provided under the plan and the manner in which the plan operates.

Participant's Benefit Statements upon Request

Upon the written request of a participant or beneficiary, the plan administrator must supply, without charge to the participant or beneficiary, a statement based on the latest available information of his or her total

---

[1] Prentice-Hall *Pension Reporter* ¶16021, et seq.

accrued benefit, and either the percentage of accrued benefits that are nonforfeitable or the date upon which benefits will become nonforfeitable.[2] The plan administrator is not required to provide more than one such benefit statement during any 12-month period.[3]

Furnishing Other Documents Relating to the Plan

The plan administrator must make available for inspection by participants and beneficiaries copies of the plan document and trust agreement, copies of any collective bargaining agreement or contract under which the plan was established or is maintained, a copy of the latest annual report filed with the Service, and a copy of the latest summary plan description.[4] No charge may be made for exercising the right to inspect these documents. If the participant or beneficiary requests copies of these documents, copies must be provided. A reasonable charge not in excess of the actual cost of reproducing the documents may be required, but no charge may be made for the postage or handling involved in providing requested documents.[5] Not later than nine months after the close of a plan year, the plan administrator must furnish each participant and each beneficiary receiving benefits with a "summary annual report" that summarizes the annual report that was sent to the Service. The format for this report is prescribed in Labor Regulations §2520.104b-10.

ADOPTION OF PLANS AND ADOPTION OF AMENDMENTS

A qualified retirement plan may be amended at any time prior to the close of the employer's taxable year and become effective retroactively on the first day of the employer's taxable year. For example, assume a calendar-year employer adopted a qualified defined benefit plan on December 31, 1981, with an effective date of January 1, 1981. The employer could contribute and deduct for 1981 the amount necessary to pay the normal cost for the entire 1981 plan year plus an amount necessary to amortize the cost of past service credit (if any) provided for in the plan. The contribution and deduction could be made at any time prior to the date for filing the 1981 tax returns, including extensions.

An employer who adopts or amends a qualified plan is permitted to file a request that the Service make a determination that the provisions of the plan as adopted or as amended satisfy the requirements of the Code for qualification; such a request is allowed during the "remedial amendment

---

[2] Section 105(a) of ERISA.
[3] Section 105(b) of ERISA.
[4] Section 104(b)(2) of ERISA.
[5] Labor Regulations §2520.104b-30.

period." The significance of filing the determination request during the remedial amendment period is that if a request is filed during that period and the Service determines that changes are necessary to cause the plan to be qualified, then the needed changes may be made *retroactive* to the effective date of the plan (or the effective date of a plan amendment) so that the plan will be qualified from its initial effective date (or remain qualified since the effective date of an amendment).[6] If a request for a determination is filed after the close of the remedial amendment period and the Service discovers deficiencies in the plan, retroactive cure of the deficiencies may not be possible. Where the plan year corresponds to the employer's taxable year, the remedial amendment period for initial qualification or for a plan amendment will extend until the date for filing the employer's tax return (including extensions) for the first taxable year of the employer in which the plan or the amendment is effective. The remedial amendment period may be extended at the discretion of the Service, but the Service does not extend the period where failure to timely file a determination letter request was due merely to oversight.

It should be remembered that the period for *adopting* a qualified retirement plan by an employer ends with the last day of the first taxable year of the employer for which the plan is effective. Although contributions may be made after the end of the employer's taxable year and may be deducted for the year to which they apply, the plan itself may not be adopted retroactive to a taxable year that ended prior to the date of adoption. In *Engineered Timber Sales*,[7] the Tax Court held that no deductions would be permitted for the first taxable year for which a plan was made effective where the employer had adopted a trust agreement, the employer's board of directors had passed a resolution to adopt the plan prior to the expiration of the employer's first taxable year for which the plan was to be effective, but no enforceable plan was drafted until the following taxable year of the employer.

A plan that satisfies all the requirements of the Code for qualification and that receives a favorable determination letter is not guaranteed to be qualified *forever*. Two distinct classes of events could occur that would disqualify the plan. First, the plan might *in operation* become disqualified. As an example, the plan administrator might improperly exclude some rank-and-file employees and thereby cause the plan to discriminate.[8] Second, the legal requirements applicable to qualified plans might change—for example, by issuance of new or modified Treasury Regulations or a new revenue ruling.[9] Generally, when there is a change in applicable law, a plan

---

[6] Treas. Regs. §1.401(b)-1.

[7] 74 T.C. No. 60 (1980).

[8] *Myron* v. *U.S.*, 550 F. 2d 1145 (9th Cir. 1977).

[9] *Wisconsin Nipple & Fabricating Co.* v. *Commissioner*, 67 T.C. 490 (1976), aff'd. 581 F. 2d 1235 (7th Cir. 1978).

will remain qualified if the plan is amended not later than the close of the plan year following the plan year in which the change in law occurred, and if the amendment is made effective as of the first day of the plan year following the plan year in which the change in law occurred. It is critical that plan administrators, or their counsel, keep abreast of changes in the laws applicable to qualified plans so that timely plan amendments may be adopted.

LOANS TO PARTICIPANTS

A loan from a qualified retirement plan to a participant of that plan is a prohibited transaction under Section 406(a)(1)(B) of ERISA and Section 4975(c)(1)(B) of the Code. However, Section 408(b)(1) of ERISA and Section 4975(d)(1) of the Code provide an exemption from the prohibited transaction rules where the following requirements are met:

1. Loans are made to all participants and beneficiaries on a reasonably equivalent basis.
2. Loans are not made available to highly compensated employees, officers, or shareholders in an amount greater than the amount made available to other employees.
3. Loans are made in accordance with specific provisions regarding such loans set forth in the plan.
4. Loans bear a reasonable rate of interest.
5. Loans are adequately secured.

The second requirement—no disproportionate amounts of loans to highly compensated individuals—will not be violated merely because the plan permits all plan participants to borrow the same percentage of their vested accrued benefits even though officers, shareholders, and highly compensated employees may, as a group, have larger vested accrued benefits than rank-and-file employees.

As a caveat, while Congress purported to establish parity between corporate and noncorporate plans in TEFRA, loans to owner-employees of proprietorships and partnerships continue to be prohibited transactions after TEFRA.

Further, effective for loans made after August 13, 1982, a direct or indirect loan from *any* qualified plan to a participant or beneficiary is treated as a distribution and, thereby, is taxable unless the loan falls within an exception specified in Code Section 72(p). A loan falls within the exception and is not treated as a distribution only if:

1. The loan must be repaid within five years, and
2. The aggregate balance of all loans from the plan made to the borrower-participant does not exceed the lesser of $50,000 or one half of the present value of the nonforfeitable accrued benefit of the employee in the plan (but not less than $10,000).

The five-year limitation does not apply if the loan is applied toward acquiring, constructing, or substantially rehabilitating any house, apartment, condominium, or mobile home (not used on a transient basis) which is used or is to be used within a reasonable time as the principal residence of the participant or a member of his or her family.

This provision of TEFRA severely restricts the availability of plan loans to participants and their beneficiaries; however, plan loans remain an invaluable advantage of qualified retirement plans. Fortunately, that a loan is treated as a distribution will not disqualify the plan.

As the funds in an existing qualified retirement plan accumulate, the employers often desire to borrow those funds so that they can, in effect, "pay interest to themselves." The availability of loans from qualified retirement plans is useful in times of inflation. The author believes that, as long as the loans are made within the exemption provided in Section 408(b)(1) of ERISA, they can provide an attractive source of financing to plan participants. Loans cannot, however, be made either directly or indirectly to the business without obtaining a specific exemption from the Department of Labor.

The author feels that loans can be made to participants if the following criteria are met:

1. Either the plan or the administrative committee of the plan sets forth the specific reasons for loans, such as medical emergencies, second mortgages, college costs, etc., and they are followed for high-paid and low-paid employees alike.

2. The interest rates charged by the plan are equivalent to rates that would be charged by local banks on similar loans and the loans themselves carry the terms that can be obtained locally from banks. Some district directors are taking the position that qualified plans cannot permit loans to extend beyond a 10-year period. While there is no authority for this position, the author recommends that loans not extend beyond the normal retirement date of the particular participant.

3. The loan must be represented by a bona fide promissory note.

4. Loans should be made only to the extent of the vested account balance of the participant, with the vested account balance acting as security. If loans in excess of the vested account balance of the participant are made, the plan should have the vested account balance as security and obtain other security, such as listed stocks, bonds, or a second mortgage. Any security taken by the plan should be segregated from the assets of the employees and held by the trustee.

5. Loans should be made in a consistent businesslike manner, and loan applications should be executed by the participant desiring to borrow.

6. Loans made by a participant should be earmarked as investments of that participant's account so that, if that participant does default on the loan, only that participant and not the other participants will suffer.

7. Although the commercially available interest rate should be charged on the loans, care should be taken that state usury laws are not violated.

8.   Loans from defined benefit plans should be made only to the extent of the accrued vested benefit.

A rather subtle problem may arise in the case of loans from a pension plan (defined benefit or money purchase plan). One of the characteristics of qualified pension plans is that such plans may not make distributions to participants prior to separation from service or attainment of normal retirement age. A *loan* from a pension plan does not violate this distribution limitation since bona fide loans are not plan distributions. A problem may arise, however, if the security for a loan from a pension plan is the vested accrued benefit of the participant. If the participant defaults on the plan loan and the only assets out of which collection may be made are the participant's vested accrued benefit, the satisfaction of the loan by reduction of the participant's accrued benefit could constitute a premature distribution that would disqualify the plan. A similar problem could arise in the case of loans from integrated profit-sharing plans, since distributions from integrated profit-sharing plans are prescribed prior to separation from service or attainment of normal retirement age. To avoid the premature distribution problem, the author suggests that pension and integrated profit-sharing plans that provide for loans to participants require adequate security for such loans *other than* the participant's accrued benefit. Loans from a cash or deferred salary reduction plan also should not be secured only by the account balance since a foreclosure of any loan by resort to the funds in an account may constitute an in-service distribution to a participant and, thereby, disqualify the plan under Section 401(k).

BONDING REQUIREMENTS OF ERISA

Section 412 of ERISA requires that every fiduciary and every person who handles funds or other property of a qualified retirement plan must be bonded and that the bond shall be not less than 10 percent of the amount of the funds handled. While such bonds, "ERISA bonds," are inexpensive and can be obtained as a rider to the general fidelity insurance of the business, they are often overlooked. Further, questions arise with regard to who "handles" funds and what are the "funds" handled. For these reasons, it is prudent to require that all trustees or members of a plan administrative committee be bonded and that the bond be in the amount of 10 percent of the funds in the plan.

INVESTMENTS

ERISA does not require any specific type of investment to be maintained by any type of qualified retirement plan. However, Section 404 of ERISA requires that fiduciaries exercise the care, skill, prudence, and diligence that a "prudent man acting in a like capacity and familiar with such matters" would use and also requires that fiduciaries diversify investments unless it is clearly prudent not to do so. These standards can normally be met by investments which are generally available, such as listed stocks and bonds. However, since a qualified trust is tax-exempt, the author feels that an effort should be made to maximize the annual income under the trust in order to take advantage of the compounding effect which the tax-exempt status provides. Obviously, tax shelters and other investments with tax-favored status provide very little benefit to a tax-exempt trust, and as such, they should generally be avoided.

Often, employers desire to leverage the ability of their qualified retirement plans to purchase various assets, such as real estate. Where the assets are purchased within a qualified retirement plan, and either funds are borrowed to acquire those assets or the assets are purchased through the use of purchase money indebtedness, the income generated from the sale of those assets will be partially taxable to the trust as if it were a regular taxable entity. This rule also applies to margin accounts.[10] There are, however, certain exceptions with regard to the purchase of real estate if the property is purchased from the owner and the owner takes back a second mortgage.

Many qualified retirement plans of small businesses will have assets of less than $500,000. Such plans may be unable to obtain the services of a registered investment advisor to handle investments. Consequently, the management of fund assets will fall to the trustee, be it a bank or the employers themselves. If employers are the trustees of the plan, they should take steps to insure that all assets held by the plan are segregated from their personal assets and from the assets of the business. Also, as trustees, the employers will be responsible for the investments of the plan.

Since, most employers either do not have the time or are not adept at investing large sums of money, the investment of assets of a qualified retirement plan of many small businesses falls to a stock broker or to an investment company. If a local stock broker is employed, it should be recognized that he will generally not be considered a fiduciary unless he exercises discretionary control or authority over the fund or renders investment advice for a fee. Most stock brokers have disclaimers which eliminate them from the fiduciary responsibility rules of ERISA. Further, many qualified retirement plans of small businesses are invested in "guaranteed investment contracts" with insurance companies. While these contracts appear to offer a good annual return, employers should be fully aware of the implications of investing in such contracts, since they usually involve some type of termination discount or some type of extended payout upon termination.

Very often, the investment ideas of the plan shareholders will differ from the ideas of the plan trustee. It is possible to provide in a qualified retire-

---

[10] *Elliot Knitwear Profit Sharing Plan,* 614 F. 2d 347 (3rd Cir. 1980) aff'g. 71 T.C. 765 (1979); Sections 511–514 of the Code; investment in partnerships (even as a limited partner) may also generate unrelated business taxable income, see Rev. Rul. 79-222, 1979-2 C.B. 236, Treas. Regs. §1.514(c)-1(a)(2) example (4).

ment plan that the participants will have the ability to earmark (direct the investment of) their accounts. Under an earmarking arrangement, the participant will have the authority to direct the trustee with regard to the vested balance of his account.

There are limitations on earmarking. First, earmarking exists only in defined contribution plans and is not available with respect to defined benefit plan assets derived from employer contributions, although defined benefit plans that permit voluntary employee contributions may permit employees to earmark their voluntary employee contribution accounts. Further, if a participant does earmark the investment of his account, the fiduciary will be relieved of liability for a loss by reason of the participant's control.[11]

Finally, it should be recognized that participants may not direct the investment of their accounts into items which are used personally, since such use would constitute a prohibited transaction and would result in the imposition of excise taxes under Section 4975 of the Code. Furthermore, effective January 1, 1982, Section 314(b)(2) of the 1981 Economic Recovery Tax Act added Code Section 408(n) which provides that the acquisition by an individually directed account under a qualified pension or profit-sharing plan of any collectible will be treated as a distribution from the account in an amount equal to the cost of the collectible. Collectibles are defined to mean any work of art, any rug or antique, any metal or gem, any stamp or coin, any alcoholic beverage, or any other tangible personal property specified by the Secretary of Treasury. This provision "grandfathers" collectibles already held by accounts as of December 31, 1981. This new law does not apply to collectibles acquired by the plan's trustee as plan assets not earmarked to the account of any participant. In addition, it may be possible to use aftertax voluntary employee contributions to make earmarked investments in collectibles, since the "deemed distribution" of an employee contribution does not give rise to gross income. Overall, it would probably be wise to await regulations in this area.

Some investment managers feel that the type of investment a plan makes should vary with the type of plan; that is, that a defined benefit pension plan with a definite fixed benefit which must be reached should be invested in interest-bearing bonds, preferred stocks, and blue chip stocks. On the other hand, they feel that since there is no definite retirement benefit provided under profit-sharing plans and money purchase plans, they may be invested in higher-risk assets. While the character of investments may vary from defined benefit to defined contribution plans, security of principal is an essential element to any investment strategy under any qualified retirement plan.

Following ERISA, it was felt that corporate trustees should be employed in order to minimize the risk of a suit against the individual employer acting

---

[11] Section 404(c) of ERISA.

as trustee. However, in the six years following ERISA, although there have been a number of suits under ERISA, there have been few suits against employees who have acted as trustees under their qualified retirement plans. For this reason, shareholder/employees should feel free to act as trustees of the qualified retirement plans established by their corporations. If shareholder/employees do choose to serve as trustees, to serve as plan administrators, or to perform other services for the plan, they normally must do so without pay other than reimbursement of expenses properly and actually incurred, since Section 408(c)(2) of ERISA prohibits persons who already receive full-time pay from an employer from receiving compensa tion from the plan other than expense reimbursement. Care should be taken, however, to assure that the investment of the plan's assets, particularly the amounts credited to the accounts of the staff employees, be done in a conservative manner.

Whether an employee of the business or a bank acts as trustee, the rights and duties of the trustee must be prescribed either in the plan itself or in a separate trust document. Although many plans and trust documents are one unified document, the author recommends establishing a plan and a separate trust agreement. In this manner, the plan need only be executed by the corporation, whereas the trust agreement must be executed by the corporation and the trustee. Consequently, if the corporation decides to amend the plan, it need only pass a board resolution and sign the amendment; the signature of the trustee is not necessary.

MASTER PLANS VERSUS INDIVIDUALLY DESIGNED PLANS

A number of banks, brokerage houses, and insurance companies offer master or prototype plans which can be adopted by a small business. These plans have received a master determination letter and can be adopted by the small business without the necessity of seeking further Service approval. Such plans can be adopted by the completion of an adoption agreement under which a number of alternatives can be selected, such as participation rules and vesting schedules.

Master plans appear to offer an attractive alternative to employers because they can be executed with very little assistance from the attorney and accountant of the business and, consequently, with a minimum fee. Employers should be aware, however, that most master plans are offered by entities which are selling a service. Banks, brokerage houses, and insurance companies all sell investment services and charge administrative fees. Master plans also have the following drawbacks:

1. Master plans usually offer less flexibility than individually designed plans since the employer only has a choice of the terms contained in the adoption agreement.

2. Master plans may contain hidden problems. The terms of the master

plan may be generally acceptable to the Service but may, in the particular situation of the small business, be unacceptable. Although the representatives of the company offering the master plan will be knowledgeable about the plan, the authors have found that they typically do not scrupulously review the plan in light of the particular situation of the small business. This is particularly true in situations where provisions in the master plan may eventually produce discrimination in operation.

3. Once a master plan is adopted, it may be difficult to terminate that plan and transfer assets to a successor trustee. Most master plans contain a provision which states that the assets may only be transferred to a plan which has received a determination letter from the Service. Consequently, if the employer desires to terminate the master plan arrangement and transfer the funds to an individually designed plan, the delay in obtaining the determination letter (at least six to eight months) will delay the transfer of the funds.

4. Master plans may have hidden administrative costs which must be borne by the plan or the employer. This is particularly true with the so-called deposit administration plans maintained by insurance companies.

5. The fees of the attorney and accountant for the small business will probably not be insubstantial if they are requested to review and comment on the master plan proposed. Problems often are identified upon a review of a master plan because master plans are not tailormade to deal with the individual needs of any specific business. Where the attorney of the small business is called upon to review and interpret provisions of master plans, the time required and, therefore, the fees charged are often significantly greater than if the attorney had drafted an individually designed plan for the corporation. This occurs because it is much easier for the attorney to work with plans with which he is familiar than to undertake a complete examination of new plans.

Employers should realize that some organizations offer plans which appear to be master or prototype plans but which are, in fact, individually designed plans. The author is aware of a number of insurance companies that engage in this practice and, in fact, draft individually designed retirement plans for small businesses. Employers encountering this arrangement should carefully assess the potential problems that may arise in adopting an individually designed plan drafted by someone other than the employer's attorney. There is a greater possibility that problems will arise under such a plan than they will arise under a master or prototype plan. Further, drafting such plans and the accompanying trust agreements is generally considered by the American Bar Association to be an unauthorized practicing of law.[12]

Because qualified retirement plans are such an important tax benefit, in most instances, employers should consider adopting individually designed

---

[12] "Final Opinion on Employee Benefit Planning" issued by the Committee on Unauthorized Practice of Law dated October 17, 1977.

plans which have been coordinated by their attorney and accountant. By adopting individually designed plans, the small business can assure that the plan initially meets its needs and creates no latent problems. Moreover, as the Service rules relating to qualified plans change in the future, the attorney and accountant will be on hand to make appropriate amendments.

PROHIBITED TRANSACTIONS

Section 406 of ERISA and parallel provisions of Section 4975 of the Code prohibit employee benefit plans from engaging in certain types of transactions. The provisions of Section 4975 of the Code only apply to qualified *retirement* plans, while the provisions of Section 406 of ERISA apply to both *retirement* plans (whether or not "qualified" under the Code) and *welfare* plans (medical, accident, layoff, etc., benefit plans). Violations of the prohibited transaction provisions of the Code can result in the imposition of a nondeductible excise tax equal to 5 percent of the "amount involved" in the transaction for each plan year that the transaction continues. An additional excise tax of 100 percent of the amount involved is imposed if correction is not made upon notice by the Service. A fiduciary who permits a prohibited transaction to which Section 406 of ERISA applies may be held personally liable under Section 409 of ERISA for any loss to the plan resulting from the transaction.

Transactions that constitute prohibited transactions are absolutely forbidden, regardless of the financial or economic soundness of the transaction and regardless of whether the transaction offers the plan a more attractive financial opportunity than is available elsewhere. Generally, the defenses of good faith, innocence, and reasonable lack of knowledge that a transaction is prohibited will not prevent imposition of the excise tax under Code Section 4975; however, violation of Section 406 of ERISA can be avoided with these defenses.

The specific transactions prohibited are certain transactions between plans and "parties in interest." ERISA Section 3(14) enumerates a rather broad class of persons who constitute parties in interest with respect to a plan. Parties in interest include all plan fiduciaries, including the plan administrator, trustee, or custodian of plan assets, any person who provides services to a plan, the employer whose employees are covered by the plan, a relative (spouse, ancestor, lineal descendant, or spouse of a lineal descendant) of any of the foregoing individuals, and any employee, officer, director or 10 percent (direct or indirect) shareholder of the employer who maintains the plan.

A prohibited transaction will occur if there is a direct or indirect:

1. Sale, exchange, or leasing of any property between a plan and a party in interest.
2. Lending of money or other extension of credit between a plan and a party in interest.

3. Furnishing of any goods, services, or facilities between a plan and a party in interest.
4. Transfer of any plan assets to or use of any plan assets by or for the benefit of a party in interest.
5. Acquisition of securities of the employer under certain circumstances or in excess of certain maximum amounts.

In addition, certain dealings by fiduciaries will constitute prohibited transactions. Specifically, a fiduciary is prohibited from dealing with assets of the plan for his own personal gain, representing any person in a transaction involving the plan in which the party represented has interests adverse to the plan, and receiving a kickback from any person in connection with a transaction involving assets of the plan.

Section 4975 of the Code and Section 408(b) of ERISA contain a number of "statutory exemptions" from the prohibited transaction provisions. For example, the statutory exemption dealing with loans to participants has been discussed. Other statutory exemptions include exemptions,

1. To provide reasonable services necessary to establish or operate the plan.
2. To permit bank trustees to invest plan assets in savings accounts and pooled investment accounts of the bank and to provide ancillary banking services to the plan.
3. To permit fiduciaries to receive reasonable compensation for services (unless they are full-time employees of the employer), and
4. To permit fiduciaries who are plan participants to receive plan benefits as they become payable.

In addition to the statutory exemptions, Section 408(a) of ERISA and Section 4975(c)(2) of the Code permit administrative exemptions from the prohibited transaction rules to be granted. Administrative exemptions may be granted in favor of a particular transaction (an "individual" exemption) or a class of transactions ("class" exemptions). Individual exemptions apply only to the specific transaction for which the exemption was granted and will not authorize an identical transaction engaged in by different parties. Class exemptions generally exempt any present, certain past, or any future transaction that satisfies the requirements of the exemption.

Requests for prohibited transaction exemptions filed with the Department of Labor. It normally takes from four to six months for an exemption request to be finally resolved, and nearly 90 percent of the requests for exemptions are *denied*. In order to obtain an administrative exemption, a plan must complete a rather tedious application in which it must be demonstrated that the exemption if granted would be: (1) administratively feasible, (2) in the interest of the plan, its participants and beneficiaries, and (3) protective of the rights of participants and beneficiaries of the plan. Chances for approval are increased if the applicant can show that, due to independent safeguards, the transaction provides a "no lose" opportunity for larger financial benefit to the plan than other available investment alternatives. Until recently, the Department of Labor was very reluctant to grant exemptions which authorized continuing transactions between the plan and parties in interest, (e.g., loans and leases). However, the Department of Labor has recently granted a number of such continuing transaction exemptions, including several that have permitted improved real property to be contributed to a plan and leased back to the employer.[13]

CONTRIBUTIONS

The determination of the deductibility of contributions to a qualified retirement plan is generally made pursuant to Section 404 of the Code. The amounts which may be deducted as contributions to a qualified pension plan (defined benefit or money purchase) are determined under Section 404(a)(1).

An employer may contribute to a pension plan (defined benefit or money purchase) and deduct the amount necessary to pay the normal cost of plan benefits plus the amount necessary to amortize past service liabilities. The normal cost of a defined benefit plan must be calculated by the plan's actuary. The normal cost of a money purchase plan is determined by the plan's benefit formula, for example, 10 percent of participants' compensation. Generally, past service liabilities are created by plan amendments that increase the rate at which benefits accrue for prior service and by plan provisions that grant past service benefits upon establishment of the plan. Past service liabilities attributable to all participants may be amortized over as many as 30 years or as few as 10 years. Alternatively, past service liabilities may be amortized over the remaining future service of each employee; but, if over 50 percent of plan costs are attributable to three or fewer individuals, past service liabilities attributable to those three or fewer individuals may not be amortized over fewer than five years.

The deductibility of contributions to profit-sharing plans is determined under Section 404(a)(3), which sets a basic deduction limit for profit-sharing contributions of 15 percent of the compensation otherwise paid or accrued during the taxable year to all beneficiaries of the plan. If an employer contributes an amount in excess of the deduction limits for a particular year, the excess payment is deductible in succeeding years. On the other hand, if a contribution made to a profit-sharing plan is less than 15 percent of the annual total compensation, the difference between the amount actually contributed and the 15 percent of annual compensation may be carried forward as a deductible amount in a succeeding taxable year.

---

[13] Prohibited Transaction Exemptions 80-78, 80-86, 80-97, and 81-1.

Of course, the total deduction in any later year may not exceed 25 percent of compensation.[14]

If amounts are deductible under both pension plans and profit-sharing plans, the employer may first deduct the entire amount deductible with respect to the pension plans. If the amount deductible on account of the pension plans is less than 25 percent of the participants' compensation for the plan year, the employer can make up the difference by making additional contributions to profit-sharing plans. If the employer's contribution to the pension plans exceeds 25 percent of the participants' compensation for the plan year, then no amount may be deducted for the profit-sharing plans.[15] Contributions must also satisfy the applicable contribution and benefit limitations of Section 415 of the Code.

Corporate contributions to qualified retirement plans are considered general business expenses. Consequently, in order for an employer to obtain a deduction for such expenses under Section 404, the expenses must be ordinary and necessary under Section 162 of the Code. In determining whether deductions to qualified retirement plans are ordinary and necessary, the question of reasonable compensation must be considered. When determining reasonable compensation for an employee, all benefits are taken into account, including contributions under qualified retirement plans. Consequently, if the reasonableness of the compensation to the employer is challenged, a challenge may also be made to the qualified retirement plan. If the challenge succeeds, a portion of the deduction for contributions may be disallowed or the Service may attempt to disqualify the plan. If discrimination results from contributions attributable to unreasonable compensation, a defined contribution plan may avoid disqualification by permitting the reallocation to other employees of any contribution determined to be unreasonable.[16]

The reasonable compensation requirement may be a particular problem where the first year of the small business is a short first year and large contributions are made. This may be especially true if large amounts of income are held over and paid during the first few months of incorporation in order to permit larger contributions to the qualified plans.[17]

Under Section 404 of the Code, deductions are generally allowed in the year in which they are made. However, under ERISA, Section 404(a)(6) of the Code was amended to permit a deduction for a particular year to be

---

[14] In one case, however, where the employer made "advance contributions" to a profit-sharing plan to enable the plan to make an investment, the Tax Court found the advance to constitute a loan, and the plan was held to have debt-financed, unrelated business income as a result of the investment. *Marprowear Profit Sharing Trust* v. *Commissioner,* 74 T.C. No. 80 (1980).

[15] Section 404(a)(7) of the Code.

[16] Rev. Rul. 67-341, 1967-2 C.B. 156.

[17] *Angelo J. Bianchi,* 66 T.C. 3234 (1976), aff'd. 553 F. 2d 93 (2d Cir. 1977). *Anthony LaMaestro,* 72 T.C. 377 (1979), *Robert A. Young,* 1979-242 T.C.M. (1979).

taken where the contribution for that year is made on or before the filing of the federal income tax return (plus extensions thereof). In order to obtain a deduction under Section 404(a)(6) of the Code, the contribution for a year must be (i) paid to the plan on or before the due date for filing the federal income tax return (plus extensions, if any), (ii) allocated on the books of the plan in the same manner as they would have been allocated if they had been actually contributed on the last day of the plan year, and (iii) deducted on the federal income tax return.[18]

The initial contributions to a qualified retirement plan may also be made during the grace period. That is, although it is absolutely necessary to adopt the plan prior to the end of the fiscal year of the employer, no contribution to that plan need be made (even though the trust may be a "dry trust" under local law) until the time for filing the corporation's federal income tax return.[19] However, the author recommends that upon the establishment of a qualified plan the trust of that plan be funded with a $100 contribution even though the remainder of the contribution will be made at a later date.

Nondeductible Voluntary Employee Contributions

Qualified retirement plans may permit nondeductible voluntary employee contributions of up to 10 percent of an employee's compensation.[20] This 10 percent limit is a maximum limitation for all plans, so that if 10 percent is contributed under a profit-sharing plan nothing may be contributed under a money purchase pension plan.[21] However, the 10 percent voluntary contribution is cumulative so that the contribution may be made equal to 10 percent of the employee's aggregate compensation for all years that he has been a participant.[22] Furthermore, the 10 percent limitation is not reduced or affected by amounts rolled over or directly transferred from another qualified plan.

Nondeductible voluntary employee contributions are also subject to the annual addition limitations under Section 415 of the Code. Notwithstanding the Section 415 limitations, a participant is always permitted to make a voluntary contribution to the plan of 6 percent of his compensation.

The ability of an employee to make voluntary employee contributions to a qualified retirement plan is an excellent benefit which creates for the employee the ability to defer income taxes on the earnings in the voluntary account. Although nondeductible voluntary employee contributions must be made with aftertax dollars (except as discussed below), the earnings on

---

[18] Rev. Rul. 76-28, 1976-1 C.B. 106.
[19] Rev. Rul. 57-419, 1957-2 C.B. 264.
[20] Rev. Rul. 80-350, 1980-51 I.R.B. 7; Rev. Rul. 59-185, 1959-1 C.B. 86.
[21] Rev. Rul. 69-627, 1969-2 C.B. 92.
[22] Rev. Rul. 69-217, 1969-1 C.B. 115, as clarified by Rev. Rul. 74-385, 1974-2 C.B. 130.

the amounts contributed voluntarily by the employee remain tax-exempt until withdrawn by him. Consequently, the employee may take advantage of the compounding effect of tax-exempt earnings through the use of voluntary employee contributions. Voluntary employee contributions are particularly useful for deferring income until later years when it will be needed, such as for the expense of a college education for children.

Deductible Voluntary Employee Contributions

Effective January 1, 1982, Section 311(a) of the 1981 Economic Recovery Tax Act amended Code Section 219 to permit participants in a plan qualified under Code Section 401(a), 403(a) or 408(k) to make voluntary deductible employee contributions (DECs) equal to the lesser of $2,000 or 100 percent of compensation. Employee contributions will not constitute "voluntary" contributions if they are required as a condition to participate or if they are matched by employer contributions as in a thrift plans. In addition, the maximum amount of DECs will be reduced dollar for dollar by the amount of any employee contributions to an individual retirement account or individual retirement annuity. This rule does not apply to the first $250 contributed to a spousal individual retirement account. DECs will not be taken into account as annual additions for purposes of determining the Code Section 415 limitations applicable to the plan.

In IRS Notice 82-3 (February 18, 1982), the IRS stated that plans which allow voluntary employee contributions need not be amended to permit DECs, but the plan administrator must manifest an intent to accept DECs. Plans that do not permit voluntary employee contributions must be amended to allow employee contributions before DECs can be accepted. Notice 82-3 states that plans that accept DECs should separately account for assets attributable to DECs. Separate accounting is necessary since the tax treatment of DECs is for the most part similar to the tax treatment of IRA contributions. For example, 10-year averaging does not apply to amounts attributable to DECs; loans may not be made to participants out of their DECs, distributions of amounts attributable to DECs prior to death, disability, or attainment of age 59½ will result in the imposition of a 10 percent excise tax; and employers may be required to comply with special reporting requirements with respect to DECs.

Because of the increased administrative requirements that DECs may create, and because employees can make IRA contributions equal to the DEC limits, most employers will probably refuse to allow DECs to their qualified plans. In some cases, however, employers may chose to allow DECs because they do allow some advantages over IRAs. For example, amounts attributable to DECs are not subject to the mandatory distribution rules at age 70½ that apply to IRAs. Also, unlike IRAs, DECs need not be trusteed by a bank, so the employer will have greater flexibility in controlling investment of DECs than an IRA participant would typically enjoy.

Employer flexibility has been increased by the Service's position that a plan may require the cash out of DECs when an employee leaves employment. This means the employer's qualified plan will not be required to keep track of amounts attributable to DECs of terminated employees.

ANNUAL ADDITION LIMITATION

Section 415 of the Code provides limitations on the annual benefits which may be provided under qualified retirement plans. Under Section 415(b)(1), the employer may not fund a defined benefit plan benefit which is greater than the lesser of $90,000 (generally for plan years beginning after December 31, 1982) or 100 percent of the participant's average compensation for his highest three consecutive calendar years.

Under defined contribution plans, the contributions and other additions with respect to a participant may not exceed the lesser of $30,000 (generally for plan years beginning after December 31, 1982) or 25 percent of the participant's compensation. For purposes of determining the annual addition, the following allocations are considered: (1) the employer contributions, (2) the lesser of the nondeductible employee contributions in excess of 6 percent of his compensation or one half of the employee contributions (deductible employee contributions are disregarded), and (3) the forfeitures allocated to his account.

QUALIFYING PLANS WITH THE INTERNAL REVENUE SERVICE

Although obtaining a determination letter with regard to a retirement plan is not a prerequisite for having a "qualified" plan, obtaining a determination letter does permit the sponsoring employer to receive advance determination of the qualified status of the plan. For this reason, the author feels that all plans which are intended to be qualified plans should be filed with the district director of the local Service office for qualification. If plans are filed for determination during the remedial amendment period discussed above and qualified status is not received, either the plans may be amended retroactively to permit qualified status or the contributions may be returned to the employer. Further, the author believes that all amendments to a plan or trust document, other than ministerial amendments like the change of the trustee or the change of the name of the plan, should be filed with the Service for continued qualification.

The receipt of a determination letter from the district director is not, however, a carte blanche to qualified status. The determination letter merely states that, on the facts and law which exist as of the date of qualification, the plan in form meets the qualification rules. Further changes in the facts relating to the employer and the employees and changes in the rules and regulations of the Service may later disqualify the plan. In Wisconsin Nipple

& Fabricating Corporation v. *Commissioner,*[23] the court upheld the commissioner's retroactive revocation of determination letters (issued in 1960 and 1962) where a later revenue ruling (issued in 1971) indicated that the plan discriminated in favor of a prohibited group. The Seventh Circuit clearly placed responsibility on the taxpayer for "keeping abreast of current developments in the law to be assured that the plan is still in compliance." For this reason, the author feels that sponsoring employers should continue to monitor the status of their retirement plans with their professional advisors to assure that they remain qualified.

Rev. Proc. 72-6, Sec. 1.04,[24] states that "a favorable determination letter on a profit-sharing plan, stock bonus plan, or bond purchase plan, or on the exempt status of a related trust, if any, is not required as a condition for obtaining the benefits pertaining to the plan or trust."

DISCRIMINATION IN OPERATION

Obviously, qualified retirement plans may be disqualified if they fail to meet the specific statutory requirements provided under Section 401, *et seq.,* of the Code such as minimum participation rules, vesting rules, etc. However, it is possible for qualified retirement plans to be disqualified due to the manner in which they have been operated, even though determination letters have been issued on those plans.

In addition to the specific statutory requirements for qualified plans, Section 401 also contains several rather vague prohibitions. For example, under Section 401(a)(2), the plan must be used for the "exclusive benefit" of participants and their beneficiaries. Further, under Section 401(a)(3), a plan may not discriminate in favor of the "prohibited group," composed of officers, shareholders, and highly compensated individuals. Regulation §1.401-1(b)(3) provides a general overview of what may constitute impermissible discrimination:

> The plan must benefit the employees in general, although it need not provide benefits for all of the employees. Among the employees to be benefitted may be persons who are officers and shareholders. However, a plan is not for the exclusive benefit of employees in general if, by any devise whatever, it discriminates either in eligibility requirements, contributions, or benefits in favor of employees who are officers, shareholders, . . . or highly compensated employees.

It is often difficult to determine the "prohibited group" in many corporations. The Service has taken the position that the term *highly compensated* is a relative term rather than an absolute term. In a small business, it is very

---

[23] *Wisconsin Nipple & Fabricating Co.* v. *Commissioner,* 67 T.C. 490 (1976), aff'd 581 F. 2d 1235 (7th Cir. 1978).

[24] 1972-1 C.B. 710.

clear that the prohibited group will include the shareholders who own the corporation.

Those situations in which a qualified retirement plan is diverted to the use of the shareholders of the small business are often obvious (for example, a loan of all qualified plan funds to the employer). However, even if the terms of a plan in *form* comply with the statutory requirements, it is possible that in *operation* the benefits and contributions provisions may discriminate in favor of the prohibited group, even though there is no intention that they do so. It is difficult to anticipate when discrimination in operation may occur, but the following are a few examples.

Erroneous Administration of Plan Provisions

In several cases, the participation provisions of qualified retirement plans were inadvertently not followed, leading to disqualification of the plans due to discrimination in operation. In *Myron* v. *U.S.*,[25] five eligible employees were excluded from coverage for two consecutive years, and the company's contributions were allocated only to the account of the corporation's sole shareholder. The lower court found that the exclusion was inadvertent but, nevertheless, concluded this innocent error justified disqualification. In affirming, the Seventh Circuit Court of Appeals agreed that even an inadvertent failure in coverage could be a proper basis for denying qualification.[26]

Several cases of erroneous administration of plan provisions specifically involve small businesses. In *Allen Ludden*,[27] a pre-ERISA case, Allen Ludden and Betty White, the famous actor and actress, formed a corporation, Albets, which adopted a money purchase pension plan and a profit-sharing plan for the benefit of the corporation's employees. The plans, as written, met the requirements for qualification, and determination letters were issued by the Service. Through a bookkeeping error, the only staff employee of Albets, a production secretary, was inadvertently excluded from participation in the plan even though she met the plan's participation requirements. The Service argued, and the court held, that the exclusion of the production secretary constituted discrimination in favor of highly compensated officers in violation of Sections 401(a)(3)(B) and 401(a)(4) of the Code and meant that the plan had failed to meet the minimum coverage provisions of Section 401(a)(3)(A).

In *Forsyth Emergency Services, P.A.*,[28] a professional corporation was engaged in emergency medical services and operated the emergency room facilities at Forsyth Memorial Hospital in Winston-Salem, North Carolina.

---

[25] *Myron* v. *U.S.*, 550 F. 2d 1145 (9th Cir. 1977).

[26] Also see *Ma-Tran Corp.*, 70 T.C. 158 (1978).

[27] 68 T.C. 826 (1977), aff'g. 620 F. 2d 700 (9th Cir. 1980).

[28] 68 T.C. 881 (1977).

The corporation was owned by three physicians who adopted a money purchase pension plan. They received a determination letter from the Service. During 1972 and 1973, certain nonprofessional employees of the corporation were inadvertently omitted from coverage under the retirement plan. However, in August of 1975, after this fact was brought to the corporation's attention by the Service, additional contributions were made so that allocations could be made for these nonprofessional employees for the years in which they were excluded. The exclusion of the nonprofessional employees resulted from a misreading of the plan by the professional advisor to the corporation.

The court held that the plan did not meet the eligibility requirements for coverage and that the plan discriminated in operation. The court further held that discrimination in operation could not be cured by retroactively funding contributions accrued but unallocated to the nonprofessional employees, even if such retroactive allocation was made voluntarily by the corporation. The court noted that, because the plan covered primarily professional employees, the plan did not cover a cross-section of all employees. In examining the question of whether a retroactive cure for discrimination was available, the court stated that it found no support in the Code, the Regulations, or the case law which would permit retroactive correction.

Cases like *Ludden* and *Forsyth* are dramatic examples of the problems which can occur due to the inadvertent errors of employers, even where they seek the advice of their professional advisors. The Service has, in some situations, relented from its position in *Ludden* and *Forsyth*. In Private Letter Ruling No. 7949001 a corporation was permitted to reallocate contributions to its money purchase pension plan and profit-sharing plan so that the plans would qualify under Section 401 of the Code. The corporation adopted a prototype plan in 1973 and made contributions in 1973, 1974, and 1975. On audit, the Service held that the eligibility requirements of the plan were not followed and that one part-time employee was erroneously included while three full-time employees were excluded from coverage. The Service ruled that the entity sponsoring the prototype plan was in error, not the corporation. Since the mistake was one of fact and not one of law, and since no distributions had been made from the plan, the corporation would be allowed to restructure the plan to meet the coverage requirements.

In 1980, the Service promulgated Document 6651, "IRS Employee Plans Restoration Guidelines." Under these guidelines, retroactive relief is available for a variety of plan deficiencies. In the case of plans that are discriminatory, restoration may be accomplished by increasing benefits to defined benefit plans or making supplemental contributions to defined contribution plans. Such corrections will reinstate the qualified status of the plan but will not restore qualified plan status treatment of employer contributions made during the plan's discriminatory period. As a result, contributions to defined benefit plans during open years in which there was discrimination will normally be disallowed, and contributions to defined contribution plans during open years in which there was discrimination will be deductible only when employees become vested in their individual accounts.[29]

Improper Exclusion of Employees

If the plan sponsor expressly attempts to categorize employees as independent contractors or employees of third-party organizations, the plan may discriminate in favor of the prohibited group by denying participation to staff employees.

Withdrawals from Qualified Plans

A profit-sharing plan may permit participants to withdraw all or part of their vested benefits provided that the underlying contributions have been allocated to their accounts for at least two years.[30] However, if withdrawals are subject to the approval of a plan administrative committee and withdrawals are permitted only by members of the prohibited group, then the plan discriminates in favor of the prohibited group and will be disqualified.[31]

Opting Out

Due to the often divergent needs of employees, some employers consider placing a provision in qualified retirement plans which permits employees to "opt out" of the plan. There appears to be little for the employer to lose by placing such a provision in a plan. However, several problems do exist. First, if the number of persons opting out is substantial, this provision may create coverage problems. Also, any opting out provision should be disclosed in the summary plan description. Moreover, if the plan is administered so that only highly paid individuals are permitted to opt out and if their compensation is correspondingly increased, then the plan may be considered a *de facto* cash or deferred profit-sharing plan. There is, however, no general prohibition against permitting highly paid employees to opt out of the plan as long as their compensation is not otherwise increased. Most district directors do not view the opting out of highly paid employees as a disqualifying event.

---

[29] Section 404(a)(5) of the Code.

[30] Rev. Rul. 71-295, 1971-2 C.B. 184.

[31] Rev. Rul. 57-587, 1957-2 C.B. 270.

On the other hand, if lower-paid employees opt out of the plan, the plan may be found to discriminate against them.[32]

Definition of the Term Compensation

Although most qualified retirement plans provide benefits based upon the compensation listed in the employee's Form W-2 (the "basic compensation"), the term, *compensation,* would normally include both contractual and voluntary bonuses paid to the employees. Such a definition normally should not cause problems. However, if the shareholders normally receive substantial bonuses and the staff employees receive small or no bonuses, the plan may be considered discriminatory if bonuses are used to figure contributions.[33]

Employee Turnover

During the pendency of a qualified retirement plan, if the staff employees of the corporation regularly terminate their service or are fired prior to their benefits becoming vested, the plan may be considered to have a discriminatory vesting schedule. This is more likely if the schedule is less favorable than the 4-40 schedule.[34]

Further, the use of so-called "last day rules" in qualified retirement plans may prove discriminatory if, due to the turnover statistics of the employer, they generally have been applied only against staff personnel. Last day rules provide that an employee will not be entitled to receive an allocation of employer contributions for the particular plan year of a defined contribution plan unless he or she is employed at the end of that plan year. Since it is generally staff personnel and not shareholders who terminate during a plan year, the rules in operation only apply to staff personnel. Last day rules should be eliminated from plans established by small businesses in order to avoid this potential discrimination in operation.[35]

Tax Consequences of Disqualification

If a plan is disqualified because it discriminates in operation, the following tax consequences will occur:

---

[32] Rev. Rul. 80-351, 1980-51 I.R.B. 7, Rev. Rul. 73-340, 1973-2 C.B. 134. Also, in *Richard F. Olmo,* 38 T.C.M. 112 (1979), pension and profit-sharing plans established by a professional corporation wholly owned by two dentists failed to qualify. The plan discriminated in favor of the prohibited group because, for the years in issue, the only participants in the plan were the two dentists. Of the two other employees who met the plan's minimum service requirements, one did not meet the minimum age requirement and the other had voluntarily waived her right to participate pursuant to provisions in the plan.

[33] *Perry Epstein,* 70 T.C. 439 (1978).

[34] Rev. Proc. 76-11, 1976-1 C.B. 550.

[35] Id.

1.   The trust will lose its tax-exempt status under Section 501(a), making the trust income taxable to the trust.

2.   Section 402(b) will govern the taxability of employer contributions to the beneficiaries of the trust. Generally, contributions will be included in the employees' income under Section 83 to the extent they have a vested right to such benefits. Employer contributions which are taxable to the employee are considered part of current compensation; thus, the withholding of taxes by the employer is required.

3.   The contributions of the employer will be deductible only to the extent that the employees are vested and only if separate accounts are maintained to record the interest of each participant.[36] As a result, deduction of employer contributions to nonqualified defined contribution plans will be delayed for the period of years necessary for employer contributions to vest, and employer contributions to nonqualified defined benefit plans will simply not be deductible. Because of the possible loss of the deduction, the author recommends that plans incorporate provisions which require employer contributions to revert to the employer within one year of the disallowance of a deduction under Code Section 404.[37]

INSURANCE

Qualified retirement plans may insure the lives of the participants. There are a number of advantages in maintaining insurance in a qualified plan.

1.   First, the possibility of an immediate and substantial benefit is secured without the necessity of relying on plan investments.
2.   Second, life insurance proceeds, like other investments, may be exempt from estate tax if they are paid to a beneficiary using a method other than the lump sum method.
3.   Third, life insurance purchased by a qualified retirement plan is purchased with "tax deductible" dollars.
4.   Finally, the proceeds of the life insurance policy are received income tax-free by the trust. The "at risk" portion of the proceeds is the excess of the face value of the policy over its cash surrender value immediately prior to death.

There are also disadvantages in maintaining insurance.

1.   First, life insurance (even whole life insurance) historically provides a low-yield investment.
2.   Second, adequate death benefits may be provided outside a qualified retirement plan through the use of other types of insurance, such as split-dollar arrangements and group term insurance.

---

[36] Section 404(a)(5) of the Code.

[37] ERISA §403(c)(2)(C) permitting this type of reversion.

3. Third, the payment of life insurance premiums by the trust will reduce the amount of cash available to pay retirement benefits.
4. Finally, the cost of term life insurance protection (the P.S. 58[38] cost) is currently taxed to the employee.

Since the purpose of a qualified retirement plan is to provide *retirement benefits,* life insurance protection may be provided only if it is "incidental."[39] As a result, specific limitations are placed on life insurance maintained in each type of qualified plan.

Profit-Sharing Plans

A profit-sharing plan is a plan primarily established to provide deferred distribution of benefits.[40] However, as previously mentioned, profit-shar-

---

[38] The P.S. 58 rate, one-year premium cost for $1,000 of life insurance protection:

Age	Cost	Age	Cost
15	$1.27	46	$ 6.78
16	1.38	47	7.32
17	1.48	48	7.89
18	1.52	49	8.53
19	1.56	50	9.22
20	1.61	51	9.97
21	1.67	52	10.79
22	1.73	53	11.69
23	1.79	54	12.67
24	1.86	55	13.74
25	1.93	56	14.91
26	2.02	57	16.18
27	2.11	58	17.56
28	2.20	59	19.08
29	2.31	60	20.73
30	2.43	61	22.53
31	2.57	62	24.50
32	2.70	63	26.63
33	2.86	64	28.98
34	3.02	65	31.51
35	3.21	66	34.28
36	3.41	67	37.31
37	3.63	68	40.59
38	3.87	69	44.17
39	4.14	70	48.06
40	4.42	71	52.29
41	4.73	72	56.89
42	5.07	73	61.89
43	5.44	74	67.33
44	5.85	75	73.23
45	6.30		

These rates are published in Rev. Rul. 57-747, 1955-2 C.B. 228.

[39] Treas. Regs. §1.401-1(b).

[40] Id.

ing plan funds may be distributed after the funds have been accumulated for a "fixed number of years," which is at least two years.[41] A distribution of funds before that time may cause a profit-sharing plan to lose its qualified status. Applying this general rule to the purchase of life insurance, premiums for life insurance certainly may be paid out of funds which have been accumulated for two or more years without causing disqualification of the plan.[42] On the other hand, insurance premiums paid out of funds which have not been accumulated for at least two years normally are considered to be distributions to the employee. An exception exists if the purchase of insurance with funds which have not been accumulated for two years is incidental. The purchase will be deemed incidental if certain requirements are met.

1. In the purchase of ordinary life insurance, the aggregate life insurance premiums for each participant must be less than one half the aggregate contributions allocated to that participant at any particular time, without regard to trust earnings and capital gains and losses. Moreover, the plan must require the trustee either to convert the entire value of the life insurance policy at or before the employee's retirement into cash, or to provide periodic income so that no portion of such value may be used to continue life insurance protection beyond retirement.[43]

2. In the purchase of term insurance, the aggregate life insurance premiums for each participant must not exceed 25 percent of the total amount of funds allocated to the participant's account.[44] The limitations on the purchase of life insurance protection do not apply to voluntary employee contributions.[45]

Notwithstanding that it is permissible for qualified profit-sharing plans to maintain life insurance on the lives of the employees, the author generally recommends that profit-sharing plans not be used as life insurance vehicles. It is possible that in certain years a profit-sharing plan may not be funded, and thus the plan may not have sufficient funds to pay the premiums without causing disqualification.

Defined Benefit Pension Plans

A defined benefit pension plan funded with life insurance will be deemed to provide an incidental (and hence permissible) preretirement death benefit if either of two sets of requirements are met.

---

[41] Rev. Rul. 54-231, 1954-1 C.B. 150.

[42] Id., note 39, *supra*.

[43] Rev. Rul. 73-501, 1973-2 C.B. 127; Rev. Rul. 69-421, 69-2 C.B. 59; Rev. Rul. 54-51, 1954-1 C.B. 147, as amplified by Rev. Rul. 57-213, 1957-1 C.B. 157, and Rev. Rul. 60-84, 1960-1 C.B. 159.

[44] Rev. Rul. 61-164, 1961-2 C.B. 99; Rev. Rul. 66-143, 1966-1 C.B. 79; Rev. Rul. 70-611, 1970-2 C.B. 89; and Rev. Rul. 73-510, 1973-2 C.B. 386.

[45] Rev. Rul. 69-408, 1969-2 C.B. 58.

1. The purchase of insurance will be incidental if less than 50 percent of the employer contributions credited to each participant's account is used to purchase ordinary life insurance policies on the participant's life, even if the death benefit consists of both the face amount of the policies and the amount of other contributions credited to the participant's retirement benefit.

2. The purchase will also be incidental if the death benefit is funded by ordinary life insurance providing 100 times a participant's anticipated monthly normal retirement benefit, and if the preretirement death benefit does not exceed the greater of: *(a)* the proceeds of the 100 times life insurance policy or *(b)* the reserve under the 100 times life insurance policy plus the participant's account in the auxiliary fund.[46]

A defined benefit pension plan will not qualify if all of the employer's contributions are used for the purchase of ordinary life insurance policies on the lives of the participants.[47]

A postretirement death benefit is considered incidental if it does not exceed 50 percent of the base salary in the year before retirement and it costs less than 10 percent of the total cost of funding other pension plan benefits.[48]

Money Purchase Pension Plans

A money purchase pension plan may provide incidental preretirement death benefits which meet either the tests for profit-sharing plans or defined benefit pension plans.[49]

Tax Treatment

Employer contributions made to a qualified retirement plan which are used to pay insurance premiums are deductible to the employer, as are other contributions. However, the cost of the insurance provided under a qualified plan is treated as a current distribution to the participant and must be included in the participant's income for the year in which the premium is paid. The result is the same without regard to the type of policy purchased. The employee is taxed on the cost of the insurance protection if either the proceeds are payable to his estate or to a beneficiary, or if the proceeds are payable to the trustee of the plan but the trustee is required by the terms of the plan to pay all proceeds over to the beneficiary of the participant. A participant is not taxed on the purchase of "key man" insurance by a

---

[46] Rev. Rul. 74-307, 1974-2 C.B. 126, clarifying Rev. Rul. 68-453, 1968-2 C.B. 163 and Rev. Rul. 73-501, 1973-2 C.B. 127.

[47] Rev. Rul. 61-164, 1961-2 C.B. 99, and Rev. Rul. 54-67, 1954-1 C.B. 149.

[48] Rev. Rul. 60-59, 1960-1 C.B. 154.

[49] Rev. Rul. 74-307, 1970-1 C.B. 194, and Rev. Rul. 69-421, 1969-2 C.B. 59.

qualified retirement plan where the proceeds of the insurance are payable into the general assets of the plan. The amount of current taxable income to the participant is measured by the pure insurance protection under Regulations §1.72-16. The rates to be used are the one-year term rates established under Rev. Rul. 55-747 or the so-called P.S. 58 rates.[50] However, if the insurance company's rates for individual one-year term policies available to all standard risk customers is lower than the P.S. 58 rates, the lower rates may be used.[51]

Where group term life insurance is provided under a qualified retirement plan, the cost of the entire amount of protection is taxable to the employee and no part is exempt.[52] It is important to note that the P.S. 58 costs which have been taxed to the employee for life insurance protection may be recovered tax-free from the benefits received under the policy.[53] Tax-free recovery of the P.S. 58 cost will be available only if the benefits are ultimately received from the insurance contract with respect to which the P.S. 58 costs were included in gross income. If, however, the life insurance policy is surrendered and the proceeds are used to purchase an annuity or the proceeds are distributed in cash, tax-free recovery of the P.S. 58 basis will be forfeited.[54]

OTHER ISSUES

One significant result of the passage of TEFRA was the establishment of approximate parity between corporate plans and noncorporate or H.R. 10 plans. Prior to TEFRA, qualified plans maintained by corporations offered significant advantages over qualified plans maintained by partnerships and proprietorships. These advantages were so great that many practitioners advised small businesses to incorporate in order to obtain the more favorable tax treatment afforded to corporate plans. TEFRA largely eliminated the advantages of corporate plans such that, after the effective date of the TEFRA parity provisions, a small business probably should not be incorporated if the only advantage of incorporation is the availability of a qualified *corporate* plan.

Nevertheless, several differences between corporate and noncorporate plans remain. First, the aggregation rules applicable to entities controlled by an owner-employee, that is a significant partner or a proprietor, are more inclusive than the aggregation rules applicable to related corporations.[55] Second, no deductions are allowed for qualified plan contributions on

---

[50] 1955-2 C.B. 228.

[51] Rev. Rul. 66-110, 1966-1 C.B. 212.

[52] Section 72 and Section 79(b)(3) of the Code.

[53] Treas. Regs. §1.72-1(b).

[54] Private Letter Rulings 7830082 and 7902083, and Rev. Rul. 67-336, 1967-2 C.B. 66.

[55] Section 401(d)(9), (10) of the Code.

behalf of self-employed individuals to the extent that the contributions are allocable to the purchase of life, accident, health, or other insurance.[56] Third, self-employed participants may *not* elect ten-year averaging for distributions "on account of" separation from service except when the separation from service is caused by disability.[57] Fourth, the $5,000 death benefit exclusion, by which an employer may pay a deceased employee's beneficiaries or his or her estate as much as $5,000 without tax to the recipient, may be paid from a self-employed individual's account, tax-free only if a lump-sum distribution as defined in Code Section 402(e)(4) is paid.[58] Fifth, a Treasury Regulation issued under pre-TEFRA law which may or may not be rescinded prohibits forfeitures in defined contribution plans from being allocated to the accounts of self-employed individuals.[59] Finally, self-employed participants may not roll Keogh plan assets over to another qualified plan, nor may self-employed participants use a conduit IRA to achieve rollovers between qualified plans.[60]

While these six differences are not the only differences between qualified corporate and noncorporate plans, they illustrate the relatively minor nature of the post-TEFRA discrimination against noncorporate plans. Assuming, however, that the small business owner wishes to incorporate, whether for the purpose of obtaining these advantages or for other purposes, the small employer's existing H.R. 10 plan or plans must be dealt with in some fashion.

DISPOSITION OF H.R. 10 PLANS UPON INCORPORATION

Freezing the H.R. 10 Plan

Many tax advisors recommend that the existing H.R. 10 plan be "frozen"; that is, no further contributions will be made to the plan, and benefits of participants are either distributed in a lump sum or held for distribution under the normal distribution provisions of the plan. As a caveat, Code Section 72(m)(5), as modified by TEFRA, imposes a 10 percent penalty tax on certain distributions to key employees who are under age 59½. The distribution method may be elected by participants in a one-time irrevocable election offered for an election period that expires prior to the date on which distributions may be made under the election. Earnings on amounts that are not distributed will continue to compound tax-free, and the frozen plan will simply constitute another deferred com-

---

[56] Section 404(a)(8)(C) of the Code.
[57] Section 402(e)(4)(A) of the Code.
[58] Section 101(b)(9) of the Code.
[59] Treas. Reg. §1.401-11(b)(3).
[60] Section 402(a)(5)(E)(ii) and Section 408(c)(3)(A)(ii) of the Code.

pensation benefit which will be payable at a later date. Generally, savings and loan institutions, as opposed to banks, offer lower minimum fees and, consequently, employers should consider transferring frozen H.R. 10 plans to savings and loan institutions.

Termination of Plan and Distribution to Participants

If a key employee of the H.R. 10 plan is over 59½, he may receive a distribution of funds along with the other employees upon its termination. However, if the key employee is under age 59½ and a distribution is made, a 10 percent penalty tax on the premature distribution will be assessed under Section 72(m)(5) of the Code unless the distribution reduced by any amounts contributed by the key employee as an employee is rolled over within 60 days into an individual retirement account or individual retirement annuity.

In addition, a termination distribution that is rolled over will not be subject to the excise tax imposed as a result of a premature distribution since Section 72(m)(5) of the Code only imposes an excise tax on amounts that are included in gross income. Given a rollover of the entire H.R. 10 distribution less employee contributions, no amount is included in gross income.[61] It should be noted, however, that a distribution from an H.R. 10 plan on behalf of any self-employed participant may not be rolled over into another H.R. 10 plan or corporate qualified plan either directly[62] or through a conduit IRA.[63] The IRS has approved a direct transfer from the trustee of one H.R. 10 plan to the trustee of another H.R. 10 plan or to the trustee of a corporate plan.[64]

Termination of Plan and Transfer of H.R. 10 Funds to Qualified Retirement Plans of the New Small Business

The assets of an existing H.R. 10 plan may be transferred from the trustee of the H.R. 10 plan directly to the trustee of the successor corporate qualified retirement plan without creating a premature distribution, as long as the special requirements of H.R. 10 plans for the owner-employees are observed and as long as the assets do not pass through the hands of participants. In Rev. Rul. 71-541,[65] the Service approved the transfer of H.R. 10 plan assets to a profit-sharing plan of a successor corporation since the profit-sharing plan provided that (1) the trustee would always be a bank; (2) separate accounts would be maintained for funds transferred on behalf

---

[61] Rev. Rul. 78-404, 1978-2 C.B. 156.
[62] Section 402(a)(5)(E)(ii) of the Code.
[63] Section 408(d)(3)(A)(ii) of the Code.
[64] See Private Letter Ruling 7733009.
[65] 1971-2 C.B. 209.

of each owner-employee; (3) no payment of benefits would be made from the separate accounts on or before the owner-employee reached age 59½ or became disabled; and (4) distribution from the owner-employee's account had to begin prior to the end of the taxable year in which he attained age 70½. As noted, TEFRA eliminated many of the distinctions between H.R. 10 plans and corporate plans, some of which are provisions of Rev. Rul. 71-541, thus, whether the Service will or should retain these four restrictions on H.R. 10 to corporate plan transfers is an open question.

Until this question is settled contrary to prior authority, care should be taken to assure that the special restrictions applicable to transferred accrued benefits of owner-employees are observed. For example, in Private Letter Ruling 8014076, the Service held that where an owner-employee's H.R. 10 account was transferred to a successor corporate plan and the former owner-employee obtained a loan from the corporate plan that reflected his transferred H.R. 10 accrued benefit, the former owner-employee had received a "benefit" attributable to the H.R. 10 plan which would be treated as a premature distribution subject to the 10 percent excise tax of Section 72(m)(5) of the Code.

Some employees desire to transfer frozen H.R. 10 accounts to the trustee of the successor qualified plans in an attempt to aggregate funds for investment purposes. The special provisions applicable to the transferred H.R. 10 plan funds need only apply to them and not to the remainder of the funds in the successor corporate plans. The aggregation of both the H.R. 10 plans and the corporate plan funds for investment purposes is permissible. In a number of private letter rulings, the Service has continued to affirm that H.R. 10 plan assets may be transferred to a successor corporate plan without creating a premature distribution.[66]

The special H.R. 10 plan requirements (bank trustees, etc.) apply only if the H.R. 10 plan covered owner-employees. If the H.R. 10 plan did not cover owner-employees, only the age 70½ restriction must be met. As a practical matter, H.R. 10 plans established by small businesses will cover owner-employees, and the staff employees' accounts will be paid out prior to the transfer of the H.R. 10 plan to the successor corporate plan.

INCOME AND ESTATE TAX CONSEQUENCES OF DISTRIBUTIONS ON TERMINATION

Qualified retirement plans are normally established because of the obvious tax advantages that they offer at the time they are adopted: the corporation is able to deduct contributions currently, and participants can defer inclusion of the contributions in this gross income until amounts are distributed or made available. The employer should not overlook the important and unique tax opportunities that are available upon the ultimate

---

[66] Private Letter Rulings 7807058, 8005022, and 8020065.

distribution of benefits. This section will deal with the unique tax aspects of benefits received upon termination of participation in a qualified retirement plan. The tax treatment of certain preretirement benefits, such as life insurance, preretirement profit-sharing plan distributions, and loan provisions has been dealt with previously and will not be repeated here.

Plan provisions govern the alternative forms in which benefits may be paid. In an individually designed plan the employer involved may assure that the benefit provisions are drafted in such a manner as to be consistent with the tax planning and business needs of the company. As explained below, certain valuable tax advantages are available only if a participant's entire accrued benefit is paid to him in a lump sum distribution. Notwithstanding the specialized tax treatment available to lump sum distributions, the employers may decide to limit the circumstances under which lump sums are paid for business reasons—for example, to prevent a departing employee from using a lump sum payment as a financial springboard for setting up a competing business. The initial step in determining the best method of minimizing tax consequences of a distribution of plan benefits is to determine the permissible benefit options that are available. If the participant's vested accrued benefit (i.e., the vested amount in the participant's profit sharing or money purchase account, or the value of the participant's vested defined benefit) is less than $1,750, the plan may, and often does, give the plan administrator the option to involuntarily "cash out" the participant at termination by paying the participant the lump sum value of the vested accrued benefit.[67]

In most situations, the retiring employee will have a choice that includes: (1) receiving a lump sum distribution of his benefit, (2) receiving payments for a fixed number of years certain, or (3) receiving payments in the form of an annuity measured by the participant's expected lifetime (a "life annuity") or the combined lifetime of the participant and some third person such as the spouse or designated beneficiary of the participant (a "joint and survivor annuity"). It is quite common for defined contribution plans (profit-sharing and money purchase) to eliminate the life annuity option so that the plan will be able to avoid compliance with the burdensome joint and survivor annuity rules; however, defined benefit plans almost always offer some form of life annuity.

Once the employer determines the options that are available, he or she should consider the following issues as they apply to each alternative:

1. What are the immediate income tax consequences of this form of distribution?
2. What are the long-term income tax consequences of this form of distribution?
3. What are the estate tax consequences of this form of distribution?

---

[67] Section 411(a)(7)(B)(i) of the Code.

4. Is this form of distribution coordinated with the employee's personal retirement planning?

Consequences of Lump Sum Distributions

A lump sum distribution, in general terms, is a distribution of the balance of a participant's account (and in certain cases more than one plan maintained by an employer must be aggregated) within one taxable year of the recipient, which distribution is made as a result of the participant's death or separation from service or after the employee attains age 59½. Complexities and potential pitfalls for the unwary abound in the area of lump sum distributions, and professional advice should normally be sought in advance if this alternative is selected. If a lump sum is received, the employee is faced with the critical decision of determining whether to "roll the distribution over" into an individual retirement plan or to retain the distribution and elect to have it taxed under the special 10-year averaging rule of Section 402(e) of the Code.

Tax Consequences of Ten-Year Averaging

A recipient of a lump sum distribution will be taxed under 10-year averaging only if this method of taxation is elected.[68] An election to use 10-year averaging is made by filing Form 4972 with the recipient's income tax return. This election can be made or revoked at any time during the period in which the income tax return for the year of receipt of the distribution can be amended; that is, within three years of the filing deadline. Ten-year averaging may be elected only once after the recipient attains age 59½ and may only be elected if the participant whose accrued benefit is distributed was an active participant in the plan including certain predecessor plans for at least five years.[69]

In general, the amount of tax imposed on a lump sum distribution will be 10 times the amount of tax that would be imposed under Section 1(c) of the Code if an unmarried individual received 1/10th of the lump sum as his or her only income during the taxable year and if the zero bracket amount or standard deduction did not apply to the individual.[70] If the distribution is less than $70,000, the tax is further reduced by a minimum distribution allowance under Section 402(e)(1)(D) of the Code. Furthermore, if the participant was an active participant prior to 1974, a portion of the lump sum equal to the fraction of the participant's total active participation that occurred prior to 1974 will be subject to tax as long-term capital gains

---

[68] Section 402(e)(4)(B) of the Code.

[69] Section 402(e)(4)(H) of the Code and Private Letter Rulings 8002078 and 8027025, with respect to using service in a predecessor plan to satisfy the five-year requirement.

[70] Section 402(e)(1)(C) of the Code.

(Section 402(a)(2) of the Code), unless the recipient elects to have the entire distribution taxed under the 10-year averaging rule (Section 402(e)(4)(L)). Table 53-1 indicates the amount of tax that would be imposed in 1982 on a lump sum distribution of various amounts (assuming that no portion is taxed as capital gains), as well as the percentage of the distribution that would be paid to satisfy the tax imposed:

Table 53-1
Tax Imposed on Lump Sum Distributions, 1982

Amount of Lump Sum	Tax Imposed	Percentage of Distribution Required to Pay Income Taxes
$ 20,000	$ 1,200	6.00%
100,000	12,767	12.77
250,000	61,670	24.67
500,000	174,680	34.94
1 million	424,680	42.47

The above table indicates that, if the amount of the distribution is small, the 10-year averaging election will create a very attractive tax rate. On the other hand, as the size of the lump sum increases, the advantage of continued deferral of tax by way of a rollover to an individual retirement account will in many cases outweigh the benefit of an immediate "reduced" tax under the 10-year averaging formula. Persons contemplating the use of 10-year averaging should consider not only the immediate tax impact but also the long-term tax consequences: once the distribution is received, earnings generated by the distribution are exposed to immediate taxation and, depending upon the investment medium selected, might be exposed to a tax rate as high as 50 percent. Once distributed, a lump sum is also subject in full to estate taxation. Finally, lump sum recipients might be tempted to increase current expenditures for unneeded or luxury items, so that a large portion of the lump sum might not be available to provide for future retirement security.

Rollover of Lump Sums

The alternative to electing 10-year averaging of a lump sum distribution is rolling over all or any part of the lump sum into an individual retirement account (IRA) or individual retirement annuity. An amount may be rolled over *no later than* 60 days after receipt of a lump sum distribution.[71] Therefore, one should plan in advance and identify the specific vehicle to

---

[71] Section 402(a)(5)(C) of the Code.

be used for the rollover prior to receipt of the distribution. If a recipient changes his mind after completing a rollover, the rollover may be revoked with a minimum financial penalty if action to revoke is taken prior to the time for filing an income tax return including extensions for the taxable year in which the lump sum was received.[72] Such timely action will avoid a 10 percent penalty tax on early receipt of the amount rolled over; however, if the recipient is younger than 59½ in the year of receipt of a revoked IRA rollover, the 10 percent penalty will still apply to income on the rollover that is returned.[73] In addition, the financial institution that maintains the IRA may impose interest or administrative cost penalties for early revocation. Once the IRA is revoked, the recipient may elect 10-year averaging of his distribution.

Rollover of a lump sum is available even if the participant whose accrued benefit is distributed was not an active participant in the plan for five years or any other minimum period. Furthermore, a rollover may be accomplished even if the recipient has previously elected 10-year averaging after age 59½.[74] The entire amount received in a lump sum distribution need not be rolled over,[75] and any amount not rolled over will be subject to tax at ordinary income rates. A recipient cannot elect to 10-year average a portion of a lump sum that is not rolled over, but he may be able to use regular income tax averaging under Section 1301 of the Code.

The amount of a lump sum that represents employee contributions may not be rolled over but will be retained by the recipient tax-free.[76] Income attributable to employee contributions may, however, be rolled over.[77] A recipient either must roll over the identical property distributed, or he or she must sell the property distributed during the period of up to 60 days between receipt of a lump sum and its rollover and roll over the proceeds of sale.[78] No gain or loss will be recognized on such sales to the extent the proceeds are rolled over. A rollover is available not only to a participant who receives a lump sum, but also to the spouse of a participant who receives a lump sum on account of the participant's death.[79]

The immediate tax consequence of a rollover is that taxation of benefits is deferred for the amount rolled over until it is actually received from the IRA. Distributions from the IRA may begin at any time after the year in which the owner of the IRA reaches age 59½. An earlier distribution would result in a 10 percent excise tax under Section 408(f) of the Code. Once age

---

[72] Section 408(d)(4) of the Code and Private Letter Rulings 8044031 and 8045026.

[73] Treas. Regs. §1.408-4(c)(3)(i).

[74] Section 402(a)(5)(D)(i)(II) of the Code.

[75] Section 402(a)(5)(A)(ii) of the Code.

[76] Section 402(a)(5)(B) of the Code.

[77] Private Letter Ruling 8037034.

[78] Sections 402(a)(5)(A)(ii) and 402(a)(6)(D) of the Code.

[79] Section 402(a)(7) of the Code.

59½ is attained and prior to reaching age 70½, distributions from the IRA are up to the discretion of the owner. Furthermore, there is no "constructive receipt" from an IRA. Thus, the owner can have the ability to demand all or any part of the IRA at any time without fear of being taxed before the money is actually received.[80] Amounts actually distributed from an IRA are taxed as ordinary income. One cannot receive a lump sum from an IRA and elect 10-year averaging on the amount received; therefore, in most cases the decision to use an IRA will foreclose use of 10-year averaging.

Once age 70½ is attained or beginning with the year of the rollover if in that year the owner is older than 70½,[81] the owner of an IRA must have an amount distributed from the IRA that is a certain fraction of the balance in the IRA at the beginning of the year. Failure to receive the minimum required distribution results in an excise tax under Section 4974 of the Code equal to 50 percent of the amount by which the required distribution exceeds the actual distribution. The fraction of the beginning year's balance in the IRA that must be distributed has a numerator equal to one and a denominator equal to the life expectancy of the owner or combined expectancies of the owner and his or her spouse as of the owner's 70th birthday minus the number of calendar years that have commenced after the owner attained age 70½.[82] The single life expectancy of a male age 70 is 12.1 years and of a female age 70 is 15 years. The joint life expectancy of a husband and wife who are both age 70 is 18.3 years.[83] Rather than receiving payments for a period certain, an annuity for the life of the participant or joint lives of a participant and his or her spouse may be purchased at age 70½. This option might be attractive to an individual who is relying on a rollover IRA as the principal source of retirement income.

TEFRA added a new level of complexity to the use of rollover IRAs. Specifically, effective for individuals dying after December 31, 1983, an individual's entire interest in an IRA must be distributed within five years of his death or, if applicable, the death of his surviving spouse, if distributions over a term certain have not commenced before the death of the individual for whose benefit the account was maintained.[84]

Summarizing the key characteristics of the alternative of using a rollover IRA, this alternative will create no initial income taxation since neither the rollover nor the return of employee contributions are subject to tax. In the long term, the IRA alternative may be used to defer taxation of benefits distributed from a qualified plan; however, since voluntary employee con-

---

[80] Private Letter Rulings 8008170, 8015093, and 8038101.

[81] Private Letter Ruling 8044059.

[82] Treas. Regs. §1.408-2(b)(6).

[83] A deferred payment over 18.3 years may be very attractive because, under the formula of Treas. Regs. §1.408-2(b)(6), the required annual distribution during the first 10 years will normally not even be equal to the interest earned on the IRA. This permits continued deferral of all the principal and some of the interest until future years.

[84] Section 408(a)(7) of the Code.

tributions cannot be rolled over, use of the IRA rollover forecloses further deferral of income earned on voluntary employee contributions. Any amount remaining in an IRA on the death of the participant will be excluded from the participant's estate, provided that the beneficiary of the IRA is not the participant's estate and distributions to the beneficiary from the IRA are made in uniform amounts over at least three years.[85] The use of a rollover IRA will undoubtedly increase the likelihood that the participant will retain his plan benefits to provide retirement income, rather than use the distribution for current expenditures as might be the case if 10-year averaging is utilized with a lump sum distribution.

Receipt of Periodic Retirement Benefits from the Qualified Corporate Plan

Rather than receiving a lump sum distribution, a participant could elect to receive a distribution over a fixed number of years from the qualified corporate plan. One advantage of this alternative is that payments may commence prior to age $59\frac{1}{2}$ and there is no inflexible requirement that distributions begin no later than age $70\frac{1}{2}$; however, the manner of distribution elected by a participant must result in distributions to the participant over his life expectancy having a present value on the date benefits commence of at least 50 percent of the present value of the participant's total vested accrued benefit.[86]

Receipt of installment benefits directly from the corporate plan provides greater flexibility in the timing of payments than receipt from an IRA. Effective January 1, 1982, the doctrine of "constructive receipt" no longer applies to qualified retirement plans. Therefore, a participant will not be subject to income tax on amounts made available to him until such amounts are actually distributed. Although the Economic Recovery Tax Act eliminated constructive receipt from qualified plans for income tax purposes, the act did not specifically address the matter of whether amounts "made available" but not distributed from a qualified plan will be subject to estate tax under Code Section 2033 as property in which the decedent had an interest at the time of his death.

It seems very unlikely that Congress intended to continue the constructive receipt doctrine in the estate tax area since that would create an estate tax trap. In addition, the Code Section 2039(c), which exempts from the gross estate certain distributions from qualified plans, is prefaced with the language: "Notwithstanding the provisions of this section or any provision of law, there shall be excluded from the gross estate. . . ." This broad exclusionary language is also found in Code Section 2039(e), which excludes from the gross estate certain distributions from IRAs. IRAs have

---

[85] Section 2039(e) of the Code.
[86] Rev. Rul. 72-241, 1972-1 C.B. 108.

always been exempted from constructive receipt for income tax purposes. Since the IRS has never argued that amounts held by IRAs should be subject to inclusion in the gross estate pursuant to the doctrine of constructive receipt, the Service should not attempt to continue to apply the doctrine of constructive receipt to the estate taxations of qualified plan benefits subsequent to December 31, 1981.

If an employee has a large amount of voluntary contributions, he might prefer electing installment payments from the plan rather than receiving and rolling over a lump sum. This is because employee contributions may not be rolled over, and therefore, earnings attributable to employee contributions would lose their tax shelter under the rollover alternative. By contrast, these contributions would remain tax-sheltered if benefits were distributed in installments from the plan.

An amount distributed from a qualified corporate plan after the death of the participant, other than an amount attributable to employee contributions, will be excluded from the participant's gross estate provided that such amount is payable to a beneficiary other than the participant's estate and provided that 10-year averaging of the distribution is not elected.[87] Again, however, TEFRA limits the advantage of qualified plans such that the amount received from a qualified plan or IRA in excess of $100,000 is included in the gross estate of the participant.[88] As an alternative, the beneficiary could elect 10-year averaging of any lump sum benefit remaining in the plan, but the amount would then be included in the participant's estate. As a third alternative the spouse of the participant may be given a lump sum distribution which could be rolled over into an IRA by the spouse.[89] Although the estate tax consequences of the surviving spouse's rollover are not certain, the author believes that a rollover by the spouse may be accomplished without loss of the participant's estate tax exclusion. In any event, appropriate tax advice should be sought with regard to the various elections and possible tax consequences which occur upon the death of an employee.

In summary, a participant may prefer receiving deferred benefits directly from a corporate plan, particularly if the participant has a large amount of voluntary employee contributions. This alternative permits continued deferral of income taxation of accrued benefits and of earnings on accrued benefits including earnings on employee contributions. This alternative also preserves the employee's estate tax exclusion on employer-derived accrued benefits. Earnings attributable to employee contributions are includible in the participant's estate under this alternative, but not under the IRA alternative to the extent such earnings are rolled over. This alternative might be best suited for a corporation that has only one shareholder since, after the

---

[87] Sections 2039(c) and 2039(f) of the Code.
[88] Section 2039(g) of the Code.
[89] Section 402(a)(7) of the Code.

shareholder participant retires, the plan could be frozen. Freezing the plan would minimize the opportunity for later events to disqualify the plan, alter the investment strategy, or modify the administration in a manner that would be to the detriment of the retired shareholder.

AFFILIATED SERVICE GROUPS

On December 28, 1980, President Carter signed into law Section 414(m) of the Code, which requires that all entities which constitute an "affiliated service group" must be treated as a single employer for purposes of determining whether a qualified retirement plan maintained by any member of the affiliated service group satisfies a number of the qualification requirements, including the nondiscrimination requirement, minimum participation rules, vesting rules, and Code Section 415 limitations. The applicability of Code Section 414(m) is specifically limited to "service organizations"—entities that have as their principal business the performance of services—and to other entities that regularly perform services for or in connection with service organizations. Because the focus of Code Section 414(m) is service organizations, the principal target of Code Section 414(m) will be professional corporations and the discussion that follows will examine the impact of Code Section 414(m) in the context of professional corporations, although it should be kept in mind that any "service organization" is within the ambit of Code Section 414(m).

Under Code Section 414(m) partnerships of professional or other service corporations will no longer be entitled to discriminate in favor of professionals in providing qualified retirement plans. There follows below an examination of the state of the law prior to the new legislation, an analysis of the new legislation, and a recommendation with regard to the new legislation and what actions should be taken while final regulations are pending.

Revenue Ruling 68-370—The IRS States Its Position

Until December 28, 1980, the rules for employee participation in the qualified retirement plans of partnerships of professional corporations were clearly stated by the Service. Through Rev. Rul. 68-370,[90] the Service ruled that a corporation that participated in a joint venture would be required to take employees of the joint venture into account in determining whether the corporation's profit-sharing plan met the requirements of Section 401(a). The Service viewed the joint venture of the two corporations as a partnership, a partnership that was not itself a taxable entity but merely the aggregate of the constituent partners. Therefore, the establishment of the requisite employment relationship between the partnership and the com-

[90] 1968-2 C.B. 174.

mon law employees of the partnership also established such relationship between each corporate partner and such employees for purposes of Section 401.

The important effect of this conclusion was to attribute to each corporate partner the common-law employment relationship that existed between the partnership and the individual employees. Thus, since the employees of the joint venture were considered employees of the corporate partners, the Service held that such employees, and a pro rata share of the compensation paid to them, must be taken into account by each corporate partner in determining whether the qualified plan of each corporate partner met the coverage and nondiscrimination requirements set forth in Section 401(a).

Packard/Burnetta Cases—The Tax Court Approves the Service Position

In *Ronald C. Packard*,[91] three dentists, practicing in a partnership, formed a service corporation to which all nonprofessional employees were transferred. The service corporation owned the office building in which the partnership was located and provided bookkeeping and general staff services and facilities to the partnership and to other dentists not in the partnership.

The Tax Court held that the profit-sharing plan adopted by the partnership (which covered only the dentists-partners) was qualified. The court reached this decision after determining that: (1) the service corporation was formed for a bona fide business purpose and was not a subterfuge and (2) the service personnel were directed and controlled by, and therefore, by the familiar common-law test, were employees of, the service corporation as opposed to the partnership. The court emphasized the following factors:

1. The service corporation marketed a complete package of services incidental to the practice of dentistry and sold this complete service not only to the partnership but also to three independent dentists.
2. The fee paid to the service corporation was not limited to a percentage of wages and expenses but rather was a percentage of gross billings with respect to subscribers.
3. The relationship between the service corporation and the subscribers was formalized in a written lease and management contract.
4. The partnership and the other subscribers were entitled to specify only the results to be accomplished by the service personnel while the service corporation maintained the right to control, hire, and fire service personnel.

It should be noted that *Packard* involved tax years prior to the enactment of Section 414(b) and (c) of the Code. If the *Packard* situation arose today,

---

[91] 63 T.C. 621 (1975).

the likely, and proper, result would be that under Section 414(c), the service employees would be treated as employed by the dental partnership, since the three dentists were in a single partnership and had the requisite degree of control in both the partnership and the service corporation.

The Tax Court again used the common-law employee attribution test in *Edward L. Burnetta, O.D., P.A.*[92] In that case, an opthalmologist and an optometrist formed separate professional corporations and adopted qualified retirement plans. Subsequently, they contracted with a service corporation, owned by the accountant for the professional corporations, to provide service personnel. As originally conceived, the service corporation was to be responsible for the selection, hiring, training, and supervision of all service personnel for a number of unrelated professional corporations. In practice, however, the selection, hiring, training, and supervision of the service personnel were maintained by the respective professional corporations. Thus, the Tax Court held that the service personnel were employees of the professional corporations for whom they worked, and consequently, the qualified retirement plans did not meet the coverage requirements of Section 401(a)(3)(A) (pre-ERISA).

The Tax Court distinguished the *Packard* decision on the basis that in *Packard* the taxpayers were able to establish under the common law employee test that control over the service personnel in fact rested in the service corporation not in the partnership. If Sections 414(b) and (c) had been in existence, their strict application to this case, without consideration of the common law employee test espoused under Rev. Rul. 68-370, would have resulted in the opposite conclusion.

The Kiddie Case—Pre-ERISA

In the pre-ERISA case of *Thomas Kiddie, M.D., Inc.,*[93] the Tax Court, discussing partnership law instead of the common law employee/employer rules, thoroughly confused the area of employee participation in qualified plans of professional partnerships. Dr. Kiddie's professional corporation provided pathological services to a hospital. In 1972, the corporation created a partnership with another professional service corporation to provide pathological services, with each corporation owning 50 percent of the partnership. The staff employees of Dr. Kiddie's corporation then became employees of the partnership, and Dr. Kiddie's corporation adopted a qualified pension plan.

The court held that the staff employees were employees of the partnership and were properly excluded from Dr. Kiddie's pension plan. The court, holding that the Section 707(b) "greater than 50 percent test" should apply for purposes of Section 401(a)(3), refused to attribute the partner-

[92] 68 T.C. 387 (1977), government appeal dismissed *nolle pros.* (10th Cir. 1978).
[93] 69 T.C. 1055 (1978).

ship's employees to Dr. Kiddie's corporation because it owned only 50 percent of the partnership and therefore did not control the partnership. Whether Dr. Kiddie's corporation controlled the partnership's employees and, thus, was their employer, was not examined by the Tax Court.

The IRS Position after Kiddie

The Service refused to follow *Kiddie* and continued to follow Rev. Rul. 68-370. For instance, in Letter Ruling 7834059, three professional corporations each held a one-third interest in the capital and profits of a law partnership with six full-time employees. One of the professional corporations proposed the adoption of a profit-sharing plan. The Service ruled that this corporation could adopt a profit-sharing plan, complying with the coverage and nondiscrimination requirements of Section 401(a), even if the other two corporations and the partnership did not adopt such a plan. Further, the employees of the partnership would be considered the full-time employees of the professional corporation and would participate in the profit-sharing plan to the extent of one third of their compensation received from the partnership. If the professional corporations included the six employees of the partnership as participants in their qualified retirement plans, if any, to the extent of one third of their compensation received from the partnership, then the participation and nondiscrimination requirements of Section 401(a) of the Code would be satisfied. The Service then stated:

> It is our conclusion that the conclusion stated in Rev. Rul. 68-370 has not been affected by the enactment of the Employee Retirement Income Security Act of 1974 and that it still may be relied upon for authority that the employees of a partnership or joint venture are considered employees of each member or partner for purposes of testing for coverage and nondiscrimination in contributions or benefits. We believe that Sections 414(b) and (c) do not establish exclusive rules for aggregation of employees for these purposes. It is our belief that Congress in enacting ERISA did not seek to erode the established rules of the Internal Revenue Service pertaining to such matters, but rather sought to extend the coverage and nondiscrimination requirements of the Code with respect to affiliated business entities regardless of whether any employee of a member of the control group performs services for another member of the control group.[94]

The Garland Case—Post-ERISA

An approach similar to that taken by the Service in Letter Ruling 7834059 was rejected by the Tax Court in its unfortunate opinion in *Lloyd*

---

[94] The Service took the same position in Letter Ruling 7902086 and Letter Ruling 7905020, the latter of which, for the most part, is restated in 13 other Letter Rulings (7905025, -026, 030, 036, -037, -038, -042, -044, -050, -053, -060, -061, -063).

M. Garland, M.D., F.A.C.S., P.A.[95] Petitioner, a professional medical corporation, formed a partnership with a physician, and each partner owned a 50 percent interest in the partnership. The professional corporation adopted a pension plan which did not cover the common law employees of the partnership. Dr. Garland felt that his professional corporation was not required by either Section 414(b) or Section 414(c) to cover the partnership's employees under the plan. Nevertheless, the Service determined that the plan did not qualify under Section 401(a) because it did not comply with the antidiscrimination provisions of Sections 401(a)(4) and 410(b)(1).

The Tax Court held, directly contrary to the position stated in Letter Ruling 7834059, that Sections 414(b) and 414(c) *are the exclusive* means for determining whether the employees of affiliated entities should be aggregated for purposes of applying the antidiscrimination provisions. Further, the Tax Court held that, since the professional corporation did not control the partnership's employees, they were properly excluded from participation in the plan. The reasoning in *Kiddie* was followed, totally ignoring the logic and desirability of using the common law employee test as used in Rev. Rul. 68-370 as an alternative means of compliance with the antidiscrimination provisions.

Effect of Section 414(m)

Section 414(m) is effective for plan years ending after November 30, 1980, for new plans and plan years beginning after that date for existing plans. Section 414(m) provides rules for the aggregation of employees of certain separate organizations for purposes of applying tests to various benefit plans. It is an emphatic response to the absurd results which have received judicial approval in *Kiddie* and *Garland* but applies *only* to service organizations.[96]

---

[95] 73 T.C. 5 (1979).

[96] A complete text of Section 414(m) is as follows:

(m) EMPLOYEES OF AN AFFILIATED SERVICE GROUP.
   (1) IN GENERAL—For purposes of the employee benefit requirements listed in paragraph (4), except to the extent otherwise provided in regulations, all employees of the members of an affiliated service group shall be treated as employed by a single employer.
   (2) AFFILIATED SERVICE GROUP—For purposes of this subsection, the term "affiliated service group" means a group consisting of a service organization (hereinafter in this paragraph referred to as the 'first organization') and one or more of the following:
     (A) any service organization which
       (i) is a shareholder or partner in the first organization, and
       (ii) regularly performs services for the first organization or is regularly associated with the first organization in performing services for third persons, and
     (B) any other organization if—
       (i) a significant portion of the business of such organization is the performance of services (for the first organization, for organizations described in subparagraph (A), or for both) of a type historically performed in such service field by employees, and
       (ii) 10 percent or more of the interests in such organization is held by persons

For purposes of defining qualified pension plans under Section 414(m), all employees of members of an "affiliated service group" will be treated as employed by a single employer. An "affiliated service group" consists of a service organization and one or more other organizations, service or not, which are related. The broad definition of organization includes a corporation, partnership or "other organization." Section 414(m)(2) defines an affiliated service group as follows:

> (2) *AFFILIATED SERVICE GROUP*—For purposes of this subsection, the term 'affiliated service group' means a group consisting of a service organization (hereinafter in this paragraph referred to as the 'first organization') and one or more of the following:
>
> (A)   any service organization which—(i) is a shareholder or partner in the first organization, and
> (ii) regularly performs services for the first organization or is regularly associated with the first organization in performing services for third persons, and
> (B)   any other organization if—
> (i) a significant portion of the business of such organization is the performance of services for the first organization (for organizations described in subparagraph (A), or for both) of a type historically performed in such service field by employees, and
> (ii) 10 percent or more of the interests in such organization is held by persons who are officers, highly compensated employees, or owners of the first organization or an organization described in subparagraph (A)(i).

In Rev. Rul. 81-105,[97] the Service provided an explanation of Section 414(m) and illustrated the application of the affiliated service group classification by way of three examples. Rev. Rul. 81-105 ruled that it obsoletes

---

who are officers, highly compensated employees, or owners of the first organization or an organization described in subparagraph (A)(i).
    (3) SERVICE ORGANIZATIONS—For purposes of this subsection, the term "service organization" means an organization the principal business of which is the performance of services.
    (4) EMPLOYEE BENEFIT REQUIREMENTS—For purposes of this subsection, the employee benefit requirements listed in this paragraph are—
    (A)   paragraphs (3), (4), (7), and (16) of section 401(a),
    (B)   sections 408(k), 410, 411, and 415,
    (C)   section 105(h), and
    (D)   section 125.
    (5) OTHER DEFINITIONS—For purposes of this subsection—
    (A)   ORGANIZATION DEFINED—The term "organization" means a corporation, partnership, or other organization.
    (B)   OWNERSHIP—In determining ownership, the principles of section 267(c) shall apply.
    (6) PREVENTION OF AVOIDANCE—The Secretary shall prescribe such regulations as may be necessary to prevent the avoidance with respect to service organizations, through the use of separate organizations, of any employee benefit requirement listed in paragraph (4).
[97] 181-1 C.B. 256.

Rev. Rul. 68-370, so that entities which must be treated as a single entity under Section 414(m) may not satisfy the minimum coverage and nondiscrimination requirements by providing a full benefit to one entity of the affiliated service group and providing a partial benefit to the rank-and-file employees in affiliated entities.

In Rev. Proc. 81-12,[98] the Service provided a procedure under which plan sponsors may request a ruling from the National Office of the IRS as to whether two or more entities are part of an affiliated service group, and may request a determination letter from the key district director as to whether plans maintained by members of an affiliated service group satisfy the qualification requirements as modified by Section 414(m). It is important that plan sponsors who believe they may be part of an affiliated service group make a specific request for the determination when submitting plans for qualification, since a determination letter will not apply to the Section 414(m) issue unless the determination letter request raises this issue. The Service has revised Item 10 of Forms 5300 and 5301 to permit plan sponsors to indicate whether they are, or believe they are, a part of an affiliated service group.

The Service has taken the position that any plan established by a member of an affiliated group must either: (1) when considered *alone* cover a classification of all the employees employed by the affiliated service group that satisfies either the percentage test or nondiscriminatory classification test of Section 410(b)(1); or (2) when considered in *combination with* other "comparable" qualified plans maintained by members of the affiliated service group cover a classification of all the employees covered by the affiliated service group that satisfies either the percentage test or nondiscriminatory classification test of Section 410(b)(1). In the typical situation, a plan established by a corporate partner that is a member of a partnership of professional corporations will cover only the individual who is the sole shareholder and sole employee of the professional corporation, and as a result, such a plan when considered alone will fail to satisfy the minimum participation and nondiscrimination requirements for qualification. As a result, it will be necessary for the partnership to establish a qualified plan which benefits the staff employees employed by the partnership, and the professional corporations which are corporate partners may then establish retirement plans which are "comparable" to the partnership's plan. Another alternative would be for the professional corporation to employ several staff employees so that coverage of the professional and several staff employees will satisfy the reasonable classification test of Section 410(b)(1)(B); in this regard see, *Federal Land Bank Associates of Asheville* v. *Commissioner*,[99] in which the Tax Court held that a plan need not cover a fair cross-section of employees to satisfy the reasonable classifica-

---

[98] 181-1 C.B. 652.

[99] 74 T.C. 1106 (1980).

tion test, and sustained the qualification of a contributory thrift plan that was open to participation for all employees but in operation covered only 2 of 23 employees one of whom was in the prohibited group and one of whom was not. The Tax Court followed the *Federal Land Bank Associates of Asheville* rationale in *Sutherland* v. *Commissioner*.[100]

If a professional corporation's plan does not qualify when considered alone, the plan may qualify when aggregated with other "comparable" plans maintained by the affiliated group. In Rev. Rul. 81-202[101] the Service provided a comprehensive set of rules for testing the comparability of contributions and benefits provided by qualified pension and profit-sharing plans. These rules permit plans which are required to be aggregated under Sections 414(b), (c) or (m) to be shown to provide either comparable contributions *or* comparable benefits and thereby satisfy the nondiscrimination test of Section 401(a)(4) and the reasonable classification test of Section 410(b)(1)(B). Generally speaking, under Rev. Rul. 81-202, two plans (whether both defined contribution or both defined benefit or one defined contribution and one defined benefit) can be shown to provide comparable benefits by projecting the straight-life annuity at age 65 which could be funded by each plan and comparing the retirement benefit at age 65 or the unit benefit rate of accrual which results in the retirement benefit, and may be shown to provide comparable contributions by comparing the actual or anticipated contribution levels under the funding provisions of each plan. Whether testing for comparability of contributions or benefits, Rev. Rul. 81-202 permits integration with Social Security to be taken into account.

Reallocation of Income

In its attempts to recharacterize transactions and arrangements for tax purposes, the Service may use statutory provisions in addition to the basic "substance over form" theory. Two sections are particularly useful to the service: Code Section 482 and new Code Section 269A which was added by TEFRA.

Section 482 permits the Service to allocate income and deductions among taxpayers in order to clearly reflect income. For example, in order for a partnership of professional corporations to achieve the desired results, it is necessary that the professional corporations be taxed on their distributive shares of partnership income and that the shareholder-employees of the professional corporations be taxable only on the compensation paid to them by their respective professional corporations. Section 482 may be asserted in an effort to reallocate income away from the professional corporation and to its shareholder-employee on the theory that the distributive share of partnership income was earned by the shareholder.

---

[100] 78 T.C. No. 27 (March 9, 1982).
[101] Rev. Rul. 81-202, 1981-2, C.B. 93.

The Service may take the position that it is the professional shareholder-employees and not the professional corporations who are, in fact, the members of the partnership because it is their personal efforts that actually create the partnership income. If such a position were to prevail, all professional income would be attributable to the individual shareholder-employees as opposed to the professional corporations. Also, in a one-man service corporation, the service may take the position that the corporation's income is actually the shareholder's personal income.

The Service has, over the years, had varying degrees of success in reallocating income under Section 482 between a sole shareholder and his corporation. For instance, in *Borge* v. *Commissioner*,[102] the taxpayer was deemed, for purposes of Section 482, to own or to control two businesses (an entertainment business and a poultry business) and a portion of the entertainment compensation paid to his corporation was reallocated to him personally. The reallocation was predicated on the finding that the taxpayer merely assigned a portion of his entertainment income to his corporation and the corporation did nothing to earn or assist in earning that income. In the case of *Richard Rubin*,[103] the controlling shareholder had corporation A enter into a management contract with corporation B, whereby the controlling shareholder, as an employee of corporation A, would provide management services for corporation B. The controlling shareholder carried on a separate trade or business of rendering managerial services and thus fell within the ambit of Section 482, and income was reallocated from corporation A to the shareholder.

In *Silvano Achivo*,[104] the Tax Court refused to sustain the Commissioner's asserted 100 percent reallocation of income under Code Section 482 from a management corporation to the controlling shareholders of the management corporation where the management corporation was established for the purposes of entering into management contracts with two other operating corporations that were controlled by the shareholders of the management corporation, and where the terms of the management contracts between the management corporation and the operating corporations were arm's-length terms, and the terms of the shareholders' employment contracts with their management corporation were arm's-length terms. The management corporation's taxable income was nominal since over 90 percent of the management fees it received were paid out for salary and pension contributions. The Tax Court held that for purposes of determining whether the shareholders' compensation was an arm's-length rate of pay or whether it was subject to reallocation under Code Section 482,

---

[102] 26 T.C.M. 816 (1967), aff'd 405 F. 2d 673 (2d cir. 1968), cert. denied sub nom. *Danica Enter., Inc.* v. *Commissioner,* 395 U.S. 933 (1969).

[103] 51 T.C. 251 (1968), reversed and remanded, 429 F. 2d 650 (2d Cir. 1970), on remand 56 T.C. 1155 (1971), aff'd per curian 460 F. 2d 1216 (2d Cir. 1972).

[104] 77 T.C. 881 (1981).

qualified plan contributions will be taken into account. The Tax Court rejected the Commissioner's position that incorporations motivated by a desire to obtain the benefits of corporate qualified plans was improper. Specifically, the Tax Court stated:

> The keynote in respondent's present position under Sections 482, 269, and 61 is his contention that incorporation for the principal purpose of taking advantage of corporate pension and profit sharing plans amounts to an evasion or avoidance of income taxes, an unclear reflection of income, and/or an assignment of income. We disagree. Of course, a mere corporate skeleton, standing alone and without any flesh on its bones, will not suffice to provide its shareholder-employees with corporate retirement benefits. See *Roubik* v. *Commissioner,* 53 T.C. 365, 382 (1969) (Tannenwald, J., concurring). Once incorporated, the personal service business must be run as a corporation. Its shareholder-employees must recognize, respect, and treat their personal service corporation as a corporation. The corporation must accept the disadvantages as well as advantages of incorporation. Once a corporation is formed and all organizational and operational requirements are met it should be recognized for tax purposes regardless of the fact that it was formed to take advantage of the richer corporate retirement plans.

In *Keller* v. *Commissioner,*[105] the Tax Court similarly rejected the Commissioner's challenge under Code Sections 482, 269, and 61 of a one-man professional corporation formed by a pathologist and used to replace the pathologist as a partner with other doctors. The Tax Court noted that: (1) the doctor's professional corporation was properly formed, (2) the corporation had entered into an arm's-length employment contract with the doctor (taking into account both cash compensation and qualified plan contributions), (3) the corporation was substituted as partners with the consent of all other partners, (4) the corporation maintained a bank account in its own name, and (5) the corporation used its own name on its office door and all stationery. Under these circumstances the Tax Court held that reallocation of income under Code Section 482 between the corporation and the doctor was improper because the total compensation, both cash and qualified plan contributions, was "essentially equivalent to that which he would have received absent incorporation." A portion of the corporation's first year's income was reallocated to Dr. Kelley for personal services he performed in his individual capacity before his corporation was substituted as partners. A strong dissent was written by six Tax Court judges, and the decision is on appeal to the Tenth Circuit. The Tax Court has followed the *Keller* line of reasoning in *Garbini Electric, Inc.,*[106] and *Pacella.*[107] In *Edwin C. Davis,*[108] the Service was unsuccessful in attempting to allocate income under Code

---

[105] 77 T.C. 1014 (1981) (appealed to the 10th Circuit).

[106] 43 T.C.M. 919 (1982).

[107] 78 T.C. 604 (1982).

[108] 64 T.C. 1034 (1975).

Section 482 from X-ray and physical therapy corporations to an orthopedic surgeon who set them up and then gave the stock to his children.

The possibility that the professional corporation may not be recognized for tax purposes under the *Roubik* rationale or that income may be allocated either away from the professional corporation partners or among them in a different fashion under Section 482 represents a formidable, but not insurmountable, obstacle to the operation of a partnership of professional corporations. Certainly the Tax Court's decisions in *Silvano Achivo* and *Keller* will provide a good deal of reassurance to tax planners, particularly if the Tax Court's *Keller* opinion is sustained on appeal. The determination of whether to apply the *Roubik* rationale or Section 482 is essentially a factual one, and proper adherence to both the form and substance of rendering professional services as a corporate partner in a professional partnership should minimize the risk in this area. At the very least, the parties should take steps to insure that the professional corporations are the actual earners of the income. The professional corporations should enter into employment agreements with the professional employees and should, in fact, retain and exercise control over the professionals' employment. The professional employees should be prohibited from entering into contracts in their individual names, and all contracts should be in the names of the professional corporations or the partnership. Also, the professional corporations must hold themselves out to the public as rendering professional services by insuring that all statements, letterheads, office signs, business cards, telephone listings, building directories, and similar business practices reflect the status of the professional corporations. A written partnership agreement should be made and consideration should be given to placing all leases, insurance policies, and other contractual agreements in the name of the professional partnership. Also, the professional partnership should hold itself out to the public as such and should also hold itself out to the Service as a partnership by obtaining an employer identification number as a partnership, by making employer tax deposits for its common law employees, and by filing partnership income tax returns.

If, in fact, the Service prevails in disregarding the corporate entities, the professional corporations' qualified retirement plans will probably be disqualified and the employees of the corporations will lose the other employee benefits, such as group term life insurance, health and medical reimbursement plans, etc. However, if income is reallocated under Section 482, it is possible that the corporations' qualified retirement plans would not be disqualified, but plan contributions could be disallowed as deductions since the corporations would not be considered as having income and would pay no compensation.

The Service also may use new Code Section 269A to reallocate income, deductions, and other tax items between a corporation and its shareholder or shareholders. Code Section 269A provides that, if substantially all of the services of a personal service corporation are performed for or on behalf of one other corporation, partnership, or other entity and if the principal purpose for forming or availing of the corporation is the avoidance or evasion of federal income tax, then the Service may allocate all income, deductions, credits, exclusions, and other allowances between such personal service corporation and its employee-owners. The report of the Conference Committee on TEFRA states that "[t]he conferees intend that the provisions [of Section 269A] overturn the results reached in cases like *Keller* v. *Commissioner*, 77 T.C. No. 70 (1981), where the Corporation served no meaningful business purpose other than to secure tax benefits which will not otherwise be available.[109] The Conference Committee's reference to *Keller* implies that Section 269A only is applicable to partnerships of professional corporations since *Keller* concerned a partnership of professional corporations formed for the purpose of maximizing the tax benefits available upon incorporation. Nonetheless, by its terms, Section 269A is applicable to any small business corporation which performs substantially all of its services for one customer, client, or patient. Obviously, Section 269A may be applicable to most hospital-based physicians who operate in corporate form.

While those service providers who now operate in corporate form may have incorporated for nontax reasons, for example, the availability of corporate limited liability, service providers who adopted and continue to maintain qualified retirement plans prior to TEFRA and who receive other corporate tax benefits may find the Service only too willing to read Section 269A broadly.

---

[109] CONF. REP. NO. 97-530, 97th Cong. 2d Sess. 634 (1982).

PART EIGHT

Issues of Special Interest in Employee Benefit Planning

The final part of the *Handbook* is devoted to issues of special interest in employee benefit planning and begins with Chapter 54, which gives a perspective on inflation including a discussion of pension adequacy and the philosophy underlying the issue of indexation.

International benefits are discussed in Chapter 55. Chapter 56 deals with public employee pension plans, and Chapter 57 takes a look at the future of employee benefit plans.

In Chapter 58, the far-reaching effects of the Tax Equity and Fiscal Responsibility Act of 1982 (TEFRA) are summarized. While these have been incorporated into the various chapters of the *Handbook* as appropriate, this summary chapter presents a concise overview of the impact of the law.

Because the taxation of group life insurance was greatly affected by TEFRA, the final two chapters of the *Handbook* were placed in the Issues of Special Interest Part following the TEFRA chapter to call attention to the major changes in this area. Chapters 59 and 60 cover federal income taxation of group life insurance and gift and estate taxation of group life insurance, respectively.

While the *Handbook* was in the final stages of production, the 1983 Amendments to the Social Security Act were passed into law. A summary of the amendments appears in Appendix A, and the reader is encouraged to refer to this appendix as an update to Chapters 5, 9, 17, and 28 as well as to other sections of the *Handbook* dealing with Social Security.

CHAPTER 54

Looking through Both Ends of the Telescope: A Perspective on Pension Plans and Inflation

LLOYD S. KAYE

PENSION ADEQUACY ISSUES

The most publicized debate in pension planning circles since the late 1970s, and still in full voice, is the issue of indexation: the responsibility for a pension plan to maintain, after retirement, the purchasing power of pension payments. This is a critical aspect of the overall pension adequacy issue which is the essence of sound pension planning. The need for pension indexation should be analyzed within the perspective of long-range pension concepts, not simply in response to immediate demands and notions of equity.

The best beginning point is not with the question of "should we index?"; rather, it is worthwhile to begin an analysis of pension plans and inflation with a brief review of how ideas on effective pension planning have evolved over the last generation. To put this another way, the issue of pension indexation is more than just experimenting with percentages and numbers. It requires a philosophy; and that may depend on whether one is looking long or short range: through the long- or short-range end of the telescope.

Career Average or Final Average?

During the 1950s and the 1960s, the most significant debate over pension adequacy was whether it is advisable for an employer's pension plan to have the pension benefit formula based on "career average" pay, measured over the employee's entire career, or on "final average" pay measured over a limited period, such as the 5 or 10 years immediately preceding retirement.

The great majority of pension plans were once based on career average pay. For example, for each year of credited service, an employee would receive credit for 1 percent of compensation recognized for that particular year. If the plan continued on this basis throughout an employee's career and retirement occurred after 30 years of service, then 30 percent of the employee's average pay throughout his or her entire career would be payable as the pension.

It is obvious that this would be far from perfect from the standpoint of adequacy. Even if there had been no inflation over that 30-year period, the amount of the pension would be adequate only if the pay level remained fairly constant. A typical employee would receive merit increases, so that in order to reflect an attained pay level fairly close to retirement, it would be necessary to "update" pension credits periodically to bring prior pension credits into line with the current pay level.

Supporters of the career average concept pointed to its inherent conservatism and the continued control by the employer to assume new updating liabilities only when and to the extent they would be financially affordable. In contrast, those in favor of the final average pay approach maintained that the assurance of an adequate pension is paramount and that the employee should be able to rely absolutely on having his or her pension based on average pay over a limited period close to retirement.

In practice, there might be little difference between a final average pay plan and a career average plan which was periodically updated to make prior pension credits adequate in terms of current pay levels. Even the modest rates of inflation which prevailed through the mid-1960s, combined with merit increases, made it necessary for financially stable, conscientious employers to operate their career average plans as if they were final average pay plans by use of updatings every three to five years. As more and more companies came to appreciate the blurring of the distinction in practice, a major trend developed during the 1960s from the career average to the final average concept.

Inflation was at the heart of this movement, even though many companies did not fully appreciate their own motivation. Increases in worker productivity during the 1950s and 1960s generated increases in pay which were clearly merit increases in the sense that they were substantially in excess of the rate of inflation, which ranged between 2 and 3 percent over that period. However, even in times when there is only a 2 or 3 percent rate of inflation, this can accumulate to a very substantial difference after 10 or 15 years. Thus, inflation was at the heart of the question, and pay scales went up regardless of merit simply because of inflationary pressures. Adoption of the final average pay concept committed companies to pay for the increased pension which derived from inflationary increases in current wages. The economics of the 1970s cautioned many companies and slowed or stopped the final average pay trend. An element that tended to dampen the enthusiasm for assuming final average pay commitments was the shock of sharper inflation at a rate not experienced within the working lifetimes of most employees. Careful analysts of the final average pay trend came to realize that it is inherent in that type of plan that the employer would commit to paying for the inflation up to the point of retirement. In effect then, a final average pay plan is a form of guaranteed indexation.

Having accomplished this, the last several years have demonstrated that this does not mean assurance of pension adequacy to the employee. An employee who retires at age 65 after 30 years of service will be relying on that pension for life. If a joint and survivor option is in effect, so will the surviving spouse. Thus, the postretirement period for measuring pension adequacy can be as long as the working career of a long-service employee. Many employers who adopted final average pay plans had been lulled into the secure feeling that there was nothing more to be done after that. It is now apparent that improvement during retirement years is essential if the same standard of adequacy which existed at the time of retirement is to be maintained thereafter.

By viewing the matter in this perspective, it is possible to identify the following issues and questions:

If the amount of the pension was adequate at the point of retirement, then it is axiomatic that the employer has underwritten the cost of inflation over the employee's working career. To what extent should the employer be responsible to continue to pay for inflation thereafter?

Is there a moral obligation? Should Congress compel indexation?

Is there a difference in the nature of a financial commitment to pay for inflation over the employee's working career, as compared to the commitment to pay for inflation in the future?

Social Security benefits are indexed with the consumer price index (CPI). To what extent should this be taken into account in future planning? Is it a model for private plans? Is the CPI a proper index, and if not, what is?

What is the potential cost impact for maintaining the purchasing power of pensions?

The Indexation Dilemma

The cost commitment for guaranteeing indexation up to the point of retirement is a different type of commitment than that of postretirement indexation. One of the often heard comments by career average plan enthusiasts is that a final average pay plan formula is like signing a blank check because it makes the employer a financial hostage to future wage scales. It seems obvious that this is an overstatement, in the sense that the employer retains an important element of financial control because the amount of that check is budgetable.

The reason is that an important aspect of actuarial planning includes an assumption as to the best estimate of increases in salaries, so the employer begins to pay for the future pension immediately by assuming pay will go up. If the increase in assumed salary proves inadequate because pay increases faster than estimated in the actuarial assumption, periodic monitoring of the adequacy of that assumption facilitates suitable measurement and adjustment. In essence, the employer can always measure the cost commitment and see an appropriate ratio between payroll and pension plan contribution. Thus, up to the point of retirement, there has always been a controlled logical progression.

The logic encounters some static at the point of retirement. A specified level of indexation could be guaranteed and the liability prefunded by including that commitment as part of the plan's actuarial assumptions. But this has only a thin surface resemblance to a salary increase assumption for active employees, which can be periodically monitored and adjusted based on actual experience. Long-range forecasts of inflation rates are likely to have a very remote relationship to the real world.

Periodic, discretionary pension indexing has been the prevailing pattern among employers. Persistent repetitions may then assume the character of the "updatings" which have been common among career average plans for active employees. Just as those updatings blur the distinction between career average and final average pay plans, so may updatings for pensioners blur the distinction between discretionary and automatic pension indexing. What impact will this have on employer costs?

When a private pension plan indexes pensions, two additional costs are assumed: first, more cash is necessary to take account of immediately increased payout rates; second, larger reserves must be accumulated to fund future increases on a sound basis. A rule of thumb is that for every 1 percent of annual increase, reserves should be strengthened by at least 6 percent and perhaps as much as 10 percent. If one assumes, somewhat pessimistically, a long-range increase in the cost of living of 10 percent per year, a doubling of pension costs could be produced. An employer whose pension contributions are now 10 percent of payroll might pay 20 percent.

Some commentators have implied that this need not be so; that this arithmetic ignores the tendency of inflation and interest rates to go up and down together. Therefore, if a plan's interest assumption is, say, 6 percent and the retired lives reserve earns 10 percent, the excess 4 percent can be applied to increase retiree benefits without additional employer contributions.

However, it is apparent the true cost must be the same no matter how neatly the index package is stapled, whether together or separately. The basic interest assumption of 6 percent was either set by taking into account the prospect for future investment yields or is maintained at 6 percent rather than a higher figure because the plan sponsor has decided to devote the higher yield to enable indexation. Either way, the cost is the same regardless of how the employer decides to provide for indexing.

If Social Security Can Do It, Why Not Private Plans?

Congress has decreed that Social Security benefits will be adjusted with the consumer price index (CPI). Why not private pension plans? What is the problem?

On a superficial level, it seems as if the Social Security system is far more effective than the private system, but as a conclusion, it ignores fundamental economics. Indexation, which looks like a solution for retired employees, is, in an important sense, part of the problem. Social Security benefits are financed by payroll taxes, and to the extent Social Security fully compensates retired employees for inflation, it takes away money from the working portion of the population. As humane as this may be, it cannot be a long-range solution. If private industry cannot afford to subsidize inflation for retired employees, then government cannot do so by siphoning taxes simply because it has the legislative and administrative mechanism to do so. Those revenues are generated by the private sector. The Social Security system is a conduit not a creator of wealth.

The most serious crisis for the Social Security system has not yet arrived. As the ratio of active to retired workers decreases, the burden on workers to support the nonworking population will increase. In the early years of the 21st century, when the post-World War II baby-boom generation begins to reach age 65, there is a serious question whether the present structure of Social Security can remain intact, much less be liberalized. To commit a public system to subsidize inflation for nonworking people by exacting increasing taxes from a gradually shrinking segment of the population—its productive workers—is a questionable long-range solution.

It is an economic mirage to assume a public system is better than a private system because the public mechanism can guarantee a portion of the population against inflation. The issue of indexation of retiree benefits must properly be dealt with, but this can only be done in an orderly economy and simply will not work unless inflation is brought under control.

THE INDEXATION STANDARD

The consumer price index is the fundamental measure of the dollar's purchasing power. How valuable a standard is it, in particular when used as a measure of pension adequacy?

It is easy to criticize the CPI. It was intended to measure price changes in a stable economy. The degree of changes experienced recently, and likely to continue for some time, warrants a new look at how inflation is measured for different purposes. This is a critical problem. Failure to come up with a rational solution could create such conflicts—between different economic groups and the almost infinite subgroups (such as those based on generation, income level, occupation, geography, and so on)—as to create serious societal problems.

The essential challenge is to determine what is really happening to spending patterns and living costs. The CPI is based on charting a market basket established on the basis of goods and services purchased in 1972–73. It is important to find out what is a current market basket; but even before this, it is vital to know how and why spending patterns change and—this is fundamentally crucial—keep up-to-date on a 12-month moving average.

What is needed is a pragmatic sample technique which will result in a vital index of living costs rather than just a measure of price increases. How have people and families been spending their money? A cross-section of people in different areas and financial circumstances could indicate through checks and credit card expenditures what they have spent on the different components of living. By utilizing sampling techniques, with cancelled checks and credit card receipts as evidence of expenditures, an exact CPI could be developed for any group segmented by income, age, geography, family situation, and so on.

For example, both common sense and personal experience would indicate a tendency that as prices of certain goods and services rise dramatically, shifts occur almost by automatic reaction. Less steak, more chicken; less driving, more walking or public transportation; less expensive vacations; more do-it-yourself repairs; more bargain hunting for clothing, etc. What would be produced is a picture on an ongoing basis of what is really happening based on actual spending patterns.

The expected conclusion would be that increases in living costs are significantly less if measured in terms of what people actually spend, as contrasted with a price index of selected goods and services, the components of which change much more slowly.

Critics of this approach may say that what is happening is a reduction in living standards. After all, a family that forgoes a vacation and buys less clothing is not living as well as previously. The difference provides a good focus on the problem.

There is a key issue here. Indexation, as now conceived, is price-oriented: it asks the question of what it takes to make everyone "whole." By concentrating on expenditures, the emphasis is changed to analyzing differences in buying and spending habits as people adjust.

It recognizes that it is an illusion to attempt to keep social groups whole against a fixed standard in the face of major economic dislocation. The development of this new approach and technique tends to share more equitably a decline in living standards made necessary by such dislocations. If society wishes to overcompensate a particular group, such as the aged, it would not be the result of an index with questionable validity. Rather, careful analysis and discussion would produce that decision.

The Close-Up Look

So much for long-range philosophy. A look through the close-up end of the telescope would concentrate on the challenge to improve benefits for retirees in some fashion and make plans for those who will retire in the next several years. Planning through models is important if a satisfactory solution is to be devised.

The key points would be these:

a. The comparative amounts of Social Security dollars between the year of retirement and the year of plan improvement is a vital element. If the objective is to maintain purchasing power in terms of income replacement ratios at the time of retirement, the amount of Social Security increases must be considered. Across-the-board, uniform percentage increases—the typical device—have a tendency to do what any nonintegrated pension plan does: either overcompensate the lower-paid or undercompensate the higher-paid.

b. It is worthwhile to think through the indexing standard to be used. One standard worth considering is to treat retired people on the same standard as active employees. (This is one of the disparities in Social Security increases which have granted higher nontaxable raises to retired people as compared to the taxable pay increases for active workers.) Thus, the pay a retired worker would be getting had he or she remained employed would be projected. If pay increases have been 8 or 10 percent per year, that rate of increase would be added to the retired worker's last rate of pay, and if the plan's pension objective were 60 percent of that pay, including Social Security, the appropriate adjustment could be made readily in recognition of the projected pay and current Social Security benefits.

It may be considered more appropriate to distinguish between the portion of active pay increases attributable to inflation compared to merit. This means that instead of hypothetically projecting a retiree's pay rate at 10 percent, a rate of 6 or 8 percent might be suitable.

What is recommended, then, for a concept of indexation for retirees is an integrated program, recognizing current Social Security payments based on the employer's recognition of living cost increases as evidenced by the inflation element of actual pay increases. Once these elements are in place, the employer will have an appropriate planning model. How much pensions are improved will then depend on how much additional liability the employer wishes to assume.

Having said this, it is appropriate to return to the initial theme: the assumption by a private employer to underwrite a significant portion of inflation over an extended period can prove to be an onerous burden for that employer.

PLANNING AHEAD

The consternation generated over the last several years by inflationary erosion of pension adequacy warrants a new look at pension planning. Some longer-range planning may be in order.

The enactment of legislation in the Economic Recovery Tax Act of 1981 (ERTA) permitting limited tax deductions for voluntary contributions by employees to individual retirement accounts or qualified plans supports expansion of the concept that employees can be encouraged and assisted to start their own retirement planning. Whether implemented through an employer's defined benefit or defined contribution plan, or through a master individual retirement account (IRA), helping employees to put aside money for their own supplemental security can serve the best interests of the employer as well as employees. Employee savings and accumulation may be the best approach to modify the employer's long-range responsibilities through the device of having employees invest currently for their own inflation hedge after retirement.

Capital accumulation through savings and thrift plans is not a scientific approach to the general problem of pension adequacy, including the issue of the postretirement inflation spectre. A typical pension plan is a so-called defined benefit plan. The plan sponsor defines the amount of the pension benefit an employee would receive and assumes the financial burden to provide that benefit. In contrast, a defined contribution plan provides benefits based on the impact of investment performance on the contributions made by and for employees. In essence, a defined contribution plan merely accumulates capital; and the adequacy of that capital accumulation to provide security in long-range pension terms may be described as typically potluck.

There are surely drawbacks to the capital accumulation approach in assuring adequacy for employees. The dependence on successful investment is critical in that a defined contribution program is based on career average pay. A contribution of, say, 5 percent of current pay may not mean much in terms of final average pay of a typical long-service employee. It is not really subject to updating, as a career average pension credit can be updated.

Yet, despite these obvious drawbacks, the concept of capital accumulation as an adjunct to a pension plan may represent an employer's best planning device. It has a major advantage in avoiding new unfunded liabilities and costs by the employer. Further, it invites the employee to participate and save, recognizing that inflation and the quest for security is a mutual problem.

In essence, the employer's message to employees is: "Within our financial capacity, we will provide an adequate pension at the point of retirement. If you are concerned about inflation protection after that, a major part of satisfying that burden will depend on your willingness to start saving now."

The ultimate capital accumulation, whatever its dimension, could be used by a retired employee as his or her counterinflationary pool in as flexible a manner as he or she desires. The employer's future responsibility may be thereby eliminated or lessened. The time to plan ahead, as ever, is as soon as practicable—before the emergency precludes long-range planning.

CHAPTER 55

International Benefits

ARTHUR C. FOLLI

The administration of international benefits has become increasingly important as the number of multinational corporations, with substantial numbers of employees overseas, has increased. There are some 500 large U.S. multinational firms with foreign operations which generate earnings important to their worldwide financial results. In the petroleum industry, for example, as much as half of the consolidated operating earnings of the parent company may be generated by foreign sources. Some large banking institutions headquartered in New York City report proportionately larger earnings from foreign sources than from operations in the United States.

As a result, international operations have warranted careful management attention. From the viewpoint of employee benefits, this includes attention to the analysis, design, and administration of employee benefit programs which make up a significant portion (30 to 40 percent) of compensation cost overseas.

BENEFIT PLAN DESIGN AND OBJECTIVES

The design of benefit programs for foreign affiliates must take into account the business and social situation prevailing in the country. No two countries are alike, and local regulations, tax laws, customs, and competitive practice vary. For example, the practice in many countries in Europe to pay lifetime retirement annuities contrasts with the practice in the Far East where, because of local custom and favorable tax treatment, retirement programs often are designed to provide lump sum benefits.

Two additional factors can influence plan design. One is the rate of inflation, and the other is the role of foreign governments in providing benefits to employees.

The international benefit environment differs from the benefit environment in the United States, and as a result, benefit programs acceptable in the United States may not be acceptable in foreign areas. However, the

951

objectives of international benefit administration will nevertheless be the same:

1. To provide benefit programs to address the "risks" of retirement, death, sickness, disability, and termination.
2. To assure that the programs are competitive.
3. To design programs which are cost effective.
4. To establish benefit programs responsive to the company's business and staffing objectives.

The attraction and retention of qualified local national employees is a challenge since there may be some reluctance on the part of local nationals to work for a multinational company with "foreign" stockholders. Local nationals, other things being equal, generally prefer to work for a local company as opposed to a subsidiary, affiliate or branch of a multinational. So the challenge to the compensation and benefits specialist advising on programs for foreign affiliates of the multinational may be greater as compared with servicing a company competing in a market with other local companies.

The material that follows deals with many of the major factors which are important considerations in the planning and administration of international benefits such as inflation, benefit plan design elements, financing, and plan evaluation methods. Inflation is addressed first because *(a)* it provides a quick flavor of the overall economic conditions in the country and *(b)* it affects benefit plan entitlements and plan costs.

INFLATION

Table 55–1 shows the inflation rates in countries located in various parts of the world. The worldwide average annual rate of inflation over the five-year period 1977–81 has been approximately 12.0 percent.

Singapore, West Germany, Malaysia, and Switzerland have experienced moderate rates of inflation. However, countries such as the United Kingdom, Egypt, Italy, and Mexico have experienced double-digit inflation. There have been very high rates of inflation in Brazil, Israel, and Turkey. A high rate of inflation has a considerable impact, over time, on plan costs and on the real value of benefits received by employees from company-provided benefit programs.

Pension Plan Design

Pension plans generally are defined benefit plans. The benefit at retirement is determined by a formula. There are three major types of pension programs: final average pay (FAP) plans, career average (CAP) plans, and lump sum plans.

A typical *final average pay pension plan* might have the following formula:

Table 55-1
Inflation Rates (percent)

	1977	1978	1979	1980	1981	5-Year Average
Switzerland	1.6	.8	3.6	4.0	6.5	3.3
West Germany	3.6	2.7	4.1	5.5	5.9	4.4
Singapore	3.3	4.7	4.0	8.5	8.2	5.7
Malaysia	4.8	4.9	3.6	6.7	9.6	5.9
Netherlands	6.4	4.1	4.2	6.5	6.8	5.6
Belgium	7.1	4.5	4.5	6.7	7.6	6.1
Japan	8.1	3.8	3.6	8.0	4.9	5.7
Canada	8.0	9.0	9.1	10.2	12.4	9.7
United States	6.5	7.6	11.3	13.5	10.4	9.9
Saudi Arabia	11.3	-1.6	1.9	3.7	2.4	3.5
France	9.4	9.1	10.8	13.3	13.3	11.2
Australia	12.3	7.9	9.1	10.1	9.7	9.8
Philippines	7.9	7.6	18.8	17.8	11.8	12.8
South Africa	11.2	10.2	13.1	13.8	15.2	12.7
Egypt	12.7	11.1	9.9	20.7	10.5	13.0
United Kingdom	15.9	8.3	13.4	18.0	11.9	13.5
Indonesia	11.1	8.1	21.9	18.5	12.2	14.4
Greece	12.2	12.6	19.0	24.9	24.5	18.6
Italy	17.0	12.1	14.7	21.2	17.8	16.6
Nigeria	21.5	18.7	11.1	11.4	20.8	16.7
Mexico	29.0	17.4	18.2	26.4	27.9	23.8
Columbia	33.1	17.8	24.7	26.5	27.5	25.9
Turkey	27.1	45.3	58.7	110.2	36.6	55.6
Brazil	43.7	38.7	52.7	82.8	105.5	64.7
Israel	34.6	50.6	78.3	131.0	116.8	82.3
Average	14.4	12.6	17.0	24.8	21.5	18.1
Worldwide Average	11.4	9.5	11.7	15.3	13.7	12.3

Source: International Monetary Fund.

1.5% × years of service × FAP-3. The multiple 1.5 percent is applied to the years of service. FAP-3 would be the average earnings over the three years prior to retirement. If an individual earned $25,000 in the last year of service and $23,000 and $21,000 in the other two years, the final average earnings over the three years would be $23,000. The annual benefit using the above formula would be $10,350 assuming 30 years of service. This would be the gross benefit before taking into account any benefits attributable to governmental social security programs. It is common practice in many countries to integrate, with the private plan, benefits provided through social security schemes or legally required termination indemnities. If the pension formula were FAP-1 instead of FAP-3 in the above example, the benefit entitlement would be $11,250, or almost 9 percent higher.

In the case of high inflation, a pension program based on an FAP-3 or FAP-5 formula often does not provide sufficient replacement income for the prospective retiree. Concern about the erosion in purchasing power caused by price inflation has resulted in a trend to higher multiple final average pay pension plans or final average pay plans based on salaries in the years or months closest to the retirement date. Generally, pension plans are designed to provide between 50 and 80 percent replacement income, after taking into consideration taxes and governmental benefits. The higher replacement ratio might be appropriate for lower-salaried employees whereas lower replacement ratios could be considered for individuals in higher salary brackets.

Career average plans, which provide benefits taking into account total earnings while employed as contrasted to final average earnings, also have been used overseas. However, during periods of high inflation and rapidly rising wages, the career average plan does not provide sufficient replacement income for employees. These programs have often been replaced by final average pay plans.

Lump-sum pension plans are common in the Far East, particularly in Hong Kong, Japan, and the Philippines. This plan design is generally used because of favorable tax laws, which tend to encourage lump sum payments, or local custom. The lump sum benefit is calculated as a multiple of final pay or the actuarial equivalent of the lifetime annuity option which also may be permitted under the plan.

It is common in European countries to provide widows'/spouses' and orphans' benefits within the pension plan. Typically, the widow's benefit is one half of the employee's entitlement. Single orphan coverage is provided when one parent survives; double orphan benefits, usually twice the single orphan benefit, may be provided when there is no surviving parent. Also disability and death benefits often are incorporated within the pension program in contrast to the usual practice in the United States where such benefits may be provided through separately insured programs.

Vesting, the guaranteed right to a benefit after a specified period of service, may not specifically be provided in foreign plans unless required by local laws. In countries such as Japan, where it is customary for an employee to work with the company for a "working lifetime," a vesting provision may not be essential.

Retirement programs may be noncontributory or contributory. In countries such as the United Kingdom, South Africa, Australia, New Zealand, and Canada, employee contributions are treated favorably as a deduction against taxable earnings under local income tax laws, and as a result, contributory programs are not unusual.

As mentioned previously, governments, in providing benefits through legislated programs, can have an important impact on plan design. Many governments, either through social security or labor legislation, provide retirement and survivor benefits. As a result, there may be less need for supplementary private company-provided benefit programs, except to meet special needs of employees.

Besides governmental influences, it is not unusual in countries in Continental Europe to have participation of Works Councils in benefit plan matters as part of the codetermination process. These Councils include blue-collar as well as white-collar representatives and can influence the employee benefit program.

Savings Plans and Provident Funds

Savings plans are defined contribution plans. The benefit at retirement or termination is based on the sum of the annual contributions made to the plan by the employer and/or employee and the accrued earnings and/or capital appreciation at the time of settlement. Employees often have a choice of investments including fixed-income securities, government bonds, company stock, etc. Employee savings plans, although currently not in common use overseas, may be included in benefit plan design in countries such as Canada, Nigeria, Mexico, and Germany. These plans supplement the benefits available from the primary retirement plan.

Provident funds are similar to savings plans and are prevalent in the Far East; e.g., Thailand, Philippines, Singapore, and Malaysia. These funds, which provide lump sum benefits at retirement or termination, also are based on the defined contribution principle, and employees as well as employers may contribute to the fund. The investment vehicle generally is restricted and often is limited to interest-bearing accounts, such as bank deposits, government bonds, or a combination.

Health Coverage

Medical care for active employees, dependents, and retirees commonly is provided through governmental programs in international areas. For example, in the United Kingdom this is accomplished through the National Health Service; in West Germany, Australia, Canada, France, Japan, and some countries in South America, medical coverage is provided through the social security system or through other programs sponsored by the government.

Some governmental health programs are more comprehensive than others. To the extent these plans lack desired health coverage or lead to delays in obtaining treatment, multinationals as well as local companies have adopted private medical programs to supplement or provide health care alternatives to governmental programs.

FINANCING THE PLAN

Unlike in the United States, where the Employee Retirement Income Security Act (ERISA) prescribes limited procedures to be followed for funding benefit programs, legislation overseas may permit many different approaches. The financing mechanisms include:

- Funded plans administered through trustees.
- Insured programs.
- Multinational pooling arrangements.
- Book reserved plans or self-insured plans.
- Pay-as-you-go programs.
- A combination of the above; i.e., split-funding.

Pension plans in countries such as the United Kingdom, South Africa, Canada, Australia, the Philippines, and New Zealand typically are funded through trusts and the assets managed by professional investment advisors. In Norway, Denmark, Finland, Belgium, the Netherlands, and Barbados, retirement plans typically are insured. In these cases, the plan costs generally are deductible for tax purposes.

Pooling arrangements can be used to provide a means of lowering benefit cost by spreading the risk. This results in administrative savings, lower reserve requirements, better investment returns, and reduced reinsurance costs. Many large insurance companies pool pension, medical, death, and disability benefit risks of multinational corporations covered by contracts with local insurers in various foreign countries.

It is not necessary, in some countries, to have funded or insured plans in order to obtain tax benefits. For example, in Germany, Austria, Japan, and Mexico retirement plans may be book reserved, and full or partial tax benefits may be obtained under the law.

The book reserve defines on the balance sheet the liability the company has undertaken for providing pensions for employees at retirement. This method may provide less security to the employee as compared with funding since no specific assets are set aside to support the pension promise. However, the book reserve procedure has worked satisfactorily in foreign countries and enables the company to retain the cash for investment in the business, which reduces the cost of borrowing funds. Also, there are advantages to this funding method during periods of high inflation when better incremental returns may be available on investments in the business as compared with investments in securities.

Although book reserved, some countries may require a company guarantee that benefits will be paid when due. For example, in West Germany, the law requires that vested benefits or benefits in the course of payment be insured against the company's insolvency through a special insurance organization (PSV). The premium paid by the company is based on a percentage of the reserve.

The choice of the financing method for benefit programs must take into account cash flow requirements, local law, investment earnings, and the tax liability, to the company as well as to the employee, on annual plan contributions and annual plan earnings. When there is high inflation, the challenge to investment managers of trusteed plans to maintain satisfactory rates of return is great. In some countries, such as Brazil, investments can be made in indexed securities. In other countries (i.e., in Latin America), pension benefits may be handled on a pay-as-you-go basis in which case liabilities normally are not accrued.

Each foreign country has different requirements to "qualify" benefit programs for purposes of obtaining corporate tax deductions as well as to assure the nontaxability of current benefit accruals to the employee.

EVALUATION OF FOREIGN BENEFIT PROGRAMS

To insure that the benefit programs designed are cost effective and responsive to the needs of the employees, the programs should be evaluated carefully, taking into account the company's objectives. A well-structured benefit program, as a part of the total compensation approach, will assist in attracting and retaining qualified personnel. To develop short- and long-range planning programs appropriate for the overseas affiliate, the multinational should establish a framework within which to evaluate the desired levels of employee benefits.

One method used to evaluate compensation and benefit programs is to establish a target ranking objective for the affiliate with respect to competition in the local market. For example, the company objective might be to maintain a position in the middle of competition, as a desired ranking for its benefit programs. Therefore, the acceptability of an employee benefit scheme would be judged on how the benefit plan meets this criterion. Determination of the desired ranking position would depend on the needs and objectives of the company; i.e., (1) whether the company is well established in the market, (2) whether the company is seeking to attract employees to foster future growth, and (3) the financial resources of the company. A ranking position in the upper quartile for compensation and benefits may be necessary in cases where the company is not well established or is seeking rapid growth in a competitive labor market. On the other hand, a less ambitious ranking may be more desirable when a new operation is started to control costs; it is far easier to improve benefit programs than to reduce them.

Once a target ranking objective is established, the ranking analysis can be made by determining the value of various employee benefit programs and developing "strawman" comparisons which rank the company's plan with the competitive community. Each competitive plan, as well as the company's present plan and alternatives, can be evaluated in terms of the benefit the employee would receive. Table 55–2 is a sample of a "strawman" comparison.

Although this table shows data for one salary and service level, a composite could be developed to show the ranking for the typical or average

Table 55-2
Strawman Comparisons

Company XYZ versus competitive community total retirement income (including social security) at age 65 as percent of employee's final three-year average salary.

Service = 30 years
Final average salary = LC65,000
LC = Local currency

Ranking	Company	Percent of Final Average Salary
1	A	75.1%
2	B	74.0
3	C	72.8
4	D	71.5
5	E	70.8
6	XYZ	70.1
7	F	69.1
8	G	68.5
9	H	67.5
10	I	67.2
Average (excluding XYZ)		70.7%

retiree. It is important, however, to determine relative rankings for various salary and service levels to assure equitable treatment is provided both at the low and high end of the salary and service range. The percentages shown for the retirement benefit take into account the value of the total retirement income received by the employee as a percentage of his or her final average pay. Total retirement income would include the company-provided pension as well as governmental social security or other legislated benefits. The table deals with the basic retirement benefit only. It does not cover other benefits which may be provided in the plan, such as death protection for widows and orphans, etc. For these important items, separate strawman analyses can be prepared.

Another method of evaluating benefit plan programs and alternatives is the relative value method. This method ties into one bundle, on a present value basis, the total value of benefits provided under the pension, savings, life insurance, disability, and health programs. The relative value method permits comparison of the entire employee benefit package versus the competitive community or versus an alternative mix of benefit programs.

In addition, the relative value method can be useful in comparing the benefit program with other types of company investments and in measuring the extent of the company's commitment. For example, the investment cost of constructing a paint factory can be readily measured. The factory might cost $25 million to build, and a present value could be developed for the investment after taking into account the corporate tax savings from depreciation. In this case, the financial outlay and company commitment and risk are relatively clear.

Development of a comparable measurement for benefit plan programs or plan improvements is more complex. Using actuarial assumptions, the present value of projected benefits for pension plans can be calculated. This liability is an estimated measurement of the company's long-term financial commitment. Welfare plans, such as medical and life insurance programs, on the other hand, are often established on a one-year term cost basis. A present value of future costs can also be developed in this case assuming an ongoing basis since, for all practical purposes, the welfare plan probably will be renewed from year to year. Although the annual cost of a welfare plan benefit might be, for example, $500,000, on an equivalent liability basis the actuarial present value of future costs could be many millions of dollars. Adoption of the welfare plan could involve a more serious financial obligation than initially apparent when the program is evaluated on the basis of annual cost alone.

The present value approach affords a reasonable measurement of the company's financial commitment. Its use can point out the need for greater care in the evaluation and design of benefit plan programs. Although construction of the paint factory involves a large financial commitment, the pension or welfare plan change could involve a commitment as large or larger. Also, with the benefit program there may be less flexibility for adjusting the commitment in the future, particularly where unions or Works Councils are involved. This contrasts with the options available for modifications in manufacturing capacity, equipment or processes.

U.S. TAX DEDUCTION—FOREIGN PENSION PLANS

Legislation enacted in the United States on December 28, 1980, (P.L. 96-603) makes available to U.S. multinational corporations certain U.S. tax advantages for pension plans of foreign branches and subsidiaries, provided the foreign plans meet the requirements of foreign law and applicable U.S. laws. Whereas in the U.S., a pension plan must be qualified under ERISA to obtain tax benefits, P.L. 96-603 imposes less stringent requirements on foreign plans. Tax deductions may now be sought for contributions made to qualified branch book reserved plans and branch funded plans, and foreign tax credits utilized for subsidiary reserve plans. The treatment for each class of plan differs under the legislation. Tax benefits were previously possible only for contributions made to subsidiary funded plans and branch funded plans qualified under ERISA.

Qualified reserve plans are plans for which a balance sheet liability is established. Additions to the reserve may be deductible under P.L. 96-603 under the following provisions:

- Plan accruals must be for the benefit of the employees with little risk of forfeiture.
- Accruals or additions to the book reserve must be tax deductible under the foreign law.

- Accruals must be computed by the unit credit method or other method prescribed by the U.S. IRS with no salary increase assumption.
- Adjustments to the reserve due to experience gains or losses, plan improvements, changes in actuarial assumptions, etc., must be amortized over a 10-year period.
- A special interest rate must be used based on the average long-term corporate bond rate over the past 15 years in the foreign country.

Qualified funded plans must meet the following requirements:

- The plan must be maintained for the exclusive benefit of the employees and beneficiaries.
- The annual contribution to the fund must be tax deductible under the foreign law and must meet limitations provided under U.S. law.
- Contributions must be made to a trust fund or its equivalent.
- The valuation of the fund assets is subject to limitations prescribed under U.S. law.

In both cases, 90 percent or more of the amounts paid into or accrued under the plan must be attributable to the services performed by nonresident aliens whose compensation is not subject to U.S. income tax. P.L. 96-603 will result in U.S. tax savings for U.S. companies doing business overseas, particularly for branch and subsidiary plans which are book reserved and meet the requirements of the law. Of course, in the case of foreign subsidiaries the extent of any U.S. tax savings depends on whether the subsidiary is in a dividend-paying position; if there are no dividends, there would not be any current savings possible under P.L. 96-603.

OTHER LEGISLATION AFFECTING PLAN DESIGN (WAGE/PRICE LEGISLATION, ANTIDISCRIMINATION LAWS, FOREIGN INSOLVENCY INSURANCE, ETC.)

From time to time, various foreign countries may adopt legislation freezing wages and prices including the level of benefits. Canada adopted a wage/price freeze between 1972 and 1979. Norway did this in 1979 and Belgium in 1981. When a foreign country imposes a freeze on wages, the freeze also may apply to benefit plan changes, although the practice has been to exempt pensioners.

Some foreign countries have ERISA-type legislation, antidiscrimination legislation, and organizations comparable to the Pension Benefit Guaranty Corporation (PBGC) in the United States. The Pension Benefits Act in Canada establishes standards for vesting of pensions, plan solvency, investments, and disclosure. There is similar legislation in other countries; e.g., Norway and West Germany. West Germany requires a company guarantee on benefits similar in some respects to the PBGC. These rules and regulations have an influence on foreign benefit plan design. Also, antidiscrimination legislation has been enacted in some foreign countries; e.g., Australia and New Zealand.

PENSION SUPPLEMENTATION

The high level of inflation in many countries has brought about an appreciable erosion in the purchasing power of the annuitant's pension. The speed at which this erosion occurs depends upon the rate of inflation. For example, a pension worth LC100 at retirement would be worth only LC50 in approximately 10 years assuming a 7 percent inflation rate. At a 10 percent inflation rate, the pension would be worth LC50 in about seven years. At a 13 or 14 percent inflation rate, the value of the pension would be halved in approximately five years. As a result, there has been increased pressure from retirees for pension supplements to offset the effects of price inflation on their annuities.

Most companies have followed an ad hoc approach to pension supplementation where this is permitted under local law. Practices vary from providing pension supplements to taking into account the full amount of the advance in consumer prices to a portion or percentage of the full amount. A regular program of fully protecting a pensioner against the erosion in purchasing power, tantamount to automatic indexing, would be expensive to the plan. If directly indexed to the movement in the consumer price index (CPI), the cost could be prohibitive at even average rates of inflation, with almost no control over the liability.

Since the spending patterns of the retired population differ from those of active employees, the usual price index or CPI may not be representative of the effect of inflation on pensioners. Also, a significant part of the pensioner's income—governmental social insurance payments—often are indexed. In some countries, a separate CPI may be developed for the retired group. The trend in average wages also can be used as a measurement since it establishes the rate at which wages of active employees have increased; this rate of increase in the wage index, if lower than the rate of change in the CPI, can indicate a possible upper limit on pensioner adjustments.

Some countries require automatic indexing of pensions. In Brazil, pensions are subject to annual increases based on an index acceptable to the government. In West Germany, there is legislation requiring that private pensions be reviewed every three years and an additional allowance paid to pensioners to restore the purchasing power eroded by inflation. This is tantamount to indexing, although West Germany has not experienced inflation rates as high as those which have been prevalent in many other parts of the world.

COUNTRY BENEFIT PROFILES

The following are brief profiles of the different benefit environments existing in some large countries where multinational companies have major operations: Canada, Mexico, Nigeria, Japan, and the United Kingdom. Canada is included because of its proximity to and similarity with the United States, Mexico as an area of the world where private benefit programs are developing, Nigeria as representative of a large African country, Japan representing the Far East, and the United Kingdom as a country with a long history of governmental and private benefit programs.

Canada

Governmental pensions are paid to annuitants primarily under two programs. The first program, the Old Age Security Act, provides to every Canadian who meets the residency test at age 65 a flat-rate pension which is indexed quarterly to protect the purchasing power of the original pension.

The second program, the Canada Pension Plan (CPP), provides an additional earnings-related benefit. (There is a separate earnings-related benefit provided under the Quebec plan in lieu of the CPP. Under Canada's constitution, the provinces have primary jurisdiction over pensions and health insurance, and Quebec chose to set up its own plan with benefits similar to the CPP.) The CPP benefit amounts to 25 percent of earnings up to a ceiling which changes each year. The benefits under this program, including survivor and disability benefits, are indexed annually which greatly enhances their value in an economy where inflation has averaged about 9 percent in the past five years. Unlike the flat rate pension, which is financed from general revenues, both employers and employees contribute to the compulsory earnings-related pension program. The benefits under both programs are taxable. An additional program, the Federal Guaranteed Income Supplement, provides additional income on a needs basis. These pensions are payable from age 65 and are also indexed with the CPI.

Medical benefits are provided in Canada for all residents regardless of age through hospital and medical programs administered by the 10 provinces. Three provinces currently require contributions from plan participants while the remainder do not. The health plans are subsidized by the federal government. Dental coverage is included in provincial plans only to a limited extent or not at all, so companies provide dental benefits through privately insured programs. Also, programs for vision care and drugs often are privately insured.

Private pension plans in Canada, which may be integrated with governmental programs, must meet the requirements of the Federal Canadian Income Tax laws as well as provincial rules and regulations to obtain tax advantages. Employee contributions to private pension plans are deductible, and therefore employee contributions are common.

Survivor benefits often are not provided within pension programs in Canada, so this need is met through life insurance contracts. Also, long-term disability benefits commonly are provided through insured plans.

The Registered Retirement Savings Plan (RRSP) permits a tax-sheltered employee contribution currently of C$3,500 per year if the employee is a member of a pension plan and C$5,500 if the employee is not a member of a pension plan. In the end result, the RRSP is not unlike the individual retirement accounts (IRAs) utilized in the United States.

Mexico

The Mexican government has legislated benefits, through enactment of various labor laws, which have lessened the need for private pension programs. The current principal provisions under the law are:

1. Cesantia: This is a basic termination indemnity equal to 3 months' pay plus 20 days' pay for each year of service. The benefit is payable on all terminations except death or termination for cause. The payment is taxable to the employee.
2. Antiguedad: This benefit is equal to 12 days' pay for each year of service. It is payable at retirement, death, disability, or termination (voluntary or involuntary, with or without cause). There is a cap (currently twice the legal minimum wage) on the earnings on which the calculation is made (unlike Cesantia for which there is no earnings limit for calculation purposes). The payment is taxable to the employee.

In both cases, the payments (lump sums) are made by the employer and are deductible for corporate tax purposes. Most employers book reserve the liability under the Antiguedad although the liability can be prefunded to obtain a current tax deduction. No deduction may be taken on a book reserve or trust fund for the Cesantia, however. Some companies have considered adoption of pension plans to approximate the Cesantia benefit, which would permit current tax deductions. The pension payment, which would be offset against the Cesantia payment, would generally not be taxable to the employee.

There are also old age, invalidity (disability), medical, and death benefits provided under the Social Insurance System. This program is financed by employee and employer contributions and governmental subsidies. Normal retirement age is 65 for males and females.

Privately insured group life, disability, and medical programs supplement the governmental benefits.

There is compulsory profit sharing in Mexico of 8 percent of before-tax profits for all employees except senior management.

Legislation enacted in 1978 included favorable tax treatment for employer and employee contributions to savings funds. These savings funds, in which participants vest immediately, permit employees to withdraw the employee and employer contributions and accrued earnings annually, tax free. The maximum that can be contributed to these savings plans is 13 percent of base pay up to 10 times the minimum wage.

Nigeria

Under the Social Security pension fund program in which most employees are covered, a lump sum equal to the employee and employer contributions plus accrued interest is paid to the employee at age 55. It also may be payable after one year of unemployment or in the case of invalidity. The survivor's benefit is equal to the benefit to which the employee would have been entitled. Pension benefits are taxable. The program is administered under the National Provident Fund.

Retirement ages in Nigeria generally are lower than the retirement ages prevailing in most non-African countries. Early retirement under some plans may start at age 45 on a discounted basis; normal retirement age generally is 55 for males and females.

In addition to benefits provided through social insurance, life insurance and disability provisions may be incorporated within private retirement plans or provided separately through insured plans. Because of relatively high rates of inflation, pension programs provided by multinationals, which are commonly funded plans, are often final average pay plans integrated with governmental benefits. Some plans may provide for full or partial commutation. Other plans provide simple gratuities at retirement based on final earnings and service.

Savings plans have been adopted by private companies in Nigeria to take advantage of favorable tax treatment on employee and employer contributions. Some companies adopt Provident funds similar to employee savings plans.

Medical benefits, particularly for subsidiaries of multinational firms, typically are provided through company clinics or on a contractual basis. Free medical care is available to residents through public dispensaries and hospitals.

Japan

The governmental pension system consists of two programs, Employee Pension Insurance and the National Pension Program. The Employee Pension Insurance program is funded by contributions from employees, employers, and the government.

The National Pension program, which covers individuals not covered by any other pension program, is funded by contributions from employees and the government. Monthly old age as well as survivor and disability benefits are provided. Benefits generally are automatically indexed and are taxable. Typical retirement age is 60 for males and 55 for females.

Health coverage is provided through the national health insurance system which may be supplemented through private health insurance societies. Certain items, such as cosmetic surgery, special dental work, and hospital expense over and above ward facilities, normally are excluded from coverage provided under the national health insurance system.

Private company provided retirement plans generally are lump sum retirement/termination plans although annuity plans are becoming more acceptable. These supplement the governmental social insurance. The lump sum or annuity benefits vary with service and salary, and in this case, there often is no provision for direct integration with statutory benefits. Book reserve plans are tax deductible up to about 50 percent of the termination benefit. If the plan is funded either through a trust or insurance company and is qualified under Japanese law, the annual plan contributions may be fully deductible. Death and disability benefits are normally included in private pension plans and paid as lump sums.

Group life insurance also may be arranged through private carriers to supplement social insurance death benefits.

United Kingdom

The British Social Security system, in one form or another, dates back many years. As a result, it has evolved into a sophisticated system incorporating automatic indexing of benefits and options for employers.

The Social Security system consists of two parts: (1) a flat rate amount and (2) an earnings-related amount. Coverage under Social Security generally is universal. Companies have been permitted to "contract out" of Social Security; i.e., to provide, through a privately funded plan, the earnings-related benefit portion. In return, employer and employee contributions to Social Security are reduced. Many multinationals have considered this option in the expectation that the earnings-related benefit can be funded through private plans at lesser cost. The decision to "contract out" is not irrevocable.

The social insurance benefits, which are taxable, include old age, sickness, disability, and survivor benefits. Normal retirement ages for Social Security and most private pension plans are 65 for males and 60 for females.

Private pension plans in the United Kingdom are often final average pay plans which reflect the influence of relatively high inflation rates (ranging up to 18 percent in the past five years). The final average pay calculation may be based on the average of the last five, three, or in some cases one year's pay. Employee contributions to pension plans are deductible for local tax purposes and, as a result, many pension plans are contributory. The benefit may be paid as a life annuity or commuted in part subject to a legislated maximum. In addition to benefits provided under social insurance, death and disability benefits generally are included within private retirement plans. This is also true for widows' and orphans' benefits subject to prescribed limits.

Comprehensive medical and dental coverage is provided through the National Health Service (NHS). Patients pay a portion of the cost for such items as dental treatment, prescriptions, eye glasses, etc. Children, new mothers, and certain low-income persons are exempt from fees. Some companies provide separately insured medical coverage through private plans as a supplement or alternative to NHS. Employer contributions to private plans are considered taxable benefits to the employee.

BENEFIT PROGRAMS FOR THIRD-COUNTRY NATIONALS (TCNs)

The development of employee benefits programs for foreign nationals (TCNs) assigned to posts outside of their home countries presents special problems. Normally, the benefit programs for expatriates are based on the benefits prevailing in the home-country affiliate. However, in some cases, the full home-country benefit package may not be available. For example, the U.K. National Health Service covers employees for medical expenses incurred only in the United Kingdom, although coverage under the home-country retirement plan may be possible. Therefore, the TCN benefit plan program may have to be augmented either by providing medical coverage under host country plans or by providing coverage through other sources. If, because of legal restrictions, the expatriate is not able to continue participation in home-country social security for accruing old age benefits, or if there are tax disadvantages to maintaining pension coverage under the home-country plan, other alternatives may have to be developed. Some multinationals have adopted the international expatriate concept in which the employee is not related to the home country for benefit plan purposes but is covered under a separate "worldwide" package. Either concept—the home-country or international expatriate approach—can be used. However, there may be advantages to the home-country approach from the viewpoint of benefit plan continuity if the expatriate is expected to return to the home country in the future for assignment or retirement.

Relating the TCN benefits to the host country can result in dissimilar benefit treatment as the TCN is reassigned to other posts. Nevertheless, this approach may be desirable in some cases to assure the availability of local tax deductions. The additional application of a "worldwide" or "umbrella" plan for such TCNs can provide a guaranteed minimum level of benefits regardless of the post or posts to which the employee may be assigned.

A number of bilateral agreements have been entered into between countries to avoid dual coverage and the double withholding of social security taxes on expatriates; i.e., payment of host-country as well as home-country social security taxes. The United States has concluded bilateral agreements with Italy, West Germany, and Switzerland, and a number of other agreements are pending. These agreements can result in significant savings to multinational companies with expatriates assigned overseas since contributions on their behalf to foreign social security plans no longer will be required. The duplicate expenditures, in most cases, did not result in any benefit to the expatriate; i.e., the assignment to the foreign country often was not of sufficient duration to qualify for benefits under local law.

The agreements generally deal with old age, survivors, and disability insurance programs of the countries involved in the agreement but not with health insurance or other social programs. In some cases, credits which may be accrued under the social security programs of both countries may be taken into account to determine eligibility for partial benefits under the home-country and/or foreign plans.

SUMMARY

Each foreign country has different cultures, laws, governmental benefit programs, and business climates; inflation rates range from low to very high. Local environments vary. These factors have an impact on the types of benefits developed and should be considered carefully in the design of benefit plan programs for the multinational.

It probably is neither possible nor desirable to adopt a standard employee benefit program for all countries. What may be acceptable or suitable in one area may not be acceptable in another; it may be too expensive or not responsive to the needs of the employees and families for whom the benefit plans are designed.

The programs should be competitive, in order to attract and retain qualified employees, and cost effective. New benefit plan packages, and improvements to current programs, should be evaluated carefully to provide optimum levels of benefits at costs within the company and employee resources.

There should be reasonable stability to employee benefit program design. Frequent changes, particularly in retirement programs, are generally not desirable. Employees are entitled to some stability in terms of expectations at retirement, and of equal importance, the programs obligate the company to future liabilities which require careful study before pension or other benefit plan improvements are made.

A wide range of methods is permitted under foreign law for financing employee benefit programs. Plans may be funded through trustees or insurance companies, book reserved, administered on a pay-as-you-go basis, or split-funded. The choice often depends on the degree of tax deductibility under local laws of annual plan contributions or accruals to the company and, as appropriate, to the employee as well.

Many foreign countries have been at the benefits business for a long time. Germany, under Bismark, was the first to introduce social security plans. The United Kingdom was among the first to introduce a comprehensive national health system; and survivors benefits for widows and orphans have a long history. The indexing of social security benefits overseas, based on changes in the consumer price index, also has a long history.

International benefits is a complex area. There is a wide variety of customs, laws, bilateral agreements between countries, and other regulations which must be taken into account in the design and administration of benefit programs. And it is a growing area because foreign source earnings have represented a very significant proportion of a multinational's consolidated worldwide earnings. As a result, it warrants careful management attention.

CHAPTER 56

Public Employee Pension Plans*

DAN M. McGILL

Pension plans operated for the employees of state and local governments are distinctive and diverse. As a group, they antedate the plans adopted by business firms to provide for the orderly and humane retirement of their employees. The first public employee retirement system was established in 1857, covering the police force of New York City. During the next half century, many other municipal employee retirement systems were brought into existence, including several whose coverage was confined to teachers. In 1911, Massachusetts established the first retirement system at the state level, the system covering the general employees of the state. Since then plans at all levels of government have proliferated until today the vast majority of all state and local government employees participate in a staff retirement system of some kind.

State and local government retirement systems function in an environment that has been well described by Thomas Bleakney in the Prologue to his book, *Retirement Systems for Public Employees.*[1] This environment gives rise to some unique problems and renders less tractable other problems commonly encountered by pension plans generally. Creatures of the political process, public employee retirement systems do not lend themselves well to the traditional constraints and disciplines that shape the structure and reinforce the foundation of pension plans in the private sector. They present challenges in plan design, funding, and financial disclosure.

The boundaries of the public retirement system universe have not been firmly established. Until recently, the universe was generally thought to be made up of about 2,300 plans or systems, ranging from gigantic to minuscule. A recent comprehensive survey by the Pension Task Force of the

---

* This material first appeared in Howard E. Winklevoss and Dan. M. McGill, *Public Pension Plans* (Homewood, Ill.: Dow Jones-Irwin, 1979). It is reproduced herein with written permission of the publisher.

[1] Thomas P. Bleakney, *Retirement Systems for Public Employees* (Homewood, Ill.: Richard D. Irwin, 1972), pp. 1–9.

House Subcommittee on Labor Standards, carried out pursuant to a mandate of the Employee Retirement Income Security Act (ERISA), has revealed that estimate to be grossly erroneous. The Pension Task Force has identified nearly 7,000 pension plans of state and local government subdivisions and estimates that there may be 10 to 15 percent more unaccounted for, presumably small in size. Over 1,400 plans have been located in the Commonwealth of Pennsylvania alone. About 75 percent of the total universe of plans are found in 10 states, including in descending order Pennsylvania, Minnesota, Illinois, Oklahoma, and Colorado. The systems range in size from the New York State Employees' Retirement System, with more than 400,000 participants, to arrangements at the township or borough level covering fewer than five employees. Nearly 75 percent of the plans have fewer than 100 active members. At the other extreme, there are 131 known plans with 10,000 or more active members, and these plans are believed to account for approximately 85 percent of the total active membership of all state and local government pension plans.[2]

State and local government retirement systems cover about 10.3 million full-time and part-time employees, roughly a fourth of the coverage of plans in the private sector. Another 2.4 million persons are receiving retirement, disability, or survivors benefits under such plans or have deferred vested benefits. Annual benefit disbursements are running between $6 and $7 billion. The plans hold assets of about $100 billion, as compared to roughly $250 billion held by private sector plans. Employer and employee contributions to the plans amount to more than $11 billion per year, a margin of at least $4 billion over annual benefit disbursements. In addition, the invested assets of the systems produce about $4 billion annually in investment income.

A profile of the retirement systems operated by states, municipalities, counties, townships, boroughs, school districts, and other public authorities is presented in this chapter. The systems or plans are examined from the standpoint of several pertinent characteristics: (1) classes of employees covered, (2) level of plan administration, (3) legal form, (4) exposure to collective bargaining, (5) legal commitment of the plan sponsor, (6) Social Security coverage, and (7) source of contributions.

CLASSES OF EMPLOYEES COVERED

Some plans cover all types of employees of the jurisdictions involved, sometimes with different benefit formulas and other pertinent plan provisions. In the great majority of jurisdictions, however, there are separate plans for different categories of employees, reflecting varying conditions of

---

[2] All of the statistical information in the foregoing paragraph and the remainder of this chapter is taken from the findings of the Pension Task Force, released in 1977 and reflecting 1976 conditions.

employment, jockeying for preferential pension treatment, political clout, and other indigenous influences.

Public school teachers frequently have their own pension plan, especially when the plan operates at the state level and covers all teachers in the state. There is a variety of arrangements for the faculty and staff of institutions of higher learning. They may have their own plan, they may participate in the plan for elementary and secondary school teachers, or they may be members of a general retirement system for all employees. The faculty and staff of many state colleges and universities participate in the individual annuity contract agreement made available by Teachers Insurance and Annuity Association (TIAA) and its sister institution, College Retirement Equities Fund (CREF), both chartered under special laws of the New York State Legislature.

In almost every jurisdiction, police and firefighters have their own plans, usually one for police officers and another for firefighters. In a few instances, these two classes of employees are combined for pension purposes and placed in their own distinctive plan. These plans are characterized by relatively generous age and service requirements for retirement, as well as other attractive features. They typically permit retirement with one half of final average salary at age 50 or 55 after 20 or 30 years of service. Some provide half pay after 20 or 25 years of service, irrespective of attained age. Such favorable retirement terms have been justified as necessary to maintain an energetic force to carry out the hazardous and physically demanding duties of these two occupations.

Other groups that often have their own pension plans are judges and legislators. Even when they do not have their own plan, they are almost certain to receive preferential treatment under the general plan in which they participate. It is common for judges to receive a pension of two thirds to three fourths of their salary at retirement with only 10 to 15 years of service. Retirement with such a benefit may be permitted as early as age 60 or at any age after 20 to 30 years of service. Under some plans for the judiciary, benefits for retired individuals are linked to the compensation of active members, being expressed as a percentage of the salary currently associated with the position occupied by the pensioner before his retirement. This practice, called recomputation, has been used in the federal military retirement system (but not since 1958) and in many plans for police and firefighters, and not only protects the purchasing power of the pension benefits but gives retired persons a share in the productivity gains of the economy (as reflected in the salaries of their successors). With Social Security, most judges receive greater aftertax income in retirement than they enjoyed while on the bench. They generally contribute to their retirement systems at a higher rate than other employees It has been considered sound public policy to place members of the judiciary in a position where they have no concern over their future economic security, freeing their minds for their judicial duties and minimizing their susceptibility to bribery and other forms of improper financial rewards.

Legislators are less likely than judges to have their own pension plan, but they are almost certain to receive preferential treatment. This preferential treatment may take the form of higher annual benefit accruals, a lower retirement age, shorter required period of service, earlier vesting, or all of these. In one state, legislators, who are also covered by Social Security, accrue a pension benefit equal to 7.5 percent of their final average salary for each year of service and may retire at age 50 with full, unreduced benefits. At the expense of an actuarial reduction, they may begin receiving their pension at any age after only six years of legislative service. Legislators who have voted more generous benefits to themselves than to rank-and-file employees have generally defended their action on the grounds that they are underpaid and are entitled to higher pensions to redress the inequity. It is less obtrusive to increase their pensions than to increase their pay. It is generally agreed that earlier vesting is justified for legislators (and members of city councils) because of their uncertain and frequently short tenure.

Perhaps the most common type of public employee retirement system is that for the general employees of the governmental unit—all employees other than teachers, police, firefighters, and other special groups who have their own plan. This plan is frequently known by the acronym PERS (Public Employment Retirement System). It tends to be the largest retirement system for a given governmental subdivision, especially if it includes the public school teachers, as it may. In many jurisdictions the teacher retirement system and the retirement system for general employees are about the same size.

LEVEL OF PLAN ADMINISTRATION

As might be expected, the great majority (80 percent according to the findings of the Pension Task Force) of public employee retirement systems are administered at the city, county, or township level. This is due in large part to the fact that plans for police or firefighters account for two thirds of the entire universe of public plans, and these tend to be local in character and sponsorship.

All states operate retirement systems for their own employees, and some operate them for employees of their political subdivisions. Most states operate at least two plans, one for public school teachers and another for all other state employees. There may be separate plans for the judiciary, state police, guards at correctional institutions, and other special groups. Some states permit the employees of their political subdivisions to participate in the appropriate state plans. In some cases, participation by local government employees is voluntary (in the sense that the local government entities elect to have their employees participate in a state-wide plan rather than operating their own plans), whereas in other cases participation is mandatory. Some states operate state-wide plans for employees of their political subdivisions in which local government employees are not commingled with state employees. Participation by the local units may be either voluntary or mandatory. It is worthy of noting that in 21 states teachers, who are typically local employees, participate in a state-wide retirement system covering state employees as well as teachers. In other states, public school teachers participate in a state-wide plan for teachers only. Except for large cities, public school teachers tend to participate in state-wide plans of some sort. In Hawaii, all state employees and all employees of the state's political subdivisions participate in a single retirement system operated by the state. This is the only state in which all public employees are covered by a consolidated system. Massachusetts has a single pension law for all new employees (since 1945) that provides a uniform set of benefits and retirement conditions for all state and local government employees, with the exception of security personnel and others in hazardous occupations, but the law is administered through 101 separate systems.

There is a trend toward merging the plans of numerous and frequently small political subdivisions into state-wide plans, either on a voluntary or mandatory basis. There are many advantages to consolidation: (1) administrative economies; (2) the potential for better investment performance through greater diversification, improved cash flow, and employment of more sophisticated investment managers; (3) pooling of mortality risk; (4) elimination of competition among systems for plan improvements; (5) protection of benefit accruals of employees who move from one locality to another; (6) sounder benefit design because of the legislature's freedom to concentrate its attention on fewer systems; and (7) improved services to plan members and their beneficiaries because of a large and more professional staff.[3]

There are some potential disadvantages in consolidation. There is clearly some loss of flexibility: a uniform plan may not accommodate local circumstances and needs. There is also the possibility that, in an effort to make the consolidated plan attractive to all groups, the plan designers will make the benefits and other substantive features too generous. There may be a tendency to build in the most appealing features of all the plans to be merged into the state-wide plan. Unless safeguards are applied, the consolidated system may attract only those groups whose benefit expectations have a greater actuarial value than their anticipated contributions. This threat can be dealt with through making participation mandatory or by adapting contributions to the population characteristics of the participating units. A final disadvantage is diminished ability to experiment and to seek answers from a diversity of approaches to problems.

Bleakney concludes that the biggest obstacle to consolidation is political, the reluctance of local authorities to relinquish any of their influence and

---

[3] Bleakney, *Retirement Systems*, p. 20.

the resistance of the administrative staffs of existing systems. "Combining two or more systems into one results in fewer titles, fewer boards and fewer persons bearing the trappings of office, minimal as they may be."[4] There may also be opposition from the local employee groups unless the consolidated plan holds out the promise of more generous benefits and other features.

LEGAL FORM

One of the distinctive features of state and local government retirement systems is that their terms and provisions are promulgated in the form of a legislative enactment of some type. The terms of a retirement system for state employees are invariably contained in a law enacted by the state legislature and, of course, approved by the governor. States that provide a state-administered system for the employees of local government units, on an optional or mandatory basis, also embody the terms of such a plan in a conventionally enacted law. The plan, as contained in the law, may permit some discretion by the local jurisdictions as to benefit levels, normal retirement age, employee contribution rate, and other critical features. The legislated plan would be duly adopted by the city council, county commission, or other legislative body of the local unit, with whatever variations might be desired and permitted. In a sense, this arrangement permits separate "plans" within a central or consolidated "system."

States that do not operate a central system or systems for local government employees still have something to say about the types of pension plans that may be adopted by their subdivisions, except for municipalities that have been granted home rule. A state with this policy enacts a law that outlines the essential features of a pension plan that can legally be adopted by municipalities and other local subdivisions, the provisions being keyed to the size of the unit. Again, the law may permit variations within prescribed limits. In these states, the pension plan actually adopted by the local unit may be contained in an ordinance or other legislative document. Retirement systems instituted by municipalities with home-rule charters will be evidenced by duly adopted ordinances.

Several of the largest cities established municipal pension plans before the state in which they are located established retirement systems for its own employees or enacted broad pension guidelines for its political subdivisions. Some of these pioneer systems continue to function under the exclusive authority of the sponsoring municipality, especially when the latter has a home-rule charter. In many jurisdictions these plans have been brought under the control of the state legislature in one way or the other. Several of the New York City pension plans predate the statewide plans established by the legislature. Despite this and the fact that New York City

---

[4] Ibid., p. 23.

has home rule in a broad sense, the state legislature reserves to itself the right to make changes in the New York City retirement systems, with two limited exceptions. However, the state constitution requires the city to consent to changes in three of its major pension plans, unless the legislature acts by general law applicable to a broad class of municipalities.

In 15 states—Alaska, Illinois, Kentucky, Louisiana, Massachusetts, Minnesota, New York, Ohio, Rhode Island, South Carolina, South Dakota, Tennessee, Washington, West Virginia, and Wisconsin—there are permanent pension commissions that evaluate all proposals for amending retirement systems subject to the state legislature and make recommendations to the legislature. These commissions have had varying success, those in Illinois and New York probably having been most effective. From time to time there have been ad hoc study commissions whose findings and recommendations had a profound effect on the structure of pension plans in those jurisdictions. Study commissions in Massachusetts and New York, some going back 60 to 70 years, have had notable impact.[5]

EXPOSURE TO COLLECTIVE BARGAINING

The Inland Steel decision of 1949[6] declared pensions to be a bargainable issue, and since that time bargaining over pensions has become standard (indeed, required) practice in those segments of the private economy subject to collective bargaining. Many states have recognized the right of public employees to bargain collectively, and in those states they bargain vigorously over wages and other conditions of employment. Yet it is the exception for public employee unions to bargain over pensions.

The explanation of this anomaly is the statutory foundation of public employee retirement systems. There is an inherent conflict over the right of the legislature to legislate and the right of organized employees to bargain collectively.

A municipality with home rule could presumably negotiate pension demands to a definitive conclusion, assuming that its negotiator has the authority to commit the municipality's legislative body. Moreover, a public authority might have enough autonomy to negotiate its own pension arrangements. In all other cases, however, it would be necessary for the legislature to approve any pension bargain that might be negotiated between a political subdivision and a public employee union. In practical effect, the pension pact would be nothing more than a recommendation to the legislature that it amend the pension law or laws in a particular manner. If the legislature refused to do so, the bargain would be of no effect. The

---

[5] See Robert Tilove, *Public Employee Pensions Funds* (New York: Columbia University Press, 1976), pp. 257–59, for a critique of permanent pension commissions.

[6] *Inland Steel Company* v. *National Labor Relations Board,* 170 F. 2d 247, 251 (1949). Certiorari denied by the Supreme Court, 336 U.S. 960 (1949).

only recourse of the union would be to take its case to the legislature and the governor. In the light of this political reality, most collective bargaining units have apparently concluded that they might as well go to the legislature in the first place, where in the past they have had considerable success.

The conflict between New York City and the New York State legislature in the early 1970s over negotiated pension increases, which for fiscal reasons the legislature refused to approve, led to strikes and ultimately amending of the Taylor Law on public employee collective bargaining to eliminate pensions as an item of bargaining. The Permanent Pension Commission was directed to develop some form of "coalition bargaining" by the various unions involved as a substitute for conventional bargaining and in an effort to avoid conflicting union demands.

Given the statutory foundation of public employee pension plans, the only way that collective bargaining over pensions could be meaningful would be for the state, through its constitution or appropriate legislation, to commit itself to implement any pension agreements reached by the collective bargaining parties. The Commonwealth of Pennsylvania has come close to making such a commitment. Since 1966 its constitution has authorized the General Assembly to enact laws that would make it mandatory for the General Assembly to take such legislative action as might be necessary to implement a collective bargaining agreement between police and firefighters and their public employers. Pursuant to this constitutional authority, the General Assembly enacted a law which states that if the appropriate lawmaking body does not approve a collective bargaining agreement (on any subject) negotiated by police and firefighters or if the bargaining reaches an impasse, the issues are to be submitted to a three-member board of arbitration. The decision of the arbitration boards is final and binding, with no recourse to the courts. Moreover, if the issue involves legislation, the decision constitutes a mandate to the appropriate lawmaking body (of the Commonwealth or a political subdivision) to enact the required legislation. In a separate law, the General Assembly has provided that for public employees generally a binding arbitration decision that would have to be implemented through legislative, as opposed to administrative, action shall be considered advisory only. The disparity in treatment of general employees and uniformed employees is another example of the political influence wielded by the latter group.

Collective bargaining over pensions could be made effective, of course, by removing the statutory foundation of public employee retirement systems. This would leave the parties free to arrive at their own pension arrangements, just as they do for wages and salaries and other conditions of employment. This would open up the possibility of plan changes with each new labor contract and more "leapfrogging" (seeking benefits superior to other groups) of pension benefits than has occurred heretofore. The various state legislatures have thus far shown no disposition to relinquish their control over the retirement systems of their political subdivisions. In view of the fiscal plight of many municipalities and the growing realization, hastened by the New York City experience, of the threat to municipal solvency posed by unwise pension expansion, it is doubtful that state legislators in the near future will be willing to grant autonomy to local government units over their retirement systems.

There is a broader question of whether pension benefits in the public sector should be subject to collective bargaining, even subject to state legislature surveillance. A pension plan is a highly technical arrangement, the terms of which with their actuarial overtones do not lend themselves well to the pressure and compromises of collective bargaining. More important, pension promises are deferred obligations that need not be funded immediately. In a budget crisis (or at any other time) it is all too easy for the incumbent public officials to relieve the pressure for higher salaries by granting pension increases that will become a charge against future budgets, the responsibility of subsequent administrations. To harried public officials it looks like a painless way to win points with public employees and their families. Unfortunately, the costs have to be met eventually, but a different generation of taxpayers will have to pay them.

It should be recognized, of course, that the same pressures and forces are at work whether or not the public employees engage in formal collective bargaining. Employees will always be seeking plan liberalizations, and public officials, who themselves may be participants in the same plan, will always be tempted to substitute deferred obligations for current ones. Public employees are adept at lobbying for their objectives at all levels of authority and can be expected to continue to pursue what they consider to be legitimate goals.

LEGAL COMMITMENT OF THE PLAN SPONSOR

There are two aspects to this question. The first is whether the sponsoring governmental unit undertakes to provide a stipulated set of benefits, as articulated in a benefit formula, to employees who meet certain age and service requirements, or whether it merely undertakes to contribute to the retirement system on behalf of each participating employee on a scale specified in the governing law or document. Plans set up under the first concept are known as *defined benefit* plans. Plans operated under the second concept are referred to as *defined contribution* plans. While many of the early plans were established on the defined contribution basis, with the sponsoring agency and the participating employees contributing at the same rate (a specified percentage of the employee's salary), the overwhelming majority of plans today observe the defined benefit principle. The Pension Task Force found only a few hundred defined contribution plans, many of them maintained by institutions of higher learning and being funded through TIAA–CREF.

The second type of commitment is concerned with the right of the sponsoring agency to change the terms of the pension bargain. It is well settled for private sector plans that, except for termination of employment before the vesting requirements have been satisfied, pension benefit rights *already accrued* cannot be rescinded, altered, or diminished without the consent of the individuals involved. This is in accordance with the concept that an accrued pension right is legally enforceable under the principles of contract law, in contrast to the older view that pensions, especially those granted by a public body, were gratuities and not enforceable at law. Unfortunately, the contract theory of benefit entitlement is not as firmly anchored in the public sector as in the private sector. In fact, the case law of the majority of states and the federal government continues to apply the gratuity theory to public sector pension plans. This theory holds that the benefits of a public pension plan are gifts of the governmental sponsor, which entity is free to confer, modify, or deny as long as it avoids arbitrary action.[7] For the participants this is an unfortunate state of affairs which should be remedied as promptly as possible by legislation if necessary. For the purpose at hand, however, the primary legal question is whether the term of a pension plan can be changed in such a manner as to adversely affect the accrual of pension benefits *in the future* by persons already in the plan.

By statute, judicial decision, or constitutional provision, a number of states have declared that pension rights under a public employee retirement system are contractual obligations of the system that cannot be diminished or impaired in respect of present members *now or in the future*. New York, Florida, and Illinois have constitutional provisions to that effect. For example, Article 5, Section 7 of the New York State Constitution provides that "membership in any pension or retirement system of the state or of a civil division thereof shall be a contractual relationship, the benefits of which shall not be diminished or impaired." This provision was adopted by the Constitutional Convention of 1938 out of concern fostered by the recent Great Depression that benefits might be cut as an economy measure. It has been construed to mean that for each individual participant the benefits in a system's law at the time that he or she first becomes a member may not in any way be diminished, not only in regard to benefit accruals based on past years of service but also with respect to future years of service. In practice the guarantee of nondiminution has the same effect as if the permanent provisions of the retirement plans were embodied in the Constitution itself.

Massachusetts has stated in its retirement statute that the rights created thereunder are contractual obligations, not subject to reduction. The courts in several states have held that pension expectations are implicit contractual obligations, the terms of which cannot be changed with respect to present members. The Supreme Court of California has ruled that the terms of a retirement plan cannot be changed with respect to present members unless the change is necessary to preserve the integrity of the system or is accom-

---

[7] For a comprehensive analysis of participants' rights under public employee retirement systems, see Robert W. Kalman and Michael T. Leibig, *The Public Pension Crisis: Myth, Reality, Reform* (Washington, D.C.: American Federation of State, County, and Municipal Employees, 1979), chap. 5.

panied by comparable new advantages to the members. Pennsylvania permits an adverse change only when it bears "some reasonable relation to enhancing the actuarial soundness of the retirement system." On the other hand, a 1969 survey found that in 35 states benefit accruals based on prospective service could be legally reduced, even for present members.[8] Even without constitutional, statutory, or judicial constraints, however, state legislatures and local councils have been extremely reluctant to reduce benefits promised to persons already in the system.[9]

SOCIAL SECURITY COVERAGE

In the beginning, employees of state and local governments were excluded from Social Security coverage because of concern that the taxation of state and local government entities by the federal government might be unconstitutional. In 1950 the Social Security Act was amended to permit states to elect Social Security coverage for such of their employees as were not already under a retirement system, and, at the option of the employing unit, the employees of all their subdivisions, thus waiving their immunity from federal taxation in their capacity as employer. In 1954 the act was further amended to permit election of coverage for employees already participating in a staff retirement system, but such an election was to be effective only if a majority of the members voted in favor of the coverage. Coverage was to be automatic for all public employees not holding membership in a retirement system on the effective date of the election and for those entering an existing retirement system thereafter. Except in specified states, members of a police retirement system do not have the privilege of electing Social Security coverage. This restriction was sought by police and the persons who administer their retirement systems.

As of October 1972, according to the Census of Governments, 70 percent of all full-time employees of state and local governments were covered by Social Security, and 70 percent of this group were also participating in an employer-sponsored staff retirement system. This is a highly significant statistic. The availability of Social Security benefits should, but frequently does not, have a material effect on the design of a staff retirement system, as will be seen in subsequent sections of this treatise. About 93 percent of all public school teachers are covered by Social Security.

The section of the Social Security Act that permits states and their political subdivisions to elect coverage under the act also permits them to revoke their election and terminate coverage of their employees. After five years of participation in the Social Security system, a state or local government unit may terminate its affiliation by giving a notice to the Social

---

[8] Report of the Governor's Committee to Study the State Employees' Retirement System, New York State, Albany, 1969.

[9] For a more detailed discussion of contractual guarantees, see Tilove, *Public Employee Pension Funds,* pp. 253–56 and 304–7.

Security Administration of its intention two years in advance of the effective date.[10] No referendum of the affected employees is required.

In recent years, a number of governmental units, mostly small and concentrated in the states of California, Texas, and Louisiana, have withdrawn from the Social Security system in a desire to avoid Social Security employer payroll taxes and in the belief that Social Security benefits can be duplicated at less cost through a staff retirement system.[11] Employees of these disaffiliating agencies continue to be entitled to some protection and some benefits under the Social Security system if they are either "currently" or "fully" insured, as these terms are defined in the act. Both New York City and the state of Alaska filed notices of withdrawal with the Social Security Administration about two years ago but revoked their notices before the proposed date of withdrawal. Congress has recently considered revoking the right of governmental units to withdraw from Social Security and extending coverage to all state and local government employees on a mandatory basis. There is a possibility that coverage of these groups will be mandatory in the future, not only to make the benefits of the system available but to force this segment of the population to bear its share of the tax burden of the system.

SOURCE OF CONTRIBUTION

State and local retirement systems have traditionally been supported by contributions from both the employing agencies and the participating employees. Employee contributions have been required to provide a steady source of income to the plan, independent of the whims of the legislature or other financing agency and the state of the public coffers, and to dampen employee demands for plan liberalizations.

The Pension Task Force found that about 75 percent of the plans that it surveyed require employee contributions. A substantial number of other plans permit voluntary contributions by employees. In the aggregate and for all the state and local government plans surveyed, employee contributions accounted for about one third of total contributions. Contributions of the employing agencies generally come out of general revenues. In some jurisdictions they are drawn from special earmarked taxes or levies.[12] Some small plans are financed on a pay-as-you-go basis through public subscriptions from an annual appeal.

---

[10] A local government unit can terminate its affiliation only with the approval of its own state authorities.

[11] On this latter point, the interested reader should consult Actuarial Note No. 95, published by the Social Security Administration in April 1978. This study shows that, except for unusual circumstances, the present value of Social Security benefits to be "gained" in the future exceed the present value of the combined employer and employee payroll taxes to be paid in the future. The results of this comparison are highly sensitive to the underlying assumptions, especially the interest assumption.

[12] For example, in one state the plan for firefighters is financed out of taxes levied on fire insurance premiums paid to out-of-state companies.

CHAPTER 57

The Future of Employee Benefit Plans

DALLAS L. SALISBURY

Predicting the future is a game of chance in which the normal laws of probability do not hold. The passage of time allows numerous unexpected events to intervene, and this has been the rule rather than the exception with employee benefits.

This chapter will first look at the accuracy of predictions made in 1970. It will then review experience and prospects for Social Security, the employees decision to retire, demographics, economic change, and government regulation. Employee benefit trends for the 1980s are then explored and implications discussed.

The field of employee benefits will be increasingly dynamic and challenging during the 80s. The greatest rewards will go to those who carefully anticipate and plan. This chapter attempts to lay a base for that purpose.

PRE-ERISA PREDICTIONS ABOUT EMPLOYEE BENEFIT PLANS (1970)

In 1970 experts made predictions concerning the future of employee benefits. The predictions were based upon specific beliefs regarding (a) the economy of the 1970s and (b) expected population change.

The economy of the 70s was expected to be strong. Median incomes were expected to rise substantially: they did. Inflation was expected to drop from the abnormally high rate of 4 percent: it didn't. The makeup of the work force (male-female) was expected to remain fairly constant: it didn't. The population over age 65 was expected to approach 23 million: it did. The average workweek was expected to move to 35 hours per week or less: it didn't.

Based upon these economic and population predictions the seers specified future benefit trends. They predicted that:

- The 70s would see dramatic increases in income replacement, reaching an average of 75 percent of final earnings (for many it did, and it's moving this way).

- The 70s would see a movement towards encouraging early retirement with the average moving to age 55 (it moved down to the 61–62 range).
- The 70s would see plans move toward shorter vesting periods and earlier participation (it happened).
- The 70s would see dramatic growth of, and pressure for, survivor benefits (it happened).
- The 70s would see liberalization of eligibility rules for disability benefits (it happened).
- The 70s would mark the beginning of active and competitive port-folio management (it happened).

The seers of 1970 were surprisingly accurate given that neither the economy nor the population cooperated in fulfilling the base assumptions.

Many things are known in 1980 about the decade of the 70s. Inflation reached its highest historical point for the United States. Median income rose dramatically but not as fast as prices. The over-65 population reached 23 million, and the proportion of women in the work force grew dramatically.

These economic and population trends of the 70s are still with us. They will help to shape what occurs in the 80s as they did in the 70s. They are relevant to a number of factors which will determine the future of benefit programs.

SOCIAL SECURITY

In 1980, on the 45th anniversary of Social Security, William Driver, then commissioner of the Social Security Administration, made bold predictions about its future. "Social security will not go bankrupt," he said. "Its benefits will continue to be the basic source of retirement income upon which people rely."

Against these predictions one must balance estimates of cash flow problems in 1982–83 and dramatic payroll tax increases necessary to meet current benefit promises over the next 40 years.

Predicting the future of Social Security or the stability of the entire employee benefit system has never been an easy task, but Social Security is in severe financial trouble.

For the plan sponsor, the participant, and the taxpayer, the stability of Social Security has far-reaching implications. The prospects for stability are affected by numerous factors, but the level of inflation, the size and makeup of the work force, and the selected age for retirement are particularly important.

There is no easy solution to Social Security's financial problems. The importance of Social Security to all elements of benefit programs and current employee compensation cannot be overstated. Should Social Security continue to absorb an ever-growing share of our nation's resources, it *will* limit the expansion of other benefit programs and take-home pay. Incremental change is likely to remain the rule. This will cause the cost of the program to go steadily upward and the resources available for other benefits to shrink.

THE EMPLOYEE'S DECISION TO RETIRE

The retirement decision is crucial for retirement income programs: it determines the amount of money required by the programs. The difference between paying benefits for 20 years versus 10 years is much greater than a doubling. Future trends, therefore, are extremely important.

What motivates a person to leave a job? What are the factors considered by an individual who has worked for 30 or 40 years and has the opportunity to decide whether to continue working or to retire? The worker must examine all sources of income, from Social Security, savings, and pensions. To the extent that the income from these sources promises to be inadequate, the worker is likely to delay retirement. This is happening more and more today.

During the 80s actions are likely to be taken which will encourage later retirement. Such changes for Social Security might include relaxing the earnings test, raising the age of eligibility for initial benefits to 68 or 70, and adjusting the level of indexing. (See Appendix A.)

Private plan changes are also possible. Changes in the tax status of benefit program contributions and benefits could alter the future pattern of benefit receipt. Should high rates of inflation persist, private plans could be required to at least partially index benefits. Government could require private plans to raise normal retirement ages as mandatory retirement is totally eliminated.

But what are the effects of a mandatory retirement age change? Studies indicate that few older workers previously subject to mandatory retirement chose to remain on the job just because the mandatory age had been lifted to 70. The effects on firms if the worker *does* remain past the previous age limit will in large part determine whether the outlawing of mandatory retirement will encourage later retirement. This unknown will have large cost implications for the 80s.

Inflation does seem to have caused persons to delay retirement. The worker may anticipate that wages will rise with prices, especially if the older worker expects several years of inflation. The worker can also anticipate that higher wages will result in higher pension benefits, so that a delay in retirement will pay off.

Other factors affecting retirement trends are health, education, personnel policies, and changes in negotiating employee benefit plans. On the whole, health has improved, and further improvements could increase the proportion of older workers in the labor force. Were the result to increase the length of retirement rather than work, the implications for plan financing would be extremely adverse.

Older workers may desire to reduce their hours of work gradually or shift to less arduous tasks while remaining employed. Whether or not unions continue to press for subsidized early retirement features will have an effect on future retirement patterns.

The consequences of retirement age are great for all benefit programs in terms of the period of coverage, the cost of coverage, and the mix of programs. Benefit professionals should watch developing trends carefully.

DEMOGRAPHIC CHANGE

The makeup of both the retired and working populations affects all public and private benefit programs. The 70s saw the World War II baby boom entering the work force for the first time. The 80s sees this group in its 30s and possibly focusing for the first time on long-term security issues.

While the Social Security program has financing problems today, they are insignificant compared to prospects for the years beyond 2010 when this group will retire. Payroll tax rates could rise to between 25 percent and 64 percent to finance the present program, dependent upon economic performance and population behavior. Should rates go this high numerous other benefit programs could find themselves crowded out.

The 80s will be the period during which the nation begins to seriously focus upon the implications of the baby boom. The implications, however, go well beyond the age mix of the population.

- Due to longer life expectancies the cost of providing health care and retirement income support to current retirees is higher than expected and rising. This will continue to be the case for future retiree groups.
- Changing family relationships are having, and will continue to have, a major effect on the stability and future development of benefit programs. The number of families headed by a woman is increasing, and the woman's labor force participation (single and married) increased by over 25 percent during the 70s. Divorce rates also hit historical highs during the 70s.

These changes will lead to greater flexibility in benefit design during the 80s. The traditional model—working husband, housewife, children—around which benefit programs have been designed in the past, is becoming less relevant.

The productive work force will continue to shrink as a proportion of the total population, increasing the proportion of each worker's income that will be needed to support the young, the old, and the infirm. As the consequences of this change become more clearly understood, decision makers will be forced to make policy changes. While this is likely to begin in the 80s, it is not likely to have its full effect until the 90s.

ECONOMIC CHANGE

The strength of the economy during the 80s will be a principal determinant of the future of employee benefits. A low-growth, high-unemployment, high-inflation economy like that of the 70s would carry with it very negative consequences. A brief look at the past allows one to understand why.

Inflation has been a persistent problem during the 70s, averaging 7.4 percent per year and topping 14 percent in 1979. Social Security and many other public benefit programs are indexed to inflation. The 14.3 percent July 1980 adjustment, attributable to 1979 inflation, increased Social Security costs by over 16 billion dollars per year. The July 1981 increase added approximately 17 billion dollars to annual program costs. The nation would have difficulty affording such a trend through the 80s.

For private pension plans a fixed pension would lose 66 percent of its value over 10 years, and 90 percent over 20 years, at 12 percent inflation: a rate which was exceeded in the 1979–80 period.

For private pension plans to index benefits against this inflation would be prohibitively expensive unless initial benefit levels are reduced. Two trends are likely in the 80s. First, ad hoc increases for retirees will become more common if inflation continues. Second, an increasing number of plans will move towards capped indexing (3 to 4 percent) and finance it through reduced initial benefits.

The only real solution for retirees is the end of inflation. The same is true for active workers. Continued inflation will jeopardize Social Security *and* private pensions. The fact that one system is indexed and the other is not does not represent a statement of success and failure. Over the long term society cannot afford the luxury of full indexing if initial benefit levels are maintained. Should inflation drop in the 80s, downward adjustments of indexing are to be expected. It is likely that Congress will take advantage of the next period of lower inflation to adjust present indexing arrangements.

GOVERNMENT REGULATION

The 70s saw a marked increase in the scope of government regulation of employee benefits—both pension and welfare programs. The movement in this area was part of a broad general expansion of the government's role in numerous areas of the economy. Many of the changes adopted were not preceded by detailed analysis of costs, benefits, or secondary consequences. Experience with the changes indicates that many carried undesired and unexpected results.

Regulatory thrusts which never succeeded were also prominent. Such was the case of national health insurance and comprehensive health care cost containment.

During the 80s it is unlikely that these initiatives will be enacted into law. In addition, it is likely that regulation imposed by ERISA will be adjusted and in some cases removed.

- Reporting and disclosure requirements are likely to be reduced in cases where no apparent gain resulted from the requirement.
- Adjustments to the program of the Pension Benefit Guaranty Corporation are likely to continue as more experience with the program is gathered.
- Emphasis is likely to be given to making all benefit components work better together—including emphasis on integration of retirement benefit programs, disability benefit programs, and health benefit programs.
- Greater equity is likely to be sought for various benefit programs in terms of tax treatment, particularly retirement programs. This is likely to include higher IRA and Keogh limits and deductible employee contributions—all with the aim of maximizing flexibility of program design so that the maximum number of people are accommodated.
- Continued attention is likely to be given to improving the quality and cost effectiveness of health care, with special emphasis on provision for the needy.
- Welfare reform will continue to be discussed, with reforms likely to place increased emphasis on state and local governments. In addition, the Supplemental Security Income program is likely to be expanded as a vehicle for income delivery.

The overall role of government is not likely to *expand* significantly in the 80s. It will, however, continue to be a very active actor. Knowledge of the regulatory environment will become no less necessary, in spite of the Reagan administration's emphasis on fairer regulation. The 80s will provide an excellent opportunity for study, review, and refinement, with the public and private sector increasingly working together as partners rather than adversaries.

EMPLOYEE BENEFIT TRENDS

The period ahead will be one of challenge and change for employee benefits. Their major role in the total compensation package will be recognized, even if the characterization of "fringe benefits" persists. The combined effects of economic, political, and population changes will not and cannot be ignored. The dynamics of change are already in progress, with much of the 80s likely to be reinforcing.

During the late 1970s a number of study groups were appointed to look at the future of components of the employee benefits world including the National Commission on Social Security (NCSS), the President's Commission on Pension Policy (PCPP), the National Commission for an Agenda for the 80s, the Minimum Wage Study Commission (MWSC), and the White House Conference On the Aging.

These groups produced well over 100 recommendations on how to "improve" employee benefit programs. The recommendations most likely to be adopted relate to Social Security and incentives to encourage savings and capital formation: they deal with recognized economic problems, and the various groups were generally in agreement regarding what should be done. In other areas action is not as likely. For example, the keystone recommendation of the PCPP was for creation of a mandatory private pension system. The NCSS recommended strongly *against* such a system. Further, such a requirement would appear to be contrary to the increasing strong spirit of deregulation present in the country.[1]

The private sector also exhibited increasing concern in the late 1970s with creation of organizations such as the Employee Benefit Research Institute (EBRI) in Washington, D.C., and development of programs such as Certified Employee Benefit Specialist (CEBS) training. Both give recognition to the growing importance of employee benefits to national and organizational policy and management.

There are already trends for the 1980s taking form which are likely to reinforce the concern noted above. They include:

- The management of employee benefits will be recognized as an important and vital business function. As such, the function will be given increasing prominence within organizations and increasing responsibility. Employee benefits will become more of a career area, rather than a stop along the management training schedule. This should lead to increasingly responsible management of benefit programs to the advantage of employers and employees.

- Efficiency in the financing of benefit programs will be increasingly emphasized: cost containment will be the watchword. For pensions, granting of past service credits will be less common. For health programs the use of employee deductibles will become more common. Some of these changes may be the result of legislative activity.

---

[1] Much of the research by MWSC is applicable to the mandatory private pension proposal since it would require a payroll expense. Discussion of the PCPP recommendations can be found in "Toward a National Retirement Income Policy: Priorities for the Eighties?" *Labor Law Journal,* May 1981, and *Retirement Income Opportunities in an Aging America: Program Coverage and Benefit Entitlement,* Employee Benefit Research Institute, 1981.

Cutbacks in federal government expenditures will lead to "cost shifting" to other levels of government and employers. Also, the debate over "health competition" legislation will tend to change behavior even if not passed. And, if passed, it will lead to greater consumer choice and the development of classes of medical care. (In addition, emphasis on better health is likely to increase.)

- Efficiency in benefit design will be increasingly emphasized in an effort to eliminate and prevent overlap and to provide participants with the particular benefits they need. Depending on economic developments, this could include benefit cutbacks during the 80s. Flexible compensation and benefits will expand as cost pressures close in and as the makeup of the work force continues to change. A continuing emphasis on employee productivity will speed this trend.

- Continued expansion of dental plans, vision care plans, group legal plans, and other benefits, which realized substantial growth during the 70s, will be experienced. The more broadly flexible compensation is adopted, the greater the speed with which extension of those benefits will occur. Should tax rates not be indexed and should "fringe benefits" continue to be taxed on only a limited basis, employee choice will increasingly lead to benefit additions rather than a compensation increase being taken primarily in salary or wages. This will serve to further reinforce the importance of benefit programs and the benefits management function.

- Relatively new employee benefits, such as group auto and group homeowners, will be offered, and preretirement counseling and financial counseling will expand as employee benefits. This will occur for the same reasons noted above.

- The trend toward providing defined contribution plans with reasonably short vesting periods will continue. Such plans provide a means of better accommodating relatively short service workers, and they help to stave off more drastic policy changes. Should uncertainty over future government requirements be reduced, however, the relative number of defined benefit creations could increase. In addition, as private plans move toward faster vesting in defined benefit plans, a major reason for the relative growth in the number of new defined contribution (DC) plans will be eliminated.

- More large pension plans will adopt vesting schedules which are more rapid than 10 years, as has already occurred among a high proportion of small pension plans. As noted above, this could lead to the creation of more defined benefit plans.

- In a response to changing family relationships there will be a trend toward improved spouses' benefits and the treatment of vested pension rights as property, subject to division in the event of divorce. These changes will become more and more likely as the percentage of women and single parents in the work force continues to grow. Such changes may well eventually apply to public *and* employer-sponsored programs for political as well as social reasons. Such changes will also provide added pressure for the development of flexible compensation and benefit programs.

* Continuation of employee benefits into retirement will be more and more common, as will part-time or contract employment of annuitants. These changes will be a natural addition to a growing emphasis on preretirement counseling and the effects of the Age Discrimination in Employment Act. Employers have increasing incentives to make retirement attractive. Retirees have now been recognized as both a growing market and as a growing political force. Both their relative numbers and life expectancies are increasing, and the market is beginning to respond. Further, flexible compensation and benefit programs make it easier to accommodate the needs of retirees by balancing pre- and postretirement benefits.

Beyond these developments we are likely to see increasing recognition of the advantages of private sector benefit provisions. The most striking advantage of providing benefits through the private sector is flexibility: the ability to adjust quickly to changing employee desires. Flexible benefit programs, whether formally structured or not, are likely to become much more common during the 80s to accommodate changes in the work force. These programs allow the employee to select the particular benefits desired. For two-earner families—now nearly 60 percent of all households—this is particularly attractive. In addition, such an approach could help achieve the goals of efficiency in financing and benefit design.

The public and private sectors will see increasing advantages in cooperation, coordination, and nonduplication. Regulatory and legislative initiatives are likely to be consistent with such recognition.

CONCLUSION

The vast majority of public and private sector workers now enjoy protection for health care. Through government programs such protection is available to nonworkers as well.

Social Security now promises a floor of income protection to most workers while nonworkers have access to Supplemental Security Income, in-kind benefits, unemployment compensation, workers' compensation, disability income, and other programs.

Supplementing these programs are an array of private income security programs. Private pensions, for example, are now participated in by over 64 percent of all steady full-time workers over age 25. A quarter of present retirees now receive private pension income, and the percentage will continue to grow. Public pensions provide coverage and benefits to many more workers. Of present 22-year-old workers, over 70 percent are likely to retire with an employer-provided pension benefit.

Employers are also providing a wide array of additional programs discussed in this book. They help to meet the needs of tens of millions of persons. They help to maintain morale, ensure family security, and maintain employee health.

Taken together, employee benefit programs provide a blanket of protection against numerous risks. For the most part they deliver with reliability, effectiveness, and efficiency. They are an integral part of our social structure, and they will continue to be.

CHAPTER 58

The Effect on Employee Benefit Plans and Executive Compensation of the Tax Equity and Fiscal Responsibility Act of 1982*

On May 19, 1982, Congressman Charles Rangel (D-N.Y.) introduced a bill (H.R. 6410) which, if enacted into law, would have had a devastating effect on private pension plans. Industry reaction to this proposed bill was both swift and strong. Although there is no way of knowing for certain, the Senate probably was influenced by this reaction. Its version of Rangel's proposals was much less severe. The final compromise bill, the Tax Equity and Fiscal Responsibility Act of 1982 (TEFRA), imposes changes upon private benefit plans—primarily pension and capital accumulation—that are tax-qualified under Section 401 of the Internal Revenue Code. As a result, most employers will be faced with:

Greater administrative burdens because taxes must now be withheld from retirement plan payments (unless the employee elects otherwise).

A rollback and temporary freeze on limitations under Section 415 of the Code on contributions and benefits.

Restrictions on amounts employees can borrow from a tax-qualified plan (although the restrictions imposed seem reasonably liberal).

Higher medical plan costs for active employees over age 65 due to the redefinition of Medicare as a secondary provider of benefits.

A new requirement that key employees must include the cost of the first $50,000 of group term life coverage in current income if the plan discriminates in their favor.

Other changes will affect different employers in different ways, if at all. Self-employed individuals, for example, will have an increased contribution (and deduction) capability for, as well as relaxed restrictions relating to, tax-

---

* This chapter is reprinted herein with the permission of Towers, Perrin, Forster & Crosby.

qualified plans. A limited number of employers will find their capability reduced to integrate defined contribution plans with Social Security. (Because most employers integrate defined benefit pension plans rather than defined contribution plans, very few companies will be affected by this change.)

For some employers, however, certain TEFRA provisions could be of major importance. These provisions introduce a new concept—that of a "top-heavy" plan—and impose significant restrictions on plans that fall into this category. In general, a plan will be considered top-heavy if key employees account for more than 60 percent of the accrued benefits (or account balances). When this is so, more rapid vesting is required, a minimum benefit applies, Section 415 limits are more restrictive, and a limit is imposed on compensation that can be considered.

The first section of this chapter reviews the changes that apply to employee-benefit plans generally as well as a change that affects the taxation of incentive stock options. The second section discusses TEFRA's provisions as they relate to top-heavy plans. The final section discusses the benefit plan issues and implications most employers face as a result of this legislation.

EMPLOYEE-BENEFIT PLAN CHANGES

The first part of this section covers changes made by TEFRA in the treatment of plans qualified under Section 401 of the Code—including pension, profit-sharing, and savings plans. The next part discusses changes affecting group term life insurance plans. The third part deals with changes in medical-expense tax deductions and in the role of Medicare for active employees over age 65. The last part describes a change in the tax treatment of incentive stock options.

Section 401 Plans

Congressman Rangel's original bill evoked much industry concern over four key areas: changes in Section 415 limitations, withholding of income taxes from retirement plan distributions, loans to employees, and integration with Social Security benefits. The following discusses what happened to each of these areas in the final bill and then concludes with a discussion of other TEFRA provisions that relate to Section 401 plans.

Section 415 Limitations. ERISA imposed limitations on the maximum benefits payable under a defined benefit pension plan and on the annual additions (primarily employer contributions) that could be made to an employee's account under a defined contribution plan. The defined benefit limitation was the lesser of 100 percent of an employee's three-year average pay or $75,000. The defined contribution limit was the lesser of 25 percent of pay or $25,000. Both dollar amounts were indexed to the CPI and in 1982 were $136,425 and $45,475, respectively. If an employer sponsored both types of plans, the combined limit was 140 percent of the individual limits (the 1.4 rule). It was not necessary to reduce the defined benefit plan limits for early retirements occurring after age 55.

The major change made by TEFRA is in the dollar limits. Beginning in 1983, these were rolled back to $90,000 for defined benefit plans and $30,000 for defined contribution plans. Though these dollar amounts will continue to be indexed in the same manner as Social Security benefits—that is, to the CPI—no such adjustments will be made until 1986 and then for only post-1984 CPI increases.

Other changes affecting the Section 415 limits are:

The defined benefit limits are actuarially reduced for retirements before age 62. However, if the early-retirement benefit begins at or after age 55, a $75,000 benefit limit is retained as a floor; if the benefit begins before age 55, the floor is the actuarial equivalent of $75,000 at age 55.

If the benefit begins after age 65, it is permissible to increase the limits on an actuarially equivalent basis.

The plan interest rate may be used in determining actuarial equivalency. However, 5 percent is the minimum rate for retirements before age 62 and the maximum for retirements after age 65.

The statute now specifies that advance funding (on a deductible basis) is not permitted for future cost-of-living adjustments.

The combined plan limit of 1.4 has been retained for the percentage limitations; however, a new 1.25 limit has been imposed when the dollar limits apply. Mechanically, this is achieved by making the overall limit 1.0, then using the 1.25 or 1.4 in the denominator of the defined benefit plan and defined contribution plan fractions.

The special limit applicable to collectively bargained defined benefit plans has been amended to continue the principle that a pension of one half the Section 415 limits will be available without regard to compensation. A permanent "grandfathered" amount of $68,212 is now available.

For existing plans, these changes generally apply to years beginning after December 31, 1982. (They are effective immediately for plans adopted after July 1, 1982.) Transitional rules are included, and benefits accrued under prior law are protected by a "grandfather" clause. The effect of these changes will vary with the type of plans involved. The formal, funded benefits of some executives, of course, are bound to be reduced, but these losses will be picked up automatically under the employer's excess benefit plan. Companies that have not yet adopted excess benefit plans might feel compelled to do so in view of these new limits.

Income Tax Withholding. The TEFRA provision requiring income tax withholding on distributions from all plans qualified under Section 401 affects all employers and creates significant additional administrative burdens for many. (Distributions from nonqualified deferred compensation plans and IRAs are also subject to withholding.) Both periodic and nonperiodic payments, including death benefit payments, are subject to withholding. These withholding provisions became effective January 1, 1983. There are limited exceptions for compliance, which are discussed later in this chapter.

The recipient of the distribution may elect not to have taxes withheld even though the payments are, in fact, taxable. The payer must notify the payee of his or her right to make such an election. In the case of periodic distributions, this notice must be given during a period that begins no more than six months before the first payment is due and ends when the first payment is made. Payers must also notify payees at least annually of their right to make and revoke withholding elections. In the case of a nonperiodic distribution, the payer must notify the payee of the right to make or revoke a withholding election at the time of distribution. (Regulations may require the notice to be issued earlier than the distribution. Regulations also may provide for an initial election to apply to subsequent distributions to the same taxpayer.)

There are two methods of determining the amount to be withheld from periodic distributions. If a withholding certificate is in effect, the number of exemptions noted on the certificate should be used for this purpose. If no certificate is in effect, the amount to be withheld will be determined by treating the payee as a married individual claiming three exemptions. The amount to be withheld for a nonperiodic distribution depends upon the nature of the distribution. Amounts withheld on lump-sum distributions will be determined by the tax on such distributions. The amount will be established under tables (or other computational procedures) that the IRS will prescribe. In the case of death benefit payments, the amount to be withheld must reflect the $5,000 exclusion from gross income provided by Section 101(b) of the Code (even though it may not be allowable).

In general, the payer of a distribution must withhold and is liable for payment of the required tax. However, if the plan is, or ever was, a tax-qualified pension, profit-sharing, savings, stock bonus, annuity, or TRASOP plan, the plan administrator must withhold and is liable for payment of the required tax. The plan administrator may avoid this requirement by directing the payer to withhold the tax and by providing the payer with information required by IRS regulations.

As noted, these new withholding rules became effective January 1, 1983. Thus, the first payment made after December 31, 1982 will be subject to the new rules. These rules require plan administrators and/or other payers to develop new information and processing systems for annual notice, first payment notice, withholding, and reporting. Because payers will have less than four months to implement the new requirements, the statute and the

Conference Report indicate two ways to postpone immediate compliance without penalty.

First, the Conference Report states that "civil and criminal penalties for failure to withhold tax will not apply to any failure before July 1, 1983, if the payer made a good-faith effort to withhold, and actually withholds from any subsequent 1983 payments sufficient amounts to satisfy the pre-July 1983 requirements." Amounts that are withheld *must* be paid to the Treasury in a timely manner.

Second, the statute provides that the IRS may grant individual extensions of up to six months, pursuant to regulations, if the payer has made good-faith efforts to comply, has a plan to ensure its ability to comply by 1983, and cannot comply on January 1, 1983, without undue hardship. If a payer receives an individual compliance waiver, amounts that were *not* withheld between January 1 and June 30, 1983, will not have to be compensated for by increasing the amounts withheld from the post-June 1983 payments.

The law adds a new provision that requires employers, plan administrators, and so forth, to make reports and returns regarding distributions to the Secretary of the Treasury, and to participants and beneficiaries of the plan (or contract). Penalties for failing to keep necessary records also have been established. A penalty will be imposed upon the payer if the data base necessary for reports is not maintained, regardless of whether reports are due for the period during which the recordkeeping failure occurs. Each year the penalty can be $50 for each individual for whom a failure occurs, up to a maximum of $50,000. Limited exceptions to the imposition of a penalty will be permitted for failures that result from reasonable cause, as long as willful neglect is not present. Penalties for recordkeeping failures will be effective as of January 1, 1985.

Loans to Employees.   At this time, many employers are considering adopting cash or deferred plans under Section 401(k) of the Code. A matter of considerable concern to these employers has been that any amounts contributed under such a plan (including any employee contributions made by way of salary reduction) can be withdrawn during active employment only as a result of severe hardship. The ability of employees to make loans has been viewed as providing some degree of relief in this situation. Thus, there has been more than a casual degree of employer interest in what restrictions might be imposed on the right to make loans that has existed since ERISA.

TEFRA's loan provisions, though imposing some restrictions, seem to provide for a reasonable degree of flexibility in allowing employees access to their vested account balances. Under TEFRA's provisions, a loan to an employee will be treated as a taxable distribution from any plan unless certain requirements are met. The requirements involve the amount of the loan (or accumulated loans) and the time period for repayment. The maximum amounts that can be borrowed without being considered a distribution depend on the amount of the employee's vested interest in his or her account balance (or in the present value of the employee's accrued benefit). If this is:

$10,000 or less, the entire vested interest is available.

Between $10,000 and $20,000, $10,000 is available.

Between $20,000 and $100,000, 50 percent of the vested interest is available.

$100,000 or more, $50,000 is available.

As to the time period for repayment, the loan, by its terms, must be repaid within five years. However, if the loan is a mortgage loan and meets the amount limitation described above, this time limit does not apply. A mortgage loan is one used to acquire, build, rebuild, or substantially rehabilitate a dwelling that is to be used as a principal residence for the employee or the employee's spouse, siblings, and lineal ascendants or descendants. The dwelling must be used as a home within a reasonable time after the loan is made. According to the Conference Report, a dwelling unit includes a house, apartment, condominium, or nontransient mobile home. If a permissible loan other than a mortgage loan is not repaid within five years, the unpaid balance will be considered a distribution at the end of five years. For this purpose:

All loans made directly or indirectly after August 13, 1982, are covered (except certain loans used to repay outstanding obligations before August 14, 1983).

The outstanding balance of any loan that is renegotiated, extended, renewed, or revised after August 13, 1982 will be treated as a new loan; a scheduled change in the interest rate will not be treated as a revision or renegotiation.

An assignment or a pledge is considered the same as a loan.

Any amount received as a loan under a contract purchased under a plan is treated as a loan, subject to these provisions, as are assignments or pledges of any such contract.

Loans from tax-deferred annuities and government plans also are subject to the same restrictions.

Existing requirements involving nondiscrimination and the alienation of plan interests continue to apply.

Regular aggregation rules apply so that all related entities are viewed as one employer and all plans of such an aggregated "employer" are treated as one plan.

It should be noted that plan loans are not prohibited. The penalty is a personal income-tax charged to the employee for the amount the loan exceeds the dollar limits or for the entire loan if it does not meet the repayment rules.

For employers who are considering a Section 401(k) plan, however, at least one question remains. Such a plan cannot make a distribution during active employment except in cases of severe hardship. If such a plan makes a loan to an employee and violates the loan rules, the loan will be taxed as a distribution. The question that remains is whether this will be considered a distribution that causes the plan to fail to meet qualification requirements. It seems reasonable that this result should not occur; however, some employers might want to have further clarification of this issue before including a loan provision in their plans.

Integration with Social Security.   Many employers integrate their private plan benefits with those provided by Social Security. This is accomplished under a very complex set of rules published by the IRS. To recognize the fact that higher levels of pay do not generate Social Security benefits, these rules allow a limited amount of additional benefits for highly paid employees. The allowable amount of additional benefit depends upon such factors as the nature of the employer's plan, the pay base used to determine benefits, and the type of ancillary benefit included. TEFRA has not changed the integration rules for defined benefit plans, but it has changed the rules for defined contribution plans for plan years beginning after December 31, 1983.

Before the enactment of the law, an employer was allowed to contribute a maximum of 7 percent of the employee's pay over the Social Security taxable wage base for the year to a defined contribution plan. Thus, in 1982, an employer could contribute 0 percent on pay up to $32,400 and 7 percent of pay in excess of this amount; or, as is more commonly the case, an employer could contribute at one rate for all pay plus 7 percent of pay over the wage base (for example, 8 percent of pay up to $32,400 plus 15 percent of pay over this amount). Under TEFRA, this integration capability has been reduced. In brief, the maximum allowable contribution that can be made on pay in excess of the Social Security taxable wage base will be equal to the tax rate applicable to employers for old age, survivors, and disability insurance (OASDI) under Social Security. Under current law, this tax rate is:

Year	Tax Rate
1984–1987	5.7
1988–1989	6.06
1990 and thereafter	6.2

Defined contribution plans, of course, will have to be modified if they now use maximum integration capability. Alternatives that might be considered include:

Reducing contributions that apply to compensation in excess of the
Social Security taxable wage base.

Increasing contribution levels for pay under the wage base to reduce the
contribution spread for pay over and under the wage base.

Changing to an integrated defined benefit alternative.

Although TEFRA spared the defined benefit plans, there is every reason to
believe that their integration with Social Security will come under study in
the near future—if for no other reason than that the current requirements
are out of date.

Other Changes.   TEFRA made many other changes that affect tax-
qualified plans under Section 401. The following briefly describes and
evaluates the most significant of these.

Parity between Corporate and Self-Employed Plans.   Federal tax law has
long contained a series of major differences between corporate plans and
those for self-employed persons. Many of these distinctions have been
eliminated in an effort to achieve parity between these plans. Although
some of the changes affect corporate plans, most liberalize the rules applicable to self-employed plans. The major changes, which are effective for plan
years beginning after December 31, 1983, are:

Corporate plans will have to provide that benefit payments must begin by
the year in which the employee reaches age 70 $\frac{1}{2}$ (or retirement, if later).
Also, any interest remaining in a plan at an employee's death must be
distributed to a beneficiary within five years, unless distribution has
already begun, and is payable over a period not greater than the joint life
expectancy of the employee and his or her spouse. (IRA rules were also
changed in the same way.)

The special deduction limits (previously the lesser of 15 percent of earned
income or $15,000) that applied to defined contribution plans for the
self-employed are repealed. The restrictions on defined benefit plans for
the self-employed are also repealed. Self-employed plans are now treated
the same as corporate plans in this regard, and maximum contributions
and benefits for the self-employed will be controlled by Section 415
limits. This will, in effect, increase allowable contributions under defined
contribution plans to the lesser of 25 percent of earned income or
$30,000—and this dollar limit will be increased by CPI changes begin-
ning in 1986.

Liberalizations for self-employed plans covering owner-employees include:

- Earned income will now be computed after subtracting deductible
  plan contributions, although other restrictions on the definition of
  this term remain.

- The requirement that the plan cover all employees with at least three
  years of service is repealed. Coverage can now be limited to a fair
  cross section of employees.

- Along with this change in coverage requirements, these plans will no longer have to provide full and immediate vesting; ERISA's regular vesting rules will apply.
- The new corporate plan rules on the integration of defined contribution plans will apply to these plans.
- The law will no longer prohibit employer contributions above deductible limits. Nor will the law prohibit or restrict either mandatory or voluntary employee contributions by an owner-employee. The 6 percent excise tax on excess contributions for an owner-employee is also repealed.
- Profit-sharing plans of self-employed individuals will no longer have to provide a definite contribution formula for nonowner employees.
- A self-employed plan will not have to require owner-employee consent for participation.
- The trustee of the plan will no longer have to be a bank or other approved financial institution.
- The prohibition against contributions for an owner-employee for five years after receiving a premature distribution is repealed.
- The $5,000 income exclusion under Section 101(b) of the Code is extended to lump-sum death benefits paid for a self-employed person.

Clearly, these parity provisions have resulted in substantial gains for the self-employed. Incorporating or forming a professional association will no longer be necessary to obtain the Section 401 tax advantages previously available only to corporate plans. In fact, TEFRA recognizes that incorporation no longer produces those tax advantages and grants relief to professionals who wish to liquidate their corporations before the end of 1984. This relief is basically in the area of avoiding current ordinary income for certain receivables distributed in liquidation.

Apart from the above, it might be noted that the self-employed are still not able to participate in "welfare" plans (group life insurance and disability and medical expense plans) on the same tax-favored basis as shareholder-employees of corporations.

Estate Tax.   Federal tax law, prior to TEFRA, granted an unlimited estate tax exclusion for certain employer-provided death benefits under Section 401 plans. This exclusion applied to all such death benefits if payable in installments and also to lump-sum benefits if the beneficiary agreed to forgo the favorable 10-year averaging income-tax treatment. This exclusion also applied to death benefits paid from an IRA in installments for at least 36 months.

For individuals dying after 1982, this exclusion will be limited to $100,000 for the aggregate value of all such death benefits. However, it should be noted that the unlimited marital deduction for amounts payable to a spouse continues to apply. Thus, any qualified plan benefits payable to a spouse, whether in installments or in a lump sum, will generally not be taxable in the employee's estate. (Of course, any amounts remaining in the spouse's estate at his or her later death could then be taxable as part of the spouse's estate.) Also, even if some part of the plan death benefit becomes includable in the employee's estate because of this new maximum, the regular estate tax credit would apply and could limit or even eliminate actual estate taxes. For those plans that provide for a death benefit only in the form of income to a surviving spouse, this change is of no significance. Benefits payable to a surviving spouse generally qualify for the unlimited marital deduction. For other plans (such as profit-sharing or savings), this change in estate taxation might require the rethinking of plan provisions and individual estate planning. For example, in most situations little is likely to be gained by having a beneficiary forgo 10-year averaging income-tax treatment.

Defined Contribution Plan Treatment of Disabled Employees. The Section 415 limitations described earlier limit the annual addition to an employee's account to the lesser of 25 percent of pay or the specified dollar amount. If a disabled employee received no compensation in a year, this provision produced a "zero" contribution limit—a result that was obviously not intended. TEFRA has corrected this oversight. An employer may elect to continue making and deducting contributions for such an employee if:

The employee is permanently and totally disabled.

The employee is not an officer, owner, or highly compensated.

The contribution is vested.

Compensation is valued as if paid for the year at the rate paid immediately before disability.

This change is retroactive and applies to taxable years beginning after 1981.

Partial Rollovers of IRA Distributions. Prior law required that the full amount in an IRA be rolled over into another IRA or a qualified plan to avoid taxation—that is, partial rollovers *from* an IRA were not permitted. TEFRA permits partial rollovers of IRA distributions to other IRAs or to qualified plans as long as the part rolled over meets the regular 60-day requirement. This change applies to distributions made after 1982 in taxable years ending after such date.

Executive Corporations. For some time now, members of affiliated personal service corporations have been aggregated for purposes of testing discrimination under qualified plans. This was primarily aimed at incorporated doctors, lawyers, and other professionals. TEFRA expands this concept to include certain organizations "performing management functions" —essentially, incorporated executives. This provision becomes effective in 1984.

In addition, the IRS is given authority to reallocate income, deductions, and credits between the personal service corporation and its employee-shareholders. This is effective in 1983.

Leased Employees.   Many employers "lease" employees—that is, retain a broker or other intermediate party to provide individuals for certain jobs. Starting in 1984, these leased employees will be treated as employees of the employer receiving their services—even if they are not "common law" employees of such employer—for "certain purposes" related to the employer's qualified plans. Such leased employees will be treated as actual employees for:

Coverage requirements.

Discrimination tests.

Limitations on contributions or benefits.

Coverage by simplified employee pensions.

The top-heavy test (Section 416 of the Code) described later in this chapter.

To determine if a leased individual has to be counted, two tests must be met: (1) the individual must have performed services for the employer receiving the services on a substantially full-time basis for at least one year, and (2) the services must be of a type historically performed by employees. As might be expected, any plan benefits provided by the intermediate party can be counted when testing for discrimination, and leased employees will not be counted at all until after they have completed one year of service. Most important, leased employees will *not* be considered employees for *deduction* purposes. If they are covered by the plans of the employer using their services, the expenses will not be deductible as long as there is no employer/employee relationship.

One way to avoid these problems is to have the intermediate party cover the leased employees with a fully vested, nonintegrated defined contribution pension plan with immediate participation and with an employer contribution of at least 7½ percent of pay. In this case, the new leased employee rules will not apply.

Church Plan Changes.   In addition to being able to use conventional tax-qualified retirement plans, churches also have been able to use tax-deferred annuities under Section 403(b) of the Code. TEFRA made a number of changes affecting church plans. These changes:

Increase the exclusion allowance under Section 403(b).

Permit segregated defined contribution retirement savings plans under the tax-deferred annuity rules.

Allow church plans special catch-up elections and additional contributions under the Section 415 limitations.

Permit a special retroactive correction period.

Although only a limited group of plans are affected, these changes are clearly beneficial to the organizations involved.

Group Term Life Insurance

The TEFRA provision dealing with discriminatory group term life insurance plans is of great interest to many employers. The taxation of the value of employer-provided group term life insurance is governed by Section 79 of the Code. In general, employees do not have to report any taxable income on the first $50,000 of employer-provided group term life insurance. If an employee is insured for more than this amount, the value of the excess (less any employee contributions) is reportable as income each year. The value of this excess insurance is determined under tables published by the IRS.

Prior law did not contain any requirements relating to nondiscriminatory coverage or benefits. Thus, it was possible to limit group term life insurance coverage to officers, the highly paid, or key employees, or (as was more commonly the case) to provide extra or higher amounts of insurance for these employees.

The change made by TEFRA does not require that all group term life insurance plans provide for nondiscriminatory coverage and benefits. What the law does provide, beginning with taxable years after 1983, is that if such a plan discriminates (in coverage or in benefits) in favor of key employees, no key employee will be able to exclude the value of the first $50,000 of insurance from current income. (This could affect even key employees who are within that classification but who do not benefit from the discriminatory coverage or benefits.) In a worst-case situation (an executive over age 60 who is in a maximum tax bracket), the additional income tax payable because of this provision would be $489. (The annual Section 79 rate for individuals over age 60 is $19.56 per $1,000 of life insurance. This amount, multiplied by 50, produces $978 of additional income. At a 50 percent tax rate, this generates $489 of additional tax.)

Two other points should be noted:

The additional income under a discriminatory plan needs to be reported only by key employees; other employees, even though highly paid, are not affected.

Group term life insurance provided for retired employees (after they have reached an age when they could have retired with unreduced benefits) does not generate any income-tax liability, regardless of the amount of insurance involved. TEFRA does not change this treatment of postretirement group term life insurance and such coverage can continue to be provided on a discriminatory basis that favors key employees without any additional income tax liability for the retirees.

For purposes of this provision, key employees basically are defined as officers (generally limited to 50 individuals or 10 percent of all employees, if less), 5 percent shareholders, certain 1 percent shareholders with more than $150,000 of annual compensation, and the 10 employees with the most shares. Obviously, an employee will have to be counted only once. These rules are more fully explained in the next section.

A group term life insurance plan will be considered to be discriminatory in coverage unless:

The plan benefits at least 70 percent of all employees of the employer.

At least 85 percent of plan participants are not key employees.

The plan is part of a "cafeteria" plan and the nondiscrimination requirements of Section 125 of the Code are met.

The plan complies with a reasonable classification found by the IRS to be nondiscriminatory.

In applying these tests, part-time and seasonal employees need not be taken into account, nor is it necessary to consider employees with fewer than three years of service. It is also possible to exclude employees who are covered by a collective bargaining agreement (where such benefits have been bargained for) and nonresident alien employees with no U.S.-source income.

A group term life insurance plan also will be considered discriminatory if the type and amount of benefits favor key employees. A plan providing a uniform percentage of salary would not be discriminatory even though the dollar amount of coverage for key employees exceeds the amount for rank-and-file employees.

Employers whose plans are considered discriminatory will have to decide whether to change their programs to make them nondiscriminatory. Other alternatives, of course, are available. For example, the plan's discriminatory features could be removed and provided under an arrangement not considered to be group term life insurance (e.g., under some form of self-insurance). Or, the pay of the affected key employees could be "grossed up" to cover their additional tax liability.

In the broad sense, it is disturbing to note this additional government regulation of employee benefit plans. Concepts of discrimination that have applied in the past to only Section 401 plans are now being applied to other employee benefit programs. And, with these additional requirements, it seems inevitable that more and more reports will have to be filed to show compliance or for other purposes. On the positive side, the Conference Report declares it is the intent of Congress that the Section 79 tables be revised periodically to reflect actual costs of group term life insurance. If the IRS heeds this statement, it might be possible that Section 79 rates will be lowered within the next year or so. Most experts feel that the current rates, particularly at older ages, are too high and are not justified by actual experience.

Medical Expenses

TEFRA made a number of changes in matters relating to medical expenses. Some of these have to do with individual tax deductions; however, most are involved with Medicare. The changes affecting individual medical tax deductions are:

The ability to deduct 50 percent of health insurance premiums (up to a maximum of $150) without regard to other medical expenses is repealed.

Medical expenses are deductible only to the extent they exceed 5 percent of adjusted gross income.

Drug expenses no longer have to exceed 1 percent of adjusted gross income to be considered part of "medical" expenses.

Drug expenses are allowable only for insulin or prescription drugs.

Most of these changes are effective in 1983 (changes concerning the treatment of drugs will not become effective until 1984).

Employees covered under employer-sponsored health insurance plans should not be affected to any great extent by the changes because their unreimbursed medical expenses rarely exceed 3 percent of adjusted gross income. For those employees who itemize deductions and who contribute to their health insurance coverage, the elimination of the deduction for health insurance premiums will cause a mild tax increase—a maximum of $75 for someone in the 50 percent tax bracket.

A change of great concern to many employers is the one that modifies the role of Medicare for active employees between the ages of 65 and 70. TEFRA amends ADEA to require private sector employers to offer these employees the choice of remaining with the employer's group health plan or moving to Medicare. If the employee chooses to stay with the employer's plan, Medicare payments will be secondary to any payments from the employer's plan. If the employee rejects the employer's plan, Medicare will be retained as the employee's primary coverage. (An exemption is provided for small businesses with fewer than 20 employees.)

The effect of this change is to transfer a significant cost burden from the government to the private sector. In a typical medical-expense plan, average employer costs for each employee over age 65 could be increased by as much as $1,800 annually. And if more and more employees continue to work beyond age 65, these costs, relative to the employer's plan as a whole, could become even more significant. This shift in costs could have even greater long-term consequences if the change were to apply to retired employees. Such an extension is, in our opinion, a possible future step. Employers would be well advised to consider at this time the design of the medical plans they provide retired employees.

In another Medicare change, the cost of Part B monthly premiums will be increased—by $.10 on July 1, 1983, and by an additional $1.30 on July 1, 1984.

In addition to the changes that make Medicare a secondary payer and increase the Part B premium, there are 25 other Medicare changes, 24 of which directly or indirectly involve cost reimbursement to hospitals for Medicare patients. (The 25th change reduces the Medicare benefit for in-hospital radiology and pathology services from 100 percent under Part A to 80 percent under Part B, after the deductible has been met.)

The many cost-reimbursement changes superficially appear to have their primary effect on hospitals and represent a significant cost saving to the government—estimated to be several billion dollars over the next three years. However, hospitals serve both Medicare patients and non-Medicare patients, and this has long-term significance. The overall economics of hospital operation are not changed when the government, by fiat, reduces what it will pay for Medicare patients. The hospital, in order to survive, will have to shift the difference between its actual costs and government reimbursed costs for Medicare patients to the non-Medicare patients. This could ultimately shift more health care costs to the private sector, driving up the already inflated premiums for health insurance plans.

One large insurer estimates that hospital cost shifting in 1982 amounted to $5.8 billion, or about 13 percent of private sector hospital revenues. In addition, physicians and other providers who no longer accept Medicare fee reimbursement as payment in full have, in effect, shifted costs for their excess fees. The new limits on Medicare reimbursement will add substantially to aggregate hospital cost shifting. The impact will, of course, vary by hospital, depending on case mix between Medicare and non-Medicare patients. But one thing is certain: Employer medical-plan costs will increase to make up some of the savings in government programs.

Minimum Tax Changes

Although the TEFRA changes in the minimum tax do not have a significant impact on employee benefit plans, they could have an effect on the treatment of incentive stock options. Hence, the following brief discussion of these changes has been included in this chapter.

Under prior law, there was both an add-on and an alternative minimum tax for individuals. TEFRA has repealed the add-on tax and revised the alternative minimum tax. This tax is now structured so the entire minimum taxable income in excess of the exemption amount is taxed at a flat 20 percent rate. Existing tax preferences (e.g., long-term capital gains) generally remain unchanged, although the spread on the exercise of an incentive stock option is added as a preference item. The annual exemption amount for married individuals filing joint returns is $40,000. This change is generally effective for taxable years beginning after 1982.

The full impact of this change is unclear because the tax is an alternative tax only. Lump-sum distributions from qualified plans could be affected to the extent of a possible 20 percent tax on the capital-gain deduction element. And, in some extreme situations, the gain from an ISO could be taxed as high as 40 percent even if the stock is held for more than a year.

TOP-HEAVY PLANS

One of the most dramatic changes made by TEFRA is the introduction of the concept of top-heavy plans and the imposition of complex and onerous rules upon such plans. These rules are applicable to qualified plans and:

Limit the amount of compensation that may be considered in providing benefits or contributions for key employees.

Call for minimum contribution and/or benefit levels for non-key employees.

Reduce the Section 415 limits on contributions and benefits for key employees.

Restrict distributions to key employees.

This section first discusses the definition of a top-heavy plan. It next discusses the definition of a key employee. The remaining material considers the qualification rules that apply to top-heavy plans and the implications of these rules.

Top-Heavy Plans Defined

A defined contribution plan is top-heavy in a plan year if, as of the determination date (generally, the last day of the preceding plan year), either:

The sum of the account balances of all key employees participating in the plan is more than 60 percent of the sum of the account balances of all covered employees.

The plan is part of a top-heavy group, as explained below.

A defined benefit plan is top-heavy in a plan year if, as of the determination date, either:

The *present value* of the accumulated accrued benefits of all key employees participating in the plan is more than 60 percent of the present value of the accumulated accrued benefits of all covered employees.

The plan is part of a top-heavy group, as explained below.

A top-heavy group is the combination of two or more plans. Under the law, it may be either required or permissible to aggregate two or more plans to determine top-heaviness. It is *required* to aggregate into a group (1) all plans covering a key employee and (2) any plan upon which a key-employee plan depends for qualification under the coverage and discrimination requirements of the Code. It is *permissible* for an employer to expand the group by aggregating other plans as long as the resulting group continues to satisfy the coverage and discrimination rules.

The 60 percent test applies to the top-heavy group. If the group is top-heavy, then each plan is also deemed to be top-heavy. However, a plan included solely at the employer's election is not necessarily considered top-heavy. In applying the top-heavy group rules, all plans of all employers who are part of the same controlled group are treated as a single plan.

To determine present value of accrued benefits and account balances, the employer may count both employer and employee contributions. Accumulated deductible employee contributions, however, must be disregarded. Also, the employer must count any amount distributed to or for a participant under the plan within the five-year period ending on the current determination date. Rollover contributions and similar transfers to a plan made after 1983 generally will not have to be part of the top-heavy plan computation. (Presumably, rollovers made before that date will have to be considered.)

If an employee ceases to be a key employee, his or her accrued benefit and/or account balance is not counted for purposes of the top-heavy plan computation for any year after the last year for which the employee was treated as a key employee.

Key Employees Defined

Key employees are defined as:

All officers (up to a maximum of 50). If the employer has between 30 and 500 employees, the number of officers included will never have to be greater than 10 percent of all employees. The Conference Report states that the determination of whether a person is an officer will be based on all the facts and circumstances, including the source of the employee's authority, the term for which he or she is elected or appointed, and the nature and extent of the employee's duties. Thus, not all individuals with the title of officer will be deemed officers for this purpose.

The 10 employees who own the largest interest in the employer.

An employee who owns more than a 5 percent interest in the employer.

An employee who owns more than a 1 percent interest in the employer and whose annual compensation is more than $150,000.

(An employee who falls into more than one category, of course, is counted only once.)

An employee is considered a key employee by falling into one of the above classifications at any time during the current plan year or the four preceding plan years. Thus, the group of key employees may be larger than the actual operating group of key employees for any period of time.

If an employer has more officers than are required to be counted, the officers to be considered are those with the highest compensation.

In determining stock ownership, an employee is treated as owning stock even if it is owned by other family members or certain partnerships, estates, trusts, or corporations in which the employee has an interest. The rules for determining ownership in noncorporate entities are similar to those for determining corporate ownership. In computing the $150,000 compensation minimum limit for a self-employed individual, compensation means earned income from the trade or business for which the plan is maintained.

Qualification Rules

A top-heavy plan must meet certain additional requirements if it is to be qualified under the Code. Moreover, the IRS is permitted to require a plan, even if it is not top-heavy, to include provisions that will automatically take effect if that event should occur. Thus, a great many plans may have to be amended significantly unless the IRS finds a method for exempting major plans from this unnecessary and burdensome requirement. The rules that apply for top-heavy plans are set forth below.

Includable Compensation. A top-heavy plan may provide benefits based on no more than the first $200,000 of an employee's compensation. This limit will be adjusted, beginning in 1986, using the same indexing (that is, changes in the CPI) that applies to Section 415 limitations.

Vesting. A top-heavy plan must meet one of two alternative "fast" vesting schedules for *all* accrued benefits. The two vesting schedules are:

100 percent vesting after three years of service.

Graded vesting of at least 20 percent after two years of service, 40 percent after three, 60 percent after four, 80 percent after five, and 100 percent after six years.

Minimum Benefits for Non-Key Employees. A top-heavy plan must provide a minimum benefit or contribution for all non-key employee participants. The minimum benefit and contribution requirements are:

For each year (maximum of 10) in which a defined benefit plan is top-heavy, each non-key employee participant must accrue an employer-provided benefit of at least 2 percent of compensation. Compensation is generally defined as the average of the five consecutive highest years of pay.

For each year in which a defined contribution plan is top heavy, an employer must contribute at least 3 percent of compensation for each non-key employee participant. However, in no case does an employer have to contribute more than the percentage contributed for key employees. For this purpose, reallocated forfeitures are counted as employer contributions.

Where a non-key employee participates in both a defined benefit and a defined contribution plan, the employer does not have to provide minimum benefits under both plans.

Limitations on Contributions and Benefits. If a key employee participates in both a defined benefit and a defined contribution plan for any year for which either plan is top-heavy, a special aggregate Section 415 limit applies. The limit is the lesser of 1.0 as applied to the dollar limit or 1.4 as determined under present law for the percentage limit. The dollar limit can be increased to 1.25, however, if the plans meet the "concentration test" and provide an extra minimum benefit for non-key employees.

The concentration test is satisfied if the present value of the key employees' accrued benefits (or account balances) is not more than 90 percent of the total value for all covered employees. The extra minimum benefits to be provided for each non-key employee are:

For defined benefit plans, a benefit accrual of 1 percent of compensation (highest five) for each year of service during which the plan is top-heavy, up to a maximum of 10 years.

For defined contribution plans, a contribution of 1 percent of compensation for each year of service during which the plan is top-heavy.

Distributions to Key Employees. Any distribution made to a key employee before age 59½ is subject to an additional income tax equal to 10 percent of the amount of the distribution attributable to service as a key employee. However, this tax will not be imposed if the distribution is made because of death or disability. Furthermore, a top-heavy plan must begin distributions to key employees no later than the taxable year in which the employee reaches age 70½. This applies even if the key employee continues to work.

Effective Dates. Generally, these provisions become effective in 1984. However, special transitional rules may apply.

ISSUES AND IMPLICATIONS

For a great many employers, the changes made by TEFRA will not cause substantial problems. Clearly, all employers will be affected to some extent; for many, though, the consequences are largely administrative. The same cannot be said for employers who are subject to the new top-heavy rules. The implications for them are significant.

All pension plans (and tax-qualified capital accumulation plans) will have to be amended to cover such matters as the new Section 415 limitations and the new requirements as to when and how benefits can be paid. Integrated defined contribution plans will have to be modified if they are now set up to use the maximum allowable integration. Plans that permit employee loans will have to be amended to incorporate the new limits if the employer wants to avoid taxable distributions. And if an employer wishes to make contributions for a disabled employee under a defined contribution plan, some amendments will probably be necessary. Also, unless the IRS exempts them, plans may have to be amended to include top-heavy provisions that automatically come into play if warranted by changing circumstances.

At least one group of employers—the self-employed—have much to consider. Increased contribution and benefit limits, along with relaxed qualification rules, suggest that many existing plans will be revised in significant ways. Those professionals who have incorporated in recent years may wish to consider the advantages of returning to an unincorporated form of doing business.

A large number of employers have group term life insurance plans that will be considered discriminatory under TEFRA's provisions. These employers have several options to consider in deciding on their response.

Because most employers now have some employees over age 65 and because this number may grow, it will be particularly important to respond to the TEFRA provisions that change Medicare to a secondary provider. This, in turn, will require a reexamination of current government policies concerning permissible changes (under ADEA) in medical plans because of age. In any event, it will be important to develop consistent and equitable handling of medical expense coverage (and employee contributions) between active employees under 65, active employees over 65, and retirees (again, both under and over 65).

In a broader sense, TEFRA imposes more administrative burdens on an already overburdened private pension system. Also, some concern can be properly expressed over the extent to which Congress is shifting the cost of medical care to the private sector.

CHAPTER 59

Federal Income Taxation of Group Life Insurance

JAMES E. ROBERTS AND
RONALD T. MARTIN

Every group life insurance plan involves four taxpayers—the employer, its employees, the employees' beneficiaries, and the insurance company insuring the employees covered under the plan. The federal taxation of life insurance companies is beyond the scope of this chapter and, therefore, is not discussed. In reviewing the federal income-tax consequences to each of the other taxpayers, the primary emphasis is on the tax benefits provided the employee under Section 79 of the Internal Revenue Code.[1]

TAX BENEFITS PROVIDED THE EMPLOYEE

Prior to the enactment of the Revenue Act of 1964, premiums paid by an employer for group term life insurance protection provided to an employee were deductible by the employer, but were not considered income to the employee even though the employee could designate the beneficiary of the insurance proceeds.[2] Premiums on permanent life insurance provided an employee by the employer, however, were considered income to the employee.[3] The introduction of Section 79 into the Internal Revenue Code in 1964 placed certain limitations upon the previous tax-free status of group term life insurance.

Section 79—In General

Under Section 79(a), an employee must include in his or her gross income for the taxable year an amount equal to the cost of group term life insurance on his or her life provided by the employer, to the extent such

---

[1] Int. Rev. Code of 1954, §79 (hereinafter cited as I.R.C.).

[2] G.C.M. 16069 (Cum. Bull. xvi–1,84); Treas. Reg. §1.61–2(d)(2) prior to its amendment in 1964.

[3] G.C.M. 16069 (Cum. Bull. xvi–1,84).

cost exceeds the sum of (1) the cost of $50,000 of such insurance and (2) the amount, if any, paid by the employee for such insurance.[4] The term *cost* refers not to the premium paid for the insurance protection, but to the cost determined under the Uniform Premium Table contained in the regulations.[5]

Section 79(b) provides three exceptions to the inclusionary rule of Section 79(a). Under the first such exception, Section 79(a) shall not apply to the cost of group term life insurance on the life of an employee provided by the employer if the employee's employment with such employer has terminated and the employee either has attained retirement age with respect to such employer or is disabled.[6]

For purposes of this exception, an employee's employment terminates when he or she ceases to render services to the employer, as such employer's employee. Therefore, an individual may retire and receive the benefits of the above exclusion from gross income while rendering consulting or other services, as an independent contractor, to the former employer. For purposes of the above exception, if the employee is covered under a written pension or annuity plan of the employer providing group term life insurance on his or her life, the term *retirement age* is the earlier of (1) the earliest age indicated by such plan at which an active employee has the right to retire, without being disabled and without the consent of his or her employer, and receive full and immediate retirement benefits under such plan, "computed at either the full rate or a rate proportionate to completed service as set forth in the normal retirement formula of the plan, i.e., without actuarial or similar reduction because of retirement before some later specified age," or (2) the age at which it has been the practice of the employer to terminate, due to age, the services of members of the class of employees to which the employee last belonged.[7] In the absence of a written pension or annuity plan, retirement age is considered to be that age at which the employer normally terminates, due to age, members of the class of employees to which the employee last belonged, provided such age is reasonable.[8] If neither of the two preceding sentences applies, retirement age is considered to be age 65.[9] An employee is considered to be disabled, for purposes of the above exception, if he or she is unable to engage in any substantial gainful activity by reason of an impairment that can reasonably be expected to be of indefinite duration or to result in the employee's death.[10]

---

[4] I.R.C. §79(a).

[5] Treas. Reg. §1.79-3(d)(2).

[6] I.R.C. §79(b)(1).

[7] Treas. Reg. §1.79-2(b)(3)(i)(a).

[8] Treas. Reg. §1.79-2(b)(3)(ii).

[9] Treas. Reg. §1.79-2(b)(3)(iii).

[10] I.R.C. §72(m)(7).

An employee who seeks the benefits provided by the above exclusion for disabled employees must file with his or her tax return, for the first taxable year for which a benefit is sought, a physician's statement concerning the impairment, together with the employee's own statement as to the date such impairment occurred and its effect on his or her substantial gainful activity.[11] Thereafter, the employee may, in lieu of the foregoing statement, attach to his or her tax return a statement declaring the continuance of the impairment, without substantial diminution, and its continued effect on the employee's substantial gainful activity.[12]

In lieu of the substantiation specified in the preceding paragraph, an insured employee may submit a statement from the insurer that he or she is disabled within the meaning of Section 72(m)(7). The insurer's statement must set forth the insurer's basis for determining the employee's disability and, for the first taxable year such statement is filed, the date such disability occurred.[13]

The second exception under Section 79(b) provides that "[Section 79(a)] shall not apply to the cost of any portion of the group term life insurance on the life of an employee provided during part or all of the taxable year of the employee under which . . . the employer is directly or indirectly the beneficiary, or . . . a [charitable organization] described in Section 170(c) is the sole beneficiary, for the entire period during such taxable year for which the employee receives such insurance."[14] Whether an employer is directly or indirectly a beneficiary of a group term life insurance policy depends on the applicable facts and circumstances. For example, if the employer, although nominally the beneficiary under the policy, is obligated to pay over the proceeds thereof to the employee's estate or beneficiary, the employer will not be the beneficiary of the policy for purposes of this exception.[15]

If the employee is to qualify for the exception, a charity must be the sole beneficiary of all or a part of the policy proceeds (under a revocable or irrevocable beneficiary designation) and there must be no contingent beneficiary thereof unless such contingent beneficiary is also a qualified charity.[16] The naming of a qualified charity as the sole beneficiary of the

---

[11] Treas. Reg. §1.79–2(b)(4)(ii)(b).

[12] Ibid.

[13] Treas. Reg. §1.79–2(b)(4)(ii)(c).

[14] I.R.C. §79(b)(2). Section 170(c) lists the following classes of exempt organizations: (1) the United States, states and possessions of the United States, and their political subdivisions; (2) if certain requirements are met, corporations, trusts, community chests, funds, and foundations organized and operated exclusively for religious, charitable, scientific, literary, or educational purposes, or to foster national or international amateur sports competition, or for the prevention of cruelty to children or animals; (3) certain organizations of war veterans; (4) certain domestic fraternal societies, orders and associations, operating under the lodge system; (5) certain cemetery companies.

[15] Treas. Reg. §1.79–2(c)(2).

[16] Treas. Reg. §1.79–2(c)(3)(ii).

proceeds of the group life insurance policy, however, does not entitle the employee to a charitable deduction under Section 170 of the Code.[17]

Under the final exception, Section 79(a) shall not apply to the cost of any group term life insurance protection provided under the trust of a qualified pensiòn, profit-sharing, or stock bonus plan, or under a qualified annuity plan if the proceeds of such insurance are payable directly or indirectly to a participant of such trust or to a beneficiary of such participant.[18] The tax consequences to the employee of such life insurance coverage are governed by the provisions of Section 72(m)(3) of the Code and the Regulations thereunder.[19]

If the proceeds of a term policy insuring the life of an employee are payable to the employee or his or her beneficiary and Section 79 is inapplicable, the full amount of the premium thereon paid by the employer will be included in the employee's gross income.[20] Therefore, notwithstanding the limitations introduced in the Revenue Act of 1964 on the previous tax-free status of group term life insurance, an employee will derive significant tax benefits if life insurance provided by the employer qualifies as group term life insurance.

Group Term Life Insurance Defined

Life insurance provided an employee can qualify as group term life insurance if it is provided under a policy carried directly or indirectly by an employer[21] and the death benefits of the policy constitute general death benefits excludible from gross income under Section 101(a) of the Internal Revenue Code.[22] In addition, such life insurance must be provided to a group of employees[23] in amounts computed under a formula that precludes

---

[17] Treas. Reg. §1.79–2(c)(3)(i).

[18] I.R.C. §79(b)(3) and Treas. Reg. §1.79–2(d).

[19] Treas. Reg. §1.79–2(d)(1).

[20] Treas. Reg. §1.61–2(d)(2)(ii)(a).

[21] Treas. Reg. §1.79–1(a)(3).

[22] Treas. Reg. §1.79–1(a)(1). Section 101(a) provides in pertinent part that "gross income does not include amounts received (whether in a single sum or otherwise) under a life insurance contract, if such amounts are paid by reason of the death of the insured." According to the courts and commentators, the major ingredients of life insurance are risk-shifting and risk-distributing. See these cases for examples: *Commissioner* v. *Treganowan*, 50–1 U.S.T.C. ¶10,770 (1949), *Tighe* v. *Commissioner*, 33 T.C. 564 (1959), *Essenfeld* v. *Commissioner*, 311 F.2d 209 (1962, 2d Cir.), *Davis* v. *U.S.*, 323 F. Supp. 861 (1971), *Kess* v. *U.S.*, 451 F.2d 1231 (1971, 6th Cir.), *Ross* v. *Odom*, 401 F.2d 470 (1968, 5th Cir.), *Evans* v. *Commissioner*, 56 T.C. 1142 (1971), *Carnation Co.*, 71 T.C. 400 (1978), Note, 66 Yale L.J. 1217 (1957), Stiller, 111-3rd T.M., *Life Insurance*. It is clear, by virtue of the reference to "general" death benefits, that accidental death benefits will not qualify for treatment under Section 79.

[23] Treas. Reg. §1.79–1(a)(2).

individual selection.[24] According to the regulations, this formula must be based on such factors as age, years of service, and compensation or position.[25] Furthermore, insurance may be provided under alternative schedules under which the amount of insurance provided an employee is based on the amount an employee elects to contribute.[26] The amount of insurance provided an employee under each such schedule must, however, be computed under a formula that precludes individual selection.[27] As no further guidance is provided concerning discrimination limits on contributory plans, perhaps pre-ERISA Revenue Rulings for contributory qualified retirement plans would be useful in plan design. The Internal Revenue Service has announced it will not issue rulings on whether life insurance under a group plan covering ten or more employees qualifies as group term life insurance if the amount of insurance is not computed under a formula that would meet the requirements under Section 1.79–1(c)(2)(ii) of the regulations if the plan covered fewer than ten employees.[28]

There are several terms in the rules concerning the qualification of life insurance as group term life insurance which must be properly defined before the restrictions contained in the rules can be fully understood. These terms include: "carried directly or indirectly," "employee," and "group of employees."

A policy is "carried directly or indirectly" by an employer if it pays, directly or through another person, any portion of the cost of such policy or arranges, alone or in conjunction with one or more other employers, for life insurance to be paid for by employees where at least one employee pays more and at least one employee pays less than the cost [determined under Table I of Treas. Reg. §1.79–3(d)(2)] of insurance provided.[29]

An "employee" is defined as a person performing services in an employer-employee relationship as defined in Section 31.3401(c)-1 of the regulations, a full-time life insurance agent as described in Section 7701(a)(2) of the Internal Revenue Code, or a person who previously performed services as an employee.[30]

---

[24] Treas. Reg. §1.79-1(a)(4). In P.L.R. 8116010 (Dec. 31, 1980), the Service ruled that an insurance plan violated Regs. §1.79-1(a)(4) because the supplemental policies were individually selected rather than according to formula based on age, years of service, compensation, or position. Factors indicating that the policies were individually selected included answering a medical questionnaire and providing coverage to the sole shareholder and his son, who was one of two managers, while the life of the other manager was not covered.

[25] Ibid. It should be noted that the Age Discrimination in Employment Act defines and prohibits certain acts of discrimination by employers against individuals who are less than 70 years of age. However, a discussion of this act is beyond the scope of this chapter.

[26] Treas. Reg. § 1.79-1(a)(4).

[27] Ibid.

[28] Rev. Proc. 80-22, IRB 1980-26,26. See Rev. Rul. 80-22, 1980-1 C.B. 654.

[29] Treas. Reg. §1.79-0.

[30] Ibid.

The term *group of employees* is defined as all employees of an employer, or less than all employees of an employer if group membership is determined solely on the basis of age, marital status, or factors related to employment.[31] Union membership, duties performed, compensation, and length of service are set forth in the regulation as examples of factors related to employment.[32] While the purchase of something other than group term life insurance is not a factor related to employment, participation in an employer's pension, profit-sharing, or accident and health plan, whether contributory or noncontributory, is a factor related to employment.[33] Although ownership of stock in the employer corporation is not a factor related to employment, participation in the employer's stock-bonus plan may be a factor related to employment and a group of employees may include an employee who owns stock in his or her employer corporation.[34]

New Rules for Discriminatory Plans

The attractiveness of group term life insurance plans has been reduced by recent changes in the tax laws. The Tax Equity and Fiscal Responsibility Act (TEFRA) provides that the exclusion from gross income of the cost of the first $50,000 of group term life insurance provided an employee will not be available with respect to a key employee insured under an employer's plan which discriminates in favor of key employees as to eligibility to participate, the type of benefits available, or the amount of benefits available. The term "key employee" is defined by reference to IRC §416(i)(1), which defines key employee in connection with top-heavy plans, with the exception that a one percent owner of an employer having an annual compensation from the employer of more than $150,000 will not be taken into account if he is not a participant in the plan.

A plan of group insurance is discriminatory unless (1) the plan benefits 70 percent or more of all employees of the employer, (2) at least 85 percent of all employees who are participants in the plan are not key employees, (3) the plan benefits such employees as qualify under a classification found by the Secretary not to be discriminatory in favor of key employees, or (4) in the case of a plan which is part of a cafeteria plan, the requirements of IRC §125 are met. In applying the above tests, employees who have not completed three years of service, part-time employees (those whose customary employment is for not more than twenty hours in any one week), seasonal employees (those whose customary employment is for not more than five months in any calendar year), employees covered under a collective bar-

---

[31] Ibid.

[32] Ibid.

[33] Ibid.

[34] Ibid. The Internal Revenue Service presently has an active regulation project on this section of the regulations.

gaining agreement under which group term life insurance benefits were the subject of good faith bargaining between employee representatives and the employer, and employees who are nonresident aliens and receive no earned income from the employer which constitutes income from sources within the United States may be excluded from consideration.

A plan will be discriminatory unless all benefits available to key employees are available to all other participants in the plan. However, a plan may, without being discriminatory, provide benefits which bear a uniform relationship to the total compensation of the employees covered under the plan or to the basic or regular rate of compensation of such employees. For purposes of the above determinations, all employees who are treated as employed by a single employer under subsection (b), (c), or (m) of Section 414 shall be treated as employed by a single employer.

The above provisions shall apply to taxable years beginning after December 31, 1983. However, neither the statute nor legislative history is clear as to whether the effective date applies to plan years beginning after that date or to the calendar year. Inasmuch as IRC §79 is directed to the exclusion of benefits from an employee's gross income, it would appear that the effective date refers to employee taxable years beginning after December 31, 1983. Because the penalty for discriminating under the new TEFRA rules is only the loss of the $50,000 exclusion for key employees, most employers would, but for proposed changes in the regulations discussed on page 1023 hereof, opt for a discriminatory plan.

However, current proposals presently before Congress would apply IRC §79(d) to both pre- and postretirement coverage.

Groups of Fewer than Ten Full-Time Employees

Even if the conditions discussed in the preceding section are met, life insurance provided to a group of employees generally cannot qualify as group term life insurance unless, at some time during the calendar year, it is provided to at least ten full-time employees who are members of the group of employees.[35] The requirement that insurance be ". . . provided to at least ten full-time employees who are members *of the group of employees* . . ."[36] (emphasis added) does not provide an escape from the under-ten restrictions via a multiple employer trust as "group of employees" as defined in Treas. Reg. §1.79-0 refers to employees of a particular employer, not to employees in general.

The general rule set forth above does not apply if:

(A) The insurance is provided to all full-time employees of the employer, or to all full-time employees who provide evidence of insurability

---

[35] Treas. Reg. §1.79-1(c)(1). The Internal Revenue Service presently has an active regulation project on this section of the regulations.

[36] Ibid.

satisfactory to the insurer, if evidence of insurability affects eligibility.[37]

(B) The amount of insurance provided is computed either as a uniform percentage of compensation[38] or on the basis of coverage brackets established by the insurer.[39] However, the amount computed under either method may be reduced in the case of employees who do not provide evidence of insurability satisfactory to the insurer.[40] In general, no bracket may exceed 2½ times the next lower bracket and the lowest bracket must be at least 10 percent of the highest bracket.[41] However, the insurer may establish a separate schedule of coverage brackets for employees over age 65, but no such bracket may exceed 2½ times the next lower bracket and the lowest such bracket must be at least 10 percent of the highest bracket in the basic schedule.[42]

(C) Evidence of insurability affecting an employee's eligibility for insurance or the amount of insurance is limited to a medical questionnaire completed by the employee that does not require a physical examination.[43]

For purposes of (A) above:

1. Employees who customarily work no more than 20 hours in any week or five months in any calendar year are considered part-time employees and may be excluded from the plan without affecting its qualified status.[44]

2. A plan will not be disqualified for failure to provide insurance coverage for all employees if, by the terms of the policy,[45] an employee must be employed for a waiting period of not more than six months before the group insurance coverage becomes effective.[46]

---

[37] Treas. Reg. §1.79-1(c)(2)(i).

[38] Computing the amount of insurance as a uniform percentage of compensation may prove most difficult to administer because compensation other than salary, e.g., bonuses, usually fluctuates from year to year, and during the year, thus changing the amount of insurance to which an employee would be entitled.

[39] Treas. Reg. §1.79-1(c)(2)(ii). *Braswell* v. *Corn.* 42 T.C.R. n. 1053 (1981).

[40] Ibid.

[41] Ibid. Although group insurance plans for ten or more employees are not required under Regs. §1.79(c)(2)(ii) to compute the amount of insurance using either of the two foregoing methods, the Internal Revenue Service has stated that it will not issue a private letter ruling as to whether such plans qualify as group term insurance unless one of the two methods is used. Section 3.011 of Rev. Proc. 80-22, 1980-1 C.B. 654.

[42] Ibid. See also discussion in footnote 25 *supra*.

[43] Treas. Reg. §1.79-1(c)(2)(iii). See discussion of Prop. Regs. on page 1023 hereof.

[44] Treas. Reg. §1.79-1(c)(4)(ii).

[45] There is uncertainty concerning the effect of provisions relating to the insurance provided employees that are not contained in the policy. Until this uncertainty is clarified, waiting periods should be contained in the policy.

[46] Treas. Reg. §1.79-1(c)(4)(i).

3. An employer may elect not to provide insurance protection for employees who continue to work full-time after they attain age 65.[47]

4. Employees who are found to be uninsurable by the insurer solely on the basis of information contained in a health questionnaire completed by the employee may be excluded from the plan without affecting its qualification.[48]

Moreover, a plan is considered to provide insurance protection for an employee who waives the right to participate in the plan.[49] In order for such a waiver to be valid, the employee waiving the life insurance coverage must be eligible for such coverage and the waiver must be voluntary. A waiver obtained by the payment of additional compensation to the employee executing the waiver would appear to be invalid.

Under (B) above, designed to prohibit discrimination in favor of higher paid employees, two issues are presented: (1) What input may an employer have in designing the coverage brackets; and (2) Must an employer, at some time during the taxable year, have at least one employee in each coverage bracket?

With respect to the first issue, a literal reading of the requirement that the insurer establish the coverage brackets would disqualify most, if not all, group insurance plans covering fewer than ten employees during an entire year. This is particularly true for plans underwritten by individual contracts. Most life insurance companies currently marketing group insurance programs underwritten with individual contracts evidently have disregarded the above requirement, for their sales literature and underwriting procedures allow each employer, without restriction, to design its own coverage brackets.[50] A few of those companies even provide sample corporate resolutions establishing the coverage brackets. Although the national office of the Internal Revenue Service has not focused on this issue in private letter rulings, it would appear that the most prudent course to follow in establishing coverage brackets for such plans is to have the insurer, as settlor of a multiple-employer trust, establish several alternative coverage brackets in the trust instrument. Coverage brackets so established could be drawn broadly enough to fit the circumstances of most employers. In addition to the brackets so established, the insurer could provide in the trust instrument that additional brackets may be established by the insurer, but only if such brackets are in conformity with the limitations set forth in the regulations.

---

[47] If the employer provides coverage for such employees, however, it must provide such coverage either on the same basis as its other employees, or under a separate schedule of coverage brackets, established by the insurer, in which no bracket exceeds two and one-half times the next lower bracket and the lowest bracket is at least 10 percent of the highest bracket in the basic schedule. See also discussion in footnote 25 *supra*.

[48] *Treas. Reg.* §1.79-1(c)(2).

[49] *Treas. Reg.* §1.79-1(c)(5).

[50] *See Braswell* v. *Com.* 42 T.C.R. n. 1053 (1981).

The second issue is more difficult. Clearly, in order to assure qualification for the benefits provided by Section 79, an employer's group insurance plan should conform in operation as well as in form to the requirements set forth in the regulations. Therefore, vacant brackets designed to circumvent the maximum differential in coverage allowed by the regulations have resulted in disqualification of the employer's plan. However, an employer's group insurance plan should not be disqualified merely because the employment of the only employee or employees in a particular coverage bracket terminates during the taxable year. Between the boundaries, common sense is the only guide. Certainly, an employer's group insurance plan should not include coverage brackets within which the employer does not reasonably expect to have employees within a relatively short period of time.[51] See, for example, Rev. Rul. 80-220, 1980-2 C.B. 35. In that ruling, a corporation established a plan to provide life insurance for its four full-time employees. The amount of coverage was computed on the basis of three coverage brackets. Three of the employees were covered under bracket one and the remaining employee was covered under bracket three. New employees had been hired since the plan was established, but no employee was ever covered under bracket two. The Internal Revenue Service determined that for all practical purposes there were only two brackets, and the coverage under the higher bracket was in excess of $2\frac{1}{2}$ times the coverage of the lower bracket. Therefore, the plan failed to meet the requirements of Regs. §1.79-1(c).

A comparison of alternatives available to an employer whose group life insurance plan will cover fewer than 10 employees for an entire calendar year must take into account both the employer's objectives and the requirements contained in the regulations.

For example, consider an employer with the following five employees:

Job Title	Annual Compensation
Physician	$150,000
Nurse	14,000
Nurse	14,000
Office Manager–Bookkeeper	12,000
Receptionist	8,400

The employer wishes to provide $300,000 in group life insurance for its physician-employee. If coverage brackets are used, the amounts of insurance shown in Table 59-1 must be provided:

---

[51] Rev. Rul. 80-220, IRB 1980-33,6.

Table 59-1

Job Title	Insurance Amount*	Number of Employees in Each Class	Total Insurance
Physicians	$300,000	1	$300,000
Nurses	$120,000	2	$240,000
Nonprofessional employees earning more than $10,000 per year	$ 48,000	1	$ 48,000
Nonprofessional employees earning $10,000 or less per year	$ 30,000	1	$ 30,000

* Note: Each bracket is no more than 2½ times the next lower bracket and the lowest bracket is at least 10 percent of the highest bracket.

Using the above brackets, the employer would have to purchase at least $318,000 of life insurance for its nonphysician-employees in order to provide $300,000 of life insurance for its physician-employee. Depending on the ages of the respective employees, the tax savings to the physician-employee may be more than offset by the cost of insurance for the non-physician-employees. Should the employer adopt a group insurance plan providing each employee with group life insurance in an amount equal to two times his or her annual compensation, only $96,800 of group insurance for nonphysician employees is required to provide $300,000 of group life insurance for the physician-employee. For example, in Rev. Rul. 80-220, 1980-2 C.B. 35, the Service ruled that a plan having three coverage brackets would not qualify where no employees were ever included in the middle bracket and the coverage of the first bracket exceeded 2½ times the coverage of the third bracket.

The requirement in (C) above prohibiting the use of medical examinations has caused more controversy within the life insurance industry than any other aspect of Section 79. The question is whether the language of the regulations justifies the position that a medical examination may be used to determine the cost of insurance once the employee's eligibility for a certain amount of insurance is established. As the regulations provide that "[e]vidence of insurability *affecting an employee's eligibility for insurance or the amount of insurance* is limited to a medical questionnaire. . . ,"[52] it would appear to be permissible to use a medical examination to determine the cost of such coverage. However, the Service has taken the position under the predecessor to Treas. Reg. §1.79-1(c)(2)(iii) that a medical examination cannot be used for any purpose in connection with an employer's plan that insures fewer than 10 employees. For example, in a private letter ruling

---

[52] Treas. Reg. §1.79-1(c)(2)(iii).

issued on August 1, 1974, which later appeared as Rev. Rul. 75-528, the insurer had agreed to underwrite the risks involved in the employee group solely on the basis of a nonmedical questionnaire completed by each proposed insured. The insurer had further agreed that the maximum premium on any policy issued under the plan would be three times the standard premium for an insured of the same age and sex. Once the insurer had committed itself to issue a specified amount of insurance on a proposed insured at a specified rate, the insurer could request additional evidence of insurability. This additional information, however, would only be used to reduce, if at all, the rate previously guaranteed with respect to the particular insured.

The ruling expressed the opinion that the type of information that may be used in an effort to reduce the guaranteed rate must be the type permitted by the regulations. The ruling further stated that whether such information is initially used to determine if an applicant is eligible for insurance or later used to determine if a premium rate arbitrarily set at three times standard should be reduced with respect to an applicant, it is still the use of such information to establish insurability. The issue of the use of evidence of insurability is presently the subject of a regulation project in the National Office. See also Private Letter Ruling 8116010, dated December 31, 1980, in which the Service referred to an insurer's request for medical information as consistent with the issuance of individual insurance policies but not group insurance.

There is another exception to the under-10 rule for insurance provided under a common plan to the employees of two or more unrelated employers.[53] To come within the exception the insurance must be restricted to, but mandatory for, all employees of the employer who belong to or are represented by an organization that carries on substantial activities in addition to obtaining insurance.[54] Moreover, evidence of insurability must not affect an employee's eligibility for insurance or the amount thereof.[55]

As with the first exception to the general under-ten rule, employees need not be taken into account if:

1. They are ineligible for insurance because they have not been employed for a waiting period, not to exceed six months, specified in the policy;[56]

2. They are part-time employees (i.e., they are customarily employed for not more than 20 hours in any week or five months in any calendar year);[57] or

---

[53] Treas. Reg. §1.79-1(c)(3)(i).
[54] Treas. Reg. §1.79-1(c)(3)(ii).
[55] Treas. Reg. §1.79-1(c)(3)(iii).
[56] Treas. Reg. §1.79-1(c)(4)(i).
[57] Treas. Reg. §1.79-1(c)(4)(ii).

3. They have attained 65 years of age.[58]

However, unlike the first exception to the general under-10 rule, for purposes of the second exception, an employer is not considered as providing insurance to an employee who waives his or her right to such coverage.[59] Therefore, life insurance provided a group of fewer than 10 employees cannot qualify for favorable tax treatment under Treas. Reg. §1.79-1(c)(3) if one of those employees voluntarily waives his or her right to such coverage.[60]

Proposed Regulations

On October 7, 1982, the Treasury Department proposed certain amendments to the regulations under Section 79 of the Internal Revenue Code. These regulations addressed four areas: the use of evidence of insurability, the definition of the term "policy," permanent benefits provided employees by their employer, and the treatment of employees who decline insurance under employer-sponsored plans covering fewer than 10 employees. Of these amendments, the proposed provisions regarding the use of evidence of insurability are the most significant.

Under the proposed regulations, if evidence of insurability provided to an insurer includes a physician's report of a physical examination or is based on a physician's records of such an examination, the insurance provided an employee is not computed under a formula that precludes individual selection. Therefore, the insurance is not group term life insurance for purposes of Section 79 to the extent that it exceeds the greater of (1) $50,000 or (2) the amount of insurance that the insurer would have issued to a member of the group of employees without evidence of individual insurability.

The above language greatly expands the restrictions on evidence of insurability which have existed under the regulations since 1969, in that the proposed prohibition applies to all employee groups. Under the existing regulations, the restrictions on the use of evidence of insurability apply only to groups in which fewer than 10 employees are covered during an entire calendar year. In addition, the proposed language would effectively preclude the use of an attending physician's statements, as any information a physician had would be based on his examination of the patient. Furthermore, as information obtained from the Medical Information Bureau would generally be "based on a physician's records" of a physical examination, the use of such information would also be precluded.

The proposed regulations state that evidence of insurability does not include information obtained before November 6, 1982. However, the

---

[58] Treas. Reg. §1.79-1(c)(4)(iii). See also discussion in note 25 *supra*.

[59] Treas. Reg. §1.79-1(c)(3).

[60] Treas. Reg. §1.79-1(c)(5).

language is unclear as to whether the exclusion applies to information obtained by a physician prior to November 6 or information obtained by the insurer prior to such date. For example, one reading of the language would preclude any information being received by an insurer after November 6, 1982, irrespective of the date the information was received by the attending physician or another third-party source. This reading would effectively preclude the use of the information insurance companies now have on their existing policyholders with respect to new applications by those policyholders, as well as information held by physicians regarding examinations made prior to November 6 and the information files of the Medical Information Bureau. Another reading of the language would allow the use of such information so long as the information was obtained by the attending physician, etc., prior to November 6. One would anticipate that the language in the proposed regulations would be modified to read information obtained "by the insurer."

The use of evidence of insurability by insurers in connection with group term life insurance plans has been a very difficult concept for the Treasury Department. Initially, the regulations under Section 79 prohibited the use of any evidence of insurability. Those regulations provided " . . . a plan will not qualify as a plan of group insurance where eligibility at the time the employee first becomes eligible for insurance protection under the plan is conditioned on evidence of insurability." This requirement was based on the theory, expressed in the regulations, that group insurance must be available to a class or classes of employees, the members of which are determined on the basis of factors which preclude individual selection. The draftsmen of this regulation evidently felt that the use of evidence of insurability would allow the employer or the insurer to determine a class or classes of employees on the basis of a factor, i.e., evidence of insurability, which would allow individual selection.

The above requirement was removed from the regulations in 1969. At that time, Section 1.79-1(b)(iii)(d) (now §1.79-1(c)) was added to the regulations which imposed certain restrictions on plans providing term insurance protection for fewer than 10 full-time employees. These restrictions were designed to "preclude individual selection." One of the restrictions was that evidence of insurability could be used to determine an employee's eligibility for, or the amount of, insurance, but only to the extent that such eligibility or amount was determined solely on the basis of a health questionnaire completed by the employee and requiring no medical examination. Thus, in 1969, evidence of insurability was allowable on all group insurance plans. However, such evidence of insurability was restricted to a health questionnaire completed by the proposed insured in plans which provided term insurance for fewer than 10 employees during an entire calendar year.

The interpretation of the language of Treas. Reg. §1.79-1(b)(iii)(d) (now Section 1.79-1(c)) led to two controversial private letter rulings, one of which was later published as Revenue Ruling 75-528. The other private letter ruling, based on a much weaker rationale, was later bolstered in 1976 when the Treasury again modified the regulations under Section 79. At that time, the language defining the reason, i.e., to preclude individual selection, for the special rules applicable to plans insuring fewer than ten lives was deleted.

The background material for the proposed regulations states that the prohibition of individual selection of amounts of insurance is an essential characteristic of group insurance. The three arguments made in the background material in justification of the position on the use of evidence of insurability taken in the proposed regulations are:

1. If evidence of insurability is allowed, the rules for determining the cost of group insurance would not produce an appropriate result as the uniform table contained in the regulations is based on group mortality and measures the cost of insurance only if the insurance company does not use evidence of insurability to determine the premiums on an individual basis;

2. If evidence of an individual's insurability is used to determine the premium for, or the amount of, insurance provided the particular employee, the insurer uses such evidence of insurability to protect itself from adverse consequences of individual selection just as it does when it sells individual life insurance; and

3. When evidence of insurability is used, it facilitates individual selection.

The rationale of the proposed regulations, as indicated in the background thereof, is based on erroneous assumptions. First, the Service assumes that the use of evidence of insurability would result in the Table 1 values not accurately reflecting the cost of insurance. Obviously, an insurance company can charge less for a known risk, i.e., a risk which it can properly evaluate through adequate evidence of insurability, than an unknown risk, which assumes group mortality. This can be demonstrated by the cost differential in the marketplace between group term life insurance issued in connection with multiple employer trusts which insure employees of employers having a small number of employees, and term life insurance which individuals can purchase on their own. The group rates are substantially higher than the individually underwritten rates. The use of additional evidence of insurability would result in a lower cost to employers and, therefore, the federal government.

Secondly, the Service has concluded that evidence of insurability is used to determine the premium for or the amount of insurance provided to particular employees. The use of evidence of insurability clearly allows an insurer to better understand the risk it is taking and therefore properly charge for the risk it accepts. However, if an insurer is unable to accurately measure the risk it is to accept, it will either reject the risk or charge a

higher premium than might otherwise be warranted, in view of the fact that
the insurance company must assume that any information that it was unable
to obtain because of the regulations would be negative and therefore
enlarge the risk that it would be exposed to. In other words, under the
proposed regulations, it is permissible for an insurer to charge a higher than
normal premium for insuring a proposed insured if its decision is based
solely on information from a health questionnaire. It would not appear
rational to force, by government regulation, an employer to purchase a
higher priced product, particularly when a portion of the increased cost
would be paid by the government through the increased deductions allowable to the employers.

Thirdly, the Service has concluded that the use of evidence of insurability other than a nonmedical health questionnaire facilitates individual
selection. While it is true that an insurer might accept a risk with adequate
evidence of insurability which it might otherwise have rejected on the basis
of a health questionnaire completed by the applicant, this does not result in
individual selection in that the individual, without providing additional
evidence of insurability to the insurer, would not have been eligible for the
coverage at all. The effect of the proposed regulations is to deny, in the
name of precluding individual selection, life insurance to employees who
might otherwise qualify for the insurance.

One result of the proposed regulations will be to deny to employees of
closely held businesses insurance coverage which would otherwise be available to similarly situated employees employed by a large concern, as group
underwriting principles only work when applied to large numbers of employees. A second result of the Treasury proposal will be that the cost of
providing employees group term life insurance will be increased for employers of small groups of employees. This will result in (1) decreasing the
amount of group term life insurance protection provided employees, which
is contrary to the legislative and prior administrative positions of encouraging such coverage, or (2) decreasing the revenues to the government in that
any increase in the cost of such coverage will be partially borne by the
federal government. Another effect will be to reduce the competitive
position of smaller companies in attracting executives.

The proposed regulations also add greater flexibility to the term "policy." Under the new regulations an employer may elect to treat two or more
policies as separate policies if neither of the policies provides a permanent
benefit and the premiums are properly allocated among the policies. In
addition, an employer may also elect to treat a policy which provides a
permanent benefit as a separate policy if the policy is (1) sold directly to the
employee, (2) the employee bears the full cost of the policy, (3) no employer-provided benefit to the employees is conditioned upon the employee's purchase of the policy, and (4) the insurer sells the policy on the
same terms and in substantial amounts to individuals who do not purchase
any other policy from the insured. In addition, the employer's participation

with respect to the sale of the policy is limited to selecting the insurer and the type of coverage, providing a list of its employees to the insurer, permitting the insurer to use the employer's premises for solicitation, and allowing the insurer to collect the premium for the policy through payroll deductions.

The proposed regulations also eliminate the requirements in Treas. Reg. §1.79-1(b)(ii) and (iv), that each employee be allowed to elect, decline, or drop the permanent benefit of a group permanent benefit without effecting his or her term benefit and that an employee's death benefit may not be reduced because of his or her election to decline or drop a permanent benefit plan.

Finally, the proposed regulations tighten the definition of covered employees for groups including fewer than 10 employees. Under the prior regulations, insurance was considered to be provided to an employee who elected not to receive the insurance. Under the proposed regulations, an employee is not considered to be provided insurance if the employee is required to contribute to the cost of benefits other than term insurance in order to qualify for the term benefit. However, an employee who elects not to participate in a group term life insurance plan, in which each employee is required to contribute to the cost of the term insurance benefit, is not taken into account in determining where the term insurance is provided to 10 or more employees.

Superimposing

For purposes of the under-10 rule, all life insurance provided under policies carried directly or indirectly by an employer must be taken into account in determining the number of employees to whom life insurance is provided.[61] This "aggregation theory," first adopted by the Service in Rev. Rul. 70-162,[62] is the foundation for the viability of superimposing, i.e., increasing, through the use of additional life insurance policies, the amount of insurance protection of certain employees under their employer's group insurance plan. Thus, an employer providing group term life insurance to 10 or more employees can increase coverage for fewer than 10 of those employees, i.e., superimpose additional coverage for those employees, without regard to the special under-10 requirements. Treating a superimposed group as a separate group would vitiate the antidiscrimination requirements set forth in the regulations, since each employer with fewer than 10 employees could then establish multiple group insurance plans. In this manner, an employer could provide large amounts of insurance for its higher-paid employees without providing a proportionate amount of insurance for its other employees. For example, a professional association em-

---

[61] Treas. Reg. §1.79-1(c)(1).

[62] 1970-1 Cum. Bull. 21.

ploying fewer than 10 employees could avoid the proportionate coverage requirements provided in Treas. Reg. §1.79-1(c)(ii) by having one group insurance plan for professional employees, providing, for example, group term life insurance in an amount equal to five times their annual compensation, and another group insurance plan for nonprofessional employees providing group term life insurance in an amount equal to one half their annual compensation. Furthermore, the tax consequences of a group insurance plan should not be governed by the fact that the insurance protection is provided under several individual policies or a single master policy, rather than a combination of a master policy and individual policies.[63]

One of the primary objectives in designing group life insurance plans for closely held corporations is to maximize the amount of life insurance provided the corporation's higher-paid employees, while minimizing the amount of life insurance provided its lower-paid employees. To achieve this objective, it is common practice for agents to superimpose large amounts of life insurance on the lives of higher-paid employees, who are frequently shareholder-employees, by amending an existing group plan. In such cases, one requirement, particularly likely to be a stumbling block, is that the amount of insurance provided to each employee be computed under a formula (based on such factors as age, years of service, compensation or position)[64] that precludes individual selection.

In the following hypothetical plan, which is not unlike the typical plan suggested by many insurance agents, it is assumed that at least 10 full-time employees are members of the group of employees at some time during the calendar year.[65]

	Existing Plan	New Plan
President	$50,000	$1,050,000
Other officers	20,000	20,000
Management personnel	12,500	12,500
Other employees	5,000	5,000

---

[63] The preamble to the regulations under Section 79 indicates that the Service is reconsidering its position in the current regulation project dealing with evidence of insurability in connection with insurance provided to a group of employees with fewer than 10 members for an entire calendar year. T.D. 7623 (Preamble), I.R.B. 1979-26,7.

[64] Caution should be used in utilizing an employee's position to determine the amount of insurance to be provided the employee. This is so even though position is listed in the regulations as a factor that precludes individual selection of the amount of insurance provided to an employee.

[65] It is assumed that at least 10 full-time employees are members of the group of employees at some time during the calendar year.

The plan is subject to Internal Revenue Service attack on several grounds. First, the Service could argue that the additional $1 million in life insurance protection provided the president and sole shareholder was based upon his or her status as a shareholder, rather than as an employee. If this argument were successful, the premium for the additional insurance coverage would not be deductible by the corporation and would be fully includible in the shareholder's gross income as a dividend from the corporation.

The Service could also assert that the amounts of insurance provided under the plan were not provided on the basis of factors which preclude individual selection; i.e., that the president was provided the additional insurance coverage only because he, as the owner of the business, would remain in that position as long as he owned the business. In *Towne* v. *Conn.*,[66] the court held that each element in a formula must apply to more than one person. Therefore, a position, such as president which applies to only one individual, should not be used in plan design. If successful, this argument, while possibly not affecting the employer's deduction for the premium paid for the term life insurance provided its employees, would result in the total premium paid by the employer with respect to each employee being includible in that employee's gross income. In other words, the employees would lose the tax benefit provided by Section 79.

The plan would also be vulnerable to attack if the total compensation paid the president, including the premium paid for the additional life insurance, were unreasonable in light of services actually performed for the corporation. Should such an attack be sustained, the premiums paid, or a portion thereof, would probably be characterized as a dividend and, while not deductible by the corporation, would be includible in the shareholder-employee's gross income.

The Service could also assert that it could ascertain no formula, as required by the regulations, under which the amounts of insurance were determined. This is, perhaps, the most likely argument to be made.[67]

To avoid the problems described above, group life insurance plans that include 10 or more full-time employees should be designed to use a formula approach, rather than coverage brackets, to determine the amount of insurance provided to each employee. This formula approach, not dissimilar to the formula approach used in benefit-oriented pension plans (e.g., unit benefit plans), could be tailored to the sponsoring employer's objectives. A sample plan is illustrated below.

Mr. Davis is the president and sole shareholder of Ace Manufacturing Company. The employees of Ace Manufacturing Company are as follows:

---

[66] 78 T.C. 791 (1982).

[67] See PLRs 7852013 and 8116010.

Officer	Years of Service	Annual Salary
President	7	$125,000
Vice President	5	20,000
Office Manager	8	15,625
Plant Manager	7	17,850
Secretary	1	10,500
Secretary	2	11,300
Secretary	3	12,500

All other personnel are commissioned salespeople and are excluded from the employee benefits available to nonsales personnel because their employee benefits are provided under a separate benefit package.[68]

In connection with his estate planning, Mr. Davis, the president, has found he needs an additional $1 million in life insurance protection. To provide this needed insurance at the lowest possible tax cost to Mr. Davis, his advisors have recommended he consider purchasing the insurance using the Section 79 concept.

Two alternatives are available in the design of Ace Manufacturing Company's plan. First, the plan could be amended to provide $1,050,000 on the president of the corporation without changing the coverage provided other employees under the master policy. However, as discussed above, this alternative would be subject to attack by the Internal Revenue Service. The second alternative would be to use the formula approach.

A formula can be designed, based on the employee census data set forth above, under which the amount of insurance each employee is entitled to is determined by multiplying his or her group insurance factor by his or her annual compensation. The group insurance factor is determined by multiplying the compensation and years of service factors from the chart (see Table 59–2). To avoid any reductions in coverage and the necessity of changing the master policy, each employee is assured a minimum of $5,000 in life insurance protection. For example, Mr. Davis has seven years of service (a factor of .7), compensation of $125,000 (a factor of 12) and is, therefore, entitled to $1,050,000 of insurance protection under the plan (12 × .7 × $125,000 = $1,050,000).

By utilizing the formula approach in determining the amounts of life insurance provided under the plan, the same amounts of life insurance have been provided under the Ace Manufacturing plan as were provided in the previously discussed plan. However, this coverage has been provided in a way that will minimize, if not eliminate, potential attacks by the Internal Revenue Service.

---

[68] Therefore, these salespeople are taken into account in determining the number of employees to whom life insurance is provided. Treas. Reg. §1.79-1(c)(1).

Table 59-2

Annual Salary	Salary Factor	Years of Service	Years of Service Factor
$150,000 or more	15	15 or more	1.5
Less than $150,000 but at least $140,000	14	Less than 15 but at least 14	1.4
Less than $140,000 but at least $130,000	13	Less than 14 but at least 13	1.3
Less than $130,000 but at least $120,000	12	Less than 13 but at least 12	1.2
Less than $120,000 but at least $110,000	11	Less than 12 but at least 11	1.1
Less than $110,000 but at least $100,000	10	Less than 11 but at least 10	1.0
Less than $100,000 but at least $90,000	9	Less than 10 but at least 9	.9
Less than $90,000 but at least $80,000	8	Less than 9 but at least 8	.8
Less than $80,000 but at least $70,000	7	Less than 8 but at least 7	.7
Less than $70,000 but at least $60,000	6	Less than 7 but at least 6	.6
Less than $60,000 but at least $50,000	5	Less than 6 but at least 5	.5
Less than $50,000 but at least $40,000	4	Less than 5 but at least 4	.4
Less than $40,000 but at least $30,000	3	Less than 4 but at least 3	.3
Less than $30,000 but at least $20,000	2	Less than 3 but at least 2	.2
Less than $20,000	1	Less than 2	.1

Treatment of Group Term Life Insurance when Combined with Other Benefits

Life insurance that otherwise qualifies as group term life insurance frequently is combined with other benefits. Whether term life insurance provided an employee under a policy containing a permanent benefit (such as a cash value) can qualify as group term life insurance has long been a matter of controversy. Because of past difficulties in separating the term and permanent benefits provided under such policies (known as "group permanent products"), the Internal Revenue Service, in drafting the existing regulations under Section 79, considered three alternatives: (1) that the term and permanent benefits be provided by different insurance carriers; (2) that such benefits be provided by separate policies, but not necessarily by different insurance carriers; (3) the elimination of all restrictions on group permanent policies so long as the insurance policy specified the amount includible in the employee's gross income as a result of permanent benefits provided thereunder.[69] The government felt that the first alternative was too burdensome and the last legally incorrect as it would leave totally within the insurance carrier's discretion the amount to be includible in an insured employee's gross income as a result of permanent benefits provided the employee under a group permanent product.[70] This left the second alternative, i.e., require that term and permanent benefits be provided under separate policies. In their deliberation of this alternative, the difficulty in defining the terms "permanent benefits" and "policy" became apparent and the separateness requirement was eliminated.

The regulations define a permanent benefit as an economic value extending beyond one policy year, such as paid-up insurance or cash value, provided under a life insurance policy.[71] Specifically excluded from the definition are (1) the right to convert or continue insurance coverage following the termination of the group term life insurance,[72] (2) a provision that provides no economic benefit other than current life insurance to the employee[73] or (3) a provision under which life insurance is provided at a level premium for a period not to exceed five years.[74]

The definition of permanent benefit together with §1.79-1(b) of the regulations, was meant to clarify the confusion surrounding the distinction under prior regulations between permanent life insurance policies and policies that combine both a term and permanent feature. In addition, the specific exclusions from the definition of permanent benefit apparently

---

[69] T.D. 7623 (Preamble). I.R.B. 1979-26,7.
[70] Ibid.
[71] Treas. Reg. §1.79-0.
[72] Ibid.
[73] Ibid.
[74] Ibid.

reverse the previous position of the Internal Revenue Service with respect to five-year renewable and convertible policies. The prior position of the IRS, as reflected in both private and published rulings, was that five-year renewable and convertible policies could not qualify as group term life insurance if the insured employee had a right to continue the coverage under the policy upon termination of his membership in the group plan.[75]

The term *policy* includes two or more obligations of an insurer or its affiliates that are sold in conjunction.[76] The term *group term life insurance,* as defined in prior regulations, denied favorable tax treatment to "the life insurance protection in a policy of permanent insurance. . . ,"[77] but allowed favorable tax treatment to the term portion of a properly allocated policy containing both term and permanent benefits.[78] Confusion regarding "proper allocation" existed with respect to both single and dual policy group permanent products. To provide uniform administration of the tax laws, the government has treated single and dual policy group permanent products alike if the elements of the dual policy are "sold in conjunction."[79] The term *sold in conjunction* encompasses a broad range of policies into the term *policy.* For example, an annually renewable term policy and a flexible premium annuity contract would be a policy for purposes of Section 79 if they were "sold in conjunction."

Obligations offered or available to a group of employees because of their employment relationship are "sold in conjunction," irrespective of whether the premium for each of the obligations is actuarially sufficient or whether the obligations are contained in one or several separate documents, each of which was separately filed and approved by the appropriate state insurance departments.[80] Therefore, the independence of one obligation from another obligation is not taken into account in determining if the obligations are sold in conjunction, even in those instances where one obligation is only available to those employees who decline the other.[81]

Life insurance provided an employee under a policy that provides permanent benefits may qualify for favorable treatment under Section 79 if (1) the policy or the employer designates in writing the portion of the death benefit that is group term life insurance;[82] (2) the part of the death benefit that is designated as group term life insurance for any policy year is not less than the difference between the total death benefit provided under the policy and the employee's deemed death benefit at the end of the policy year

---

[75] Rev. Rul. 75-91, 1975-1 CB 39.

[76] Treas. Reg. §1.79-0.

[77] Treas. Reg. §1.79-1(b)(1)(i) (prior regulations).

[78] Treas. Reg. §1.79-1(b)(1)(ii) (prior regulations).

[79] Treas. Reg. §1.79-0.

[80] Ibid.

[81] Ibid.

[82] Treas. Reg. §1.79-1(b)(1)(i).

determined under Treas. Reg. §1.79-1(d)(3);[83] (3) an employee may elect to decline or drop the permanent benefit;[84] and (4) the death benefit designated as group term life insurance is not reduced because of the employee's election to decline or drop the permanent benefit.[85]

The requirement discussed at (1) above merely requires that death benefits for the term and permanent portion of the policy be separately stated; that is, the benefits under the policy must be allocated.[86] By setting forth a minimum death benefit for the term portion of the policy,[87] and establishing a deemed death benefit for the permanent portion of the policy, the regulations preclude one potential manipulation of the formula. Without such requirement, the term and permanent cost of a particular product could be altered by varying the amount of the death benefit allocable to the term and permanent portions of the policy.

The requirements that an employee be permitted to decline or drop the permanent benefit under the policy[88] without affecting the amount of term insurance provided the employee[89] will necessitate careful product design by companies who market single-policy group permanent products in order to minimize the potential for adverse selection against the company. The continuation of a portion of a whole life or other permanent policy without continuing the entire policy would be impossible under the insurance laws of many states. The regulations, however, do not require that the employee be able to continue the actual coverage under the policy, but only the amount of group term life insurance provided under the policy.[90] From informal discussions with government personnel, the authors understand that it is not even intended that the premium for the term insurance remain the same.

The primary issue left unresolved by Treas. Reg. §1.79-1(b)(1), discussed above, is whether all employees must be offered permanent benefits if any employee is offered such coverage. Prior regulations initially contained such a requirement.[91] A subsequent amendment,[92] however, merely required that all employees in the same class with an employee offered permanent benefits also be offered such benefits. The current regulations do not speak directly to the issue, although all of the examples in Treas. Reg. §1.79-1(b)(2) state that "each employee" has an option with respect to

---

[83] Treas. Reg. §1.79-1(b)(1)(ii).
[84] Treas. Reg. §1.79-1(b)(1)(iii).
[85] Treas. Reg. §1.79-1(b)(1)(iv).
[86] Treas. Reg. §1.79-1(b)(1)(i).
[87] Treas. Reg. §1.79-1(b)(1)(ii).
[88] Treas. Reg. §1.79-1(b)(1)(iii).
[89] Treas. Reg. §1.79-1(b)(1)(iv).
[90] Ibid.
[91] Treas. Reg. §1.79-1(b)(1)(ii), T.D. 6888, 1966-2 CB 23.
[92] Treas. Reg. §1.79-1(b)(1)(ii), T.D. 7132, 1971-2 CB 89.

permanent benefits. These references are, however, to employees covered under a policy and not to insurance provided by separate carriers, as would be the case where additional coverage insured by another carrier is added to existing coverage.

Determining the "Cost" of Group Term Life Insurance

Once it has been determined that life insurance provided by a policy qualifies, in whole or in part, as group term life, determining the cost of such group term life insurance becomes necessary. The cost of it that must be included in the employee's gross income is determined by computing the cost of the portion of such insurance "to be taken into account" for each "period of coverage," aggregating such costs and reducing the amount so determined by the amount paid by the employee toward the purchase of such insurance.[93] A "period of coverage" is any "calendar month period, or part thereof, during the employee's taxable year during which the employee is provided group term life insurance on his or her life to which . . . Section 79(a) applies."[94]

For each "period of coverage" the portion of the group term life insurance "to be taken into account" is the sum of the proceeds payable upon the employee's death under each group term life insurance policy on his or her life reduced by the sum of (1) $50,000 of such insurance and (2) the amount of the proceeds payable under each group term life insurance policy on his or her life that qualifies for one of the exceptions contained in Section 79(b).[95] Where the proceeds payable under a group term life insurance policy vary during a period of coverage, the proceeds payable during such period are, for purposes of Section 79, considered to be the average of the amount payable under the policy at the beginning and at the end of such period.[96] In the event the policy proceeds are payable in other than a lump sum, and a lump-sum payment is not an alternative method of payment, the proceeds are considered to be equal to the present value of the right to receive the payments under the policy.[97] For each period of coverage such present value is determined as if the first and last day of the period of coverage is the date of the employee's death.[98] The regulations provide special rules for the determination of such present value.[99]

Once the portion of the group term life insurance on the employee's life to be taken into account for each period of coverage has been determined,

---

[93] Treas. Reg. §1.79-3(a).
[94] Treas. Reg. §1.79-3(c).
[95] Treas. Reg. §1.79-3(b)(1).
[96] Treas. Reg. §1.79-3(b)(2).
[97] Treas. Reg. §1.79-3(c)(3)(i).
[98] Ibid.
[99] Treas. Reg. §1.79-3(b)(3)(ii)–(iv).

the cost of such coverage is determined by multiplying the number of thousands of dollars of such coverage, rounded to the nearest tenth, by the appropriate uniform premium contained in Table I in the regulations.[100] Then, as stated above, the cost of such insurance for each period of coverage is aggregated and reduced by the amounts, if any, paid by the employee for the purchase of such insurance. The resulting amount is includible in the employee's gross income and reportable by the employer on Form W-2 as other compensation.[101]

In determining the amount paid by an employee toward the purchase of group term life insurance, any amounts paid by the employee for such insurance which qualifies for one of the exceptions contained in Section 79(b) or for group term life insurance protection to be provided during a subsequent taxable year (other than amounts applicable to compensation periods which may extend to such taxable year) are not taken into account.[102] Special rules in the regulations determine the amount paid by an employee toward the purchase of group term life insurance provided under an insurance policy or policies providing benefits in addition to group term life insurance, where the amounts paid by the employee for group term life insurance cannot be determined from the insurance policy or plan under which the benefits are provided.[103]

Determining the Amount Includible in Income by Employees Receiving Permanent Benefits

If a policy provides only group term life insurance coverage, the amount includible in an employee's gross income can be determined solely by reference to the preceding section. If, however, the policy also provides a permanent benefit, the cost of the permanent benefit must also be determined.

An employee insured under a policy providing permanent benefits, in addition to group term life insurance benefits qualifying for favorable tax treatment under Section 79, must include in his gross income the cost of such permanent benefits provided to him, reduced by the amount, if any, he paid for the permanent benefits.[104] The cost of permanent benefits provided an employee must be no less than: the sum of (1) the product of the net single premium for $1 of paid-up whole life insurance at the employee's attained age at the beginning of the policy year multiplied by the increase in

---

[100] Treas. Reg. §1.79-3(d). Proposed revisions to Table 1 were published in the Federal Register on July 7, 1983.

[101] Ann. 74-4, I.R.B. 1974-29, 23, and Rev. Proc. 75-19, I.R.B. 1975-14, 24.

[102] Treas. Reg. §1.79-3(e)(2).

[103] Treas. Reg. §1.79-3(e)(3).

[104] Treas. Reg. §1.79-1(d)(1).

the deemed death benefit during the policy year[105] plus (2) that portion of the dividends actually or constructively received by the employee which are includible in the employee's gross income.[106] The net single premium for one dollar of paid-up whole life insurance is determined by using the 1958 Commissioner's Standard Ordinary Mortality Table and an interest factor of 4 percent.[107] The deemed death benefit at the end of a policy year is determined by dividing (1) the greater of the cash value of the policy at the end of the policy year, or the net level premium reserve at the end of the policy year for all permanent benefits provided the employee under the policy; by (2) the net single premium for $1 of paid-up whole life insurance at the employee's age at the end of the policy year.[108] Both the net level premium reserve and the net single premium discussed above are determined by using the 1958 CSO Mortality Table and a 4 percent interest factor.[109]

Expressed actuarially, the cost of permanent benefits provided under a policy which otherwise meets the requirements of Treas. Reg. §1.79-1 is as follows:

$$\text{Cost} = X\ (DDB_2 - DDB_1)$$

where:

X is the net single premium for $1 of paid-up whole life insurance at the employee's age at the beginning of the policy year determined by using the 1958 CSO Mortality Table and a 4 percent interest assumption.

DDB$_1$ is the employee's deemed death benefit at the end of the preceding policy year,[110] and

DDB$_2$ is employee's deemed death benefit at the end of the current policy year, or

$$\text{Cost} = X \left(\frac{R_2}{Y_2} - \frac{R_1}{Y_1} \right)$$

where:

X is the net single premium for $1 of paid-up whole life insurance at the employee's attained age at the beginning of the policy year.

R_1 is the greater of the cash value of the policy at the end of the immediately preceding policy year or the net level premium reserve at the end of the immediately preceding policy year of all permanent benefits provided the employee under the policy.

R_2 is the same as R_1 above but at the end of the current policy year.

---

[105] Treas. Reg. §1.79-1(d)(2).
[106] Treas. Reg. §1.79-1(d)(5).
[107] Treas. Reg. §1.79-1(d)(4).
[108] Treas. Reg. §1.79-1(d)(3).
[109] Treas. Reg. §1.79-1(d)(4).
[110] Treas. Reg. §1.79-1(d)(2).

Y_1 is the net single premium for \$1 of paid-up whole life insurance at the employee's age at the end of the immediately preceding policy year, and

Y_2 is the same as Y_1 above but at the end of the current policy year.[111]

In policy years with no cash value, the permanent portion of the policy will have no actual death benefit but will have a deemed death benefit and, therefore, a premium.

In addition to the amounts determined above, an employee insured under a participating group permanent policy qualifying for favorable taxation under Section 79 may have all or a portion of the dividends paid or made available to him under the policy includible in his gross income.[112] If the employee does not contribute to the cost of the permanent benefits provided him under the policy, all dividends provided him under the policy are includible in his gross income.[113] Where an employee insured under a qualifying group permanent product contributes a portion of the cost of permanent benefits provided him under the policy only a portion of the dividends paid to him, actually or constructively, is includible in his gross income.[114] The portion of the dividends includible in his gross income is determined under the following formula:

$$I = (D + C) - (PI + DI + AP)$$

where:

I is the amount of the dividend includible in the employee's gross income for the current year.

D is the sum of all dividends received, actually or constructively, under the policy by the employee during the current and all prior taxable years of the employee.

C is the total cost of all permanent benefits provided under the policy (whether to the employee or the employer) for the current and all prior taxable years of the employee. The cost of such benefits is to be determined under the formula discussed above and set forth in §1.79-1(d)(2) and (3) of the Regulations.

PI is the sum of the cost of the permanent benefits provided the employee under the policy which were included in the employee's gross income under Treas. Reg. §1.79-1(d)(1) for the current and all preceding taxable years of the employee.

DI is the sum of the dividends included in the employee's gross income under Treas. Reg. §1.79-1(d)(5) for all preceding taxable years of the employee; and

---

[111] Treas. Reg. §1.79-1(d)(2) and (3).

[112] Treas. Reg. §1.79-1(d)(5).

[113] Ibid.

[114] Ibid.

AP is the sum of the amounts paid (during the current and all preceding taxable years) by the employee for permanent benefits provided him under the policy.[115]

Although the regulations recognize that an insured employee may contribute toward the purchase of the term or permanent benefits, or both, provided under the policy,[116] the regulations do not set forth a means of allocating employee contributions between term and permanent benefits if no allocation method is set forth in the policy or related documents. As the shifting of employee contributions between the elements of a qualifying group permanent product would not yield an income tax advantage to the employee, the absence of a method of allocation is insignificant.

If, as will usually be the case, the policy year begins in one taxable year of the employee and ends in another, the cost of permanent benefits provided the employee will be allocated first to the taxable year of the employee in which the policy year begins.[117] This is done by multiplying the cost of permanent benefits for the policy year by the fraction of the premium for that policy year that is paid on or before the last day of the employee's taxable year. The remaining cost of permanent benefits is allocated to the taxable year of the employee in which the policy year ends. The cost of permanent benefits for any taxable year of the employee will equal the sum of the costs of permanent benefits allocated to that year.[118]

The computations of the amounts to be includible in an employee's gross income may be illustrated by the following example from the regulations:[119]

> An employer provides insurance to employee A under a policy that meets the requirements of [the regulations under Section 79]. Under the policy, A, who is 47 years old, received $70,000 of group term life insurance and elects to receive a permanent benefit under the policy. A pays $2 for each $1,000 of group term life insurance through payroll deductions and the employer pays the remainder of the premium for the group term life insurance. The employer also pays one half of the premium specified in the policy for the permanent benefit. A pays the other one half of the premium for the permanent benefit through payroll deductions. The policy specifies that the annual premium paid for the permanent benefit is $300. However, the amount of premium allocated to the permanent benefit by the formula in paragraph (d)(2) of this section is $350. A is a calendar year taxpayer; the policy year begins on January 1. In 1980, $200 is includible in A's income because of insurance provided by the employer. This amount is computed as follows:

---

[115] Ibid.

[116] Treas. Reg. §1.79-1(d)(1).

[117] Treas. Reg. §1.79-1(d)(5).

[118] Ibid.

[119] Treas. Reg. §1.79-1(d)(7). Proposed amendments to this example were published in the Federal Register on July 7, 1983, to reflect the proposed changes in the Table 1 notes.

(1)	Cost of permanent benefits	$350
(2)	Amounts considered paid by A for permanent benefits (1/2 of $300)	150
(3)	Line (1) minus line (2)	$200
(4)	Cost of $70,000 of group term life insurance under Table I of §1.79-3	$336
(5)	Cost of $50,000 of group term life insurance under Table I of §1.79-3	240
(6)	Cost of group term life insurance in excess of $50,000 (line (4) minus line (5))	96
(7)	Amount considered paid by A for group term life insurance (70 × $2)	140
(8)	Line (6) minus line (7) (but not less than 0)	0
(9)	Amount includible in income (line (3) plus line (8))	$200

Effect of State Issue Limits

Section 79 does not apply to "life insurance in excess of the limits under applicable state law on the amount of life insurance that can be provided to an employee under a single policy of group term life insurance."[120] Of course, in states that do not place a ceiling on the amount of term insurance that can be provided to an employee, this limitation will not be significant. Where state issue limits exist, however, the employee will be taxed each year on the premium, not the Table I cost, attributable to life insurance in excess of the applicable limit. It should be noted that there may be serious income-tax consequences at retirement to an employee entitled to post-retirement coverage under a Retired Lives Reserve plan if such coverage exceeds the applicable state issue limit. This is because the excess would not be group term life insurance so that, as to such excess, the argument, made infra,[121] that Section 79(b) should override Sections 83 and 61 could not be made.

Effective Dates and Transitional Rules

The current regulations under Section 79 were issued on May 4, 1979, and, generally, apply to insurance provided in employee taxable years beginning on or after January 1, 1977.[122] However, prior regulations continue to apply to insurance provided in employee taxable years beginning before January 1, 1978, for group term life insurance plans in effect on November 4, 1976, if the insurer was providing, or was contractually bound to provide, insurance under the plan.[123] This limited grandfathering is only

---

[120] Treas. Reg. §1.79-1(e).
[121] See text at notes 21–24 in Chapter 7.
[122] Treas. Reg. §1.79-1(g).
[123] Treas. Reg. §1.79-1(g).

available for insurance that could have been provided under the terms of the plan as in effect on November 4, 1976.[124] Thus, grandfathering would not apply to any additional insurance made available to an employee as a result of post-November 4, 1976, plan amendments. However, additional coverage available to an employee due, for example, to a change in the employee's status under the terms of a grandfathered plan would qualify for grandfathering.[125]

Under another grandfathering provision, certain plans providing a permanent benefit have additional time to incorporate certain policy modifications mandated by the regulations. Under Treas. Reg. §1.79-1(b)(1)(iii) employees must have the right to decline or drop the permanent benefit. Under Treas. Reg. §1.79-1(b)(1)(iv), group term life insurance provided an employee cannot be reduced as a result of the employee's declining or dropping the permanent benefit. The regulations provide that these requirements do not apply to employee taxable years beginning before January 1, 1983, for insurance that could have been provided an employee under a plan meeting the requirements for grandfathering discussed in the preceding paragraph.[126] Furthermore, the third, fourth, and fifth sentences of the definition of "group of employees" are not effective for taxable years beginning before January 1, 1979.[127]

Other Benefits

Dependent Life Coverage. Several life insurance companies have now started to market dependent life coverage, in substantial amounts, under employer-sponsored group term life insurance plans. While the tax consequences to the employer are relatively simple, those to the employee are somewhat complex. An employer can deduct the cost of dependent life coverage under Section 162(a) of the code, so long as such coverage is provided an employee as compensation for services actually rendered to the employer and the total compensation paid the employee is reasonable in light of the services performed by him. The tax treatment on the employee's side, however, is a bit more involved.

Except for those items specifically excluded from gross income, an

---

[124] Treas. Reg. §1.79-1(g)(i).

[125] Ibid.

[126] Treas. Reg. §1.79-1(g)(2).

[127] Treas. Reg. §1.79-1(g)(3). The sentences referred to read as follows:

Ordinarily the purchase of something other than group term life insurance is not a factor related to employment. For example, if an employer provides credit life insurance to all employees who purchase automobiles, these employees are not a "group of employees" because membership is not determined solely on the basis of age, marital status, or factors related to employment. On the other hand, participation in an employer's pension, profit-sharing, or accident and health plan is considered a factor related to employment even if employees are required to contribute to the cost of the plan.

employee must include in gross income all income, from whatever source derived.[128] The special includibility provision of Section 79 for group term life insurance provided an employee by the employer is inapplicable to dependent life coverage because such coverage is not on the life of an employee.[129] The regulations under Section 61 provide that the cost (determined under Treas. Reg. §1.79-3(d)(2)) of group term life insurance on the life of an employee's spouse and/or children, provided that an employee by the employer is includible in the gross income of the employee.[130] However, such cost is not required to be included in the employee's gross income if the amount of such insurance, payable upon the death of the spouse or child, does not exceed $2,000.[131] In other words, the regulations under Section 61 provide that the amount to be included in an employee's gross income as the result of the employer providing group term life insurance on the life of the spouse and/or children, is to be computed on the basis of the Table I values reflected in the regulations under Section 79 and not the premium paid by the employer for such coverage. There is, however, no exclusion, such as the $50,000 exclusion available under Section 79, for dependent life coverage. In the event such coverage does not exceed $2,000 no amounts are includible in the employee's gross income.[132] However, in those instances where coverage for dependents exceeds $2,000, the economic value, i.e., "term cost" thereof, for the entire amount of insurance provided is includible in the employee's gross income. The inclusion of the "term cost" rather than the premium paid by the employer can result in not insubstantial tax savings to employees with dependents who cannot purchase life insurance at standard rates due to health impairments, etc. Assume, for example, an employer provides group term life insurance coverage in the amount of $2,000 for an employee's spouse, whose attained age is 43. Pursuant to Treas. Reg. §1.61-2(d)(2)(ii)(b), no amount is includible in the employee's gross income. However, if the employer were to provide $10,000 of such coverage, the employee would include in gross income for the year in question the Table I cost of $10,000 (not $8,000) of group term life insurance coverage for the spouse for that year (i.e., $27.60).

The above regulations under Section 61 are not as straightforward as they might seem, however, because they refer to "group term life insurance" on the life of an employee's spouse or children without defining the term. The only definition of group term life insurance is contained in the regulations under Section 79, which state that life insurance, to qualify as group term life insurance, must provide a general death benefit excludible

---

[128] I.R.C. §61(a). *N.W.D. Investment Co.* v. *Conn.* 1982 T.C.R. n. 1246 (1982).
[129] Treas. Reg. §1.79-3(f)(2).
[130] Treas. Reg. §1.61-2(d)(2)(ii)(b).
[131] Ibid.
[132] Ibid.

from gross income under Internal Revenue Code Section 101(a) and must be provided to a group of employees under a policy carried directly or indirectly by an employer in amounts computed under a formula which precludes individual selection.[133] Therefore, in order for dependent coverage to qualify as "group term life insurance," it would appear that the employees eligible for such coverage must be members of a group of employees and that the amounts of such coverage must be computed under a formula which precludes individual selection. Contrary to many sales approaches now in use, simply providing large amounts of term life insurance on the life or lives of a shareholder-employee's spouse and/or children will not qualify such insurance as group term life insurance for purposes of Section 61(a). If an employee's eligibility for dependent life coverage and the amount thereof are not determined in accordance with the requirements of Section 79, the entire premium paid for such coverage, rather than the term cost thereof, must be included in the employee's gross income.

There is an additional problem with dependent life coverage provided employees under an employer's plan which insures fewer than 10 employees for an entire calendar year. This is that the coverage provided such spouses and/or dependents would appear subject to the same restrictions as employee coverage in such plans. Although the regulations are not clear on this point, the most prudent course to follow in the under-10 area is to provide dependent life coverage for all employees if such coverage is provided for any employee and to provide such coverage on the basis of a uniform percentage of the employee's compensation, or a fractional share of the coverage provided the respective employees under coverage brackets which meet the parameters set forth in the regulations.[134]

Accidental Death Benefits. It is not uncommon for employers to provide accident insurance on the lives of their employees. Such coverage may be provided in conjunction with life and/or health insurance or as a separate benefit, and may provide lifetime coverage, death benefits, or both.

Generally, the premiums paid by an employer for insurance on the life of an employee are includible in the employee's gross income where the proceeds of such insurance are payable to the beneficiary of such employee.[135] Exceptions to this general rule can be found in the provisions applicable to the incidental life insurance protection provided under a qualified plan and in those applicable to group term life insurance.[136] The exception for qualified plans is obviously not applicable to accidental death benefits. Furthermore, since Section 79 applies only to life insurance providing general death benefits, that section does not apply to accidental

---

[133] Treas. Reg. §1.79-1(a).
[134] Treas. Reg. §1.79-1(c).
[135] I.R.C. §61(a) and Treas. Reg. §1.61-2(d)(2)(ii)(a).
[136] I.R.C. §79(a) and Treas. Reg. §1.79-2(d).

death insurance (including amounts payable under a double indemnity clause or rider).[137] Therefore, the portion of employer paid premiums under a group term life insurance plan that are allocable to accidental death benefits will not be excludible from an employee's gross income under Section 79. The Service has also taken the position that premiums allocable to accidental death insurance are not excludible from an employee's gross income under Section 106.[138]

Section 106 provides that an employee's gross income does not include contributions by an employer to an accident or health plan for compensation (through insurance or otherwise) to its employees for personal injuries or sickness. When combined with the Section 162(a) deduction generally available to an employer for such premium payments, the effect of these two provisions is to allow an exclusion from the employee's gross income for such premiums on the one hand, and a corresponding employer deduction on the other. If correct, the Service's position would continue to allow the employer to deduct premiums allocable to accidental death insurance, whether provided under a separate insurance policy or as a rider to a group insurance policy, while disallowing the exclusion of such premiums from the gross income of the employee. However, the correctness of this position is in doubt.

Treas. Reg. Section 1.106-1 provides, in part, that an employer may contribute to an accident or health plan by paying the premium on a policy of accident or health insurance. The issue, then, which the Service resolved in the negative, is whether accidental death benefits are within the scope of the term *accident* or *health insurance* for purposes of Section 106. In arriving at the conclusion that accidental death insurance is not accident or health insurance within the meaning of Section 106, the Service appears to have overlooked the cross-reference regulations under Section 79. As stated, Section 79 does not apply to life insurance that provides a death benefit other than a general death benefit. Examples of insurance that provide a death benefit other than a general death benefit are travel insurance, accident insurance, and health insurance. The death benefits provided under these types of policies arise from the insurer's assumption of specifically limited risks, and from the happening of specifically delineated contingencies. The regulations under Section 79 state clearly that reference should be made to Section 106 and the regulations thereunder ". . . for the rules relating to certain insurance that does not provide general death benefits, such as travel insurance or accident and health insurance (including amounts payable under a double indemnity clause or rider)."[139] Although this reference could be interpreted as referring to Section 106 for rules relating to the treatment of insurance which provides no death bene-

---

[137] Treas. Reg. §1.79-1(a)(1).

[138] Letter Rulings 8025100R and 8038207.

[139] Treas. Reg. §1.79-1(f)(3).

fit, as opposed to a limited or specific type of death benefit, this interpretation would appear to be incorrect. In referring to accident and health insurance, the regulations parenthetically include amounts payable under a double indemnity clause or rider. In practice, double indemnity benefits are purchased to increase the amount of the death benefit which would otherwise be payable upon the death of the insured from specified causes. In view of the rarity of double indemnity provisions relating to other occurrences than death, it is unlikely that the parenthetical reference would have been included in the regulations if the term *accident* and *health insurance* had been meant to exclude death benefit provisions. Moreover, travel insurance, a type of limited coverage accident insurance, most typically includes, and is most typically purchased, for the death benefits payable thereunder.

The rationale employed by the Service in excluding accidental death insurance from Section 106 was one of comparison to Section 105. It was determined on unstated authority that the term *accident* or *health plan* has the same meaning for purposes of Sections 105 and 106, and that accidental death benefits are not considered benefits received by employees through an accident or health plan within the meaning of Section 105. Section 105 however, which generally requires an employee to include in his gross income amounts received under an accident or health plan to the extent attributable to employer contributions, refers only indirectly to accidental death benefits. The reference thereto is contained in the regulations pertaining to Section 105(c), which presents an exception to the Section 105 general rule of inclusion, and states only that the Section 105(c) exception will not apply to amounts paid by reason of the death of the employee. To the extent that such benefits are excluded from gross income under the provisions of Section 101,[140] it is not necessary that these amounts also be excludible from the gross income of an employee under Section 105. Moreover, the legislative history of Section 106 does not exclude accidental death insurance from the scope of Section 106, nor do the legislative histories of Section 105 and Section 106 equate the provisions of those sections for definitional purposes. Instead, the legislative history of Section 106 has revealed ". . . that the intent of Congress was to interpret as liberally as possible the provisions relating to the exclusion from gross income of employer contributions."[141]

The regulations under Section 101 lend further support to the position that accidental death benefits should be included within the meaning of the term *accident* or *health insurance* for the purposes of Section 106. Such regulations provide that "[d]eath benefit payments having the characteristics of life insurance proceeds payable by reason of death under contracts such as . . . *accident and health insurance contracts*, are covered by this

---

[140] Treas. Reg. §1.101-1(a)(1).
[141] Letter Ruling 7922082.

provision."[142] The existence and use of this language indicates the recognition of the common understanding that accident or health insurance contracts include death benefit provisions.

Therefore, although the Service has, through private letter rulings, taken a position to the contrary, an employee should be able to exclude from his gross income the full amount of the premium paid by his employer for accidental death benefit riders, in addition to premiums applicable to any other accident insurance provided him by his employer through a plan of accident or health insurance.

Generally, the premium paid or incurred by an employer for accident insurance on the lives of its employees will be deductible under Section 162(a) as an ordinary and necessary business expense, whether providing accidental death benefits or not. However, Section 264(a) provides that no deduction shall be allowed for premiums paid on any life insurance contract insuring the life of any officer, employee, or other person financially interested in any trade or business carried on by the taxpayer when the taxpayer is, directly or indirectly, a beneficiary under the policy. Therefore, in the event the employer is the beneficiary under an accidental death benefit provision, any premium paid by it for such insurance protection is nondeductible.

TAX BENEFITS TO THE EMPLOYER

The deductibility of premiums paid by an employer for group insurance on the lives of its employees is governed primarily by Section 162(a)(1). That Section allows a deduction for all ordinary and necessary business expenses paid or incurred during a taxable year in carrying on a trade or business, including a reasonable allowance for salaries and other compensation for personal services actually rendered.[143]

The regulations under Section 162 provide that:

[T]he test of deductibility in the case of compensation payments is whether they are reasonable and are in fact payments purely for services.[144]

This two-part test—the amount test (whether the amount paid is reasonable in view of the services actually performed) and the purpose test (whether the payments were both intended and made as compensation for services rendered)—presents questions of fact, not law, to be determined by the facts and circumstances in each particular case.

---

[142] Treas. Reg. §1.101-1(a)(1) (emphasis added).

[143] The deduction provided by Section 162(a)(1) is available to all employers, including proprietorships, partnerships, and corporations. However, as a proprietor is not his or her own employer, and few partners are employees of the partnerships of which they are members, the exclusion provided by Section 79 is unavailable to them.

[144] Treas. Reg. §1.162-7(a).

Factors likely to be considered in determining the reasonableness of an employee's compensation are: (1) the employee's personal qualifications, such as intelligence, education, experience, and judgment, as well as the time devoted to the performance of duties; (2) the nature and scope of the employee's duties and responsibilities; (3) the employee's salary history; (4) the compensation currently being paid for comparable services by similarly situated employers within the employer's industry; (5) the employer's compensation policy toward other employees, particularly its nonshareholders; (6) the dividend history of the employer and the relationship of compensation to dividends paid by the employer; (7) the size and complexity of the employer's business; (8) general economic conditions as well as the economic conditions in the employer's industry; (9) the relationship of compensation to the gross and net income of the employer; and (10) the timing and formality of the employer's action with respect to payment of the compensation.[145]

Even if the two-part test of the regulations is met, and a deduction for premium payments would be allowable under Section 162(a)(1), Section 264(a) may preclude such deduction.

That Section provides that no deduction shall be allowed for premiums paid on an insurance policy or policies insuring the life of an officer, employee, or other person financially interested in any trade or business carried on by the employer when such employer is, directly or indirectly, a beneficiary under such policy or policies.

There is a common marketing practice, used by some life insurance agents in connection with stock redemption agreements, that illustrates how Section 264(a) may cause an employer's deduction for premium payments for group insurance on the lives of its employees to be disallowed. Since premiums paid or incurred by a corporation to fund its obligations under a stock redemption agreement are nondeductible pursuant to Section 264(a), some insurance agents suggest that the corporation and its shareholder-employees agree to a reduction in the redemption price. This reduction is then accompanied by a like increase in the group life insurance protection offered the shareholder-employees by the corporation. The anticipated result of this marketing approach is to provide, with deductible dollars, the members of each shareholder-employee's family with the same amount of money they would have received through the stock-redemption arrangement that the corporation had been providing with nondeductible dollars. Unfortunately, this desired result is unattainable because the corporation remains the indirect beneficiary of the insurance contract by virtue of the reduction in the redemption price and, therefore, the premium for the increase in group life insurance is nondeductible under Section 264(a).

---

[145] *Holden* and *Suwalsky*, T.M. 202-3rd, p. A-7 et. seq., Reasonable Compensation.

Beneficiary

Generally, life insurance proceeds, whether paid under a personally owned policy, a group life policy, a split-dollar policy, or any other form of policy, are specifically excluded from the beneficiary's gross income by Section 101(a)(1). This exclusion applies whether payment is made directly or in trust, or whether it is made to the insured's estate or to any beneficiary.[146] As discussed below, the exclusion is not applicable to (1) the proceeds of an insurance policy that has been transferred for a valuable consideration; (2) proceeds includible in the gross income of a spouse under Section 71 of the code (relating to alimony and separate maintenance payments) or Section 682 of the code (relating to income of an estate or trust in case of a divorce); or (3) interest paid the beneficiary by the insurer.

Transfer for Value

In the case of a policy, or any interest therein, which has been transferred for a valuable consideration, the exclusion from gross income of life insurance proceeds payable by reason of the insured's death is limited to the sum of (1) the value of the consideration paid for such transfer, and (2) the premiums and other amounts subsequently paid by the transferee.[147]

A transfer for a valuable consideration is any absolute transfer, by assignment or otherwise, of a right to receive all or a portion of the proceeds of a life insurance policy in exchange for something of value.[148] However, merely pledging a policy as security is not a transfer for value and Section 101(a) does not exclude from the pledgee's gross income any proceeds received by the pledgee.[149]

There are two exceptions to the application of the transfer for value provision: (1) where the transferee's basis is determinable, in whole or in part, by reference to the transferor's basis in the policy or interest (except in certain cases where a series of transfers is involved); and (2) where the transfer is made to the insured, a partner of the insured, or a partnership in which the insured is a partner or a corporation in which the insured is an officer or shareholder.[150]

If the policy has been the subject of a series of transfers, the last of which was for a valuable consideration, the transfer for value provision generally applies to limit the proceeds excludible from the gross income of the final transferee.[151] If, however, the final transferee is the insured, a partner of the insured, a partnership in which the insured is a partner, or a corporation in which the insured is an officer or shareholder, the general rule of Section

---

[146] Treas. Reg. §1.101-1(a)(1).

[147] I.R.C. §101(a)(2).

[148] Treas. Reg. §1.101-1(b)(4).

[149] Ibid.

[150] I.R.C. §101(a)(2).

[151] Treas. Reg. §1.101-1(b)(3).

101(a)(1) applies.[152] On the other hand, if the final transferee's basis in the policy is determined in whole or in part by reference to his transferor's basis therein, the amount excludible from the final transferee's gross income is limited (unless the final transferee is a person described in the preceding sentence so that the proceeds are entirely tax-free) to the sum of (1) the amount that would have been excludible from gross income by his transferor if the transfer had not taken place, and (2) any premiums and other amounts paid by the final transferee subsequent to the transfer.[153]

Interest Payments and Deferred Payments of Insurance Proceeds

Interest Payments.   Pursuant to Section 101(c), if insurance proceeds excluded from gross income by Section 101(a) are "held under an agreement to pay interest thereon," the interest payments will be included in the gross income of the recipient.[154] Proceeds are deemed to be "held under an agreement to pay interest thereon" if held without substantial diminution during the period such payments are made.[155] Section 101(c) applies irrespective of who made the election to have the proceeds so held and whether or not an interest rate was specified in the agreement.[156]

Deferred Payments to Beneficiaries Other than the Insured's Spouse.   It is not uncommon for an insured to require, or a beneficiary to request, that life insurance proceeds be paid by the insurer in installments, either for a fixed period or for life, rather than in a lump sum. In such event, pursuant to Section 101(d)(1)(A), proceeds otherwise excludible from gross income by Section 101(a)(1) will remain so, while amounts attributable to the earnings thereon will be includible in the gross income of the beneficiary.[157] To determine the amount excludible from a beneficiary's gross income, the "amount held by an insurer" with respect to that beneficiary is prorated over the period during which the payments are to be made.[158] The "amount held by an insurer" with respect to all beneficiaries is generally the amount that would be payable in a lump sum on the date of death of the insured in full discharge of the policy.[159] The prorated amounts are excludible from gross income irrespective of the year in which they are received.[160] Any excess is taxable as interest except to the extent of the additional exclusion (discussed below) for life insurance proceeds paid to the surviving spouse of an insured. For example, if a beneficiary of

---

[152] Treas. Reg. §1.101-1(b)(3)(ii).
[153] Treas. Reg. §1.101-1(b)(3)(iii).
[154] I.R.C. §101(c).
[155] Treas. Reg. §1.101-3(a).
[156] Ibid.
[157] Treas. Reg. §1.101-4(a)(1)(i).
[158] Ibid.
[159] Treas. Reg. §1.101-4(b)(1).
[160] Treas. Reg. §1.101-4(a)(1)(i).

$150,000 in life insurance proceeds elected to receive the proceeds over a 10-year period in equal annual installments of $16,500, the beneficiary would exclude $15,000 ($150,000 divided by 10) of each $16,500 payment. The balance of each payment, $1,500, would be includible in the beneficiary's gross income. In the event two installments were received within a single taxable year, the beneficiary would exclude $30,000 ($15,000 for each installment) and include $3,000 in his gross income.[161]

If life insurance proceeds are payable for the life of a beneficiary, the prorated amount is determined by dividing the lump-sum death benefit[162] by the beneficiary's life expectancy.[163] If payments are to be made for a period certain or in a certain amount and life thereafter, the lump sum must be reduced, before making the proration, by the present value (on the date of the insured's death) of the contingent beneficiaries' interest.[164] The prorated amounts are excludible from the beneficiary's gross income, even if he lives beyond the life expectancy used in making the proration.[165] If the beneficiary dies during any period certain or prior to receiving any certain amount, guaranteed payments to the contingent beneficiary or beneficiaries are excludible from the gross income of the recipient(s).[166]

Special rules apply in the case of installment or annuity-type payments to two or more beneficiaries.[167]

Deferred Payments to the Insured's Spouse. An additional exclusion from gross income is provided by Section 101(d)(1)(B) where life insurance proceeds are paid to the insured's surviving spouse.[168] Such payments are includible in gross income only to the extent they exceed, in any taxable year of the spouse, the sum of (1) the amounts prorated in accordance with Section 101(d)(1)(A); and (2) $1,000.[169] If the beneficiary, in the example in the text at footnote 161, had been the surviving spouse of an insured, he or she would have included in gross income only $500 of each annual installment, that is, the amount of the installment ($16,500) less the sum of (1) the prorated amount ($15,000) and (2) the additional exclusion provided a surviving spouse ($1,000). However, if two installments were received within a single taxable year, the spouse would exclude $31,000 ($15,000 for each installment plus $1,000), not $32,000. This is because a spouse is entitled to only one exclusion of $1,000 in any taxable year.

---

[161] Treas. Reg. §1.101-4(a)(2) example 2.

[162] If one of the alternative methods of payment under the contract is not a lump-sum payment upon the death of the insured, the present value of the payments receivable by the beneficiary is used in lieu of a lump sum.

[163] Treas. Reg. §1.101-4(c).

[164] Ibid.

[165] Ibid.

[166] Treas. Reg. §1.101-4(d)(3).

[167] Treas. Reg. §1.101-4(d).

[168] I.R.C. §101(d)(1)(B).

[169] Treas. Reg. §1.101-4(a)(1)(ii).

CHAPTER 60

Federal Gift and Estate Taxation of Group Life Insurance

JAMES E. ROBERTS AND
RONALD T. MARTIN

Because the federal gift and estate taxation of group life insurance generally involves principles applicable to the federal gift and estate taxation of life insurance in general, the focus here is on policies providing only group term life insurance coverage.

Gift Tax

Section 2501 imposes a tax on the "transfer of property by gift" by an individual. Section 2501 applies "whether the transfer is in trust or otherwise, whether the gift is direct or indirect, and whether the property is real or personal, tangible, or intangible."[1] A "transfer of property by gift" will not occur unless the following factors are present:

"Property" Is Transferred. The term encompasses "every species of right or interest protected by law and having an exchangeable value."[2]

The Transfer Is Wholly or Partially Gratuitous. The gift tax is imposed upon the transfer of property for less than adequate and full consideration in money or monies' worth. When property is so transferred, the amount by which the value of the property exceeds the value of the consideration received therefor is deemed a gift, and is included in computing the amount of the gifts made.[3]

The Transfer Is Complete. The gift tax is imposed upon transfers in which the donor has so parted with dominion and control as to leave him or her with no power to change its disposition, whether for his or her own benefit or for the benefit of another.[4]

---

[1] I.R.C. §2511.

[2] S. Rep. 665, 72nd Cong., 1st Sess. (1932) 1939-1 CB Part 2, 496, 524.

[3] I.R.C. §2512(b).

[4] Treas. Reg. §25.2511-2(b).

The Property Interest Transferred Is Susceptible to Valuation.
The Internal Revenue Service has taken the position that if a reasonably
accurate value cannot be ascertained when the "gift" becomes complete, the
time of the gift will be deferred until the amount of the gift first becomes
susceptible to valuation.[5]

The tax imposed by Section 2501 is a tax on "taxable gifts." The term
taxable gifts means the total amount of gifts made during the calendar year,
reduced by the gift tax marital and charitable deductions.[6] In determining
the total amount of gifts made, the first $10,000 in gifts of present interests
made to any one donee during the calendar year is excluded.[7] No exclusion
is permitted on account of gifts of future interests.[8]

The regulations define a "present interest" as "an unrestricted right to
the immediate use, possession, or enjoyment of property or income from
property."[9] In contrast, the term *future interest* has reference to a reversion,
remainder, or other interest, vested or contingent, which is limited to
commence in use, possession, or enjoyment at some future time.[10]

When an employee assigns the entire interest in his or her employer's
group term life insurance plan, an interest in the policy has been assigned.
The transfer of an interest in a group term life insurance policy may be a gift
subject to tax.[11] Assuming the employee's health is not substantially impaired or, if impaired, the premium accurately reflects such impairment, the
gift tax value of the insurance benefits transferred is the proportionate part
of the annual premium last paid before the date of the gift which covers the
period extending beyond that date.[12] In other words, the value of the
insurance benefits at the time of the transfer generally is the amount of
unearned premium thereon. Of course, insurance on the life of a person
with impaired health would have a value in excess of the unearned premium
thereon unless the premium took into account the health impairment.[13]

Each time a premium is paid by the employer, directly or indirectly, an
additional benefit is conferred on the employee. By assigning the insurance
benefits and continuing participation in the plan, the employee causes these
benefits to inure to the benefit of the donee. Accordingly, each premium
payment made by the employer for group term life insurance on the life of

---

[5] Rev. Rul. 69-346 1969-1 CB 227.

[6] I.R.C. §2503(a).

[7] I.R.C. §2503(b).

[8] Ibid.

[9] Treas. Reg. §25.2503-3(b).

[10] Treas. Reg. §25.2503-3(a).

[11] I.R.C. §2511 and the regulations promulgated thereunder; Rev. Rul. 76-490, 1976-2 CB
300.

[12] Treas. Reg. §25.2512-6(a).

[13] In this circumstance, the unearned premium may be helpful only as a criterion of
minimum value. Cf. *Estate of Prichard* 4 T.C. 204.

the employee is deemed an indirect transfer by the employee to the donee[14] and is subject to the gift tax imposed by Section 2501.[15] If the premium for group insurance is calculated on an average premium basis, the actual premium attributable to an employee, and not the average premium, is deemed to be the amount of the indirect transfer from the employee to the assignee.

Contractual rights under an insurance policy are not future interests, even though the obligations thereunder are to be discharged by payments in the future.[16] However, a future interest may be created by limitations in a trust or other instrument of transfer used in making a gift of a policy or interest therein.[17] Assuming the employee transfers his or her rights under the employer's plan to an individual or to a trust in such manner as to avoid the transfer being a gift of a future interest, the payment by the employer of each premium for that employee is not a gift of a future interest in property. Accordingly, the annual exclusion would be available on the initial transfer and subsequent premium payments.[18]

Some group term life insurance plans provide for the continuation of insurance coverage on the life of a retired employee until death.[19] Generally, the employer obligates itself, either under a separate document or under the master policy, to continue the insurance for its retired employees. In such a case, a retired employee's benefits are not forfeitable.[20] Additionally, if the employee has assigned his or her interest in the plan, the donee, as a third-party beneficiary, may enforce the obligation of the employer.

Assuming an employer's plan provides postretirement group term life insurance and the employer has obligated itself to continue the insurance upon the employee's retirement, the value of the indirect transfer by the employee to the donee upon his or her retirement is more than the annual premium payment with respect to the employee for that year. The value of the gift, at this time, would be the value of all future premiums due under the policy for the employee; that is, the value of a nontransferable paid-up term life insurance policy on the life of the retired employee.[21] The value of

---

[14] I.R.C. §2511.

[15] Rev. Rul. 76-490, 1976-2 CB 300.

[16] Treas. Reg. §25.2503-3(a).

[17] Ibid.

[18] Rev. Rul. 76-490, 1976-2 CB 300.

[19] For a discussion of the income-tax aspects of retired lives reserves, see discussion in text at footnotes 1 through 41 in Chapter 7.

[20] *Sheehy* v. *Seilon, Inc.*, 10 OS 2d 242, 39 OO 2d 374, 227 N.E. 2d 229 (1967), *Matter of Erie Lackawanna Ry. Co.*, 548 F.2d 621 (1977). See, also, *Cantor* v. *Berkshire Life Ins. Co.*, 171 OS 405, 14 OO 2d 157, 171 N.E. 2d 518 (1960) (Retirement Pay), and *Dangott* v. *ASG Industries, Inc.*, 558 P.2d 379 (OKL., 1976) (Severance Pay).

[21] See generally, Treas. Reg. §§25.2512-1 and 25.2512-6; Rev. Rul. 76-490, 1976-2 CB 300.

such a policy would be approximately 42 to 62 percent of the amount of the insurance benefit provided the employee. This result is the same, regardless of whether the employer's obligation is prefunded or not, unless the employer does not appear financially able to discharge its obligation to the employee, in which event its unfunded obligation would be worth less than a fully funded obligation. The increased unified credit, increased annual exclusion, and unlimited marital deduction under the Economic Recovery Tax Act of 1981 (ERTA) have substantially reduced the gift tax impact of most postretirement group term life insurance benefits.

Estate Tax

The principal sections of the Internal Revenue Code (IRC) relating to the estate taxation of life insurance are Sections 2042 and 2035.[22]

Section 2042. It provides that the proceeds of an insurance policy on a decedent's life are includible in his or her gross estate if they are: (1) receivable by the executor; or (2) receivable by beneficiaries other than the decedent's executor and if the decedent had, at the time of death, any incidents of ownership in the policy.[23]

The amount includible in the gross estate with respect to insurance on the life of the decedent is the full amount receivable under the policy. However, if the proceeds are payable in the form of an annuity for life or for a term of years, the amount includible in the decedent's gross estate is the lump sum that could have been received (in lieu of the annuity payments) or, if a lump sum could not have been received, the sum used by the insurance company in determining the amount of the annuity.[24]

Proceeds are "receivable by the executor" if they are "receivable by or for the benefit of the estate."[25] Thus, proceeds receivable by a beneficiary subject to a legally binding obligation to pay taxes, debts or other charges enforceable against the decedent's estate are includable to the extent of those obligations.[26] If insurance on the decedent's life is assigned to a creditor as collateral security for the decedent's loan, the insurance is "receivable by the executor," even though the creditor is the beneficiary, since the estate has benefited from the discharge of the decedent's liability to the creditor.[27] Conversely, if the decedent's executor or estate is the named beneficiary under a life insurance contract, but state law requires the proceeds to inure exclusively to the benefit of the decedent's children and

---

[22] Although Sections 2042 and 2035 do not operate upon life insurance to the exclusion of all other sections, it frequently occurs that these sections overlap with others that may be applicable, rendering resort to such other sections unnecessary.

[23] I.R.C. §2042.

[24] Treas. Reg. §20.2042-1(a)(3).

[25] Treas. Reg. §20.2042-1(b)(1).

[26] Ibid.

[27] Ibid.

surviving spouse, the insurance is not "receivable by the executor."[28] In this situation, the estate will not benefit from the insurance proceeds.

The proceeds of an insurance policy are includible in the insured's gross estate under Section 2042(2) if he or she possessed at death any incidents of ownership in the policy, exercisable alone or in conjunction with any other person, irrespective of the beneficiary designation thereunder. Possession of any incident of ownership will invoke inclusion of the entire proceeds— full ownership of all the rights and privileges pertaining to the policy is not required.[29] The term *incident of ownership,* as defined by the regulations, relates to the right of the insured or of his or her estate to the economic benefits of the policy. Specifically, incidents of ownership include the right to: (1) change the beneficiary, (2) surrender or cancel the policy, (3) assign the policy, (4) revoke an assignment, (5) pledge the policy as collateral for a loan, or (6) obtain from the insurer a loan against the cash surrender value of the policy.[30] However, the language of the regulations is not intended to be inclusive. Consequently, other powers may constitute an incident of ownership.[31]

The IRC specifically provides that the term *incident of ownership* includes a reversionary interest in the insurance policy or its proceeds.[32] A reversionary interest is defined by the regulations to include a possibility that the insurance policy or its proceeds may return to the decedent or to his or her estate, and a possibility that the policy or its proceeds may become subject to a power of disposition by the insured.[33] The interest may arise by the express terms of the policy or other instrument of transfer, or by operation of law.[34] However, an important qualification exists—the value of the reversionary interest must exceed 5 percent of the value of the policy valued immediately before the death of the insured.[35] In arriving at this value there must be taken into consideration any incidents of ownership held by others, immediately before the decedent's death, which would affect the value of the decedent's reversionary interest.[36] Therefore, it is possible to design a group insurance policy that the insured could assign to another and reserve the right to recover the policy rights upon the occurrence of certain events (e.g., divorce and the like) without having the policy proceeds includible in the gross estate in the event he or she were to die prior to the policy reverting to him or her.

---

[28] *Webster* v. *Commissioner,* 120 F.2d 514, 41-1 USTC ¶10,059 5, (1941).

[29] Stephens, Maxfield and Lind, *Federal Estate and Gift Taxation,* ¶4.14(4)(a), at 4-294 (4th ed. 1978).

[30] Treas. Reg. §20.2042-1(c)(2).

[31] Treas. Reg. §20.2042-1(c).

[32] I.R.C. §2042(c).

[33] Treas. Reg. §20.2042-1(c)(3).

[34] Ibid.

[35] Ibid.

[36] Ibid.

In addition, the regulations provide that the insured is considered to have an "incident of ownership" in an insurance policy held in trust if he or she has the power as trustee, exercisable either alone or in conjunction with another, to change the beneficial owner of the policy or its proceeds, or the time or manner of enjoyment thereof, even though he or she has no beneficial interest in the trust.[37]

In view of the foregoing, if the group term life insurance provided under an employer's plan is payable to the employee's estate, or if the employee at the time of death possessed an incident of ownership in the policy, the entire policy proceeds are includible in the gross estate.[38]

Assuming the employee transfers all interests in the group term life insurance benefits provided under the employer's plan and the insurance proceeds are not payable to or for the benefit of the estate, Section 2042 will not require the policy proceeds to be includible in the employee's gross estate unless (1) the employee's right to terminate employment and, thus, cancel the insurance, constitutes an incident of ownership, or (2) in the case of a shareholder-employee, the employer's power to surrender or cancel the policy is attributed to the employee through his or her stock ownership.

In Revenue Ruling 69-54,[39] the IRS conceded that an employee may transfer all incidents of ownership in a group term life insurance policy if these requirements are met:

1. The policy may be converted to a separate policy on the employee's termination of employment.
2. The policy and state law permit the employee to assign absolutely all incidents of ownership in the policy, including the conversion right.
3. The employee irrevocably assigns all incidents of ownership in the policy, including the conversion right.

Under the ruling, if the foregoing requirements are met, the employee's power to terminate employment is not an incident of ownership because the assigned conversion right enables the assignee to prevent such termination from effecting a cancellation of the insurance.[40]

Revenue Ruling 72-307[41] modifies Revenue Ruling 69-54. Pursuant to Revenue Ruling 72-307, an employee's right to cancel the insurance coverage solely by terminating employment is not an incident of ownership but, rather, is "a collateral consequence of the power that every employee has to terminate his employment."[42] Thus, Revenue Ruling 72-307 provides, in effect, that an employee may effectively assign a nonconvertible policy and

---

[37] Treas. Reg. §20.2042-1(c)(4).
[38] I.R.C. §2042 and the regulations promulgated thereunder.
[39] 1969-1 C.B. 221.
[40] Ibid.
[41] 1972-1 C.B. 307.
[42] Ibid.

avoid inclusion of the proceeds under Section 2042(2), if he or she assigns all rights therein.[43] However, if the employee has a conversion right that he or she fails to assign, Section 2042(2) will apply.[44]

Pursuant to Treasury Regulation §20.2042-1(c)(6), a corporation's incidents of ownership in a life insurance policy on the life of its sole or controlling shareholder will be attributed to the shareholder through stock ownership to the extent the proceeds of the policy are not payable to or for the benefit of the corporation. The regulation provides the following exception to this rule:

> In the case of group term life insurance . . . , the power to surrender or cancel a policy held by a corporation shall not be attributed to any decedent through his stock ownership.[45]

The exception applies even though the shareholder is a sole or controlling shareholder[46] and notwithstanding that the proceeds of the policy are not payable to or for the benefit of the corporation.[47] Thus, if a sole or controlling shareholder-employee irrevocably assigns a group term life insurance policy, the fact that the corporation, through its power to terminate its group term life insurance plan, has the power to surrender or cancel the policy, will not cause inclusion of the policy proceeds in the employee's gross estate.[48]

Because the exception applies only "[i]n the case of group term life insurance,"[49] it may be impossible for a sole or controlling shareholder-employee to make an estate tax saving assignment of the portion of a group permanent policy that provides a permanent benefit if the employer possesses the right to terminate the policy.[50]

Section 2035. Even if Section 2042 is inapplicable to an employee's transfer of group term life insurance benefits, it may require inclusion of the policy proceeds in the employee's gross estate.

Section 2035 states that a decedent's gross estate "shall include the value

---

[43] Ibid.

[44] Rev. Rul. 69-54, 1969-1 C.B. 221. The group term life insurance plans described in Rev. Rul. 69-54 were noncontributory plans. Since, in the case of a contributory plan, (1) the employee arguably has a right to cancel the policy by discontinuing his or her premium payments, and (2) a termination of coverage due to a failure to pay premiums generally does not give rise to a right of conversion, the IRS might argue that an employee under a contributory plan who complies with the requirements of Rev. Rul. 69-54, as modified by Rev. Rul. 72-307, has nevertheless retained an incident of ownership. This possible argument seemingly would be avoided if the plan gives the employee's donee the right to pay premiums.

[45] Treas. Reg. §20.2042-1(c)(6).

[46] There would seem to be no basis, in any event, for attributing corporate incidents of ownership to a noncontrolling shareholder.

[47] Treas. Reg. §20.2042-1(c)(6).

[48] Query whether Section 2036 or 2038, or both, will be applicable.

[49] Ibid.

[50] See, Keydel, "Irrevocable Insurance Trusts: The Current Scene," U. Miami 10th Inst. on Est. Plan. ¶509.1 n. 74 (1976).

of all property to the extent of any interest therein of which the decedent has at any time made a transfer, by trust or otherwise, during the three-year period ending on the date of the decedent's death."[51] In addition, pursuant to subsection 2035(c), any gift tax paid on the transfer is also includable in the decedent's gross estate.[52] There is an exception under subsection 2035(b)(2) for any gift to a donee that was "made during a calendar year if the decedent was not required by Section 6019 . . . to file any gift tax return for such year with respect to gifts to such donee."[53] However, this exception does not apply "to any transfer with respect to a life insurance policy."[54]

Section 2035 was amended by the Economic Recovery Tax Act of 1981, which added new subsection 2035(d). Pursuant to this new provision, the general rule of Section 2035 (inclusion of transfers within three years of death) generally will not apply to the estate of a decedent dying after December 31, 1981. However, in light of subsection 2035(d)(2), the rules discussed in the preceding paragraph nevertheless will continue to apply under the new law. This is because subsection 2035(d) does not apply to a transfer of an interest in property that would have been included in the decedent's estate under Section 2042 if the transfer had not been made.

In view of the subsection 2035(d)(2) exception, and the limitation to the subsection 2035(b)(2) exception,[55] it is possible to reach the following conclusions concerning the estate tax consequences under Section 2035 of the transfer of a life insurance policy:

1. Where a decedent transfers a life insurance policy (other than a renewable policy) more than three years prior to death, no portion of the death proceeds will be included in the decedent's gross estate, even though he or she pays the premiums on the policy until death. Section 2035 is inapplicable since, by its terms, it applies only to transfers made within three years of the decedent's death.

2. Where a decedent transfers a life insurance policy within three years of death and continues to pay the premiums, the entire proceeds of the policy will be included in the decedent's gross estate, even though the transfer of the policy was not required to be shown on a gift tax return. However, according to one case, if the decedent transfers the policy within three years of death and the transferee pays the premiums after the date of transfer, the policy proceeds, less a pro rata share thereof attributable to the

---

[51] I.R.C. §2035(a).

[52] I.R.C. §2035(c).

[53] I.R.C. §2035(b)(2).

[54] Ibid.

[55] Pursuant to I.R.C. §2035(d)(2), as amended by the Technical Corrections Act of 1982, §2035(b)(2) will be inapplicable in any event.

transferee's premium payments, will be included in the decedent's gross estate.[56]

3. Where a decedent transfers a renewable policy more than three years prior to death and continues to pay the premiums thereon, directly or indirectly, concern has been expressed by many with respect to the tax consequences under Section 2035; that is, a question arises: Will the IRS argue that all rights in the policy are transferred when the policy is renewed and that Section 2035 applies if the policy is renewed within three years of the decedent's death? Since (1) group term life insurance is generally annually renewable term insurance, and (2) each premium payment made by the employer is an indirect transfer by the employee to the donee for purposes of Section 2511, this argument, if successful, would make it impossible for an employee to avoid inclusion in the gross estate of the proceeds of an annually renewable group term life insurance policy. A recent Revenue Ruling makes it clear, however, that, in the case of a typical group term life insurance policy, the argument will not be made.[57]

In Revenue Ruling 82-13,[58] decedent's employer covered him and its other employees under a noncontributory group term life insurance policy. The policy was renewable at standard rates, without evidence of insurability, upon payment of the annual premium. In 1975, decedent gratuitously assigned to a third party all his rights under the policy, including any conversion privilege. Decedent's employer continued making premium payments until decedent's death in 1980. The issue was whether the policy proceeds should be included in decedent's gross estate under Section 2035. After making it clear that Section 2035 would apply if the employer's premium payment was deemed to purchase a new insurance policy each year,[59] the IRS held that the premiums here "merely effectuated the continuation of an existing agreement." The factors cited by the IRS in making this determination are:

1. The policy was renewable automatically upon payment of the annual premium.
2. Evidence of insurability was not necessary for renewal.
3. So long as the policy was renewed each year, all rights and obligations thereunder continued without interruption.

---

[56] *Estate of Silverman* v. *Commissioner*, 521 F.2d 574 (C.A.2d 1975). The case seems to be wrongly decided and has been criticized by several commentators. See, for example, Kahn and Waggoner, "Federal Taxation of the Assignment of Life Insurance, 1977 *Duke L.J.* 941 at 969 *et. seq.*

[57] *Rev. Rul. 82-13, 1982-2 I.R.B.,* 9.

[58] *1982-2 I.R.B.,* 9.

[59] *See Bel* v. *United States,* 452 F.2d 683 (CA5, 1971) and Rev. Rul. 71-497, 1971-2 C.B. 329.

Thus, said the IRS, "the payment of the premium at the time of the policy's renewal did not create new rights, nor was such payment a repurchase of insurance." Therefore, Section 2035 did not apply.

Notwithstanding Revenue Ruling 82-13, an insured employee who irrevocably assigns, more than three years prior to death, all rights in his or her employer's group term life insurance plan may have the entire insurance benefit included in the gross estate as a result of the employer's change of insurance carriers.

In Revenue Ruling 79-231,[60] the decedent, in 1971, assigned to his spouse his entire interest in his employer's group term life insurance plan. Prior to making the assignment, decedent executed a written agreement with his spouse stating the assignment also would vest in his spouse his entire interest in any other arrangement for life insurance coverage established by his employer. In 1977, less than a year before the decedent's death, decedent's employer terminated its existing insurance arrangement and entered into a virtually identical arrangement with a different insurance carrier. Pursuant to the written agreement with his spouse, decedent assigned to his spouse his entire interest in his employer's new group term life insurance plan. The IRS held that the decedent-employee had transferred his rights under his employer's group term policy in 1977, within three years of his death. According to the IRS, the anticipatory assignment in 1971 was not effective as a present transfer of the decedent's rights in the group term life insurance policy acquired by the employer in 1977. Rather, if such anticipatory assignment constituted a binding promise under local law, the transfer for purposes of Section 2035 occurred when the employer changed insurance carriers. Otherwise, said the IRS, such transfer occurred when decedent actually assigned his interest in his employer's new group term life insurance plan.

Revenue Ruling 79-231 was revoked by the IRS in Revenue Ruling 80-289.[61] The new ruling holds as follows:

> Rev. Rul. 79-231 . . . concluded under identical facts that the anticipatory assignment in 1971 was not effective as a present transfer of the decedent's rights in the group term life insurance policy issued [in 1977] and that the time of transfer for purposes of Section 2035 was in 1977. The Internal Revenue Service maintains the view that the anticipatory assignment was not technically effective as a present transfer of the decedent's rights in the policy issued [in 1977]. Nevertheless, the Service believes that the assignment in 1977 to [the decedent's] spouse, the object of the anticipatory assignment in 1971, should not cause the value of the proceeds to be includible in the gross estate of the decedent under Section 2035 where the assignment was necessitated by the change of the employer's master insurance plan carrier and the new arrangement is *identical in all relevant aspects* to the previous arrangement. [Italics added for emphasis.]

---

[60] 1979-2 CB 323.
[61] I.R.B. 1980-43.

Thus, based on Revenue Ruling 80-289, if, more than three years prior to death, an employee irrevocably assigns his or her entire interest in the employer's group term life insurance plan, and makes such assignment effective to cover all substituted insurance coverage, the employer's change of insurance carriers nevertheless will start the running of a new three-year period, unless the employer's new group term life insurance plan is "identical in all relevant aspects" to the previous plan.[62]

The language of the limitation to the subsection 2035(b)(2) exception (discussed briefly, above) would seem to apply to the payment of premiums on a life insurance policy by the donor within three years of death as well as to the transfer of the policy itself during that period.[63] However, the Senate Report on the amendments in the Revenue Act of 1978 to Section 2035 provides:

> The exception [of Section 2035(b)(2)] does apply to any premiums paid (or deemed paid) by the decedent within three years of the death to the extent that such payment would not have resulted in the inclusion of the proceeds of the policy in the decedent's gross estate under prior law. On the other hand, the exception does not apply to any transfer which would have resulted in inclusion in the gross estate of the proceeds of the policy under law prior to the 1976 Act if the transfer were made within three years of death.[64]

Thus, based on the foregoing language, it would seem if a decedent's payment of premiums within three years of death on a life insurance policy will not cause any of the policy proceeds to be included in the gross estate under the three-year rule, the premiums themselves will be included in the gross estate only if a gift tax return is required because, for example, they (together with any other present interest gifts to the donee) exceed $10,000 for the calendar year,[65] or because they are gifts of future interests.

---

[62] If an employee's group term life insurance coverage is increased, the IRS may argue that the increase in coverage is transferred at the time of the increase or, in the absence of an anticipatory assignment of all increased insurance coverage (or if such an assignment is ineffective under local law), at the time of an actual assignment of such increase.

[63] I.R.C. §2035(b)(2).

[64] S. Rep. on HR 6715, p. 87.

[65] If a gift tax return is required for this reason, the entire value of the premium, and not merely the excess over $10,000, will be included in the gross estate.

APPENDIX A

The Effects of the 1983 Social Security Amendments*

ROBERT J. MYERS

Two years of extensive legislative efforts to resolve the financing problems of the Social Security program reached culmination when President Reagan signed into law on April 20 the Social Security Amendments of 1983. The principal part of this legislation, which reflected the recommendations of the National Commission on Social Security Reform, dealt only with the financing problems of the Old-Age, Survivors, and Disability Insurance program (OASDI) and did not address those of the Hospital Insurance portion of Medicare (HI) to any significant extent. The problems of the latter program were not as immediate as were those of the OASDI system, but rather they will arise four or five years from now, and will then steadily become worse.

Actually, the legislation had tacked onto it certain provisions with regard to both the HI and the Unemployment Insurance (UI) programs. As to HI, a gradual phasing-in of a new method of providing reimbursements to providers of services is established. The HI cost basis is to be changed to a system of uniform sums (but varying as among nine different geographical areas and as between urban and rural facilities) for each of 467 different Diagnosis Related Groups. The amendments to the UI system essentially involve extending the duration of federally financed supplemental benefits, on a temporary basis, and providing more lenient treatment of loans to the various state systems from the federal UI Trust Fund.

The remainder of this appendix will deal only with the changes in the OASDI program and their effect on its financial status and a change in the Supplemental Security Income program (SSI) to conform with the change in the OASDI COLA provision.

By and large, the changes made very closely follow the basic recommendations of the National Commission on Social Security Reform—neither adding to them nor taking away from them to any significant extent.

---

* Reprinted with minor revisions by the author with permission of Meidinger, Inc., Compensation and Benefit Services, 2600 Meidinger Tower, Louisville Galleria, Louisville, Kentucky 40202.

COVERAGE PROVISIONS

Mandatory coverage is extended to all newly hired federal employees and to all existing members of Congress, judges, and political appointees in the Executive Branch, beginning in 1984. Currently, only temporary civilian employees and members of the armed forces are covered under OASDI and HI (although all others are covered under HI).

All employees of nonprofit charitable, educational, and religious organizations (including both those who were never covered and those who had been covered but whose organization had terminated coverage) will be mandatorily covered, beginning in 1984. Current employees aged 55 and over will have special, more lenient conditions for qualifying for benefits. For example, persons aged 60 or over at the beginning of 1984 will need only 6 quarters of coverage (acquired after 1983) to be fully insured (as against a normal requirement of 35 quarters of coverage for other persons aged 60 then), but the benefit amount for a person with only 6 quarters of coverage will be relatively small.

State and local government entities which are currently covered as a result of their past election to do so will not be allowed to terminate coverage in the future (even though they may have a termination notice now pending).

Certain other smaller coverage extensions were made. Broadened coverage is made possible for employees of foreign affiliates of American employers and for self-employed persons working abroad. Certain fringe benefits were made taxable and creditable for OASDI-HI purposes—standby pay after age 62 when it is expected that, at some future time, services will be rendered; and employer contributions under "cash-or-deferred" plans (Sec. 401[k]), whether or not part of a "cafeteria" plan (but with a "grandfather" clause for deferral elections made before 1984). Cafeteria plans under Section 125 are not affected. The previous treatment of tax-sheltered annuities (Sec. 403[b]), under which the gross salary (before salary reduction) is covered for OASDI-HI purposes, would be continued as long as they are true salary-reduction plans which are individually negotiated. Deferrals under a nonqualified deferred compensation plan will not be covered for OASDI-HI purposes until the later of the time when the services are performed or when there is no longer a substantial risk of forfeiture of the deferred compensation.

BENEFIT CHANGES

Paralleling, and consistent with, the changes in the coverage provisions, the method of computing benefits for certain persons with pensions from noncovered employment is revised. Such changes will not be applicable to newly covered persons in types of employment that were previously not covered (although they will be applicable to those who had been covered while working for a nonprofit organization which withdrew from coverage at some time in the past). Also, these windfall-benefit restrictions will not apply to persons who have 30 or more years of substantial covered employment or to persons who first become eligible for benefits (by attaining age 62, or dying or becoming disabled before then) before 1986. The new method of benefit computation for those so affected will tend to result in the payment of proportionate benefits, rather than those which are heavily weighted for persons with low average earnings. This new method will be gradually phased in for those becoming newly eligible in the first few years. Also, it will apply in a more limited manner for those who have slightly less than the 30 years of coverage which would exempt them from its operation.

The major immediate benefit change is a 6-month delay in the payment of the automatic-benefit increases (COLAs). Instead of being for the June checks, payable at the beginning of July, the COLAs will be for the December checks, payable in early January. It is important to note that this does not have merely a one-time cost effect, but rather it impacts for all beneficiaries each year into the future. (The increases in the enrollee premium rates for the Supplementary Medical Insurance program [part B] will be coordinated with the COLAs, so as to show up first in the January OASDI benefit checks; the present standard premium rate of $12.20 will continue for July–December 1983.)

The major long range benefit change is a deferred, gradually phased-in increase in the normal retirement age (i.e., the minimum age at which unreduced benefits are payable, currently age 65). Such age will be gradually increased to 66 for those who attain it in 2009, beginning the phase-in with those who attain age 62 in 2000. The normal retirement age will then be held at 66 until again being gradually increased (to 67 for those who attain that age in 2027), beginning with those who attain age 62 in 2017.

It is important to note that the eventual increase in the normal retirement age for the OASDI program does not apply to the Medicare program as to its initial eligibility age (logical, and even desirable and necessary, as that might be), which will remain at 65 for aged persons.

Early-retirement benefits at ages down to 62 will continue to be available, but the actuarial-reduction factors will be changed in an appropriate manner. When the normal retirement age is 66, the factor will be 75 percent (as compared with the present 80 percent), while it will be 70 percent when the normal retirement age is 67. In the latter case, the factor will be 75 percent at age 63 and 80 percent at age 64, with graded-in amounts at older ages up to age 67.

The minimum age for full spouse's benefits will be increased in the same manner, while early benefits will continue to be available at age 62. The reduction factors will change from the present 75 percent at age 62—to 70 percent when the normal retirement age is 66, and to 65 percent when it is 67. In the latter case, the factor will be 70 percent at age 63 and 75 percent at age 64, with graded-in amounts at older ages up to age 67.

Similarly, the age for receipt of full widow(er)'s benefits will gradually rise in the future from 65 to 67 (but with a two-year lag in the increases behind those for retired workers. However, the amount payable at age 60 will continue at 71½ percent of the primary benefit, with the factor for intervening ages at initial claim before the normal retirement age being obtained by linear interpolation. Further, disabled widow(er)s first claiming benefits at ages 50–59 will receive the same 71½ percent rate (as compared to 50 percent at age 50 under the old law, and graded-in amounts at older ages).

Under the old law, persons who attain age 62 after 1978 and who delay retirement beyond the normal retirement age receive larger benefits, at the rate of 3 percent for each year of delay. The new law increases this credit, in a phased-in manner, to 8 percent. The phase-in begins for persons who attain age 65 in 1990, and the 8 percent rate will apply for those reaching the normal retirement age in 2009 (when such age is 66).

The retirement-earnings test in the old law results in reductions of $1 of benefits for each $2 of earnings in excess of a prescribed exempt amount (in 1983, $6,600 for persons aged 65–69 and $4,920 for younger persons), with those aged 70 and over having no limitation. The exempt amount rises automatically each year when the general wage level rises. Beginning with those who reach the normal retirement age in 1990 (then 65), the reduction basis will be changed to $1 of benefits for each $3 of excess earnings (but will not change for younger persons).

A number of minor benefit liberalizations were made. These include the following:

1. Several which primarily affect women—e.g., indexing deferred widow(er)'s benefits by the *better* of wage or price increases; continuing benefits to widow(er)s who are divorced spouses even though remarriage occurs in certain cases (just as for other widow(er)s; paying spouse's benefits to divorced spouses who are of retirement age even though the ex-spouse has not retired, although eligible to do so; and permitting one month's benefit retroactivity (to the month of death of the worker) for widow(er)'s benefits even though this results in a reduced benefit rate when initially claimed before age 65 (which retroactivity is prohibited in other cases).
2. Liberalization of insured-status requirements for persons who become disabled before age 31, who then recover, and who shortly later again become disabled.
3. The offset of a pension based on noncovered employment of a person against his or her spouse's benefit or widow(er)'s benefit is to be based on two thirds of such pension, instead of on all of it as under old law.

All gender-based distinctions in the Social Security law are eliminated. This has practically no real effect because such distinctions which were not previously eliminated by legislation have already been overturned by the courts.

An important stabilizing mechanism that will go a long way to offset adverse economic conditions was added. Beginning with the December 1984 checks, if the trust-fund ratio (fund balance compared with the outgo in the next 12 months) is less than 15 percent, the COLA will be the *lower* of the wage increase for the preceding calendar year or the CPI increase usually used (in the future to be measured from third quarter to third quarter). Beginning for the December 1989 checks, the trigger for the fund ratio is increased to 20 percent. If the fund ratio later rises above 32 percent, then prospectively any decrease in the COLA due to using wage increases, rather than CPI increases, will be restored.

The new law introduces certain restrictions on payment of benefits to aliens living abroad and to prisoners. Unless prevented by treaties with other countries, benefits will not be payable to dependents—spouses, widow(er)s, dependent parents, and children—becoming eligible after 1983 who are aliens living outside of the United States for six consecutive months and who had not resided in the United States during their relationship with the insured worker for at least five years (with a special alternative requirement for children, based on the residence duration of both parents). Despite the lack of knowledge of many in the public, benefits for prisoners were terminated by legislation in 1980 with respect to disability and student benefits; the new law extends such restrictions to all other types of benefits (which involves relatively few persons).

REVENUE PROVISIONS

The OASDI employer and employee tax rate of 5.7 percent scheduled under previous law for 1985 (versus 5.4 percent in 1983–1984) is moved up to 1984 insofar as the employer is concerned, but with no change for the employee. However, the OASDI tax rate going to the trust funds in 1984, will be 5.7 percent in both cases. This means that the difference of .3 percent in the employee rate will, undesirably, come from general revenues. A clear case of "doing it with mirrors"! Thus, the OASDI-HI tax rate in 1984 will be 6.7 percent for the employee and 7.0 percent for the employer, but with the trust funds receiving 14.0 percent (see table on page 1068).

The OASDI-HI employer and employee tax rates in previous law for 1985–87 will remain unchanged (7.05 percent each in 1985 and 7.15 percent in 1986–87). Most of the increase in the 1990 OASDI tax rate is moved up to 1988, so that the employer and employee rates are each 6.06 percent for OASDI and 7.51 percent for OASDI-HI in 1988–89. The corresponding rates for 1990 and after are left unchanged at 6.20 percent and 7.65 percent, respectively.

Self-employed persons paid 75 percent of the combined employer-employee rate for OASDI and 50 percent thereof for HI under the previous law. Now they will pay the full combined employer-employee rate, but with certain tax credits during 1984–89. The net effect is that the self-

OASDI-HI Tax Rates and Amounts Going to Trust Funds
in Various Years

Year	Employee Rate	Employer Rate	Combined Rate	Rate Going to Trust Funds
1983	6.70%	6.70%	13.40%	13.40%
1984	6.70	7.00	13.70	14.00
1985	7.05	7.05	14.10	14.10
1986–87	7.15	7.15	14.30	14.30
1988–89	7.51	7.51	15.02	15.02
1990 and after	7.65	7.65	15.30	15.30

Self-Employed Basis

Year	Employee Rate	Employer Rate	Combined Rate	Rate Going to Trust Funds
1983	*	*	9.35%	9.35%
1984	*	*	11.30	14.00
1985	*	*	11.80	14.10
1986–87	*	*	12.30	14.30
1988–89	*	*	13.02	15.02
1990 and after	*	*	14.13†	15.30

* Not applicable.
† See text.

employed will pay an OASDI-HI tax rate of 11.3 percent for 1984 (versus 13.7 percent for the employer and employee combined), 11.8 percent for 1985 (versus 14.1 percent), 12.3 percent for 1986–87 (versus 14.3 percent), and 13.02 percent for 1988–89 (versus 15.02 percent). The OASDI-HI trust funds, however, will be credited with the full employer-employee rate; the difference will come from general revenues—which will have about the same effect on general revenues in the aggregate as if all self-employed persons were to incorporate and count 50 percent of the resulting employer-employee tax as a business-expense deduction for income-tax purposes.

After 1989, the taxation basis for the self-employed will change. They will pay the combined employer-employee rate on a lower amount of self-employment income than under the present basis (lower by the amount of the employee tax on their net earnings), except that those well above the maximum taxable earnings base would be taxed on such amount. As a result, their total OASDI-HI tax will tend to be lower, but so, too, will be their earnings which are used in computing benefits. In addition, they will receive a credit against their net earnings from self-employment in the computation of their income tax which will be equal to 50 percent of the OASDI-HI tax that they pay. The foregoing complicated procedure approximates the overall treatment applicable to persons who incorporate their businesses. The net result, expressed as a net percentage payroll tax for OASDI-HI, will depend to some extent on the individual's top income-tax bracket.

Private employers have, for many years, been required to deposit their (and their employees') payroll taxes quite promptly. The larger the tax amounts involved, the more rapidly deposit is required. State and local governments were given much more latitude—making payments within 30 days after the end of the month; under the new law, they must do so twice a month, with a half-month lag permitted.

The payroll taxes are to be credited to the OASDI and HI Trust Funds at the *beginning* of each month (when the vast majority of OASDI benefits are sent out), instead of as received during the month, as under previous law. This so-called normalized tax procedure would be a form of general revenue subsidy, except that interest (at the rate earned by the trust funds) is to be paid by the trust funds to the General Fund for the advance payments, with appropriate adjustment at the end of each month. Thus, over the long run, the trust funds will neither gain nor lose, but they will have a much better cash-flow position. The procedure may properly be described as short-term loans to the trust funds by the General Fund, on a continuing basis, but repayable each month.

Part of OASDI benefits will be subject to income taxes, beginning in 1984. This will occur only for persons with relatively high incomes (about 8 percent of the beneficiaries in 1984). The resulting income taxes will be transferred to the OASDI Trust Funds. In the author's opinion, taxing Social Security benefits is good tax policy, but putting the proceeds in the trust funds is merely undesirable general-revenue financing (even though somewhat indirect). One might well ask why this is not done when private pensions are taxed (i.e., putting the resulting income taxes back in the pension fund)!

The specific procedure for taxing OASDI benefits is to compare the sum of (a) Adjusted Gross Income, (b) tax-exempt municipal bond interest, and (c) 50 percent of OASDI benefits with the threshold amount ($25,000 for single persons, $32,000 for married persons filing joint returns, and zero for other married persons—unless they lived apart from each other during the entire year, in which case they are considered as single persons). There is then added to the Adjusted Gross Income, in computing income-tax liability, the *smaller* of (d) 50 percent of the excess of the foregoing sum over the threshold amount or (e) 50 percent of OASDI benefits. (Railroad Retirement Tier-I benefits, the Social Security component, are taxed in a similar manner.)

It is important to note that the threshold amounts are not indexed (unlike most other economic elements in the OASDI program). This means that, over the years, an ever-growing proportion of beneficiaries will have 50 percent of their benefits included in their taxable income for income-tax purposes.

The estimated additional income taxes from taxing OASDI benefits are placed in the trust funds as the taxes are incurred, not as they are paid—a general-revenue subsidy, because people generally lag their tax liabilities in their tax payments. Even more of a general-revenue subsidy occurs because the transfers involved are made at the *beginning* of each quarter, instead of (more logically and equitably) during the quarter as the liability arises. (The Senate version of the bill did adopt the proper approach, but this was dropped in the conference between the House and the Senate.)

Another source of revenue will be the transfer in 1983 of about $21 billion to the OASDI Trust Funds (and $3 billion to the HI Trust Fund) from general revenues as representing primarily the present value of certain military-service wage credits which had been given for past service. Under the previous law, the costs of these benefits were to be paid for from general revenues only at the time that benefits resulting therefrom will actually be disbursed. It seems proper that such costs should be met by the federal government (from general revenues) as the "employer." Payment in a current lump sum seems reasonable and equitable—and probably such payment should have been made previously, when the service was rendered. Somewhat less than $1 billion of the $24 billion transfer from the General Fund will be for uncashed benefit checks which have not been returned (and accumulated interest thereon that would have accumulated if they had not been debited against the trust funds when they were issued); quite inequitably, the amounts of such checks were, in essence, credited to the General Fund in the past.

The allocation of the OASDI tax rate in the future between the OASI and DI Trust Funds is altered, so as to place both such trust funds in about the same relative financial position over future years (as can best be estimated).

OTHER FINANCING PROVISIONS

Interfund borrowing among the three payroll-tax-supported trust funds (OASI, DI, and HI) had been temporarily authorized for 1982 only. In practice, OASI borrowed $5.1 billion from DI and $12.4 billion from HI. The new law permits such borrowing (repayable with proper interest) for 1983–87. However, restrictions are established such that HI cannot make loans if its fund ratio would fall below 10 percent, and OASDI must repay the loans if its fund ratio exceeds 15 percent, and in any event during 1988–89. Furthermore, interest on any outstanding loans must be paid monthly. Similar provisions will apply in the event that HI borrows from OASDI.

Both the House and Senate bills had contained provisions for significantly revising the investment procedures for the trust funds. Under previous law, investments were almost entirely made (at a fair market interest rate) in special issues with arbitrary long maturity periods (even though redeemable at par when the proceeds were needed). The proposed new procedure would have been similar to money-market funds with varying market interest rates each month.

This revised investment procedure would have added to the general public's understanding of the investment situation, even though, over the long run, it would likely have had a neutral cost effect. The proposed new basis was dropped in the joint conference between the House and the Senate, because of the belief that there will apparently be a declining trend in interest rates in the next few years. If that does occur, the trust funds would have lower investment returns. But, if the reverse occurs, a bad choice will have been made by dropping the new procedure!

The members of the Boards of Trustees of the several trust funds have always been three cabinet members (political appointees, and generally of the same party). The new law provides for the addition of two public members, of different political parties, nominated by the President and confirmed by the Senate. This new composition of the Boards of Trustees should be of some value in the public-confidence area by introducing more bipartisanship in the general operation of the trust funds.

The Trustees Reports are, by permanent law, to be submitted each year by April 1. The new law extends the period of submittal of the 1983 reports, so that the deadline is 45 days after the date of enactment. This was done so that these reports can be based on the program as it is changed by the new law.

The Senate bill had contained a fail-safe device based on adjusting (or even eliminating) the COLAs when the OASDI trust fund balances became dangerously low. This "powerful medicine" would have virtually assured that benefit checks would continue to go out under even the worst of economic circumstances. However, this provision was dropped in the joint conference between the House and the Senate. The interfund-borrowing provision and the stabilizing device of the COLAs being based on the lesser of the wage or price increases in times of adverse experience are very helpful, but they do not *assure* that a financial crisis cannot again occur.

The only provision in the nature of a fail-safe device in the new law is, in essence, only a statement of intent. It is provided that the Board of Trustees shall report to Congress whenever the fund ratio of any of the four trust funds (OASI, DI, HI, and SMI) will become less than 20 percent after once having been more than 20 percent (which OASI and DI now are not). Under such circumstances, the Board of Trustees shall give recommendations as to how statutory changes could be made to restore a fund ratio of 20 percent over time. The report would be required to give a specific method as to how this result could be achieved, either by benefit changes or tax increases (or a combination of both).

The operations of the four trust funds (OASI, DI, HI, and SMI) will in the future be displayed as separate functions within the Federal Budget. Beginning with the fiscal year 1993, the operations of the OASI, DI, and HI Trust Funds will be removed from the unified budget.

NEW STUDIES REQUIRED

The new law requires that the Executive Branch should make several studies, as follows:

1. Length of time between issuance of benefit checks and their redemption.
2. Feasibility of daily transfers based on benefit checks paid by the Federal Reserve Banks.
3. Feasibility and implementation of the establishment of the Social Security Administration as an independent agency (outside of the Department of Health and Human Services).
4. Earnings-sharing proposals for OASDI benefit purposes (as between spouses, during the period of their marriage).

CHANGES IN SUPPLEMENTAL SECURITY INCOME PROGRAM

The new law postpones the date when COLAs are payable under the SSI program, so that they coincide with those under the OASDI program. In order to compensate SSI beneficiaries for the delay in the next COLA (to January 1984), the federal SSI benefit standard will be increased by $20 for single persons and by $30 for couples, effective on July 1. The amounts then will be $304.30 and $456.40 per month, respectively. Future COLAs under the SSI program will continue to be based on the CPI, even though at times the OASDI program may use the lesser of wage or price increases as the basis for the COLA. This SSI change represents a real increase in the level of payments.

ARE THE FINANCING PROBLEMS OF THE OASDI PROGRAM NOW REALLY SOLVED?

There is no question but that the very significant financing problems of the OASDI program—identified and agreed to by the National Commission on Social Security Reform—have been greatly alleviated by the new legislation.

The cost estimates as to the short range (the 1980s) are based on fairly pessimistic economic assumptions, and they show that there will be sufficient financial resources to make the program viable then—as a result of the presence of a number of elements, including COLA delays, additional income from several sources, the so-called normalized tax procedure, and reduced COLA adjustments under certain adverse conditions.

If economic conditions are somewhat better, the result will be a desirable buildup of the all-too-low current trust-fund balances. However, it is not inconceivable that there could be significantly worse economic conditions than assumed in the pessimistic cost estimates, and—quite unlikely—there could be financing problems for the OASDI program in 1985-87.

After 1987, because of the large tax-rate increase scheduled in 1988, and because of the favorable demographic picture then (due to the relatively small number of births annually in 1925-39), the financing situation for OASDI will be favorable *if economic conditions are reasonably good* (i.e., if wages increase significantly more each year than do prices—say, by a differential of 1½ percent per year). However, if wages increase only slightly more than prices, the bright situation of large annual excesses of income over outgo will not materialize—and, under certain circumstances, income and outgo might be, at best, only in close balance (or, conceivably, even worse).

If conditions in the 1990s are as favorable as shown by the intermediate estimate, it may be possible—and desirable, as well—to reduce slightly the OASDI tax rates for that decade, so as to prevent too large a fund buildup.

However, lurking in the wings is the serious financing problem of the HI program. Despite its improved financial situation as a result of the new law (due to the hoped-for favorable effect of the new reimbursement basis for hospitals and to the increased tax income with respect to self-employed persons), it is estimated to have continuing cash flow problems by 1990 under the intermediate cost estimate and perhaps two years earlier under the pessimistic cost estimate.

COST-OF-LIVING INCREASE

A 3.5 percent cost-of-living increase—the smallest ever—will be paid to nearly 36 million Social Security beneficiaries effective December 1983 and payable on January 3, 1984. Prior to the legislation enacted on April 20, this increase would have been effective for the month of June and payable in July. The six-month delay was part of the cost reduction objectives of the new law. The January payment date will be used for all future years, but the calculation period will change.

The forthcoming increase will be based on a comparison of the average consumer price index (CPI) for the first calendar quarter of 1983 with that for the first calendar quarter of 1982. In subsequent years, the comparison will be between the preceding third calendar quarter and the same period one year earlier.

ADVISORY COUNCIL MEETS

The statutory Advisory Council on Social Security (which was to have been appointed during 1981, but was actually named in August 1982 and first met November 7-8, 1982) has focused its work on the Medicare program and not at all on the OASDI program. Its members largely have expertise in medical economics and health-care problems.

The Advisory Council has been holding monthly meetings, open to the public, and has been proceeding at a deliberate speed in its study. No important decisions or conclusions have as yet been made. Undoubtedly, the new method of hospital reimbursement—based on Diagnosis Related Groups, established by the Social Security Amendments of 1983—will have an important effect on its conclusions.

Index